Marta,
I'm glad we had the opportunity
to meet and hope we can work
together. Mike Moll f

Editorial Staff

Editors .... Wolters Kluwer Editorial Staff

ISBN 978-1-5438-0534-5

Wolters Kluwer
2700 Lake Cook Road,
Riverwoods, Illinois, 60015
866 529 6600
www.WoltersKluwerLR.com

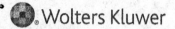

To Karen Melbinger,
my wife and best friend, without whose patient support this book would not have been possible,

to Peter, Charlotte and Lucy Melbinger,
for allowing me to miss a few regattas, recitals and games to complete this gargantuan project, and

to my parents Don and Joyce Melbinger,
for teaching me the values and rewards of hard work.

Preface

Executive compensation is a complicated mix of market forces, personalities, business strategies, accounting principles and the law. The portions of this volume that focus on plan design are based on the terms and provisions that are, were or might become "market" for executive compensation arrangements. Of course, those terms and conditions must comply with a seemingly endless list of laws, including portions of the Internal Revenue Code of 1986, the Employee Retirement Income Security Act of 1974, the Securities Act of 1933, the Securities Exchange Act of 1934, the Sarbanes-Oxley Act of 2002, the American Jobs Creation Act of 2004, Pension Protection Act of 2006, the Dodd-Frank Act of 2010, the Tax Cuts and Jobs Act of 2017, state corporation and business laws, federal and state case law, and applicable regulations and rulings under each of them. Executive compensation programs also must be designed to pass muster with entities and interest groups as diverse as stock exchanges, shareholder organizations and accountants.

New in the Third Edition. The Third Edition of *Executive Compensation* contains extensive analysis of many critical new developments that have occurred since publication of the second edition. Among these are:

- The Tax Cuts and Jobs Act of 2017, signed into law in December 2017;
- The release of SEC rules on several sections of the Dodd-Frank Wall Street Reform and Consumer Protection Act of 2010;
- The evolution of different forms of compensation and best practices for companies' compensation committee; and
- Numerous court decisions in the area, including a surge in litigation over the fiduciary duty of boards of directors when setting their own compensation and a revival of lawsuits over "excessive executive compensation."

Indeed, executive compensation has never been more in the spotlight than it is today. It is critical for executives, directors, companies and their advisers to understand the new laws, the evolving legal environment, and the duties and responsibilities (and potential liabilities) that courts and the government are imposing on companies, executives, and boards of directors.

Hence, this volume is structured to provide a basic framework for executives, board members, in-house and external lawyers, compensation consultants, and other compensation and human resources professionals to design, draft and apply executive compensation programs. Although I am a lawyer, the focus of this volume is not solely on legal compliance. Instead, I intend that readers should be able to analyze the effects, advantages, disadvantages and potential pitfalls of nearly all of the applicable legal, market and other factors when designing, drafting and administering their executive compensation programs.

Michael S. Melbinger

September 2018

About the Author

Michael S. Melbinger is a partner in the law firm of Winston & Strawn LLP and former Chair of the firm's Executive Compensation and Employee Benefits Practice Group. Mr. Melbinger works out of the firm's Chicago office and has practiced for more than 35 years exclusively in the area of executive compensation and employee retirement benefit issues for corporations, partnerships, executives, boards of directors, and fiduciaries. He also handles employee benefits and compensation litigation matters and the benefits and compensation aspects of change in control and public offering transactions.

Mr. Melbinger is also an adjunct professor of law at Northwestern University School of Law and the University of Illinois College of Law. He is considered one of the country's foremost experts in the area of executive compensation and has spoken extensively on all types of executive compensation and employee benefit plan issues. He is the author of the American Bankers Association's *Compliance Guide to Employee Benefit Trusts* and more than 75 articles on executive compensation and employee benefits topics. In addition, he writes the Compensation Blog for *CompensationStandards.com*, the oldest and most widely-read blog of its kind, and is an editor of *The Corporate Executive, mynqdc.com*, and *mystockoptions.com*. He was inducted as a fellow into the American College of Employee Benefit Counsel in 2005.

Mr. Melbinger is frequently quoted on executive compensation topics in the national press, has appeared as a commentator on numerous national television programs, and has testified before Congressional Committees on executive compensation topics.

Mr. Melbinger received a B.A. from the University of Notre Dame in 1980 and a J.D. from the University of Illinois College of Law in 1983.

Acknowledgments

Numerous current and former lawyers from Winston & Strawn LLP contributed to this volume, in particular, members of the Executive Compensation and Employee Benefits Department.

Winston & Strawn clients contributed more than they know with their challenging assignments and questions, and also by giving me a base to determine what issues employers most frequently encounter.

In short, despite the single name on the cover, this volume, like all others, is not the work of one person.

Table of Contents

Chapter 2: Change in Control Agreements

Chapter 3: Consulting Agreements

Chapter 12: Securities Law Compliance Issues Relating to Executive Compensation Plans

Chapter 18: Split-Dollar and Other Life Insurance Arrangements

Chapter 29: Ethical Issues, Conflicts and Privilege in Executive Compensation

Chapter 1

EXECUTIVE EMPLOYMENT AGREEMENTS

¶101 Overview—Executive Employment Agreements

An employment agreement is a legal contract between an employer and an executive that sets forth the terms of the employment relationship. No law requires an employer and an employee to set forth the terms of their relationship in a written agreement, and some employers do not use employment agreements for even their most senior executive officers. However, employers without any employment agreements are in the minority, as most employers feel it is necessary to have some form of written agreement for the employer's protection.

The employer may enter into employment agreements with as many or as few employees as it desires (subject to market forces, *i.e.*, many executives would not come to an employer without a written agreement). Although most employers limit employment agreements to senior executive officers, the majority of employers require all officers and nearly all employees to sign a confidentiality, noncompete or other agreement imposing restrictive covenants on the employees.

.01 Goals of the Parties

The employer and the executive have several goals in common in connection with the design and negotiation of compensation arrangements and employment agreements. Generally, both parties desire an arrangement that is compliant with all applicable laws, cost-effective and tax-effective to the employer, and tax-effective to the executive. Both parties also should seek an arrangement that is competitive with other employers and not frightening to regulators, investors, or potential acquirers.

.02 Common Provisions

The employment agreement could cover as many or as few aspects of the employment relationship as the parties desire. Among the terms and conditions that employment agreements commonly address are the following:

- Title(s) (see ¶185);
- Duties (see ¶185);
- Employment Term (see ¶185);
- Base Salary (see ¶125);
- Bonus(es) (see ¶125 and ¶145);
- Equity Compensation (see ¶135);

- Other Incentive Compensation (see ¶145);
- Retirement Plan Benefits (see ¶155);
- Health and Welfare Benefits (see ¶155);
- Perquisites (see ¶175);
- Severance Benefits (see ¶160);
- Change in Control Protection (see ¶160);
- Noncompete and Other Restrictive Covenants (see ¶165);
- Representations by the Executive;
- Arbitration Provision;
- Legal Fees to Negotiate Agreement;
- Legal Expenses of Litigation of Arbitration;
- Choice of Law and/or Forum (see ¶185);
- Successors;
- Notices; and
- Amendment.

The determination to use such agreements is a matter of business judgment for the board of directors and the members of senior management. See Practice Tool ¶10,020 for a checklist of employment agreement provisions and ¶10,010 for a sample executive employment agreement.

.03 The Negotiation

Like most negotiations, negotiating executive employment agreements is more of an art than a science. One of the most important factors of negotiating an executive employment agreement is that, at the conclusion of the negotiations, the parties' interests are inextricably intertwined for the near-term and, possibly, the long-term future. The employer and the executive will need to work together and trust each other to the highest possible degree for the immediate future and, likely, for at least the duration of the agreement.

Counsel for the executive and counsel for the employer should arrive at the negotiation with data and supporting information on comparable pay and benefits levels for similar executives at similar companies. This is the science part of the negotiation. Counsel should also understand and account for the direction of the market for executive talent. For example, during the boom years of 1998-2000, executives and their counsel could (and some did) demand and receive almost any amount or form of compensation or perquisites they wanted. Some of those executives ended up in a different kind of "big house" after the crash.

The Sarbanes-Oxley Act of 2002 ("SOX") began a push for better corporate governance in the area of executive compensation. However, in my judgment, 2004 was the real turning point where executive reforms began to take root. A conference sponsored by CompensationStandards.com in Fall 2004, which thereafter would become an annual conference on best practices, proved to be an important catalyst. A speech by the Chief of the SEC's Division of Corporation

Finance, on more fulsome disclosure of compensation arrangements was the SEC's opening salvo on this front, and seemed to energize attendees, who were the nation's leading compensation attorneys and consultants, to promote the adoption of best practices throughout corporate America.

The execution, amendment, or termination of management contracts and compensation plans involving directors or named executive officers must be disclosed on Form 8-K. Since August 2004, companies have been required to file a Form 8-K within four days of certain executive compensation and employment events (see ¶197). Significant rulemaking changes in 2006 and 2009 greatly expanded the amount and detail of executive compensation required to be reported by companies in their annual proxy statements.

Counsel must also understand the relationship element of the negotiations, and should endeavor to conduct the negotiation in a way that preserves the parties' ability to work together and trust each other. This is the art of the negotiation.

> **Comment:** The kind of approach and demand that may have worked for (1) an incoming executive, (2) at a public company, and (3) in 2000, could result in an employment termination when made by counsel for a current executive seeking to renew his agreement with a family-owned business in 2011.

It should be noted that while negotiating salary, bonus and equity compensation elements of the employment agreement can be somewhat exciting, sometimes the most important protection the executive and the employer will receive is in the so-called "boilerplate" provisions of the agreement (see ¶185).

Where an employer has a policy of not offering employment agreements (for whatever reason), the executive's counsel may be able to negotiate all the protections the executive needs into an offer letter (see ¶195).

¶115 Best Practices and Poor Pay Practices and Why They Matter

In July 2010, President Obama signed into law the Dodd-Frank Wall Street Reform and Consumer Protection Act (the "Dodd-Frank Act"). Section 951 of the Dodd-Frank Act added a new Section 14A to the Securities and Exchange Act of 1934 (the "Exchange Act"), entitled "Shareholder Approval of Executive Compensation" (referred to as "Shareholder Say on Pay") which provides that, not less frequently than once every three years, a company's annual proxy statement must include a separate resolution, subject to shareholder vote, to approve the compensation of the company's named executive officers (NEOs).

The Shareholder Say on Pay vote is a single "For" or "Against" vote on the total compensation package provided to the named executive officers, as disclosed in the company's Compensation Discussion and Analysis (CD&A), compensation tables, and any related material. If the overall packages of the NEOs are reasonable – even below market – but there is one perceived blemish, such as a gross-up on perquisite payments or a single-trigger golden parachute agreement, many shareholders may vote "no" on the package. *There is no other way for shareholders to register disapproval.* They cannot criticize or object to that one provision or practice only.

Shareholder advisory firms, such as Institutional Shareholder Services ("ISS") scrutinize the compensation packages of public companies and issue voting recommendations to institutional investors. These advisory firms and can often be a "swing vote" factor in the success of a vote on Shareholder Say on Pay.

.01 Shareholder Say on Pay

Dodd-Frank Act Section 951 added a new Section 14A to the Exchange Act, entitled "Shareholder Approval of Executive Compensation," which requires that, not less frequently than once every three years, a company's annual proxy statement must include a separate resolution, subject to non-binding shareholder vote, to approve the compensation of the company's named executive officers, as disclosed in the company's CD&A, compensation tables, and any related material. Section 951 also requires that, not less frequently than once every six years, the proxy statement must include a separate resolution subject to a non-binding shareholder vote to determine whether future votes on the resolutions required under the preceding paragraph will occur every one, two, or three years (see ¶3115).

The Shareholder Say on Pay vote is a single "yes" or "no" vote on the total compensation package provided to the NEOs, as described in the proxy statement. One questionable action, payment, or practice could cause shareholders to vote "Against," regardless of the reasonableness of the overall packages. Therefore, most public companies have focused on developing and implementing a strategy to maximize the likelihood of achieving a favorable vote on Shareholder Say on Pay. Many compensation committees have added one more factor to their consideration of each compensation issue or contract provision: How will we explain this provision or payment in the proxy statement CD&A, and will it increase the risk that shareholders will vote "Against" us on Shareholder Say on Pay?

.02 Compensation Clawback

Section 954 of the Dodd-Frank Act added new Section 10D, entitled "Recovery of Erroneously Awarded Compensation Policy," to the Exchange Act. Under Section 954, a company's compensation recovery policy **must** provide that:

> "in the event that the issuer is required to prepare an accounting restatement due to the material noncompliance of the issuer with any financial reporting requirement under the securities laws, the issuer will recover from any current or former executive officer of the issuer who received incentive-based compensation (including stock options awarded as compensation) during the 3-year period preceding the date on which the issuer is required to prepare an accounting restatement, based on the erroneous data, in excess of what would have been paid to the executive officer under the accounting restatement."

The SEC issued proposed rules under Section 954 in 2015, but has not issued final rules. Therefore, Section 954 and new Section 10D are not yet effective.

However, many companies now add a sentence to their executive employment agreements similar to the following: "Notwithstanding any provision in this Agreement to the contrary, compensation and awards paid or provided to the Executive under this Agreement will be subject to any Compensation Recovery Policy established by the Corporation and amended from time to time."

.03 Institutional Shareholder Services

ISS is a provider of proxy voting and corporate governance services. It analyzes public companies proxy statements and compensation programs and issues research and vote recommendations to institutional investors. The underlying premise of ISS is that good corporate governance ultimately results in increased shareholder value. ISS is currently considered the most influential of the proxy advisory firms and can often be a "swing vote" factor in the success of a vote on Shareholder Say on Pay.

In order for a company to get a "FOR" vote recommendation from ISS on Shareholder Say on Pay, a company's executive compensation package must pass a variety of tests. Each year ISS issues its U.S. Corporate Governance Policy Guidelines. These guidelines cover a variety of topics and include a list of "problematic pay practices," which may warrant recommendations of "AGAINST" or "WITHHOLD" votes.

.04 Best and Worst Pay Practices and Policies

Among the problematic pay practices, best pay practices and issues that ISS and other advisory firms focus on are the following:

1. Pay-for-performance, including samples of pay versus performance disclosure:
   a. ISS looks at the long-term (at least five years) alignment of the CEO's total direct compensation with the company's total (or relative) shareholder returns, with particular focus on the most recent three years. Looking for "disconnect" between performance and CEO pay.
   b. Glass Lewis gives an A-F curved grade (*i.e.*, 10% receive an A, 10% receive an F) to each company based on the link between pay and performance relative to each company's top five peer companies.

2. Whether the CEO's pay has increased or decreased, and the magnitude of the change, and the reason for the change in pay with respect to the pay mix (*i.e.*, performance- versus non-performance-based elements).

3. Whether the company prohibits hedging company stock ownership by executives.

4. Multi-year guarantees for salary increases, non-performance based bonuses, and equity compensation.

5. Overly generous new-hire packages, such as excessive "make whole" provisions without sufficient rationale.

6. Abnormally large bonus payouts without justifiable performance linkage or proper disclosure, including performance metrics that are

changed, canceled or replaced during the performance period without adequate explanation of the action and the link to performance.

7. Payment of dividends or dividend equivalents paid on unvested performance shares or units.

8. Change in control payments, including:

   a. A liberal change in control definition that could result in payments to the executive without an actual change in control occurring.

   b. Change in control payments exceeding three times of base salary and bonus.

   c. Change in control payments without loss of job or substantial diminution of job duties (single-trigger or walk-away).

   d. Agreements that provide for single or modified-single triggers, under which an executive may voluntarily leave for any reason and still receive the change-in-control severance package.

   e. Agreements that provide for an excise tax gross-up. Modified gross-ups would be treated in the same manner as full gross-ups.

9. Generous SERP or other non-qualified retirement plan benefits, including additional years of service not worked that result in significant benefits and/or inclusion of performance-based equity awards in the pension calculation.

10. Overly generous perquisites, including but not limited to: personal use of corporate aircraft, personal security systems maintenance and/or installation, car allowances, or executive life insurance.

At one time, ISS would not challenge the existence of problematic pay practices such as excise tax gross-ups, if the problematic provision had been in the employment agreements since before ISS began to object to it as problematic. However, ISS changed its approach in 2016, announcing:

> Would a legacy employment agreement that is automatically extended (e.g., has an evergreen feature) but is not otherwise amended warrant an adverse vote recommendation if it contains a problematic pay practice?

> Automatically renewing/extending agreements (including agreements that do not specify any term) are not considered a best practice, and existence of a problematic practice in such a contract is a concern. However, if an "evergreen" employment agreement is not materially amended in manner contrary to shareholder interests, it will be evaluated on a holistic basis, considering a company's other compensation practices along with features in the existing agreement.

Companies and committees should be conscious of the fact that ISS takes a firm approach to problematic pay practices in "grandfathered" agreements, including "evergreen" agreements with problematic pay practices. In fact, more recent ISS guidance does not even include the phrase "grandfathered."

¶115.04

¶125 Base Salary and Bonus(es)

The employment agreement should specify the executive's annual base salary or other mechanism of compensation. Many agreements also state whether the executive's base salary increases automatically and, if so, by how much or according to what measurement. The agreement could base an automatic increase in annual base salary on such measures as (1) an annual cost of living increase, (2) a flat percentage increase, or (3) an increase equal in amount to the percentage increase granted to other senior officers of the employer. The desirability of automatic annual increases depends on the party's point of view: one can view the increase as either requiring a minimum increase, or as capping the maximum increase.

> **Example:** ABC Corporation's employment agreement with Executive D could provide that: "Each year, the Executive's Base Salary shall be increased by an amount equal to the percentage of change in the Consumer Price Index (CPI) as indicated by 'The Consumer Price Index for All Urban Consumers (CPI-U) for the U.S. City Average for All Items,' published by the U.S. Department of Labor, Bureau of Labor Statistics (BLS) in the preceding calendar year."

Most employers believe that an annual review to determine increases is more appropriate than building in automatic increases. For the CEO, and perhaps other top-level executives, the board of directors (or compensation committee) conducts the review and determines the change in base salary. If increases are not automatic, the employment agreement should specify: (1) who will review the executive's performance and base salary, (2) when they will review it (generally at least annually, as of a specified date), and (3) when the first review will occur.

Finally, most employment agreements also provide that:

- The employer will pay the executive's base salary according to payroll practices in effect for all senior executive officers of the employer;
- The employer may increase the executive's annual base salary, but cannot reduce the executive's base salary without the executive's consent; and
- Any adjusted annual salary then becomes the executive's "base salary" for all other purposes of the agreement.

One of the unintended consequences of SOX and other legislation and agency rulemaking since then, was that executives tend to seek a greater percentage of their annual compensation paid as salary rather than bonus. Under SOX, if a public company is required to restate its accounting results due to material noncompliance, as a result of misconduct, with financial reporting requirements, the company's CEO and CFO are required to reimburse the company for any bonus or other incentive-based compensation or equity-based compensation and profits from the sale of the company's securities during the 12-month period following initial publication of the financial statements that had to be restated.[1]

---

[1] Act Section 304 of the Sarbanes-Oxley Act.

Many employment agreements also provide that the executive will be eligible to participate in the company's bonus and incentive programs, according to criteria set by the company's CEO, compensation committee or board of directors, and subject to the terms, conditions, restrictions and forfeiture provisions, if any, of such programs. Some agreements are more explicit about the executive's bonus opportunity, including more detail about the company's bonus program(s) and the executive's target annual bonus. However, very few employment agreements incorporate the specific terms and provisions of the company's bonus plan. Most agreements simply refer to the bonus plan and set forth the general parameters (see ¶ 145.)

¶ 135 Equity Compensation

An employment agreement will sometimes reference a specific equity grant to be awarded to the executive. Alternatively, the agreement will simply require the executive to participate in the employer's equity compensation plan on the same basis as other executives at his or her level. In either case, the employer ordinarily makes the actual grant of equity compensation through its regular equity compensation plan.

.01 Stock Options

Before 2005, stock options were by far the most common form of equity compensation. To ensure favorable accounting treatment, as well as the approval of institutional investors, employers nearly always granted options to purchase a fixed number of shares at an exercise price equal to fair market value of a share of employer stock on the grant date. Many employment agreements will specify the number of option shares that the employer will award to the executive, at least for the initial option award, and the applicable vesting schedule (see Chapter 7 [¶ 701 *et seq.*] for a detailed discussion of stock options).

Since 2005, FAS 123R (now known as Accounting Standards Codification Topic 718 or "ASC 718") has required employers to recognize an accounting expense for stock option awards just as for any other stock-based award, and the types of stock awards employers make vary greatly. Some of the most vocal proponents of stock options as the ideal method for aligning management's interests with those of stockholders have become the most vocal critics of options.

For example, Executive D's employment agreement with privately held ABC Corporation could provide as follows:

> On the Effective Date, ABC Corporation shall grant the Executive a nonquali-
> fied stock option ("Option") to purchase an aggregate of five percent (5%) of
> the issued and outstanding shares of common stock of ABC ("Option
> Shares"). The per share exercise price for the Option Shares to be issued
> pursuant to the exercise of the Option shall be the fair market value of a share
> of ABC's common stock ("Share") as of the Effective Date. The Option shall
> become vested immediately upon the Effective Date with respect to twenty
> percent (20%) of the Option Shares and shall become vested with respect to an
> additional one and two-thirds percent (1 2/3%) of the Option Shares on each
> subsequent first day of each subsequent month. Notwithstanding the preced-

ing sentence, the Option shall become vested immediately upon a Change of Control (as hereinafter defined). The Option shall be granted pursuant to an option agreement in the form attached hereto as Exhibit A. ABC may grant additional options to the Executive in the future.

Alternatively, the employment agreement could provide only the following promise:

The Executive shall be eligible to participate in any annual performance bonus plans, long-term incentive plans, and/or equity-based compensation plans established or maintained by ABC Corporation for its senior executive officers, including, but not limited to, the ABC Corporation Management Incentive Plan and the ABC Corporation Long-Term Incentive Plan.

.02 Restricted Stock, RSUs and Performance Shares

Restricted stock awards are the second most common equity compensation tool. In the basic restricted stock or performance shares scenario, the employer grants the executive a specified number of shares of stock, subject to forfeiture by the executive if he or she (1) leaves the employer before the shares vest or (2) fails to satisfy the performance criteria. Restricted stock units (RSUs) became a popular substitute for restricted stock award in the 1990s. Many employment agreements will specify the applicable vesting or performance criteria, at least for the initial award. When stock option expensing became required, employers' use of restricted stock and performance shares awards increased dramatically. See Chapter 8 (¶801 *et seq.*) for a detailed discussion of restricted stock, RSUs, and performance shares.

.03 Other Equity-Based Compensation

Other popular forms of equity-based compensation, particularly for private companies, include awards of stock appreciation rights or phantom stock. Stock appreciation rights ("SARs") are essentially the right to a payment in cash or shares of any increase in the value of the employer's shares from the time of grant to the time the SARs expire. Employers sometimes grant SARs in tandem with stock options. Phantom stock is a form of equity-based compensation similar to SARs (the terms are sometimes used interchangeably), but more closely resembling a restricted stock award. The phantom stock recipient has the right to receive, generally in cash, a payout equal to the full value of the underlying share of employer stock on a future date. See Chapter 9 (¶901 *et seq.*) for a detailed discussion of SARs and phantom stock.

In the context of a privately owned company, executives and the company will sometimes negotiate a right of first refusal in the event the owners decide to sell the company.

Example: Family-owned ABC Corporation could agree to the following language with Executive D:

ABC hereby grants to the Executive a right of first refusal on any Sale of the Company. In the event the Company receives a good faith *bona fide* offer for purchase, then the Company shall deliver to the Executive a certified written copy of such purchase offer. Thereafter, the Executive shall have sixty (60) days either to match the outstanding purchase offer by agreeing to purchase the Company or to decline to exercise his right of first refusal to purchase the Company. If the Executive agrees to purchase the Company, the Executive may accomplish such purchase either individually or as part of a group of investors, partners, or other financial business arrangements as the Executive, in his discretion, may deem necessary to complete the purchase transaction.

¶145 Bonuses and Other Incentive Compensation

Most employment agreements also address short and long-term incentive compensation, sometimes referred to as "bonus." Employers usually pay short-term incentive compensation in cash. Employers generally make long-term incentive compensation payouts in cash or employer stock. Neither type of incentive payout is taxable until the actual date of payment. See Chapter 15 (¶1501 *et seq.*) for a detailed discussion of non-equity incentive compensation.

.01 Signing Bonus

Some first time employment agreements for newly hired executives provide for a "signing bonus." This is a lump sum payable at the time the executive joins the employer. Employers often pay a signing bonus to compensate the executive for something he or she is leaving behind at the previous employer, such as a bonus for the current year. Employment agreements that provide for a substantial signing bonus often require the executive to repay all or part of the bonus if he or she leaves the employer before a specified date.

For example, Executive D's employment agreement with ABC Corporation could provide as follows:

> You will also receive a sign-on bonus of $100,000. ABC Corporation will pay you $50,000 within 30 days of your start date and pay you the remaining $50,000 after the Corporation has secured the first round of equity financing. If your employment is terminated by ABC for Cause (defined below) or if you terminate employment for reasons other than a Constructive Termination (defined below) within one year of your start date, you agree to make a prorated repayment of the total amount of sign-on bonus you have received.

Signing bonuses are sometimes referred to as "golden hellos." Among the significant signing bonuses paid in past years was the $45 million golden hello paid to Gary Wendt upon joining Conseco Inc. in 2000, and the $14,522,827 in restricted stock units and guaranteed bonus awarded to Gary Forsee on his joining Sprint in 2003.[2]

Rev. Rul. 2004-109[3] held that amounts an employer pays as a "signing bonus" are wages for purposes of the Federal Insurance Contributions Act (FICA), the Federal Unemployment Tax Act (FUTA), and the Collection of Income Tax at Source (Federal income tax withholding). In Rev. Rul. 2004-109, a baseball club had negotiated an employment agreement with a player under which the club would pay the player a signing bonus if he reports for spring training on time. The agreement provided that the signing bonus was not contingent on the player's future performance of services. The IRS ruled that the

---

[2] Paul Hodgson, "Sprint Hires Forsee as New CEO with a Golden Hello of More Than $14.5M," THE CORPORATE LIBRARY, April 2003.

[3] Rev. Rul. 2004-109, IRB 2004-50.

individual receives the signing bonus in connection with establishing the employer-employee relationship. The individual does not provide clear, separate, and adequate consideration for the payment that is not dependent upon the employer-employee relationship and its component terms and conditions. Thus, the signing bonus is part of the compensation the baseball club pays as remuneration for employment, making it wages regardless of the fact that the contract provides that the bonus is not contingent on the performance of future services.

The Code and regulations provide that amounts an employer pays an employee as remuneration for employment are wages, unless a specific exception applies.[4] The regulations also provide that the name by which the remuneration is designated is immaterial. Salaries, fees, and bonuses, for example, are all wages, if paid as compensation for employment.[5] The Code and the regulations also provide that any service of whatever nature performed by an employee for the person employing him is employment, unless a specific exemption applies.[6] Employment encompasses the establishment, maintenance, furtherance, alteration, or cancellation of the employer-employee relationship or any of the terms and conditions thereof. However, if an employee provides clear, separate, and adequate consideration for the employer's payment that is not dependent upon the employer-employee relationship and its component terms and conditions, the payment is not wages for purposes of FICA, FUTA, or Federal income tax withholding.

Many agreements that provide for a signing bonus also provide for a "clawback" of the signing bonus, applicable in certain circumstances in which the executive's employment is terminated before a certain date. Where the clawback clause is triggered, the tax consequences to the company and the executive are governed by the "claim of right" doctrine. Under the claim of right doctrine, the executive should be required to include in taxable income the amount of the signing bonus he or she receives. Since the executive is an individual and is therefore a cash method taxpayer, the amount is included in income in the year received.

The claim of right doctrine was set forth by the U.S. Supreme Court in *North American Oil Consolidated v. Burnet*:[7]

> If a taxpayer receives earnings under a claim of right and without restriction as to its disposition, he has received income which he is required to [report], even though it may still be claimed that he is not entitled to retain the money, and even though he may still be adjudged liable to restore its equivalent.

Under the claim of right doctrine, the executive will be taxable on the signing bonus as if it were not subject to restriction, and the company will receive a deduction for the amount of the signing bonus it pays pursuant to the agreement. If the executive is then required to return any portion of the signing

---

[4] Code Sec. 3121(a), Code Sec. 3306(b) and Code Sec. 3401(a); Reg. §31.3121(a)-1(b), Reg. §31.3306(b)-1(b) and Reg. §31.3401(a)-1(a)(1).

[5] Reg. §31.3121(a)-1(c), Reg. §31.3306(b)-1(c) and Reg. §31.3401(a)-1(a)(2).

[6] Code Sec. 3121(b) and Code Sec. 3306(c); Reg. §31.3121(b)-3(b) and Reg. §31.3306(c)-2(b).

[7] *North American Oil Consolidated v. Burnet*, 286 U.S. 417, 424 (1932).

bonus, the company would include the amount received in taxable income. The tax consequences to the executive of repayment of any portion of the signing bonus depends on the timing of the repayment and the events giving rise to the obligation to repay. If the executive repays any portion of the signing bonus to the company in the same calendar year it is received, the amount repaid is subtracted from the amount received for purposes of determining taxable income, since taxable income is determined as of year end.

The tax treatment applicable where a taxpayer restores a substantial amount held under a claim of right is set forth in Code Sec. 1341. This section provides an option for calculating the tax for the year such amount is returned, but it only applies if:[8]

- an item was included in gross income for a prior tax year because it appeared that the taxpayer had an unrestricted right to the such item;

- a deduction is allowable under another section of the Code because it was established after the close of such prior tax year that the taxpayer did not have an unrestricted right to the item or to a portion thereof; and

- the amount of such deduction exceeds $3,000.

If the above-listed requirements are met, then the taxpayer may do either of the following, whichever is more favorable for the taxpayer:[9]

- take the deduction in the amount of the repayment allowed by the other section of the Code; or

- calculate tax for the year of repayment without the deduction, but subtract the amount by which the tax (not taxable income) for the prior year would have decreased if the amount received under claim of right (or the portion of that amount subsequently repaid) was excluded from income.

The claim of right doctrine will not apply in all situations. In *Griffiths v. U.S.*,[10] the U.S. Court of Federal Claims denied the deduction sought by a former executive under the claim of right doctrine. The former executive sought a deduction on her tax return for a settlement she paid to her former employer, alleging that it was a return of consulting payments that she had reported as income over a period of years. The court disagreed. The fact that she had reported the consulting payments as income for each year supported the first step in the analysis — that the taxpayer have an unrestricted right to the income. However, the court found that the circumstance did not support the second part of the test - that the obligation to repay the funds must arise from the same circumstances that gave rise to the original inclusion in income. In this case, the court found, the taxpayer's obligation to pay was attributable to her having authorized improper, unsecured loans to her son while she was CEO, rather than the consulting payments.

---

[8] Code Sec. 1341(a)(1), Code Sec. 1341(a)(2) and Code Sec. 1341(a)(3).

[9] Code Sec. 1341(a)(4) and Code Sec. 1341(a)(5).

[10] *Griffiths v. U.S.*, 90 AFTR 2d 5609 (Ct. Fed. Cl. 2002).

.02 Target Bonus and Bonus Plan Structure

The structure and terms of bonus plans varies as much as any element of an executive compensation package. However, a common form of bonus plan is one that provides for varying payments equal to specified percentages of the executive's base salary, depending on whether the executive and/or the employer attain certain levels of performance. Often the employment agreement of a newly hired executive will specify a bonus guarantee for the first year of employment, equal to some minimum percentage of base salary.

For example, Executive D's employment agreement with ABC Corporation could provide as follows:

> The Executive shall be entitled to participate in an annual cash bonus program based on performance and calculated as a percentage of Annual Base Salary. Under the annual bonus program, the Executive's Target Bonus level shall be no less than 50% of the Executive's Annual Base Salary and the Executive's maximum bonus level shall be no greater than 80% of the Executive's Annual Base Salary. The annual cash bonus shall be paid no later than March 1 of the year following the year to which the bonus relates. The specific bonus program for the Executive and the Threshold, Target and Maximum performance levels under the bonus program for each fiscal year shall be established by the Board in its good faith determination after consultation with the Executive. Notwithstanding the foregoing, the Executive shall receive for 2010, no later than March 1, 2011, a bonus of at least 25% of her highest Annual Base Salary during 2010.

Very few employment agreements incorporate the specific terms and provisions of the employer's bonus plan. Instead, most agreements simply refer to the bonus plan and set forth the general parameters.

.03 Long-Term Incentive Plan

Increasingly, employers sponsor incentive plans that pay according to the performance of the executive, his or her division, the employer as a whole, or some combination of those factors, measured over a period of anywhere from two to five years. Again, although few employment agreements incorporate the specific terms and provisions of the employer's long-term plan, most agreements refer to the plan and set forth the general parameters. Typically, in a long-term incentive plan, the company retains a degree of discretion over the ultimate grant of the award. Many employers do not maintain a long-term incentive plan that is separate from their stock incentive plan.

¶155 Employee Retirement and Insurance Benefits

Most employment agreements simply provide that the executive will be entitled to participate in the qualified retirement plans (401(k) plans, pension plans, money purchase plans, profit sharing plans, ESOPs and the like) according to the terms of those plans. Qualified retirement plans are subject to various rules that, in combination, (1) require participation by nearly all employees on the same terms, and (2) ensure that highly compensated employees may not accrue a larger benefit under these plans. See Chapter 16 (¶1601 *et seq.*) for a detailed discussion of qualified retirement plans.

Life and long-term disability insurance coverage are arguably the most important benefits provided under any employment agreement. Severance benefits are important, because they can help an executive provide for his or her family during a rough patch. However, if the executive becomes permanently and totally disabled, the family not only needs funds to replace the employee's income, but also to care for a disabled family member. If the executive employee dies, the life insurance proceeds would be essentially for his or her family members to replace the executive's income and maintain their lifestyle. Recognizing this, the Code offers favorable tax treatment to employers that provide life and long-term disability insurance.[11] Large numbers in the salary, bonus and equity compensation area are more exciting, but the executive and his or her counsel need to be certain the employer provides this coverage. (See also ¶ 1945 for a general discussion of life and long-term disability insurance as an executive benefit.)

Nonqualified retirement plans, on the other hand, permit the employer to pick and choose among who will participate and what benefit they will accrue. Benefits under the employer's nonqualified retirement plan are frequently described in an employment agreement. See Chapter 17 (¶ 1701 *et seq.*) for a detailed discussion of nonqualified retirement plans.

.01 Nonqualified Plan Provisions in Employment Agreements

Many employment agreements provide simply that the executive will be permitted to participate in any nonqualified retirement plans maintained by the employer on the same terms and conditions that apply to similarly situated executives. Sometimes, the agreement will name the specific nonqualified plan or plans of the employer for which the executive will be eligible.

Because of the eligibility and benefit design flexibility of nonqualified plans, many employment agreements will use the employer's nonqualified plan, or require establishment of a new nonqualified plan, to make whole a newly hired executive for some benefit or amount the executive left behind at his or her previous employer. Sometimes, the employment agreement itself will contain all of the terms and conditions of the employer's promise to provide nonqualified retirement benefits to the executive.

For example, an executive employment agreement might provide as follows:

> ABC Corporation shall provide the Executive with an annual supplemental executive retirement benefit of one hundred thousand dollars ($100,000) per year payable in monthly installments commencing when the Executive attains age 65, and continuing for ten years. This supplemental executive retirement benefit is fully and immediately vested as of the date hereof. If the Executive dies before receiving payments for ten complete years, the Executive's designated beneficiary or, if no beneficiary has been designated, his spouse shall receive benefits in the same amount and at the same time as the Executive would have received if he had remained alive until age 75. Upon the Executive's termination of employment following a Change in Control (as hereinafter defined), termination of the Executive's employment by the Company

---

[11] Code Sec. 101.

other than for Cause (as hereinafter defined) or the Executive's termination of employment for Good Reason (as hereinafter defined), the present value of the supplemental executive retirement benefit shall be paid to the Executive. Such supplemental retirement benefit shall not be payable if the Executive's employment is terminated for Cause or if the Executive terminates his employment other than for Good Reason.

Because nonqualified plans are not subject to the required vesting provisions of the Internal Revenue Code and the Employee Retirement Income Security Act (ERISA), employers sometimes use the amounts accrued under these plans as enforcement tools for noncompete agreements.

.02 Funding Nonqualified Plan Promises

An occasional source of negotiation in executive employment agreements is the extent to which the employer will informally fund its promise to pay nonqualified retirement benefits. The essential tension in nonqualified plan design lies between the need to maintain the plan as unfunded (so that benefits are not currently taxable and the plan is not subject to most of Title I of ERISA), but secure executives' benefits. The most common solution to this dilemma is a rabbi trust. Although a rabbi trust has several advantages to the covered executive, for the employer, it primarily has disadvantages. See Chapter 17 (¶1701 *et seq.*) for a detailed discussion of rabbi trusts.

For executives at some companies, informal funding through a rabbi trust is not enough. Unlike a qualified plan, benefits under a nonqualified plan would be completely lost if the company files for bankruptcy. For this reason, according to its 2003 proxy statement, the board of directors of Delta Air Lines, Inc. approved the funding of employee grantor trusts to secure the nonqualified retirement benefits of 33 management personnel. Amounts held in these so-called secular trusts were not available to Delta's creditors in its insolvency. See ¶2435 for a detailed discussion of Delta's use of so-called "secular trusts."

.03 Insurance and Welfare Benefits

Most employment agreements simply provide that the executive will be entitled to participate in the health and welfare benefits and insurance arrangements according to the terms of those plans. See Chapter 19 (¶1901 *et seq.*) for a detailed discussion of welfare benefit plans.

For example, an executive employment agreement might provide as follows:

The Executive shall be entitled to participate in and receive the benefits of ABC Corporation's benefit plans, programs, policies, and practices for senior executives, as adopted from time to time and as amended or modified from time to time by the Board. The benefits under the benefit plans, programs, policies, and practices available to the Executive shall be no less favorable than those available to other senior executives and commensurate with his position and salary.

However, many employment agreements will expressly provide for special insurance arrangements for the executive.

.04 Supplemental Life or AD&D Insurance

The most common additional welfare benefit provided for in executive employment agreements is additional life insurance coverage. Sometimes, the insurance takes the form of "split-dollar" life insurance. See Chapter 18 (¶ 1801 *et seq.*) for a detailed discussion of life insurance and split-dollar life insurance.

In the employment context, a split-dollar life insurance arrangement is an arrangement between the owner of a life insurance policy and a non-owner, under which the employer pays all or part of the premiums and the beneficiary of all or part of the death benefit is designated by the executive or is any person the executive would reasonably be expected to name as beneficiary. (Split-dollar is not involved if the insurance is merely group-term life insurance coverage.) Between them, the employer and the executive split the other benefits of the policy (*i.e.*, dividends, cash surrender value, and so forth) as they see fit. SOX, coupled with regulations issued by the IRS, decreased public companies' use of split-dollar arrangements.

.05 Executive Physicals

Some executive employment agreements will provide for supplemental, executive-only medical coverage. This coverage may provide for the full payment by the employer of all of the executive's deductible, co-payments and other out-of-pocket expenses, or it may provide coverage for special benefits such as an annual physical. Some companies require their key executives to obtain annual physicals. The annual physical is "medical care" within the meaning of Code Sec. 213(d), and is therefore excludible from the executive's income. If the employer's medical plan is self-insured, the plan may not cover only executives without creating a discrimination issue. The portion of a self-insured medical plan that provides for diagnostic procedures is exempt from discrimination testing, so long as the procedures are performed at a facility that performs only medical (and ancillary) services.[12]

.06 Long-Term Care Insurance

The aging of baby boomers has led to an increase in demand for long-term care insurance coverage. Insurance companies have responded by developing a new kind of insurance aimed at helping to offset the high cost of long-term care. Insurance companies offer both individual policies and employer-sponsored group products. Employer-sponsored policies offered to a large group of people can provide coverage on a more affordable basis.

¶160 Severance and Change in Control Provisions

Among the most negotiated provisions of any executive employment agreement are the provisions on severance and change in control. The terms of severance are the single most important provision of the employment agreement for many executives because they represent the executive's main protection in the "worst-case scenario." Salary, bonuses and stock prices can go up and down, but

---

[12] Reg. § 1.105-11(g).

the sudden loss of compensation and health benefits would be the most person-ally devastating to many executives.

Fortunately for executives, severance provisions have become commonplace in most agreements, in most industries. In fact, to remain competitive in the ongoing struggle to hire and retain executive talent, most employers need to provide severance benefits—and many need to provide change in control protection as well.

An employer should periodically study what the "market" is for executive severance in its industry segment—both as to amount of severance and circumstances under which severance is and is not paid. Public companies may be able to obtain a quick idea of the severance market by reviewing the most recent proxy statements of companies in their peer group. The media and institutional shareholder groups have sharply criticized large severance amounts paid to failed executive officers.[13] See Chapter 14 (¶1401 *et seq.*) for a detailed discussion of severance benefits.

.01 Release of Claims

An employment agreement that provides severance typically will require the executive to execute a release of claims in return for severance benefits. Although it is nearly always a good idea for an employer to seek a release of claims from terminating employees, the fact that a waiver of claims under the Age Discrimination in Employment Act is only valid if the employee receives consideration for it is another good reason to include a provision making the receipt of severance contingent on the executive's executing a release of claims.[14]

The terms of the release itself are important. In 2016, a federal district court case faced an issue we see all too often. In *Willis Re, Inc. v. Hearn*[15], a chief executive officer announced his "retirement" from his long-time employer – and went to work for a competitor. The company sought repayment from the former CEO of a portion of a $1.75 million incentive award made to him during the three years before his retirement. According to the former CEO, the governing award agreement allowed him to retain the award if he retired.

In March 2013, 2014, and 2015, the parties signed letter agreements making "AIP Awards" to the CEO of $1,750,000 each for 2012, 2013, and 2014, subject to:

> If your employment with Willis ends prior to December 31, [2015] [2016] [2017] for any reason other than your incapacity to work due to your permanent disability (as "disability" or a substantially similar term is defined within an applicable Willis long term disability plan/policy), death, your redundancy (as redundancy is determined by Willis in accordance with its usual human resource administration practices) or your retirement, you will be obligated to repay to Willis a pro-rata portion of the net amount . . . of the Willis Retention Award (the "Repayment Obligation").

---

[13] See Floyd Norris, "Dynergy Chief Is Much Richer for Being Forced Out," New York Times, May 30, 2002.

[14] 29 U.S.C. §626(f).

[15] 200 F.Supp.3d 540 (E.D Pa. 2016).

To define "retirement" the award agreements referred to (i) "your employment agreement" or (ii) "a written retirement policy applicable to you as a Willis employee" or (iii) "by reference to the ending of your employment at such mandatory age as may apply in the applicable employment jurisdiction" or (iv) "as may be determined by Willis in its absolute discretion." The pension plan provided for retirement benefits, including an "Early Retirement Benefit" for a participant who retires on his "Early Retirement Date," which the plan defined as the first day of any month following the date the participant attains age 55 and has completed at least 10 years of service.

In May 2015, when he was 59-years old and employed by the company for 21 years, the CEO announced his "decision to retire from Willis Re Inc., effective May 15, 2015 to explore other options and pursue other interests." The company agreed that the CEO was eligible for an "Early Retirement Benefit" under the pension plan, but argued that the pension plan was not a "written retirement policy" under the AIP Award letters. Instead, the company claimed that the AIP Awards allowed it to define "retirement under in its absolute discretion under subsection (iv) and that it had determined that the CEO did not retire.

Rather than construing the ambiguous contract terms against the drafter of the agreement, as many courts would do, the court instead announced that it would not assume the contract's language "was chosen carelessly" or "that the parties were ignorant of the meaning of the language employed."

> The words used in subsection (ii) are "written retirement policy," not "Pension Plan." If these sophisticated parties negotiated incentive payments for a chief executive officer intended the term "written retirement policy" to be defined as eligibility for benefits under the Pension Plan, they were free to include it. The parties could have done so in the same way the parties expressly defined "disability" in the phrase "incapacity to work due to your permanent disability" as the definition "within an applicable Willis long term disability plan/policy" and "redundancy" as "determined by Willis in accordance with its usual human resource administration practices." The parties could have referred to the Pension Plan in subsection (ii), but did not do so.

The court held that the company was entitled to define "retirement under the AIP Awards in its absolute discretion" and upheld the company's decision that the CEO did not retire. At this stage, the company won. However, because the court's decision was a fairly close run thing, the CEO is likely to appeal it – unless the parties negotiate a settlement. Either way, it will lead to more legal costs and headaches for the company, which could have been avoided through better drafting.

Finally, we note that because the CEO left to work for a competitor, it seems like the case should have been an easy one. The court observed that the CEO had acknowledged his obligation to "comply with certain terms and conditions applicable to time after his retirement from Willis, including an obligation not to compete with Willis for a period of [12] months beginning May 15, 2015." However, apparently those provisions also were not clear.

¶160.01

.02 Change in Control

Change in control provisions typically cover only a handful of executives at the top of company management. As with severance, it is useful to know what the "market" is in the employer's industry for change in control provisions. Because of the number of issues and terms necessary in a change in control agreement, including the definition of "change in control," the type of trigger, the protected period, the form and amount of benefits, and whether payouts will be subject to a "gross-up payment," these agreements are often set forth in a legal document separate from the executive's employment agreement. See Chapter 2 (¶ 201 *et seq.*) for a detailed discussion of change in control agreements.

.03 Defining a "For Cause" Termination

Many executive agreements and severance plans include a provision that provides for severance payments for a termination by the company without cause. The problem is that many companies have not reviewed or revised the definition of "cause" in their plans and agreements, and the definition is too narrow. Companies should consider revisions to the definition of "cause" in their plans and agreements in the following specific respects.

"Cause" should include such items as filing a fraudulent CEO/CFO certification under Section 302 or 906 of SOX. SOX requires companies to adopt a Code of Conduct.[16] Thus, publicly traded companies might want to include the language similar to the following:

'Cause' means . . . the Executive violates the Company's Code of Ethics or any of the Company's internal controls, procedures, and/or policies, including, but not limited to the Company's policy on sexual harassment.

Plans and agreements should clarify that, an executive's employment shall be deemed to have terminated for cause if, after the executive's employment has terminated, facts and circumstances are discovered that would have justified a termination for cause. Upon finding "misconduct" relating to filing financials with the SEC, SOX Section 304 permits the SEC to force a CEO or CFO to pay back any bonuses, incentive-based and equity-based compensation, and profits from stock sales that were paid or received during the twelve-month period following the initial filing of the incorrect SEC filing. A potential trap under SOX Section 304 is that a CEO or CFO who engages in misconduct that results in a restatement of the corporation's financial reports could potentially leave the corporation before the restatement and retain his or her bonus and/or severance benefits. To fix this problem, "cause" should be defined to ensure that benefits can be "clawed" back from the CEO and CFO who caused the incorrect filing to be made.[17]

---

[16] See SEC Release Nos. 33-8177; 34-47235; Disclosure Required by Sections 406 and 407 of the Sarbanes-Oxley Act of 2002. "We are adopting rules and amendments requiring companies, other than registered investment companies, to include two new types of disclosures in their annual reports filed pursuant to the Securities Exchange Act of 1934 . . . Second, the rules require a company to disclose whether it has adopted a code of ethics that applies to the company's principal executive officer, principal financial officer, principal accounting officer or controller, or persons performing similar functions."

[17] For example, in 2005, International Paper added a provision to its long-term incentive compen-

> For example: "A Participant's Service shall be deemed to have terminated for Cause if, after the Participant's Service has terminated, facts and circumstances are discovered that would have justified a termination for Cause."

Many companies include a definition of cause that specifically refers to violations of securities laws in their equity incentive plans and employment agreements. Some companies require that the executive cooperate with internal or government investigations. The following are two examples of the definition of "cause" taken from various incentive plans and employment agreements.

> "Cause" shall be limited to: . . . (b) Indictment or a violation of a federal or state law or regulation which indictment or violation is for a crime which is a felony under federal or state law, or any violation of state or federal securities laws involving securities of MarketWatch which would result in a civil penalty being imposed by the U.S. Securities and Exchange Commission or similar state securities law authority.[18]

> "Cause" shall mean any one or more of the following: . . . (vi) An uncurable loss by Executive of any license or registration that is necessary for Executive to perform the duties of President, or the imposition by a self-regulatory organization of special supervision or other special requirements as prerequisites for maintaining any license or registration that is necessary for Executive to perform the duties of President, or the commission of any act or occurrence of any event that could result in the statutory disqualification of Executive from being employed or otherwise associated with a broker-dealer . . . [19]

Companies in regulated industries, such as gaming, energy, defense, banking or other financial services, should include special provisions in their definitions of for cause termination. For example, a gaming company might want to include the language similar to the following:

> "Cause" means . . . being denied a gaming license by any state gaming board or any other gaming authority having jurisdiction over the operations of the Company or its subsidiaries or affiliates ('Gaming Body'), or if the Executive's individual license issued by any Gaming Body is suspended, revoked, sanctioned or reprimanded for any period of time or for any conduct; or if the Executive knowingly violates any statute, rule or regulation of any Gaming Body, the United States Coast Guard, or any other governmental body having jurisdiction over the business activities of the Company.

Companies also might want to include the language providing that reasons for a "cause" termination include the executive's failure to cooperate with the company in any internal investigation or administrative, regulatory or judicial proceeding. Some employment agreements require that an executive cooperate with internal or government investigations not in the definition of "cause," but elsewhere in the agreement. For example:

> During the Employment Period and thereafter, Executive shall cooperate with the Company and its Subsidiaries in any internal investigation or administrative, regulatory or judicial proceeding as reasonably requested by the Company (including, without limitation, Executive being available to the

---

(Footnote Continued)

sation plans that explicitly give the company the right to "recover compensation paid to a participant in cases of a restatement of the company's financial statements, due to errors, omissions or fraud."

[18] From BigCharts Inc. 1999 Employment Agreement.

[19] From Charles Schwab Corp. 2002 Employment Agreement.

Company upon reasonable notice for interviews and factual investigations, appearing at the Company's request to give testimony without requiring service of a subpoena or other legal process, volunteering to the Company all pertinent information and turning over to the Company all relevant documents which are or may come into Executive's possession, in all cases by providing truthful and accurate information and all at times and on schedules that are reasonably consistent with Executive's other permitted activities and commitments). In the event the Company requires Executive's cooperation in accordance with this paragraph, solely in recognition of Executive's time and expenses he may incur, the Company shall pay Executive a per diem reasonably determined by the Board and reimburse Executive for reasonable expenses incurred in connection therewith (including lodging and meals, upon submission of receipts, and reasonable attorneys' fees, except in relation to matters as to which Executive is liable for negligence or misconduct).[20]

Cooperation. The Executive agrees, upon reasonable notice, to cooperate fully with the Corporation and its legal counsel on any matters relating to the conduct of any litigation, claim, suit, investigation or proceeding involving the Corporation in connection with any facts or circumstances occurring during the Executive's employment with the Corporation in which the Corporation reasonably determines that the Executive's cooperation is necessary or appropriate.[21]

All well drafted employment agreements, equity award plans, and executive retirement programs provide for forfeiture in the event of a "for cause" termination. However, what happens when the company does not discover an executive's malfeasance until after he or she has left? Several court cases have held that companies could not rely on after-acquired evidence of executive misconduct to justify a "for cause" termination and forfeiture of compensation. While every case is unique, these cases highlight the need for companies to draft the "for cause" termination provisions in their plans and agreements to specifically allow for the use of after-acquired evidence.

In *Dell Computer Corp. v. Rodriguez*[22], the Fifth Circuit Court of Appeals refused to allow Dell to recover option exercise profits in excess of $2.7 million when it discovered financial irregularities three months after signing a separation agreement that treated Rodriguez as an employee for option vesting and exercise purposes. In *Teter v. Republic Parking Systems Inc.*[23], a Tennessee State Court held that the company could not rely on information learned after it discharged the executive that he had used his company computer to view pornographic web sites during work hours to deny him more than $900,000 in severance payments. In *Rinaldi v. CCX Inc.*[24], the Fourth Circuit Court of Appeals decided that a former executive was entitled to severance benefits despite that company's assertion that it would have fired the executive for "cause," and therefore would not have been liable for severance benefits under his employment agreement, if it had known that the executive had been obtaining cash reimbursements for business travel on which he used frequent flyer miles.

---

[20] From Samsonite Corp. 2004 Employment Agreement.

[21] From Intersections Inc. 2004 Employment Agreement.

[22] 390 F.3d 377 (5thCir. 2004).

[23] 181 S.W.3d 330 (2005).

[24] 49 EBC 1785 (4th Cir. 2010).

The unfortunate reality is that many companies do not discover the inappropriate or illegal conduct of a former employee until after he has voluntarily left the company. Employers could add the following sentence at the end of the "for cause" definition: "For purposes of this Agreement, a Participant's Service shall be deemed to have terminated for Cause if, after the Participant's Service has terminated, facts and circumstances are discovered that would have justified, in the opinion of the Board, a termination for Cause."

Finally, some companies provide that, for new hires, where applicable, a termination "for cause" also shall include termination by the company of the executive based on the executive's failure to satisfactorily complete any part of the company's pre-employment screening process being performed in connection with the execution of the Agreement.

.04 Other Required Provisions for Regulated Industries

As noted briefly above, companies in regulated industries, such as gaming, energy, defense, banking or other financial services, may need to include special provisions in their employment agreements. For example, all FDIC-insured institutions are required to include a provision that automatically terminates all obligations under the employment agreement if the institution is in default.[25]

This requirement became the subject of litigation in *Lanigan v. Resolution Trust Corp.*[26] In *Lanigan*, the plaintiff/former executive argued that the Resolution Trust Corp. had breached the severance provision in his employment agreement with Olympic Savings because the applicable regulation and the agreement provision, each provide that the termination of the agreement obligations does not effect any of the employee's vested rights: "if (Olympic]is in default, as said term is defined at Section 401(d) of the National Housing Act (12 U.S.C.A. § 1724[d]) all obligations under this Agreement shall terminate as of the date of such default. However, vested rights of [plaintiff] and [Olympic] shall not be thereby effected."[27] The Resolution Trust Corp. argued that the employment agreement terminated as a matter of law when Olympic was placed into receivership and that therefore, plaintiff's right to severance pay was not protected under regulation and the agreement provision.

The court noted that, although only a few courts have addressed the issue of whether severance agreement provisions vest so as to survive a §563.39 default termination, "These cases have held, almost uniformly, that §563.39 operates to terminate the employment contract by operation of law upon default. [Citations omitted] Therefore, these cases go on to reason, severance or termination benefits conditioned upon termination without cause never vest prior to the termination of the employment contract."[28]

---

[25] 12 C.F.R. § 563.39

[26] *Lanigan v. Resolution Trust Corp.*, 1993 U.S. Dist. LEXIS 7485 (N.D. Ill., June 1, 1993).

[27] 12 C.F.R. § 563.39(b)(4).

[28] *Lanigan v. Resolution Trust Corp.*, 1993 U.S. Dist. LEXIS 7485 (N.D. Ill., June 1, 1993).

.05 Contract Cancellation Payment

In Rev. Rul. 2004-110[29] the IRS attempted to resolve the issues of whether an amount paid to an employee as consideration for the cancellation of an employment contract and relinquishment of contract rights is ordinary income, and wages for purposes of FICA, FUTA, and federal income tax withholding. The IRS ruled that an amount paid to an employee as consideration for cancellation of an employment contract and relinquishment of contract rights is ordinary income, and wages for purposes of FICA, FUTA, and federal income tax withholding.

The IRS described a situation in which an employee performs services under a written employment contract providing for a specified number of years of employment. The contract does not provide for any payments to be made by either party in the event the contract is cancelled by mutual agreement. Before the end of the contract period, the employee and the employer agree to cancel the contract and negotiate a payment from the employer to the employee in consideration for the employee's relinquishment of his contract rights to the remaining period of employment.

The Code and regulations provide that amounts an employer pays an employee as remuneration for employment are wages, unless a specific exception applies.[30] The regulations also provide that the name by which the remuneration is designated is immaterial.[31] Furthermore, the remuneration is wages even though at the time paid the relationship of employer and employee no longer exists.[32]

The Code and the regulations also provide that any service of whatever nature performed by an employee for the person employing him is employment, unless a specific exemption applies.[33] Employment encompasses the establishment, maintenance, furtherance, alteration, or cancellation of the employer-employee relationship or any of the terms and conditions thereof. If the employee provides clear, separate, and adequate consideration for the employer's payment that is not dependent upon the employer-employee relationship and its component terms and conditions, the payment is not wages for purposes of FICA, FUTA, or Federal income tax withholding.

Under the facts presented in the ruling, the employee receives the payment as consideration for canceling the remaining period of his employment contract and relinquishing his contract rights. As such, the payment is part of the compensation the employer pays as remuneration for employment. The employee does not provide clear, separate, and adequate consideration for the employer's payment that is not dependent upon the employer-employee relationship and its component terms and conditions. Thus, the payment provided by the employer to the employee is wages for purposes of FICA, FUTA, and

---

[29] Rev. Rul. 2004-110, IRB 2004-50.

[30] Code Sec. 3121(a), Code Sec. 3306(b) and Code Sec. 3401(a); Reg. §31.3121(a)-1(b), Reg. §31.3306(b)-1(b) and Reg. §31.3401(a)-1(a)(1).

[31] Reg. §31.3121(a)-1(c), Reg. §31.3306(b)-1(c) and Reg. §31.3401(a)-1(a)(2).

[32] Reg. §31.3121(a)-1(i), Reg. §31.3306(b)-1(i) and Reg. §31.3401(a)-1(a)(5).

[33] Code Sec. 3121(b) and Code Sec. 3306(c); Reg. §31.3121(b)-3(b) and Reg. §31.3306(c)-2(b).

Federal income tax withholding. This conclusion applies regardless of how the parties characterize the remuneration or whether the employment relationship still exists at the time the payment is made.

Additionally, the IRS ruled that the payment received by the employee is taxable as ordinary income and not a payment for property that could qualify for taxation as capital gain. To qualify as capital gain, eligible for the reduced rates in Code Sec. 1(h), a payment must be received in connection with a "sale or exchange" of "property," as those terms are used in Code Sec. 1221, Code Sec. 1222 and Code Sec. 1231. Consideration received for the transfer or termination of a right to receive income for the past or future performance of services is a substitute for ordinary income, taxable as such.

The IRS stated that, with respect to the application of FICA and Federal income tax withholding, Rev. Rul. 55-520[34] and Rev. Rul. 58-301[35] erred in their analysis by failing to apply the Code and regulations appropriately to the question of whether the payments made in cancellation of the employment contract were wages. Accordingly, the IRS modified and superseded Rev. Rul. 55-520 and Rev. Rul. 58-301, and modified Rev. Rul. 74-252[36] and Rev. Rul. 75-44[37] to the extent their holdings regarding FICA, FUTA, RRTA, and federal income tax withholding rely on distinguishing Rev. Rul. 58-301. The IRS observed that the specific holdings in Rev. Rul. 58-301 and Rev. Rul. 75-44 that payments were ordinary income remain correct.

¶165 Noncompetes and Other Restrictive Covenants

Most employers will agree to provide substantial compensation to their senior executives without much of a fight. However, employers want to know (and ensure) that those executives will not use the knowledge and experience gained in their employ to compete with, or solicit employees or customers from, the employer. Therefore, most executive employment agreements include noncompete provisions and other restrictive covenants. Restrictive covenants are not enforceable in every state or under all circumstances. However, the majority of states permit enforcement of restrictive covenants that are reasonable. See Chapter 4 (¶401 *et seq.*) for a detailed discussion of restrictive covenants.

.01 Nondisclosure and Nondisparagement

Most employment agreements require the executive to agree that during his or her employment with the employer, and for a period thereafter, the executive will not use, divulge or make accessible to any person any of the employer's confidential information. Additionally, well-drafted agreements often provide that the executive will not make disparaging comments about the employer or its officers, directors or employees during or following employment. Finally, the employment agreement should provide that the executive, following employment termination for whatever reason, will deliver to the employer all property

---

[34] Rev. Rul. 55-520, 1955-2 CB 393.
[35] Rev. Rul. 58-301, 1958-1 CB 23.

[36] Rev. Rul. 74-252, 1974-1 CB 287.
[37] Rev. Rul. 75-44, 1975-1 CB 15.

of the employer and will not take or copy property or information of the employer.

The Dodd-Frank Act amended the Exchange Act by adding Section 21F, "Whistleblower Incentives and Protection." Section 21F only applies to publicly-traded companies governed by the Exchange Act. The Congressional purpose underlying these provisions was "to encourage whistleblowers to report possible violations of the securities laws by providing financial incentives, prohibiting employment-related retaliation, and providing various confidentiality guarantees." In 2011, the SEC adopted Rule 21F-17, which provides in relevant part:

> (a) No person may take any action to impede an individual from communicating directly with the Commission staff about a possible securities law violation, including enforcing, or threatening to enforce, a confidentiality agreement . . . with respect to such communications.

Rule 21F-17 became effective on August 12, 2011.

In April 2015, the SEC announced its first enforcement action against a company for using improperly restrictive language in confidentiality agreements with the potential to stifle the whistleblowing process. The SEC charged a Houston-based company with violating Rule 21F-17 by requiring witnesses in certain internal investigations interviews to sign confidentiality statements with language warning that they could face discipline and even be fired if they discussed the matters with outside parties without the prior approval of KBR's legal department. Since these investigations included allegations of possible securities law violations, the SEC found that these terms violated Rule 21F-17. Without admitting or denying the charges, the company agreed to pay a $130,000 penalty to settle the SEC's charges and the company voluntarily amended its confidentiality statement by adding language making clear that employees are free to report possible violations to the SEC and other federal agencies without company approval or fear of retaliation.

The language used by the company read:

> I understand that in order to protect the integrity of this review, I am prohibited from discussing any particulars regarding this interview and the subject matter discussed during the interview, without the prior authorization of the Law Department. I understand that the unauthorized disclosure of information may be grounds for disciplinary action up to and including termination of employment.

The SEC demanded the addition of the following additional language:

> Nothing in this Confidentiality Statement prohibits me from reporting possible violations of federal law or regulation to any governmental agency or entity, including but not limited to the Department of Justice, the Securities and Exchange Commission, the Congress, and any agency Inspector General, or making other disclosures that are protected under the whistleblower provisions of federal law or regulation. I do not need the prior authorization of the Law Department to make any such reports or disclosures and I am not required to notify the company that I have made such reports or disclosures.

Companies should consider adding a paragraph similar to the foregoing in any employment agreement that contains a confidentiality or non-disclosure provision.

.02 Noncompete

Many executive employment agreements include noncompete provisions. Most employment agreements require the executive to agree that during his or her employment with the employer, and for a period thereafter, the executive will not engage in any employment, consulting or other business activity that is competitive with the employer's business or usurp or take advantage of any business opportunity relating to the employer's business. Noncompete provisions are not enforceable in every state or under all circumstances. However, the majority of states permit enforcement of noncompete provisions that are reasonable as to geographic scope and duration, particularly if they are linked to severance payments.

.03 Nonsolicit

Many executive employment agreements also include provisions that prohibit the executive from directly or indirectly soliciting any employee of the employer to leave employment and join or become affiliated with any business that is competitive with the employer's business within the geographic area. Well-drafted employment agreements often also include provisions that prohibit the executive from directly or indirectly soliciting any supplier, customer, or other person or entity that had a business relationship with the employer from continuing to do business with or entering into business with the employer.

.04 Licensing the Right to Publicity

A company that has a "rock star" executive, should consider licensing the executive's right to the executive's image for publicity. The company could do this by providing in the employment agreement that the company owns the right to use the executive's image. This could be particularly useful in California, where non-competes generally are not enforceable.

This theory was played out in litigation between Microsoft and Google. Microsoft lost a high profile executive (labeled by some as the "father of the internet in China") to Google. To add insult to injury, Google began using the executive's familiar image in much of its local advertising and in recruiting posters. However, Google claimed that the executive was not involved in actual hiring and other duties that could have violated his non-compete agreement. Microsoft argued that the executive was the engineering equivalent of a rock star, and that Google's use of his image in its recruiting was conduct that arguably violated the executive's obligations to Microsoft. The court disagreed, saying if Microsoft wanted to restrict the use of the executive's likeness, it should have written that restriction into the employment agreement.

.05 Remedies and Enforceability

Most executive employment agreements provide that if a former executive violates the noncompete or other restrictive covenants of the agreement, the employer either may seek to: (1) obtain an injunction preventing the former executive from continued violation, or (2) forfeit some form of severance or retirement payment or equity compensation award otherwise payable to the former executive. Courts are more likely to enforce a noncompete or other restrictive covenant that provides for the former employee to forfeit some form of compensation than one that seeks to prevent the former employee from earning a living. See ¶475 for a detailed discussion of the enforceability of restrictive covenants.

Moreover, most states allow a judge to modify a noncompete or other restrictive covenant to reduce its scope to a level that may be enforced. However, some states only permit a judge to modify the written covenant where the employment agreement explicitly permits such modification (a so-called "blue-pencil" provision).

> **Planning Note:** The restrictive covenant section of an employment agreement should invite and encourage the court to modify any provision the court deems invalid or unenforceable to the extent and in the manner necessary to render the same valid and enforceable.

¶175 Perquisites and Other Compensation

The salary, bonus and equity compensation provisions in an executive's employment agreement make up the bulk of the value of the overall employment package offered by the employer. However, nearly all executive employment agreements also include some forms of perquisites and/or other compensation. While the recent excesses of the compensation packages for CEOs at Tyco, WorldCom and other scandal-ridden companies have cast an unwelcome light on many executive perquisites, employers have not eliminated the manifold forms of legitimate and appropriate compensation and perquisites.

.01 Special Tax-Favored Benefits and Perquisites

Companies can provide executives with certain benefits and perquisites on a tax-favored basis. Among these benefits are the following:

1. Relocation expenses and benefits.

2. Employer-provided automobile: The value or reimbursement to an executive for business use is excludable as a working condition fringe benefit. The executive's personal use of the automobile would be taxable, generally based on the "annual lease value." Chauffeurs or drivers provided or reimbursed by the employer must be valued separately from the vehicle they drive.

3. *Bona fide* business-oriented security concern:[38] Car, plane, home, family and travel.

4. Employer-provided meals: Meals furnished in-kind, from an eating facility owned or leased by the employer, located on the employer's prem-

---

[38] Reg. § 1.132-5(m).

ises, for the employer's convenience, during or immediately before or after the employees' workday, may be excludable from income.

5. Outplacement services generally can be excludable from an executive's income as a working condition fringe.

6. The use of on-premises athletic facilities is not taxable to the executive.

7. Gifts to charities in the executive's name are generally not taxed to the executive, and are deductible by the employer.

.02 Outplacement and Career Transition Services

Many employment agreements provide for the company to provide the executive with outplacement and career transition services. However, many other agreements overlook this benefit, which the company generally can provide at little cost, but which can be extremely valuable to the former executive.

Some C-level executives believe that the best way to find a new position is through word of mouth. This works well for some of them, but many other executives would be better served by the evolving area of career transition services. Today, these services include more than advice on preparing a resume and finding a new job.

For example, an executive employment agreement could contain the following language regarding outplacement and career transition services:

> The Company will pay the full cost of professional executive career transition services (*e.g.*, outplacement and life planning services) to be provided to the Executive by an outplacement firm with Master Coaches who have been former Presidents and CEOs with P&L experience. The Executive will select the outplacement firm and the Company the costs upon the Executive's presentation of an invoice describing the services to be provided, equal to twenty percent (20%) of the Executive's prior year's total cash compensation (base salary and annual bonus) with minimum fee of $100,000 and a maximum fee of $200,000.[39]

.03 Stock or Home Purchase Loans

Many public companies require top executives to own a certain amount of company stock. Until SOX, it was common for a company to help an executive purchase the stock by granting him or her a loan. Another common reason for an employer to loan money to an executive is to help him or her purchase a home, particularly if the executive must relocate in order to join the employer.

Before SOX,[40] loans to executives were a very popular form of executive compensation. SOX Section 402 prohibits publicly-traded companies from directly (including through a subsidiary) extending or maintaining credit, arranging for the extension of credit, or renewing an existing extension of credit, in the form of a personal loan, to or for any director or executive officer of the company. However, privately held employers can continue to provide for execu-

---

[39] Thank you to Doreen Lent from SSP for assistance in developing this model language.

[40] P.L. 107-204, 107th Cong., 2d Sess., 2002.

tive loans. See Chapter 11 (¶1101 *et seq.*) for a detailed discussion of executive stock purchase loan issues.

Executive loan provisions still appear in the employment agreements of private company executives. Often the executive's employment agreement might tie the term of the loan to the vesting period for the stock, and/or tie the executive's yearly bonus to the annual repayment required. In this manner, the executive could purchase the shares with no cash outlay.

For example, Executive D's employment agreement with ABC Corporation could provide as follows:

> Upon signing, ABC Corporation will loan the Executive one million dollars ($1,000,000.00), at an interest rate of five percent (5.0%) per annum, compounded annually, in accordance with the terms of a Promissory Note and Security Agreement between ABC and the Executive Loan Agreement attached hereto as Exhibit A (the "Executive Loan"). If the Executive's employment with ABC terminates for any reason during the Employment Term, the remaining principal balance and accrued interest of the Executive Loan shall be repaid to ABC by the Executive in annual two hundred fifty thousand dollar ($250,000.00) installments beginning with the first anniversary of the Employment Date that is coincident with or next following the Executive's employment termination.

If the employment agreement links the executive's annual bonus too closely to the repayment obligation, IRS may deem the full amount of the loan as an advance payment of compensation, taxable as ordinary income.[41]

Similarly, some employment agreements that provide for executive loans provide for the forgiveness of the loan under certain circumstances. If the terms of the employment agreement or the related documents provide for forgiveness of the loan, the executive will generally recognize ordinary income.

For example, the agreement might provide as follows:

> The Executive Loan, including the Executive's obligation to pay both principal and interest, shall be forgiven as follows: on each of the fourth, fifth, sixth and seventh anniversaries of the Effective Date, two hundred fifty thousand dollars ($250,000.00) of principal and all interest accrued to date shall be forgiven, provided that the Executive is employed by ABC Corporation on such anniversary. If the Executive's employment with the ABC Corporation terminates for any reason before the seventh anniversary of the Effective Date, the remaining principal balance and accrued interest of the Executive Loan shall be repaid to the Company by the Executive in annual two hundred fifty thousand dollar ($250,000.00) installments beginning with the first anniversary of the Effective Date that is coincident with or next following the Executive's employment termination.

.04 Below-Market Loan Issue

A loan from an employer to an executive that exceeds $10,000 will be subject to the below-market loan rules of the Internal Revenue Code.[42] Under these rules, if the interest payable on the loan is not sufficiently high, the executive will be taxable on the difference between the amount loaned to him or her and the

---

[41] IRS Letter Ruling 200040004 (June 12, 2000).   [42] Code Sec. 7872.

present value of all payments to be made under the loan, determined at the time of the loan, at a rate of interest specified in the Code.

.05 Executive Relocation Expenses

Prior to 2018, the Code provided favorable tax treatment for employment-related relocation expenses, under certain circumstances. The legislation known as the Tax Cuts and Jobs Act ("TCJA") signed into law by President Trump in December 2017, repealed the Code Sec. 217 deduction provisions and the Code Sec. 132 income exclusion provisions related to moving expenses for taxable years 2018 through 2025.

Until the TCJA, Code Sec. 82 and Code Sec. 132(a)(6) provided that, if an employer reimburses an employee for moving expenses or pays the expenses directly, the employee does not have to report the reimbursements or payments as income if the employee could have deducted the expenses on his or her tax return. Code Sec. 82 and Code Sec. 162 generally permitted employers to claim any reimbursements for employee moving expenses as ordinary and necessary business expenses.

Similarly, until the TCJA, Code Sec. 217 allowed an employee/taxpayer to deduct his or her moving expenses, provided that the employee satisfied the minimum distance and period-of-employment tests. The new job must have been located at least 50 miles farther from the employee's old residence than his or her former job was located. (For someone first entering the workforce, the new job must be at least 50 miles from his or her old residence.) The employee then had to work full-time in the new area for at least 39 weeks, consecutive or otherwise, in the first 12 months after arrival.

Companies that previously reimbursed moving expenses may need to update their payroll reporting and controls, so that moving expenses are properly reported. Companies also may need to revise their model employment agreements, new hire process, compensation packages, and any policies or arrangements that relate to moving expenses to conform with legal requirements.

.06 Travel Expenses

In a June 2004 information letter, the IRS laid out some guidelines for the proper tax treatment of travel expense reimbursements paid by a company to an employee who works out of his residence in one state but who regularly travels to the company's office in another state, where he stays in a corporate apartment provided by the taxpayer.[43]

An employer's payments to an employee, including fringe benefits, generally are included in the employee's gross income, and the employer must treat the payments as wages subject to withholding and employment taxes. However, a fringe benefit that qualifies as a working condition fringe is not treated as taxable wages. Code Sec. 132(d) defines working condition fringe as "any property or services provided to an employee of the employer to the extent that, if the

---

[43] Information Letters, INFO 2004-0166, Document Date: June 24, 2004.

employee paid for such property or services, such payment would be allowable as a deduction under Code Sec. 162 or 167."

Code Sec. 162(a)(2) allows deductions for traveling expenses (including amounts expended for meals and lodging other than amounts that are lavish or extravagant under the circumstances) paid or incurred while away from home in the pursuit of a trade or business. To be deductible under Code Sec. 162(a)(2), an employee's traveling expenses must be: (1) ordinary and necessary, (2) incurred in pursuit of a trade or business, and (3) incurred while away from home.[44] Code Sec. 162(a)(2) and Rev. Rul. 93-86[45] provide that traveling expenses with respect to an assignment in a single location that exceeds one year are not deductible.

In *Comm'r v. Flowers*, the Court determined that travel undertaken by a lawyer from his residence in Jackson, Mississippi, to his office for a railroad company based in Mobile, Alabama, was not incurred in pursuit of his trade or business. The traveling expenses, the Court found, were incurred solely for personal purposes and did further the employer's business: "The exigencies of business rather than the personal conveniences and necessities of the traveler must be the motivating factors. Such was not the case here."[46]

If the factors indicate that the vicinity of the employee's residence is the employee's principal place of business (and hence the employee's tax home), then the employee's use of the corporate apartment while traveling in the pursuit of the trade or business will be considered a working condition fringe, and the value will not be treated as taxable wages. If the employee's "tax home" is located in the vicinity of the taxpayer's office, or if the employee's travel is not in the pursuit of the trade or business, then the use of the corporate apartment is not a working condition fringe; the taxpayer would be required to treat as taxable wages the value of the employee's use of the apartment.

.07 Other Benefits and Perquisites

Most employment agreements provide simply that the executive will be entitled to the same perquisites available to other officers of the company. Some of the benefits and perquisites an executive may enjoy include:

1. Supplemental medical insurance;

2. Supplemental long and short-term disability insurance;

3. Employee stock purchase plan;

4. Retiree medical and life insurance;

5. Company car, limousine or chauffeur;

6. Use of company aircraft;

7. Spouse travel (not deductible by employer);

8. Income tax preparation, financial counseling/planning, estate planning;

---

[44] *Comm'r v. Flowers*, 46-1 USTC ¶9127, 326 U.S. 465 (1946).

[45] Rev. Rul. 93-86, 1993-2 CB 71.

[46] *Comm'r v. Flowers*, 326 U.S. at 474.

9. Club dues/fees (employer's deduction disallowed for dues it pays to social, athletic, sporting and luncheon clubs, and airline, hotel and business clubs);

10. Professional organization fees;

11. Cell phone and/or home office equipment; and

12. Executive dining room.

Code Sec. 132(a) specifically excludes the value of *de minimis* benefits from an employee's wages. The Code defines *de minimis* benefits as any property or service an employer provides to an employee that has so little value (taking into account how frequently the employer provides similar benefits to employees) that accounting for it would be unreasonable or administratively impracticable.[47] The IRS has specifically excluded the occasional theater or sporting event ticket from income as a *de minimis* fringe.[48] The IRS specifically includes in income (and thus not excludable as a *de minimis* fringe) season tickets to sporting or theatrical events. Therefore, if an executive only uses tickets for personal reasons on occasion (and are not given season tickets), it could be considered a *de minimis* fringe per the IRS regulations. On the other hand, if the facts show that the executive used the tickets more frequently, it could prevent the application of the exclusion.

SEC Item 402(c)(ix) requires disclosure of perquisites and personal benefits unless the aggregate of such compensation is less than $10,000. The instructions require that each perquisite or personal benefit that exceeds the greater of $25,000 or 10% of the total perquisites and other personal benefits reported for a named executive must be identified by type. The GE enforcement action order includes an itemized list of the perks, which could be read as an example of what the Staff now expects to see in proxy statements for disclosing company's perks.

Following a period during which executives' use of company-owned aircraft had come under intense scrutiny and criticism,[49] the American Jobs Creation Act of 2004[50] revised Code Sec. 274(e) to limit the amount of a corporation's deduction for non-business use of company-owned aircraft by an executive who is a Section 16 insider to the amount reported as income to that executive. Previously, some corporations were able to report only a small amount of income to executives for vacation, entertainment or other non-business use of aircraft under the base aircraft valuation formula known as the Standard Industry Fare Level formula, or SIFL,[51] while deducting the corporation's full cost for the aircraft use.

.08 Company Paid Legal Fees

Code Sec. 132 provides that fringe benefits that qualify as working condition fringe benefits are excluded from gross income. Treasury regulations under Code Sec. 132 define a "working condition fringe" as any property or services pro-

---

[47] Code Sec. 132(e)(1).
[48] Reg. § 1.132-6(e).
[49] See, for example, "Plane Perks," from Perfectly Legal, by David Cay Johnston, NY Times Reporter cited at www.compensationstandards.com.

[50] American Jobs Creation Act of 2004 (P.L. 108-357).
[51] Reg. § 1.61-21(g).

¶175.08

vided to an employee of the employer to the extent that, if the employee paid for such property or services, such payment would be allowable as a deduction under Code Sec. 162. Thus, to the extent that the legal fees paid by the company on the executive's behalf would be allowable as a deduction by the executive under Code Sec. 162, then the payment of such fees by the company should be excludable under the working condition fringe exception of Code Sec. 132.

A cash payment made by a company to an employee will not qualify as a working condition fringe under Code Sec. 132 unless the company requires the employee to (i) use the payment for expenses in connection with a specific or prearranged activity or undertaking for which a deduction is allowable under Code Sec. 162, (ii) verify that the payment is actually used for such expenses, and (iii) return to the employer any part of the payment not so used.[52]

Code Sec. 162 allows a deduction for ordinary and necessary expenses paid in carrying on any trade or business. Legal fees incurred in connection with a taxpayer's trade or business are generally deductible under Code Sec. 162.[53] The performance of services as an employee and the business of being an employee of the employer each constitute a trade or business under Code Sec. 162. For example, the IRS has held that expenses incurred by a taxpayer in seeking new employment are deductible under Code Sec. 162 as ordinary and necessary business expenses.[54] Additionally, the Tax Court, in *Primuth v. Comm'r*, allowed a deduction of outplacement service fees because they were incurred in connection with the taxpayer's trade or business of being a corporate executive.[55] The court noted, "[U]nder the facts before us, because the legal expenses were incurred by an employee in carrying on his or her trade or business of being a corporate executive, they would be deductible by the employee under Code Sec. 162."

However, to be excludable under Code Sec. 132 as working condition fringe, the payment of legal fees must satisfy two requirements in addition to being deductible under Code Sec. 162. First, the payment must be made to provide services to an employee who is currently employed by the employer.[56]

Second, the payment must be incurred in connection with the employee's trade or business of being an employee of the employer, rather than the employee's general trade or business of performing services as an employee.[57] This requirement is generally satisfied if, under all of the facts and circumstances, the employer derives a substantial business benefit from the provision of the services, which is distinct from the benefit that the employer would derive from the mere payment of additional compensation. In Revenue Ruling 92-69, the IRS determined that payment for outplacement services in seeking new employment in the same trade or business would be allowed as a deduction under Code Sec. 162 and, if the employer derived a substantial business benefit from the provision of such outplacement services that was distinct from the benefit it would derive from the mere payment of additional compensation, then the services may

---

[52] 26 C.F.R. § 1.132-5(a)(1)(v).
[53] 72 T.C.M. 1443 (1996).
[54] See IRS Rev. Rul. 75-120.

[55] 54 T.C. 374, 377 (1970).
[56] 26 C.F.R. § 1.132-1(b)(2).
[57] 26 C.F.R. § 1.132-5(a)(2).

be treated as a working condition fringe. The substantial business benefit arguably derived by the employer in paying an employee's legal fees incurred in the amendment of his employment agreement could include a positive corporate image, maintaining corporate morale, and avoiding wrongful termination suits (since having an employment agreement with clear and mutually agreed upon terms in place is beneficial to the employer), in addition to ensuring compliance with Code Sec. 409A.

¶185　Other Employment Agreement Provisions

It can be fun and exciting to negotiate the salary, bonus and equity compensation elements of the employment agreements, and designing the long-term compensation element (and tax deferral aspects) can test counsel's creativity. However, sometimes the most important protection the executive and the employer will receive is in the so-called "boilerplate" provisions of the agreement. Counsel cannot ignore these important issues.

.01　Title(s) and Duties

Most employment agreements will specify the office or position to which the executive is appointed. For example:

> ABC Corporation hereby employs the Executive and the Executive hereby accepts employment with the Corporation as President and Chief Executive Officer. During the Employment Term (as hereinafter defined), the Executive shall have the title, status and duties of President and Chief Executive Officer and shall report directly to the Corporation's Board of Directors.

Where applicable, the agreement should explicitly provide that the company will appoint the executive to be a director of the company.

Most employment agreements will also specify the executive's duties, to avoid any misunderstanding or drastic change:

> The Executive will perform duties assigned by the Corporation's Board of Directors (the "Board"), from time to time; provided that the Board shall not assign the Executive tasks inconsistent with those of President and Chief Executive Officer.

However, the employment agreement should give the company the flexibility to change the executive's reporting relationship and assign him additional responsibilities. The agreement should specify that the executive will perform the duties and serve in any other office or position of the company assigned to him, or her, with no additional compensation.

An employment agreement should also require the executive to devote his or her full time and best efforts, talents, knowledge and experience to serving the employer. Although it may seem obvious and axiomatic, to protect the employer an employment agreement should provide that the executive will perform his or her duties diligently and competently, act in conformity with the employer's written and oral policies and act within the limits, budgets and business plans set by the employer. The agreement should specify any special set of rules or regulations, *e.g.*, banking or securities laws, to which the employer's executives are required to adhere.

However, employment agreements also generally permit the executive to devote reasonable time to activities such as supervision of personal investments and activities involving professional, charitable, educational, religious and similar types of activities. Speaking engagements and membership on other boards of directors, provided such activities do not interfere in any material way with the business of the employer, may also be permitted. Most employment agreements expressly provide that the employer will not treat the time involved in such activities as vacation time. Many employment agreements permit the executive to keep any amounts paid to him or her in connection with these outside activities (*e.g.*, director fees and honoraria). Most employment agreements prohibit the executive from serving on the boards of directors of a publicly traded company without the employer's written consent, or limit the number of boards on which the executive can serve. Most employment agreements also prohibit the executive from engaging in consulting work or any trade or business outside of the executive's employment with the employer.

.02 Indemnification and Insurance

Every well-drafted executive employment agreement should explicitly require the employer to indemnify the executive and provide directors and officers' liability insurance coverage for the executive.

For example, Executive D's employment agreement with ABC Corporation might provide as follows:

> For the period from the date hereof through at least the sixth anniversary of the Executive's termination of employment from ABC Corporation, the Corporation agrees to maintain the Executive as an insured party on all directors' and officers' insurance maintained by the Corporation for the benefit of its directors and officers on at least the same basis as all other covered individuals and provide the Executive with at least the same corporate indemnification as its officers.

However, bankruptcy courts in some jurisdictions have found that D&O coverage is an asset of the bankruptcy estate, thereby subordinating directors' and officers' claims to those of other creditors. Suggestions made by some compensation professionals include: (i) separate policy limits for the individuals, (ii) negotiate a clause in the policy requiring the insurer to pay the individuals first for unindemnified claims, or (iii) carrying separate Side A coverage for the officers and directors.[58]

.03 Term of Employment Agreement

Both the executive and the employer have an interest in specifying the duration or term of the employment agreement and any provisions for continuation of renewal.

Planning Note: Employers generally should not sign executives to an employment agreement that expires on a fixed day in the future with no

---

[58] See "Negotiating D&O Policies: Key Terms And Conditions," Carolyn Rosenberg, Duane Sigelko, Kit Chaskin, Neil Posner, and Venus Mc- Ghee, Review of Securities & Commodities Regulation - Vol. 37, No. 4, pp. 31-43.

provision for renewal. The employer should not put itself in the position, a few years later when the agreement is about to expire, of not knowing whether it can count on the executive to run the business after the expiration date. Similarly, the executive should not put herself in the position of not knowing whether she will have a job with the employer after the expiration date. While the uncertainty will likely improve the negotiation strength of one party or the other on the eve of expiration, when the agreement is drafted and signed, neither the executive nor the employer is generally sure which party that will be. For this reason, many employment agreements will provide for an "evergreen" employment term or automatic renewal.

An alternative approach that some employers use is to provide that, after the expiration of the initial contract term, the employment relationship converts to an "at will" employment relationship, with survival of specified terms such as confidentiality, arbitration and restrictive covenants, for the balance of the employment relationship. In this manner, the employer retains the benefits of its initial bargain, without retaining the severance pay obligations.

.04 Vacation

Most employment agreements provide that the executive will be entitled to paid vacation in accordance with the company's vacation policy for senior executive officers, but in no event less than a specified number of weeks or days per calendar year. Some companies use the concept of paid-time-off rather than vacation. For example, an agreement could provide that the executive will be entitled to 30 days of paid time off in accordance with company policy. The company should bear in mind that the executive may be entitled to Family and Medical Leave Act (FMLA) leave under various circumstances. While FMLA leave may be unpaid, the company should be able to count the PTO it provides for this purpose toward satisfying the FMLA requirements, if it specifically references this fact in the employment agreement.

.05 Location

Some agreements provide for specifying the location of the executive's principal office. If the agreement specifies a location, it also could clarify that the executive will engage in business travel as reasonably required in the performance of his duties, and specify whether the company may relocate the executive's principal office to another city. Agreements that allow relocation also typically provide for the reimbursement of relocation expenses.

.06 Protection Against Code Sec. 409A

Code Sec. 409A, added by the American Jobs Creation Act of 2004, is entitled "Inclusion in Gross Income of Deferred Compensation Under Nonqualified Deferred Compensation Plans." However, Code Sec. 409A, can apply to *employment agreements*, in addition to deferred compensation plans, which were the original target of Congress. "Deferred compensation" means compensation:

- To which an employee or other service provider has a legally binding right during a taxable year (*i.e.*, it is "earned and vested");

- That has not been previously taxed; and

- That is payable pursuant to the applicable agreement in a later year.

The failure to comply with Code Sec. 409A results in immediate income on deferrals, an excise tax of 20% and other penalties

Code Sec. 409A applies to any plan or arrangement that provides for the deferral of compensation. Regulations under Code Sec. 409A[59] state that an arrangement provides for the deferral of compensation if, under the terms of the agreement and the relevant facts and circumstances, the employee has a legally binding right during a taxable year to compensation that, (i) has not been actually or constructively received and included in gross income, and (ii) pursuant to the terms of the agreement, is payable to (or on behalf of) the employee in a later year. Since an employment agreement creates a legally binding right to payments on the executive's signing of the agreement – payments that will be made in a later year – it fits this definition.

The principal effect of Code Sec. 409A on employment agreements depends on whether any stock of the employer is publicly traded on an established securities market.

- For public companies, if an employee is a "key employee" of the company (generally, one of the top 50 highest paid for the preceding calendar year) as of the date of the employee's separation from service, a six-month delay applies to payments made due to a "separation from service" (as defined in the regulations), unless an exception applies.

- For private and public companies, separation payments made over time will be subject to Sec. 409A and the timing and form of the payments cannot be changed without following the restrictions of Sec. 409A.

The final regulations clarify that separation pay is only subject to Code Sec. 409A if it is conditioned upon separation from service. Amounts that would be paid upon other events, like change in control or a date certain, are not separation pay (although they still could be subject to Sec. 409A).

Separation Pay and Public Companies

For public companies, the application of Sec. 409A to separation pay is crucial because Sec. 409A requires a six-month delay in payments, if as of the date of the employee's separation from service, the employee is a "key employee" (discussed below). The final regulations provide certain exceptions from Sec. 409A for separation payments. The exceptions apply to payments made only on an involuntary separation that are:

1. Made in a lump sum following an involuntary separation;

2. Less than the Code Sec. 401(a)(17) amount;

3. Made under certain foreign plans or agreements;

---

[59] The Treasury and IRS issued 397 pages of final regulations under Code Section 409A on April 10, 2007.

4. Certain reimbursements and in-kind payments;

Example: If an employment agreement with a public company CEO provided that the company would pay it's CEO $1 million in a lump sum immediately following a termination of the CEO without cause, this lump sum payment ordinarily would not be subject to Sec. 409A, because it qualifies for the short-term deferral exception (payment is made in the same year as the right to payment becomes vested).

Separation pay from an employment agreement will not qualify as "involuntary" if the agreement provides for payments upon a separation for "good reason" – even if the actual termination was involuntary – unless the definition of "good reason" satisfies a safe harbor in the final regulations or otherwise is tough enough to satisfy the IRS. Separation pay rules also apply to private companies, in the event of (i) payments on a voluntary separation or (ii) payments on involuntary separation that continue for longer than two years *or* exceed two times the lesser of the employee's annual pay or the Code Sec. 401(a)(17) limit.

Separation for Good Reason

Under the safe harbor definition of separation for good reason in the final regulations, the separation from service must occur during a pre-determined, limited period not to exceed two years following the initial existence of one or more of the following conditions, arising without the consent of the executive:

1. A material diminution in the employee's base compensation.
2. A material diminution in the employee's authority, duties, or responsibilities.
3. A material diminution in the authority, duties, or responsibilities of the supervisor to whom the employee is required to report, including a requirement that an employee report to a corporate officer or other employee instead of reporting directly to the board of directors of a corporation (or similar governing body with respect to an entity other than a corporation).
4. A material diminution in the budget over which the employee retains authority.
5. A material change in the geographic location at which the employee must perform the services.
6. Any other action or inaction that constitutes a material breach by the employer of the agreement under which the employee provides services.

The amount, time, and form of payment upon the separation from service for good reason must be substantially identical to the amount, time and form of payment payable due to an actual involuntary separation from service (to the extent such a right exists). Additionally, the agreement must require the employee to provide notice to the employer of the existence of the condition described above within a period not to exceed 90 days of the initial existence of the condition. The agreement also must give the employer a period of at least 30 days following receipt of the notice during which it may remedy the condition and not be required to make separation payments.

Other Exceptions for Separation Payments

The final regulations provide a few other useful exceptions for separation pay under Sec. 409A. Moreover, the final regulations clarify that employers may use *more than one of the separation pay exceptions* for each payment or separation (so-called "stacking" of the separation payments).

The final regulations provide an exception for certain limited payments made following an involuntary separation from service, to the extent the payments do not exceed two times the lesser of the Code Sec. 401(a)(17) limit ($275,000 for 2018) or employee's annual compensation for the year prior to the year of separation, and the agreement provides that the separation pay must be paid no later than the last day of the second taxable year of the employee following the taxable year of the employee in which he or she incurred the separation from service. If the employer pays *more than* two times the lesser of the employee's annual pay or the Code Sec. 401(a)(17) limit, the exception still applies to the amount paid *up to* the limit. No similar rule applies for payments continuing for longer than two years. Such payments would be completely subject to Code Sec. 409A.

The final regulations also clarify that non-taxable benefits provided following separation from service are not subject to 409A. Continuing health plan coverage is the most common non-taxable benefit provided under employment agreements. However, continuing health plan coverage is not always a non-taxable benefit (for example, if it is provided on a discriminatory basis). Taxable medical benefit reimbursements still may be able to qualify for an exception, to the extent they are paid over a period no longer than the applicable COBRA coverage period (18 or 36 months), under the exception discussed next below.

Reimbursements and In-Kind Benefits

The final regulations provide that to the extent an employment agreement (including an agreement providing payments upon a *voluntary separation* from service) entitles an employee to payment of reimbursements:

(a) that are not otherwise excludible from gross income, for expenses that the employee otherwise could deduct under Code Sec. 162 or 167 as business expenses incurred in connection with the performance of services (ignoring any applicable limitation based on adjusted gross income), or

(b) of reasonable outplacement expenses and reasonable moving expenses actually incurred by the employee and directly related to the termination of services for the employer.

An agreement does not provide for a deferral of compensation to the extent such rights apply during a limited period (regardless of whether such rights continue beyond the limited period). The reimbursement of reasonable moving expenses includes the reimbursement of all or part of any loss the employee actually incurs due to the sale of a primary residence in connection with a separation from service.

The final regulations provide that a "limited period of time" in which expenses may be incurred, or in which in-kind benefits may be provided by the employer or a third party that the employer will pay, does not include periods beyond the last day of the second taxable year of the employee following the employee's taxable year in which the separation from service occurred, provided that the period during which the reimbursements for such expenses must be paid may not extend beyond the third taxable year of the employee following the taxable year in which his or her separation from service occurred.

The final regulations provide that a terminating employee's entitlement to in-kind benefits, such as the continued use of a car or corporate aircraft, membership dues or payment for financial or tax advice, from the employer, or a payment by the employer directly to the person providing the goods or services to the employee, will not be treated as providing for a deferral of compensation under Code Sec. 409A to the extent such rights apply during a limited period of time (regardless of whether such rights extend beyond the limited period of time).

Finally, the final regulations provide an exception for amounts less than the Code Sec. 402(g) limit - $18,500 in 2018.

Specified Employees

Code Sec. 409A provides that distributions to a "specified employee" may not be made before the date that is six months after the date of the employee's separation from service or, if earlier, the date of the employee's death (the "six-month delay rule"). The six-month delay rule applies to payments under deferred compensation and other non-qualified plans, but also payments under employment agreements. The final regulations provide that the employer must write into the agreement the six-month delay rule.

Code Sec. 409A and the final regulations provide that the term "specified employee" means an employee who, as of the date of his or her separation from service, is a key employee of an employer whose stock is publicly traded on an established securities market or otherwise. An employee is a "key employee" if the employee meets the requirements of Code Sec. 416(i)(1)(A)(i), (ii), or (iii) (the top-heavy plan rules) at any time during the 12-month period ending on a "specified employee identification date" (generally, December 31). If an employee is a key employee as of a specified employee identification date, the employee is treated as a key employee for purposes of Sec. 409A for the entire 12-month period beginning on the specified employee effective date (or for a different 12-month period beginning within three months of that date).

Code Sec. 416(i)(1)(A) provides that the term "key employee" means an employee who, at any time during the year, is —

   (i) an officer of the employer having an annual compensation greater than $175,000 (as adjusted at the same time and in the same manner as under Code Sec. 415(d)),

(ii) a 5-percent owner of the employer, or

(iii) a 1-percent owner of the employer having an annual compensation from the employer of more than $150,000.

Sec. 416(i)(A) also provides that no more than 50 employees (or, if lesser, the greater of 3 or 10 percent of the employees) are treated as officers. The definition of compensation under Treas. Reg. § 1.415(c)-2(a) applies, unless the agreement or employer specifies another definition.

The final regulations provide that, like the six-month delay rule, an agreement must specify the method for determining key employees and for applying the six-month delay rule. To meet the six-month delay requirement, an agreement may provide that:

- Any payment pursuant to a separation of service due within the six-month period is delayed until the end of the six-month period, or

- Each scheduled payment that becomes payable pursuant to a separation from service is delayed six months, or

- A combination thereof.

.07 Choice of Law; Choice of Forum

Nearly all forms of contract, including employment agreements, include a provision specifying which state laws will govern the validity, interpretation, construction, and performance of the agreement. Many companies now include a provision in their employment (and other) agreements, which specifies the forum in which litigation may be brought, e.g., "The jurisdiction and venue for any disputes arising under, or any action brought to enforce (or otherwise relating to), the Plan will be exclusively in the courts in the State of Illinois, County of Cook, including the Federal Courts located therein (should Federal jurisdiction exist)." Courts nearly always enforce these provisions when the forum specified is in or near the headquarters of the company. This provision can prevent the company from being forced to defend claims made by former employees in a distant forum or one that has excessively protective provisions in favor of employees (e.g., California).

.08 Other Boilerplate Provisions

Both the executive and the employer have an interest in including the miscellaneous or so-called "boilerplate" provisions in the employment agreement, including provisions:

- specifying that the agreement will be binding upon the employer and its successors, and that neither party may assign the agreement without the other's written consent. Some agreements require the company to require any successor to all or substantially all of the business or assets of the company to assume and agree to perform the employment agreement in the same manner that the company would be required to perform it if no such succession had taken place;

- specifying in which federal or state courts the parties must bring an action relating to the agreement;
- that the employer may withhold from any payments amounts sufficient to satisfy applicable withholding requirements under any federal, state or local law;
- that the agreement may be amended only by written agreement between the employer and the executive;
- for the proper delivery of notices required by the agreement;
- stating that the written employment agreement sets forth the entire agreement and understanding between the employer and the executive and supersedes all prior agreements and understandings, written or oral;
- stating that no failure or delay by the employer or the executive in enforcing or exercising any right under the agreement will operate as a waiver of that right;
- requiring the executive to represent and warrant to the company that he or she is not a party to or subject to any restrictive covenants, legal restrictions or other agreements that would preclude or limit his or her ability to perform his or her obligations under the agreement;
- requiring the executive to represent and agree that he or she has reviewed and fully understands all provisions of the Agreement, and is voluntarily entering into the Agreement;
- providing that, if the executive dies, any monies that are due and owing to the executive under the agreement as of the date of his or her death will be paid to his or her estate; and
- clarifying that the parties may execute the agreement in one or more counterparts, all of which together shall constitute but one agreement.

When updating or replacing a current employment agreement with a new one, the new employment agreement should expressly cancel or replace the previous agreement. Otherwise, the old agreement may continue to bind the employer. In *Ford v. American Express Financial Advisors Inc.,*[60] the Utah Supreme court held in favor the plaintiffs who were financial planners working for American Express as independent contractors. American Express and the financial planners had executed an agreement providing that American Express would make contributions for a planner's welfare benefits if the planner met certain contractually specified production levels. Eventually, American Express terminated the agreement and implemented a business franchise agreement, under which it would not pay contributions towards a planner's welfare benefits. The court found that the financial planners had earned the benefits contributions pursuant to the terms of the original agreement and that the second agreement did not constitute a substituted contract that replaced the original agreement because it did not indicate any intent by the planners to extinguish their right to

---

[60] *Ford v. American Express Financial Advisors Inc.,* 98 P.3d 15 (2004).

welfare benefits contributions that they had already earned under the original agreement.

¶195 Offer Letters

Employers generally use offer letters either to (1) establish a preliminary, binding employment agreement with an executive, subject to the negotiation of a comprehensive employment agreement, or (2) set forth the general terms of the executive's employment in lieu of entering into a comprehensive employment agreement. Where an employer has a policy of not offering employment agreements (for whatever reason), the executive's counsel may be able to negotiate all the protections the executive needs into an offer letter.

.01 Offer Letters as Contracts

Although offer letters have been infrequent subjects of litigation, when the employee signs or acknowledges the offer letter, either orally or in writing, the courts consistently treat offer letters as contracts and enforce them as such. Therefore, careful drafting, a detailed review of the signed offer letter, and follow-up on the terms of the letter are imperative components of the informed use of offer letters.

Courts have found enforceable or have directly enforced offer letters as contracts, although most have done so without citation or any discussion of the relationship between offer letters and contracts.[61] Although questions regarding offer letters arise occasionally in litigation, no reported cases have directly questioned the idea that accepted offer letters are contracts and enforceable as such. Courts universally regard employment offer letters signed by both parties as contracts. Courts often refer to offer letters as contracts without discussion and without citation to authority.[62]

For example, in *Coll v. PB Diagnostic Systems, Inc.*,[63] the court referred to termination in accordance with the terms of the employee's offer letter as "in accordance with his employment contract." In *Stafford v. Conn. General Life Ins. Co.*,[64] the court stated: "Stafford is correct that the January 27 letter constituted an offer of employment. He accepted that offer. Therefore, that letter is the contract between the parties."

Not only do courts simply refer to offer letters as contracts, but parties willingly concede that signed offer letters constitute contracts.[65] Even offer letters

---

[61] See *Watson v. Champion Computer Corp.*, 2000 U.S. Dist. LEXIS 17086, at *10 (N.D. Ill. 2000); *Huffman v. Premis Corp.*, 1998 Minn. App. LEXIS 770, at *6 (Minn. App. 1998).

[62] See *McGurn v. Bell Microproducts, Inc.*, 284 F3d 86, 90 (1st Cir. 2002) addressing whether an employer's silence regarding an employee's alteration of his offer letter constituted acceptance and referring to the alteration as "an offer to enter into a contract."

[63] *Coll v. PB Diagnostic Systems, Inc.*, 50 F3d 1115, 1121 (1st Cir. 1995).

[64] *Stafford v. Conn. General Life Ins. Co.*, 1997 U.S. Dist. LEXIS 1475, at *10 (N.D. Ill. 1997).

[65] See *Hubka v. Mobil Corp.*, 2002 U.S. App. LEXIS 2714, at *5 (4th Cir. 2002) ("the parties agreed that the 1991 offer letter was a contract"); and *Conway v. Saudi Arabian Oil Co.*, 867 F.Supp. 539, 543 (S.D. Tex. 1994) ("Even Plaintiffs maintain that the offer letter was a contract.")

that have not been signed by the parties may be enforceable as contracts. Oral acceptance of an offer letter can constitute acceptance.[66]

Whether an offer letter constitutes the entire agreement between the employer and employee depends upon the terms of the offer letter. Where an offer letter included a passage indicating that the employer would establish an incentive compensation plan "to make it possible for [the employee] to earn substantially greater incentive compensation payments than the guarantee" provided for in the letter, that plan was deemed incorporated into the agreement between the parties.[67] Where an offer letter provided that the employer "intend[ed] to jointly explore with [the employee] appropriate methods of compensation to reflect [his] contribution to the success of the venture," the employer was obligated to do no more than the joint exploration called for in the offer letter.[68] Any arrangement later reached as to that additional compensation was not considered a part of the employment agreement, as the offer letter "was an integrated and final expression of the parties' agreement with respect to compensation matters." Whether the offer letter constitutes the entire agreement when the letter references other documents depends upon the particular language utilized in the referencing remark.

As contracts, offer letters are subject to contractual restrictions. For example, just as a party may waive conditions precedent in a contract by conduct indicating that compliance is unnecessary, a party also may waive conditions precedent in an offer letter.[69] Thus, it is unlikely that an employer can force an employee to strictly comply with the terms of the offer letter if the employer's behavior has indicated that strict compliance is not required. For example, in one case, the employee began work without having signed an employment agreement that would have provided terms of employment, including an at-will clause. According to the terms of the offer letter, signing the employment agreement was a condition precedent to employment. The court concluded that, since the employee began and continued her employment with Champion Computer without a signed employment agreement, she could reasonably believe that signing the agreement was not necessary, and that only the terms in the offer letter would govern the terms of her employment.[70]

In *Hopmayer v. Aladdin Indus. LLC*,[71] a Tennessee state court held that a company owed a fired executive $160,000 plus prejudgment interest for phantom shares promised in his employment contract. The court recognized that phantom shares are a type of executive compensation used by limited liability companies to provide an equity stake in the company without providing voting rights or corporate dividends and rejected the company's arguments that the phantom

---

[66] *Hoffman v. Structural Research & Analysis Corp.*, 1993 U.S. Dist. LEXIS 15051, at *9-10 (E.D. Mich. 1993). The Hoffman court concluded that "an express bilateral employment contract" was formed between employer and employee when "Hoffman communicated his acceptance via telephone."

[67] *Stafford v. Conn. General Life Ins. Co.*, 1997 U.S. Dist. LEXIS 1475, at *10 (N.D. Ill. 1997).

[68] *Coll v. PB Diagnostic Systems, Inc.*, 50 F3d 1115, 1119 (1st Cir. 1995).

[69] *Watson v. Champion Computer Corp.*, 2000 U.S. Dist. LEXIS 17086, at *10 (N.D. Ill. 2000).

[70] *Watson v. Champion Computer Corp.*, 2000 U.S. Dist. LEXIS 17086, at *12 (N.D. Ill. 2000).

[71] *Hopmayer v. Aladdin Indus. LLC*, 2004 Tenn. App. LEXIS 364 (Tenn. App. 2004).

shares had not vested and that the letter offering employment to Hopmayer was not a valid contract.

The company's CEO had mailed an offer-of-employment letter to Mr. Hopmayer stating that, in addition to his base salary, "[a]phantom unit plan will be adopted by the Board of Managers in which you will be granted 4,000 phantom units with an initial value of $40.00 per unit." The court found that (1) the provision describing the phantom units was sufficiently definite to be a valid contract, and (2) the contract contained no vesting or appreciation requirements.

In *Savage v. PricewaterhouseCoopers LLP*,[72] PricewaterhouseCoopers LLP agreed to pay $1.8 million to approximately 270 recent college graduates who did not receive promised signing bonuses and management consulting jobs, under the terms of a settlement given final approval. According to the complaint, recruiters working for PricewaterhouseCoopers and assigned to major colleges and universities in the eastern United States made written offers of employment to students slated to graduate in spring 2001. The graduates alleged that after accepting the company's job offer, they stopped looking for other jobs, turned down job offers from other companies, and incurred expenses in preparing to begin work for PricewaterhouseCoopers. Some even moved to the cities where they expected to begin working. As the economy declined in 2001, the recruiters allegedly made repeated assurances to the graduates that the jobs were secure. However, the approximately 270 graduates never received jobs and were not paid the bonuses.

In another case involving an offer letter, a California state court ruled that conflicting terms in a company's offer letter meant that an employee could be terminated only for good cause.[73] The letter sent to the employee stated that he would be employed "at will" and then added:

> This simply means that Arnold Communications has the right to terminate your employment at any time just as you have the right to terminate your employment with Arnold Communications at any time.

The court found that, "If the contract contained only the first sentence stating Dore's employment was 'at will' there would be no question it meant Arnold could terminate Dore at any time without cause." Elsewhere in the offer letter it mentioned a 90-day assessment and evaluation period. The court held that, "The two provisions taken together, along with the rule [that] any ambiguities in the terms of a contract are to be construed against the party who drafted it, convince us the term 'at will' as used in Dore's contract did not mean 'at any time for any reason' but only 'at any time.'"

.02 Legal Effect of an Employment Agreement that Both Parties Did Not Sign

Although there is scant law on the subject, occasionally we are forced to consider the legal effect of an employment agreement that one or both of the

---

[72] *Savage v. PricewaterhouseCoopers LLP*, No. 02-8167 (D.C. Super. Ct. 2003) (settlement approved August 1, 2003).

[73] *Dore v. Arnold Worldwide Inc.*, 2004 Cal. App. Unpub. LEXIS 2687 (2004).

parties never signed. We believe that the courts probably would discuss whether the unsigned agreement (i) is a writing memorializing an oral contract, or (ii) has no contractual value because the parties intended that there would be no deal in the absence of a signed written contract. We believe that some courts would find the unsigned agreement to be enforceable under certain circumstances, particularly where the parties worked under conditions that closely followed the agreement's terms. After all, an oral contract is enforceable. An oral contract is just harder to prove. Since an oral employment agreement could be enforceable, the unsigned document could be evidence of what the parties in fact agreed to, depending upon the reasons the document was never signed.

.03 Benefits Handbook as an Enforceable Contract

The courts generally have held that a benefits handbook does not constitute a contract between the employer and its employees. For example, in *Wilkes v. Electronic Data Systems Corp.*, the court found that the handbook did not constitute a binding contract and, thus, EDS did not breach a contract by denying an employee's claim for short-term disability benefits that were listed in the handbook.[74] Importantly, the court observed that the benefits handbook contained a clear and unambiguous disclaimer that could not have given the employee a reasonable expectation that the handbook constituted a commitment on the part of the employer.

¶197 SEC Reporting

.01 Form 8-K

Since August 2004, U.S. public companies have been required to file a Form 8-K within four days of certain executive compensation and employment events. A public company must file Form 8-K with the SEC for the appointment of certain new executive officers, under Item 5.02(c). A public company also must file Form 8-K with the SEC if it enters into a material contract or arrangement with certain executive officers, under Item 5.02(e). These contracts are reportable because they are deemed to be material agreements not made in the ordinary course of business, even if the amount involved would not otherwise be considered material to the company. In addition, contracts or plans involving any other executive officer must be disclosed, unless the amount or significance of the contract is immaterial.

A public company must file Form 8-K with the SEC, under Item 5.02(c) if it "appoints a new principal executive officer, president, principal financial officer, principal accounting officer, principal operating officer, or person performing similar functions." In its filing, the company must disclose the following information with respect to the newly appointed officer:

(1) the name, age, and all positions with the company held by the newly appointed officer and the date of the appointment;

---

[74] *Wilkes v. Electronic Data Systems Corp.*, D. Ariz., No. CIV 04-341 TUC JMR, March 2006.

(2) the term of office as officer, any previous period during which he or she has served as such, and any arrangement or understanding between the officer and any other person(s) (naming such person) pursuant to which he or she was or is to be selected as an officer;

(3) any family relationship between the executive officer and any director or executive officer;

(4) the business experience during the past five years of the executive officer, including his or her principal occupations and employment during the past five years; the name and principal business of any corporation or other organization in which such occupations and employment were carried on; and whether such corporation or other organization is a parent, subsidiary or other affiliate of the corporation or other organization; and

(5) a brief description of any material plan, contract or arrangement (whether or not written) to which the covered officer is a party or in which he or she participates that is entered into or material amendment in connection with the triggering event or any grant or award to any such covered person or modification thereto, under any such plan, contract or arrangement in connection with any such event.

The Form 8-K requirement applies even if the new CEO is appointed from inside the company. For example, if a company were to promote its CFO to CEO, the Form 8-K would report that promotion and any new awards or agreements entered into in connection with the promotion.

Section B of the instructions to Form 8-K states that when the company appoints a new executive officer, "a report is to be filed or furnished within four business days after occurrence of the event." This four-day period runs from the date the company appoints the new executive officer. However, according to the SEC's Compensation Disclosure and Interpretation Question 117.05 for Form 8-K, if the company intends to make a public announcement of the appointment other than by means of a report on Form 8-K, it may delay disclosure until the date of the announcement. If the terms of a new officer's employment agreement have not been settled by the time disclosure is required, a company may state that fact in the Form 8-K filing, then file an amendment to the Form 8-K containing the required information within four business days of the date it becomes known.

Until the board of directors or a committee thereof, appoints an individual as an executive officer, there is no obligation or requirement to file a Form 8-K. Discussions, expectations, and negotiations are not sufficient to trigger an 8-K filing requirement. If the company and candidate reach an understanding that, if everything goes according to plan over the next few months the company will employ the candidate under certain terms, *but nothing is signed and the board has not approved or appointed him or her*, and either party could back out at any time – and may well back out, given the length of time between "understanding" and the onset of a legal obligation – then an appointment requiring disclosure has *not* occurred and generally no Form 8-K is required.

The result could be different in the situation where a candidate actually comes to work for the company before an agreement is signed or terms fully agreed, where he or she could be deemed to have accepted his appointment by performing duties.

.02 Form 10-K

In addition to the immediate filing requirements of Form 8-K, public companies must list and attach all material agreements to their Annual Report Form 10-K. However, the SEC permits companies to incorporate most material agreements, including employment agreements, by reference to previous filings. Thus, when you look at the exhibits to a company's Form 10-K, you will not find actual employment agreements attached (unless the company entered into the agreement that year), but rather a reference to the previous SEC filing when that agreement was first attached.

Chapter 2

CHANGE IN CONTROL AGREEMENTS

¶201 Overview—Change in Control Agreements

Change in control agreements between companies and executives, so-called "golden parachute agreements," have become a ubiquitous part of the executive compensation scene. Congress added the golden parachute provisions to the Internal Revenue Code in the Deficit Reduction Act of 1984.[1] Code Sec. 280G prohibits a corporation from taking a deduction for any excess parachute payments.[2] An "excess parachute payment" is an amount equal to the excess of the aggregate present value of all "parachute payments" paid to a disqualified individual ("DI") over the DI's "base amount."[3]

In August 2003, the U.S. Treasury Department and IRS issued final regulations for Code Sec. 280G (the "final regulations"). The IRS previously had issued proposed regulations relating to parachute payments under Code Sec. 280G in February 2002 and in May 1989 (the "1989 regulations"). From 1989, the IRS had issued a smattering of private letter rulings on various issues left unclear in the statute. However, the dollar amounts and increasing prevalence of golden parachute payments left employers, executives and their lawyers clamoring for more.

.01 Code Sec. 280G and Code Sec. 4999

Code Sec. 280G provides that any payments or distributions in the nature of compensation to a DI that are contingent on a change in control of a corporation will be deemed "excess parachute payments" if the aggregate present value of the payments or distributions exceeds three times the DI's "base amount."[4] The consequences of any payments being deemed "excess parachute payments" are that:

1. Code Sec. 280G prohibits the corporation from taking a deduction for any excess parachute payments.

2. Code Sec. 4999 imposes an excise tax on the DI who receives an excess parachute payment, equal to 20 percent of the amount above his or her

---

[1] P.L. 98-369. As enacted, Code Sec. 280G applied to agreements entered into or renewed after June 14, 1984. Any agreement that was entered into before June 15, 1984 but that was renewed after June 14, 1984 was treated as a new contract entered into on the date the renewal took effect. (1989) Reg. §1.280G-1, Q&A-47. Even if an agreement was entered into before June 14, 1984, and not renewed

after that date, Code Sec. 280G applied if the contract was amended or supplemented after June 14, 1984, in a significant relevant respect.

[2] Code Sec. 280G(a).

[3] Code Sec. 280G(b)(1).

[4] Code Sec. 280G(b)(2)(A)(i) and Code Sec. 280G(b)(2)(A)(ii).

base amount. (The corporation would normally withhold this tax, in addition to income taxes for which the DI would be liable.)

The excess parachute payment provisions of Code Sec. 280G and Code Sec. 4999 only apply to payments made to, or for the benefit of, a DI, as defined in Code Sec. 280G(c). Officers, shareholders, or highly compensated individuals who are employees or independent contractors of the corporation are considered DIs (see ¶215).

The final regulations clarified that the limits of Code Sec. 280G and Code Sec. 4999 operate independently of each other.[5] In other words, the denial of a deduction under Code Sec. 280G is not contingent on the imposition of an excise tax under Code Sec. 4999, and vice versa (see ¶245).

.02 Compensation Paid as a Result of a Change in Control

Code Sec. 280G and Code Sec. 4999 only apply to payments of compensation that are contingent on a change in the ownership of a corporation (see ¶225).

.03 Payment in Excess of Three Times the Disqualified Individual's Base Amount

Not all payments made to a disqualified individual as a result of a change in control are subject to the penalties of Code Sec. 280G and Code Sec. 4999. The penalties only apply to "excess parachute payments," which occur when the aggregate present value of all payments made to the DI as a result of the change in control equals or exceeds an amount equal to three times the DI's "base amount."[6] The DI's base amount is the average annual compensation payable by the corporation and includible in the DI's gross income, over the DI's five most recent taxable years ending before the date of the change in control (see ¶215 and ¶265).

.04 Application to Corporations and Small-Business Corporations

By its terms, Code Sec. 280G applies only to "corporations." However, the regulations clarified that Code Sec. 280G applies to corporations, publicly traded partnerships treated as corporations under Code Sec. 7704(a), real estate investment trusts under Code Sec. 856(a), corporations with mutual or cooperative ownership, such as a mutual insurance company, a mutual savings bank, or a cooperative bank, and a foreign corporation, as well as all members of the same affiliated group as such corporations.[7]

Code Sec. 280G contains an exemption for "small business corporations," which includes subchapter S corporations and privately held corporations that satisfy certain shareholder disclosure and approval requirements as to any payments to DIs (see ¶235).

---

[5] Reg. § 1.280G-1, Q&A-1(b).

[6] Code Sec. 280G(b)(2)(A); Reg. § 1.280G-1, Q&A-2.

[7] Reg. § 1.280G-1, Q&A-45 and 46.

.05 Code Sec. 409A

Code Sec. 409A, can apply to change in control agreements, in addition to deferred compensation plans, which were the original target of Congress. The failure to comply with 409A results in immediate income on deferrals, an excise tax of 20% and other penalties (see ¶265).

.06 Caps, Gross-Ups and Other Parachute Agreement Terms

Additionally, because the consequences of a payment that exceeds the limits of Code Sec. 280G and Code Sec. 4999 by even one dollar are so punitive, both the corporation and the executive generally have a strong incentive to deal with the possibility of an excess parachute payment in advance. Some change in control agreements are silent on the impact of payments resulting in excess parachute payments. There are ways to draft an agreement and deal with the Code limits (see ¶275).

.07 Litigation Over Change in Control Agreements

Perhaps not surprisingly, given the monetary amounts involved, change in control agreements have led to a significant amount of litigation. Generally, the litigation over change in control agreements has involved one of three issues:

1. whether a change in control occurred under the terms of the agreement;
2. whether the covered executive's voluntary resignation was on account of "good reason;" or
3. whether the company terminated the covered executive's employment for "cause."

Like most litigation over executive compensation or severance, the resolution of the change in control agreement cases has been very fact-specific (see ¶285).

.08 Change of Control in Bankruptcy Context

Recently, practitioners have received guidance on Code Sec. 280G issues in the context of a corporate bankruptcy from both the IRS and the federal courts (see ¶285).

¶215 Does a Payment Constitute a Parachute Payment?

Not all benefits paid in connection with a change in control are subject to Code Sec. 280G. To be deemed a "parachute payment," a payment must satisfy each the following four conditions:

1. the payment is paid to, or for the benefit of, a disqualified individual ("DI");
2. the payment is in the nature of compensation;
3. the payment is contingent on a change in the ownership of a corporation, the effective control of the corporation, or a substantial portion of the corporation's assets (a "change in control"); and

4. the aggregate present value of all payments that satisfy the first three conditions equals or exceeds an amount equal to three times the DI's "base amount."[8]

There is no requirement that a legally enforceable agreement is a necessary predicate to a determination that the payments constitute a golden parachute for purposes of Code Sec. 280G.[9] Note also that a golden parachute agreement may or may not constitute an employee benefit plan under ERISA, depending upon whether there is an ongoing administrative scheme.[10]

.01 Determining Who is a Disqualified Individual

A corporation may pay severance and other benefits to a large number of its employees following a change in control. However, the excess parachute payment restrictions only apply to "disqualified individuals." DIs include certain officers, shareholders, or highly compensated individuals who are employees or independent contractors of the corporation or of any corporation connected to the corporation by a parent-subsidiary relationship through 80 percent or more ownership (an "affiliated group member").[11] The regulations modify the DI definition so that fewer individuals will fall within the definition.

Shareholders. A shareholder is considered a DI if he or she owns stock with a fair market value that exceeds one percent of the total fair market value of the outstanding stock of the corporation or an affiliated group member [all classes of the corporation's stock.][12]

Officer. Whether an individual is an officer of the corporation is determined on the basis of all the facts and circumstances of the individual's situation, such as his or her authority and the nature of his or her duties.[13] An officer generally means an administrative executive who is in regular and continuous service with the corporation or an affiliated group member. No more than 50 employees (or, if less, the greater of three employees or 10 percent of the employees [rounded up]) will be treated as officers who are DIs.

Highly Compensated Individual. A highly compensated individual is an individual (1) whose compensation, on an annualized basis, is at least equal to the limit set forth in the definition of "highly compensated employee" under

---

[8] Code Sec. 280G(b)(2)(A); Reg. §1.280G-1, Q&A-2.

[9] *Cline v. Comm'r*, 100 TC 331, CCH Dec. 48,976, 34 F3d 480, 486 (7th Cir. 1994).

[10] See, e.g., *Lettes v. Gold*, CCH Pension Plan Guide Transfer Binder ¶23,968U (10th Cir. 2001), holding that a golden parachute agreement did not constitute an ERISA plan because there was no ongoing administrative scheme. In *U.S. v. Hemingway*, 99-2 ustc ¶50,667, 81 F.Supp.2d 1163 (D. Utah 1999), the District Court rejected a taxpayer's argument that payment had to be made by a target corporation in order to constitute a parachute payment. According to the court, the excise tax liability

applies to all payment agreements contingent upon a change in control, without regard to the payor.

[11] Code Sec. 280G(c); Reg. §1.280G-1, Q&A-15.

[12] Reg. §1.280G-1, Q&A-17(a). Under the 1989 regulations, a shareholder was considered a DI if he or she owned stock with a fair market value that exceeded the lesser of (i) one million dollars or (ii) one percent of the total fair market value of the outstanding stock of the corporation or an affiliated group member. The preamble to the 2002 regulations indicated that the one million dollar test was removed because it included individuals who did not possess significant influence over a company.

[13] Reg. §1.280G-1, Q&A-18.

Code Sec. 414(q),[14] and (2) who was part of the group consisting of the highest paid one percent of the employees (or, if less, the highest paid 250 employees) of the corporation and its affiliated group members.[15] For 2018, the Code Sec. 414(q) limit, which is adjusted periodically for cost-of-living increases, is $120,000.

DI Determination Period. An individual is considered a DI with respect to a corporation during the 12-month period prior to and ending on the date of change in control.[16] For example, if a corporation with a calendar year tax year incurs a change in control on July 31, 2009, the DI determination period would begin on August 1, 2008, and end on July 31, 2009.[17] The determination period for any change in control will be the 12 months immediately preceding the change in control, regardless of when the change occurs during a year.

In a 2006 private letter ruling, the IRS considered whether an individual in a complicated relationship on both sides of a transaction was a "disqualified individual" for purposes of Code Sec. 280G and Code Sec. 4999.[18] The IRS ruled that neither his role as chairman of the board nor his role as trustee of an affiliated real estate investment trust (REIT) made him a "disqualified individual" under the circumstances.

.02 Three Times Base Amount

If the aggregate present value of payments contingent on a change in control is *less than* three times the DI's base amount, then none of the payments are considered excess parachute payments.[19] If the aggregate present value of payments contingent on a change in control *equals or exceeds* three times the DI's base amount, then all of the payments in excess of one times the base amount are excess parachute payments.

Contingent Payments. The regulations modified the rules for determining the present value of a payment that is contingent upon an uncertain event, such as a severance agreement under which an individual must be involuntarily terminated within a specified period of time after a change in control before the DI is entitled to the payment (*i.e.*, a typical double trigger agreement). If there is at least a 50 percent probability that the uncertain payment will be made, the entire present value of the payment is included for purposes of determining if there is an excess parachute payment. However, if there is less than a 50 percent probability that the uncertain payment will be made, the present value of the payment is excluded from the three-times base amount test.[20]

---

[14] Reg. § 1.280G-1, Q&A-19. The 1989 regulations defined a highly compensated individual as an individual whose compensation was at least $75,000 and was part of the highest paid one percent of employees.

[15] Reg. § 1.280G-1, Q&A-19. Under the 1989 regulations, the period of time during which an individual was considered a DI was the portion of the year ending on the date of the change in control plus the immediately preceding twelve months. 1989 Reg. § 1.280G-1, Q&A-20.

[16] Reg. § 1.280G-1, Q&A-20.

[17] Under the 1989 regulations, if a company with a calendar year tax year incurred a change in control on July 31, 2002, the DI determination period would begin on January 1, 2001 and end on July 31, 2002, a period of 20 months.

[18] IRS Letter Ruling 200607006 (November 17, 2005).

[19] Reg. § 1.280G-1, Q&A-30(a).

[20] Reg. § 1.280G-1, Q&A-33(a).

If the initial determination on the probability of the uncertain payment was incorrect, the three-times base amount test generally must be reapplied.[21] However, if the three-times base amount test resulted in a determination that an individual received (or would receive) an excess parachute payment, without regard to the contingent payment at issue, and no base amount is allocated to the uncertain payment, then the three-times base amount test does not have to be reapplied.[22] In this situation, the total amount of the uncertain payment would be treated as an excess parachute payment.

Base Amount. The method of calculating a DI's "base amount" under Code Sec. 280G snares many more executives than one would expect. A DI's base amount equals the average annual compensation payable by the corporation and includible in the DI's gross income, computed over the DI's five most recent taxable years ending before the date the change in control occurs (the "base period").[23] Because most DIs' compensation increases from year to year, the five-year averaging has the effect of artificially lowering the DI's base amount figure, as compared to the DI's current annual compensation. For example, a change in control agreement that pays severance equal to 2.99 times the DI's annual compensation as of his or her employment termination would exceed three times the executive's base amount if the executive had received even modest raises during the preceding five years.

Another trap that can ensnare DIs is the fact that Code Sec. 280G calculates the base amount without reference to the DI's nonqualified plan deferrals. For example, the base amount of a DI who earned $180,000, $190,000, $200,000, $210,000, and $220,000 per year during the base period, but made nonqualified deferrals of 10% each year, would be $180,000, rather than $200,000.

In IRS Letter Ruling 200430019,[24] the IRS considered a strategy to reduce parachute amounts. The facts of the ruling request included a corporate merger that would result in certain executives receiving severance pay. The company amended the executives' salary continuation agreements, to provide accelerated payments before a merger. The accelerated payments will be reported on each executive's Form W-2 and applicable income and FICA tax will be withheld from such payments. Once the accelerated payments are made, the executives will not be required to return the accelerated payments under any circumstance, including termination of the merger.

---

[21] This approach differs substantially from the approach taken in the 1989 regulations, which required the taxpayer to make a reasonable estimate of the time and amount of any future payment, with the present value of the payment determined on the basis of the estimate. For example, assume that there was a 50% possibility that an individual will be terminated by the company, in which event he or she would be entitled to a payment of $100,000. Under the proposed and the final regulations, the amount taken into account for purposes of the three-times base amount test is $100,000, while

under the 1989 regulations the amount is $50,000. In these circumstances, it could be advantageous to continue to apply the 1989 proposed regulations.

[22] Reg. § 1.280G-1, Q&A-33(b).

[23] If the DI has been employed by the company less than five years, the portion of this five-year period during which the DI performed services for the company is the base period. Code Sec. 280G(d). If the base period includes a short tax year, then compensation paid during the short year is annualized. Reg. § 1.280G-1, Q&A-34(b).

[24] IRS Letter Ruling 200430019, April 7, 2004.

The IRS found that, if the merger is completed, the accelerated payments would constitute compensation to a disqualified individual due to a change in the ownership or effective control of the company within the meaning of Code Sec. 280G(b)(2)(A)(i)(I). However, the IRS also found that the accelerated payments would count toward determining each executive's base amount, since they were includible in the gross income of the executive for taxable years in the "base period." Thus, the accelerated payments are included in the base amount under Code Sec. 280G for the purpose of determining whether participants are subject to an excise tax under Code Sec. 4999 and the company is subject to any deduction limit under Code Sec. 280G.

Other Benefits. In addition, a DI's base amount includes every bit of additional compensation paid to the DI as a result of the change in control. For example, a change in control agreement that pays severance equal to 2.99 times the DI's annual compensation as of his or her employment termination would exceed three times his or her base amount if the DI receives any benefit continuation or acceleration of benefits.

One of the most common features of executive employment and/or change in control agreements is a requirement that the corporation continue to provide group health plan coverage for the executive and his or her family over a specified period of months. The regulations provide guidance on determining the present value of this benefit to the executive. Generally, the present value of the corporation's obligation to continue group health plan coverage must be determined in accordance with generally accepted accounting principles ("GAAP"). The corporation can measure this obligation by projecting the cost of premiums for purchased health care insurance, even if no health care insurance is actually purchased. If the obligation to provide health care coverage is made in coordination with the corporation's group health plan, then the premium used for determining present value may be the group premiums.[25]

Benefits payable to a DI under a nonqualified deferred compensation plan would not be counted if the DI is already fully vested in such benefits at the time of the change in control. However, if the change in control accelerates the vesting of such benefits, a portion would be treated as parachute payment according to the rules for vested versus unvested payments described below.[26]

.03 Compensation Paid

Not all benefits paid or bestowed upon employees following a change in control constitute "compensation" for purposes of the excess parachute tax. A payment is compensation if it arises out of the employment relationship or is associated with the performance of services for the corporation or a member of the corporation's controlled group. Compensation includes wages, salary, bonuses, severance pay, fringe benefits, other deferred compensation, and transferred property (such as stock or stock options).[27] The regulations clarify that compensation includes cash, the right to receive cash, or a transfer of property.[28]

[25] Reg. § 1.280G-1, Q&A-31(b)(2).
[26] Reg. § 1.280G-1 Q&A-24(d)(1).
[27] Reg. § 1.280G-1, Q&A-11.
[28] Reg. § 1.280G-1, Q&A-11(a).

The regulations also make clear that transfers of property include both incentive stock options (qualified under Code Sec. 421) and nonqualified stock options.[29] The IRS presumes that any payments the corporation (or a member of its controlled group) makes to an employee are compensation.

The value of a corporation's promise to continue the DI's compensation for a specified period of months is worth less, on a present value basis, than a DI's right to a lump sum cash payment.

Determining the Value of Stock Options. The regulations and Rev. Proc. 2002-13 provide extensive guidance on determining the value of options for purposes of Code Sec. 280G and Code Sec. 4999. In particular, the value of an option with no ascertainable fair market value at the time the option vests is based on all the facts and circumstances. Factors to take into account include the spread between the exercise price and the value of the property at the time of vesting, the probability that the value of the property will increase or decrease, and the length of time during which the option can be exercised.[30]

Under Rev. Proc. 2002-13, the value of an option may be determined by using any valuation method that is consistent with generally accepted accounting principles ("GAAP") and that takes into account the factors listed in the regulations. The Revenue Procedure also sets forth a safe-harbor valuation method that is based on the Black-Scholes method of valuing options and that takes into account, as of the valuation date, the following factors:

1. The volatility of the underlying stock;[31]

2. The exercise price of the option;

3. The value of the stock at the time of the valuation (the "spot price"); and

4. The term of the option on the valuation date, *e.g.*, the number of full months between the date of the valuation and the latest date on which the option will expire.[32]

The safe-harbor value of the option is calculated as the number of options multiplied by the spot price of the stock multiplied by a valuation factor set forth in an Appendix to the Revenue Procedure, which Appendix also reflects other elements of the Black-Scholes method, including the risk-free rate of interest and assumptions related to dividend yield. The IRS also requires, as a condition for reliance upon the Revenue Procedure, that the assumptions made and the determination of each factor be reasonable and consistent with assumptions made with respect to the options valued in connection with the change in ownership or control.

---

[29] Reg. § 1.280G-1, Q&A-13(a). The regulations provide that incentive stock options and nonqualified stock options are treated in the same manner, *i.e.*, payments in the nature of compensation.

[30] Reg. § 1.280G-1, Q&A-13(a).

[31] With respect to volatility, the taxpayer must determine whether the volatility of the underlying stock is low, medium or high, and follow a series of other rules set forth in the Revenue Procedure.

[32] If the term of the option exceeds ten years, then the safe harbor valuation method cannot be used.

The regulations clarify that a Code Sec. 83(b) election to recognize income in an earlier year will be disregarded in determining the value of accelerated vesting and the timing of a payment relating to restricted stock.

In Rev. Proc. 2002-45, the Internal Revenue Service clarified that accelerated options should be valued using a Black-Scholes or similar model for purposes of determining their parachute value. Valuing options on a Black-Scholes basis could result in an optionee being subject to the parachute tax on an *underwater option* that may be worthless. In light of this required option parachute valuation method, some companies have implemented shorter option or restricted stock vesting periods, or monthly, rather than annual vesting increments. Shorter or more frequent vesting periods would tend to reduce the parachute value attributable to option or restricted stock acceleration upon a change in control.

Generally, the parachute value of performance-based vesting awards is not measured in the same way as time-based vesting awards, since, for purposes of Code Sec. 280G, the general rule is that the full amount attributable to the accelerated payment of performance awards is treated as contingent on the change of control. Most companies do not design their equity compensation awards solely with an eye toward mitigating the potential negative tax consequences under Code Sec. 280G. However, companies need to understand how these design features affect other areas, including Code Sec. 280G and disclosure.

¶225 Payments Not Considered Parachute Payments

Code Sec. 280G expressly exempts certain types of payments from the definition of parachute payment (meaning a deduction may be taken for these payments, these payments are not subject to the 20 percent excise tax under Code Sec. 4999, and not included in the three-times base amount test).[33] Among the payments that Code Sec. 280G exempts from the definition of parachute payment are the following:

1. Payments with respect to a small business corporation or a corporation no stock of which is readily tradable on an established securities market.[34]

2. Amounts that the taxpayer establishes, by clear and convincing evidence, is reasonable compensation for personal services to be rendered *on or after* a change in control.[35]

3. Amounts that the taxpayer establishes, by clear and convincing evidence, is reasonable compensation for personal services actually rendered *before* the change in control.[36]

4. Payments to or from a tax-qualified plan, including a retirement plan described in Code Sec. 401(a), an annuity plan described in Code Sec. 403(a), a simplified employee pension plan described in Code Sec. 408(k)

---

[33] Reg. § 1.280G-1, Q&A-5.
[34] Code Sec. 280G(b)(5); Reg. § 1.280G-1, Q&A-6.

[35] Code Sec. 280G(b)(4)(A); Reg. § 1.280G-1, Q&A-9.
[36] Code Sec. 280G(b)(4)(B); Reg. § 1.280G-1, Q&A-3.

or a simple retirement account described in Code Sec. 408(p).[37] (Another one of the many reasons companies should make sure they have maximized benefits under their qualified plans).

The regulations include a detailed discussion of each of the foregoing types of exempt payments.

.01 Reasonable Compensation for Services Rendered Before or After a Change in Control

Reasonable compensation the corporation pays to the executive for services actually rendered to the corporation (1) before the change in control, or (2) on or after the change in control will not be counted as parachute payments. Although the statement of this concept seems fair, reasonable and straightforward, because many corporations, executives and lawyers have attempted to stretch it to protect payments from Code Sec. 280G and Code Sec. 4999, the Code and regulations require, to avoid any payment being treated as a parachute payment, that the taxpayer establish by clear and convincing evidence that such payment is reasonable compensation for services actually rendered before or after a change in control.[38]

Factors for determining whether the compensation is reasonable include (1) the nature of the services to be rendered, (2) the disqualified individual's (DI's) historic compensation for rendering such services, and (3) the compensation of individuals performing comparable services where the compensation is not contingent on a change in control. To qualify for the exemption for compensation paid for services rendered on or after the change in control, the regulations require that such compensation (a) only be paid for the period the DI actually performs services, (b) is not significantly greater than the DI's compensation prior to the change in control, and (c) is for duties and responsibilities that are substantially the same as before the change in control.[39]

Finally, the regulations reaffirm that reasonable compensation for personal services rendered includes reasonable compensation for holding oneself out as available to perform services, such as under a consulting agreement, and refraining from performing services (such as under a covenant not to compete).[40]

.02 Covenants Not to Compete

Code Sec. 280G(b)(4)(A) states that parachute payments do not include reasonable compensation for personal services to be rendered on or after the date of change in control. The regulations provide that reasonable compensation for personal services includes reasonable compensation paid for refraining from performing services.[41] The regulations specifically use a covenant not to compete as an example. Thus, as long as the payments made to an individual pursuant to

---

[37] Code Sec. 280G(b)(6); Reg. § 1.280G-1, Q&A-8. See Chapter 16 (¶ 1601 et seq.) for an extensive discussion of each of these types of qualified plans.

[38] Code Sec. 280G(b)(4)(B); Reg. § 1.280G-1, Q&A-3.

[39] Reg. § 1.280G-1, Q&A-42.

[40] Reg. § 1.280G-1, Q&A-42(b).

[41] See Reg. § 1.280G-1, Q&A-40(b).

¶225.01

the non-compete agreement are reasonable, they will not be parachute payments subject to Code Sec. 280G and Code Sec. 4999.

For a corporation and executive to use the exemption for payments made to a DI under an agreement to refrain from performing services, such as under a covenant not to compete, they must demonstrate by clear and convincing evidence that the agreement substantially constrains the individual's ability to perform services and there is a reasonable likelihood that the agreement will be enforced against the individual.[42] If the corporation has previously enforced similar restrictive covenants against former employees, the requirement that there is a reasonable likelihood that the agreement will be enforced would most likely be satisfied, though this requirement will need to be analyzed under each jurisdiction's limitations on the permissible scope of covenants not to compete. If the covenant not to compete does not satisfy these criteria, any payments made with respect to the covenant may be treated as severance payments[43] (which are never treated as reasonable compensation exempt from the parachute payment rules).

In a series of private letter rulings, the IRS explained that "compensation for services rendered following a change in control includes compensation in exchange for an agreement not to perform services." The regulations attempt to limit the ability of savvy accountants and lawyers to attribute a portion of the payments made under a change in control agreement to the covenant not to compete, thus qualifying for Code Sec. 280G's exemption for services performed after a change in control.

> **Planning Note:** By including noncompete, nonsolicitation and other restrictive covenants in the change in control agreement, counsel will allow accountants to attribute a portion of the severance payments to the covenant, thus qualifying for Code Sec. 280G's exemption for services performed after a change in control.

Whether the compensation is reasonable requires a facts and circumstances test that includes, but is not limited to, the nature of the services rendered, the individual's historic compensation for performing such services, and the compensation of individuals performing comparable services in situations where the compensation is not contingent on a change in ownership or control.[44] There is no requirement that a non-compete agreement be entered into prior to the change in control or subject to a pre-change employment agreement. Thus, if an acquiring company, for example, wishes to terminate an executive and pay him to refrain from performing certain services after termination, as long as the payment to the executive for post-change services is reasonable, it will not be subject to Code Sec. 280G and Code Sec. 4999. The timing of the non-compete agreement is irrelevant.

---

[42] Reg. § 1.280G-1, Q&A-42(b).
[43] Reg. § 1.280G-1, Q&A-42(b).

[44] Reg. § 1.280G-1, Q&A-40(a).

.03 Compensation Paid as Damages for a Breach of Contract

The regulations allow a taxpayer to demonstrate that certain payments should not be deemed parachute payment because they are damages for a breach of contract.[45] If a DI's employment agreement is involuntarily terminated before the end of its term, the regulations state that a showing of the following factors generally would be considered clear and convincing evidence that the payment is reasonable compensation for personal services to be rendered on or after the change in control:

1. The contract was not entered into, amended or renewed in contemplation of a change in control;

2. The compensation the DI would have received under the agreement would have qualified as reasonable under Code Sec. 162;

3. The damages do not exceed the present value of the compensation the DI would have received under the agreement had he or she continued to perform services for the employer until the end of the term;

4. The damages are received because the DI offered to provide personal services and the employer rejected the offer; and

5. The damages are reduced to the extent the DI earns income during the remainder of the term the agreement would have been in effect.[46]

Examples under the regulations indicate that the foregoing five factors could be used to shield payments made to an executive either where the acquiring corporation (a) terminates and pays the executive a damages amount no more than the present value of the remaining payments under the employment agreement (with a reduction for earnings from other employment), or (b) retains and pays the executive the same amount required under his or her existing employment agreement for services after the change in control.[47]

.04 Securities Violation Parachute Payments

Another category of payments made in connection with a change in control that are not exempt from Code Sec. 280G and Code Sec. 4999 are so-called securities violation payments.[48] The regulations define securities violation payments as payment made or to be made "pursuant to an agreement that violates any generally enforced Federal or State securities law or regulations."[49]

.05 Agreements Entered into After a Change in Control

Generally, agreements entered into after the change in control are not treated as contingent on a change in control and, thus, payments made under such agreements do not count as excess parachute payments.[50] However, an agreement executed after a change in control pursuant to a legally enforceable agree-

---

[45] Reg. §1.280G-1, Q&A-42(c). This issue is also discussed in the Severance and Retention Benefit Plans chapter, at ¶1435.

[46] Reg. §1.280G-1, Q&A-42(c).

[47] Reg. §1.280G-1, Q&A-42(d), Examples 1-4.

[48] Code Sec. 280G(b)(2)(B).

[49] Reg. §1.280G-1, Q&A-37.

[50] Code Sec. 280G(b)(4)(B); Reg. §1.280G-1, Q&A-23.

ment entered into before the change in control will not qualify for this exemption. More importantly, the regulations make clear that if a DI has a right to receive parachute payment under an agreement entered into before a change in control and gives up that right as bargained-for consideration for compensation and benefits under a post-change in control agreement, the payments to be made under the post-change agreement will qualify for the exemption only to the extent that the value of the payments under the post-change agreement exceed the value of the parachute payments under the pre-change agreement.[51]

Square D Co. v. Comm'r,[52] one of the most significant court decisions on the application of Code Sec. 280G, ruled on this issue. Square D was a publicly held company whose stock was traded on the New York Stock Exchange. In 1991, Square D was acquired by Schneider S.A., a French corporation and became indirectly owned by Schneider. In 1990, prior to the acquisition, Square D entered into employment agreements with certain executives who were "disqualified individuals" under Code Sec. 280G. The agreements provided for lump sum payments upon a change in control if an executive chose to terminate employment during the 13th month after the acquisition or if the company terminated the executive's employment within three years of the acquisition.

Schneider's acquisition of Square D triggered the executives' rights to the parachute payments. However, Schneider sought to retain the executives' services for Square D beyond the 13th month after the acquisition. As you might expect, the executives used their rights to parachute payments under the existing agreements as leverage to negotiate new agreements that also provided for significant lump-sum payments. The new agreements provided for lump-sum payments that were even larger than the parachute payments under the original agreements, and required an executive to remain employed with Square D for an additional three years (through 1994). However, the parties then amended the new agreements to accelerate the payment of the lump sums to December 1992 in exchange for an extension of the employment terms through 1995.

The IRS challenged the payments under Code Sec. 280G and Code Sec. 4999. The Tax Court agreed, holding that the lump-sum payments made in 1992 under the post-acquisition agreements were "contingent on a change in ownership or effective control" within the meaning of Code Sec. 280G(b)(2)(A)(i), because the payments *would not have been made but for the change in ownership or control.*

Companies and their counsel face this issue in many change in control transactions. The crux of the inquiry is whether a payment is contingent on a change in control. In other words:

- Would the payment have been made if no change in control occurred?
- Is it substantially certain that the payment will be made whether or not the change in control occurs?

---

[51] Reg. § 1.280G-1, Q&A-23.

[52] *Square D Co. v. Comm'r*, 121 TC No. 11, CCH Dec. 55,308 (2003).

As noted above, the regulations under Code Sec. 280G provide that a payment generally is not treated as contingent on a change of control if the payment is made pursuant to an agreement entered into after the change in control. However, the regulations also provide that if an individual gives up a right to receive a parachute payment in exchange for benefits under a post-change agreement, the benefits under the post-change agreement are a parachute payment up to the amount the individual would have received under the pre-change agreement. Simply entering into a new agreement after the change in control in exchange for giving up parachute payments under an existing agreement is not enough.

¶235 The Small Business Exemption

Code Sec. 280G(b)(5) contains an exemption for "small business corporations," including a corporation that, immediately before the change in control:

1. is an S corporation under Code Sec. 1361, or

2. has no stock that was readily tradable on an established securities market or otherwise,[53] and that satisfies certain shareholder approval requirements with respect to the payments to DIs.

For purposes of the shareholder approval requirement, the term "stock" does not include any stock that: (a) is not entitled to vote, (b) is limited and preferred as to dividends and does not participate in corporate growth to any significant extent, (c) has redemption and liquidation rights that do not exceed the issue price of such stock (except for a reasonable redemption or liquidation premium), (d) is not convertible into another class of stock, and (e) has redemption and liquidation rights that are not adversely affected by the parachute payments.[54]

Code Sec. 280G(b)(5)(B) provides that a corporation satisfies the shareholder approval requirements if: (1) the payment was approved by a vote of the persons who owned, immediately before the change in control, more than 75 percent of the voting power of all outstanding stock of the corporation, and (2) there was adequate disclosure to shareholders of all material facts concerning all payments that, but for this exception, would be parachute payments to a DI. Stock held by a DI is disregarded in determining whether the "more than 75 percent" approval requirement has been met.[55]

Inexplicably, the regulations impose a number of conditions that make it harder to satisfy these conditions.

.01 The Holding Company Exception

The regulations provide that the exemption for corporations with "no stock that was readily tradable on an established securities market" does *not* apply "if a substantial portion of the assets of a corporation undergoing a change in

---

[53] Reg. § 1.280G-1 Q&A-6(e) provides that stock is "readily tradable" if it is regularly quoted by brokers or dealers making a market in such stock.

[54] Reg. § 1.280G-1 Q&A, 6(d). Senate Com. Report Technical and Miscellaneous Revenue Act of 1988 ("TAMRA") (P.L. 100-647).

[55] Reg. § 1.280G-1, Q&A-7(b)(5).

ownership or control consists (directly or indirectly) of stock in another entity (or any ownership interest in such entity) and stock of such entity (or any ownership interest in such entity) is readily tradable on an established securities market or otherwise."[56]

.02 Voting Requirement

According to the regulations, the shareholder vote must determine the right of the DI to receive the payment, or, if the payment was made before the vote, the right of the DI to retain the payment.[57] This regulation clearly departs from the plain language of the statute. There is no evidence in the statute or legislative history that Congress intended the shareholder approval requirements to include the requirement that the separate shareholder vote must determine *the right* of an individual to receive or retain a parachute payment. Before the regulations, many practitioners held the view that once an executive had a contractual right to the payments, a shareholder vote could be taken to determine whether or not the payments could be deductible by the corporation, since the shareholders could no longer be asked whether or not the executive had a right to the payments. The regulations indicate that the vote cannot be framed as whether or not the corporation will be entitled to deduct the payments it is contractually obligated to make, which puts an inordinate amount of pressure on an executive. The regulations also state that the vote cannot indicate that approval of the change in control is contingent upon approval of the payments.[58]

The regulations also require that the payments must be approved in a separate vote of the shareholders. That is, the total payment submitted for shareholder approval must be separately approved by the shareholders.[59] However, the regulations indicate that the shareholders can approve, in a single vote, all payments submitted to the vote, including payments to more than one DI. However, not all payments to DIs must be subject to a shareholder vote to satisfy the voting requirement. It is permissible to submit to a vote only a portion of the payments that would otherwise be made to a DI.[60] For example, assume a DI has a base amount of $150,000 and would receive the following payments: (1) a bonus payment of $200,000, (2) vesting in stock options with a fair market value of $500,000, $200,000 of which is contingent on the change in control, and (3) a $100,000 severance payment. In this situation, the corporation may submit to the shareholders for approval (a) all of the payments, (b) any one of the three payments, or (c) $50,001 of any one of the payments (which would cause the total aggregate value of parachute payments to be less than three times the DI's base amount).

.03 Adequate Disclosure Requirement

The regulations provide that the adequate disclosure requirement of Code Sec. 280G(b)(5)(B) will not be met unless there is "full and truthful disclosure of the material facts and such additional information as is necessary to make the

---

[56] Reg. § 1.280G-1, Q&A-6(c).
[57] Reg. § 1.280G-1, Q&A-7(b)(1).
[58] Reg. § 1.280G-1, Q&A-7(b)(1).

[59] Reg. § 1.280G-1, Q&A-7(b)(1).
[60] Reg. § 1.280G-1, Q&A-7(b)(1).

disclosure not materially misleading . . . made to every shareholder of the corporation entitled to vote."[61] Before the regulations, some practitioners believed that disclosure could be limited to shareholders with 75 percent of the voting power. The regulations specify that the material facts that must be disclosed include the total amount of payments that would be parachute payments (absent the shareholder approval) and a brief description of each payment (*e.g.*, accelerated vesting of options, bonus or salary).[62]

.04 Tax-Exempt Entities

Payments made by a tax-exempt entity, which would otherwise constitute parachute payments, will not be considered parachute payments if two conditions are satisfied. First, the payment must be made by a tax-exempt organization. The regulations define a tax-exempt organization as any organization described in Code Sec. 501(c) that is subject to an express statutory anti-inurement provision, such as a Code Sec. 501(c)(3) charitable or educational institution, a social welfare organization under Code Sec. 501(c)(6), a VEBA under Code Sec. 501(c)(9), as well as other specified organizations such as qualified tuition programs under Code Sec. 529, black lung trusts, federal instrumentalities, and certain religions and apostolic organizations.[63] Second, the entity must meet the definition of a tax-exempt organization both immediately before and immediately after the change in control.[64]

¶245 Contingent on Change in Control

Generally, Code Sec. 280G treats a payment as contingent on a change in control only if the payment would not have been made unless the change in control occurred.[65] However, the Code also treats a payment as contingent on a change in control if the change in control accelerates the time at which the payment is made.[66] Thus, for example, if a change in control accelerates the vesting of options or the payment of a long-term incentive award, Code Sec. 280G treats the value of the acceleration as parachute payment.

There are two exceptions to this general rule, under which only a portion of the payment is treated as contingent on the change in control: one for vested payments, and one for unvested payments.

.01 Contingent

The regulations provide that a payment is treated as "contingent" on a change in ownership or control if "the payment would not, in fact, have been made had no change in ownership or control occurred."[67] A payment generally is treated as one that would not, in fact, have been made in the absence of a change in ownership or control unless it is substantially certain that, at the time of the change, the payment would have been made whether or not the change occurred.

---

[61] Reg. § 1.280G-1, Q&A-7(c).
[62] Reg. § 1.280G-1, Q&A-7(c).
[63] Reg. § 1.280G-1, Q&A-5(a)(4).
[64] Reg. § 1.280G-1, Q&A-6(a)(3).

[65] Reg. § 1.280G-1, Q&A-22(a).
[66] Reg. § 1.280G-1, Q&A-22(c).
[67] Reg. § 1.280G-1, Q&A-22(a).

The regulations also provide that agreements entered into within one year of the change in ownership or control are presumed to be on account of a change in ownership or control.[68] Under Code Sec. 280G(b)(2), parachute payments include "any" payment made on account of a change in ownership or control. The regulations merely create a presumption in the case of payments made pursuant to an agreement entered into within one year from the change in ownership or control. Agreements made more than one year before a change in control are still subject to Code Sec. 280G.[69]

A payment is treated as contingent on a change in control, even if the payment is also contingent on a second event.[70] For example, employment agreements often condition parachute payments on the termination of a DI's employment within a certain period of time after the change in control (a so-called "double trigger" agreement). The requirement of this second event would not prevent the payments from being treated as being made contingent on a change in control.

The general rule is that the entire amount of any payment made contingent on a change in control is treated as a parachute payment.[71] This general rule applies to payments due under a change in control agreement upon a termination of employment or change in control that, had there been no change, would have been paid for the continued performance of services after the termination of employment or change in control.[72] The general rule also applies to the accelerated payment of an amount that is otherwise payable only on the attainment of a performance goal or is contingent on an event or condition other than the continued performance of services for a period of time.[73]

.02 Vested Payments

A payment that is already vested is treated as contingent on a change in control if the time at which the payment is paid is accelerated. In this situation, the portion of the payment that is contingent on a change in control is the amount by which the accelerated payment exceeds the present value of the payment absent acceleration. If the amount of the payment without acceleration is not reasonably ascertainable, and the acceleration does not significantly increase the value of the payment, then the accelerated payment is equal to the present value of the payment absent acceleration. As a result, since the value of the accelerated payment is equal to the value of the payment absent acceleration, no portion of the payment is treated as contingent on a change in control. If the value of a payment absent acceleration is not reasonably ascertainable and the acceleration significantly increases the value of the payment, the future value of the payment is equal to the amount of the accelerated payment. In this situation, the portion of the payment that is treated as contingent on a change in control

---

[68] Reg. § 1.280G-1, Q&A-25.
[69] Chief Counsel Advice Memorandum 200944049.
[70] Reg. § 1.280G-1, Q&A-22(a).

[71] Reg. § 1.280G-1, Q&A-24(a).
[72] Reg. § 1.280G-1, Q&A-24(d)(2).
[73] Reg. § 1.280G-1, Q&A-24(d)(3).

equals the amount by which the future value of the payment exceeds the present value of the payment absent acceleration.[74]

.03 Unvested Payments

An unvested payment is treated as contingent on a change in control if the payment becomes vested as a result of a change in control, but only to the extent the payment was contingent only on the performance of services for a specified period of time and the payment is attributable in part to the performance of services before the date the payment is made. In this situation, the portion of the payment treated as contingent on the change in control is the lesser of (1) the amount of the accelerated payment or (2) the amount determined under the vested payment rules, above, plus an amount reflecting the lapse of the obligation to perform additional services. The amount reflecting the lapse of the obligation to perform services equals one percent of the amount of the accelerated payment multiplied by the number of full months until the payment would have become fully vested, absent the acceleration.[75]

The following example is illustrative of these principles. Assume that an employee receives a grant of 10,000 stock options on January 1, 2018. The stock options vest in 25% increments each year over the next four years, but become fully vested upon a change in control. On January 1, 2020, when 5,000 of the options are already vested, a change in control occurs. The other 5,000 stock options become vested as a result of the change in control, and, at this time, have a fair market value of $100,000. The portion of the $100,000 payment that is treated as contingent on the change in control is determined in two parts. First, the amount by which the $100,000 payment exceeds the present value, as of the date of the change in control, of the payment absent the acceleration must be determined. If we assume the present value is $75,000 for this example, the amount that is treated as contingent on a change in control is $25,000. Second, the amount representing the lapse in the obligation to continue to perform services in order for the 5,000 stock options to become fully vested must be determined. This amount must equal, at a minimum, $24,000 (1% times 24 months (until full vesting) times $100,000).

.04 Determining Whether a Change in Control Occurred for Purposes of Code Sec. 280G

Just because a corporate transaction triggers payments to certain executives does not necessarily mean that the Code's parachute limits apply. Code Sec. 280G only applies to payments that are "contingent on a change—(I) in the ownership or effective control of the corporation; or (II) in the ownership of a substantial portion of the assets of the corporation."[76]

A change in control includes a change in the ownership of a corporation. Generally, a change in ownership occurs on the date that any one person, or more than one person acting as a group, acquires ownership of a corporation's

---

[74] Reg. § 1.280G-1, Q&A-24(b).
[75] Reg. § 1.280G-1, Q&A-24(c).
[76] Code Sec. 280G(b)(2)(A).

stock that constitutes more than 50 percent of the total fair market value or total voting power of the corporation's stock. The regulations clarify that, for purposes of determining whether a group of individuals owns or has acquired more than 50 percent of the total fair market value or voting power of an entity, a person who owns stock in both entities involved in the transaction is considered acting as a group only with respect to other shareholders in that corporation and only to the extent of his or her ownership in that corporation, and not with respect to his or her ownership in the other corporation. This rule applies to both individuals and institutional entities, such as mutual funds, and will cause transactions to be treated as constituting a change in control or ownership in circumstances in which one reasonably could have concluded under the 1989 payment regulations that there was not a change in control.[77]

The regulations also provide guidance and examples of three distinct situations that trigger the limitations on parachute payments: (1) a change in ownership or control, (2) a change in effective control, and (3) a change in the ownership of a substantial portion of a corporation's assets.[78]

In most acquisitions, and in case of a so-called "merger of equals," it should be impossible for there to be a change in control as to both parties to the merger, since only one of the parties would acquire more than 50 percent of the other. Consistent with this interpretation of the regulations, the IRS has privately ruled that no "change in ownership or control" occurred as to Company Y when, after a merger, the shareholders of Company Y received *over* 50 percent of the value and voting power of the new entity. Additionally, the IRS found no "change in ownership or control" when all of Corporation X's assets were transferred to Corporation Y and Corporation Y was renamed.[79] Since Corporation X's shareholders received more than 50 percent of Corporation Y's stock in the transaction, no change in ownership or control of Corporation X occurred.

According to the regulations, a "change in effective control" is presumed to have occurred in two particular situations:

1. When "a majority of members of the corporation's board of directors is replaced during any 12-month period by directors whose appointment or election is not endorsed by a majority of the members of the corporation's board of directors prior to the date of the appointment or election."

2. When "any one person, or more than one person acting as a group, acquires (or has acquired during the 12-month period ending on the date of the most recent acquisition by such person or persons) ownership of stock of the corporation possessing 20 percent or more of the total voting power of the stock of such corporation."[80]

The first scenario of "change in effective control" will not occur in most negotiated transactions because a majority of the target's current board of direc-

---

[77] Reg. § 1.280G-1, Q&A-27(b).
[78] Reg. § 1.280G-1 Q&A-27 & 28.
[79] IRS Letter Ruling 9719003 (Dec. 24, 1996).
[80] Reg. § 1.280G-1 Q&A-28.

tors will endorse the election or appointment of the board of the surviving corporation.

The presumption created by a change in the ownership of 20% of the stock of a corporation may be rebutted. To rebut the presumption, the taxpayer must establish that "such acquisition or acquisitions of the corporation's stock . . . does not transfer the power to control (directly or indirectly) the management and policies of the corporation from any one person (or more than one person acting as a group) to another person (or group)."

Note that many agreements are drafted so that parachute payments are triggered by certain events that would not constitute a change in control under Code Sec. 280G. For example, a severance agreement could entitle a DI to severance payments upon the shareholders' approval of a merger, even if the merger does not close.[81] These payments may not trigger parachute payment taxes under Code Sec. 280G, but shareholders will not be pleased.

With respect to the timing of the payment of the 20% excise tax, it is generally paid in the tax year that the parachute payment is includible in the DI's gross income or, with respect to benefits excludible from gross income, in the year in which the benefit is received. However, the regulations permit a DI, for purposes of the excise tax, to treat certain payments as made in the year of change in ownership or control (or the first year for which a payment contingent on a change in ownership or control is certain to be made) even though the payment is not yet includible in income. The regulations further provide, however, that this treatment is unavailable if either the present value is not reasonably ascertainable or the payment relates to health benefits or coverage.

In IRS Letter Ruling 200348012,[82] the IRS considered whether a split-off/spin-off transaction and a merger transaction cause a change in ownership or effective control of, or a change in a substantial portion of assets of any of the corporations involved. As the IRS described it, Corporation 1 will incorporate Corporation 2 and immediately split-off/spin-off Corporation 2. Then Corporation 2 will merge with Corporation 3 and Corporation 4. The IRS viewed the split-off/spin-off and the merger as two separate transactions. After the split-off/spin-off, Corporation 1 will have transferred to Corporation 2 certain assets and will, therefore, have surrendered ownership of a substantial portion of its assets, as described in Q & A 29(a) of the regulations. However, Corporation 1 shareholders will still own over 50% of the stock of the entity to which ownership of those assets has passed, Corporation 2. Thus, according to Q & A 29(b)(3) and (4), and Example 3 of Q & A 29(d), this transfer will not be considered a change in ownership of a substantial portion of the assets of Corporation 1 for purposes of Code Sec. 280G. Q & As 27 and 28 will not apply to this transaction because Corporation 1 will not have parted with any of its stock and because there will be not be a change in the composition of Corporation 1's board of directors as a result of the transaction.

---

[81] See, for example, the aborted U.S. Airways Group, Inc. and Sprint Corporation mergers.

[82] IRS Letter Ruling 200348012, August 20, 2003.

After the merger, Corporation 2 will have surrendered its stock in exchange for Corporation 4 stock. According to Q & A 27, this would result in a change of ownership of Corporation 2. However, the former shareholders of Corporation 2 will still own, after the merger, greater than 50% of the stock of Corporation 4. Thus, Corporation 2 does not undergo a change of control.

Based on these facts the IRS ruled that (i) the split-off/spin-off will not cause a change in ownership, a change in effective control, or a change in the ownership of a substantial portion of the assets of Corporation 1; (ii) the provisions of Code Sec. 280G and Code Sec. 4999 will not apply to any payments made contingent upon the split-off/spin-off from Corporation 1 or Corporation 2 to the employees of Corporation 1 or Corporation 2; (iii) the merger will not cause a change in ownership, a change in effective control, or a change in the ownership of a substantial portion of the assets of Corporation 2; (iv) the provisions of Code Sec. 280G and Code Sec. 4999 will not apply to any payments made contingent upon the merger by Corporation 2 or Corporation 1 to the employees of Corporation 1 or Corporation 2; and (v) Corporation 3, however, will undergo a change in control.

In Revenue Ruling 2005-39,[83] the IRS applied an expansive interpretation for determining whether certain individuals owned stock with respect to which they had made an 83(b) election. The IRS ruled that an employee should be considered the owner of unvested shares of restricted stock for which he has made an 83(b) election for purposes of Reg. § 1.280G-1, Q & A-27 because the regulations under Code Sec. 83(b) treat stock transferred to an employee in connection with the performance of services as substantially vested when the employee makes an election under Sec. 83(b), and the employee is considered the owner of the stock for that purpose. The IRS also ruled that restricted stock with respect to which the employee has not made an 83(b) election is not considered outstanding for purposes of determining whether a change in ownership or control occurred.

In *Yocum v. U.S.*, Fed. Cl., No. 03-84 T (July 1, 2005) the U.S. Court of Federal Claims found that the transfer of a corporation's assets to a new joint venture could constitute a change "in the ownership of a substantial portion of the assets" of the employer making the transfer and, thus, the executive's $5.7 million payment, an "excess parachute payment" subject to excise tax under Code Sec. 4999.

A transaction where a corporation merged with a wholly owned subsidiary of a buyer and survived as a subsidiary of the buyer, resulted in a change of ownership of a substantial portion of the corporation's assets for purposes of Code Sec. 280G, but the IRS found that the removal of a book value restriction on the stock in the transaction was a non-compensatory cancellation of a non-lapse restriction under Code Sec. 83 and no portion of the consideration payable with respect to vested stock would constitute a parachute payment under Code Sec. 280G.[84]

---

[83] Rev. Rul. 2005-39, I.R.B. 2005-27, July 5, 2005. [84] IRS Letter Ruling 200840015 (June 26, 2008).

.05 Sale of Assets or Sale of a Subsidiary

For purposes of Code Sec. 280G, a change in the ownership of a substantial portion of a corporation's assets occurs on the date that any one person, or more than one person acting as a group acquires (or has acquired during the 12-month period ending on the date of the most recent acquisition) assets from the corporation that have a total gross fair market value equal to or more than one-third of the total gross fair market value of all of the assets of the corporation immediately prior to such acquisition or acquisitions. For this purpose, gross fair market value means the value of the corporation's assets, or the value of the assets being disposed of, determined without regard to any liabilities associated with such assets.

This rule would not apply to a transaction involving the transfer of stock (or issuance of stock) in a parent corporation, where stock in such corporation remains outstanding after the transaction. However, Code Sec. 280G applies to the sale of stock in a subsidiary (when that subsidiary is part of a controlled group of corporations with the parent) and to mergers involving the creation of a new corporation or with respect to the corporation that is not a surviving entity.[85] The regulations provide an example of how a sale of stock could trigger a change in control under the sale of assets test. Under the example, a company sells all of the stock of its wholly-owned subsidiary to another corporation. The fair market value of the affiliated group, determined without regard to its liabilities, is $210 million. The fair market value of the subsidiary, determined without regard to its liabilities, is $80 million. Because there is a change in more than one-third of the gross fair market value of the total assets of the affiliated group, there is a change in the ownership of a substantial portion of the assets of the affiliated group.[86]

¶255 Calculating the Amount of Excess Parachute Payments

To determine whether an excess parachute payment exists, add together all parachute payments to a DI. If this sum is at least three times the DI's base amount, there are excess parachute payments equal to the amount by which the total amount of all parachute payments exceeds the DI's base amount. This means the amount of a DI's excess parachute payment equals the amount by which the aggregate amount of all parachute payments exceeds one times (not three times) the DI's base amount.

If parachute payments are made at different times, the portion of the executive's base amount allocated to each parachute payment must be calculated. The portion of the base amount allocated to each parachute payment is determined by multiplying the base amount by a fraction, the numerator of which is the present value of the parachute payment at issue and denominator of which is the aggregate present value of all parachute payments.

The following three examples illustrate how to calculate the amount of an excess parachute payment.

---

[85] Reg. § 1.280G-1 Q&A-29.

[86] Reg. § 1.280G-1 Q&A-29, Example 4.

Example 1: Assume a DI's base amount equals $200,000, and the aggregate present value of the DI's payments that are contingent on a change in control total $599,999. In this situation, the DI's total parachute payments are less than three times the DI's base amount, so there are no excess parachute payments, and no excise tax is due.

Example 2: Assume a DI's base amount equals $200,000, and the aggregate present value of the payments is contingent on a change in control total $600,000. In this situation, since the parachute payments equal at least three times the DI's base amount, there are excess parachute payments. The excess parachute payment equals $400,000 ($600,000 minus $200,000). The excise tax on the DI is $80,000 (20% of $400,000). When we add the DI's basic federal income taxes of $234,000 on the full $600,000 (assuming a 39% tax rate), the DI must pay a total of $314,000 in federal taxes on the $600,000 in payments. Even before paying state income taxes, the DI takes home net payments of far less than if his or her parachute payments had been limited to 2.99 times his or her base amount.

Example 3: A DI's base amount equals $200,000, and the DI receives two parachute payments: a $200,000 payment at the time of the change in control, and a $700,000 payment at a future date. Assume that the present value of the future $700,000 payment is $600,000 at the time of the change in control. In this situation, the portion of the base amount allocated to the $200,000 parachute payment is $50,000 ($200,000 base amount times $200,000/$800,000). Since the $200,000 parachute payment is more than three times the $50,000 base amount allocated to it, the excess parachute payment with respect to this $200,000 parachute payment equals $150,000 ($200,000 less $50,000). The portion of the base amount allocated to the $700,000 parachute payment is $150,000 ($200,000 base amount times $600,000/$800,000). Since the $700,000 parachute payment is more than three times the $150,000 base amount allocated to it, the excess parachute payment with respect to this $700,000 parachute payment equals $550,000 ($700,000 less $150,000).

Planning Note: One strategy for preventing excess parachute payment is to increase the DI's base amounts as much as possible. This strategy is not available when the change in control is sudden and unexpected. However, many companies have a good idea that a change in control is imminent before the end of the last tax year that will be included in its DI's base period.

Increasing the DI's base amounts is as simple as increasing his or her taxable income in the last full tax year before the change in control, which will be the last year included in the DI's base periods. Among the tactics for increasing the DIs' taxable income in the last year of the base period are the following:

- Accelerate bonuses and deferred payments into the last base year;
- Accelerate the vesting of restricted stock or other taxable equity-based awards into the last base year;

- Exercise nonqualified stock options during the last base year; or
- Avoid deferring compensation during the last base year.

For the foregoing to be effective, the corporation cannot make any bonuses or accelerated payments contingent on the change in control.

Even accelerating into the last base year any one-time payments the corporation would have made to the executive after the change in control could have a significant beneficial effect. While the accelerated payment would be considered a parachute payment, it will also increase the executive's base amount. The net effect of accelerating the payment is to increase the executive's base amount by $0.20 for every dollar that was accelerated, which could shield additional amounts from the excess parachute payment.

¶265 Code Sec. 409A

Code Sec. 409A, added by the American Jobs Creation Act of 2004, is entitled "Inclusion in Gross Income of Deferred Compensation Under Nonqualified Deferred Compensation Plans." However, Code Sec. 409A, can apply to *change in control agreements*, in addition to deferred compensation plans, which were the original target of Congress. The failure to comply with Code Sec. 409A results in immediate income on deferrals, an excise tax of 20% and other penalties.

Code Sec. 409A applies to any plan or arrangement that provides for the deferral of compensation. Regulations under Code Sec. 409A[87] state that an arrangement provides for the deferral of compensation if, under the terms of the agreement and the relevant facts and circumstances, the executive has a legally binding right during a taxable year to compensation that, (i) has not been actually or constructively received and included in gross income, and (ii) pursuant to the terms of the agreement, is payable to (or on behalf of) the executive in a later year. Since a change in control agreement creates a legally binding right to payments on the executive's signing of the agreement — payments that will be made in a later year - it fits this definition.

The effect of Code Sec. 409A on change in control agreements depends on whether any stock of the employer is publicly traded on an established securities market.

- For public companies, if an executive is a "key employee" of the company (generally, one of the top 50 highest paid for the preceding calendar year) as of the date of the executive's separation from service, a six-month delay applies to payments made due to a "Separation from Service" (as defined in the regulations), unless an exception applies.

- For private and public companies, separation payments made over time will be subject to Sec. 409A and the timing and form of the payments cannot be changed without following the restrictions of 409A.

---

[87] The Treasury and IRS issued 397 pages of final regulations under Code Section 409A on April 10, 2007.

The final regulations clarify that separation pay is only subject to Code Sec. 409A if it is conditioned upon separation from service. Amounts that would be paid upon other events, like change in control or a date certain, are not separation pay (although they still could be subject to Code Sec. 409A).

.01 Change in Control Separation Pay and Public Companies

For public companies, the application of Code Sec. 409A to separation pay is crucial because Code Sec. 409A requires a six-month delay in payments, if, as of the date of the executive's separation from service, the executive is a "key employee" (discussed below). The final regulations provide certain exceptions from 409A for separation payments. The exceptions apply to payments made only on an involuntary separation that are:

1. Made in a lump sum following an involuntary separation;

2. Less than the Code Sec. 401(a)(17) amount;

3. Made under certain foreign plans or agreements; or

4. Certain reimbursements and in-kind payments.

> **Example:** If a change in control agreement with a public company CEO provided that the company would pay it's CEO $1 million in lump sum immediately following a termination of the CEO without cause, this lump sum payment ordinarily would not be subject to Code Sec. 409A, because it qualifies for the short-term deferral exception (payment is made in the same year as the right to payment becomes vested).

Separation pay from a change in control agreement will not qualify as "involuntary" if the change in agreement provides for payments upon a separation for "good reason" — even if the actual termination was involuntary — unless the definition of "good reason" satisfies a safe harbor in the final regulations or otherwise is tough enough to satisfy the IRS. Separation pay rules also apply to private companies, in the event of (i) payments on a voluntary separation or (ii) payments on involuntary separation that continue for longer than two years *or* exceed two times the lesser of the executive's annual pay or the Code Sec. 401(a)(17) limit.

.02 Separation for Good Reason

Under the safe harbor definition of separation for good reason in the final regulations, the separation from service must occur during a pre-determined, limited period not to exceed two years following the initial existence of one or more of the following conditions, arising without the consent of the executive:

1. A material diminution in the executive's base compensation.

2. A material diminution in the executive's authority, duties, or responsibilities.

3. A material diminution in the authority, duties, or responsibilities of the supervisor to whom the executive is required to report, including a requirement that an executive report to a corporate officer or other employee instead of reporting directly to the board of directors of a

corporation (or similar governing body with respect to an entity other than a corporation).

4. A material diminution in the budget over which the executive retains authority.

5. A material change in the geographic location at which the executive must perform the services.

6. Any other action or inaction that constitutes a material breach by the employer of the agreement under which the executive provides services.[88]

The amount, time, and form of payment upon the separation from service for good reason must be substantially identical to the amount, time and form of payment payable due to an actual involuntary separation from service (to the extent such a right exists). Additionally, the change in control agreement must require the executive to provide notice to the employer of the existence of the condition described above within a period not to exceed 90 days of the initial existence of the condition. The agreement also must give the employer a period of at least 30 days following receipt of the notice during which it may remedy the condition and not be required to make separation payments.

.03 Other Exceptions for Separation Payments

The final regulations provide a few other useful exceptions for separation pay under Code Sec. 409A. Moreover, the final regulations clarify that employers may use *more than one of the separation pay exceptions* for each payment or separation (so-called "stacking" of the separation payments).

The final regulations provide an exception for certain limited payments made following an involuntary separation from service, to the extent the payments do not exceed two times the lesser of the Code Sec. 401(a)(17) limit ($275,000 for 2018) or the executive's annual compensation for the year prior to the year of separation, and the agreement provides that the separation pay must be paid no later than the last day of the second taxable year of the executive following the taxable year of the executive in which he or she incurred the separation from service.[89] If the employer pays *more than* two times the lesser of the executive's annual pay or the Code Sec. 401(a)(17) limit, the exception still applies to the amount paid *up to* the limit. No similar rule applies for payments continuing for longer than two years. Such payments would be completely subject to Code Sec. 409A.

The final regulations also clarify that non-taxable benefits provided following separation from service are not subject to Code Sec. 409A. Continuing health plan coverage is the most common non-taxable benefit provided under change in control agreements. However, continuing health plan coverage is not always a non-taxable benefit (for example, if it is provided on a discriminatory basis). Taxable medical benefit reimbursements still may be able to qualify for an exception, to the extent they are paid over a period no longer than the applicable

---

[88] Treas. Reg. § 1.409A-1(n)(2).   [89] Treas. Reg. § 1.409A-1(b)(9)(iii).

COBRA coverage period (18 or 36 months), under the exception discussed next below.

.04 Reimbursements and In-Kind Benefits

The final regulations provide that to the extent a change in control agreement (including an agreement providing payments upon a *voluntary separation from service*) entitles an executive to payment of reimbursements:

(a) that are not otherwise excludible from gross income, for expenses that the executive otherwise could deduct under Code Sec. 162 or 167 as business expenses incurred in connection with the performance of services (ignoring any applicable limitation based on adjusted gross income), or

(b) of reasonable outplacement expenses and reasonable moving expenses actually incurred by the executive and directly related to the termination of services for the employer.[90]

An agreement does not provide for a deferral of compensation to the extent such rights apply during a limited period (regardless of whether such rights continue beyond the limited period). The reimbursement of reasonable moving expenses includes the reimbursement of all or part of any loss the executive actually incurs due to the sale of a primary residence in connection with a separation from service.

The final regulations provide that a "limited period of time" in which expenses may be incurred, or in which in-kind benefits may be provided by the employer or a third party that the employer will pay, does not include periods beyond the last day of the second taxable year of the executive following the executive's taxable year in which the separation from service occurred, provided that the period during which the reimbursements for such expenses must be paid may not extend beyond the third taxable year of the executive following the taxable year in which his or her separation from service occurred.

The final regulations provide that a terminating executive's entitlement to in-kind benefits, such as the continued use of a car or corporate aircraft, membership dues or payment for financial or tax advice, from the employer, or a payment by the employer directly to the person providing the goods or services to the executive, will not be treated as providing for a deferral of compensation under Code Sec. 409A to the extent such rights apply during a limited period of time (regardless of whether such rights extend beyond the limited period of time).

Finally, the final regulations provide an exception for amounts less than Code Sec. 402(g) limit - $18,500 in 2018.

.05 Specified Employees

Code Sec. 409A provides that distributions to a "specified employee" may not be made before the date that is six months after the date of the executive's

---

[90] Treas. Reg. § 1.409A-3(i)(1)(iv)(A) and (B).

separation from service or, if earlier, the date of the executive's death (the "six-month delay rule"). The six-month delay rule applies to payments under deferred compensation and other non-qualified plans, but also payments under change in control agreements. The final regulations provide that the employer must write into the agreement the six-month delay rule.[91]

Code Sec. 409A and the final regulations provide that the term "specified employee" means an employee who, as of the date of his or her separation from service, is a key employee of an employer whose stock is publicly traded on an established securities market or otherwise.[92] An employee is a "key employee" if the executive meets the requirements of Code Sec. 416(i)(1)(A)(i), (ii), or (iii) (the top-heavy plan rules) at any time during the 12-month period ending on a "specified employee identification date" (generally, December 31).[93] If an executive is a key employee as of a specified employee identification date, the executive is treated as a key employee for purposes of Code Sec. 409A for the entire 12-month period beginning on the specified employee effective date (or for a different 12-month period beginning within three months of that date).

Code Sec. 416(i)(1)(A) provides that the term "key employee" means an employee who, at any time during the year, is —

    (a) an officer of the employer having an annual compensation greater than $175,000 (for 2018) (as adjusted at the same time and in the same manner as under Code Sec. 415(d)),

    (b) a 5-percent owner of the employer, or

    (c) a 1-percent owner of the employer having an annual compensation from the employer of more than $150,000.

Sec. 416(i)(A) also provides that no more than 50 employees (or, if lesser, the greater of 3 or 10 percent of the employees) are treated as officers. The definition of compensation under Treas. Reg. § 1.415(c)-2(a) applies, unless the agreement or employer specifies another definition.

The final regulations provide that, like the six-month delay rule, an agreement must specify the method for determining key employees and for applying the six-month delay rule.[94] To meet the six-month delay requirement, an agreement may provide that: (a) any payment pursuant to a separation of service due within the six-month period is delayed until the end of the six-month period, or (b) each scheduled payment that becomes payable pursuant to a separation from service is delayed six months, or (c) combination thereof.

.06 Code Sec. 409A and Excise Tax Gross-Up Payments

Excise tax gross-ups can meet Code Sec. 409A distribution requirements if the agreement provides that payments will be made by the end of the year following the year in which the taxes are remitted.[95] Counsel might want to add the following language to a change in control agreement for this purpose:

---

[91] Treas. Reg. § 1.409A-1(c)(3)(v).

[92] Treas. Reg. § 1.409A-1(i)(1).

[93] Treas. Reg. § 1.409A-1(i)(3).

[94] Treas. Reg. § 1.409A-3(i)(2)(ii).

[95] Treas. Reg. § 1.409A-3(i)(1)(v).

Payment will be made by the end of the executive's taxable year next following the executive's taxable year in which the executive remits the related taxes, in accordance with Code Section 409A and Treas. Reg. § 1.409A-3(i)(1)(v) (or any similar or successor provisions).

¶275 Caps, Gross-Ups and Other Parachute Agreement Terms

Because the consequences of a payment that exceeds the limits of Code Sec. 280G and Code Sec. 4999 by even one dollar are so punitive, both the corporation and the executive generally have a strong incentive to deal with the possibility of an excess parachute payment in advance.

.01 Dealing with the Possibility of Excess Parachute Payments

Some change in control agreements are silent on the impact of payments resulting in excess parachute payments. However, better-drafted agreements generally deal with the Code limits in one of the following ways:

1. The employment or change in control agreement limits the corporation's payments to the DI's to an amount that, when combined with all other payments to the DI under any other corporate plans, policies or arrangements, would be $1 less than the amount that would constitute an excess parachute payment. Under this design, the DI often has the right to choose which benefits or payments to forego.

2. The agreement requires the corporation to make a "gross-up payment" to the DI if payments under the agreement result in excess parachute payments and the DI is liable for the payment of an excise tax under Code Sec. 4999. This gross-up provision would generally require payments sufficient to make the DI whole for the excise tax he or she is required to pay due to both the excess parachute payment and the gross-up payment.

3. The agreement contains a so-called "best after-tax amount" provision, which will pay the DI either (a) $1 less than the amount that would constitute an excess parachute payment, or (b) the uncapped amount with no gross up, whichever results in a greater net after-tax benefit to the DI.

4. The agreement provides that, if the aggregate "after-tax amount" (as defined below) of the total payments and the gross-up payment that would be payable to the DI does not equal or exceed 110% of the "after-tax floor amount" (as defined below), then no gross-up payment shall be payable to the DI and the aggregate amount of payments payable to the DI shall be reduced to the "floor amount" (as defined below).

"After-tax amount" means the portion of a specified amount that would remain after payment of all federal, state, and local taxes, and excise tax paid or payable by DI in respect of such specified amount. "After-tax floor amount" means the after-tax amount of the floor amount. "Floor amount" means the greatest pre-tax amount of payments that could be paid to the DI without causing the DI to become liable for any excise tax liability.

In nearly all agreements that address the consequences of an excess parachute payment, the agreement requires a public accounting firm to perform the calculations. For a more detailed discussion of these calculation issues, see the checklist in ¶10,010.

> **Comment:** Because executives do not want to have their benefit and/or payments reduced (or pay excise taxes), and corporations do not want to make large, non-deductible gross-up payments, it is in all parties' best interests to find ways to avoid having the payments characterized as parachute payments or reduce the amount of payments subject to the limits.

Most change in control agreements provide that all determinations required to be made under the tax gross-up provisions, including whether and when a gross-up payment is required, the amount of the gross-up payment and the assumptions to be used in arriving at the determinations, will be made by an independent public accounting firm agreed to by the corporation and the executive. Well-drafted agreements require the accounting firm to provide detailed supporting calculations to both the corporation and the executive within a specified number of business days after receiving notice that there have been payments under the agreement (or at some earlier time requested by the corporation). Some agreements will provide that if the accounting firm is serving as accountant or auditor for the acquirer or any of its affiliates, the executive will designate another nationally recognized accounting firm to make the determinations required. All agreements provide that the fees and expenses of the accounting firm will be borne solely by the corporation. If the accounting firm determines that no excise tax is payable by the executive, it should give the executive a written opinion that the failure to report an excise tax on the executive's applicable federal income tax return would not result in the imposition of a negligence or similar penalty.

Most change in control agreements recognize that, as a result of the uncertainty in the application of Code Sec. 4999, it is possible that the IRS or other agency will claim that a greater excise tax is due, and thus a greater amount of gross-up payment should have been made by the corporation than originally determined. Most agreements provide that if the executive is required to make a payment of any such excise tax, the accounting firm will determine the amount of the underpayment that has occurred, if any, and the corporation will promptly pay the underpayment to the executive. The agreement should require the executive to notify the corporation of any claim by the IRS or other agency that, if successful, would require payment by the corporation of the gross-up payment or an underpayment.

.02 Menu of Common Provisions

The following chart lists the most common benefits payable under change in control agreements and the status of each:

Type of Payment	Counted as Parachute Payment?
Payment equal to a multiple of the executive's annual salary or total compensation (or compensation/salary continuation)	Yes
Severance payment	Yes
Automatic bonus payments. For example: (1) a payment equal to two times an executive's largest bonus, or (2) a *pro rata* portion of target bonus for year in which employment terminates	Yes
Acceleration of long-term performance plan payments	Yes (to the extent of the acceleration)
Continuation of welfare benefits (*e.g.*, medical, dental, life, and disability insurance), other than as required by law	Yes
Qualified retirement plans (including defined benefit pension, money purchase pension, profit sharing, 401(k), and employee stock ownership plans):	
Distributions from a qualified retirement plan following termination of employment	No
Lump sum amount equal to the present value of the additional benefit the executive would have accrued under the qualified retirement plans had he or she continued to participate through the last day of the severance period	Yes
Full vesting of all benefits under the qualified retirement plans (to the extent not vested upon the change in control)	Yes (to the extent of the acceleration)
Cash payment equal to any unvested benefits under a qualified plan	Yes
Adding three years to the executive's age and years of service for purposes of determining the executive's eligibility for and benefits under the qualified retirement plan	Yes
Payment equal to any unvested matching contributions that the executive forfeits upon termination after a change in control	Yes
Payment equal to matching contributions that would have been made on the executive's behalf during the severance payout period had the executive made the maximum 401(k) contribution	Yes
Nonqualified supplemental executive retirement plans (*e.g.*, SERP, excess plan, etc.):	Yes
Distribution from a nonqualified plan following termination of employment	No
Lump sum amount equal to the present value of the additional benefit the executive would have accrued under a nonqualified plan had he or she continued to participate through the last day of the severance period	Yes
Full vesting of all benefits under the nonqualified plan (to the extent not vested upon the change in control)	Yes (to the extent of the acceleration)

Type of Payment	Counted as Parachute Payment?
Cash payment equal to any unvested benefits under the nonqualified plan	Yes
Adding three years to the executive's age and years of service for purposes of determining the executive's eligibility for and benefits under a nonqualified plan	Yes
Payment equal to any unvested matching contributions that the executive forfeits upon termination after a change in control	Yes
Cash out or liquidation of vested stock options, restricted stock or other equity awards	No
Accelerated vesting of stock options, restricted stock or other equity awards	Yes (to the extent of the acceleration)
Credit for additional years of service toward eligibility for retiree medical or life insurance benefits	Yes
Outplacement services	Yes
Continued coverage under indemnification agreement and/or directors' and officers' liability coverage	No
Employee stock purchase plan (Code Sec. 423 Plan)	No (Payments are not contingent on a change in control and not accelerated)
Continuation of executive prerequisites (*e.g.*, company car, country club dues)	Yes
Promise to pay executive's out-of-pocket expenses, including attorneys' fees, in the event the executive successfully enforces any provision of the agreement in any action, arbitration, or lawsuit	Most likely No

.03 Designing, Drafting and Acting to Mitigate the Code Sec. 280G Excise Tax Hit

For many executives, the total payments provided under their severance or change in control agreements, when combined payments and benefits under the company's omnibus stock incentive plan and other compensation or benefit plans ("total payments") in connection with a change in control would be subject to the "excess parachute payment" excise tax under Code Secs. 4999 and 280G. Over time, we have developed or utilized a variety of strategies for reducing the amount of such payments that would be subject to the tax, which are accepted by the IRS.

1. *Link Change in Control Payment to Compliance with Restrictive Covenants.* As discussed in ¶225.02 above, linking severance payments under the change in control agreement to non-compete, non-solicit, and other restrictive covenants would cause all or a part of the linked payments to be excluded from the calculation of "excess parachute payments" as reasonable compensation for personal services actually rendered by the executive after the date of the change in control. IRS regulations under Code Sec. 280G expressly provide that the performance of services includes holding oneself out as available to perform

services and refraining from performing services (such as under a covenant not to compete or similar arrangement).

Some companies will seek the assistance of their accounting firm to estimate a reasonable value for the non-compete provision, which would be supportable for use in the determination of "reasonable compensation for services." However, as a rule of thumb, an enforceable one-year non-compete provision should reduce the amount included in the calculation of "excess parachute payments" by the full amount of the executive's total annual compensation (including salary, annual bonus, and equity award value).

2. *Modify the Vesting Provisions of Equity Awards.* Code Sec. 280G does not count toward the calculation of "excess parachute payments," payments to an executive that derive from vested equity awards. In fact, any equity awards that had become taxable unrelated to the change in control would be counted on the base amount side of the equation, making it less likely that other payments to the executive would become excess parachute payments (as discussed below). Generally, full value (stock price) of a performance-based award for which vesting is accelerated will count toward the calculation of "excess parachute payments." The parachute value of stock options, restricted stock, and RSUs is measured differently, based on the percentage of time remaining in the vesting period, resulting in somewhat less value being counted toward the calculation of "excess parachute payments."

3. *Increase the Base Amount.* An effective strategy for reducing the amount of excess parachute payment is to increase each executive's base amount as much as possible. This strategy may not be available when the change in control is sudden and unexpected. However, when the company has an idea that a change in control is likely to occur in a following tax year, *e.g.*, after December 31 of the current year, this strategy can be very beneficial. Increasing an executive's base amount can be as simple as increasing his or her taxable income in the last full tax year before the change in control (which will be the last year included in the executive's base periods).

Among the commonly used methods for increasing an executive's base amount are the following: (a) accelerate bonuses and deferred payments into the current base year, (b) accelerate the vesting of restricted stock or other taxable equity-based awards into the last base year, and (c) exercise non-qualified stock options during the last base year.

4. *Shifting the Close Date.* If the transaction is set to close near the end of the calendar year, delaying the closing date to the following calendar year may increase the base amount in a period of increasing taxable income to each executive or the base amount may increase when an executive has not captured full cycles of taxation on equity awards, *i.e.*, a recently hired employee.

5. *Change Single-Trigger Payments to Double-Trigger.* Double-trigger payments still count toward the calculation of excess parachute payments, but the amount is less because the acceleration is not certain. This strategy may not be available

to the company's executives, since payments under the change in control agreements already are double trigger.

6. *Transaction Bonus Payment.* As noted above, payments to an executive are not counted toward the calculation of excess parachute payments to the extent such payments are attributable to services performed before the change in control. A company could provide a cash bonus amount to the executive under a separate agreement, which is directly linked to the significant additional workload attributable to closing a change in control transaction.

7. *Consulting Agreement.* As noted above, the regulations under Code Sec. 280G exclude reasonable compensation for personal services actually rendered by the executive after the date of the change in control. It is probably premature to discuss this method, but companies often use it to exempt a portion of the total payment.

8. *Shift Nonqualified Plan Benefits to a Qualified Plan.* Code Sec. 280G counts certain nonqualified plan payments that are made on account of a change in control in the calculation of "excess parachute payments." However, it does not count payments to or from a tax-qualified plan toward that calculation. This method may not be available to the company, but the company could evaluate the possibility of reducing the amount payable to the executives from its nonqualified plans upon a change in control. This could be accomplished by shifting a portion of the benefits accrued by the executive under the nonqualified plans to the qualified plans through a process often referred to as a SERP-switch, SERP-swap or QSERP. This action also has other benefits to the executive, such as making promised retirement benefits more secure.

¶285 The Prevalence of Parachute Agreements; Litigation and Bankruptcy

The proliferation of change in control agreements has raised a variety of practical and legal issues in addition to the tax issues under Code Sec. 280G and Code Sec. 4999.

.01 Prevalence of Change in Control Agreements

Despite the punitive limits of Code Sec. 280G and Code Sec. 4999, corporations have increasingly adopted golden parachute and severance agreements for their executive employees. There are at least two reasons for this. First, continued merger and acquisition activity has caused executives to demand change in control protection from their employers. Golden parachute agreements not only pay out handsome benefits to executives terminated following a change in control, but also help retain the executives prior to any potential change in control by reassuring them that if their employment is terminated following a change, they will receive severance and benefits. An executive can continue to concentrate on his or her daily duties without worry.

Additionally, the spread of parachute agreements is a trend that feeds itself. As each employer and each newly public company provides golden parachute agreements to its executives, this fact appears in surveys and boardrooms across the country. The number and percentage of executives with golden parachute agreements, and the generosity of those agreements, has risen steadily over the years. Agreements and features that were limited to the top 5 or 10 percent of agreements ten years ago may appear in the 50 percent range today.

Finally, the increase in initial public offerings ("IPOs") during the last several years has fuelled the growth in parachute agreements. Golden parachute agreements are more common among public companies than private. Often, the corporation will adopt such agreements at the time of the IPO.

An early reminder of the prevalence and use of change in control or golden parachute agreements came in November 2004. Following the decision of Merck & Co., Inc. to withdraw its blockbuster painkiller Vioxx in light of information suggesting that it may lead to increased risk of heart attack, Merck filed a Form 8-K to report the adoption of the Merck & Co., Inc. Change in Control Separation Benefits Plan. According to the 8-K, participants in the plan include approximately 230 members of Merck's management committee and other vice president-level managers. The plan provides for a participant to receive severance pay equal to a multiple of the sum of his or her base salary plus a target bonus amount upon a qualifying termination of employment in connection with or within two years following a change in control of the company. The multiples under the plan are three, two, or one-and-one-half, depending on tier of participation under the plan. A participant is entitled to receive a *pro rata* annual cash bonus at target levels, paid in a lump sum at termination, continuing medical, dental and life insurance benefits at active-employee rates for a period of years equal to the multiple, enhanced retirement benefits, continued financial planning benefits and outplacement benefits. Management committee members are entitled to full indemnification for any excise taxes that may be payable under Section 4999 of the Internal Revenue Code of 1986, as amended, in connection with the change in control. The Merck board adopted an amendment to the company's 2004 incentive stock plan to provide for the full vesting of all outstanding stock options and restricted stock units upon a change in control of the company.

.02 Perceptions of the Public and Acquirers

In *Cline v. Comm'r*,[96] the U.S. Court of Appeals of the Seventh Circuit provided a succinct summary of the congressional purpose underlying the enactment of Code Sec. 280G:

> The golden parachute provisions . . . were added to the Internal Revenue Code by the Deficit Reduction Act of 1984 in order to discourage the use of golden parachutes payments to senior executives of a company in the event of a corporate takeover. Congress found that agreements to make such payments hindered "acquisition activity in the marketplace" by making target corporations less attractive to prospective investors. The prospect of a handsome payment tends to encourage management personnel of the target corporation

---

[96] *Cline v. Comm'r*, 94-2 ustc ¶50,468, 34 F3d 480 (7th Cir. 1994), affirming *Balch v. Comm'r*, 100 TC 331, CCH Dec. 48,976 (1993).

to favor a proposed takeover, regardless of whether the takeover would be in the best interest of the target corporation's shareholders.

Notwithstanding the general concern about golden parachutes payments, the argument that they are against public policy has been rejected by the U.S. Court of Appeals for the Sixth Circuit.[97] As the existence of change in control agreements has become commonplace in corporate America, acquirers and potential acquirers have grown accustomed to them. Instead of "making target corporations less attractive to prospective investors," as the *Cline* court and Congress may have feared, prospective acquirers now simply calculate the potential cost of the change in control agreement as part of the transaction.

However, some of the provisions found in change in control agreements are more repugnant to prospective acquirers than others. One of acquirers' least favorite provisions in change in control agreements is the single trigger. Acquirers dislike single trigger provisions in agreements because the single trigger significantly reduces the acquirers' ability to retain key management after the acquisition, and makes it virtually certain that the acquirer will have to pay the full cost of the agreement. Even modified single trigger provisions, *e.g.*, giving the executive the right to leave employment and receive payment for any reason or no reason, after a fixed period, are less repugnant to acquirers because at least those agreements give the acquirer some period to convince the executive to stay or negotiate another arrangement. (See, also, the discussion in ¶ 295.03.)

Acquirers generally do not like to see tax gross-up provisions in the agreements of a target company. Although these provisions have become more and more common, they represent a huge increase in costs, virtually all non-deductible, for the acquirer.

.03 Litigation Over Change in Control Agreements

As the prevalence and value of change in control agreements has increased, so has the litigation over payments to be made under such agreements. Certainly the gross-up payments required under many change in control agreements and the nondeductibility of excess parachute payments has increased the stakes for companies, along with their willingness to fight disputes in court.

Was the Executive's Termination Voluntary? A majority of the cases in this area have involved former employees' claims for severance benefits despite the apparent voluntary termination of their employment. Companies have prevailed in nearly all of these cases, as courts have eagerly looked to extrinsic evidence to determine the parties' intent in forming the severance or change in control agreement.

In *Collins v. Ralston Purina Co.*,[98] a former employee claimed that his employment with the company was effectively terminated (1) upon sale of company, (2)

---

[97] See *Campbell, et al v. Potash Corporation of Saskatchewan, Inc.*, 238 F3d 792 (6th Cir. 2001).

[98] *Collins v. Ralston Purina Co.*, 147 F3d 592 (7th Cir. 1998). Similarly, in *Televantos v. Lyondell Chemical Co.*, 31 Fed Appx 63 (3d Cir. 2002) (unpublished

opinion) the company apparently offered the employee employment in the same position in another location to which the company was moving, and advised him that he would be entitled to change in control severance if he declined the offer. The court when his job responsibilities were reduced, or (3) upon the acquirer's attempt to transfer him to another region. The court found the language of Mr. Collins' retention agreement to be ambiguous as to whether compensation and benefits were payable upon the sale of the company, or only upon the actual termination of employment. Upon an examination of extrinsic evidence, however, the court concluded that neither the company nor Collins intended that the mere sale of the company would trigger a payout. The court further held that, although Collins anticipated his reassignment to a less attractive position in another region, he voluntarily left employment with the company before the time the acquirer actually made the reassignment, and thus, he was not entitled to payments under the agreement.

In *Epps v. NCNB Texas National Bank*,[99] the agreement provided for payment if the employee "should cease to be employed by the bank for any reason other than termination for cause or voluntary termination." Mr. Epps claimed that he was effectively terminated from his job because the duties that he was initially hired to perform were no longer needed. The court found that nothing in the agreement provided for payment upon a change in the employee's job duties. Therefore, when the employee left the bank to accept another job, he voluntarily terminated his employment. The court also rejected the employee's argument that the change in job responsibilities constituted a constructive discharge, finding that Texas' strict, objective standard of constructive discharge was not met in this case. Under Texas law, a constructive discharge only occurs when an employer makes conditions so intolerable that an employee reasonably feels compelled to resign.

In *Grun v. Pneumo Abex Corp.*,[100] the agreement stated that benefits would be payable if, following a change in control, a relocation of the company's principal executive offices or a relocation of the employee's place of employment occurred. Mr. Grun claimed although his work location was unaffected, the agreement required payments to him because the company moved its principal executive office after the change in control. Again, despite the language of the agreement, the court found that because the intended purpose of the agreement was to induce Grun to remain employed by the company following a change in control, and the relocation "had minimal, if any, effect on Grun's work-related activities," a payments of benefits upon relocation of the company's principal office only would not achieve the purpose of the agreement.

(Footnote Continued)

held the employee was not entitled to payment where he resigned and took another job before the date of the relocation. See also, *Shipner v. Eastern Air Lines, Inc.*, 868 F2d 401 (11th Cir. 1989), where the former employee claimed that the termination of his status as an officer of corporation following a takeover constituted "termination following change in control." The court agreed with the company that the phrase "termination of your employment" was clear and unambiguous and meant a complete termination of the employment relationship with company.

[99] *Epps v. NCNB Texas National Bank*, 838 F.Supp. 296 (N.D.Tex. 1993).

[100] *Grun v. Pneumo Abex Corp.*, 808 F.Supp. 632 (N.D. Ill. 1992).

In *Godfrey v. Eastman Kodak Co.*,[101] the relevant provision of the agreement stated that one "good reason" for resignation was "a significant diminution of . . . your status, duties or responsibilities in effect on the date of this Agreement." Mr. Godfrey claimed that his business responsibilities had been reduced or altered, constituting "good reason" for resignation under his golden parachute agreement. The employee admitted that his duties were not diminished from those he enjoyed on the date of agreement, but as he rose to a higher level in the company, his duties were diminished. The court found that the language of the agreement was unambiguous, and held that Mr. Godfrey was not entitled to terminate employment for "good reason" because the reduction in responsibilities occurred at a higher level than the one at which the employee worked on the date of the agreement, and he did not terminate employment for "good reason" in accordance with the agreement.

Finally, in *Kolkowski v. Goodrich Corp.*,[102] the Sixth Circuit Court of Appeals held that a former employee was entitled to severance pay and benefits under a change in control severance plan maintained by Goodrich because the company that acquired part of Goodrich's business did not offer him employee benefits "comparable" to what he had received from Goodrich.

Other Alleged Failures to Follow the Terms of the Agreement. As with any other executive agreement, despite counsel's best efforts to clearly resolve the outcome of every possible issue in the four corners of the agreement, some unforeseen issues arise.

Well-drafted change in control agreements provide that the calculation of whether or not payments under the agreement trigger an excise tax (and, thus, either a cutback in payments or a gross-up payment) will be performed by a public accounting firm (see ¶10,030, Checklist for Change in Control Agreements). In *Manzon v. Stant Corp.*,[103] the executive's change in control agreement required the calculation of severance pay to be made by an independent auditor and examined by tax counsel. Despite the fact that the company had engaged Deloitte & Touche to perform the calculations, the court found that the company had failed to comply with the agreement, because it had not submitted the calculations to tax counsel for examination.

In *Sanchez v. Verio Inc.*,[104] an employee of an internet service provider who left the company four months before it was acquired by another firm argued that she was entitled to accelerated vesting of her stock options, because the stock option agreement provided that the vesting of her options would accelerate if her employment was terminated "without cause or voluntarily with good reason within 12 months of a change in control." The court rejected Sanchez's contention that the stock option agreement was ambiguous and found that "within 12 months of" clearly meant "within 12 months after" a change in control.

---

[101] *Godfrey v. Eastman Kodak Co.*, 1991 U.S. Dist. LEXIS 4803 (S.D.N.Y. 1991).

[102] *Kolkowski v. Goodrich Corp.*, 6th Cir., No. 05-3339 (May 18, 2006).

[103] *Manzon v. Stant Corp.*, 202 F.Supp. 2d 851 (S.D.Ind. 2002).

[104] *Sanchez v. Verio Inc.*, 2004 U.S. App. LEXIS 27171 (5th Cir. 2004) (unpublished).

Calculating the Change in Control Consideration. The case of *Duffy v. Vision Hardware Group*,[105] illustrates the importance of drafting. In *Duffy*, the parties had signed a detailed employment contract in 1993. One provision of the contract provided that Duffy would receive a bonus "if and when the Company sells all or substantially all of the outstanding stock or of the assets of VSI Fasteners, Inc.," if the sale "result[ed] in the Company receiving consideration in excess of Eight Million Dollars." The contract also provided that "To the extent the consideration . . . is paid in other than cash, the proportionate share of the VSI Bonus shall be paid to the executive in kind." The bonus was to be 2.5% of the total consideration received by Vision Hardware for the sale of VSI Fasteners. In 1996, Duffy and Vision Hardware signed a written resignation agreement. Duffy remained eligible for the bonus if VSI Fasteners was sold before December 31, 1997. In December 1996, VSI Fasteners sold substantially all of its assets for $6.9 million in cash. The buyer also agreed to assume liabilities of VSI Fasteners totalling some $2.3 million. Duffy demanded payment of the bonus on the theory that the liabilities assumed by the buyer were part of the consideration received for the assets of VSI Fasteners. The court upheld Vision Hardware's refusal to pay him, finding that VSI received consideration of $6,900,000 from the sale of VSI, since the assumption of VSI's liabilities could not be paid in kind to Duffy.

Misinformation? In *Marks v. Newcourt Credit Group Inc.*,[106] the Sixth Circuit Court of Appeals held that ERISA does not preempt a former employee's claim that his employer breached his employment contract by deceiving him about his job responsibilities, which ultimately "lulled" him into not exercising his right to receive benefits under the employer's change in control severance plan. Marks participated in a severance plan that entitled him to approximately $1.5 million in benefits if, in the event of a change in control, he suffered a "qualifying termination." The plan defined "qualifying termination" as including a reduction and/or elimination in job responsibilities. In January 1998, Newcourt Credit Group Inc. acquired AT&T Capital. Marks accepted employment with Newcourt and agreed to purchase 14,665 shares of the company's stock as part of his employment contract. According to the court, Marks borrowed more than $450,000 to finance the stock purchase. Pursuant to AT&T's severance plan, Marks had until October 1, 1998, to make a claim for benefits. In March 1999, Marks learned Newcourt had awarded him a bonus that was significantly lower than bonuses he typically received from AT&T. Marks alleged the decrease in his bonus was caused by Newcourt's change in its method of calculating perform-ance goals and that Newcourt did not communicate these changes to him because the changes were intended to materially reduce his job responsibilities. Marks' lawsuit alleged that Newcourt deceived him about his job responsibi-lities, thus inducing him to accept employment with the company and purchase Newcourt stock, which ultimately lulled him into not exercising his rights under AT&T's severance plan.

---

[105] *Duffy v. Vision Hardware Group*, 2000 U.S. Dist. LEXIS 18694 (D. Md. 2000).

[106] *Marks v. Newcourt Credit Group Inc.*, 342 F3d 444 (6th Cir. 2003).

Termination Before a Change in Control. It appears clear that terminating an employee subject to a change in control agreement in anticipation of a change in control would subject the employer to a claim for breach of implied covenant of good faith and fair dealing. An implied covenant of good faith and fair dealing is included in every employment contract made under the laws of Delaware.[107] In *Hills Stores Co. v. Bozic,*[108] a Delaware court specifically recognized that change in control agreements are subject to the implied covenant. The Delaware courts have explained that the implied covenant requires a party in a contractual relationship to refrain from arbitrary or unreasonable conduct which has the effect of preventing the other party to the contract from receiving the fruits of the bargain. Thus, parties are liable for breaching the covenant when their conduct frustrates the "overarching purpose" of the contract by taking advantage of their position to control implementation of the agreement's terms.[109] A different circuit noted in dicta that termination in anticipation of a change in control may give rise to an implied covenant claim.[110]

No Automatic Vesting. One of the most significant trends in equity plan design in the 2010s, fuelled largely by investors and proxy advisors, is to eliminate single trigger vesting upon a change in control. Most folks seem to shrug off the impact of this change and assume all employees will end up vested anyway. A 2015 case demonstrates painfully that this is not always the case: *Timian v. Johnson & Johnson.*[111] In January 2006, Ms. Timian commenced employment with the company as a patent attorney, providing legal services to one of its subsidiaries, OCD. The company had awarded restricted stock units to Timian under its long-term incentive plan for several years. The RSUs had a vesting period of three years, which required Timian to be employed by the company on the third anniversary of the vesting date in order to receive the value of the RSUs.

In early 2013, the company began discussions to sell OCD. The patent attorneys supporting OCD, including Timian, were included as assets to the sale and were not allowed to look for work within the company or any of its other subsidiaries. The patent attorneys were forced to either leave the company's employment or become an employee of OCD after the sale. In January 2014, the company announced its formal intention to sell OCD. In February 2014, the company awarded RSUs to Timian based on her 2013 work performance. On June 29, 2014, the company's sale of OCD became final, Timian's employment with the company was terminated, and she became an employee of OCD. Upon the sale of OCD, the company terminated the RSUs granted to Timian in 2012, 2013, and 2014, on the basis that these RSUs had not vested prior to the termination of her employment. Timian lost the full value of the RSUs awarded

---

[107] *Marks Merrill v. Crothall-American, Inc.,* 606 A.2d 96, 101 (1992).

[108] *Hills Stores Co. v. Bozic,* 769 A.2d 88, 108 (Del.Ch. 2000).

[109] *Dunlap v. State Farm Fire and Cas. Co.,* 878 A.2d 434, 442 (Del.2005); see also *Aspen Advisors LLC v. UA Theatre Co.,* 861 A.2d 1251, 1260 (Del. 2004) ("The implied covenant is only breached when the

defendant [has] engaged in arbitrary or unreasonable conduct which has the effect of preventing the other party to the contract from receiving the fruits of the contract.").

[110] *Fenoglio v. Augat,* 254 F.3d 368 (1st Cir. 2001).

[111] *Timian v. Johnson & Johnson,* __F.Supp__ , (W.D.NY 2015).

in 2012, 2013, and 2014, and sued the company for a breach of the LTIP, breach of the implied contract between employee and employer, breach of the implied covenant of good faith and fair dealing, and breach of ERISA.

The federal court ruled against Timian on each of her claims. First, the court found that the LTIP was not subject to ERISA, as has every other court that has ever considered the issue. Second, the court found that the language of the LTIP was clear. There could be no legal dispute that Timian's employment with the company had terminated, even though she continued to sit at the same desk and perform the same job functions on the day after the sale of OCD as she did on the day before the sale. The LTIP did not provide for accelerated vesting of Timian's RSUs. The provisions of the LTIP on change in control simply did not apply to the sale of a division of the company.

Finally, the claims for breach of the implied contract between employee and employer and breach of the implied covenant of good faith and fair dealing are based on a notion that some rules apply to the relationships among parties, even though they are not written into a contract or agreement. Courts sometimes find a breach of these implied covenants in cases of egregious conduct. However, the terms of the LTIP addressed situations like the one at issue and were clear on the outcome.

The court's decision in *Timian v. Johnson & Johnson* is consistent with that of nearly every other federal court that has considered a similar issue. Some companies' LTIPs would provide for accelerated vesting for an employee terminated solely because of a sale of a division of the company. However, this LTIP did not. Executive compensation professionals should take care in considering all of the terms of a stock plan or employment or other agreements, because the courts will uphold those terms for better or worse.

Executive Relinquished Right to Payments. A 2013 case, *Yarber v. Capital Bank Corporation*[112], involved a factual situation that many private company executives and companies find themselves in from time to time. Mr. Yarber worked for Capital Bank as its president and chief executive officer. Yarber had an employment agreement with Capital Bank, which provided for severance payments equal to a multiple of his salary in the event of his employment termination following a change in control.

Another financial institution offered to purchase a controlling interest in Capital Bank in 2010. During negotiations, all parties agreed that Yarber would remain the president of Capital Bank after the purchase, according to the court's opinion. However, the acquirer threatened to withdraw its offer to purchase Capital Bank unless Yarber and other bank executives signed amendments to their employment agreements relinquishing their right to the change in control severance payments. The chairman of the board of Capital Bank told Yarber that he "had no option but to give up any payments due under his employment contract," and that the board of directors could and would terminate Yarber for

---

[112] *Yarber v. Capital Bank Corporation*, 944 F.Supp.2d 437 (E.D.N.C. 2013).

cause if he refused to give up his right to change in control severance payments. According to the opinion, the chairman also told Yarber that Capital Bank's shareholders could sue Yarber for breach of fiduciary duty if he refused to amend his employment contract and his refusal caused the acquirer to withdraw its offer. Yarber signed an amendment to his employment contract (the "2011 Amendment") that effectively eliminated his right to severance payments and created a term of employment that expired on November 4, 2011.

The acquirer closed the deal to purchase Capital Bank. It then removed Yarber from his position as president and chief executive officer, and terminated his employment ten days after the term of his contract expired. Yarber received no change in control severance payments. Yarber sued, claiming, among other things, that (i) Capital Bank violated ERISA by refusing to pay his change in control severance payments, and by terminating his employment upon false grounds with the intent of denying his right to severance benefits, and (ii) the 2011 Amendment was void for lack of consideration.

Unfortunately for Mr. Yarber, the court saw this as an open and shut case. The employment agreement and the 2011 Amendment were crystal clear on Yarber's rights. The 2011 Amendment had deleted the language providing for change in control severance payments, and created a term of employment ending on November 4, 2011. After November 4, 2011, Yarber became an at-will employee with no employment contract. Because ERISA allows employers to amend or eliminate employee welfare benefit plans, such as a severance plan, and preempts any state law contract claims the court also dismissed his claim that the 2011 Amendment was void for lack of consideration. Mr. Yarber relinquished his contractual right to severance, then lost his job, lost his lawsuit, and got nothing.

.04 Change in Control in Bankruptcy Context

Payments in the bankruptcy context are often appropriate. Recently, practitioners have received guidance on Code Sec. 280G issues in the context of a corporate bankruptcy from both the IRS and the federal courts.

In Rev. Rul. 2004-87,[113] the IRS analyzed different fact patterns under Code Sec. 280G. In scenario 1, a publicly held company traded on the New York Stock Exchange files a voluntary petition for relief under Chapter 11 of the Bankruptcy Code. Under a plan of reorganization approved by the bankruptcy court, all of the existing shares of the company are cancelled and new shares are issued. The unsecured creditors of the company receive 75% of the new common stock, distributed proportionately to their claims, but none of the creditors receive 20% or more of the outstanding shares of the reorganized company. Under the plan of reorganization, the existing board of directors is replaced by a new board of directors that is pre-endorsed by the pre-reorganization board of directors. Under the golden parachute regulations, a transfer of ownership of 75% of the voting stock of a corporation to more than one person acting as a group would trigger a change of control for purposes of Code Sec. 280G. However, the IRS concluded

---

[113] Rev. Rul. 2004-87, IRB 2004-32.

that, under the circumstances, the creditor's committee was not acting as a group to acquire the stock of the company. Therefore, there was no change of control.

The facts of scenario 2 were the same as scenario 1, except that the largest creditor owned 25% of the reorganized company. In this context, because one creditor acquired 20% or more of the corporation's stock within a 12-month period, there is a presumptive change in control for purposes of Code Sec. 280G. However, the presumption may be rebutted by a showing that the largest creditor will not act to control the management and policies of the corporation.

In scenario 3, a corporation files a voluntary petition under Chapter 11 of the Bankruptcy Code. Its stock is subsequently de-listed from the New York Stock Exchange and is thereafter no longer traded on any other market. Another corporation then proposes to buy more than one-third of its assets in a transaction that will trigger a change in control benefit to an executive of the bankrupt corporation. The bankruptcy court approves the sale of assets and the payment of benefits to the executive. According to the IRS, a sale of more than one-third of a corporation's assets would be a change in ownership for purposes of Code Sec. 280G. However, because the corporation whose assets were sold was de-listed and no longer tradable on any exchange, it qualifies for the shareholder approval exception to the application of the golden parachute rules. That exception would generally require adequate disclosure to shareholders, and then approval by at least 75% of the voting power immediately before the change in control. In the bankruptcy context, the IRS concluded that the approval of the bankruptcy court served the same purpose as the 75% shareholder approval. The IRS therefore deemed the shareholder approval and disclosure requirement of Code Sec. 280G to be satisfied, the result of which was that the payments to the executive were not treated as parachute payments under Code Sec. 280G. The IRS also indicated that a subsequent trading of the bankrupt corporation's stock on an over-the-counter market, when the corporation was still a debtor in a case under the Bankruptcy Code, did not cause the stock to be "readily tradable" and, thus, the bankrupt corporation still qualified for the 75% shareholder approval exception.

The case of *Fix v. Quantum Industries Partners LLC*, indicates the importance of precise plan drafting to avoid an unintended expansion (or, in other instances, an unintended contraction) of that which the parties intended in the employment agreement. *Fix* involved a somewhat unusual change in control provision. The employment agreement provided that the sale of all or substantially all of the assets of the company would constitute change in control event. However, the agreement effectively gave that company a second bite at the apple, in that a change in control would not be triggered if the board of directors decided by a majority vote that the event did not constitute a change in control in the 30-day period immediately before the event.

The employment agreement provided that Fix, the executive in question, was to receive a cash payment equal to the difference between $5,000,000 and the exercise value of his stock options upon a change in control. When the company lost its financial support, the board approved the sale of all or substantially all of the assets of the company. The board did not specify that the sale would not constitute a change in control. Nonetheless, the company refused to make the change in control payments, arguing that the agreement's intent was to pay benefits only upon a profitable sale of the company. The court found that the plan language was specific, and did not incorporate the "spirit and intent" claimed by the company. The court noted that the agreement could have included language that excluded from the definition of change in control a sale of assets in connection with a bankruptcy liquidation. It is not the general intent of a contractual provision that is dispositive; but rather the specific language of the agreement that determines (i) whether the change of control provision is triggered, and (ii) if so, the amount of the payments to which the executive is entitled.

¶295 Dodd-Frank, TARP and Shareholder Pushback

The financial crisis beginning in 2008 added strength and legislation to the effort to curb change in control payouts.

.01 EESA, ARRA and TARP

In response to the financial crisis that began in 2008, President Bush signed into law the "Emergency Economic Stabilization Act" ("EESA"),[114] in October 2008. EESA created the "Troubled Assets Relief Program" ("TARP"), which made available federal funds to financial institutions and set forth certain requirements, including detailed limitations on compensation for executives of financial institutions that received TARP funds. President Obama then signed into law the "American Recovery and Reinvestment Act" ("ARRA"),[115] in February 2009, which included amendments to the executive compensation provisions of the EESA.

Section 111 of EESA, as amended by ARRA,[116] imposed a variety of new limitations and restrictions on the executive compensation plans and arrangements of any entity that received financial assistance under TARP. These restrictions and standards apply throughout the period during which any obligation arising from financial assistance provided under TARP remains outstanding (the "TARP obligation period"). The Treasury Department published an interim final rule interpreting Section 111 of EESA, in the Federal Register in June 2009,[117] which is still in effect as of this writing.

The TARP limitations apply only to the financial institution's "senior executive officers" (SEOs), which TARP defines as "an individual who is 1 of the top 5 most highly paid executives of a public company, whose compensation is required to be disclosed pursuant to the Securities Exchange Act of 1934, and any regulations issued thereunder, and non-public company counterparts."[118]

---

[114] Emergency Economic Stabilization Act of 2008, Pub. L. No. 110-343, 122 Stat. 3765 (2008).

[115] American Recovery and Reinvestment Act of 2009, Pub. L. No. 111-5, 123 Stat. 115 (2009).

[116] 12 U.S.C. § 5221 (2010).

[117] TARP Standards for Compensation and Corporate Governance, 74 Fed. Reg. 28394 (June 15, 2009) (to be codified at 31 C.F.R. pt. 30).

[118] Id.

TARP prohibited affected institutions from making "golden parachute payments," or severance payments, to a SEO or any of the next five most highly compensated employees during the TARP obligation period.[119] Importantly, EESA and ARRA expand the original definition of the term "golden parachute payment" to include "any payment to a senior executive officer upon departure from a company for any reason, except for payments for services performed or benefits accrued."[120]

TARP also prohibited financial institutions that received funds from providing (formally or informally) tax gross-ups to any of the SEOs and next twenty most highly compensated employees during the TARP period, except in extremely limited circumstances.[121] The interim final rule clarified that the term "gross-up" means any reimbursement of taxes owed with respect to any compensation (other than a payment under a tax equalization agreement to take into account foreign taxes).[122] The prohibition on gross-ups includes a right to a payment of such a gross-up at a future date, even if it is after the TARP period.[123]

.02 Annual Disclosure of Potential Payments upon Termination of Employment or Change in Control

The SEC's 2006 rewrite of the proxy disclosure rules added Item 402(j), "Potential payments on termination or change in control." This provision requires disclosure regarding each agreement, plan, or arrangement, whether written or unwritten, that provides for payment(s) to a named executive officer at, following, or in connection with any termination of employment, including without limitation resignation, severance, death, disability, retirement, or a constructive termination of a named executive officer, or a change in control of the company or a change in the named executive officer's responsibilities. With respect to each named executive officer, the company must describe, in each annual proxy statement:

(1) The specific circumstances that would trigger payment(s) or the provision of other benefits, including perquisites and health care benefits;

(2) The amount of the estimated payments and benefits that would be provided in each covered circumstance, whether they would or could be lump sum, or annual, disclosing the duration, and by whom they would be provided;

(3) How the appropriate payment and benefit levels are determined under the various circumstances that trigger payments or provision of benefits;

(4) Any material conditions or obligations applicable to the receipt of payments or benefits, including but not limited to non-compete, non-solicitation, non-disparagement or confidentiality agreements, including the duration of such agreements and provisions regarding waiver of breach of such agreements; and

---

[119] American Recovery and Reinvestment Act of 2009, Pub. L. No. 111-5, § 7001, 123 Stat. 115, 517 (2009).

[120] American Recovery and Reinvestment Act § 7001, 123 Stat. 115, 517.

[121] TARP Standards for Compensation and Corporate Governance, 74 Fed. Reg. at 28417.

[122] TARP Standards for Compensation and Corporate Governance, 74 Fed. Reg. at 28409.

[123] TARP Standards for Compensation and Corporate Governance, 74 Fed. Reg. at 28417.

(5) Any other material factors regarding each such contract, agreement, plan or arrangement.

The company must provide quantitative disclosure under these requirements, applying the assumptions that the triggering event took place on the last business day of the company's last completed fiscal year, and the price per share of the company's stock is the closing market price as of that date. The SEC rules do not require or provide a table for reporting potential payments upon termination of employment or change in control.[124]

.03 Dodd-Frank Act Disclosure and Vote

In July 2010, President Obama signed into law the "Dodd-Frank Wall Street Reform and Consumer Protection Act" ("Dodd-Frank"). Section 951 of Dodd-Frank added a new Section 14A to the Exchange Act, entitled "Shareholder Approval of Executive Compensation," which provides that, not less frequently than once every three years, a company's annual proxy statement must include a separate resolution subject to shareholder vote to approve the compensation of executives, as disclosed in the company's CD&A, the compensation tables, and any related material.

Exchange Act Section 14A also provides for "Shareholder Approval of 'Golden Parachute' Compensation," which requires in any proxy or consent solicitation material for a meeting of the shareholders *at which shareholders are asked to approve an acquisition, merger, consolidation, or proposed sale or other disposition of all or substantially all the assets of the company*, the party soliciting the proxy or consent **must disclose** in the proxy or consent solicitation material, in accordance with regulations to be promulgated by the SEC, any agreements or understandings that the party soliciting the proxy or consent has with any named executive officers of the company (or of the acquiring company) concerning any type of compensation (whether present, deferred, or contingent) that is based on or otherwise relates to the acquisition, merger, consolidation, sale, or other disposition of all or substantially all of the assets of the company and the aggregate total of all such compensation that may (and the conditions upon which it may) be paid or become payable to or on behalf of such executive officer. This requirement is effective for any shareholders' meeting that occurs after January 21, 2011.

This shareholder vote is **not** binding on the company or the company's board and, according to the statute, may not be construed as (1) overruling their decision, (2) creating or implying any addition or change to their fiduciary duties, or (3) restricting or limiting shareholders' ability to make proposals for inclusion in proxy materials related to executive compensation. The impact of this disclosure and shareholder voting requirement since its inception in 2011 has been minimal. Shareholders seldom vote against a sale or merger transaction, especially where the buyer is paying a premium to the target's stock market price. And even if they do, the vote is not binding.

---

[124] § 229.402(j) (Item 402).

The proxy statement also must include a separate resolution subject to shareholder vote to approve such agreements or understandings and compensation, as disclosed, unless shareholders already have approved such agreements or understandings in a "Say on Pay" (under Exchange Act, subsection 14A(a) described above). This requirement was intended to make it more difficult for companies to add or improve their payouts at the eleventh hour before a change in control.

Finally, Dodd-Frank also requires every institutional investment manager subject to Section 13(f) of the Exchange Act to report at least annually how it voted on any shareholder vote pursuant to Say on Pay generally and this provision, unless such vote is otherwise required to be reported publicly by rule or regulation of the SEC.

.04 Shareholder Advisory Firm Pushback

Shareholder advisory firms, such as Institutional Shareholder Services ("ISS"), have long sought to influence public company shareholders' voting for directors and the approval of compensation plans based on the executive compensation and corporate governance profile of the company in question. With the promulgation of shareholder Say on Pay in the Dodd-Frank Act, their influence became more pronounced.

At least annually, ISS publishes guidance listing executive pay practices that could cause it to recommend a vote against directors up for elections or compensation plans up for approval. Among the pay practices ISS labels as "problematic," are the following:

- Change in control payments exceeding three times of base salary and bonus;
- Change in control payments without loss of job or substantial diminution of job duties (single-triggered);
- New or materially amended employment or severance agreements that provide for modified single triggers, under which an executive may voluntarily leave for any reason and still receive the change in control severance package;
- New or materially amended employment or severance agreements that provide for an excise tax gross-up. Modified gross-ups would be treated in the same manner as full gross-ups; and
- Liberal change in control definition that could result in payments to executives without an actual change in control occurring.

Therefore, many companies will need to review and re-evaluate their change in control agreements and consider eliminating these provisions in order to receive an ISS recommendation in favor of the shareholder Say-on-Pay vote.

Even before the promulgation of shareholder Say on Pay, surveys showed that more than one-half of Fortune 500 companies had revised their change in control agreements to curtail excise tax gross-up provisions, reduce the severance multiple, eliminate continuation of perquisites and/or enhance non-compete provisions.

Chapter 3
CONSULTING AGREEMENTS

¶301 Overview—Consulting Agreements

A consulting agreement is a legal contract between a company and a nonemployee consultant or independent contractor, which sets forth the terms of the consulting relationship between the parties. No law requires a company and a consultant to set forth the terms of their relationship in a written agreement. However, most companies recognize that some form of written agreement helps to protect the company from unwanted liabilities and problems.

.01 Correctly Categorizing Individuals as an Employee or a Consultant

For decades, disputes have been arising between the IRS and various companies (and entire industries) over whether the companies are employing certain individuals in a capacity as employees or as independent contractors/consultants. The reason for these disputes is that the Internal Revenue Code requires a company to make matching Federal Insurance Contributions Act ("FICA") payments for employees, but does not require payments for independent contractors. In 2018, the company's matching contribution is 1.45% of an employee's total wages and an additional 6.20% of the employee's wages up to $128,400 (see ¶315).

.02 Common Contract Provisions

A consulting agreement is very much like an employment agreement in its terms and conditions (see Chapter 1 [¶101 *et seq.*] for a detailed discussion of employment agreements). The consulting agreement could cover as many or as few aspects of the consulting relationship as the parties desire (see ¶10,040 for a model consulting agreement). However, every consulting agreement should address a few critical issues, such as the following:

- Duties;
- Consulting term;
- Compensation;
- Status as an independent contractor, including liability for taxes;
- Incentive compensation, if any;
- Lack of retirement and welfare benefits plan coverage; and
- Noncompete and other restrictive covenants.

The most important terms and provisions of a consulting agreement are different from those of an employment agreement (see ¶325).

.03 Company and Consultant Tax Issues

Like an employee, a consultant would recognize most payments made to him or her as ordinary income. Similarly, a company would be entitled to a compensation deduction for most payments it makes to a consultant, in the same manner as it is for employees. The main difference in the taxation of employees and independent contractors relates to the obligation to pay Federal Insurance Contributions Act ("FICA") and Federal Unemployment Tax Act ("FUTA") taxes. However, in cases where the consultant is a former employee of the company who was covered by an employment agreement, the parties may face the issue of whether the payments are for consulting, employment, or damages for termination of the contract (see ¶ 335).

.04 Code Sec. 409A

Yes, dear reader, I am afraid it is true. Code Sec. 409A, the scourge of all executive compensation professionals, also applies to consultants and other independent contractors. Code Sec. 409A would apply to any arrangement to defer compensation by a consultant or other independent contractor. The failure to comply with 409A results in immediate income on deferrals, an excise tax of 20% and other penalties (see ¶ 345).

¶315 Correctly Categorizing Individuals as an Employee or an Independent Contractor

Using temporary workers or independent contractors, including leased employees, raises several significant legal issues. For decades, disputes have been arising between the IRS and various companies over whether the companies are employing certain individuals in a capacity as employees or as independent contractors/consultants.

Most workers fall into one of two categories: independent contractors and common-law employees. This classification is critical because employers must withhold income taxes, withhold and pay Social Security and Medicare taxes, and pay unemployment tax on wages paid to an employee. Moreover, other tax issues, such as the inclusion of certain individuals in employee benefit plans, depend on the proper classification of workers. In contrast, employers generally do not have to withhold or pay any federal taxes on payments to independent contractors, although they are subject to a self-employment tax.

.01 Factors That Determine Whether an Individual is an Employee or an Independent Contractor

In general, the most important factor in determining how to classify a worker is the degree of control the employer has over the individual. The more control an employer has over a worker, the more likely it is that the worker is an employee rather than an independent contractor. An employer must base its classification determination on all available facts and circumstances of its relationship with the worker.

¶301.03

The relevant facts fall into three main categories: behavioral control, financial control, and relationship of the parties. Behavioral control includes facts that show if the business has a right to direct and control what work is accomplished and how the work is done, through instructions, training, or other means. Financial control relates to facts that show if the business has a right to direct or control the financial and business aspects of the worker's job. This includes five factors:

(i) The extent to which the worker has unreimbursed business expenses;

(ii) The extent of the worker's investment in the facilities or tools used in performing services;

(iii) The extent to which the worker makes his or her services available to the relevant market;

(iv) How the business pays the worker; and

(v) The extent to which the worker can realize a profit or incur a loss.

Finally, the relationship of the parties explores facts that show the type of relationship the parties had. This includes four factors:

(i) Written contracts describing the relationship the parties intended to create;

(ii) Whether the business provides the worker with employee-type benefits, such as insurance, a pension plan, vacation pay, or sick pay;

(iii) The permanency of the relationship; and

(iv) The extent to which services performed by the worker are a key aspect of the regular business of the company.

If an employer incorrectly classifies a worker as an independent contractor, the employer still would be responsible for paying the employee's federal income tax withholding and the employee's share of FICA, even if the employer did not withhold those amounts from the employee's wages. Penalties and interest also may apply. However, the IRS provides some relief when an employer incorrectly classifies an employee as an independent contractor. Code Sec. 3509 provides reduced rates for the employee's share of FICA taxes and for the federal income tax that the employer should have withheld. An employer still is responsible for the full amount of its share of FICA taxes. In addition, an employer may not owe employment taxes for misclassified workers if it meets the three requirements of Code Sec. 530:

1. The employer must have had a reasonable basis for not treating the workers as employees,

2. The employer must have treated the workers and any similar workers as independent contractors for all applicable periods as of December 31, 1977, and

3. The employer must have filed a Form 1099 for each worker, if such form was required.

The IRS summarizes its position on the distinction between employees and independent contractors in Tax Topic Number: 762 - Independent Contractor vs. Employee,[1] and provides a variety of resources for making the determination on its web site, including a detailed summary of the relevant factors in Publication 1779, Independent Contractor or Employee[2] and Publication 15-A, Employer's Supplemental Tax Guide[3]. An employer also can ask the IRS to make a classification determination for it, by using Form SS-8, Determination of Worker Status for Purposes of Federal Employment Taxes and Income Tax Withholding.[4]

.02 Federal Insurance Contributions Required of Company

The Internal Revenue Code requires companies to make matching Federal Insurance Contributions Act ("FICA") payments and Federal Unemployment Tax Act ("FUTA") payments for employees, but does not require such payments for independent contractors. The company's contributions are currently:

- 6.20% of an employee's "wages" for the Old Age, Survivors and Disability Insurance ("OASDI") tax portion of FICA, up to the Social Security wage base ($128,400 in 2018); and

- 1.45% of all of the employee's wages for the Medicare Hospital Insurance ("HI") tax portion.

Under the Affordable Care Act ("ACA"), employees, but not employers also must pay an additional 0.9% tax on wages, compensation, and self-employment income that exceeds a threshold amount based on the individual's filing status. The threshold amounts are $250,000 for married taxpayers who file jointly, $125,000 for married taxpayers who file separately and $200,000 for all other taxpayers. An employer is responsible for withholding the additional Medicare tax from wages or compensation it pays to an employee in excess of $200,000 in a calendar year, without regard to the employee's filing status.

Employers also must pay FUTA taxes, a federal tax on employers covered by a state's unemployment insurance (UI) program, currently 6% on the first $7,000 of wages. However, employers typically receive a credit of 5.4% on IRS Form 940, reducing the FUTA rate to 0.6 percent, or $42 per employee per year. Only the employer makes FUTA contributions.

Example 1: ABC Corporation employs Executive D as its senior vice president of marketing and pays her $300,000 in 2018. For 2018, ABC and Executive D *each* must pay $7,960.80 in Social Security taxes ($128,400.00 x 6.20%) and $4,350.00 in Medicare taxes ($300,000 x 1.45%). Executive D also must pay approximately $900 in additional Medicare tax. ABC pays a total of $12,310.80 in federal insurance contributions for D in 2018.

If the individual works for the company as an independent contractor or consultant, he or she must pay 100% of FICA taxes.

---

[1] www.irs.gov/taxtopics/tc762.
[2] www.irs.gov/pub/irs-pdf/p1779.pdf.
[3] www.irs.gov/pub/irs-pdf/p15a.pdf.
[4] www.irs.gov/pub/irs-pdf/fss8.pdf.

Example 2: Effective January 1, 2018, ABC terminates D's employment, but retains D as an independent marketing consultant. ABC agrees to pay D a flat amount of $300,000 for unlimited consulting services in 2018. For 2018, Consultant D must pay approximately $25,521 in FICA taxes: $15,921.60 in Social Security taxes ($128,400 × 12.40%), $8,700.00 in Medicare taxes ($300,000 × 2.90%), and $900 in ObamaCare taxes. ABC pays nothing.

The federal government stands to receive nearly as much from independent contractors paying insurance contributions separately as it does from the combined company and employee contributions. However, the government is usually not as successful in recovering the full amount of insurance taxes due from individuals paying on their own, as it is when companies withhold funds from employees' wages weekly or bi-weekly and pay them directly to the government. Therefore, the Internal Revenue Service is strongly biased in favor of finding an employer-employee relationship, rather than independent contractor status.

.03 Government Challenges to Companies' Characterization of Workers

In the 1980s, the Internal Revenue Service began aggressively challenging the employment tax status of physicians and other health care professionals it believed companies had misclassified as independent contractors. By 1991, increased enforcement activity on the part of the IRS had produced an almost 500% increase over a three-year period in the taxes paid by tax-exempt organizations due to misclassification. In the 1980s, hospitals were able to realize substantial tax savings (as companies are today) if they engaged a physician as an independent contractor rather than an employee.

In the late 1990s, the U.S. Department of Labor ("DOL") joined the IRS in challenging companies' worker characterizations by suing Time Warner, Inc. The DOL claimed that Time Warner illegally used temporary workers and independent contractors to reduce employee benefit costs. The allegation was similar to that in the infamous case of *Vizcaino v. Microsoft Corporation.*[5] In *Vizcaino*, a group of independent contractors sued Microsoft, claiming entitlement to benefits under Microsoft's retirement and stock-based benefit plans.

The IRS now issues fact sheets and news releases nearly every year reminding businesses to ensure they treat their workers properly for purposes of meeting various tax obligations.

.04 Employee Benefit Plan Claims

Misclassified employees can also seek to recover retroactive employee benefits for which they are otherwise eligible, including health care, paid and unpaid leave, retirement benefits, disability benefits, and other incidental benefits provided by the employer to its employees. For example, an employer may face substantial liability if misclassified contractors, who are otherwise entitled to coverage under an ERISA employee benefit plans, have not been provided with

---

[5] *Vizcaino v. Microsoft Corporation,* 97 F3d 1187 (9th Cir. 1996).

group health, disability and life insurance coverage. Similar liability may attach with respect to 401(k) plan contributions and other pension and profit-sharing plan.

Neither the Employee Retirement Income Security Act of 1974 ("ERISA"), as amended, nor the Internal Revenue Code requires that a company cover an independent contractor under its retirement, health, life and disability insurance plans. However, ERISA and the Code impose strict nondiscrimination rules on qualified retirement and 401(k) plans. (The Code imposes less strict rules on health and life insurance plans.) Among these rules, ERISA and the Code prohibit discrimination against employees' eligibility to participate in plans. Thus, if a company's plans exclude from coverage a significant number of workers who the DOL (or the IRS) thinks it should treat as employees, the plans could be violating ERISA and/or the Code. (This was part of the DOL's primary charge against Time Warner.)

Employee benefit plans that are not subject to the Code's nondiscrimination rules, such as stock option and stock purchase plans still may be vulnerable to claims by misclassified workers if the terms of the plan documents are not absolutely clear about the exclusion of these workers. Workers in the *Microsoft* case sued for retroactive participation in Microsoft's stock-based compensation programs, as well as its qualified retirement plans. Code Sec. 423, which confers tax-favored status on qualifying employee stock-purchase plans, requires (among other things) the company to offer eligibility to participate in the plan to all employees.

The ACA increased the potential adverse consequences to employers of misclassifying employees as independent contractors. A large employer will be liable for the employer shared responsibility no-coverage penalty for each month in which the employer does not offer minimum essential coverage to at least 95 percent of its full-time employees (and their dependents), and at least one of the employer's full-time employees receives a premium assistance tax credit when purchasing coverage on a health insurance marketplace. The penalty is equal to the number of full-time employees multiplied by $193.33 per month ($2,320 per year (for 2018)). The reclassification of one or more workers misclassified as independent contractors may, in some instances, cause an employer to fail to satisfy the 95 percent threshold, thereby triggering an employer-shared responsibility excise tax penalty based not only on the misclassified workers, but the employer's entire full-time workforce.

Moreover, a large employer that satisfies the 95 percent coverage threshold may still be subject to an excise tax penalty of $290.00 per month ($3,480 per year (for 2018)) for each full-time employee who is either not offered coverage by the employer or who is offered insufficient coverage (coverage that does not provide minimum value or is not considered affordable), and who enrolls in subsidized marketplace coverage. Thus, if an employer misclassifies a full-time worker as an independent contractor and does not offer the worker coverage under the employer's health plan, and the worker purchases subsidized marketplace coverage, the employer is subject to an excise tax penalty of $290.00 per month for the worker.

Other employment laws, such as laws governing employment discrimination and wages and hours, may impose liability on corporations that they deem "employers" or "joint employers" of temporary workers or independent contractors. For example, Title VII of the Civil Rights Act of 1964, the Americans with Disabilities Act, the Age Discrimination in Employment Act, and the Fair Labor Standards Act have their own statutory definitions of "company." These definitions, as interpreted by the courts, can sometimes cover temporary workers or independent contractors that a company may not consider its employees. Often, the question of whether a company will be found a "company" or "joint company" will turn on such issues as whether the company exercises direction and control over temporary workers or independent contractors, determines the terms and conditions of their employment, and/or integrates them into the company's operations.

.05 *Vizcaino v. Microsoft Corporation*

The IRS investigation of Microsoft's employment records in 1989 and 1990 was the genesis of *Vizcaino*. The result of that investigation was Microsoft's concession to the IRS that it had misclassified workers as independent contractors. Microsoft agreed to give W-2 forms to the independent contractors *cum* employees and pay the company's share of Social Security and Medicare taxes for past years. Smelling blood in the water, the plaintiffs' lawyers sued Microsoft in federal court, claiming that, as employees, they were entitled to participate in Microsoft's Savings Plus Plan (a 401(k) and profit-sharing plan) and Employee Stock Purchase Plan (a discounted stock-purchase plan under Code Sec. 423).

At first blush, the case looked like a David-versus-Goliath struggle between the little workers and the giant Microsoft Corporation. However, the workers' case became far less sympathetic when they acknowledged that each of them had signed an agreement specifying that he or she was an independent contractor, not covered under Microsoft's employee-benefit plans, and was responsible for paying all Social Security and withholding taxes. Instead of providing benefits, Microsoft paid the contractors at a higher hourly rate of pay than its regular employees.

Vizcaino is not the only federal case to have ruled on this issue. In *Trombetta v. Cragin Federal Savings Bank*,[6] the Seventh Circuit Court of Appeals, based in Chicago, upheld the interpretation of "employee" made by the administrative committee of an employee stock ownership plan. In *Trombetta*, the plan excluded independent contractors from participation. Following the 1989 U.S. Supreme Court decision in *Firestone Tire & Rubber Co. v. Bruch*,[7] the Seventh Circuit held that the courts could overturn the ESOP administrative committee's decision only if that decision was arbitrary and capricious. In *Firestone v. Bruch*, the Supreme Court held that if the governing plan documents reserved for the plan

---

[6] *Trombetta v. Cragin Federal Savings Bank*, 102 F3d 1435 (7th Cir. 1996).

[7] *Firestone Tire & Rubber Co. v. Bruch*, 489 US 101 (1989).

administrator or trustee the authority and discretion to interpret the plan's terms, then the courts should not overturn such interpretations unless it finds them to be arbitrary and capricious. Since *Trombetta* and *Vizcaino*, each of the other federal courts of appeals that have considered the issue has sided with the *Trombetta* decision.[8]

> **Planning Note:** Counsel should carefully examine a company's benefit-plan documents and employment policies in light of the *Vizcaino* decision and DOL's enforcement activity. This is especially true if the company uses any of the following types of workers:
>
> - temporary workers;
> - independent contractors;
> - leased employees;
> - part-time employees; or
> - seasonal employees.

Companies can evaluate their potential exposure to government or individual claims similar to those in the *Vizcaino* and Time Warner cases by asking, together with their counsel, the following specific questions:

1. Has the company properly classified workers as "temporary," "leased," or as "independent contractors"? Does the company's documentation (for example, consulting or employee-leasing agreements) support its classification of workers as temporary employees or independent contractors?

2. Has counsel drafted employee benefit and executive compensation plan documents to exclude from coverage any workers classified as temporary or independent contractors, while reserving to the plan administrator sole and absolute discretion to interpret the plan's terms? One reason Microsoft has had so little success in defending the plaintiffs' claims in *Vizcaino* is that its benefit-plan documents unambiguously extend coverage to all employees. Thus, Microsoft essentially lost the war when it agreed with the IRS, and conceded to the court, that the individuals it classified as independent contractors and temporary employees were actually common-law employees. The lesson for companies and their counsel is that the company can improve its chances to exclude independent contractors from benefit-plan coverage by using two specific plan design strategies.

   a. Ensure that counsel has drafted employee benefit and executive compensation plan documents to exclude from coverage explicitly any workers who the company classifies as temporary or leased employees, or independent contractors.

---

[8] See *Montesano v. Xerox Corp. Retirement Income Guarantee Plan*, 256 F3d 86 (2d Cir. 2001); *Yak v. Bank Brussels Lambert*, 252 F3d 127 (2d Cir. 2001); *Mulzet v. R.L. Reppert Inc.*, 2002 U.S. App. LEXIS 27369 (3d Cir. 2002) (unpublished opinion); *McDonald v. Southern Farm Bureau Life Insurance Co.*, 291 F3d 718 (11th Cir. 2002).

    b. Ensure that counsel has drafted the employee benefit-plan documents to reserve to the plan administrator the sole and absolute discretion to interpret the terms of company plans.

3. Could the company's qualified retirement plans pass the Code's nondiscrimination tests even if the company counted temporary workers, independent contractors and/or leased employees? Does the use of leased employees endanger the qualified status of the company's retirement plan? One of Microsoft's responses to the 1990 IRS enforcement action was to rehire, using many of the same contract workers through a temporary employment agency. However, the Ninth Circuit ordered a lower federal court to consider these individuals as employees, for purposes of determining damages.

4. Has the company made decisions about hiring, training, supervising and terminating temporary workers and independent contractors, whenever possible, with an eye toward shielding the company from claims that it is the "employer" or "joint employer" of these workers?

Companies face the possibility of lawsuits from two different sources. Individuals that the company classified as independent contractors or leased employees may decide to sue over lack of benefit-plan coverage, and the IRS or DOL may launch an enforcement action over the benefit plan or tax issues, or both. The differing results in *Vizcaino* and *Trombetta* raise the distinct possibility that the U.S. Supreme Court will weigh in on the issue. In assessing the likely outcome of such a case, a handicapper would have to consider the fact that the Ninth Circuit, which decided *Vizcaino*, has the unenviable distinction of being the federal court that the U.S. Supreme Court most often overrules.

.06 Legal Issues and Potential Consequences of Independent Contractor Misclassification

Using temporary workers or independent contractors, including leased employees or part-time employees, raises several significant legal issues. There has been an uptick in cases and government action over misclassification in the new "gig economy." The DOL has stated it believes most contractors are really employees and will focus on "economic realities." In 2016, both the California Labor Commission and the California Employment Development Department have held that Uber drivers are employees. Also in 2016, the New York Department of Labor held that two former Uber drivers were not independent contractors and were therefore eligible for unemployment compensation. However, this holding conflicts with a federal court decision in the Southern District of New York holding that "black car" for-hire livery service drivers are independent contractors.

A number of federal and state statutes impose civil penalties and provide misclassified workers with recourse to civil suit. Indeed, employers that use independent contractors have increasingly been targeted by plaintiffs' class action lawyers. The following is an overview of the array of tax penalties and other potential liabilities an employer may face for misclassifying an employee as an independent contractor.

Wage & Hour Claims. Under the federal Fair Labor Standards Act ("FLSA"), employers are obligated to pay minimum and overtime wages to workers who are not exempt from certain of the FLSA's regulations. Many states, including Illinois, have similar or additional laws regulating wages. Where an individual is improperly classified as an independent contractor and does not otherwise fall within any of the overtime exemptions, the employee may be awarded wages, overtime, and additional compensation for up to three years with a possibility of doubling the amount as liquidated damages. In such situations, employers are generally hamstrung by a lack of records of hours worked, opening up the employer to significant and potentially class-wide liability.

National Labor Relations Act Claims. The National Labor Relations Act ("NLRA"), which governs employees' rights to organize, select a bargaining representative, and engage in other concerted activity, specifically excludes from its coverage and protection independent contractors. 29 U.S.C. § 152(3). Not only will misclassification increase the risk of actions under the NLRA, it also heightens the risk of union organizing efforts.

Employment Discrimination Claims. Misclassified employees will also be able to bring actions under Title VII of the Civil Rights Act of 1964 which protects "employees" from unlawful discrimination based on inclusion in a protected class. Most states have parallel or similar statutes.

¶325 Consulting Agreement Provisions

A well-drafted consulting agreement will be like an employment agreement in many respects. However, the terms and provisions that are most important in a consulting agreement are not the same as the terms and provisions that are critical to an employment agreement. Additionally, the types of provisions found in the consulting agreement may vary significantly depending on whether the agreement is for an ordinary consultant, or a former chief executive officer moving to consulting status.

Planning Note: Always include the miscellaneous or so-called "boilerplate" provisions in the consulting agreement, including provisions:

- specifying that the agreement will be binding upon the company and its successors, and that neither party may assign the agreement without the other's written consent;
- specifying which state laws will govern the validity, interpretation, construction, and performance of the agreement;
- that the company may withhold from any payments amounts sufficient to satisfy applicable withholding requirements under any federal, state or local law;
- that the agreement may be amended only by written agreement between the company and the consultant;
- for the proper delivery of notices required by the agreement;

- stating that the written consulting agreement sets forth the entire agreement and understanding between the company and the consultant and supersedes all prior agreements and understandings, written or oral;

- stating that no failure or delay by the company or the consultant in enforcing or exercising any right under the agreement will operate as a waiver of that right; and

- clarifying that the parties may execute the agreement in one or more counterparts, all of which together shall constitute but one agreement.

.01 Consultant's Duties

Few consulting agreements will specify an office or position to which the consultant is appointed. However, most consulting agreements will specify the consultant's duties. For example, ABC Corporation's agreement with Consultant D might include the following paragraph:

> The Company hereby retains the Consultant and the Consultant hereby agrees to be retained by Company, as an independent consultant, and not as an employee. Consultant will provide consulting service to the Company in the area of direct product marketing.

Unlike an employment agreement, which generally requires the executive to devote his or her full time and best efforts, talents, knowledge and experience to serving the company, many consulting agreements expressly acknowledge that the consultant has other clients, and permit the consultant to devote reasonable time servicing those clients. To protect the company, where the consultant will be performing services on the company's premises, some consulting agreements will provide that the consultant will act in conformity with the company's code of conduct and other written policies (*e.g.*, sexual harassment), and act within the limits, budgets and business plans set by the company. The agreement should specify any special set of rules or regulations, *e.g.*, banking or securities laws, to which the company's consultants are required to adhere. However, these types of provisions create a risk that the IRS would argue that the individual is an employee.

> **Planning Note:** The consulting agreement should require the consultant to exercise a reasonable degree of skill and care in performing services for the company.

.02 Consulting Term

Because a consulting relationship is less formal than an employment relationship, many consulting agreements will not specify the term or duration of the agreement. One of the main purposes of a "term" is to provide for severance or other benefits in the event of early termination. However, some consulting agreements will specify the duration of the agreement.

Example: ABC Corporation has retained its former CEO as a consultant following her retirement: "*Term.* The term of this Agreement shall begin on the Retirement Date and shall continue through December 31, 2019."

.03 Time Commitment

Most consulting agreements will specify the amount of time the parties expect the consultant to devote to performing services to the company. A number of factors will determine exactly how the consulting agreement expresses this time commitment.

1. Some consulting agreements will express this time commitment as a very modest hour-per-month or open-ended matter. Generally, the parties to this sort of an agreement contemplate that the company seldom, if ever will ask the consultant to provide services. In this situation, the parties are more interested in continuing payments to the individual named as a consultant or binding the individual to noncompete and/or other restrictive covenants.

   Example: ABC Corporation acquires 100% of the stock of Littlecorp, Inc. ABC believes that it will be critical to the success of the acquisition to keep Mr. D, Littlecorp's founder and former CEO, happy, involved and available to make appearances at trade shows, etc., for ABC Corporation. Therefore, ABC signs a three-year consulting agreement with D, under which ABC pays D $10,000 per month and D commits to spend up to five hours per month consulting for ABC.

2. Some consulting agreements will express this time commitment in an open-ended manner, but precisely describe the consultant's duties. A company might take this approach where it is attempting to support its position that the individual is an independent contractor, not an employee. This approach supports the company's position that it is not supervising the individual or directing the day-to-day performance of his or her duties—(factors that would suggest an employer-employee relationship) but only retaining the individual to handle a specific project.

3. Some consulting agreements expressly acknowledge that the consultant has other clients, and permit the consultant to devote reasonable time servicing those clients. This provision supports the company's position that its relationship with the individual is not one of an employer-employee, because the individual in fact provides consulting services to other companies. However, consulting agreements generally prohibit the consultant from working for the company's competitors, suppliers, or customers.

.04 Status as an Independent Contractor

Experienced legal counsel will always draft provisions into a consulting agreement that explicitly set forth the individual's status as an independent contractor. While this self-serving language alone would not convert an employer-employee relationship into one as an independent contractor, it serves to clarify that the parties to the agreement understood and intend to create an independent contractor relationship.

> **Planning Note:** Legal counsel should consider adding language similar to the following:

> Company hereby retains Consultant, and Consultant hereby agrees to be retained by Company, as an independent consultant, and not as an employee.

> Consultant shall not be entitled to participate in or receive benefits under any of the Company programs maintained for its employees, including, without limitation, life, medical and disability benefits, pension, profit sharing or other retirement plans or other fringe benefits. If the IRS subsequently classifies the Consultant as a common law employee, Consultant expressly waives his or her rights to any benefits to which he or she was, or might have become, entitled.

> As an independent contractor, Consultant will be solely responsible for all taxes, withholdings, and other similar statutory obligations, including, but not limited to, Workers' Compensation Insurance laws.

.05 Compensation

The consulting agreement should specify the consultant's rate of pay or other mechanism of compensation. Some consulting agreements also will reference a specific equity grant the company will award to the consultant or allow the consultant to participate in the company's equity compensation plan. During the technology boom/bubble of the 1990s, many companies made stock option grants to consultants. Although stock option grants to nonemployees do not qualify for the favorable accounting treatment available for grants to employees, many companies nonetheless concluded that option grants were easier to make than cash payments.

.06 Retirement and Welfare Benefit Plan Participation

Most consulting agreements expressly provide that the consultant will not be entitled to participate in the company's qualified retirement plans (*e.g.*, 401(k) and pension plans), nonqualified retirement plans, and health and welfare benefits and insurance arrangements. The Internal Revenue Code limits participation in qualified retirement plans to a company's common law employees. Most insurance arrangements expressly limit coverage to "full-time" or "regular" employees of the company (see Chapters 16 [¶ 1601 *et seq.*], 17 [¶ 1701 *et seq.*] and 19 [¶ 1901 *et seq.*] for a detailed discussion of qualified retirement plans, nonqualified retirement plans and welfare benefit plans, respectively).

.07 Noncompetes and Other Restrictive Covenants

Experienced legal counsel will always draft provisions into a consulting agreement that explicitly set forth noncompete provisions and other restrictive covenants. Companies want to know (and ensure) that their consultants will not use the knowledge and experience gained in their service to the company to compete with, or solicit employees or customers from, the company. Restrictive covenants are not enforceable in every state or under all circumstances. However, the majority of states permit enforcement of restrictive covenants that are reasonable (see Chapter 4 [¶ 401 *et seq.*] for a detailed discussion of noncompetes and other restrictive covenants).

The company and counsel should consider adding some or all of the following restrictive covenants to the consulting agreement:

1. *Inventions or Developments*. The consultant agrees that he or she will disclose to the company all discoveries, improvements, inventions, formulas, ideas, processes, designs, techniques, etc. made, conceived or developed by the consultant, either alone or jointly with others, while consulting with the company. All inventions and developments are to be the sole property of the company. This provision would not apply to any inventions or developments that the consultant developed entirely on his or her own time, and did not use any equipment, supplies, facility, or trade secret information of the company to develop.

2. *Nondisparagement*. The consultant will not make disparaging comments about the company or its officers, directors or employees during or following the consulting period.

3. *Nondisclosure*. The consultant agrees that during his or her consulting with the company (and usually for a period thereafter), the consultant will not use, divulge or make accessible to any person any of the company's confidential information. The consultant will not engage in any consulting or other business activity that is competitive with the company's business, or usurp or take advantage of any business opportunity relating to the company's business. The consultant, following consulting termination for whatever reason, will deliver to the company all property of the company and will not take or copy property or information of the company.

4. *Noncompetition*. Many consulting agreements include noncompete provisions. Noncompete provisions are not enforceable in every state or under all circumstances. However, the majority of states permit enforcement of noncompete provisions that are reasonable as to geographic scope and duration.

   Example: ABC Corporation's consulting agreement with Consultant D might provide as follows: The Consultant agrees that so long as he is providing services to the company and for a period of two (2) years thereafter (the "Period"), he shall not, without the prior written consent of ABC Corporation, participate or engage in, directly or indirectly (as an owner, partner, employee, officer, director, independent contractor, consultant, advisor or in any other capacity calling for the rendition of services, advice, or acts of management, operation or control), any business that, during the Period, is competitive with the business conducted by ABC or any of its affiliates within the United States.

5. *Nonsolicitation of Employees.* The consultant may not directly or indirectly solicit any employee of the company to leave employment and join or become affiliated with any business that is competitive with the company's business within the geographic area.

6. *Nonsolicitation of Customers.* The consultant may not directly or indirectly solicit any customer, supplier, or other person or entity that had a business relationship with the company from continuing to do business with or entering into business with the company.

Most consulting agreements provide that if a former consultant violates the noncompete or other restrictive covenants of the agreement, the company either may seek to: (1) obtain an injunction preventing the former consultant from continued violation, or (2) forfeit some form of severance or retirement payment or equity compensation award otherwise payable to the consultant. Courts are more likely to enforce a noncompete or other restrictive covenant that provides for the former employee or consultant to forfeit some form of compensation, than one that seeks to prevent the former employee or consultant from earning a living. The restrictive covenant section of a consulting agreement should invite and encourage the court to modify any provision the court deems invalid or unenforceable to the extent and in the manner necessary to render the same valid and enforceable.

Legal counsel should consider adding language similar to the following:

Consultant shall give Company a list of all other companies, organizations or persons for whom Consultant currently performs services and shall continually update that list during the consulting relationship provided for by this Agreement.

.08 Standard Employment Agreement Provisions Not Found in Consulting Agreements

Consulting agreements do not contain many of the provisions that would be standard in an employment agreement, including some or all of the following:

- Title;
- Bonus and incentive compensation;
- Retirement and welfare benefits plan coverage;
- Severance benefits; and
- Change in control protection.

.09 Special Provisions Found in Some Consulting Agreements

A consulting agreement for a former chief executive or other senior executive officer will often contain several provisions not found in the agreements of an ordinary consultant.

1. Severance and change in control provisions. Consulting agreements seldom provide for severance and change in control payments. The exception would be for former senior executive agreements.

2. Indemnification and insurance.

¶325.09

Example 1: ABC Corporation might include the following provision in the consulting agreement for Consultant D, the former CEO: To the fullest extent permitted by law, Consultant shall indemnify and hold harmless Company against all claims, damages, losses (including but not limited to the loss of use of property) and expenses (including but not limited to attorneys' fees) arising out of or resulting from the performance of consulting services covered by this Agreement caused in whole or in part by any negligent or willful act or omission of Consultant.

3. Some consulting agreements will specify an office or position to which the company intends to appoint the consultant upon the successful completion of his or her consulting assignment.

Example 2: ABC Corporation might include the following provision in the consulting agreement for Consultant D, to whom it expects to offer a permanent position in the future:

No later than January 1, 2018, the Company will offer Consultant the position of senior vice president, marketing, according to the terms and conditions specified in Exhibit A to this Agreement.

.10 Support, Supplies and Office Space

For very favored consultants such as the former CEO, the consulting agreement may require the company to provide the consultant with suitable administrative support during the term of the agreement, including, among other things, secretarial support, photocopying and facsimile services, voice mail access, remote e-mail access, message taking services, mail receipt, office furniture, utilities, office equipment, and office supplies.

¶335 Company and Consultant Tax Issues

The tax issues for a company and its consultants are straightforward. The Internal Revenue Code does not require the company to withhold federal income, employment or any other taxes from the compensation it pays to the consultant. Rather, the company pays the agreed amount to the consultant, and reports the amount it paid on IRS Form 1099. The consultant alone is responsible for calculating and paying his or her income and other taxes.

Legal counsel should consider adding language to the consulting agreement similar to the following:

Taxes and Statutory Obligations. As an independent contractor, Consultant will be solely responsible for all taxes, withholdings, and other similar statutory obligations, including, but not limited to, Workers' Compensation Insurance laws.

Because Consultant is an independent consultant and not an employee of the Company, there shall be no withholdings or deductions from these payments. Consultant will be responsible for payment of all personal income, employment and other taxes due in connection with payments made pursuant to this Agreement.

The company generally would be entitled to a deduction for the payments it made to the consultant.

.01 Consulting Payments or Cancellation of Employment Agreement

The payment of compensation to an employee, including payments following the employee's termination of employment, generally would be subject to income and employment tax withholding as "wages" for purposes of federal income tax ("FIT") withholding, FICA and FUTA taxes.

The Code defines wages broadly as all remuneration for services performed by an employee for his or her employer.[9] However, not all payments made by an employer to an employee are considered wages.[10] In determining whether payments made in connection with the cancellation of an employment contract are wages for purposes of income and employment tax withholding, the Internal Revenue Service has developed two lines of authority. Under the first line of authority, the IRS does not consider payments made to cancel or relinquish contractual rights wages. Under the second, dismissal payments made to compensate involuntarily terminated employees are considered wages.

However, with the exception of two rulings from the 1950s,[11] the IRS has routinely attempted to characterize all such payments as dismissal payments. Before 2004, while the IRS was expending a significant amount of energy drawing increasingly narrow distinctions between dismissal payments and cancellation payments, the IRS had not reversed its earlier taxpayer favorable rulings and had repeatedly acknowledged that the distinction is still viable.[12]

.02 Rev. Rul. 2004-110

In Rev. Rul. 2004-110,[13] the IRS attempted to resolve the issues of whether an amount paid to an employee as consideration for the cancellation of an employment contract and relinquishment of contract rights is ordinary income, and wages for purposes of FICA, FUTA and FIT withholding. The IRS ruled that an amount paid to an employee as consideration for cancellation of an employment contract and relinquishment of contract rights is ordinary income, and wages for purposes of FICA, FUTA, and FIT withholding.

The IRS described a situation in which an employee performs services under a written employment contract providing for a specified number of years of employment. The contract does not provide for any payments to be made by either party in the event the contract is cancelled by mutual agreement. Before the end of the contract period, the employee and the employer agree to cancel the

---

[9] Reg. §31.3121(a)-1(b) and Reg. §31.3121(b)-3(b) (FICA); Reg. §31.3306(b)-1(b) and Reg. §31.3306(c)-2(b) (FUTA); Reg. §31.3401(a)-1(a) (FIT).

[10] Examples of payments by employers to employees that are not considered wages include, but are not limited to, the following: lunch allowances paid to utility workers during day trips (*Central Illinois Public Service Co. v. U.S.*, 435 US 21 (1978); reimbursement of moving expenses (*Humble Oil & Refining Co. v. U.S.*, 71-1 USTC ¶9402, 442 F2d 1362

(Ct. Cl. 1971); signing bonuses paid to baseball players (Rev. Rul. 58-145, 1958-1 CB 360); liquidated damages, interest and attorneys' fees in connection with settlement agreements (Rev. Rul. 72-268, 1972-1 CB 313 and Rev. Rul. 80-364, 1980-2 CB 294).

[11] Rev. Rul. 55-520, 1955-2 CB 393 and Rev. Rul. 58-301, 1958-1 CB 23.

[12] GCM 37784 (1978); GCM 38098 (1979); GCM 38534 (1980).

[13] Rev. Rul. 2004-110, IRB 2004-50.

contract and negotiate a payment from the employer to the employee in consideration for the employee's relinquishment of his contract rights to the remaining period of employment.

The Code and regulations provide that amounts an employer pays an employee as remuneration for employment are wages, unless a specific exception applies.[14] The regulations also provide that the name by which the remuneration is designated is immaterial.[15] Furthermore, the remuneration is wages even though at the time paid the relationship of employer and employee no longer exists.[16]

The Code and the regulations also provide that any service of whatever nature performed by an employee for the person employing him is employment, unless a specific exemption applies.[17] Employment encompasses the establishment, maintenance, furtherance, alteration, or cancellation of the employer-employee relationship or any of the terms and conditions thereof. If the employee provides clear, separate, and adequate consideration for the employer's payment that is not dependent upon the employer-employee relationship and its component terms and conditions, the payment is not wages for purposes of FICA, FUTA, or FIT withholding.

Under the facts presented in the ruling, the employee receives the payment as consideration for canceling the remaining period of his employment contract and relinquishing his contract rights. As such, the payment is part of the compensation the employer pays as remuneration for employment. The employee does not provide clear, separate, and adequate consideration for the employer's payment that is not dependent upon the employer-employee relationship and its component terms and conditions. Thus, the payment provided by the employer to the employee is wages for purposes of FICA, FUTA, and FIT withholding. This conclusion applies regardless of how the parties characterize the remuneration or whether the employment relationship still exists at the time the payment is made.

Additionally, the IRS ruled that the payment received by the employee is taxable as ordinary income and not a payment for property that could qualify for taxation as capital gain. To qualify as capital gain, eligible for the reduced rates in Code Sec. 1(h), a payment must be received in connection with a "sale or exchange" of "property," as those terms are used in Code Sec. 1221, Code Sec. 1222 and Code Sec. 1231. Consideration received for the transfer or termination of a right to receive income for the past or future performance of services is a substitute for ordinary income, taxable as such.

The IRS stated that, with respect to the application of FICA and FIT withholding, Rev. Rul. 55-520 and Rev. Rul. 58-301[18] erred in their analysis by failing

---

[14] Code Sec. 3121(a), Code Sec. 3306(b), and Code Sec. 3401(a); Reg. §31.3121(a)-1(b), Reg. §31.3306(b)-1(b), and Reg. §31.3401(a)-1(a)(1).

[15] Reg. §31.3121(a)-1(c), Reg. §31.3306(b)-1(c), and Reg. §31.3401(a)-1(a)(2).

[16] Reg. §31.3121(a)-1(i), Reg. §31.3306(b)-1(i), and Reg. §31.3401(a)-1(a)(5).

[17] Code Sec. 3121(b) and Code Sec. 3306(c); Reg. §31.3121(b)-3(b) and Reg. §31.3306(c)-2(b).

[18] Rev. Rul. 55-520, 1955-2 CB 393 and Rev. Rul. 58-301, 1958-1 CB 23.

to apply the Code and regulations appropriately to the question of whether the payments made in cancellation of the employment contract were wages. Accordingly, the IRS modified and superseded Rev. Rul. 55-520 and Rev. Rul. 58-301, and modified Rev. Rul. 74-252 and Rev. Rul. 75-44 to the extent their holdings regarding FICA, FUTA, RRTA, and federal income tax withholding rely on distinguishing Rev. Rul. 58-301. The IRS observed that the specific holdings in Rev. Rul. 58-301 and Rev. Rul. 75-44 that payments were ordinary income remain correct.

.03 Pre-2004 Analysis

In the IRS's repeated attempts to distinguish cancellation payments from dismissal payments prior to 2004, and the courts' attempts to interpret those distinctions, three factors have been probative in determining whether a payment made by an employer to an employee upon his or her termination of employment will be deemed to be wages:

- Whether the employee was covered by an individual employment agreement with a fixed term or employed at-will;

- Whether the termination was voluntary or involuntary; and

- Whether the company made the payments pursuant to an existing agreement or separately negotiated at the time of termination.

Individual Contract with a Fixed Term. The most important factor appears to have been whether the terminating employee is covered by an individual employment agreement that specifies a fixed term of employment. In both Rev. Rul. 55-520 and Rev. Rul. 58-301,[19] the IRS concluded that payments received by a terminating employee were amounts received on cancellation or relinquishment of an employment contract and not wages for income and employment tax withholding purposes. In each ruling, the company made payments upon the premature cancellation of the original contract of employment under which the parties were bound for a specified period.

In Rev. Rul. 75-44,[20] however, the IRS distinguished the payments described in the earlier rulings from certain payments received in consideration for an employee's relinquishing his seniority rights and agreeing to terminate employment in a particular position. The IRS explained that, unlike the payments described in Rev. Rul. 58-301,[21] these payments were made under an employment contract that "contemplated a relation between the parties that was to continue indefinitely, but that, except as might otherwise be specially provided under certain circumstances, was generally terminable by either party without liability to the other solely for the failure to maintain the relationship for a specified period." Accordingly, the IRS concluded that the payment was for the past performance of services and did not treat the payment as one for the cancellation of contract rights.

---

[19] Rev. Rul. 55-520, 1955-2 CB 393 and Rev. Rul. 58-301, 1958-1 CB 23.

[20] Rev. Rul. 75-44, 1975-1 CB 15.

[21] Rev. Rul. 58-301, 1958-1 CB 23.

The IRS has repeatedly drawn a distinction between payments made to an employee upon the cancellation of a contract under which the employee had a right to remain employed for a fixed term and payments made to an at-will employee or to an employee covered by a contract under which he or she could be terminated, either upon notice or at any time. For example, in IRS Letter Ruling 9711001,[22] the IRS distinguished the payments made in Rev. Rul. 58-301 from payments made to tenured faculty members because the payments in Rev. Rul. 58-301 involved the cancellation of an employment contract that bound the parties for a specific period. By way of contrast, the IRS reasoned that because tenure is based on a faculty member's past performance of services to a university, not on negotiated contract rights, payments made to terminated faculty were wages.[23]

Similarly, in IRS Letter Ruling 8808019,[24] the IRS bifurcated a severance payment made to a terminating employee who waived his right under an employment agreement to receive written notice before his termination of employment. Citing Rev. Rul. 58-301, the IRS reasoned that to the extent the payment was in lieu of the employee's contractual right to receive 90 days' notice before termination of his employment, such payment would not be treated as wages, but that any amounts received in excess of the value of the 90 days' notice would be considered paid in exchange for certain other rights acquired as a result of employment and would be treated as remuneration for the past performance of services.

In *North Dakota State University v. U.S.*,[25] the Eighth Circuit attempted to apply the distinctions promulgated by the IRS before 2004, holding that payments made under an early retirement program were not wages when paid to tenured faculty but were wages when paid to senior administrators. Citing Rev. Rul. 58-301, the Eighth Circuit reasoned that payments to the professors were not wages because such payments represented the professors' relinquishment of their contractual rights to tenure. In other words, while the professors received a negotiated amount of money in exchange for what they were entitled to under their contracts (*i.e.*, continued employment), the administrators were at-will employees entitled only to extended notice before termination. Thus, the IRS deemed the payments to the administrators to be wages.

Involuntary Termination vs. Voluntary Termination. A second significant factor was whether the employee's termination is voluntary or involuntary. In Rev. Rul. 74-252,[26] the IRS held that payments made to an employee following his involuntary termination of employment were in the nature of dismissal payments and thus were wages for purposes of income and employment tax with-

---

[22] IRS Letter Ruling 9711001 (Jan. 23, 1995).

[23] But cf., *North Dakota State University v. U.S.*, 2001-2 USTC ¶50,485, 255 F3d 599 (8th Cir. 2001) (tenured professors had a recognized property interest in their tenure and the payments made to them were in exchange for the relinquishment of their

property or contract interest and were not subject to withholding taxes).

[24] IRS Letter Ruling 8808019 (Nov. 24, 1987).

[25] *North Dakota State University v. U.S.*, 2001-2 USTC ¶50,485, 255 F3d 599 (8th Cir. 2001).

[26] Rev. Rul. 74-252, 1974-1 CB 287.

holding.[27] The IRS distinguished Rev. Rul. 58-301, since, in this case, the company made the payments to the employee upon his involuntary separation from service as opposed to in consideration for the cancellation of an employment contract.

Similarly, in Rev. Rul. 71-408,[28] the IRS found that dismissal payments made to former employees by a company that had terminated its operations were wages for income and employment tax purposes. The IRS explained that the amounts paid by the company to its former employees were dismissal payments because the company made them upon the involuntary separation of the employees from the service of the employer.

In *North Dakota State University*,[29] the Eighth Circuit declined to treat as wages payments made to tenured faculty where the terminations involved "were totally voluntary by both parties." In another case, a district court in New York determined that a lump sum payment made to an employee under a severance agreement was a dismissal payment constituting wages.[30] Citing a decision by the Second Circuit, the court explained that when determining whether a payment is a "dismissal payment, the ultimate inquiry is into the 'basic reason' for the company's payment."[31] In *Greenwald*, the court ultimately determined that the payment was a dismissal payment because the employer made the payment because it wanted to replace the employee with new management.[32]

Payments Made Under the Original Contract. Another basis upon which the IRS had distinguished nonwage cancellation payments from dismissal payments considered wages was whether the payments were made pursuant to the terms of the original agreement. In Rev. Rul. 74-252,[33] the IRS concluded that payments made to an employee following his or her involuntary termination of employment under the terms of a three-year contract were wages for purposes of income and employment tax withholding. Under the terms of the employment contract, the company could terminate the relationship at any time if it paid the employee an amount equal to an additional six months of salary. Distinguishing these payments from the amounts described in Rev. Rul. 58-301, the IRS explained that the company made payments in Rev. Rul. 74-252 pursuant to the provisions of the contract rather than as consideration for the relinquishment of interests the employee had in his employment contract in the nature of property.

The case of *Greenwald v. U.S.*,[34] expanded the distinction made by the IRS in Rev. Rul. 74-252. In this case, the district court characterized as wages certain

---

[27] Reg. §31.3401(a)-1(b)(4) (for purposes of income tax withholding, all payments made by an employer to an employee on account of dismissal, that is, involuntary separation from the service of the employer, constitute "wages" regardless of whether the employer is legally bound by contract, statute, or otherwise to make the payments).

[28] Rev. Rul. 71-408, 1971-2 CB 340.

[29] *North Dakota State University v. U.S.*, 2001-2 USTC ¶50,485, 255 F3d 599 (8th Cir. 2001).

[30] *Greenwald v. U.S.*, 2000-1 USTC ¶50,197, 2000 U.S. Dist. LEXIS 102 (2000).

[31] *Agar v. Comm'r*, 61-1 USTC ¶9457, 290 F2d 283 (2d Cir. 1961).

[32] But cf., Rev. Rul. 55-520, 1955-2 CB 393 (payments not wages although made in connection with the cancellation of an employment agreement following the employer's demand and receipt of the employee's resignation).

[33] Rev. Rul. 74-252, 1974-1 CB 287.

[34] *Greenwald v. U.S.*, 2000-1 USTC ¶50,197, 2000 U.S. Dist. LEXIS 102 (2000).

payments made under a severance agreement that were made to an employee covered by a separate employment agreement. Under the terms of the employment agreement, the employer was obligated to pay the employee all of the remaining salary and bonus due to him under the agreement unless the company terminated his employment. The court based its conclusion, in part, on the employee's concession that the payment under the severance agreement was essentially a "discount of the future income [he] anticipated earning pursuant to the employment agreement." Also problematic was the fact that the severance agreement provided that the employer was entitled to withhold all applicable taxes.

.04 Compensation of Independent Contractors Linked to Pension Plan Funding

In June 2010, President Obama signed into law the so-called "Preservation of Access to Care for Medicare Beneficiaries and Pension Relief Act of 2010," which, among other things, extended the time period over which ERISA and the Internal Revenue Code require an employer to fully fund its defined benefit pension plan. (Pension plan funding became a major problem for many employers after the market crash reduced the value of the assets accumulated in their pension trust accounts.)

However, the Act also adds a new Section (7) to Code Sec. 430(c) (ERISA Section 303(c)), which provides that an employer's required pension contribution using these funding rules will be increased in any year by the amount of "excess employee compensation" it pays in that year, plus the amount of any extraordinary dividends and redemptions.

Code Sec. 430(c)(7) also provides that the term "employee" includes, with respect to a calendar year, a self-employed individual who is treated as an employee under section 401(c) of such Code for the taxable year ending during such calendar year, and the term 'compensation' shall include earned income of such individual with respect to such self-employment.

Code Sec. 430(c)(7) defines "excess employee compensation" as the aggregate amount includible in income for any employee for any plan year over $1 million. Sec. 430(c)(7) also includes assets set aside or reserved (directly or indirectly) during the year in a trust (or other arrangement as determined by the Secretary of the Treasury), or transferred to such a trust or other arrangement, by a plan sponsor for purposes of paying deferred compensation of an employee.

Code Sec. 430(c)(7) applies to compensation for services performed by the employee for the employer after February 2010. Notably, new Code Sec. 430(c)(7) excludes from the definition of "excess employee compensation:"

1. Amounts includible in income as a result of the grant, after February 2010, of employer stock options, restricted stock or certain other stock-based compensation with at least a five-year vesting schedule.

2. Remuneration payable on a commission basis solely on account of income directly generated by the individual performance of the individual to whom such remuneration is payable, and

3. Any nonqualified deferred compensation, restricted stock, stock options, or stock appreciation rights payable or granted under a written binding contract that was in effect on March 1, 2010, and which is not modified in any material respect before such remuneration is paid.

.05 Tax Penalties for Misclassification

Federal Taxes. Under federal tax law, an employer that misclassifies an employee as an independent contractor will be required to pay back taxes owed for that employee, including income, FICA, and unemployment taxes. The employer may also be subject to interest and penalties, all of which become due at the same time.

If an employer incorrectly treats an employee as an independent contractor due to an unintentional misclassification, the employer's penalty for failing to deduct and withhold income taxes is equal to 1.5% of wages paid to that employee. The employer is also assessed an amount equal to 20% of the employee's share of FICA taxes that should have been deducted and withheld. Furthermore, if, during the period that the employer erroneously treated the employee as an independent contractor, the employer also failed to report the compensation to the worker by filing Form 1099-MISC, the penalty for failure to withhold income taxes becomes 3% of the worker's earnings (instead of 1.5%) and 40% of the FICA amount that should have been withheld (instead of 20%. In limited circumstances, the IRS will allow an employer to treat a worker as an independent contractor, even if the worker is an employee under common law standards. This so-called "Section 530 Safe Harbor" hinges on the company's reasonable reliance on certain recognized authorities, such as a prior IRS audit, judicial precedent, or industry practice.

These specific "failure-to-withhold penalties" apply where the employer is merely negligent; they do not apply if the employer is found to have intentionally disregarded the withholding requirements. In addition to the employer still being liable for its share of FICA taxes as well as for the employee's income and FICA taxes, the Code imposes interest on those amounts at the variable federal short-term rate. The Code also imposes a penalty equal to 100% of the taxes due for a willful failure to collect or account for employment taxes. The 100% penalty may be asserted against anyone the IRS determines may be a "responsible corporate officer." A responsible corporate officer could be any officer, shareholder, director or employee who had the responsibility to withhold and remit taxes, but failed to do so, or had authority over the payment of wages and other corporate obligations.

These significant tax burdens will be carried by the employer alone, as employers that are liable for back taxes and penalties may not recover any portion of these taxes from their misclassified employees.

¶335.05

State Taxes. In addition to federal tax consequences, states generally impose penalties for failure to properly withhold and remit taxes. In most instances, additional penalties will depend on whether the failure was willful or not.

Unemployment Insurance Taxes. Employment is a requirement of eligibility for state unemployment benefits. Because unemployment tax payments are made to the state for "employees" based upon the formula established by the state, employers are liable for failure to remit unemployment insurance tax premiums on behalf of workers improperly classified as independent contractors and may be fined.

¶345 Code Sec. 409A

Code Sec. 409A, added by the American Jobs Creation Act of 2004, is entitled "Inclusion in Gross Income of Deferred Compensation Under Nonqualified Deferred Compensation Plans." The failure to comply with 409A results in immediate income on deferrals, an excise tax of 20% and other penalties.

Code Sec. 409A can apply to consulting agreements and other arrangements with independent contractors, in addition to deferred compensation plans, which were the original target of Congress. Code Sec. 409A applies to any plan or arrangement that provides for the deferral of compensation by a "service provider." Regulations under Code Sec. 409A[35] state that an arrangement provides for the deferral of compensation if, under the terms of the agreement and the relevant facts and circumstances, the service provider has a legally binding right during a taxable year to compensation that, (i) has not been actually or constructively received and included in gross income, and (ii) pursuant to the terms of the agreement, is payable to (or on behalf of) the service provider in a later year.

.01 Code Sec. 409A Limited to Those Who Provide Services to Only One Entity

Generally, Code Sec. 409A does not apply to an amount deferred under a plan between a service provider, such as a consultant, and a service recipient with respect to a particular trade or business, if each of the following applies:

(A) The service provider is actively engaged in the trade or business of providing services, other than as an employee or as a member of the board of directors (or similar position with respect to an entity that is not a corporation).

(B) The service provider provides significant services to two or more service recipients to which the service provider is not related and that are not related to one another.

(C) The service provider is not related to the service recipient.[36]

An exception to the general rule applies to consultants and other service providers that provide management services to a service recipient. Under Code

---

[35] The Treasury and IRS issued 397 pages of final regulations under Code Section 409A on April 10, 2007.

[36] Treas. Reg. § 1.409A-1(f)(2).

Sec. 409A, the term "management services" means services that involve the actual or *de facto* direction or control of the financial or operational aspects of a trade or business of the service recipient, or investment management or advisory services provided to a service recipient whose primary trade or business includes the investment of financial assets (including investments in real estate), such as a hedge fund or a real estate investment trust.[37]

.02 Termination of Employment and Move to Consultant Status

Code Sec. 409A provides that a deferred compensation plan or arrangement may permit distributions only upon certain dates or events, such as the employee's death, disability, retirement, or termination of employment with the employer. Final regulations under Code Sec. 409A, seek to prevent employers and employees from accelerating distributions by causing a retirement or other termination of employment, which should allow a distribution, followed by rehire of the employee as a consultant or other independent contractor. Under Code Sec. 409A, whether a termination of employment has occurred is determined based on whether the facts and circumstances indicate that the employer and employee reasonably anticipated that no further services would be performed after a certain date or that the level of bona fide services the employee would perform after such date (whether as an employee or as an independent contractor) would permanently decrease to no more than 20 percent of the average level of bona fide services performed (whether as an employee or an independent contractor) over the immediately preceding 36-month period (or the full period of services to the employer if the employee has been providing services to the employer less than 36 months).[38] The regulations provide that an employee is presumed:

- to have separated from service where the level of bona fide services performed decreases to a level equal to 20 percent or less of the average level of services performed by the employee during the immediately preceding 36-month period, and

- not to have separated from service where the level of bona fide services performed continues at a level that is 50 percent or more of the average level of service performed by the employee during the immediately preceding 36-month period.[39]

Either presumption is rebuttable by facts or circumstances demonstrating that the employer and the employee anticipated changing the level of services as of a future date.[40]

With respect to an individual who truly is an independent contractor, the regulations under Code Sec. 409A, provide that such individual is considered to have a separation from service with the service recipient:

- upon the expiration of the contract under which services are performed for the service recipient,

---

[37] Treas. Reg. § 1.409A-1(f)(2)(iv).
[38] Treas. Reg. § 1.409A-1(h)(1)(ii).

[39] Treas. Reg. § 1.409A-1(h)(1)(ii).
[40] Treas. Reg. § 1.409A-1(h)(1)(ii).

- if the expiration constitutes a good faith and complete termination of the contractual relationship.[41]

The regulations provide further that an expiration does not constitute a good faith and complete termination of the contractual relationship if the service recipient anticipates a renewal of a contractual relationship or the independent contractor becomes an employee.

---

[41] Treas. Reg. § 1.409A-1(h)(2)(i).

Chapter 4

NONCOMPETES AND OTHER RESTRICTIVE COVENANTS

¶401 Overview—Noncompetes and Other Restrictive Covenants

Most employers will agree to provide substantial compensation to their senior executives without much of a fight. However, employers want to know (and ensure) that if an executive later leaves the employer, the executive will not use the knowledge and experience gained during his or her employment to compete with, or solicit employees or customers from, the employer. In today's highly competitive market, an employer needs to preserve confidential information that gives it a competitive advantage and protect unique relationships between employees and customers. Therefore, most executive employment agreements include post-employment restrictive covenants.[1]

Such covenants typically relate to confidentiality, noncompetition, nonsolicitation, and nondisparagement. In general, employers use these restrictive covenants to prevent the spread of trade secrets or other confidential information, to restrict the flight of employees to competitors, to protect against the loss of client and customer bases, and to restrain employees from leaving to start a competing company. By the nature of their positions, executives usually have access to sensitive proprietary information, maintain relationships with important company clients and customers, and have extensive knowledge of the company's inner workings. Therefore, it is hardly surprising that executives are frequently required to execute employment agreements containing restrictive covenants.

.01 Nondisclosure

Nondisclosure clauses are the most prevalent of all restrictive covenants. Nondisclosure or "confidentiality" clauses are intended to prohibit the executive from using the information he or she learned during service with the company to benefit another business venture following his or her employment termination—particularly a business venture that competes with the business of the company. Nondisclosure clauses are common in all executive employment agreements and many companies use them as a stand-alone agreement with all employees (see ¶425).

---

[1] *See* ¶10,010 for a sample executive employment agreement.

.02 Nonsolicitation

After nondisclosure, nonsolicitation clauses are the most prevalent of all restrictive covenants. Employers use nonsolicitation clauses to prevent two distinct types of behavior:

1. *Nonsolicitation of Customers.* These nonsolicitation clauses are intended to prohibit the executive from seeking to convince the customers of the executive's former employer—particularly the customers with whom the executive worked while with the former employer—to leave the former employer and begin doing business with the executive's new employer.

2. *Nonsolicitation of Employees.* These clauses are intended to prohibit the executive from seeking to convince the employees of the executive's former employer—particularly the employees with whom the executive worked while with the former employer—to leave the former employer and begin working for the executive's new employer.

Some companies view a nonsolicitation clause as more important than a noncompete, because the clause can prevent the former executive from using the unique relationship he or she developed with employees and customers during the executive's service with the company to benefit a business venture that competes with the business of the company (see ¶ 415).

.03 Noncompete

Most executive employment agreements include a noncompete clause. Employers use this clause to prohibit the executive from using the knowledge and experience gained during his or her service with the company in a business venture that competes with the business of the company, following his or her employment termination. Noncompete clauses are more common in employment agreements with executives employed in sensitive areas, such as marketing or operations, and among executives possessing particular knowledge and skills (see ¶ 415).

If you think non-compete provisions are not enforceable, look at the highly publicized battle between Motorola, Inc. and Nortel Networks Corporation over Nortel's attempt to hire away Motorola's chief operating officer as its CEO. Mike Zafirovski left Motorola and become "available" in 2005, after being passed over for the CEO position at Motorola. In addition to the costly, public litigation, uncertainty and placing Mr. Zafirovski on ice during pendency of the litigation, Mr. Zafirovski forfeited at least $11.5 million in payments he had received from Motorola, for which Nortel agreed to reimburse him, and agreed not to contact certain customers or shape Nortel's strategy to compete against Motorola until July 1, 2006.

.04 Nondisparagement

Many executive employment agreements include a nondisparagement clause. Employers use this clause to prohibit the executive from making derogatory comments about the company following his or her employment termination.

Nondisparagement clauses are more common in employment agreements with senior executive officers and public companies (see ¶425).

.05 Enforceability

Although most states permit enforcement of restrictive covenants, they are not enforceable in every state or under all circumstances. For example, in California, a state statute prohibits enforcement of nearly all restrictive covenants except in the narrowest of circumstances. States that do not have a blanket prohibition on restrictive covenants in the employment context will typically enforce such provisions as long as they are "reasonable."

An employer should intermittently remind employees, especially departing ones, of their obligations. Simply executing an employment agreement, with no follow-up, may not be adequate. An exit interview is also a valuable opportunity to remind a departing employee of his or her continuing obligations under a restrictive covenant agreement (see ¶485).

Most agreements also provide that limitations do not apply to any inventions or developments unrelated to the business of the employer, that the executive developed entirely on his or her own time, and for which the executive did not use any equipment, supplies, facility or trade secret information of the employer (see ¶445).

Where an employer has sought in good faith to protect a legitimate business interest, most (but not all) states allow a court to modify an unreasonable aspect of a restrictive covenant to an acceptable level that may be enforced, *i.e.*, "blue penciling" (see ¶455).

Most executive employment agreements provide that if a former executive violates the noncompete or other restrictive covenants of the agreement, the employer either may seek to: (1) obtain an injunction preventing the former executive from continued violation, or (2) forfeit some form of severance or retirement payment or equity compensation award otherwise payable to the former executive (see ¶475).

¶415 Noncompete

Many employment agreements include noncompete provisions that prohibit a departing executive from competing against his or her employer for a specified time in a defined geographic area. Although they are not enforceable in every state or under all circumstances, a majority of states will enforce noncompete provisions that are reasonable as to both geographic scope and duration. There are only a few states that completely prohibit noncompete provisions in the employment realm, prohibit noncompete provisions in only specific professions, or limit the period for which the restriction will be upheld. For example, Delaware bans noncompete agreements that restrict a physician's right to practice medicine,[2] and South Dakota enforces noncompete provisions only if they are limited to two years from the date of termination.[3]

---

[2] *See* 6 Del. C. §2707. Massachusetts has a similar law for nurses. Mass. Gen. Laws ch.112 §74D.

[3] *See* S.D. Codified Laws §53-9-11.

A majority of states apply a balancing test to determine whether a noncompete provision is "reasonable" and thus, enforceable. In those states, a court must determine that the covenant meets the following requirements: (1) protects a legitimate interest of the employer; (2) is reasonable in scope and duration; (3) is not overly burdensome to the employee; and (4) does not harm the public interest. When reviewing a noncompete provision, the threshold question for a court is whether the employer is attempting to protect a legitimate business interest. If a legitimate interest cannot be identified, then the covenant will not be enforced. Examples of legitimate business interests include protecting against the diversion of a substantial number of clients by a former employee and preventing a former employee from divulging or using company trade secrets.

A New York court refused to enforce a noncompete provision in an employment agreement because it did not serve a legitimate business interest.[4] The court stated that a noncompete covenant would be enforced to protect an employer from unfair competition, such as when a former employee could reveal confidential information or where the employee's services are unique or extraordinary. In striking down the noncompete provision, the court reasoned that:

> [The noncompete provision's] broad-sweeping language is unrestrained by any limitations keyed to [the employee's] uniqueness, trade secrets, confidentiality or even competitive unfairness. It does no more than baldly restrain competition. This it may not do.[5]

In the following example of a noncompete provision, ABC Corporation's employment agreement with Executive D provides:

> The Executive agrees that so long as he is employed by the employer and for a period of two (2) years thereafter (the "Period"), he shall not, without the prior written consent of ABC Corporation, participate or engage in, directly or indirectly (as an owner, partner, employee, officer, director, independent contractor, consultant, advisor or in any other capacity calling for the rendition of services, advice, or acts of management, operation or control), any business that, during the Period, is competitive with the business conducted by ABC or any of its affiliates within the United States.

Although many executive employment agreements contain a version of the foregoing noncompete provision, a court may view it as overbroad and thus, unenforceable. For example, the geographic scope of the provision covers the entire United States. To avoid having it struck down by a court, it should be limited to the employee's prior geographic area of doing business (*e.g.*, within a 50-mile radius of the company office where the employee worked). Similarly, the duration of the noncompete provision should not be longer than necessary. Although the two-year time frame in the above provision may be reasonable, it is within the outer limits of reasonableness and the employer should have sound business reasons to support its length. A noncompetition period of six or twelve months would be upheld more readily and be easier to justify.

Most non-compete provisions contain fairly standard language that the employee or former employee cannot directly or indirectly own any interest in,

---

[4] *Columbia Ribbon & Carbon Mfg. Co., Inc. v. A-1-A Corp.*, 369 N.E.2d 4, 6 (N.Y. 1977).

[5] *Columbia Ribbon & Carbon Mfg. Co., Inc. v. A-1-A Corp.*, 369 N.E.2d 4, 6 (N.Y. 1977).

operate, control or participate as a partner, director, principal, officer, or agent of, enter into the employment of, act as a consultant to, or perform any services for, any company, person, or entity engaged in a competitive business. However, most non-competes also provide that: "Notwithstanding anything herein to the contrary, this Section shall not prevent the Employee from acquiring securities representing up to [1% - 5%] of the outstanding voting securities of any publicly held corporation." Lest you wonder whether this provision ever applies in the real world, March 2006 saw LCA-Vision Inc. remove its chief executive officer and chairman after the executive acquired a 7.7% of the stock of its closest competitor.[6]

¶425 Nondisclosure and Nondisparagement

Nondisclosure provisions are designed to maintain the confidentiality of private information, which can range from trade secrets to customer lists, while nondisparagement provisions prohibit former employees from making negative remarks about the company.

.01 Nondisclosure or Confidentiality

Nondisclosure provisions are typically easier to enforce than noncompete provisions because they do not affect an individual's livelihood and often involve identifiable proprietary information. Additionally, most states have statutes that explicitly protect trade secrets from disclosure. Most employment agreements require the executive to agree that during his or her employment with the employer (and sometimes for a period thereafter):

- The executive will not use, divulge or make accessible to any person any of the employer's confidential information.

- The executive, following employment termination for whatever reason, will deliver to the employer all property of the employer and will not take or copy property of information of the employer.

- The executive will not make disparaging comments about the employer or its officers, directors or employees during or following employment.

Whether a court will deem certain information as "confidential" depends primarily on the extent to which it is known outside of the company, its value to the company, and the extent of the measures taken by the company to guard its secrecy. Certain information, such as trade secrets and marketing plans, is typically deemed confidential as long as the company has made reasonable attempts to protect against its dissemination. Other information, such as the general knowledge of industry insiders and publicly available facts, will not be deemed confidential.

> **Planning Note:** The employment agreement should define important terms such as "Confidential Information" and the "Business Conducted by the Company" broadly, and should make clear that it applies to information

---

[6] SEC Rules require that an individual or entity that acquires 5% or more of the stock of a public company to report that acquisition to the SEC on Form 13D.

or business of all company affiliates. Additionally, the company should make sure that it can demonstrate actions it took to mark and protect information it characterizes as "trade secrets."

The Dodd-Frank Wall Street Reform and Consumer Protection Act ("Dodd-Frank") amended the Securities and Exchange Act of 1934 ("Exchange Act") by adding Section 21F, "Whistleblower Incentives and Protection." Section 21F only applies to public companies governed by the Exchange Act. The congressional purpose underlying these provisions was "to encourage whistleblowers to report possible violations of the securities laws by providing financial incentives, prohibiting employment-related retaliation, and providing various confidentiality guarantees." In 2011, the SEC adopted Rule 21F-17, which provides in relevant part:

> (a) No person may take any action to impede an individual from communicating directly with the Commission staff about a possible securities law violation, including enforcing, or threatening to enforce, a confidentiality agreement . . . with respect to such communications.

Rule 21F-17 became effective on August 12, 2011.

In April 2015, the SEC announced its first enforcement action against a company for using improperly restrictive language in confidentiality agreements with the potential to stifle the whistleblowing process. The SEC charged a Houston-based company with violating Rule 21F-17 by requiring witnesses in certain internal investigations interviews to sign confidentiality statements with language warning that the witness could face discipline and even be fired if he or she discussed the matters with outside parties without the prior approval of the company's legal department. Since these investigations included allegations of possible securities law violations, the SEC found that these terms violated Rule 21F-17. Without admitting or denying the charges, the company agreed to pay a $130,000 penalty to settle the SEC's charges and the company voluntarily amended its confidentiality statement by adding language making clear that employees are free to report possible violations to the SEC and other federal agencies without company approval or fear of retaliation.

The language originally used by the company, to which the SEC objected, read:

> I understand that in order to protect the integrity of this review, I am prohibited from discussing any particulars regarding this interview and the subject matter discussed during the interview, without the prior authorization of the Law Department. I understand that the unauthorized disclosure of information may be grounds for disciplinary action up to and including termination of employment.

The SEC demanded the removal of the foregoing language and the addition of the following:

> Nothing in this Confidentiality Statement prohibits me from reporting possible violations of federal law or regulation to any governmental agency or entity, including but not limited to the Department of Justice, the Securities and Exchange Commission, the Congress, and any agency Inspector General, or making other disclosures that are protected under the whistleblower provi-

sions of federal law or regulation. I do not need the prior authorization of the Law Department to make any such reports or disclosures and I am not required to notify the company that I have made such reports or disclosures.

Companies should consider adding a paragraph similar to the foregoing in any employment or other agreement that contains a confidentiality or non-disclosure provision.

.02 Nondisparagement

The inclusion of a nondisparagement clause in an executive's employment agreement can help an employer avoid having to sue a former employee for defamation, a claim that is much more difficult to prove than a basic breach of contract. In a recent case decided under Connecticut law, a court relied on a nondisparagement provision to enjoin two former executives of a consulting firm from making negative remarks about the company and its employees.[7] Although the former executives had not technically breached the nondisparagement clause, the court found that some of their comments bordered on disparagement and prohibited any future negative remarks.

In *Kamfar v. New World Restaurant Group, Inc.,*[8] the court found that the company may have breached a provision in a settlement agreement with the former CEO that forbade the company from making disparaging comments about the CEO, when it issued news releases characterizing the CEO's $1.6 million bonus payment as "unauthorized." However, the court held that the company did not defame the former CEO in the news release.

Ramin Kamfar, the founder, CEO, and chairman of New World Restaurant Group Inc. left the company in April 2002 amid questions about the propriety of bonus payments he and two other officers had received. In 2000, while attempting to acquire the Einstein/Noah Bagel Corp., Kamfar proposed to New World's board of directors a bonus plan that would pay himself $1.6 million and two other officers who had worked on the Einstein acquisition received a nearly $2 million bonus. According to the court, the board of directors never discussed or approved the bonus plan until it was discovered in February 2002 by a law firm hired to advise the company on unrelated matters. In April 2002, Kamfar and New World entered a settlement agreement under which Kamfar agreed to repay the $1.6 million in return for $1.4 million in severance payments he had been promised in his employment agreements. Among other things, the settlement agreement included mutual covenants not to make disparaging statements. However, shortly after Kamfar's departure from the company, a New Jersey newspaper published an article, based on comments from a New World official, which stated Kamfar was the recipient of an unauthorized bonus.

The court dismissed Kamfar's defamation claim, because it found that he failed to demonstrate that the company acted in a grossly irresponsible manner by releasing information that characterized his bonus payment as "unauthorized." However, the court refused to dismiss Kamfar's claim that the company

---

[7] *Rogerscasey Inc. v. Nankof,* 2002 U.S. Dist. LEXIS 7165 (S.D.N.Y. 2002).

[8] *Kamfar v. New World Restaurant Group, Inc.,* 347 FSupp2d 38 (S.D.N.Y. 2004).

breached the settlement agreement's nondisparagement provision by characterizing the bonus payment as unauthorized.

.03 Licensing the Right to Publicity

A company that has a "rock star" executive should consider licensing the executive's right to the executive's image for publicity. The company could do this by providing in the employment agreement that the company owns the right to use the executive's image. This could be particularly useful in California, where non-competes generally are not enforceable.

This theory was played out in litigation between Microsoft and Google. Microsoft lost a high profile executive (labeled by some as the "father of the internet in China") to Google. To add insult to injury, Google began using the executive's familiar image in much of its local advertising and in recruiting posters. However, Google claimed that the executive was not involved in actual hiring and other duties that could have violated his non-compete agreement. Microsoft argued that the executive was the engineering equivalent of a rock star, and that Google's use of his image in its recruiting was conduct that arguably violated the executive's continuing obligations to Microsoft. The court disagreed, saying if Microsoft wanted to restrict the use of the executive's likeness, it should have written that restriction into the employment agreement.

¶435 Nonsolicitation

Many executive employment agreements also include provisions that prohibit the executive from directly or indirectly soliciting customers and employees. For example, an employment agreement may prohibit the executive from soliciting:

- any employee of the employer to leave employment and join or become affiliated with any business that is competitive with the employer's business within the geographic area; and

- any supplier, customer, or other person or entity that had a business relationship with the employer from continuing to do business with or entering into business with the employer.

Although a nonsolicitation provision must protect the employer's legitimate interests and not unduly burden the employee, they are more likely to be enforced than noncompete provisions because they typically do not restrain an individual's ability to earn a living.[9] To avoid being invalidated as overbroad, however, a nonsolicitation provision should define important terms, such as "customer," and contain reasonable geographic and temporal restrictions. For example, an 18-month time restriction in a nonsolicitation clause may be reasonable when it takes the employer one to two years to establish a major account.

---

[9] *See, e.g., Digital Corp. v. DeltaCom, Inc.,* 953 F.Supp. 1486, 1495 (M.D. Ala. 1996) (holding that prohibition against soliciting customers whose identities become known to the employee as a result of an employment relationship is not the same as prohibition against engaging in lawful profession or trade).

With respect to nonsolicitation provisions addressing customers or clients, the provision will likely only be applied to those whom the employee had significant contact while employed and whose relationship with the customer or client was developed at the employer's expense. Additionally, courts have drawn a distinction between *soliciting* and *accepting* business from former customers or clients. A nonsolicitation provision should not prohibit a former employee from accepting unsolicited business from company customers or clients.

Prohibiting nonsolicitation of company employees by a former executive can also be a valuable safeguard for the employer. In a recent case,[10] a vice-president of a large insurance company solicited 17 co-workers to leave the company when he joined a competitor. The employees' mass departure caused significant operational problems for the company. By virtue of a nonsolicitation clause in the executive's employment agreement, the company successfully sued the former vice-president for breach of contract and collected significant monetary damages.

¶445 Inventions or Developments

Under many employment agreements, the executive agrees that he or she will disclose to the employer all discoveries, improvements, inventions, formulas, ideas, processes, designs, techniques, know-how, data and computer programs (whether or not patentable, copyrightable or susceptible to any other form of protection), made, conceived, reduced to practice or developed by the executive, either alone or jointly with others, during the executive's employment with the employer. All inventions and developments are to be the sole property of the employer. However, most agreements also provide that the foregoing limitations do not apply to any inventions or developments unrelated to the business of the employer, that the executive developed entirely on his or her own time, and for which the executive did not use any equipment, supplies, facility or trade secret information of the employer.

¶455 Blue Pencil Provision

Where an employer has sought in good faith to protect a legitimate business interest, most states allow a court to modify an unreasonable aspect of a restrictive covenant to an acceptable level that may be enforced, *i.e.*, "blue penciling." However, a few states, such as Georgia, do not blue pencil agreements to rewrite their terms, but may enforce severable provisions.[11] Other states only permit a judge to modify the written covenant where the employment agreement explicitly permits such modification. Accordingly, the employment agreement should invite and encourage the court to modify any provision the court deems invalid or unenforceable to the extent and in the manner necessary to render the same valid and enforceable.

For example, the agreement might provide as follows:

---

[10] *GAB Business Services Inc. v. Lindsey & Newsom Claim Services Inc.*, 2000 Cal. App. LEXIS 687 (Cal. Ct. App. 2000).

[11] *See New Atlanta Ear, Nose and Throat Assoc., P.C. v. Pratt*, 560 S.E. 2d 268 (Ga. App. 2002) ("the blue pencil marks, but it does not write") (quoting *Hamrick v. Kelly*, 392 S.E.2d 518) (Ga. 1990)).

If any provision(s) of this section shall be found invalid or unenforceable, in whole or in part, then such provision(s) shall be deemed to be modified or restricted to the extent and in the manner necessary to render the same valid and enforceable, or shall be deemed excised from this Agreement, as the case may require, and this Agreement shall be construed and enforced to the maximum extent permitted by law, as if such provision(s) had been originally incorporated herein as so modified or restricted, or as if such provision(s) had not been originally incorporated herein, as the case may be.

In the absence of a modification or severability clause, any invalidity of a restrictive covenant could render it wholly unenforceable. On the other hand, the inclusion of such a clause in an employment agreement does not guarantee that a court will accept the invitation to blue pencil, or partially enforce, the restrictive covenant. For example, the states of New York and Illinois have long permitted courts to modify otherwise invalid restrictive covenants, but judges occasionally decline to exercise their discretion to blue pencil an agreement.[12]

¶465 Remedies

Most executive employment agreements provide that if a former executive violates the noncompete or other restrictive covenants of the agreement, the employer either may seek to: (1) obtain an injunction preventing the former executive from continued violation, or (2) forfeit some form of severance or retirement payment or equity compensation award otherwise payable to the former executive. Injunctive relief is considered an extreme remedy, however, and courts refuse to grant such relief unless the employer can make a strong showing of ultimate success and the probability of immediate, irreparable harm. Moreover, courts are more likely to enforce a noncompete or other restrictive covenant that provides for the former employee to forfeit some form of compensation, than one that seeks to prevent the former employee from earning a living.

In a leading case, the court observed that "Illinois disfavors noncompete provisions in employee contracts."[13] However, the court continued:

This is not a case that involves a facially anti-competitive provision; nothing in the agreements at issue actually restricted Tatom's ability to work for Ameritech's competitors. Federal cases draw a distinction between provisions that prevent an employee from working for a competitor and those that call for a forfeiture of certain benefits should he do so. [citations omitted]. An anti-competitive clause, if that is what the forfeiture provision here is, may still be enforced in Illinois as long as it is reasonable. [citations omitted]. A provision that calls for the forfeiture of a bonus in the form of stock options does not strike us as an unreasonable restraint on competition. Stock options, in contrast to other types of regular and bonus compensation, give an employee the right to acquire an ownership interest in a company; that interest in turn gives the employee a long-term stake in the company and supplies him an incentive to contribute to the company's performance. [citations omitted]. A provision calling for the forfeiture of such options in the event that the holder goes to

---

[12] *See, e.g., Heartland Securities Corp. v. Gerstenblatt,* 2000 U.S. Dist. LEXIS 3496 (S.D.N.Y. 2000) ("this court declines to exercise its discretion to 'blue pencil' the provisions at issue in an effort to make them enforceable"); *Dryvit Systems v. Rushing,* 77 N.E.2d 35, 39 (1st Dist. 1985) (refusing to modify restrictive covenants because agreement's broad geographical scope was unreasonable).

[13] *Tatom v. Ameritech,* 305 F3d 737 (7th Cir. 2002).

work for a competitor thus serves to keep the option holder's interests aligned with the company's. In this respect, the LTIP's forfeiture provision is not unreasonable.[14]

In *Fraser v. Nationwide Mutual Insurance Co.*,[15] a federal court upheld a forfeiture-for-competition provision in an independent contractor agreement between Nationwide Mutual Insurance Co. and an insurance agent, causing the agent to forfeit his deferred compensation plan benefits when he began to work for a Nationwide competitor. According to the court, when his independent contractor agreement terminated with Nationwide, Fraser faced two options: he could choose to compete and forfeit his deferred compensation, or he could choose not to compete for one year and receive his deferred compensation. "Nationwide did not impede Fraser from working for another company by threat of injunction—rather, Fraser was simply faced with the decision of whether or not to disqualify himself from a monetary benefit."

¶475 Restrictive Covenants in Nonqualified Plans, Severance Plans, and Equity Award Agreements

.01 Employee Choice Doctrine

As noted above, courts are more likely to enforce a noncompete or other restrictive covenant that provides for the former employee to forfeit some form of compensation, than one that seeks to prevent the former employee from earning a living. As a matter of public policy, courts are loathe to enforce a provision that prevents an individual from earning a living in his or her chosen profession. However, when the restrictive provision gives the former employee a choice of (a) working for a competitor and forfeiting severance, equity, or nonqualified deferred compensation and (b) keeping the compensation but not competing, most courts will enforce the provision (this is known as the "employee choice doctrine").

We most often place restrictive covenants in nonqualified or deferred compensation plans, severance plans and agreements, and equity award plans and agreements. With respect to each type of compensation, the former employee has the choice between competing with the business, for example, or accepting the payment or distribution otherwise provided for under the plan or agreement.

.02 Restrictive Covenants in Equity Compensation Award Agreements

Based on experience with clients and frequent discussions with the other leading executive compensation practitioners, we estimate that nearly 50% of companies outside of California include restrictive covenants in their equity awards to some executives. Some companies simply make the covenants part of their form agreement. Others restrict application to officer employees and others who could do harm (*e.g.*, tech, operations, strategy, or sales employees), even though not necessarily highly paid.

---

[14] *Tatom v. Ameritech*, 305 F3d 737, 744 (7th Cir. 2002).

[15] *Fraser v. Nationwide Mutual Insurance Co.*, 334 FSupp2d 755 (E.D. Pa. 2004).

Other issues arise, but none are insurmountable. Therefore, if you have not already done so, you might consider adding these provisions to your severance, equity, and nonqualified deferred compensation plan. Note, state laws generally prohibit applying a non-compete to lawyers, so be careful about the agreements, plans and awards to legal staff.

Generally, a company should draft the plan document to give the compensation committee the authority to include restrictive covenants in any award agreement and place the detailed restrictive covenants in the award agreements themselves. In addition to all of the usual questions about restrictive covenants, *e.g.*, geographic scope and duration, the following drafting and design issues arise in the context of equity award agreements:

1. Will the restrictive covenants apply to all employees? Only to executives? Only to at-risk employees, such as information security/technology or sales force employees.

   (a) Courts are more likely to enforce restrictive covenants against executives and employees who could do harm.

   (b) In many states, including Illinois and New Jersey, non-compete restrictions may not be available for in-house lawyers, unless they perform significant "business" functions (violates Rules of Professional Conduct).

2. Will the restrictive covenants provide for all available remedies, including injunction, or only for the forfeiture and clawback of awards?

   (a) More comprehensive remedies, *i.e.*, injunction, are more common in industries where these is brutal competition for and poaching of talent, *e.g.*, financial services.

   (b) The extent of the remedies provided for in the award agreement is an important design decision for the company. We have seen some award recipients refuse to sign the agreement because it contained restrictive covenants with remedies beyond forfeiture. We also have seen companies decline to add such broad remedies because they believed them to be contrary to their company culture (of fairness).

   (c) Many courts have enforced restrictive covenants in stock award agreements under the so-called "employee choice doctrine." Most state and federal courts considering whether to enforce restrictive covenants, particularly non-compete provisions, in stock award agreements begin their decision by observing that the law of the governing state strongly disfavors the enforcement of restrictive covenants as a matter of public policy because enforcement could prevent the individual (often a citizen of that state) from earning a living in his or her chosen profession. [*Tatom*] The employee choice doctrine holds essentially, that the restrictive covenants in the award agreement does not violate (or even implicate) the state's public policy against restrictive covenants because the remedy set forth in the award agreement for violating the restrictive covenant is merely the forfeiture of the outstanding stock award. Thus, the employee has the choice of adhering to the covenants and keeping the valuable award or earning a living in his or her chosen profession at a competitor, but forfeiting the award.

(d) Consider whether to make available a range of sanctions depending on how egregious the violation was. Consider providing for all remedies and allowing the committee to determine the level of enforcement in its discretion.

(e) Be certain to include all state-of-the-art provisions, such as blue penciling and tolling.

3. What restrictive covenants should the company include: non-compete, non-solicit of employees, non-solicit of clients, non-solicit of prospective customers, non-disclosure, non-disparagement, IP assignment, and non-interference? Courts generally are more likely to enforce a prohibition on disclosure of confidential information or trade secrets.

(a) Consider including a non-exhaustive list of competitors.

(b) Consider what entities "company" should include.

4. Consider the differences in applying the restrictive covenants to (i) vested but unexercised options and SARs, (ii) restricted stock, RSUs, or performance shares that have vested (*i.e.*, stock distributed), and (iii) stock that the former employee has sold.

5. To enhance enforceability, should the company also adopt post-employment holding requirements or require a "holdback" of owned company stock if it does not do so already?

(a) Such a provision/requirement may be in the award agreement, a company policy, a separate written agreement, or all of the above.

(b) Consider requiring each former employee to sign an attestation to the effect that he or she has not breached the restrictive covenants before releasing the held-back shares.

6. Consider electronic delivery, acceptance, and acknowledgement issues.

(a) Courts enforce electronic agreements. Electronic "acceptance" of an award may be as good as a signature on a written document.

(b) The structure and wording of electronic delivery and acceptance websites is important. Award agreements, written or electronic, should explicitly state that the grant awards have not been accepted until the recipient executes the agreement or takes other specific actions through the website.

(c) Courts are more likely to enforce a click-wrap form of electronic delivery and acknowledgement of agreements than a browse-wrap form.

(d) Opacity may not prevent "actual notice." The lack of what many folks would consider "notice" is not a legal barrier.

7. Specify the choice of law and the choice of forum for the resolution of disputes. This is particularly relevant for employees in California (or any other state that does not enforce noncompetes and other restrictive covenants) and/or employees who move to California for new employment. Generally, the company will want to draft the plan or agreement to specify the county and state of its headquarters as the governing law and required site of litigation or arbitration, to give it the "home court" advantage.

   (a) The first step in getting a court outside of California to enforce a restrictive covenant against an employee based in California is to get that court (*i.e.*, the court *not* in California) to take jurisdiction of the lawsuit - or to get that court to transfer jurisdiction to the jurisdiction specified in the plan or agreement).

   (b) The second step is to get the court to apply the law of a more favorable state with which the company *has a close connection*. Thus, for example, a company based in New York, NY should consider specifying the state and county of New York as the forum for disputes, rather than Delaware, even if the company is incorporated in Delaware.

   (c) Generally, it is difficult to enforce restrictive covenants on employees outside the US, unless they are US citizens. In most countries, non-compete, non-solicit, non-hire provisions are not enforceable. In some, *e.g.*, the UK "garden leave, the company must pay monetary consideration to the employee during the post-employment non-compete period.

8. Consider how to communicate the new restrictive covenants. Do not overlook the *in terrorem* effect. Consider what to do about employees who refuse to accept the awards.

   (a) Just because one award agreement does not impose restrictive covenants, does not mean that the next one will not or cannot. It is never too late for a company to begin imposing restrictive covenants through its stock award agreements. In *Newell Rubbermaid, Inc. v. Storm*, the 2011 and 2012 award agreements did not contain a confidentiality or non-solicitation provision, although it did refer to the 2010 RSU plan, which explicitly stated that the company's board of directors, in its sole discretion, could condition the grant of an award upon those provisions.

9. Does the company wish to attempt to impose the restrictive covenants on all past awards by way of a retroactive amendment with recipient consent?

10. Special issues may apply in California. Specify the state of the company's non-California headquarters as the choice of *law* and choice of forum. The company also should make its trade secret language state of

the art and emphasize the enforcement of those provisions as a forfeiture trigger.

11. Other design, drafting, and implementation issues:

    (a) If the award agreement or plan requires arbitration of disputes, be sure to provide a carve-out allowing the company to file suit over violation of the restrictive covenants.

    (b) Verify that the company's nonqualified and severance plans contain the restrictive covenants.

    (c) Continued employment generally is sufficient consideration to impose restrictive covenants, but a stock award definitely is sufficient consideration.

    (d) Plan documents should give the company or committee the authority to add restrictive covenants to any stock award agreements.

.03 Restrictive Covenants in Electronically-Delivered Equity Award Agreements

A 2014 decision out of the Delaware Chancery Court contains important lessons for (i) companies that make awards with restrictive covenants, particularly by electronic delivery, (ii) executives who receive the awards, and (iii) stock plan administrators who design and implement electronic delivery and acceptance procedures.

The conventional wisdom had been that it was better to have a hard copy award agreement, signed by the award recipient/executive, in order to be able to enforce the restrictive covenants in the stock award agreement. However, this was contrary to the trend among both private and publicly traded companies to handle the entire award agreement delivery and acceptance process electronically.

In *Newell Rubbermaid Inc. v. Storm*[16], the court granted the company a temporary restraining order against a former executive for actions that the court believed may violate the non-solicitation and confidentiality covenants of RSU agreements to which she assented through a third-party website. The critical facts in the case were as follows: Sandy Storm had worked for the company and its subsidiaries as an employee in various capacities from June 2000, until her voluntary resignation in January 2014. She was part of a 17-person office in Minneapolis, Minnesota, which was dedicated to servicing Target Corporation (also based in Minneapolis).

In 2011, Storm received RSUs granted under the company's stock plan. She received written notice that she had been awarded RSUs from Fidelity Investments, which maintained the investment and retirement accounts of the company's employees. The notice directed her to the website site operated by Fidelity where she could accept the RSUs awarded to her. On a webpage of the Fidelity

---

[16] No. CV 9398-VCN, 2014 WL 1266827, at *2 (Del. Ch. Mar. 27, 2014).

site related to Storm's RSU awards under the company's stock plan, a box, titled "Grant Terms and Agreement," provided that she must read the "Grant Agreement" and review the terms to continue. And below this box was a hyperlink to a "Grant Agreement (PDF)" that she could click to review the agreement. Underneath that hyperlink, was another checkbox accompanied by text in bold reading: "I have read and agree to the terms of the Grant Agreement." The instructions on this webpage prompted Storm to accept the 2011 RSUs by clicking on an "Accept" button.

The 2011 award did *not* contain a confidentiality or non-solicitation provision. Those provisions first appeared in the 2013 Agreement. However, the Terms and Conditions of the 2011 award did refer to the stock plan, which explicitly stated that the company's board of directors, in its sole discretion, could condition the grant of an award upon those provisions.

In February 2012, Storm again received written notice from Fidelity that she had been awarded RSUs. She again returned to the Fidelity website to accept them. As before, the provisions of this 2012 award did *not* contain non-solicitation or confidentiality clauses.

In February 2013, Storm was granted her third award of RSUs. She again clicked the "Accept" button on the Fidelity website. The RSUs, as accepted, were subject to the stock plan and the "2013 Restricted Stock Unit Award Agreement." However, the 2013 Agreement, unlike the prior RSU agreements, contained confidentiality, non-solicitation, and non-compete provisions. The 2013 Agreements also included boilerplate language through which the assenting party acknowledged that: (a) the confidentiality, non-solicitation, and non-compete restrictions are reasonable; (b) her ability to work and earn a living are not impaired by the restrictions; and (c) that the company will suffer substantial damage for which no adequate remedy at law exists as a result of a breach of the restrictions.

Under the 2013 Agreements, performance-based RSUs vest three years from the award date and time-based RSUs vest ratably in one-third increments on the first, second, and third anniversaries of the award date. However, if the recipient of the RSUs is terminated from employment by the company for any reason other than death, disability, or retirement, then the RSUs will be forfeited and no portion will vest. The time-based 2013 Agreement also granted the recipient a cash equivalent to the value of the dividends she would have received had she been the actual owner of the number of shares of common stock represented by the time-based RSUs in the recipient's account on that date. Storm actually received cash equivalent awards from dividends paid in 2013.

Finally, the 2013 Agreements also contained Delaware choice of law provisions and a forum selection clause requiring that suits between the company and Storm be litigated in Delaware.

Storm resigned from the company in January 2014 and began working for a direct competitor of the company. The company sent her two letters that month reminding her that she had assented to confidentiality and non-solicitation

¶475.03

provisions in the 2013 Agreements. The company also sent a letter to the competitor advising it of Storm's obligations under the 2013 Agreements.

RSU Award Agreements Made Electronically. The court began its opinion with a discussion and contrasting of so-called "click-wrap" agreements, which are online agreements that require a webpage user to manifest assent to the terms of a contract by clicking an "Accept" button in order to proceed, and "browse-wrap" agreements, which typically involve a situation where notice on a website conditions use of the site on compliance with certain terms or conditions, which may be included on the same page as the notice or accessible by a hyperlink. With a browse-wrap agreement, the employee (or other party) gives assent to the agreement's terms simply by using the website.

The derivation of these terms appears to have come from consumer law cases relating to so-called "shrink-wrap" agreements, which Delaware courts have upheld, in which contract terms (such as a disclaimer of the implied warranty of merchantability or arbitration requirement) appear on or inside a product's packaging and become enforceable after a consumer opens it.

The RSU agreements that the company sought to enforce were electronic click-wrap agreements. The issues before the court were the enforceability of click-wrap agreements and whether RSUs that would not vest for one year constituted adequate consideration for the restrictive covenants when the company, without cause, could terminate the award holder's employment, which would result in the forfeiture of the RSUs. Importantly, the restrictive covenant provisions permitted the company to seek an injunction against any violation or threatened violation of the provisions. Award agreements with restrictive covenants often provide that the employer's only remedy for the employee's breach of the covenants is a forfeiture of the awards made under the agreement. The restrictive covenants under the company's award agreement granted it much broader remedies, including the ability to enjoin the former employee from working for a competitor.

The Fidelity Website. The court carefully reviewed a series of screenshots from the Fidelity website, which demonstrated the process by which an award recipient could accept the award grants. The court's opinion describes the screenshots in detail to explain the process.

- For a person to accept the awards, he or she must first select [indicate by clicking on a box] that she will accept the grant from a list of "Unaccepted Grants."

- The award recipient would then navigate to a page that explained more fully how to accept the awards. On this page, a box, titled "Grant Terms and Agreement," provided that "[y]ou must read your Grant Agreement and review the terms to continue."

- Below this box is a hyperlink to a "Grant Agreement (PDF)" that the user can click to review the agreement. Underneath that hyperlink, a checkbox is accompanied by text in bold reading: "I have read and agree to the terms of the Grant Agreement."

- Below this checkbox and above the "Accept" button, bold text provides: "To complete your Grant Agreement online, you must read and accept the terms outlined in the document posted above . . . . Your grant acceptance will be final once you click Accept." "Previous" and "Accept" buttons also appear below the checkbox, as does a link allowing the user to "Cancel."

- Text under the "Accept" button reads "Submit Grant Acceptance" and "To cancel the transaction, click the Cancel link."

We note that some stock plan administrators' websites do not even allow the user to advance to "Accept" without having opened the award agreement or award terms and conditions. (You cannot force an employee/user to read the full document, but you can force him or her to at least open it.)

Issues and Decision. The court observed that the company's motion for a TRO presented two novel questions for the Delaware courts:

1. Whether a company can enforce an agreement to which an employee assented online, such as the 2013 Agreements and, if so, whether Storm assented to the post-employment restrictive covenants in the 2013 Agreements.

2. Whether RSU grants are sufficient consideration if the employer is able to terminate the employee at will and thereby cause the employee to lose her award.

The court concluded that the click-wrap 2013 Agreements were enforceable under Delaware law. The court concluded further that Storm voluntarily accepted the RSU awards she received in 2013 and she had reasonable notice that she was manifesting her acceptance of the terms of the 2013 Agreements by clicking "Accept" on the Fidelity web portal.

The court also concluded that the company had "more than a colorable claim that Storm has violated the restrictive covenants and that it will suffer irreparable harm in the absence of interim injunctive relief." Thus, the court granted the company's motion for a TRO preventing Storm from working for the company's competitor.

Can a Company Enforce an Agreement to which an Employee Assented Online? The company argued that click-wrap agreements, such as the 2013 Agreements that Storm had accepted, are routinely recognized by courts and, thus, Storm's belief that the 2013 Agreements were like the 2011 and 2012 RSU award agreements to which she had assented does not create a defense to enforcement. Storm countered that the parties to the 2013 Agreements did not mutually assent to their terms because of the company's failure to indicate on the Fidelity website that Storm was modifying her post-employment rights.

"Agreements may, of course, be made online" was the first sentence of the court's opinion. A contract is valid if it manifests mutual assent by the parties and they have exchanged adequate consideration. The use of the internet as the vehicle for contract formation "has not fundamentally changed the principles of contract." The threshold issue is the same: did the party who assented online have reasonable notice, either actual or constructive, of the terms of the agreement and did that party manifest assent to those terms.

Arguments Against Enforcement that the Court Rejected. Storm cited Delaware case law stating that the acceptance of a benefit may constitute assent, but only where the offeree makes a decision to take the benefit with actual or constructive knowledge of the terms of the offer. She argued that an offeree cannot be bound by inconspicuous contractual provisions of which she is unaware, contained in a document whose contractual nature is not obvious. In support of her arguments, Storm asserted (and the court acknowledged) that:

- Storm believed that when she clicked the "Accept" button, she was only agreeing to terms relating directly to the RSUs and that her agreement would not impact her post-employment obligations to the company.

- The company's treatment of other similarly situated employees or higher-level employees might have been a more appropriate method of putting her on notice of post-employment restrictions. The company had asked other employees more directly to sign post-employment restrictive covenants. The company also had given paper copies of the 2013 RSU award agreements, which also contained answers to frequently asked questions, to some employees who were similarly situated to Storm. The company imposed similar restrictive covenants on higher-level employees through employment contracts, instead of through RSU award agreements. Other employees also agreed to similar provisions in separation agreements.

- When Storm was contemplating leaving the company, she had searched both her personnel file and her "Employee Connections" page, which contains employment-related information such as compensation and company policies. Since neither location stored a copy of the 2013 Agreements, Storm apparently concluded that there were no restrictions on subsequent employment.

Nonetheless, the court found that a party may assent to an agreement on the internet without reading its terms and still be bound by it if she is on notice that she is modifying her legal rights, just as she may with a physical written contract.

The court emphasized that, to accept her RSUs, Storm was directed to a screen that informed her in several places that she was agreeing to the 2013 Agreements. Storm had admitted that she clicked the checkbox next to which were the words "I have read and agree to the terms of the Grant Agreement." The court found that this functioned as an acknowledgement that she had the opportunity to review the 2013 Agreements upon which the company was entitled to rely, even if she later said that she did not read the 2013 Agreements.

Her actions of clicking the checkbox and "Accept" button were manifestations of assent. The court concluded that this constituted Storm's assent after being provided with, and acknowledging, actual notice. The court further concluded that the company's method of seeking Storm's agreement to the post-employment restrictive covenants, "although certainly not the model of transparency and openness with its employees," was not an improper form of contract formation.

Actual Notice? Storm's Failure to Read the Agreement. The court found that "the contractual nature of the 2013 Agreements was obvious and the restrictive provisions were not inconspicuous," and provided Ms. Storm with "actual notice." The court also found that it was not "determinative" that the 2013 Agreements were part of a "lengthy scrolling pop-up." Storm's failure to review fully the terms (on a ten-page readily accessible agreement) to which she assented also did not invalidate her assent.

The court also observed that Storm was not entirely helpless and that the company had justification for seeking such restrictions. She was an experienced employee who managed a significant client relationship worth over $100 million annually and the company apparently believed the retention of her services merited RSU grants for three years.

The court commented that "Storm is understandably unhappy that she did not read the 2013 Agreements." It found, however, that she was presented with a fair opportunity to read the terms, opened up the appropriate pop-up from which she could do so, and even indicated through the checkbox that she did so. Piling on, the court added that she had "altered her post-employment rights in a manner she appears to regret now, but it was her choice to modify her rights without fully investigating the terms to which she agreed." The well-settled principles of offer and acceptance remain applicable even when two parties utilize technology to distribute agreements and to assent to them online.

The court acknowledged that the "result may appear somewhat harsh given Storm's seemingly genuine belief that she had no post-employment restrictive covenants in place with her employer." However, the court concluded that parties under Delaware law have the same ability, prevalent in other jurisdictions, which they have with respect to paper agreements: to assent to such agreements even without reading them and to bear the consequences. The courts will enforce such agreements as it would an agreement written on paper.

Award Forfeiture vs. Restraining Order. The non-compete and confidentiality restrictions in the 2013 Agreements permitted the company to seek an injunction against any violation or threatened violation of the restrictions. Award agreements with restrictive covenants often provide for a forfeiture of the awards as the employer's exclusive remedy in the event of a breach by the employee/recipient, utilizing the so-called "employee choice doctrine." The employee choice doctrine essentially holds that a restrictive covenant in the award agreement does not violate (or even implicate) the state's public policy against non-compete provisions if the remedy set forth in award agreement for violating the non-compete provision is merely the forfeiture of the outstanding award. Thus, the employee has the choice between (i) adhering to the covenants and keeping the valuable award or (ii) earning a living in his or her chosen profession at a competitor, but forfeiting the award.

Many courts have enforced restrictive covenants in stock award agreements under the employee choice doctrine. Most state and federal courts considering whether to enforce restrictive covenants, particularly non-compete provisions, in stock award agreements begin their decision by observing that the law of the governing state strongly disfavors the enforcement of restrictive covenants as a matter of public policy because enforcement could prevent the individual (often a citizen of that state) from earning a living in his or her chosen profession.

However, the case law draws a distinction between provisions that prevent an employee from working for a competitor and those that call for a forfeiture of certain benefits should he do so. Courts have found that a provision that calls for the forfeiture of stock awards is not an unreasonable restraint on competition. Stock awards, in contrast to other types of regular and bonus compensation, give an employee the right to acquire an ownership interest in a company. That interest in turn gives the employee a long-term stake in the company and supplies an incentive to contribute to the company's performance. A provision calling for the forfeiture of stock awards in the event that the holder goes to work for a competitor thus serves to keep the option holder's interests aligned with the company's.

The court's decision to enforce broader restrictions and grant a temporary restraining order against a former employee in *Newell* is significant. In this case, if the 2013 Agreements had limited the company's remedies to forfeiture of the outstanding awards, the restrictive covenants would have been useless. Ms. Storm automatically forfeited the RSU awards upon her voluntary termination of employment before vesting. Thus, the company would have had no remedy for the breach of the covenants.

The company argued that Storm either had breached, or inevitably would breach, the terms of those non-compete and confidentiality provisions of the 2013 Agreements during her employment in a sales position for a competitor. The court accepted the inevitable breach argument, which further expands the reach of the non-compete and confidentiality provision, but may not be applicable to employees less highly placed and intimately involved.

The extent of the remedies provided for in the award agreement is an important design decision for the company. We have seen some award recipients refuse to sign the agreement because it contained restrictive covenants with remedies beyond forfeiture. We also have seen companies decline to add such broad remedies because they believed them to be contrary to the company's culture.

Was the Consideration for the Non-Competition Covenants Illusory? As a secondary issue, the court considered whether the consideration for the non-compete and other covenants was illusory, because the 2013 Agreements would cause Storm to forfeit her awards if the company terminated her, which it could do at its sole discretion and without cause.

The court acknowledged that at least one other jurisdiction had rejected consideration as illusory if it would be forfeited in the event that the employer fired the employee before vesting occurred. However, the court distinguished the leading case finding that RSUs were illusory consideration, because it was in part based on Texas law that, in an at-will employment context, "consideration for a promise, by either the employee or the employer, cannot be dependent on a period of continued employment." Delaware law permits continued employment to "serve as consideration for an at-will employee's agreement to a restrictive covenant." The court also cited other authority holding that RSUs awards are not illusory even if the RSUs may be forfeited through termination without cause and upholding restrictive covenants granted in the context of stock option awards that are entirely at the discretion of the board in an at-will employment context.

The court also recognized that Storm had received actual consideration in the form of cash dividends on the RSUs in 2013.

Finally, the court rejected Storm's claim that the RSUs were awarded before Storm visited Fidelity's website to accept them and that her acceptance of the RSUs on the Fidelity website was only ministerial. The language of the Fidelity website explicitly stated that the grant awards had not been accepted until certain specific actions were taken by the employee through the website.

Lessons Learned. Finally, we offer the following summary of the lessons that employers, employees, and stock plan administrators can learn from this case, in list format.

Enforcement Is Not in Question. Courts will enforce restrictive covenants contained in stock award agreements. The court never even considered or discussed the possibility that the company could not enforce restrictive covenants contained in stock award agreements. Rather, it only considered and discussed whether the employee's electronic assent to the terms of the restrictive covenants in the agreements was effective.

Remedies Can Go Beyond Mere Forfeiture of the Awards. Courts may enforce all remedies set forth in the stock award agreement, including remedies that go beyond simply the forfeiture of the stock award, such as an injunction against the former employee.

Many courts have enforced restrictive covenants in stock award agreements under the so-called "employee choice doctrine." As we noted above, most state and federal courts considering whether to enforce restrictive covenants in stock award agreements, particularly non-compete provisions, begin their decision by observing that the law of the governing state strongly disfavors the enforcement of restrictive covenants as a matter of public policy because enforcement could prevent the individual (often a citizen of that state) from earning a living in his or her chosen profession. The employee choice doctrine holds essentially, that the restrictive covenant in the award agreement does not violate (or even implicate) the state's public policy against restrictive covenants because the remedy set forth in award agreement for violating the restrictive covenant is merely the forfeiture of the outstanding stock award. Thus, the employee has the choice of adhering to the covenants and keeping the valuable award or earning a living in his or her chosen profession at a competitor, but forfeiting the award. The court "sympathized" with and seemed to believe that Storm thought she was agreeing to certain terms relating specifically to her grant of RSUs. The extent of the remedies provided for in the award agreement is an important design decision for the company. We have seen some award recipients refuse to sign the agreement because it contained restrictive covenants with remedies beyond forfeiture. We also have seen companies decline to add such broad remedies because they believed them to be contrary to their company culture (of fairness).

Award Agreements Can Include Restrictive Covenants. Warning to executives and other employees: the company may place restrictive covenants in any form of agreement. The court was not persuaded by the fact that Storm did not find the restrictive covenants in her efforts to ascertain their existence (as noted above, Storm searched her personnel file and the company's internal employee website for the covenants). The fact that she didn't think to check her award agreements for the covenants turned out to be her loss.

Courts Enforce Electronic Agreements. Electronic "acceptance" of an award may be as good as a signature on a written document. The first sentence of the court's opinion states flatly: "Agreements may, of course, be made online." The conventional wisdom had been that it is better to have a hard copy award agreement signed by an employee in order to be able to enforce the restrictive covenants in the agreement. The court observed that a party may assent to an agreement on the internet without reading its terms and still be bound by it if she is on notice that she is modifying her legal rights, just as she may with a physical written contract.

Click-wrap Is Preferable to Browse-wrap. Companies and stock plan administrators should use the "click-wrap" form of electronic delivery and acknowledgement of agreements rather than the browse-wrap form. The court found that another case upon which Storm relied was distinguishable, as it involved a browse-wrap license, "which often fails to provide adequate notice before assent." The court's extensive discussion of the Fidelity screenshots suggests that its analysis could be limited to click-wrap agreements including this level of detail.

Read Before Signing. Parties to an agreement must read it, no matter how mundane and boilerplate it appears. How many times have we all—even the lawyers—seen such a box and how many times have any of us actually read the terms (since this morning, even)? The court held unequivocally that Storm's failure to review fully the terms to which she assented did not invalidate her assent. The court was unmoved by the fact that the 2013 Agreement was part of a lengthy scrolling pop-up. The lesson is - you may think it is only "boilerplate" and we may think it is only boilerplate, but the courts will enforce it.

Opacity may not prevent "actual notice." The lack of what most folks would consider "notice" is not a legal barrier. The court expressly rejected Storm's argument, based on prior, unrelated case law, that the mere acceptance of a benefit may constitute assent only where the offeree makes a decision to take the benefit with actual or constructive knowledge of the terms of the offer. The court found that "the contractual nature of the 2013 Agreements was obvious and the restrictive provisions were not inconspicuous."

Plan Should Authorize Restrictive Covenants. Plan documents should give the company or committee the authority to add restrictive covenants to any stock award agreements. The court mentioned several times that the company's stock plan document included this authority, partly as the basis for "actual notice."

Language Counts. The structure and wording of electronic delivery and acceptance websites is important. Award agreements, written or electronic, should explicitly state that the grant awards have not been accepted until the recipient executes the agreement or takes other specific actions through the website. The court scrutinized the structure and wording of the electronic delivery and acceptance website. The court rejected Storm's claim that the RSUs were awarded before Storm visited Fidelity's website to accept them and that her acceptance of the RSUs on the Fidelity website was only ministerial. The language of the Fidelity website explicitly stated that the grant awards had not been accepted until certain specific actions were taken by the employee through the website.

Stock Awards Are Sufficient Consideration for Restrictive Covenants. Continued employment generally is sufficient consideration to impose restrictive covenants, and a stock award definitely is sufficient consideration. The courts in some jurisdictions have held that the mere right to continued employment is not sufficient consideration to support the execution of a restrictive covenant agreement by a current employee (*i.e.*, if you don't sign the agreement, you will not be allowed to continue your employment with us, we will fire you). This court held that continued employment generally is sufficient consideration to impose restrictive covenants, and a stock award definitely is sufficient consideration.

Forfeiture Restrictions Don't Negate Consideration. The consideration of a stock award is not diminished or made illusory by the company's right to terminate the employee at any time for any reason after making the award, which would cause the employee to forfeit the award.

It Is Never Too Late to Include Restrictive Covenants in Future Awards. Just because one award agreement does not impose restrictive covenants, does not mean that the next one will not—and its corollary—it is never too late to for a company to begin imposing restrictive covenants through its stock award agreements. The 2011 and 2012 award agreements did not contain a confidentiality or non-solicitation provision, although the court did refer to the 2010 RSU plan which explicitly stated that the company's board of directors, in its sole discretion, could condition the grant of an award upon those provisions.

Confidentiality Considerations Can Strengthen Non-Competes. An employer's case for enforcement of a non-compete provision will be stronger if the former employee's work for a competitor also threatens a violation of the covenants of confidentiality and protection of trade secrets. The court observed that Storm was directly responsible for over $100 million in sales to Target in 2013. She was the "face" of the company at Target for the sale of infant and juvenile goods and that during Storm's last two years of employment she was involved primarily in selling to, developing sales strategy for, and maintaining the company's relationship with Target. Storm had access to confidential information and trade secrets regarding product pricing, marketing strategies, platform innovation, and business incentives, among other things. She also had access to information about the company's relationship with Target and access to information relating to the sale of the company products to other retailers and distributors.

Thus, the court applied the doctrine of inevitable disclosure, which essentially holds that no matter how solid the former employee's promises not to disclose confidential information are or how pure his or her intentions not to disclose confidential information are, the former employee's knowledge of the former employer is so extensive that such disclosure would be inevitable. The concept of breach by inevitable disclosure further expands the reach of the confidentiality restrictions and nullifies the former employee's sincere promises not to share confidential information or trade secrets. However, not all former employees to whom confidentiality restrictions apply are likely to have knowledge that is comprehensive and intimate.

Choice of Law Provisions Can Be Key. Courts generally will enforce forum selection clauses and choice of law provisions. The 2013 Agreements also contained Delaware choice of law provisions and forum selection clauses requiring that suits between the company and Storm be litigated in Delaware.

An interesting question is whether this case would have been decided the same way under California law, which expressly forbids non-compete provisions in most situations. While it is not clear, a California court may have decided the case similarly due to the importance of the trade secrets and confidential information risks posed by Storm's new employment.

Similarly, in *ADP v. Lynch*,[17] the Third Circuit Court of Appeals affirmed a federal district court's holding that restrictive covenants in electronically delivered equity award agreements were enforceable. In *ADP*, the two plaintiffs/former employees had on five occasions accepted stock awards by accessing a webpage containing the award documents. The webpage stated, "you must select the checkbox to indicate you have read all associated documents before you can proceed" and provided a checkbox next to the statement "I have read all the documents below." Next to the checkbox was a link to open a 19-page PDF document, which included (i) the plan document, (ii) the award agreement, and (iii) the noncompete agreement. The first page of the award agreement stated that the employee would have 90 days to review the terms and decide whether to accept. It also specifically advised employees that the acceptance of the award was conditioned on agreement to the noncompete. The first page of the noncompete reiterated this condition. After they checked the "I have read all the documents" box, employees had to enter their personal password and click the "Accept Grant" or "Reject Grant" buttons.

---

[17] No. 16-3617 (3rd Cir. February 7, 2017).

The court easily rejected plaintiffs' argument that they had never checked a box stating they "agreed to" or "accepted or acknowledged" the terms of the agreements. The court observed that they had checked a box affirming that they "read" the documents, and the documents explicitly advised them that the noncompetes were a condition of accepting the stock award. The court also found the plaintiffs' contention that they did not recall reading the documents, irrelevant.

¶485 Enforcement

When an employer has expended time and money to negotiate restrictive covenants with its executives, it should intermittently remind employees, especially departing ones, of their obligations. Simply executing an employment agreement, with no follow-up, may not be adequate. The employer should annually review with the employee any duties of confidentiality required by an agreement. An exit interview is also a valuable opportunity to remind a departing employee of his or her continuing obligations under an agreement.

Another critical key to having enforceable restrictive covenants in executive employment agreements is a favorable choice-of-law provision. Unfortunately, employers who do not consult legal counsel beforehand often choose a state as the controlling jurisdiction with respect to restrictive covenants merely because the company's principal office is located there. However, legal consultation may have revealed that the law of the state where the company was incorporated or where the executive is employed is more favorable to the employer. Legal counsel should also keep employers informed of recent developments and changes in the applicable state's law.

.01 How Much Consideration is Required?

The courts are split on whether an employer can require a current employee to sign a restrictive covenant at any time. Some courts have held that such a requirement would lack consideration and the noncompete or other covenant would, therefore, be unenforceable. However, other courts have held that the consideration is the employee's ability to retain his or her job. For example, in *Lake Land Employment Group v. Columber*,[18], the Ohio Supreme Court found that an Ohio temporary employment service owner was bound by a noncompetition agreement he signed with his former employer because his continued employment after the agreement represented the necessary consideration to show he had agreed to the clause. The court reasoned that: "The presentation of a noncompetition agreement by an employer to an at-will employee is, in effect, a proposal to renegotiate the terms of the parties' at-will employment. . . . Where an employer makes such a proposal . . . and the employee assents to it, thereby accepting continued employment on new terms, consideration supporting the noncompetition agreement exists." In contract law, an essential component of an enforceable contract is that each party receives something of value—or consideration—in exchange for agreeing to the terms of the contract.

---

[18] *Lake Land Employment Group v. Columber*, 804 NE2d 27 (Ohio 2004).

¶485

.02 Can the Employer Enforce the Covenant?

Before running to court to seek enforcement of a noncompetition agreement, especially in the form of an injunction, experienced legal counsel will ask the employer the following questions, which the court will ask of counsel:

- Does the proposed employment actually violate the Agreement?
  - Does the executive's new employer "compete" with the former employer, as that term is defined in the Agreement?
  - What job will the employee perform for the competitor? Do those activities violate the Agreement?
  - Could it be argued that the Agreement was meant for another type of employee than the person in question? (*E.g.*, the Agreement was clearly intended to apply to a salesperson, but this individual was not in sales.)
- Is enforcement of the Agreement necessary to protect the former employer's trade secrets?
  - Is there risk of exposure of a secret that the employee developed or learned while at the former employer? (*E.g.*, names of clients, names of vendors, contract terms, business methods, marketing plans.)
  - If the employee were to disclose the secret to the competitor, would the former employer be harmed?
  - Is it truly a secret or could the competitor figure it out themselves? (Publicly available or readily ascertainable information is not a trade secret.)
  - Did the former employer make it clear to the employee that it considered the information secret? (*E.g.*, was it stamped "confidential," kept in locked files?)
- Is enforcement of the Agreement necessary to protect the employer's goodwill?
  - Did the employee have a relationship with customers or vendors?
  - Would those customers or vendors have associated the goodwill of the former employer with the employee?
- Is the Agreement reasonable in time and scope?
  - A duration of more than a year may not be reasonable.
  - Defining geographic scope as the entire country may not be reasonable.
- Does the Agreement essentially prevent the employee from working in his or her chosen profession?
  - Does the Agreement prevent the employee from using his or her general skills and knowledge, even if those were developed at the former employer?

— Does the Agreement prevent the employee from doing that which he or she has been trained to do?

— Could the employee get a comparable job without competing? To avoid violating the Agreement, would the employee essentially have to re-start his or her career from scratch?

• Would enforcement of this Agreement cause the employee undue hardship?

— Did the former employer offer the employee any alternatives to leaving?

— Is the employee being paid anything to refrain from competing?

• Is the employee's employment with the competitor truly an emergency?

— Did the former employer do everything it could to prevent the harm?

— Did the former employer remind the employee of the noncompetition obligations soon after learning of the employee's plans to work for a competitor?

— Did the former employer send out demand letters to the employee and the competitor?

— Does the former employer let other employees get away with violating their noncompetition agreements?

• Exactly how would the former employer be damaged by the employee's employment with the competitor?

— Are there any real damages besides the loss of a good employee to a competitor?

— Is it possible to point to specific damages the former employer would suffer if the employee were to work for the competitor? (*E.g.*, loss of customers, loss of information that cost large amounts of money to develop.)

— Would these damages be "irreparable"? (*E.g.*, could a money judgment after trial make the former employer whole?)

• Is the Agreement valid?

— Did the employee actually sign it? Is it the employee's signature? Did a representative of the company sign it?

— Was the employee forced to sign it under duress?

— Was the employee induced to sign it by fraud? (*E.g.*, was the employee told, "Don't worry about signing it. The courts never enforce these things anyway. If you want to leave, we'll be nice.")

— Did the employee get anything in return for signing it? (Continued employment may be enough, but a special signing bonus adds protection.)

• Is the Agreement still in force?

¶485.02

— Was the employee given any agreements (*e.g.*, stock options, employment contracts) after the date of the Agreement that supersede it?

— Were there any major changes in the terms of the employee's employment? (*E.g.*, switching to another subsidiary or division.)

• Would the public interest be served by the injunction?

— Is there something horrible that might happen if the Agreement is/is not enforced? (*E.g.*, loss of services to the public.)

• Does the former employer have "clean hands"?

— Has the former employer itself ever hired employees who were subject to a noncompetition agreement?

— Has the former employer complied with labor laws regarding the employee? (*E.g.*, was the employee paid everything owed to him or her? Was the employee subjected to any discrimination?)

• Is the former employer truly prepared to accept the significant costs and burdens associated with pursuing litigation?

— Injunction proceedings alone can cost $10,000 or more. If the case proceeds to trial, the employer may have costs in excess of $150,000.

— The employee may file counterclaims, which can take on an expensive life of their own.

— Litigation is very time-consuming and distracting.

— There may be negative press about the case.

— Discovery could result in revelation of the very secrets the former employer is trying to protect.

.03 Litigation

As long as there are employers and employees, it seems we will have litigation over non-competition provisions. Every day, all over the country, courts decide cases involving non-competes and other restrictive covenants. Most of these cases are very fact-specific. However, those of us who read all of these cases can spot trends and learn lessons.

In *Olander v. Compass Bank*,[19] the Court of Appeals for the Fifth Circuit ordered a former executive to repay his employer nearly $225,000, pursuant to a clause in his stock option agreements requiring the executive to return such funds in the event a court declares the agreements' noncompete clause unenforceable. As discussed elsewhere, many stock awards require the award recipient to forfeit his or her award if the recipient competes with the awarding company—and the courts have enforced those provisions. However, the stock option agreements from Compass Bank also contained what the court called a "remarkable provision" stating that if a court declared the noncompete clause invalid or unenforceable then Compass was entitled to receive from an employee

---

[19] *Olander v. Compass Bank*, 363 F3d 560 (5th Cir. 2004).

all common stock held by the employee, along with any profits the employee received by selling his or her stock.

The court found that a noncompete clause in the stock option agreements was void and unenforceable. The court went on to find that because the noncompete clauses were unenforceable, the former executive was required to repay Compass for all profits he earned under the option agreements.

In one surprising case, *McGough v. Nalco Company*, a federal district judge declined to enjoin a former employee from working for a direct competitor because the employee had signed the non-compete agreement in 1978.[20] Companies would be wise to update their non-compete agreement as the employee's position and responsibilities evolve and/or to include non-compete provisions in every new compensation agreement or award.

The case of *Estee Lauder v. Batra*[21] illustrates a few important lessons for employers. The first lesson, which, judging by the number of non-compete cases decided each week, many employees and their lawyers still have not yet learned, is that courts do enforce non-compete provisions. In May 2006, a federal district court in New York upheld a substantial portion of a non-compete provision against a former employee, including the portion that prohibited competition *anywhere in the world*. However, the company's victory was far from complete. Although the court agreed that Estee Lauder could apply the provision to competition anywhere in the world, it reduced the prohibition to five months from 12, and limited its application to Estee Lauder's trade secrets.

The second lesson is that courts are more likely to enforce a non-compete provision where the company is paying the former employee/executive some form of severance during the period of the non-compete. In this case, the court went out of its way to indicate that the fact that Estee Lauder contracted to pay Batra his salary of $375,000 per year for the duration of the 12 months helped the court to find that the clause was not overbroad: "the concern that the breadth of such a prohibition would make it impossible for him to earn a living is assuaged by the fact that he will continue to earn his salary from Estee Lauder."

Another interesting fact in this case was that the federal court declined to defer to a state court action the former employee and his new employer filed in California. Although Mr. Batra was a resident of California and the court acknowledged California's well-known public policy against enforcement of noncompetition agreements, it also found the interests of the New York based employer to be compelling:

> "Just as California has a strong interest in protecting those employed in California," Judge Sweet wrote, "so too does New York have a strong interest in protecting companies doing business here in keeping with 'New York's recognized interest in maintaining and fostering its undisputed status as the preeminent commercial and financial nerve center of the Nation and the world.'"

---

[20] *McGough v. Nalco Company* (N.D. W.Va. 2006).   [21] *Estee Lauder v. Batra*, S.D.N.Y., No. 06-civ.-2035, May 4, 2006.

In *Hearns v. Interstate Bank*,[22] the federal court for the Northern District of Illinois held that the unambiguous non-competition clause in the salary continuation agreement for retirement benefits that Interstate Bank had made with Mr. Hearns allowed it to cancel the agreement and benefits after Hearns helped form and served on the board of a new competing bank.

Finally, in *Lakeview Tech. v. Robinson*, the federal appellate court granted an employer an injunction to enforce a noncompetition agreement against a former sales executive even before the former executive had violated the provisions.[23] The court found four factors as significant to its holding:

1. The former executive had stated that he did not believe the noncompete was enforceable and threatened to ignore the noncompetition agreement with the employer.

2. The former executive had a history of deceitful behavior.

3. The employer would clearly suffer great damage if the former executive revealed its confidential information.

4. The former executive would not be financially able to satisfy a judgment against him if he violated the agreement. "A judgment-proof defendant is not deterred by the threat of money damages, so some other remedy (such as the contempt power) may be essential."

¶495 Noncompetes and the Internal Revenue Code

Covenants not to compete are occasionally used as a means of affecting taxation. Under Code Sec. 280G, so-called "parachute payments" do not include reasonable compensation for personal services to be rendered on or after the date of change in control.[24] The Treasury regulations under Code Sec. 280G provide that reasonable compensation for personal services includes reasonable compensation paid for refraining from performing services.[25] The regulations specifically use a covenant not to compete as an example. Thus, as long as the payments made to an individual pursuant to the non-compete agreement are reasonable, they will not be parachute payments subject to Code Sec. 280G and Code Sec. 4999.

A covenant not to compete does not create a substantial risk of forfeiture for purposes of Code Sec. 409A. Thus, a payment or benefit that is or could be received by an employee, former employee or other individual subject to his or her complying with a covenant not to compete is not deemed subject to a substantial risk of forfeiture and is, therefore, fully taxable.

---

[22] *Hearns v. Interstate Bank*, N.D. Ill., No. 05 C 175, March 31, 2006.

[23] *Lakeview Tech. v. Robinson*, 7th Cir., No. 05-4433, May 1, 2006.

[24] Code Sec. 280G(b)(4)(A).

[25] *See* Reg. § 1.280G-1, Q&A-40(b).

Chapter 5
RETENTION AND COMPENSATION
OF NON-EMPLOYEE BOARD
MEMBERS

¶501 Overview—Retention and Compensation of Non-Employee Board Members

Serving as an outside director for a corporation has changed dramatically over the past century. In the early 1900s, board members received no direct compensation. In the 1950s, states began authorizing boards to set their own compensation, as is now the norm.[1] Today, outside board members at public corporations receive varying amounts of compensation, as much as six and seven-figure amounts, arranged in packages including cash, equity, and various benefits.[2] As directors' responsibilities and potential liability continue to increase, the compensation figures are certain to rise as well.

The clear trend in non-employee director compensation has been toward a mixture of cash and equity. The use of other, less direct compensation, such as life insurance and pensions, has declined. For example, in 1999, only ten percent of companies offered a defined benefit pension plan to their board members, down from forty-eight percent in 1995.[3] In 1995, the National Association of Corporate Directors called for a shift away from benefits and pensions and toward equity.[4] The rationale was to align the interests of stockholders and directors and to reward performance rather than longevity. Today, almost no public companies offer pensions or other benefits to directors.

Throughout the 2000s, the requirements concerning director compensation have been getting stricter while the demands on directors and the directors' potential for liability has been growing. One way in which the demands on directors have increased is by the directors spending more time in meetings. Under NYSE guidelines, each company must have an audit committee, a corporate governance committee, and a compensation committee, all comprised solely of independent directors.[5] In the face of heightened scrutiny of director compen-

---

[1] Charles M. Elson, Director Compensation and the Management-Captured Board-The History of a Symptom and a Cure, 50 SMU L. Rev. 127, 138, 145-46 (1996).

[2] The highest-paid board members in 2000 were directors at Tibco Software, Inc., garnering $3.5 million apiece. Joseph B. Treaster, Directors' Compensation: Cash Laughs Last, Corp. Board Member (Jan./Feb. 2002).

[3] Joseph B. Treaster, Directors' Compensation: Cash Laughs Last, Corp. Board Member (Jan./Feb. 2002).

[4] Charles M. Elson, Director Compensation and the Management-Captured Board-The History of a Symptom and a Cure, 50 SMU L. Rev. at 166 (1996).

[5] See New York Stock Exchange Corporate Accountability and Listing Standards Committee, Recommendations to the NYSE Board of Directors 6, 9-11 (June 6, 2002).

sation, it could become increasingly difficult to compensate directors sufficiently for their greater responsibilities.

Since there are few legal limits (see ¶535), the types and amounts of compensation and benefits that corporations pay to their non-employee directors vary widely (see ¶525). However, most corporations provide at least the following to their outside board members:

- Directors' liability insurance;
- Annual board retainer fee;
- Fees for committee service;
- Meeting fees;
- Deferred directors' fee plan; and
- Reimbursement of expenses.

As noted above, nearly all publicly traded companies pay a significant amount of non-employee directors' compensation in the form of stock. Even more so than the executives, the members of the board of directors directly represent the company's stockholders. The greater the percentage of the directors' compensation that the company pays in stock, the more the directors will think and act like stockholders. These stock awards generally take the form of stock options, restricted stock or restricted stock units ("RSUs") (see ¶545).

Corporations subject to the reporting and shareholder approval requirements of the Securities Exchange Act of 1934 (the "Exchange Act") (see ¶555) must disclose to stockholders what they pay their directors. The SEC requires "clear, concise and understandable disclosure of all compensation" paid to directors for their services to the corporation. Public companies need to consider whether shareholders might find the type or amount of directors' compensation objectionable. However, corporations that do not provide sufficient compensation to non-employee directors will likely have great difficulty attracting and retaining qualified directors.

.01 Advisory Boards

Some corporations will create a separate "board" to advise or assist the corporation or the regular board of directors in some way. Members of these "advisory" or "technology" boards generally receive significantly less compensation than true board members receive, because they do not enjoy the same legal status or suffer the same potential legal liability as true board members (see ¶575).

.02 Sarbanes-Oxley Act of 2002

President Bush signed into law the Sarbanes-Oxley Act of 2002 ("SOX") in June 2002. SOX added significant new responsibilities for public corporations' audit committees, while further restricting the individuals eligible to serve on such committees (see ¶565).

¶501.01

.03 Code Sec. 409A

Code Sec. 409A, added by the American Jobs Creation Act of 2004, is entitled "Inclusion in Gross Income of Deferred Compensation Under Nonqualified Deferred Compensation Plans." Most companies make some form of deferred fee plan or arrangement available to their non-employee directors. Like the deferred compensation of corporate officers, directors' deferred fees are subject to Code Sec. 409A (see ¶ 585).[6]

.04 Surge in Litigation over Directors' Compensation

Litigation against companies and boards of directors over non-employee directors' compensation began to increase dramatically after 2012. In these lawsuits, the plaintiffs typically allege that the compensation of the non-employee directors was excessive, unauthorized, or otherwise improper. Some plaintiffs' lawyers have figured out a new strategy to circumvent the demand requirement and the business judgment rule with respect to non-employee director compensation, which increases the potential for a nuisance settlement with the company and busy board members (see ¶ 595).

.05 Increasing Requirements for Directors

Some commentators and politicians have blamed companies' directors for the financial scandals and compensation excesses of the last fifteen years. Thus, regulation and legislation promulgated during this period has often increased the requirements applicable to directors. Specifically, SEC disclosure rules have required and the Dodd-Frank Wall Street Reform and Consumer Protection Act, signed into law by President Obama in July 2010 (the "Dodd-Frank Act") imposed additional requirements on board compensation committees (see ¶ ¶ 555 and 565).

¶515 Agreements with Outside Board Members

Most corporations use a written agreement to appoint individuals to serve as outside members of their boards of directors and to specify their compensation and other terms and conditions of service. Companies often retain outside board members through a detailed, written offer letter or letter agreement.

.01 Status of Board Members

Outside board members are not employees of the corporation. The status of an outside board member to the corporation is that of an independent contractor. Outside board members are solely responsible for the payment of all taxes related to their board compensation. For this reason, the company's regular retirement, health or other employee benefit plans do not cover the board members.

Non-employee directors must make estimated tax payments to the IRS on all compensation and fees, including equity compensation, the corporation pays to

---

[6] See Chapter 17 (¶ 1701 et seq.) for a detailed discussion of all aspects of deferred compensation.

them. Generally, the corporation should not withhold income or FICA taxes on non-employee director stock transactions, such as the vesting of restricted stock.

.02 Appointment to the Board and Board Committees

One of the most fundamental provisions of an agreement with a non-employee director is the offer of, or appointment to, service on the board. Because the corporation's stockholders must approve an appointment to the board of directors, offer/appointment letters are often conditioned on stockholder approval. The exception to this situation occurs where the stockholders have already approved the individual's appointment to the board (generally true with private companies) and all that remains is to negotiate or memorialize the terms of the appointment. Additionally, as the duties and responsibilities of board committee members, particularly audit and compensation committee members, have increased, an agreement on appointment to these committees has become more important.

.03 Amount and Form of Compensation

Most agreements with non-employee directors will specify the compensation to be paid. Directors' compensation packages generally are much simpler than executives' packages, often consisting of only meeting fees and equity awards (see ¶ 525 below).

.04 Indemnification and Insurance

More important to outside board members than compensation is the corporation's indemnification provisions and directors' liability insurance. Most likely, no corporation could find individuals willing to serve as directors without providing directors' liability insurance. Indeed, some companies use strong D&O coverage as a selling point to prospective directors (and officers). Nearly all corporations' bylaws explicitly provide for the indemnification of directors to the maximum extent legally permitted. The corporation's articles of incorporation also should provide for director indemnification, exculpation, and immunity from liability.[7] Further, compensation committees may be assigned responsibility for corporate indemnity matters.[8] However, such indemnification is only as good as the corporation itself. A promise of indemnification from an insolvent corporation is not worth much to a director facing litigation.

> **Caution:** If an individual is considering board service, he or she should ask about the company's director liability insurance coverage first. Even the largest retainer and meeting fees would be exhausted in a couple of weeks of expensive litigation, and a comprehensive indemnification from an insolvent company would also be worthless.

Bankruptcy courts in some jurisdictions have found that D&O coverage is an asset of the bankruptcy estate, thereby subordinating directors' and officers' claims to those of other creditors. Suggestions made by some compensation

---

[7] American Bar Association, The Lawyer as Director of a Client, 57 BUS. LAW 387 (November 2001).

[8] Joseph Hinsey IV, The Buck Starts Here: The Who, What & How of a Compensation Committee, BUS. L. TODAY, at 32, 36 (Mar./Apr. 1993).

professionals include: (i) separate policy limits for the individuals; (ii) negotiate a clause in the policy requiring the insurer to pay the individuals first for unindemnified claims; or (iii) carrying separate Side A coverage for the officers and directors.[9]

Directors are at significant risk of having to contribute their own assets to a settlement or judgment if D&O insurers succeed in rescinding the policy. From the company's perspective, rescission means that the company will wind up having to pay more to its directors and officers pursuant to its indemnification obligations. In addition, if the company goes bankrupt, then the officers and directors are left naked.

A Delaware Chancery Court case highlights a potential trap for directors. In *Schoon v. Troy Corp.*[10], the Delaware Chancery Court upheld the rights of a corporation to amend its by-laws after the departure of a director to eliminate the critical director protections of fee advancement and indemnification rights for claims related to his service on the board, brought after the director's departure from the board. In this era of increasing liabilities, directors need this protection more than ever.

So how do we protect our directors from such an *ex post facto* elimination of their rights? One commentator has suggested three possibilities:[11]

1. Draft the by-laws to state explicitly that they cannot be amended retroactively to apply to actions taken during the directors' tenure;

2. Provide for fee advancement and indemnification in the corporate charter, which can only be amended by shareholder vote; and

3. Provide for fee advancement and indemnification rights in a separate written agreement between the corporation and the director, which cannot be amended except by written agreement.

Most corporations favor individual agreements between the director and the corporation, which set forth the rights and responsibilities of the parties, much like an employment agreement. However, we now will be exploring all three possible methods of protection.

¶525 Compensation of Non-Employee Board Members

Most corporations use a written agreement to appoint individuals to serve as outside members of their boards of directors and to specify their compensation and other terms and conditions of service. More so than with senior executive officers, companies retain outside board members through a detailed, written offer letter or letter agreement. Unlike executives, board members' annual compensation period typically runs from the date of the company's annual shareholders meeting (where board members are elected) through the date of the next following annual shareholders meeting.

---

[9] Chaskin, Neil Posner, and Venus McGhee, Review of Securities & Commodities Regulation—Vol. 37, No. 4, pp. 31-43.

[10] 948 A.2d 1157 (2008).

[11] American Bar Association's Business Law Today, November/December 2008, Steven H. Goldberg and Michael B. Jacobson.

.01 Retainer Fees

The Nominating and Corporate Governance Committee usually is responsible for conducting an annual assessment of non-employee director compensation and benefits. As part of this assessment, the committee generally considers the amount of director compensation and the mix of compensation instruments. The committee usually uses benchmarking data related to director compensation at other, similar companies. Often it will seek the input and assistance of the independent compensation consultant or counsel.

An intrinsic part of the appointment to the board and specified board committees is compensation, generally paid as retainer fees, for service. Again, as the responsibilities and *liabilities* of board and board committee members have increased, so have the retainer fees necessary to attract qualified individuals. Typically, a corporation will pay an outside board member a specified, minimum retainer fee for board service and specified additional fees for service on one or more committees.

Some boards confer certain titles on individual outside board members, including one or more of the following:

- Chairman/Chairwoman of the Board/Chair;
- Lead Director;
- Chair of the Audit Committee;
- Financial Expert of the Audit Committee;[12] and
- Chair of the Compensation Committee.

These titles come with additional responsibilities, additional potential liabilities and, therefore, separate and additional retainer fees.

.02 Meeting Fees

Most corporations traditionally paid a separate, additional fee to outside board members for their attendance at quarterly, annual, or special meetings. These corporations would pay outside board members serving on one or more committees additional fees for attendance at each committee meeting as well. This provided an incentive to the board members to attend the meetings. Today, many corporations are dropping the practice of paying separate meeting fees under the theory that effective and proper board service requires attendance at every meeting, and no additional incentive should be necessary.

.03 Equity-Based Compensation

For more than two decades, the overwhelming trend in director compensation has been to emphasize company stock.[13] Institutional investors and others promoting this trend reasoned that board members, like corporate officers, were

---

[12] This corporation or board must confer this title in accordance with Section 407 of the Sarbanes-Oxley Act of 2002, P.L. 107-204.

[13] For some reason, many of the same groups that wholeheartedly supported more equity-based compensation for officers and directors now seem to believe that focusing these individuals on short-term stock price performance is the root of all evil.

more likely to pay attention to the concerns of stockholders if they themselves had significant stock ownership. As is the case for executive officers, stock options, restricted stock, and restricted stock units (RSUs) are the most common form of equity-based compensation for non-employee directors (see ¶545 for a detailed discussion of outside directors' stock plans).

Restricted stock and RSUs generally are preferred over stock options because of their tendency to reward steady performance. That is, stock options only reward the recipient for substantial gain in the stock price, which tends to encourage risk-taking. Stock options can lose their value completely in a down market. Risk taking is good for executives, but many feel that board members should manage for long-term growth, even in times of declining stock prices. Most companies require that directors have a stake in the company by instituting stock ownership guidelines, with more companies adding this requirement each year.

.04 Benefits

Corporations often make available certain additional, generally modest, benefits and perquisites to their outside board members, including some of the following:

- *Expense Reimbursement.* Expense reimbursement is not really a benefit so much as it is a policy of paying the outside directors' direct costs for traveling to and attending meetings. However, expense reimbursement also often includes attendance at seminars on issues such as corporate governance and, occasionally, spouse travel.

- *Retirement Benefits.* Defined benefit pension plans were a very popular form of directors' benefits until the mid-1990s, when they fell out of favor with institutional investors and, thus, corporations.[14]

- *Charitable Award Programs.* Compensation professionals also know these programs as "CAPs" or "Director Legacy" donations. Under these plans, the corporation purchases a large life insurance policy on a director, the beneficiary of the policy being one of the director's favorite charities,[15] such as an educational institution (*e.g.*, University of Notre Dame).[16]

- *Other Perquisites.* A perquisite can be described as an expected benefit aside from one's regular compensation, a fringe benefit, or a perk. Some director perquisites include augmented pensions and annual physicals, luncheon and country club memberships, and cars and drivers. One director even had his state income tax paid every year by his company.[17]

---

[14] See ¶1635 for a more detailed discussion of defined benefit pension plans.

[15] Lynn Brenner, Are Directors Overpaid?, CFO: The Magazine for Senior Financial Executives, at 32 (February 1996) ("The premium [on such an insurance policy] is not tax deductible, but the corporation takes a deduction for the policy proceeds when the beneficiary is paid.")

[16] The Associated Press State & Local Wire, Alumnus Leaving $1 Million to Support MSU Engineering, November 16, 1998.

[17] Martha Groves, Special Report: Executive Pay in California; Riding the Wave; Annual Survey Shows How the Soaring Stock Market is Driving up Compensation, Los Angeles Times, May 26, 1996, at D1.

Examples: Directors of Apple Computer receive up to two free computer systems per year and are eligible to purchase additional equipment and products at a discount.

A Carnival Corporation Proxy Statement provides:

"All non-executive directors are encouraged to take a cruise for up to 14 days per year for product familiarization and pay a fare of $35 per day for such cruises. Guests traveling with the non-executive director in the same stateroom will each be charged a fare of $35 per day. All other charges associated with the cruise (*e.g.*, air fares, government fees and taxes, gratuities, ground transfers, tours, etc.) are the responsibility of the non-executive director."

Because outside directors are not employees of the corporation, they generally are not eligible to participate in the retirement, health, insurance and other benefit plans the corporation makes available to its employees. The terms of most qualified retirement and group health benefit plans expressly prohibit participation by non-employees.

.05 Deferred Fee Arrangements

As a practical matter, many outside board members do not need their retainer and meeting fees to live on. Outside board members are often the chief executive or chief financial officers of other large companies where they are well compensated. Therefore, nearly every company makes some form of deferred fee plan or arrangement available to its non-employee directors. Like the deferred compensation of corporate officers, directors' deferred fees are subject to Code Sec. 409A (see ¶ 585).

.06 Change in Control Protection

Many board of director agreements specifically provide that any equity-based compensation or other benefits subject to time-based or performance-based vesting or forfeiture restrictions will become fully vested and nonforfeitable in case of a change in control of the corporation. Many other equity awards to non-employee directors simply will provide that the award is fully vested at all times. The reasoning behind these provisions is simply that their existence will ensure that board members will not be concerned about how a potential transaction will affect their service or compensation, but instead will focus solely on the benefits of the potential transaction to the stockholders. While an acquirer may retain some executive officers following a change in control, it is virtually certain that the acquirer will not retain any board members.

Many companies' stock incentive plans and other arrangements reserve to the board of directors the ability to cause full vesting on the eve of a change in control.[18] However, no plan or arrangement should put board members in the position of having to decide the acceleration of vesting of their own compensation. To do so would expose the directors to a terrible conflict of interest.

---

[18] Before 2001, reserving this discretion to the board of directors could prevent the use of favorable "pooling of interest" accounting for a transaction, so these provisions were uncommon.

Comment: Consider making all forms of director compensation fully vested at the time of payment or award. A vesting schedule may be necessary to retain officers in the marketplace for executive talent. However, although good directors are always in high demand, there is very little movement of directors from one company to another.

.07 The Call for Increasing Compensation

Following SOX, nearly everyone began to agree that corporations should increase directors' compensation in light of the dramatically increased liabilities faced by corporate directors. In his special report to the court concerning MCI, Inc., Richard C. Breeden concluded as follows:

> The compensation for service on compensation committees is typically very low, and in some companies is purely nominal. While the risk of serving on this committee may be perceived as lower than that of the Audit Committee, service on the Compensation Committee is likely to require substantial work, and significant pressure. Low compensation is likely to lead to insufficient time commitments by members. The Company should make a substantial investment in careful oversight of its human resources department and compensation programs.

> Recommendation 7.04. Members of the Compensation Committee should receive a retainer to be established by the board, but which should not be less than \$35,000 for members of the Committee, and not less than \$50,000 for the chairman of the Committee.[19]

Over time, companies have increased the fees they pay to their non-employee directors and diversified stock-based pay to directors by decreasing their reliance on stock options and increasing use of full-value shares (restricted stock and RSUs).

.08 The Coca-Cola Company Directors Compensation Plan

In 2006, the Board of Directors of The Coca-Cola Company adopted an unusual compensation plan for its non-employee directors.[20] The plan consisted entirely of equity-based compensation, equal to a flat fee of \$175,000, payable only when the company meets pre-defined performance targets (except for the option for the board to make a one-time cash award to any new director). When the performance target is met at the end of the performance period, the share units would be payable in cash. Should the performance target not be met, all share units and hypothetical dividends would be forfeited in their entirety.

The plan replaced a compensation structure under which the directors received an annual retainer of \$125,000, of which \$50,000 was paid in cash and \$75,000 accrued in share units. This structure also provided additional fees for such duties as chairing board committees and attending board and committee meetings. The new plan eliminated all those fees. For 2006, the initial year of the

---

[19] Recommendation 7.04, p. 117, RESTORING TRUST, Report to The Hon. Jed S. Rakoff, The United States District Court For the Southern District of New York, On Corporate Governance For The Future of MCI, Inc., Prepared By Richard C.

Breeden, Corporate Monitor, August, 2003, http://www.nysd.uscourts.gov/rulings/02cv4963_082603.pdf.

[20] Form 8-K filed April 4, 2006.

plan, the board set an initial three-year performance target of 8 percent compounded annual growth in earnings per share.

It is quite rare for directors to have an "all-or-nothing" pay package and a number of commentators expressed concerns over its design, such as "the approach would make directors fixated on earnings and undermine their role as watchdogs." Director stock options have been criticized as providing directors an incentive to look the other way (*see* Enron and WorldCom). This criticism is aimed generally at all incentive plan participation because directors are fiduciaries for stockholders, not the operators of the company. Linking their pay directly to financial results, the traditional domain of executives, is inconsistent with their duties and responsibilities.

.09 Intangible Compensation - Support of the Company

Individuals who accept a directorship with a public company need to be assured that the company will support their future re-election as directors (absent malfeasance or other performance problems, of course). Section 951 of the Dodd-Frank Act added a new Section 14A to the Exchange Act, entitled "Shareholder Approval of Executive Compensation," which provides that, not less frequently than once every three years, a company's annual proxy statement must include a separate resolution, subject to a non-binding shareholder vote, to approve the compensation of executives, as disclosed in the company's Compensation Discussion and Analysis (CD&A), the compensation tables, and any related material. This resolution applies only to the named executive officers ("NEOs"), although the Act does not contain this explicit limitation.

A collateral effect of losing the Shareholder Say on Pay vote - or only narrowly winning the vote - is that directors who are members of the compensation committee are likely to receive substantially more "Withhold" votes than other directors in future elections. This is not only embarrassing for the directors, it may make it harder for the company to recruit and retain directors willing to serve on the compensation committee in the future. For example, after SOX imposed significant new responsibilities and potential liabilities on members of the audit committee, we began to see directors (i) express reluctance to serve on, and (ii) ask to "cycle off," the audit committee. Companies will find it more difficult to recruit new board members to serve on the compensation committee if the potential directors know that they will be subject to greater scrutiny by outsiders and that the company does not have an explicit strategy for maximizing the likelihood of (i) their future retention as directors, and (ii) achieving a favorable vote in Shareholder Say on Pay.

¶535 Legal Limits on Director Compensation

State law allows compensation of boards of directors to take many forms. Delaware, for example, authorizes payment in stock, stock options, pensions, benefits, and incentive plans.[21] A board member's compensation package might include an annual cash retainer, fees for attending board and committee meet-

---

[21] Del. Code Ann. tit. 8, § 122(15).

ings, stock options or grants, a retirement plan, life and medical insurance, future donations to the director's designated charity, or the option of deferred compensation in order to gain more favorable tax treatment. A corporation also may provide a director with consulting fees and/or gifts in kind of company services such as free cars, computers, cell phone service, and first-class air travel for providing advice to the company on particular issues.[22] General Motors' directors, for example, can receive the use of a new car every three months for simply filling out a product evaluation form.[23]

Outside board members are not employees. Thus, they cannot receive certain forms of compensation that are limited to employees. For example, an outside board member cannot receive stock options that qualify for tax-advantaged treatment as incentive stock options under Code Sec. 422.[24] Outside board members also cannot participate in an employee stock purchase plan qualified under Code Sec. 423.[25] Generally, board members cannot be covered under an employee group health insurance plan or make pre-tax contributions under the corporation's cafeteria or flexible benefits plans.

.01 Amount of Compensation

Other than the negative effect that lavish director compensation can have on stock price via the public stock markets, the primary constraints on director compensation are the laws embodied by the doctrine of corporate waste, and enforced through stockholder derivative suits. Stockholder derivative suits can be thought of as claims by so-called "strike suit" lawyers, ostensibly representing stockholders, that amounts paid out as director compensation constitute a waste of corporate assets.

According to Delaware case law, the standard for determining waste is whether the services provided by the director were "so inadequate in value that no person of ordinary, sound business judgment would deem [them] worth what the corporation has paid."[26] To determine whether the compensation meets the standard, courts sometimes compare the compensation of directors at similar companies.[27] Courts have toyed with the notion of turning waste of corporate assets into a proportionality standard, *i.e.*, mandating that there must be a reasonable relationship between the value of the benefits passing to the corporation and the value of the compensation granted to the director.[28] However, the Delaware Supreme Court has affirmed that the classic waste standard is appropriate.[29]

---

[22] Charles M. Elson, Director Compensation and the Management-Captured Board-The History of a Symptom and a Cure, 50 SMU L. Rev. at 154-156 (1996).

[23] Susan Caminiti, Are You Paid Enough?, Corp. Board Member (Autumn 1999).

[24] See Chapter 7 (¶701 et seq.) for a detailed discussion of incentive stock options.

[25] See Chapter 10 (¶1001 et seq.) for a detailed discussion of ESPPs.

[26] *Saxe v. Brady*, 184 A2d 602, 610 (Del. Ch. 1962).

[27] Eric L. Johnson, Note, Waste Not, Want Not: An Analysis of Stock Option Plans, Executive Compensation, and the Proper Standard of Waste, 26 Iowa J. Corp. L. 145, 156 (2000).

[28] E.g., *Beard v. Elster*, 160 A2d 731, 737 (Del. 1960).

[29] *Brehm v. Eisner*, 746 A2d 244 (Del. 2000).

.02 Valuation of Stock Option Plans

Other Delaware cases have dealt with more specific aspects of shareholder suits alleging wasteful director compensation. For example, *Lewis v. Vogelstein*[30] involved a plan, approved by stockholders, granting stock options to the directors of Mattel, Inc. The "stockholder" plaintiffs alleged that the proxy statement describing the plan was materially incomplete and misleading because it did not include an estimate of the present value of the stock options. In addition, the plaintiffs alleged that the grants were each worth as much as $180,000, representing excessive compensation for the directors and a waste of corporate assets.

The stock option plan provided for a one-time grant of 15,000 shares of Mattel common stock with an exercise price equal to the market price on the day granted, exercisable immediately and valid for ten years. In addition, the plan granted 5,000 to 10,000 shares annually to each board member upon his or her re-election. These options were set at the market price on the day granted, vested fully over four years, and expiring after ten years. The court held that when a board is seeking stockholder approval of an option compensation plan, it satisfies its duty of disclosure by disclosing all of the relevant terms of the plan along with any material extrinsic facts within its knowledge. The existing option-pricing models (*e.g.*, the Black-Scholes method), moreover, do not provide reliable estimates of the value of option plans with as many uncertain factors as the Mattel plan. Thus, the board had no duty to disclose to stockholders an estimated value of the options.

For the plaintiffs' waste claim, the court applied the classic waste standard, *i.e.*, corporate assets exchanged for consideration so insignificant that no reasonable person would have agreed to the transaction. The court said that it would need to hear evidence on the value of the one-time option grants to determine whether they constituted corporate waste and refused to dismiss the plaintiffs' claim.[31]

> **Comment:** The dramatic increase in scrutiny from investors, the SEC, and law enforcement following the Enron, Tyco and other scandals of recent decades has made it even harder to attract qualified directors. The days of even a highly qualified individual like Vernon Jordan sitting on eleven different public company boards are over. (We refer to this as "overboarded.") In addition to rock-solid indemnification and liability insurance, companies should expect to pay more cash and equity compensation to qualified directors to make up for the smaller number of boards on which a qualified individual can sit and the increased liability of each.

.03 Accurate Disclosure

In Re 3COM Corp. Shareholders Litigation,[32] involved an option compensation plan ratified by the stockholders. The plan expanded the pool of shares available

---

[30] *Lewis v. Vogelstein*, 699 A2d 327 (Del. Ch. 1997).

[31] *Lewis v. Vogelstein*, 699 A2d 327, 338-39 (Del. Ch. 1997).

[32] *In Re 3COM Corp. Shareholders Litigation* (Del. Ch. 1999), contained in 25 Del. J. Corp. L. 1060 (2000).

to directors through the current stock option plan from 2,000,000 to 3,000,000 shares. The plaintiffs argued that the proxy materials describing the option plan were misleading because they contained the statement, "No gain to an optionee is possible without an increase in stock price, which will benefit all stockholders commensurately. A zero percent gain in the stock price will result in zero dollars for the optionee."[33] The plaintiffs argued that it was misleading not to include a statement saying that directors could sell their option contracts for cash. The court, however, dismissed the allegation, stating that the corporation does not have to disclose every possible use of the compensation granted, especially when the use depends on the personal decisions and risk aversion of the individual being compensated.

In *3COM*, the plaintiffs also argued that since the directors had created the plan for their own compensation, it was an "interested" transaction and the directors would have to show entire fairness. The court noted, however, that since the shareholders approved the plan, the directors were merely subject to the business judgment rule. The plaintiffs also argued that since the court in *Lewis* had found that $180,000 of options might be wasteful, the options in this case (alleged to be worth $650,000 per director) were surely wasteful. The court refused, however, to make a direct comparison between the numbers in *Lewis* and the numbers in the present case, stating that the facts of another case were not to be the benchmark for what dollar amounts constituted excessive compensation.[34]

¶545 Non-Employee Directors' Stock Incentive Plans

Corporations provide most of their non-employee directors' compensation in the form of company stock. Conventional wisdom is that directors should hold, and receive all or part of their fees in, shares of company stock to ensure their interests are aligned with those of the company's stockholders. Corporations generally decide whether to compensate non-employee directors with stock options, restricted stock, RSUs, or some other type of stock-based compensation, based on the same considerations applicable to employees.[35]

Though federal securities laws no longer require it, some corporations will establish and maintain a separate stock incentive plan for non-employee directors. Generally, the stock incentive plan provisions applicable to non-employee directors are similar to those that apply to the company's executives and other employees. However, stock option or restricted stock awards to non-employee directors nearly always have a shorter (or no) vesting schedule. The exercise price of any stock options awarded to non-employee directors is generally related to the fair market value of the stock at the date of grant. Non-employee directors cannot receive an award of incentive stock options.[36]

---

[33] *In Re 3COM Corp. Shareholders Litigation*, 25 Del. J. Corp. L. 1060, 1073 (2000).

[34] *In Re 3COM Corp. Shareholders Litigation*, 25 Del. J. Corp. L. 1060, 1070-71 (2000).

[35] This topic will be discussed further in Chapters 6 through 13.

[36] See Chapter 7 (¶701 *et seq.*).

Before 1997, stock incentive awards to directors had to be made under a plan administered solely by "disinterested persons," or pursuant to a self-administered plan, to provide protection from the short-swing trading restrictions of Section 16 of the Exchange Act.[37] Many corporations satisfied this requirement by making equity awards to directors under so-called "formula plans" that provided for an automatic award to directors each year. The SEC rewrote Rule 16b-3 of the Exchange Act in 1996[38] to eliminate the disinterested administration requirement. Thus, directors can now authorize and approve awards to themselves and participate in the same equity award plans as executive employees. However, many stock incentive plans still provide for administration by disinterested persons and/or for automatic awards to non-employee directors.

.01 Restricted Stock Units

Restricted stock units ("RSUs") can be a useful tool for awarding restricted stock to non-employee members of the employer's board of directors. Companies want their board members to hold company stock. Board members are very often interested in deferral of taxation, and not interested in being seen selling shares into the market. RSUs can be an ideal vehicle for achieving both of these goals (see Chapter 8 [¶ 801 *et seq.*] for a detailed discussion of RSUs).

RSUs allow each director to control the timing of his or her recognition of income. For the recipient to avoid constructive receipt of the vested RSUs, counsel must structure the plan and award agreement to provide that the RSUs are subject to "a substantial risk of forfeiture" and meet the other requirements of Code Sec. 409A. To prevent a constructive receipt of income by the RSU holder, while complying with Code Sec. 409A, the employers can provide that RSU amounts will be distributed in shares of stock no earlier than six months following the date the director/RSU holder terminates service on the board. The director must make a deferral election, if any, at least one year in advance of the time the award vests.

> **Example:** Assume ABC Corporation awarded 10,000 restricted stock units to Director D on July 1, 2017, vesting 25% per year, and payable in shares of stock on the first anniversary of D's separation from service with the ABC board. D would not recognize any income on the July 1, 2018, 2019, 2020, or 2021, vesting dates of the RSUs and, thus, D could retain the full value and appreciation of her RSUs during this period. Although D would become fully vested in her RSUs on July 1, 2021, because D is not holding real share certificates in her hands (figuratively), the risk exists that ABC Corporation could become insolvent and pay her nothing. Moreover, because D cannot receive a distribution of her vested RSUs until one full year after ending her service on the board, that risk of insolvency continues until

---

[37] Section 16 requires forfeiture of any profits of officers, directors, and ten percent shareholders resulting from matched purchases and sales of company stock within any six-month period.

[38] Ownership Reports and Trading by Officers, Directors and Principal Security Holders Release No. 34-37260 (May 30, 1996). Rule 16b-3(b)(3) retains the concept of approval by a committee of two or more "nonemployee directors" as one of the transactional exemptions to the provisions of 16b-3.

the day D actually receives a distribution of ABC stock. If D ended her service on the board on July 1, 2023, and ABC's stock is trading at $50.00 per share on July 1, 2021, the date ABC distributes the shares to D, she will recognize ordinary income of $500,000 on that date.

If ABC had awarded Director D 10,000 shares of restricted stock, and ABC's stock was trading at $50.00 per share on July 1, 2018, Director D will recognize ordinary income of $125,000 on that date. At a 39% federal tax rate, D would owe, and ABC would need to withhold, approximately $48,750, which D may need to satisfy by selling some of the 250 shares of restricted stock that just vested. This event would be repeated on each of July 1, 2019, 2020, and 2021.

¶555 SEC Disclosure and Stock Exchange Rules

The SEC requires a corporation to disclose to shareholders what it pays its directors. In particular, the SEC requires "clear, concise and understandable disclosure of all compensation" paid to directors for their services to the corporation.[39] That disclosure must include the amount of the standard directors' fee, per-meeting and committee participation fees, and any stock grants. In addition, the corporation must describe the material terms of any nonstandard compensation arrangements, such as consulting contracts.

.01 Form 8-K

Over the years, the SEC has changed the immediate disclosure requirements imposed on U.S. public companies by expanding the number of disclosure items that trigger a Form 8-K filing requirement and by tightening the filing deadline. Companies are required to file a Form 8-K within four days of certain executive compensation and employment events.

The retirement, resignation, termination, or refusal to stand for re-election by directors creates a Form 8-K disclosure obligation for the corporation. The information the corporation must disclose depends on the circumstances, and is extensive in the case of a director who is leaving as a result of a disagreement about operations, policies, or practices. Similarly, the election of a new director (except by shareholder vote) must be disclosed on a Form 8-K.

Form 8-K disclosure is not needed for director compensation unless in conjunction with the director's appointment or departure. The SEC requires a brief description of any material plan, contract or arrangement (or grant or award made to any covered person thereunder) that is entered into or amended in connection with an appointment or election. The corporation still must file any compensatory arrangements with directors, and any amendments to such arrangements, whether or not material, with the applicable periodic report.

.02 Proxy Statement Disclosure

In August 2006, the SEC published final rules governing the disclosure of executive and director compensation. The rules require companies to disclose the

---

[39] 17 C.F.R. § 228.402(a).

compensation of their directors in a format similar to the Summary Compensation Table applicable to the corporation's named executive officers. The directors' table must list the following forms and amounts of compensation:

  (a) Fees Earned or Paid in Cash

  (b) Stock Awards

  (c) Options Awards

  (d) Non-Equity Incentive Plan Compensation

  (e) Change in Pension Value and Nonqualified Deferred Compensation Earnings

  (f) All Other Compensation

  (g) Total

However, directors with identical compensation may be listed and disclosed on one line.

Additionally, companies must provide (i) footnote disclosure of aggregate option and stock awards held at prior fiscal year end, and (ii) a narrative description of any material factors necessary to an understanding of director compensation, including:

• Description of standard compensation arrangements

• Whether any director has a different compensation arrangement

.03 Form 4 and 5 Filings

Directors, as Section 16 insiders, are required to file a Form 4 under the Section 16 reporting rules when they defer fees in the form of company stock. The SEC has released Final Rule: Ownership Reports and Trading by Officers, Directors and Principal Security Holders, File No. S7-31-02, in which the Commission states, "transactions pursuant to non-qualified deferred compensation plans or other dividend or interest reinvestment plan transactions (such as acquisitions pursuant to voluntary contributions of additional funds) will be reportable on Form 4 within two business days after the date of execution. However, to the extent that such a transaction satisfies the affirmative defense conditions of Rule 10b5-1(c), the date of execution for Form 4 reporting purposes may be calculated on the modified basis." Under the limited extension provided by Rule 10b5-1(c), the two business day deadline is counted from a "deemed" transaction date, which is the earlier of (i) the date the insider receives notice that the transaction was executed, or (ii) the third business day after the date the transaction is executed. Consequently, the latest a Form 4 can be timely filed for these transactions is on the fifth business day after the transaction. The extended time for reporting these transactions is not available if the insider has selected the date for transaction execution. While this exception does allow for extended filing, it is important to note that the filing is still required.

Included in the transactions that now require accelerated reporting on Form 4 are routine deferrals of director compensation under a nonqualified deferred compensation plan where the deferrals are credited to an investment account

¶555.03

whose value is derived from the value of the sponsoring company's stock. Typically, such an investment account would involve phantom stock units (including the use of the stock's performance as the index for crediting investment returns to the deferrals). As a result, the crediting of phantom stock units with respect to contributions to a nonqualified deferred compensation plan by directors or officers is now reportable on Form 4 within two business days of each date compensation withheld is credited to the company stock investment account (generally, at the end of each pay period). Previously, a full year's worth of these recurring acquisitions could be aggregated and reported as a single item on a year-end Form 5 report.

.04 Stock Exchange and Other Disclosure Rules

For more than a decade, the trend in director compensation has been toward increasing amounts of equity in the compensation package. In 2000, for example, stock and stock options made up almost sixty percent of the average overall compensation—compared to thirty-six percent just four years before—and ninety-five percent of companies included some stock in their director compensation.[40] The Nasdaq and NYSE generally require that the corporation submit these stock and stock option plans for shareholder approval.[41]

Besides requiring shareholder approval for more stock-based plans, the NYSE rules include several other guidelines for director compensation. First, the NYSE requires boards to have a majority of their members be independent directors.[42] In addition, the independent directors who serve on the audit committee can receive from the company only normal directors' fees, which include equity-based awards, additional per-meeting fees, and pensions or other forms of deferred compensation.[43] Finally, the NYSE warns that charitable contributions, consulting contracts, and other forms of indirect compensation may raise concerns about the amount of compensation awarded and the independence of the director receiving the award.[44]

> **Comment:** Apply the "kiss" principle to director compensation: Keep it simple, stupid. A simple package of retainer and meeting fees, coupled with stock-based compensation awards and the ability to defer taxation on all of it will be satisfactory to most directors who are serious about the job of corporate governance. A director candidate seeking unusual perquisites may not be dedicated to the concept of good corporate governance.

---

[40] Joseph B. Treaster, Directors' Compensation: Cash Laughs Last, Corp. Board Member (Jan./Feb. 2002).

[41] See Chapter 6 (¶601 et seq.) for a detailed discussion of the Nasdaq and NYSE rules.

[42] New York Stock Exchange Corporate Accountability and Listing Standards Committee, Recommendations to the NYSE Board of Directors 6 (June 6, 2002).

[43] New York Stock Exchange Corporate Accountability and Listing Standards Committee, Recommendations to the NYSE Board of Directors 11, n.7 (June 6, 2002). The Recommendations do not mention whether they would consider less-direct forms of compensation, such as consultation arrangements and charitable contributions, normal fees.

[44] New York Stock Exchange Corporate Accountability and Listing Standards Committee, Recommendations to the NYSE Board of Directors 18-20 (June 6, 2002).

.05 Director and Nominee Disclosure in the Proxy Statement

SEC rules require public companies to make specific disclosures as to the compensation paid to non-employee directors in the annual proxy statement.

Compensation Disclosure. Item 402(k) of Regulation S-K requires public companies to provide certain information concerning the compensation of the directors for the company's last completed fiscal year, in a tabular format, similar format to that of Summary Compensation Table (including value for equity awards recognized during the fiscal year under ASC 718).

Like the treatment of NEO awards in the Summary Compensation Table, stock awards and stock options granted to directors are reported in separate columns of the Director Compensation Table. The amount reported for these awards is to be the aggregate grant date fair value as computed in accordance with ASC 718.[45] Unlike the Summary Compensation Table, however, the Instruction to Item 402(k)(2)(iii) and (iv) requires companies to disclose—in footnotes to the appropriate columns—the full grant date fair value of each equity award as computed in accordance with ASC 718, on a director-by-director basis, as well as the aggregate number of stock awards and stock options outstanding for each director at the end of the last completed fiscal year.

Director Compensation Table

Name (a)	Fees Earned or Paid in Cash ($) (b)	Stock Awards ($) (c)	Options Awards ($) (d)	Non-Equity Incentive Plan Compensation ($) (e)	Change in Pension Value and Nonqualified Deferred Compensation Earnings ($) (f)	All Other Compensation ($) (g)	Total ($) (h)
A							
B							
C							
D							
E							

Also reportable in the Director Compensation Table is:

- The dollar value of all earnings for services performed during the fiscal year pursuant to non-equity incentive plans and all earnings on any outstanding awards (column (e));

- The aggregate change in the actuarial present value of the director's accumulated benefit under all defined benefit and actuarial pension plans (including supplemental plans) for the prior completed fiscal year and any above-market or preferential earnings on compensation that is de-

[45] Item 402(k)(iii) and (iv) of Regulation S-K.

ferred on a basis that is not tax-qualified, including such earnings on nonqualified defined contribution plans (column (f));

- All other compensation for the fiscal year that the company could not properly report in any other column of the Director Compensation Table (column (g)), including:

  - Perquisites and other personal benefits, or property, unless the aggregate amount of such compensation is less than $10,000;

  - All "gross-ups" or other amounts reimbursed during the fiscal year for the payment of taxes; and

  - The amount paid or accrued to any director pursuant to a plan or arrangement in connection with the resignation, retirement or any other termination of such director, or a change in control of the company;

- Company contributions or other allocations to vested and unvested defined contribution plans;

- Consulting fees earned from, or paid or payable by the company and/or its subsidiaries (including joint ventures);

- The annual costs of payments and promises of payments pursuant to director legacy programs and similar charitable award programs;

- The dollar value of any insurance premiums paid by, or on behalf of, the company during the covered fiscal year with respect to life insurance for the benefit of a director; and

- The dollar value of any dividends or other earnings paid on stock or option awards, when those amounts were not factored into the grant date fair value required to be reported for the stock or option award in column (c) or (d).

Other Disclosure. The SEC's final rule on executive compensation disclosure and corporate governance requires companies to disclose for each director and any nominee for director the particular experience, qualifications, attributes or skills that led the board to conclude that the person should serve as a director for the company. (The same disclosure, with respect to any nominee for director put forward by another proponent, would be required in the proxy soliciting materials of that proponent.) This disclosure will be required for all directors, including those not up for re-election in a particular year. The final rule requires that companies make this disclosure annually because the composition of the entire board is important information for voting decisions.

The final rule does *not* require companies to disclose the specific experience, qualifications or skills that qualify a person to serve as a committee member (as the proposed rules would have required). Notably, the SEC deleted the reference to "risk assessment skills" that was included in the proposed rules. However, the final rule provides that if the board chose an individual to be a director because of a particular qualification, attribute or experience related to service on a specific committee, such as the audit or compensation committee, then it should disclose this fact under the requirements as part of the individual's qualifications to serve on the board.

The final rules also require disclosure of any directorships at public companies or registered investment companies held by each director and nominee *at any time during the past five years.* The SEC believes that expanding this disclosure will allow investors to better evaluate the relevance of a director's or nominee's past board experience, as well as professional or financial relationships that might pose potential conflicts of interest.

The final rule also lengthens the time during which disclosure of legal proceedings involving directors, director nominees and executive officers is required from five to ten years, "as a means of providing investors with more extensive information regarding an individual's competence and character." The SEC also expanded the list of legal proceedings for which it requires disclosure to include:

- Any judicial or administrative proceedings resulting from involvement in mail or wire fraud or fraud in connection with any business entity;
- Any judicial or administrative proceedings based on violations of federal or state securities, commodities, banking or insurance laws and regulations, or any settlement[114] to such actions; and
- Any disciplinary sanctions or orders imposed by a stock, commodities or derivatives exchange or other self-regulatory organization.

The SEC believes that certain legal proceedings can reflect on an individual's competence and integrity to serve as a director, and that this additional disclosure will provide investors with valuable information for assessing the competence, character and overall suitability of a director, nominee or executive officer.

Finally, the final rule amends Item 407(c) of Regulation S-K to require companies to disclose whether, and if so how, a nominating committee considers diversity in identifying nominees for director. If the nominating committee (or the board) has a policy with regard to the consideration of diversity in identifying director nominees, the company must disclose how this policy is implemented, as well as how the nominating committee (or the board) assesses the effectiveness of its policy. For purposes of this disclosure requirement, the SEC allows companies to define diversity in ways that they consider appropriate. The final rule does not define diversity.

.06 Evolving Best Practices in Non-Employee Director Compensation Disclosure

As director compensation has increased, so has investor scrutiny of it (and litigation over it, see ¶595, below). Certain best practices for setting executives' compensation have become more commonplace in the process for setting directors' compensation.

Most importantly, every company's equity incentive plan should have a meaningful limit on the number or value of shares that may be awarded to a non-employee director under the plan in any year. Companies also should impose a limit on the total compensation payable to a non-employee director in any year. Companies may place this limit in the company's equity incentive plan or a separate directors' compensation plan, but they must be sure to have the limit approved by shareholders.

Other best practices for setting non-employee director pay include the following:

Independent Review. If the board has not done so recently, it should request - or have the company request - a review of the boards' compensation by a consultant that is not retained by the board. Independent review should alert the board to any anomalies and make it easier to defend the board compensation levels.

Benchmarking. Part of an independent review is, of course, benchmarking the non-employee directors' compensation against that of the company's peer group. The board (and its consultant) generally should benchmark board compensation against the same peer group of companies as the board has chosen for benchmarking executives' pay, unless the board has a very good reason for choosing a different peer group, which it should discuss in the proxy statement.

Charter Language. The charter of the board's compensation committee (or such other committee as is assigned the responsibility for setting non-employee director compensation) should specify the committee's responsibilities for reviewing and setting non-employee directors' compensation, as well as clarifying its authority to retain an independent compensation consultant.

Disclosure. Finally, the proxy statement should discuss the process for setting non-employee directors' compensation and proudly disclose the fact that the board has retained an independent review of its compensation program and benchmarked it against the company's peers. If the board's compensation is at or near the high end of the peer group, the disclosure can explain the reason why the board believes this level is appropriate.

Investors' scrutiny of non-employee director (NED) compensation was further increased in 2017, when ISS announced a policy that provides for adverse vote recommendations for board and committee members who are responsible for approving/setting NED compensation when there is a recurring pattern (*i.e.*, two or more consecutive years) of excessive NED pay magnitude without a compelling rationale or other mitigating factors. This new policy will not impact vote recommendations in 2018. However, in future years, negative recommendations would be triggered only after a pattern of excessive NED pay is identified in consecutive years. ISS states that it has "identified some extreme outliers that pay directors substantially more than their peer companies without providing a clear explanation for these discrepancies."

.07 Proxy Access Rule

In 2010, the SEC adopted proxy access rules at an open Commission meeting by a 3-2 vote. Neither the adopting release nor proxy access generally has an automatic or direct impact on executive compensation. However, one of the announced purposes of proxy access is to enhance shareholders' abilities to hold directors feet to the fire on executive compensation, as indicated in the introductory and background statements from the release:

> We recognized at that time that the financial crisis that the nation and markets had experienced heightened the serious concerns of many shareholders about the accountability and responsiveness of some companies and boards of directors to shareholder interests, and that these concerns had resulted in a loss of investor confidence. These concerns also led to questions about whether boards were exercising appropriate oversight of management, whether boards were appropriately focused on shareholder interests, and whether boards need to be more accountable for their decisions regarding issues such as compensation structures and risk management.

> A principal way that shareholders can hold boards accountable and influence matters of corporate policy is through the nomination and election of directors.

However, in 2015, the U.S. Court of Appeals for the D.C. Circuit vacated the SEC's controversial proxy access rule, SEC Rule 14a-11, which would have permitted the inclusion of shareholder nominees in the company's proxy statement.

.08 Directors' Compensation Payable to a Third Party

As private equity firms and their funds became major investors in private and public companies beginning in the 1990's, many members and employees of private equity firms began serving on the board of directors of their portfolio companies. Since these individuals are already compensated as members or employees of their private equity firm, the parties desire to provide that any board of directors fees paid to such individual be paid directly to the private equity firm instead.

The common scenario is where a company, in which the private equity or venture capital firm invests, becomes scheduled to go public in the near future. Consistent with the investor's standard practice, an employee of the investor is a director of the company. The company designs a compensation package for its directors, which includes cash and awards of company stock. Since the employee/director is a only a director of the company in his or her capacity as an employee of the investor, any amount paid by the company to him or her should be the property of the investor, not of the employee/director individually. In this situation, companies generally follow one of the following alternative approaches:

- Cause the portfolio company to make cash payments and grant stock awards directly to the investor as a fee for services pursuant to a contract, such as a consulting agreement; or
- Allow the portfolio company to make cash payments and grant stock awards to the director and execute a written agreement between the employee/director and the investor under which:
  - The employee/director agrees to (i) accept the investor company direction on the exercise of the option and sale of the stock, and (ii) turn

over to the investor company any cash received and any gain realized on the sale of the stock, and

- The investor company agrees to make the employee/director whole for tax consequences and other expenses of the compensation arrangement.

.09 "Golden Leash" Disclosure

When an investor has the right to appoint one of its employees/partners to the board of a corporation and the investor provides a separate compensation arrangement to that director, it is referred to as a "golden leash." Nasdaq imposes a disclosure requirement on corporations that have golden leash arrangements. The rule is aimed at the potential for perceived conflicts that may arise when a third-party investment group appoints a director and maintains a separate or additional compensation arrangements for that director, which "may lead to conflicts of interest among directors, call into question their ability to satisfy their fiduciary duties [and] tend to promote a focus on short-term results at the expense of long-term value creation." Nasdaq Rule 5250(b)(3), which the SEC approved in 2016, provides as follows:

> Rule 5250(b)(3) requires listed companies to publicly disclose the material terms of all agreements and arrangements between any director or nominee and any person or entity (other than the Company) relating to compensation or other payment in connection with that person's candidacy or service as a director. The terms "compensation" and "other payment" as used in this rule are not limited to cash payments and are intended to be construed broadly.

> Subject to exceptions provided in the rule, the disclosure must be made on or through the Company's website or in the proxy or information statement for the next shareholders' meeting at which directors are elected in order to provide shareholders with information and sufficient time to help them make meaningful voting decisions. A Company posting the requisite disclosure on or through its website must make it publicly available no later than the date on which the Company files a proxy or information statement in connection with such shareholders' meeting (or, if they do not file proxy or information statements, no later than when the Company files its next Form 10-K or Form 20-F). Disclosure made available on the Company's website or through it by hyperlinking to another website, must be continuously accessible. If the website hosting the disclosure subsequently becomes inaccessible or that hyperlink inoperable, the company must promptly restore it or make other disclosure in accordance with this rule.

Rule 5250(b)(3) does not separately require the initial disclosure of newly entered into agreements or arrangements, *e.g.*, on Form 8-K, provided that disclosure is made pursuant to the rule for the next shareholders' meeting at which directors are elected.

¶565 Sarbanes-Oxley Act of 2002 and Dodd-Frank Act of 2010

In any financial scandal or financial collapse, a certain percentage of commentators and politicians blame companies' directors. Subsequent legislation usually increases the requirements applicable to directors.

.01 Sarbanes-Oxley Act of 2002

In an effort to restore investor confidence in the wake of widely publicized corporate scandals such as Enron, WorldCom, and Global Crossing, President Bush signed into law the Sarbanes-Oxley Act of 2002 ("SOX") in July 2002.[46] SOX contains several provisions affecting boards of directors.

SOX Section 301 adds a new paragraph (m) to Section 10A of the Exchange Act, providing that the SEC must direct the national securities exchanges and the NASD to prohibit the listing of any security of a company that does not have an Audit Committee composed entirely of independent directors. SOX does not consider a director who receives any consulting, advisory or other compensatory fee from the company other than director and committee fees as independent. As discussed below, all public companies (not just listed companies) must disclose in their SEC filings whether the Audit Committee has at least one member who is a financial expert or explain the reasons for not having such a member. For a non-listed company, this requirement will in effect require the public company to disclose whether it has an Audit Committee.

SOX Section 407 required the SEC to adopt rules requiring corporations to disclose whether at least one member of the Audit Committee is a "financial expert," as that term is ultimately defined by the SEC and, if not, the reasons therefor. The factors to be considered by the SEC in defining "financial expert" include a member's education and experience generally in accounting and auditing matters, experience in preparing or auditing financial statements of generally comparable public companies, and experience with the application of accounting principles in connection with accounting for estimates, accruals and reserves.

Under SOX, the Audit Committee, rather than the board of directors, is responsible for the appointment, compensation (appropriate funding to be provided by the public company), and oversight of the auditor. These duties include resolution of disagreements between management and the auditor. The Audit Committee must have the authority to engage independent counsel and other advisors whose fees the corporation must pay. The auditor must issue a report to the Audit Committee that discusses all critical accounting policies and practices to be used, all alternative GAAP treatments of financial information that have been discussed with management, the ramifications of the use of such alternatives, and the treatment preferred by the auditor. The corporation must submit all other material written communications between it and the auditor, such as the management letter and any schedule of unadjusted differences, to the Audit Committee. The report to the Audit Committee must also include the auditor's report on the public company's system of internal controls, as discussed above. Finally, SOX requires Audit Committees to establish procedures for the confidential, anonymous submission by employees of concerns regarding questionable accounting or auditing matters.

SOX does not create new bases for D&O suits, but does increase exposure to criminal fines, penalties and sanctions for non-compliance. Generally, it is not

---

[46] P.L. 107-204.

expected that SOX, in and of itself, will increase frequency or severity of civil claims against directors and officers.

.02 Dodd-Frank Act Imposes Compensation Committee Independence Requirements

President Obama signed into law the Dodd-Frank Act in July 2010. The Dodd-Frank Act imposed additional requirements on compensation committees.

Section 952 of the Dodd-Frank Act added a new section 10C to the Exchange Act, which requires the SEC to promulgate rules that direct the NYSE, Nasdaq, and other national securities exchanges and associations to prohibit the listing of any equity security of a company that does not have an independent compensation committee. In determining the definition of the term "independence," the national securities exchanges and associations must consider relevant factors to be determined and published by the SEC, including: (A) the source of compensation of a member of the company's board of directors, including any consulting, advisory, or other compensatory fee paid by the company to such member; and (B) whether a member of the company's board is affiliated with the company, or a subsidiary or affiliate of the company.

Most public companies will already satisfy the independent compensation committee requirement, due to their compliance with Code Sec. 162(m) and the current stock exchange rules. Companies that most likely will be affected by this requirement are those with significant investments from private equity funds. The SEC may apply its traditional definition of "affiliate," which is: "a person that directly or indirectly controls, or is controlled by, or is under common control with, the issuer, with a presumption that more than 10% direct or indirect ownership of a an issuer creates affiliate status." If so, then a representative of a private equity fund owning more than 10% (or of a group of private funds acting in concert and owning in the aggregate more than 10%) of a public portfolio company would be precluded from serving on the company's compensation committee, subject to the "controlled company" exception of the statute. However, this is very much up in the air awaiting final SEC rules, because, in its proposed rules from March 2011, the SEC expressly declined to adopt a definition of "affiliate," so as to give the stock exchanges the flexibility to define the term and acknowledged that "directors affiliated with significant investors (such as private equity funds or venture capital firms) . . . are highly motivated to rigorously oversee compensation and are well-positioned to exercise independent judgment regarding compensation."

The SEC's rules must provide a procedure for a listed company to cure any "independence" defects before it is de-listed. The SEC's rules also will permit the national securities exchange or association to exempt a particular relationship from the compensation committee independence requirements, taking into consideration the listed company's size and any other relevant factors.

Note, this requirement will not apply to a controlled company, a limited partnership, an open-ended management investment company that is registered under the Investment Company Act of 1940, a foreign private issuer that provides annual disclosures to shareholders of the reasons that the foreign private issuer does not have an independent compensation committee, or a company that is in bankruptcy proceedings.

.03 Dodd-Frank Disclosure of Hedging by Directors Requirement

Dodd-Frank Act Section 955 added a new subsection 14(j) to the Exchange Act, "Disclosure of Hedging by Employees and Directors." This section requires the SEC to require companies to disclose in their annual proxy statement whether the company permits any employee or director (or any designee of such employee or director) to purchase financial instruments (including prepaid variable forward contracts, equity swaps, collars, and exchange funds) that are designed to hedge or offset any decrease in the market value of equity securities (1) granted to the employee or director by the company as part of the compensation; or (2) held, directly or indirectly, by the employee or director. The obvious aim of this provision is to encourage companies to adopt policies that prohibit hedging transactions. Investors want execs to own large amounts of company stock [not hedged] so they will manage for long-term gains, not just a short-term pop with devastating long-term effect. Section 955 does not require any company to adopt such a policy, but we expect that most will do so.

.04 Elimination of Discretionary Voting by Brokers on Executive Compensation (and other) Matters

Section 957 of the Dodd-Frank Act amended Section 6(b) of the Exchange Act to provide that national securities exchanges must prohibit brokers from voting shares they do not beneficially own in connection with the election of directors and other executive compensation matters, unless the beneficial owner of the security has instructed the broker to vote the proxy in accordance with the voting instructions of the beneficial owner. Previously, the approval of equity plans were non-routine matters upon which brokers were not permitted to vote uninstructed shares and beginning in 2009, the NYSE amended its Rule 452 to eliminate broker voting of uninstructed shares in uncontested director elections. Inasmuch as every public company has some portion of its outstanding equity securities held in "street name" on behalf of their beneficial owners, this new provision affects all public companies.

¶575 Advisory Board Members

Some corporations will create a separate "board" to advise or assist the corporation or the regular board of directors in some way. These may be referred to as "advisory boards" or "technology boards." These advisory or technology boards do not have the special legal status and responsibilities accorded to true boards of directors under U.S. corporate law. The members of these boards also do not face the same potential liability as true corporate board members. Accordingly, members of advisory or technology boards generally receive significantly less (or no) compensation. The corporation generally pays these board members solely in stock or stock equivalent awards.

Advisory boards are common with corporations based outside of the United States with significant operations in the United States. Technology boards are common with corporations involved in extremely technical or scientific areas that individuals serving on the regular board may not understand. Individuals appointed to a corporation's advisory board have neither the responsibilities nor the liabilities of true board members.

Example: ABC Corporation is a start-up technology company. ABC's board consists solely of its founders and an investor representative. Although ABC's founders are experts in their field of technology, they decide that they could use some "adult supervision." For this reason, and to create networking opportunities with potential customers and suppliers, ABC creates an advisory board and appoints several experienced technology company executives. To incent these advisory board members to offer advice and present networking opportunities, ABC awards each member of the advisory board 1,000 shares of restricted stock.

¶585 Directors' Deferred Compensation

Most companies make some form of deferred fee plan or arrangement available to their non-employee directors. Like the deferred compensation of corporate officers, directors' deferred fees are subject to Code Sec. 409A.

Code Sec. 409A, added by the American Jobs Creation Act of 2004, is entitled "Inclusion in Gross Income of Deferred Compensation Under Nonqualified Deferred Compensation Plans." Code Sec. 409A applies to any plan or arrangement that provides for the deferral of compensation by a "service provider." The failure to comply with 409A results in immediate income on deferrals, an excise tax of 20% and other penalties.

Under Code Sec. 409A, the director generally must elect to defer the receipt of his or her retainer and/or fees before the start of the year for which the retainer and fees are payable to avoid taxation. As with the deferred compensation of corporate officers, directors' deferred fee accounts must remain an unfunded, unsecured promise to pay benefits in the future. In addition, like the deferred compensation of corporate officers, directors' deferred fee plans often provide for immediate distribution upon a change in control of the company. However, no plan or arrangement should put board members in the position of having to decide the acceleration of vesting of their own compensation. Similarly, if deferred compensation or other retirement benefit amounts are to be funded in a rabbi trust, the decision on whether to prefund non-employee directors' benefits in this manner should be made separately from the decision for other employees and, preferably, not by the affected directors.

¶595 Surge in Litigation Over Directors' Compensation

For decades, there was little litigation over directors' compensation. In an early case, *Steiner v. Meyerson*,[47] the non-employee directors received an annual

---

[47] *Steiner v. Meyerson*, No. 13,139 (Del. Ch. 1995), contained in 21 Del. J. Corp. L. 320 (1995).

retainer of $20,000, between $1,250 and $2,500 for each meeting attended, consulting fees ranging from $10,000 to $30,000 per year, an option to purchase 25,000 shares upon election to the board, and 10,000 shares per year while a board member—all amounting to perhaps $100,000 a year. In dismissing the plaintiffs' claim of excessive compensation, the court noted that there is no single format that corporations must follow to pay their directors, and that the dollar amount is not the most important aspect of director compensation.[48]

However, litigation against companies and boards of directors over non-employee directors' compensation began to increase dramatically after 2012. In these lawsuits, the plaintiffs typically allege that the compensation of the non-employee directors was excessive, unauthorized, or otherwise improper.

In the past, plaintiffs' lawyers brought lawsuits against companies, boards of directors, and executives alleging waste or excessive executive compensation, without much success. The reason these lawsuits never gained much traction is because of the protections of the demand requirement and the business judgment rule. Recently, some plaintiffs' lawyers have employed a new strategy to circumvent the demand requirement and the business judgment rule with respect to non-employee director compensation.

By circumventing the demand requirement and the business judgment rule, the odds of a lawsuit surviving a defendant's motion to dismiss is greatly increased, which, in turn, greatly increases the potential for a nuisance settlement with the company and busy board members. Nuisance settlements occur because after the motion to dismiss stage, the costs to the targeted company and its directors in legal fees and directors' time rapidly begin to exceed the costs to settle the matter. Of course, the biggest costs to companies in most nuisance settlements (and sometimes the only cost, other than its own attorneys' fees) are paying for the plaintiffs' attorneys fees.

Four lawsuits against the directors at Republic Services, Inc., Unilife Corporation, Facebook Inc., and Citrix Systems, Inc., illustrate the key factors in this increase in litigation. As discussed further below, in each of these lawsuits, the Delaware Court of Chancery declined to dismiss a lawsuit against the company's directors. However, the current state of the law is described in *In re Investors Bancorp, Inc. Shareholder Litigation*, discussed below.[49]

How Did We Get Here? In 1996, the Securities and Exchange Commission updated regulations under Section 16(b) of the Exchange Act, as amended, in order to relax the requirements under Section 16(b) for awards issued to insiders.[50] As part of this update, the SEC provided a general exemption for equity award grants to insiders, provided, among other alternatives, the terms of the disposition are approved in advance by the board of directors or a non-employee director committee. The SEC stated that part of the rationale for the SEC's changes to the Section 16(b) requirements was because in 1995 the Treasury

---

[48] *Steiner v. Meyerson*, No. 13,139 (Del. Ch. 1995), 21 Del. J. Corp. L. 320, 332 (1995).

[49] 2017 WL 6374741 (Del. Dec. 19, 2017).

[50] *See Ownership Reports and Trading by Officers, Directors and Principal Security Holders*, Release 34-37260 (1996) (adopting release for 1996 rule changes).

Department finalized rules regarding Code Sec. 162(m), as amended. The SEC felt that the prior Section 16(b) requirements were too onerous in light of the amendments to the Code Sec. 162(m) requirements.

Prior to this update, among other requirements, most companies had director-only plans that provided for grants to directors under a formula plan requirement. These plans were structured in this way in order to make sure the transaction was exempt from the prior Section 16(b) requirements. As discussed in *Calmara*, most of these plans were protected from non-employee director compensation litigation because they contained specific non-employee director compensation limits, which were approved by shareholders.

Since the SEC adopted the changes in 1996, companies generally migrated towards providing for equity awards to non-employee directors from the same equity incentive plan that the company uses to provide awards to officers and employees. This makes sense from an administrative perspective and transaction cost perspective, as there is no need for the company to maintain two plan documents, seek shareholder approval of two plans, create two prospectuses, file two Form S-8s, etc.

In the migration into one equity incentive plan, the director-specific limit that was in the director-only plans was no longer required, so they were slowly dropped in the process. Rather, most equity plans contained one limit in the plan that applied to all participants. This was typically the limit that was consistent with the requirement under Code Sec. 162(m), which had its regulations finalized in December 1995.[51]

Securities Plaintiffs' Attorneys' Template for Surviving a Motion to Dismiss. However, a plaintiff's attorney can get around both the demand requirement and nullify the protection of the business judgment rule when an equity incentive plan does not provide for a meaningful limit on non-employee director compensation when alleging companies excessively paid their directors.

Because the shareholders' ability to institute an action on behalf of a corporation inherently impinges upon the directors' power to manage the affairs of the corporation the Delaware corporate law imposes certain prerequisites on a stockholder's right to sue derivatively. For that reason, under Delaware corporate law (and the law of most other jurisdictions), a condition precedent to filing a shareholder derivative suit is to file a demand with the company's board of directors that the board of directors investigate and/or bring legal action to remedy an alleged wrong against the company, *e.g.*, paying excessive compensation to its officers and directors.

Under Delaware law, a "demand" is excused if a plaintiff pleads facts with particularity that demonstrates the futility of making a demand on the board.

---

[51] As background, it is important to note that this limit is drafted to help the plan provide qualified performance based compensation under Code Sec. 162(m). Treas. Reg. 1.162-27(e)(e)(vi) states that in order for stock options and stock appreciation rights to qualify as performance-based compensation, among other requirements, there must be a limit as to the maximum number of shares that a participant may be granted. Since Code Sec. 162(m) does not provide a realistic ceiling on this limit, typically, plans are drafted in anticipation of never actually being reached.

Unfortunately for companies, getting the demand excused in derivative claims regarding director compensation is relatively easy because Delaware law is skeptical as to whether an individual can fairly and impartially consider whether to have the corporation initiate litigation challenging his or her own compensation, regardless of whether or not that compensation is material on a personal level. The vernacular for this sort of allegation is self-dealing. In general, because the demand typically revolves around whether or not a majority of the entire board received appropriate compensation, it becomes perfunctory for the plaintiff to show that the majority of the board was interested in the alleged transaction, and therefore, the court can rather easily find that the demand is excused.

What About the Business Judgment Rule? Delaware courts examine the merits of a claim for breach of fiduciary duty (and similar claims) through one of two standards relative to director compensation litigation: (i) business judgment rule and (ii) entire fairness test.

For boards, the beauty of the business judgment rule is that plaintiffs must show that the board's decision was not attributed to any rational business purpose. This standard is notoriously difficult to meet. However, if a plaintiff can adequately allege that the directors' should not be granted the benefits of the business judgment rule, the burden of flips to the directors to prove to the court's satisfaction that the transaction was the product of both fair dealing and fair price (otherwise known as the entire fairness test).

The problem in the area of non-employee director compensation, is that when directors are approving compensation to themselves, there is self-dealing involved, which means the directors are interested in the transaction (as discussed above). When directors are interested in the disputed transaction, they cannot seek the protections of the business judgment rule, unless the transaction is approved by shareholders. Instead, the directors must meet the strict requirements of the entire fairness test, which normally precludes the court from granting a motion to dismiss. The inability to be granted a motion to dismiss means a windfall to plaintiffs' attorneys in the form of nuisance settlements.

First Case of Its Kind. Plaintiffs' lawyers first discovered the possibility of avoiding the demand requirement in an executive compensation lawsuit almost accidentally, when the Delaware Court of Chancery in *Seinfeld v. Slager*[52] reviewed the plaintiffs' final cause of action (which plaintiffs' counsel seemed to have added to the complaint as an afterthought). In *Seinfeld*, plaintiffs sued each member of Republic's board of directors alleging that the defendant directors paid themselves excessive compensation, in addition to other claims regarding the compensation Republic paid its executives.

The court dismissed the executive compensation claims because of the plaintiffs' failure to file a demand with the company's board of directors, reaffirming numerous earlier decisions on executive compensation. However, the court did not outright dismiss the plaintiffs' claim about the director's compensa-

---

[52] 2012 WL 2501105 (Del. Ch. June 2012).

tion because the directors were interested in the granting of awards to themselves.

The court stated that the equity plan lacked sufficient definition to afford the directors the benefits of the business judgment rule because the stockholders did not impose a meaningful limit on the directors via the equity plan. The court went on to say that if a board is free to use its absolute discretion under even a stockholder-approved plan, with little guidance as to the total pay that can be awarded, a board will ultimately have to show that the transaction is entirely fair because the directors are inherently interested in the transaction.

Therefore, the court held the board's self-interested decision to award bonuses to each director must be evaluated for entire fairness and the motion to dismiss related to this count was denied.

Immediately after *Seinfeld v. Slager*, we began recommending that clients amend their incentive stock plans from which non-employee director awards were made to add a meaningful limit on the value or the number of shares awarded under such plans.

Lawsuit Against Unilife's Directors. In *Cambridge Retirement System v. Bosnjak*[53], the aggrieved plaintiffs brought shareholder derivative claims for breach of fiduciary duty and corporate waste against Unilife's directors concerning stock awards and cash compensation the directors had paid to themselves dating back to November 2010. Unilife and the directors had moved to dismiss the complaint for failure to make a pre-suit demand. However, the plaintiffs successfully alleged that the demand was excused because five of the six members of the Unilife board at the time the action was filed were personally interested in their own compensation for their service as directors, which was the subject of the claims in this litigation.

While the court did excuse the pre-suit demand, the court found that the claims regarding the non-employee directors' stock awards grants to themselves should be dismissed because Unilife followed the unusual procedure of conditioning all equity grants to board members on obtaining shareholder approval, which the shareholders had provided. With that being said, the court did allow the plaintiffs' allegations regarding cash compensation paid to one of the directors to proceed because that compensation was not predicated on shareholder approval. On June 4, 2015, the parties entered into a Memorandum of Understanding agreeing to the basic terms of a non-monetary settlement of the action.

Lawsuit Against Facebook's Directors. The shareholder derivative complaint against Facebook and each of its directors, *Espinoza v. Zuckerberg, et al.*[54], alleged breach of fiduciary duty, waste of corporate assets, and unjust enrichment against Facebook and its directors. As in *Seinfeld*, the court found that the plaintiff adequately alleged that the demand requirement was excused and the business judgment rule did not apply because the directors were interested parties when they granted awards to themselves and the decision to grant the

---

[53] 2014 WL 2930869 (Del. Ch. June 2014). [54] 124 A. 3d 47 (Del. Ch. 2015).

equity awards lacked proper shareholder approval. In this case, the total limit on the amount of stock issuable under the equity plan was 25 million shares and the annual limit to any one individual was 2.5 million shares. At the then-current trading price, 2.5 million Facebook shares were worth approximately $145 million, which theoretically meant the directors could have awarded themselves that much in compensation.

Interestingly, the defendants did not elect to dispute whether the demand was excused and conceded this point (apparently, the defendants felt they would not be able to successfully argue this point in light of the *Seinfeld* case discussed above). Rather, Facebook argued that its controlling shareholder Mark Zuckerberg properly provided the shareholder approval to ratify the compensation paid to its directors, which, if true, meant that the board would be granted the benefit of the business judgment rule. The court found that neither Mr. Zuckerberg's affidavit nor his deposition testimony ratified the directors' decision to approve the directors' compensation in 2013 because such ratification attempts failed to follow the corporate formalities required by Delaware law. Accordingly, the court denied defendants' motion for summary judgment with respect to plaintiff's allegations that the directors breached their fiduciary duties and were unjustly enriched in granting equity awards to themselves.

The defendants agreed to the following settlement with the plaintiff:

1. Submit to a stockholders vote at its 2016 annual meeting, the following separate proposals for stockholder approval (that the non-employee directors abstain from voting on):

   a. A proposal to approve the 2013 grants to the non-employee directors and

   b. A proposal to approve the annual compensation program for non-employee directors, which includes a specific amount for annual equity grants and delineates the annual retainer fees, for use by the board going forward;

2. Make certain governance reforms, by amending the Compensation & Governance Committee Charter; and

3. Pay an award of attorneys' fees and expenses to plaintiff's counsel not to exceed $525,000.

Lawsuit Against Citrix's Directors. In *Calma*, the court produced a lengthy opinion that summarized and reaffirmed the relevant case law. The plaintiff challenged equity awards made to non-employee directors of Citrix, under an equity plan, approved by shareholders that stated no participant could receive more than one million shares per calendar year (this comes out to be a limit of roughly $55 million when the action was filed) as excessive. Therefore, the plaintiff sought recovery due to: (i) the directors' breach of fiduciary duty and (ii) the directors' unjustly enriching themselves, among other allegations. As in *Seinfeld*, the court found that the demand requirement was excused because of the alleged self-dealing and the lack of a meaningful limit on non-employee director compensation in the equity incentive plan.

Interestingly, in *Calma*, the defendants forcefully argued that there was well over 60 years of precedent indicating that the shareholder's approval of the equity plan limit was proper. And because of the shareholder approval of that limit, the approval of the equity awards to the directors should be granted the benefits of the business judgment rule due to shareholder ratification. The court reviewed the case law and felt differently.

The court stated that it was pretty clear that stockholder approval was only appropriate if meaningful limits were provided regarding the awards to the directors. Specifically, the court cited the *Seinfeld* opinion to buttress this opinion.

Accordingly, the court stated that the defendants did not carry the burden of establishing shareholder ratification as an affirmative defense to having to prove the entire fairness of the transaction. Therefore, the court denied the defendants' motion to dismiss the breach of fiduciary duty and unjust enrichment claims.

Citrix agreed to the following settlement with the plaintiff:

1. Submit to a stockholders vote at its 2016 annual meeting a proposal that the equity plan will be amended to cap equity compensation to non-employee directors at $795,000 per year;

2. Enhance disclosure in the Citrix's 2017 director compensation practices portion of the proxy;

3. Make certain governance reforms, by amending the Compensation Committee Charter; and

4. Pay an award of attorneys' fees and expenses to plaintiff's counsel not to exceed $425,000.

Entire Fairness. In *Williams v. Ji*,[55] the plaintiff sued the directors of Sorrento Therapeutics for breach of fiduciary duty over the directors' decision to grant themselves options and warrants for the stock of five subsidiary companies. Shortly before or after the options grants, the board transferred valuable assets and opportunities of the corporation to the subsidiaries. The board members sought a dismissal of the lawsuit, claiming that their actions were protected by the business judgment rule. In June 2017, the Delaware Chancery Court disagreed, finding that the more rigorous entire fairness standard applied to the equity awards.

Every member of the board at the time of the grants was interested in them, as each received options. Thus, entire fairness review applied, as long as the plaintiff had pled some specific facts suggesting unfairness in the options and warrant grants. The court found that the plaintiff's allegations gave rise to a reasonable inference of unfair dealing. Consequently, the burden at trial was shifted to the board to show that the grants were both:

- fair in terms of how they were disclosed and structured, and

- fair compensation for services rendered to the company.

---

[55] C.A. No. 12729-VCMR (Del. Ch. 2017).

Fair Dealing: According to the court, the fair dealing inquiry must address the questions of when the transaction was timed, how it was initiated, structured, negotiated, and disclosed to the directors, and how the approvals of the directors were obtained. As to process, the plaintiff had alleged that no one other than the interested directors independently approved the grants. Stockholder approval of the grants or a limited plan allowing such grants could have removed the taint of self-interest. However, the company had not requested stockholders' approval of the grants or any plan to make them. The grants were also made around the same time as the company transferred valuable assets or opportunities to the subsidiaries. The directors had argued that the grants were "routine compensation pursuant to the subsidiaries' stock option plans." However, the grants were not disclosed as non-executive directors' compensation in the company's 2016 proxy statement. Instead, they were disclosed as related-party transactions. Only five days before director nominations were due to the board, the company disclosed for the first time that it had caused the subsidiaries to issue the grants. Those allegations gave rise to at least a reasonably conceivable inference of unfair process.

Fair Price: The fair price aspect of the test ensures that the transaction was substantively fair by examining the economic and financial considerations. As to this test, the court observed that the complaint had alleged that one of the directors, Henry Ji, alone was granted the right to acquire 25% of the voting power of LA Cell and 18% of its economic value (in excess of $170 million). Taken as true, the value of that compensation was large enough to plead sufficiently that the grants were excessive. The directors must prove that the grants were entirely fair to the company, which they had not done at this stage.

The court acknowledged that directors may be compensated for additional service in managing subsidiaries. The court also stated that a mere disagreement cannot serve as grounds for imposing liability based on alleged breaches of fiduciary duty where there is no reasonable doubt as to the disinterest of or absence of fraud by the board. However, the court rejected the defendant/board members' argument that the award of options and warrant in this case were typical compensation decisions subject to business judgment review.

Williams v. Ji seems to be a surprisingly bald case of self-interested overreach by the directors and the CEO and, therefore, may not be instructive to readers. However, an axiom among lawyers is that "bad facts make bad law." In this case, the court helped fine-tune the entire fairness review process. This was not a final decision in the case, but it allowed the plaintiff to proceed to trial over its allegations.

Related Development. During the same period that plaintiffs and the Delaware courts were expanding the litigation risks for the compensation decisions of non-employee directors, the Delaware courts were expanding their scrutiny of the disinterested status of directors. Two of the earliest (or at least most widely publicized) lawsuits to challenge the disinterested status of non-employee directors, involved Martha Stewart Living and Oracle Corporation. In *Beam v. Stew-*

art,[56] the Delaware Supreme Court declined to hold that certain board members lacked independence due to personal friendships (*e.g.*, Martha Stewart and certain of the non-employee directors attended the same weddings and parties) and outside business interests.

In December 2016, the Delaware Supreme Court, sitting *en banc* reversed the decision of the Delaware Court of Chancery, which had dismissed a shareholder derivative suit for the failure to satisfy the demand requirement. In *Sandys v. Pincus*,[57] the court found that at least five of the non-employee directors were not necessarily independent, and therefore, the burden to prove independence shifted to the defendants. Of these, two had been involved in the transaction that was the subject of the lawsuit (these two were easy), one was the co-owner of a private airplane and "close family friends" with Pincus (the controlling stockholder and former Chairman and CEO), and two were partners at a large private equity firm that had "a mutually beneficial network of ongoing business relations with Pincus and [another director named in the lawsuit] that they are not likely to risk by causing Zynga to sue them." With respect to these last two, the court also found it persuasive that the company's own public disclosures stated that the board had determined that they did not qualify as independent directors under the Nasdaq Listing Rules.

Neither of these cases involved executive or director compensation. However, the independence of non-employee directors is at the core of many of the defendants' motions to dismiss.

What Does All of This Mean to Boards? No one who can spell "equity" believes that the Facebook non-employee directors would award themselves anything approaching $145 million (especially, considering that it has a majority controlling shareholder in Mr. Zuckerberg who probably would not "like" that decision). Presumably, at the very least, ISS would have a similar problem in Citrix's situation. However, based on current Delaware case law, all that matters to excuse the Delaware demand requirement and usurp the protection of the business judgment rule, is that they *could* make such an award under the terms of the equity incentive plan.

Based on our analysis, it seems that the Delaware courts have decided that they want the ability to second-guess limits that shareholders have approved. Implicitly, it seems that Delaware courts would like equity incentive plans to have limits more similar to the prior Section 16(b) limits, as opposed to the current Code Sec. 162(m) limits. In our opinion, this sort of second-guessing is what the business judgment rule is designed to protect against. However, regardless of our views, it seems that not adopting a meaningful limit with respect to non-employee director compensation is an unnecessary risk to carry.

Investors Bancorp. In 2017, the Delaware Supreme Court reversed an earlier decision of the Chancery Court in favor of directors, *In re Investors Bancorp, Inc. Shareholder Litigation. Investors Bancorp* represents the current state of the law. Also, the court implicitly overturned much of the analysis in the *Bosnjak* (Unilife),

---

[56] 845 A.2d 1040 (Del. 2004).   [57] 2016 Del. LEXIS 627 (Del. 2016).

Citrix (Calma), and other cases, reversing the trend of decisions in favor of directors, and casting doubt on whether any decision of directors as to their own compensation is protected from court review.

The Equity Incentive Plan ("EIP") at Investors Bancorp contained explicit limits on awards to non-employee directors and had been disclosed to and approved by stockholders. The Chancery Court had observed that "[c]ritically, this plan included director-specific limits that differed from the limits that applied to awards to other beneficiaries under the plan." Citing the decisions in *Calma on Behalf of Citrix Systems, Inc. v. Templeton* ("Citrix") and *In re 3COM Corp. Stockholders Litig.*, the Chancery Court held that the fully informed stockholder vote that approved the plan extended to the awards themselves, which indisputably fell within the limits set by the plan.

However, foreshadowing the Supreme Court's reversal, the Chancery Court indicated that it would not automatically waive through all non-employee director awards under stockholder approved equity compensation plans – even plans with limits on awards to non-employee directors. The court noted that in some cases, it has determined that the purported limit on the total amount of equity compensation allowed under a plan approved by stockholders "was, in fact, no limit at all." In such cases, the court warned, it would refuse to deem approval of the overall plan as an approval of any specific awards directors might give themselves and, instead, review the awards under the entire fairness standard of review.

The Delaware Supreme Court essentially found that the purported limit on equity awards under the EIP approved by stockholders was, in fact, no limit at all. The Supreme Court explained that director action is "twice-tested," first for legal authorization, and second by equity. The Investors Bancorp stockholders had granted the directors the legal authority to make awards. But the directors still must exercise that authority consistent with their fiduciary duties.

> Given that the actual awards are self-interested decisions not approved by the stockholders, if the directors acted inequitably when making the awards, their "inequitable action does not become permissible simply because it is legally possible" [fn]under the general authority granted by the stockholders.

The court seems to approve explicitly two forms of non-employee director compensation for which stockholder approval will serve as a defense in support of a motion to dismiss.

- First, when the directors submit specific compensation decisions for approval by fully informed, uncoerced, and disinterested stockholders; and

- Second, self-executing plans, meaning plans that make awards over time based on fixed criteria, with the specific amounts and terms approved by the stockholders.

In contrast, when stockholders approve an equity incentive plan that "gives the directors discretion to grant themselves awards within general parameters, *and* a stockholder properly alleges that the directors inequitably exercised that discretion, then the ratification defense is unavailable to dismiss the suit, and the directors will be required to prove the fairness of the awards to the corporation." [Emphasis added.]The *"and"* is important for the reasons set forth below.

Bad Facts. Importantly, *Investors Bancorp* was a "bad facts" case (and bad facts make bad law). The awards at issues *were not your usual director awards* – and the plan's limits were not typical of those we would recommend. The Supreme Court observed the following:

- The equity plan left it to the discretion of the non-employee directors to allocate up to 30% of all option or restricted stock shares available as awards to themselves. There was no annual or per-director limit.

- Each non-employee director was paid more than *$2,100,000* in 2015, the year being challenged. This amount was higher than the director pay at every Wall Street firm that year. This amount also significantly exceeded the non-employee directors' compensation in 2014, which ranged from $97,200 to $207,005.94. It also far surpassed the $198,000 median pay at similarly sized companies and the $260,000 median pay at much larger companies.

- The awards were more than twenty-three times the $87,556 median award granted to other companies' non- employee directors after a mutual-to-stock conversion similar to that which the company had completed.

- The directors "held a series of nearly contemporaneous meetings that resulted in awards to both the non-employee directors and the executive directors" which led the court to declare that it was "implausible to us that the non-employee directors could independently consider a demand when to do so would require those directors to call into question the grants they made to themselves."

The Supreme Court's decision in *Investors Bancorp* could easily be read as a smack-down of egregious conduct rather than a giant step back from the line of cases that had approved awards to non-employee directors under a stockholders-approved equity plan that included limits on the amount of shares that could be awarded to the directors.

How to Interpret *Investors Bancorp*. Some have argued that the *Investors Bancorp* decision may be read to preclude the Delaware courts from dismissing any claim of fiduciary breach involving self-interested discretionary director self-compensation decisions. Meaningful limits in an equity (or other) plan approved by stockholders will not protect compensation awards within those limits. We believe that reading is too narrow. Instead, we believe the *Investors Bancorp* decision should be read to clarify that, in the words of the court, the Delaware doctrine of stockholder ratification does not embrace a "blank check" theory.

In its own words, the court sought to "balance the competing concerns—utility of the ratification defense and the need for judicial scrutiny of certain self-interested discretionary acts by directors—by focusing on the specificity of the acts submitted to the stockholders for approval." The court found that "generic limits" on director compensation, even if later approved by stockholders, are not enough. Put another way, "meaningful" means meaningful.

¶595

The Supreme Court's decision did not actually find the directors liable for a breach of fiduciary duty or corporate waste. The decision only allows the plaintiff to avoid the stockholder demand requirements of state law and proceed with their claims to trial (or settlement).

Chapter 6
STOCK INCENTIVE PLAN DESIGN AND ISSUES

¶601 Overview—Stock Incentive Plan Design and Issues

Stock incentive plans are among the most complicated types of compensation plans for a company and its advisors to design. Few plans will mean so much to the company, its employees, and its stockholders as a stock incentive plan. Additionally, a plethora of tax and securities laws, as well as accounting considerations, will affect nearly every provision of the plan. Among the design and structural issues the company and its legal counsel will face are the following:

- The type of stock-based awards to make available under the plan;
- The number of shares authorized for awards under the plan;
- Who will administer the stock plan;
- What employees and other persons or entities will be eligible for awards under the plan; and
- Vesting of awards.

The company and its counsel also may need to consider a number of issues that are unique to stock option plans and to private companies' plans.

.01 Types of Awards

Even if the company's intent is to only award stock options under the plan, experienced legal counsel generally suggests drafting the plan more broadly to authorize other stock-based awards, such as restricted stock and stock appreciation rights. Many companies also draft their stock incentive plans to permit the company to grant both incentive stock options ("ISOs") and non-incentive stock options ("NISOs") (see ¶615).

.02 Number of Shares Authorized Under the Stock Plan

The company should determine the number of shares to authorize for awards under the plan. The plan document would specify the number or percentage of shares that the company's board of directors or stockholders has authorized for awards.

This is an important decision for all companies, but particularly for public companies. Public companies generally must seek and receive the approval of stockholders for a number of shares authorized for awards under the plan. Both public and private companies face important stockholder dilution issues when authorizing shares for award under a plan (see ¶625).

.03 Plan Administration

Every stock incentive plan must address the issue of who will have discretionary authority over, and otherwise administer, the plan. The duties of the plan administrator include determining who will receive awards, determining the types of awards and the terms of those awards, providing for the payment or settlement of awards, interpreting the provisions of the plan and seeing to the day-to-day administration of the plan (see ¶635).

.04 Eligibility for Awards

No plan document would be complete without a clear definition of who is eligible to participate in and/or receive awards under the plan. Code Sec. 422 provides that only employees can receive incentive stock options, and Code Sec. 162(m) provides that a stock incentive plan must specify the class of individuals that is eligible to receive awards under the plan. Additionally, federal securities laws and stock exchange regulations may require a public company to describe the individuals eligible to receive stock awards (see ¶645).

.05 Vesting of Stock Awards

For retention purposes, most companies provide for stock options, restricted stock, and other awards to vest over a period of three to five years. Companies and their advisors also need to consider the impact on vesting of a change in control, or the death or disability of the award recipient. Vesting also has an impact on taxation for certain types of awards (see ¶655 and ¶665).

.06 Plan Provisions Unique to Stock Option Plans and Awards

In addition to the plan design features described elsewhere in this chapter, stock option plans must cover issues such as the permitted methods for paying the option exercise price and for how long the option will remain exercisable after the optionee terminates employment (see ¶675).

.07 Dilution and Overhang Problems

"Overhang" refers to the total amount of shares awarded and authorized for award under all of a company's stock-based plans, as a percentage of the company's total outstanding stock. Stockholders generally dislike overhang because it dilutes the value of their stockholdings. Companies have several alternatives for dealing with overhang problems, each with certain advantages and disadvantages (see ¶685).

.08 Special Issues for Private Company Stock Plans

By their nature, private companies are less likely to award restricted stock or options to purchase stock. More often, these companies award phantom stock or stock appreciation rights (see Chapter 9 [¶901 et seq.] for a detailed discussion of phantom stock and stock appreciation rights). In addition to the issues described above, privately held companies face a variety of special issues, mostly related to the fact that there is no market for the companies' stock once an employee or other award recipient acquires it. Among these issues are:

¶601.03

- Put rights;
- Call rights;
- Tag along rights;
- Drag along rights; and
- Registration rights.

(See ¶695 for a detailed discussion of plan provisions unique to private company stock plans.)

¶615 Types of Awards

One of the most critical plan design issues for companies and their advisors is the type of stock awards the plan should permit. Fortunately, a company can avoid, or at least postpone, the decision of what types of stock-based awards to make by drafting and adopting a so-called "omnibus plan." An omnibus plan gives a company significant flexibility as to the type of awards or grants it makes to participants. Among the types of stock and stock-based awards that an omnibus stock plan may provide are:

- Incentive stock options;
- Nonincentive stock options;
- Restricted stock;
- Restricted stock units;
- Performance shares; and
- Stock appreciation rights (settled in cash or in stock).

.01 ISOs vs. NSOs

An ISO generally produces better tax results to the optionee by providing the optionee with long-term capital gain at the time the optionee eventually sells the stock acquired through exercise of the option, if the plan and award meet certain Code requirements. However, since the optionee does not recognize ordinary income at the time he or she exercises the incentive stock option, the company is not entitled to a corresponding tax deduction at that time (or ever), as it would be for a nonqualified option. Under the circumstances, this may not be a problem for the company (see Chapter 7 [¶701 *et seq.*] for a detailed discussion of the ISO requirements).

Additionally, stock options (either ISOs or NSOs) produce dramatically different results from restricted stock or performance share awards. Whereas stock options only provide value to an employee (or other recipient) if the company's stock price goes up, restricted stock awards have value to the employee regardless of whether or not the stock price increases (see Chapter 8 [¶801 *et seq.*] for a detailed discussion of restricted stock and performance share awards).

Companies typically establish a process and guidelines for making stock grants to executives. Approaches may include:

1. Granting a fixed number of stock awards based simply on position;

2. Establishing a target grant by position, with adjustments made within a range of performance;

3. Awarding stock or options based purely on company and/or individual performance; and/or

4. Evaluating dilution as a guideline for making grants.

Companies must decide whether to establish an annual stock grant program, or make a one-time "mega-grant." An annual program encourages executives to build ownership at different grant prices via a steady stream of grants over a number of years. A mega-grant allows the executives to realize appreciation on a larger number of shares, assuming continued stock price appreciation.

.02 Code Sec. 162(m)

Before 2018, nearly all public companies designed their stock compensation plans to comply with the requirements of Code Sec. 162(m) (the $1 million deduction limitation), specifically, the "performance-based compensation" exception to Code Sec. 162(m). It was easy for stock option and SAR awards to qualify for the performance-based compensation exception, if a committee of outside directors awarded the option and the exercise price was at least equal to the fair market value of the underlying stock on the date of grant. On the other hand, restricted stock and RSUs could only qualify for the exception if the vesting or award of the shares was based on the achievement of objective performance goals that comply with the requirements of Code Sec. 162(m).

However, the Tax Cuts and Jobs Act of 2017 ("TCJA") repealed the performance-based compensation exception, rendering such design considerations moot. Until the grandfathering protection allowed to certain stock awards by the transition rules of the TCJA expires, most stock plans will continue to include provisions necessary to comply with Code Sec. 162(m). But stock awards made in 2018 and after will not need to include such provisions. The following requirements no longer will apply:

- The requirement that the compensation committee establish performance goals in advance;

- The requirement that the performance goals be based solely on objective factors;

- The requirement that the compensation committee has no ability or discretion to increase payout above those dictated by the pre-established performance goals;

- The requirement that the compensation committee be comprised *solely of two or more outside directors;*

- The requirement that the compensation committee certify that performance goals were achieved, before payment is made; and

- The requirement that the material terms of any performance goals be disclosed to and subsequently approved by the company's stockholders before the compensation is paid.

.03 Tax Treatment of Different Awards

The primary difference among the various types of stock awards available under most stock incentive plans is the tax result to the executive. The most fundamental distinction is between awards that are taxed as transfers of property, such as restricted stock and RSUs, and awards that are taxed as future promises, such as stock options and SARs. Promises generally are taxed when the promised amounts -shares of stock - are paid or made available, according to the constructive receipt rules of Code Secs. 61, 409A, and 451.

Transfers of property are subject to taxation under Code Sec. 83, "Property Exchanged for Services." Generally, the value of property is taxed at the later of: (1) transfer of property; or (2) vesting of the property, that is, when it is no longer subject to substantial risk of forfeiture.

¶625 Number of Shares Authorized Under the Stock Plan

Another of the most critical plan design issues is the number of shares of company stock to authorize for issuance under the plan, including whether to use an "evergreen" provision for the plan's authorized share limit, and the dilution or "overhang" problems the plan's authorized share limit could cause. Another issue the company and its legal counsel may face is whether to allow reload options and awards. Publicly held companies must seek stockholder approval of the number of shares authorized, and register the offer to "sell" those shares with the U.S. Securities and Exchange Commission.

.01 Reasons for Limit

The establishment of a share reserve is necessary and/or desirable for several reasons.

1. *Incentive Stock Options.* A stock incentive plan that provides for the grant of incentive stock options must specify the number of shares that the plan may issue upon the exercise of incentive stock options.

2. *Stockholder Relations.* Specification of the number of reserved shares is important for maintaining good relations with stockholders, particularly institutional stockholders for whom the issue of dilution is a concern.

3. *Self-Regulatory Organizations.* The New York Stock Exchange, the American Stock Exchange and Nasdaq rules require that the stockholders approve the number of shares reserved for issuance under a stock incentive plan if awards of newly issued shares are to be issued to directors and officers.

4. *One Million Dollar Deductible Compensation Cap.* Code Sec. 162(m) limits to $1 million the company's deduction for compensation paid to the CEO and each of the four most highly paid officers. Until 2018, qualified performance-based compensation was not subject to or counted towards the limit. For this reason, experienced legal counsel made sure all plan awards qualify as incentive compensation under Code Sec. 162(m).

For plan awards to qualify for the "performance-based compensation" exemption from the $1 million limit under Code Sec. 162(m), the plan must specify the maximum number of shares with respect to which rights or options may be granted *to any one participant during a specified period (typically, one year)*. Counsel should draft the plan to provide a fixed limit on the number of shares that the company or plan may award per participant per year.

.02 Manner of Specifying Limit

Two commonly used methods of specifying the limit on reserved shares are (1) as a fixed number or (2) as a percentage of outstanding shares of the company from time to time. When deciding which method to use to specify the share reserve, the application of the share limit is administratively more complicated if the plan bases the reserve on a percentage of the outstanding shares of the company, as opposed to using a fixed number. Nevertheless, using a fixed number of shares may require the company to go back to seek approval from its stockholders to increase the share reserve.

.03 Evergreen Limits

A popular compromise is to draft a plan's share reserve limit to provide an evergreen limit. An evergreen limit is a self-adjusting formula for determining the number of shares available for plan awards. Plans typically express evergreen limits as a percentage of the number of company shares outstanding from time to time. As the number of outstanding company shares changes, so does the limit. At its simplest, an evergreen limit might say:

> At any given time, the maximum number of shares that may be issued or transferred to participants under the plan will be 5% of the number of Company shares outstanding (on a fully diluted basis) at the end of the plan year preceding the then-current plan year.

A properly designed evergreen limit will reduce the frequency with which the company must ask the stockholders to authorize shares for granting under the plan. Not all companies adopt evergreen share limits in their stock compensation plans, because this type of limit raises certain legal and practical issues.

The NYSE and Nasdaq have imposed significant restrictions on companies' ability to use an evergreen limit. For example, Nasdaq IM-4350-5 provides "However, if a plan contains a formula for automatic increases in the shares available (sometimes called an 'evergreen formula'), or for automatic grants pursuant to a dollar-based formula (such as annual grants based on a certain dollar value, or matching contributions based on the amount of compensation the participant elects to defer), such plans cannot have a term in excess of ten years unless shareholder approval is obtained every ten years. However, plans that do not contain a formula and do not impose a limit on the number of shares available for grant would require shareholder approval of each grant under the plan."

Moreover, proxy advisory firms and institutional stockholders do not like evergreen provisions of any sort, because they believe a plan with an evergreen limit can result in too much dilution. There is no sure way to address these stockholders' concerns, other than by keeping the percentage of outstanding shares subject to the plan relatively low.

Other institutional stockholders tend to be more concerned about the total potential "cost" of the plan, than about the total number of shares that the company could issue under the plan. These stockholders will assume, if the plan does not otherwise say so, that the most expensive types of awards available under an omnibus stock incentive plan (for instance, restricted stock, rather than options) are the awards most likely to be made with shares reserved under the plan. The company could address this type of concern by placing fixed limits on the number of shares of so-called full value awards, like restricted stock, that will be available under the plan.

Establish a Limit on the Number of Shares Available Under the Plan. Under a typical evergreen limit, the number of shares available for plan awards varies with the number of company shares outstanding. This works so long as the number of outstanding shares remains constant or increases. If, however, the number of company shares outstanding decreases, the number of awards authorized under the plan also decreases. It would present problems if that happened and the number of awards already issued exceeded the new limit. To avoid such a situation, a company may place a fixed floor on the maximum number of shares authorized for issuance under the plan. The company could express the floor as a number or as a percentage of the company shares outstanding on a particular date.

> **Example:** ABC Corporation could draft its stock incentive plan to provide that at any given time the maximum number of shares that may be issued or transferred to participants under the plan would be 5% of the number of company shares that were outstanding at the end of the preceding plan year or 5% of the number of company shares outstanding on January 1, 2018, whichever is larger.

The limit should state how often the number of shares subject to the plan would be determined. If the limit is silent on this point, personnel administering the plan would have to look up the number of outstanding shares every time they sought to make a plan award. The most common way to avoid this annoyance is to state that the number will be determined each year, based on the number of shares outstanding at the end of the preceding year.

Sample Evergreen Limit Language. Putting all of the above considerations together, experienced legal counsel might draft evergreen limit language along the following lines:

> At any given time, the maximum number of shares that may be issued or transferred to Participants under the Plan will be x% of the number of Company shares outstanding (on a fully diluted basis) at the end of the plan year preceding the then-current plan year, or on January 1, 2018, whichever is greater. Notwithstanding the foregoing, the maximum number of shares that the Plan may award or transfer to Participants as Incentive Stock Options is y, and the maximum number of shares that the Plan may award or transfer to Participants as Restricted Stock is z. The maximum number of Shares and Share equivalent units that may be granted during any calendar year to any

one Participant under all types of awards available under the plan is *a* (on an aggregate basis); the foregoing limit will apply whether the awards are paid in Shares or in cash.

When determining whether to draft a stock incentive plan to provide for automatic annual increases in the reserve of shares available for awards, *i.e.*, evergreen provisions, companies need to be mindful of stock exchange listing issues, unfavorable reactions from proxy advisory firms, and eliminating the plan's ability to grant ISOs.

.04 Incentive Stock Option ("ISO") Issues

As discussed above, if the plan allows the award of incentive stock options ("ISOs"), the plan document must describe the maximum number of shares available for ISO awards so that the actual number can be determined at the date as of which the limit is adopted. A plan with a floating limit on the number of shares available for ISOs does not satisfy the Internal Revenue Code requirements for ISOs. The typical way of solving this problem is to place an overarching maximum number (or maximum formula determinable at the time of adoption) on the number of shares available under the plan. For example, the plan would say that the maximum number of shares available for all plan awards will be 5% of the number of shares outstanding from year to year, or 5% of the number of shares outstanding on January 1, 2018, whichever is less. This approach does not solve the problem of having to go back to stockholders every couple of years to have them authorize a larger number of plan shares.

A company can comply with the Code's requirements by adopting a narrower fixed limit: one that applies *only* to the number of ISOs that it can grant under the plan, rather than to *all* types of plan awards. If the company picks a large enough number for ISO-only awards, it can still avoid having to ask the stockholders to increase the number of ISOs authorized under the plan too often. Therefore, the plan's share limit could provide that 5% of the company's shares outstanding from year to year will be available for all plan awards, but the plan could issue no more than 5,000,000 of those shares as ISOs.

Few companies award ISOs, primarily because of the Code Sec. 422 restrictions applicable to ISOs, but also due to the fact that the company receives no deduction for the award or exercise of ISOs. However, the repeal of the performance-based compensation exception to the $1 million limit on the deductibility of compensation by the TCJA, seems likely to lead to a revival in the popularity of ISOs, at least among companies that pay more than $1 million in total compensation (cash, equity, *etc.*) to executive employees. Generally, ISOs do not result in a tax deduction for the company. But many companies will not be entitled to a deduction for stock awards because of the $1 million limit. And ISOs provide favorable tax consequences for the employee recipients. As long as the company will not be able to deduct the gain on some stock awards, why not provide better tax treatment to the employees?

.05 Return of Shares to the Pool

Most plans will include language indicating whether shares that the plan awards to participants but does not actually issue under the plan, *i.e.*, because the participant forfeits the award, will count against the share reserve. Experienced legal counsel will draft the share reserve provisions to specify that:

1. Shares that are actually delivered to a participant (for example, upon exercise of an option) will be treated as having been issued; and

2. Shares that are subject to awards that are forfeited, canceled, settled in cash or expire will not be deemed to have been issued and thus will be returned to the share reserve.

Planning Note: A plan that seeks to include the maximum number of shares in the authorized pool could read as follows:

The total number of shares of Common Stock reserved and available for issuance in connection with Awards under the Plan shall be equal to the sum of: (i) X million shares of Common Stock; (ii) any shares of Common Stock available for future awards under the 2016 Equity Incentive Award Plan or any other prior equity incentive plan of the Company (the "Prior Plans") as of the May 1, 2018, effective date of the Plan; (iii) any shares of Common Stock that are represented by awards granted under any Prior Plans that are forfeited, expire or are canceled without delivery of shares of Common Stock or that result in the forfeiture of the shares of Common Stock back to the Company; and (iv) without duplication for shares of Common Stock counted under clauses (ii) and (iii) of this subparagraph (a), a number of shares of Common Stock equal to the number of shares repurchased by the Company in the open market or otherwise and having an aggregate repurchase price no greater than the amount of cash proceeds received by the Company from the sale of shares of Common Stock under the Plan. Shares of Common Stock subject to an Award under the Plan or a Prior Plan that are forfeited, canceled, settled or otherwise terminated without a distribution of Common Stock to the Participant will again be available for Awards under the Plan, as will (A) shares of Common Stock that are tendered (either actually or by attestation) to the Company in satisfaction of the Exercise Price of, or in payment of any required income tax withholding for, a Stock Option awarded under the Plan or a Prior Plan, and (B) shares of Common Stock repurchased on the open market with remittances from the exercise of Stock Options granted under the Plan or a Prior Plan.

Included in the series of FAQs on Equity Compensation Plans published by the New York Stock Exchange is a question on plans that provide for a return or recapture of shares, which reads as follows:[1]

Section D. Formula Plans:

D-1. How do the rules apply to a plan that provides for adding shares back to the pool of available shares in various situations?

---

[1] http://www.nyse.com.

In some cases, increasing the pool of available shares by adding back shares may be considered a "formula" that implicates the formula plan rules.

A rule to add back shares that have never in fact been issued is not a "formula." Examples of this include (1) shares that are subject to an option that expires without being exercised, or another award that is forfeited without the shares having been issued, and (2) shares that are held back upon exercise of an option or settlement of an award to cover the exercise price or tax withholding.

On the other hand, a rule to add back shares that have actually been issued (regardless of how long they were outstanding) generally is considered a formula. For example, adding back shares that an optionee already owns that are tendered to pay the exercise price of an option is a "formula," as is adding back shares that are repurchased by the company using the cash paid upon exercise of options. The only exception to this rule is that shares of restricted stock that are forfeited rather than vesting is not a formula, even though technically the restricted stock is issued upon grant. However, a rule to add back shares that are withheld from restricted stock upon vesting to cover taxes is a formula.

If a plan has a fixed number of shares available, but for one or more formula addback rules, the latter may be treated as separate from the fixed share pool for purposes of our rules. Thus, if a "formula" rule is included in a plan, the term during which the formula may be operative must be limited to 10 years from the last shareholder approval of the plan, but that term need not be applied to the fixed share pool itself. Similarly, if such a plan was in effect as of the effective date of our rules but had not been approved by shareholders, the company may continue to use the fixed share pool after expiration of the limited transition period without seeking shareholder approval, even though it will not be able to continue to use the formula addback rules without shareholder approval.

Thus, a plan could add back all of the following to the plan's authorized share pool (assuming the plan so provides):

(1) Shares that are subject to an option that expires without being exercised, or another award that is forfeited without the shares having been issued;

(2) Shares that are held back upon exercise of an option or settlement of an award to cover the exercise price or tax withholding;

(3) Shares of restricted stock that are forfeited rather than vested (even though technically the restricted stock is issued upon grant);

(4) Shares that are withheld from restricted stock upon vesting to cover taxes;[2]

(5) Shares that an optionee already owns that are tendered to pay the exercise price of an option; and

(6) Shares that are repurchased by the company using the cash paid upon exercise of options.

---

[2] Subject to the "formula" plan limitation that the plan's duration cannot exceed 10 years from stockholder approval.

When determining whether to draft a stock incentive plan to provide that shares subject to cancellation, expiration, or forfeiture become available for new grants, companies need to be mindful of unfavorable reactions from proxy advisory firms.

.06 Adjustments

A well-drafted stock incentive plan will provide that, if the company's shares are changed into or exchanged for a different number or kind of shares of stock or other securities of the company or of another corporation (whether because of merger, consolidation, recapitalization, reclassification, split, reverse split, combination of shares, or otherwise) or if the number of shares is increased through the payment of a stock dividend, then the board or compensation committee will substitute for or add to each share previously appropriated, later subject to, or which may become subject to, an award, the number and kind of shares of stock or other securities into which each outstanding share was changed, for which each such share was exchanged, or to which each such share is entitled, as the case may be. Stock incentive plans also generally permit the board or compensation committee to amend outstanding awards as to price and other terms, to the extent necessary to reflect the events described above. For instance, a plan may provide that in the event of a stock split, the share reserve and the number of shares subject to outstanding awards will increase automatically while in the event of a reverse stock split, the share reserve and the number of shares subject to outstanding awards will decrease automatically.

In 2006, some of the "Final Four" accounting firms came out with an interpretation of FAS 123R (since renamed as Financial Accounting Standards Board (FASB) Accounting Standards Codification (ASC) Topic 718, Stock Compensation) that required many corporations to amend the authorized share adjustment provisions of their stock compensation plans. Under the interpretation, an antidilution adjustment provision that is discretionary rather than automatic could result in an expense charge to earnings if the adjustment occurs because of an equity restructuring (*e.g.*, a stock dividend, stock split, spin-off, rights offering, recapitalization through a large, non-recurring cash dividend, or other similar non-reciprocal transaction). In many cases, this required us to amend plans to substitute the word "shall" for the word "may" in the authorized share adjustment section of the plan. Plans could continue to reserve to the board or compensation committee the discretion to adjust the number of authorized shares for reciprocal transactions such as mergers, acquisitions and other business combinations.

With more companies paying dividends because of the lower tax rate on "qualified dividends," companies may want to consider whether this places options and RSUs at a disadvantage, and how to adjust for it. In theory, when a company pays a dividend, particularly a large special dividend, its stock value declines by this amount after the ex-dividend date. For stockholders, the cash they receive offsets this decline. However, the company does not pay dividends to holders of stock options and may not pay dividends to holders of RSUs (companies generally pay dividends to holders of restricted stock). For example,

Microsoft amended its stock plan to adjust outstanding options, unvested RSUs, and performance awards for the huge special dividend it paid in 2004. With more companies paying dividends because of the lower tax rate on qualified dividends, companies may want to consider whether this places options and RSUs at a disadvantage, and how to adjust for it.

.07 Fungible Share Counting

Investors and proxy advisory firms also look favorably on stock plans that use fungible share counting. Fungible share counting recognizes that different types of awards are more or less dilutive and have different "costs." Full value awards, such as restricted stock and RSUs are more dilutive than stock option or SAR awards. Thus, a stock plan could provide, for example, that each option granted will use up one share from the authorized share pool, whereas each RSU or share of restricted stock awarded would use up 1.5 shares from the stockholder approved share pool.

.08 Limits on Awards to Non-Employee Directors

In light of the recent surge in litigation over stock awards to non-employee directors, any stock plan that allows for stock awards to non-employee directors should include meaningful limits on the number or fair value of stock awards that may be made to any non-employee director in any year. (See ¶595 for a more detailed discussion of this issue.)

> **Sample Language:** ABC Corporation could draft its stock incentive plan to read as follows: Notwithstanding the foregoing, in no event may any number of Shares be granted during any one Directors' Compensation Year to any one Director with a grant date fair value that, when aggregated with all cash compensation for service as a Director of the Company during such period, exceeds $450,000.

¶635 Plan Administration

Every stock incentive plan must address the issue of who will have discretionary authority and otherwise administer the plan. The administrative duties of these individuals typically include determining who will receive awards, determining the types of awards and the terms of those awards, providing for the payment or settlement of awards, interpreting the provisions of the plan and seeing to the day-to-day administration of the plan.

Most public companies will designate the compensation committee of the board of directors as the entity responsible for administering the plan, though in some instances the board of directors will retain administrative authority with respect to the plan. In selecting the members of a committee to administer a stock incentive plan, the company and legal counsel must take into consideration the following issues.

.01 One Million Dollar Limit

Before 2018, to satisfy the "performance-based compensation" exception to the $1 million limit under Code Sec. 162(m), stock awards must have been made by a committee comprised solely of two or more "outside directors." The TCJA repealed the performance-based compensation exception, rendering such design considerations moot. However, until the grandfathering protection allowed to certain stock awards by the transition rules of the TCJA expires, most stock plans will continue to include provisions necessary to comply with Code Sec. 162(m). See Chapter 22 (¶2201 *et seq.*) for a detailed discussion of Code Sec. 162(m) issues.

.02 Rule 16b-3

For an award to satisfy the exemption from Section 16(b) of the Securities Exchange Act of 1934, as amended, either (1) a committee of "nonemployee directors" or (2) the full board of directors generally must make the award. Generally, a "nonemployee director" is a director who:

1. is not currently an officer of the company (or a parent or subsidiary thereof), or otherwise currently employed by the company (or a parent or subsidiary thereof);

2. does not receive compensation, either directly or indirectly, from the company (or a parent or subsidiary thereof), for services rendered as a consultant or in any capacity other than as a director, except for an amount that does not exceed the dollar amount for which disclosure would be required pursuant to Item 404(a) of Regulation S-K;

3. does not possess an interest in any other transaction for which disclosure would be required pursuant to Item 404(a) of Regulation S-K; and

4. is not engaged in a business relationship for which disclosure would be required pursuant to Item 404(b) of Regulation S-K.

In addition to the need to satisfy corporate formalities, adoption by the board of directors is critical to satisfy Rule 16b-3(d), which will exempt the grant from short swing trading liability. Rule 16b-3(d) provides as follows:

> (d) Acquisitions from the issuer. Any transaction, other than a Discretionary Transaction, involving an acquisition from the issuer (including without limitation a grant or award), whether or not intended for a compensatory or other particular purpose, shall be exempt if:
>
> > (1) The transaction is approved by the board of directors of the issuer, or a committee of the board of directors that is composed solely of two or more Non-Employee Directors;
> >
> > (2) The transaction is approved or ratified, in compliance with section 14 of the Act, by either: the affirmative votes of the holders of a majority of the securities of the issuer present, or represented, and entitled to vote at a meeting duly held in accordance with the applicable laws of the state or other jurisdiction in which the issuer is incorporated; or the written consent of the holders of a majority of the securities of the issuer entitled to vote; provided that such ratification occurs no later than the date of the next annual meeting of shareholders; or
> >
> > (3) The issuer equity securities so acquired are held by the officer or director for a period of six months following the date of such acquisition, provided that this condition shall be satisfied with

respect to a derivative security if at least six months elapse from the date of acquisition of the derivative security to the date of disposition of the derivative security (other than upon exercise or conversion) or its underlying equity security.

Rule 16b-3(e) describes the requirements for approval of a disposition to the issuer:

(e) Dispositions to the issuer. Any transaction, other than a Discretionary Transaction, involving the disposition to the issuer of issuer equity securities, whether or not intended for a compensatory or other particular purpose, shall be exempt, provided that the terms of such disposition are approved in advance in the manner prescribed by either paragraph (d)(1) or paragraph (d)(2) of this section.

.03 Delegation of the Authority to Make Awards

Delaware General Corporation Law § 157(c) allows the board of directors of a Delaware corporation to delegate to one or more officers the authority to designate officers and employees of the corporation to receive options and to determine the number of rights or options that the plan issues to those officers and employees. Many other states have similar laws.

Recognizing the need to make stock awards more frequently than the board's compensation committee is likely to meet, many corporations have drafted this authority into their plan documents. Typically, these plans authorize either the company's chief executive officer or senior vice president of human resources to award a limited number of shares to newly hired or promoted individuals who are not Section 16 officers. Section 16 rules don't allow for the CEO to make grants to the Section 16 officers. This will need to be done by the board or the compensation committee.

Sample Language: Notwithstanding the foregoing, the Board may delegate authority to the Company's Chief Executive Officer to grant a specified number of Stock Options (as determined by the Board from time to time and during such time periods determined by the Board) to existing or prospective Employees (other than those individuals who are subject to Section 16(a) of the 1934 Act at the time of the grant) as the Chief Executive Officer determines appropriate without further action from the Board.

Although this provision transfers some decision-making authority to officers, important decisions remain with the board. These decisions include establishing (1) an exercise price, and (2) the total number of rights or options that an officer may award to other officers or employees. The board may establish the exercise price by designating a formula for determining the price, *e.g.*, fair market value on the date of grant. In addition, a designated officer may not award himself or herself rights or options, nor may the designated officer award rights or options to board members.

Planning Note: A stock incentive plan should provide for administration by the company's board of directors, but permit the board to appoint a committee to administer the plan.

.04 Discretion to Interpret Plan Terms

Courts will generally enforce the terms set forth in plan documents and award agreements, including a highly deferential standard of review if that is what the plan or award agreement requires. Therefore, a stock incentive plan should give the plan administrator the power and duty to interpret ambiguous plan terms. Many stock plan drafters will incorporate the so-called "*Firestone* language," which is the standard for ERISA plans, in their non-ERISA plans. The "*Firestone* language" is a plan provision that expressly gives the plan administrator the power, right and duty to interpret and construe the plan, in its sole discretion, and determine all questions of law or fact or mixed questions of law and fact. The "*Firestone* language" derives from the case of *Firestone Tire & Rubber Co. v. Bruch*,[3] in which the Supreme Court held that if the governing plan documents reserved for the plan administrator or trustee the authority and discretion to interpret the plan's terms, then the courts should overturn such interpretations only if it finds them to be arbitrary and capricious.

Stock incentive plans are not subject to ERISA. However, drafters incorporate the "*Firestone* language" in stock incentive plans hoping for a similar result. More often, courts have applied a good faith standard to the plan administrator's interpretation of ambiguous plan terms, which may not differ in substance that much from arbitrary and capricious. However, the difficulty with applying *Firestone* in the non-ERISA context is that *Firestone* has trust antecedents, and a non-ERISA plan such as a stock incentive plan will not. Most drafters conclude that there is little downside in having both standards, *i.e.*, the administrator has the discretion to interpret and construe the plan and determine all questions of law or fact or mixed questions of law and fact, and any determination made by the committee in good faith shall be binding.

A case from the influential Seventh Circuit Court of Appeals provided precedent for applying the *Firestone* deferential standard of review beyond qualified retirement plans, but only to the relevant language as set forth in the plan.[4] However, the company also should be careful to follow proper procedures and to develop records showing reasonable determinations whenever plan participants question determinations.

.05 Influence of Proxy Advisory Firms on Plan Design

Proxy advisory firms, such as Institutional Shareholder Services Inc. (ISS) and Glass Lewis have acquired an outsized influence in stock plan design due to their ability to recommend that investors vote "Against" a company's stock plan. This influence was further enhanced by the so-called "Shareholder Say on Pay" provisions of the Dodd-Frank Wall Street Reform and Consumer Protection Act (the "Dodd-Frank Act"). ISS has labeled certain plan design features and practices as problematic, including stock plan provisions that would allow a company to reprice outstanding underwater stock options and add back to the authorized share pool certain shares already awarded.

---

[3] *Firestone Tire & Rubber Co. v. Bruch*, 489 U.S. 101, 109 S. Ct. 948, 103 L. Ed. 2d 80 (1989).

[4] *Comrie v. IPSCO Inc.*, 50 EBC 2473 (7th Cir. 2011).

Liberal Share Counting: If the stock plan provides that shares delivered or withheld in connection with the exercise of an award or payment of taxes shall again be available for awards under the plan (shares are being recycled and are available to be granted again), ISS considers this "liberal share counting," which causes ISS to value the entire share authorization as being grantable as full-value awards. This results in a much higher stockholder value transfer cost. To avoid liberal share counting, a company's stock plan could be drafted as follows:

> **Sample Language:** Notwithstanding the foregoing, the following Shares shall **not** again be available for grant under the Plan: (i) Shares that are withheld from issuance with respect to an Award in satisfaction of any tax withholding or similar obligations, (ii) Shares purchased on the open market with the cash proceeds from the exercise of Options or SARs, and (iii) Shares tendered to the Company by the Participant or withheld by the Company in payment of the Exercise Price of an Option or SAR.

Fungible Share Counting: ISS assigns a much higher value to "full market value" share awards, like restricted stock and RSUs. Therefore, for some companies, we draft stock plans to count the use of restricted stock and RSUs at a higher rate for purposes of depleting the total shares available/remaining for future awards. For example, a fungible share counting provision might read as follows:

> **Sample Language:** The total number of shares of Common Stock of the Company subject to issuance under the Plan, subject to adjustment upon occurrence of any of the events indicated in the next paragraph, may not exceed 1,000,000, reduced by one (1) share of Common Stock for every one (1) share that is subject to an Option or Stock Appreciation Right granted under the Plan after the Effective Date, and two and one-half (2 1/2) shares of Common Stock for every one (1) share that was subject to an award other than an Option or Stock Appreciation Right granted after the Effective Date.

Performance and Vesting Periods: ISS and other stockholder advisers prefer (and often demand) a minimum vesting or performance period of at least one-year, sometimes more. They also prefer (and sometimes demand) that stock plans limit the maximum exercise term of an option or SAR to no more than 10 years from the date of grant.

For its minimum vesting requirement, ISS will only award points if the plan mandates a vesting period of at least one year for all equity award types issuable under the plan, which applies to no less than 95% of the shares authorized for grant. No points are awarded if the minimum vesting requirement does not apply to all equity award types, if the plan allows for individual award agreements or other mechanisms to reduce or eliminate the requirement, or provides any other exceptions beyond the 5%.

For CEO vesting of time-based options, time-based restricted stock, and/or performance-based equity compensation, ISS will only award "points" under its Employee Plans Scorecard if the plan provides at least three years from the grant date until all shares from the award vest. Partial vesting could occur earlier, *e.g.*, one-third on each anniversary of the grant date.

> **Sample Language:** Awards granted under the Plan shall vest no earlier than the first anniversary of the date the Award is granted and no Award may provide for partial or graduated vesting beginning before the first anniversary of the Date of Grant; provided that, notwithstanding the foregoing, Awards that result in the issuance of an aggregate of up to five percent (5%) of the shares of Common Stock available pursuant to Article IV may be granted to any one or more Participants without respect to the minimum Award Period requirements of this sentence; provided, however, that, notwithstanding the foregoing, Awards that result in the issuance of an aggregate of up to five percent (5%) of the Shares available pursuant to Section X may be granted to any one or more eligible individuals without respect to such minimum vesting provision.

For change in control vesting, ISS will award points *only if the equity plan contains both* of the following:

(a) for performance-based awards, acceleration is limited to (A) *actual* performance achieved, (B) prorate of target based on the elapsed proportion of the performance period, (C) a combination of both actual and pro-rata, or (D) the performance awards are forfeited or terminated upon a change in control; and

(b) for time-based awards, acceleration cannot be automatic single-trigger or discretionary. Where there are no performance-based awards, points will be based solely on the treatment of time-based awards.

If the plan is *silent* as to treatment of awards upon a change in control, the treatment will be considered discretionary.

If a plan would permit accelerated vesting of **performance** awards upon a change in control (either automatically upon the change in control, at the board's discretion, *or only if they are not assumed*), ISS will consider whether the amount of the performance award that would be payable/vested is (a) at target level, (b) above target level, (c) prorated based on actual performance as of the change in control date and/or the time elapsed in the performance period as of the change in control date, or (d) based on board discretion.

Many corporations would benefit from the use of a proxy solicitation firm in the design and implementation of their equity incentive plans. For some corporations an aggressive and coordinated proxy solicitation campaign could be essential to getting stockholders to approve a new plan or authorize additional shares for award under an existing plan. However, even a corporation that has reason to believe that its stockholders will easily approve a new plan or additional shares may find it beneficial to involve a proxy solicitation firm at the earliest stages. Even if the majority of stockholders vote in favor of a new plan or shares, a significant number of "no" votes can create embarrassing publicity.

For a modest cost, the proxy solicitation expert can review the early draft of the equity incentive plan document and point out to the corporation specific terms or provisions that may draw a negative vote from certain institutional investors. Often the corporation does not intend to use the provision that is offensive to the institutional investors and can simply remove it. Occasionally, the solicitor can broker a discussion between the corporation and the investor to iron out any potential issues before they arise. Because institutional investors such as mutual funds now must disclose how they vote proxies, they must be careful to follow the recommendations of investor services to which they subscribe, or else justify a deviation from those recommendations. A proxy solicitor can help investors understand the corporation's position on certain issues and, possibly, avoid a "no" vote.

.06 Code Sec. 409A

Code Sec. 409A can apply to stock incentive awards.[5] Failure to satisfy the requirements of Code Sec. 409A could result in significant penalties to the award recipient.

Code Sec. 409A applies differently to different types of stock incentive awards, and to stock incentive awards made by public and private companies. Generally, Code Sec. 409A applies to various stock incentive awards, as follows:

- Restricted Stock is not subject to Code Sec. 409A. Restricted stock awards are taxed under Code Sec. 83 immediately upon vesting, so it is akin to a short-term deferral. However, a plan could permit an individual to elect to defer the receipt of restricted stock subject to an award, subject to the deferral requirements of Code Sec. 409A.

- Restricted Stock Units generally are subject to Code Sec. 409A. An RSU is a current promise to transfer stock later. RSUs could be exempt as a short-term deferral if they require distribution of stock upon vesting.

- Phantom Stock generally is subject to Code Sec. 409A, since it is a promise to pay an amount in the future based on the value of stock at that time. Like RSUs, it could be exempt as a short-term deferral if payment is made upon vesting.

- Stock Options and stock appreciation rights ("SARs") will be exempt from Code Sec. 409A if the option or SAR awards meet the "Stock Right" exception under Code Sec. 409A and the final regulations. A stock option or SAR will be exempt from Code Sec. 409A if:

  –The exercise price is not less than fair market value,

  –The award is service recipient (employer) stock,

  –The award is not extended or modified, and

  –The award does not contain any feature allowing for further deferral.

Counsel should design stock incentive plans to incorporate or avoid the requirements of Code Sec. 409A. For example, counsel may want to insert language similar to the following:

---

[5] Added by the American Jobs Creation Act of 2004 (P.L. 108-357).

Notwithstanding any provision of this Plan to the contrary, all Awards made under this Plan are intended to be exempt from or, in the alternative, comply with Code Sec. 409A and the interpretive guidance thereunder, including the exceptions for stock rights and short-term deferrals. The Plan shall be construed and interpreted in accordance with such intent.

The Committee may provide for payment to the Participant of amounts representing dividend equivalents, either currently or in the future, or for the investment of such amounts on behalf of the Participant; provided that the Committee shall design such payment to be exempt from or, in the alternative, comply with Code Sec. 409A and the interpretive guidance thereunder.

The Committee may not amend any Award to extend the exercise period beyond a date that is later than the earlier of the latest date upon which the Award could have expired by its original terms under any circumstances or the tenth anniversary of the original date of grant of the Award, or otherwise cause the Award to become subject to Code Sec. 409A. However, if the exercise period of an Option is extended at a time when the exercise price of the Option equals or exceeds the Fair Market Value of the Stock that could be purchased (in the case of an Option) or the Fair Market Value of the Stock used to determine the payment to the Participant (in the case of a stock appreciation right), it is not an extension of the original Award.

¶645 Eligibility for Awards

Several factors will affect the determination of the group that is eligible to participate in a stock incentive plan and how the company and legal counsel describe that group in the plan.

Planning Note: If individuals other than employees will be eligible to receive awards, the plan should not define the eligible group as "Eligible Employees" but rather "Eligible Individuals."

Type of Awards. If a stock incentive plan is going to provide for the grant of "incentive stock options" that qualify for favorable tax treatment to the employee under Code Sec. 422, employees of the company must be eligible to participate in the stock incentive plan because only employees are eligible to receive incentive stock options. The plan can allow other types of awards (*i.e.*, nonqualified stock options and restricted stock awards) for nonemployees (*i.e.*, nonemployee board members, consultants, advisors or other independent service providers to the company).

Securities Law Considerations. Typically, the issuance of shares of stock under a stock incentive plan is considered a sale under the securities laws and as such, the shares must either be registered on a Form S-8 Registration Statement (for public companies) or satisfy the requirements of Rule 701 of the Securities Act of 1933, as amended (for privately held companies). The rules governing the use of the Form S-8 Registration Statement and the availability of Rule 701 restrict the issuance of shares to a company's employees, directors and certain advisors and consultants.

Experienced legal counsel will draft a stock incentive plan's provisions on eligibility to participate and receive awards as broadly as possible to preserve the company's ability to make awards to employees, nonemployee board members and consultants, advisors or other independent service providers to the company or an affiliate.

> **Planning Note:** The plan and award agreement also should use the term "service" in place of "employment" and define the term broadly to include the services of these potential participants. A plan that links key provisions to termination of "employment" could create uncertainties in cases where an employee moves to independent contractor, consultant, or board member status.

However, regarding eligibility by consultants, note that the General Instructions to Form S-8 provide that the short Form S-8 is available for the issuance of securities to consultants or advisors only if:

(i) they are natural persons;

(ii) they provide bona fide services to the registrant; and

(iii) the services are not in connection with the offer or sale of securities in a capital-raising transaction, and do not directly or indirectly promote or maintain a market for the registrant's securities.

.01 Impact of the Dodd-Frank Act

In July 2010, President Obama signed into law the Dodd-Frank Act. The Dodd-Frank Act included 11 separate changes in the area of executive compensation, many of which are likely to influence companies' design and administration of their stock incentive plans (see Chapter 31 for a detailed discussion of all provisions of the Dodd-Frank Act).

Shareholder Say on Pay: Section 951 of the Dodd-Frank Act added Section 14A to the Securities and Exchange Act of 1934, entitled "Shareholder Approval of Executive Compensation," which provides that, not less frequently than once every three years, a company's annual proxy statement must include a separate resolution, subject to non-binding stockholder vote, to approve the compensation of executives, as disclosed in the company's Compensation Discussion and Analysis (CD&A), the compensation tables, and any related material. This Shareholder Say on Pay requirement did not require any specific changes to the design or administration of stock plans, but it did force companies to pay more attention to "best practices" in plan design and administration in order to receive the approval of stockholders and proxy advisory firms.

Policy on Recovery of Erroneously Awarded Compensation: Section 954 of the Dodd-Frank Act added Section 10D, entitled "Recovery of Erroneously Awarded Compensation Policy," to the Exchange Act. This section requires the SEC to direct the national securities exchanges to prohibit the listing of any security of an issuer that does not develop and implement a clawback policy. This provision caused most companies to add to their stock plans language similar to the following: "Notwithstanding any provision in the Plan or in any Award Agreement to the contrary, Awards granted or paid under the Plan will be subject to any Compensation Recovery Policy established by the Corporation and amended from time to time." (See also, the discussion at ¶665.06 below.)

¶645.01

Disclosure of Hedging by Employees and Directors: Section 955 of the Dodd-Frank Act, "Disclosure of Hedging by Employees and Directors," added subsection 14(j) to the Exchange Act, which requires the SEC to require companies to disclose in their annual proxy statement whether the company permits any employee or director to purchase financial instruments that are designed to hedge or offset any decrease in the market value of equity securities (1) granted to the employee or director by the company as part of the compensation; or (2) held, directly or indirectly, by the employee or director. Most public company executives have a significant portion of their total wealth held in shares of their company's stock and, therefore, have a (prudent) desire to hedge that position. While not leading to any direct changes in the design or administration of stock plans, this change has led many companies to explicitly prohibit hedging transactions on company stock.

Disclosure of Pay Versus Performance: Section 953(a) of the Dodd-Frank Act, "Disclosure of Pay Versus Performance," added 14(i) to the Exchange Act, which requires each public company to disclose in its annual proxy statement "information that shows the relationship between executive compensation actually paid and the financial performance of the issuer." While not leading to any direct changes in the design or administration of companies' stock plans, over time this change seems likely to lead more companies to emphasize performance-based stock awards.

Enhanced Disclosure and Reporting of Compensation Arrangements: Section 956 of the Dodd Frank Act only applies to financial institutions with assets of $1 billion of more. It required the federal regulators to jointly prescribe regulations that require each covered financial institution to disclose to the appropriate federal regulator the structures of all incentive-based compensation arrangements offered by the institution, sufficient to determine whether the compensation structure (A) provides an executive officer, employee, director, or principal stockholder of the covered financial institution with excessive compensation, fees, or benefits; or (B) could lead to material financial loss to the covered financial institution. In March 2011, the Office of the Comptroller of the Currency, FDIC, Office of Thrift Supervision, SEC, Board of Governors of the Federal Reserve System, National Credit Union Administration, and Federal Housing Finance Agency (collectively, the "Agencies") jointly issued proposed rules pursuant to Section 956, which, if finalized without revision, would force nearly every financial institution in the United States to redesign its executive compensation program.

The proposed rules would require that at least 50% of the annual incentive-based compensation, including most forms of stock compensation, of each executive officer at a financial institution with total consolidated assets of $50 billion or more be deferred over a period of no less than three years, with the institution allowed to release (or allow vesting of) the full deferred amount in a lump-sum at the end of the deferral period in equal increments, pro rata, for each year of the deferral period. The proposed rules seem likely to push institutions and their officers toward more fixed compensation, such as base salaries, and less incentive compensation, such as stock awards. This result would be counterproductive at a time when stockholders are demanding more performance-based compensation.

¶655 Vesting of Stock Awards

Vesting refers to the point at which a participant's right to receive an award under the stock incentive plan becomes nonforfeitable. With respect to options, plans often use the term "vesting" to describe when the option becomes exercisable. In general, an option can vest upon either the passage of time and/or the achievement of a predetermined performance goal. Vesting is a useful tool for retaining key employees and service providers and for motivating those individuals to perform well.

For retention purposes, most companies provide for stock options, restricted stock, and other awards to vest over a period of three to five years. In determining the vesting requirements that will apply to awards granted under a stock incentive plan, most companies and their advisors consider a variety of issues.

> **Planning Note:** Experienced legal counsel will draft the plan to give the company flexibility to set different vesting schedules for each stock award. The stock option or other award agreement delivered to each award recipient would specify the precise vesting provisions applicable to that award.

.01 Limits in the Plan

Most companies and their legal counsel will draft stock incentive plans to provide very broad discretion to the administrator of the plan (*e.g.*, the board of directors, the compensation committee) to establish the vesting schedule. Accordingly, most plan documents will not contain the actual vesting schedule. Instead, the details regarding the vesting schedule will be set forth in each individual award agreement.

.02 Time-Based or Performance-Based Vesting

A company will need to consider whether awards will vest upon the completion of a period of service or upon the achievement of performance requirements. When the plan uses time-based vesting, the company must decide whether the award should vest all at one time (*e.g.*, cliff vesting) or over time (*e.g.*, gradual or installment vesting). A typical vesting schedule might provide for cliff vesting of a portion of the award one year after the date of grant and then installment vesting on a monthly or quarterly basis over the next three to four years.

If the plan uses performance to determine vesting, a company will need to establish the targets, the period during which it measures performance and whether the plan administrator will have the authority to alter those targets during the performance period. Performance-based vesting no longer will subject an award to variable accounting treatment for financial accounting purposes, since the effective date of FAS 123R (now known as "ASC 718").

Some companies design and draft their stock plans and award agreements to provide for more frequent (periodic) vesting. The two problems that some companies see with annual (or longer) vesting are that:

1. Highly mobile employees need to have a retention element in front of them every moment. If such an employee must wait one full year (or more) for the next tranche of awards to vest, he or she might decide to leave for another employer immediately rather than wait. These companies may provide for monthly vesting of awards.

2. If the company terminates an employee with a huge amount of value in his/her unvested award, the employee is more likely to bring a lawsuit for that value.

.03 Impact of a Change in Control of the Company on Award Vesting

Many companies and plans provide for the full or partial acceleration of award vesting in the event of a change in control of the company. Companies provide acceleration to both reward and protect participants. However, companies increasingly draft their plans' change in control vesting provisions to require participants to remain with the company for some period (often one year) following the change in control, to improve a buyer's ability to retain key employees and, thus, increase the value of the business. To protect the participant, the plan and/or agreement typically will provide that the participant fully vests if the acquirer terminates his or her service, without cause, before the end of the "stay" period.

Example: Corporation awards stock options to key employees with the following change in control vesting provision:

If a Change in Control of the Company occurs, fifty percent (50%) of the then unvested portion of the Option will become fully vested on the closing date of the Change in Control, if the Participant has remained in Service with the Company continuously until that date. The remaining fifty percent (50%) of the then unvested portion of the Option will become vested on a monthly basis, 1/12 as of the last day of each of the successive calendar months that begin after the closing date of the Change in Control, so that the Option will be fully vested on the last day of the last calendar month that begins on or before the first anniversary of the closing date of the Change in Control, if the Participant has remained in Service continuously until that date. Notwithstanding the foregoing, the Option will fully vest as of any date following the Change in Control, if the Company terminates the Participant's employment without Cause or the Participant terminates employment for Good Reason, death or Disability.

Those companies and plans that do not provide for full vesting of all outstanding awards automatically upon a change in control usually provide that all outstanding awards will fully vest immediately unless the company's successor at the time of the change in control irrevocably assumes the company's obligations under the stock incentive plan or replaces each participant's outstanding award with an award of equal or greater value and having terms and conditions no less favorable to the participant than those applicable to the participant's award immediately prior to the change in control.

To maximize the company's value, the stock plan probably should provide for double trigger vesting upon a change in control. That is, a participant would not become fully vested and entitled to payout automatically upon a change in control. However, if after the change in control, the successor company/acquirer terminates the participant's employment without "cause," or gives the participant "good reason" to terminate his or her employment (such as a demotion or cut in pay), the participant would become fully vested in all outstanding stock awards. This is intended to allow the successor company/acquirer to retain the key employee/participant, if it desires, but protects the participant if the successor company/acquirer does not retain him.

Timian v. Johnson & Johnson[6] involved questions of vesting on a change in control. In January 2006, Ms. Timian commenced employment with the company as a patent attorney, providing legal services to one of its subsidiaries, Ortho-Clinical Diagnostics, Inc. ("OCD"). The company had awarded Restricted Stock Units to Timian under its Long-Term Incentive Plan for several years. The RSUs had a vesting period of three years, which required Timian to be employed by the company on the third anniversary of the vesting date in order to receive the value of the RSUs.

In early 2013, the company began discussions to sell OCD. The patent attorneys supporting OCD, including Timian, were included as assets to the sale and were not allowed to look for work within the company or any of its other subsidiaries. The patent attorneys were forced to either leave the company's employment or become an employee of OCD after the sale.

In January 2014, the company announced its formal intention to sell OCD. In February 2014, the company awarded RSUs to Timian based on her 2013 work performance. On June 29, 2014, the company's sale of OCD became final, Timian's employment with the company was terminated, and she became an employee of OCD. Upon the sale of OCD, the company terminated the RSUs granted to Timian in 2012, 2013, and 2014, on the basis that these RSUs had not vested prior to the termination of her employment. Timian lost the full value of the RSUs awarded in 2012, 2013, and 2014, and sued the company for a breach of the LTIP, breach of the implied contract between employee and employer, breach of the implied covenant of good faith and fair dealing, and breach of ERISA.

The federal court ruled against Timian on each of her claims. First, the court found that the LTIP was not subject to ERISA, as has every other court that has ever considered the issue. Second, the court found that the language of the LTIP was clear. There could be no legal dispute that Timian's employment with the company had terminated, even though she continued to sit at the same desk and perform the same job functions on the day after the sale of OCD as she did on the

---

[6] *Timian v. Johnson & Johns*, No. 6:15-cv-06125(MAT), W.D. New York, October 26, 2015.

day before the sale. The LTIP did not provide for accelerated vesting of Timian's RSUs. The provisions of the LTIP on change in control simply did not apply to the sale of a division of the company.

Finally, the claims for breach of the implied contract between employee and employer, and breach of the implied covenant of good faith and fair dealing, are based on a notion that some rules apply to the relationships among parties, even though they are not written into a contract or agreement. Courts sometimes find a breach of these implied covenants in cases of egregious conduct. However, the terms of the LTIP addressed situations like the one at issue and were clear on the outcome.

The court's decision in *Timian v. Johnson & Johnson* is consistent with that of nearly every other federal court that has considered a similar issue. Some companies' LTIPs would provide for accelerated vesting for an employee terminated solely because of a sale of a division of the company. However, this LTIP did not. Executive compensation professionals should take care in considering all of the terms of a stock plan or employment or other agreements, because the courts will uphold those terms for better or worse.

.04 Impact of Service Termination

The plan and/or award agreements should address the effect of a participant's termination of service on award vesting. Many plans and award agreements provide for fully or slightly accelerated award vesting in the event a participant terminates service due to death or disability.

> **Comment:** Acceleration is generally more common with larger companies that can more easily bear the loss of a participant's services. Smaller companies and start-up ventures are often highly dependent on the services of each employee and, therefore, can ill afford to compound the loss of an employee by accelerating the vesting of his or her stock award.

Stock plan documents should be clear on the effect of all employment termination scenarios on vesting, including termination for death, disability, "cause," *etc.* Many large companies' stock plans provide for full or slightly accelerated vesting if a participant terminates employment due to death or disability. Most smaller companies do not provide for accelerated vesting on death, disability, retirement or any other employment termination, because of the importance of each employee to the company. Most plans provide that the participant will forfeit any outstanding stock options, even if vested, if the company terminates the participant's service for cause.

Some plans even provide for acceleration if the participant retires or the company constructively terminates the participant or terminates him or her without cause.

¶665 Other Provisions Common to Stock Incentive Plans

Despite the wide variety of stock incentive plans that a company may establish and awards that it may grant thereunder, almost all companies that decide to implement a stock incentive plan must address the issues set forth below.

.01 Purpose

Most stock incentive plans contain a provision explaining why the company has established the plan. The most common reasons for implementing a stock incentive plan are to attract and retain key employees, to motivate employees to perform well and to align the interests of key employees with those of a company's stockholders. When drafting the "Purpose" language for a stock incentive plan, experienced legal counsel will take into consideration stockholder relations, employee relations and corporate waste. The statement of purpose should be consistent with the description of eligibility described below.

.02 Noncompete and Other Restrictive Covenants

Today, many companies explicitly incorporate the covenants of nondisclosure, noncompetition, and nonsolicitation in their plans and/or award agreements (see Chapter 4 [¶ 401 *et seq.*] for a detailed discussion of noncompetes and other restrictive covenants). To give these restrictive covenants teeth, the plans and/or agreements provide that the participant will forfeit:

1. all awards granted to him or her under the agreement, including vested awards (this remedy is easier to enforce in the case of options); and

2. the profit on any option the participant exercised either after terminating service or within the six-month period immediately preceding his or her termination of service.

   Planning Note: Experienced legal counsel will suggest that the plan give the company flexibility to impose different restrictive covenants on different employees and awards. The stock option or other award agreement delivered to each award recipient would specify the precise vesting provisions applicable to that award.

.03 Design Changes Responsive to Accounting Rules

For decades, a variety of plan design provisions revolved around ensuring that plan awards would qualify for favorable (that is, "fixed") account treatment under APB Opinion No. 25. Since FAS 123R (now known as ASC 718) became effective in 2006, many of the rules of plan design have changed. First and foremost, stock options no longer enjoy "too-good-to-be-true" accounting treatment. In this respect, ASC 718 leveled the playing field for other stock awards. With companies no longer able to award stock options without any accounting expense, each company could design its stock compensation plan and awards to create its own incentives and achieve its own goals - by focusing on the economic incentives that the awards create and the behavior that these incentives elicit.

Among the design changes many companies made were the following:[7]

---

[7] "Top Ten List: Things You Can Do Under FAS 123(R) That You Couldn't Do Under APB 25," The NASPP Advisor, March-April 2006.

1. Awarding restricted stock instead of stock options. The advantages and disadvantages of restricted stock are discussed elsewhere in this Chapter. However, a board of directors or compensation committee that concluded that its goals were more likely to be achieved through the award of restricted stock could do so without dramatically different accounting treatment.

2. Awarding stock-settled SARs. Stock appreciation rights offer the same economic benefits as stock options but result in the issuance of fewer shares, reducing plan dilution and overhang. Under ASC 718, stock-settled SARs receive the same accounting treatment as stock options.

3. Eliminating the six-month hold requirement for shares used to pay the exercise price. The payment methods are sometimes referred to as pyramid exercises, net exercises, and immaculate exercises. Each method allows the employee/optionee to tender his/her exercised shares back to the company in payment of the option price and taxes.

4. Awarding performance-based stock options. Under APB 25, stock options with performance-based vesting did not qualify for fixed (favorable) accounting treatment, which was a significant disincentive for companies to award them. True performance-based grants were subject to variable-plan accounting under APB 25. Therefore, many companies granted awards where vesting accelerates upon the achievement of performance goals but which vested anyway after a specified period (such as five years) if the targets were not achieved. Under ASC 718, there is no need for this fail-safe vesting event, allowing companies to award options that are purely performance-based.

   For example, Midas, Inc. made restricted stock awards that vest in seven years. However, one-third of the award shares would vest early in any year that Midas' total stockholder return exceeds the S&P 500 index. Similarly, H.J. Heinz Co. made restricted stock awards that vest in five years. However, one-third of the award shares would vest early in any year that the company meets specified earnings per share targets.

5. Address the problem of underwater options by requiring employees to either (a) tender the underwater options in exchange for a new award, or (b) exchange their underwater options for new at-market options.

6. Shortening the option term (that is, the period during which the employee/optionee may exercise the stock option). Before ASC 718, the standard term of stock option awards was ten years. Some companies award stock options with terms of five to seven years. Under ASC 718, a shorter option term means a shorter period during which the underlying stock may appreciate and, thus, a lesser accounting charge. Among the companies awarding options with a seven-year term were Intel, Yahoo Inc., XTO Energy, Union Pacific Corp., Manhattan Associates, Inc., Corning Inc., CIT Group, Inc., and eBay, Inc.

.04 Dividends and Dividend Equivalents

Most equity compensation plans provide that the individual award agreement will govern whether dividends are paid on the shares underlying the award. Other plans provide that some awards, typically restricted stock, automatically will receive dividend rights while other awards, such as stock options, do not. With respect to an award that is not vested, plans or agreements typically will provide that either (a) the plan will hold any dividends for the award recipient until the award vests, and then will pay it, or (b) no dividend will be earned or paid until the award vests.

Some plans and agreements provide for "dividend equivalents," typically during the period before a restricted stock award vests or a stock option is exercised. For example, one public company's proxy statement provides: "If minimum performance share award measures are met, executive officers who receive performance awards will obtain cash dividend equivalents equal to the cash dividends that would have been paid on the shares had the recipient owned the shares during the performance period. Typically, a plan would not pay dividend equivalents until the performance period has ended and performance results are known. The Committee believes that this feature is appropriate to put the executives on an equal footing with other stockholders."

Code Sec. 409A throws a curve ball at plans and agreements that provide dividend equivalents. The final regulations adopt the rule that a right to a payment of accumulated dividend equivalents at the time of the exercise of a stock option or SAR generally will be treated as a reduction in the exercise price of the option or SAR, causing it to be deferred compensation subject to the requirements of Code Sec. 409A.[8] However, an arrangement to accumulate and pay dividend equivalents that are not contingent upon the exercise of the option or SAR may be treated as a separate arrangement for purposes of Code Sec. 409A, which will not affect whether the related option or SAR qualifies for the exclusion from coverage under Code Sec. 409A.

Stock plan drafters should provide the company/committee with discretion to grant dividend equivalents only with respect to awards other than stock options and SARs. Giving the company/committee discretion to grant dividend equivalents with respect to stock options and SARs or "any awards," will result in ISS assigning a higher cost attributable to the option and SAR awards under the plan.

Investors and proxy advisory firms want companies' stock plans to state unequivocally that (a) dividends or dividend equivalents on unvested awards will only be paid if/when the underlying award shares vest, and (b) no dividend or dividend equivalents may be paid on options or SARs. Dividend equivalents may be accumulated and paid once the underlying stock award vests. Until then, dividends are held. Finally, dividend payouts on RSUs should not be linked to vesting, in case there is an election to defer.

---

[8] Treas. Reg. 1.409A-3(e).

.05 Prohibition on Repricing

Very few companies would dare to consider a stock option repricing, given the investor backlash that would follow. However, institutional stockholders and their advisors often demand that the stock incentive plan document expressly preclude repricing. Therefore, many companies and plans will include language similar to the following:

> Repricing of Options or Rights shall not be permitted without stockholder approval. For this purpose, a "repricing" means any of the following (or any other action that has the same effect as any of the following): (A) changing the terms of an Option or Right to lower its Exercise Price; (B) any other action that is treated as a "repricing" under generally accepted accounting principles; and (C) repurchasing for cash or canceling an Option or Right at a time when its Exercise Price is equal to or greater than the Fair Market Value of the underlying stock in exchange for another Option or Right, restricted stock or other equity award, unless the cancellation and exchange occurs in connection with an Equity Restructuring. Such cancellation and exchange would be considered a "repricing" regardless of whether it is treated as a "repricing" under generally accepted accounting principles and regardless of whether it is voluntary on the part of the Participant.

Stock plan drafters might consider further enhancing the "no repricing without prior stockholder approval provision" to prohibit the canceling of outstanding stock options or SARs in exchange for cash. If not, ISS could interpret the plan as allowing repricings without prior stockholder approval, which would result in an automatic AGAINST vote recommendation. The plan document could prohibit both: (i) "repricing" (without prior stockholder approval) by lowering the exercise/grant price of an Option/SAR or canceling an Option/SAR and substituting with another Award(s), and (ii) cancellation in exchange for cash.

.06 Boilerplate

Lawyers sometimes dismissively refer to the miscellaneous provisions at the end of a plan document or agreement as "boilerplate" implying that it is "standard stuff" that may not be worth reading. However, we commonly place some very critical terms and conditions in the miscellaneous or boilerplate section of documents.

Clawback Provisions. All compensation plans and agreements should include a recoupment or "clawback" provision, which allows the company to recover compensation paid in the event subsequent actions (*e.g.*, a violation of the restrictive covenants) or calculations (*e.g.*, a financial restatement) indicate that the amount should not have been paid.

> **Sample Language:** Anything in this Plan to the contrary notwithstanding, it is intended that, this Plan, and any compensation described herein or made hereunder, comply with any legislative or regulatory limitations or requirements that are or may become applicable to the Employer or any of its affiliates or to any such payments, including, but not limited to, the Dodd-Frank Wall Street Reform and Consumer Protection Act and any rules or regulations issued thereunder (collectively, the "Regulatory Require-

ments"). The Employee acknowledges that any cash or stock-based bonus or incentive compensation payments or awards which may be granted or paid to Employee will be subject to any such clawback provisions and to possible change due to applicable Regulatory Requirements.

In *Marsh Supermarkets, Inc. v. Marsh,*[9] the company had terminated the employment of its CEO, Mr. Marsh, and begun making severance and retirement plan payments to him under the terms of his employment agreement. However, the company stopped all payments and benefits to Mr. Marsh when it discovered a pattern of highly irregular expense reimbursements to him (according to an earlier jury verdict in favor of the company on this point). Thus, the company argued that Mr. Marsh had:

> "snookered [it] into terminating [his] employment without cause and then paying him over $2 million in Salary Continuation Benefits when, by any reasonable analysis of facts now proven, Mr. Marsh should have been terminated for cause and would have been but for his fraud."

In turn, Mr. Marsh countersued the company for $2,171,261.48 as equitable relief under ERISA Section 502(a)(3) and other breach of contract claims. Both parties asked the court for an award of attorneys' fees and costs under ERISA Section 502(g)(1).

As happens all too often, the company terminated Mr. Marsh "without cause," and then sought to recharacterize the termination as "for cause" after discovering the fraud. Despite the jury verdict in favor the company on the question of fraud by Mr. Marsh, the court found in favor of the Mr. Marsh on the ERISA and contract claims. The court based its decision on the unambiguous wording of the employment agreement, which provided for payments and benefits to Mr. Marsh if the company terminated his employment "without cause," which it inarguably did. The employment agreement included no clawback provisions, no exception for "fraud," and no provision for after-discovered cause.

The parties had previously agreed that part of Mr. Marsh's employment agreement was subject to ERISA, presumably as an ERISA severance benefit plan. This appears to have been a major mistake by the company for several reasons. First, the court found that the provisions of the employment agreement that were subject to ERISA were segregable from the others. Second, with respect to the provisions subject to ERISA, the court found that ERISA compelled it to confine its inquiry to "the face of written plan documents." The court observed that the written plan documents (the employment agreement) provided: "Each and every payment made hereunder by the Company shall be final, and the Company shall not seek to recover all or any part of such payment from [Mr. Marsh] or from whosoever may be entitled thereto, for any reasons whatsoever."

Finally, the company's agreement that part of the employment was subject to ERISA opened the door for the court to order the reimbursement of the legal fees of the prevailing party – Mr. Marsh - as ERISA permits.

---

[9] 56 EBC 2965 (SD IN 2013).

The bottom line for the company was that, despite a jury verdict finding that Mr. Marsh had breached his employment agreement and committed fraud against the company, the court ordered the company to pay $2,171,261.48 to Mr. Marsh and held that Mr. Marsh is entitled to recover attorneys' fees and costs as incurred in litigating the ERISA claims.

Choice of Forum/Venue Provision. All compensation plans and agreements should include a choice of forum/venue provision, which specifies the location and court for the resolution of any dispute under the plan.

Sample Language: To the extent they are not preempted by federal law, the laws of the State of Illinois, other than its conflict of law principles, will govern in all matters relating to this Agreement. The Company and the Executive agree that the jurisdiction and venue for any disputes arising under, or any action brought to enforce (or otherwise relating to), this Agreement shall be exclusively in the courts in the State of Illinois, County of Cook, including the Federal Courts located therein (should Federal jurisdiction exist), and the Company and the Executive and hereby submit and consent to said jurisdiction and venue.

Coordination/Consistency. Most compensation plans should include a provision that specifies which document would govern in the event of an inconsistency.

Sample Language: Unless otherwise determined by the Committee at the grant date and set forth in the Award Agreement covering the Award or otherwise in writing or determined thereafter in a manner more favorable to the Participant, or otherwise as may be provided in an agreement between a Participant and the Company, if a Participant's employment or service terminates for any reason other than Cause . . .

Tax Withholding for Stock Compensation. All compensation plans and agreements should include provisions that give the company the right to withhold taxes from payments or distributions of stock. ASC 718 allow companies to withhold shares for taxes up to the maximum individual tax rate in the applicable jurisdiction, rather than the minimum statutory withholding amount. Withholding taxes at a rate higher than the minimum may not appeal to many companies, who then would have to come up with cash to pay the tax. However, most companies (and many executives) will want to preserve to themselves the flexibility to withhold taxes at a higher rate in some circumstances. Therefore, we are suggesting plan amendments that make a simple language change that gives the company flexibility in tax withholding within the confines of ASC 718's liability accounting provision.

Sample Language: The Company shall withhold a number of whole Shares having a Fair Market Value, determined as of the date of withholding, *not exceeding the maximum individual statutory tax rate in a given jurisdiction (or such lower amount as may be necessary to avoid liability award accounting, or any other accounting consequence or cost,* as determined by the Committee, and in any event in accordance with Company policies), and any remaining amount shall be remitted in cash or withheld; and provided, further, that with respect to any Award subject to Section 409A, in no event shall Shares be withheld pursuant to this Section (other than upon or immediately prior to settlement in accordance with the Plan and the applicable Award Agreement) other than to pay taxes imposed under the U.S. Federal Insurance Contributions Act (FICA) and any associated U.S. federal withholding tax imposed under Code Section 3401 and in no event shall the value of such Shares (other than upon immediately prior to settlement) exceed the amount of the tax imposed under FICA and any associated U.S. federal withholding tax imposed under Code Section 3401.

Notice - Electronic Delivery. Many companies still require award recipients to sign and return a copy of their stock award agreement in order for the award to be effective. Most companies are moving toward electronic delivery of award agreements. However, many of those companies still require the recipient to acknowledge his or her receipt of the award in order to enhance the likelihood that a court will enforce the agreement's terms. When drafting or amending stock plans document, companies and their counsel should take care to note in each place where the plan document requires "written" instrument or "delivery," that electronic delivery is acceptable. Alternatively, some companies and plan drafters may add a catch-all provision like the following:

> **Sample Language:** Electronic Delivery of Plan Information and Electronic Signatures. To the extent permitted by applicable law, the Company may deliver by email or other electronic means (including posting on a web site maintained by the Company or by a third party under contract with the Company) all documents relating to the Plan or any Award thereunder (including without limitation, prospectuses required by applicable securities law) and all other documents that the Company is required to deliver to its security holders (including without limitation, annual reports and proxy statements). To the extent permitted by applicable law, the Participant's execution of an Award Agreement may be made by electronic facsimile or other method of recording of the Participant's signature in a manner that is acceptable to the Committee.

¶675 Plan Provisions Unique to Stock Option Plans and Awards

.01 Expiration of Awards at Termination

Stock incentive plans that provide for the grant of stock options typically specify a fixed number of years during which a stock option may be exercised (*i.e.*, ten years), and often the plan or the stock option agreement will provide that a stock option will expire prior to the end of that period under certain circumstances (*i.e.*, after service termination). In designing a plan's expiration provisions, the company and legal counsel should consider the following issues.

Incentive Stock Options. The Internal Revenue Code limits the time after employment termination during which a participant (or the participant's beneficiary) can exercise an incentive stock option. Code Sec. 422(a)(1) requires that, for an option to qualify as an incentive stock option, the individual to whom the company grants the option must exercise the option no more than three months after his or her cessation of status as an employee (see Chapter 7 [¶701 *et seq.*] for a detailed discussion of the rules relating to incentive stock options).

> **Planning Note:** Some companies' incentive stock option agreements allow the participants more time to exercise after an employment termination, provided that, once the ISO limits are exceeded, the option will no longer qualify as an ISO.

To receive favorable tax treatment as an ISO, the ISO award recipient must not dispose of the shares acquired upon exercise of the ISO until at least two years after receipt of the ISO award and at least one year after exercise of the ISO (and receipt of actual shares). Despite the favorable tax treatment available, many employees cannot wait to sell their shares and do so immediately after (or upon) exercise. This is a disqualifying distribution, which converts the ISO to an NSO, and allows the company a tax deduction for the amount of income recognized by the employee/optionee upon exercise. Because of this deduction, the company has an interest in knowing whether the employee/optionee receives a disqualifying distribution. A well drafted plan and award agreement will require the employee/optionee to notify the company if he or she makes a disqualifying distribution.

> **Drafting Tip:** The Employee must notify the Company of any disposition of any Shares issued pursuant to the exercise of the Option under the circumstances described in Code Section 421(b) (relating to certain disqualifying dispositions) (any such circumstance, a "Disqualifying Disposition"), within 10 days of such Disqualifying Disposition.

Termination of Employment. Most companies design stock options to expire before the end of the regularly scheduled term if the participant's service with the company terminates. In most instances, the option plan or agreement provides a period of time after the date of termination for exercise, with the length of time dependent on the reason for termination. For example, the plan may give a participant who the company involuntarily terminates without cause three months following termination in which to exercise his or her option, whereas it gives a participant who voluntarily quits to work for another company only 30 days' post-termination in which to exercise. Many plans provide that a participant will forfeit any outstanding awards, including vested awards, if the company terminates his or her service for cause.

Death or Disability. The beneficiary of a deceased participant typically will be given a year in which to exercise an option in order to afford the estate sufficient time to get organized after the participant's death. Some plans provide for accelerated vesting in the event of the participant's death or disability. Code Sec. 422 and the regulations thereunder extend the three-months exercise rule for incentive stock options (noted above) to one year, if the individual to whom the company granted the incentive stock option dies or becomes disabled.[10]

Retirement. From time to time, we see companies tripped up by conflicting definitions of the term "retirement" among their qualified retirement plans, nonqualified retirement plans, stock incentive plans, and other benefit plans. Stock plans often distinguish retirements from other employment terminations for purposes of whether unvested options vest and/or the period after termination within which vested options may be exercised.

The case of *Jones v. Bank of America*[11] illustrates some of the problems that can arise in this situation. Upon termination of employment due to "retirement," the stock incentive plan at Bank of America ("BOA") gave an employee the full remaining term of the stock option (*i.e.*, until the 10-year expiration date) to exercise vested options. However, the BOA stock plan gave employees terminated for other reasons only 90 days to exercise any vested options. (Employees terminated due to death or disability were allowed 12 months to exercise vested options.)

The BOA stock plan defined "retirement" as a termination of employment after the employee has: (1) attained at least age 50; (2) completed a minimum of fifteen years of "vesting service;" and (3) attained a combined age and years of "vesting service" equal to at least 75. Mr. Jones worked at a company that had a "Rule of 70" before BOA acquired it, which BOA carried forward to its pension plan. One year after Mr. Jones lost his job in a reduction in force, he tried to exercise options, which BOA personnel had led him to believe would be exercisable for the remainder of their term, due to his eligibility for retirement under the pension plan. However, BOA informed him that his options had expired because he had not terminated due to retirement as defined in BOA's stock plan. Thus, his termination came under "all other terminations," with the 90-day exercise-or-canceled rule.

The court took a strict interpretation of the stock plan. The stock plan's definition of "retirement" was clear. The court found that Jones treatment as "retired" for purposes of the pension plan did not make his termination a retirement under the stock plan. Jones clearly did not meet the conditions for "retirement" under the stock plan.

In another federal court case involving the definition of retirement, *Willis Re, Inc. v. Hearn*,[12] a chief executive officer announced his "retirement" from his longtime employer – and went to work for a competitor. The company sought repayment from the former CEO of a portion of $1.75 million incentive awards made to him during the three years before his retirement. According to the former CEO, the governing award agreement allowed him to retain the award if he retired.

---

[10] Code Sec. 422(c)(6); Reg. §14a.422A-1, Q&A-2(b).

[11] *Jones v. Bank of America*, 311 F. Supp.2d 828 (D.C. Az. 2003).

[12] 200 F.Supp.3d 540 (E.D. Pa. 2016).

In March 2013, 2014, and 2015, the parties signed letter agreements making "AIP Awards" to the CEO of $1,750,000 each for 2012, 2013, and 2014, subject to:

If your employment with Willis ends prior to December 31, [2015] [2016] [2017] for any reason other than your incapacity to work due to your permanent disability (as "disability" or a substantially similar term is defined within an applicable Willis long term disability plan/policy), death, your redundancy (as redundancy is determined by Willis in accordance with its usual human resource administration practices) or your retirement, you will be obligated to repay to Willis a pro-rata portion of the net amount . . . of the Willis Retention Award (the "Repayment Obligation").

To define "retirement" the award agreements referred to (i) "your employment agreement" or (ii) "a written retirement policy applicable to you as a Willis employee," (iii) "by reference to the ending of your employment at such mandatory age as may apply in the applicable employment jurisdiction" or (iv) "as may be determined by Willis in its absolute discretion." The pension plan provided for retirement benefits, including an "Early Retirement Benefit" for a participant who retires on his "Early Retirement Date," which the plan defined as the first day of any month following the date the participant attains age 55 and has completed at least 10 years of service.

In May 2015, when he was 59 years old and employed by the company for 21 years, the CEO announced his "decision to retire from Willis Re Inc., effective May 15, 2015 to explore other options and pursue other interests." The company agreed that the CEO was eligible for an "Early Retirement Benefit" under the pension plan, but argued that the pension plan was not a "written retirement policy" under the AIP Award letters. Instead, the company claimed that the AIP Awards allowed it to define "retirement" in its absolute discretion, and that it had determined that the CEO did not retire.

Rather than construing the ambiguous contract terms against the drafter of the agreement, as many courts would do, the court instead announced that it would not assume the contract's language "was chosen carelessly" or "that the parties were ignorant of the meaning of the language employed."

The words used in subsection (ii) are "written retirement policy," not "Pension Plan." If these sophisticated parties negotiated incentive payments for a chief executive officer intended the term "written retirement policy" to be defined as eligibility for benefits under the Pension Plan, they were free to include it. The parties could have done so in the same way the parties expressly defined "disability" in the phrase "incapacity to work due to your permanent disability" as the definition "within an applicable Willis long term disability plan/policy" and "redundancy" as "determined by Willis in accordance with its usual human resource administration practices." The parties could have referred to the Pension Plan in subsection (ii), but did not do so.

The court held that the company was entitled to define "retirement under the AIP Awards in its absolute discretion" and upheld the company's decision that the CEO did not retire. At this stage, the company won. However, because the court's decision was a fairly close run thing, the CEO is likely to appeal it - unless the parties negotiate a settlement. Either way, it will lead to more legal costs and headaches for the company, which could have been avoided through better drafting.

Because the CEO left to work for a competitor, it seems like the case should have been an easy one. The court observed that the CEO had acknowledged his obligation to "comply with certain terms and conditions applicable to time after his retirement from Willis, including an obligation not to compete with Willis for a period of [12] months beginning May 15, 2015." However, apparently those provisions also were not clear.

.02 Allow for the Extension of the Option Expiration Period

An all too common situation we see is where an option or SAR is due to expire, but the holder cannot exercise it because the company is in a trading blackout period. Code Sec. 409A explicitly allows a company or agreement to automatically extent the exercise period of an option or SAR if making the payment would violate federal securities laws or other applicable law, provided that the period during which the option or SAR may be exercised is not extended more than 30 days after the exercise first would no longer violate an applicable federal, state, local, and foreign laws.[13]

.03 Payment of the Option Exercise Price

Plans that allow stock option awards should specify (or the award agreements should specify) the methods the company makes available for participants to pay their option exercise price. The most common types of payment methods are set forth below.

Cash or Check. Companies that require a participant to tender payment in cash or by check will also require that such payment accompany the exercise election. Often, the company will also collect payment of the withholding taxes triggered by the exercise at the time of exercise.

Payment with Stock. Most public companies' plans will permit a participant to use some form of stock to satisfy the exercise price of an option. One method is to permit participants to tender previously owned shares of the company's stock to pay the exercise price. This type of payment can be effected either by delivery of actual shares or by attestation (where the participant assigns his or her right to the shares to the company). If the optionee uses previously owned shares to pay the exercise price, the plan (or agreement) may provide that only "mature" shares (*e.g.*, shares held at least six months) be used in order to avoid incurring a charge to earnings for financial reporting purposes.

Most companies use automatic share withholding to cover tax payments due on their restricted stock and RSU transactions and do not even allow taxes to be paid in cash to avoid the possibility of an insider trading issue.

Another method for using shares to satisfy the exercise price is through broker-assisted cashless exercise procedures. Under a typical cashless exercise program, a participant will provide written instructions to the company and the

---

[13] Treas. Reg. § 1.409A-1(b)(5)(v)(C)(1).

broker indicating the participant's cashless exercise election and instructing the company to deliver to the broker the stock issuable upon exercise. The broker will then sell the shares, withhold from the sale proceeds, and deliver to the company an amount, in cash, equal to the option exercise price.[14] Most plans and companies no longer permit simultaneous exercise and sale by anyone other than senior officers, because such an exercise could trigger a compensation expense charge to the company's earnings for financial reporting purposes under current accounting rules.

The company or its plan administrator generally will establish and maintain a program and procedures to allow employees/optionees to exercise their exercisable options, and to pay the exercise costs of such option exercise, as follows:

1. *Exercise and Sell to Cover.* An "Exercise and Sell to Cover" exercise means an option exercise in which the optionee sells that portion of the optioned stock necessary to yield sufficient proceeds to pay (a) the exercise cost of the option, (b) applicable taxes and deductions as specified by the company, and (c) any brokerage fees or commissions.

2. *Exercise and Sell Balance.* An "Exercise and Sell Balance" or "Cashless" exercise means an option exercise in which the optionee sells all the stock acquired upon exercise, and applies a portion of the proceeds to pay (a) the exercise cost of the option, (b) applicable federal, state and local taxes and deductions, and (c) any brokerage fees or commissions. Cashless exercises may be market or limit orders.

3. *Exercise and Hold.* An "Exercise and Hold" exercise means an option exercise in which the optionee wishes to receive and hold all the optioned stock. It requires the payment by the optionee to the company (or its plan administrator) of the exercise cost of the option as well as all applicable taxes and deductions and any other applicable charges.

4. *Exercise with Stock (Stock-for-Stock).* A "Stock for Stock Exercise" means an option exercise in which the optionee wishes to deliver by attestation shares of stock owned by the optionee for at least six months (as certified by the optionee in writing) to pay the exercise cost of the option. The optionee may elect to pay applicable taxes and deductions by cash or check or by share withholding (from additional shares issued upon exercise of the option).

.04 Reload Options and Awards

A "reload" or "restorative" option is a feature that companies can add to stock option plans and awards to encourage company stock ownership. The concept of a reload option is that, when an individual uses in-the-money options or owned shares to pay the exercise price or satisfy the withholding obligation

---

[14] In order to avoid being treated as a prohibited loan to an executive under the Sarbanes-Oxley Act of 2002, experienced legal counsel will advise a company that its cashless exercise program must comply with the following steps: the broker must comply with Regulation T of the Federal Reserve System, the broker must verify that the company will deliver the shares of stock promptly, and the participant must designate his or her brokerage account with the broker as the account into which the securities are to be deposited.

for his or her stock options (*e.g.*, cashless exercise), the plan will automatically award the individual reload options to replace the stock or options he or she used for the exercise price. Typically, the exercise price for the reload option is equal to the fair market value of the underlying stock on the date that the plan grants the reload option. A reload option is a tool that permits an optionee to lock in an increase in share price on one date, and still have an option that he or she can exercise later, if the shares continue to increase in value. However, because of problems with adding reload features to a company's options, only a minority of companies' stock option plans and awards provide for reload options.

> **Example:** In 2015, ABC Corporation issued Executive D an option to purchase 30,000 shares of ABC Corporation's stock, with an exercise price of $10.00 per share. The option agreement provides for automatic award reload options.
>
> In 2018, the option is fully vested and exercisable and ABC's stock is trading at $30.00 per share. D exercises the stock option, in a simultaneous purchase and sale (cashless exercise) transaction, which results in D receiving 30,000 shares of stock and simultaneously selling 10,000 of the shares to pay the $300,000 exercise price. Pursuant to the automatic reload feature, ABC's stock incentive plan will immediately award D an option to purchase 10,000 shares of ABC stock.

Reload options may comfort an executive who is concerned that his or her options are about to go underwater, but it does not help when options are already underwater. To obtain a reload option, the executive must first exercise an existing option. If that option is underwater, he or she will not want to exercise.

In addition, granting options with reload features may pose more of an overhang threat than conventional options. This is because, when an executive exercises all of his or her conventional options, the overhang attributable to those options disappears—the options cease to exist. If the plan automatically grants an executive a certain number of options in connection with exercising the options, however, the exercise does not reduce the number of options he or she holds to zero, it just reduces the number of options he or she holds. Some commentators argue that reloads help alleviate overhang, because they encourage executives to exercise options earlier, thus at least reducing the number of options outstanding at any given time.

> **Planning Note:** If the stock incentive plan allows the company to provide for reload options in any award agreement evidencing an option, the reload feature should be subject to the following requirements:
>
> (1) The company may not add reload options to an already outstanding option. Any reload feature must be part of the option as originally granted.

(2) The reload must be automatic, not subject to the discretion of the company, board of directors, compensation committee or anyone else.

(3) The reload option must have an exercise price at least equal to the fair market value of the company stock at the time of reload.

(4) It may be granted with respect only to previously owned company stock used to pay the exercise price of the original option, only if the individual has owned the stock used to pay the exercise price for at least six months, and only with respect to individuals who are actively in service at the time of the grant.

(5) The award agreement that contains the reload feature must not permit multiple reloads (*i.e.*, no reload options may be granted on stock acquired through reload options) and must subject any option granted on reload to a vesting period of at least six months.

(6) Unless expressly stated in the award agreement reload options will not be granted in connection with payment of tax withholding by tendering company stock owned by the individual.

(7) The company must limit the duration of any reload options, by providing that an option granted on reload expires at the same time as the initial option would have.

Few, if any companies still include a reload feature in their option awards. Institutional investors frown on reload features, because they view them as permitting optionees to lock in gain in an unfair way. The optionee, presumably with superior inside information, can exercise and then sell, and is now off the hook as to his or her future performance. In addition, if reloads are automatic, rather than in the discretion of the plan administrator, the plan does not tie additional grants to the performance of the optionee or the organization. Finally, because an option with a reload feature can ultimately give an optionee more shares than an option without a reload feature, reloads are dilutive.

> **Sample Language:** We recommend adding an express prohibition for reload options. "In no event shall the Committee have the power or authority to include provisions in an Award Agreement that provides for the reload of the Option or Stock Appreciation Rights upon exercise or settlement."

.05 Plan Amendments

The stock plan must permit the company to amend the plan document. However, the amendment provision should address whether an amendment will require the consent of participants or the approval of stockholders.

Most plans require that participants consent to any potentially adverse change to outstanding stock awards. However, many plans permit the amendment of outstanding awards without the consent of participants, provided the company's board of directors or the plan's administrative committee determines that the amendment is in the best interest of affected participants. This subtle change has significance in part because of the SEC's tender offer rules, which could require a Schedule TO filing and full prospectus disclosure if more than a few participants must consent to a particular change in the terms of their awards. Additionally, plan documents should give the company the unilateral ability to amend the plan for Code Sec. 409A compliance, stock exchange listing requirements, and changes in applicable laws or other regulatory matters.

Most plan documents require stockholder approval for amendments only when required by law or because of the board's decision to seek it (*e.g.*, to satisfy stock exchange listing requirements).

Most plan documents also give the company the ability to terminate the plan or outstanding awards in certain change in control situations. For example, a stock plan could provide that:

> "In the event of a Change in Control that is a merger or consolidation in which Company is not the surviving corporation or which results in the acquisition of substantially all the Company's outstanding Stock by a single person or entity or by a group of persons or entities acting in concert, or in the event of a sale or transfer of all or substantially all of Company's assets (a 'Covered Transaction'), the Committee shall have the discretion to provide for the termination of all outstanding Options as of the effective date of the Covered Transaction; provided, that, if the Covered Transaction follows a Change in Control or would give rise to a Change in Control, no Option will be so terminated (without the Participant's consent) prior to the expiration of 20 days following the later of (i) the date on which the Award became fully exercisable and (ii) the date on which Participant received written notice of the Covered Transaction."

Among the scenarios under which this discretion is particularly useful to all parties are the following (keep in mind that most option agreements do not permit the company to simply terminate the option if it is not exercised):

- ABC Corporation buys XYZ Corporation. XYZ is a technology company with millions of options outstanding. Most are underwater. ABC does not want the stockholder dilution that will come by acquiring so many outstanding options and advises XYZ that: "We will assume the outstanding options for your top ten employees (by substituting options to purchase ABC stock). We will *not* assume the other options."

- A sale of assets occurs when some or all of the outstanding options are underwater. Seemingly, no optionee will want to exercise the options. However, absent some affirmative action, the legal contract formed by the option agreement does not go away.

¶685 Dilution and Overhang Problems

"Overhang" refers to the total amount of shares awarded and authorized for award under all of a company's stock-based plans, as a percentage of the company's total outstanding stock.[15] Stockholders generally dislike overhang because it dilutes the value of their stockholdings; that is, once the value of the

---

[15] For example, as of September 9, 2002, Microsoft Corporation had 1,402,000,000 shares awarded and authorized for awards under its stock-based plans, and 5,363,475,897 shares of publicly held stock outstanding, for an overhang percentage of approximately 26%.

shares appreciates, option holders may exercise, diluting the value of previous stockholders' holdings. Companies have several alternatives for dealing with overhang problems, each with certain advantages and disadvantages.

.01 Award Restricted Stock

Because an award of restricted stock is thought to be worth as much as five times the value of the award of a stock option, a company concerned about overhang can convey an equal amount of value to its executives at approximately one-fifth the rate of dilution. The disadvantage of restricted stock awards is that under current law they are taxable to recipients when they vest, whether or not the employee sells the stock (see Chapter 8 [¶801 *et seq.*] for a complete discussion of restricted stock awards).

.02 Award Stock-Settled SARs

By awarding stock-settled stock appreciation rights, a company can provide employees and other award recipients with the same value, while issuing significantly less shares. For example, if a company awarded an employee 10,000 stock-settled SARs with an exercise price of $10 per share and the employee exercised the stock-settled SARs three years later when the stock was trading at $20 per share, instead of the plan delivering to the employee 10,000 shares, it only would deliver to the employee 5,000 shares, the number of shares equal to the appreciation ($20 -$10 = $10. 10,000 × $10 = $100,000. $20 × 5,000 = $100,000).

Most stock incentive plans should permit the award of stock-settled SARs. Importantly, if a stock plan allows the award of restricted stock, the company should be able to add a provision allowing awards of RSUs without stockholder approval.

.03 Disclosure Requirements for Adopting a Separate Stock Option Plan—Not Approved by Stockholders

Although stockholder approval may not be required to issue shares under some plans, new disclosure rules inevitably result in stockholders finding out about such plans. The disclosure rules for employee benefit plans applicable to annual reports filed on Forms 10-K and 10-KSB and to proxy and information statements, require companies to disclose, at least annually, information about two categories of employee benefits plans: (1) plans approved by stockholders; and (2) plans not approved by stockholders. For each plan category, information must be disclosed in tabular form regarding:

- The number of employer securities to be issued upon the exercise of outstanding awards granted to participants;
- The weighted-average exercise price of outstanding awards granted to participants; and
- The number of employer securities remaining available for future issuance under employee benefits plans.

When the company is seeking stockholder approval to amend an existing employee benefit plan, the table should include information about the employer securities previously authorized for issuance under the plan. The rules permit companies to aggregate information about individual arrangements and plans in each disclosure category.

The rules also require a company to identify and describe briefly, in narrative form, the material features of each employee benefit plan in effect as of the end of the last completed fiscal year that was adopted without stockholder approval. The SEC will permit companies to satisfy their disclosure requirement by cross-referencing to the portion of their required ASC 718 disclosure containing descriptions of their non-stockholder-approved plans. The cross-reference should identify the specific plan or plans in the required ASC 718 disclosure that stockholders have not approved.

In addition, companies are required to file as an exhibit to their Form 10-K, any employee benefit plan adopted without the approval of stockholders in which any employee (whether or not an executive officer or director of the registrant) participates, unless immaterial in amount or significance.

¶695 Special Issues for Private Company Stock Plans

Privately held companies face certain issues when it comes to designing and operating a stock incentive plan that are of no concern to publicly held companies. Primarily, private companies must contend with the fact that no market exists for the securities underlying awards granted under their stock incentive plans. As such, participants often have no means of recognizing the benefits of owning company stock. Some of the ways in which this issue presents itself are set forth below.

.01 Shares Authorized for Awards

Where the plan specifies the number of shares authorized for awards as a percentage of the company's outstanding shares, a private company should specify whether that amount is expressed on a fully diluted basis or not.

> **Example:** ABC Corporation, a private company, has 100,000 shares outstanding in 2018. ABC's board approves a plan to award shares equal to 10% of the company's equity to executive employees. If the ABC Corporation 2018 Stock Incentive Plan authorizes 10,000 shares for awards, executives would end up holding only 9% of ABC's outstanding stock (10,000 ÷ 110,000).

> **Planning Note:** Experienced legal counsel will ask the company whether it is calculating the percentage of shares or equity it wishes to award under the plan on a "fully diluted" basis. In the Example above, if ABC wants to award fully 10% of its outstanding equity ownership to executives, it might draft the plan to read as follows: "The number of Shares available for Awards under the Plan will be ten percent (10%) of the Company's aggregate outstanding Shares on the Effective Date, on a fully diluted basis, treating all Shares authorized for Awards under this Plan as issued and outstanding, subject to adjustment as provided below."

.02 Fair Market Value

Unlike public company stock, the value of which typically is the stock's trading price on the public markets, private company stock does not always have a readily ascertainable fair value. A private company must consider how to value the stock underlying awards granted to participants under its stock incentive plan. In general, many private company plans will provide that the company's board of directors, in its sole discretion, will determine the fair market value of the company's stock. Other alternatives include drafting the plan to provide a formula for determining value or to provide for periodic appraisals by an outside party. (See ¶745 for a detailed discussion of fair market value for private companies.)

.03 Company Repurchase Rights

Private companies are often reluctant to share ownership with others, especially former employees. Accordingly, most private company stock incentive plans will give the company the right (a "call right") to purchase at fair market value on the date of such purchase the shares acquired by the participant through an award. Most plans limit a company's ability to exercise its call rights to the period after a participant terminates service and before an initial public offering.

In order to preserve favorable stock-based accounting treatment, counsel needs to draft repurchase and/or put option rights carefully and monitor the exercise of these rights. A practice of cashing-out awards could trigger liability-based accounting, which essentially involves ongoing "mark-to-market" adjustments to reflect the potential cost of redeeming outstanding awards.

.04 Participant Put Rights

Similar to call rights, put rights provide participants with the ability to require and/or request that a company repurchase shares acquired by the participant pursuant to an award at fair market value on the date of repurchase. Put rights give participants in a private company stock plan a liquidity opportunity even if the company does not eventually go public.

.05 Drag-Along and Tag-Along Rights

Some private company plans give the company "drag-along rights" and participants "tag-along rights." (Also sometimes referred to as "come along" and "bring along" rights in some plans.) Drag-along rights give a company the right to require participants to sell a proportionate amount of any shares acquired by the participants through awards on the same terms and under the same conditions as any significant sale contemplated by the company's principal stockholders, thus protecting the liquidity of the principal stockholders. Similarly, tag-along rights protect the liquidity of participants by giving them the right to require a company to include in any significant sale contemplated by the company's principal stockholders a proportionate amount of the shares acquired by the optionees through an award.

.06 Other Provisions

Consider adding a specific disclaimer to private company equity award agreements. In *Bors v. Duberstein*,[16] the controlling stockholders and the CEO convinced an executive to exchange her shares of phantom stock, for which she then was entitled to a cash payment, for shares of restricted stock. The restricted stock became worthless when the company filed for bankruptcy.

The executive sued, argued that by failing to disclose to her important facts about the poor financial prospects of the company, various stockholders and officers committed "fraud by omission." The court dismissed the executive's complaint because it concluded that the stockholders and officers owed the executive no duty to speak under Illinois law. The court based its holding primarily on two findings. First, the defendants' statements referred to future events, and statements that relate to contingent events, expectations or probabilities, rather than to present facts, will not support a claim of fraud under Illinois law.

Second, and more importantly to readers, the court found that the stockholders and officers had no duty to speak because the executive's restricted stock agreement specifically disclaimed any such duty, providing that neither the company nor its directors and officers had "any duty or obligation to disclose to [the executive] any material information regarding the business of [the company] or affecting the value of the stock." Thus, the court found, the executive was not justified in relying on oral statements made prior to her signing the restricted stock agreement. Companies should consider adding to their equity compensation plan and award agreements the type of language that proved helpful in *Bors*.

---

[16] *Bors v. Duberstein*, 3 EBC 1893 (N.D. Ill. 2004).

Chapter 7

STOCK OPTIONS AND STOCK APPRECIATION RIGHTS

¶701 Overview—Stock Options and Stock Appreciation Rights

Stock options and stock appreciation rights ("SARs") are each a form of equity-based incentive compensation under which a company gives the recipient the right to receive any appreciation or increase in value in the company's stock between the date it grants or awards the option or SAR and the date the recipient exercises it. Stock options and SARs are sometimes referred to as "appreciation-only awards."

A stock option is a contract that gives an employee, director, or other person (the "optionee") the right to purchase a specific number of shares of the company's stock at a fixed price (the "exercise price") at some future date or dates. A SAR is a contract that gives an employee, director, or other person the right to receive a payment equal to the increase in the value between the award date and the exercise date of a specific number of shares of the company's stock. Generally, the company's board of directors and the company's stockholders adopt a stock option or SAR plan to provide the company's employees with an opportunity to earn additional income beyond their salary and to provide an incentive to increase the value of the company and the price of the company's stock. The board of directors or compensation committee then awards stock options or SARs to employees (and others) according to the provisions of the plan (see ¶725).

Example 1: ABC Corporation's stock is trading at $10.00 per share on January 1, 2018. ABC Corporation awards Executive D (its chief executive officer) an option to purchase 1,000 shares of ABC common stock at $10.00 per share, exercisable by D at any time during the next ten years. If the market price of ABC's stock increases to $20.00 per share over the next few years (presumably, at least in part, due to Executive D's efforts), then D may decide to exercise the option to purchase ABC's stock at the bargain price of only $10.00.

Example 2: The same facts as in Example 1, except that ABC Corporation awards Executive D 1,000 SARs at $10.00 per share, exercisable by D at any time during the next ten years. If the market price of ABC's stock increases to $20.00 per share over the next few years, D may decide to exercise the SARs and receive $10,000 (1,000 x $10.00).

Although corporations most often award stock options and SARs, business entities other than corporations, including partnerships and limited liability companies, also can award options to purchase equity interests or SARs to their employees or others. These awards might be more properly referred to as "unit options" or "UARs."

.01 Stock Option/SAR Plan Basics

Companies award stock options or SARs to employees (and others) to compensate them for services in a manner that links the employees' interests to those of the stockholders. Stock options and SARs are only valuable to the employee or other recipient if the company's stock price increases. In this manner, the theory is, the employee will be strongly motivated to work to increase the company's value and stock price, thus aligning the employee's interests with those of the company's stockholders. Stock options and SARs also offer flexibility and favorable tax treatment to the employee/award recipient (see ¶715).

Stock options and SARs are generally awarded pursuant to a written plan. However, it is possible to award a stock option or SAR to one or more recipients by an individually designed agreement.

.02 Types of Stock Options

The two main types of stock options[1] are incentive stock options ("ISOs" also referred to sometimes as "qualified" or "statutory" stock options) and nonqualified or non-incentive stock options ("NSOs," "NISOs" or "NQSOs"). An ISO is an option awarded to an employee under a plan that meets the requirements of Code Sec. 422. An NSO is any stock option awarded under a plan or option agreement that does *not* meet the requirements of Code Sec. 422. NSOs do not qualify for the favorable tax treatment accorded ISOs. However, NSOs are not subject to the requirements for ISOs. Thus, the company has greater flexibility in setting the terms of an NSO.

The main difference between ISOs and NSOs, in addition to complying with the requirements of Code Sec. 422, is the tax consequences to the recipient and the company (discussed in ¶735 and ¶755 below). ISOs generally have significantly more favorable tax consequences for the employee/recipient, than do NSOs.

.03 SARs and a Comparison to Stock Options

A SAR gives an employee the right to receive the appreciated value of the company's stock when the right vests and the employee exercises it. Normally, the employee will receive the difference between the fair market value of the underlying stock on the SAR award date and the value of the stock on the date the employee exercises the SAR. SARs are like stock options in this respect. Once used only by private companies that did not want to issue real stock, SARs have enjoyed a resurgence in popularity among public companies in the form of stock-settled SARs (see ¶745).

---

[1] Under the ISO regulations, as a result of the $100,000 limitation (see ¶735.06), an option may be bifurcated into an ISO and NQSO. Reg. § 1.422-4(c).

.04 Treatment as Deferred Compensation—Code Sec. 409A

Code Sec. 409A[2] defines nonqualified deferred compensation to include any stock options or SARs unless the option or SAR is issued with an exercise price at least equal to fair market value, and the option or SAR satisfies certain other requirements. Failure to satisfy the requirements of Code Sec. 409A could result in significant penalties to the recipient (see ¶755).

.05 Accounting Treatment

Stock option and SAR awards result in a compensation expense for the company like other forms of stock-based and other compensation (see ¶765).

.06 Stock Options Compared to Warrants

Warrants are treated like options in many respects. Warrants are often referred to or defined as options. Many regulations, including the final regulations dealing with ISOs,[3] and laws classify warrants and options together. Warrants differ from options due to their purpose and function as a financing tool. Generally, warrants differ in form and function from the options used as equity compensation, but do not receive significantly different tax treatment (see ¶775).

.07 Stock Options to Charity

Some companies will award stock options to a newly-formed charitable organization immediately prior to the company's initial public offering. This raises certain legal issues (see ¶785).

.08 State Taxation of Gains on Stock Options and SARs

Most states conform to the federal method of taxing income derived from stock options or SARs. However, states must deal with the taxation of nonresidents and resident individuals who leave the state. Moreover, some states employ variations of the federal plan, or tax income derived from stock options and SARs differently. Finally, some states exclude income derived from stock options or SARs in certain specified cases as an incentive to lure certain industries to locate and remain within their state (see ¶795).

.09 Award Timing Issues, Including Option Backdating

In May 2005, an academic study found that many companies had awarded stock options on the same day as their stock price hit its low for the year or quarter.[4] In March 2006, this story hit the big time (despite a blog post by this author in November 2005) when *The Wall Street Journal* published a front page story concluding that the odds of certain option awards occurring at historic market lows (as they had been at several companies) were between 1 in 1 million and 1 in 300 billion[5]. Although the news media characterized this as the

---

[2] Added by the American Jobs Creation Act of 2004 (P.L. 108-357).

[3] Reg. § 1.421-1(a)(1).

[4] "On the Timing of CEO Stock Option Awards," by University of Iowa Professor Erik Lie.

[5] "The Perfect Payday," Charles Forelle and James Bander, March 18, 2006, *The Wall Street Journal*, page 1.

"backdating" of stock options, for companies that award stock options, the issue is much more complex. However, the variety of parties involved in investigating option award practices and pursuing their own interests creates significant potential problems for any company that awards stock options. Stock option timing issues are discussed in detail in Chapter 13.

¶715 Basics of Stock Options and SARs

A stock option is a contract that gives the recipient the right to purchase a specific number of shares of the company's stock at a fixed price (the "exercise price") at some future date or dates. A SAR is a contract that gives an employee, director, or other person the right to receive a payment equal to the increase in the value between the award date and the exercise date of a specific number of shares of the company's stock. Generally, the company's board of directors and the company's stockholders adopt an option or SAR plan to provide the company's employees with an opportunity to earn additional income beyond their salaries and to provide an incentive to increase the value of the company and its stock price. The board of directors or compensation committee then grants or awards stock options or SARs to employees (and others) according to the provisions of the plan.

.01 Rationale for Compensatory Stock Options and SARs

Proponents of stock options generally make the following well-supported arguments in favor of awarding compensatory stock options:

1. Stock options align the employee/award recipients' interests with those of stockholders, *i.e.*, an increasing stock price. Virtually no one disagrees with that general proposition. However, some have offered the criticism that stock options really reward employees for run-ups in the stock market, not their individual performance. This is because, they argue: how many employees can really create a difference in their employer's stock price through their performance? A similar, more clearly stated criticism of stock options is that, with respect to the majority of employees at the majority of companies, stock options fail to create a "line of sight" for the employee between his or her performance and compensation.

2. Stock options and SARs can compensate the employee for past and/or future services. Depending on how a company structures its option awards and communicates them, it can fairly state that the option is either a reward for past meritorious service or an incentive to perform well in the future, or both.

> **Comment:** An award with a shorter vesting schedule would be more characteristic of the reward for past service model. A "mega-award" with a longer vesting schedule would be more appropriate as an incentive for future performance. A series of annual awards with regular vesting schedules would have a strong retention effect.

Planning Note: As a general rule, retroactive compensation is not favored. Compensation may be awarded for past services, however, where an implied contract was shown, or where the amount awarded is not unreasonable in view of the services rendered.[6] An option award that emphasizes past service as its rationale could also create difficulty in enforcing vesting and claw-back provisions.

3. Stock options and stock-settled SARs allow the company to compensate employees and other persons without a cash outlay. However the company will recognize an accounting expense for option awards, and a secondary "cost" in the dilution of existing stockholders.

4. When an employee exercises a stock option, not only must he or she pay the option exercise price to the company, but also, in the case of NSOs, the company is entitled to a deduction for the amount of ordinary income recognized by the employee on the option exercise (see ¶725 and ¶735 for discussions of the income tax consequences of stock options). Thus, in theory, the option results in a net inflow of cash to the company. In practice, however, virtually all option exercises are "cashless," meaning that the company withholds the number of shares equal in value to the exercise price and any taxes due. Upon the exercise of an SAR, there is no exercise price, but the company would be entitled to a deduction.

5. Stock options and SARs are a tax-favored method of compensating employees (and others). A stock option or SAR award does not result in tax to the recipient at the time of the award or even when the award becomes vested and exercisable. The recipient will only recognize taxable income when he or she exercises the option or SAR or, in the case of incentive stock options, at the time the employee sells the stock acquired through the option[7] (as discussed in greater detail in ¶725 and ¶735.)

6. Prior to 2018, stock options and SARs were generally deductible under Code Sec. 162(m) without the need to establish additional performance goals if the strike price was equal to fair market value on the award date.

7. Stock options and SARs are generally not subject to Code Sec. 409A if (a) the exercise price is equal to fair market value on the award date, (b) the option is to purchase stock of the employer, and (c) the option contains no other deferral feature (see ¶745).

8. Because neither stock options nor SARs are considered outstanding shares until exercised, they are not counted in the denominator for calculating earnings per share.

---

[6] In *Zupnick v. Goizueta*, 698 A.2d 384 (Del. Ch. 1997), the court held that Coca-Cola's action in awarding its CEO, Roberto Goizueta, one million stock options based "on the substantial performance of the Company . . . and remarkable increase in market value of the Company during this period (nearly $69 billion)" was a valid exercise of the board's business judgment. The court determined that reasonable, disinterested directors properly concluded that the CEO's past services resulted in such an extraordinary benefit to the company, that, as a matter of law, the situation fell into the recognized exception to the common law rule that usually prohibits retroactive executive compensation.

[7] Note, however, that there may be alternative minimum tax consequences. See ¶725.12.

9. Before 2006, stock options allowed the company to compensate employees without reflecting an accounting charge against earnings on its financial statements, if the company drafted and operated its stock option plan and made awards in a manner that satisfied the accounting requirements set forth in APB No. 25.

Among the criticisms leveled against stock options and SARs are the following:

1. Under ASC 718, an expense charge must be recognized following the option or SAR award even though no economic benefit is derived by the recipient at that time - or at any time, if the stock price does not increase or the recipient does not exercise the options are SARs. Stock options and SARs create a potential disconnect between the amount of remuneration the employee receives and the amount of expense charged to the company.

2. Because employees have a long period during which to exercise their options or SARs, a well-timed exercise can result in significant gain even where the company's stock does not provide commensurate long-term gain for stockholders.

3. The award of stock options results in an increase of so-called "overhang," which ultimately can result in dilution of existing stockholders if the options are exercised. Institutional stockholders often measure dilution based on outstanding options or even reserved option shares.

4. In a falling stock market, underwater options or SARs may lose retentive value for employees who could switch employers to receive new options or SARs at the then-current market price.

5. Because options and SARs only have value if the company's stock price increases (and only have significant value if the company's stock price increases significantly), critics argue that they create too much incentive to take imprudent risks to increase the stock price rapidly. Stated differently, the options or SARs create an incentive to "hit a home run" rather than to achieve slow and steady growth.

Not surprisingly, given the remarkable tax and accounting advantages described above, before 2002, few voices were raised against the widespread use of compensatory stock options.[8] As noted above, one of the only criticisms of stock options before 2002 was that, with respect to the majority of employees at the majority of companies, stock options failed to create a "line of sight" for the employee between his or her performance and compensation.[9] The criticism follows that stock options really reward employees for run-ups in the stock market, not their individual performance.

---

[8] For a notable exception, *see* James A. Knight, *Value Added Management*, McGraw Hill, New York, 1998.

[9] James A. Knight, *Value Added Management*, page 221.

.02 Awarding Options and SARs

A company usually awards options or SARs by delivering a form of award agreement, which is an enforceable contract between the employee/award recipient and the company. An option award agreement will set forth the number of shares of stock with respect to which the company has awarded to the recipient an option to purchase, and the exercise price for those shares. A SAR award agreement will set forth the number of shares for which the appreciation payable to the recipient is measured, and the exercise price against which the appreciation will be measured.

An option or SAR award agreement will also set forth the period after which the recipient can exercise the SAR or option to purchase the stock ("vesting"), the time period within which the recipient must exercise the option or SAR, if at all (referred to as the "award term"), and any limitations on the recipient's right to exercise the stock option or SAR. A stock option agreement also will indicate whether it is an ISO or an NSO (ISOs are eligible for more favorable tax treatment for an employee than NSOs or SARs). While an ISO is contractual arrangement and, thus, can be amended, certain modifications could cause it to lose its status as an ISO. If the terms of an option that has lost its status as an ISO are changed with the intent to again qualify it as an ISO, such change will result in the awarding of a new ISO on the date of the change.[10]

Companies nearly always award options or SARs with an exercise price equal to the fair market value of the company's stock on the award date. For a public company, that typically is the closing price on the stock exchange or market where the company's stock is traded on the date of the award (or, sometimes, the closing price on the day before the award). At private companies, the board of directors generally determines the exercise price. Code Sec. 409A establishes rules and procedures private companies should follow in setting fair market value and exercise price.

.03 Value of a Stock Option or SAR

A stock option gives the employee the right to purchase shares of the company's stock at an exercise price during the term of the stock option. A stock option is valuable[11] because if the shares of the company's stock increase in price after the company awards the option, the employee will be able to purchase the stock at the lower exercise price and recognize an immediate gain (or "profit"). If the company is not publicly traded, there may be no market to sell the stock at the time of exercise, so the gain may be only "on paper." If the price of the

---

[10] Reg. § 1.422-2(a)(3) and Reg. § 1.424-1(e).

[11] In the context of the golden parachute rules of Code Sec. 280G (and the corresponding excise tax under Code Sec. 4999), special valuation rules apply. Rev. Proc. 2003-68, 2003-34 IRB 398 allows the use of Black-Scholes and other valuation methods, but provides flexibility to make adjustments for early termination of employment or changes in volatility of the stock price. Section 3.04 of Rev. Proc. 2003-68 provides for an 18-month window after a change in ownership or control during which option values can be recalculated based upon changes in the terms of employment or volatility of stock. The one valuation method that is specifically prescribed by Rev. Proc. 2003-68 is to value the option solely by reference to the spread between the exercise price and the value of the stock at the time of the change in ownership or control.

company's stock decreases after the company awards the option, the employee will not have suffered a loss so long as he or she has not exercised the option.

A SAR gives the employee the right to receive cash or shares of stock equal to the number of shares underlying the award, multiplied by the amount of appreciation in the stock price since the award date. A SAR is valuable[12] because if the shares of the company's stock increase in price after the company awards the SAR, the employee will be able to receive cash or shares in the amount of the increase and recognize an immediate gain (or "profit"). If the price of the company's stock decreases after the company awards the SARs, the employee will not have suffered any loss.

.04 Exercising a Stock Option or SAR

When an employee/award recipient "exercises" a stock option, the recipient purchases the company's stock and owns a number of shares equal to the number of options he or she exercised. An employee may purchase the stock subject to the stock option at any time during the option's term, so long as the limitations on the employee's right to exercise the stock option have not expired. These limitations are referred to as "vesting."

Similarly, when an employee/award recipient "exercises" a SAR, the recipient receives cash or stock equal in value to the number of shares underlying the SAR award, multiplied by the amount of appreciation. An employee may exercise the SAR at any time during its term, so long as the limitations on the employee's right to exercise have not expired.

The stock option or SAR agreement (or a related award notice) will contain a provision setting forth when the recipient may exercise the option or SAR. Generally, an employee will not be able to exercise the option or SAR when he or she first receives it. Often, however, on each anniversary of the award date, the employee will become entitled to exercise a portion of the stock option or SAR. A company places vesting restrictions on its stock options or SARs because it intends the award to provide the recipient with a benefit that covers a number of years during the recipient's employment or service. The employee is not required to exercise the option and buy the stock when it vests. After an option or SAR becomes vested, the employee chooses when (and whether) to exercise it, so long as the employee exercises the option or SAR before it expires.

.05 Premium and Discounted Options

Both ISOs and NSOs may be awarded at a premium (exercise price greater than fair market value on award date). Some companies issue premium options

---

[12] In the context of the golden parachute rules of Code Sec. 280G (and the corresponding excise tax under Code Sec. 4999), special valuation rules apply. Rev. Proc. 2003-68, 2003-34 IRB 398 allows the use of Black-Scholes and other valuation methods, but provides flexibility to make adjustments for early termination of employment or changes in the volatility of the stock price. Section 3.04 of Rev. Proc. 2003-68 provides for an 18-month window after a change in ownership or control during which option values can be recalculated based upon changes in the terms of employment or volatility of stock. The one valuation method that is specifically prescribed by Rev. Proc. 2003-68 is to value the option solely by reference to the spread between the exercise price and the value of the stock at the time of the change in ownership or control.

or SARs to create a higher hurdle for employee/recipients to achieve. However, because the Black-Scholes option pricing model does not fully discount the value of premium-priced options (*i.e.*, the Black-Scholes value is not reduced dollar-for-dollar with the amount of the premium), companies taking a charge under ASC 718 based on the Black-Scholes value will experience a higher charge than may be expected. Conversely, Black-Scholes tends to undervalue discount options. Given that some companies' employees already hold underwater options, the award of a premium-priced option (essentially an option that is underwater on the award date) may not be the most universally attractive compensation tool.

For example, in 2006, 3Com Corporation awarded premium priced options to its chief executive officer ("CEO"). One-fourth of the options had an exercise price that was 11% higher than the company's stock price on the award date and another fourth had an exercise price that was 33% higher than the company's stock price on the award date. Similarly, in 2005, Federal Signal Corporation awarded premium options to its president. The options' exercise price was $16.01, which was 12% higher than the stock's trading price on that date of $14.26. Also in 2005, Computer Associates awarded premium options to ten executives. The options' exercise price was $32.80, which was 20% higher than the stock's trading price on that date of $27.23.

In 2016, IBM awarded premium priced options to purchase a total of 1.5 million shares to its CEO, in four tranches. Each tranche would cliff vest in three years and have a different exercise price, ranging from $129.08 to $153.66 (premiums ranging from 5% to 25% of the award date stock price). In 2017, FreightCar America awarded premium priced options to its incoming CEO, one-third of which would vest when the stock price exceeds the award date price by $5.00; another one-third of which would vest when the stock price exceeds the award date price by $10.00; and the remaining one-third of which would vest if and when the stock price exceeds the award date price by $15.00 (premiums ranging from approximately 7% to 80% of the award date stock price).

NSOs may be awarded at a discount (exercise price less than fair market value on award date), although as discussed below, discount options would have certain negative tax and accounting consequences. A company might want to give discounted options to provide an employee with immediate value or to make up for awards that the company wishes it had made to the employee earlier, when the stock price was lower. Discount options generally require a smaller award to attain the same award value and therefore result in less dilution than premium-priced or at-the-money options. However, discount options (1) result in tax penalties under Code Sec. 409A unless the options are designed to comply with the strict requirements of Code Sec. 409A,[13] and (2) are generally not favored by institutional investors. Unless discounted options are properly accounted for and disclosed to investors and the SEC, liability for option "backdating" could result.

---

[13] Reg. § 1.409A-1(b)(5)(i)(A)(1).

.06 Stock Options as Performance-Based Compensation

Code Sec. 162(m) prohibits a publicly held company from deducting more than $1 million of compensation paid to certain covered employees in any tax year. However, prior to 2018, Code Sec. 162(m) contained a significant exception for so-called "performance-based compensation." Chapter 22 discusses Code Sec. 162(m) in more detail.

Prior to 2018, Code Sec. 162(m) and the regulations treated stock options and SARs more favorably than other types of performance-based compensation. In order to qualify as performance-based compensation, the stock option or SAR must satisfy the following requirements:

- The compensation committee must make the award;

- The plan under which the company awards the option or SAR must state the maximum number of shares with respect to which the company may award options or SARs during a specified period to any employee;

- The terms of the option or SAR must provide that the amount of compensation that the employee could receive is based solely on an increase in the value of the stock after the date of the award; and

- Certain stockholder approval and disclosure requirements must be satisfied.

If the amount of compensation was not based solely on an increase in the value of the stock after the date of the award, none of the compensation attributable to the award would have been qualified performance-based compensation. The only exception to this rule was that the award would have qualified as performance-based compensation if it was made on account of, or if the vesting or exercisability of the award was contingent on, the attainment of a performance goal that satisfied the performance goal requirements.[14]

The legislation known as the Tax Cuts and Jobs Act of 2017 ("TCJA") signed into law by President Trump in December 2017, eliminated the performance-based compensation exception from Code Sec. 162(m). The performance-based compensation exception was far and away, the most frequently used and most helpful exception, as it allowed public companies covered by Code Sec. 162(m) to deduct tens to hundreds of millions of dollars in compensation expense each year.

.07 Proxy Advisors' View of Stock Options

The proxy advisory firms (generally, Glass Lewis and ISS) regard stock options with disdain. Improvements in corporate governance and stock award practices have led more corporations to emphasize awards that link pay to performance. One would think that no form of stock-based compensation is more linked to performance than a stock option, since the stock option only rewards future increases in the company's stock price and has absolutely no value unless the company's stock price increases. But the proxy advisory firms

---

[14] Reg. § 1.162-27(e)(2)(vi)(A).

ignore this truth and argue that stock options tend to reward overall increases in the stock market (as if other stock-based awards did not).

Other stock option features that the proxy advisory firms find repugnant are single-trigger vesting upon a change in control (that is, without a termination of employment), provisions for reload options, and plans that permit a repricing or cash buyout of underwater options without stockholder approval.

.08 Federal Securities Law Reporting of Stock Options and Option Awards

Section 16(a) of the Securities Exchange Act of 1934 (the "Exchange Act") requires that an insider electronically file a Form 4 Statement of Changes of Beneficial Ownership of Securities with the SEC on or before the second business day after any transaction involving company stock, including transactions that are exempt from Section 16(b) of the Exchange Act. Examples of transactions that an insider must report include awards of stock options or SARs and the cashless exercise of stock options (and any sale of stock acquired through option exercises). Chapter 12 discusses federal securities law disclosure and Chapter 31 discusses proxy statement disclosure in more detail.

Additionally, public companies must report in their annual proxy statement the award of stock options or SARs to any named executive officer ("NEO"), the vesting of options or SARs held by a NEO, and any outstanding options or SARs held by a NEO, as follows:

- A company must disclose and discuss any stock option or SARs awards it made to an NEO in the most recently concluded fiscal year in the Compensation Discussion and Analysis ("CD&A") section of the proxy statement.[15]

- A company must disclose any option or SARs awards it made to an NEO in the most recently concluded fiscal year in the Summary Compensation Table of the proxy statement.[16]

- A company must disclose any stock option or SARs awards it made to an NEO in the most recently concluded fiscal year in the Awards of Plan-Based Awards Table of the proxy statement.[17]

- A company must disclose any option or SARs awards it made to an NEO in a previous year and held by an NEO as of the last day of the most recently concluded fiscal year, whether vested or not, in the Outstanding Equity Awards at Fiscal Year-End Table of the proxy statement.[18]

- A company must disclose any stock options or SARs that were exercised by an NEO in a previous year in the Option Exercises and Stock Vested Table of the proxy statement.[19]

---

[15] Regulation S-K, Item 402(b), 17 CFR 229.402.
[16] Regulation S-K, Item 402(c), 17 CFR 229.402.
[17] Regulation S-K, Item 402(d), 17 CFR 229.402.
[18] Regulation S-K, Item 402(f), 17 CFR 229.402.
[19] Regulation S-K, Item 402(g), 17 CFR 229.402.

.09 Using a Non-Recourse Loan to Exercise Stock Options

Many employees who want to exercise vested stock options lack the funds to pay the exercise price in cash. Usually, the company or its stock plan allows employees to use a cash-less or net-exercise mechanism to exercise stock options without paying the exercise price in cash. However, some companies and stock plans allow employees to pay the exercise price for stock options using a promissory note. Promissory notes can provide employees a means of exercising options and starting their capital gains holding periods without coming up with cash. However, the use of a full recourse or non-recourse loan/note to exercise stock options can raise issues for both employees and the company. Note that the Sarbanes-Oxley Act forbids public companies from making loans (or materially modifying existing loans) to executive officers.

A promissory note is "full recourse" if the note is a general obligation of the employee in the event of default, as opposed to recourse being limited to recovery the stock purchased. The company/lender has "recourse" to other assets of the employee/borrower, not just the stock as collateral, so that the company can make a full recovery in case of default. A "non-recourse" note or loan is secured only by the stock itself, and may be satisfied, for example, if the stock price declines, by simply turning back the stock. The note holder has "no recourse" to any assets of the borrower, other than the stock, in case of default.

If an employee uses a promissory note to pay the exercise price for stock options and the note is not substantially full recourse, then the option is not deemed to be exercised for federal income tax purposes. The IRS likely would deem the exercise transaction to be the award of another option, rather than the receipt of property/stock, until the employee pays down the note. (The IRS likely would treat the pay-down of the note as the exercise of the option, with the ordinary income tax consequences that result from regular option exercise.)

A promissory note used to exercise stock options must be substantially full recourse to start the capital gains holding period. Exercise using a full recourse note creates a real obligation for the employee even if the stock eventually becomes worthless. A bankruptcy trustee likely would attempt to collect on a full recourse note in the event the company goes bankrupt.

Payment of the stock option exercise price with a full recourse note generally results in a completed exercise for tax and accounting purposes. Payment with a non-recourse note does not. Generally, accountants view the exercise of an option with a non-recourse note as the award of a new option, which results in the need to calculate a new accounting expense on that date. Additionally, if the interest accrued on the loan/note also is a full-recourse obligation (or, apparently, if any interest paid is not refundable), then the terms of interest payments do not convert an otherwise fixed award to a variable award. Worse yet, the use of a non-recourse note could cause "variable" (as opposed to fixed) accounting expense treatment for the options.

Finally, any dividends paid on stock issued for a non-recourse note would not be accounted for as real dividends on stock but rather as additional compensation expense. This follows from treating a non-recourse note as a new option since dividends (or dividend equivalents) on an option are deemed compensation.

A company might be able to make a promissory note "substantially" full recourse and start the capital gains holding period by making the note automatically forgivable (i) in the event of a change in control or (ii) if the company terminates the employee without cause (the parties should check this with bankruptcy counsel). If the company were to forgive the note, this would create debt forgiveness income to the employee, which would be taxable at ordinary income rates. If the employee repaid the note in the future and there is a difference between the purchase price and fair market value at that time, the employee also may have a taxable event.

.10 IRS May be Able to Enforce a Tax Levy by Seizing and Selling Employee's Stock Options

In 2009, the IRS released a memorandum from the Office of the Chief Counsel declaring that the IRS can seize and sell executive stock options held by a taxpayer regardless of restrictions on the transferability of the options. The taxpayer had received and held both ISOs and nonqualified stock options. His employer's stock plan and the option award agreements unambiguously provided that the options could not be transferred except by will, the laws of descent or distribution, or pursuant to a QDRO, and during the employee's life, could only be exercised by the employee, his guardian or legal representative.

The employee had terminated employment with all options fully vested, and the IRS served a Notice of Levy on Wages, Salary and Other Income (Form 668-W) on the employer about that time. The Chief Counsel found that (i) a federal tax lien that arises upon assessment of the tax and notice and demand for payment attaches to all of the taxpayer's property and rights to property, according to Code Secs. 6321 and 6322, and (ii) Congress broadly defined "property" to reach every interest a taxpayer might have in property.

Regarding the nonqualified options, the IRS' Chief Counsel concluded that contractual restrictions on transferability (*e.g.*, in the plan or award documents) do not bar the IRS from seizing and selling property under the procedures of Code Sec. 6335. Regarding the ISOs, the IRS acknowledged that to be a qualified ISO, the option by its terms must not be "transferable by such individual otherwise than by will or the laws of descent and distribution," under Code Sec. 422(a)(5). However, the IRS also concluded here that it "is not bound by the restrictions on transferability applicable to the employee and levy may be enforced by the sale of the incentive stock options to a third party."

Obviously, it is good to be the King (or the IRS). In response, some companies have amended their stock plans and option award agreements to provide explicitly that any Notice of Levy or other attempt to transfer the options will result in the immediate forfeiture of the options. This may offer the employer the satisfaction of sticking it to the IRS, but may increase its risk of liability without rendering benefit at all to the employee (at least the transfer of options would reduce his tax liability somewhat).

¶725 Incentive Stock Options

An ISO is an option granted or awarded an employee under a plan that meets the requirements of Code Sec. 422. ISOs have very favorable tax consequences to employees. The primary purpose for awarding ISOs is the favorable tax treatment accorded them under the Code. Specifically, under Code Sec. 422, neither the award nor the exercise of an ISO results in tax consequences to the company or the employee/recipient. This deferral of tax consequences occurs even though the employee exercised the option at a price that is significantly less than the market value of the stock at the time of exercise. The employee recognizes taxable income only at the time of the sale of the stock acquired through the ISO and then at the long-term capital gains rate, subject to compliance with certain minimum holding period requirements.

To qualify for this favorable tax treatment, the ISO must meet the requirements of Code Sec. 422, as described in the following paragraphs. Assuming that these conditions are satisfied, the option will not fail to be an ISO merely because (i) it provides for cashless exercise;[20] (ii) the employee has the right to receive additional compensation, in cash or in property, when the option is exercised, provided such additional compensation is includible in income;[21] or (iii) the option is subject to a condition, or awards a right, that is not inconsistent with the ISO regulations.[22]

.01 Written Plan Requirement

The company must award the ISO pursuant to a written plan[23] (which may be in an electronic form.)[24] The plan document must specify the aggregate number of shares that the plan may issue as ISOs. Typically, a company maintains an omnibus incentive plan under which it may make ISO, NSO, and other stock based awards. The plan must set forth the maximum aggregate number of shares that the company may award as ISOs, but need not set forth the maximum number that the company may issue pursuant to NSOs or other awards.[25] Under the ISO regulations, only the net number of shares that the company issues pursuant to the exercise of an ISO is counted against the maximum aggregate number of shares. For example, if the exercise price of an ISO to purchase 100 shares equals the value of 20 shares, and the company permits the employee to use those 20 shares to pay the exercise price of the ISO, so that the company only issues 80 shares to the employee, then only 80 shares, rather than 100 must be counted against the maximum aggregate number of shares.[26] The plan also must specify the employees (or class of employees) who are eligible to receive ISOs under it. The plan could satisfy the requirement even though it gives the board of

---

[20] Reg. § 1.422-5(b).

[21] Reg. § 1.422-5(c).

[22] Reg. § 1.422-5(d).

[23] Code Sec. 422(b)(1).

[24] Reg. § 1.422-2(b)(1). The option itself may be in paper or electronic form. Reg. § 1.421-1(a)(3).

[25] Preamble to Fed. Reg. (August 3, 2004).

[26] Fed. Reg. (August 3, 2004).

directors, compensation committee, or an individual the authority to select the particular employees who are to receive ISOs.[27]

.02 Corporations Only

Only a corporation[28] can award ISOs. A corporation can only award ISOs to the employees of a corporation or its parent or subsidiary corporation, and the ISO can only be to purchase stock[29] of any of such corporation.[30] ISOs are not available to the employees of a partnership or LLC. However, the IRS has permitted certain employees of non-corporate entities to receive ISOs, where their employer is part of a chain of corporations.[31]

.03 Stockholder Approval

The stockholders of the awarding company must approve the option plan within 12 months before or after the date the company's board of directors adopts the plan.[32]

.04 Employees Only

In general, a company can only award ISOs to individuals who are its employees on the date the company awards the ISO. Nonemployee board members, partners, or other self-employed persons, independent contractors, outside service providers, and business entities cannot receive ISOs. A company could award an ISO to a potential employee conditioned upon the commencement of employment. In such a case, law would treat the option as awarded on the date that employment begins, and would test the award date requirements necessary to be an ISO as of the day that employment commences.[33] However, under the final ISO regulations, in the case of an assumption or substitution of options, an option will be treated as awarded to an employee of the awarding company if the employee is an individual who is in the three month period following the termination of the employment relationship.[34]

For an option to remain an ISO, the individual to whom the company awards the option must remain an employee at all times from the award date to the day three months before the date of exercise.[35] Stated another way, if the employee terminates employment with the company that awarded the ISO, the employee must exercise the ISO, if it is to qualify for ISO treatment, no later than three months after the date he or she terminated employment. For this purpose,

---

[27] Reg. § 1.422-2(b)(4).

[28] For these purposes, a corporation includes an S corporation, a foreign corporation, and a limited liability company that is treated as a corporation for all federal tax purposes. Reg. § 1.421-1(i)(1).

[29] Because corporations include foreign corporations and limited liability companies, the definition of stock includes ownership interests other than capital stock. Reg. § 1.421-1(d)(3).

[30] Code Sec. 422(b).

[31] IRS Letter Ruling 200112021 (Dec. 15, 2000).

[32] Code Sec. 422(b)(1). As a general rule, a plan is adopted when it is approved by the awarding cor-

poration's board of directors. However, if the board's action is subject to a condition, such as stockholder approval or the happening of a particular event, the plan is adopted on the date the condition is met or the events occur, unless the board's resolution fixes the date of approval by the board as the date of the board action. Reg. § 1.422-2(b)(2). By virtue of this regulatory position, the stockholder approval requirement can effectively be mooted.

[33] Reg. § 1.421-1(c)(2).

[34] Reg. § 1.421-1(h)(1).

[35] Code Sec. 422(a)(2).

the law considers the employment relationship to continue intact while an individual is on military leave, sick leave or other bona fide leave of absence, if the period of leave does not exceed three months or, if longer, the individual's right to reemployment is provided by statute or contract.[36]

.05 Exercise Period

To qualify as an ISO, the option must require the employee to exercise the option, if at all, within ten years after it is awarded.[37] As noted above, consistent with the requirement that a company can only award ISOs to employees, to qualify for ISO treatment, an employee must exercise the ISO, if at all, no later than three months after the date of the employee's termination of employment.[38] Code Sec. 422 and the regulations thereunder create a special exception in the cases of an employee terminated due to death or disability, who may exercise an ISO for up to one year after such termination.[39] Additionally, the holding period requirements ordinarily applicable to ISOs do not apply in the case of an employee terminated due to death or disability.[40]

.06 Limitations

To qualify as an ISO, the company must award the option within 10 years from the date it adopted the plan, or the date the stockholders approved the plan, whichever is earlier.[41] The option's exercise price also must be not less than the fair market value of the stock at the time the company awards the ISO.[42] The fair market value may be determined in any reasonable manner, including the valuation methods for estate taxes. Moreover, even if the exercise price is less than the fair market value, the option may still qualify as an ISO if there was a good faith attempt to satisfy this requirement. One condition for qualifying as a good faith attempt is to determine fair market value with regard to nonlapse restrictions, but without regard to lapse restrictions. In addition, for nonpublicly traded stock, the fair market value at the award date must be based upon the average of the fair market values as of such date, as set forth in the opinions of "completely independent" and well-qualified experts. Such opinions may take into account the employee's status as a majority or minority stockholder.[43] However, if the awardee is a more than ten percent stockholder, then the rules with respect to good faith determination are inapplicable.[44]

The fair market value of the stock with respect to which the incentive stock options are exercisable for the first time may not exceed $100,000 during any calendar year.[45] IRS regulations consider an ISO to be first exercisable during a calendar year if the ISO will vest and become exercisable at any time during the year. However, if an employee's ability to exercise the ISO in a year is subject to an acceleration provision, then the regulations consider the option first exercisa-

---

[36] Reg. § 1.421-1(h)(2).
[37] Code Sec. 422(a)(3).
[38] Code Sec. 422(a)(2).
[39] Code Sec. 422(c)(6); Reg. § 1.422-1(a)(3); Reg. § 1.421-2(c).
[40] Reg. § 1.421-2(c).

[41] Code Sec. 422(b)(2).
[42] Code Sec. 422(b)(4).
[43] Reg. § 1.422-2(e)(2).
[44] Reg. § 1.422-2(f).
[45] Code Sec. 422(d).

ble in the calendar year in which the acceleration provision is triggered.[46] Also under the final regulations, an option (or portion thereof) is disregarded if, prior to the calendar year during which it otherwise would have become exercisable for the first time, or the option is modified, cancelled, or transferred. If, however, an ISO (or portion thereof) is modified, cancelled, or transferred at any other time, such ISO (or portion thereof) is treated as outstanding according to its original terms until the end of the calendar year during which it otherwise would have become exercisable for the first time.[47] To the extent an option award exceeds the $100,000 limit, the remaining options are treated as NSOs.[48]

> **Example 1:** If ABC Corporation's stock is trading at $100.00 per share on January 1, 2018, and ABC Corporation awards Executive D (its chief executive officer) an option to purchase 10,000 shares of ABC common stock at $100.00 per share exercisable by D at any time during the next ten years, only 1,000 of the options could qualify as ISOs ($100.00 × 1,000 = $100,000). If the option becomes vested and exercisable 1/5 per year over five years, e.g., 2,000 options per year, one-half of the options vesting in each year could qualify as ISOs ($100.00 × 1,000 = $100,000).

.07 ISO Holding Period

The ISO holding periods are the length of time that the employee needs to hold the shares of stock purchased when he or she exercises the stock option. To qualify for the favorable tax treatment of Code Sec. 422, the employee must hold and may not dispose of the stock acquired under the ISO until after the later of (1) one year from the date the employee exercised the ISO, or (2) two years from the date the company awarded the ISO.[49] If the employee does not hold the shares long enough, the employee will have made a "disqualifying disposition."

A "disqualifying disposition" is the sale or disposition (including making a gift of purchase shares) of stock acquired upon the exercise of an ISO before the end of the holding periods. Upon a disqualifying disposition, the employee would recognize taxable ordinary income (like salary), measured as the difference between the fair market value of the shares on the date the employee exercised the stock option and the exercise price. Any additional gain would be long or short-term capital gain depending on how long the employee held the shares. If the sales price is higher than the exercise price, but not higher than the market price on the exercise date, the amount between the exercise price and sales price would be ordinary compensation income and there would be no capital gain or loss. If the sales price is lower than the employee would have no compensation income and a short-term capital loss. The company must include the taxable income on the employee's Form W-2 (or Form 1099) for the year in which the disqualifying disposition occurs.

---

[46] Reg. § 1.422-4(b)(4).

[47] Reg. § 1.422-4(b)(5).

[48] Reg. § 1.422-4(a).

[49] Under Code Sec. 421(d), if a share of stock is transferred to an eligible person under Code Sec. 1043(b)(1) pursuant to the exercise of an ISO, and that person disposes of the shares pursuant to a certificate of divestiture under Code Sec. 1043(b)(2), such disposition is treated as satisfying the holding period requirements.

Planning Note: Experienced legal counsel will draft the option agreement to require the employee to notify the company if he or she makes a disqualifying disposition.

Code Sec. 422 and the regulations thereunder waive the holding period requirement, in the case of the death or disability of the individual to whom the company awarded the incentive stock option.[50]

.08 Special Rules Applicable to Ten Percent Stockholders

If the plan awards an option to a 10%-or-more stockholder,[51] Code Sec. 422(c)(5) provides that the exercise price must be at least 110% of the fair market value of the stock subject to the option. Additionally, an option awarded to a 10%-or-more stockholder must provide that it is not exercisable after the expiration of five years from the option's award date.

.09 Duration of the Plan

The plan must award the option within ten years from the date the board of directors adopts the plan or, if earlier, the date the stockholders approve the plan.

.10 Transferability

The ISO must not be transferable (other than by will or the laws of descent and distribution) by the employee to whom the ISO was awarded, and must be exercisable, during the lifetime of the employee, only by the employee.[52] This statutory requirement does not preclude pledging the stock purchasable under the ISO as security for a loan the employee uses to pay the exercise price. However, if an ISO is transferred incident to a divorce or pursuant to a domestic relations order, it would no longer qualify as an ISO as of the date of transfer.[53]

.11 Tax Treatment of the Employee

Under the current tax rules, if the option plan and the award satisfy the ISO requirements, the employee will not recognize income when the company awards him/her the ISO or when he or she exercises the ISO. At the time of exercise, the difference between the ISO's exercise price and the fair market value of the company's stock is not taxed (unless the employee is subject to the alternative minimum tax—as explained in ¶725.12). With an ISO, the employee does not incur any taxable income until the employee sells or otherwise disposes of the shares of stock purchased under the option. If the employee holds the shares of stock long enough, the difference between the option exercise price and the price at which the employee sells or otherwise disposes of the stock will be long-term capital gain or loss. Currently, long-term capital gain gets a preferential tax rate. In addition, an employee may be able to offset capital gains by capital losses.

---

[50] Reg. § 1.422-2(c)(1).

[51] For purposes of determining whether a stockholder is a 10% or more stockholder, certain attribution rules apply. Reg. § 1.424-1(d). However, any stock that the optionee may purchase under outstanding options is not treated as stock owned by the individual. Reg. § 1.422-2(f).

[52] Code Sec. 422(b)(5); Reg. § 1.421-1(b)(2).

[53] Reg. § 1.421-1(b)(2). But, see IRS Letter Ruling 200519011, May 19, 2005.

Example 2: Assume ABC Corporation's stock is trading at $10.00 per share on January 1, 2017. On that date, ABC Corporation awards Executive D an incentive stock option to purchase 1,000 shares of ABC common stock at $10.00 per share. On March 15, 2018 (at least one year after the option award date), Executive D exercises the option to purchase all 1,000 shares, at a time when the market price of ABC's stock is $20.00 per share. Because Executive D only had to pay $10,000 for shares worth $20,000, Executive D made $10,000 "on paper" simply by exercising her stock option.

Since the option is an ISO, D will recognize no taxable income at the time of exercise (although the $10,000 paper gain may be subject to the alternative minimum tax).

If the stock option had been a NSO, Executive D would owe taxes on the $10,000 spread as though it had been paid to D as salary. D also would be required to pay the company approximately 34% of the $10,000 spread (or $3,400) at the time of exercise to cover income tax withholding, and an additional amount to cover FICA taxes.

If Executive D were to hold the ABC stock acquired upon exercise of the ISO for at least one year after the exercise date, and sell all 1,000 shares at a time when ABC's market price was $25.00 per share, D's $15,000 gain ($25,000 sales price, less $10,000 option exercise price) would be taxable at long-term capital gains rates.

.12 Alternative Minimum Tax

Congress added the Alternative Minimum Tax ("AMT") provisions to the Internal Revenue Code in 1969, in response to media reports over 21 millionaires who legally paid no income tax (because their clever tax lawyers helped them take advantage of numerous deductions and other provisions). Subsequent legislation has either increased or decreased the AMT rates, depending on the political party in power.

The Code imposes an AMT on an individual taxpayer to the extent the taxpayer's alternative minimum tax liability exceeds his or her regular income tax liability. An individual's alternative minimum tax is the sum of (i) 26 % of so much of the taxable excess as does not exceed $175,000, and (ii) 28 % of the remaining taxable excess. The taxable excess is the amount by which the alternative minimum taxable income ("AMTI") exceeds an exemption amount. An individual's AMTI is his or her taxable income increased by certain preference items and adjusted by determining the tax treatment of certain items in a manner that negates the deferral of income resulting from the regular tax treatment of those items.

The item of AMT income that most often surfaces in the executive compensation area is the bargain element an employee receives upon the exercise of an ISO. An employee does not recognize taxable income on the spread between the ISO's exercise price and the fair market value of the stock on the date of the exercise. However, the AMT rules treat the exercise of an ISO like the exercise of a non-qualified option. The spread constitutes a tax preference[54] item requiring computation of the AMT[55] on the difference between the fair market value of the stock and the option price. The employee would be required to complete and file IRS Form 6251 to determine whether the employee owed AMT. If the tax amount calculated under the AMT was greater than the amount of ordinary income tax the employee owed for the year, the employee would need to pay the greater AMT amount.

> **Example:** In Example 2, Executive D would need to include her $10,000 "paper" gain upon the exercise of her option in March 2018, as a tax preference item for purposes of calculating whether she owes AMT. D would need to complete and file Form 6251 with her 2018 federal income tax return.

When the employee eventually sells the stock, for purposes of computing capital gain or loss for purposes of AMTI, the adjusted basis of the stock includes the amount taken into account as AMTI. The adjustment relating to incentive stock options is a deferral adjustment and therefore generates an AMT credit in the year the taxpayer sells the stock.

The AMT is calculated at the time of the ISO exercise. It matters not that the stock acquired upon the ISO exercise declines in value. Accordingly, when the internet stock bubble burst in early 2000, many internet executives who had exercised ISOs and enjoyed substantial paper gains incurred devastating liabilities under the AMT. Moreover, in many cases, the value of the executive's stock holdings had decreased so significantly that the executive could not even sell the stock to cover the tax liability.[56]

Code Sec. 6039 requires an employer to file an information return with the IRS, in addition to providing information to the employee, regarding the transfer of stock pursuant to exercise of an incentive stock option, and to certain stock transfers regarding employee stock purchase plans.

Under Code Sec. 63, an individual's minimum tax credit allowable for any taxable year beginning before January 1, 2013, is not less than the "AMT refundable credit amount." The "AMT refundable credit amount" is the greater of (1) the lesser of $5,000 or the long-term unused minimum tax credit, or (2) 20% of the long-term unused minimum tax credit. The long-term unused minimum tax credit for any taxable year means the portion of the minimum tax credit attributable to the adjusted net minimum tax for taxable years before the third taxable year immediately preceding the taxable year (assuming the credits are used on a first-in, first-out basis). In the case of an individual whose adjusted gross income for a taxable year exceeds the threshold amount (within the meaning of Code Sec. 151(d)(3)(C)), the AMT refundable credit amount is reduced by the applicable percentage (within the meaning of Code Sec. 151(d)(3)(B)). The additional credit allowable due to this provision is refundable.

---

[54] Code Sec. 56(b)(3).
[55] Code Sec. 55.

[56] *See, for example,* Damien Cave and Amy Standen, *"Death to the AMT!"* Salon.com, April 18, 2001, describing an internet employee whose tax bill exceeded his gross income.

Example: If an employee exercised 1,000 ISOs with an exercise price of $10.00 per share at a time when the stock was trading on the market for $20.00, the employee would not recognize ordinary income on the $10,000 "paper gain," but that $10,000 would be AMTI. If the income tax calculated on the employee's total income, including AMTI for the year, is greater than that imposed on his or her regular income alone, the employee must pay tax on the AMTI. However, because the employee did not actually receive the AMTI, the Code also provides a tax credit attributable to his or her AMT liability. This is where the Act made a crucial change.

An example from the Explanation of the Tax Relief and Health Care Act, which amended Sec. 63, by the Joint Tax Committee reads as follows:

Assume in 2010 an individual has an adjusted gross income that results in an applicable percentage of 50% under Code Sec. 151(d)(3)(B), a regular tax of $45,000, a tentative minimum tax of $40,000, no other credits allowable, and a minimum tax credit for the taxable year (before limitation under Code Sec. 53(c)) of $1.1 million — of which $1 million is a long-term unused minimum tax credit. The AMT refundable credit amount for the taxable year is $100,000 (20% of the $1 million long-term unused minimum tax credit reduced by an applicable percentage of 50%). The minimum tax credit allowable for the taxable year is $100,000 (the greater of the AMT refundable credit amount or the amount of the credit otherwise allowable). The $5,000 credit allowable without regard to this provision is non-refundable. The additional $95,000 of credit allowable by reason of this provision is treated as a refundable credit. Thus, the taxpayer has an overpayment of $55,000 ($45,000 regular tax less $5,000 non-refundable AMT credit less $95,000 refundable AMT credit). *The $55,000 overpayment is allowed as a refund or credit to the taxpayer.* The remaining $1 million minimum tax credit is carried forward to future taxable years.

If, in the above example, the adjusted gross income did not exceed the threshold amount under Code Sec. 151(d)(3)(C), the AMT refundable credit amount for the taxable year would be $200,000, and the overpayment would be $155,000.

The TCJA temporarily increased the AMT exemption amounts and raised the so-called phase-out thresholds for these exemptions, effective after December 31, 2017, and before January 1, 2026. In 2018, the AMT exemption amounts for taxpayers:

- Filing as a single or head of household, increased to $70,300, from $54,300,
- Married filing jointly, increased to $109,400, from $84,500, and
- Married filing separately, increased to $54,700, from $42,250.

A taxpayer's ability to utilize these exemptions phases out as the taxpayer's annual income increases. For 2018, the TCJA substantially increased the income levels at which the phase-outs begin to apply to $1,000,000 for joint filers and $500,000 for single filers, from $160,900 and $120,700, respectively.

.13 Tax Treatment of the Company

The company is not entitled to a deduction upon the employee's exercise of an ISO, or upon the employee's subsequent sale of stock, unless the exercise or sale causes the option to fail to qualify as an ISO. In case of a disqualifying disposition or other failure, the option would essentially be converted to a NSO, and the company would be entitled to a deduction according to the law applicable to NSOs. The company does not send a Form W-2 to an employee who exercises an ISO.[57]

As noted above, to receive favorable tax treatment as an ISO, the ISO award recipient must not dispose of the shares acquired upon exercise of the ISO until at least two years after receipt of the ISO award and at least one year after exercise of the ISO (and receipt of actual shares). Despite the favorable tax treatment available, many employees cannot wait to sell their shares and do so immediately after (or upon) exercise. This is a disqualifying distribution, which converts the ISO to an NSO, and allows the company a tax deduction for the income recognized by the employee/award recipient upon exercise. Because of this deduction, the company has an interest in knowing whether the recipient receives a disqualifying distribution. A well drafted plan and award agreement will require the recipient to notify the company if he or she makes a disqualifying distribution.

> **Example:** The Employee must notify the Company of any disposition of any Shares issued pursuant to the exercise of the Option under the circumstances described in Code Sec. 421(b) (relating to certain disqualifying dispositions) (any such circumstance, a "Disqualifying Disposition"), within 10 days of such Disqualifying Disposition.

.14 Possible Impact of the Tax Cuts and Jobs Act of 2017

As discussed in ¶715, the TCJA signed into law by President Trump in December 2017, eliminated the performance-based compensation exception from Code Sec. 162(m). In light of the limitation on covered employees' deductible compensation, some companies are likely to award ISOs to covered employees. As discussed, generally ISOs do not result in a tax deduction for the company, but they do provide favorable tax consequences for the employee/recipients. As long as the company will not be able to deduct the gain on some equity awards, why not provide better tax treatment to the executives?

¶735 Nonqualified Stock Options

A nonqualified stock option is simply a stock option granted or awarded to an employee under a plan or option agreement that does not meet the requirements of Code Sec. 422. NSOs do not qualify for the special tax treatment accorded ISOs, but neither are they subject to the requirements for ISOs. Thus, the employer has greater flexibility in setting the terms of an NSO. Business entities other than corporations can award NSOs, and companies are free to award NSOs to nonemployee directors, independent contractors, and even other business entities. The Code Sec. 422 rules on stockholder approval, holding

---

[57] The American Jobs Creation Act of 2004 (P.L. 108-357) modified the definition of wages for purposes of FICA, FUTA and the Railroad Retirement Act to exclude from the definition of wages remuneration on account of a transfer of a share of stock pursuant to an ISO of an account of a disqualifying disposition of an ISO. Code Sec. 3121(a), Code Sec. 3306(b) and Code Sec. 3231(e).

periods, duration of the plan, and exercisability after employment termination do not apply.

Code Sec. 83 generally governs the taxation of NSOs. Pursuant to Reg. § 1.83-7(a), an issuance of an NSO that does not have a readily ascertainable value is not included in the recipient's income until the option is exercised or disposed of, even if in the interim the value of the option becomes readily ascertainable.

.01 Tax Treatment of the Recipient

Generally, an employee is not taxed on the award of an NSO or the vesting of the NSO (the exception would be if the option has a readily ascertainable fair market value and is transferable or is publicly traded). The employee recognizes taxable income only when he or she exercises the NSO.[58] When the employee exercises the NSO, the employee will recognize ordinary income on the difference between the option's exercise price and the fair market value of the company's stock on the date of exercise. After the exercise, future appreciation in the value of the stock owned by the employee could be taxable at capital gain rates.

> **Example 1:** Assume ABC Corporation's stock is trading at $10.00 per share on January 1, 2018. ABC Corporation awards Executive D a NSO to purchase 1,000 shares of ABC common stock at $10.00 per share. If D exercises the option to purchase all 1,000 shares at a time when the market price of ABC's stock is $20.00 per share, D will recognize ordinary income of $10,000 at exercise ($10.00 × 1,000 shares). If D holds the ABC stock acquired upon exercise of the option for at least one year after the exercise date, and sells all 1,000 shares at a time when ABC's market price is $25.00 per share, D's $5,000 gain would be taxable at long-term capital gains rates.

Code Sec. 83(a), entitled "Property transferred in connection with performance of services," provides, in pertinent part:

(a) General rule

If, in connection with the performance of services, property is transferred to any person other than the person for whom such services are performed, the excess of—

(1) the fair market value of such property ... at the first time the rights of the person having the beneficial interest in such property are transferable or are not subject to a substantial risk of forfeiture, whichever occurs earlier, over

(2) the amount (if any) paid for such property, shall be included in the gross income of the person who performed such services in the first taxable year in which the rights of the person having the beneficial interest in such property are transferable or are not subject to a substantial risk of forfeiture, whichever is applicable ....

---

[58] In *Miller v. United States*, 345 FSupp2d 1046 (N.D. Cal 2004) a federal district court rejected a taxpayer's argument that he should not be taxed upon exercise but rather when his shares were liquidated by a broker under the terms of a margin loan agreement pursuant to a cashless exercise program.

Reg. § 1.83-1(a)(1) explains that property is not taxable under Code Sec. 83(a) until (1) it has been "transferred" and (2) has become "substantially vested" in the taxpayer. "[A] transfer of property occurs when a person acquires a beneficial ownership interest in such property . . . "[59] "Property is substantially vested . . . when it is either transferable or not subject to a substantial risk of forfeiture."[60] "The rights of a person in property are subject to a substantial risk of forfeiture if such person's rights to full enjoyment of such property are conditioned upon the future performance of substantial services by any individual."[61] The determination of "whether a risk of forfeiture is substantial or not depends upon the facts and circumstances." The "risk that the value of the property will decline during a certain period of time does not constitute a substantial risk of forfeiture."

The rights of a person in property are transferable only if the rights in such property of any transferee are not subject to a substantial risk of forfeiture.[62] For example, "property is transferable if the person performing the services or receiving the property can sell, assign, or pledge (as collateral for a loan, or as security for the performance of an obligation, or for any other purpose) his interest in the property to any person other than the transferor of such property and if the transferee is not required to give up the property or its value in the event the substantial risk of forfeiture materializes."[63]

In Notice 2004-28,[64] the IRS warned taxpayers against making frivolous claims for avoiding income tax or alternative minimum tax on the exercise of stock options. The five positions that the IRS considered frivolous were:

- Options should have been taxed at their award date rather than the exercise date;
- The fair market value of the stock acquired upon exercise of an option is reduced by an employer restriction that prohibits the employee from selling the stock for a specified period of time;
- A broker's sale of stock purchased under a NSO due to a margin call, where the stock was pledged as security for a loan to pay the exercise price, is a forfeiture of the stock causing an ordinary loss rather than a capital loss;
- The purchase of stock using borrowed funds is not, in substance, a purchase if the employee does not have the ability to repay the loan; and
- Options are the economic equivalent of the underlying stock and are not subject to tax of the spread upon exercise.

Interests in nonqualified stock options transferred as part of a divorce are subject to tax, withholding and reporting requirements when the transferee exercises the options rather than when the transfer occurs. In Rev. Rul. 2002-22[65] and Notice 2002-31,[66] the IRS held that neither party to a proposed settlement

---

[59] Reg. § 1.83-3(a).

[60] Reg. § 1.83-3(b).

[61] Code Sec. 83(c)(1); *see also* Reg. § 1.83-3(c)(1).

[62] Code Sec. 83(c)(2); *see also* Reg. § 1.83-3(d).

[63] Reg. § 1.83-3(d).

[64] Notice 2004-28, 2004-16 IRB 783.

[65] Rev. Rul. 2002-22, IRB 2002-19, 849.

[66] Notice 2002-31, IRB 2002-19, 908.

agreement is required to recognize income when a party transfers nonstatutory stock options to the other party. However, the transferee former spouse recognizes income when he or she exercises the options. While generally, the income on exercise would be taxed to the transferor under the assignment of income doctrine, that doctrine does not apply to divorces. However, because the payments are wages for FICA tax purposes, they are reportable by the employer as Social Security and Medicare wages on the employee's Form W-2, as are the Social Security and Medicare taxes withheld. This can produce the anomalous result of employment taxes being reported on the employee's Form W-2, but being withheld from amounts received by the nonemployee spouse upon exercise.

.02 Options with a Readily Ascertainable Value

Under the Code Sec. 83 regulations, an option can have a readily ascertainable value in one of two ways. First, an option has a readily ascertainable value if it is traded on an established market.[67] Second, an option has a readily ascertainable value if (a) the option is transferable by the recipient; (b) the option is exercisable immediately in full; (c) the option or the property subject to the option is not subject to any restriction that would significantly affect its fair market value; and (d) the fair market value of the option privilege is readily ascertainable in accordance with Reg. § 1.83-7(b)(3).[68]

There may be an exception to the foregoing tax rule for an employer's award of "in-the-money" options. The IRS has taken the position that if a company were to award an NSO with an exercise price significantly below the then fair market value of the company's stock, the company would have made a taxable transfer of value and the employee would recognize ordinary income. In *Morrison v. Comm'r*, the taxpayer was the part owner of Sig Laboratories, Inc. ("Sig").[69] Intra Products Inc. ("Intra") subsequently acquired Sig and the taxpayer agreed to become an employee of Intra and, as a result, received a freely transferable option to acquire 75 shares of Intra for $1 a share (a fraction of the market value). In determining whether the option had a readily ascertainable value under the tests prescribed in the predecessor to Reg. § 1.83-7(b)(3), the court found that because the option had a nominal exercise price, its option privilege had a readily ascertainable value. The court reasoned that the value of the option privilege was readily ascertainable because the low exercise price meant the option was substantially equivalent to the underlying stock.[70]

In Revenue Ruling 82-150, the IRS ruled that for purposes of determining whether a corporation is a foreign personal holding company, a taxpayer who held an option to acquire $100,000 in stock for $30,000 was in substance the owner of the stock. The IRS based its ruling on the general form over substance

---

[67] Reg. § 1.83-7(b).
[68] Reg. § 1.83-7(b)(2).

[69] *Morrison v. Comm'r*, 59 TC 248, CCH Dec. 31,602 (1972).
[70] *Morrison v. Comm'r*, 59 TC 248, 260, CCH Dec. 31,602 (1972).

doctrine and specifically stated that the ruling would apply wherever an option was substantially equivalent to stock.[71]

Notwithstanding the importance of the issue, there is little authority on point. However, based on Revenue Ruling 82-150, an option with an exercise price below 30 percent of the price for the underlying stock could be subject to challenge. Additionally, one commentator has suggested that if the exercise price is less than 10 percent of the underlying stock price, there is a significant risk that this authority will apply; if the exercise price is between 10 percent and 25 percent of the underlying stock price, the risk of the authority applying is moderate; and if the exercise price is above 50 percent of the underlying stock price, the risk of the authority applying is low.[72]

Although there is little authority on point, it is doubtful that an option with an exercise price of 50 percent or more of the price of the underlying stock would be treated as the equivalent of stock or as having an ascertainable value. Further, since Revenue Ruling 82-150 addresses a situation in which there are no specific regulations covering the tax consequences of issuing an option and *Morrison* only addresses an option with a nominal exercise price, the better position is that the award of an option with an exercise price above 30 percent of the price of the underlying stock (or the substitution of an option with an exercise price above 30 percent of the price of the stock for another option) is not a taxable event pursuant to Treasury Regulation §1.83-7. It appears that the doctrine of "substance over form," upon which Revenue Ruling 82-150 was based, continues to serve as the source of guidance within the context of discounted stock options.[73]

.03 Tax Treatment of the Company

Generally, the company that awarded the option will be entitled to a deduction for compensation paid for services at the same time as the employee recognizes ordinary income, and in the same amount as the employee recognized. The company is not entitled to a deduction at the time of the option award. The Code conditions the employer's deduction on proper withholding for federal income taxes.

> **Example 2:** In Example 1, where Executive D recognized ordinary income of $10,000 upon exercise of the NSO ($10.00 × 1,000 shares), ABC Corporation would also become entitled to a $10,000 deduction at that time. ABC will not receive any further deduction when D later sells the shares, regardless of the sales price.

---

[71] Rev. Rul. 82-150, 1982-2 CB 110.

[72] *See* Ginsburg and Levin, *Mergers, Acquisitions, and Buyouts*, §1314.1.2 (Little Brown and Company 1995).

[73] The application of this doctrine to the discount option context is that "if it is substantially certain that a taxpayer will exercise an option, the form of the option should be disregarded and the agreement should be treated, in substance, as the direct purchase of the stock." Harry J.J. O'Neill and David A. Schenck, *Using Discount Stock Options as Executive Compensation*, 72 J. Tax'n 348, 351 (1990) (estimating that to avoid a claim that a discount option should be deemed exercised, the exercise price should be 25% or more of the underlying stock price).

.04 Whether to Award ISOs or NSOs

ISOs have advantages[74] and disadvantages. The employee has the advantage of deferring taxation until he or she sells the stock. However, the company does not receive a tax deduction for a compensation expense equal to the amount of ordinary income recognized by the employee absent a disqualifying disposition by the employee. As a result, awarding ISOs may cost a company more than other arrangements that are not tax qualified.

NSOs are generally more popular with employers for several reasons. First, the employer has greater flexibility in the option terms, including the ability to award in-the-money options, although as discussed below, Code Sec. 409A has restricted that ability. Second, the employer may deduct the amount included in the employee's income when he or she exercises the option. Third, the employer may award NSOs to non-employees, such as outside directors, independent contractors and advisors. Finally, the NSO has no value to the employee unless the market price of the employer's stock increases. However, the more the stock price increases, the more the option rewards the employee.

The popularity of ISOs rises and falls from time to time. Between 1986 and 1992, companies seldom awarded ISOs because the spread between ordinary income tax rates and capital gain rates was minimal. In 1992, Congress lowered the rate on long-term capital gains. In 1993, Congress increased the tax rates on ordinary income. Beginning in 1992, ISOs quickly grew in popularity. During the dot.com bubble, ISOs were extremely popular because the primary disadvantage of ISOs, the lack of a deduction to the company, was not a concern to start-up ventures with no taxable earnings. However, when the bubble burst, many of the individuals who had exercised ISOs near the market's peak faced huge alternative minimum tax liabilities, despite the fact that the actual market value of their stock had plummeted.

.05 Tax Withholding

When an employee exercises a NSO, the company must withhold income taxes at the supplemental withholding rates. The TCJA of 2017 reduced individuals' rates, repealed the personal exemption, and increased the standard deduction, which required companies to change their tax withholding procedures. In 2018, the IRS released Notice 1036, which updated the income-tax withholding tables for 2018 reflecting changes made by the TCJA.

Prior to 2018, the law required an employer that makes supplemental wage payments (e.g., equity award vesting, annual bonus payments, etc.) to an employee in excess of $1 million during a calendar year to withhold on the amount above $1 million (or on the entire payment) at a rate equal to the highest individual income tax bracket in effect for the year. In 2017, this flat rate was 39.6%. The TCJA lowered the top marginal tax rate to 37%, effective January 1, 2018.

---

[74] ISOs are also not subject to the excise tax on stock compensation of insiders in expatriated corporations. Code Sec. 4985(e)(3)(B)(i). Code Sec. 4985 was added to the Code by the American Jobs Creation Act of 2004 (108-357).

For supplemental wage payments to an employee for less than $1 million in a calendar year, companies may withhold at the supplemental flat rate. Prior to 2018, that rate was 25%. Notice 1036 reduced that rate to 22%. A company can choose to use the supplemental rate or the W-4 method, although the employee often makes a request. Because of the increase to the standard deduction and the change to the tax rates, if an employer chooses to use the W-4 method, it should use the tax tables provided in Notice 1036.

A company also needs to make sure that its withholding practices comply with its plan document, which typically provides language on required withholding in order to avoid matters arising under ASC 718.

With respect to stock options, the company or its plan administrator generally will establish and maintain a program and procedures to allow optionees to exercise their exercisable options, and to pay the exercise costs of such option exercise, as follows:

1. *Cashless or Net Exercise.* A "Cashless or Net Exercise" means an option exercise in which the company withholds from the number of shares that would be deliverable to the option upon exercise, a number of shares with a value equal to the exercise price and the required tax withholding, and delivers to the optionee the net proceeds from the exercise. No broker is involved. For example, if an employee exercised an option to purchase 1,000 shares with an exercise price of $10.00 per share, at a time when the market price of the stock was $20.00 per share, instead of delivering to the employee 1,000 shares of stock, the company would withhold 500 shares to pay the purchase price and approximately 200 shares to pay the withholding taxes. The company would deliver 300 shares of stock to the employee.

2. *Exercise and Sell to Cover.* An "Exercise and Sell To Cover" means an option exercise in which the optionee sells that portion of the optioned stock necessary to yield sufficient proceeds to pay (a) the exercise cost of the option, (b) applicable taxes and deductions as specified by the company, and (c) any brokerage fees or commissions.

3. *Exercise and Sell Balance.* An "Exercise and Sell Balance" or "Cashless" exercise means an option exercise in which the optionee sells all the stock acquired upon exercise, and applies a portion of the proceeds to pay (a) the exercise cost of the option, (b) applicable federal, state and local taxes and deductions, and (c) any brokerage fees or commissions. Cashless exercises may be market or limit orders.

4. *Exercise and Hold.* An "Exercise and Hold" exercise means an option exercise in which the optionee wishes to receive and hold all the optioned stock. It requires the payment by the optionee to the company (or its plan administrator) of the exercise cost of the option as well as all applicable taxes and deductions and any other applicable charges.

5. *Exercise with Stock (Stock-for-Stock).* A "Stock for Stock Exercise" means an option exercise in which the optionee wishes to deliver by attestation

shares of stock owned by the optionee for at least six months (as certified by the optionee in writing) to pay the exercise cost of the option. The optionee may elect to pay applicable taxes and deductions by cash or check or by share withholding (from additional shares issued upon exercise of the option).

.06 Individuals' Efforts to Avoid Taxation on the Exercise of Stock Options—and the IRS's Consistent Demolition of Those Efforts

Like tax protesters who continue to fight the U. S. Government's ability to impose an income tax more than a century after it was first enacted, every few months another case arises in which an individual argues that he or she should not be taxed upon the exercise of vested stock options - sometimes under a new theory, sometimes under an old one — and the court rejects the claim. The bust of the dot.com bubble, which left many individuals with only worthless shares of stock to pay their hefty tax bill following option exercises, led to a fresh round of these claims.

In Revenue Ruling 2005-48,[75] the IRS held that an employee recognizes income under Code Sec. 83 at the time of the exercise of a NSO, even though he is subject to restrictions on his ability to sell the stock obtained through exercise of the option under both (i) Rule 10b-5 under the Securities Exchange Act of 1934, and (ii) contractual provisions applicable to the employee under a standard Underwriting Agreement signed when the company went public. Similarly, see:

- *Merlo v. Commissioner of Internal Revenue*, T.C.,[76] in which the tax court held that incentive stock options exercised by an executive were subject to the alternative minimum tax, despite his claim that the stock was not freely transferable because the company's insider trading policy caused the stock to be "blacked out from trading."

- *Palahnuk v. United States*,[77] where Mr. Palahnuk argued that he should not have been taxed at the time of the exercise of his stock options because he exercised the options using a margin account, a form of indebtedness, pledging the stock as collateral. Instead, he argued, he should be taxed at the value of the stock at the time he eventually paid off the margin loan years later, when the stock was worth substantially less.

.07 Qualified Equity Award Deferrals Under the TCJA

The TCJA added a new Code Sec. 83(i), effective beginning in 2018. Code Sec. 83(i) permits a "qualified employee" of an "eligible corporation" to elect to defer the inclusion in income of amounts attributable to the exercise of a stock option or the distribution of a restricted stock unit ("RSU"). Sec. 83(i) contains no reference to SARs. Deferral elections are only available for options and RSUs awarded to employees by a company if the stock of the company has not been readily tradable on an established securities market during any preceding calen-

---

[75] I.R.B. 2005-32, Aug. 8, 2005.

[76] *Merlo v. Commissioner of Internal Revenue*, No. 21538-03, T.C. Memo. 2005-178 (2005).

[77] *Palahnuk v. United States*, 70 Fed. Cl. 87 (2006).

dar year. To determine whether any stock of the company has been readily tradable on an established securities market during any preceding calendar year, any predecessor to the company is included, as well as any member of the controlled group of companies that includes that company or group of trades or businesses under common control with the company.

Awards made on after January 1, 2018, under an existing equity award plan could qualify for the deferral election even if the rights and privileges of awards under that plan were not the same before that date, so long as any awards after that date satisfy the equal rights and privileges requirement.

New Code Sec. 83(i) is designed primarily for the benefit of smaller and start-up companies. It draws on employee eligibility and tax treatment elements of Code Sec. 423 (employee stock purchase plans) and Code Sec. 422 (incentive stock options). The key feature of new Code Sec. 83(i) is that a company's written equity plan must award stock options or RSUs to at least 80% of all employees who provide services to the company in the U.S. And all stock options and RSUs must have the same "rights and privileges" to receive qualified stock.

Although this income deferral election is only available to employees of privately-held corporations, the change is significant enough that it warrants further discussion.

Awards of Qualified Stock of an Eligible Corporation: A deferral election only may be made on stock received by an employee in connection with the exercise of an option or the settlement of an RSU. The options or RSUs must be awarded under the terms of a written plan document. The employee must be performing services as an employee for the company that awards the option or RSU and the option or RSU must apply to the stock of the company that employs the employee. An option or RSU will not be qualified under Code Sec. 83(i) if it permits the employee to sell the stock to, or receive cash in lieu of stock from, the company at the time that the employee's rights in the stock first become transferable or not subject to a substantial risk of forfeiture.

Qualified Employee: The company's equity plan must award stock options or RSUs to at least 80% of all employees who provide services to the company in the U.S., including employees in any U.S. possession. Certain employees are not eligible to elect a deferral, including the company's chief executive officer and chief financial officer ("CFO"), any family member of the CEO or CFO, any one of the four highest compensated officers for any of the company's 10 prior taxable years, and an individual who is or has been a 1% owner of the company at any time during the individual's 10 prior calendar years. Part-time employees customarily employed for fewer than 30 hours per week also are not eligible. For purposes of determining a family relationship, Code Sec. 83(i) refers to the rules under Code Sec. 318(a)(1). For purposes of determining the company's highest compensated officers for any of the 10 preceding taxable years, Code Sec. 83(i) refers to the SEC's stockholder disclosure rules (applied as if those rules applied to the company).

Tax Treatment: If an employee makes the deferral election under new Code Sec. 83(i), the employee would recognize taxable income on the earliest of (i) the date the stock becomes transferable (including becoming transferable to the company), (ii) the date the employee becomes an excluded employee, (iii) the date any stock of the company becomes readily tradable on an established securities market, (iv) the date that is five years after the first date the rights of the employee in such stock are transferable or are not subject to a substantial risk of forfeiture (whichever occurs earlier), or (v) the date on which the employee revokes the qualified election with respect to the stock.

After the deferral period, the employee would recognize taxable income on the fair market value of the stock on the vesting date, regardless of whether the value of the stock had increased or decreased between the time of the vesting date and the end of the deferral period. The deferred award would be subject to FICA tax at the time of vesting.

The TCJA also amended Code Sec. 409A to provide that "qualified stock" is not subject to Code Sec. 409A, and RSUs and options subject to the deferral elections will not be considered non-qualified deferred compensation.

Notice and Election Requirements: To defer income, an employee must make an election with respect to qualified stock received upon an option exercise or RSU vesting no later than 30 days after the first date the employee rights in the stock are transferable or are not subject to a substantial risk of forfeiture, whichever occurs earlier. In the deferral election, the employee must agree to certain tax withholding requirements, described further below. A qualified employee could make a deferral election with respect to qualified stock attributable to an ISO in which case the option would be treated as a non-incentive stock option.

A company offering qualified employees the elections to defer income on qualified stock must provide certain information to such employees. At or before the time that the employee would recognize income on the award, but for the employee's deferral election the company must notify the employee that he or she may be eligible to elect to defer income on the stock under Code Sec. 83(i). As part of this notice, the company also must explain that:

- if the employee makes a deferral election, the amount of income recognized at the end of the deferral period will be based on the value of the stock at the time at which the rights of the employee in such stock first become transferable or not subject to substantial risk of forfeiture, regardless of whether the value of the stock has declined during the deferral period,

- the amount of the income the employee would recognize at the end of the deferral period would be subject to federal income tax withholding at not less than the maximum rate, and

- the employee would remain responsible for his or her portion of the required withholding taxes.

The company also must certify to the employee that the stock the employee is about to receive, absent a deferral election, is qualified stock.

Same Rights and Privileges: Code Sec. 83(i) expressly provides that the determination of rights and privileges with respect to stock is to be made in a similar manner as under Code Sec. 423(b)(5). Rights and privileges with respect to the exercise of an option are not treated as the same as rights and privileges with respect to the settlement of a restricted stock unit. Where a company wants RSUs or stock options to be treated as qualified equity awards, 80% of employees must receive that same type of award. It is not sufficient, for example, if 40% of employees receive stock options and 40% to receive RSUs.

Regulations under Code Sec. 423 offer significant guidance on the meaning of "equal rights and privileges" and, presumably, that guidance will apply to new Code Sec. 83(i). An employee will not fail to be treated as having the same rights and privileges to receive stock solely because the number of shares available to all employees is not equal in amount, so long as the number of shares available to each employee is more than a *de minimis* amount. The amount of stock that is awarded to employees may vary, as long as it bears a uniform relationship to the total compensation or the basic or regular rate of compensation of the employees.

The new qualified equity award deferral feature appears to have limited applicability due to the fact that the options or RSUs must be made available to 80% of employees in a privately held company. The fact that significant owners and certain officers are not eligible further limits the utility of the provision. However, many employees at eligible corporations could benefit from this opportunity to defer income recognition on common forms of equity awards.

¶745 SARs and a Comparison to Stock Options

There is not a precise definition of an SAR. Early regulatory guidance based on a 1975 General Counsel Memorandum ("GCM") pertaining to a tandem SAR and option program and the application of the concept of constructive receipt,[78] described the SAR arrangement as an economic right to receive a payment in cash, stock, or a combination of both calculated as the appreciation in a unit, or phantom share, of stock.[79] Essentially, the SAR is similar to an option but without the requirement, and related cost, of an exercise price.

> **Example:** ABC Corporation hires Executive D as CEO. One of the likely exit strategies for ABC's owners is to sell the company. ABC awards SARs to D, equal to 10% of the company, valued as of D's hire date, January 1, 2018. ABC has 10,000 shares outstanding. An independent valuation firm determines ABC's value to be $50 million. ABC sets the exercise price for D's SARs at $5,000.
>
> D is successful in preparing ABC for sale and negotiating a favorable purchase price. Megacorp agrees to purchase the stock of ABC for $90

---

[78] *See* Chapter 17 (¶1701 *et seq.*) for a detailed discussion of constructive receipt.

[79] GCM 36456, Oct. 8, 1975; *see also*, Rev. Rul. 80-300, 1980-2 CB 165 (defined the SAR as the excess of fair market value at the date of grant versus the fair market value at the date of exercise).

million on January 15, 2020. D will receive 10% of the increase in value since the date of her hire, or $4,000,000.

A SAR is generally a long-term incentive based on company, not individual, performance. The executive/recipient of a SAR derives benefit or value from the SAR based on appreciation. Therefore, a SAR requires the company to establish an initial benchmark value or "exercise price." For public companies, the exercise price will be the market price on the day of the award. Private companies need to determine the exercise price according to a procedure that satisfies Code Sec. 409A (see ¶755.02).

Private companies generally design SARs as a compensation vehicle that provides cash payments. Some companies provide a more flexible alternative under which the executive or company (or either) may elect the form of settlement of the SAR. Obviously, a private company that wants to minimize minority stockholder issues should avoid giving discretion to the executive.

.01 Tandem SARs

Generally, the SAR is not paired, or linked, to other forms of stock-based compensation but functions as a stand-alone award, like a stock option. However, some companies award so-called tandem SARs, although the award of a SAR in tandem with a stock option would make the entire award subject to Code Sec. 409A. This arrangement involves the use of the SAR as a funding mechanism for the exercise price required by the option. Upon exercise of the SAR, the employee uses the cash payment to pay the exercise price of the remaining options. Upon exercise of the option and tandem SAR, the total gain is subject to ordinary income tax.[80]

A company can grant a SAR by itself or in addition, or as an alternative to, an incentive stock option (ISO) or a nonqualified stock option (NSO). When a company issues SARs at the same time, and in like amounts, as stock options, it is issuing tandem SARs. Companies issue SARs in conjunction with options to provide the executive with these benefits:

1. The choice between exercising the option and receiving the stock, or simply receiving cash equal to the appreciation;

2. Cash with which to exercise the option; and

3. Cash to assist the executive in paying taxes.

.02 Stock Settled SARs

SARs were originally designed for and used by privately held companies that wanted to provide an incentive to executives or employees to grow the value of the company, but did not want to issue actual shares of stock to them. As discussed, a SAR provides very similar economic benefits to stock options. Traditionally, upon exercise of the SAR, the holder received a payment equal to the amount the company's stock had appreciated since the SAR was granted.

---

[80] § 16(b) of the Securities Exchange Act of 1934, 15 U.S.C. § 78p(b).

However, because a SAR award generally reduces the number of shares that a company is authorized to issue less than an award of options, public companies began to award stock settled SARs.

> **Example:** ABC Corp. awards 10,000 stock settled SARs to executive D, with an exercise price of $10.00 per share (the market price of ABC's stock on that award date). Three years later, after the stock-settled SARs have vested and ABC's stock is trading at $20.00, D exercises all 10,000 of the stock-settled SARs. D will receive 5,000 shares of stock upon exercise, calculated as follows: The spread between $10 and $20 multiplied by 10,000 shares equals $100,000. The plan must award 5,000 shares, worth $20 per share, to provide the $100,000 gain.

Stock-settled SARs will provide less dilution and overhang problems than stock options. Additionally, stock-settled SARs reduce the number of shares sold into the market to finance exercise transactions, and can reduce or eliminate the need for costly and administratively burdensome stock repurchase programs. Stock-settled SARs also encourage long-term ownership by eliminating employees' need to sell stock to pay taxes on the exercise price. Employees are more likely to hold shares when they are not required to pay cash out-of-pocket to do so. Finally, stock-settled SARs can also reduce the need for the company to maintain (or facilitate, through a broker) a same-day sale program. Preventing this constant flow of shares into the market helps the stock plan to better achieve the company's objective of delivering stock to employees and may make it more palatable to stockholders. It also may help reduce the myriad recurring issues that apply to insider sales.

.03 Other Advantages and Disadvantages of SARs

The advantages and disadvantages of awarding SARs generally are the same as granting stock options, except:

- **Advantage:** The exercise of SARs does not require the holder to pay an exercise price for which he or she may need to borrow against the exercise proceeds or engage in a cashless exercise.

- **Advantage:** SARs settled in cash instead of stock would not result in subsequent "sales" required to be reported on Form 4.

- **Advantage:** SARs settled in cash instead of stock will not result in dilution.

- **Disadvantage:** SARs settled in cash instead of stock will require an outlay of cash by the company.

- **Disadvantage:** SARs settled in cash instead of stock will not increase the employee's holdings of company stock,

- **Disadvantage:** SARs settled in cash are treated as liability awards under FAS 123R (requiring quarterly adjustments to the compensation charge based on the price of the stock underlying the SAR).

¶755 Treatment as Deferred Compensation—Code Sec. 409A

For purposes of ERISA, stock option plans are generally not regarded as pension plans.[81] However, Code Sec. 409A defines the term "nonqualified deferred compensation agreement" broadly to include any stock option or SAR issued with an exercise price that is less than fair market value. Failure to satisfy the requirements of Code Sec. 409A may result in significant penalties to the affected party.

.01 Code Sec. 409A and Stock Options

Code Sec. 409A applies differently to different types of equity compensation grants and awards, and to equity compensation awards made by public and private companies. Under Code Sec. 409A, stock options and SARs will be exempt from 409A if the option or SAR award satisfies the requirements of the "Stock Right" exception under Code Sec. 409A and the final regulations. An option or SAR will satisfy these requirement and be exempt from Code Sec. 409A if:

- The exercise price is no less than fair market value,[82]
- The award is service recipient (employer) stock,[83]
- The award is not extended or modified, and[84]
- The award does not contain any feature allowing for further deferral.[85]

Note that the definition of "stock right" does not include ISOs. ISO are covered by a separate exception.

Code Sec. 409A does not prohibit option or SAR awards that fail to satisfy the requirements of the stock right exception, but such awards would have comply with all of the other requirements of Code Sec. 409A to avoid tax penalties.

.02 Exercise Price No Less Than Fair Market Value

For an option or SAR to be exempt from Code Sec. 409A, the exercise price must be no less than fair market value.[86] The regulations allow a public company to use the closing market price on the day of or the day before the award, as long as the company is reasonable and consistent in setting the price. The regulations also allow a public company to use an average fair market value, so long as the company has made an irrevocable commitment to award the option or SAR before the averaging period begins.

For private company valuation, the regulations allow the employer to use the reasonable application of a reasonable valuation method. However, the regulations clarify that this standard is higher than the good faith standard

---

[81] *Houston v Aramark Corp.*, 2004 US App LEXIS 20642 (3rd Cir. 2004) (unpublished opinion); *Oatway v American International Group, Inc.*, 325 F3d 184 (3rd Cir. 2003). Stock option plans also are not treated as nonqualified deferred compensation plans for purposes of FICA withholding. Reg. § 31.3121(v)(2)(b)(4)(iii).

[82] Reg. § 1.409A-1(b)(5)(i)(A)(1).

[83] Reg. § 1.409A-1(b)(5)(iii).

[84] Reg. § 1.409A-1(b)(5)(v).

[85] Reg. § 1.409A-1(b)(5)(i)(C), (D) and (E).

[86] Reg. § 1.409A-1(b)(5)(i)(A)(1) and Reg. § 1.409A-1(b)(5)(iv).

applicable under the Code Sec. 422 incentive stock option rules. The determination of whether a valuation method is reasonable, or whether an application of a valuation method is reasonable, is made based on the facts and circumstances as of the valuation date. The regulations indicate that the factors to be considered under a reasonable valuation method, include the following:[87]

- The value of tangible and intangible assets of the corporation,

- The present value of anticipated future cash-flows of the corporation,

- The market value of stock or equity interests in similar corporations and other entities engaged in trades or businesses substantially similar to those engaged in by the corporation the stock of which is to be valued, the value of which can be readily determined through nondiscretionary, objective means (such as through trading prices on an established securities market or an amount paid in an arm's length private transaction),

- Recent arm's length transactions involving the sale or transfer of the corporation's stock,

- The extent to which the corporation has *consistently* used the valuation method to determine the value of its stock or assets for other purposes, including for purposes unrelated to compensation of service providers,

- Whether the valuation method is used for other purposes that have a material economic effect on the corporation, its stockholders, or its creditors, and

- Other relevant factors such as control premiums or discounts for lack of marketability.

The regulations also provide that the use of a valuation method is not reasonable if it does not take into consideration *all available information* material to the value of the corporation in applying its methodology. Along those same lines, the final regulations provide that the use of a value *previously calculated* under a valuation method is not reasonable as of a later date if:

(i) the calculation fails to reflect *information available after the date of the calculation* that may materially affect the value of the corporation (*e.g.*, the resolution of material litigation or the issuance of a patent), or

(ii) the value was calculated with respect to a date that is *more than 12 months earlier* than the date for which the valuation is being used.[88]

The regulations give private companies a safe harbor of sorts—providing that the use of one of three specified valuation methods gives rise to a rebuttable presumption in favor of the company that its valuation is reasonable:

First method. The first valuation method that creates a presumption of reasonableness is one determined by an independent appraisal as of a date that is no more than 12 months before the award date (or other relevant valuation

---

[87] Reg. § 1.409A-1(b)(5)(iv)(B)(1) and (2).   [88] Reg. § 1.409A-1(b)(5)(iv)(2)(A) and (B).

event). (The independent appraisal must meet the same requirements that apply to ESOP valuations under Code Sec. 401(a)(28)(C) and the regulations.)[89]

Second method. The second valuation method that creates a presumption of reasonableness, which may be very useful to start-up companies, is a valuation of the *"illiquid stock of a start-up corporation"* that made reasonably and in good faith and evidenced by a written report that takes into account the relevant factors described above.[90]

For this purpose, an "illiquid stock of a start-up corporation" is stock:

- Of a business that has been conducted for a period of less than 10 years;

- Stock that is not subject to any put or call right or obligation of the company, (or other person) to purchase such stock, other than: a right of first refusal upon an offer to purchase by a third party; and

- Stock that is not publicly traded and not reasonably anticipated (as of the time of valuation) to be subject to an IPO within 180 days or a change in control within the 90 days following the time of valuation.

This valuation will not be treated as made reasonably and in good faith unless the valuation is performed by a person that the company reasonably determines is qualified to perform such a valuation based on the person's significant knowledge, experience, education, or training. Generally, a person will be qualified to perform such a valuation if a reasonable individual, upon being apprised of such knowledge, experience, education, and training, would reasonably rely on the advice of such person with respect to valuation in deciding whether to accept an offer to purchase or sell the stock being valued. For this purpose, significant experience generally means at least five years of relevant experience in business valuation or appraisal, financial accounting, investment banking, private equity, secured lending, or other comparable experience in the line of business or industry in which the company operates.

Third method. The last valuation method that creates a presumption of reasonableness is one based upon a formula that, if used as part of a nonlapse restriction with respect to the stock (*e.g.*, as part of a stockholders agreement), would be considered to be the fair market value of the stock, provided that:[91]

i. such stock is valued in the same manner for purposes of any transfer of shares to the issuer or any person that owns stock possessing more than 10% of the issuer, other than an arm's length transaction involving the sale of all or substantially all of the outstanding stock of the issuer, and

ii. such valuation method is used consistently for all such purposes.

A company may use a different valuation method for each separate action for which a valuation is relevant, provided that a single valuation method is used for each separate action and, once used, may not retroactively be altered. The regulations state explicitly that an independent valuation is not necessary.

---

[89] Reg. § 1.409A-1(b)(5)(iv)(B)(2)(i).
[90] Reg. § 1.409A-1(b)(5)(iv)(B)(2)(ii).
[91] Reg. § 1.409A-1(b)(5)(iv)(B)(2)(iii).

.03 Service Recipient Stock

The regulations elaborate on the issue of: what stock is service recipient stock? The final regulations state that service recipient stock is any class of common stock (as defined in Code Sec. 305).[92] Common stock may have restrictions on transfer and liquidity preferences. However, common stock may not have dividend preference. The employer/service recipient can be privately owned or publicly traded.

The regulations also clarify that "service recipient stock" may be stock of direct service recipient (*e.g.*, the employer) or stock of entity that is above the direct service recipient in the ownership chain. Stock of a subsidiary of the direct service recipient or other entity below the service recipient in the ownership chain does not qualify. Stock of a related brother/sister entity also does not qualify. For determining entities up the chain, the final regulations lower the ownership threshold from 80% to 50%. The final regulations even allow as little as 20% ownership interest in the service recipient chain, if the employer can show there are legitimate business (non-tax) purposes to justify awarding the stock award.

.04 No Extension or Modification

As noted above, an option or SAR that satisfied the requirements of the stock right exception at issuance could nonetheless become subject to Code Sec. 409A if the award was modified or the terms of the award extended. The regulations provide guidance on what constitutes an impermissible modification or extension. The regulations provide that an extension of the post-employment exercise period of a stock option or SAR does not make the option subject to Code Sec. 409A if the exercise period is extended to a date no later than the earlier of (i) the latest date upon which the option or SAR could have expired by its original terms under any circumstances or (ii) the 10th anniversary of the original award date of the option or SAR.[93] This is important, because many negotiated separation agreements promise an extended period for exercise of the employee's options or SARs.

The regulations also provide that it is *not* an extension of the original stock option or SAR if the exercise period of the option or SAR is extended at a time *when the exercise price of the option or SAR equals or exceeds the fair market value of the company's stock* that could be purchased. Instead, the regulations treat the original option or SAR award as modified rather than extended and a new option or SAR as having been awarded for this purpose.

The regulations under Code Sec. 409A also provide that it is not an extension of a stock right if the expiration of the stock right is tolled while the holder cannot exercise the stock right because such an exercise would violate an applicable federal, state, local, or foreign law, or would jeopardize the ability of the service recipient to continue as a going concern, provided that the period during which the stock right may be exercised is not extended more than 30 days after

---

[92] Reg. § 1.409A-1(b)(5)(iii).   [93] Reg. § 1.409A-1(b)(5)(v).

the exercise of the stock right first would no longer violate an applicable federal, state, local, and foreign laws or would first no longer jeopardize the ability of the service recipient to continue as a going concern.[94]

The "modification" of a "stock right" also could cause it to become subject to Code Sec. 409A. The regulations provide that a stock right is modified if any change in the terms of the stock right (including any change to the plan under which the right was issued) may result in a *reduction in the exercise price*. The regulations provide that certain actions are not modifications of a stock right:

- Shortening the exercise period
- Adding the ability to use previously acquired stock to pay the exercise price

Finally, a stock option or SAR could become subject to Code Sec. 409A if it allows dividend equivalents to accumulate until the exercise of the option. The regulations would treat accumulated dividend equivalents as a reduction of the exercise price.

.05 Code Sec. 457A

Code Sec. 457A, effectively eliminates the ability to defer compensation for taxpayers that provide services to "nonqualified entities." Nonqualified entities are typically foreign companies in "tax-indifferent" jurisdictions (colloquially, tax havens) or domestic partnerships and other pass-through entities that are owned more than 20% by tax-exempt entities. Sec. 457A imposes tax on deferred compensation at vesting, rather than on payment as under Sec. 409A. Section 457A most commonly applies to hedge funds and U.S. citizens working outside the U.S. for a non-U.S. employer in a tax-indifferent jurisdiction.

When Code Sec. 457A became effective in 2009, some compensation professionals were concerned that Code Sec. 457A and its 20% penalty tax would apply to any stock option or SAR awarded to a service provider of a nonqualified entity. This concern arose from the explicit language of the statute, which defines nonqualified deferred compensation by referring to the definition in Code Sec. 409A(d) but then adds, "except that such term shall include any plan that provides a right to compensation based on the appreciation in value of a specified number of equity units of the service recipient." The IRS allayed this concern with IRS Notice 2009-8 and Revenue Ruling 2014-18, confirming that Code Sec. 457A does not apply to stock options and SARs that are stock-settled so long as they met the stock right exemption in Code Sec. 409A.

Revenue Ruling 2014-18 is an interesting example of statutory interpretation. Despite the plain language of the statute, the IRS used the legislative history to find that 409A-exempt stock options were not intended to be subject to Code Sec. 457A. Further, the IRS stated that stock-settled SARs are functionally identical to stock options in all material respects and thus are similarly exempt. Perhaps constrained by the language of the statute, the IRS could not extend the exemption to SARs settled in cash.

---

[94] Reg. § 1.409A-1(b)(5)(v)(C).

.06 Code Sec. 409B

In 2014 and 2017, legislation passed by at least one house of Congress would have added a new Code Sec. 409B. In each case, the legislation ultimately passed and signed into law did not contain the proposed Section 409B. Each of the proposed Tax Reform Act of 2014 and the proposed Tax Cuts and Jobs Act of 2017, would have added a new Code Sec. 409B with language similar to that of Code Sec. 457A. Additionally, unlike 409A or 457A, proposed Code Sec. 409B would have defined deferred compensation to include "any plan that provides a right to compensation based on the appreciation in value of a specified number of equity units of the service recipient or stock options," extending its reach to stock options and SARs. In each case, the proposed Sec. 409B would have effectively eliminated stock options, SARs, and deferred compensation for all U.S. taxpayers.

¶765 Accounting for Stock Options and SARs

Before 2006, one of the most beneficial features of stock options and SARs was the fact that a company could award them to employees without reflecting a financial expense or cost. Under prior accounting rules, the accountants measured the compensation expense for options and SARs at the time when both the number of shares and the price per share was known. For "fixed" plan awards, the compensation expense would be measured as zero.

> **Example:** In lieu of cash bonuses, on December 31, 2002, ABC Corporation awards each of its top-paid 100 employees an option to purchase 10,000 shares of its common stock. ABC sets the exercise price of all options at $50.00 per share, the market price of ABC's stock on the award date. ABC's financial statements for the 2002 fiscal year will reflect a compensation cost of $0.00 attributable to the massive option award.

.01 ASC 718

In December 2004, the Financial Accounting Standards Board ("FASB") issued Statement of Accounting Standards No. 123 (revised 2004), Share Based Payments (referred to as "FAS 123R" and now known as ASC 718), which required companies to expense the value of employee stock options that they issue. For most public companies, ASC 718 required expensing of employee stock options for annual and quarterly reporting periods beginning in 2006.

ASC 718 covers the accounting for Share Based Payments ("SBP") transactions with employees, including:

- stock options;
- stock appreciation rights;
- restricted stock;
- phantom stock;
- performance shares; and
- employee stock purchase plans (ESPPs or "423 Plans.")

ASC 718 does not cover ESOPs or awards made in connection with business combinations.

The general concept of ASC 718 is that a company must recognize as a compensation expense on the income statement the "fair value" of SBP awards beginning on the date the company makes the award.[95] A company must recognize the expense over the vesting period and adjust it for actual forfeitures that occur before vesting. That is, there is a "true up" of the compensation expense at the end of the vesting period based on the number of options or awards that actually vest. Previously recognized expense can be reversed for awards that do not vest (but not for options that expire unexercised).

- For stock awards with graded vesting (*i.e.*, 25% per year over four years), ASC 718 provides that expense may be recognized either on a straight line or an accelerated basis. If vesting is linked to attainment of a performance condition such as net income or revenue target, this is not factored into the award's award-date fair value. However, because failure to achieve the performance condition precludes vesting of the award, a company records no compensation expense (that is, the previously recorded charge is reversed) if the performance condition is not met.

- In contrast, if vesting is linked to a market condition, such as the company's stock price or a market index, this is factored into the award's award-date fair value. This reduces fair value compared to a similar award that does not contain a market contingency. However, the company must record a compensation expense regardless of whether the condition is ever met or the option becomes exercisable. That is, no true-up of compensation charge for awards that do not vest.

ASC 718 requires companies to incorporate six standard assumptions, including the option's expected term and exercise price, and the current price, expected volatility and expected dividends of the company.

- Under ASC 718, repricing of unvested options or SARs results in a one-time expense. Additionally, companies will not have to wait six months after cancelling underwater options or SARs to award new options or SARs. Because repricing of underwater options no longer results in variable accounting for those options, it could come back into vogue in the event of another market downturn, subject to stockholder pressure on public companies not to allow it.

- We commonly use a ratio of 3:1 as a rule of thumb for comparing the value to an employee of restricted stock and stock options or SARs (that is, an option to purchase three shares was equal in value to one share of restricted stock).

- Companies will recognize the cost for SBP awards as they vest, including the related tax effects (expected). Upon settlement of the SBP awards, the

---

[95] Prior to 2006, the general rule had been that fair value was calculated at the award, and never again remeasured.

tax effects will be recognized in the company's income statement or
additional paid in capital.

.02 ASC 718 May Favor Performance-Based Awards

When stock awards are subject to performance conditions based on internal
metrics such as revenues or return on assets, the company does not recognize an
accounting expense under ASC 718 for the awards if the performance conditions
are not met.

ASC 718 recognizes three basic types of conditions:

- Service conditions based on an employee's service with the company,
  usually measured by length of employment.
- Performance conditions based on specific targets derived from a company's own operations or activities, such as revenues, EBIDTA, or market
  share.
- Market conditions derived from the company's share price or another
  market index related to the company's share price.

For stock awards tied *only* to service or performance conditions, ASC 718
permits the company to reverse previously recognized expenses if the company
does not meet the conditions during the "requisite service period" (which is
usually the same as the vesting period). However, ASC 718 does not permit
reversal if an award includes one or more market conditions, even if the award
does not become exercisable (because the market condition was not fulfilled), if
the employee stays with the company throughout the requisite service period.

.03 More Recent Guidance on Accounting for Equity-Based Compensation

In May 2017, the FASB issued Accounting Standards Update No. 2017-09,
Stock Compensation (Topic 718), Scope of Modification Accounting (the "ASU").
FASB issued the ASU to provide clarity and reduce the "diversity in practice"
among companies and accountants in applying ASC 718 to changes to the terms
or conditions of share-based payment awards. When a company makes a substantive change to a share-based payment award, it must apply modification
accounting (which is usually undesirable). However, ASC 718 offered little
guidance as to what changes are substantive, thereby leading to the diversity in
practice among accounting firms.

The ASU should reduce the instances that an entity is required to apply
modification accounting to a share-based payment award. For accounting purposes, a modification is viewed as the exchange of the original award for a new
award. If a company modified an award, ASC 718 generally would require it to
(i) calculate the incremental fair value of the new award, (ii) assess the effect of
the modification on the number of award shares expected to vest, including a
reassessment of the probability of vesting, and (iii) immediately recognize the
incremental difference between the fair value of the modified award and the fair
value of the original award as a compensation cost. The ASU became effective for
all companies for fiscal years beginning after December 15, 2017.

¶765.02

Some of the impetus for the ASU was the question of whether a change to the maximum withholding rate permitted under ASU 2016-09 would be considered a "modification" under ASC 718. However, companies change the terms of outstanding award agreements for a variety of reasons, including to provide for continued vesting following an employee's change in status to an independent contractor/consultant or to extend the expiration date of options held by a terminated employee (*e.g.*, to one year from 90 days).

The ASU streamlines the application of modification accounting by stating that when making a change to the terms or conditions of a share-based payment award, a company should apply modification accounting to the award, unless each of the following conditions is met:

1. The fair value (or calculated value or intrinsic value, if such an alternative measurement method is used) of the modified award is the same as the fair value (or calculated value or intrinsic value, if such an alternative measurement method is used) of the original award immediately before the original award is modified. If the modification does not affect any of the inputs to the valuation technique that the entity uses to value the award, the entity is not required to estimate the value immediately before and after the modification.

2. The vesting conditions of the modified award are the same as the vesting conditions of the original award immediately before the original award is modified.

3. The classification of the modified award as an equity instrument or a liability instrument is the same as the classification of the original award immediately before the original award is modified.

Helpfully, ASC 718, as amended by the ASU, provides some examples of changes to an award that generally require modification accounting and changes that do not require modification accounting. The former category includes:

- Repricing of share options that results in a change in value of the options (as most would),
- Changes in a service condition,
- Changes in a performance condition or a market condition (*e.g.*, to increase the likelihood of vesting or payout),
- Changes in an award that result in a reclassification of the award (equity to liability or vice versa), or
- Adding a provision for accelerated vesting of the award in the event of employment termination, in anticipation of a sale of a business unit.

Examples of changes to an award that generally do not require modification accounting include the following:

- Changes that are administrative in nature, such as a change to the company name, company address, or plan name, or
- Changes in an award's net settlement provisions related to tax withholdings that do not affect the classification of the award.

The ASU cautions that these examples "are educational in nature, are not all-inclusive, and should not be used to override the guidance in paragraph 718-20-35-2A."

¶775 Comparing Stock Options to Warrants

Occasionally, a company will issue warrants to employees, directors, or others instead of stock options. Warrants and options are essentially treated the same. Warrants differ from options in form and function but do not receive differing treatment under laws or regulations. The inappropriate classification of certain options and warrants as equity rather than debt has become a significant issue for the SEC staff. The subject of liability versus equity classification of certain instruments is complicated under ASC 718. Warrants, more so than options, are often settled in cash, triggering classification as a liability.

.01 Analysis

Stock purchase warrants are often defined as "stock options issued by a company which are traded like stock."[96] Warrants are usually treated the same way[97] and regulated by the same provisions as options.[98] "The stock purchase warrant is purely an option (generally, but not always awarded by the company itself) to purchase shares of stock of the company at a fixed price" and for a specified period.[99]

Case law and scholarly articles both reference the similarities between options and warrants but contain little, if any, citation to differing treatment under laws or regulations.[100] One notable example is that some provisions of the Code treat warrants to acquire stock as options.[101] The Internal Revenue Service generally treats warrants as "not realistically different" from options when determining the constructive ownership of stock for income tax purposes. Furthermore, warrants and options both use the same method of valuation.[102]

---

[96] 6A William Meade Fletcher et al., FLETCHER CYCLOPEDIA OF THE LAW OF PRIVATE CORPORATIONS §2641 (perm. ed., rev. vol. 1997).

[97] For example, in a contract interpretation case concerning warrants the Tennessee District Court noted that "in corporate jargon, a warrant is an option to purchase stock at a given price." The court interpreted the warrant "strictly in accordance with its terms." thus borrowing from the standard for exercising options.

[98] A typical example of this occurs in 17 C.F.R. §240.16a-1(c) which defines "derivative securities" as "any option, warrant, convertible security, stock appreciation right, or similar right with an exercise or conversion privilege at a price related to an equity security, or similar securities with a value derived from the value of an equity security."

[99] 19 William Meade Fletcher et al., FLETCHER CYCLOPEDIA OF THE LAW OF PRIVATE CORPORATIONS §2:60 (1997); See Robert Half Int'l, Inc. v. Franchise Tax Bd., 78 Cal. Rptr. 2d 453, 454 (Cal. Ct. App. 1998).

[100] One of the only situations an option was distinguished from a warrant was a New York case

that held a "call" option was not a security within the 1968 version of the Uniform Commercial Code Article 8 definition. In *Cohn, Ivers & Co. v. Gross*, 289 N.Y.S.2d 301 (N.Y.App. Term. 1968) the court held that since the call option was not a sale of the security itself, it did not meet the definition of security. "The court distinguished the call option from a warrant to purchase stock." 11 A.L.R. 4th 1036 §4. The court explained that a warrant is issued by the company whose stock is involved. It is the obligation of that company to issue its own shares upon exercise of the warrant. The court noted that the seller of a call option was not the corporation whose stock the option is issued upon. Furthermore, the person selling the call option need not even own the stock underlying the transaction. Calls are not written by the issuer and were not considered securities like other options. The court held call stock options were instead covered under Article 1.

[101] Rev. Rul. 68-601, 1968-2 CB 124; Rev. Rul. 77-250, 1977-2 CB 309.

[102] "An option [or warrant] has two values: an intrinsic value and a time value. The intrinsic value is the difference between the exercise price and the

.02 Warrants Differ from Options in Function and Purpose

The issuing party and purpose of warrants are the major distinctions of stock purchase warrants. The company usually[103] issues warrants to investors as a financing tool.[104] Companies often offer warrants to make the purchase of debt or securities more attractive. When issuing debt securities, a company may reduce its interest costs by also issuing warrants for common stock along with bonds or debentures.[105] The warrants usually have a life of five years and an exercise price fixed above the market price. The purchaser gets an "equity play not unlike that afforded to a purchaser of convertible securities." Companies also sometimes sell warrants at a nominal price to purchasers of junk bonds to facilitate a leveraged buyout. Selling warrants will also "provide an equity incentive to purchase the debt securities."[106]

Finally, companies issue warrants as an inducement to purchase shares of preferred or common stock. A warrant with an exercise price above the current market price may be included in the sale of a specified number of shares. This offering is described as a "unit offering."[107] A company may use a unit offering to encourage the sale of its preferred stock by also issuing a warrant that is redeemable for several shares of common stock.[108] Depending on the terms of each warrant, a company may be able to obtain considerable financing by issuing warrants.[109]

.03 Considerations When Issuing Warrants

Because a company issues warrants redeemable for its stock and the warrants usually trade as separate securities,[110] several considerations are important when issuing warrants. Some commentators have even noted that issuing stock

---

(Footnote Continued)

market price of the stock." *Custom Chrome, Inc. v. Comm'r*, 2000-2 USTC ¶ 50,566, 217 F3d 1117 (9th Cir. 2000); *See* 6A William Meade Fletcher et al., FLETCHER CYCLOPEDIA OF THE LAW OF PRIVATE CORPORATIONS § 2641 (1997), (the time value "reflects the expectation that, prior to expiration, the price of [the] stock will increase by an amount that would enable an investor to sell or exercise the option at profit.") "The privilege [conferred by a warrant upon its holder] constitutes a call upon the future prosperity of the company, and its value will depend upon the hope that the market price of the stock will rise above the stipulated subscription price before the right expires." *Niagara Hudson Power Corp. v. Leventritt*, 340 U.S. 336, 345 (1951) (citing Guthmann & Dougall, CORPORATE FINANCIAL POLICY (2d ed. 1948)), 145.

[103] Controlling stockholders may also issue warrants. *See* 69 Am. Jur. 2d *Securities Regulation-Federal* § 20 (1993).

[104] 6A William Meade Fletcher et al., FLETCHER CYCLOPEDIA OF THE LAW OF PRIVATE CORPORATIONS § 2641 (1997).

[105] Charles J. Johnson, Jr., CORPORATE FINANCE & THE SECURITIES LAWS 680 (1990).

[106] Charles J. Johnson, Jr., CORPORATE FINANCE & THE SECURITIES LAWS 680 (1990).

[107] Charles J. Johnson, Jr., CORPORATE FINANCE & THE SECURITIES LAWS 680, 683 (1990).

[108] For example, a purchaser may buy a warrant and five shares of stock which, has a market price of $10 per share, for $55. The warrant has essentially been sold for $5.

[109] Charles J. Johnson, Jr., CORPORATE FINANCE & THE SECURITIES LAWS 680, 683 (1990); 6A William Meade Fletcher et al., FLETCHER CYCLOPEDIA OF THE LAW OF PRIVATE CORPORATIONS § 2641 (1997).

[110] Warrants are within the Uniform Commercial Code's revised Article 8 definition of security or security entitlement. 6A William Meade Fletcher et al., FLETCHER CYCLOPEDIA OF THE LAW OF PRIVATE CORPORATIONS § 2641 (1997). The comments to Article 8 of the 1962 Uniform Commercial Code explain that "transferable warrants evidencing rights to subscribe for shares in a corporation will normally be 'securities' within the definition." U.C.C. § 8-102 cmt. (1962). An option to purchase corporate securities is itself a security within the definition of the Exchange Act. 69 Am. Jur. 2d *Securities Regulation-Federal* § 20 (1993) (citing definition within § 3(a)(10) of 15 U.S.C. § 78c(a)(10)).

purchase warrants in connection with the sale of securities may involve "serious problems."[111] The problem arises from the nature of a warrant as a continual offer to sell stock. One concern is that the issuing company must authorize and set aside a sufficient number of shares of common stock to meet all the possible demand from the warrant holders.[112] In a "unit offering, both the primary securities and the warrants must be registered, as must the common stock underlying the warrants."[113] Normally, an issuer must give each warrant holder a prospectus that meets the requirements of Section 10(a) of the 1933 Securities Act. The issuer must also keep the prospectus current so as not to violate the Act. Upon exercise of the warrant, the holder is entitled to this prospectus, referred to as an "evergreen" prospectus, which the company has updated at regular intervals or when any material change occurs.

"Transferable warrants to purchase corporate stock are [also] securities within the meaning of the Securities Act, and if they are to be distributed to the public, are subject to the registration provisions thereof."[114] Nontransferable warrants are usually exempt from the registration requirements of the 1933 Securities Act. Moreover, "[w]arrants that expire in 90 days or less are exempt from registration under § 12(a) of the exchange act."[115]

A company may have the duty to give notice to warrant holders of any proposed dissolution or liquidation.[116] Unlike bondholders, warrant holders may have the contractual protection requiring the company to express a record date on which the right to exercise the warrants will expire.

Further, federal regulations restrict a company's ability to repurchase its own stock if the company issued warrants that are not yet exercised. This guards against the repurchase of stock causing the share price to increase and holders of warrants to think they should exercise their warrants. However, a company may repurchase the warrants directly without triggering any regulatory prohibitions.[117]

Warrants have a different function from traditional equity compensation. Warrants also differ slightly from options in the terms contained within the warrant. As noted above, most warrants are intended to be traded separately from the underlying stock on an exchange. Warrants, like options, usually allow the holder to purchase common stock at a given price before a specified time. Warrants usually have a much longer period in which the holder may exercise the right. One commentator distinguished warrants from "call"[118] or "stock

---

[111] 6A William Meade Fletcher et al., FLETCHER CYCLOPEDIA OF THE LAW OF PRIVATE CORPORATIONS § 2641 (1997).

[112] 6A William Meade Fletcher et al., FLETCHER CYCLOPEDIA OF THE LAW OF PRIVATE CORPORATIONS § 86 (1997).

[113] Charles J. Johnson, Jr., CORPORATE FINANCE & THE SECURITIES LAWS 680, 684 (1990).

[114] 69 Am. Jur. 2d Securities Regulation-Federal § 20, p. 88 (1993).

[115] 69 Am. Jur. 2d Securities Regulation-Federal § 581 (1993).

[116] 6A William Meade Fletcher et al., FLETCHER CYCLOPEDIA OF THE LAW OF PRIVATE CORPORATIONS §§ 12-13 (1997).

[117] 6A William Meade Fletcher et al., FLETCHER CYCLOPEDIA OF THE LAW OF PRIVATE CORPORATIONS § 13 (1997).

[118] Calls are options given by individuals to sell a stock to another individual at a stated price within a certain period of time. 6A William Meade Fletcher et al., FLETCHER CYCLOPEDIA OF THE LAW OF PRIVATE CORPORATIONS § 12 (1997).

rights"[119] by noting that warrants are usually for a longer period and are issued in connection with the sale of other securities.

¶785 Contribution of Stock Options to a Charitable Organization

Some companies have awarded stock options to a newly-formed charitable organization immediately prior to the company's initial public offering. This raises certain legal issues.

.01 Income Tax Deduction

In addition to the intangible benefits of making a charitable contribution, the company should obtain a corresponding deduction for federal income tax purposes. An award of stock options should enable the company to maximize the deduction. By awarding the options to a related charitable organization, the company should be able to time the deduction to arise in a year (or years) in which the deduction is most useful.

A deduction for federal income tax purposes is generally allowed to corporations that make contributions to organizations recognized as tax-exempt under Code Sec. 501(c)(3) (a "501(c)(3) organization.") A contribution of cash or stock gives rise to a deduction in the year in which the contribution is made. However, a contribution of stock options gives rise to a deduction in the year in which such options are exercised by the 501(c)(3) organization, not when they are awarded. Deductions for charitable contributions made by a corporation are limited to 10% of the corporation's taxable income. Such deductions may be carried forward, to a limited extent, for up to five years. For planning purposes, the company will want to time its charitable deduction, to the extent possible, to arise in the year in which the deduction will be used.

A corporation's deduction for a charitable contribution of stock options is equal to the fair market value of the stock at the time of exercise, less the exercise price paid to the corporation. In contrast, a contribution of cash or stock would result in a deduction equal to the value of the cash or stock contributed. A charitable contribution of stock options allows a corporation to take advantage of future increases in its stock value for purposes of the federal income tax deduction, especially if the corporation can control the timing of exercise of the options.

.02 Creation of the Foundation

The company will obtain the same federal income tax deduction, regardless of which 501(c)(3) organization it selects to receive its charitable contribution. However, it would be to the company's advantage to award stock options to a newly-created 501(c)(3) organization related to the company (the "foundation"). This will allow the company to control when and how many of the stock options

---

[119] "Rights" are "privileges given by a corporation to its stockholders to subscribe to a new, or an increased, issue of stock of the corporation in proportion to the present holdings of such stockholder." 6A William Meade Fletcher et al., FLETCHER CYCLOPEDIA OF THE LAW OF PRIVATE CORPORATIONS § 12 (1997).

are exercised, which will determine the timing and amount of the company's tax deduction.

Due to certain provisions of federal tax law, it may be necessary for the foundation to transfer the stock options to another 501(c)(3) organization, which would then exercise them. The value of the stock options could be divided between the two organizations, as agreed upon by the parties. The foundation would be a viable 501(c)(3) organization that would continue to exist beyond the initial option award to it. The foundation could facilitate the company's future charitable activities and serve as the company's mechanism for community outreach.

The earnings charge with respect to a charitable contribution of stock options can be discounted, without affecting the amount of the future federal income tax deduction, by reducing the fair market value of the options at the time of the award. This may be accomplished, for example, by restricting transferability of the options solely to 501(c)(3) organizations and by not having a registration statement in effect at the time of the award. Although in-the-money stock options may be contributed to a 501(c)(3) organization, most companies do not follow that course of action because it increases the earnings charge. However, since it would eventually give rise to a larger tax deduction, it may be appropriate in certain circumstances.

¶795 State Taxation of Stock Options

The IRS requires employers to report as ordinary income the discount portion of the stock acquired by the exercise of a non-qualified stock option or the cash or stock received upon the exercise of a SAR. The IRS also requires employers to report the difference between the exercise price and the fair market value of the stock at the time of exercise (the "spread") upon a disqualifying disposition of stock acquired by the exercise of an incentive stock option. An individual's gains from stock disposed of after the holding period mandated by Code Sec. 422 are treated as capital gains rather than as ordinary income.

Most states (with the exception of those that do not have an income tax[120]) tax all of the income of each resident, regardless of the source of the income, based on the individual's adjusted gross income computed for the individual's federal tax return with certain modifications.[121] Consequently, most states' treatment of income derived from the exercise of stock options or SARs, or the disposition of stock acquired upon the exercise of an option or SAR, mirrors the policies of the federal Internal Revenue Code. However, most states also tax non-residents on income that is from sources, *e.g.* services performed, within their state. And some states apply different timing and taxation rules than the Code. For example, Pennsylvania does not recognize incentive stock options. (Of

---

[120] Seven states currently have no state income tax: Alaska, Florida, Nevada, South Dakota, Texas, Washington and Wyoming. Two others, New Hampshire and Tennessee, currently tax only dividend and interest income. *http://www.taxadmin.org.*

[121] See, e.g. Ariz. Rev. Stat. §43-1001; 35 Ill. Comp. Stat. Ann. 5/203; 79 Kans. Stat. Ann. 32,117; 206 Mich. Comp. Laws 206.12; 44 R.I. Gen. Laws 30-12; 12 S.C. Code Ann. §6-560.

course, city or local tax also may be due on income from the exercise of stock options or SARs.)

State tax withholding complications arise when an individual lives in one state and works in another, lived and worked in one state, but then moved to another, either during or after employment, or works in more than one state each year or during the relevant years. As you might expect, traditionally high tax states like New York, California, New Jersey, and Massachusetts are the most aggressive in taxing the option and SAR income of residents and former residents alike. Moreover, state statutory approaches to taxation of option or SAR income must deal with the problems of individuals who are resident within the state for only a portion of the intervals between the award of the stock option or SAR, its exercise, and the disposition of the stock (if applicable). Some states have held that the value of a stock option or SAR may be taxed when exercised. Other states have, or have attempted to, make income derived from the exercise of options or SARs, or the disposal of the stock so obtained (if applicable), nontaxable in limited circumstances.

Aggressive and varying state tax laws frequently create double taxation. Some states provide a tax credit to avoid double taxation. Usually, but not always, it is the resident state that will provide the tax credit, if one is allowed. And some states, *e.g.*, Indiana, have reciprocity agreements with neighboring states to prevent double taxation, with the resident state usually dominant. During employment, employers are generally responsible for tracking their employees' movements and withholding accordingly.

States often change their tax withholding laws and it is difficult to keep up with the developments in each of the 50 states. But a few examples should help to illustrate the complications.

.01 New York

New York generally follows the federal scheme, imposing a personal income tax on a nonresident's taxable income that is derived from New York sources. In general, a nonresident would have New York source income from compensation received from stock options, stock appreciation rights, or restricted stock if at any time during the "allocation period," the nonresident performed services in New York State for the corporation awarding such options, rights, or stock. When stock option compensation is received by a nonresident of New York, a determination must be made as to whether some portion of the income is taxable in New York.

In New York, the allocation period is the number of days between the *award of the option until it vests* (as opposed to when the option is exercised). However, other states may apply a sourcing rule that applies the ratio of the number of days worked in that state during the period between the award date and the date of exercise, over the total number of days worked during that period.[122] This is the rule that New York employed for many years.

.02 California

Generally, California taxes the income recognized on the exercise of a nonqualified stock option by an individual who was awarded the option while a California resident but exercises the option while a nonresident, to the extent that the services to which the option is attributed were performed in California.[123] If the individual performed services entirely within California, but the individual exercises the option after terminating employment and becoming a nonresident, the difference between the option price and the price of the stock on the exercise date, has a source in California, where the services were performed, and is therefore taxable as California income.[124]

For an option awarded to an individual not resident in California, who then becomes a California resident before exercising the option, California generally would still tax the difference between the option price and the FMV of the shares on the exercise date, because the individual is a resident of California when the income is recognized.[125] If an individual is employed by a California corporation and performs services both within and outside of California (the individual is a nonresident), California generally would tax the portion of the income on exercise that is reasonably attributed to California. Similar to New York, the method of allocation is generally based on the ratio between the days worked in California after the award of the option and the total number of workdays between the date of the award and the date of the exercise. That ratio is then multiplied by the total stock option income to determine the income taxable by California.

.03 New Jersey

Nonresidents exercising NSOs are subject to taxation by New Jersey from sources arising within the state.[126] Included in this definition is any income earned in connection with a trade, profession, or occupation carried on in New Jersey, or for the rendition of personal services performed in the state. According to the New Jersey State Tax News, stock options received by a taxpayer while working in New Jersey, or for a New Jersey company, are taxable as New Jersey source income when exercised.

.04 Massachusetts

Massachusetts considers the income recognized on the exercise of an NSO as taxable in Massachusetts if the option is awarded or exercised in connection with employment or conduct of a trade or business in Massachusetts, regardless of

---

[122] California and Arizona appear to use this method-*i.e.*, day count from award to exercise (*see*, Stock Option Guidelines, Calif. Franchise Tax Bd. Pub. 1004 [Rev. 03-2005] at 6; Arizona HR 02-50).

[123] Stock Option Guidelines, Ca. Franchise Tax Board Pub. 1004, 2 (Revised, January 2005). *Appeal of Charles W. and Mary D. Perelle*, 1958 WL 1283 at *4 (Cal.St.Bd.Eq. December 17, 1958).

[124] Stock Option Guidelines, Ca. Franchise Tax Board Pub. 1004, 2 (Revised, January 2005).

[125] *Appeal of Earl R. and Alleene R. Barnett*, 1980 WL 5091 at *4 (Cal.St.Bd.Eq. October 28, 1980).

[126] New Jersey State Tax News, Vol. 34 (3), 2 (Fall 2005) available at http://www.state.nj.us/treasury/taxation/pdf/pubs/stn/fall05.pdf.

whether the taxpayer is a Massachusetts resident at the time the income is recognized.[127] Similarly, income is treated as Massachusetts source income whether or not the taxpayer remains employed by the issuer of the option in the year the income is recognized. Subsequent gain or loss resulting from disposition of the stock is generally not taxable to non-residents.

Massachusetts does not explicitly allow an apportionment of the income allocated between days worked in Massachusetts or for a Massachusetts company, but recognizes any gain realized at the award or exercise of the option as ordinary income taxable by Massachusetts.

.05 Pennsylvania

Pennsylvania's personal income tax policy with respect to stock option income differs from that of the Internal Revenue Service. In Pennsylvania, the taxable event in connection with an ISO requiring an employer to withhold Pennsylvania income tax is the date when the option is exercised, sold, or exchanged (rather than the stock).[128] Pennsylvania does not delay the imposition of income tax to the date when stock is sold in a disqualifying disposition.

Pennsylvania makes no distinction between ordinary income and capital gain. Income from all eight recognized categories (including capital gains) is taxed at the same rate of 2.8%. Moreover, Pennsylvania does not differentiate between ISOs and all other stock option plans. According to the Pennsylvania Code, compensation in the form of any stock option plan shall be considered to be received: (1) when the option is exercised if the stock subject to the option is free from any restrictions having a significant effect on its market value; (2) when the restrictions lapse if the stock subject to the option is subject to restrictions having a significant effect on its market value, and; (3) when exchanged, sold, or otherwise converted into cash or other property.[129] Income is thus recognized at the exercise of the stock option and the tax should be withheld by the employer.[130]

When the stock is later sold by the taxpayer, the taxpayer reports the gain or loss as net taxable gain or loss from the disposition of property, which is taxed at a different rate under Pennsylvania law.[131]

Income recognized at the exercise of a stock option is taxable to nonresidents under Pennsylvania law if it is "compensation . . . to the extent that it is earned, received or acquired from sources within this Commonwealth . . . [i]n connection with a trade, profession, occupation carried on in this Commonwealth or for the rendition of personal services performed in this Commonwealth."[132] Income

---

[127] Taxation of Income earned by Non-Residents after St. 2003, Mass. Dept. of Revenue, 6. available at: https://www.mass.gov.

[128] Pennsylvania Personal Income Tax: Compensation/Witholding/Stock Options/Disqualifying Disposition Income, Pennsylvania Dept. of Revenue, No. PIT-03-037 (December 20, 2003 available at: www.revenue.state.pa.us.

[129] 61 Penn. Code § 101.6(f).

[130] Pennsylvania Personal Income Tax: Compensation/Withholding/Stock Options/Disqualifying Disposition Income, Pennsylvania Dept. of Revenue, No. PIT-03-037 (December 20, 2003) available at: www.revenue.state.pa.us.

[131] 72 Penn. Stat. Ann. § 7303(a)(3).

[132] Pennsylvania Personal Income Tax: Compensation — Severance Pay for Services Within and Outside Pennsylvania, Pennsylvania Dept. of Reve-

that does not result from employment within Pennsylvania or as compensation for services rendered in that state is not taxable under Pennsylvania law. Thus, for a nonresident individual who received stock options while employed within Pennsylvania and who left employment upon moving out of the state, and who later exercised the stock option, only that portion of the interval between award of the option and the exercise of the option allocated to Pennsylvania is subject to Pennsylvania income tax. Again, such allocation is typically determined by dividing the days worked in Pennsylvania by the total days worked in the interval between the award and exercise of the option and multiplying the quotient by the gain recognized at exercise of the option. The resulting product is the income allocable to Pennsylvania sources.

(Footnote Continued)

nue, No. PIT-01-038 (July 27, 2001) available at: www.revenue.state.pa.us.

Chapter 8
RESTRICTED STOCK, PERFORMANCE SHARES AND RSUs

¶801 Overview—Restricted Stock, Performance Shares and RSUs

Companies award restricted stock, performance shares and restricted stock units ("RSUs") to employees, directors and other service providers to compensate them for services in a manner that links the interests of the award recipients to those of the stockholders. A share of restricted stock is a real share of stock—not merely an option to purchase stock—that a company awards to its employees, directors or others. However, the employee (or other recipient) may not sell, transfer or dispose of the stock, and may forfeit the stock if he or she leaves employment or otherwise fails to satisfy the requirements or restrictions on the stock. Thus, the stock is "restricted." Practitioners generally refer to share awards that vest solely based on the passage of time as "restricted stock," and share awards that vest only upon the attainment of specific performance goals as "performance shares." For most purposes other than vesting, restricted stock and performance shares are the same thing.

Restricted stock and performance share awards are also sometimes referred to as "full value" awards.

Although corporations most often award restricted stock or performance shares, business entities other than corporations, including partnerships and limited liability companies, also can award restricted equity interests to their employees or others. We could more properly refer to these awards as "restricted units" or "restricted interests."

The percentage of companies granting restricted stock or RSUs has more than doubled over the last ten years. The increase in popularity of RSUs has been especially pronounced, as the percentage of companies granting RSUs instead of restricted stock has increased by a factor of ten over the last ten years.

.01 Contrasted with Stock Options

Unlike stock options, which are valuable only if the company's stock price increases, restricted stock and RSUs have immediate value and will continue to be valuable even if the company's stock price declines. If the chosen performance standards are satisfied, performance shares will also be valuable even if the company's stock price declines (see ¶815).

.02 Restricted Stock

The recipient of an award of restricted stock cannot sell, transfer, or dispose of the stock until he or she satisfies the restrictions set forth in the award.

Typically, the restriction is an employment requirement, *i.e.*, the recipient must remain employed with the company for a specified number of years (see ¶ 825).

.03 Performance Shares

Performance shares are a form of restricted stock under which the recipient only vests after certain performance requirements have been satisfied. A typical requirement could include the completion of a specified period of employment and the company's attainment of a particular level of earnings or revenues. Once the specified requirements or goals have been satisfied or obtained, the executive would acquire full ownership rights in the stock (see ¶ 835). More companies are awarding performance shares since FAS 123R (now known as Accounting Standards Codification Topic 718 or "ASC 718") ended the negative accounting for performance share awards.

.04 Restricted Stock Units

Restricted stock units ("RSUs") are a form of restricted stock award that has grown in popularity over the years. RSUs have nearly all of the characteristics of restricted stock, except that an RSU is not an award of actual shares. However, an award of RSUs can accomplish many of the same objectives of an award of restricted stock. Some companies have even converted awards of restricted stock into awards of RSUs (see ¶ 845).

.05 Taxation of Awards

An individual who receives restricted stock or performance shares will recognize income only when his or her stock ownership is no longer subject to a substantial risk of forfeiture or becomes transferable, *e.g.*, when the restrictions lapse or the company attains the performance goals. The amount included in income on that date is the difference between the fair market value of the stock on that date and the amount, if any, paid by the employee for the stock. However, an employee who receives stock subject to a risk of forfeiture may elect to recognize income at the time of the award by making a so-called "83(b) election." An 83(b) election would cause the employee to recognize taxable income on the difference between the stock's fair market value at the time of the award and the amount paid for the stock, if any (see ¶ 855).

Restricted stock units are considered deferred compensation, subject to the rules of Code Sec. 409A (see ¶ 875). No 83(b) election is available with respect to RSU awards.

.06 Securities Law Issues

The Securities Act of 1933 requires a publicly held company to register offers or sales of its securities, including offers to its own employees. Generally, a publicly held company must file a Form S-8 Registration Statement with the SEC for a restricted stock, performance share, or RSU plan. The company must report the value of any restricted stock awarded to a named executive officer in the "Restricted Stock" column of its proxy statement for the year of the award (see ¶ 865).

¶801.03

.07 Code Sec. 409A

Code Sec. 409A can apply to stock incentive awards, including restricted stock, performance shares, and RSUs. Failure to satisfy the requirements of Code Sec. 409A could result in significant penalties to the award recipient. Code Sec. 409A applies differently to different types of stock incentive awards. Code Sec. 409A will not apply to most restricted stock or performance share awards. However, most RSU awards will be subject to Code Sec. 409A (see ¶ 875).

¶815 Restricted Stock Basics

A restricted stock award is a grant of actual shares of stock by a company to its employees, directors or other service providers. The stock is "restricted" in two respects: the award recipient's ability to sell, transfer, or dispose of the stock is limited; and the stock will be forfeited if he or she leaves employment or otherwise fails to satisfy the requirements or restrictions on the stock. The term "restricted stock" refers to stock awarded by corporations. Business entities other than corporations, including partnerships and limited liability companies, can also award restricted equity interests to their employees or other service providers. We would generally refer to these awards as "restricted units" or "restricted interests."

.01 Awarding Restricted Stock

Companies generally make restricted stock awards through equity compensation plans that the company's board of directors and its stockholders have approved. The board of directors or compensation committee awards restricted stock to employees (and other service providers) according to the provisions of the plan, usually by delivering a form of award agreement, which is a specific contract between the employee and the company. The restricted stock award agreement will set forth the number of shares of restricted stock that the company has awarded to the employee, as well as the vesting or other restrictions applicable to those shares.

The award recipient will acquire full ownership of the stock after a specified period of time (e.g., five years of employment) or when the company and/or the employee attain specific performance goals (e.g., the company's return on equity is 15% or higher). Restricted stock plan and/or award agreements often contain some exceptions to the general vesting rules if the executive terminates employment because of death, disability, or in the event of a change in control of the company.

> **Example:** On January 1, 2018, ABC Corporation awards 10,000 shares of restricted stock to Executive D. On the award date, ABC's stock price is $20.00. The restricted stock becomes 25% vested on January 1, 2019, the first anniversary of the award date. It then becomes 50% vested on January 1, 2020, 75% vested on January 1, 2021, and 100% vested on January 1, 2022.
>
> On January 1, 2019, ABC Corporation's stock price is $15.00 per share. However, Executive D vests in 2,500 shares of ABC stock on that date. D is free to sell those shares in the open market if she wishes.

On January 1, 2020, ABC Corporation's stock price is back at $20.00 per share. ABC's stockholders have not seen any gains, but Executive D becomes vested in another 2,500 shares of ABC stock on that date. D is free to sell those shares in the open market if she wishes.

.02 Voting and Dividend Rights

Whether and how to pay dividends and give voting rights to holders of unvested restricted stock is a plan design issue for the company. Holders of restricted stock generally are treated as stockholders for all purposes except transferability and, accordingly, have the right to vote their restricted shares and receive dividends. Some companies, however, will impose restrictions on dividends. The company may legend the stock certificates for the shares of restricted stock to reflect the restrictions, and/or the company, or its transfer agent, may hold the stock in escrow. When the executive has satisfied the restrictions, *i.e.*, the restrictions lapse, the company would remove any restrictive legend and release the shares to the executive. Some companies credit any dividends paid on the restricted stock to an account on behalf of the executive and hold the account until the executive vests in the stock. (Note that Institutional Shareholder Services ("ISS") has commented that dividends or dividend equivalents paid on unvested performance shares or units may result in negative recommendations on a stand-alone basis.)

.03 Payment for Restricted Stock

Generally, the executive does not pay anything for the restricted stock. However, most plans permit the board or compensation committee to make awards that require the executive to pay some amount (generally nominal) for the stock. Such provisions reflect the possibility that some states might require executives to pay a nominal price for the restricted stock, such as par value.

.04 Entities That May Award Restricted Stock

Restricted stock awards are available as a form of executive compensation to both publicly traded and privately held corporations. Similarly, partnerships and LLCs can implement "restricted unit" or "restricted interest" plans that award actual partnership interests or membership rights. However, partnerships and LLCs utilize these types of plans less often than corporations, largely because of the fact that generally, the consequences of becoming a partner in a partnership or a "member" of an LLC are more significant than the consequences of receiving a minority interest in the shares of a corporation. For example, the death or voluntary withdrawal of a member of an LLC may cause the technical dissolution of the entity, while the death of a minority shareholder or the redemption of all of his or her stock will not affect the continued existence of the corporation.

¶825 Comparison to Stock Options—Advantages and Disadvantages

Traditionally, companies have utilized stock options much more frequently than restricted stock. Unlike stock options, which are only valuable to the executive if the company's stock price increases, a restricted stock award is valuable to the executive recipient *even if the company's stock price declines*. For this reason, most institutional (and other) investors have generally discouraged companies from awarding restricted stock.

However, due to the corporate and accounting scandals of the 1990s, stock options received a lot of criticism for giving executives an inappropriate incentive to increase artificially the company's stock price in order to create value for their options. As a result, there is now more interest in restricted stock awards.

The following discussion compares and contrasts stock options with restricted stock, and highlights the advantages and disadvantages of each.

1. Stock options and restricted stock both generally align the recipient's interests with those of stockholders, *i.e.*, an increasing share price. However, the cyclical nature of the stock market leads to different critiques of the two forms of compensation. Stock options can reward executives for increases in stock price that are attributable to a general run-up in the stock market, rather than to the executive's performance. On the other hand, commentators often criticize restricted stock for rewarding employees even if the stock price goes down. Restricted stock proponents respond that sharing the upside and the downside of an increase or decrease of share price, more closely aligns the interests of restricted shareholders and shareholders. Additionally, proponents point to the need to compensate executives in a down market, which stock options generally cannot do. Undeniably, restricted stock has greater retentive value than options in a down market.

2. Restricted stock awards enable the company to provide the executive with nearly all of the benefits of stock ownership, including voting and dividend rights. In contrast, stock options convey neither voting nor dividend rights. In this respect, restricted stock awards more closely align the executive's interests with those of stockholders.

3. Unlike stock options, the recipient of a restricted stock award generally cannot control the timing and amount of his or her tax liability for the award. The basic rule is that restricted stock is taxable as ordinary income to the recipient on the day of vesting.

   Example 1: In the Example in ¶815, when Executive D vested in 2,500 shares of ABC stock, worth $15.00 per share, on January 1, 2019, she recognized ordinary income of $37,500. When D vested in another 2,500 shares of ABC stock, worth $20.00 per share, on January 1, 2020, she recognized ordinary income of $50,000.

   However, an employee may elect to recognize income when the company awards her restricted stock by making a so-called "83(b) election." An 83(b) election would cause the employee to recognize taxable income on the difference between the stock's fair market value at the time of the award and the amount paid for the stock, if any. Any appreciation in the value of the stock from the date of the restricted stock award to the date the employee sells the stock would be taxed at capital gain rates (see

¶855 below for a detailed discussion of taxation and 83(b) election issues).

Example 2: On July 1, 2018, ABC Corporation, a start-up venture, awards 100,000 shares of restricted stock to Executive D. The restricted stock becomes 25% vested on July 1, 2019, the first anniversary of the award date, and becomes vested an additional 25% on each of July 1, 2020, 2021 and 2022. ABC's stock price is $0.15 on the July 1, 2018 award date. Executive D files an 83(b) election within 30 days of July 1, 2018, to recognize income on the full value of the award. D recognizes $15,000 of ordinary income on that date. ABC Corporation becomes a public company. On July 1, 2020, the stock is trading at $20.00 per share and Executive D sells the 50,000 shares that have vested into the open market. D's gain of $985,000 would be taxable as long-term capital gain, reported on Schedule D, as with the sale of any stock.

4. The company is entitled to a deduction that corresponds in timing and amount to the income recognized by the employee for both options and restricted stock.

Example 3: In Example 1 above, when Executive D recognized ordinary income of $37,500 on January 1, 2019, ABC Corporation became entitled to a corresponding deduction. Similarly, when D recognized another $50,000 of ordinary income on January 1, 2020, ABC became entitled to a corresponding deduction.

5. Like stock options, restricted stock awards allow the company to compensate employees and other service providers without a cash outlay. The primary "cost" to the company of restricted stock awards and options is the dilution of existing stockholders.

6. Before 2006, an award of restricted stock would result in an immediate compensation expense to the company, unlike stock options, which allowed a company to compensate employees without reflecting a compensation charge against earnings on its financial statements. However, when ASC Topic 718, Stock Compensation (formerly, FASB Statement 123R) became fully effective, the extraordinarily favorable treatment accorded to stock options ended (see ¶735 for a discussion of the evolving rules on accounting for stock options). Since 2006, stock options have not had that accounting advantage over restricted stock or RSUs.

7. Using Black-Scholes, one restricted share is typically equal in value to three or four options shares. However, one restricted share is equal to the "perceived value" of four to six option shares."[1] Thus, some professionals reason that restricted stock is a more efficient compensation tool from a stockholder dilution perspective.

---

[1] "Restricted Stock Over Options: An Overreaction?" Paul Gilles, NACD Directors Monthly, January 2006.

¶825

8. For companies with "overhang" or dilution problems, restricted stock is more useful than options because the company can award more value to its executives, while using fewer shares of stock authorized for awards (see Chapter 13 [¶1301 *et seq.*] for a detailed discussion of overhang problems).

   Overhang percentages and annual share allocations declined for many companies beginning in 2006. One of the reasons for this was that companies awarded more restricted stock than options, which resulted in the award of a fewer number of shares with the same approximate value.[2]

9. Some corporate governance groups view restricted stock awards more favorably than stock options. The belief/fear is that stock option awards may cause executives and directors to approve riskier strategies to increase the value of their options, whereas full value stock awards like restricted stock tend to encourage a steady, long-term focus that is more like that of an ordinary shareholder.

10. From the perspective of the recipient, restricted stock usually represents a more tangible benefit than options. Additionally, stock options are inherently a much higher risk instrument than restricted stock from an investment analyst standpoint. By moving toward restricted stock, companies are moving executives into a vehicle that is less risky. Finally, since many companies awarded only stock options for years, the award of restricted stock helps spread the risk out among several different vehicles.

11. Until 2018, stock options granted under a plan approved by stockholders would generally qualify as "performance-based compensation," which is exempt from the $1 million cap on deductible compensation under Code Sec. 162(m). Although a company could design its restricted stock to qualify for Code Sec. 162(m)'s "performance-based compensation" exception, only stock options qualify for nearly automatic exemption (see Chapter 22 [¶2201 *et seq.*] for a detailed discussion of Code Sec. 162(m) issues).

    However, the legislation known as the Tax Cuts and Jobs Act of 2017 ("TCJA") signed into law by President Trump in December 2017, eliminated the performance-based compensation exception from Code Sec. 162(m). The performance-based compensation exception was far and away the most frequently used and most helpful exception to Code Sec. 162(m).

Except as otherwise noted in ¶835 (which discusses performance shares) and ¶845 (which discusses RSUs), performance shares and RSUs have the same

---

[2] The other two reasons were: (1) many companies responded to the effective date FAS 123R by reducing the number of options awarded and eliminating awards entirely for non-executive employees, and (2) significantly increased pressures for good governance caused some companies to reduce their equity compensation awards.

advantages and disadvantages as does restricted stock when compared to stock options.

¶835 Performance Shares

The term "performance shares" can be used to describe at least two different types of equity-based compensation arrangements. On the one hand, "performance share" plans can refer to restricted stock plans that contain performance-based forfeiture restrictions. In these plans, performance share awards represent actual distributions of shares of company stock to the executive that vest only after certain performance requirements have been satisfied, such as the company attaining a particular level of earnings or revenues. For tax and operational purposes, this type of performance share plan functions just like restricted stock plans that have an employment restriction as the sole forfeiture restriction.

The other types of performance share plans are more similar to RSUs than to restricted stock. A grant under this type of performance share plan does not involve an actual issuance of shares to the recipient, but is instead a grant of a right to receive a specified number of shares if certain performance criteria are satisfied. If the performance standards are not completely satisfied, the company/plan will only issue a portion or none of the granted performance shares. Some plans set discrete thresholds and issue shares whenever any of the thresholds are met, while other plans do not issue any shares until the end of the performance period. In addition, many plans of this type permit distributions in cash, stock or a combination of the two, although the company measures the value of the performance award solely by reference to its stock. Plans that permit cash distributions are also sometimes referred to as "performance unit" or "performance award" plans.

The latter type of performance share plans is taxed liked RSUs in that the executive recognizes income only when the plan makes a distribution to him or her and only in the amount that the plan actually distributed. The company is entitled to a deduction at the same time and at the same amount. No election is permitted under Code Sec. 83(b) (see ¶855 below for a detailed discussion of taxation and 83(b) election issues).

The main benefit of performance share awards, in contrast to normal restricted stock and RSU awards, is that the company can give an executive compensation incentives that it has tailored to his or her job. Institutional stockholders, who sometimes refer to restricted stock as "pay for pulse" because it can provide a significant benefit to executives even if the company's stock price does not increase, strongly prefer performance shares over restricted stock or RSUs.

¶845 Restricted Stock Units ("RSUs")

Restricted stock units ("RSUs") are a popular form of executive compensation that in certain circumstances is preferable to true restricted stock. Except for the fact that it is not an award of actual shares, an award of RSUs has nearly all of the characteristics, and can accomplish most of the objectives, of a restricted stock award. Another important difference, and potential drawback, is that RSUs are taxed more like deferred compensation than restricted stock (see Chapter 17 [¶1701 *et seq.*] for a discussion of nonqualified retirement plans, including deferred compensation).

.01 Structure of RSUs

Companies structure an award of RSUs like an award of restricted stock. RSUs consist of awards in the form of phantom shares or units, which are valued based on company stock. RSUs may be settled in cash, stock, or both. As is the case with restricted stock, vesting of RSUs may be service-based, performance-based, and/or performance-accelerated.

The company's stock incentive plan must permit the company or its board of directors or compensation committee to award RSUs. The award agreement specifies the number of shares awarded, the vesting restrictions and any other terms and conditions the company deems necessary or appropriate for its award agreements.

Example 1: Pursuant to the ABC Corporation Stock Incentive Plan, ABC awarded 10,000 RSUs to Executive D on July 1, 2018, vesting at 25% per year. The terms of the award agreement provide that D can elect to receive a distribution of a like number of shares of ABC stock (in increments of at least 1,000 shares) at any time after the RSUs become vested, by filing a written election with ABC at least 12 months before the designated distribution date.

One of the most common provisions in an RSU plan and/or award agreement is that the value of the RSUs is to be measured solely by reference to the company's share price and the recipient must receive a distribution of his or her RSUs in shares of stock. While not legally required, these provisions were once necessary to obtain favorable accounting treatment (discussed below) for the RSUs. A company could decide to forego favorable accounting treatment for the RSUs and permit an executive/recipient to elect to:

1. "diversify" his or her RSU holdings into other investment choices— much like a participant in a nonqualified deferred compensation plan may diversify his or her holding among various investment choices (see Chapter 17 [¶1701 *et seq.*] on nonqualified retirement plans); and/or

2. receive a distribution of the value of his or her RSUs in cash rather than shares of stock.

.02 Taxation of RSUs

One advantage of RSUs compared to restricted stock is that the recipient of RSUs does not recognize taxable ordinary income at the time the RSUs vest. If properly drafted, RSUs are not to be taxable to the recipient until he or she ultimately elects and receives a distribution of the stock underlying the RSUs, which often is not until after the recipient leaves employment. (Note, however, this distribution election must be made in advance, subject to the rules of Code Sec. 409A.)

Example 2: Assume ABC Corporation awarded 10,000 shares of restricted stock to Executive D, vesting 25% per year, on July 1, 2017. If ABC's stock is trading at $50.00 per share on July 1, 2018, Executive D would recognize ordinary income of $125,000 on that date. At a 37% federal tax rate, D would owe, and ABC would need to withhold, approximately $46,000, which D may need to satisfy by selling some of 2,500 shares of restricted stock that just vested. This event would be repeated on July 1 of 2019, 2020, and 2021.

If ABC had instead awarded 10,000 RSUs to Executive D, D would not recognize any income on July 1, 2018, or on any of the three other vesting dates, if she did not receive a distribution with respect to the vested RSUs.

In order to prevent the vesting of RSUs from causing taxation for the award recipient under the constructive receipt doctrine, the plan and award agreement must subject the RSUs to "a substantial risk of forfeiture," and the award recipient must elect the ultimate distribution date in advance. The company accomplishes this by not issuing a stock certificate to the award recipient until an extended period (generally one year) after the date that the RSU award recipient files an irrevocable written election to receive a distribution. Until the company issues a stock certificate, the award recipient has received nothing more than a promise from the company, under the plan and award agreement, to distribute shares of stock in the future. In the event of the company's insolvency, the company's promise would be treated in the same manner as claims of general creditors. Therefore, under constructive receipt principles, the RSU recipient is subject to a substantial risk of forfeiture until the plan actually makes a distribution to him or her (see ¶1725 for a detailed discussion of the doctrine of constructive receipt).

Example 3: In Example 2 above, Executive D fully vested in her RSUs on July 1, 2021. However, until ABC Corporation actually issues share certificates to D, there is a risk that the corporation could become insolvent and pay her nothing. Moreover, because D cannot receive a distribution of her vested RSUs until the date D specified in a written election previously filed with ABC, the risk of insolvency continues until the day D actually receives a distribution of ABC stock. If D's written election specified a distribution date of July 1, 2025, ABC would distribute 100,000 shares to D on July 1, 2025. If ABC's stock is trading at $50.00 per share on July 1, 2025, D would recognize ordinary income of $5,000,000 on that date.

The company will be entitled to a tax deduction in the same amount and at the same time as the executive recognizes taxable ordinary income—upon distribution of the shares. This is a disadvantage to companies of RSUs as compared to restricted stock, which produce a tax deduction at the time the awarded shares vest. Because an RSU award is not a transfer of property, the executive cannot make a Code Sec. 83(b) election to begin the running of the long-term capital gain rate holding period.

The tax treatment of any dividends paid on the shares of company stock to which the RSUs pertain depends on the design of the plan and the RSU award.

To ensure equal treatment of RSU holders and restricted stockholders, many companies provide that RSU holders will receive a cash payment of a "dividend equivalent" in the amount of any dividend payable on company stock. Dividend equivalents payable on unvested RSUs generally would be taxable to the recipient and deductible by the company, while dividend equivalents payable on vested RSUs would be taxable to the recipient, but not deductible by the company until actually paid.

Some companies structure their RSUs differently than the norm. These companies structure the RSUs to vest in equal installments over a period of years (possibly with acceleration upon the achievement of certain performance goals or a change in control). As the RSUs vest, they are payable to the executives in "unrestricted" shares of the company's common stock. Generally, however, the company gives the executive the opportunity to elect to defer receipt of the unrestricted common stock through a deferred compensation plan.

The tax treatment of RSUs is similar to the treatment of nonqualified deferred compensation with respect to the application of the constructive receipt doctrine, Code Sec. 409A, and FICA and Medicare taxation (see ¶1735 for a detailed discussion of the FICA and Medicare taxation of deferred compensation).

.03 Accounting Treatment

The unfavorable accounting treatment of RSUs relative to stock options had made RSUs less desirable for many companies. However, FAS 123R (now known as ASC 718) eliminated the favorable accounting treatment of stock options for all companies in 2006, causing this artificial advantage for stock options to disappear. Thus, RSUs and restricted stock are on the same footing as stock options from an accounting perspective.

> **Planning Note:** Always incorporate the following three provisions in a plan that includes RSUs and/or RSU award agreements: (1) RSU recipients' holdings and/or gain will always be measured solely by reference to the market price of the company's stock; (2) RSU recipients will receive a distribution of their RSU value solely in shares of company stock; and (3) the value of any vested RSUs will be distributed no earlier than one year following the date the RSU holder files an irrevocable written election to receive a distribution.

Since RSUs are considered common stock equivalents, they sometimes are included in the denominator for purposes of computing basic and diluted earnings per share.

.04 Why RSUs?

The primary advantage of RSUs over true restricted stock is that RSUs give the award recipient significant flexibility to defer taxation. The holder of restricted stock recognizes ordinary income on the fair market value of the stock at the time of vesting. Often the restricted stock holder will not have a sufficient amount of available cash to cover his or her tax liability, and will be required to sell some of the vested shares to pay taxes. In contrast, as discussed above, the holder of RSUs will not be taxed until he or she elects to receive, and then actually does receive, a distribution.

A number of large multinational corporations have awarded RSUs, including McDonalds Corporation, Motorola, Inc., and W.W. Grainger, Inc. Many multinational corporations will award RSUs instead of restricted stock for employees in countries (such as Canada) that would treat restricted stock as taxable on the date of award.

RSUs can also be a useful tool for compensating members of the company's board of directors, particularly for directors who might have to sell shares to pay the taxes. Since RSUs allow each director to control the timing of his or her recognition of income, directors can avoid the potential negative repercussions of the market seeing them sell the company's shares (see Chapter 5 [¶ 501 et seq.] for a more detailed discussion of compensating directors with RSUs).

In addition, most companies that award RSUs have drafted (or revised) their stock ownership guidelines for employees and directors so that RSUs count toward the required holdings. The fact that recipients of RSUs will not be tempted or required to sell some of their holdings to meet tax obligations at the time of vesting makes it easier for RSU recipients to meet any ownership guidelines.

Because RSUs are not "property" under Code Sec. 83 and merely represent a general unsecured promise to pay a future amount, the employee may postpone taxation beyond vesting (the company's deduction is similarly delayed) until such time as the RSUs are settled. Accordingly, RSUs can allow employees to retain an interest in company stock, and consequently, company performance, for an extended period. Some of the other advantages of RSUs are the following:

- A company could use RSUs to minimize the impact of the $1 million deduction limit under Code Sec. 162(m). The annual $1 million deduction limit applies only to the taxable compensation of the five highest paid officers of a publicly held corporation who are employed by the corporation as of the last day of the year. Therefore, an executive can delay receiving an RSU-related stock distribution until after retirement, and thereby ensure the corporation's ability to deduct fully the value of the stock distribution. However, the TCJA eliminated the performance-based compensation exception from Code Sec. 162(m) (see Chapter 22 [¶ 2201 et seq.] for a detailed discussion of Code Sec. 162(m)).

- There is no administrative burden with respect to stock certificates until shares are paid. Because no shares are paid or distributed until vesting, maintaining unit accounts is more administratively simple.

- RSUs that provide for settlement in cash instead of stock will not result in shareholder dilution.

- RSUs may be preferable for employees outside the United States because many countries would tax restricted stock immediately upon award, regardless of vesting restrictions.

RSUs have disadvantages as well. An RSU award that provides for settlement in cash instead of stock will require the company to make a cash outlay. Additionally, RSUs that are settled in cash instead of stock will not increase the employee's holdings of company stock. Finally, RSUs settled in cash are treated as liability awards under ASC 718 (requiring quarterly adjustments to the compensation charge based on the price of the stock underlying the RSU). Among the other perceived disadvantages of RSUs are the following:

- Unless settled within two and a half months of the end of the year in which they vest, RSUs must comply with Code Sec. 409A.

- Because an RSU award is not a transfer of property, the recipient cannot make a Code Sec. 83(b) election. (Note that some companies view this as an advantage because they do not have the difficulty of administering employees' elections.)

- RSUs are included in the denominator for computing "diluted" earnings per share.

- RSU holders generally do not enjoy voting rights with respect to the underlying shares.

- RSUs are not deductible under Code Sec. 162(m) unless performance-based or the receipt of income from the award is deferred until the executive is no longer subject to Code Sec. 162(m). However, if payment on the RSUs is postponed until employment termination, the payment would be deductible under Code Sec. 162(m).

.05 Converting Restricted Stock to RSUs

Some companies have even converted awards of restricted stock into awards of RSUs. A variety of circumstances might cause a company to consider converting an outstanding award of restricted stock to an award of RSUs. However, the most frequent circumstances would be the company's desire to (1) permit its executives to defer taxation and (2) avoid putting the executives in a position of having to sell some of their newly vested stock just to pay taxes.

> **Example 4:** In Example 2 above, if ABC Corporation decided to convert the entire restricted stock award to an award of RSUs before July 1, 2018, Executive D would not recognize any income at the time of the conversion, or on July 1, 2018, 2019, or 2020. D could retain the full value and appreciation of her RSUs during this period.

The incentive to convert outstanding awards of restricted stock to awards of RSUs could become particularly acute in a situation where a substantial number of shares of restricted stock that are held by a number of different executives are scheduled to vest on the same date. If the executives have to sell a significant amount of their newly vested shares to pay the taxes from the vesting, there would be an appearance of mass insider selling, which the stock market probably would not receive well.

The rules would not require a company to disclose in its proxy statement that it had converted, or allowed executives to elect to convert, outstanding restricted stock awards into RSUs, as long as the terms and conditions of the awards remain the same. Similarly, if the conversion does not alter the material terms and conditions of the awards, the RSUs could continue to qualify for favorable (*i.e.*, fixed) accounting treatment.

.06 Adding RSUs

Generally, shareholder approval would not be required to add RSUs to an equity compensation plan that allows for the issuance of restricted stock. An award of RSUs typically results in the issuance of restricted stock on a deferred basis after vesting requirements are met. As such, this type of award is substantially equivalent to the award of restricted stock, and if the plan allows for the award of restricted stock, the addition of RSUs is not a material modification that requires shareholder approval. Shareholder approval would be required, however, to add RSUs to a plan that does not provide for restricted stock awards because the revision would expand the types of awards available.

.07 Qualified Equity Grant Deferrals Under the TCJA

The TCJA added a new Code Sec. 83(i), effective for 2018. Code Sec. 83(i) permits a "qualified employee" of an "eligible corporation" to elect to defer the inclusion in income of amounts attributable to the distribution of an RSU or the exercise of a stock option. Deferral elections are only available for RSUs and options awarded to employees by a company if the stock of the company has not been readily tradable on an established securities market during any preceding calendar year. To determine whether any stock of the company has been readily tradable on an established securities market during any preceding calendar year, any predecessor to the company is included, as well as any member of the controlled group of companies that includes that company or group of trades or businesses under common control with the company.

Awards made on after January 1, 2018, under an existing equity award plan could qualify for the deferral election even if the rights and privileges of awards under that plan were not the same before that date, so long as any awards after that date satisfy the equal rights and privileges requirement.

New Code Sec. 83(i) is designed primarily for the benefit of smaller and start-up companies. It draws on employee eligibility and tax treatment elements of Code Sec. 423 (employee stock purchase plans) and Code Sec. 422 (incentive stock options). The key feature of new Code Sec. 83(i) is that a company's written equity plan must grant stock RSUs or options to at least 80% of all employees who provide services to the company in the U.S. And stock RSUs and options must have the same "rights and privileges" to receive qualified stock.

Although this income deferral election is only available to employees of privately held corporations, the change is significant enough that it warrants further discussion.

Awards of Qualified Stock of an Eligible Corporation: A deferral election only may be made on stock received by an employee in connection with the exercise of an option or the settlement of an RSU. The RSUs or options must be awarded under the terms of a written plan document. The employee must be performing services as an employee for the company that awards the RSU or option and the RSU or option must apply to the stock of the company that employs the employee. An RSU or option will not be qualified under Code Sec. 83(i) if it permits the employee to sell the stock to, or receive cash in lieu of stock from, the company at the time that the employee's rights in the stock first become transferable or not subject to a substantial risk of forfeiture.

Qualified Employee: The company's equity plan must grant RSUs or stock options to at least 80% of all employees who provide services to the company in the U.S., including employees in any U.S. possession. Certain employees are not eligible to elect a deferral, including the company's chief executive officer and chief financial officer ("CFO"), any family member of the CEO or CFO, any one of the four highest compensated officers for any of the company's 10 prior taxable years, and an individual who is or has been a 1% owner of the company at any time during the individual's 10 prior calendar years. Part-time employees customarily employed for fewer than 30 hours per week also are not eligible. For purposes of determining a family relationship, Code Sec. 83(i) refers to the rules under Code Sec. 318(a)(1). For purposes of determining the company's highest compensated officers for any of the 10 preceding taxable years, Code Sec. 83(i) refers to the SEC's shareholder disclosure rules (applied as if those rules applied to the company).

Tax Treatment: If an employee makes the deferral election under new Code Sec. 83(i), the employee would recognize taxable income on the earliest of (i) the date the stock becomes transferable (including becoming transferable to the company), (ii) the date the employee becomes an excluded employee, (iii) the date any stock of the company becomes readily tradable on an established securities market, (iv) the date that is five years after the first date the rights of the employee in such stock are transferable or are not subject to a substantial risk of forfeiture (whichever occurs earlier), or (v) the date on which the employee revokes the qualified election with respect to the stock.

After the deferral period, the employee would recognize taxable income on the fair market value of the stock on the vesting date, regardless of whether the value of the stock had increased or decreased between the time of the vesting date and the end of the deferral period. The deferred award would be subject to FICA tax at the time of vesting.

The TCJA also amended Code Sec. 409A to provide that "qualified stock" is not subject to Code Sec. 409A, and RSUs and options subject to the deferral elections will not be considered non-qualified deferred compensation.

Notice and Election Requirements: To defer income, an employee must make an election with respect to qualified stock received upon an option exercise or RSU vesting no later than 30 days after the first date the employee rights in the stock are transferable or are not subject to a substantial risk of forfeiture, whichever occurs earlier. In the deferral election, the employee must agree to certain tax withholding requirements, described further below.

A company offering qualified employees the elections to defer income on qualified stock must provide certain information to such employees. At or before the time that the employee would recognize income on the award, but for the employee's deferral election the company must notify the employee that he or she may be eligible to elect to defer income on the stock under Code Sec. 83(i). As part of this notice, the company also must explain that:

- if the employee makes a deferral election, the amount of income recognized at the end of the deferral period will be based on the value of the stock at the time at which the rights of the employee in such stock first become transferable or not subject to substantial risk of forfeiture, regardless of whether the value of the stock has declined during the deferral period,

- the amount of the income the employee would recognize at the end of the deferral period would be subject to federal income tax withholding at not less than the maximum rate, and

- the employee would remain responsible for his or her portion of the required withholding taxes.

The company also must certify to the employee that the stock the employee is about to receive, absent a deferral election, is qualified stock.

Same Rights and Privileges: Code Sec. 83(i) expressly provides that the determination of rights and privileges with respect to stock is to be made in a similar manner as under Code Sec. 423(b)(5). Rights and privileges with respect to the exercise of an option are not treated as the same as rights and privileges with respect to the settlement of a restricted stock unit. Where a company wants RSUs or stock options to be treated as qualified equity grants, 80% of employees must receive that same type of award. It is not sufficient, for example, if 40% of employees receive stock options and 40% receive RSUs.

Regulations under Code Sec. 423 offer significant guidance on the meaning of "equal rights and privileges" and, presumably, that guidance will apply to new Code Sec. 83(i). An employee will not fail to be treated as having the same rights and privileges to receive stock solely because the number of shares available to all employees is not equal in amount, so long as the number of shares available to each employee is more than a *de minimis* amount. The amount of stock that is awarded to employees may vary, as long as it bears a uniform relationship to the total compensation or the basic or regular rate of compensation of the employees.

The new qualified equity grant deferral feature appears to have limited applicability due to the fact that the RSUs or options must be made available to 80% of employees in a privately held company. The fact that significant owners and certain officers are not eligible further limits the utility of the provision. However, many employees at eligible corporations could benefit from this opportunity to defer income recognition on common forms of equity awards.

¶855 Taxation of Awards

Under the Code,[3] an employee who receives restricted stock will not recognize any income as long as the stock is subject to a "substantial risk of forfeiture" *and* is nontransferable. According to Code Sec. 83, a "substantial risk of forfeiture" exists if the plan or award conditions the executive's rights to the restricted stock on the executive's future performance of services and the services that the executive is required to perform are substantial. Imposing the requirement of continued employment will generally create a substantial risk of forfeiture and will delay taxation if the restricted stock remains nontransferable until the employment restrictions lapse.

> **Example 1:** On July 1, 2017, ABC Corporation awarded 10,000 shares of restricted stock to Executive D. D's ownership interest in the stock vests at a rate of 25% per year to the extent that D continues to be employed by ABC Corporation. If ABC's stock is trading at $50.00 per share on July 1, 2018, Executive D will recognize ordinary income of $125,000 on that date. At a 37% federal tax rate, D would owe, and ABC would need to withhold, approximately $46,000 for federal income tax purposes. This event would be repeated on each of July 1, 2019, 2020, and 2021.

Dividends earned on unvested restricted stock are usually considered compensation income, which the company must report on Form W-2. However, if the recipient made a timely 83(b) election to be taxed according to the value of the shares at the time of grant and not at vesting, any dividend payments would be dividend income reported on 1099-DIV.

.01 Company's Deduction

The company is entitled to a compensation deduction that corresponds in timing and amount to the compensation income recognized by the employee. If the employee makes an 83(b) election, the employee treats dividends on the restricted stock as dividend income. The company cannot deduct the dividends. If the employee does not make an 83(b) election, dividends on unvested shares of restricted stock will be treated as compensation income to the employee and be deductible as such.

.02 Withholding

The company has the obligation, and the plan or award documents should give it the right, to withhold, or to require the executive to remit to the company, an amount sufficient to satisfy federal, state and local income or other taxes required by law to be withheld, including the executive's FICA obligation, before the restricted stock is distributed to the executive. Experienced legal counsel can draft a plan to allow an executive to choose the manner in which the company will satisfy its withholding obligation. Alternatives include the following:

1. **Withhold to Cover.** The company or plan administrator can withhold shares that have an aggregate fair market value, on the date the tax is to

---

[3] Code Sec. 83.

be determined, equal to the amount required to be withheld. This method is known as "withhold to cover." If the company or plan uses a third-party administrator or broker, the withhold to cover amount also generally would include any applicable commissions or fees. The company then would provide the net amount of shares to the plan administrator or broker to deposit into the individual executive's restricted stock account.

2. **Sell to Cover.** If the parties use the sell to cover method, the company or plan administrator will calculate the number of shares to be sold to satisfy the individual's tax obligation, and any applicable commissions or fees. The plan administrator or broker then will sell such shares following receipt of the entire gross share amount from the company. The parties may do this sale transaction through a market transaction, a block sale or through an average priced trade per the company's instruction, in consultation with the plan administrator. Commissions and fees generally will apply to executives in the sell to cover method.

3. **Sell All Shares.** If the sell all shares method is used, the company or plan administrator will, upon the settlement of the sale transaction, deduct from the gross sale proceeds an amount to cover the executive's tax obligation (and any applicable commissions or fees).

4. **Payroll Deduction or Cash.** If the parties use the payroll deduction or cash method, the company or plan administrator will calculate the taxes required to satisfy the tax obligation. The company could withhold from any cash compensation (*e.g.*, salary or bonus) the amount it is required to withhold. Alternatively, the executive could remit to the company a cash payment for the amount of the withholding.

5. **Tendered Shares.** The executive could remit to the company shares of company stock already owned by the executive that have an aggregate fair market value equal to the amount to be withheld, provided that the executive has owned the stock for the period of time required by applicable securities law transfer restrictions.

Regardless of the withholding method chosen, the amount the company withholds must satisfy the minimum statutory withholding rates for federal, state, and local income or other taxes. Some companies permit executives to elect a higher percentage of tax withholding.

Example 2: ABC Corporation awarded Executive D 60,000 shares of restricted stock on July 1, 2017. The award provided that the restricted stock would vest in equal monthly installments over a five-year period beginning on August 1, 2017, if D remained in ABC's employ on the applicable vesting dates. ABC's stock incentive plan provides that grantees may elect to satisfy their tax-withholding obligation upon the vesting of restricted stock by surrendering a number of vested shares having a value on the date of vesting equal to the tax-withholding obligation. D elected to utilize this method of withholding. On August 1, 2017, when the 1,000 shares of restricted stock vested, the market price of ABC's stock was $20 per share.

The vested shares therefore had a value of $20,000, and tax withholding (at an estimated combined federal and state rate of 40%) amounted to $8,000. In accordance with D's election, ABC withheld 400 of the 1,000 vested shares ($8,000 ÷ $20 = 400 shares) and paid the then current value of those shares to state and federal tax authorities for D's account. ABC generally will apply D's tax withholding election for all subsequent portions of the restricted stock as and when they vest, until and unless D changes his withholding tax election method.

.03 Code Sec. 83(b) Election

Under Code Sec. 83(a), if a company transfers property, such as stock, to an employee or other service provider in connection with the performance of services, the excess of the fair market value of the property as of the first day that the transferee's rights in the property are transferable or are not subject to a substantial risk of forfeiture, whichever occurs earlier, over the amount (if any) paid for the property is included in the service provider's gross income for the taxable year that includes that day. However, Code Sec. 83(b) permits the employee or other service provider to elect to include in gross income the excess (if any) of the fair market value of the property at the time of transfer over the amount (if any) paid for the stock (or other property), as compensation for services.[4] If the service provider makes this election, the substantial vesting rules of Code Sec. 83(a) do not apply to the property, and any subsequent appreciation in the value of the property is not taxable as compensation to the service provider.

This is an "83(b) election." Although an 83(b) election causes the employee to recognize taxable income on the market value of the stock immediately upon the award, any appreciation in the stock from the date the company awards the stock to the date the employee sells the stock may then be eligible for taxation at lower, long-term capital gain rates. Capital gains or losses are reported on Schedule D.

The IRS does not provide a specific tax form for an 83(b) election. However, most companies where an 83(b) election might make sense have developed a form. Many companies even will make the required IRS filings for electing employees or directors. Before 2016, an individual who made an 83(b) election was required to attach a copy of the election form when the individual filed his or her annual tax return. No additional filing was necessary when the stock vests. In July 2016, the IRS finalized new regulations to ease the filing of Section 83(b) elections. The regulations eliminated the requirement that a taxpayer/employee submit a copy of a Code Sec. 83(b) election with his or her income tax return for the year in which the property was transferred (for example, a restricted stock award). An employee/taxpayer must maintain records sufficient to demonstrate a timely 83(b) election, but need not file a copy of the election with the IRS. This change was particularly helpful to individuals who electronically file (e-file) their annual income tax returns and non-US residents making an 83(b) election.

---

[4] See also Reg § 1.83-2(a).

A recipient of restricted stock should make an 83(b) election only if (1) the stock has a low fair market value on the date of grant, (2) the recipient expects the fair market value to increase substantially, and (3) there is a low likelihood that the recipient will forfeit the restricted shares. The advantage of an 83(b) election is that the appreciation of the restricted stock after the grant date may be taxed at capital gains tax rates, rather than at ordinary income tax rates. The disadvantage is that the employee cannot obtain a refund of the taxes paid at the time of the 83(b) election if the employee subsequently forfeits the stock before the employment restriction or other restriction lapses.

An executive should always consult with his or her financial or tax advisor regarding the election. If an executive decides to make the election, he or she must file the election with the Internal Revenue Service within 30 days after the date that the property is transferred to the service provider (e.g., the date the company's board or compensation committee granted the restricted stock).[5]

Because an RSU award is not a transfer of property, the recipient cannot make an 83(b) election as to it.

.04 Revoking an 83(b) Election

An 83(b) election can be risky. If the company's stock price decreases in value after the holder makes the election, the holder will have accelerated taxation without receiving any benefit. Additionally, the holder could forfeit the stock after making the 83(b) election. In this case the holder should be able to deduct the amount he or she actually paid for the stock (subject to capital loss limitations), but would get no deduction for the ordinary compensation income the holder recognized when he or she made the election.

Code Sec. 83(b)(2) provides that an individual may not revoke an 83(b) election without the consent of the Commissioner of Internal Revenue.[6] The regulations provide that such consent will only be granted where the person filing the election is under a mistake of fact as to the underlying transaction and requests revocation within 60 days of the date on which he or she first became aware of the mistake of fact. The regulations make clear that the mistake of fact exception is narrow in its scope. "A mistake of fact is an unconscious ignorance of a fact that is material to the transaction."[7] The following are not mistakes of fact under the regulations:[8]

- A mistake as to the value (or decline in the value) of the property for which the election was made.
- A failure of anyone to perform an act that was contemplated at the time of transfer of the property.
- The failure of a service provider to understand the substantial risk of forfeiture associated with the transferred property.

---

[5] Code Sec. 83(b)(2).
[6] See also Reg. § 1.83-2(f).
[7] Rev. Proc. 2006-31, citing 27A AmJur 2d, Equity § 10. By contrast, a mistake of law occurs where a

person is ignorant of, or comes to an erroneous conclusion as to, the legal effect of the facts. See 27A AmJur 2d, Equity § 15.
[8] Reg. § 1.83-2(f).

- The failure of a service provider to understand the tax consequences of making an 83(b) election.

IRS Rev. Proc. 2006-31 provides guidance concerning the factors that must be present in order for a taxpayer to receive consent to revoke an election previously filed under Code Sec. 83(b) and procedures for submitting a request for consent to revoke a valid 83(b) election.

.05 Adding New Vesting Restrictions to Previously Vested Stock

In July 2007, the IRS issued Rev. Rul. 2007-49, discussing whether restrictions imposed on substantially vested stock would cause the substantially vested stock to become substantially nonvested. Specifically, the IRS considered the impact of situations where additional vesting and forfeiture restrictions were imposed on an individual's vested stock.

Rev. Rul. 2007-49 begins with investors forming Corporation X by contributing $1,000 each to Corporation X in exchange for 100 shares of stock. Corporation X then issues 100 shares of its stock to Executive A in exchange for A's agreement to perform services for Corporation X. The fair market value of the Corporation X stock on that date is $10 per share. The amount included in A's income under Code Sec. 83(a) is $1,000 (the fair market value of the stock ($10 × 100 shares) less the amount paid ($0)). A's basis in the stock is $1,000.

Corporation X sought financing from a new investor on July 9, 2007. The new investor insisted that Executive A agree to subject his shares to a restriction that will cause the stock to be "substantially nonvested" within the meaning of Reg. § 1.83-3(b). Under this new restriction, if A terminated employment with Corporation X before July 9, 2009, A would have to sell the shares to Corporation X in exchange for the lesser of $150 per share (the fair market value of Corporation X stock on July 9, 2007) or the fair market value at the time of forfeiture. A's shares are nontransferable before that date. A remained employed with Corporation X, and on July 9, 2009, the fair market value of Corporation X stock was $250 per share.

Regarding this situation, the IRS held that because A already owned the substantially vested shares of Corporation X stock for purposes of Code Sec. 83, there was no taxable "transfer" under Code Sec. 83. Thus, the imposition of new restrictions on the substantially vested shares had no effect for purposes of Code Sec. 83. Moreover, when A again vested in the substantially nonvested Corporation X stock on July 9, 2009, A did not recognize compensation income under Code Sec. 83(a). A's basis in the stock continued to be $1,000.

.06 Handling the Taxation Issue

As discussed above, one problem with restricted stock is that vesting of the restricted stock results in ordinary income to the employee but no cash to pay the income tax. As a response to this problem, some companies have "hard-wired" restricted stock awards to require withholding of a portion of the restricted shares that vest to satisfy tax withholding requirements. Withholding a portion of a vested stock award is a commonly used method of satisfying tax withholding requirements. However, there are conditions and restrictions on a company's decision to withhold shares of vested restricted stock.

Securities Exchange Act of 1934 Section 16. Generally, foregoing the delivery of a portion of shares acquired under a stock compensation scheme to settle tax withholding requirements constitutes a "sale" under the Securities Exchange Act of 1934 ("Exchange Act.") Section 16(b) of the Exchange Act restricts the sale of stock by certain beneficial owners. Withholding vested shares for the purpose of satisfying all or a portion of a recipient's estimated federal, state and local taxes arising from the award and vesting of shares is exempt from the restrictions of Section 16(b) of the Exchange Act pursuant to Rule 16b-3.[9] In a number of No-Action letters written by the Securities Exchange Commission ("SEC") with regard to withholding shares of restricted stock upon vesting, the SEC noted that an amendment to the plan that would allow an election to withhold need not be approved by the shareholders pursuant to Rule 16b-3.

Withholding of stock must be reported on Securities Exchange Commission Form 4, "Statement of Changes of Benefit Ownership of Securities," which is due within two business days of the transaction.[10]

Financial Accounting Standards Board. A withholding transaction will not result in the recognition of additional compensation cost for companies as long as the amount withheld does not exceed the minimum required federal, state, and payroll statutory withholding minimums.[11] If the amount withheld exceeds the minimum required rate, companies must recognize compensation cost for the total number of shares withheld, not just on the excess withheld. In addition, if the company does allow for withholding excess shares, the award will be subject to variable accounting treatment.

Tax. The Internal Revenue Service issued two private letter rulings that discuss the employer satisfying its withholding obligation by delivering a reduced number of shares to the recipient upon vesting.[12] The plan at issue in the private letter rulings required a recipient to submit a "Notice of Withholding Election" at least six months prior to the date the stock vests or in any "window period" (as defined in the option agreement) prior to the vesting date. Recipients who are Section 16(b) "insiders" under the Exchange Act must make a timely a Code Sec. 83(b) election with respect to their awards of restricted stock, otherwise the full market value of all of the shares transferred to them will be included in income, even if the employer delivers fewer shares due to its withholding process.[13]

Rule 10b-5. The SEC does not provide an exception to the prohibition on insider trading for an insider who would like to sell a portion of the shares of

---

[9] See 17 C.F.R. §240.16b-3; Ownership Reports and Trading by Officers, Directors, and Principle Security Holders, Exchange Act Release No. 34-37260, Fed. Sec. L. Rep. (CCH) ¶85,810 (May 31, 1996); see also Securities Exchange Commission No-Action Letter to NCNC Corporation (Feb. 12, 1991).

[10] See Ownership Reports and Trading by Officers, Directors, and Principle Security Holders, Ex-

change Act Release No. 34-37260, Fed. Sec. L. Rep. (CCH) ¶85,810 (May 31, 1996).

[11] See FASB Interpretation No. 44 ¶75-80 (2004).

[12] IRS Letter Ruling 9025078 (March 28, 1990); IRS Letter Ruling 9030015 (April 25, 1990).

[13] See Utz, 383-3rd T.M., Nonstatutory Stock Options (2001).

restricted stock upon vesting to cover his or her tax liability, when the vesting occurs during a blackout period. The withholding of a portion of restricted stock that has vested may implicate the insider trading restrictions of Rule 10b5-1.

However, if the restricted stock award qualifies as a Rule 10b5-1 Plan, then the employer may withhold shares of stock to satisfy tax withholding requirements without regard to limitations imposed by a company insider trading policy and the recipient has an affirmative defense against allegations of insider trading. A Rule 10b5-1 plan must (1) be in writing, (2) state the number of shares to be bought or sold, which can be stated as a number of shares, as a percentage of holdings, a number of shares needed to produce a specific dollar amount (presumably it may be stated as a number of shares necessary to satisfy the tax withholding requirements as well), (3) state the price at which the shares will be bought or sold, whether at a stated price, at market price, or otherwise, and (4) state the time of the purchase or sale, either a specific date or at the time of a specific event (this should include the vesting date of restricted stock). If the restricted stock award satisfies these requirements, then there should be no difficulty satisfying Rule 10b-5.

.07 Restricted Stock, RSUs, and Accelerated Vesting Upon Retirement

In general, awards of restricted stock made in connection with the performance of services are not subject to federal income tax until restrictions imposed on the stock lapse or the stock becomes fully transferable. Some equity compensation plans and award agreements provide that the restricted stock or RSU award would fully vest if the recipient terminated employment after attaining normal retirement age (generally defined as between age 60 and 65). This provision might cause the restricted stock or RSU award to fully vest and become taxable immediately upon the recipient's eligibility for retirement, even though he or she has not terminated employment.

Taxation would be based on the fact that the retirement-eligible recipient has performed all the services that he or she will need to perform in order to receive an award free of restrictions once the recipient becomes retirement-eligible. Thus, the rights of a retirement-eligible recipient are not conditioned upon the performance of continued services, but rather on his or her decision to retire the ordinarily scheduled lapse of the vesting restrictions.

The IRS has indicated that the voluntary termination of employment as a prerequisite to receiving an award does not rise to the level of a substantial risk of forfeiture. For example, the IRS has ruled that if an employee must both meet a service vesting condition and terminate employment to receive a benefit, the termination requirement does not delay vesting after an employee has met the service requirement. In Technical Advice Memorandum 199903032, the IRS examined an arrangement where employees became entitled to a benefit of $26,000 upon reaching a specified sum of years of service and age. An employee received the benefit upon retirement, unless terminated for cause between the time he or she satisfied the specified sum of years of service and age and the date of the employee's actual retirement. Citing § 1.82-3(c)(2) of the regulations, which provide that a requirement that an employee return property if discharged for cause does not rise to the level of a substantial risk of forfeiture, the IRS concluded that because the employee's rights to compensation were not conditioned on any future performance of services and no other conditions created a substantial risk of forfeiture, no substantial risk of forfeiture existed beyond the time a recipient met the plan's service requirements.

However, the IRS has provided contradictory guidance in its application of the definition of substantial risk of forfeiture. For example, in Private Letter Ruling 9628011, the IRS examined a Section 457(f) plan that created a risk of forfeiture by providing that a recipient would vest in the recipient's deferred benefits only upon their retirement or attainment of age $70^{1}/_{2}$. The IRS concluded that benefits under the plan would be included in the gross income of the recipient in the taxable year in which the recipient retired from continuous service. Similarly, in Private Letter Ruling 9050037, recipients were not taxed until benefits under a deferred compensation plan were actually received or made available.

Importantly, the IRS has not specifically held that a requirement that a recipient retire within a specified period in order to vest restricted stock does not constitute a substantial risk of forfeiture. The regulations provide an example of voluntary actions taken by the recipient that nonetheless create a substantial risk of forfeiture. For example, § 1.83-3(c)(2) of the regulations provides that the imposition of a refund provision based on compliance with a noncompetition clause may constitute a substantial risk of forfeiture under some circumstances. Presumably, whether to compete or not is wholly within the recipient's discretion.

While these examples support an interpretation that a substantial risk of forfeiture extends until the time a recipient fulfills all the requirements necessary to vest restricted stock (*i.e.*, a recipient retires), the determination of whether a substantial risk of forfeiture exists for any particular retirement-eligible recipient of restricted stock or RSU awards, most likely hinges on the employer's practices with respect to retirement and retirement-eligible employees.

The regulations provide that a determination of whether a risk of forfeiture is substantial is ultimately made by examining the applicable facts and circumstances. The regulations provide that a restriction requiring an employee to return property if discharged "for cause" is not a substantial risk of forfeiture. Therefore, the mere fact that a retirement-eligible recipient may terminate employment for a reason other than retirement during the period used to measure performance-based vesting conditions is not enough to create a substantial risk of forfeiture. For example, an employer might be able to show a substantial risk of forfeiture exists under the following circumstances:

- The company (and award agreement) required that the board of directors approve the early termination as a "retirement," and could demonstrate that such approval was not always given;

- The company (and award agreement) imposed a non-compete provision on individuals taking "retirement," and could demonstrate that it had enforced that provision by forfeiting awards; or

- Few retirement-eligible recipients took advantage of the opportunity to accelerate the vesting of performance-based restricted stock by retiring (particularly if some awards then lapsed).

For example, in Private Letter Ruling 8326151, the IRS found that the requirement that an employer consent to an employee's termination of employment created a substantial risk of forfeiture until the employer consented. The IRS noted that a substantial risk existed because the employer had only consented to such awards on a few occasions in the past. In Private Letter Ruling 9615023, the IRS examined a plan that permitted the employer to refuse to deliver shares in settlement of vested stock options and to reclaim the spread on any stock options exercised by the recipient within a specified time before termination of employment. The IRS found that these provisions did not constitute a substantial risk of forfeiture because the employer had indicated that the employer was not likely to inhibit the full enjoyment of awards, the employer had no pattern of enforcement and did not present any other indication as to the likelihood of forfeitures under the plan. In Private Letter Ruling 9712029, the IRS examined a restricted stock plan that required retired employees to forfeit their restricted stock if they engaged in material competition with the employer and found that "[w]hether the stock will continue to be not vested beyond an employee's retirement age will depend on the facts and circumstances of each case."

The argument that RSUs should not be taxable to a recipient becoming eligible for retirement (and accelerated vesting) is even stronger. Generally, vested RSUs constitute an unsecured promise to distribute stock in the future. The IRS has frequently declined to treat the transfer of phantom stock rights and plan units as a transfer of property for purposes of Code Sec. 83.[14] Instead, the IRS has examined restricted stock units using the principles of actual and constructive receipt under Sections 61 and 451 of the Code.

.08 FICA/FUTA Tax

Generally, an employer takes into account compensation for FICA tax purposes at the time the employee actually or constructively receives the compensation.[15] However, a special timing rule exists for amounts deferred under a nonqualified deferred compensation plan. An award of restricted stock is generally not a form of deferred compensation for purposes of FICA taxes.[16] Restricted stocks are wages for FICA purposes at the time employees actually or constructively receive them free from restrictions.[17]

---

[14] See Private Letter Rulings 9609019, 7946072, 8642025 and 8019053.

[15] Treas. Reg. § 31.3121(v)(2)-1.

[16] See Treas. Reg. § 31.3121(v)(2)-1(b)(4)(iii) (providing that restricted property under Section 83 of the Code that is not includible in the year of receipt by virtue of being nontransferable and being subject to a substantial risk of forfeiture is not deferred compensation).

[17] Treas. Reg. § 31.3121(a)-2(a).

Revenue Ruling 79-305 provides the best guidance available with respect to the timing of taxation of restricted stock for purposes of FICA. In Revenue Ruling 79-305, the IRS held that in situations where an employee is awarded stock subject to a substantial risk of forfeiture under a restricted stock bonus plan, FICA taxes are assessed and wages are paid when the risk of forfeiture lapses. The IRS noted that it is at this time that the "stock is made available to the employee without any substantial limitation or restriction as to the time or manner of payment or condition upon which payment is made, and could be drawn upon at any time and brought within the employee's own control and disposition." The IRS has cited Revenue Ruling 79-305 for this proposition as recently as Revenue Ruling 2007-48.

RSUs generally constitute contributions or benefits from a nonqualified deferred compensation plan, and thus are subject to FICA taxes when they are no longer subject to a substantial risk of forfeiture.[18] Regulations provide that "stock options, stock appreciation rights and other stock value rights" do not constitute a deferral of compensation for purposes of Code Sec. 3121(v)(2).[19] The regulations provide that deferred compensation under a nonqualified deferred compensation plan "must be taken into account as wages for FICA tax purposes as of the later of the date on which services creating the right to the amount deferred are performed, or the date on which the right to the amount deferred is no longer subject to a substantial risk of forfeiture" (internal parenthesis omitted).[20]

.09 Accelerating Performance-Based Compensation - Code Sec. 162(m)

Code Sec. 162(m)(4)(C) and Treas. Reg. § 1.162-27(e)(1) provide that the $1,000,000 deduction limit does not apply to "qualified performance-based compensation." Treas. Reg. § 1.162-27(e)(1) provides that qualified performance-based compensation is compensation that meets all of the requirements of Treas. Reg. § 1.162-27(e)(2) through (5). Treas. Reg. § 1.162-27(e)(2)(i) provides, in part, that qualified performance-based compensation must be paid solely on account of the attainment of one or more preestablished, objective performance goals. Treas. Reg. § 1.162-27(e)(2)(v) provides that compensation does not satisfy the *"solely on account of the attainment of one or more preestablished, objective performance goals"* requirement if the facts and circumstances indicate that the employee would receive all or part of the compensation regardless of whether the performance goal is attained. If the payment of compensation under a grant or award is only nominally or partially contingent on attaining a performance goal, none of the compensation payable under the grant or award will be considered performance-based.

Treas. Reg. § 1.162-27(e)(2)(v) further provides that compensation does not fail to be qualified performance-based compensation merely because the plan allows the compensation to be payable upon death, disability, or change of ownership or control, despite the fact that compensation actually paid on ac-

---

[18] Code Sec. 3121(v)(2)(A) and Treas. Reg. § 31.3121(v)(2)-1(a)(2)(ii).

[19] Treas. Reg. § 31.3121(v)(2)-1(b)(4).

[20] Treas. Reg. § 31.3121(v)(2)-1(e)(1).

count of those events prior to the attainment of the performance goal would not satisfy the requirements of Treas. Reg. § 1.162-27(e)(2).

In a private letter ruling released in 2008, the IRS reversed its long-standing position and ruled that employment agreement terms providing for the accelerated vesting of performance-based awards upon termination of the executive by the company without cause or termination by the executive for good reason, and payment at target performance levels, regardless of actual performance, *would cause the awards to fail to satisfy 162(m)'s performance-based exception - even if the accelerated vesting and payout is never triggered.*[21]

The critical section of the ruling reads as follows:

> "The provision in the Agreement allowing for payment of performance share or performance unit awards under the Plan upon Executive's termination by Company without cause or by Executive with good reason does not meet the exception in section 1.162-27(e)(2)(v) of the regulations that allows compensation to be payable upon death, disability or change of ownership or control. Thus, compensation paid to Executive with respect to performance share or performance unit awards is not payable solely upon attainment of a performance goal, for purposes of section 162(m)(4)(C) of the Code."[22]

Accordingly, the IRS ruled that any compensation paid to an executive who completes the performance period under the performance share or performance unit awards agreement cited and attains the performance goal, would not be considered performance-based compensation under Code Sec. 162(m)(4)(C). The IRS confirmed its position in Revenue Ruling 2008-13.

The TCJA eliminated the performance-based compensation exception from Code Sec. 162(m) effective in 2018, so these issues are less likely to be important in the future.

.10 Dividends on RSUs - Code Sec. 162(m)

Rev. Rul. 2012-19 describes when dividends and dividend equivalents related to restricted stock and RSUs can be treated as performance-based compensation for purposes of Code Sec. 162(m)(4)(c). Rev. Rul. 2012-19 contains two fact patterns, regarding publicly held corporations X and Y. Both have restricted common stock and RSU plans based on the common stock of each. The restricted stock and RSUs granted under the plans of both corporations vest upon reaching certain pre-established, objective performance goals and otherwise meet the requirements of Treas. Reg. § 1.162-27(e). Therefore, compensation received due to the vesting of the restricted stock and vesting and payment of the RSUs would qualify as performance-based compensation and be excluded from the applicable employee's compensation subject to the Code Sec. 162(m) limitation.

Treas. Reg. § 1.162-27(e)(2)(iv) provides that, except with regard to stock options and SARs, whether a grant of restricted stock or other stock-based compensation satisfies the "performance goal" requirements of Code Sec. 162(m) is determined without regard to whether dividends, dividend equivalents, or other similar distributions with respect to stock, on such stock-based compensa-

---

[21] Private Letter Ruling 200804004.   [22] Id.

tion are payable prior to the attainment of the performance goal. Dividends, dividend equivalents, or other similar distributions with respect to stock that are treated as separate grants under Treas. Reg. § 1.162-27(e)(2)(iv) are not performance-based compensation unless they separately satisfy the performance goal requirements. The IRS cited this provision in stating that the grants of the dividends and dividend equivalents must separately satisfy the requirements of Treas. Reg. § 1.162-27(e) to be qualified performance-based compensation.

The TCJA eliminated the performance-based compensation exception from Code Sec. 162(m) effective in 2018, so these issues are less likely to be important in the future.

¶865 Securities Law Reporting and Disclosure of Awards

The Securities Act of 1933 requires a publicly held company to register offers or sales of its securities, including offers to its own employees. The U.S. Securities and Exchange Commission would consider any offer or sale of securities not made under an effective registration statement a violation of the Securities Act, absent an available exemption. A company that offers or sells unregistered securities may be subject to civil liability under both federal and state securities laws, as well as enforcement actions by both the SEC and state regulators. Chapter 12 discusses federal securities law disclosure and Chapter 31 discusses proxy statement disclosure in more detail.

.01 Securities Exchange Act of 1934 Section 16

The company's board of directors or compensation committee must approve the grant of restricted stock and RSUs (and the forms of the awards, including vesting and share withholding terms), so that the grants are exempt from matching under Section 16 of the Securities Exchange Act of 1934 (the "Exchange Act"). An executive officer subject to Section 16(a) reporting under the Exchange Act must report the restricted stock grant on Form 4 within two business days of the transaction. No additional Section 16(a) reporting is required when the restricted stock subsequently vests. When the restricted stock vests, if shares are withheld to satisfy the tax, then a Form 4 is due within two business days of the vesting. When RSUs vest and settle into stock or cash, a Form 4 is due within two business days of the vesting.

.02 Registration Statement on Form S-8

Typically, a registration statement covering an employee benefit plan is prepared on Form S-8. The Form S-8 Registration Statement is simple and includes the following information:

- the incorporation of certain documents by reference, such as the company's latest annual report on Form 10-K;
- interests of named experts and counsel;
- a description of director and officer indemnification;
- a description of the specific exemption from registration for any restricted securities to be reoffered or resold pursuant to the registration statement;

- exhibits; and
- certain undertakings.

Registration on Form S-8 requires payment of a filing fee that varies with the aggregate offering price (*e.g.*, fair market value) for the maximum amount of securities registered.[23] In addition, the company must furnish plan recipients with all the communications that go to stockholders (*e.g.*, annual reports, proxy statements).

.03 Section 10(a) Prospectus

In addition to filing a Form S-8 Registration Statement, an effective registration requires that a company deliver to each recipient in a restricted stock plan, documents, and information constituting a prospectus that meets the requirements of Section 10(a) of the Securities Act. The company must keep the information contained in the prospectus current, whether by supplements or restatements. The prospectus documents and information summarize the plan, the company's stock offered, the eligible recipients, procedures relating to the purchase and sale of the stock, and the federal tax consequences of an investment in the stock offered (see ¶1235 for a more detailed description of the information the SEC requires in a prospectus).

Unlike other types of prospectuses, the company does not need to file the prospectus material used in connection with an employee benefit plan with the SEC. However, the company must retain the documents constituting a part of the prospectus. A registration statement on Form S-8 and any post-effective amendment become effective immediately upon filing with the SEC. Upon filing, they become publicly available.

.04 Proxy Statement Disclosure

A company must report the value of any restricted stock awarded to a named executive officer in its proxy statement for the year of the award, in any year for which the award is outstanding but not vested, and in the year the award vests. If the recipient of a restricted stock award is an executive officer, the SEC will consider the executive to own the shares beneficially. The company must include the shares in the beneficial ownership table of its proxy statement.

Additionally, public companies must report in their annual proxy statement the award of restricted stock or RSUs to any named executive officer ("NEO"), the vesting of restricted stock or RSUs held by an NEO, and any outstanding restricted stock or RSUs held by an NEO, as follows:

- A company must disclose and discuss any restricted stock, RSU, or performance share grants it made to an NEO in the most recently concluded fiscal year in the Compensation Discussion and Analysis ("CD&A") section of the proxy statement.[24]

---

[23] If the registration statement also covers participation interests in the plan that constitute separate securities, no separate fee is required with respect to the plan interests. Rule 457(h)(2) of the Securities Act.

[24] Regulation S-K, Item 402(b), 17 CFR 229.402.

- A company must disclose any restricted stock, RSU, and performance share grants it made to an NEO in the most recently concluded fiscal year in the Summary Compensation Table of the proxy statement.[25]

- A company must disclose any restricted stock, RSU, and performance share grants it made to an NEO in the most recently concluded fiscal year in the Grants of Plan-Based Awards Table of the proxy statement.[26]

- A company must disclose any restricted stock, RSU, and performance share grants it made to an NEO in a previous year and held by an NEO as of the last day of the most recently concluded fiscal year in the Outstanding Equity Awards at Fiscal Year-End Table of the proxy statement.[27]

- A company must disclose any restricted stock, RSUs, and performance shares that vested in an NEO in a previous year in the Option Exercises and Stock Vested Table of the proxy statement.[28]

.05 SEC Reporting Issues Unique to Performance Shares

This growing prevalence of performance shares presents some unique SEC reporting issues. Executive compensation professionals know that grants of stock awards must be reported on a Form 4 within two business days of the grant. However, grants of performance-based stock awards are reportable as derivative securities *only if the performance condition relates solely to the stock price.* In most cases, performance awards are based at least in part on other factors, such as an increase in net earnings, earnings per share, or other financial measures. In such cases, the performance shares are not deemed to have been acquired by the grantee until the performance criteria have been satisfied, *i.e.,* the vesting date. Thus, a performance share award that vests upon the stock price hitting, for example, $25 per share, would be reportable on a Form 4 within two days of grant, while a performance share award that vests, for example, based on EPS would not be reportable until the award vests (and the stock is delivered).

The SEC staff has stated that an instrument whose exercisability is subject to a material condition (other than the passage of time or continued employment) that is not tied to the market price of an equity security of the corporation is not a derivative security until the condition is satisfied. From a reporting standpoint, instruments such as performance rights and earn-out rights, which generally are subject to material conditions that are not based on the market price of the corporation's securities (*e.g.,* the reaching of performance goals or the attainment of earnings targets) will not be deemed beneficially owned until the number of shares that can be acquired under the rights is determined.

An award that vests or becomes exercisable only if the corporation achieves a specified level of "total shareholder return" (defined as stock price appreciation plus dividends) may (or may not) be considered to be tied solely to the price of the corporation's stock, depending on the significance of dividends as a component of the issuer's total shareholder return. If, for example, the corporation pays

---

[25] Regulation S-K, Item 402(c), 17 CFR 229.402.

[26] Regulation S-K, Item 402(d), 17 CFR 229.402.

[27] Regulation S-K, Item 402(f), 17 CFR 229.402.

[28] Regulation S-K, Item 402(g), 17 CFR 229.402.

no dividends or only a *de minimis* dividend, conditioning vesting of an award on total shareholder return would be equivalent to conditioning vesting on the corporation's stock price, and therefore the condition would not prevent the award from being reportable at the time of grant. The SEC staff has not provided guidance regarding the circumstances under which a dividend should be considered *de minimis*.

Additionally, most plans provide that performance shares vest on the last date of the fiscal year if the specified performance criteria are satisfied. However, since the determination whether the performance criteria have been satisfied generally requires that the company's financial statements be prepared and then reviewed by the compensation committee, the audit committee and/or independent accountants, many companies deem the vesting date for reporting and liability purposes to be the date on which the company (*e.g.*, the audit committee or the compensation committee) in good faith determined that the awards in fact vested.

For awards that vest based on performance, but remain subject to an additional service period (*e.g.*, one year) before shares are delivered, the corporation would report the acquisition of performance units in Table II upon the measurement date, and then report the acquisition of actual shares on Table I when the units convert to shares, *e.g.*, one year later. When a performance share unit award becomes a fixed number of units at measurement that tracks the stock price, it would then meet the definition of a "derivative security."

Performance share awards made in a fiscal year are reportable in the Summary Compensation Table for that year. According to Instruction 3 to Item 402(c)(2)(v) and (vi), the corporation should report the grant date value of any awards that are subject to performance conditions *based upon the probable outcome* of such conditions. This amount should be consistent with the estimate of aggregate compensation cost to be recognized over the service period determined as of the grant date under ASC Topic 718 (excluding the effect of estimated forfeitures). However, if the corporation discloses an amount less than the maximum in the Summary Compensation Table, the corporation must disclose the value of the award assuming that the highest level of performance conditions will be achieved, in a footnote to the table.

Generally, performance share awards vest at the end of a fiscal year, if the requisite performance criteria are met. However, as noted above, shares are not distributed until after the compensation committee has certified that the criteria have been met, usually after audited financials are complete. In this typical situation, the performance shares in question would be reportable in the "Stock Vested Table" for the completed fiscal year and not in the "Outstanding Equity Awards at Year End Table," despite the fact that the shares were not actually delivered until after the fiscal year end.

.06 Potential Exemption from Registration

Section 12(g) of the Exchange Act requires a corporation having total assets of more than $10 million and a class of equity securities "held of record" by 2,000 or more persons (or 500 persons who are not accredited investors) to register such securities. Private companies (and their counsel) granting stock options or other stock awards must recognize that a proposed stock plan or awards could cause the company to exceed the stockholder limit after an offering period, thus forcing the company to register with the SEC and become a "reporting company" under Section 12(g).

However, when determining whether Section 12(g) requires a company to register a class of equity securities with the SEC, the company may exclude from the definition of "held of record," securities that are held by persons who received them under an employee compensation plan in transactions exempt from, or not subject to, the registration requirements of Section 5 of the Securities Act and in certain circumstances, held by persons who received them in exchange for securities received under an employee compensation plan.[29]

Additionally, Rule 12g5-1 includes a non-exclusive safe harbor for determining the holders of record. The safe harbor provides that a company may deem a person to have received the securities under an employee compensation plan if the plan and the person who received the securities under the plan met conditions of Securities Act Rule 701(c), and the company may, solely for the purposes of Section 12(g), deem the securities to have been issued in a transaction exempt from, or not subject to, the registration requirements of Section 5 of the Securities Act if the issuer had a reasonable belief at the time of the issuance that the securities were issued in such a transaction.

In terms of registration, counting and SEC reporting, the treatment of performance shares and RSU awards parallels that of restricted stock awards (see Chapter 12 [¶ 1201 *et seq.*] for a detailed discussion of securities law issues). The SEC staff also has issued exceptions and no-action letters on a case-by-case basis for other forms of equity compensation, including letters to Facebook in 2008[30] and Twitter in 2011, for restricted stock units (RSUs).

¶875 Code Sec. 409A

Code Sec. 409A can apply to stock incentive awards, including restricted stock, performance shares, and RSUs. Failure to satisfy the requirements of Code Sec. 409A could result in significant penalties to the award recipient. Code Sec. 409A applies differently to restricted stock, performance shares, and RSUs.

.01 Restricted Stock

Restricted stock is not subject to Code Sec. 409A. A restricted stock award is taxed under Code Sec. 83 immediately upon vesting, so it is akin to a short-term deferral. However, if an individual could elect to defer the receipt of restricted stock subject to the award, the award and deferral would be subject to all of the deferral election and distribution requirements of Code Sec. 409A (see Chapter 17 [¶ 1701 *et seq.*] for a detailed discussion of Code Sec. 409A).

---

[29] Rule 12g5-1.

[30] The Rule 12h-1(f) exemption for stock options was in Release No. 34-56887, December 7, 2007.

The regulations state that if an employee receives restricted stock under an employer plan, there is no deferral of compensation merely because the value of the stock is not includible in income in the year of receipt by reason of the stock being substantially nonvested or restricted, even if the stock becomes includible in income due to a valid election under Code Sec. 83(b).[31]

The regulations clarify that a vested right to receive nonvested property in a future year does not constitute deferred compensation, since a right to receive nonvested property is not truly vested. For example, an incentive plan that, upon satisfaction of certain performance criteria, will give employees the right to receive restricted stock that will be subject to a substantial risk of forfeiture until the employee completes three years of future services is not a vested right.

The regulations also clarify the circumstances under which an executive may elect to be paid a bonus or other payment in the form of restricted stock, rather than cash. Generally, an election between compensation alternatives, none of which provides for a deferral of compensation within the meaning of Code Sec. 409A, will not cause the election to be subject to the Code Sec. 409A timing restrictions. Thus, the 409A election timing rules will not govern a choice between an award of restricted stock or stock options that are not subject to Code Sec. 409A. However, where any of the alternatives involves a deferral of compensation subject to Code Sec. 409A, the election must comply with the provisions of Code Sec. 409A. Such an election must comply with other federal tax rules such as Code Sec. 83, Code Sec. 451, the constructive receipt doctrine, or the economic benefit doctrine.

For example, where a bonus plan provides an election between a cash payment or restricted stock units with a present value that is materially greater (disregarding the risk of forfeiture) than the present value of the cash payment and that will be forfeited absent continued services for a period of years, the right to the restricted stock units generally will be treated as subject to a substantial risk of forfeiture.[32]

An executive's agreement after receiving an award of restricted stock but before the restrictions have lapsed, to postpone the vesting of restricted stock by an additional year or two would not implicate Code Sec. 409A because restricted stock is a transfer of property tax under Code Sec. 83, not Code Sec. 409A.

.02 Performance Shares

Since performance shares are essentially just restricted stock that vests according to performance criteria rather than continued service, performance shares are not subject to Code Sec. 409A. Like restricted stock, performance share awards are taxed under Code Sec. 83 immediately upon vesting and, thus, akin to a short-term deferral. However, if an individual could elect to defer the receipt of performance shares subject to an award, the award and deferral would be subject to the deferral requirements of Code Sec. 409A.

---

[31] Reg § 1.409A-1(b)(6)(i).   [32] Reg § 1.409A-1(d)(1).

.03 Restricted Stock Units

Restricted stock units generally are subject to Code Sec. 409A. An RSU is a current promise to transfer stock later. RSUs could be exempt as a short-term deferral if they require distribution of stock upon vesting.

Chapter 9
PHANTOM STOCK AND PROFITS INTERESTS

¶901 Overview—Phantom Stock and Profits Interests

Many companies cannot, or do not want to, award real stock ownership to executives, directors or others. Nearly everyone agrees that the best way to link directly management's interests with those of the company's stockholders is through stock ownership. A private company may have several valid reasons for not wanting to award real stock interests to its executives. However, privately held companies have the same need to attract, retain, and motivate talented executive employees, as do public companies. Therefore, private companies and their counsel will frequently look to phantom stock or profits interests to provide the link.

.01 Private Company Issues

Stock-based compensation programs are successful and widely used among publicly held companies. However, among privately held companies, compensating executives with company stock gives rise to various ancillary concerns. Most state laws give minority stockholders of a privately held company significant rights, including:

- the right to review the company's financial records;
- the right to vote the stock; and
- dissenter rights.

State laws generally give executives who become minority stockholders a variety of rights that many private company owners would prefer the executives did not have. In the family-owned business context, family members may be loath to permit ownership outside the family. Subchapter S limitations on the number of stockholders also can be a factor in restricting the ownership of real stock (see ¶915).

.02 Profits Interests

A profits interest is similar to a stock appreciation right ("SAR") in that it gives an executive the right to receive a portion of the appreciated value of the company when the right vests and the executive exercises it. However, profits interests are only available to a business entity that is organized as a partnership or limited liability company ("LLC"). Normally, the executive will receive the difference between the fair market value of the underlying LLC units on the profits interest award date and the value of the units on the date the executive exercises the profits interest (see ¶925).

.03 Phantom Stock

Companies, executives, and even compensation professionals may label a wide variety of plans and programs that seek to provide executives with an interest in the future value of the company without giving the executive the right to actual shares of stock, as phantom stock plans. Under phantom stock programs, executives do not receive any actual shares of stock, only the right to payment based on the value of the company's stock. Often, a phantom stock plan will confer benefits that are similar to restricted stock. That is, the recipient of a share of phantom stock will receive the full value of the phantom share, not just appreciation. Sometimes, the company will tie the value of a share of phantom stock to the appreciation in the stock of the company between the date the company awards the share to the executive and the settlement date (as with profits interests). The initial value of each share, however, could be determined as of some prior date, so that the executive would be entitled to appreciation that occurred before the award (see ¶935).

.04 Profits Interest and Phantom Stock Plan Design

Because profits interest and phantom stock plans or awards are essentially a contractual arrangement established unilaterally by the company, the company has significant flexibility in their design (see ¶945).

.05 Accounting Issues

Because companies design phantom stock to pay executives in cash instead of stock, the accounting rules would require a company that awards phantom stock to reflect a compensation expense on its financial statements at the time it makes such awards (see ¶955).

.06 Securities Law Issues

Although the company will never be giving real stock to the executive as payment for the executive's phantom stock or profits interests, the federal securities laws would still generally treat a company's award of phantom stock or profits interests as an offer to sell securities under the Securities Act of 1933. However, the federal securities laws also make available to private companies several exemptions to the registration requirements that apply to public companies (see ¶965).

.07 Code Sec. 409A

Code Sec. 409A can apply to profits interests and phantom stock awards.[1] Failure to satisfy the requirements of Code Sec. 409A could result in significant penalties to the award recipient (see ¶975).

¶915 Private Company Issues

Companies recognize that stock-based compensation is a significant incentive and a binding force between the interests of executives and the interests of

---

[1] Added by the American Jobs Creation Act of 2004 (P.L. 108-357).

stockholders. Stock-based programs are successful among publicly held companies. However, among privately held companies, stock compensation gives rise to various ancillary concerns. For numerous reasons, often related to the various rights available under state law to minority stockholders, many private companies are reluctant to utilize actual awards of stock as an incentive compensation vehicle. While state laws differ, most states give minority stockholders the following rights:

1. The right to review corporate records and financial information;

2. The right to attend all stockholder meetings;

3. The right to vote on all matters; and

4. So-called "dissenter rights," which may include the right to have stock repurchased by the company if the stockholder disagrees with a majority decision.

From the perspective of the closely held company, family considerations can range from an estate planning need, or desire, for intergenerational transfers and associated issues as well as the related tax considerations, which are estate, individual and corporate in nature. Family businesses often also have a psychological reluctance to include "outsiders" in the stockholder group. While participation in management may be acceptable, participation in the ownership structure may seem intrusive. In addition, many closely held companies utilize a subchapter S election to accommodate tax issues and, therefore, must consider the seventy-five-stockholder limitation in the design of any stock-based compensation program. Since stock-based incentive programs are designed to provide benefits to upper and middle management or are broad-based, depending upon the size of the business operation, the stockholder limitation can create a restrictive, not incentive, atmosphere, which is counter-productive to profitability and growth.

Example: Family-owned ABC Corporation needs to hire a CEO from outside the family for the first time. To secure the services of Executive D, who has many other executive employment opportunities, ABC offers D a phantom stock interest equal to one percent of the company. In 2025, Megacorp acquires ABC for $50 million. D will receive a payout of $500,000.

While recognizing the ancillary issues of family considerations, stockholder rights and tax accommodations, many companies realize that the primary benefit of a stock-based incentive program is to correlate incentive compensation more directly to performance measures. Unfortunately, while discretionary bonuses may satisfy executive compensation issues, the lack of correlation to profitability, growth or other performance measures cannot always provide incentives tied to the overall success of the business operations.

In lieu of tangible stock-based compensation, such as options, outright awards of stock or employee stock purchase plans, a private company can implement a cash-based program that defines executive incentive compensation by reference to the growth in the value of a unit. An alternative program can be designed to provide incentive compensation based on an imaginary, or phantom, share providing the same economic benefit as an actual share of stock, appreciation plus the underlying value, but without voting privileges or minority stockholder rights. In addition, the phantom stock arrangement, which is hypothetical in nature, would not be subject to stockholder limitations.

Whether the company designs the awards as profits interests or phantom stock, the company is directly tying the interests of management to the interests of the stockholders. In a sense, the company can provide the cash equivalent of an equity interest, and achieve the same objectives, without the inherent risks of minority ownership or costs associated with the regulatory compliance applicable to stock-based compensation.

¶925 Profits Interests

A profits interest is similar to a stock appreciation right ("SAR") in that it gives an executive recipient the right to receive a portion of the appreciated value of the company when the right vests and the executive exercises it. However, profits interest awards receive unique and favorable tax treatment under current law.

Profits interests are only available to a company that is organized as a limited liability company or a partnership. Normally, the executive will receive the difference between the fair market value of the underlying LLC units on the award date of the profits interest and the value of the units on the date the executive exercises the profits interest.

A profits interest is an LLC or partnership interest other than a capital interest.[2] Reg. § 1.721-1(b)(1) provides that the receipt of a partnership capital interest for services is taxable compensation. A capital interest is any interest that entitles the holder to a share of partnership assets if the partnership sells its assets at fair market value and liquidates the partnership.[3] The IRS generally makes this determination when the company distributes the interest. The IRS views an interest that is not a capital interest as a "profits interest."

A profits interest represents an actual interest in the profits (both operating and appreciation) of the LLC or partnership. However, a holder cannot share in any profits realized prior to an issuance or in any appreciation in the value of the assets (whether realized or unrealized) of the LLC or partnership that occurs.

.01 Taxation of Profits Interests

The tax consequences of the receipt of a profits interest had been subject to litigation and still is not entirely resolved.[4] In earlier years, the issue turned, in large part, on whether the profits interest had a readily ascertainable value on receipt by the provider of the services. The Tax Court held that a "special limited partner interest" (which represented an interest in future appreciation and $150

---

[2] Revenue Procedure 93-27 (1993-27 C.B. 343).

[3] Rev. Proc. 93-27, 1993-2 CB 343.

[4] *See, e.g., Campbell v. Comm'r*, 59 TCM 236, CCH Dec. 46,493(M), TC Memo 1990-162, *rev'd and aff'd,*

91-2 USTC ¶50,420, 943 F2d 815 (8th Cir. 1991); *St. John v. U.S.*, 84-1 USTC ¶9158, (D.C. Ill. 1983); *Diamond v. Comm'r*, 56 TC 530, CCH Dec. 30,838 (1971), *aff'd* 74-1 USTC ¶9306, 492 F2d 286 (7th Cir. 1974).

of capital) was property within the meaning of Code Sec. 83.[5] The court noted that, under the Uniform Limited Partnership Act, a limited partner interest is personal property. The award of a mere contractual right to receive compensation in the future, based on the performance of a partnership unit, but which does not make the holder a partner, should not be "property" for these purposes. Instead, such a right should be viewed as a mere unfunded promise to pay money in the future.[6]

The IRS's current position is that the receipt of a profits interest in a partnership (including an LLC created as a partnership for tax purposes) is not taxable unless at least one of the following is satisfied:

1. The profits interest relates to a "substantially certain and predictable" stream of income from the assets of the partnership (e.g., from high quality debt or a high quality net lease);

2. The profits interest is disposed of within two years of receipt; and

3. The profits interest is a limited partner interest in a publicly traded limited partnership within the meaning of Code Sec. 7704(b).[7]

The taxation of profits interest is set forth in IRS Rev. Proc. 93-27 and 2001-43. The award of an LLC interest to an executive or other service provider for compensatory purposes is generally treated as a transfer of property under Code Sec. 83 and governed by the same tax rules that apply to the award by a company of restricted stock. That is, if an LLC awards a "capital" interest to an executive in connection with the performance of services, an amount equal to the fair market value of the LLC capital interest transferred constitutes compensation (less any amount paid for such interest). If the transfer of the LLC capital interest is "restricted" by a vesting schedule, then the award of the LLC capital interest is not immediately taxable; rather, taxation is deferred until the lapse of the restrictive provisions.

Where the LLC award is not a capital interest, but rather a profits interest to an executive or other service provider, the IRS generally still will treat the award as a transfer of property under Code Sec. 83. A capital interest would entitle the holder to a share of the proceeds of any liquidation of the entity. However, under a profits interest, if the LLC were liquidated on the award date, the executive would not be entitled to any liquidating distribution. Because the profits interest has no value on the award date, generally the IRS will treat neither the award of the profits interest nor the lapse of any vesting restrictions on the profits interest as a taxable event.

Only when the LLC earns a profit would the executive/holder of the profits interest be entitled to profits proportionate to such interest. As with a restricted stock award, the recipient should make a "protective" election to recognize income under Code Sec. 83(b).

---

[5] *Campbell v. Comm'r*, 59 TCM 236, CCH Dec. 46,493(M), TC Memo 1990-162, *rev'd and aff'd*, 91-2 USTC ¶50,420, 943 F2d 815 (8th Cir. 1991).

[6] *See* Reg. § 1.83-3(d).

[7] Section 4.02 of Rev. Proc. 93-27, 1993-2 CB 343.

By far the best feature of a profits interest is the uniquely favorable tax treatment of the distribution proceeds to the executive/holder. Although generally, no distribution or payment is made to the executive/holder until a liquidation event such as a sale of the company, if the executive meets the one-year holding period requirement, the full amount of the distribution would be taxable to him or her at the lower long-term capital gains rates.

Example: ABC LLC hires Executive D as CEO. One of the likely exit strategies for ABC's owners is to sell the company. ABC awards profits interests to D, equal to 10% of the company, valued as of D's hire date, January 1, 2018. ABC has 10,000 shares outstanding. An independent valuation firm determines ABC's value to be $50 million. ABC sets the exercise price for D's profits interests at $5,000.

D is successful in preparing ABC for sale and negotiating a favorable purchase price. Megacorp agrees to purchase the stock of ABC for $90 million on January 15, 2020. D will receive 10% of the increase in value since the date of her hire, or $4,000,000.

Prior to 2018, the holding period requirement for long-term capital gains rates was one year from the award date. The legislation known as the Tax Cuts and Jobs Act of 2017 ("TCJA") signed into law by President Trump in December 2017, increased the holding period to three years from the award date for profits interests awarded in connection with performance of certain investment services. This change target so-called "carried interests," which are often used by private equity funds, hedge funds and similar investment partnerships

As with SARs the executive/recipient of a profits interest derives benefit or value based on the appreciation in the value of the profits interest. Therefore, a profits interest requires the company to establish an initial benchmark value or "exercise price."

.02 Advantages and Disadvantages of Profits Interests

The primary advantage of profits interests is that the payout to the executive/recipient generally would be taxable at the lower long-term capital gains rates. Additionally, the exercise of profits interests does not require the recipient to tender an exercise price for which he or she may need to borrow against the exercise proceeds or engage in a cashless exercise.

The primary disadvantage of profits interest awards is that after receipt of a profits interest, the executive/recipient would be treated as a partner and receive allocations (and appropriate tax distributions). The LLC likely would be required to furnish the executive/recipient with a Form K-1 for income from the LLC. This can be complicated to explain to executives. Additionally, a company would not receive a deduction for the award (or upon the exercise of) a profits interest.

Prior to vesting, the executive/recipient's rights as a member of the LLC or partnership (*e.g.*, voting and review of LLC books and records) may be restricted. However, the executive-recipient would immediately become a "member" of the LLC (or partner of the partnership) for federal income tax purposes upon award of the interest to him or her. Thereafter, a member would be allocated his or her distributive share of LLC taxable income each year, including prior to vesting. Typically, the LLC funds any tax liability in respect of the restricted interests by making a distribution for taxes to all its tax members (including those holding the restricted interests). Since the taxable income allocated to the restricted members otherwise would have been allocated to non-restricted members, then as long as the restricted and unrestricted members have essentially the same tax rate, no inefficiencies are created.

.03 Use of Profits Interests by REITs

A Real Estate Investment Trust ("REIT") is a company that owns or finances income-producing real estate in a range of property sectors, which can offer unique benefits to investors. These companies have to meet a number of requirements to qualify as REITs. A REIT may be publicly traded or privately held. Because a REIT includes an operating partnership, the REIT can award profits interests.

Generally, a REIT executive can elect to convert his or her interests or units into cash or REIT shares at any time after they become vested. When the executive elects to convert the units into shares or cash, he or she will be taxed at capital gains rates based on the full value received upon conversion.

¶935 Phantom Stock Arrangements

A phantom stock plan can be an excellent executive compensation program for a closely held corporation. The company can give an executive the economic benefits of being a stockholder without giving the executive the rights of a stockholder under state law. The executive does not have to pay anything to acquire his or her phantom stock, as they would if they purchased stock.

Holders of phantom stock receive the economic benefits of being stockholders, without the rights and privileges of stockholders. The executives share the proceeds, to the extent of appreciation, if the company sells all of its stock or assets to a third party. Since the executives do not actually hold any shares, however, they are not entitled to vote on stockholder matters.

> **Example 1:** Privately held ABC Corporation is competing with numerous public companies for the talented Executive D. For a variety of reasons, ABC is unwilling to give real stock ownership to executive employees. However, ABC must create a compensation package that resembles those the public companies are offering to D.
>
> ABC has 10,000 shares of stock outstanding. ABC offers D 1,000 shares of phantom stock, with a ten-year vesting period. If D remains with ABC for ten years, she will own 9.1% of the company (1,000/11,000).

.01 Comparison to Other Stock-Based Awards

As noted above, phantom stock generally takes the form of a hypothetical share or unit. Unlike an option, SAR, or profits interest, which provide a benefit measured by an appreciation in value of the company stock, phantom stock is usually a full value award. The hypothetical share is designed to provide the economic benefits associated with stock ownership without diluting current stockholders or extending ownership rights to minority stockholders. A phantom stock plan or award could give the executive a conversion right, so that the executive, at a later date, could convert the phantom share into an actual stock interest.

As with most stock-based awards, the executive's taxable event is deferred until payment on the phantom stock.[8] From the perspective of the company, the holding period associated with the hypothetical interest provides the economic tie to the stockholders. Like options or SARs interests, but unlike actual shares, the phantom stock can be "cashed in" upon demand.

> **Example 2:** In Example 1 above, if ABC Corporation had awarded Executive D a SAR with respect to 1,000 shares, and D remained with ABC for ten years, she would have been entitled to 10% of the increase value, if any, of ABC from her hire date until the end of the ten-year period. That amount may be zero or it may be significant, but it will almost certainly not be equal to 9.1% of the value of the entire company.

.02 Dividend Rights

The phantom stock program can, however, have dividend rights, which can be paid and taxed currently, credited to the executive with or without interest or paid in-kind, *i.e.*, paid as additional shares of phantom stock. The treatment of dividends associated with phantom stock is a business decision of the company since each alternative has economic ramifications, *e.g.*, accruing dividends can be costly over time.

A phantom stock plan may provide that the units credited to a participant's account have dividend rights equivalent to those of actual stock. The company may pay the dividend equivalents to the participant at the same time it pays dividends on actual shares to stockholders. However, the company also may credit the dividends to the participant's phantom stock account. The company would hold in the account a cash amount equal to dividends actually declared. The company could make payment of the equivalent dividends when the participant chooses or it could defer payment until the date it actually pays out the phantom stock account. The company could credit deferred dividend equivalents with interest at a fixed rate, which it then accumulates in the participant's account, or the company could convert the dividend equivalents to additional phantom stock units.

.03 Types of Phantom Stock

There are at least three types of phantom stock arrangements. One common form of a phantom stock plan is an arrangement that mirrors the actual stock issued by the company without creating a second class of stock.[9] A private company that wants to provide stock-based compensation similar to that of a

---

[8] Reg. § 1.83-1(a).   [9] GCM 39750, May 18, 1988.

public company, without actually giving away any stock, could adopt a phantom stock plan like this.

An incentive-based phantom stock plan is a bonus-oriented plan. The company has no underlying obligation to provide the benefit until the actual award. This form of phantom stock plan is more incentive-oriented, recapturing the benefit at a date earlier than retirement.

An alternative is a deferred compensation arrangement under which the company and the executive agree to defer a portion of the executive's compensation. The company or plan would credit the executive with phantom shares as if the executive had used cash for the purchase. This form of phantom stock plan is retirement-oriented, requiring a longer period to establish the benefit.

The choice of whether to design a phantom stock arrangement as a deferred compensation or incentive program will ultimately depend upon the purpose of the arrangement.

.04 Tax Treatment to the Executive

Since phantom stock is nothing more than a contractual right between a company and an executive, the IRS will not take the view that the company has made a taxable transfer of property under Code Sec. 83. Instead, the IRS will treat the award as an unfunded and unsecured promise to pay an amount in the future.[10] Generally, an executive will not be taxed until the phantom stock pays him or her a benefit at a specific date. The company must report that amount on the executive's Form W-2.[11] The settlement price in connection with phantom stock includes the appreciation plus the underlying value of the share or unit.[12] The executive does not have to raise cash to "exercise" a phantom stock right. The executive will receive cash sufficient to cover taxes due upon exercise.

In addition to the general taxing concepts, an issue for companies and executives to consider in connection with intangible stock-based awards is the doctrine of constructive receipt. Generally, an award of a phantom stock right or interest does not result in constructive receipt to the executive.[13] However, the IRS might determine that the executive constructively received the amounts at the point that he or she can request payment.[14] To eliminate constructive receipt issues under Code Sec. 451 as it pertains to a phantom stock program, the company may find it necessary to create a substantial risk of forfeiture, *i.e.*, a conversion date that will establish the executive's right to the benefit. In addition, if the program provides for dividends, any executive election as to settlement of the dividend should occur before the record date or constructive receipt may be applicable to the dividend stream. The constructive receipt issue in connection with a phantom stock program depends not only on the ability of the executive to demand the settlement, but also on the concept of substantial limitation on the executive's right to receive the compensation.

---

[10] Reg. § 1.83-3(e) [taxing property transferred in connection with the performance of services]; IRS Letter Ruling 9501032 (Oct. 5, 1994).

[11] Code Sec. 6051.

[12] Code Sec. 61 and Code Sec. 83; Rev. Rul. 82-121, 1982-1 CB 79; Rev. Rul. 80-300, 1980-2 CB 165.

[13] Rev. Rul. 80-300, 1980-2 CB 165.

[14] Code Sec. 451.

Generally, if the executive is credited with phantom stock but the stock is not available until a later date, *i.e.*, the program utilizes a term of years during which employment must be maintained or the rights would be forfeited, there will not be constructive receipt.[15] If the stock is available, constructive receipt could be applicable since there is no risk of forfeiture.[16]

Planning Note: Experienced legal counsel should be able to draft a phantom stock plan under which the executive faces enough downside risk and upside reward to avoid constructive receipt.

.05 Tax Treatment to Company

Upon the settlement of a phantom share, the company will be entitled to a compensation deduction.[17] A complication could arise as to whether Code Sec. 404 or Code Sec. 83(h) should govern unfunded deferred compensation arrangements that include phantom stock plans.[18]

The law imposes no funding requirement on a phantom stock plan. The participant to whom the company has awarded phantom stock has in effect received a contractual promise that at a future date the company will convert the phantom shares into real shares of stock or cash. The participant is not subject to tax until he or she actually converts the phantom stock to cash or stock, at which time the company can take its tax deduction. If the settlement is in cash, generally, the payment is treated like bonus compensation. Cash payments to current executives are deductible in the tax year that includes the year in which the executive recognizes the income.[19] If the plan is unfunded and the company pays cash to a former executive, the company can deduct it at the point when paid and not on a subsequent date.[20]

A phantom stock arrangement, which provides a right to receive payment for the underlying share and not merely appreciation, is treated as a nonqualified deferred compensation plan with respect to the imposition of FICA and FUTA taxes. As such, the taxes are imposed on the latter of (1) the date the services were performed to create the underlying right or (2) the date upon which there is no substantial risk of forfeiture.[21]

The company can treat income recognized by the executive as supplemental wages.[22] Current law requires an employer that makes supplemental wage payments (*e.g.*, equity award vesting, annual bonus payments, etc.) to an executive in excess of $1 million during a calendar year to withhold on the amount above $1 million (or on the entire payment) at a rate equal to the highest

---

[15] Reg. § 1.451-2.

[16] IRS Letter Ruling 8829070 (April 27, 1988).

[17] Code Sec. 162(a).

[18] Reg. § 1.83-6(a)(3) provides that Code Sec. 83(h) is not applicable to transfers to employee benefit plans described in Reg. § 1.162-10(a) or to transfers to trust or annuities under Code Sec. 404(a)(5). Although unfunded plans are described in the latter, such plans are neither trust nor annuities, and it would appear that Code Sec. 83 could be applicable.

Notwithstanding, the exception in Reg. § 1.83-6(a)(3) applies the timing described in Reg. § 1.404(a)-12(b)(1) and Reg. § 1.404(a)-12(b)(2).

[19] Reg. § 1.404(b)-1; Code Sec. 404(a)(5); Reg. § 1.404(a)-12.

[20] *See generally*, Reg. § 1.404(a)-12(b).

[21] Code Sec. 3121(v)(2); Reg. § 31.3121(v)(2)-1(b)(4)(ii) and Reg. § 31.3121(v)(2)-1(b)(5), Example 8.

[22] Reg. § 31.3402(g)-1(a)(2).

individual income tax bracket in effect for the year, which is 37% in 2018. For supplemental wage payments to an executive for less than $1 million in a calendar year, companies may withhold at the supplemental flat rate of 22%. A company can choose to use the supplemental rate or the W-4 method, although the executive often makes a request. Because of the increase to the standard deduction and the change to the tax rates by the TCJA, if an employer chooses to use the W-4 method, it should use the tax tables provided in Notice 1036.

If sums are being withheld for other services, it can be included as part of regular wages.[23] Withholding would not be required for independent contractors. As a general rule, however, the underlying plan document should include such provisions as required by the company to facilitate application of the withholding requirements either when part of the settlement is noncash or the executive has an election as to whether the supplemental or regular rate will be used for purposes of withholding. If the company pays stock to the executive as part of the settlement, withholding is required at the fair market value.[24] If the settlement is part of normal wages, the Code requires withholding at the same rate applicable to the cash salary.[25]

¶945 Plan Design

Because profits interest and phantom stock plans or awards are essentially a contractual arrangement established unilaterally by the company, the company has flexibility in their design (subject to Code Sec. 409A, as described in ¶975 below). The profits interest/phantom stock plan or award agreement could measure appreciation by the fair market value of the company's assets or the underlying company stock. The profits interest/phantom stock plan or award agreement could set the settlement date as the date of the executive's termination of employment or some other time in the future. The plan need not fix the settlement date. The company may pick and choose among employees, and even nonemployees, in eligibility for and awards under a profits interest or phantom stock plan. The Code's nondiscrimination rules do not apply.

Nearly all profits interest/phantom stock plan awards provide for a vesting period, such as five years. A profits interest can require a "cliff" vesting, i.e., the executive cannot exercise the profits interest until expiration of the five-year period, or a ratable vesting period where the award vests proportionately over the period of years. Some profits interest/phantom stock awards also provide for a limited exercise period, such as two years after the award date or the vesting date.

A phantom stock program should include specific conversion provisions that state whether the exercise of the award can be for stock, cash, or a combination. Open-ended conversion rights can have a significant economic impact on the company and as such, the company should tie the exercise of the phantom stock award to a period of years. Regardless of the form of settlement, the tax consequences will be the same for the executive, i.e., ordinary income[26] and the

---

[23] Reg. § 31.3402(g)-1(a)(2).
[24] Reg. § 1.3401(a)-1(a)(4).
[25] IRS Pub. No. 15 (Circular E).
[26] See ¶955.

company will receive a deduction equal to the fair market value of the benefit.[27] These provisions must also accommodate changes in the employment status of the executive and can provide a pro rata conversion right that is triggered on the original conversion date and not the date of separation.

.01 Administration

A profits interest/phantom stock plan is usually administered by a committee appointed by the board of directors or administered by the board itself. The plan gives either the board or the committee authority to determine the number of profits interests or phantom stock units to award, the time at which it will award the profits interests or units, and who will participate under the plan. The board or committee has the authority to interpret the plan and to adopt rules and regulations thereunder.

If the profits interest/phantom stock plan provides for deferral of payments until the executive's retirement or employment termination, the plan may be an employee benefit plan subject to the Employee Retirement Income Security Act ("ERISA").[28] If so, counsel must design the plan to fall under the ERISA exception for unfunded plans covering only a select group of management or highly compensated employees.

The profits interest/phantom stock plan will ordinarily provide for payments in cash, either in a lump sum or in installments. The company makes payments from its general assets. The executive ordinarily is taxed on the payments (attributable to the stock appreciation) only when the company makes such payments to him or her. The company gets a compensation deduction at the time, and in the amount, of the payments.

.02 Litigation

If there is a downside to the flexibility in design of phantom stock plans, it is that the lack of legal requirements can sometimes give rise to ambiguous, vague or even sloppy drafting that leaves the parties uncertain of their rights and leads to litigation.

In *Emmenegger v. Bull Moose Tube Co.*,[29] the court upheld a jury award in excess of $7 million to two employees who the company denied phantom stock compensation. Mr. Emmenegger and another senior executive were participants in a phantom stock plan the company established in 1988. The plan obligated the company to repurchase a participant's phantom shares when the participant terminated employment, either at "book value" or at a specified "redemption value" which was significantly higher. When the company terminated Mr. Emmenegger and the other senior executive in 1996, it refused to redeem their phantom shares on the grounds that the company terminated them for cause. Later the company decided to pay them only the book value for their shares. The

---

[27] *See* ¶965.

[28] *See* Chapter 17 (¶1701 *et seq.*) for a detailed discussion of deferred compensation and nonqualified plans subject to ERISA.

[29] *Emmenegger v. Bull Moose Tube Co.*, 324 F3d 616 (8th Cir. 2003).

jury found, and the court of appeals agreed, that the company had a significant financial incentive to argue that the terminations were "with cause" and the circumstances did not support such an argument. Thus, the court ordered the company to pay Mr. Emmenegger and the other senior executive the full redemption value for their phantom shares.

Courts have found an obligation of good faith in the administration of phantom stock appreciation plans. In *Feldman v. National Westminster Bank*,[30] the court noted that, as a matter of common law, good faith is not a defense to a breach of contract claim. Although the court did not agree with the plan administrator's interpretation of the plan, it nonetheless believed the interpretation was well within the discretion the plan afforded it, to construe the plan and make all other determinations and take all other actions deemed necessary or advisable for the proper administration of the plan.

Both the *Emmenegger* and *Feldman* courts also held that the companies' phantom stock plans were not employee pension plans within the meaning of ERISA.[31]

In *Hopmayer v. Aladdin Indus. LLC*,[32] the state court held that a manufacturer owes a former employee $160,000 plus prejudgment interest for phantom shares promised in his employment contract. Aladdin gave Mr. Hopmayer an offer-of-employment letter. The letter stated that the company would adopt a phantom unit plan "in which you will be awarded 4,000 phantom units with an initial value of $40.00 per unit." When the company terminated Hopmayer's employment, it advised him that he was not entitled to any compensation for the phantom shares because the shares had neither vested nor appreciated in value. The court found that the offer letter was enforceable and that it contained neither vesting nor appreciation requirements.

As noted above, some plans that are intended to create a phantom stock interest can become subject to ERISA. See ¶ 1585 for a detailed discussion of this issue.

¶955 Accounting Issues

The accounting treatment of a profits interest or phantom stock essentially turns on whether it will be settled in cash or in stock. Stock-settled profits interests enjoy the same accounting treatment as stock options. Profits interests and phantom stock that may be settled in cash are subject to variable accounting,[33] and the measurement date is considered the date of exercise or the time that the amount of the settlement, whether cash or stock, is completely ascertainable.[34]

---

[30] *Feldman v. National Westminster Bank*, 2003 NY App Div LEXIS 2759 (Sup Ct NY 2003).

[31] *Emmenegger v. Bull Moose Tube Co.*, 197 F3d 929 (8th Cir. 1999).

[32] *Hopmayer v. Aladdin Indus. LLC*, 2004 Tenn App LEXIS 364 (Tenn Ct App 2004).

[33] Financial Accounting Standards Board ("FASB") Interpretation No. 28 (AC § 4062-1).

[34] AC §§ 4062.10 and 4062-1 Fn. 2.

.01 Accounting for Phantom Stock Awards

Variable accounting requires interim calculations of the amount of compensation expense. The compensation expense can fluctuate based on market conditions. Adjustments due to such market fluctuations occur in subsequent periods before the measurement date (but not below zero) and are applied to the period in which the market fluctuation occurred.[35] For purposes of variable accounting, if the award is for past services, compensation accrues during the period that company awarded the awards. If the company or the plan does not define the service period, it is presumed to be the vesting period.[36]

From an accounting perspective, vesting requires that the awards be noncontingent and generally require a stated period between the award and the initial permissible exercise date.[37] If a plan utilizes vesting at designated periods, *i.e.*, five years, the company must recognize the compensation expense *pro rata* over the five-year period,[38] based on the market price at the end of each one-year period (and not the average price during the year).

> **Planning Note:** Using a five-year example, the compensation expense will be calculated at the rate of 1/5 in the first year with each subsequent year calculated as the *pro rata* amount, *e.g.*, 3/5, 4/5, minus the amount previously recognized.

If ratable vesting is utilized, providing a right to vest based on a percentage per year as opposed to a "cliff-type" vesting, an award over five years will be treated as five separate profits interests with compensation expense recognized in each year proportionate to the rate of the vesting. Since in all years subsequent to the first year, services will be deemed performed in the current as well as prior years, compensation expense, which accrues proportionately, would be accelerated.

.02 Accounting for Profits Interest Awards

As a form of compensation, profits interests are subject to various financial reporting requirements in order to comply with US GAAP. Most profits interests are accounted for as share-based payment awards. Specific provisions relating to share-based payments in private companies are provided under ASC 718 (the successor to FAS 123R) for profits interests awarded to employees and directors. ASC 505-50 provides accounting guidance for profits interests awarded to other service providers.

The profits interest must be classified as subject to either equity or liability treatment. The classification of the award as equity or liability determines its accounting requirements. Generally, equity awards are settled (paid) in equity interests and liability awards are paid (settled) in cash.

For equity awards, the fair value of the profits interests will be established as of the award date, and recognized as an expense over the corresponding service period. The service period frequently is the vesting period. The fair value of an

---

[35] AC § 4062-1.04.
[36] AC § 4062-1.03.

[37] AC § 4062-1, Fn. 3.
[38] FASB Interpretation No. 28.

equity award is not adjusted for changes in fair value over the expense period. The expense may be adjusted for forfeitures or certain modifications. The offsetting entry for the compensation expense is recognized as an increase in members' equity.

For liability awards, private companies can make an accounting policy election to measure the value of the award at either fair value or intrinsic value. The corresponding value of the profits interest is initially determined as of the award date and an estimated expense is established for the service period. In addition, a liability for the associated total value of the award is recorded on the balance sheet. Thereafter and until the obligation is settled or retired, the liability and expense are adjusted ("marked to market") at each future reporting date reflecting any changes in value, forfeitures, or certain modifications.

¶965 Securities Law Issues

Although the company will never be giving real stock to the executive as payment for the executive's phantom stock or profits interests, the federal securities laws would still generally treat a company's award of phantom stock or profits interests as an offer to sell securities under the Securities Act of 1933. However, the federal securities laws also make available to private companies several exemptions to the registration requirements that apply to public companies.

.01 Intrastate Offerings Exemption

The intrastate offerings exemption applies if, at the award date, all offerees and purchasers are residents of the same state in which the corporation is incorporated and the corporation does substantially all of its business. There is no limit as to the number of employees or the size of the option award.

.02 Rule 701

Rule 701 provides an exemption from registration for securities issued by private companies pursuant to compensatory benefit plans and arrangements. The aggregate sales price or amount of securities "sold" during any consecutive 12-month period may not exceed the *greatest* of the following:

1. $1,000,000;

2. 15% of the company's total assets (or of the company's parent if the company is a wholly-owned subsidiary and the securities represent obligations that the parent fully and unconditionally guarantees), measured at the company's most recent balance sheet date (if no older than its last fiscal year end); or

3. 15% of the outstanding amount of the class of securities being offered and sold in reliance on this exemption, measured at the company's most recent balance sheet date (if no older than its last fiscal year end).

The aggregate sales price is determined when the company awards the option, without regard to when the option becomes exercisable.

However, Rule 701 includes a specific disclosure requirement for all transactions in which sales of securities exceed $10,000,000 in a 12-month period.[39] The company would need to provide this specific disclosure to all participants within a reasonable period before the date of exercise. Transactions involving sales of less than $10,000,000 need only provide participants with a copy of the plan document and the respective award agreement and any other disclosure necessary to satisfy the antifraud provisions of the federal securities laws.

¶975 Code Sec. 409A

Code Sec. 409A can apply to phantom stock awards, but does not currently apply to profits interests. Failure to satisfy the requirements of Code Sec. 409A could result in significant penalties to the award recipient (see Chapter 17 [¶1701 et seq.] for a detailed discussion of Code Sec. 409A).

.01 Profits Interests

Code Sec. 409A may apply to arrangements between a partner and a partnership, which provide for the deferral of compensation under a nonqualified deferred compensation plan. However, IRS Notice 2005-1 explicitly provides that, until additional guidance is issued, taxpayers may treat the issuance of a partnership interest (including a profits interest) awarded in connection with the performance of services under the same principles that govern the issuance of stock.[40] To date, no additional guidance has been issued. For purposes of Code Sec. 409A, taxpayers may treat an issuance of a profits interest in connection with the performance of services that is properly treated under applicable guidance as not resulting in inclusion of income by the service provider at the time of issuance, as also not resulting in the deferral of compensation.

.02 Phantom Stock

Phantom Stock generally is subject to Code Sec. 409A, since it is a promise to pay an amount in the future based on the value of stock at that time. However, if the phantom stock award is paid out in cash (or otherwise) immediately upon vesting, it could be exempt as a short-term deferral.

---

[39] In May 2018, President Trump signed into law the Economic Growth, Regulatory Relief, and Consumer Protection Act, Public Law No. 115-174, which directed the SEC to revise Rule 701, so as to increase from $5,000,000 to $10,000,000 the aggregate sales price or amount of securities sold during any consecutive 12-month period in excess of which

the issuer is required under such section to deliver an additional disclosure to investors. In July 2018, the SEC approved an amendment of Rule 701 to accomplish this. Release No. 33-10520.

[40] Notice 2005-1, 2005-2 I.R.B. 274 (January 10, 2005).

Chapter 10
EMPLOYEE STOCK PURCHASE PLANS

¶1001 Overview—Employee Stock Purchase Plans

An employee stock purchase plan ("ESPP"), or Section 423 plan, is a type of stock option plan that permits employees of a company to purchase company stock at a discount to the prevailing market value on the date of the exercise of the option. The "option" to the employee is an election to contribute from his or her compensation, on an after-tax basis, toward the purchase of company stock, at a favorable price. The option exercise is automatic at the end of the specified offering period (also sometimes referred to as the "purchase period").

> **Example::** On the first business day of each semi-annual purchase period, the ABC Corporation employee stock purchase plan grants each eligible employee an option to buy company stock on the last business day of such purchase period. The ESPP specifies a purchase price that is 85% of the average market price of ABC's stock on either the first or last business day of the purchase period, whichever is less. After the last business day of the purchase period, the company or a third party administrator will purchase for the employee that number of full or fractional shares of ABC stock that it can pay for with the employee's payroll deductions accumulated through the last month of the purchase period.

Code Sec. 423 imposes significant requirements on ESPPs, and grants significant tax benefits to plans that meet those requirements. If the ESPP satisfies the requirements of Code Sec. 423, the company stock purchased by employees will qualify for favorable taxation under Code Sec. 421.

ESPPs that qualify for favorable tax treatment under Code Sec. 421 and Code Sec. 423 are available to both public and privately held companies. However, only common-law employees (as opposed to directors or independent contractors) can participate in a qualified ESPP.

.01 Tax Treatment

An employee who receives "options" under an ESPP is not taxed on the date the company grants the option to participate, or on the date the employee is deemed to exercise the option to purchase the stock. The taxable event occurs only when the employee sells the stock purchased through the ESPP. The tax treatment of options under an ESPP is similar to the tax treatment of incentive stock options ("ISOs") under Code Sec. 422.[1] If the employee holds the stock purchased under the ESPP for the required period, any gain on the sale or

---

[1] *See* Chapter 7 (¶701 *et seq.*) for a detailed discussion of stock options, and ¶725 for a detailed discussion of the tax treatment of incentive stock options.

transfer of stock will be taxed in two parts. The discount the employee received off the purchase price would be ordinary income and any excess gain between the purchase price would be long-term capital gain. The company will not be entitled to a deduction for ESPP shares that the employee holds for the required period. However, the employee would recognize ordinary income and the company would be entitled to a deduction if the employee were to dispose of the ESPP shares before the end of the holding period (see ¶1025 and ¶1035 for detailed discussions of the tax effects of ESPPs to employees and companies).

In contrast to a 401(k) plan, employees make payroll deductions and contributions to purchase stock under an ESPP on an after-tax basis. The contributions, although generally made on a payroll reduction basis, are included in an employee's gross income.

The final regulations under Code Sec. 409A expressly provide that the grant of an option under an ESPP described in Code Sec. 423 (including the grant of an option with an exercise price discounted in accordance with Code Sec. 423(b)(6) and the accompanying regulations), does not constitute a deferral of compensation.[2]

.02 Internal Revenue Code Requirements

Code Sec. 423 imposes a variety of requirements with which the company and the ESPP must comply to qualify for favorable tax treatment, including:

- The company's shareholders must approve the ESPP;
- The company must offer participation in the ESPP to all employees (with some exceptions);
- Five percent owners cannot participate;
- The participation rights and options must be identical for all employees;
- The purchase price discount cannot be more than a specified percentage;
- The offering period cannot exceed a specified duration; and
- The ESPP cannot permit employees to transfer their purchase rights.

(See ¶1015 for a detailed discussion of the Internal Revenue Code requirements applicable to ESPPs.)

.03 Design and Operational Issues

Code Sec. 423 does not provide for employee payroll deductions. However, many ESPPs contain such provisions. Unlike a 401(k) plan, however, such payroll deductions are not excluded from an employee's gross income. Rather, the employee is taxed on the entire amount of the payroll deduction when it is earned. The tax advantage of an ESPP is the deferral of the recognition of taxable gain on the difference between the option price and the market value of the stock on the date of exercise (see ¶1045).

---

[2] Reg. §1.409A-1(b)(5)(ii).

.04 Advantages of an ESPP

While many companies utilize nonqualified and incentive stock options in equity-based compensation arrangements for managerial and executive categories of employees, the culture of the company may also dictate a broad-based program designed to provide such equity opportunities to all members of the workforce, not merely senior management (see ¶ 1055).

.05 Accounting Treatment

The accounting rules generally categorize plans that provide equity-based compensation as either compensatory or noncompensatory. Compensatory plans require that the plan sponsor recognize compensation expense while plans that meet the requirements for a noncompensatory plan, such as a qualified ESPP, do not require a charge to earnings. FASB Accounting Standards Codification Topic 718, Compensation—Stock Compensation (referred to as "ASC 718"), reduced the attractiveness of employee stock purchase plans by limiting the discount and other features an ESPP could offer without being deemed "compensatory (see ¶ 1065).

.06 Federal Securities Law Issues

The Securities Act of 1933 requires a company to register offers or sales of its securities to employees under an ESPP. Any offer or sale of a plan sponsor's securities not made under an effective registration statement would be considered a violation of the Securities Act, absent an available exemption (see ¶ 1075).

.07 Non-qualifying Stock Purchase Plans

Some companies are willing to forego the favorable tax treatment of Code Sec. 423 in order to create and implement a stock purchase plan that achieves other objectives. Some of the reasons for creating a nonqualified ESPP are discussed in ¶ 1085.

¶ 1015 Statutory Requirements

To qualify for favorable tax treatment under Code Sec. 421 and Code Sec. 423, the ESPP must satisfy the many requirements of Code Sec. 423. The plan's compliance—or failure to comply—with these requirements, however, impacts the qualified tax treatment of the overall plan and the options the plan grants to employees to varying degrees. Violation of certain requirements, *e.g.*, the 5% owner exclusion, would only affect the treatment of those options granted to the 5% owner. On the other hand, if the plan does not have identical rights and privileges applicable to all options, the plan in its entirety, and all options under it, would fail to be eligible for the favorable treatment of Code Sec. 421(a).[3]

If the ESPP satisfies each of the nine statutory requirements listed below, an employee will not recognize taxable income until the disposition of the stock. The employee stock purchase plan not only must satisfy the specific requirements of Code Sec. 423, but the ESPP must specifically set forth each of the

---

[3] Reg. § 1.423-2(a)(2).

statutory requirements, except shareholder approval, in the document in order for the plan to be eligible for favorable tax treatment under Code Sec. 423.[4] While the document can, and should, include other provisions regarding the administration and operations of the plan, as dictated by the design of the program to meet the needs of the company, the following substantive provisions are mandatory.

.01 Shareholder Approval

Shareholder approval is required within twelve months before or after adoption of the plan by the board of directors. The approval must specifically reference (1) the aggregate number of shares that the plan can issue, and (2) the company (or companies) to whose employees the plan will offer stock purchase rights.[5] The company must obtain shareholder approval of the ESPP according to applicable state law provisions. However, if state law does not designate an approval method, approval must either be (1) by a majority of the voting shares at a meeting that meets the state law quorum requirements; or (2) by a method that, under state law, would be adequate to satisfy general shareholder approval requirements.[6] Additionally, the shareholders must approve the specific plan, not merely a generic approval of a concept or proposed program.[7]

Code Sec. 423 would require the company to seek shareholder approval of a material amendment. The IRS has shed some light on what types of amendments require shareholder approval in a private letter ruling, in which it held that a company's amendment of an ESPP to (i) comply with SEC restrictions, and (ii) provide the company with a method of tracking the exercise of purchase options under the plan in order to meet its employment tax obligations, did not require shareholder approval.[8]

Regulations under Code Sec. 423 clarify that new shareholder approval is required if there is a change in the shares with respect to which a purchase option is offered or a change in the granting company. With respect to a subsidiary company that establishes an ESPP, the shareholders from whom approval must be sought include both the parent company and any other shareholders of the subsidiary.[9] If shares of an acquiring company are substituted for shares of a target company subject to a purchase option in the context of an acquisition, the

---

[4] Generally, Code Sec. 423(a) referencing Code Sec. 421(a), provides, in the event of a qualifying transfer, that employees will not recognize ordinary income on the discount and companies are not entitled to a deduction. If the requirements of Code Sec. 423 are not met, ordinary income must be recognized based on the difference between the fair market value of the stock on the date of grant and the price of the option and the company receives a deduction for the amount recognized as income by the employee.

[5] Code Sec. 423(b); Reg. § 1.423-2(c)(3). To alleviate continuing administrative issues and facilitate the shareholder approval process, plan provisions can be designed to refer to classes of corporations and incorporate automatic adjustments in the aggregate number of shares, commonly referred to as an "evergreen provision." Reg. § 1.423-2(c)(4); IRS Letter Ruling 9531031 (May 8, 1995) (approving evergreen share reserve in ISO).

[6] Reg. § 1.423-2(c)(1).

[7] Reg. § 1.423-2(c).

[8] IRS Letter Ruling 200418020 (November 25, 2003).

[9] Reg. § 1.423-2(c)(5), Example 1(iii).

acquiring company (instead of its shareholders) must approve the amendment of the stock purchase plan to issue parent stock instead of subsidiary stock.[10]

.02 Participation and Permitted Exclusions

Only employees of the company, or designated affiliates, may participate in the ESPP.[11] Consultants to the company, independent contractors and members of the company's board of directors cannot participate in a qualified ESPP.

Generally, all employees of any company designated under the ESPP must be included. However, the plan can exclude certain employees, including the following:

- employees who the company has employed less than two years;
- employees who work twenty hours a week or less;
- employees who work no more than five months in a calendar year; and
- highly compensated employees (as defined in Code Sec. 414(q)).[12]

A company may utilize these exclusions to ensure that it focuses the rewards of the ESPP on its long-term, full-time employees (in the case of the exclusions of temporary and part-time employees) or to promote the plan as a means of passing stock ownership to lower level employees (if the exclusion of highly compensated employees or officers is utilized).

The regulations provide that the terms of an ESPP or an offering may exclude highly compensated employees with compensation above a certain level or who are officers or subject to the disclosure requirements of Section 16(a) of the Securities Exchange Act of 1934 (the "Exchange Act"), provided the exclusion is applied in an identical manner to all highly compensated employees of every company whose employees are granted a purchase option under the ESPP or purchase offering.[13] The regulations offer some flexibility by providing that, with respect to the exclusion of highly compensated employees, the terms of each purchase offering made under an ESPP need not be identical with respect to the highly compensated employees, provided the highly compensated employees are excluded as permitted and within the limitations of the regulations.[14] An ESPP cannot exclude "executives" as a category.

The determination of whether the terms of an ESPP and any offering satisfy the requirements of Code Sec. 423 and the regulations is made on an *offering-by-offering* basis.[15] The terms of each offering may provide different exclusions of employees, within the limits of the regulations. The exclusions established with respect to a particular offering must be applied in an identical manner to all employees of every company whose employees are granted options under that particular offering. The terms of each offering under an ESPP may be different,

---

[10] Reg. § 1.424-1(a)(10), Example 9.

[11] Code Sec. 423(b)(1); Reg. § 1.423-2(e)(1)(iv).

[12] Code Sec. 423(b)(4); Reg. § 1.423-(e)(1). The classification of employees eligible to participate is critical since inadvertent exclusion of one or more employees may negatively affect the tax-qualified status of the entire plan.

[13] Reg. § 1.423-2(e)(2)(ii).

[14] Reg. § 1.423-2(e)(2)(ii).

[15] Reg. § 1.423-2(e)(6), Examples 7 and 8.

provided the ESPP and the offering together satisfy the requirements of Code Sec. 423 and the regulations.

It is not necessary to allow employees of foreign entities to participate, provided that the foreign entity is considered to be a separate corporate entity from the U.S. employer. A company can exclude employees working outside of the U.S. in a foreign entity. The company may simply not designate the entity as one of the corporate entities participating in the ESPP. Code Sec. 423 does not provide exclusions for non-resident aliens (or employees under a specified age).

Some multinational companies extend ESPP participation to their employees working outside of the U.S. This is complicated, because most foreign countries have tax and other laws that are substantially different than those of the U.S. Companies that offer a stock purchase plan to their employees working outside of the U.S. nearly always do so in a separate plan document. A company that is offering or evaluating whether to offer an ESPP to employees working outside of the U.S. should consider local law as to withholding and reporting issues, securities restrictions, exchange controls, future plan entitlement issues, data privacy limitations, and the availability of deductions to foreign subsidiaries.

.03 Exclusion of 5% Owners

An employee who will have more than five percent of either (1) the company's voting securities or (2) the value of all shares of the company's stock (including any parent or subsidiary of the company) after the grant of an ESPP option, will not be entitled to favorable tax treatment on any options granted under the plan. This could be significant for a closely held company. All of the employee's outstanding stock options will be considered as stock held by the employee in determining the percentage of ownership, even if the exercise is in installments or after a fixed period.[16] The total number of shares used in the calculation is based on the issued and outstanding shares immediately after the grant, not including treasury shares.[17]

.04 Equal Rights and Privileges

Code Sec. 423 requires that all employees granted options under an ESPP have the same rights and privileges. The purchase price discount, payment options and related provisions under the ESPP must be identical for all employees. However, the amount of stock that any employee may purchase under the ESPP or option may bear a uniform relationship to the total compensation, or the basic or regular rate of compensation, of employees.

Additionally, an ESPP may provide that no employee may purchase more than a maximum amount of stock fixed under the plan.[18] The ESPP may limit employees' grants to a specific dollar amount or a certain percentage of compensation. For example, an ESPP could limit the amount of options granted to any employees to a ratio of the employee's compensation, such as one option per $1,000.00 of compensation. A limitation is not the same as an exclusion. A

---

[16] Code Sec. 423(b)(3); Reg. § 1.423-2(d)(1).
[17] Reg. § 1.423-2(d)(2).

[18] Code Sec. 423(b)(5).

formula limiting a grant is acceptable, while a formula that has the effect of excluding a group is generally not acceptable. A variation on the one option for $1,000 dollars of compensation, which is only applicable for compensation amounts in excess of $25,000, would be impermissible since it excludes a group of employees from participating in the plan.[19]

The regulations provide flexibility by permitting a company to make multiple offerings with different rights and privileges applicable to the participants of each offering under a plan. The determination of whether the terms of an offering satisfy the "equal rights and privileges" requirement is made on an *offering-by-offering* basis.[20] The terms of each offering under an ESPP may be different, provided the ESPP and offering together satisfy the requirements of Code Sec. 423 and the regulations. However, the rights and privileges established with respect to a particular offering must be applied in an identical manner to all employees of every company whose employees are granted options under that particular offering.

.05 Purchase Price

Code Sec. 423 allows a company to offer stock under the ESPP at a discount. An ESPP may allow participating employees to elect to purchase company stock **at a price equal to** the lesser of 85% of the fair market value of the stock on (1) the first day of the purchase period, or grant date, or (2) the last day of the purchase period, or exercise date.[21]

The ESPP may express the stock purchase price as a percentage or as a dollar amount. However, expressing the purchase price as a dollar amount could result in the loss of favorable tax treatment for the plan if the amount is less than 85% of fair market value at the time the ESPP grants the purchase option, regardless of the fair market value at time of exercise.[22]

Example: The ABC Corporation ESPP allows each eligible employee of ABC to make a semi-annual election to contribute a portion of his or her compensation toward the purchase of ABC common stock. The purchase price for participating employees will be 85% of the market price of ABC's stock on (1) the first day of the semi-annual offering period (the grant date) or (2) the last day of the semi-annual offering period (the exercise date), whichever is less.

If ABC's stock is trading at $10.00 per share on January 1, 2018, and at $15.00 per share on June 30, 2018, employees' contributions will be used to purchase stock at $8.50 per share for them on the June 30 exercise date.

.06 Establishing the Grant Date

Generally the "grant date" under an ESPP is the start of the purchase or offering period. However, this is not always so. Because of the various limita-

---

[19] Code Sec. 423(b)(5); Reg. § 1.423-2(f)(2).

[20] Reg. § 1.423-2(f)(7), Examples 4 and 5.

[21] Code Sec. 423(b)(6); Reg. § 1.423-2(g)(1). To the extent that the purchase price does not meet this requirement, the stock will not be treated as having been granted under an ESPP regardless of whether the plan satisfies the requirements.

[22] Reg. § 1.423-2(g)(2).

tions placed on a qualified ESPP and tax reporting requirements, the company must be able to establish the "grant date." (See also ¶ 1035.02, below.)

The regulations provide that the grant date will be the first day of an offering period if the terms of the ESPP or offering designate a maximum number of shares that may be purchased by each employee during the offering period. Similarly, the grant date will be the first day of an offering period if the terms of the plan or offering require the application of a formula to establish, on the first day of the offering, the maximum number of shares that may be purchased by each employee during the offering.

If the maximum number of shares that can be purchased under an option is not fixed or determinable until the date the option is exercised and shares purchased, then the grant date will not occur until the date of exercise and purchase.

.07 Limitation on Grants

An ESPP must provide that no employee may be granted an option that permits his or her rights to purchase stock to accrue at a rate that exceeds $25,000 of fair market value of such stock (determined at the time such option is granted) for each calendar year during which the purchase right or option is outstanding.[23] The regulations provide that the limit increases by $25,000 for each calendar year that an option is outstanding.[24] An employee may actually purchase more than $25,000 worth of stock in a calendar year, as long as the overall rate of purchase does not exceed $25,000 per year for each year in which the option is outstanding.[25]

No particular number of shares is necessary to satisfy the requirement that the plan designate a maximum number of shares that may be purchased during the offering in order for the first day of the offering period to be the grant date. The regulations provide that the designation of any maximum number of shares is sufficient to establish the first day of the offering period as the grant date for the option. However, the regulations do not require that an ESPP or offering designate a maximum number of shares that may be purchased by each employee during the offering or incorporate a formula to establish a maximum number of shares that may be purchased by each employee during the offering.

Importantly, the $25,000 limit and the limit on the aggregate number of shares that may be issued under an ESPP are not sufficient to establish the maximum number of shares that can be purchased by an employee under an option so that the grant date will be the first day of the offering.[26]

> **Example:** The ABC Corporation ESPP allows each eligible employee to make a semi-annual election to purchase ABC common stock at a price equal to 85% of the market price of ABC's stock on (1) the first day of the semi-

---

[23] Code Sec. 423(b)(8).

[24] Reg. § 1.423-2(i)(5), Example 5.

[25] Code Sec. 423(b)(8); Reg. § 1.423-2(i)(2) and Reg. § 1.423-2(i)(3); application of the limitation including carry-forward and multiple grant treatment. All

plans that qualify as an ESPP are aggregated for purposes of the $25,000 limitation; however, options (whether nonqualified or incentive) and nonsection 423 plans are not aggregated in calculating the limit.

[26] Reg. § 1.423-2(h)(4), Examples 1, 2, 3 and 4.

annual offering period (the grant date) or (2) the last day of the semi-annual offering period (the exercise date), whichever is less. Executive D wishes to purchase the maximum amount of stock permitted. If ABC's stock is trading at $10.00 per share on January 1, 2018, and at $15.00 per share on June 30, 2018, D can elect to purchase 2,500 shares for $21,250 on the June 30 purchase date, and no more for the remainder of the calendar year.

.08 Offering Period

If the ESPP expresses the stock purchase price as a percentage of the stock's fair market value (at least 85%) at the time of exercise, Code Sec. 423 imposes a maximum offering period (also sometimes referred to as the "purchase period") of five years from the grant date. If the ESPP expresses the stock purchase price in any other manner, such as a flat dollar amount or the lesser of a percentage and a flat dollar amount, the ESPP must require employees to exercise the option within twenty-seven months from the date the plan grants the option.[27] Thus, an ESPP that allows participants to purchase at 85% of the market price of the company's stock on (1) the first day of the semi-annual offering period (the grant date) or (2) the last day of the semi-annual offering period (the exercise date), whichever is less, could not have an offering period in excess of twenty-seven months.

One or more purchase offerings may be made under an ESPP and the offerings may be consecutive or overlapping.[28] The terms of each offering need not be identical. If overlapping offerings are made under an ESPP, then each offering may contain different terms, provided that the terms of each offering (together with the ESPP) satisfy the requirements of Code Sec. 423 and the regulations. When a parent company adopts an ESPP, it may establish separate purchase offerings with different terms under the ESPP and designate which subsidiary companies of the parent may participate in a particular offering.

> **Example:** The ABC Corporation ESPP allows each eligible employee to make an election to purchase ABC common stock at a price equal to 85% of the market price of ABC's stock on (1) the first day of the offering period (the grant date) or (2) the last day of the offering period (the exercise date), whichever is less. The maximum duration of the offering period for this design is twenty-seven months. If ABC wanted to have an offering period of five years, it must design the ESPP to allow each eligible employee to make an election to purchase ABC common stock at a price equal to 85% of the market price of ABC's stock on the last day of the offering period (the exercise date), without the look-back feature.

.09 Transferability

The ESPP must provide that the employee cannot transfer the purchase rights granted to him or her under the ESPP, other than through inheritance. The ESPP must provide that the purchase rights can only be exercisable during the

---

[27] Code Sec. 423(b)(7); Reg. § 1.423-2(h).　　[28] Reg. § 1.423-2(a)(1).

employee's lifetime by the employee. These restrictions on transfer are similar to the restrictions applicable to an ISO.[29]

¶1025 Tax Treatment of the Employee

As with incentive stock options (ISOs), the favorable tax consequences of an employee stock purchase plan accrue mainly to the employee. If the ESPP and the employee satisfy all of the Code's requirements, the company will have received cash from employees as the purchase price, albeit discounted, for the stock, but the company will not receive any tax deductions.

In contrast to a 401(k) plan, employees make payroll deductions and contributions to purchase stock under an ESPP on an after-tax basis. The contributions, although generally made on a payroll reduction basis, are not excluded from an employee's gross income. Rather, the employee is taxed on the entire amount of the payroll deduction as regular compensation.

.01 Tax Treatment at Grant

An employee will not recognize federal income tax upon the grant of a purchase right under an employee stock purchase plan if the ESPP meets the requirements of Code Sec. 423.[30] As with an ISO, if the ESPP does not meet the statutory requirements, the individual will recognize ordinary income on the difference between the fair market value of the stock on the date of grant and the fair market value on the date of purchase. Similarly, if the ESPP allows an individual who is not an employee to participate (or allows a former employee to exercise an option to purchase stock more than three months after terminating employment), the individual would recognize ordinary income on the market value spread at purchase.[31] In general, the rules of Code Sec. 421(a), which result in no recognition of income by the employee, apply to company stock transfers that qualify under Code Sec. 423, and the rules of Code Sec. 421(b), which result in the immediate recognition of income by the employee, apply to disqualifying dispositions.

Additionally, to qualify for nonrecognition treatment, any discount in the stock purchase the ESPP offers to employees must be within the limits of Code Sec. 423(b)(6) (described above).

> **Example:** The ABC Corporation ESPP allows each eligible employee of ABC to make a semi-annual election to contribute a portion of his or her compensation toward the purchase of ABC common stock. The purchase price for participating employees will be 85% of the market price of ABC's stock on (1) the first day of the semi-annual offering period or (2) the last day of the semi-annual offering period, whichever is less.
>
> If ABC's stock is trading at $10.00 per share on January 1, 2018, and at $15.00 per share on June 30, 2018, employees' contributions will be used to purchase stock at $8.50 per share for them on the June 30 exercise date. An

---

[29] Code Sec. 423(b)(9); Reg. § 1.423-2(j).　　[31] Code Sec. 421(a); Code Sec. 423(a).

[30] Code Sec. 421(a)(1).

employee would not recognize any income on the difference between the $8.50 per share he or she paid for the stock on June 30, 2018, and the stock's $15.00 market value on that date.

A 2017 survey indicated that, among plans offering a discount, 70 percent of companies offered a 15 percent discount, with the remaining 30 percent of companies offering either a 5 percent or 10 percent discount.[32]

.02 Tax Treatment at Sale or Other Disposition of the Stock

The tax implications of an employee's disposition of stock depend upon the timing of the disposition. The statutory holding period for ESPP shares is two years after the date of the grant of the option or purchase right, and one year from the date of exercise of the option or purchase right.[33] If the employee disposes of the stock after expiration of the holding period (or after the employee's death), it is considered a qualifying disposition and the employee recognizes ordinary income equal to the lesser of the amount (1) by which the market price of the stock on the purchase right grant date exceeds the exercise price, or (2) the market price on the date of sale exceeds the exercise price,[34] plus any applicable capital gain or loss recognized in the disposition.

If the employee disposes of his or her ESPP stock before the expiration of the holding period, it will be considered a disqualifying disposition and the employee will recognize ordinary income equal to the excess of the stock's fair market value over the exercise price the employee paid,[35] plus any applicable capital gains or losses.

The transfer of a purchase right to an estate by virtue of the employee's death does not result in a disqualifying disposition.[36] Similarly, an estate may exercise a purchase right held by a decedent if the plan provisions specifically authorize such exercise.[37] On the other hand, a transfer by an estate does constitute a disposition triggering the recognition of ordinary income[38] without a corresponding increase in basis.[39]

.03 Determining the "Grant Date" and "Holding Period"

As noted above, the statutory holding period for ESPP shares is two years after the grant date of the purchase right, and one year from the date of exercise or purchase. What constitutes the "grant date" depends on the design of the ESPP. Generally, we think of the grant date as the first day of the offering period. However, for purposes of Code Sec. 423 (as well as the ISO rules of Code Sec. 422), the date of granting of the option "refers to the date or time when the granting company completes the corporate action constituting an offer of stock

---

[32] "Our Updated Survey of Employee Stock Purchase Plans," originally published in the January 2017 issue of the Ayco Compensation & Benefits Digest, The Ayco Company L.P., a Goldman Sachs Company.

[33] Code Sec. 423(a)(1).

[34] Code Sec. 423(c). Notwithstanding the foregoing, if the purchase price is determined on a "look back" basis, the grant date is used even if the

purchase price was calculated using the exercise date.

[35] Reg. § 1.421-6(d).

[36] Code Sec. 421(c)(1)(A) [holding period does not apply].

[37] Code Sec. 421(c)(1).

[38] Code Sec. 421(c)(1)(B).

[39] Code Sec. 421(c)(3); Reg. § 1.423-2(k)(2).

for sale to an individual under the terms and conditions of a statutory option. A corporate action constituting an offer of stock for sale is not considered complete until the date on which the maximum number of shares that can be purchased under the option and the minimum option price are fixed or determinable."[40]

> **Example:** ABC Corporation's ESPP allows participants to elect to reduce their compensation during the offering period by a whole number percentage between one and ten. The ESPP will use the amount withheld to purchase ABC stock at the end of the offering period at 85% of the market price of ABC's stock on (1) the first day of the offering period or (2) the last day of the offering period, whichever is less. Because the number of shares of ABC stock that the participant will purchase will not be known until the purchase date at the end of the offering period, the twenty-four month holding period will not begin until that date.

> If ABC's ESPP allowed participants to purchase ABC stock at the end of the offering period at 85% of the market price of ABC's stock on the first day of the offering period, the number of shares of ABC stock that any participant will purchase generally would be known based on the participant's election and the stock's market price on the offering date, and the twenty-four month holding period would not begin until that date.

However, the IRS has allowed some flexibility in determining the date on which the maximum number of shares can be purchased. The IRS has allowed the holding period to begin under ESPPs that limit the number of shares that any participant may purchase in any offering period, even if a participant's election is well below that limit (and, thus, arguably the number of shares that the participant can purchase is not determinable).[41]

¶1035 Tax Treatment of the Company

From the company's perspective, if an ESPP meets the definition of a qualified plan under Code Sec. 423, there is generally no deduction available for the difference between the option and the exercise price.[42] If the ESPP did not meet the Code Sec. 423 requirements, or an employee engages in a disqualifying disposition, the company would be entitled to a deduction equal to the amount of income recognized by the employee as ordinary income,[43] if the company has complied with the statutory reporting requirements.

.01 Filing Requirements

Code Sec. 6039 requires a company to file an information return with the IRS and provide employees with an information statement, following a stock transfer. The company must furnish employees with the required information state-

---

[40] Reg. § 1.421-1(c)(1).

[41] *See Rev. Rul.* 68-317, 1968-1 C.B. 186, clarified by *Rev. Rul.* 73-223. *But See* PLR 9414042.

[42] Code Sec. 421(a)(2).

[43] Code Sec. 421(b). The amount and timing of the deduction is determined under the rules applicable to Code Sec. 83(h) which actually states that a com-

pany will be entitled to a deduction in its taxable year in which the employee actually recognizes income. Reg. § 1.83-6(a)(2) provides that if a company timely complies with the filing requirements for forms W-2 or 1099, the employee will be deemed to have included that amount in the taxable year reported by the company.

ments on or before January 31 of the year following the year for which the statement is required.

Code Sec. 6039(a) requires every company that transfers stock acquired under an employee stock purchase plan at a discount between 85 percent and 100 percent of the value of the stock to file a return setting forth the information required by IRS regulations (listed below).[44] This return is required only with respect to the first transfer of such stock by the person who exercised the option.[45] The regulations provide that the return and information statement requirements of Code Sec. 6039(a)(2) and (b) also apply to the transfer of shares acquired pursuant to an option where the exercise price is not fixed or determinable on the date of grant, *as well as to* the transfer of shares acquired pursuant to a purchase option where the exercise price is less than 100 percent of the value of a share on the date of grant.

Code Sec. 6039(b) requires every company filing a return under Code Sec. 6039(a)(2) to furnish to each employee named in such return a written statement with respect to the transfer or transfers made to the employee during a particular year. The company must provide the written statement to each employee on or before January 31 of the year following the calendar year for which it filed the return. One of the primary purposes of this requirement is to provide information to employees for purposes of computing their tax liability with respect to the disposition of shares acquired under an ESPP. The statement must include:

 (i) The name, address, and identifying number of the transferor;

 (ii) The name, address and employer identification number of the company whose stock is being transferred;

 (iii) The date the option was granted to the transferor;

 (iv) The fair market value of the stock on the date the option was granted;

 (v) The actual exercise price paid per share;

 (vi) The exercise price per share determined as if the option were exercised on the date the option was granted to the transferor (to be provided only if the exercise price per share is not fixed or determinable on the date the option was granted);

 (vii) The date the option was exercised by the transferor;

 (viii) The fair market value of the stock on the date the option was exercised by the transferor;

 (ix) The date the legal title of the shares was transferred by the transferor; and

 (x) The number of shares to which legal title was transferred by the transferor.[46]

If the exercise price per share of an option is not fixed or determinable on the date the option was granted to the employee, the company must include in the

---

[44] Code Sec. 6039(a)(2).
[45] Code Sec. 6039(c)(2).

[46] Reg. § 1.6039-1(b)(1).

return and information statement the exercise price per share determined as if the option were exercised on the grant date.[47]

The return requirement of Code Sec. 6039(a)(2) is not applicable to the first transfer of legal title of a share of stock by an employee who is a nonresident alien and to whom the company is not required to provide a Form W-2 for any calendar year within the time period beginning with the first day of the calendar year in which the option was granted to the employee and ending on the last day of the calendar year in which the employee first transferred legal title to shares acquired under the option.[48]

Any time a participant transfers ESPP shares, the company is required to provide an IRS Form 3922 to the participant after the calendar year-end. Form 3922 is required whenever a "transfer of legal title" has occurred under Code Sec. 6039.

.02 Other Income Reporting

The American Jobs Creation Act of 2004 (P.L. 108-357) added an express exclusion to the definition of "wages" for FICA purposes for the nontaxable discount on company stock purchased under an employee stock purchase plan. Historically, there had been significant confusion with respect to the ESPP in connection with the required withholding as well as the treatment for purposes of FICA and FUTA employment taxes. The ISO rules had long applied to an ESPP, so that companies were not required to pay FICA or FUTA taxes at either the grant or exercise of a right under a Code Sec. 423 plan or at the time the employee recognized income upon a disqualifying disposition.[49]

Additionally, some states require the reporting and taxation of the ESPP benefit. Any discount on share purchases in a non-qualified ESPP are subject to federal and FICA payroll tax withholding on the purchase date, and reporting on Form W-2.

IRS Publication 15-B, "Employer's Tax Guide to Fringe Benefits" suggests that the company must report income recognized upon a disqualifying disposition on Form W-2.[50] Because of federal income tax requirements, the company may place a legend on any certificates issued to an employee requiring that the employee notify the company if he or she sells shares within two years of the date the employee acquired the shares.

¶1045 Design and Operational Issues

In addition to the statutory provisions listed in ¶1015, employee stock purchase plans typically include certain provisions that reduce administrative complexity and facilitate compliance with the statutory provisions.

---

[47] Reg. § 1.6039-1(b)(vi).

[48] Reg § 1.6039-1(e).

[49] Rev. Rul. 71-52, 1971-1 CB 278; IRS Letter Ruling 8225050 (March 23, 1982); IRS Letter Ruling 8351020 (Sept. 13, 1983).

[50] "Employer's Tax Guide to Fringe Benefits," page 12, https://www.irs.gov/pub/irs-pdf/p15b.pdf

.01 Business Issues

An increase in the aggregate number of shares that the plan may issue would require shareholder approval. Similarly, a change in the company sponsoring the plan would be considered a new plan, requiring renewed shareholder approval.[51] Therefore, an ESPP should include broad provisions regarding certain business decisions affecting the ESPP, to reduce the possibility that the company will need to amend the plan and again seek shareholder approval. In that the shareholder approval is limited to the two categories of information—the pool of shares and participating entities—experienced legal counsel can design a plan to minimize the approval requirement using proactive provisions to anticipate the potential, and future, modifications that may be required under the program. Although not all modifications trigger the shareholder approval process, experienced legal counsel should review any change from the perspective of this statutory requirement.

.02 Participating Companies and Class of Stock

As with incentive stock options under Code Sec. 422, the stock offered under an ESPP must be the capital stock of the company or any company in the parent-subsidiary chain. The stock may be of any class, common or preferred, voting or nonvoting, treasury stock, or a special class authorized solely for employees. The valuation problems associated with special classes of stock within a closely held company when used in connection with an ISO, however, also apply in the context of the ESPP.

As noted above, the company must make the ESPP available to all employees of the company, with limited exceptions. This provision can create problems when the company has employees working for it (not for a foreign subsidiary) who reside in a foreign country, the laws of which make participation impractical. An ESPP can extend eligibility to employees of subsidiaries of the sponsoring company.

.03 Authorized Shares

Evergreen provisions that automatically increase the aggregate number of shares available under the plan on an annual basis and/or provisions adjusting the aggregate number of shares upon a stock split or stock dividend will eliminate the need to obtain shareholder approval as the aggregate pool of shares is adjusted. Similarly, using categories of entities, as opposed to specific names of companies, will accommodate the merger or acquisition activity of a parent, and permit the company to make the plan available to employees of newly acquired subsidiaries without triggering shareholder approval.

.04 Plan Administration

Most employee stock purchase plans provide that the company's board of directors, an existing benefit plan committee, or a new committee the board appoints will administer the ESPP. The plan administrator has the authority to

---

[51] Reg. § 1.423-2(c)(4).

interpret the ESPP and to establish rules and regulations. Additionally, nearly every company that establishes an ESPP will retain a third-party administrator, such as a bank or brokerage firm, to handle participants' accounts and stock transactions.

.05 Handling Employee Payroll Deductions

Code Sec. 423 does not expressly provide for employee payroll deductions. However, nearly all ESPPs contain such provisions. Unlike a 401(k) plan, employees make payroll deductions and contributions to purchase stock under an ESPP on an after-tax basis. The tax advantage of an ESPP is the deferral of the recognition of taxable gain on the difference between the option price and the market value of the stock on the date of exercise.

Code Sec. 423 also does not provide any requirements for the handling of employees' payroll deductions. The company may set aside the contributed amount each pay period in an interest-bearing or other account, or simply treat the amount as part of general assets. Some companies credit employees' contributions to a daily access money market fund maintained by a third-party administrator in the employee's name. These amounts would then earn interest at the rate earned by the money market fund. The company then may use the interest amounts to purchase additional shares of company stock. For federal income tax purposes, the interest credited to an employee's account would be considered ordinary income and would be taxed to the employee each year.

When the company uses a third party administrator, the third party administrator would allocate to a brokerage account established in the employee's name the number of shares of stock purchased from the company on the last business day of the purchase period. The employee could leave his or her share in the brokerage account, sell them within the brokerage account, or take a distribution of share certificates. In most cases, the employee would not necessarily need to close his or her brokerage account if the employee left the company.

> **Planning Note:** Companies generally cover the custody costs of employees' brokerage accounts. Some companies will use the short-term investment earnings from contributions held in employees' accounts to defray these costs. Most companies would require the employee to pay the brokerage costs of selling the company stock from the account.

In most cases, a third-party administrator will hold the company stock purchased by the employee under the ESPP in an account in the employee's name. The company would not actually issue stock certificates for the shares the employee owns unless the employee requests it, for which the TPA generally will charge a fee.

The company would not issue certificates for fractional interests in shares. Fractional interests in shares may be paid to the employee in cash if the employee so requests or may be accumulated in the employee's account until they equal one whole share, for which the employee may elect to receive a stock certificate.

.06 Stock Ownership

As a result of owning company stock purchased under the ESPP, the employee should automatically receive the annual report, quarterly reports, proxy materials and any other materials the company issues for the benefit and information of its stockholders. The employee will be entitled to vote the company stock in accordance with the employee's written proxy instructions, or otherwise in accordance with the applicable rules of the Securities and Exchange Commission. If the company pays dividends on its stock, an employee holding stock purchased under the ESPP will automatically receive dividends.

Generally, there are no limitations on the sale of an employee's stock purchased under the ESPP. Although companies usually intend an ESPP to provide the employee with an ownership interest in the company as an investment, most companies permit employees to sell purchased stock at any time the employee chooses.

.07 Changes in Payroll Deduction and Purchase Election

Some companies will draft their ESPP to allow employees to change or stop their payroll deduction at any time before the end of the purchase period. However, most ESPPs provide that an employee can increase or decrease his or her percentage deduction only at the beginning of a purchase period. ESPPs also typically provide that if an employee stops contributions in mid-period, the employee will not be able to participate in the ESPP before the beginning of the next purchase period, and must complete a new payroll deduction authorization form.

.08 Employment Termination

Most companies' employee stock purchase plans provide that if the employee/participant terminates employment for any reason before the end of a purchase period, all payroll deductions not already used to purchase company stock will be refunded to the employee (or to the employee's estate). Some plans allow the employee to elect to have his or her accumulated contributions used to purchase stock in the current purchase period, as long as the purchase will occur within three months of the employee's termination.

.09 Other Design Issues

In addition, the inclusion of provisions pertaining to the operation of the plan in the event of a merger or acquisition, including but not limited to the expansion of the program to additional employee groups, may reduce requirements to amend the plan to accommodate the revised business structure, thereby avoiding potential shareholder approval or accounting issues.

Similarly, an integration provision may address any potential conflict between the rights described in the ESPP and other compensation-based agreements, such as employment or severance contracts.

While many of the provisions are designed for flexibility, the company also must consider whether the language or operation of a provision may inadvertently give rise to other issues. A six-month "look back" price feature[52] may meet the Code Sec. 423 requirements; however, it may also affect the accounting treatment resulting in the plan being categorized as compensatory. The issue is whether the potential for large discounts would violate the requirement that the discount not be greater than that available to others.

Other helpful design features include the following:

1. A company sponsoring an ESPP should consider prohibiting participants from increasing their contribution rates at any point during the offering period. Increases in contribution rates are subject to modification accounting, which results in additional accounting expense.

2. The ESPP sponsor should consider prohibiting decreases in contribution rates and withdrawals. Decreases in either contribution rates or withdrawals from the plan can be costly to administer.

3. Sponsors should consider maintaining strict contribution limits. By controlling contributions to the plan, the company can more accurately forecast plan expense. This is because any changes in the purchase price are accompanied by a proportionate change in the number of shares employees can purchase, resulting in the same overall expense.

4. Sponsors should consider imposing eligibility restrictions, including a prohibition against highly compensated employees,[53] employees in foreign subsidiaries[54] and employees who receive other stock awards.

5. Consider allowing purchases only from salary - or from salary and bonus only. If participants are allowed to make purchases with other types of compensation, it could be difficult to predict plan expense.

6. Consider eliminating the "automatic reset" provision. Some ESPPs that have multiple purchases within a single offering period include a "reset" provision that automatically withdraws and reenrolls all participants in a new offering period at a lower price when the fair market value of the company's stock has declined during the period. Automatic resets are subject to modification accounting under ASC 718, producing additional incremental cost.

7. Consider shorter offering periods with more frequent purchases. Longer offering periods can be very beneficial to employees, but very costly in terms of ASC 718 expense, since most of the expense is attributable to the look-back over this period. Shortening the offering period can have a greater impact on per-share fair value than reducing the discount or other changes.

---

[52] Such a feature gives the employee the right to purchase shares at 85% of the lesser of fair market value on the first or last day of a six (6) month period. A variation of the "look-back" provisions can provide that the fair market value is determined

as the lesser amount on the date of grant or the date of exercise.

[53] Code Sec. 423(b)(4).

[54] ESPPs generally don't receive preferential tax treatment abroad and the plan may be subject to costly local compliance regulations.

.10 Excess Contributions

Excess contributions invariably occur under an ESPP. Three factors can cause "excess" contributions or payroll withholdings:

- **Fractional shares.** Each participant's contribution election almost certainly will result in a dollar amount insufficient to purchase a whole number of shares. Thus, an ESPP should have provisions that specify whether it will purchase and hold fractional shares. Some ESPPs will hold fractional shares in participants' accounts.

- **Contributions that exceed the $25,000 limitation.** These contributions or payroll withholdings simply cannot be used to purchase stock under the ESPP for that offering period.

- **Contributions that exceed the fixed share limitation (used to set the "date of grant" and beginning of the holding period).** As discussed in ¶ 1025.03 above, some plans will set the number of shares that may be purchased based on the participant's contribution election and the market price of the stock on the first day of the purchase period. If the stock price declines during the offering period, the company will have withheld more dollars from the participant's payroll than can be used to purchase stock for that offering period.

In each case, the ESPP should specify what it will do with the leftover cash - the payroll withholdings that are in excess of what can be used to purchase stock - unless the ESPP will hold fractional shares in participants' accounts. Will the ESPP refund the amounts or hold them and apply them toward the purchase of shares in the next purchase periods?

¶ 1055 Advantages of an ESPP

While many companies utilize nonqualified and incentive stock options in equity-based compensation arrangements for managerial and executive categories of employees, the culture of the company may also dictate a broad-based program designed to provide such equity opportunities to all members of the workforce, not merely senior management. Such company-sponsored programs are not limited to high-tech or start-up ventures but can be implemented in a large variety of business enterprises. An ESPP can be an alternative to an incentive stock option ("ISO") plan, which also provides favorable tax treatment for employees.[55]

Both the ISO as well as the ESPP are considered qualified plans; the former subject to Code Sec. 422, the latter to Code Sec. 423. An ISO plan is distinguished from an ESPP in that the company must make the ESPP available to a broad base of employees, while an ISO plan has no minimum participation requirements. To minimize administrative costs, however, ESPPs utilize payroll deductions to enable employees to purchase stock at a discount pursuant to purchase rights granted under the plan, which are similar to options.[56]

---

[55] See ¶ 1025 for a discussion of the tax implications for employees.

[56] Unlike the ISO, which requires 100% "purchase price," the ESPP can offer purchase rights at the

Generally, a company designs its ESPP to provide equity incentives for all employees but it is not treated as a compensatory plan for accounting purposes.[57] Compensatory plans require that the company recognize compensation expense upon the grant of a purchase right or an issuance of stock. Stock issued in connection with a noncompensatory plan is treated for accounting purposes as any other sale of stock transaction.[58] However, unlike an ESPP, most stock plans do not meet the requirements to be treated as a noncompensatory plan, which include (1) an issuance of stock; (2) available to all employees, with limited exceptions; (3) grants made on a uniform basis; (4) a discount no greater than if made to shareholders, generally 85% of fair market value; and (5) a limited exercise period, generally five or less years.

An ESPP is not subject to ERISA; that is, there are no reporting requirements and no need for a summary plan description.[59]

An ESPP is beneficial to a company for several reasons. Because the financial rewards of the company's earnings belong to its stockholders in direct proportion to their stockholdings, employees who become stockholders of the company under an ESPP will likely be more motivated to see the company succeed. This should have a positive effect on productivity. Additionally, the plan provides a source of "market demand" for the stock. If the plan provides for the purchase of newly issued shares, the company will be able to raise additional capital without incurring the substantial cost normally associated with a public offering.

.01 Disadvantages

There are several disadvantages to an ESPP. Shareholders of the company must approve the plan, a process that can be costly to the company. In general, the plan permits employees to exercise stock options without recognizing any income until the time of disposition of the option stock. As a result, the company cannot take a current deduction at the time of the exercise of the option. Instead, the company must wait until the employee disposes of the ESPP stock. In addition, although the plan is a nontax-qualified plan, the company cannot discriminate in favor of highly compensated employees. Finally, another disadvantage of an ESPP is that the company generally must register the options issued under an ESPP under the federal and state securities laws.

¶1065 Accounting Treatment

The accounting rules regarding share-based compensation plans and stock purchase plans create the potential for significant expenses. ASC 718 generally categorizes plans that provide equity-based compensation as either compensatory or noncompensatory. Compensatory plans require that the plan sponsor recognize compensation expense while plans that meet the requirements for a

---

(Footnote Continued)

lesser of 85% of fair market value at the time of grant or 85% of the fair market value at the time of purchase.

[57] See ¶1035 for a discussion of the tax implications for companies.

[58] See ¶1065 for a discussion of the accounting treatment for companies.

[59] See generally DOL Advisory Opinion 77-23 (February 14, 1977).

noncompensatory plan do not require a charge to earnings. Until 2005, Code Sec. 423 plans could be deemed "noncompensatory" for financial accounting purposes under an exception for "broad-based employee stock purchase plans," contained in APB Opinion No. 25, Accounting for Stock Issued to Employees.[60] A Code Sec. 423 plan could qualify for this exception if: (1) the stock options issued under the plan are available to substantially all full-time employees equally or based on a uniform percentage of pay; (2) the plan limits the time period for the exercise of the option or purchase right; and (3) stock is offered at no more than a reasonable discount.

.01 The Impact of FAS 123R

The promulgation of Statement of Accounting Standards No. 123 (revised 2004), Share Based Payments (referred to as "FAS 123R"), reduced the attractiveness of employee stock purchase plans. FASB updated and replaced FAS 123R with ASC 718 in 2014. Under ASC 718, an ESPP plan can only be considered noncompensatory if it meets the following requirements:

1. The plan cannot incorporate any option-like features. The common option-like feature that is prohibited under this requirement is a "lookback" provision, under which the purchase price is based on the lower of the market value of the stock on the enrollment date or the purchase date.

2. Where the terms of the plan are more favorable than those available to all shareholders, any discount offered under the plan must be equal to or less than the company's costs of raising capital through a public offering. A safe-harbor discount of 5% is allowed without further justification, but companies wishing to offer a higher discount must offer either that same discount to all shareholders or demonstrate that their costs of undergoing a public offering would be greater.

3. The plan must permit substantially all employees to participate on an equal basis.

Thus, many ESPPs that were considered noncompensatory under APB Opinion No. 25 are considered compensatory under ASC 718. The stock purchase rights given to employees are treated as stock options, which produce an accounting expense. The stock options are deemed granted on the enrollment date and exercised on the purchase date.

Companies have been using certain design strategies to reduce the accounting expense charge attributable to ESPPs. These strategies include, for example,

---

[60] Historically, APB Opinion No. 25 ("APB 25") provided guidance on the generally accepted methods of accounting for compensatory stock-based compensation awards. The compensation expense to be recognized was the difference between the fair market value of the stock and the exercise price on the measurement date. The measurement date is the date upon which the number of shares awarded and the purchase price of those shares can be identified. The measurement date concept includes fixed and variable plan accounting. If the number of shares and corresponding price per share are known at the grant date, the measurement date is the grant date and the accounting treatment is considered fixed, meaning there are no subsequent adjustments. Most stock option programs are fixed plans. If the measurement date does not occur on the date of grant because the number of shares or purchase price or cash payment cannot be determined at that date, the plan would be considered a variable plan.

eliminating the look-back period and shortening the offering period and eliminating multiple purchase options in an offering period.[61] Before 2005, the typical ESPP would grant each eligible employee an option to buy company stock on the last business day of a six-month purchase period at a purchase price that is 85% of the average market price of the company's stock on either the first or last business day of the purchase period, whichever is less. The typical ESPP now grants each eligible employee an option to buy company stock on the last business day of a six-month purchase period at a purchase price that is 95% or 100% of the market price of the company's stock on the last business day of the purchase period.

The original version of FAS 123 had provided a choice for Code Sec. 423 plan sponsors that would result in the recognition of compensation expense upon grant. FAS 123 changed the limitations that determine whether a Code Sec. 423 plan will be deemed noncompensatory for financial accounting purposes. FAS 123 created a safe harbor for determining whether the ESPP is offering stock at no more than a "reasonable discount." FAS 123 provided that if the purchase discount is 5 % or less, the Code Sec. 423 plan will be deemed noncompensatory for financial accounting purposes. FAS 123 also would treat Code Sec. 423 plans with a look-back option as compensatory.

Thus, Code Sec. 423 plans offering a purchase discount in excess of 5%—which most did, because the Code permits a discount of up to 15%—could create a compensation expense for the company. A discount in excess of 5% still could be deemed noncompensatory if the plan sponsor could demonstrate that the amount of the discount does not exceed the greater of: (1) a per-share discount that would be reasonable in an offer of stock to stockholders or other; or (2) the "per-share amount of stock issuance costs avoided" by not having to raise a significant amount of capital in a public offering. If the plan sponsor could not make this showing, the amount of compensation expense attributable to the Code Sec. 423 plan would be the amount by which the per-share discount exceeds 5%.

However, certain triggering events may result in the recognition of compensation expense. If the company delays shareholder approval, it may be required to reflect a compensation expense for the period of delay. Similarly, FASB imposes a requirement for compensation expense if the reserve is not sufficient for an offering and subsequent, shareholder-approved, additional shares use the original purchase price.[62] Optional language in the plan such as evergreen provisions or other limitations can alleviate these issues for many companies.

---

[61] Where a plan allows for multiple purchases during a single offering, each individual purchase is valued as a separate option. For example, a 24-month offering that provides for four purchases to occur at six-month intervals throughout the offering is treated as four options (a six-month option, a 12-month option, an 18-month option, and a 24-month option), with a separate fair value computed for each option.

[62] EITF Issue No. 97-12 (Sept. 18, 1997) requiring compensation expense equal to the difference between the fair market value on the date of purchase and the purchase price if the price is less than 85% of fair market value on the date of the approval of the additional shares.

.02 Companies' Reactions to ASC 718

Despite the accounting treatment of ASC 718, companies have enunciated several reasons for keeping their ESPPs, including:[63]

- Many companies remain convinced that broad-based equity plans tend to improve employees' performance, thus improving the company's performance.

- ESPP purchases provide cash flow and capital for the company.

- Employees "self-select" participation in the ESPP, so the company can be confident it has spent the expense on the "right people."

- The ASC 718 expense is still less than other vehicles, such as stock options, that provide for broad-based stock ownership among employees. Many companies have reduced the number of employees to whom they award stock options, so the ESPP remains the only vehicle for creating broad-based stock ownership.

However, as a concession to the ASC 718 expense, ESPPs tend to be less generous in terms of discount and look-back than before ASC 718. The most common changes made by companies to their ESPPs were to eliminate the look back feature, followed by reduction of the discount on the stock purchase price.

¶1075 Federal Securities Law Issues

The Securities Act of 1933 requires a company to register offers or sales of its securities to employees under an employee stock purchase plan. Any offer or sale of a plan sponsor's securities not made under an effective registration statement would be considered a violation of the Securities Act, absent an available exemption. A company that offers or sells unregistered securities under the company's employee benefit plans may be subject to civil liability under both federal and state securities laws, as well as enforcement actions by both the SEC and state regulators.

.01 Registration Statement on Form S-8

Typically, a registration statement covering an ESPP is prepared on Form S-8. The Form S-8 Registration Statement is relatively simple, and includes the following information:

- the incorporation of certain documents by reference (*i.e.*, the company's latest annual report on Form 10-K, other reports filed since the end of the last fiscal year, all documents filed subsequently pursuant to Sections 13(a), 13(c), 14 or 15(d) of the Exchange Act and the description of the company's common stock);

- interests of named experts and counsel;

- a description of director and officer indemnification;

---

[63] As reported in Equilar newsletter February 16, 2006.

- a description of the specific exemption from registration for any restricted securities to be reoffered or resold pursuant to the registration statement;
- exhibits; and
- certain undertakings.

Registration on Form S-8 requires the company to pay a filing fee that varies with the aggregate offering price (*e.g.*, fair market value) for the maximum amount of securities registered.[64] The company also must give plan participants all communications that go to shareholders (*e.g.*, annual reports, proxy statements).

.02 Section 10(a) Prospectus

In addition to filing a Form S-8 Registration Statement, an effective registration requires that a company deliver to each participant in the employee stock purchase plan documents and information constituting a prospectus that meets the requirements of Section 10(a) of the Securities Act. The company must keep the information contained in the prospectus current, whether by supplements or restatements. The prospectus documents and information generally consist of:

- a statement of general information that summarizes: (1) general plan information; (2) the securities to be offered; (3) plan participants; (4) purchase procedures; (5) resale restrictions on the securities offered; (6) the material federal tax consequences of an investment in the securities offered; (7) the terms and conditions under which an employee may withdraw from the plan or withdraw funds or investments from the employee's account; (8) any event under the plan that could result in a forfeiture by or a penalty to an employee and the consequences thereof; (9) any charges and deductions that may be made against employees participating in the plan or against funds, securities or other property held under the plan; and (10) whether any person has or may create a lien on any funds, securities or other property held under the plan;

- the documents that are incorporated by reference into the Form S-8 Registration Statement, including the company's annual report filed on Form 10-K, the plan's latest annual report (if interests in the plan are being registered), and any other company reports filed pursuant to Section 13(a) or 15(d) of the Exchange Act since the end of the fiscal year covered by the company's annual report; and

- a statement of the availability, without charge, of documents filed by the plan sponsor under the Exchange Act and incorporated by reference into the prospectus or otherwise required to be delivered to plan participants.

Unlike some other types of prospectuses, the company does not need to file the prospectus material used in connection with an ESPP with the SEC. However, the company must retain the documents constituting a part of the prospec-

---

[64] If the registration statement also covers participation interests in the plan that constitute separate securities, no separate fee is required with respect to the plan interests. See Rule 457(h)(2) of the Securities Act of 1933.

tus. A registration statement on Form S-8 and any post-effective amendment become effective immediately upon filing with the SEC. Upon filing, the documents become publicly available.

.03 Section 16 Reporting and Short-Swing Trading Liability

The regulations under Section 16(b) of the Securities Exchange Act of 1934 (the "Act") provide, "Any transaction (other than a Discretionary Transaction) pursuant to a Qualified Plan, an Excess Benefit Plan, or a Stock Purchase Plan shall be exempt without condition [from Section 16(b) of the Act.]"[65] Further, a "Stock Purchase Plan shall mean an employee benefit plan that satisfies the coverage and participation requirements of sections 423(b)(3) and 423(b)(5), or section 410, of the Internal Revenue Code of 1986 . . . ."[66] Therefore, ESPPs are exempt from Section 16(b) of the Act.

The regulations under 16(b) of the Act go on to state that "Section 16(a) reporting requirements applicable to transactions exempt pursuant to this section are set forth in § 240.16a-3(f) and (g) . . . ."[67] Since ESPPs are exempt from Section 16(b) of the Act pursuant to Section 240.16b-3(c), ESPPs are exempt from Section 16(a) of the Act and exempt from the Form 4 filing requirements.

Finally, if the ESPP purchases shares directly from the company, rather than on the open market, the purchase should be exempt from insider trading under Rule 10b-5, even if the employee purchases while in possession of material nonpublic information.

¶1085 Non-qualifying Stock Purchase Plans

Some companies are willing to forego the favorable tax treatment of Code Sec. 423 in order to create and implement an employee stock purchase plan that achieves other objectives. Some of the reasons for creating a nonqualified employee stock purchase plan are as follows:

- A company may wish to offer the stock at a greater discount;
- The company may wish to limit eligibility to purchase stock to certain employees;
- The company may wish to give directors or consultants the ability to purchase stock;
- The company may need to incorporate certain provisions that would not satisfy Code Sec. 423, but are required by the law of a foreign country; and
- Code Sec. 423 and final regulations thereunder.[68]

Among companies offering some form of stock purchase plan in 2017, 75 percent offered an ESPP qualified under Code Sec. 423.[69] The remaining offered a non-qualifying purchase plan or a direct purchase plan.

---

[65] 17 C.F.R. § 240.16b-3(c).
[66] 17 C.F.R. § 240.16b-3(b)(5).
[67] 17 C.F.R. § 240.16b-3(b)(5), note 2.

[68] 26 CFR 1.423-2; Amendment of final regulations—Employee stock purchase plan defined, (Jan. 01, 1979), T.D. 7645, 1979-2 CB 198.
[69] "Our Updated Survey of Employee Stock Purchase Plans," originally published in the January 2017 issue of the Ayco Compensation & Benefits

Some companies implement a non-qualifying ESPP for their non-U.S. employees, which roughly mirrors their qualifying ESPP for U.S. employees, but is flexible enough to qualify under local laws.

Digest, The Ayco Company L.P., a Goldman Sachs Company.

¶1085

Chapter 11
COMPANY LOANS TO EXECUTIVES

¶1101 Introduction—Company Loans to Executives

Companies make loans to executives, and executives seek loans from companies for many reasons, including for the purchase of company stock or a new home, relocation to the company's headquarters or other location, or simply as an advance payment of compensation. The Internal Revenue Code will treat certain loans to executives (and other employees) as compensation, generally where the interest rate and/or other loan terms are less than market rate or the parties otherwise evidence little intention to actually make a loan.

.01 Executive Loan and Stock Purchase Programs

Investors, companies and compensation professionals nearly all agree that one of the best ways to link an executive's interests to those of the company's stockholders is by making the executive a significant stockholder. Stock options and other forms of executive stock-based compensation help make the executive a stockholder, but often do not require the executive to spend any of his or her own money to purchase the stock. Companies believe that executive stock purchase programs send a message to investors that executive leadership is committed to the company's future success. Under an executive loan and stock purchase program the executive is borrowing money to buy company stock (see ¶1115 for a more detailed discussion of executive loan and stock purchase programs).

.02 Sarbanes-Oxley Act of 2002

Before the Sarbanes-Oxley Act of 2002 ("SOX"),[1] executive loan and stock purchase programs were relatively new and companies' interest in them was increasing significantly. Section 402 of the Sarbanes-Oxley Act prohibits publicly traded companies from directly (including through a subsidiary) extending or maintaining credit, arranging for the extension of credit, or renewing an existing extension of credit, in the form of a personal loan, to or for any director or executive officer of the company.

Executive loan and stock purchase programs were not limited to public companies. However, among the well-known public companies that had implemented an executive loan and stock purchase program were: Allegiance Healthcare; Baxter International Inc.; Budget Group, Inc.; Comdisco; Conseco, Inc.; CSX Corporation; Herman Miller, Inc.; Illinois Tool Works Inc.; Jostens Inc.; Monsanto Company; and W.W. Grainger, Inc.

In March 2013, the SEC issued a no action letter describing the extent to which a company may permit its directors and officers to participate in a plan

---

[1] Pub. L. No. 107-204, 107th Cong., 2d Sess., 2002.

without the company being deemed to "extend or maintain credit" in the form of a personal loan. In this private letter ruling the SEC also indicated that public companies may provide a type of equity-based financing to employees through a loan program without violating SOX Section 402 (see ¶ 1125 for a more detailed discussion of the Sarbanes-Oxley Act of 2002 and SEC's guidance on equity-based financing through loan programs).

.03 Other Loans to Executives

In addition to company stock purchases, executives seek loans from companies, and companies make loans to executives, for reasons such as the purchase of a new home or second home, for relocation expenses to the company's headquarters or another location, and other reasons. Some companies and executives attempt to pass off compensation advances, signing bonuses or other payments as *bona fide* loans (see ¶ 1135 for a more detailed discussion of other types of loans to executives and the tax consequences of each).

.04 "Loans" Treated as Compensation Advances

The IRS has expressed its view that certain payments made by a company to an employee, which the parties attempt to characterize as loans, are immediately taxable as "up-front payments" of compensation. The IRS has found these up-front payments occur when the company and the employee simultaneously enter into two contracts: a "bonus agreement" and a "promissory note" (see ¶ 1145 for a more detailed discussion of "loans" treated as compensation advances).

.05 Special Rules for Loans to Executives at Financial Institutions

Special rules apply to loans by banks to their executive officers, directors, and principal shareholders (see ¶ 1155 for a more detailed discussion).

¶1115 Executive Loan and Stock Purchase Program

Under an executive loan and stock purchase program the company arranges the opportunity for eligible executives to obtain a loan to fund the purchase of company stock. Some companies have established such a program and have themselves loaned the funds to the executives. An executive may elect to pay cash for the company stock using his or her own resources. However, most companies arrange for loans to the executives through a specified bank. Once the bank makes the loan, the executive is obligated to repay to the bank principal and interest when due.

.01 Program Objectives

Executive stock purchase programs send a clear message to investors that the management team and executive leadership is confident in the company's future. These programs also help executives meet the executive stock ownership requirements that many companies have adopted or recommended. Companies implementing an executive loan and stock purchase program seek to:

- Encourage senior managers to act more like owners;
- Further align the interests of management with those of the stockholders;

- Encourage stock ownership among senior management; and
- Assist executives in meeting stock ownership guidelines.

.02 Program Mechanics and Participation

The company will arrange the opportunity for each executive to obtain a loan through a specified bank (or syndicate of banks agented by one bank) to fund the purchase of company stock. Each executive must sign a "letter of direction" that directs all loan proceeds to be payable directly to the company in payment for the purchased stock. Each executive is responsible for satisfying all of the lending requirements specified by the bank to qualify for the loan. Each executive is fully obligated to repay to the bank principal and interest (and any prepayment or other fees, if applicable) when due and payable.

Companies generally issue the stock purchased by executives under the program from treasury stock. Most companies issue a certificate of the purchased stock and register the stock in the name of the executive. The certificates will bear a legend referring to the program and the restrictions that apply to the stock. Generally, either the bank or the company hold the certificates for the purchased stock until the pledge and any other restrictions have lapsed. The executive must deliver to the bank (or the company) a stock power endorsed in blank with respect to the purchased stock.

In our experience, companies do not require executives to participate in its executive loan/stock purchase program, even when the executives are below the company's stock ownership requirements. However, executives may feel a certain amount of peer pressure to participate in the executive loan/stock purchase program, even if participation is strictly voluntary.

.03 Company Guarantee of the Loans

Most banks will not lend executives the amounts of money necessary for significant company stock purchases using only the company stock as collateral. Most banks, furthermore, will not participate in an executive loan/stock purchase program arranged by a company without the company guaranteeing the executives' repayment of the loans. Occasionally, however, some banks will make stock purchase loans to very well-heeled executives of companies whose stock price and financial condition are beyond question.

.04 Regulation U

Regulation U of the Federal Reserve Board[2] contains a potential trap for banks and companies making loans to executives to purchase stock. Regulation U applies to a bank or nonbank lender that makes a "purpose credit loan" that is secured, directly or indirectly, by "margin stock." Regulation U provides that a lender cannot make a purpose credit loan secured directly or indirectly by margin stock unless it has "adequate collateral coverage." Under Regulation U:

- "Adequate collateral coverage" means securities of a value equal to twice the amount of the loan.

---

[2] 12 C.F.R. § 221.1 (2005).

- "Purpose credit" means any credit extended for the purpose, whether immediate, incidental or ultimate, of buying or carrying margin stock.

- "Margin stock" is any equity security registered on a national securities exchange or market system (*i.e.*, publicly traded securities), any debt security convertible into a margin stock, and includes most mutual fund shares.

Regulation U would apply to a company, if they (1) loaned money to the executive, or (2) guaranteed repayment of the bank's loan to the executive and had a direct or indirect security interest in the margin stock. Generally, Regulation U would prevent the company from holding or restricting the securities of an executive to protect itself from liability under the guarantee to the bank. Regulation U also requires a filing by the lender and the executive.

Regulation U provides an exception for certain company-sponsored stockholder-approved plans. An "eligible plan" under this exception is any employee stock option, purchase or ownership plan adopted by a company and approved by its stockholders. Regulation U does not apply to a company that extends credit to finance the acquisition of margin stock of the company or its affiliates under an eligible plan.

.05 Executives' Repayments of the Loans

Most companies arrange with the banks for executives to make only minimal repayments in the early years of the loan with a large balloon payment due at the end of the fifth year. Internal Revenue Code regulations provide that the payment of both principal and interest may be made in arrears at the end of a repayment schedule of up to five years. To avoid ordinary income to executives, the executives must repay the loans over a definite period and interest must accrue at least annually.

This balloon payment arrangement causes increased risk and concern to both the bank and the company that an executive will be unable to repay the loan. For this reason, some companies consciously schedule loan repayments to coincide with the payment date for cash bonuses under the company's annual or long-term incentive bonus plan.

Executives may be able to deduct their interest payments on the loan as interest on investment indebtedness. An executive's deduction for interest on investment indebtedness is limited to their net investment income.

.06 Sale, Transfer, Pledge or Other Disposition of the Purchased Stock

Generally, an executive may not sell, transfer, pledge or otherwise dispose of the purchased stock until the stock has been released from security for the loan. The pledge and security agreement may, however, permit the executive to sell stock still subject to pledge as long as the sale proceeds are paid directly to the bank, subject to federal securities law restrictions (*e.g.*, the prohibition against sale when the executive has material nonpublic information). The pledge and security agreement may also permit the executive to use purchased stock for an "attestation" form of cashless option exercise.

.07 Employment Termination Before Repaying the Loan

To protect the company, most executive loan/stock purchase programs provide that if an executive terminates employment with the company for any reason (including death, disability or retirement) *before* he or she has fully repaid the loan, the full amount of the loan will become immediately due and payable.

.08 What If the Executive Cannot Continue Loan Repayments?

Even if the company were to guarantee the loans from the bank to the executives, the bank would generally be required to proceed first against the executive. If the value of the purchase stock pledged as collateral (and any other collateral pledged by the executive) was less than the amount of principal and interest payments due the bank, and the executive had no other assets, the company would be liable for such repayments. (This (1) assumes the company has guaranteed the loans and (2) depends on the nature and extent of such guarantee.) The company would then have the right to take any action against the executive or the executive's assets the company deems reasonable or necessary to obtain reimbursement for amounts it paid to the bank.

.09 Effect of the Company's Insolvency

Because the loan is between the bank and the executive, the executive would remain liable for principal and interest repayments even if (1) the company became insolvent; (2) its stock declined in value; or (3) its stock became worthless. The company would not be in a position to forgive the loan or otherwise waive repayment.

All investments in securities involve risk. Securities may lose part or even all of their value. Company stock is no exception. The numerous corporate bankruptcies of 2001 and 2002, following the burst of the 1990s bubble, further illustrate the risks of an executive concentrating his or her investments, or over weighting, in any one security—no matter how successful the company behind that security seems.

> **Planning Note:** Most financial planning professionals would advise an executive not to put his or her retirement "eggs" in the same basket as his or her current employment "eggs." When communicating an executive stock purchase program, the company should make no recommendations to purchase or optimistic statements regarding the company's future. For every executive loan and stock purchase program success story like Baxter International and W.W. Grainger, there were failures, such as Comdisco and Conseco, Inc.[3]

---

[3] In the years preceding their bankruptcy filings, Comdisco arranged for loans to 106 managers totalling approximately $109 million and Conseco executives borrowed more than $162 million to purchase company stock.

.10 Effect of the Sale or Merger of the Company

Generally, the executive loans would require full and immediate payment if the company's stock ceased to be publicly traded. The loan agreements also would permit the executive to (1) substitute a new security, acceptable to the bank (*e.g.*, that of the surviving company in a merger), for the company stock pledged as security for the loan, and (2) sell his or her stock in connection with an acquisition, provided the proceeds are applied to repayment of the loan.

.11 Participating Executive's Rights as a Stockholder

During the period in which the purchased stock is subject to restrictions on transfer, each executive will have all of the rights of a stockholder with respect to the stock, including the rights to vote the stock and receive dividends paid on the stock. In some cases, the loan agreements with the bank may require the company to deliver all dividends directly to the bank for payment of principal or interest on the loans. In this situation, the company would pay out to the executive any dividends that exceed the required principal or interest payments on the loans, or deposit such dividends in an account maintained on the executive's behalf at the bank. Dividends would continue to be taxable to the executive as investment income.

> **Caution:** Where a company has historically paid dividends on its stock, neither the company nor the executive should assume that the company will continue to pay dividends. The company itself should take care to communicate to executives considering participation in the program that the company's board of directors determines the payment of dividends, in its sole discretion. A company that has historically paid dividends on its stock, and expects to continue doing so, could add something like: "However, at this time, the company has no reason to believe that dividends will be eliminated."

.12 Communicating the Program

The sale of treasury stock to executives would be a "sale of securities" for federal securities law purposes. Accordingly, a company implementing an executive loan and stock purchase program must offer to sell the securities by preparing and distributing a formal prospectus. Most companies also prepare and distribute a detailed description of their program.

> **Planning Note:** The program summary prepared by counsel for the board's compensation committee can often be adapted to satisfy the securities law prospectus requirement, inasmuch as that summary should cover virtually all of the issues relevant to executives.

.13 Additional Securities Law Considerations

An executive loan and stock purchase program does not require stockholder approval. Depending on the structure of the program, however, the company might likely be required to report the program to its stockholders. If the company (1) sells treasury stock to participating executives, or (2) provides a guarantee to the bank for the loans to executives' loans, the sale or guarantee would need to be disclosed in the "related party transactions" section of the company's reports. Additionally, the company must disclose stock owned and acquired by executives in the ownership section of its securities law filings. If the executive loan and stock purchase program lacks a compensation element, which most programs do, the federal securities laws would not require stockholder disclosure in the executive compensation section of the company's reports.

> **Planning Note:** One of the main purposes of an executive loan and stock purchase program is to send a message to investors that the management team and executive leadership is confident in the company's future. Therefore, most companies that adopt such a program eagerly disclose the program to investors and the public.

For executives to later be able to sell the stock acquired under the program on the open market, the company must register the stock on a Form S-8 Registration Statement. Alternatively, the company could require executives to sell their stock subject to Rule 144 of the Securities Exchange Act of 1933. Since some of the eligible executives are likely to be "affiliates" of the company for federal securities law purposes, their ability to sell stock on the open market may be subject to the restrictions of Rule 144[4] (other than the holding period requirement) regardless of whether the company files a registration statement.

The company's board of directors or compensation committee should approve the program in advance so that sales to executives who are Section 16 insiders are exempt transactions for purposes of the short-swing profit requirements of Section 16(b) of the Securities Exchange Act of 1934 (the "1934 Act").

.14 The Stock Purchase Loan's Effect on the Executive's Credit Rating

Generally, as long as the stock value is equal to or greater than the amounts owed and the executive is otherwise creditworthy, participation in the executive loan and stock purchase program should not affect the executive's ability to obtain an unrelated loan.

¶1125 Sarbanes-Oxley Act of 2002

In response to the corporate and accounting scandals of the 1990s, President George W. Bush signed into law the Sarbanes-Oxley Act of 2002 ("SOX") on July

---

[4] The five conditions of Rule 144 are as follows: (1) *a holding period* before restricted securities may be sold in the marketplace (of either six months or one year depending, respectively, on whether the company is or is not a "reporting company" subject to the Securities Exchange Act; (2) an *adequate public disclosure* requirement which for reporting companies generally means that they have complied with the periodic reporting requirements of the Securities Exchange Act and for non-reporting companies generally means the public disclosure of current information regarding the nature of the business, the identity of its officers and directors, and financial statements; (3) a *trading volume limit* of no more than 1% of outstanding shares of the same class being sold in any three-month period, or if the classes of shares listed on a stock exchange, whichever is greater between (a) no more than the greater of either 1% of outstanding shares of the same class being sold in any three-month period and (b) the average reported weekly trading volume during the four weeks preceding the filing; (4) sales must be handled as an *ordinary trading transaction* in which sellers/brokers cannot solicit orders to buy the securities and the broker may not receive more than a "normal" commission; and (5) *filing a notice of proposed sale* with the SEC for sales that involve more than 5,000 shares or the aggregate dollar amount for any three-month period exceeding $50,000.

30, 2002. SOX Section 402 prohibits publicly traded companies from directly (including through a subsidiary) extending or maintaining credit, arranging for the extension of credit, or renewing an existing extension of credit, in the form of a personal loan, to or for any director or executive officer of the company.

SOX Section 402 added a new Section 13(k) to the 1934 Act under the heading "Enhanced Conflict of Interest Provisions." New Section 13(k) provides as follows:

> (k) PROHIBITION ON PERSONAL LOANS TO EXECUTIVES—
>
> (1) IN GENERAL—It shall be unlawful for any issuer (as defined in Section 2 of the Sarbanes-Oxley Act of 2002), directly or indirectly, including through any subsidiary, to extend or maintain credit, to arrange for the extension of credit, or to renew an extension of credit, in the form of a personal loan to or for any director or executive officer (or equivalent thereof) of that issuer. An extension of credit maintained by the issuer on the date of enactment of this subsection shall not be subject to the provisions of this subsection, provided that there is no material modification to any term of any such extension of credit or any renewal of any such extension of credit on or after that date of enactment.

.01 Companies Affected by SOX Section 402

On or after its July 30, 2002, effective date, SOX Section 402 prohibits public companies from making loans to their senior executives and board members. SOX defines "issuer" to include any company that:

- has a class of securities listed on a national securities exchange in the United States;
- otherwise has securities registered under Section 12 of the 1934 Act;
- is required to file reports under Section 15(d) of the 1934 Act; or
- has a registration statement pending under the Securities Act of 1933.

Importantly, this definition includes companies in addition to those that have made an initial public offering of equity securities. For example, companies that have filed to sell debt into the public market are included. Moreover, SOX does not distinguish between U.S. and non-U.S. companies. Its prohibition on loans to officers and directors applies to a "lender" that is a non-U.S. company, director or executive officer located outside the U.S., or loans made outside the U.S.

For example, the SEC issued a cease and desist order against Stelmar Shipping Ltd., a foreign private issuer, for making personal loans to its Chief Executive Officer and Chief Financial Officer in 2003, in violation of Section 13(k).[5] In connection with the order, the SEC accepted the settlement offers of the CEO and CFO, each of whom had resigned from Stelmar in connection with its acquisition by Overseas Shipholding Group, Ltd. (also a publicly traded company).

---

[5] Securities and Exchange Act of 1934, Release No. 52865 (December 1, 2005).

.02 Individuals Affected by SOX Section 402

SOX prohibits a company from making loans to a "director or executive officer (or equivalent thereof)," but does not define that term. However, Rule 3b-7 of the 1934 Act defines "executive officer" of a registrant as:

> its president, any vice president of the registrant in charge of a principal business unit, division or function (such as sales, administration or finance), any other officer who performs a policy making function, or any other person who performs similar policy making functions for the registrant. Executive officers of subsidiaries may be deemed executive officers of the registrant if they perform such policy-making functions for the registrant.

Rule 3b-7 suggests that SOX Section 402 applies only to directors of the issuer, not directors of any subsidiary.[6] To date, the best interpretation of who is an executive officer of a company includes anyone who is an executive officer within the meaning of Rule 3b-7 of the 1934 Act. This includes:

- the company president;
- any company vice president in charge of a principal business unit, division or function;
- any other officer of the company who performs a policy-making function;
- any other person who performs similar policy-making functions for the company; or
- an executive officer of a subsidiary of the company, if he or she performs policy-making functions for the company.

.03 "Loans" Affected by SOX Section 402

SOX Section 402 does not define the term "personal loan." The SEC has not addressed interpretive issues involving the permissibility of these transactions that may involve an extension of credit or "loan" under Section 402. Companies and their legal counsel need to be concerned that the prohibition may ban many common corporate practices, including:

1. *Cashless exercise of stock options.* The nation's top corporate law firms published their consensus view that broker-assisted cashless exercise is not a prohibited personal loan as long as:

   - The brokerage firm complies with Regulation T of the Federal Reserve System,
   - The brokerage verifies that the issuer will deliver the stock promptly, and
   - The optionee designates his/her brokerage account with the brokerage firm as the account into which the securities are to be deposited.[7]

2. *Cash advances, company credit cards, and indemnification advances.* Consensus has developed that SOX Section 402 will not treat cash advances,

---

[6] Unless executive officers of a company's subsidiary are performing policy-making functions for the company.

[7] *See* "Leading Law Firms Provide Interpretation of Sarbanes-Oxley Act Prohibition on Insider Loans (PDF)." (Winston & Strawn, Alston & Bird LLP, 23 More Firms), BenefitsLink, October 28, 2002.

company credit cards, and indemnification advances as prohibited personal loans, as long as:

- In the case of cash advances and credit cards, the company's policy clearly states that the executive is to use such advances and cards for reimbursable expenses only.

- In the case of indemnification advances, it appears that the officer or director will not be required to pay back the advance, except in the most egregious circumstances.

> **Planning Note:** Companies should check and/or revise their cash advance, company credit card, and indemnification advance policies to ensure such policies could not be abused in a manner that would also result in a violation of Section 402.

3. *Retirement and 401(k) plan loans.* The nation's top law firms have developed a consensus that retirement and 401(k) plan loans are not prohibited personal loans from the issuer to the executive for several reasons, including:

- The retirement/401(k) plan is a separate legal entity from the issuer.

- The issuer established the plan, but certainly not for the purpose of arranging credit.

- The loan to the executive is from his or her own account under the plan.

4. *Split-dollar life insurance arrangements.* The news is not as good for split-dollar life insurance arrangements. In Notice 2002-8,[8] and the proposed and final regulations that followed, the IRS indicated that it would provide for the taxation of split-dollar life insurance under one of two "mutually exclusive regimes," (1) the economic benefit regime and (2) the loan regime, depending on whether the company or the employee is the owner of the life insurance policy. The loan regime generally would apply to collateral assignment split-dollar arrangements—where the employee (or a trust designated by the employee) owns the policy. Under the loan regime, the IRS treats the nonowner of the life insurance contract as loaning premium payments to the owner of the contract (see Chapter 18 [¶ 1801 *et seq.*] for a detailed discussion of split-dollar life insurance). Thus, most practitioners believe that SOX Section 402 prohibits equity split-dollar life insurance arrangements where the executive (or a trust) owns the policy, which would be taxed under the loan regime.

.04 Existing Loans and Private Companies

The SOX prohibition on loans to executives and directors does not apply to private companies. The extent to which a private company that "goes public" will be able to continue to grant loans to executives and directors will likely

---

[8] I.R.S. Not. 2002-8, 2002-1 C.B. 398.

depend on how regulations under SOX treat loans made after July 30, 2002, but in existence at the time a company becomes an "issuer" subject to SOX.

SOX Section 402 contains three exceptions to the prohibition of personal loans to directors and executive officers, including an exception for loans made before July 30, 2002, provided there is no material modification to any terms of loan or renewal of the loan after July 30, 2002.

Therefore, loans made by a public company "issuer" before July 30, 2002, are still good, provided there is no material modification to any terms of the loan or renewal of the loan after July 30, 2002. SOX Section 402 did not describe what would be a material modification. However, experience tells us that the SEC could consider the following modifications to be material:

- A change in interest rate of the loan;
- A change in the loan's repayment period;
- A change in amount of the loan; or
- A change in any other material term of the loan.

.05 SEC's 2013 Interpretative Guidance on Equity-Based Financing

More than a decade after its enactment, the SEC finally issued is first interpretative guidance regarding SOX Section 402 in March 2013. In a request by Michael Oxley—former Congressman and co-author of the Sarbanes-Oxley Act—on behalf of public company RingsEnd Partners, LLC ("RingsEnd"), the SEC issued a private letter ruling. In its letter, RingsEnd sought permission to allow company executives to participate in their equity-based incentive compensation program (the "EBIC Program") without RingsEnd being deemed to violate SOX Section 402.[9] RingsEnd sought confirmation that through their EBIC Program the company would not be deemed to either extend/maintain credit or arrange for the extension of credit, in the form of a personal loan.

Under RingsEnd's proposed EBIC Program, participating executives would receive company stock as a form of incentive compensation and then transfer those shares to an independently managed Delaware statutory trust. The trust could then obtain term loans, secured by shares, from an independent banking institution. The trust would then distribute borrowed funds to the executives to pay taxes on the shares. Ultimately, when the loans matured, the trustee would sell off sufficient shares to pay the loans and then distribute any remaining shares and cash to the executives.

RingsEnd acknowledged that in order to effectuate the EBIC Program, the company would be required to perform a number of ministerial acts—such as "delivering the share awards to the trust, as directed by participants and the stock awards; and delivering to the lending institution a prospectus and registration statement covering the shares under the plan"—that were necessary to allow executives to participate in the EBIC Program. RingsEnd emphasized that they

---

[9] RingsEnd Partners, LLC, Incoming Letter of No Action (Feb. 28, 2013), *available at* https:// www.sec.gov/divisions/corpfin/cf-noaction/2013/ringsend030413-13-incoming.pdf

would not play any role in, among other things, (1) the loan between the lending institution and the trust; (2) encouraging or discouraging executives from participating in the program; (3) guaranteeing repayment or otherwise supporting the loan; and (4) reimbursing participants for income taxes payable by the participant.

Ultimately the SEC responded by approving of RingsEnd's actions with respect the proposed EBIC Program. In its guidance, the SEC stated that a company permitting its executives to participate in a plan "would not be deemed . . . directly or indirectly, to be extending or maintaining credit, in the form of a personal loans or for such individuals for purposes [that otherwise violate SOX Section 402]."[10] The SEC went on to write that a company undertaking certain ministerial/administrative functions to allow its executives to participate in the EBIC Program[11] would not be deemed, either directly or indirectly, to have extended/arranged for the extension of credit as a personal loan in violation of SOX Section 402.

.06 Exceptions to Section 13(k) and SOX Section 402

Section 13(k) does not prohibit home improvement and manufactured home loans, consumer credit, or any extension of credit under an open end credit plan or a charge card that is, (A) made or provided in the ordinary course of the consumer credit business of such issuer; (B) of a type that is generally made available by such issuer to the public; and (C) made by such issuer on market terms, or terms that are no more favorable than those offered by the issuer to the general public for such extensions of credit.

Section 13(k) also does not prohibit an extension of credit by a registered broker or dealer to an employee of the broker or dealer to buy, trade, or carry securities, which is permitted under Federal Reserve System rules or regulations, other than an extension of credit that would be used to purchase the stock of the registered broker or dealer.

Section 13(k) does not apply to any loan made or maintained by an insured depository institution[12] if the loan is subject to the insider lending restrictions of Federal Reserve Act Section 22(h) (see, also ¶ 1155).

Finally, SEC rules provide an exemption to Section 13(k) for a foreign bank that has a home jurisdiction other than the United States in which it is regulated as a bank.[13]

¶1135 Other Types of Company Loans

Before SOX, loans to executives were a very popular form of executive compensation. SOX Section 402 prohibits publicly traded companies from loan-

---

[10] RingsEnd Partners, LLC, SEC No-Action Letter, 2013 WL 860508 (Mar. 4, 2013).

[11] The SEC's guidance was limited strictly to the RingsEnd EBIC Program and did not comment upon other similar programs.

[12] As defined in Section 3 of the Federal Deposit Insurance Act (12 U.S.C. 1813).

[13] § 240.13k-1.

ing money to a director or executive officer of the company. However, privately held companies can continue to provide for executive loans for any reason.

Code Sec. 61 provides, in part, that gross income includes compensation for services. The proceeds of a *bona fide* loan are not includible in gross income because the receipt of money is offset by a corresponding obligation to pay.[14] Code Sec. 83(a) generally provides that the excess (if any) of the fair market value of property transferred in connection with the performance of services over the amount paid (if any) for the property is includible in the gross income of the person who performed the services for the first taxable year in which the property becomes transferable or is not subject to a substantial risk of forfeiture.

A loan from a company to an executive that exceeds $10,000 may be subject to the below-market loan rules of Code Sec. 7872. Under these rules, if the interest payable on the loan is not sufficiently high, the executive will be taxed on the difference between the amount loaned to him or her and the present value of all payments he or she will make under the loan. The IRS would determine the taxable amount at the time of the loan, and at a rate of interest specified in the Code.

.01 Compensation-Related Loans

The Internal Revenue Code provides that a compensation-related loan is a below-market loan that a company makes in connection with the performance of services, directly or indirectly, by an employer to an employee, independent contractor, or partner.[15] The Code will treat the imputed transfer by the employer/lender to the employee/borrower as compensation for service, which is taxable as ordinary income. The Code clarifies that a loan from a qualified retirement or 401(k) plan to a plan participant is not a compensation-related loan.

Code Sec. 7872 would treat a loan that an employer made in part in exchange for services and in part for other reasons as a compensation-related loan only if more than 25 percent of the amount loaned is attributable to the performance of services.[16] If 25 percent or less of the amount loaned is attributable to the performance of services, the loan is not subject to Code Sec. 7872 because of being a compensation-related loan. If a loan is characterized as a "compensation-related" loan under Code Sec. 7872(c), but less than 100 percent of the amount loaned is attributable to the performance of services, and the portion of the amount loaned that is not attributable to the performance of services is not subject to Code Sec. 7872, then the amounts of imputed transfer (as defined in Proposed Reg. § 1.7872-1(a)(2)) and imputed interest (as defined in Proposed Reg. § 1.7872-1(a)) are determined only with respect to that part of the loan that is attributable to services. The company and its counsel must (because the IRS will) take into account all of the facts and circumstances surrounding the

---

[14] *See C.I.R. v. Tufts,* 461 U.S. 300, 307 (1983).

[15] 26 U.S.C. § 7872(c)(1)(B).

[16] Proposed Reg. § 1.7872-4(c)(2). Although these regulations were only proposed and not finalized,

many practitioners tend to follow them. *See,* for example, 2 Mertens Law of Fed. Income Tax'n § 12C:101 (updated Jan. 2018) and Tax Asp. Real Est. § 9:25 (updated Dec. 2017)).

loan agreement and the relationship between the lender and the borrower in determining the portion of the loan made in exchange for services.[17]

A below-market loan by an unrelated third-party lender to an employee is treated as attributable to the performance of services if, taking into account all the facts and circumstances, the transaction is in substance a loan by the employer made with the aid of a third-party lender acting as an agent of the employer. Among the facts and circumstances that indicate a company has made such a loan is whether the company bears the risk of default when and immediately after the third-party lender makes the loan.[18]

A below-market loan also may be subject to Code Sec. 7872 other than as a compensation-related loan, for example, as a corporation-stockholder loan or tax-avoidance loan. Special rules apply to *de minimis* compensation-related loans and employee relocation loans.

.02 Corporation-Stockholder Loans

The Code would treat a below-market loan as a "corporation-stockholder loan" if a company makes a loan directly or indirectly to any of its stockholders. The amount of money treated as transferred by the company/lender to the stockholder/borrower is a distribution of money (characterized according to Code Sec. 301 or, in the case of an S corporation, Code Sec. 1368) if the company is the lender, or a contribution to capital if the stockholder is the lender.

.03 Demand Loans vs. Term Loans

The Code taxes compensation-related demand loans differently from term loans.[19] If the company makes a demand loan to an executive, Code Sec. 7872 treats the company-lender as having received imputed interest from the executive-borrower for any day that the loan is outstanding and as having paid an identical amount in taxable compensation to the executive. Thus, Code Sec. 7872 will require the company to include in income the amount of imputed interest deemed received for each year of the loan. The company will be entitled to a business deduction for compensation paid in an amount equivalent to the interest income. Code Sec. 7872 will treat the executive as having paid the company imputed interest for any day that the loan is outstanding and as having received an identical amount from the company as additional, taxable compensation.

Under a compensation-related term loan, the Code would treat the executive as receiving current compensation from the company in an amount equal to the excess of the amount of the loan over the present value of all principal (and any interest payments required under the loan agreement) due under the loan. The Code would treat the executive as having received this taxable compensation on the date the company made the loan. The company would be entitled to an immediate compensation deduction. However, the Code would treat a compen-

---

[17] Proposed Reg. § 1.7872-4(c)(2).

[18] Proposed Reg. § 1.7872-4(c)(3).

[19] *See also*, Stnd. Fed. Tax. Rep. (CCH) ¶ 43,960.026, Loans with Below-Market Interest Rates: Compensation-related loans (2013).

sation-related term loan as a demand loan if the benefit derived by the executive from the interest arrangement is (1) nontransferable and (2) conditioned on the future performance of substantial services by the executive.[20]

> **Planning Note:** Companies and their counsel drafting executive loan agreements should take care to condition the loan benefit on the executive's future performance of substantial services. For example, the loan agreement could provide that, on termination of the executive's employment, the loan is immediately due and payable, or the interest rate is increased.

The Code provides an exception to the below-market loan rules for certain loans between a company and an employee (or independent contractor) where the aggregate outstanding amount of the loans between the employee/borrower and the company/lender is $10,000 or less (unless one of the principal purposes of the loan arrangement is the avoidance of any federal tax).[21]

.04 Employee Relocation Loans

Under the regular below-market interest rules, the applicable federal rate (the "AFR") for the month in which the company made the term loan is the test rate to be used to determine whether the loan is to be treated as a below-market interest loan. However, with respect to a term loan from a company to an executive to purchase a principal residence in connection with the commencement of work at a new principal place of work, the test rate is the AFR for the month in which the executive enters into the written contract for the purchase of the principal residence.[22] This employee relocation rule applies only to a relocation move subject to Code Sec. 217, which allows the deduction of certain moving expenses if the move is closely related, both in time and place, to the start of work at a new job location and if two tests are met.

Certain employee relocation loans are exempt from the below-market loan provisions because the IRS has determined that the interest arrangements do not have a significant effect on the tax liability of either the borrower or the lender. The exemption does not apply to tax avoidance loans. The regulations provide that if a compensation-related loan to an employee is secured by a mortgage on the executive's new principal residence that the executive acquired in connection with his or her transfer to a new principal place of work, the loan will be exempted from the below-market loan provisions if the loan satisfies certain conditions.[23]

The legislation known as the Tax Cuts and Jobs Act ("TCJA") signed into law by President Trump in December 2017, repealed the Code Sec. 217 deduction provisions and the Code Sec. 132 income exclusion provisions related to moving expenses for taxable years 2018 through 2025. The IRS has not issued guidance on whether or how this temporary repeal will affect the below-market interest loan rules.

---

[20] Code Sec. 7872(f)(5).
[21] Code Sec. §7872(c)(3)(A).
[22] Code Sec. 7872(f)(11).

[23] Temp. Reg. §1.7872-5T(c)(1)(ii). Certain bridge loans to employees are also exempt as provided in Temp. Reg. §1.7872-5T(c)(1)(ii).

¶1145 "Loans" Treated as Compensation Advances

The IRS has expressed its view that certain payments made by a company to an employee, which the parties attempt to characterize as loans, are taxable as "up-front payments" of compensation.[24] In a private letter ruling, the IRS reviewed a series of interrelated transactions between a company and certain new stockbroker employees. As a means of recruiting the new employees, the company offered an arrangement under which they would receive certain up-front payments. When the company made up-front payments, the company and the employee simultaneously entered into two contracts: a "bonus agreement," and a "promissory note."

> **Planning Note:** A typical participating employee might receive an up-front payment of $x. Under the Note, this principal sum ($x) is repayable with interest at z% in five annual installments of $y due on the last day of August each year. The company will forgive the entire remaining unpaid principal and accrued interest upon the death or disability of the employee while employed by the company or upon termination of employment with the company other than for cause. At the option of the company, any unpaid principal and interest will become immediately due and payable in the event the employee defaults on a payment of an installment when due. The company takes a security interest in all the company common stock owned or acquired by a participating employee during the term of the promissory note as collateral for the note.

Under the Bonus Agreement the company might agree to pay annual bonuses (plus interest at the rate of z%) to a participating employee in five annual installments of $y (based on the above example) on the last day of August each year. The bonus agreement provides that an employee "acknowledges the contemporaneous execution of a promissory note in the amount of $x payable to" the company and that "all bonus payments made pursuant to this agreement shall be applied to the payment of the promissory note until paid in full." The bonus agreement states that the employee "understands that bonuses paid under this agreement shall not be considered 'recognized compensation' and shall be disregarded for purposes of the company's retirement plans."

In this private letter ruling, the IRS first addressed the issue of whether the up-front payments from the company to participating employees constituted compensation or loan proceeds. The IRS concluded that the purported loan lacked the indicia of *bona fide* indebtedness (*i.e.*, that there is an unconditional and personal obligation on the employee to repay the loan).

In reaching this conclusion, the IRS was unconvinced there was an unconditional and personal liability on the part of the participating employees. Unconditional and personal obligations to repay the loans were not present in this case, because the loans were to be repaid with guaranteed "bonus payments" to be

---

[24] I.R.S. Priv. Ltr. Rul. 200040004 (June 12, 2000).

made by the company—in an amount precisely matching the payments due under the loans. The employees were to be required to repay a portion of the up-front payment only if they left the company's employ before the end of the required period of service. Provided the employees performed all of the contracted services, they would not be required to repay any portion of the up-front payments. In its ruling the IRS distinguished this case from others such as *Gales v. Comm'r* in which the IRS did find a *bona fide* loan between the company and the executive.[25] In Gales *v. Comm'r* there was—at the time the insurance salesperson borrowed funds from the company—substantial uncertainty as to the amount of insurance commissions he would receive in the future. Thus, the parties did not know whether the commissions would be sufficient to satisfy the employee's obligation to the company, and the employee was personally responsible for repayment of any shortfall.

Planning Note: Companies and employees often enter into arrangements where the company loans money or sells stock (or other property) to the employee to be paid or repaid in installments, while simultaneously offering or continuing a plan or program that is intended to result in annual payments to the employee in amounts sufficient to make loan payments. When counsel memorializes such arrangements, he or she should ensure that there is an element of uncertainty to the annual payment, such as a performance requirement, and that the repayment obligation does not simply disappear if the employee leaves employment for any reason.

When the parties enter into such an arrangement, they should take into account the tax consequences to the employee of the annual payouts when estimating the amount of such payments. If the full amount of any annual payouts goes to pay or repay the obligation, the employee could have a significant tax liability without the dollars to pay it.

Example 1: ABC Corporation loans $1 million to newly hired Executive D to assist her in relocation and transition to employment with ABC. The parties anticipate that D will be able to repay the loan during the first five years of her employment with ABC with the annual bonus payments negotiated into her employment agreement. Although the annual bonus arrangement specifies a "target" bonus at the exact amount necessary to repay the loan, the arrangement also provides that D must hit certain objective performance measures to receive the "target" annual bonus payment. The employment agreement also provides that if D leaves employment for any reason other than death or disability, D must repay the loan in full within two years.

Example 2: Partner A of AB&C Partnership is retiring and has agreed to sell 10% of the partnership interests he holds to new partner D for $1 million, payable in installments, with interest, over a five-year period. Although the parties expect that the annual distribution of AB&C's partnership profits to D will be sufficient for her to make the payment to retiring partner

---

[25] *Gales v. Comm'r*, 77 T.C.M (CCH) 1316 (1999).

A, the actual partnership distributions in any year are based on the partnership's profits for the year.

Further, the IRS determined that the purported loans did not require cash payments in accordance with a specific repayment schedule. Despite the form of the transaction, the employee's obligations were satisfied, in substance, by performing services over five years, rather than by a cash payment. For each year the employees performed services, the company forgave one-fifth of their debts. Thus, there was a forgiveness of the debt, rather than a payment of the debt by cash.

The IRS concluded that the up-front payments were advance payments for services and not loan proceeds. Only the up-front payment had a tax effect. The IRS would not treat the "bonus" payments as compensatory payments to the employees in the year made.

.01 Timing of the Company's Deduction

In the case described above, the IRS concluded that the company could not deduct the full amount of the up-front payments in the year of payment. The IRS held that the company incurred the expenses as participating employees performed services over the five-year term of the note and bonus agreement and, therefore, the company could deduct the amount incurred in each year.

¶1155 Special Rules for Loans to Executives at Financial Institutions

As noted above, Section 13(k) of the 1934 Act does not apply to any loan made or maintained by an insured depository institution if the loan is subject to the insider lending restrictions of Federal Reserve Act Section 22(h). Special rules apply to loans by financial institutions to their executive officers, directors, and principal shareholders under the Federal Reserve Act,[26] the Federal Deposit Insurance Corporation Improvement Act of 1991,[27] the Home Owners' Loan Act,[28] and the Dodd-Frank Wall Street Reform and Consumer Protection Act.[29]

The insider lending restrictions do not prohibit an extension of credit made pursuant to a benefit or compensation program that is widely available to employees of the bank and do not give preference to any officer, director, or principal shareholder of the bank, or to any related interest of such person, over other employees of the member bank.[30]

Finally, nothing in Section 13(k) or any provisions of the banking law prohibits a bank from allowing its insiders to obtain a loan or extension of credit from another bank. The insider lending provisions of Section 22(h) and Regulation 0 thereunder apply only to loans or extensions of credit made by a bank to an insider of that same bank.

---

[26] Federal Reserve Act Sections 11(a), 22(g), and 22(h) (12 U.S.C. 248(a), 375a, and 375b).

[27] Federal Deposit Insurance Corporation Improvement Act of 1991 Section 306 (Pub. L. 102—242, 105 Stat. 2236 (1991)).

[28] Home Owners' Loan Act Section 11 (12 U.S.C. 1468).

[29] Dodd-Frank Wall Street Reform and Consumer Protection Act Section 312(b)(2)(A) (12 U.S.C. 5412).

[30] Federal Reserve Act Section 22(h)(2)(B).

Chapter 12

SECURITIES LAW COMPLIANCE ISSUES RELATING TO EXECUTIVE COMPENSATION PLANS

¶1201 Overview—Securities Law Compliance Issues Relating to Executive Compensation

Most companies appreciate the value of offering employees an ownership interest in the company. In addition to providing an alternative means of compensating employees, company stock is useful to motivate employees, to align employees' interests with the interests of the company's shareholders and to retain valuable employees. The prevalence of company stock as a means of compensating, motivating, and retaining employees and the variety of employee benefit plans established in order to deliver company stock to employees continue to multiply.

Federal securities laws including, specifically, the Securities Act of 1933 (the "Securities Act") and the Securities Exchange Act of 1934 (the "Exchange Act"), affect employee benefit plans, including executive compensation arrangements and tax-qualified retirement plans, in several ways. Self-regulatory organizations (*e.g.*, the New York Stock Exchange ("NYSE") and Nasdaq Stock Market ("Nasdaq")) impose requirements with respect to the issuance of shares to executive officers and directors by companies whose securities are listed with the applicable exchange or national market. Companies with registered securities must disclose compensation of executive officers in their proxy statements. The required proxy disclosure includes information about incentive compensation retirement plans and other employee benefit arrangements, in addition to salary and bonus information. Stock issued pursuant to employee benefit plans as well as interests in employee benefit plans may have to be registered. There may be limitations or restrictions on an employee's ability to resell stock acquired pursuant to an employee benefit plan. Finally, "insiders" with respect to a publicly held company are subject to further requirements and limitations, including a requirement that they report their company stock holdings and disgorge any profits from short-swing trading.

The Exchange Act established the Securities and Exchange Commission ("SEC") with a mission to protect investors, maintain fair, orderly, and efficient markets, and facilitate capital formation. It has extensive rulemaking, enforcement and quasi-judicial powers with respect to the primary federal securities laws. Its decisions are subject to review by the U.S. Court of Appeals. The SEC also must approve rules adopted by stock exchanges and self-regulatory organization ("SROs"), such as FINRA and the NYSE. The SEC operates through four main Divisions: Corporation Finance, Enforcement, Investment Management and Trading and Markets. Each has its own web pages which are very useful resources.

.01 Types of Employee Compensation and Benefits Plans

The following is a list of several common types of employee compensation and benefit plans under which employees may have an opportunity to receive company stock:

- stock incentive plans (options, restricted stock, RSUs, performance shares, etc.);
- employee stock purchase plans qualified under Code Sec. 423;
- retirement plans qualified under Code Sec. 401(a) (*e.g.*, Section 401(k) plans and employee stock ownership plans);
- nonqualified deferred compensation plans; and
- supplemental executive retirement plans.

.02 Approval Process (Board and Shareholder), Filings, and Disclosures

Nearly all stock-based compensation plans must be approved by the company's board of directors. Securities and tax law requirements make it advisable to seek shareholder approval of stock-based plans as well. Federal securities laws also impose a variety of disclosure requirements on executive compensation arrangements, including written proxy statements, Form 11-Ks and beneficial ownership reporting (see ¶ 1225).

.03 Registration

Federal securities laws prohibit the offer or sale of unregistered securities, including company stock offered under a stock-based compensation plan. The SEC also requires registration of offers or sales of an employer's securities to participants under any voluntary, contributory employee benefit plan. In addition, the ability to participate in a plan may also be considered a security and require registration.

A company offering to sell its securities can only do so through a prospectus that meets the requirements of federal securities law—even if the prospective sale is to its own employees. Section 10(a) of the Securities Act requires that a prospectus being used more than nine months after the effective date of a registration statement contain information as of a date within 16 months of the date the prospectus is used, "so far as such information is known to the user of such prospectus or can be furnished by such user without unreasonable effort or expense" (see ¶ 1235).

.04 Resales by Employees

In general, shares of stock acquired under an employee benefit plan that have been registered on Form S-8 are unrestricted securities and may be freely resold. In certain cases, shares acquired under an employee benefit plan by affiliates (*e.g.*, executive officers or directors) will be subject to restrictions on resale, notwithstanding the fact that the shares acquired under the plan are registered. We refer to these shares as "control securities" (see ¶ 1245).

.05 Rule 10b5-1

Rule 10b-5 under the Exchange Act prohibits individuals from trading stock based on nonpublic, or "inside," information. Employee benefit plans may be structured so that corporate insiders can satisfy the conditions set forth in Rule 10b5-1. This rule provides that a purchase or sale of securities is not on the basis of material, nonpublic information where the individual or entity making the purchase or sale can show that prior to becoming aware of the material, nonpublic information, the individual or entity had (1) entered into a binding contract for the purchase or sale of the security; (2) instructed a third party to purchase or sell the security for its account; or (3) adopted a written plan for trading securities (see ¶ 1255).

.06 Section 16 of the Exchange Act

Section 16(a) of the Exchange Act contains reporting requirements and Section 16(b) contains trading restrictions. Section 16(a) requires a company's insiders to file reports with the SEC disclosing the ownership of, and certain transactions involving, company stock. The Sarbanes-Oxley Act requires corporate insiders to file a Form 4 within two business days of any purchase or sale of company stock. There are some exemptions to this section (see ¶ 1265).

.07 Compensation Clawback Policies

Compensation clawbacks first became a matter of law under Section 304 of the Sarbanes-Oxley Act of 2002 ("SOX"). Section 954 of the Dodd-Frank Wall Street Reform and Consumer Protection Act (the "Dodd-Frank Act") signed into law by President Obama in July 2010, would expand the compensation clawback requirement applicable to public companies. As of this date, Section 954 is not fully effective because the SEC has not adopted the required regulations. However, compensation clawback policies have become a best practice and nearly every public company in America has adopted a compensation clawback policy (see ¶ 1275).

.08 Private Company Securities Law Issues

Generally, private companies are exempt from both federal and state registration requirements with respect to compensatory benefit plans, including stock incentive plans (see ¶ 1285). However, these exemptions are not automatic and larger private companies can easily run afoul of them.

¶ 1215 Benefit Plan Disclosure Requirements

Companies are required to disclose, at least annually, information about two categories of employee benefits plans: (1) plans approved by shareholders; and (2) plans not approved by shareholders. For each plan category, the company must disclose information in tabular form regarding:

- the number of shares of company stock to be issued upon the exercise of outstanding awards granted to participants;

- the weighted-average exercise price of outstanding awards granted to participants; and

- the number of shares of company stock remaining available for future issuance under employee benefits plans.

When the company seeks shareholder approval to amend an existing employee benefit plan, the table should include information about the company stock previously authorized for issuance under the plan. The rules permit companies to aggregate information about individual arrangements and plans in each disclosure category.

The amendments also require a company to identify and describe briefly, in narrative form, the material features of each employee benefit plan in effect as of the end of the last completed fiscal year that it adopted without shareholder approval. The SEC will permit companies to satisfy their disclosure requirement by cross-referencing to the portion of their required FASB Accounting Standards Codification Topic 718, Compensation—Stock Compensation (referred to as "ASC 718")[1] disclosure containing descriptions of their nonshareholder-approved plans. The cross-reference should identify the specific plan or plans in the required ASC 718 disclosure that shareholders have not approved.

In addition, companies are required to file as an exhibit to their Form 10-K, any employee benefit plan adopted without the approval of shareholders in which any employee (whether or not an executive officer or director of the registrant) participates, unless immaterial in amount or significance.

¶1225 Shareholder Approval, Filings, and Disclosures

The company's board of directors must approve nearly all stock-based compensation plans. Stock exchange and certain Internal Revenue Code rules require shareholder approval of stock-based plans as well.

.01 Board Approval

The issuance of shares of a public company's stock under an employee benefit plan requires the approval of the company's board of directors. Typically, the board's authorization may be evidenced by:

- written resolutions adopted by a majority of the members of the board at a meeting; or

- the unanimous written consent of the members of the board without a meeting.

In addition to the need to satisfy corporate formalities, adoption by the board of directors is critical in order to satisfy Rule 16b-3(d), which will exempt the grant from short swing trading liability. Rule 16b-3(d) provides as follows:

---

[1] Formerly known as Statement of Financial Accounting Standards ("FAS") No. 123.

(d) *Acquisitions from the issuer.* Any transaction, other than a Discretionary Transaction, involving an acquisition from the issuer (including without limitation a grant or award), whether or not intended for a compensatory or other particular purpose, shall be exempt if:

> (1) The transaction is approved by the board of directors of the issuer, or a committee of the board of directors that is composed solely of two or more Non-Employee Directors;
>
> (2) The transaction is approved or ratified, in compliance with section 14 of the Act, by either: the affirmative votes of the holders of a majority of the securities of the issuer present, or represented, and entitled to vote at a meeting duly held in accordance with the applicable laws of the state or other jurisdiction in which the issuer is incorporated; or the written consent of the holders of a majority of the securities of the issuer entitled to vote; provided that such ratification occurs no later than the date of the next annual meeting of shareholders; or
>
> (3) The issuer equity securities so acquired are held by the officer or director for a period of six months following the date of such acquisition, provided that this condition shall be satisfied with respect to a derivative security if at least six months elapse from the date of acquisition of the derivative security to the date of disposition of the derivative security (other than upon exercise or conversion) or its underlying equity security.

Rule 16b-3(e) describes the requirements for approval of a disposition to the issuer:

> (e) *Dispositions to the issuer.* Any transaction, other than a Discretionary Transaction, involving the disposition to the issuer of issuer equity securities, whether or not intended for a compensatory or other particular purpose, shall be exempt, provided that the terms of such disposition are approved in advance in the manner prescribed by either paragraph (d)(1) or paragraph (d)(2) of this section.[2]

.02 Shareholder Approval

In most cases, a public company will need to obtain shareholder approval for the issuance of shares under an employee benefit plan. The four primary technical purposes for seeking shareholder approval of an employee benefit plan are to:

- have compensation qualify as performance-based under Code Sec. 162(m);

- satisfy stock exchange listing requirements;

- receive protection from short-swing profit liability under Section 16(b) of the Exchange Act; and/or

- enable the company to grant qualified stock options (*i.e.,* incentive stock options pursuant to Code Sec. 422 or options granted under an employee stock purchase plan pursuant to Code Sec. 423).

---

[2] The Exchange Act refers to "issuer equity securities" and "equity-compensation plans," but we generally use the terms company stock or stock-based compensation in this Chapter for consistency.

Generally, the stock exchanges require shareholder approval prior to the issuance of any shares when a company establishes or materially amends a stock incentive plan or other stock compensation arrangement under which company stock may be acquired by officers, directors, employees, or consultants.[3] Shareholders must be given the opportunity to vote on all stock-based compensation plans and material revisions thereto, with limited exemptions listed below.[4]

A stock-based compensation plan is a plan or other arrangement that provides for the delivery of company stock (either newly issued or treasury shares) of the listed company to any employee, director or other service provider as compensation for services. However, the following are not stock-based compensation plans even if the brokerage and other costs of the plan are paid for by the listed company:

- Plans that are made available to shareholders generally, such as a typical dividend reinvestment plan.
- Plans that merely allow employees, directors or other service providers to elect to buy shares on the open market or from the listed company for their current fair market value, regardless of whether:
  - the shares are delivered immediately or on a deferred basis; or
  - the payments for the shares are made directly or by giving up compensation that is otherwise due (for example, through payroll deductions).

Receiving shareholder approval is not automatic, as ISS and other shareholder advisory firms will closely scrutinize the stock proposed for approval and recommend a vote "Against" if the shares authorized for issuance would create overhang issues or the plan document includes provisions the advisory firms find offensive (such as liberal share counting or evergreen features).

A public company may be able to obviate the need to obtain shareholder approval for its stock-based compensation plan in certain limited circumstances. For example, protection from Section 16 short-swing profit liability can be secured by obtaining the approval of the company's board of directors or a committee of two or more "nonemployee" directors for the issuance of company stock under an employee benefit plan.

.03 Definitive Proxy Statements

As part of its annual proxy statement, a company with registered securities must disclose (1) the compensation of executive officers, (2) information about retirement plans and other employee benefit arrangements, and (3) stock issued to executive officers from employee benefit plans (including phantom stock interests). When a company seeks shareholder approval of an employee benefit plan (or certain amendments to such plan), a definitive written proxy statement containing the information specified in Item 10 of Schedule 14A of the Exchange Act must be furnished to each shareholder and filed with the SEC. This informa-

---

[3] Nasdaq Stock Market Listing Rule 5635(c).

[4] NYSE Listed Company Manual Sec. 303A.08 Shareholder Approval of Equity Compensation Plans.

tion includes the types of stock compensation awards available under the plan, the employees eligible for awards and the tax consequences to the company and the executive of each type of award. (See Chapter 31 for a more detailed discussion.)

.04 Forms 10-K and 10-Q

Annual reports on Form 10-K must be filed within 60 days after a company's fiscal year end by large accelerated filers, within 75 days after fiscal year end by accelerated filers, and within 90 days after fiscal year end for all other filers. Accelerated filers are companies that have a public equity "float" of at least $75 million but less than $700 million, have been subject to the Exchange Act reporting requirements for at least 12 months, and previously have filed at least one annual report on Form 10-K. Float is calculated as share price times shares outstanding, as of the last business day of the second fiscal quarter of the company's previous fiscal year, less shares held by insiders. A company should monitor its market capitalization for a possible move up (or down) among "non-accelerated filer," "accelerated filer," and "large accelerated filer," determined as of the last day of the preceding fiscal year.

Large accelerated filers and accelerated filers must file quarterly reports on Form 10-Q within 40 days after the end of fiscal quarter (other than the last fiscal year quarter). All other filers must file quarterly reports on Form 10-Q within 45 days after the end of each fiscal quarter.

A company must file compensatory arrangements with executive officers and directors as exhibits to Form 10-K or Q,[5] even an immaterial amendment to a material contract. A company also must file any amendment or modification to a previously filed exhibit to a Form 10-K or 10-Q document as an exhibit to its next Form 10-Q and Form 10-K, except that the company need not file such amendment or modification where such previously filed exhibit would not be currently required.[6] This is true even though no Item 8-K triggering event had occurred. However, when an 8-K reportable event occurs within four business days of the company's 10-K filing, the company may report the event in Form 10-K.[7]

Executive compensation professionals and others are familiar with the executive compensation disclosure requirements of Item 402 of Regulation S-K. These disclosure requirements actually apply to a company's Form 10-K annual report, rather than the company's proxy statement and notice of annual meeting on Schedule 14A. Part III, Item 11 of Form 10-K requires a company to "Furnish the information required by Item 402 of Regulation S-K . . . and paragraph (e)(4) and (e)(5) of Item 407 of Regulation S-K . . . ." However, general instruction G(3) provides: "The information required by Part III (Items 10, 11, 12, 13 and 14) may be *incorporated by reference from the registrant's definitive proxy statement* . . . which involves the election of directors, if such definitive proxy statement . . . is filed with the Commission not later than 120 days after the end of the fiscal year

---

[5] Item 601 of Regulation S-K.
[6] Item 601(a)(4).

[7] Item 9B on form 10-K.

covered by the From 10-K." If the company misses that deadline, it must file an amended Form 10-K.

.05 Form 8-K

The SEC requires U.S. public companies to file a Form 8-K within four days of certain executive compensation and employment events. Since most companies do not want to file any more executive compensation information than the law requires, companies and their advisors need to understand exactly what the 8-K rules require - and what the rules no longer require.

What Must You Report? The SEC shifted the disclosure requirement to Section 5.02 of Form 8-K from Section 1.01. Section 5.02 is more specific about what public companies must disclose, including information regarding:

- Appointment of Certain Officers
- Compensatory Arrangements of Certain Officers
- Departure of Directors or Certain Officers
- Election of Directors

These more specific rules require companies to make fewer determinations about "materiality."

For Whom Reporting is Required. The rules continue an unfortunate distinction between Named Executive Officers ("NEOs") and Specified Principal Officers ("SPOs").

- Named Executive Officers are those who the company listed in its last Proxy Statement.
- Specified Principal Officers are the company's principal executive, financial, accounting, and operating officers, or individuals performing a similar function.

The individuals in these two categories may be the same for many companies. However, some of the reporting requirements apply to NEOs and not SPOs and vice versa.

Commencement or Material Amendment of Material Compensatory Plans, Agreements, or Arrangements, or of Material Grants or Awards for Officers. The SEC does not presume compensatory plans, agreements, and arrangements to be material. If the company determines that a plan, agreement, or arrangement is truly material, then the company must disclose it, along with the amount to be paid to an NEO under the plan, agreement, or arrangement according to Item 5.02(e). Note that the rules would not require the company to disclose any award or modification that is consistent with the previously disclosed terms of a plan or agreement. For example, the company would not be required to file an award agreement for stock options, restricted stock or other stock award if the company previously filed a model award agreement on Form 8-K.

Note also that no 8-K disclosure is required for directors under Item 5.02(e). However, the company will need to disclose entering into plans or arrangements for directors on its next periodic report.

¶1225.05

Departure of NEO or SPO. The rules require public companies to file Form 8-K for the departure of an NEO or SPO.

Appointment or Election of a New SPO or Director. The rules also require public companies to file Form 8-K for the appointment or election of a new SPO and disclose the following information:

- Any material plan, agreement, or arrangement to which the individual is a party or in which he or she participates.
- Any award or grant under, or material amendment to, a plan, agreement or arrangement that the appointment or election triggers.

For example, if a company were to promote its CFO to CEO, the Form 8-K would report that promotion and any new awards or agreements entered into in connection with the promotion.

.06 Form 8-K Reporting of Recurring Awards or Payments

Grants or awards (or modifications thereto) made pursuant to a plan, contract or arrangement (whether involving cash or stock), that are materially consistent with the previously disclosed terms of such plan, contract or arrangement, need not be disclosed under Item 5.02(e), provided the company has previously disclosed such terms and the grant, award or modification is disclosed when Item 402 of Regulation S-K requires such disclosure.

For example, a company need not disclose annual bonus awards/targets set in 2018, and paid out in 2019, if they are consistent with the awards/targets the company has set in prior years. If the company disclosed in a prior year that the CEO's target annual incentive was 100% of her base salary, based on achievement of certain total shareholder return metrics, and the target and metrics for the 2018 fiscal year are not materially different from prior years, there should be no need for an 8-K filing.

Similarly, annual bonuses paid in 2019 for 2018 performance do not need be disclosed if they are consistent with awards reported in a prior year. For example, if the company disclosed the target and metrics for the 2018 fiscal year in early 2018 when the awards were made (or years ago, per #1 above), the company should not need to file an 8-K disclosing that it just made a 105% of base salary payout based on those targets and metrics. However, if the committee were to decide to pay an annual bonus despite the fact that the metrics were not achieved in 2018, that payout, if material, generally should be disclosed in an 8-K filing.

Reporting of stock grants made by a compensation committee in 2018 is essentially the same. Instruction 2 to Item 5.02(e) of 8-K states: Grants or awards (or modifications thereto) made pursuant to a plan, contract or arrangement (whether involving cash or stock), that are materially consistent with the previously disclosed terms of such plan, contract or arrangement, need not be disclosed under this Item 5.02(e), provided the registrant has previously disclosed such terms and the grant, award or modification is disclosed when Item 402 of Regulation S-K (17 CFR 229.402) requires such disclosure.

.07 Form 11-K

Unless a company furnishes certain information, financial statements and exhibits as part of its annual report filed on Form 10-K or Form 10-KSB, Section 15(d) of the Exchange Act requires the company to file with the SEC an annual report on Form 11-K with respect to employee stock purchase, savings and similar plans under which plan interests are separate securities registered under the Securities Act. The information required to be filed, either on Form 11-K or as part of the company's annual report on Form 10-K or Form 10-KSB, includes:

- the full title of the plan;
- the name of the company;
- the name of the securities held pursuant to the plan; and
- certain audited financial statements for the plan.

If required, a Form 11-K must be filed within 90 days after the end of the employee benefit plan's fiscal year, *provided* that financial statements for plans subject to the Employee Retirement Income Security Act of 1974 ("ERISA") are not required to be filed until 180 days after the plan's fiscal year end.

.08 Special Rules for Smaller Reporting Companies and Emerging Growth Companies

SEC rules provide exceptions and scaled-down disclosure obligations for smaller reporting companies and emerging growth companies.

Smaller Reporting Companies. A "smaller reporting company" is an operating company (*i.e.*, one that is not an investment company, an asset-backed issuer, or a majority-owned subsidiary of a parent that is not a smaller reporting company) that: (i) had a public float of less than $250 million; or (ii) had annual revenues of less than $100 million for the most recently completed fiscal year for which audited financial statements are available, and either: (A) no public float; or (B) a public float of less than $700 million.[8]

The determination is made based on the information as to shares outstanding as reported in the Form 10-Q relating to the second fiscal quarter of the issuer's previous fiscal year, *e.g.*, June 30 for calendar year companies, *but excluding shares held by affiliates on that date*. Affiliates include directors, executive officers and shares held by other significant shareholders that may be deemed to be affiliates of the issuer (*i.e.*, they "control, are controlled by, or are under common control with" the issuer). "Control" is "the possession, direct or indirect, of the power to direct or cause the direction of the management and policies of the issuer, whether through the ownership of voting securities, by contract, or otherwise."

For newly public companies, the public float is measured as of a date within 30 days of the date of the filing of the registration statement and computed by multiplying the aggregate worldwide number of shares of its voting and non-

---

[8] § 229.10(f)(1) and (2). Prior to amendments published by the SEC in 2018, the public float test was $75 million. "Smaller reporting company" also is defined in § 230.405 and § 240.12b-2.

voting common stock held by non-affiliates before the registration plus, in the case of a Securities Act registration statement, the number of shares of its voting and non-voting common equity included in the registration statement by the estimated public offering price of the shares.

Emerging Growth Companies. In 2012, the Jumpstart Our Business Startups Act (the "JOBS Act") added a section (19) to the definitions in Section 2(a) of the Securities Act, which reads, in part, as follows:

> (19) The term "emerging growth company" means an issuer that had total annual gross revenues of less than $1,000,000,000 (as such amount is indexed for inflation every 5 years by the Commission to reflect the change in the Consumer Price Index for All Urban Consumers published by the Bureau of Labor Statistics, setting the threshold to the nearest 1,000,000) during its most recently completed fiscal year.

The JOBS Act also amended Section 14A(e) of the Exchange Act to provide generally, that emerging growth companies are permitted to follow requirements for smaller reporting companies. Additionally, an emerging growth company is not required to provide for the shareholder say on pay vote until it loses its emerging growth company status and (i) three years after the company's IPO, if the company was an emerging growth company for less than two years after the IPO, or (ii) one year after losing its emerging growth company status for other companies.

¶1235 Registration

The SEC, pursuant to the Securities Act, requires registration of offers or sales of the company's stock by the company or its affiliates to participants under any voluntary, contributory employee benefit plan. In addition, the ability to participate in a plan may also be considered a security and require registration.[9] Any offer or sale of a plan sponsor's securities not made under an effective registration statement would be considered a violation of the Securities Act, absent an available exemption. A company that offers or sells unregistered securities under the company's employee benefit plans may be subject to civil liability under both federal and state securities laws, as well as enforcement actions by both the SEC and state regulators.

Any offer or sale of a security not made under an effective registration statement would be considered a violation of the Securities Act, absent an exemption. A company that offers or sells unregistered securities under the company's employee benefit plans may be subject to civil liability under both federal and state securities laws, as well as enforcement actions by both the SEC

---

[9] In 1980, the SEC issued an extensive release discussing the issue of when employee benefit plan participation interests are securities. SEC Release No. 33-6188 (February 1, 1980). According to the Release, whether a plan involves the sale of a security depends on whether employee participation is voluntary and whether employees contribute their own money to the plan. Section 3(a)(2) of the Securities Act generally exempts from registration interests in tax-qualified retirement plans, unless employee contributions are allocated to investment in company stock. Similarly, most employee stock purchase plans are not deemed to create separate participation interests that must be registered in addition to the shares of company stock. (SEC Release No. 33-6188).

and state regulators. In addition, participants who purchase unregistered securities may have rescission rights.

.01 Registration Statement on Form S-8

Typically, a registration statement covering an employee benefit plan is prepared on Form S-8. The Form S-8 Registration Statement is quite simple and includes the following information:

- the incorporation of certain documents by reference (*i.e.*, the company's latest annual report on Form 10-K, other reports filed since the end of the last fiscal year, all documents filed subsequently pursuant to Sections 13(a), 13(c), 14 or 15(d) of the Exchange Act and the description of the company's common stock);
- interests of named experts and counsel;
- a description of director and officer indemnification;
- a description of the specific exemption from registration for any restricted securities to be reoffered or resold pursuant to the registration statement;
- exhibits; and
- certain undertakings.

Registration on Form S-8 requires payment of a filing fee that varies with the aggregate offering price (*e.g.*, fair market value) for the maximum amount of securities registered.[10] In addition, the company must furnish plan participants with all the communications that go to shareholders (*e.g.*, annual reports, proxy statements).

.02 Section 10(a) Prospectus

In addition to filing a Form S-8 Registration Statement, an effective registration requires that a company deliver to each participant in an employee benefit plan documents and information constituting a prospectus that meets the requirements of Section 10(a) of the Securities Act. The company must keep the information contained in the prospectus current, whether by supplements or restatements. The prospectus documents and information generally consist of:

- a statement of general information that summarizes: (1) general plan information; (2) the securities to be offered; (3) plan participants; (4) purchase procedures; (5) resale restrictions on the securities offered; (6) the material federal tax consequences of an investment in the securities offered; (7) the terms and conditions under which an employee may withdraw from the plan or withdraw funds or investments from the employee's account; (8) any event under the plan that could result in a forfeiture by or a penalty to an employee and the consequences thereof; (9) any charges and deductions that may be made against employees participating in the plan or against funds, securities or other property

---

[10] If the registration statement also covers participation interests in the plan that constitute separate securities, no separate fee is required with respect to the plan interests. Rule 457(h)(2) of the Securities Act.

held under the plan; and (10) whether any person has or may create a lien on any funds, securities or other property held under the plan;

- the documents that are incorporated by reference into the Form S-8 Registration Statement, including the company's annual report filed on Form 10-K, the plan's latest annual report (if interests in the plan are being registered), and any other company reports filed pursuant to Section 13(a) or 15(d) of the Exchange Act since the end of the fiscal year covered by the company's annual report; and

- a statement of the availability, without charge, of documents filed by the plan sponsor under the Exchange Act and incorporated by reference into the prospectus or otherwise required to be delivered to plan participants.

Unlike other types of prospectuses, the company does not need to file the prospectus material used in connection with an employee benefit plan with the SEC. However, the plan sponsor must retain the documents constituting a part of the prospectus.

.03 Electronic Delivery

The rules require the issuer to send the Prospectus to all participants or holders of outstanding stock awards (and in the future to all new award recipients) under the plan, along with (i) a copy of the plan and (ii) a copy of the latest annual report or 424(b) prospectus (with audited financial statements). Under SEC rules, the issuer may deliver the prospectus and other documents electronically (*e.g.*, by e-mail), if these following requirements are satisfied:

(1) All employees who would receive the e-mail delivering the prospectus documents use e-mail in the ordinary course of performing their duties and are expected to log on to e-mail routinely. For those employees who do not use e-mail, they must have alternative means to receiving electronic messages (*e.g.*, secretaries or other co-workers deliver e-mail messages to them).

(2) The company must attach the prospectus documents to the e-mail. Alternatively, the prospectus documents can be placed on the issuer's intranet, and the e-mail must announce that these documents are available and provide information on how to access these documents (*e.g.*, include the URL).

(3) The e-mail informs employees that they can receive a hard copy of any or all of the documents that constitute the prospectus free of charge, on request.

A registration statement on Form S-8 and any post-effective amendment become effective immediately upon filing with the SEC. Upon filing, they become publicly available.

.04 Prospectus Delivery and Updating Obligations

Section 10(a) of the Securities Act requires that a prospectus being used more than nine months after the effective date of a registration statement contain information as of a date within 16 months of the date the prospectus is used, "so far as such information is known to the user of such prospectus or can be furnished by such user without unreasonable effort or expense." This requirement means that the company must periodically update the financial data given on investment funds described in a prospectus for a 401(k) plan, unless it is unreasonable to do so. For example, if a prospectus contains financial data for investment funds that is dated as of March 31, 2016, the company should update this financial data by the end of July 2017 (16 months after March 31, 2016). Generally, most other information is updated through incorporation by reference of the plan sponsor's SEC filings in the prospectus.

Further, in accordance with SEC rules, any material change in the employee benefit plan information provided in a prospectus must be updated to reflect such changes as soon as practicable. In the case of an employee benefit plan subject to ERISA, most of this information also will be described in the updated summary plan description (the "SPD").

A company may update the prospectus information in different ways. For example, the company could republish the entire prospectus document with the new data. Alternatively, the company could produce and distribute separate updates or supplements as necessary. All separate updates would have to contain the legend required under SEC rules stating that the information is part of a prospectus. Whatever method the company uses, it must keep copies of all documents that constitute a part of a prospectus for a period of five years after they are last used as part of a prospectus.

An additional updating requirement involves the registration with the SEC of shares offered under an employee benefit plan. In this respect, the aggregate number of shares acquired by participants under an employee benefit plan may not exceed the number of registered shares. Thus, monitoring of total shares of company stock purchased under an employee benefit plan is important. The company may register additional shares with the SEC on a new Form S-8 Registration Statement as required.

¶1245 Resales by Employees

In general, shares of stock acquired under an employee benefit plan that have been registered on Form S-8 are unrestricted securities and may be freely resold. In certain cases, shares acquired under an employee benefit plan by affiliates (*e.g.*, executive officers or directors) will be subject to restrictions on resale, notwithstanding the fact that the shares acquired under the plan are registered. These shares are referred to as "control securities." In addition, shares acquired by a participant under an employee benefit plan prior to the registration on Form S-8 will be subject to restrictions on resale imposed by Rule 144 under the Securities Act ("Rule 144"). These shares are called "restricted securities." In both cases, Rule 10b-5 prohibits the purchase or sale of securities while in possession of material nonpublic information.

.01 Reoffer Prospectus

Control and restricted securities may be reoffered and resold under a Form S-8 Registration Statement if the company files with the SEC a separate "reoffer prospectus." The reoffer prospectus generally contains the same information that would be required to be included in a prospectus contained in a Form S-3 Registration Statement, including summary information about the company, risk factors, the ratio of combined fixed charges and preference dividends to earnings (if applicable), information regarding use of proceeds, the determination of the offering price, dilution, selling security holders and the plan of distribution, as well as a description of the securities to be registered, the disclosure of any interests of named experts and counsel, disclosure of any material changes, the incorporation of certain information by reference and the disclosure of the SEC's position on indemnification for Securities Act liabilities. A reoffer prospectus would allow the holder of control or restricted securities to sell shares without regard to the manner of sale and volume limitations imposed by Rule 144.

The reoffer prospectus may be used for any amount of securities if the company meets the requirements for use of Form S-3 under the Securities Act. However, if at the time of filing, the company does not satisfy the requirements for use of Form S-3, then the amounts of control securities and restricted securities acquired under an employee benefit plan that may be reoffered and resold by each selling shareholder may not exceed, during any three-month period, the amount of securities specified in Rule 144(e)[11] under the Securities Act. The SEC has stated that a holder does not need to aggregate his or her employee benefit plan shares with other shares to be resold under Rule 144 in determining compliance with the volume limitations.

With respect to control securities, the reoffer prospectus must disclose the names of the holders who are reoffering and reselling these control securities. If the names of the sellers of control securities are unknown at the time of the filing of the registration statement, they may be referred to generically. Otherwise, all such holders eligible to resell must be named and the maximum number of securities that may be resold by them must be indicated, regardless of their intent to sell such securities. As the names of generically described or additional sellers of control securities become available, they must be disclosed in supplements to the reoffer prospectus filed with the SEC.

With respect to restricted securities, the reoffer prospectus must also disclose the names of the holders who are reoffering and reselling restricted securities, provided, however, that any nonaffiliate who holds less than 1,000 shares or 1% of the shares issuable under the employee benefit plan to which the Form S-8 Registration Statement relates need not be named if the reoffer prospectus indicates that certain unnamed nonaffiliates, each of whom may sell up to the excepted amount, may use the reoffer prospectus for reoffers and resales.

---

[11] The amount of securities that can be sold under the rule during any three-month period is limited to the greater of one percent of the outstanding securities of the class or the average weekly trading volume of the class during the four calendar weeks preceding the date of the sale.

A reoffer prospectus covering control securities may be filed with the initial registration statement on Form S-8, or by means of a post-effective amendment thereto. A reoffer prospectus covering restricted securities must be filed with the initial registration statement, and may not be filed by means of a post-effective amendment thereto.

.02 Rule 144

Generally, shares of stock acquired under an employee benefit plan, which have been registered on Form S-8 (as all should be) are unrestricted securities and may be resold freely. However, shares acquired under an employee benefit plan by "affiliates" of the company will be subject to restrictions on resale under Rule 144, as "control securities."

Rule 144 applies to sales or resales of company stock by "affiliates." Affiliates must "register" sales of stock by filing Form 144. Rule 144 provides a safe harbor that allows for the resale of restricted securities by affiliates, if certain conditions are satisfied. An "affiliate" of the company is a person that, directly or indirectly, controls, is controlled by or is under common control with the company. The term "affiliates" also includes directors, executive officers, and shareholders owning more than 10% of the company's common stock.

Most companies do not file a reoffer prospectus. Thus, holders of control or restricted securities acquired under an employee benefit plan must sell their securities in accordance with Rule 144. In general, Rule 144 provides a safe harbor from the registration requirements of the Securities Act for resales of control securities if the following conditions are met:

- *Current Public Information:* The company must have securities registered pursuant to the Exchange Act, have been subject to SEC reporting requirements for a period of 90 days immediately preceding the sale and have filed all reports required to be filed during the 12 months preceding such sale.
- *Volume limitation:* The amount of securities that may be resold in any three-month period is limited to the greater of 1% of the company's outstanding stock and the average weekly trading volume during the four calendar weeks preceding the resale.
- *Manner of sale:* The securities must be sold in an unsolicited "brokers' transaction" or directly to "market makers."
- *Holding period:* The affiliate must have held the restricted securities for at least six months.
- *Notice of sale:* The affiliate/seller must file a Form 144 "Notice of Proposed Sale of Securities," with the SEC if more than 500 shares or securities with a value in excess of $10,000 are to be sold.

SEC Compliance and Disclosure Interpretation 532.06 provides that with regard to restricted securities received under an individually negotiated employment agreement, the Rule 144 holding period commences when investment risk for the securities passes to the employee (which is the date that the employee is deemed to have paid for them). For full value awards, such as restricted stock or RSUs, if the vesting of the securities is conditioned on continued employment and/or company performance (*i.e.*, not tied to the employee's individual performance) and the employee pays no further consideration for the securities, the commencement date would be the date of the agreement. For awards that require additional payment upon exercise, conversion or settlement, the commencement date would be the date that payment is made.

Compliance with insider trading policies/laws and Section 16 reporting also is required. In all cases, Rule 10b-5 of the Exchange Act prohibits the purchase or sale of securities while in possession of material nonpublic information. Company insider trading policies and stock ownership guidelines may impose further restrictions on sales by directors and executive officers.

¶1255 Rule 10b-5

Rule 10b-5 under the Exchange Act prohibits individuals from trading stock based on nonpublic, or "inside," information.

.01 Rule 10b5-1

Rule 10b5-1 under the Securities Exchange Act of 1934 provides that a purchase or sale of securities is not on the basis of material, nonpublic information where the individual or entity making the purchase or sale can show that prior to becoming aware of the material, nonpublic information, the individual or entity had (1) entered into a binding contract for the purchase or sale of the security; (2) instructed a third party to purchase or sell the security for its account; or (3) adopted a written plan for trading securities. With respect to (3), this type of plan must have the following characteristics:

- It must specify the "amount"[12] of securities to be purchased or sold, and the "price"[13] at which the securities were to be purchased or sold and the "date"[14] on which the securities were to be purchased or sold; or

- It must include a written formula for determining the amount, price and date of the transaction; or

- It must not permit the individual or entity to exercise any subsequent influence over how, when and whether to conduct the purchases or sales, and to delegate those decisions to a person who does not possess material, nonpublic information; and

- The purchase or sale at issue must occur "pursuant to the contract, instruction or plan," meaning that the individual or entity that entered into the trading plan did not alter or deviate from it, or enter into or alter a corresponding or hedging transaction with respect to the securities.

---

[12] The rule defines "amount" as either a specified number of shares or other securities or the dollar value of securities.

[13] The rule defines "price" as the market price on a particular date, a limit price, or a particular dollar price.

[14] The rule defines "date," in the case of a market order, as the specific day of the year on which the order is to be executed (or as soon thereafter as possible under principles of best execution) and, in the case of a limit order, as any day of the year on which the limit order is in force.

However, an insider may modify a trading plan at a time when the insider is not in possession of material, nonpublic information.

There is no requirement that issuers (or executive officers) disclose the entry into a 10b5-1 plan. However, most companies choose to disclose insiders' plans, either in a press release or in an 8-K. The reason for the filings is twofold: first, issuers want the market to know that an insider will be trading (usually selling) on a regular basis for a period of time, so the market won't be spooked every time a Form 4 gets filed showing that the insider is selling. Second, many issuers fear that an insider's plan to sell might be considered material nonpublic information about the issuer's securities, making Regulation FD applicable to the issuer's discussion of the plan with analysts. Because issuers often like to inform analysts of the proposed sales and to explain how the plan will work, they file an 8-K to assure adequate public dissemination of the information for purposes of Regulation FD.

Acquisitions of company stock through payroll deductions under these types of plans could qualify under the rule if the acquisitions were made pursuant to either oral or written instructions as to plan participation or a written plan. The transaction amount could be based on a percentage of salary to be deducted under the plan, and the transaction price could be based on the market price. The date could be determined in accordance with a formula contained in a written plan, or could be controlled by the administrator or investment manager of the benefit plan. Where the date of acquisition is controlled by the administrator or investment manager, that person must not be aware of material, nonpublic information at the time of executing the transaction, and the employee must not exercise influence over the timing of the transaction.

.02 Insider Trading Cases

In a decision on May 15, 2008, *In Re Countrywide Financial Corp. Derivative Litigation*, a federal district court judge in California found that former CEO Angelo Mozilo's changes to his 10b5-1 plans were "probative of scienter," which is the knowledge necessary to support a charge of insider trading.[15] The former CEO established his original 10b5-1 plan on April 26, 2004. The original plan provided for the sale of roughly 200,000 to 250,000 shares each month, and expired in May 2006. The former CEO subsequently implemented two additional plans on October 27, 2006 and December 12, 2006. The October plan was implemented only days after the company announced a stock repurchase offer, which typically increases the price of the stock. He then amended the December plan to double the number of shares sold, on February 2, 2007, which coincided with the date on which Countrywide stock reached an all time high of $45.03 a share. Interestingly, the court found it irrelevant that the former CEO held on to over seven million shares of Countrywide stock through the end of 2007, even as the market was falling, quoting from *Nursing Home Pension Fund, Local 144 v. Oracle Corp.*, "where, as here, stock sales result in a truly astronomical figure, less

---

[15] 554 F. Supp.2d 1044 (C.D.CA 2008).

weight should be given to the fact that they may represent a small portion of the defendant's holdings."[16]

In 2009, the SEC filed a complaint in the federal district court in Los Angeles charging the former CEO and two other former Countrywide executives with securities fraud for deliberately misleading investors about the significant credit risks being taken in efforts to build and maintain the company's market share. The SEC also charged the former CEO with insider trading for selling his Countrywide stock based on non-public information for nearly $140 million in profits.

> "During the course of this fraud, Mozilo engaged in insider trading in Countrywide's securities. Mozilo established four sales plans pursuant to Rule 10b5-1 of the Securities Exchange Act in October, November, and December 2006 while in possession of material, non-public information concerning Countrywide's increasing credit risk and the risk that the poor expected performance of Countrywide-originated loans would prevent Countrywide from continuing its business model of selling the majority of the loans it originated into the secondary mortgage market. From November 2006 through August 2007, Mozilo exercised over 5.1 million stock options and sold the underlying shares for total proceeds of over $139 million, pursuant to 10b5-1 plans adopted in late 2006 and amended in early 2007."

In October 2010, the former CEO reached a settlement with the SEC, agreeing to pay $67.5 million in fines and accepting a lifetime ban from serving as an officer or director of any public company.

¶1265 Section 16 of the Exchange Act

Section 16 of the Exchange Act provides that directors, certain executive officers, and 10-percent shareholders of a publicly held company are subject to obligations and restrictions relating to their ownership and trading of the company's equity securities. Section 16(a) of the Exchange Act contains reporting requirements and Section 16(b) contains trading restrictions. Equity securities include the company's common stock and all options to purchase such stock.

.01 Executives and Directors Subject to Section 16

The reporting and short-swing profit provisions of Section 16 apply to all stock owned by a 10-percent shareholder, director or executive officer (referred to as "insiders" or "reporting persons") of a public company. Section 16 applies to all stock beneficially owned by a reporting person, even if the person is not the record owner. A person is deemed to own stock beneficially if he or she has the ability to vote or dispose of, or to direct the voting or disposition of, the stock, or if he or she has the right to acquire such power within 60 days. Under Section 16, a person is deemed to own beneficially securities held by members of his or her "immediate family" who share his or her residence (including children, stepchildren, grandchildren, parents, step-parents, grandparents, spouses, siblings and in-laws, and all adoptive relationships). However, a member of a group is required to report only the stock in which the person has a "pecuniary interest,"

---

[16] 380 F.3d 1226, 1232 (9th Cir. 2004).

or the opportunity, directly or indirectly, to profit or share in any profit derived from a transaction in the equity securities.

The term executive officer means the company's president, any vice president in charge of a principal business unit, division or function (such as sales, administration or finance), and any other officer who performs a policy-making function or any other person who performs similar policy-making functions for the company. Executive officers of subsidiaries may be deemed executive officers of the parent company if they perform such policy-making functions for the company. Executive officers must be listed in the Form 10-K (or the proxy statement). If an individual is listed as an executive officer in the 10-K, there is a presumption that the individual is also a Section 16 officer. A company's board of directors usually appoints Section 16 executive officers.

.02 Reporting Requirements

Section 16(a) of the Exchange Act requires a company's insiders (*i.e.*, officers, directors and owners of more than 10% of the company's outstanding securities) to file the following reports with the SEC disclosing the ownership of, and certain transactions involving, company stock.

- *Initial Statement of Beneficial Ownership (Form 3)*: Must be filed within 10 days of becoming an insider of a company that has a class of equity securities registered under Section 12 of the Exchange Act.

- *Statement of Changes of Beneficial Ownership of Securities (Form 4)*: Must be filed on or before the second business day after any transaction involving company stock, including transactions that are exempt from Section 16(b) of the Exchange Act.

- *Annual Statement of Beneficial Ownership of Securities (Form 5)*: Must be filed on or before the 45th day after the end of the company's fiscal year. In general, Form 5 must include information regarding transactions not previously reported and total beneficial ownership as of the end of the company's fiscal year.

Gifts or donations of securities by insiders may be reported on a delayed basis on a Form 5, although many companies voluntarily choose to report such gifts on a Form 4. In addition, the SEC has created two other exceptions to the requirement for Form 4 reporting within two business days of any officers' or directors' transactions involving company stock.

The first exception is for 10b5-1(c) transactions, where the officer or director does not select the date of execution. For example, a 10b5-1(c) arrangement where the price movement in the market determines the date of execution of a transaction as opposed to a 10b5-1(c) arrangement where the transaction is to occur on the first business day of each month.

The second exception exists for "discretionary transactions" where the officer or director does not select the date of execution (*i.e.*, fund-switching elections under a tax-qualified individual account retirement plan). Transactions that qualify for one of these two exceptions do not need to be reported until the "deemed date of execution." The deemed execution date is the earlier of: (1) the date on which the officer or director is notified that the transaction has occurred or (2) the third business day following the transaction.

.03 Exemptions

Certain exemptions to Section 16(a) reporting and 16(b) liability are contained in Rule 16b-3 under Section 16 of the Exchange Act.

- *Tax Qualified Plans.* A transaction pursuant to a "qualified plan," "stock purchase plan," or an "excess benefit plan" is generally exempt from Section 16(b), unless the transaction is a "discretionary transaction." A "discretionary transaction" is generally defined to include volitional intra-plan transfers of equity securities of the company or a cash distribution funded by a volitional disposition (such as a loan) of equity securities of the company.

- *Acquisitions from and Dispositions to the Company.* A transaction (other than a "discretionary transaction") between a company and an employee is exempt from Section 16(b) if: (1) the transaction is approved by the company's board of directors or a committee of the board of directors composed solely of two or more "nonemployee" directors;[17] (2) the transaction is approved or ratified by a majority of the company's shareholders; or (3) the employee holds the securities for a period of six months following the date of acquisition.

.04 Form 4 Issues

Form 4 is due within two business days after compensation committee approval of an award (unless the grant is made effective as of a future date.) For example, if a compensation committee were to grant awards on Saturday, the Form 4 must be filed on Tuesday.[18] When options are exercised or restricted stock vests, if shares are withheld to satisfy the tax, then a Form 4 is due within two days of the vesting or exercise. When RSUs vest and settle into stock or cash, a Form 4 is due within two days of the vesting. If all of these grants and the terms are approved, then all of these events are exempt from matching - but the company still needs to file the Forms.

The types of transactions reportable on Form 4 include:

- Grants of Stock Options
- Cashless Exercise of Stock Options (and sale of shares)
- Grants of Restricted Stock or RSUs

---

[17] A nonemployee director is a director who: (1) is not currently an officer of the company (or a parent or subsidiary thereof), or otherwise currently employed by the company (or a parent or subsidiary thereof); (2) does not receive compensation, either directly or indirectly, from the company (or a parent or subsidiary thereof), for services rendered as a consultant or in any capacity other than as a director, except for an amount that does not exceed the dollar amount for which disclosure would be required pursuant to Item 404(a) of Regulation S-K; and (3) does not possess an interest in any other transaction for which disclosure would be required pursuant to Item 404(a) of Regulation S-K. See Rule 16b-3(b)(3) of the Exchange Act.

[18] Very small acquisitions, cumulatively less than $10,000 in a rolling six-month period, do not need to be filed on Form 4 (but would need to be reported on Form 5, eventually).

- Grants of RSUs
- Vesting (Settlement) of RSUs
- Open Market Purchase of Stock
- Open Market Sale of Stock

Form 4 specifies the following "Transaction Codes," which companies and other filers must use:

General Transaction Codes

- P — Open market or private purchase of non-derivative or derivative security
- S — Open market or private sale of non-derivative or derivative security
- V — Transaction voluntarily reported earlier than required

Rule 16b-3 Transaction Codes

- A — Grant, award or other acquisition pursuant to Rule 16b-3(d) **(these are "compensatory awards")**
- D — Disposition to the issuer of issuer equity securities pursuant to Rule 16b-3(e)
- F — Payment of exercise price or tax liability by delivering or withholding securities incident to the receipt, exercise or vesting of a security issued in accordance with Rule 16b-3
- I — Discretionary transaction in accordance with Rule 16b-3(f) resulting in acquisition or disposition of issuer securities
- M — Exercise or conversion of derivative security exempted pursuant to Rule 16b-3

Derivative Securities Codes (Except for transactions exempted pursuant to Rule 16b-3)

- C — Conversion of derivative security
- E — Expiration of short derivative position
- H — Expiration (or cancellation) of long derivative position with value received
- O — Exercise of out-of-the-money derivative security
- X — Exercise of in-the-money or at-the-money derivative security

Other Section 16(b) Exempt Transaction and Small Acquisition Codes (Except for Rule 16b-3 codes above)

- G — Bona fide gift
- L — Small acquisition under Rule 16a-6
- W — Acquisition or disposition by will or the laws of descent and distribution
- Z — Deposit into or withdrawal from voting trust

Other Transaction Codes

- J — Other acquisition or disposition (describe transaction)
- K — Transaction in equity swap or instrument with similar characteristics
- U — Disposition pursuant to a tender of shares in a change of control transaction

All Form 4 statements must be filed electronically with the SEC and posted on a company's website no later than the next day after filing. A company whose officers and directors do not file the appropriate Form 4s in a timely manner will be required to disclose the failure in its proxy statement.

.05 Form 4 Issues for Restricted Stock and RSU Awards

Companies should report a grant of restricted stock in Table I (Non-Derivative Securities), using code A. No separate filing is made at vesting for restricted stock, unless any shares of stock are withheld or surrendered to cover withholding. Shares automatically withheld to pay taxes are reported on a different line in Table I with transaction code F. When dividends are paid on restricted awards and held until vesting, if the dividends are distributed in stock, they must be reported on Form 4.

Ordinarily, a company will report a grant of RSUs in Table I (Non-Derivative Securities), using code A. When the RSUs can be settled only in stock and the grant was reported in Table I, the company does not need to file a separate Form 4 at vesting, unless any stock is withheld or surrendered to cover withholding. Shares automatically withheld to pay taxes are reported on a different line in Table I with transaction code F. If instead the RSUs were reported at grant as derivative securities in Table II (they technically represent the right to receive securities in the future), then no more than two business days after vesting the company must report this on Table I for the conversion into actual shares and Table II for the disposition of the RSUs. For awards approved under Rule 16b-3, this is reported with transaction code M ("Exercise or conversion of derivative security exempt pursuant to Rule 16b-3").

.06 Form 4 Issues for Performance Share Awards

Performance share awards with vesting that is contingent upon any metrics other than a stock price target are not reportable on a Form 4 until earned. The SEC considers total shareholder return ("TSR") to be the equivalent of a stock price target only when the TSR target is absolute, not relative, and then only if dividends are not paid on the underlying stock or the dividends paid are nominal.

A participant will be deemed to acquire a derivative security on the date the performance criteria are satisfied and should report the acquisition on Form 4 within two business days thereafter. Similarly, to the extent that satisfaction of the performance criteria results in delivery to the participant of stock or other equity securities, the participant must report the acquisition of those securities as of the date the number earned is determined. In those instances in which delivery of the underlying securities (or the cash value thereof) is made at the same time the number of securities earned is determined, the performance right would not be reportable at all, based on the SEC staff's position that an instrument that has terms that become fixed only at the time of exercise is not a derivative security.

.07 Proxy Statement Disclosure of Late Form 4s

Item 405 of Regulation S-K requires a company to review the Forms 3, 4 and 5 filed by its insiders (directors, officers and 10% owners) for the preceding fiscal year and disclose in its proxy statement all known instances where a corporate insider failed to make a Section 16(a) filing, or filed one late. In September 2014, the SEC announced a major enforcement action against 34 individuals and companies for violations of the beneficial ownership reporting requirements of Sections 16(a) and 13(d) and (g) of the Exchange Act and the companies' violations of the Item 405 disclosure requirement of Reg. S-K (the proxy statement).[19]

It appears that some of the companies subject to the enforcement action had not reviewed or revised their Item 405 disclosures for several years. A number of the violations seem to be attributable to an over-reliance on boilerplate. For example, two of the companies in the enforcement action had included boilerplate Item 405 disclosures to the effect that all reports were timely filed. However, it was clear even from EDGAR filings that dozens of their required Form 4s were filed late. Another company had filed numerous late reports, and all it said under Item 405 was that certain directors or executives filed late, which is not enough. Another company indicated that its compliance with Section 16 reporting requirements was based on written certifications from insiders, when in fact it had not obtained any such certifications.

Four of the companies cited for Item 405 violations were also charged with causing their insiders to violate Section 16(a), by undertaking to file the Section 16 reports for the insiders - which is the common practice among companies - by filing them late. This is notable, because it is the first time to our knowledge that the SEC has brought enforcement actions like this against a company since the adoption of Section 16. For companies that file Section 16 reports on behalf of their officers and directors, this could mean that Section 16(a) compliance is now part of the company's legal compliance risk. We do not expect companies to push this responsibility back onto officers and directors, but boards of directors now have more of a stake in making sure the compliance process is adequate. In addition to the insiders, companies are now possible enforcement targets when the company's processes and systems fail.

.08 Short-Swing Profit Liability

Section 16(b) of the Exchange Act requires the mandatory recovery by the company of any "short-swing" profit attributed to a reporting person or members of his or her immediate family as a result of the matched purchase and sale, or sale and purchase, of company stock that occurs within a period of less than

---

[19] https://www.sec.gov/news/press-release/2014-190.

¶1265.07

six months, unless an exemption applies to one or both of the matched transactions.

In determining whether there has been a purchase and sale within the meaning of Section 16(b), it is not necessary that the same shares were purchased and sold, or sold and purchased, within the six-month period. The identity of the particular shares is irrelevant for determining Section 16(b) liability. There have even been cases where the reporting person actually lost money but was held accountable for "profits."

To compute the statutory short-swing profit, the highest sale price and lowest purchase price during the six-month period are matched, regardless of whether the sale and purchase involved the same shares. For a series of transactions, the difference between the highest sale price and the lowest purchase price during the period is computed (regardless of the order in which they occur), then the difference between the next highest sale price and next lowest purchase price, and so forth.

The recovery for short-swing profits belongs to the company and the company cannot waive it. If the company fails or refuses to collect or sue a reporting person for short-swing profits within 60 days of a demand by a shareholder, the shareholder may sue in the company's name for recovery within two years after such profits were realized. Courts have often awarded attorneys' fees to the plaintiff's counsel in these actions based upon the amount recovered. The failure of a director or executive officer to comply with Section 16 requirements could also require the company to make adverse disclosures in its proxy statements.

> **Planning Note:** The regulations governing short-swing trading liability are extremely complex and subject to continuing modification by the SEC. It is imperative that any trading in company stock be coordinated with someone who is familiar with these regulations. Nearly all public companies have adopted a compliance program that requires executive officers and directors to pre-clear all transactions involving company stock with the corporate secretary's or general counsel's office.

.09 Compliance Programs

Because of the complexity of and high stakes surrounding securities law compliance by a reporting person, most public companies maintain a compliance and pre-clearance program. Public companies' compliance programs typically require all reporting persons to pre-clear transactions in company stock (including the exercise of stock options and certain benefit plan transactions) with the office of the corporate secretary or general counsel. Companies' pre-clearance programs also generally apply to (1) transactions conducted by members of a reporting person's immediate family who share the same household, (2) shares of company stock held in "street name," (3) shares of company stock held in other accounts (*e.g.*, individual retirement accounts and trust accounts), and (4) company stock owned by companies and partnerships over which the reporting person exercises control.

Among the key elements of most public companies' compliance programs would be the following:

1. Section 16 Filings. The company will prepare SEC Form 3 upon an individual's assumption of reporting person status. Additionally, the company will automatically prepare the appropriate SEC Form 4 on behalf of all reporting persons upon being informed of transactions in company stock (including certain benefit plan transactions) pursuant to the pre-clearance requirement. The company will require each reporting person to execute a power of attorney authorizing the corporate secretary to sign SEC Forms 3 and 4 on his or her behalf.

2. Short-Swing Profit Preventative Procedures. Prior to clearing a reporting person's transaction in company stock, the corporate secretary or general counsel's office would review with the individual any Section 16(b) matchable transactions that may have occurred within the preceding six months as well as any transactions that may occur within the coming months. Matchable transactions conducted by members of the reporting person's immediate family who share his or her household also would be reviewed.

3. "Window Periods." Most compliance programs permit open market purchases or sales of company stock and the exercise and sale (or cashless exercise) of stock options by reporting persons only during a specified "window period." Typically the "window period" would begin on the fourth trading day following the release of the company's quarterly or annual financial information via public earnings release (usually the second week of January, April, July and October for a calendar year company) and end sometime between the first day of the last month of each calendar quarter or ten days prior to the end of the calendar quarter. Other benefit plan transactions are also limited to this period (*i.e.*, transfers to or from the company stock fund, cash distributions funded by company stock fund sales). Generally, directors, officers, employees and other insiders who have regular access to material nonpublic information are forbidden from trading outside of the "window periods."

4. "Blackout Periods." Most compliance plans permit the board of directors, chief executive officer, or general counsel to suspend trading during a window period in the event of a material, nonpublic occurrence or event (*e.g.*, an acquisition, stock offering, earnings variance, or similar development).

5. Insider Trading Procedures. As part of most companies' pre-clearance procedures, the corporate secretary or general counsel will determine whether any material information relating to the company or the company stock is nonpublic before clearing a director's or executive officer's transaction in company stock. Additionally, if the company has recently released material information, the corporate secretary or general counsel will evaluate whether sufficient time has elapsed to enable the information to be adequately disseminated to, and considered by, investors and the general public. Many companies will assist the reporting person in establishing an effective Rule 10b5-1(c) trading plan.

6. Rule 144 and Rule 145 Procedures. Prior to clearing a reporting person's transaction in company stock, the corporate secretary's office will determine whether the conditions of the safe harbor of Rule 144 and, if applicable, Rule 145, have been satisfied.

.10 Section 16b Litigation

A company's board or compensation committee approves restricted stock and RSU grants (and the forms of the awards, including vesting and share withholding terms) so that they are exempt from matching. Whether insiders are allowed to have the company withhold some shares to pay their taxes on restricted stock that vests during a closed window period may depend on whether the company's insider trading policy allows it. Most practitioners do not consider withholding of shares for taxes during a closed window or blackout period to violate Rule 10b-5 insider trading restrictions, primarily because the company and the employee have equal access to the nonpublic information.

There is no "legal" prohibition on tax withholding where an insider elects to have shares withheld upon the vesting of restricted stock for the purpose of tax withholdings, even if the vesting date happens to coincide with the first day of a company mandated blackout period. The issue is only whether the insider can engage in tax withholding during a blackout period without violating the company's policy. Most policies do not prohibit tax withholding transactions during a blackout period, because transactions directly with the issuer do not raise the same Rule 10b-5 concerns as sales into the open market (because the issuer, unlike market purchasers, has the same access to nonpublic information as the insider). In 2016, several public companies received a letter from a single "shareholder" demanding that they seek to recover alleged short-swing profits from insiders under Section 16(b) of the Exchange Act. The letters alleged that the insiders had made non-exempt purchases of stock within six months of having shares withheld either (i) for payment of the exercise price of employee stock options or (ii) to satisfy tax liabilities upon the vesting of restricted stock, restricted stock units, or stock appreciation rights, or upon the exercise of employee stock options.

The companies had reported the withholding transactions on Form 4s, indicating the dispositions were exempted from matching for purposes of Section 16(b) liability by SEC Rule 16b-3(e) because the transactions were between the company and its officers and directors and the withholding right was a term of the initial award as approved by the board or a committee of non-employee directors. The shareholder argued that Rule 16b-3(e) exemption for withholding is not available unless (i) the company has no discretion to accept or reject the withholding, and (ii) the withholding is "automatic" in that the insider must pay the tax or exercise price with shares and cannot elect to pay the tax or exercise price with cash instead.

In April 2017, the United States District Court for the Southern District of Texas granted a motion to dismiss this type of claim, with prejudice. In *Jordan v. Flexton, et al.*,[20] the court held that dispositions of restricted stock units to cover

---

[20] No. 4:16-CV-03316 (S.D. Tx. 2017).

tax withholding were compensation related transactions and were designed to be exempt under Section 16b-3(e) of the Exchange Act.

At this time, the shareholder/plaintiff seems to have given up on this issue. However, to minimize the risk of future claims and litigation over the issue, some companies have made all share withholding in forms of stock award agreements for Section 16 officers automatic and have the compensation committee approve the withholding.

.11 Potential Trap for Executives at Dividend-Paying Companies

Most companies have a firm handle on the stock ownership and trades made by their officers and directors (referred to as "insiders"). This knowledge is essential for the company and its insiders to comply with the reporting and short-wing profit rules of Section 16. However, a scenario in which we have occasionally seen a slip-up is when the insider enters into a dividend reinvestment plan (DRIP) with respect to shares of company stock held by his or her broker (especially where the insider has transferred company stock to a trust and it has become even further removed from the company's oversight).

One problem that can arise in this scenario is that the company does not timely file a Form 4 for the acquisition of new stock - by way of a dividend - by the insider because it is not aware of the DRIP (and the insider forgets to inform the company). The only way to address this problem is through enhanced communication and follow up with the insider as to all of his or her company stock holdings, perhaps with a specific question about any outside DRIPs that the insider may have established.

A second problem that can arise is that the insider sells company stock in a separate transaction, such as under a Rule 10b5-1 plan, which becomes a matchable transaction to the DRIP acquisition. Rule 16a-11 provides for an exemption for DRIP acquisitions made pursuant to a plan providing for the regular reinvestment of dividends or interest and the plan provides for broad-based participation, does not discriminate in favor of employees of the company, and operates on substantially the same terms for all plan participants. However, if the DRIP is maintained by the insider's broker and not the company, we cannot automatically assume that it satisfies the 16a-11 exemption.

Again, the answer to this problem is enhanced communication and follow up with the insiders. If the company learns of a DRIP maintained by an insider's broker, in-house or outside counsel can review it for compliance with the 16a-11 exemption. Most DRIPs established by large brokerage firms will be designed to mirror the DRIP maintained by the company and, thus will satisfy the 16a-11 exemption.

¶1275 Compensation Clawback Policies

Nearly every public company in America has adopted a compensation clawback policy. Compensation clawbacks first became a matter of law under Section 304 of SOX. Section 954 of the Dodd-Frank Act signed into law by

President Obama in July 2010, would expand the compensation clawback requirement applicable to public companies.

As of this date, Section 954 is not fully effective because the SEC has not adopted the required regulations. However, compensation clawback policies were becoming a best practice even before the Dodd-Frank Act, which accelerated this development.

.01 SOX Section 304 Clawbacks and SEC Enforcement

Under SOX Section 304, effective July 30, 2002, if a public company is required to prepare an accounting restatement due to the material noncompliance of the company, as a result of misconduct, with any financial reporting requirement under the securities laws, the CEO and CFO must reimburse the company for (1) any bonus or other "incentive-based" or "equity-based" compensation received during the 12-month period following the first public issuance or filing with the SEC (whichever occurs first) of the financial document embodying the financial reporting requirement; and (2) any profits realized from the sale of securities of the company during that 12-month period.

The SEC has vigorously enforced the clawback provisions of SOX Section 304 in many cases over the years for compensation received by executives following the filing of misstated financial statements.[21] Generally, the SEC has found no amount too small to pursue. In one case from 2016, the SEC forced a CEO to reimburse the company for $15,234 and the former CFO to reimburse the company for $11,789, for incentive-based compensation they received following the filing of misstated financial statements.[22]

Importantly, in most of the cases, the executive from whom the SEC forced a clawback was not accused of any wrongdoing. Additionally, in many cases, the executives had voluntarily reimbursed their respective companies and, therefore, the SEC concluded that it was not necessary to pursue a clawback action under SOX Section 304.[23] In one case, the CEO and former CFO, reimbursed the company $3,165,852 and $728,843, respectively, for cash bonuses and certain stock awards they received during the period when the company committed accounting violations.[24]

In *SEC v. Michael A. Baker and Michal T. Gluk*,[25] United States District Court for the Western District of Texas, the SEC sued to recover the bonuses and stock profits earned by two former executives during a period that an accounting fraud was taking place at their company, despite the fact that the executives were not involved in the fraud. Both in the complaint and the release announcing its filing of the lawsuit, the SEC emphasized that the defendants, the former CEO and CFO of surgical products manufacturer ArthroCare Corp., were not charged personally with misconduct.

---

[21] *See, SEC v. McGuire; SEC v. Schroeder; SEC v. Brooks; SEC v. Sabhlok & Pattison.*

[22] https://www.sec.gov/news/pressrelease/2016-32.

[23] https://www.sec.gov/news/pressrelease/2016-25.

[24] *Id.*

[25] https://www.sec.gov/litigation/complaints/2012/comp22315.pdf.

"The Commission does not allege that Baker and Gluk participated in the wrongful conduct. Defendants, however, have not reimbursed ArthroCare for the SOX 304 compensation and stock sale profits they received during this time period, as the law requires them to do."

Nonetheless, the SEC's complaint asserted that SOX Section 304 requires the two former executives to reimburse their company for bonuses and stock profits received for 2006, 2007, and the first quarter of 2008, during which ArthroCare filed fraudulent financial statements.

In another case, the SEC announced[26] that the former chairman and CEO of CSK Auto Corporation had agreed to return $2.8 million in bonus compensation and stock profits that he received while the company was committing accounting fraud to O'Reilly Automotive, which has since acquired CSK Auto. The SEC never alleged that CSK former CEO Maynard Jenkins had engaged in misconduct. However, the SEC still sued Jenkins, claiming that the clawback provisions of SOX Section 304 required him to reimburse CSK Auto for incentive-based compensation and stock sale profits that he received during the company's fraudulent period. This was the SEC's first SOX clawback case against an individual who was not alleged to have otherwise violated the securities laws. The SEC previously charged four former CSK Auto executives who perpetrated the accounting fraud, and separately charged the company for filing false financial statements for fiscal years 2002 to 2004. The company settled the charges, and the litigation against three of the former executives is continuing (CSK's former chief operating officer has since died). The U.S. Department of Justice brought a criminal indictment against those same executives, who have pleaded guilty to various charges. CSK Auto recently entered into a non-prosecution agreement with the DOJ in which it agreed to pay a $20.9 million penalty.[27]

In 2010, the SEC filed an action against the former CEO of Diebold, Inc. seeking reimbursement for bonuses and other incentive-based and stock-based compensation under SOX Section 304.[28] The SEC's complaint alleged that Diebold was required to restate its annual financial statements for 2003, as well as other reporting periods, as a result of fraud and other misconduct. The complaint further alleged that the CEO received cash bonuses, shares of Diebold stock, and stock options during the 12-month period following the issuance of Diebold's 2003 financial statements. The complaint did not allege that the CEO engaged in the fraud. Without admitting or denying the SEC's allegations, the CEO agreed to consent to a final judgment ordering him to reimburse $470,016 in cash bonuses, 30,000 shares of Diebold stock, and stock options for 85,000 shares of Diebold stock.

---

[26] https://www.sec.gov/news/press/2011/2011-243.

[27] https://www.sec.gov/litigation/litreleases/2009/lr20933a.

[28] https://www.sec.gov/litigation/complaints/2010/comp21543-diebold.pdf, *SEC v. Diebold, Inc.*, Civil Action No. 1:10-CV-00908 (D.D.C.); *SEC v. Walden O'Dell*, Civil Action No. 1:10-CV-00909 (D.D.C.); and *SEC v. Gregory Geswein, Kevin Krakora, and Sandra Miller*, Civil Action No. 5:10-CV-01235 (N.D. Ohio).

In *SEC v. Anthony J. Nocella and J. Russell McCann*,[29] filed in the United States District Court for the Southern District of Texas, Houston Division, the executives are alleged to have "engaged in a disclosure and accounting fraud that misled investors about Franklin's financial condition and concealed the extent of its exposure to loan delinquencies" (although a class action lawsuit making that same allegation was dismissed). The SEC's complaint seeks an order requiring the former executives "to repay Franklin for the bonuses they received during the time period of the misconduct and Franklin's materially misstated financial results, as required by SOX Section 304 of the Sarbanes-Oxley Act" among other things.

.02 Dodd-Frank Act Requirements

Section 954 of the Dodd-Frank Act added Section 10D, entitled "Recovery of Erroneously Awarded Compensation Policy," to the Exchange Act. Under Section 954, a company's compensation recovery policy *must* provide that:

> "in the event that the issuer is required to prepare an accounting restatement due to the material noncompliance of the issuer with any financial reporting requirement under the securities laws, the issuer will recover from any current or former executive officer of the issuer who received incentive-based compensation (including stock options awarded as compensation) during the 3-year period preceding the date on which the issuer is required to prepare an accounting restatement, based on the erroneous data, in excess of what would have been paid to the executive officer under the accounting restatement."

Like all of the compensation provisions the Dodd-Frank Act, Section 954 was not immediately effective. This section requires the SEC to direct the national securities exchanges to prohibit the listing of any security of an issuer that does not develop and implement a clawback policy. The SEC has yet to issue final rules under Section 954.

Once Section 10D becomes effective, companies must disclose their policy on the recovery of incentive-based compensation that is based on erroneous financial information, presumably in the proxy statement, if not before then. However, currently, nearly all public companies already disclose their compensation clawback provisions.

.03 Individuals and Compensation Covered

SOX 304 applies only to the company's CEO and CFO, and requires those officers to reimburse the company for (1) any bonus or other "incentive-based" or "equity-based" compensation received during the 12-month period following the first public issuance or filing with the SEC (whichever occurs first) of the financial document embodying the financial reporting requirement; and (2) any profits realized from the sale of securities of the company during that 12-month period.

Under Dodd-Frank Act Section 954, a company's compensation clawback policy must apply at least to the individuals who are subject to Section 16 of the

---

[29] http://amlawdaily.typepad.com/ 040912FRANKLIN.pdf.

Exchange Act (usually referred to as "Section 16 officers" and including the president, any vice president in charge of a principal business unit, division or function (such as sales, administrations or finance or other officer performing a policy-making function)) and individuals who formerly were Section 16 officers.

We expect the compensation clawback policy required by Section 10D to apply to all annual and long-term incentive compensation plans and arrangements, and stock options. However, Section 954 is ambiguous, providing that it applies to:

- Incentive-based compensation that is based on financial information required to be reported under the securities laws, and

- Incentive-based compensation (including stock options awarded as compensation) in excess of what would have been paid but for the erroneous data in the reported financial information.

Whether the SEC attempts to extend the policy requirements to stock-based awards other than options remains to be seen.

The clawback policy must provide for a potential recovery period of three years, measured from the date the company is "required to prepare the accounting restatement." Until the SEC publishes final rules, we will not know whether that means three years from the discovery of the error, three years from the filing of the restatement (which could be much later), or something else.

The compensation clawback policy must be triggered in the event that the company is required to restate its financial statements as the result of material noncompliance with applicable accounting principles and the original financial statements resulted in an erroneous payment to a current or former executive officer. The policy must apply regardless of whether (i) the noncompliance was accidental or intentional, and/or (ii) the executive was at fault.

.04 Whistleblower Bounties and Protections

Section 922 of the Dodd-Frank Act added Section 21F to the Exchange Act, "Securities Whistleblower Incentives and Protection." Section 21F requires a payment of between ten percent and thirty percent (10% - 30%) of the amount of monetary sanctions to "1 or more whistleblowers who voluntarily provided original information to the Commission that led to the successful enforcement." Previously, the SEC could only pay bounties to informants for insider trading violations. (Note that the SEC settlement with AIG was $800 million, which would have produced a bounty of *at least $80 million* to some lucky winner and his or her lawyer.)

In June 2011, the SEC issued final rules under the "Whistleblower Incentives and Protection" provisions, making the provisions fully effective on August 12, 2011. The final rules made modest changes in response to some business community concerns, but expressly declined to require whistleblowers to report violations or concerns under the company's internal policies first in order to be eligible to receive a bounty, which was the primary concern of the business community.[30] Instead of requiring whistleblowers to report violations or concerns under the company's internal program first, in order to be eligible to receive a bounty, the SEC's final rules provide "incentives" for whistleblowers to use the internal reporting program, including:

- A whistleblower's voluntary participation in an internal compliance program is a factor that can increase the amount of the award;

- A whistleblower who reports original information to the company's compliance and reporting program will get credit for all information that is provided to the SEC by the company, regardless of whether such information was included in the whistleblower's report to the company; and

- A whistleblower will be deemed to have reported information to the SEC on the date that he or she made an internal report to the company, as long as the whistleblower or the company then reports that information to the SEC within 120 days of the initial internal report.

Whistleblower incentives are relevant to executive compensation because more "whistle blowing," accurate or not, could lead to more SEC enforcement actions and more financial restatements, which could require enforcement of more companies' compensation clawback provisions under Dodd-Frank Act Section 954.

The obvious problem with the whistleblower bounties is that people make mistakes. Until now, an employee who discovered an accounting or reporting error would promptly report it to the company, which would then address it, possibly even with a financial restatement. However, the bounty provisions create a very powerful financial incentive to individuals to report potential accounting or securities law issues directly to the SEC, rather than internally.

¶1285 Private Company Securities Law Issues

Generally, private companies are exempt from both federal and state registration requirements with respect to compensatory benefit plans, including stock incentive plans. The federal securities laws make available several exemptions for private company stock incentive plans.

.01 Intrastate Offerings Exemption

The intrastate offerings exemption applies if, at the date of grant, all offerees and purchasers are residents of the same state in which the company is incorporated and the company does substantially all of its business. There is no limit as to the number of employees or the size of the option grant.

.02 Rule 701

Rule 701 provides an exemption from registration for securities issued by private companies pursuant to compensatory benefit plans and arrangements.

---

[30] David Hirschmann, president and CEO of the U.S. Chamber's Center for Capital Markets Competitiveness, and Lisa Rickard, president of the Institute for Legal Reform, had commented that: "In approving this whistleblower rule, the SEC has chosen to put trial lawyer profits ahead of effective compliance and corporate governance."

The aggregate sales price or amount of securities sold during any consecutive 12-month period may not exceed the greatest of the following:

1. $1,000,000;

2. 15% of the issuer's total assets, measured at the issuer's most recent balance sheet date (if no older than its last fiscal year end); or

3. 15% of the outstanding amount of the class of securities being offered and sold, measured at the issuer's most recent balance sheet date (if no older than its last fiscal year end).

The aggregate sales price is determined when an option grant is made, without regard to when the option becomes exercisable.

However, Rule 701 includes a specific disclosure requirement for all transactions in which sales of securities exceed $10,000,000 in a 12-month period.[31] The company would need to provide this specific disclosure to all participants within a reasonable period before the date of exercise. Transactions involving sales of less than $10,000,000 need only provide participants with a copy of the plan document and the respective award agreement and any other disclosure necessary to satisfy the antifraud provisions of the federal securities laws.

Legal counsel should monitor whether registration is required in connection with the grant of awards under a private company's stock incentive plan.

In March 2018, the SEC announced that internet-based financial technology company Credit Karma, Inc., headquartered in San Francisco, had agreed to settle charges that it unlawfully offered securities to its employees and failed to provide them with timely financial statements and risk disclosures. According to the SEC's order instituting cease-and-desist proceedings, the company issued stock options worth millions of dollars to its employees from October 1, 2014, through September 30, 2015. Credit Karma did not register its offer of stock options. It sought instead to rely on Securities Act Rule 701, which allows privately-held companies to compensate their employees with securities without incurring the obligations of public registration and reporting as long as, once the company issues $5 million worth of securities, it provides essential information about the investment to employees. Here, Credit Karma issued almost $14 million in stock options to employees over a one-year period. Even though financial statements and risk disclosures were available and confidentially provided to potential institutional investors, Credit Karma failed to provide this information to its own employees.

Without admitting or denying the allegations in the order, Credit Karma agreed to pay a $160,000 penalty and consented to the SEC's order finding that the company violated Section 5 of the Securities Act by failing to comply with the

[31] In May 2018, President Trump signed into law the Economic Growth, Regulatory Relief, and Consumer Protection Act, Public Law No. 115-174, which directed the SEC to revise Rule 701, so as to increase from $5,000,000 to $10,000,000 the aggregate sales price or amount of securities sold during any consecutive 12-month period in excess of which the issuer is required under such section to deliver an additional disclosure to investors.

registration requirements or to meet the requirements of an exemption to the registration requirements when it offered securities to its employees.

.03 State Blue Sky Laws and Exemptions

All 50 states also regulate the offering and sale of securities to some extent. The state laws are referred to as "blue sky" regulations. Before 1996, a public company offering to sell securities needed to comply with applicable blue sky laws in addition to rules of the Securities Act. In 1996, Congress amended the Securities Act to preempt state regulation of any security listed or approved for listing on the NYSE, the Nasdaq, and certain other recognized exchanges.[32]

However, the state blue sky laws continue to apply to offers and sales of securities by privately held companies. Although every state law is different, and subject to change at any time, most state laws closely track the exemptions from registration and filing under the Securities Act. For example, Illinois state law provides an exemption from registration for any offer to purchase stock made under a compensatory benefit plan.[33] If the plan and the awards under the plan qualify under the terms of the Illinois exemption, there are no additional actions, such as filing of notice or payment of fees, required in connection with this exemption.

On the other hand, California law provides that an offer or sale of any security issued pursuant to a stock purchase plan or agreement, or issued pursuant to a stock option plan or agreement, where the security is exempt pursuant to Rule 701 from registration in California only if (1) the stock plan complies with certain requirements of the California Code of Regulations, and (2) the issuer files a notice of transaction and a filing fee within 30 days after the initial issuance under such plan.[34] The California Code of Regulations[35] requires that:

1. the stock option plan is approved by shareholders within 12 months of the plan's adoption;

2. the issuer provide all plan participants with financial statements at least annually; and

3. the stock option plan provide, among other items: (a) the total shares available; (b) eligible persons; (c) a term of no more than 10 years; (d) nontransferability of options; (e) a period of at least 30 days after termination within which to exercise (unless terminated for cause, and at least six months for death or disability); and (f) options must be granted within 10 years from the date the plan is adopted or approved by stockholders, whichever is earlier.

Finally, companies issuing unregistered securities should make that fact clear to employees and others who receive shares or awards. Some state blue sky

---

[32] The National Securities Markets Improvement Act of 1996 (NSMIA), Pub.L. No. 104-290, 110 Stat. 3416, amending Section 18 of the Securities Act.

[33] 815 ILCS 5/3(n).

[34] § 25102(o), CCH Blue Sky Reporter ¶ 11, 133.

[35] California Code of Regulations, 10 CCR §§ 260.140.4; 260.140.42; 260.140.45; 260.140.46.

laws require a particular legend. In the absence of a particular restrictive legend mandated by state statute, the following traditional private security legend could be used:

> THE SECURITIES REPRESENTED BY THIS CERTIFICATE HAVE NOT BEEN REGISTERED UNDER THE SECURITIES ACT OF 1933, AS AMENDED, OR THE SECURITIES LAWS OF ANY STATE, AND THUS MAY NOT BE TRANSFERRED UNLESS SO REGISTERED OR UNLESS AN EXEMPTION FROM REGISTRATION IS AVAILABLE.

Chapter 13

OTHER STOCK OPTION PLAN ISSUES

¶1301 Overview—Other Stock Option Plan Issues

Stock options were the most popular form of executive compensation for more than a decade. The popularity of stock options was diminished in 2006 when changes to the accounting rules required companies to recognize expense upon the award of options. Nonetheless, many companies still award stock options and many ancillary issues and innovations have arisen in connection with the award, exercise, and transfer of options. Among the significant issues and innovations relating to stock options are the following:

- Option award timing issues, including backdating;

- Executives' ability to transfer their unexercised stock options to family members;

- Companies' ability to reprice outstanding underwater stock options;

- Companies' ability to grant stock options with a "reload" feature (also sometimes referred to as "restorative options");

- Companies' decisions to grant "premium priced" stock options; and

- Executives' ability to defer the gains on their stock option exercises.

Note that when the exercise price of a stock option is below the market price of the underlying stock (so that the optionee could exercise the option at a gain), we say the option is "in-the-money." When the exercise price of a stock option is above the market price of the underlying stock, we say the option is "underwater."

.01 Option Award Timing Issues, Including Backdating

The so-called "stock option backdating" scandal broke in March 2006 when *The Wall Street Journal* published a front page story concluding that the odds of certain option grants occurring at historic market lows when they did were between 1 in 1 million and 1 in 300 billion[1]. Although the news media and others concerned with the issue characterize it as the "backdating" of stock options, for companies that award stock options, the issue is much more complex. However, the variety of parties involved in investigating option award practices and pursuing their own interests creates significant potential problems for any company that awards stock options (see ¶1315).

---

[1] "The Perfect Payday," Charles Forelle and James Bander, March 18, 2006, *The Wall Street Journal*, page 1.

.02 Transferable Stock Options

Unexercised stock options can become a significant portion of an executive's total wealth. As with all forms of accumulated wealth, many executives have a desire to transfer that wealth to family members or to charity. The IRS and the U.S. Securities and Exchange Commission have approved a method for allowing the holder of unexercised stock options to transfer those options to family members, a charity, or a trust for the benefit of either, with favorable tax consequences to the transferees (for a detailed discussion of transferable stock options, see ¶1325).

.03 Underwater Stock Options

For many years, nearly everyone agreed that stock options were one of the best ways to link executives' interests to the interests of the company's stockholders. However, when the exercise price of a stock option is far below the current market price of the company's stock, the option seems unlikely to have any value and, thus, ceases to be a motivating factor. A company with underwater options has several alternatives available to it for renewing the options' incentive effect, including:

- Reprice the underwater options;
- Award new options at the current market price without canceling the underwater awards;
- Cancel the underwater options and grant new options at the current price;
- Repurchase the options;
- Cancel or repurchase the options and award restricted stock; and
- Use synthetic repricing.

(See ¶1335 for a detailed discussion of handling underwater stock options.)

.04 Reload Option Feature

A "reload" or "restorative" option is a feature that companies can add to stock option plans and awards to encourage company stock ownership. The concept of a reload option is that, when an individual uses in-the-money options or owned shares to pay the exercise price for his or her stock options (*e.g.*, cashless exercise), the plan will automatically award the individual "reload" options to replace the stock or options he or she used for the exercise price. Only a minority of companies' stock option plans and awards provide for reload options (see ¶1345 for a detailed discussion of reload options).

.05 Premium Priced Options

A premium price stock option is one with an exercise price that is higher than the current market price of the company's stock. This is thought to emphasize "pay for performance." IBM introduced premium-priced stock options for executives in 2004. IBM and many other corporations have awarded premium priced options since then (see ¶1355).

.06 Qualified Equity Grant Deferrals

The legislation known as the Tax Cuts and Jobs Act of 2017 ("TCJA") added a new Section 83(i) to the Code. Code Sec. 83(i) permits a "qualified employee" of an "eligible corporation" to elect to defer the inclusion in income of amounts attributable to the exercise of a stock option or the distribution of an RSU (see ¶ 1365).

.07 Deferral of Stock Option Election Gains

Practitioners had developed a method for allowing the executive to exercise his or her in-the-money stock options before expiration, but defer the taxable gain on such exercise directly into a nonqualified deferred compensation plan. However, the IRS made it clear in the final regulations under Code Sec. 409A that it considers a deferral of stock option gain to be a violation of Code Sec. 409A (for a detailed discussion of the deferral of stock option gains, see ¶ 1375).

¶ 1315 Option Award Timing Issues, Including Backdating

In May 2005, an academic study by University of Iowa Professor Erik Lie, "On the Timing of CEO Stock Option Awards," found that many companies had awarded stock options on the same day as their stock price hit its low for the year or quarter. However, not until March 2006 did this story hit the big time when *The Wall Street Journal* published a front page story concluding that the odds of certain option grants occurring at historic market lows when they did were between 1 in 1 million and 1 in 300 billion[2].

.01 Backdating Scandal

The SEC, Department of Justice, State Attorneys General, Investors, and, of course, plaintiffs' lawyers soon followed up and discovered that many companies, primarily on the West Coast and in the technology sector had in fact "backdated" their stock option awards so that the exercise price was set on an earlier date when the company's stock price was at a low point.

For example, see the following from the Analog Devices, Inc. Form 10-K, filed with the SEC on November 30, 2004.

> The Company has received notice that the SEC is conducting an inquiry into the Company's granting of stock options over the last five years to officers and directors. The Company believes that other companies have received similar inquiries. Each year, the Company grants stock options to a broad base of employees (including officers and directors) and in some years those grants have occurred shortly before Analog's issuance of favorable annual financial results. The SEC has requested information regarding Analog's stock option grants and the Company intends to cooperate with the SEC. The Company is unable to predict the outcome of the inquiry.

Backdating was possible because there was no requirement to report the award of options to the SEC on a Form 4 within two business days, as is now the

---

[2] "The Perfect Payday," Charles Forelle and James Bander, March 18, 2006, *The Wall Street Journal*, page 1. For an earlier discussion of this issue, see "SEC Investigates Timing of Option Grants," November 10, 2005, Mike Melbinger, CompensationStandards.com.

rule. Because of the new rule a public company could no longer get away with backdating an option award.

The scandal played out over the next few years as there occurred many SEC and corporate investigations, executive terminations, lawsuits, and even criminal prosecutions involving companies with suspiciously-timed option awards.

.02 Other Option Timing Issues

Some companies have more innocent problems with the timing and documenting of option grants. For example, one such problem may occur where management presents a spreadsheet of proposed option grants to the compensation committee, the committee formally approves the grants at its next meeting, and management uses the terms and date of the original spreadsheet (including the price on that date).

In addition to backdating (*i.e.*, specifying a grant date in the option award agreement that is before the actual grant date — a grant date when the stock's market price was below the price on the actual grant date), other potential issues with the timing and documenting of option grants include:

1. *Misdating* - Honest but sloppy paperwork, *e.g.*, delay in obtaining all signatures to a Unanimous Written Consent.

2. *Spring-loading* - The company grants options just prior to the release of material non-public information that is likely to result in an increase in its stock price.

3. *Bullet-dodging* - The opposite of spring-loading. The company delays granting options until after the release of material non-public information that is likely to result in a decrease in its stock price.

In September 2006, the SEC's Chief Accountant issued guidance on determining measurement dates for option grants under applicable accounting principles (now contained in ASC Topic 718). The letter reaffirmed that the measurement date for determining the compensation cost of a stock option is the first date on which both of the following are known: (1) the number of options that an individual employee is entitled to receive and (2) the option or purchase price. The letter then discusses the accounting consequences under APB 25 of several scenarios, including the following:

Dating an Option Award to Predate the Actual Award Date. The SEC observed that even if documents related to an option award are dated as of an earlier date, the measurement date cannot occur until the date the terms of the award and its recipient are actually determined. The measurement date is the actual date of the award and an in-the-money award with variable accounting may be the result.

Option Grants with Administrative Delays. In this circumstance, the SEC adopted an open-minded (some would say "charitable") approach, observing that,

> "where a company's facts, circumstances, and pattern of conduct evidence
> that the terms and recipients of a stock option award were determined with

finality on an earlier date prior to the completion of all required granting actions, it may be appropriate to conclude that a measurement date under Opinion 25 occurred prior to the completion of these actions. This would only be the case, however, when a company's facts, circumstances, and pattern of conduct make clear that the company considered the terms and recipients of the awards to be fixed and unchangeable at the earlier date."

However, if a company operated as if the terms of its awards were not final prior to the completion of all required granting actions (such as by retracting awards or changing their terms), the SEC staff believes the company should conclude that the measurement date for all of its awards (including those awards that were not changed) would be delayed until the completion of all required granting actions. Any earlier-date awards would be considered "back-dated."

Uncertainty as to the Validity of the Option Grants. This situation could arise where, for example, the company's stock option plan only permits the award of at-the-money options. In this case, the SEC staff opined that the option award still would be valid, but the accounting treatment would depend on the market price at the measurement date.

Uncertainty as to Individual Award Recipients. In these situations, a company may have approved a number of option awards, but may not have specified the exact number of shares to award to each individual recipient. Again, the SEC staff adopted an open-minded approach, observing that:

"In certain circumstances, the approved award may contain sufficient specificity to determine the number of options to be allocated to individual employees, notwithstanding the absence of a detailed employee list. If management's role was limited to ensuring that an allocation was made in accordance with definitive instructions (*e.g.*, the approved award specified the number of options to be granted based on an individual's level within the organization), the measurement date could appropriately be the date the award was approved. However, if management was provided with discretion in determining the number of options to be allocated to each individual employee, a measurement date could not occur for such options prior to the date on which the allocation to the individual employees was finalized."

Exercise Price Set by Reference to a Future Market Price. This describes the situation where a company awards options with provisions designed to protect the employee from immediate declines in the stock price.

"For example, an award may establish an exercise price as the lowest market price of the company's stock over a 30-day period beginning with the award approval date. If the market price of the company's stock increases following the award approval date, the exercise price will be equal to the price of the company's stock on the award approval date. If the market price of the company's stock declines following the award approval date, the exercise price will be equal to the lowest price of the company's stock during the 30-day period following the award approval date."

If the original terms of a stock option provide for a reduction to the exercise price if a specified future condition occurs, variable accounting would be required from the award approval date until that uncertainty is resolved. Then, a measurement date would occur and variable accounting would cease at the date the contingency is resolved. "In the fact pattern described above, the amount of compensation cost related to the option would be the difference between the market price of the underlying stock at the end of the 30-day contingency period and the lowest market price of the stock during the contingency period, which would be the exercise price of the option."

If the original terms of an award do not include terms that would cause an adjustment of the exercise price upon the occurrence of a contingent event and the exercise price is nonetheless reduced after the award approval date, a repricing of the award has occurred and variable accounting would be appropriate.

Documentation of Option Granting Activities is Incomplete or Cannot be Located. The SEC staff indicates an open mind to considering the facts and circumstances of each case where a company cannot locate full documentation. However, the staff also observes that

> "the existence of a pattern of past option grants with an exercise price equal to or near the lowest price of the entity's stock during the time period surrounding those grants could indicate that the terms of those grants were determined with hindsight. Further, in some cases, the absence of documentation, in combination with other relevant factors, may provide evidence of fraudulent conduct."

Changes to Option Grants Due to the Release of New Information. This would be a repricing resulting in variable accounting.

Income Tax Benefits Related to Options. In this situation, the company documents option exercises as though the exercise occurred on a date other than the actual date of exercise. A company might do this because the stock price has dropped suddenly, and using a date with a lower price allows the employee to pay less income tax. The SEC staff opines that a repricing of the option has occurred and, therefore, variable accounting must apply to the option. (While this is not a favorable result, I suspect that the IRS might have an even harsher opinion of this practice.)

.03 Potential Board of Directors Liability

In *Ryan v. Gifford*,[3] the plaintiff alleged that the director defendants breached their duties of due care and loyalty by approving or accepting backdated options that violated the shareholder-approved stock option plan and stock incentive plan. Even though *Ryan* was not a decision on the merits, but rather a ruling on a motion to dismiss, the implication of Chancellor Chandler's opinion is that the board of directors violated their duty of loyalty by intentionally backdating options. The Chancellor stated, "I am convinced that the intentional violation of a shareholder approved stock option plan, coupled with fraudulent disclosures regarding the directors' purported compliance with that plan, constitute conduct that is disloyal to the corporation and is therefore an act in bad faith."[4] He continued, "I am unable to fathom a situation where the deliberate violation of a shareholder-approved stock option plan and false disclosures, obviously intended to mislead shareholders into thinking that the directors complied hon-

---

[3] *Ryan v. Gifford*, 918 A.2d 341 (Del.Ch. 2007).   [4] *Ryan v. Gifford*, 918 A.2d 341, 358 (Del.Ch. 2007).

estly with the shareholder-approved option plan, is anything but an act of bad faith. It certainly cannot be said to amount to faithful and devoted conduct of a loyal fiduciary."

The significance of Chancellor Chandler's implication that the directors acted in bad faith by intentionally backdating the options in violation of a shareholder-approved stock option plan, is that the directors lose the protection of the business judgment rule. The business judgment rule is a "presumption that in making a business decision the directors of a corporation acted on an informed basis, in good faith and in the honest belief that the action taken was in the best interest of the company."[5] However, directors lose the protection of the business judgment rule if they breach their fiduciary duties of due care or loyalty. One way to show such a breach is to demonstrate that the board acted in bad faith.[6]

The *Ryan* decision also suggests that positive proof of option backdating is not a necessary element for a cause of action as long as the plaintiff supports his allegations with empirical evidence which suggests that backdating occurred (like the Merrill Lynch analysis which measured the extent to which stock price performance subsequent to options pricing events diverged from stock price performance over a longer period of time to measure the aggressiveness of the timing of option grants).[7] In *Ryan*, every challenged option grant coincided with the lowest market price of the month or year in which it was granted. Even though there was no positive proof of backdating and the Merrill Lynch report could not conclusively determine that the options were backdated, the Chancellor said, "[g]iven the choice between improbable good fortune and knowing manipulation of option grants, the Court may reasonably infer the latter."[8]

In *Ryan*, Chancellor Chandler observed that the directors' concerns do not end with considerations of the duty of loyalty.[9] In proxy statements filed pursuant to Section 14(a) of the Exchange Act, half the board verified that they bore direct responsibility for granting options and that they granted all options according to the options plan. Furthermore, these same directors were also members of the audit committee, and as such, directly responsible for approving any false financial statements that resulted from the mischaracterization of the option grants. Thus, they might be exposed to potential criminal liability for securities fraud, tax fraud, and mail and wire fraud.

Spring-Loading. Spring-loading means that a company is issuing stock options right before the announcement of good news. In other words, the company issues options just before the stock price increases, resulting in a quick gain to the holders of the options. In *In re Tyson Foods, Inc. Consolidated Shareholder Litigation*,[10] plaintiffs alleged that defendants knowingly spring-loaded options to key executives and directors, while maintaining in public disclosures that it

---

[5] *Aronson v. Lewis*, 473 A.2d 805, 812 (Del. 1984).

[6] *Malpiede v. Townson*, 780 A.2d 1075, 1093-97 (Del. 2001).

[7] *Ryan v. Gifford*, 918 A.2d 341, 346-7 (Del.Ch. 2007).

[8] *Ryan v. Gifford*, 918 A.2d 341, 355 (Del.Ch. 2007).

[9] *Ryan v. Gifford*, 918 A.2d 341, 356 (Del.Ch. 2007).

[10] *In re Tyson Foods, Inc. Consolidated Shareholder Litigation*, 919 A.2d 563, 592 (Del.Ch. 2007).

issued the options at market rates.[11] Like *Ryan*, the *Tyson* case was not a decision on the merits, but rather a ruling on a motion to dismiss. However, the case serves as a good indication of the court's stance on spring-loading.

There is no law against spring-loading options. Nonetheless, Chandler held that the directors breached their fiduciary duty by spring-loading options. "Granting spring-loaded options, without explicit authorization from shareholders, clearly involves an indirect deception. A director's duty of loyalty includes the duty to deal fairly and honestly with the shareholders for whom he is a fiduciary. It is inconsistent with such a duty for a board of directors to ask for shareholder approval of an incentive stock option plan and then later to distribute shares to managers in such a way as to undermine the very objectives approved by shareholders. This remains true even if the board complies with the strict letter of a shareholder-approved plan as it relates to strike prices or issue dates."[12]

Chandler concluded that spring-loading options deceives the shareholders. This should be alarming to directors, because a finding of deceptive practice ultimately leads to a finding of bad faith, and therefore to the loss of the business judgment rule protection. Indeed, Chandler continued, "[t]he relevant issue is whether a director acts in bad faith by authorizing options with a market-value strike price, as he is required to do by a shareholder-approved incentive option plan, at a time when he *knows* those shares are actually worth more than the exercise price. A director who intentionally uses inside knowledge not available to shareholders in order to enrich employees while avoiding shareholder-imposed requirements cannot, in my opinion, be said to be acting loyally and in good faith as a fiduciary."[13]

In *DeSimone v. Sycamore Networks, Inc.*,[14] a shareholder brought a derivative breach of fiduciary duty action against directors and officers regarding the backdating of stock options. Defendants moved to dismiss and the court granted the motion. By distinguishing *DeSimone* from *Ryan* and *Tyson*, Vice Chancellor Strine offered ways in which directors can avoid liability.

The first important distinction is that Sycamore Networks' stock option plans allowed the company to award options with strike prices below the current market price. This is important because in *Ryan* and *Tyson*, the court based its disloyalty analysis on the intentional violation (or circumvention) of a shareholder-approved stock option plan. Since Sycamore Networks' stock option plan allowed the company to award options with strike prices below the current market price, doing so did not violate the shareholder-approved stock option plan. However, Strine cautioned that even in a situation where the directors are expressly permitted by the shareholder-approved stock option plan to award options with strike prices below the current market price, "a director could not,

---

[11] *In re Tyson Foods, Inc. Consolidated Shareholder Litigation*, 919 A.2d 563, 590 (Del.Ch. 2007).

[12] *In re Tyson Foods, Inc. Consolidated Shareholder Litigation*, 919 A.2d 563, 592-3 (Del.Ch. 2007).

[13] *In re Tyson Foods, Inc. Consolidated Shareholder Litigation*, 919 A.2d 563, 593 (Del.Ch. 2007).

[14] *DeSimone v. Sycamore Networks, Inc.*, No. 2210-VCS, Del.Ch. LEXIS 75, at *75 (Del.Ch. June 7, 2007).

with impunity, secretly backdate the option grants while falsely representing that they were made at fair market value on the dates of the grants or account for them as such . . . [because] by consciously causing the corporation to violate the law, a director would be disloyal to the corporation and could be forced to answer for the harm he has caused."[15]

The second important distinction is that the plaintiff in *DeSimone* failed to prove that the directors were aware that management was awarding the employees backdated options. In other words, "plaintiff Desimone has pled no facts to suggest even the hint of a culpable state of mind on the part of any director."[16] In fact, "Sycamore's stockholder-approved option plans contemplated delegation of the option-granting function to non-director executive officers, and the complaint itself alleges that much of Sycamore's backdating operation was carried out by a single executive officer and was actively concealed from the board and from Sycamore's auditors."

As an illustration, Strine offered two scenarios. In Scenario I, the compensation committee approves the option grants without realizing that the grants violate the terms of the stock option plan and without realizing that the corporation is accounting for them improperly.[17] In Scenario II, the committee approves the option grants despite the fact that they are aware that the stockholder-approved option plan requires the company to issue options at fair market value on the date of the grant. The first set of directors probably have not violated their fiduciary duties (unless their failure to realize the impropriety of the option grants rose to a level of gross negligence or resulted from their knowing abdication of their directorial duties). On the other hand, the directors in Scenario II (the situation presented in *Ryan* and *Tyson*) probably have violated their fiduciary duties because they issued below market options, despite agreeing not to, and then lied to the shareholders about it. Importantly, Strine also rejects the claim that "knowledge on the part of any one board member can be imputed to other board members as a result of their shared board or committee service."[18] Therefore, even if a court found individual board members liable, that liability does not necessarily correspond to liability for the entire board of directors collectively.

An additional factor aiding the defendants' motion to dismiss was that only two of the six Sycamore directors were insiders, and those two had no options. This fact led Strine to the conclusion that "it is difficult to infer any motive on [the inside directors'] part to enrich Sycamore's executive officers at the expense of its stockholders."[19]

---

[15] *DeSimone v. Sycamore Networks, Inc.*, No. 2210-VCS, Del.Ch. LEXIS 75, at *77-79 (Del.Ch. June 7, 2007).

[16] *DeSimone v. Sycamore Networks, Inc.*, No. 2210-VCS, Del.Ch. LEXIS 75, at *59 (Del.Ch. June 7, 2007).

[17] *DeSimone v. Sycamore Networks, Inc.*, No. 2210-VCS, Del.Ch. LEXIS 75, at *63 (Del.Ch. June 7, 2007).

[18] *DeSimone v. Sycamore Networks, Inc.*, No. 2210-VCS, Del.Ch. LEXIS 75, at *96 (Del.Ch. June 7, 2007).

[19] *DeSimone v. Sycamore Networks, Inc.*, No. 2210-VCS, Del.Ch. LEXIS 75, at *106 (Del.Ch. June 7, 2007).

.04 Abusive Option Transfers

In February 2005, the IRS announced a settlement initiative for executives and companies that participated in an abusive tax avoidance transactions involving the transfer of stock options or restricted stock to family controlled entities.[20] Under this scheme, executives, often facilitated by their corporate employers, transferred stock options to family controlled partnerships and other related entities typically created for the sole purpose of receiving the options and avoiding taxes on compensation income normally taxed to the executive. The tax objective was to defer for up to 30 years taxes on the compensation and, in many cases, resulted in the company deferring a legitimate deduction for the same compensation.

According to the IRS, it had identified more than 40 companies, many more executives and unreported income of more than $700 million involved in this scheme. Executives who engaged in these transactions had until May 2005 to accept an IRS settlement offer to resolve their tax issues. The offer also extended to companies that issued the options to executives and directors as part of their compensation. This IRS action appears to have eliminated the practice.

¶1325 Transfers of Stock Options

Unexercised stock options can become a significant portion of an executive's total wealth. As with all forms of accumulated wealth, some executives have a desire to transfer that wealth to family members or charity. The IRS and the SEC have approved a method for allowing the holder of unexercised stock options to transfer those options to family members, charity or a trust for the benefit of either, with favorable tax consequences to the transferees. Only nonqualified stock options ("NSOs") can be transferred.

.01 Rationale for Transferring Stock Options

The transfer of NSOs by an executive to family members, at a time when the options have little current value, may be a useful estate planning tactic. A transfer would remove a potentially appreciating asset from the executive's estate, minimize gift tax and avoid future estate tax on any appreciation in the value of the asset.

.02 Tax Effect

Counsel may be able to structure the transfer of stock options to family members during the executive's lifetime as a tax-free gift, because of the low value of the options at the time of the gift. When the family member later exercises the transferred options, the income tax on the difference between the fair market value of the stock options on the date of exercise and the exercise price would be payable by the executive rather than the donee, thereby enabling the executive to further increase the value of the transferred option to the donee.

---

[20] Announcement 2005-19, I.R.B. 2005-9, February 28, 2005.

When the transferred options are exercised, the executive who transferred the options will recognize ordinary taxable income without receiving any cash (or new stock to sell), which could create tax or cash flow problems for the executive and withholding issues for the company. A mandatory tax withholding provision in the plan is one way to deal with this concern.

The company would receive an income tax deduction in the same amount the executive recognizes as income. The donee would hold the option stock at a stepped-up basis equal to its fair market value on the date of exercise. The executive could make the gift of options to family members in trust rather than outright.

Example: ABC Corporation issued Executive D an option to purchase 150,000 shares of ABC Corporation's stock, with an exercise price of $20.00 per share (which was the then market price of ABC's stock). D transfers all 150,000 options to a trust for her heirs. The chart below shows the net proceeds available to the heirs after 20 years from the options, which the trust exercises and sells after $4^1/2$ years.

Option to Purchase 100,000 Shares of ABC Stock at Then-current Market Price of $30.00 per Share [a]

Years After Grant		Scenario 1: Executive Exercises Option, Sells Stock and Reinvests Proceeds	Scenario 2: Executive Gifts the Option Immediately upon Grant	
			Cash Flow to:	
			Heirs	Executive
0	Gift tax paid:	$0.00 (Executive does not transfer)		($15,000)[b]
Year 5	Options exercised at $60.34 and stock sold immediately.			
	Gross proceeds on exercise and sale:	$3,034,072	$3,034,072	
	Less: Income tax upon exercise:[c]	($1,338,936)		($1,338,936)
	Net cash available for reinvestment:	$1,695,136		
	Assumed after-tax reinvestment rate:[d]	5.59%	6.04%	5.59%
Year 25	Value of the reinvested cash:	$5,028,211	$9,804,381	($4,030,022)
	Estate tax payable (or saved):[e]	($3,016,927)		$2,418,013
	Net wealth transferred to heirs:	$2,011,284	$9,804,381	($1,747,141)
	Net Wealth Transferred to Heirs:	**$2,011,284**	**$8,192,373**	
	Difference:		**$6,181,089**	

[a] Chart prepared by J.P. Morgan Private Wealth Management.
[b] Value of options transferred for gift tax purposes = $5.00.
[c] Effective rate of federal and state income tax = 44.1%.
[d] Net proceeds reinvested at 10% pre-tax for an investment period of 20 years.
[e] Effective rate of federal and state estate tax = 60%.

.03 Plan Provisions

Companies may want to include in their stock incentive plans provisions permitting specific NSOs to be made transferable, at least to family members, trusts or partnerships or to charities. Most stock option plans expressly provide that options:

- Are not transferable other than by will or the laws of descent and distribution;
- Are not subject to execution, attachment or similar process;
- May be exercised during the grantee's lifetime, only by the grantee or his or her guardian or legal representative; and
- May not be transferred to a third-party financial institution without prior shareholder approval.

However, counsel may amend the option plan to provide that the option agreement for a grant of NSOs may permit the employee who received the option, at any time prior to the employee's death, to assign all or any portion of the option granted to him or her to one or more of the following:

1. The individual's spouse or lineal descendants;

2. The trustee of a trust for the primary benefit of the individual, the individual's spouse or lineal descendants, or any combination thereof;

3. A partnership of which the individual, the individual's spouse and/or lineal descendants are the only partners;

4. Custodianships under the Uniform Transfers to Minors Act or any other similar statute; or

5. Upon the termination of a trust by the custodian or trustee thereof, or the dissolution or other termination of the family partnership or the termination of a custodianship under the Uniform Transfers to Minors Act or other similar statute, to the person or persons who, in accordance with the terms of such trust, partnership or custodianship are entitled to receive options held in trust, partnership or custody.

Thereafter, option agreements reflecting awards under the plan could either expressly permit transfers, or give the committee the discretion to allow an optionee to transfer his or her options.

In the event of a transfer, the spouse, lineal descendant, trustee, partnership, or custodianship would be entitled to all of the individual's rights with respect to the assigned portion of such option. The assigned portion of the option will continue to be subject to all of the terms, conditions, and restrictions applicable to the option, as set forth in the plan document and the related option agreement.

The company and its plan should permit the assignment or transfer of an option only if the individual does not receive any consideration therefor, and the assignment is expressly permitted by the applicable option agreement (and any amendment to it). The company's grant of an option agreement with assignment rights, or amendment of an option agreement to allow for assignment rights for any one individual, would not require the company to include such assignment rights in the option agreements of any other individual.

.04 Legal Considerations and Requirements

The SEC has amended Form S-8 to cover option exercises by family member transferees. However, the transferring officer or director still must report the transferee's exercise of the option on Form 4.

IRS rulings clarify that an executive may make a transfer only to the executive's spouse or lineal descendants, trusts or partnerships for their benefit, or tax-exempt charitable organizations. Following the transfer, the transferee must be entitled to all of the rights of the executive with respect to the stock option, and the option must continue to be subject to all of the terms, conditions, and restrictions applicable when the stock option was granted.

The executive cannot receive any consideration for the transfer. A transfer is available only with respect to nonqualified stock options. Internal Revenue Code Section 422 expressly prohibits the transfer of an incentive stock option.

Revenue Ruling 98-21 provided that a transfer of a compensatory nonqualified stock option is a completed gift for U.S. gift tax purposes only upon the later of: (1) the transfer, or (2) the time when the donee's right to exercise the option is no longer conditioned on the performance of services by the transferor (that is, the option vests).

> **Planning Note:** Legal counsel should draft (or amend) the company's stock option plan to include provisions permitting employees to transfer nonqualified stock options. Even if no executive currently intends to make a transfer or the company currently does not intend to allow transfers, this provision will give the plan and the company the flexibility to allow transfers in the future.

.05 Liquidity Transfers of Stock Options

Over the years, some companies have developed programs that assign values to employee stock options for two distinct purposes: (i) to allow employees to sell their options for their current value, and (ii) to create an option valuation mechanism for accounting purposes. The SEC has recently allowed a few companies to implement stock option liquidity programs that are designed to allow current and/or former employees to realize value for their (mostly) underwater stock options. Microsoft was the first company to implement such a liquidity program. Comcast Corporation also has implemented a program, for former employees only. JPMorgan Chase Bank assisted both companies in the implementation of their programs.

¶1335 Underwater Stock Options

When the exercise price of a stock option is so far below the current market price of the company's stock that the option seems unlikely to have any value, the option ceases to be an incentive. Companies occasionally faced this situation even before the technology bubble burst in 2000, although the "tech-wreck" and resulting market crash created an unprecedented number of underwater options.

Underwater options pose at least two problems for a company. First, when options are underwater, they no longer serve their purpose of retaining and motivating the employees who hold them. Second, because the options are not being exercised, the number of outstanding, unexercised options becomes large, compared to the number of outstanding shares of company stock. Stockholders generally dislike this condition (called "overhang," because it dilutes the value of their stockholdings); that is, once the shares come up in value, option holders may exercise, diluting the value of previous stockholders' holdings.

A company with underwater options has available to it several alternatives for renewing the options' incentive effect, including:

- Reprice the options;
- Award new options at the current market price without canceling the underwater awards;
- Cancel the underwater options and grant new options at the current price;
- Repurchase the options;
- Cancel or repurchase the options and award restricted stock; and
- Synthetic repricing.

.01 Reprice the Options

The most straightforward alternative would seem to be for the company to reset the exercise price of its outstanding underwater options to the current market price. Because repricing would not require the company to issue new options, it would not exacerbate the overhang problem. However, this alternative is problematic for the following reasons:

Accounting Issues. Under current accounting rules,[21] repricing stock options will cause the options to be subject to variable accounting treatment, resulting in an immediate charge to earnings and quarterly accounting charges.

Plan Document Issues. Many stock incentive plan documents require the company to obtain the consent of the stockholders to reprice any nonqualified stock options. Almost no plans allow the company to lower the exercise price of an incentive stock option and, in any event, a repricing would disqualify the option from ISO treatment.

Section 16 Issues. The board of directors, a committee of nonemployee directors, or the stockholders must approve a repricing before it occurs, in order to obtain protection from the Rule 16b-3 short-swing profits rules. Federal securities law would treat the repricing as a cancellation of outstanding options, followed by a grant of new options at the current price. The grant of new options may be exempt, if the stockholders already approved the plan. However, federal securities law may treat the cancellation itself as a sale of securities.

---

[21] ASC Topic 718.

Rule 16b-3(e) exempts *dispositions to* the issuer of equity securities. In its release adopting the 1996 revisions of the Rule, the SEC stated that this exemption will apply to the cancellation or surrender of a stock option in connection with the grant of a replacement option,[22] but only if the transaction is approved in advance by the board of directors, a committee of nonemployee directors,[23] or the stockholders of the company.

Proxy Issues. The company would have to include in its next proxy statement a table (titled "Ten Year Option/SAR Repricings") displaying the option repricing as it applies to the named executive officers. The compensation committee's report in the next proxy statement also would have to discuss the option repricing.

Taxation Issues. Repricing the options should not be a taxable event to either the company or the executives. However, repriced options would no longer qualify for the exemption from the Code Sec. 162(m) limits,[24] which was extremely important prior to the 2018 TCJA changes.

State Law Issues. The company's stockholders could challenge the repricing on one of two grounds. First, if the plan document did not permit repricing, stockholders could allege that the repricing was *ultra vires*. Second, stockholders could challenge the repricing as lacking consideration. Thus, legal counsel generally recommends making the repriced options somewhat less valuable than the canceled option, *e.g.*, by offering fewer shares, or providing for an earlier expiration date or longer vesting. Directors may better protect themselves by seeking stockholder ratification. Additionally, if the repriced options are made less valuable than the canceled option, the company may be required to obtain each optionee's consent to the repricing.

Institutional Investors Issues. Institutional investors despise option repricing and typically vote against stock option plans that permit repricing.

.02 Award New Options Without Canceling the Underwater Awards

This is another simple alternative. It solves the motivational problem, but clearly exacerbates the overhang problem. In a sense, the company will use this alternative when it makes any annual option grants in the future. In many cases, companies will accelerate the timing of grants scheduled in the future to maintain the integrity of their existing grant programs, while still sending a positive message to employees.

.03 Cancel the Underwater Options and Grant New Options at the Current Price

This is functionally the same as repricing the options, and raises all of the same issues, with one exception: if the company waits to issue the new options for at least six months after canceling the underwater options, the company's

---

[22] SEC Release 34-37260 (May 31, 1996), text following Note 82.

[23] The assumption is made that the committee consists of only nonemployee directors.

[24] *See* Chapter 22 (¶ 2201 *et seq.*) for a detailed discussion of the Code Sec. 162(m) limits.

accountants may not be required to treat the award of new options as a repricing. Under most plans, any shares attributable to expired or canceled options would be available for new awards. Thus, this alternative would help the overhang problem.

.04 Repurchase the Options

The company could repurchase the outstanding options from employees and other optionees for a nominal amount (*e.g.*, $0.50 or $1.00), with no legal commitment to make future grants. Most plans would allow the shares attributable to the repurchased options to be available for regrant after six months. This alternative is attractive to stockholders, because it reduces overhang. However, this alternative raises other issues:

Accounting Issues. Generally, the company must report the aggregate amount paid to optionees on its financial statements as a compensation expense. However, the amount of the expense would be much smaller than the expense recorded on repricing.

Plan Document Issues. Most plan documents would require the company to obtain the optionees' written consent to a repurchase. If the company can make the optionees understand that it does not intend to stop making option grants altogether, and that it recognizes that the compensation it is paying for the options is very small, the optionees may be more willing to agree to the repurchase.

Section 16 Issues. The sale to the company of the options would be a disposition of equity securities for Section 16. Because the repricing transaction was not specifically approved at the time of grant, the board, the committee or the stockholders should approve the repurchase in advance to qualify for the Rule 16b exemption.

Proxy Issues. Although this purchase would not require stockholder approval or separate proxy statement disclosure (assuming the transaction is approved in advance by the board or committee), the proxy statement generally must list all amounts paid to executives.

Taxation Issues. The payment for the options would be taxable income to recipients. The payment for the options could not be treated as incentive compensation, and would therefore be counted towards and subject to the $1 million limit on deductible compensation payable to the CEO and each of the four most highly paid officers.

.05 Cancel or Repurchase the Options and Award Restricted Stock

The company could cancel the underwater options or repurchase them for a nominal amount, and indirectly replace the options with restricted stock. Under most plans, the shares attributable to expired or canceled options would be available for new awards. This alternative is attractive because it decreases overhang. Additionally, restricted stock can motivate executives and is acceptable to institutional investors. The exact nature of the securities, proxy statement, and state law issues would depend on whether the options were repurchased or simply exchanged.

Accounting Issues. The company would have to record a compensation expense equal to the fair market value of the restricted stock on the date of grant. If the company paid for the canceled options, it also would have to record the cost of repurchase as a compensation expense.

Plan Document Issues. The company would have to obtain the optionees' consent to cancel the options. However, it might not be too difficult to obtain the consent of the option holders, because restricted stock is, in many ways, more valuable than options. There is no exercise price, so the holder does not have to pay any money to own company shares. Even if the value of the shares drops after grant, the holder still has a benefit that has a positive dollar value to him or her. The terms of the stock incentive plan may require the company to obtain the stockholders' consent.

Taxation Issues. Restricted stock awards would be taxable to recipients when they vest. If the company repurchased the options, the price paid would be taxable to employees on receipt.

.06 Synthetic Repricing

The term "synthetic repricing" is a buzzword that applies to a variety of strategies under which the company changes the terms of an underwater stock option in such a way that the change creates a result similar to a direct repricing, but without the negative consequences of a direct repricing. Some of the strategies described above could be called synthetic repricings. For example, a repurchase followed by a grant of new awards is a form of synthetic repricing. Any synthetic repricing that the company's accountants judge to be too close to a direct repricing would result in a compensation charge to the company's financial statements. Moreover, optionees would have to consent in writing to most synthetic repricing alternatives, because they would be giving up certain rights.

¶1345 Reload Options and Awards

A "reload" or "restorative" option is a feature that companies can add to stock option plans and awards to encourage company stock ownership. The concept of a reload option is that, when an individual uses in-the-money options or owned shares to pay the exercise price for his or her stock options (*e.g.*, cashless exercise) the plan will automatically award the individual reload options to replace the stock or options he or she used for the exercise price. Only a minority of companies' stock option plans and awards provide for reload options.

Institutional investors dislike reload features almost as much as they dislike option repricing, because they view them as permitting optionees to lock in gain in an unfair way. The optionee, presumably with superior inside information, can exercise and then sell, and is now off the hook as to his or her future performance. In addition, if reloads are automatic, rather than at the discretion of the plan administrator, the plan does not tie additional grants to the performance of the optionee or the organization. Finally, because an option with a reload feature can ultimately give an optionee more shares than an option without a reload feature, reloads are dilutive.

Reload stock options are replacement options that are issued when an optionee uses previously owned shares to pay the exercise price, or satisfy the withholding obligation, for an option. Upon exercise of the original option, the plan automatically grants the optionee a new option to purchase a number of shares equal to the number of shares he or she used to satisfy the exercise price and/or withholding obligation. Typically, the exercise price for the reload option is equal to the fair market value of the underlying stock on the date that the plan grants the reload option. A reload option is a tool that permits optionees to lock in an increase in share price on one date, and still have an option that he or she can exercise later, if the shares continue to increase in value. Another reason given for providing reload options is that they assist executives in retaining shares and, thus, meet the company's stock ownership guidelines.

> **Example:** In 2010, ABC Corporation issued Executive D an option to purchase 30,000 shares of ABC Corporation's stock, with an exercise price of $10.00 per share. The option agreement provides for automatic award reload options.
>
> In 2017, the option is fully vested and exercisable and ABC's stock is trading at $30.00 per share. D exercises the stock option, in a simultaneous purchase and sale (cashless exercise) transaction, which results in D receiving 30,000 shares of stock and simultaneously selling 10,000 of the shares to pay the $300,000 exercise price. Pursuant to the automatic reload feature, ABC's stock incentive plan will immediately award D an option to purchase 10,000 shares of ABC stock.

Reload options may comfort an executive who is concerned that his or her options are about to go underwater, but it does not help when options are already underwater. To obtain a reload option, the executive must first exercise an existing option. If that option is underwater, he or she will not want to exercise.

In addition, granting options with reload features may pose more of an overhang threat than conventional options. This is because, when an executive exercises all of his or her conventional options, the overhang attributable to those options disappears—the options cease to exist. If the plan automatically grants an executive a certain number of options in connection with exercising the options, however, the exercise does not reduce the number of options he or she holds to zero, it just reduces the number of options he or she holds. Some commentators argue that reloads help alleviate overhang, because they encourage executives to exercise options earlier, thus at least reducing the number of options outstanding at any given time.

If the company amends an outstanding option to include a reload feature, a company may be required to recognize variable accounting with respect to the award. Options that include a reload feature at the time of grant, however, do not trigger negative accounting consequences for a company.

Planning Note: If the stock incentive plan allows the company to provide for reload options in any award agreement evidencing an option, the reload feature could be subject to the following requirements:

1. The company may not add reload options to an already outstanding option. Any reload feature must be part of the option as originally granted.

2. The reload must be automatic, not subject to the discretion of the company, board of directors, compensation committee or anyone else.

3. The reload option must have an exercise price at least equal to the fair market value of the company stock at the time of reload.

4. It may be granted with respect only to previously owned company stock used to pay the exercise price of the original option, only if the individual has owned the stock used to pay the exercise price for at least six months, and only with respect to individuals who are actively in service at the time of the grant.

5. The award agreement that contains the reload feature must not permit multiple reloads (*i.e.*, no reload options may be granted on stock acquired through reload options) and must subject any option granted on reload to a vesting period of at least six months.

6. Unless expressly stated in the award agreement reload options will not be granted in connection with payment of tax withholding by tendering company stock owned by the individual.

7. The company must limit the duration of any reload options by providing that an option granted on reload expires at the same time as the initial option would have.

The proxy statement disclosure for a company's stock option plan providing reloads could read as follows:

To encourage stock ownership by executives and other key employees, replacement stock options ("replacement options") may be granted simultaneously with the exercise of the original stock option. Replacement options are intended to encourage executives and other key employees to exercise a stock option earlier than might otherwise occur, thus resulting in increased share ownership. Replacement options are granted when an executive or other key employee exercises an option by surrendering (or attesting to) currently owned shares to purchase the shares subject to the option as well as to satisfy tax withholding obligations related to the exercise of the option. Replacement options are subject to the same terms and conditions as the original options, including the expiration date, except that the option price of a replacement option is the fair market value on the date of its grant rather than the option price of the original option and replacement options do not become exercisable until one year after award. The grant of replacement options does not result in an increase in the total combined number of shares and options held by an employee.

¶1355 Premium-Priced Stock Options and Other Issues

A premium price stock option is one with an exercise price that is higher than the current market price of the company's stock. This is thought to emphasize "pay for performance." IBM introduced premium-priced stock options for executives in 2004. IBM and many other corporations have awarded premium priced options since then.

Some companies have responded to shareholders' demands for more performance-based compensation by awarding premium-priced options to their executives. A premium-priced option is one with an exercise price that is *higher* than the market price at the time of the award.

.01 Companies Awarding Premium-Priced Options

According to its 2004 Proxy Statement, IBM introduced premium-priced options for senior executives in 2004, and rolled them out to the broader executive population in 2005. According to its proxy statement, the change in equity grant practice represents a stronger focus on corporate governance and putting shareholders first, while emphasizing "pay for performance." IBM specifically cited the following attributes of premium-priced options:

- Transparency: The ability to be clear with shareholders that this design strongly demonstrates pay-for-performance.

- Long-term thinking: The 10% premium promotes an even longer-term perspective than at-the-money options.

- Put shareholders first: Demonstrate more clearly to shareholders that they benefit before executives profit from IBM's equity programs.

- Minimize the overall financial impact of IBM's equity awards: reduce overhang over time.

- Commitment to stock price growth: In contrast to restricted stock or RSUs, the option value is purely contingent on growing the value of IBM stock. IBM still grants restricted stock and RSUs, but views these instruments as a better choice for retention needs, or value replacement for new hires.

- Simplicity: First, executives are familiar with the instrument; second, premium-priced options avoid the need for complex financial performance metrics, which often cannot be communicated to a broad population of executives (which means they may not know where they stand until payout); third, the infrastructure is already in place to manage them, and the tax and legal implications are generally the same.

According to its proxy statement, the 10% premium is reasonable because it is in line with the company's guidance on earnings. If the premium were much higher, the motivational aspect of the awards might be diminished. IBM did not grant more options to offset the premium price.

In April 2005, Federal Signal Corporation granted a premium option to its president. The option's exercise price was $16.01, which was 12% higher than the stock's trading price on that date of $14.26. Also in April 2005, Computer Associates granted premium options to ten executives. The options' exercise price was $32.80, which was 20% higher than the stock's trading price on that date of $27.23. In January 2006, 3Com Corporation granted options to its CEO, one-fourth of which had an exercise price that was 11% higher than the company's stock price on the grant date and another fourth of which had an exercise price that was 33% higher than the company's stock price on the grant date.

Other companies awarded options that accelerate vesting upon performance-based criteria. Keane, Inc. awarded options that cliff vest on the fifth anniversary of the award date, except 50% of the options would vest upon the company achieving one CEPS target and the other 50% of the options would vest upon the company achieving another, higher CEPS target.[25] Wal-Mart Stores, Inc. instituted a program of granting shares that vest depending on the company's performance against two separate pre-established performance measures: average return on investment, and average revenue growth over the relevant performance cycle.[26]

.02 ASC Topic 718 Issues

The conventional wisdom is that ASC Topic 718 favors performance-based awards. This is true, but only to a limited extent. When stock awards are subject to performance conditions based on internal metrics such as revenues or return on assets, the company does not recognize an accounting expense under ASC Topic 718 for the awards if the performance conditions are not met. Thus, ASC Topic 718's new requirements can make performance-based equity awards a more efficient incentive vehicle than service-vested ones.

The new rules for expensing awards linked to performance and market conditions provide that companies will not incur an expense greater than what they would have incurred if the awards had simply been vested over time. ASC Topic 718 recognizes three basic types of conditions:

- Service conditions based on an employee's service with the company, measured either by length of employment (most often) or by the amount of service rendered in a specified time frame (less common);

- Performance conditions based on specific targets derived from a company's own operations or activities, such as revenues, EBIDTA, or market share; and

- Market conditions derived from the company's share price or another market index related to the company's share price.

---

[25] As reported in Equilar newsletter, March 1, 2006.

[26] As reported in Equilar newsletter, May 27, 2005.

For equity compensation tied only to service or performance conditions, companies are permitted to reverse previously recognized expenses if the conditions are not met during the "requisite service period" (usually the same as the vesting period). However, if the award is based on market conditions, ASC Topic 718 does not permit reversal of the cost even if the award does not become exercisable (because the market condition was not fulfilled), if the employee stays with the company throughout the requisite service period. Thus, market conditions have the disadvantage of creating an expense even for awards that do not become exercisable. Awards subject to market conditions usually have a significantly lower grant-date fair value than awards subject only to service or performance conditions. However, because the Black-Scholes option pricing model does not fully discount the value of premium-priced options (*i.e.*, the Black-Scholes value is not reduced dollar-for-dollar with the amount of the premium), companies taking a charge under ASC Topic 718 based on the Black-Scholes value may experience a slightly higher charge than they expected.

¶1365 Option Grant Deferrals

The TCJA signed into law by President Trump in December 2017, added a new Section 83(i) to the Code. Code Sec. 83(i) permits a "qualified employee" of an "eligible corporation" to elect to defer the inclusion in income of amounts attributable to the exercise of a stock option (or the distribution of an RSU). Deferral elections are only available for options awarded to employees by a company if the stock of the company has not been readily tradable on an established securities market during any preceding calendar year. To determine whether any stock of the company has been readily tradable on an established securities market during any preceding calendar year, any predecessor to the company is included, as well as any member of the controlled group of companies that includes that company or group of trades or businesses under common control with the company.

New Code Sec. 83(i) is designed primarily for the benefit of smaller and start-up companies. It draws on employee eligibility and tax treatment elements of Code Sec. 423 (employee stock purchase plans) and Code Sec. 422 (incentive stock options). The key feature of new Section 83(i) is that the company's written equity plan must grant stock options (or RSUs) to at least 80% of all employees who provide services to the company in the U.S. And all stock options must have the same "rights and privileges" to receive qualified stock.

The new qualified equity grant deferral feature appears to have limited applicability due to the fact that the options must be made available to 80% of employees in a privately held company. The fact that significant owners and certain officers are not eligible further limits the utility of the provision. However, many employees at eligible corporations could benefit from this opportunity to defer income recognition on common forms of equity awards.

Awards of Qualified Stock of an Eligible Corporation. The options must be awarded under the terms of a written plan document. The employee must be performing services as an employee for the company that awards the option and the option must apply to the stock of the company that employs the employee. An option will not be qualified under Code Sec. 83(i) if it permits the employee to sell the stock to, or receive cash in lieu of stock from, the company at the time that the employee's rights in the stock first become transferable or not subject to a substantial risk of forfeiture.

Qualified Employee. The company's equity plan must grant stock options to at least 80% of all employees who provide services to the company in the U.S., including employees in any U.S. possession. Certain employees are not eligible to elect a deferral, including the CEO, the CFO, any family member of the CEO or CFO, any one of the four highest compensated officers for any of the company's 10 prior taxable years, and any individual who is or has been a 1% owner of the company at any time during the individual's 10 prior calendar years. Part-time employees customarily employed for fewer than 30 hours per week also are not eligible. For purposes of determining a family relationship, Code Sec. 83(i) refers to the rules under Code Sec. 318(a)(1). For purposes of determining the company's highest compensated officers for any of the 10 preceding taxable years, Code Sec. 83(i) refers to the SEC's shareholder disclosure rules (applied as if those rules applied to the company).

Tax Treatment. If an employee makes the deferral election under new Code Sec. 83(i), the employee would recognize taxable income on the earliest of (i) the date the stock becomes transferable (including becoming transferable to the company), (ii) the date the employee becomes an excluded employee, (iii) the date any stock of the company becomes readily tradable on an established securities market, (iv) the date that is five years after the first date the rights of the employee in such stock are transferable or are not subject to a substantial risk of forfeiture (whichever occurs earlier), or (v) the date on which the employee revokes the qualified election with respect to the stock.

After the deferral period, the employee would recognize taxable income on the fair market value of the stock on the vesting date, regardless of whether the value of the stock had increased or decreased between the time of the vesting date and the end of the deferral period. The deferred award would be subject to FICA tax at the time of vesting. The TCJA also amended Code Sec. 409A to provide that "qualified stock" is not subject to Code Sec. 409A, and RSUs and options subject to the deferral elections will not be considered non-qualified deferred compensation.

Notice and Election Requirements. To defer income, an employee must make an election with respect to qualified stock received upon an option exercise no later than 30 days after the first date the employee rights in the stock are transferable or are not subject to a substantial risk of forfeiture, whichever occurs earlier. In the deferral election, the employee must agree to certain tax withholding requirements, described further below. A qualified employee could make a deferral election with respect to qualified stock attributable to a statutory option ("ISO") in which case the option would be treated as a nonqualified stock option.

A company offering qualified employees the elections to defer income on qualified stock must provide certain information to such employees. At or before the time that the employee would recognize income on the award, but for the employee's deferral election, the company must notify the employee that he or she may be eligible to elect to defer income on the stock under Code Sec. 83(i). As part of this notice, the company also must explain that:

- if the employee makes a deferral election, the amount of income recognized at the end of the deferral period will be based on the value of the stock at the time at which the rights of the employee in such stock first become transferable or not subject to substantial risk of forfeiture, regardless of whether the value of the stock has declined during the deferral period;

- the amount of the income the employee would recognize at the end of the deferral period would be subject to federal income tax withholding at not less than the maximum rate; and

- the employee would remain responsible for his or her portion of the required withholding taxes.

The company also must certify to the employee that the stock the employee is about to receive, absent a deferral election, is qualified stock.

Same Rights and Privileges. Code Sec. 83(i) expressly provides that the determination of rights and privileges with respect to stock is to be made in a similar manner as under Code Sec. 423(b)(5). Regulations under Code Sec. 423 offer significant guidance on the meaning of "equal rights and privileges" and, presumably, that guidance will apply to new Code Sec. 83(i). An employee will not fail to be treated as having the same rights and privileges to receive stock solely because the number of shares available to all employees is not equal in amount, so long as the number of shares available to each employee is more than a *de minimis* amount. The amount of stock that is awarded to employees may vary, as long as it bears a uniform relationship to the total compensation or the basic or regular rate of compensation of the employees.

Rights and privileges with respect to the exercise of an option are not treated the same as rights and privileges with respect to the settlement of a restricted stock unit. Where a company wants RSUs or stock options to be treated as qualified equity grants, 80% of employees must receive that same type of award. It is not sufficient, for example, if 40% of employees receive stock options and 40% receive RSUs.

Awards made on after January 1, 2018, under an existing equity award plan could qualify for the deferral election even if the rights and privileges of awards under that plan were not the same before that date, so long as any awards after that date satisfy the equal rights and privileges requirement.

¶1375 Deferral of Stock Option Gains

Before Code Sec. 409A, many companies' stock option plans allowed an executive to exercise his or her in-the-money stock options and defer the taxable gain on such exercise directly into a nonqualified deferred compensation plan.[27] However, the IRS made it clear in the final regulations under Code Sec. 409A, that it considers a deferral of stock option gain to be a violation of Code Sec. 409A. The final regulations provide that a stock option award that permitted the holder to elect to defer the gains on exercise of the option would be deemed to include an "additional deferral feature" and, thus, be subject to Code Sec. 409A. Presumably, a stock option award that permitted the holder to elect to defer the gains on exercise of the option also could be drafted and administered so as to comply with the requirements of Code Sec. 409A.

.01 Before Code Sec. 409A

Both the stock option plan and the nonqualified plan would need to permit this method of exercise and deferral. The holder of an in-the-money stock option with the expiration date approaching would have to exercise the option, but may not want to pay the ordinary income tax that would result from such exercise. The plans generally could only allow deferral elections for nonqualified stock options ("NSOs").

> **Example 1:** In 1993, ABC Corporation issued Executive D an option to purchase 10,000 shares of ABC Corporation's stock, with an exercise price of $10.00 per share, which was the then market price of ABC's stock. In 2003, D is still employed by ABC and holds the option, which is now fully vested and exercisable. ABC's stock is trading at $30.00 per share. The option's expiration date is three months away.

If D exercises the stock option, she will recognize $200,000 of ordinary income. If D does not exercise the stock option, she will lose all of its value and gain nothing. If ABC's stock option plan and nonqualified plan each allow, D could use owned shares to exercise the option, but defer the $200,000 gain into her vested account in ABC's nonqualified plan. Executive D would recognize no taxable gain on the exercise of the options.

The IRS did not explicitly approve the mechanism for deferring tax on the gain from exercising stock options. However, practitioners looked to the IRS's analysis in Private Letter Ruling 199901006 for support.[28] In Private Letter Ruling 199901006, the IRS ruled that executives given the chance to surrender options in exchange for a deferral compensation plan account balance equal to the options' "spread" were not in constructive receipt of the spread.

To the extent permitted under the terms of the stock option plan, an individual to whom the company has granted an NSO would elect to defer any income or gain that the individual would otherwise recognize upon the exercise of the option.

1. An optionee would irrevocably elect, with respect to any NSO granted to him or her under the plan, to defer receipt of a number of shares of stock

---

[27] For example, Daimler Chrysler, AT&T Corporation, Wyeth/American Home Products and Sky Financial Group, Inc.

[28] IRS Letter Ruling 199901006 (Sept. 28, 1998).

representing the excess of (a) the number of shares of stock purchased pursuant to the exercise of such option, over (b) a number of shares of stock with a fair market value equal to the exercise price of such option.

2. The optionee would make a deferral election with respect to the NSO pursuant to a written instrument delivered by the optionee to the company at least 180 days before the exercise of such option.

3. The optionee could make an election to defer only if the optionee pays the exercise price of the applicable stock option by the use of stock acquired by the optionee at least 180 days before the exercise date of such option.

4. Upon exercise of a stock option (as described in 3 above), the optionee would provide a notarized statement to the company that he or she is the sole owner of the shares of stock used to pay the exercise price of such option, and that he or she acquired such shares of stock at least 180 days prior to the exercise date. Rev. Rul. 80-244[29] permits an optionee to exercise a nonqualified stock option with shares of company stock previously acquired, without taxation. In Rev. Rul. 80-244, the IRS separated the option exercise into two parts:

    a. a tax-free exchange of the previously held shares for a like number of the "new" shares under Code Sec. 1036; and

    b. the optionee's receipt of shares equaling the spread as a taxable receipt of property.

5. Upon exercise of a stock option that was subject to a deferral election, the company would credit the optionee's stock option deferral account established under the company's nonqualified retirement plan with a number of stock units equal to the fair market value on the date of exercise of the number of shares of stock the optionee elects to defer.

6. An optionee would make a deferral election with respect to one or more specific NSOs granted to him or her under the plan on or before the date of the deferral election. Alternatively, the optionee would make a blanket election applicable to all NSOs granted to the optionee on or before the date of the deferral election and all NSOs the company grants to the optionee under the plan after the date of the deferral election.

7. A deferral election must be irrevocable with respect to the stock options specified.

8. An individual's deferral election would defer receipt of the stock units related to the deferred shares of stock to a date designated by the optionee in his or her deferral election. The election form would only permit the individual to select distribution dates allowed by the nonqualified plan.

---

[29] Rev. Rul. 80-244, 1980-2 CB 234.

9. The company would hold, administer, invest and distribute all deferred stock units according to the terms of the company's nonqualified deferred compensation plan.

.02 Exercise of Options by Attestation: Generally

As noted above, Rev. Rul. 80-244 permits an optionee to exercise a nonqualified stock option with shares of company stock previously acquired, without taxation. To do so, the optionee must provide a notarized statement to the company (or its administrator) that he or she is the sole owner of the shares of stock being used to pay the exercise price of such option, and that he or she acquired such shares of stock at least 180 days prior to the exercise date. With respect to shares acquired through the exercise of an option, the employee/optionee must wait 180 days (6 months) before "reusing" the already-owned stock to exercise additional shares of the option.

For example, if Executive D had an option for 3,000 shares with a strike price of $20 per share, the total exercise price would be $60,000. If Executive A wanted to do a cashless exercise by attestation, he or she would need to own, and have owned for at least six months, $60,000 worth of company stock outside of any retirement accounts.

IRS Letter Ruling 9629028 also discusses the basis treatment for shares received through the constructive tender of previously held shares, stating that using previously held stock to exercise an option results in the same tax treatment as that which would result if there had been physical tender of the shares.

An optionee who constructively pays the exercise price of an NQSO with Payment Shares that are Mature ISO Stock, Immature ISO Stock, NQSO Stock, or stock that was purchased on the open market would receive the same tax treatment as if the optionee had physically surrendered the shares, specifically:

(a) The optionee will recognize as compensation income the fair market value of the shares that exceed the number Payment Shares used to exercise the NQSO, less cash, if any, paid on the transfer;

(b) The optionee will not recognize income upon the constructive exchange of the Payment Shares for those shares of stock received that are equal in number to the Payment Shares;

(c) The optionee will have a carryover basis with respect to those shares of stock received that are equal in number to the Payment Shares and a basis in any additional stock equal to the difference between the fair market value of the shares received pursuant to the NQSO and the exercise price of the NQSO, plus any cash actually paid; and

(d) The optionee will have a carryover holding period with respect to those shares of stock received that are equal in number to the Payment Shares, whereas the holding period of any additional shares of stock received will begin on the date that the NQSO is exercised.

Example 2: Option: 3,000 shares with an exercise price of $5 per share and fair market value of $15 per share. Owned: 1,000 shares with a fair market value of $15 per share and a basis of $2 per share. If the optionee constructively tenders the 1,000 shares to exercise the 3,000 share option, the basis in 1,000 of the shares "tendered" will be carried over from those previously owned shares to 1,000 of the shares exercised in the option and will be $2 for those shares. The basis in the other 2,000 shares is the fair market value of the shares ($15) and the optionee must include that amount in income (unless it is deferred). Put another way, the old shares that the executive constructively tenders to pay the exercise price continue with the same tax basis. There is no tax on this part of the transaction. This is considered a like-kind exchange under the tax rules and there is no change in the basis on these shares, which the executive continues to hold. The shares the executive receives upon exercising the options will have a tax basis of the fair market value of the stock on that date. The executive is selling a portion of these shares to the company to pay the tax withholding. However, since this is all one simultaneous transaction, the executive is selling these shares to the company at the same price as his or her tax basis in the shares — so there is no tax on the sale.

¶1395 Mismatch of Tax Obligations Related to Employee Stock Options

In 2007, Congress began to take interest in the "gap" between the accounting and tax treatment of employee stock options. Critics argue that the disparity between the two methods distorts the financial picture of public companies, and reportedly costs the IRS billions of dollars in lost tax revenue. This issue typically concerns the profitability of tech companies because those businesses utilize compensatory options more frequently.

The perceived problem stems from ASC Topic 718, which requires companies to estimate the long term value of stock options at the time those options are granted, and then subtract that amount from income over the period the options become exercisable. Companies then estimate a provision for income taxes and include taxes related to the options. However, those taxes are never paid. For tax purposes, the stock options must be exercised before they appear on the return. At that point, the tax burden shifts to the employees, and companies receive a tax deduction for employee compensation. These tax deductions reduce the total amount of taxes owed on the tax return, but never decrease the income tax expense amount in the financial statements. Thus, companies are accruing a large provision for income taxes that does not really exist.[30]

Because investors supposedly cannot tell what the exact tax liability of a company is, the end result is a distorted picture of a company's financial performance. For companies with rising stock prices, profits may be higher because the company's tax liability is less than what the financials indicate. Of course, the opposite is possible if a company's stock price falls. It is also plausible that companies can appear more profitable because they are giving away income using stock option gains that are not recognized in their income statements.

---

[30] *See* Jesse Drucker, *Tech Titans' Tax Picture Is Clouded by Options*, THE WALL STREET JOURNAL, Apr. 16, 2007, at C1.

This problem is not new. As far back as 2000, *The Wall Street Journal* reported that Cisco reaped $2.67 billion in profits, but paid little or no taxes because of a $2.5 billion tax benefit related to employee stock options.[31] In 2001, firms still had the choice of whether to report the fair value of options in the financials or merely disclose the data in the notes. They found that because of this option, two firms could report widely different provisions for taxes, yet owe very similar amounts to the IRS.

As of publication, there has been no legislative activity taken on this issue, and FASB has declined to take action. Its current position is that allowing companies to report options similarly for financial and tax purposes would impermissibly permit a company to recognize changes in its stock price in its financial statements. Some scholars have suggested doing the opposite, and advocate bringing the tax code in line with the accounting rules.[32]

[31] Rebecca Buckman, *Cisco, Mircosoft Get Income Tax Break on Gains From Employee Stock Options*, THE WALL STREET JOURNAL, Oct. 10, 2000, at B8. A year later, two accounting professors analyzed the potential investor misinformation related to the tax benefits of options. TERRY SHEVLIN AND MICHELLE HANLON, ACCOUNTING FOR TAX BENEFITS OF EMPLOYEE STOCK OPTIONS AND IMPLICATIONS FOR RESEARCH, (University of Washington, Working Paper April 2001), *available* *at* http://papers.ssrn.com/sol3/papers.cfm?abstract_id=271310.

[32] Mihir Desai, *Leveling the Executive Options Playing Field*, Harvard Business School - Working Knowledge, Jun. 18, 2007, *available at* http://hbswk.hbs.edu/item/5706.html.

This problem is not new. As far back as 2000, The Wall Street Journal reported that Cisco reaped $2.67 billion in profits but paid little or no taxes because of a $2.5 billion tax benefit related to employee stock options. In 2005 firms still had the choice of whether to report the fair value of options in the financials or merely disclose the data in the footnotes. They found that because of this option, two firms could report widely different provisions for taxes, yet owe very similar amounts to the IRS.

As of publication, there has been no legislative activity major on this issue, and FASB has declined to take action. Its current position is that allowing companies to report options differently for financial and tax purposes would impermissibly permit a company to recognize changes in its stock price in its financial statements. Some scholars have suggested doing the opposite, and advocate bringing the tax code in line with the accounting rules.

Robert Tannenwald, "Measuring Corporate Income Tax and Unmeasured Tax Benefits of Options," The Wall Street Journal, Oct. 10, 2002, at B6a. A year later, two accounting professors analyzed the potential tax implications of options related to the tax treatment of options. Terry Shevlin and Michelle Hanlon, "Accounting for Tax Benefits of Employee Stock Options and Implicit Taxes," Journal of American Taxation Association ... University of Washington, Working Paper, April 2001, available at SSRN (ssrn.com) 264313; paper unnumbered id. 264313.

John Deal, Reviewing the Law of Employee Stock Plans, Cambridge, Harvard Business School Working Knowledge, June 18, 2001, available at http://hbswk.hbs.edu/item/2536.html.

Chapter 14

SEVERANCE AND RETENTION BENEFIT PLANS

¶1401 Introduction—Severance and Retention Benefit Plans

Severance benefit plans have become extremely common among companies of all sizes. Companies use severance benefit plans to provide pay and benefits to employees who they have had to terminate. No law or regulation requires a company to provide severance benefits to former employees. However, the marketplace has come to dictate that severance benefits are part of the regular compensation package that all mid-sized and large companies, and many small companies that can afford it, offer to their employees. Companies offer severance benefits not only for fairness and for humanitarian reasons, but also because they need to be competitive with other companies offering similar benefits. Many executive employees will not accept a position at a company that does not expressly incorporate severance benefits into their employment agreements.

Companies generally only adopt retention plans during times of uncertainty or crisis. A company that has put itself up for sale or received bad financial news may decide to implement a retention plan to ensure that its key executive (and other) employees do not seek or accept new employment before the company can complete its sale or recovery.

.01 Severance Plan Design

Severance pay policies generally fall within one of three basic types of arrangements, depending upon the type of employees the plan covers and the company's reasons for establishing the plan:

- The salaried policy format;
- The executive contract format; and
- The event format.

(See ¶1415 for a detailed discussion of severance plan design issues.)

.02 Retention Plan Design

Retention plans tend to come in two flavors: (1) a retention plan adopted by a company facing a period of uncertainty or transition, such as an acquisition or bankruptcy, and (2) a retention plan adopted by a company following the occurrence of a significant event of uncertainty. In either case, the company faces several critical design decisions in drafting the plan (see ¶1425 for a detailed discussion of retention plan design issues).

.03 Taxation of Severance Payments

Generally, the Internal Revenue Code will tax severance and/or retention payments as ordinary income. The Code also would require the company to withhold applicable taxes from severance payments, since the employment relationship was the basis for the payments. Practitioners and the Internal Revenue Service have engaged in a long-running battle over whether FICA and FUTA taxation applies to all forms of severance payments. In 2004, the IRS tried to put an end to the battle with Rev. Rul. 2004-100 (see ¶1435 for a detailed discussion of the taxation of severance payments).

.04 ERISA Coverage

The Employee Retirement Income Security Act of 1974, as amended, ("ERISA") applies to severance plans more often than not. Most companies view ERISA coverage as a good thing, in that it preempts state law claims that former employees might make against the company. The burdens of ERISA compliance are light. ERISA applies less frequently to retention plans (see ¶1445 for a detailed discussion of ERISA coverage issues).

.05 Advantages of a Legal Plan Document

A severance plan that an employer has established in a written plan document is likely to become subject to ERISA. However, unrelated to ERISA, there are several benefits to having severance benefits set forth in a clear and detailed written plan document (see ¶1455).

.06 The Application of Code Sec. 409A to Severance Plans

Code Sec. 409A, added by the American Jobs Creation Act of 2004, is entitled "Inclusion in Gross Income of Deferred Compensation Under Nonqualified Deferred Compensation Plans." However, Code Sec. 409A can apply to separation payments under a plan or agreement, in addition to deferred compensation plans, which were the original target of Congress (see ¶1465).

.07 Implementation Steps for a Severance Plan

There are a number of steps that a company could take to implement a new severance benefit plan that will be subject to ERISA (see ¶1475). Taking these steps in the proper order should help protect the company and ensure the company provides the benefit it intended to provide.

¶1415 Severance Plan Design

The terms, conditions, and benefits that a company includes in its severance benefit plan depend on the type of employees the plan covers and the company's reasons for establishing the plan. Fortunately for executives, severance provisions have become commonplace in most agreements in most industries. In fact, to remain competitive in the ongoing struggle to hire and retain executive talent, most companies need to provide some severance benefits (and many need to provide change in control protection as well). Companies may need to periodically study what the market is for executive severance in its industry segment— both as to the amount of severance and circumstances under which severance is paid. Public companies may be able to obtain a quick idea of the severance market by reviewing the most recent proxy statements of companies in their peer group.

.01 Executive Severance Benefits

Most companies provide severance benefits to executive employees. Many companies have a severance plan that expressly applies to senior executives. However, many senior executives negotiate individual severance arrangements into their employment agreements or separately. This type of severance pay policy is known as the "executive contract format." The executive and the company usually negotiate the amount of severance pay under the executive contract format. Thus, the amount generally depends upon the executive's rank and bargaining strength.

> **Planning Note:** When drafting severance provisions into an executive employment agreement or drafting the terms of a severance plan, be certain to clarify that the executive's eligibility for severance pay under the agreement automatically renders the executive ineligible for any severance pay under otherwise applicable plans or policies.

Among the most negotiated provisions of any executive employment agreement are the provisions on severance (and change in control). For many executives, the terms of severance are the single most important provision of the employment agreement because they represent the executive's sole protection in the "worst case scenario." Salary, bonuses, and stock prices can go up and down, but the sudden loss of compensation and health benefits could be personally devastating to the executive.

> **Example 1:** ABC Corporation's employment agreement with Executive D provides as follows:
>
> Termination by the Company Without Cause, or Voluntary Termination by the Executive for Good Reason. If the Company terminates the Executive's employment other than for Cause, or the Executive voluntarily terminates his employment for Good Reason, the Company will continue the Executive's coverage under the Company's medical, dental and life insurance benefit plans until the third anniversary of the termination of employment.

.02 Broad-Based Severance Plans

No law or regulation requires a company to provide severance benefits to employees that it terminates. However, many companies maintain severance benefit plans covering salaried and management employees. These companies are motivated by a desire to offer an overall compensation package, including severance benefits, which is competitive in the marketplace. Under the salaried policy format of severance benefit plans, the company provides severance benefits to nearly all salaried employees who involuntarily terminate employment. The amount of severance pay under the salaried policy format is generally determined by taking into account the terminated employee's annual compensation and length of service with the company.

Example 1: ABC Corporation's severance plan for salaried employees provides as follows:

The amount of an eligible employee's severance pay will be based on the employee's total years of service and then-current pay grade. Severance pay for exempt employees in pay grades 10 through 14 will be equal to two weeks' pay for each full year of service with a minimum of 12 weeks and a maximum of 36 weeks' pay and pay grades 15 and above will be equal to two weeks' pay for each full year of service with a minimum of 16 weeks' pay and a maximum of 52 weeks' pay.

.03 Event-Based Severance Plans

Companies typically offer severance pay under the event format type of severance policy to employees whose employment is terminated due to a plant closing, reduction in force or similar event. The event format type of policy generally determines the amount of severance pay by taking into account the same factors as under the salaried policy format. Event format severance plans also typically offer continuing health insurance to the employees terminated due to the event.

.04 Eligibility for Benefits

Because the nondiscrimination and coverage rules applicable to qualified retirement plans do *not* apply to severance plans, a company can specify any eligibility requirements it desires. Some companies' plans contain different eligibility criteria and multiple benefit formulas applicable to different subsidiaries or locations (generally in separate plan supplements). Most plans set forth certain fundamental criteria for eligibility.

Example 3: ABC Corporation's severance plan for salaried employees provides as follows:

Subject to the provisions set forth in this Plan, a terminated regular employee who worked on a full-time or part-time basis (the "Employee") and to whom the Company gave written notice of eligibility for severance pay benefits, will become entitled to severance pay benefits provided that the Employee meets the following conditions:

1. The Employee remains an active employee with the Company until the ultimate date established by the Company as the Employee's termination date, relocation date, "work through" date or other similar date specified by the Company.

2. The Employee properly executes and submits to the Company the form of release, waiver and covenants prepared by the Company, within the time specified in the form, and does not thereafter revoke the release.

3. The Company does not offer the Employee "reasonable alternative employment" (as defined) with the Company or an affiliate.

4. In connection with a reduction in force, outsourcing, closing, sale or relocation of a Company facility or component within a Company

facility, or a restructuring effort, the Employee (a) terminates employment with the Company and is not hired, retained or employed by a successor company to the Company (including, but not limited to, a purchaser, spin-off, or outsourcing provider), or (b) continues employment with the Company in other than reasonable alternative employment.

Some severance plans define the situations where the company's termination of an eligible employee's employment will make him or her entitled to severance, including such events as the following:

1. A reduction in the work force;
2. The relocation of a company facility or component within a company facility;
3. The closing or sale of a company facility; or
4. The tendering of the employee's resignation in response to a written release presented by the company, as part of the company's restructuring efforts, provided the company approves the resignation in writing.

Finally, many plans also expressly exclude certain employees from eligibility for benefits, including some or all of the following:

- An employee who accepts any offer of employment with the company or an affiliate.
- An employee who refuses to accept an offer of "reasonable alternative employment" from the company or any affiliate.
- In the case of a sale of a company subsidiary, facility or operation, an employee who is offered employment by the "buyer," "transferor" or other "successor employer" of employees of a subsidiary, facility or operation.

.05 Amount of Severance Payments and Benefits

As noted above, most companies use a formula based on the eligible employee's compensation and years of service with the company. Other issues under this section include:

1. Whether to count all compensation (*e.g.*, including bonus and/or commission) in calculating severance payments;
2. How to define "years of service" for benefit purposes; and
3. Whether to provide for payments in a lump sum or according to regular payroll practices. (The company can use periodic payments to give it a continuing check on the former employee's behavior.)

Many companies' severance plans give former employees the opportunity to continue group health plan coverage at active employee contribution rates. Health benefits are a crucial issue for many employees (and their dependents). Issues arise if the company decides to continue benefits under health and welfare plans, particularly if such plans are insured.

.06 Other Severance Plan Terms

Many terms and conditions are "standard"' or found in many companies' severance plans, including:

1. Full or partial vesting of outstanding stock awards;

2. Outplacement assistance;

3. Continuation of payments and/or benefits for the promised period, if the former employee dies or becomes disabled during the severance period;

4. Provisions making the payment of benefits conditioned on compliance with certain restrictive covenants. Most plans impose the covenants of noncompete, nonsolicitation (employees or customers) and nondisclosure. Some also include nondisparagement;

5. Return of company property and cooperation with the company in the defense of claims (generally only for executives);

6. A requirement that the employee execute a company-prepared release of claims in order to receive severance benefits;

7. A reduction in severance payments from the plan to the extent the former employee receives any other pay or benefits from the company;

8. To comply with ERISA, the plan document contains claims procedures. If the company or plan administrator complies with ERISA's claims procedures in denying an employee's claim for benefits, the courts generally will only overturn that denial if it was arbitrary and capricious;

9. A provision allowing the company to clawback severance payments and benefits if the former employee is found to have committed misconduct or breaches restrictive covenants, or in the event of a financial restatement that changes the performance metrics upon which certain compensation payments may have been based;

10. A provision that specifies the forum and venue for the resolution of all disputes related to the plan; and

11. Amounts owed. Companies generally provide for certain payments upon an employee's (especially an executive's) termination of employment for any reason, including:

    a. Earned but unpaid base salary through the date of termination;

    b. Any annual incentive plan bonus, or other form of incentive compensation, for which the performance measurement period has ended, but which is unpaid at the time of termination;

    c. Any accrued but unpaid vacation;

    d. Any amounts payable under any of the company's executive benefit plans in accordance with the terms of those plans, except as may be required under Code Sec. 401(a)(13); and

e. Unreimbursed business expenses incurred by the executive on the company's behalf.

Finally, a few severance plans also contain these provisions, or provide for some of these benefits:

1. Continued directors' and officers' insurance coverage and indemnification (generally only for executives).

2. Mandatory arbitration instead of litigation.

3. Some companies' plans require mitigation and suspend payment and/or benefits upon other employment.

4. Counting severance pay (and/or the severance period) for qualified retirement plan purposes.

The case of *Rosenberg v. CNA Financial Corp.*[1], illustrates how a carelessly drafted provision can harm an employer. The CNA Severance Plan required the company to give notice of a change in benefits within "a reasonable amount of time." The court decided that the company could not enforce a plan amendment when it waited seven months after adopting the amendment and only four days before terminating the employees before it notified them.

A Provision Public Companies Cannot Include. In August 2016, the SEC announced the settlement of two actions against companies over provisions in the companies' severance and release agreements. The SEC announced an enforcement action against BlueLinx, in which the company agreed to pay $256,000 and to: (1) amend its severance agreements to make clear that employees may report possible securities law violations to the SEC and other federal agencies without the company's prior approval and without having to forfeit any resulting whistleblower award, and (2) make reasonable efforts to contact former employees who had executed severance agreements after August 2011 to notify them that the company does not prohibit former employees from providing information to the SEC staff or from accepting SEC whistleblower awards. Similarly, Health Net agreed to pay a $340,000 penalty to the SEC for "illegally using severance agreements requiring outgoing employees to waive their ability to obtain monetary awards from the SEC's whistleblower program" and agreed to notify certain former employees.

These actions were based on Section 21F, "Whistleblower Incentives and Protection," added to the Securities and Exchange Act of 1934 (the "Exchange Act") by the Dodd-Frank Wall Street Reform and Consumer Protection Act (the "Dodd-Frank Act"). In 2011, the SEC adopted Rule 21F-17, which provides in relevant part:

(a) No person may take any action to impede an individual from communicating directly with the Commission staff about a possible securities law violation, including enforcing, or threatening to enforce, a confidentiality agreement ... with respect to such communications.

Rule 21F-17 became effective on August 12, 2011.

---

[1] *Rosenberg v. CNA Financial Corp.* (N.D. Ill. 2005).

For decades, employers had required terminating employees to advise them of any facts of which the employee is aware that constitute or might constitute a violation of any ethical, legal, or contractual standards or obligations of the company. The following language is typical:

> You represent that you have been given an adequate opportunity to advise the Company's human resources, legal, or other relevant management division, and have so advised such division in writing, of any facts that you are aware of that constitute or might constitute a violation of any ethical, legal, or contractual standards or obligations of the Company or any subsidiary. You further represent that you are not aware of any existing or threatened claims, charges, or lawsuits that you have not disclosed to the Company.

The foregoing language still should be acceptable. Arguably, that was the employee's fiduciary duty to the company during employment. However, where some employers seem to have gone too far is by asking that the former employee not take part in or benefit from any litigation of governmental actions involving such matters. The following is the offending language from the BlueLinx action as revised by the SEC to make it acceptable:

> Employee further acknowledges and agrees that nothing in this Agreement prevents Employee from filing a charge with . . . the Equal Employment Opportunity Commission, the National Labor Relations Board, the Occupational Safety and Health Administration, <u>the Securities and Exchange Commission</u> or any other administrative agency if applicable law requires that Employee be permitted to do so; <u>however, Employee understands and agrees</u> <u>that Employee is waiving the right to any monetary recovery in connection</u> <u>with any such complaint or charge that Employee may file with an adminis-</u> <u>trative agency.</u> (Emphasis added by the SEC.)

Public companies should consider adding a paragraph similar to the foregoing in any severance agreement that contains a confidentiality or non-disclosure provision.

.07 Litigation Over Severance Plan Terms and Operation

An employment termination often means the relationship between the company and the employee has soured. As you might expect, where cash payments are at stake in the termination context, litigation frequently ensues.

Severance Payments Denied. In *Allen v. Baxter International Inc.,*[2] the court held that a former executive was not entitled to severance benefits because his employment was not "terminated" as defined in the company's severance plan, which paid severance only in the event an employee's position was eliminated. Similarly, in *Magin v. Monsanto Co.,*[3] the court held that Monsanto was not required to pay severance to a former executive who it had involuntarily terminated. The Monsanto severance plan only paid enhanced severance benefits to executives from whom the company requested a waiver of claims. Since Mon-

---

[2] *Allen v. Baxter International Inc.* (N.D. Ill. 2006).   [3] *Magin v. Monsanto Co.* (7th Cir. 2005).

santo had requested a waiver from this executive when it terminated his employment, the plan did not entitle him to enhanced benefits.

In *Johnson v. U.S. Bancorp. Broad-Based Change in Control Severance Pay Program*[4], the Eighth Circuit Court of Appeals held that a severance plan administrator did not abuse its discretion by denying severance to an employee because she was fired for "cause" after she accessed unrestricted files in a computer drive shared by bank employees. Although the employee had access to these files, the company's severance plan defined "cause" to include a violation of company policy. (The files she accessed were a senior manager's wedding invitation, guest list, and directions to the wedding.) Neither the company nor the court commented on the appropriateness of the senior manager maintaining such information on shared files within the company's computer system.

Lest you think the Eighth Circuit is always hard-hearted, in *McGrann v. First Albany Corporation*[5], it upheld an $840,000 arbitrator's award to a former managing director who was fired after he refused to forego a contractually guaranteed bonus. When the executive refused to renegotiate his contract, the company attempted to manipulate his employment requirements and fire him for "cause." Among other things, the company gave him written notice that it would terminate him for cause if he did not generate at least $400,000 in revenue each month for the next three months. (The company's top producer generated only $300,000 in revenue for the company during any given month.) This is a good reason to be very careful when including a phrase such as "failure to follow the written directions of the Board/CEO" in the definition of "cause" in an employment agreement or severance plan. At least add the term "reasonable directions, consistent with executive's current responsibilities and/or the responsibilities of similarly situated executives at similar companies."

Reader might contrast the case of *Picard v. Best Source Credit Union*,[6] with the *Johnson v. U.S. Bancorp* case above, for a better standard of "cause." The court in *Picard* held that an employer did not act arbitrarily and capriciously when it classified the termination of its former CEO as "for cause" and forfeited his deferred compensation benefits. Picard had violated company policy and Michigan regulations governing credit unions by extending 28 loans totaling $3 million to a single credit union member.

In *Miniace v. Pacific Maritime Association*,[7] the court allowed the company to forfeit an executive's right to severance benefits where the executive had caused an amendment of his executive compensation package without the approval of the company's board.

In *Agenbright v. Zix Corporation*,[8] the court held that after-discovered cause was sufficient to allow a company to deny severance benefits to a former

---

[4] *Johnson v. U.S. Bancorp. Broad-Based Change in Control Severance Pay Program* (8th Cir. 2005).

[5] *McGrann v. First Albany Corporation* (8th Cir. 2005).

[6] *Picard v. Best Source Credit Union* (E.D. Mich. 2006).

[7] *Miniace v. Pacific Maritime Association* (N.D. Cal. 2006).

[8] *Agenbright v. Zix Corporation* (N.D. Texas 2005), citing *Moos v. Square D Company*, 72 F.3d 39 (6th Cir. 1995).

employee. The court found that the "after-acquired" evidence doctrine made the former employee ineligible to receive benefits under the plan. The summary judgment evidence showed that the former employee had violated the Zix business policy during December 2003, and was subject to immediate termination, well before he voluntarily resigned his employment.

In *Rowell v. BellSouth Corporation*,[9] the court held that even if potential termination is one possible outcome for an employee who does not accept a severance package, that situation does not create "intolerable conditions" equivalent to a constructive termination. The plaintiff had accepted a voluntary retirement severance amid a reduction in force - then sued for damages under the Age Discrimination in Employment Act, claiming he was constructively terminated. The court held that, under the circumstance, a reasonable person would not assume that he or she was in a "quit or be fired" situation.

As more employers added to or tightened forfeiture provisions in their employment agreements and compensation and benefit plans in the event of a "for cause" termination, more lawsuits have resulted over the interpretation and application of those forfeiture provisions. Again, employers following best practices almost always win these cases. In *Marsh Supermarkets, Inc. v. Marsh*,[10] the company had terminated the employment of its CEO, Mr. Marsh, and begun making severance and retirement plan payments to him under the terms of his employment agreement. However, the company stopped all payments and benefits to Mr. Marsh when it discovered a pattern of highly irregular expense reimbursements to him (according to an earlier jury verdict in favor of the company on this point). Thus, the company argued that Mr. Marsh had:

> "snookered [it] into terminating [his] employment without cause and then paying him over $2 million in Salary Continuation Benefits when, by any reasonable analysis of facts now proven, Mr. Marsh should have been terminated for cause and would have been but for his fraud."

In turn, Mr. Marsh had countersued the company for $2,171,261.48 as equitable relief under ERISA Section 502(a)(3) and other breach of contract claims. Both parties had asked the court for an award of attorneys' fees and costs under ERISA Section 502(g)(1).

As happens all too often in the business world, the company terminated Mr. Marsh "without cause," and then sought to recharacterize the termination as "for cause" after discovering the fraud. Despite the jury verdict in favor the company on the question of fraud by Mr. Marsh, the court found in favor of Mr. Marsh on the ERISA and contract claims. The court based its decision on the unambiguous wording of the employment agreement, which provided for payments and benefits to Mr. Marsh if the company terminated his employment "without cause," which it inarguably did. The employment agreement included no clawback provisions, no exception for "fraud," and no provision for after-discovered cause.

---

[9] *Rowell v. BellSouth Corporation* (11th Cir. 2005).   [10] 56 EBC 2965 (S.D. IN 2013).

The parties had previously agreed that part of Mr. Marsh's employment agreement was subject to ERISA, presumably as an ERISA severance benefit plan. This appears to have been a mistake by the company for several reasons. First, the court found that the provisions of the employment agreement that were subject to ERISA were segregable from the others. Second, with respect to the provisions subject to ERISA, the court found that ERISA compelled it to confine its inquiry to "the face of written plan documents." The court observed that the written plan documents (the employment agreement) provided: "Each and every payment made hereunder by the Company shall be final, and the Company shall not seek to recover all or any part of such payment from [Mr. Marsh] or from whosoever may be entitled thereto, for any reasons whatsoever."

Finally, the company's agreement that part of the employment was subject to ERISA opened the door for the court to order the reimbursement of the legal fees of the prevailing party - Mr. Marsh - as ERISA permits.

The bottom line for the company was that, despite a jury verdict finding that Mr. Marsh had breached his employment agreement and committed fraud against the company, the court ordered the company to pay $2,171,261.48 to him and held that Mr. Marsh was entitled to recover attorneys' fees and costs as incurred in litigating the ERISA claims.

Can a New Statute or Regulation Override an Existing Employment Agreement? A question that arises in discussions about adopting or updating a clawback policy is whether a new statute or SEC rule can override an existing employment or severance agreement. For example, if an employment agreement requires a severance payment; can a new law forbid the company from paying severance? Based on recent case law, the answer seems to be: Yes.

Issues like this began to arise after the Troubled Assets Relief Program ("TARP")[11] prohibited a variety of common executive compensation practices that companies had included in employment, severance, change in control, and other legally binding agreements. The clawback provisions of the Dodd-Frank Act have further highlighted (and will continue to highlight) the issue.

In a case decided in August 2016, *Piszel v. United States*,[12] a federal appellate court considered the question of whether a governmental prohibition on making golden parachute payments to terminated employees of a company constitutes a "taking" of the former employee's property interest, which is prohibited by the "Takings Clause" of the Fifth Amendment to the U.S. Constitution ("nor shall private property be taken for public use, without just compensation").

It is not often that executive compensation matters raise Constitutional issues. In *Piszel*, the Housing and Economic Recovery Act of 2008 was signed two years after Piszel's hire date and the signing of his employment agreement. The Act limited severance payments (which it misleading labeled "parachute payments"). Two months after the Act was signed into law, the government placed

---

[11] Added by the Emergency Economic Stabilization Act of 2008, P.L. 110-343, signed into law by President Bush on October 3, 2008.

[12] 833 F.3d 1366 (Federal Circuit Court of Appeals, 2016).

Piszel's employer into conservatorship. When the employer eventually terminated Piszel, it refused to pay the severance required under his employment agreement, based on the new law.

Piszel sued the U.S. government rather than his former employer. (The court found that no law mandates that a claimant pursue a remedy against a private party before seeking compensation from the government.) The court found that Piszel had a "cognizant Fifth Amendment property interest." However, the court also found that "Congress did not outright prohibit all golden parachute payments, but rather left it to the Director of the [Federal Housing Finance Agency] to develop regulations determining which payments should, and should not, be made." This created a bizarre Catch 22 for Piszel. The Act did not take away his ability to pursue a breach of contract claim against his employer, but the Act ensured that his claim would be of little value because the claim would be subject to an impossibility defense.

In a similar case from 2016, *Hampton Roads Bankshares, Inc. v. Harvard*,[13] the Supreme Court of the state of Virginia considered whether a financial institution participating in TARP, created by the Emergency Economic Stabilization Act of 2008 ("EESA"), could assert the federal prohibition on "golden parachute payments" as a defense to a breach of contract action brought by one of its former officers, and whether said officer could collaterally attack the prohibition as an unconstitutional "taking" without just compensation. The court then concluded that EESA § 111, as implemented by the interim final rules issued by the Department of the Treasury, rendered "*HRB's payment of the severance allowance impossible*" [emphasis added].

> Because federal law prohibits the golden parachute payment under these circumstances, Section 3(b)(iii) of the Employment Agreement is void and unenforceable. Accordingly, we reverse the judgment of the circuit court and vacate the award of damages in favor of Harvard. Moreover, because federal law also bars any payment pursuant to Section 11 of the Employment Agreement, we also reverse the judgment of the circuit court with respect thereto and vacate the award of attorney's fees in favor of Harvard.

In *Von Rohr v. Reliance Bank*,[14] Von Rohr was the chairman, president, and chief executive officer of the bank for 13 years until 2011, when the bank notified him it would not renew his employment agreement when the agreement expired on September 1, 2011. Von Rohr correctly pointed out that his contract did not expire for another year and claimed he was entitled to compensation for the full year. The FDIC, in response to an inquiry from the bank, advised it that Von Rohr sought a "golden parachute payment," which the bank could not make without prior FDIC approval (the FDIC also was a named defendant in the lawsuit). The bank refused to make the payment. A federal district court upheld the FDIC's determination and entered summary judgment for the bank, finding that the FDIC's determination made the bank's performance under the contract impossible. On appeal, the Eight Circuit affirmed the district court's decision against Von Rohr.

---

[13] 291 Va. 42,781 S.E.2d 172 (2016).

[14] (8th Cir. 2016).

Under Missouri law, "[i]f a party, by contract, is obligated to a performance that is possible to be performed, the party must make good unless performance is rendered impossible by an Act of God, the law, or the other party." *Farmers' Elec. Co-op., Inc. v. Missouri Dep't of Corr.*, 977 S.W.2d 266, 271 (Mo. banc 1998). Here, the bank's obligation to pay Von Rohr was rendered impossible when the FDIC determined the payment was a golden parachute.

Many states have similar laws or court precedents. In addition to the Fifth Amendment, which we noted above, the "Contract Clause" [Article I, Section 10, Clause 1] of the U.S. Constitution provides that "No State shall . . . pass any Bill of Attainder, ex post facto Law, or *Law impairing the Obligation of Contracts*" [emphasis added]. No mention is made of the federal government.

Shareholder Lawsuits Alleging that Severance Should Not Have Been Paid. A relatively recent development in the area of severance payments are shareholder lawsuits alleging that severance should not have been paid.

In *City of Tamarac Firefighters Pension Fund Trust v. Corvi*,[15] plaintiffs sued the directors of United Continental claiming that the directors breached their fiduciary duties of loyalty and care by failing to claw back compensation amounts from the outgoing CEO, and instead paying him $37 million in equity, severance, and benefits. The company ousted its CEO, Jeffrey Smisek, in September 2015, after a government investigation into a bribery scheme under which the Port Authority of New York and New Jersey approved development projects at Newark Airport in exchange for United's agreement to institute and continue a money-losing direct flight to Columbia, South Carolina, where the Port Authority Chairman had a vacation home. United was forced to pay more than $4.5 million in government penalties as a result of the investigation.

It does not appear that United clawed back any compensation from Smisek. According to an 8-K filing in 2015, United and Smisek entered into a separation agreement and general release under which he received a separation payment in the amount of almost $4.9 million, the title to his current company vehicle, flight benefits (plus tax indemnification payments on such flight benefits) and parking privileges for the remainder of his lifetime, and continued coverage under the company's welfare benefit plans until he becomes eligible for Medicare coverage, plus tax indemnification payments on any income imputed to him from such coverage. He also retained over 60,000 shares of United's stock, a portion of his outstanding long-term incentive awards for fiscal years 2013, 2014 and 2015, and remained eligible for a pro-rated annual cash incentive award for fiscal year 2015.

Under the separation agreement, the company "may terminate and require repayment of certain severance payments and benefits provided to Mr. Smisek" if he fails to comply with the cooperation provisions of the separation agreement or is convicted or pleads guilty or *nolo contendere* to any felony or any crime involving moral turpitude, which conviction or plea relates to or arises from his service with the company. The separation agreement also provided that "all

---

[15] No. 2017-0341, Delaware Chancery Court, May 10, 2017.

compensation recovery, forfeiture and clawback related provision in any policy, plan, award or award notice . . . will continue in full force and effect after the Separation Date, including to the extent necessary to comply with applicable law as such may be adopted or modified after the Separation Date." The company has not disclosed the terms of the compensation clawback policy, if any, in affect at the time, although the lawsuit filed by the shareholders against the directors in May 2017 alleged that the company's policies empowered the board to claw back compensation.

In May 2017, a shareholder filed a shareholder derivative action in Delaware. The complaint also alleged that the United directors:

- Diverted corporate assets for improper and unnecessary purposes, in that the consideration received by the company could not be viewed as a fair exchange for the corporate assets and monies expended, and
- Wasted corporate assets by refusing to claw back compensation paid to the senior executives involved in the bribery scheme.

The plaintiffs also sued Smisek for unjust enrichment.

Following Delaware law, the shareholder previously had made a demand on the board that it claw back all or a portion of the compensation paid or payable under the separation agreement. The board formed a special committee to investigate the matter and the special committee did not find fault in the directors' decisions to pay severance and not seek a clawback. In March 2017, the board rejected the demand. According to the complaint, the board's reasoning in denying the shareholder's demand to claw back compensation was that if the board has unlimited authority to recoup compensation whenever it finds that misconduct has occurred it would be difficult for United to recruit and retain top talent.

No decision has been made in this case and so far, we only have the allegations from the complaint. We also do not know the reason why United's board did not try to claw back any of Smisek's compensation; it could be that United had not adopted a compensation clawback policy that would have allowed it to claw back certain compensation or United might have had a policy that the board chose not to enforce.

However, this shareholder demand and the lawsuit may be indicative of what companies and boards can expect if they do not (i) adopt a compensation clawback policy that gives them the legal right to withhold or claw back a variety of forms of compensation or (ii) vigorously enforce such a policy.

.08 Corporate Governance Issues

ISS, Glass Lewis and other shareholder advocates have targeted "excessive" severance payout provisions for more than 20 years now. Among the pay practices that ISS has identified as contrary to a performance-based pay philosophy and, therefore "problematic," are excessive severance and/or change in control provisions. Specifically, ISS includes the following as excessive severance and/or change in control provisions:

- Change in control cash payments exceeding three times base salary plus target/average/most recent bonus (or that include equity gains or other pay elements into the calculation basis).

- New or materially amended arrangements that provide for change-in-control payments without loss of job or substantial diminution of job duties (single-triggered or modified single-triggered), where an executive may voluntarily leave for any reason and still receive the change-in-control severance package).

- New or materially amended employment or severance agreements that provide for an excise tax gross-up. Modified gross-ups would be treated in the same manner as full gross-ups.

- Excessive payments upon an executive's termination in connection with performance failure.

- Liberal change in control definition in individual contracts or equity plans which could result in payments to executives without an actual change in control occurring.

The SEC required reporting discussed below allows investors and proxy advisers to calculate the potential amount of severance payments that may become due from any public company.

.09 SEC Reporting - Annual Disclosure of Potential Payments upon Termination of Employment or Change in Control

Item 402(j) of Regulation S-K, "Potential payments upon termination or change in control," requires public companies to disclose each agreement, plan, or arrangement, whether written or unwritten, that provides for payment(s) to a named executive officer at, following, or in connection with any termination of employment, including without limitation resignation, severance, death, disability, retirement, or a constructive termination of a named executive officer, or a change in control of the company or a change in the named executive officer's responsibilities. With respect to each named executive officer, the company must describe, in each annual proxy statement:

1. The specific circumstances that would trigger payment(s) or the provision of other benefits, including perquisites and health care benefits;

2. The amount of the estimated payments and benefits that would be provided in each covered circumstance, whether they would or could be lump sum, or annual, disclosing the duration, and by whom they would be provided;

3. How the appropriate payment and benefit levels are determined under the various circumstances that trigger payments or provision of benefits;

4. Any material conditions or obligations applicable to the receipt of payments or benefits, including but not limited to non-compete, non-solicitation, non-disparagement or confidentiality agreements, including the duration of such agreements and provisions regarding waiver of breach of such agreements; and

5. Any other material factors regarding each such contract, agreement, plan or arrangement.

The company must provide quantitative disclosure under these requirements, applying the assumptions that the triggering event took place on the last business day of the company's last completed fiscal year, and the price per share of the company's stock is the closing market price as of that date. The SEC rules do not require or provide a table for reporting potential payments upon termination of employment or change in control.

¶1425 Retention Benefit Plans

Companies that need to retain key employees through periods of uncertainty often establish retention payment programs. Retention payment programs, also sometimes referred to as "golden handcuffs" or "stay bonus" plans, generally provide a cash incentive for eligible employees to continue their employment with the company through a specified date or event, such as the completion of a change in control or company restructuring.

> **Example 1:** ABC Corporation has just signed a letter of intent to be acquired by MegaCorp. ABC recognizes that it needs to continue running its business while ABC and MegaCorp complete the acquisition. To prevent executives and other key employees from seeking other employment during this lengthy and uncertain period, ABC might promise to pay the executives and key employees a bonus equal to 50% of their annual salary if they remain continuously employed by ABC until the closing of the MegaCorp acquisition (or beyond).

Only a minimum number of legal requirements apply to retention payment programs. To ensure that it is enforceable, a retention payment program should be contained in a written legal document. The retention payment program may be subject to ERISA. The Internal Revenue Code will not generally require covered employees to recognize taxable income on any retention payment until they actually receive the payments.

The most critical issues surrounding a retention payment program relate to the design of the program. If the company does not design its retention payment program to satisfy covered employees' concerns, or extend coverage to the right employees, the company could find its ability to run its business crippled by early departures. Among the design issues the company needs to consider are the following:

1. Which executives and employees are eligible for retention payments?

2. The dollar amount of payments.

3. Until what time should the company require employees to stay to receive payments, *e.g.*, until closing, or for a period of months after closing?

4. Whether to provide different amounts and different structures for employees in different positions.

5. Whether to prefund the program, *e.g.*, through a letter of credit, escrow account, VEBA or rabbi trust.

6. Whether to make retention payments in cash or some other form of payment.

7. Whether to provide protection against termination without cause or termination for good reason prior to end of required stay period.

8. Whether to try to convince the buyer to pay some of the retention payment costs.

.01 Retention Plan Design

With any executive compensation program, the company should carefully consider its goals and objectives, in addition to the tax and other legal consequences, when designing the program. However, in no other type of executive compensation program is this need more imperative than with retention payment programs. When a company prepares and establishes a retention payment program, it is not simply because these programs are a normal form of executive compensation and every other company is offering them. Rather, if a company is establishing a retention payment program, it most likely faces the very real risk that executive employees and other key employees will leave the company for more certain employment positions.

.02 Retention in Bankruptcy

One of the common situations where a company would establish a retention payment program is where the company is contemplating or has filed for Chapter 11 bankruptcy. Executives and other key employees are faced with significant uncertainty as to their future employment with the company at a time when the company's survival depends upon each executive working above and beyond the call of duty to trim costs, negotiate concessions, and/or find new sources of capital. Additionally, the executives have almost certainly lost any of the equity investment they had in the company and any deferred compensation or other unfunded benefit plan promises (see Chapter 24 [¶2401 *et seq.*] for a detailed discussion of executive compensation issues in bankruptcy). However, if the company is to have any chance of emerging from bankruptcy as a viable company, it must retain and motivate its key employees.

Most companies that are contemplating or have filed for Chapter 11 bankruptcy will establish a retention payment program designed to induce executives and other key employees to remain with the company at least until it emerges from bankruptcy proceedings. The bankruptcy court would not need to approve this program. In most cases, the court readily approves retention payment programs without significant objection from the creditors' committees, because all parties recognize the need to retain management.

Example 2: ABC Corporation is in severe financial difficulty and preparing to file for bankruptcy protection, a fact that is well known among the executives. ABC's executives face an uncertain employment future. As part of its pre-packaged application for bankruptcy protection, ABC proposes a retention payment program that will pay executives and other key employees a cash bonus equal to 100% of their then-current base salary if the executive/employee remains continuously employed by the company until ABC emerges from bankruptcy. Thus, the executives and other employees are highly motivated to work for a successful emergence from bankruptcy proceedings.

.03 Retention in an Acquisition Situation

A company also may establish a retention payment program when it has put itself up for sale, agreed to be acquired or facing a hostile takeover attempt. Executives will recognize that the completion of the acquisition may mean the loss of their jobs. However, the company will expect and require the executives to work long hours under stressful conditions, either fending off the hostile offer or accepting the offer and negotiating the terms of a binding purchase agreement, seeking governmental approval, obtaining financing and closing the transaction—all of which could easily take six months or more (see Chapter 2 [¶201 *et seq.*] for a detailed discussion of change in control agreements).

Where the company is putting itself up for sale or is otherwise facing an acquisition, it would be more likely to design its retention payment program to:

1. require continued employment beyond the specific event to ensure a smooth transition; and/or

2. link the amount of the retention payments to the purchase price to motivate executives to maximize the value of the company for its stakeholders.

If the company is to retain its value during the negotiation and consummation of the transaction, it must retain and motivate its key employees. Moreover, a significant percentage of negotiated transactions never close for one reason or another, and the targeted company must continue as an ongoing concern. Even a friendly acquirer will recognize the need to retain the focus of key employees during the acquisition, and most likely for some transition period after the acquisition.

Example 3: On July 1, 2018, ABC Corporation enters into preliminary discussions to be acquired by a larger competitor, XYZ, Inc. Soon ABC's executives learn of the discussions and eventually the word gets out to executive search firms and ABC's competitors. The executives recognize that an acquisition by XYZ most likely will mean the loss of their jobs. However, consummation of the acquisition is by no means certain, and a grueling six to twelve months of negotiations, government approvals, and transitioning awaits these executives. To ensure that the key executives remain focused on a successful acquisition rather than polishing up their resumes, and to protect against the possibility that the transaction will never be consummated and ABC will continue on as an independent company, ABC implements a retention payment program. The program promises to allocate (1) a $5 million retention bonus pool among all executives who remain continuously employed by ABC until the earlier of December 31, 2018, or the date the acquisition closes and, (2) if the acquisition closes, a $3 million retention bonus pool among all executives who remain continuously employed by ABC until six months after the date the acquisition closes. (Executives who are involuntarily terminated before the end of the six months would be entitled to share.)

.04 Preliminary Design Considerations

The most critical plan design decisions for the company generally relate to which executives and employees to cover under its retention payment program and how much to offer each employee or group. The answer most likely will depend upon several factors, including:

1. The company's need for that specific employee or group of employees.
2. The acquirer's need for that employee or group of employees.
3. The likelihood that the specific employee or group of employees will lose employment following or in connection with the pending event.
4. The demand and availability of other opportunities for the employee or group of employees.

.05 Which Executives and Employees Are Eligible for Retention Payments

One of the first plan design issues the company faces is which executives and employees to cover under its retention payment program. An analysis of the four factors listed in ¶1425.04 will produce different results in different situations at different companies, with different types of transactions, and even in different years.

For this reason, many companies will establish and offer a combination of individual retention agreements and retention payment plans. Individual agreements for the most senior executives and irreplaceable employees, and a broad-based plan for other groups of important management and key employees.

.06 Amount of Payments

The amount and form of retention payment the company should offer to affected employees also depends largely on an analysis of the four factors listed in ¶1425.04, and will vary among different employees in different groups and under different circumstances. The company's decision on how much to offer as retention depends partly on how badly the company wants to retain the employees, partly on the current "market" for such payments, but also on that company's philosophy of retention. Put another way, each company decides whether it wants to offer (1) an amount under which it would be "stupid for the employee to leave," or (2) only an amount that will cause the employee to "think twice" before leaving.

Some companies wish to offer their executives and key employees a generous retention/severance amount so employees can continue performing their duties assured that if they lose their jobs, they would be adequately paid while they look for new ones. These types of payments or arrangement are often more appropriately described as change in control agreements (see Chapter 2 [¶ 201 *et seq.*] for a detailed discussion of change in control agreements).

Many companies that are putting themselves up for auction or sale, particularly privately held companies, will add the notion of a success fee to their retention payment formula. These companies offer a payment based on the sales price, to motivate the executives to work toward the best deal and the highest price for shareholders.

Example 4: The Smith family has owned ABC Corporation for generations. The Smith family has employed professional, nonfamily management for the last decade and now has decided to sell ABC. As part of the process of readying the corporation for sale and retaining investment bankers, the Smith family offers a written agreement to pay ABC's top five executives shares from a pool equal to five percent of the proceeds of the sale of ABC Corporation. The shares will be payable in the same form and at the same time as the Smith family members receive their consideration for the purchase.

Some companies base their retention payments on the covered employees' base salary, total compensation, and/or years of service with the company before the transaction.

Example 5: On August 1, 2018, XYZ Corporation announces that it will be closing its Cleveland facility on or about November 30, 2018, as part of a company restructuring. To retain critical management employees until the shutdown, XYZ establishes a retention program that would pay each management employee who remains with XYZ until November 30, 2018 (or the employee's "scheduled completion date," if earlier), a lump sum amount equal to two weeks of "Base Salary" for each year of the employee's continuous (and satisfactory) employment with XYZ before the shutdown. The program will pay a minimum retention payment of 10 weeks of Base Salary and a maximum retention payment of 52 weeks of Base Salary. For example, if a management employee with 15 years of service with XYZ and a Base Salary of $2,000 per week continued working until his or her scheduled completion date of October 31, 2018, the employee would receive a retention payment of $60,000.00 (15 × 2 × $2,000). If the employee leaves before October 31, 2018, the employee would receive nothing.

For employees who would stand to lose bonus or commission compensation because of the transaction or shutdown, the company should consider: (1) a guaranteed compensation amount, or (2) a bonus amount that is offset by any bonus or commission income they receive in the ordinary course.

.07 Until What Time Should the Company Require Employees to Stay to Receive Payments?

In change in control transactions, the question arises of whether to make all or part of a retention payment contingent on the executive's remaining with the company for some transition period after the change in control date. The answer is usually based on one or more of the following factors:

- whether the seller believes that it will make the company more attractive to prospective buyers if its executives are tied up for a period beyond the sale;
- whether the acquirer has demanded that any retention program ties up the seller's executives for a period beyond the sale; and
- whether the acquirer is a "financial" buyer who will require the services of key executives and employees after the purchase, or a "strategic" buyer, who may not.

The amount of time an executive is required to stay with the acquirer after the acquisition is generally between three and 12 months.

To protect covered employees, any well-drafted retention program that required employees to remain employed for a period beyond the closing of a transaction would also provide for payment if the acquiring company terminates the employee (without cause) before the end of that period.

Planning Note: ABC Corporation's retention payment program may promise each covered executive a payment equal to 50% of his or her base salary on the closing date of a transaction and a second payment equal to 50% of his or her base salary on the date that is six months after the date the acquisition closes, if the executive remains employed by the acquirer until that date. Counsel should make certain to draft the retention program document to provide that an executive will be entitled to the second payment if the executive remains employed by the acquirer until six months after the acquisition closing date, or the acquirer terminates the executive's employment without cause before that date.

.08 Whether to Make Payments in Cash or Some Other Form of Payment

Nearly all retention payment programs provide for cash payments. Many programs also provide some or all of the following to employees who qualify for retention payments:

- Continuing coverage under the company's health benefits and/or other welfare benefit plans, such as life or disability insurance.
- Accelerated vesting of qualified and/or nonqualified retirement plan amounts.
- Stock options or other equity-based awards.
- Additional service or benefit credit under the company's qualified and/or nonqualified retirement plans.

With the exception of stock-based compensation, providing some or all of these other benefits causes the retention payment program to look increasingly like its cousin, the severance benefit program.

.09 Whether to Prefund the Retention Program

Many companies that create retention payment programs will prefund the program. Prefunding is most common in the following situations:

- where the company is in financial difficulty—and thus its unfunded promise to pay may not carry much weight;
- the company is putting itself up for sale or auction, and has the luxury of preparing for all contingencies in advance; and
- the company is subject to a hostile takeover attempt and protecting the executive employees is critical.

Among the methods available to prefund retention payments are letters of credit, an escrow account, VEBA, or a rabbi trust. If properly established, none of these prefunding mechanisms should cause covered employees to recognize taxable income until such time, if ever, as they actually receive retention payments.

.10 Whether the Buyer Pays Some of the Retention Payment Costs

In many transactions, the buyer's desire to retain executives and other key employees is even stronger than the seller's desire to do so. In these transactions, the buyer may push for the creation of the retention program and assume the full payment obligation. Where the buyer controls the retention program design, the program is more likely to require covered employees to work for a period beyond the closing date to receive their full benefits. A buyer is also more likely to draft the retention program to require that covered employees execute a release of claims against the company before receiving payments.

¶1435 Tax Consequences

As a general matter, severance pay is considered compensation for services rendered and as such is subject to federal income tax, Federal Insurance Contributions Act ("FICA") and Federal Unemployment Tax Act ("FUTA") withholding. For purposes of federal income tax withholding, however, a special rule applies to supplemental unemployment compensation benefits. Code Sec. 3402(o)(2) defines such benefits as:

> amounts which are paid to an employee pursuant to a plan to which the employer is a party, because of the employee's involuntary separation from employment (whether or not such separation is temporary), resulting directly from a reduction in force, the discontinuance of a plant or operation, or other similar conditions, but only to the extent that such benefits are includible in an employee's gross income.

Even though supplemental unemployment compensation benefits are not characterized as wages for federal income tax purposes, they are subject to federal income tax withholding in order to avoid unexpected final tax burdens for recipients.

.01 Rev. Rul. 90-72 and the *Quality Stores* Case

In a 1990 Revenue Ruling,[16] the IRS took the position that the characterization of supplemental unemployment compensation benefits as nonwages under Code Sec. 3402(o) applied only for purposes of federal income tax withholding

---

[16] Rev. Rul. 90-72, 1990-2 CB 211.

but not for purposes of FICA and FUTA withholding. Rather, the FICA and FUTA exclusion for supplemental unemployment compensation benefits was created through a series of administrative exclusions beginning in the 1950s. As modified by Revenue Ruling 90-72, these administrative exclusions provide that in order to avoid characterization as wages for purposes of FICA and FUTA, the company must link benefits to state unemployment compensation benefits.

In IRS Letter Ruling 200322012,[17] the IRS issued a more thorough analysis of the federal employment tax consequences of a plan intended to be a supplemental unemployment benefits plan. According to the information submitted, a company and its union agreed to establish a plan to provide eligible employees who are on layoff with supplemental unemployment benefits, which were intended to supplement state unemployment compensation. The company also established a section 501(c)(17) trust to pay benefits under the plan.

The IRS acknowledged that the definition of supplemental unemployment compensation benefits ("SUB pay") under Code Sec. 3402(o) had never dictated the proper tax treatment to be accorded to a payment for FICA or FUTA purposes. The IRS observed that, for FICA and FUTA purposes, SUB pay is defined solely through a series of administrative pronouncements published by the IRS dating back to the 1950s, when SUB pay plans were first adopted. The IRS then confirmed that the principles set forth in Rev. Rul. 90-72 continue to govern.

The IRS then concluded that the plan under review was a SUB plan because it was similar in all material respects to the plan described in Rev. Rul. 56-249,[18] as modified by Rev. Rul. 90-72; *i.e.*, the plan was designed to supplement state unemployment benefits and the benefits are linked to the receipt of state unemployment compensation. Specifically, the IRS concluded that regular benefits paid because of layoffs and tied to the receipt of state unemployment compensation are not wages for FICA and FUTA purposes. This exclusion also applies to regular benefits paid to a laid off employee who is ineligible to receive state unemployment compensation because the employee (1) does not have sufficient employment to be covered under the state system, (2) has exhausted the duration of state unemployment benefits, or (3) has not met the requisite waiting period (provided the employee otherwise becomes eligible and receives state benefits once the waiting period expires.) The IRS also concluded that the FICA and FUTA exclusion extends to the de minimis amount of regular benefits contained in the plan that have no tie to state unemployment benefits (as in Rev. Rul. 56-249). Finally, the IRS observed that separation payments available at the election of certain employees who have been on layoff for a continuous period of at least twelve months and payable in a lump sum would continue to constitute wages for FICA and FUTA purposes.

In 2012, the Sixth Circuit Court of Appeals held that SUB payments made by Quality Stores were not "wages" for FICA tax purposes (and the IRS must repay both the employee and the employer portions of the tax paid on the SUB

---

[17] IRS Letter Ruling 200322012 (Feb. 12, 2003). [18] Rev. Rul. 56-249, 1956-1 CB 488.

payments).[19] The *Quality Stores* case created a split with the Federal Circuit and its 2008 decision in *CSX Corporation v. United States*,[20] which held that severance payments were both wages for FICA tax purposes and compensation for Railroad Retirement Tax Act (RRTA) tax purposes.

In March 2014, the U.S. Supreme Court held in a unanimous 8-0 decision in the case of *U.S. v. Quality Stores Inc.*,[21] that severance payments to laid-off workers are subject to Social Security and Medicare taxes. The Supreme Court's decision was consistent with the conclusion reached by the Federal Circuit in the *CSX* case.

In the years leading up to the Supreme Court's decision, the IRS received claims for refund of FICA, RRTA, and FUTA taxes paid with respect to severance payments from over 3,000 taxpayers. Consistent with its position in the litigation, the IRS disallowed all such claims for refund from taxpayers located outside of the jurisdiction of the Sixth Circuit. Many of these taxpayers submitted a request to appeal the disallowed claim for refund to the IRS Office of Appeals. The IRS suspended action on these appeal requests pending the resolution of the *Quality Stores* litigation. The IRS also suspended action on the claims for refund filed by taxpayers located within the Sixth Circuit's jurisdiction pending the resolution of the *Quality Stores* litigation.

In February 2015, the IRS issued Announcement 2015-8, which stated simply and flatly, that it would take no further actions on any claims or appeal for refund of employment taxes in light of the Supreme Court's decision, as "there is no basis for taxpayer to appeal the disallowance to the IRS Office of Appeals with respect to that issue."

Following the Supreme Court's holding in *Quality Stores*, the IRS disallowed all claims for refund of FICA or RRTA taxes paid with respect to severance payments that do not satisfy the narrow exclusion contained in Revenue Ruling 90-72. This included all claims for refund that were held in suspense pending the resolution of *Quality Stores*. Since the definition of wages contained in Code Sec. 3121(a) is generally the same as the definition of wages in Code Sec. 3306(b) with respect to the FUTA, the IRS also disallowed claims for refund of FUTA taxes paid with respect to such severance payments.

¶1445 Status as an ERISA-Governed Plan

Determining the applicability of ERISA to a company's severance or retention benefit program depends on whether the arrangement is an "employee benefit plan" under ERISA Section 3(3) and, if so, whether the plan is a welfare plan or a pension plan under ERISA. On balance, most companies would be better off if their severance plan is covered by ERISA.

No law explicitly delineates what constitutes a "severance plan." However, Code Sec. 409A and the regulations under it apply to any "separation pay plan" that does not qualify for an exception, *e.g.*, for involuntary termination or as a

---

[19] *In re Quality Stores, Inc.*, 693 F.3d 605, 616 (6th Cir. 2012).

[20] 518 F.3d 1328 (Fed. Cir. 2008).

[21] 134 S. Ct. 1395 (2014).

collectively-bargained separation pay plan or window program, and set forth specific criteria necessary to qualify for an exemption.

"Employee welfare benefit plans," as defined in ERISA Section 3(1), includes any plan, fund or program that provides benefits such as severance pay, medical care, dental care, disability coverage, death benefits, vacation pay, unemployment benefits, and educational and dependent care. "Employee pension benefit plans," as defined in Section 3(2) of ERISA, includes any plan, fund, or program that provides retirement income to employees, or results in a deferral of income by employees for periods extending to the termination of employment or beyond. The ERISA requirements that apply to welfare benefit plans are minimal (and discussed further below). The ERISA requirements that apply to "pension benefit plans," however, can be significant and onerous. Generally, companies do not want their severance plan to be subject to ERISA as a pension benefit plan.

Although ERISA defines classes of plans, it provides little guidance as to whether a particular program or arrangement is a "plan" for purposes of ERISA, as opposed to a compensation policy that would not be subject to ERISA. Courts typically apply one of two related lines of reasoning in making this determination.

Under the first test, a severance or other pay policy will be an ERISA plan if, from the surrounding circumstances, a reasonable person could ascertain the existence of intended benefits, intended beneficiaries, a source of financing and a procedure to apply for and collect benefits. Courts have found an ERISA plan to exist even where (1) there was no formal plan document, (2) payments were discretionary, and (3) the company did not communicate the plan to all employees. Furthermore, the cases have made it clear that payments out of a company's general assets are enough to support the "source of financing" requirement.

A second related test focuses on whether the severance or other arrangement involves on-going administration or the exercise of discretionary administrative authority. For example, several courts have found a one-time lump sum payment to terminated employees triggered by a single event not to constitute an ERISA plan, because the program required no administrative scheme for processing claims and paying benefits, and the company assumed no responsibility to pay benefits on a regular basis, which would entail financial coordination and control. Similarly, courts have found that companies' one-time undertakings to give employees additional pay upon termination of employment do not constitute an ERISA plan.[22] The undertakings occurred over a short period, they did not require an administrative scheme to meet the companies' obligation, and the companies had no responsibility to pay benefits on a regular basis.

On the other hand, courts have applied this reasoning to hold that payments requiring a company's analysis on a case-by-case basis entail a discretionary, administrative scheme and thus constitute a plan under ERISA. For instance, a company that expected to sell its business agreed to provide retention payments

---

[22] See, e.g., Fort Halifax Packing Co. v. Coyne, 482 U.S. 1 (1987).

to its executives if their job responsibilities were "substantially reduced."[23] Because the company's obligation to assess each employee's new job duties to determine whether they were substantially equivalent to his or her former job duties required the application of an ongoing and discretionary administrative scheme, the court held that the arrangement was an ERISA plan.

A determination as to a plan's ERISA status ultimately depends on an analysis of the particular plan and the context in which the company uses it. Because case law has not always consistently applied the principles articulated above, it can be difficult to determine the exact parameters of an ERISA-covered plan. However, to the extent the arrangement is of more than limited duration, involves discretion in determining eligibility for severance, and pays benefits on more than an ad hoc basis, it will more likely than not constitute an ERISA plan.

.01 Status as a Welfare or Pension Plan

The extent to which ERISA applies to a specific plan depends on whether it is a welfare plan or a pension plan. If a plan is a welfare plan, only the reporting and disclosure, fiduciary duty and administration and enforcement provisions of ERISA are applicable. If the plan is a pension plan, however, all of Title I of ERISA is applicable and the plan will be subject to ERISA's participation, vesting, and funding provisions.

ERISA regulations provide that a severance pay arrangement will not be considered to be a pension plan if (1) payments are not contingent upon the employee's retirement, (2) the total amount of such payment does not exceed twice the employee's annual compensation during the year preceding his or her termination of service and (3) all such payments are generally completed within 24 months after the employee's termination. The 24-month requirement includes a special rule for reductions in force. This rule requires that payments be completed within the later of 24 months after the termination or 24 months after the employee reaches normal retirement age.

.02 Advantages of Being Subject to ERISA

Companies often want to have their severance, retention, and other benefit plan arrangements declared subject to ERISA for several reasons.

Federal Preemption. ERISA explicitly and broadly preempts state laws. The U.S. Supreme Court decision in *Pilot Life Ins. Co. v. Dedeaux*,[24] makes it clear that federal law does not permit the judge to consider state law claims of any type. Because ERISA provides the exclusive remedies to participants in plans falling within its coverage, employees and former employees cannot successfully bring a lawsuit for payments under state laws. As a result, punitive or extra-contractual damages (*e.g.*, emotional distress damages) typically available under state law causes of action are not recoverable in ERISA cases. The U.S. Supreme Court

---

[23] *Collins v. Ralston Purina Co.*, 147 F3d 592 (7th Cir. 1998); *see also Bogue v. Ampex Corp.*, 976 F2d 1319 (9th Cir. 1992) (retention program where benefits would be paid if employees were not offered

"substantially equivalent employment" obligated employer to apply "ongoing, particularized, administrative" analysis).

[24] 481 U.S. 41, 54 (1987).

case of *Mass. Life Ins. Co. v. Russell*,[25] further supports federal law limits on claims that may be advanced and the damages that can be awarded.

Federal Courts. ERISA lawsuits are nearly always handled by the federal courts, which many believe are of a higher quality. The federal courts have defined quite well the rights and duties of employees, companies, and plan administrators under ERISA benefit plans. In addition to consistently upholding the principles described in the two preceding paragraphs, the body of ERISA case law has clarified a company's right to amend, modify or terminate any ERISA benefits (except for benefits provided under an "employee pension benefit plan"). ERISA does not limit the amount of discretion a company can reserve to itself under the terms of a welfare benefit plan.

Claims Process. A covered employee or participant cannot bring a lawsuit under ERISA until the employee/participant has exhausted his or her administrative remedies under ERISA's claims procedures. The claims process gives the parties an opportunity to exchange information and communicate in a setting outside of litigation. A participant or beneficiary first must present any disputes or claims to the plan administrator for review under ERISA "claims procedures."

Additionally, the record evidence presented to a reviewing court may be limited to the evidence presented to the plan administrator.[26]

Deference to Plan Administrator Decisions. The federal courts will uphold the plan administrator's decision on review unless the court finds the decision to be arbitrary and capricious, under the standard set forth in the Supreme Court case of *Firestone Tire & Rubber Co. v. Bruch*.[27] If the plan administrator denies the employee's benefit claim, and any appeal, and the employee brings a lawsuit, the federal court will review the plan administrator's decision, and will not overturn the decision unless it finds the decision to be arbitrary and capricious. A properly drafted severance plan will provide that the plan administrator has the power, right, and authority to interpret and apply the plan's terms, in its sole discretion.

The arbitrary and capricious standard of review is the "least demanding" level of judicial scrutiny. Therefore, a court's review of an administrator's decision is "extremely" deferential.[28] In contrast, if the plan is not subject to ERISA, a *de novo* standard of review would apply, and the court will not simply review the reasonableness of the decision, but will examine whether it was a correct decision.[29] Also important is the fact that these claims procedures help make it easier to resolve disputes before going to court in the first place.

Discretion. The federal courts have well defined the rights and duties of employees, employers, and plan administrators under ERISA benefit plans. In addition to consistently upholding the principles described in the preceding paragraphs, the body of ERISA case law has clarified an employer's right to amend, modify, or terminate any ERISA benefits. ERISA does not limit the

---

[25] 473 U.S. 134, 147 (1985).

[26] *Wang Labs, Inc. v. Kagan*, 990 F.2d 1126, 1128-29 (9th Cir. 1993).

[27] 489 U.S. 101, 115 (1989).

[28] *Brean v. Carpenters Pension Fund*, 202 F3d 272 (7th Cir. 1999).

[29] *Buchholz v. General Elec. Employee Benefit Plan*, 720 F.Supp. 102, 105 (N.D. Ill. 1989).

amount of discretion an employer can reserve to itself under the terms of a welfare benefit plan.

No Jury Trials. Jury trials generally are not available under ERISA. Only federal judges (and not juries) decide disputes, except that the plan sponsor/plan document could provide that all claims or disputes are subject to arbitration.

.03 Disadvantages of Being Subject to ERISA

As a practical matter, there are only a few possible disadvantages of being subject to ERISA. First, ERISA benefit plans must comply with ERISA's reporting and disclosure requirements, fiduciary requirements and administrative and enforcement rules. The reporting and disclosure requirements provide that the plan sponsor or administrator must: (1) provide each participant with a summary plan description ("SPD"), summary of material modifications ("SMM") and summary annual report and, if requested, copies of annual reports and the plan documents; and (2) file the appropriate annual report from the Form 5500 series with the Internal Revenue Service. ERISA does not require the company to file an annual report form if the plan covers less than 100 participants, or only covers a select group of management or highly compensated employees, and is funded from the company's general assets. Additionally, most employers would not need to file a new or separate Form 5500, as a severance plan could be added to the current filing for the employer's welfare benefit plans by simply checking a box on the Form 5500.

Under ERISA's civil penalty provisions, a participant or beneficiary, a plan fiduciary or the U.S. Department of Labor can bring a civil suit to enjoin violations of the reporting and disclosure or fiduciary requirements of ERISA or the terms of the plan or to obtain other equitable relief to redress a violation or enforce ERISA or the terms of the plan. In addition, the DOL may bring an action to collect any civil penalty owed for failure to provide information requested by a participant or beneficiary or failure to file the annual report. The civil penalty for a failure to provide requested information is imposed on the plan administrator in an amount of up of $110 for each day the administrator failed or refused to provide the requested information. As a practical matter, these actions are unheard of except in situations where the company or plan administrator fails to respond to an individual's written request for documents.

ERISA Section 502(g) gives a court the discretion to award reasonable attorneys' fees and costs to either party in an action brought by a participant, beneficiary, or fiduciary. Generally, a court examines five factors to decide whether it should award fees. These factors are: (1) the culpability or bad faith of the offending party; (2) the ability of the offending party to satisfy a fee award; (3) whether an award of fees would deter others from acting similarly; (4) the benefit conferred on the members of the plan as a whole; and (5) the relative merits of the parties' positions.[30] Although this provision of ERISA may cause some plaintiffs' attorneys to accept cases and bring lawsuits they otherwise

---

[30] See *Eaves v. Penn*, 587 F2d 453 (10th Cir. 1978) (enunciating the five-factor test).

might not have, courts have not routinely awarded attorneys' fees in ERISA cases. Additionally, courts have recently awarded fees to prevailing defendants in a few well-publicized cases. Thus, this is not a major disadvantage.

Finally, the decision to deny a claim for benefits described in the preceding section would be a fiduciary function, subject to the requirements of ERISA. Thus, plaintiffs could try to recharacterize their simple claims disputes as claims for a breach of fiduciary duty.

¶1455 Advantages of a Legal Plan Document

A severance plan that an employer has established in a written plan document is likely to become subject to ERISA. However, unrelated to ERISA, there are several benefits to having severance benefits set forth in a clear and detailed written plan document.

Recruitment and Retention. The trend in corporate governance has been against the establishment of long-term employment agreements. However, for many employers, it may be impossible to recruit the quality of employee they seek without offering severance protection. A single written severance plan can incorporate all of the protections most potential employees would seek, without creating a bunch of separate employment agreements. Thus, a written severance plan should help recruit and retain quality employees by providing the substantial certainty of severance protection in the event the employer terminates the employee.

Uniformity and Control. Using a single plan document offers the advantages of uniformity and control. When one document controls, the employer can ensure that the document clearly sets forth its intent and thoroughly protects the employer and employees.

Clawbacks. A severance plan document, including a plan subject to ERISA, can incorporate clawback provisions that would allow the employer to halt or even recover severance payments made to a former employee who breaches restrictive covenants incorporated into the plan or is found to have committed misconduct. Even states that "disfavor" non-compete provisions generally will enforce a forfeiture of severance under the employee choice doctrine.

Jurisdiction. Most courts that have considered the issue have affirmed that the employer/plan sponsor can specify in the plan document which state's law governs the interpretation of the plan's provisions and, perhaps more importantly, the forum in which litigation, if any, must be brought. For example, an employer based in the Chicagoland area might provide in its plan, "The jurisdiction and venue for any disputes arising under, or any action brought to enforce (or otherwise relating to), the Plan will be exclusively in the courts in the State of Illinois, County of Cook, including the Federal Courts located therein (should Federal jurisdiction exist)." In this way, an employer can assure itself of the "home court advantage" and not have to worry about responding to litigation brought in some far away, inconvenient, or hostile jurisdiction using unfamiliar counsel.

Time Limits. A severance plan document, including a plan subject to ERISA, can incorporate a time limit within which a covered employee or participant must file a lawsuit (*e.g.*, within one year of employment termination). Although it may not be possible to override state statutes of limitations in all situations (*e.g.*, fraud or breach of fiduciary duty), most courts have upheld reasonable periods for asserting contractual and ERISA claims.

¶1465 Application of Code Sec. 409A to Severance Plans

Code Sec. 409A, added by the American Jobs Creation Act of 2004,[31] is entitled "Inclusion in Gross Income of Deferred Compensation Under Nonqualified Deferred Compensation Plans." However, Code Sec. 409A, can apply to separation payments under a plan or agreement, in addition to deferred compensation plans, which were the original target of Congress. "Deferred Compensation" means compensation:

- To which an employee or other employee has a legally binding right during a taxable year (*i.e.*, it is "earned and vested");

- That has not been previously taxed; and

- That is payable pursuant to the applicable agreement in a later year.

The failure to comply with 409A results in immediate income on deferrals, an excise tax of 20% and other penalties.

.01 Code Sec. 409A Basics

Code Sec. 409A applies to any plan or arrangement that provides for the deferral of compensation. Regulations under Code Sec. 409A[32] state that an arrangement provides for the deferral of compensation if, under the terms of the plan or agreement and the relevant facts and circumstances, the employee has a legally binding right during a taxable year to compensation that, (i) has not been actually or constructively received and included in gross income, and (ii) pursuant to the terms of the plan or agreement, is payable to (or on behalf of) the employee in a later year. Since many severance plans create a legally binding right to payments on the employees' eligibility — payments that will be made in a later year — they fit this definition.[33]

The principal effect of Code Sec. 409A on severance plans and agreements depends on whether any stock of the employer is publicly traded on an established securities market.

- For public companies, if an employee is a "key employee" of the company (generally, one of the top 50 highest paid for the preceding calendar year) as of the date of the employee's separation from service, a six month delay applies to payments made due to a "Separation from Service" (as defined in the regulations), unless an exception applies.

---

[31] P.L. 108-357.

[32] The Treasury and IRS issued 397 pages of final regulations under Code Section 409A in April 2007.

[33] Treas. Reg. § 1.409A-1(b)(9).

- For private and public companies, separation payments made over more than one calendar year generally will be subject to Code Sec. 409A and the parties will be unable to change the timing or form of the payments without following the restrictions of 409A.

The final regulations clarify that separation pay is only subject to Code Sec. 409A if it is conditioned upon separation from service. Amounts that would be paid upon other events, like change in control or a date certain, are not separation pay (although they still could be subject to 409A).

.02 Separation Pay and Public Companies

For public companies, the application of Code Sec. 409A to separation pay is crucial because 409A requires a six-month delay in payments, if, as of the date of the employee's separation from service, the employee is a "key employee" (discussed below). The final regulations provide certain exceptions from 409A for separation payments. The exceptions generally apply to payments made only on an involuntary separation that are made in a lump sum following an involuntary separation or less than the Code Sec. 401(a)(17) amount.

> **Example:** If an employment agreement with a public company CEO provided that the company would pay its CEO $1 million in a lump sum immediately following a termination of the CEO without cause, this lump sum payment ordinarily would not be subject to Sec. 409A, because it qualifies for the short-term deferral exception (payment is made in the same year as the right to payment becomes vested).

Separation pay from an employment agreement will not qualify as "involuntary" if the agreement provides for payments upon a separation for "good reason"—even if the actual termination was involuntary—unless the definition of "good reason" satisfies a safe harbor in the final regulations or otherwise is tough enough to satisfy the IRS.

.03 Separation for Good Reason

Under the safe harbor definition of separation for good reason in the regulations, the separation from service must occur during a pre-determined, limited period not to exceed two years following the initial existence of one or more of the following conditions, arising without the consent of the executive:

1. A material diminution in the employee's base compensation.

2. A material diminution in the employee's authority, duties, or responsibilities.

3. A material diminution in the authority, duties, or responsibilities of the supervisor to whom the employee is required to report, including a requirement that an employee report to a corporate officer or other employee instead of reporting directly to the board of directors of a corporation (or similar governing body with respect to an entity other than a corporation).

4. A material diminution in the budget over which the employee retains authority.

5. A material change in the geographic location at which the employee must perform the services.

6. Any other action or inaction that constitutes a material breach by the employer of the agreement under which the employee provides services.[34]

The amount, time, and form of payment upon the separation from service for good reason must be substantially identical to the amount, time and form of payment payable due to an actual involuntary separation from service (to the extent such a right exists). Additionally, the agreement must require the employee to provide notice to the employer of the existence of the condition described above within a period not to exceed 90 days of the initial existence of the condition. The agreement also must give the employer a period of at least 30 days following receipt of the notice during which it may remedy the condition and not be required to make separation payments.

.04 Other Exceptions for Separation Payments

The final regulations provide a few other useful exceptions for separation pay under Code Sec. 409A. Moreover, the final regulations clarify that employers may use *more than one of the separation pay exceptions* for each payment or separation (so-called "stacking" of the separation payments).[35]

The final regulations provide an exception for certain limited payments made following an involuntary separation from service, to the extent the payments do not exceed two times the lesser of the Code Sec. 401(a)(17) limit ($275,000 for 2018) or employee's annual compensation for the year prior to the year of separation, and the agreement provides that the separation pay must be paid no later than the last day of the second taxable year of the employee following the taxable year of the employee in which he or she incurred the separation from service.[36] If the employer pays *more than* two times the lesser of the employee's annual pay or the Code Sec. 401(a)(17) limit, the exception still applies to the amount paid *up to* the limit. No similar rule applies for payments continuing for longer than two years. Such payments would be completely subject to Code Sec. 409A.

The final regulations also clarify that non-taxable benefits provided following separation from service are not subject to Code Sec. 409A. Continuing health plan coverage is the most common non-taxable benefit provided under employment agreements. However, continuing health plan coverage is not always a non-taxable benefit (for example, if it is provided on a discriminatory basis). Taxable medical benefit reimbursements still may be able to qualify for an exception, to the extent paid over a period no longer than the applicable COBRA coverage period (18 or 36 months), under the exception discussed next below.

The regulations also provide that the following plans, agreements, or provisions do not provide for a deferral of compensation under Code Sec. 409A:

---

[34] Treas. Reg. § 1.409A-1(n)(2).
[35] Treas. Reg. § 1.409A-1(b)(9)(i).
[36] Treas. Reg. § 1.409A-1(b)(9)(iii).

¶1465.04

- Provisions for indemnification or liability insurance protecting the employee from claims, costs, and liability for actions or failures to act by the employee in his or her capacity as an employee of the employer.[37]

- An agreement that provides for amounts paid as settlements or awards resolving bona fide legal claims based on wrongful termination, employment discrimination, the Fair Labor Standards Act, or worker's compensation statutes, or for reimbursements or payments of reasonable attorneys' fees or other expenses incurred by the employee related to such bona fide legal claims does not provide for a deferral of compensation under Code Sec. 409A, regardless of whether such payments are treated as compensation or wages for tax purposes.[38] However, the regulations also make clear that this exception does not apply to any deferred amounts that did not arise as a result of an actual bona fide claim for damages under applicable law, such as amounts that would have been deferred or paid regardless of the existence of such claim, even if such amounts are paid as a part of a settlement.

- A separation pay plan (including a plan providing payments upon a voluntary separation) required to be provided under the applicable law of a foreign jurisdiction.[39]

- A collectively bargained separation pay plan that provides for separation pay only upon an involuntary separation from service or pursuant to a window program.[40] Only the portion of the separation pay plan attributable to employees covered by a bona fide collective bargaining agreement is considered to be provided under a collectively bargained separation pay plan.[41]

- A window program to the extent the payments do not exceed two times the lesser of the Code Sec. 401(a)(17) limit ($275,000 for 2018) or employee's annual compensation for the year prior to the year of separation, and the agreement provides that the separation pay must be paid no later than the last day of the second taxable year of the employee following the taxable year of the employee in which he or she incurred the separation from service:[42]

---

[37] Treas. Reg. § 1.409A-1(b)(10).

[38] Treas. Reg. § 1.409A-1(b)(11).

[39] Treas. Reg. § 1.409A-1(b)(9)(iv).

[40] Treas. Reg. § 1.409A-1(b)(9)(ii).

[41] Treas. Reg. § 1.409A-1(b)(9)(ii). The regulation provides that a collectively bargained separation pay plan is a separation pay plan that meets the following conditions: (A) the separation pay plan is contained within an agreement that the Secretary of Labor determines to be a collective bargaining agreement; (B) the separation pay provided by the collective bargaining agreement was the subject of arm's length negotiations between employee representatives and one or more employers, and the agreement between employee representatives and one or more employers satisfies Code Sec. 7701(a)(46); and (C) the circumstances surrounding the agreement evidence good faith bargaining between adverse parties over the separation pay to be provided under the agreement.

[42] Treas. Reg. § 1.409A-1(b)(9)(iii). Under the Code Sec. 409A regulations, the term "window program" refers to a program established by the employer to provide for separation pay in connection with a separation from service, for a limited period of time (no greater than one year), to employees who separate from service during that period or to employees who separate from service during that period under specified circumstances.

.05 Reimbursements and In-Kind Benefits

The regulations under Code Sec. 409A provide that to the extent a plan or agreement (including a plan or agreement providing payments upon a *voluntary separation* from service) entitles an employee to payment of reimbursements:

    (a) that are not otherwise excludible from gross income, for expenses that the employee otherwise could deduct under Code Secs. 162 or 167 as business expenses incurred in connection with the performance of services (ignoring any applicable limitation based on adjusted gross income), or

    (b) of reasonable outplacement expenses and reasonable moving expenses actually incurred by the employee and directly related to the termination of services for the employer.[43]

An agreement does not provide for a deferral of compensation to the extent such rights apply during a limited period (regardless of whether such rights continue beyond the limited period). The reimbursement of reasonable moving expenses includes the reimbursement of all or part of any loss the employee actually incurs due to the sale of a primary residence in connection with a separation from service. The regulations provide that a "limited period of time" in which expenses may be incurred, or in which in-kind benefits may be provided by the employer or a third party that the employer will pay, does not include periods beyond the last day of the second taxable year of the employee following the employee's taxable year in which the separation from service occurred, provided that the period during which the reimbursements for such expenses must be paid may not extend beyond the third taxable year of the employee following the taxable year in which his or her separation from service occurred.[44]

The final regulations provide that a terminating employee's entitlement to in-kind benefits, such as the continued use of a car or corporate aircraft, membership dues or payment for financial or tax advice, from the employer, or a payment by the employer directly to the person providing the goods or services to the employee, will not be treated as providing for a deferral of compensation under Code Sec. 409A to the extent such rights apply during a limited period of time (regardless of whether such rights extend beyond the limited period of time).

Finally, the final regulations provide an exception for amounts less than the Code Sec. 402(g) limit—$18,500 in 2018.[45]

.06 Specified Employees

Code Sec. 409A provides that distributions to a "specified employee" may not be made before the date that is six months after the date of the employee's separation from service or, if earlier, the date of the employee's death (the "six-month delay rule"). The six-month delay rule applies to payments under de-

---

[43] Treas. Reg. § 1.409A-3(i)(1)(iv)(A) and (B).
[44] Treas. Reg. § 1.409A-1(c)(3)(v).
[45] Treas. Reg. § 1.409A-1(b)(9)(v)(D).

ferred compensation and other non-qualified plans, but also payments under employment agreements. The final regulations provide that the employer must write into the agreement the six-month delay rule.[46]

Code Sec. 409A and the final regulations provide that the term "specified employee" means an employee who, as of the date of his or her separation from service, is a key employee of an employer whose stock is publicly traded on an established securities market or otherwise.[47] An employee is a "key employee" if the employee meets the requirements of Code Sec. 416(i)(1)(A)(i), (ii), or (iii) (the top-heavy plan rules) at any time during the 12-month period ending on a "specified employee identification date" (generally, December 31).[48] If an employee is a key employee as of a specified employee identification date, the employee is treated as a key employee for purposes of Code Sec. 409A for the entire 12-month period beginning on the specified employee effective date (or for a different 12-month period beginning within three months of that date).

Code Sec. 416(i)(1)(A) provides that the term "key employee" means an employee who, at any time during the year, is —

  (i) an officer of the employer having an annual compensation greater than $175,000 (for 2018) (as adjusted at the same time and in the same manner as under Code Sec. 415(d)),

 (ii) a 5-percent owner of the employer, or

(iii) a 1-percent owner of the employer having an annual compensation from the employer of more than $150,000.

Code Sec. 416(i)(A) also provides that no more than 50 employees (or, if lesser, the greater of three or 10 percent of the employees) are treated as officers. The definition of compensation under Treas. Reg. § 1.415(c)-2(a) applies, unless the agreement or employer specifies another definition.[49]

The final regulations provide that, like the six-month delay rule, an agreement must specify the method for determining key employees and for applying the six-month delay rule.[50] To meet the six-month delay requirement, an agreement may provide that:

- Any payment pursuant to a separation of service due within the six-month period is delayed until the end of the six-month period, or

- Each scheduled payment that becomes payable pursuant to a separation from service is delayed six months, or

- A combination thereof.

.07 Code Sec. 409A and Retention Bonus Programs

Most retention bonus programs should satisfy Code Sec. 409A. To the extent that the program requires eligible employees to remain employed through the last day of the retention period to receive a payment, such payments would

---

[46] Treas. Reg. § 1.409A-1(c)(3)(v).

[47] Treas. Reg. 1.409-1(c)(i).

[48] Treas. Reg. 1.409-1(c)(i)(3).

[49] Treas. Reg. 1.409-1(c)(i)(2).

[50] Treas. Reg. § 1.409A-3(i)(2)(ii).

qualify for the short-term deferral exception to 409A. The STD exception applies to amounts that are paid within 2 1/2 months after the close of the year in which they vest.

If the program could be interpreted (or is modified/clarified) to provide "vesting" to participants after their completion of one or more of the various "incentive program periods," the payments may not qualify for the STD exception. However, the payments should still satisfy 409A, because the program provides for a fixed future payment date that (it appears) cannot be accelerated for any reason.

¶1475 Implementation Steps for a Severance Plan

The following is a summary of the steps that a company could take to implement a new severance benefit plan that will be subject to ERISA:

1. The company's board of directors, or a committee appointed by the board, should adopt the severance plan, since it is a legal document. (Some plans require an affiliated company (*e.g.*, any company other than the parent company) that wants to extend the plan to its employees to adopt the plan expressly.)

2. Unrelated to ERISA, a public company that establishes a severance plan covering any of its named executive officers, generally must file a Form 8-K within four business days of adopting or amending the plan, pursuant to Item 5.02(e) of Form 8-K.

3. The company (or plan administrator, if different) should prepare and distribute to participants a form of summary plan description ("SPD") for the plan. If the company amends the plan in the future, it must give participants a summary of material modifications ("SMM") or new SPD.

4. The company (or plan administrator) should file an Annual Report Form 5500 with the IRS for the plan, as it does for its other welfare benefit plans. In lieu of filing a separate Form 5500 for the plan, however, the company may be able to simply indicate on (page one of) the Form 5500 it files for its general welfare benefits program that the company maintains a severance benefit plan.[51]

5. The company does not need to file the plan document or SPD with the IRS, DOL or any other governmental agency. No determination letter or other approval is required.

6. The company does not need to "post" the plan or SPD or otherwise notify employees of its existence in any way other than distribution of the SPD. However, most companies announce their implementation of a severance plan as a significant employee benefit.

---

[51] ERISA does not require the employer to file an annual report form if the plan covers less than 100 participants, or covers only a select group of management or highly compensated employees, and is funded from the employer's general assets.

7. If a plan participant requests, in writing, a copy of the plan document or Form 5500, the company (or plan administrator) must give the participant a copy.

The foregoing assumes that the severance plan will be a welfare plan under ERISA, not a pension plan.[52] If the severance plan is a welfare plan, only the reporting and disclosure (described above), fiduciary duty and administration and enforcement provisions of ERISA apply.

---

[52] ERISA regulations provide that a severance pay arrangement will *not* be considered to be a pension plan if (a) payments are not contingent upon the employee's retirement, (b) the total amount of such payment does not exceed twice the employee's annual compensation during the year preceding his termination of service and (c) all such payments are generally completed within 24 months after the employee's termination.

Chapter 15

NONEQUITY-BASED INCENTIVE COMPENSATION

¶1501 Introduction—Nonequity-Based Incentive Compensation

Many have repeated the aphorism: "Cash is king." In the late 1990s, with the economy strong and the stock market booming, stock options were the incentive of choice for executives.[1] Commentators and consultants alike heralded stock options as the most effective way to align an executive's interests with the continued success of his or her company. The incredibly favorable accounting treatment and cash flow benefits of stock options made them impossible for companies to ignore (see Chapter 7 [¶701 *et seq.*] for a detailed discussion of stock options).

However, even at the time, some commentators criticized the practice of using company stock as incentive compensation. For example, some pointed out that most executives sell their shares immediately after exercising their options.[2] Commentators and cranks alike have also criticized stock options as causing executives to boost stock prices in the short term at the expense of long-term stock success, resulting in poorer product quality and layoffs.[3] Despite these criticisms, stock options remain attractive to many companies and their executives.

Anything a company offers or provides to employees in return for their membership, commitment and/or contribution can be considered an incentive. Perhaps long-term incentive plans with a better line of sight will reemerge as the dominant form of incentive compensation, resulting in a clearer connection between the corporation's strategic goals and the executive's performance.

.01 Advantages of Incentive Compensation

Many companies have short-term and long-term incentive plans designed to motivate executives toward specific goals. Yet, even at the height of the internet bubble/stock option craze, a few voices in the wilderness called for more

---

[1] By 1999, about 60% of chief executives' annual pay was comprised of stock and options. Daniel Altman, *How to Tie Pay to Goals, Instead of the Stock Price*, N.Y. TIMES, Sept. 8, 2002, at C4. In 2001, "[o]ver 90% of the compensation many CEOs received . . . came as a result of gains in stock options . . . ." James A. Knight, *Performance*, J. OF BUS. STRATEGY, July/Aug. 2002, at 24. Currently, over 96% of public companies award stock options to their executives.

James A. Knight, *Performance*, J. OF BUS. STRATEGY, July/Aug. 2002, at 26.

[2] Sarah Anderson et al., *A Decade of Executive Excess: The 1990s Sixth Annual Executive Compensation Survey*, UNITED FOR A FAIR ECONOMY PRESS ROOM 6.

[3] Sarah Anderson et al., *A Decade of Executive Excess: The 1990s Sixth Annual Executive Compensation Survey*, UNITED FOR A FAIR ECONOMY PRESS ROOM 6.

attention to and focus on pure incentive compensation. Their reasoning, stated simply, was that: How much control over the company's stock price does the average executive really have? Thus, wiser compensation consultants argued for an executive compensation structure that provided incentives for particular behavior and results by the executive—with different behaviors, results and goals specified for different executives (see ¶1515 for a more detailed discussion of the advantages of nonequity-based incentive compensation).

> **Example:** ABC Corporation, a publicly traded telecommunication company, awards Executive D stock options of 100,000 shares in 2010, when ABC's stock is trading at $15.00. By April 2018, ABC's stock price has risen to $250.00. By April 2020, ABC's stock price is $12.00. Did Executive D's exceptional job performance from 2010 to 2018 lead to ABC's phenomenal stock performance? Did D do a terrible job beginning in April 2018, causing ABC's price to plummet? Did D perform his duties at approximately the same level from 2010 through 2020, while other factors led to the phenomenal increase and precipitous drop in ABC's stock price?

.02 Taxation of Nonequity Compensation

Some forms of equity-based compensation offer significant tax advantages and opportunities. Incentive compensation paid in cash is taxable to the executive as ordinary income. However, companies do not have to pay incentive compensation solely in cash, and they can offer executives tax deferral opportunities (see ¶1525 for a more detailed discussion of the taxation of nonequity-based incentive compensation).

.03 Structuring Incentive Compensation

This chapter does not argue that companies should pay executives *less*, only that companies may want to consider paying their executives *differently*. In actuality, executives who can make a company successful in not only the short-term, but also in the medium and long-term, may make *more*. Each company should tailor its executive compensation plan to fit its own special needs and goals. Employers should strive to create incentive compensation packages that incentivize executives to achieve results that will most likely guarantee the company's success. Because stock value is sometimes more reflective of the market itself rather than a company's performance, granting stock options to executives may not be the best method by which an employer can realize its goals. This structure places the burden of strategic thinking firmly in the hand of the board of directors, the compensation committee, and the chief executive officer. In sum, if a company structures its incentive compensation in a way that is tailored to a company's goals and mindful of short, medium, and long-term performance, the result may be increased payoffs for investors, customers, employees, and executives (see ¶1535 for a more detailed discussion of structuring nonequity-based incentive compensation).

.04 Securities Law Reporting Requirements

Public companies are required to file a Form 8-K within four days of certain executive compensation and employment events, including the adoption of a cash incentive plan and/or the making of payments under such a plan (see ¶1545).

.05 Litigation Over Nonpayment

As you might expect, numerous cases have involved employees' disputes over whether an employer should have made an annual or long-term incentive bonus payment. The decisions in these cases are very fact specific. About the only conclusion that one can draw from a review of these cases is that, as in most areas of executive compensation litigation, the court will uphold the plain wording of the plan or arrangement (see ¶1555).

.06 Supplemental Withholding

The Code imposes on employers a mandatory income tax withholding obligation at the highest rate of income tax in effect under the Code (currently 37%) to the extent an employee's total supplemental wages from an employer (and other businesses under common control with the employer) exceed $1,000,000 during the calendar year. For many highly compensated employees, the incentive compensation bonus is what puts them into the "supplemental" wage category (see ¶1565).

.07 Litigation Based On State Wage Payment Laws

In recent years, there has been a striking rise in the number of lawsuits brought under the state wage and hour laws. Many of these cases have challenged deferred compensation and other incentive plans (see ¶1575).

¶1515 Advantages of Nonequity-Based Incentive Compensation

Simply stated, the advantage of an incentive compensation program that makes cash (or even stock) awards based on executives' achievements of specific goals and objectives is that the program will better reward an executive for his or her actual performance and better serve the company by driving executives to achieve its strategic goals.

> **Comment:** In the example in ¶1501, few sentient beings would argue that Executive D's job performance alone led to the phenomenal increase and precipitous drop in ABC Corporation's stock price from 2010 through 2020. Most observers would attribute the rise to irrational exuberance over stocks in general and the telecommunications industry in particular, and to the bursting of the artificial bubble.

.01 Superior Line of Sight

Stock options align the optionees' interests with those of stockholders, *i.e.*, an increasing share price. Virtually no one disagrees with that general proposition. However, some have offered the criticism that stock options actually reward employees for run-ups in the stock market, not for individual performance. This is because, they argue, most employees cannot really create a difference in their employer's stock price through their performance. In other words, with respect to the majority of employees at the majority of companies, stock options have failed to create a "line of sight" for the employee between his or her performance and compensation.[4] This means that, because individual employee performance usually has little effect on the price of company stock, stock option-based incentives do not give optionees much incentive to perform better.

Situations such as one where an executive is in charge of a subsidiary or division of a company create an obvious example of how a better line of sight between performance and compensation can benefit both company and executive. In this situation, rewarding the executive with stock options may not tie the incentive to his or her performance. After all, the executive only controls the operation of his or her division, not the whole company. In this case, a long-term incentive arrangement that is nonequity-based can link the incentive to the success of the business for which the executive is responsible. That way, if the stock market falls, but the executive's division thrives, he or she would be rewarded, instead of punished.

> **Example:** Executive D works in the distressed debt division of ABC Corporation, a publicly traded, diversified financial services company. In 2018, business is booming for Executive D's division, while ABC's stock trading and investment banking operations are moribund.
>
> If ABC compensates Executive D solely with stock option awards, it will not be rewarding her for the burgeoning success of her division (or incentivizing her to continue performing at the highest levels for ABC).
>
> If, instead, ABC designed its compensation program to reward D for the revenue and profitability of her division, D should be highly motivated to continue delivering superior results for the duration of the economic downturn.

Line of sight may also be hindered by using stock options as incentive compensation because the executive may not perceive the options to be as valuable as other forms of compensation.[5] This is especially true in times when the stock market is not strong. In sum, creating a superior line of sight for executives is likely to increase productivity and performance.

.02 Flexibility

Related to and intertwined with the line of sight rationale is the fact that stand-alone stock awards are a blunt instrument for compensating executives. The company's stock price goes up, the company's stock price goes down, often irrespective of any individual executive's performance. More effective incentive compensation programs present individual (or similarly situated) executives

---

[4] James A. Knight, *Value Added Management: Developing A Systematic Approach To Creating Stockholder Value*, 221 (1998).

[5] *See, e.g.*, Graef Crystal, *General Electric, Others May Have New Pay Option* (Aug. 13, 2002), at http://bloomberg.com.

with individually tailored performance goals. The company designs those goals so that each executive is working toward a result that furthers the company's overall strategic plan. If the company needs to change one piece of its strategic plan, it can modify the performance goals of certain executives to orient them in a new direction.

Of course, many companies have short-term and long-term incentive plans designed to motivate executives toward specific goals. Some companies integrate these plans with stock-based compensation so that the company will make a fixed equity award if the executive achieves his or her short-term or long-term performance goals. Other short-term and/or long-term incentive plans stand alone, separate from the company's equity award programs.

.03 Tax Consequences

While equity compensation awards offer executives (and other employees) favorable tax consequences and planning opportunities, the tax consequences to the company are not as favorable (see ¶1525 for a comparison of the tax consequences of equity versus cash compensation to executives). With nearly all forms of executive compensation, the company becomes entitled to a tax deduction only when the compensation becomes taxable to the executive as ordinary income.[6] The company will be entitled to a deduction for short-term and long-term cash compensation awards at the time it pays the awards.

.04 Favorable Accounting Treatment Disappeared

Until 2006, stock options allowed a company to compensate employees without spending cash or reflecting an accounting charge against earnings on its financial statements. If a company drafted and operated its stock option plan, and made awards in a manner that satisfied the accounting requirements set forth in Accounting Principles Board (APB) Opinion Number 25, the option award qualified for highly favorable, "fixed" accounting treatment.[7] This unique way of compensating executives without a cash flow effect or accounting expense charge was simply too good for companies not to use.

The United States Financial Accounting Standards Board (the "FASB") ended this extraordinary treatment with FAS 123R (now known as "ASC 718"). Critics of this favorable accounting treatment had long asserted that companies should expense stock options because they use them to pay employees, plain and simple. After all, the companies expense the salaries they pay to employees—that is, count the salaries as expenses—thereby reducing company earnings. Thus, the argument follows that companies should not treat stock options differently than salary in this respect. As favorable accounting practices disappear, and the perception of stock option incentive plans as being abused and ineffective spreads, stock options have become less attractive.[8]

---

[6] The one notable exception to this general rule is for companies' contributions to qualified retirement plans on behalf of employees. See Chapter 16 (¶1601 et seq.) for a detailed discussion of qualified retirement plans.

[7] See Chapter 7 (¶701 et seq.) for a detailed discussion of stock options.

[8] Stock options have also been criticized as an "'externality,' an outside factor that creates a market inefficiency . . . .[T]he distortion boosts the attrac-

.05 Sarbanes-Oxley Act of 2002

If a public company is required to prepare an accounting restatement due to the material noncompliance of the company, and this noncompliance is the result of misconduct under any financial reporting requirement under securities laws, the CEO and CFO must reimburse the company for compensation gains attributable to the misconduct. Specifically, Section 304 of the Sarbanes-Oxley Act ("SOX") would require the CEO and CFO to reimburse the company for:

- Any bonus or other "incentive-based" or "equity-based" compensation the executive received during the 12-month period following the first public issuance or filing with the SEC (whichever occurs first) of the financial document embodying the financial reporting requirement; and

- Any profits realized from the sale of the company's securities during that 12-month period.[9]

One possible result of this provision is that public companies will pay more of their executives' compensation in cash salary. There are other issues raised by this provision as well. For example:

- There is no necessary relationship between the amount of the restatement and the amount the executive is required to reimburse.

- The CEO or CFO need not be the party responsible for the misconduct.

- No state of mind is required for "misconduct" (*i.e.*, intent, recklessness, negligence, strict liability, *etc.*).

- It is unclear what SOX considers "incentive-based" compensation.

- It is unclear when SOX considers compensation to be "received."

Therefore, it is possible that SOX would force a CEO or CFO to forfeit these bonuses and profits regardless of whether the executive himself or herself was at fault in the misconduct at issue, even in a case where the company hired the executive after the occurrence of the misconduct. The SEC can grant exemptions to the forfeiture requirement.[10] Thus, an innocent executive may successfully obtain an exemption from these penalties. In addition, while the Sarbanes-Oxley Act does mandate that CEOs and CFOs reimburse their companies in the aforementioned circumstances, SOX does not authorize companies to carry out such reimbursement on their own. Hence, it is unclear whether employers can withhold CEO and CFO compensation in this situation.

¶1525 Taxation of Incentive Compensation

Some forms of equity-based compensation offer significant tax advantages and opportunities. Incentive compensation paid in cash is taxable to the executive as ordinary income. However, companies can structure their incentive

---

(Footnote Continued)

tiveness of options over other forms of compensation, even though these [other forms] may offer more powerful performance incentives." Michael Casey, *Stock Options Didn't Work; What Will?*, WALL ST. J., Aug. 26, 2002, at A2.

[9] H.R. Con. Res. 3763 § 304(a), 107th Cong. (2002) (enacted).

[10] H.R. Con. Res. 3763 § 304(b).

compensation programs so they do not pay solely in cash, and so that the programs offer executives tax deferral opportunities. Before 2018, companies could more easily design incentive compensation programs to protect the deductibility of payout from Code Sec. 162(m)'s $1 million deductibility limit.

.01 Comparison to Equity Compensation

When a company grants stock options to an executive, the executive does not recognize taxable income on either the grant or vesting of the award. The executive will only recognize income when he or she exercises the option and purchases stock—and the amount of income will only be the difference between the option exercise price and the stock's fair market value on that date. Thus, stock options give the executive the ability to control the time when he or she recognizes income. The company will only receive a tax deduction for the amount the executive recognizes as ordinary income, and at the time he or she recognizes that income.

An executive's tax treatment of incentive stock options is even better. The executive does not recognize taxable income on the grant, vesting, or even the exercise of the incentive stock option. The executive will only recognize income when he or she sells the stock purchased with the incentive option. The income the executive recognizes on sale will be taxable at more favorable long-term capital gains rates if the executive meets the holding requirements for the option and the stock.[11] The company does not receive any deduction at any time when it awards incentive stock options.

.02 "Performance-Based" Compensation Under Code Sec. 162(m)

Code Sec. 162(m) limits a publicly traded company's ability to deduct the annual compensation of its top five executive officers to $1 million.[12] Before 2018, Code Sec. 162(m) contained an exception to the deductibility limit for performance-based compensation. Under this provision, the deductibility limit did not apply to:

> any remuneration payable solely on account of the attainment of one or more performance goals, but only if (i) the performance goals are determined by a compensation committee of the board of directors of the taxpayer which is comprised solely of 2 or more outside directors, (ii) the material terms under which the remuneration is to be paid, including the performance goals, are disclosed to stockholders and approved by a majority of the vote in a separate stockholder vote before the payment of such remuneration, and (iii) before any payment of such remuneration, the compensation committee referred to in clause (i) certifies that the performance goals and any other material terms were in fact satisfied.[13]

Therefore, an employer could design its incentive compensation plan to qualify for the "performance-based" exception, thereby avoiding the $1 million deductibility cap.[14]

---

[11] See ¶735 for a detailed discussion of the taxation and requirement of incentive stock options.

[12] See Chapter 22 for a detailed discussion of Code Section 162(m).

[13] Code Sec. 162(m)(4)(C).

[14] See Chapter 22 (¶2201 et seq.) for a detailed discussion of Section 162(m) issues.

However, the legislation known as the Tax Cuts and Jobs Act of 2017 ("TCJA") signed into law by President Trump in December 2017, eliminated the performance-based compensation exception from Code Sec. 162(m), rendering such design considerations moot. Until the grandfathering protection allowed to certain compensation awards by the transition rules of the TCJA expires, most plans will continue to include provisions necessary to comply with Code Sec. 162(m). But awards made in 2018 and after will not need to include such provisions. The following requirements no longer will apply:

- The requirement that the compensation committee establish performance goals in advance;

- The requirement that the performance goals be based solely on objective factors;

- The requirement that the compensation committee has no ability or discretion to increase payout above those amounts dictated by the pre-established performance goals;

- The requirement that the compensation committee be comprised *solely of two or more outside directors*;

- The requirement that the compensation committee certify that performance goals were achieved, before payment is made; and

- The requirement that the material terms of any performance goals be disclosed to and subsequently approved by the company's stockholders before the compensation is paid.

.03 Compensation Deferral Opportunities

Often short-term and long-term incentive compensation plans pay out in cash only. Generally, these amounts will be taxable to the employee and deductible for the employer at the time of payment. However, a company could easily design its incentive compensation program to make payouts in the form of company stock.

> **Example 1:** Executive D has earned a cash payout of $500,000 for 2018 under ABC Corporation's short-term incentive compensation program. ABC's program gives eligible executives the ability to elect to take the payout in cash or in shares of company stock, or partly in each. For senior executives, the program will automatically make one-half of the payout in company stock, and for any senior executive who has not yet satisfied ABC's stock ownership guidelines, the program will pay out 100% in company stock.

Similarly, a company could easily design its incentive compensation program to give executives the opportunity to defer the receipt and taxation of cash or stock payments.[15]

---

[15] *See* Chapter 17 (¶1701 *et seq.*) for a detailed discussion of deferred compensation.

Example 2: In Example 1 above, ABC Corporation's incentive compensation program could allow eligible executives to elect to defer the receipt and taxation of both cash or of company stock payouts. By establishing a parallel nonqualified deferred compensation plan, ABC could allow Executive D to defer all or a portion of her $500,000 payout to employment termination or beyond. If the program would make one-half of the payout in shares of restricted stock, Executive D could elect to defer the receipt of the stock beyond vesting.

This is one of the design features of a restricted stock unit ("RSU") plan. The executive's deferrals are converted to RSUs held in an unfunded deferred compensation plan. The value of the executive's RSU account is measured solely by the value of the underlying shares of company stock, and the plan ultimately will pay the value of Executive D's account to her in company stock.

.04 Timing of Annual Bonus Payments

Many annual bonus and long-term incentive plans provide for payments to participants within 2 1/2 months of the end of the employer's tax year, so the employer can deduct the payments in the prior tax year (for example, for a calendar-year employer, payment by March 15, 2019, for a 2018 deduction). However, the company and the plan must meet other requirements in order to achieve this retroactive deductibility. Under Code Sec. 461 and the regulations, an accrual-basis taxpayer generally can deduct expenses that meet the "all-events" or "fact of liability" test. The all-events test has three requirements: (i) all events have occurred that determine the fact of the liability, (ii) the amount of the liability can be determined with reasonable accuracy, and (iii) the "economic performance" has occurred (*e.g.*, the employee's performance that triggered the bonus payout).

For companies and plans that pay awards within 2 1/2 months of the company's year end, the terms of the plan or the governing corporate action determine whether the company can deduct the awards for the year just ended or in the payment year. To satisfy the all-events test, the award amounts and the obligation to pay must be fixed by year end. A plan based entirely on financial performance should meet the requirement that bonus amounts be fixed as of year-end, because the information needed for calculating the bonus is available at year end (even if the numbers still need to be audited).

The requirement that participants' rights to bonuses be vested (that is, the obligation to pay the bonuses be fixed) as of year end generally can be met in one of two ways. An individual participant's right to a bonus may be vested at year end. That is, even if the person quits early in the following year, before the bonus is actually paid to him or her, the person would be entitled to the bonus. Alternatively, a company could meet the all-events test by creating a fixed-dollar bonus pool and provide for it to be allocated among and paid to employees who satisfy the plan's terms as of the payment date. If the company has to pay out the bonus pool even if only one employee ultimately meets the requirements—the all-events test should be satisfied.

Some companies require employees to remain employed until the date the annual bonus is paid in order to receive it. This can be problematic. First, for companies that seek to take the deduction in a prior tax year for bonuses paid within 2 1/2 months of the subsequent year, requiring employment beyond the last day of the bonus year could cause the plan to fail the "all-events" test for deductibility in the prior year.

Second, an employee who is denied an annual bonus because his or her employment terminated in the subsequent year before the bonus was paid, could allege a violation of state wage payment laws. Although these laws vary from state to state, some state wage payment laws would deem the employee to have irrevocably earned the annual bonus payment on the last day of the bonus year (usually December 31). A company may be able to address this second problem by drafting the bonus plan to provide clearly that it is a retention device in addition to a bonus plan, and continuing employment is required.

The IRS has provided guidance on this issue in a number of forms. In IRS Field Attorney Advice 20134301F, the taxpayer/employer maintained a variety of annual bonus plans. Each plan provided that covered employees must be employed as of the last day of Year 1 to receive the bonus in Year 2. The IRS Chief Counsel addressed three other issues:

1. Do amounts paid under the terms of the taxpayer's cash bonus plans, which plans provide that the taxpayer retains the unilateral right to modify or eliminate the bonuses at any time prior to payment, meet the all events test any earlier than the date the amounts are paid?

2. Do amounts paid under the terms of the taxpayer's plans, which amounts must be approved by a committee of the taxpayer's board of directors before being paid; meet the all events test any earlier than the date the amounts are approved?

3. Do amounts paid under the terms of certain of the taxpayer's plans, the computation of which are dependent, in part, on subjective employee performance appraisals, meet the all events test any earlier than the date the employee performance appraisals are completed?

The IRS Chief Counsel concluded that neither the fact of liability prong nor the amount of liability prong was met with respect to bonuses so long as (i) the taxpayer retains the unilateral right to modify or eliminate the bonuses at any time prior to payment, (ii) the bonuses are subject to board or committee approval, or (iii) subjective calculation needs to be made to calculate the amount of the bonuses.

These conclusions are generally consistent with previous IRS interpretations of the all events test. In late 2011, the IRS issued Revenue Ruling 2011-29, which held that: (1) an employer can satisfy the "fact of the liability" test and achieve early deductibility under Code Sec. 461 for bonuses payable to a group of employees even though the employer does not know the identity of any particular bonus recipient and the amount payable to that recipient until after the end of the taxable year. Put another way, Revenue Ruling 2011-29 indicated that an employer would meet the "all events test" for purposes of determining when a bonus pool amount is deductible if the company were obligated at the end of the current year to pay the full bonus pool amount without any contingencies.

Under the bonus program of Rev. Rul. 2011-29, any bonus amount allocable to an employee who is not employed on the date on which the employer pays bonuses is reallocated among other eligible employees. Thus, the aggregate minimum amount of bonuses the employer pays to its group of eligible employees is not reduced by the departure of an employee after the end of the taxable year but before the employer pays bonuses for that year.

- The employer's liability to pay a minimum amount of bonuses to the group of eligible employees is fixed at the end of the year in which the services are rendered;
- The employer is obligated under the program to pay to the group the minimum amount of bonuses determined by the end of the taxable year; and
- Any bonus allocable to an employee who is not employed on the date on which bonuses are paid is reallocated to other eligible employees.

Thus, this bonus program established the employer's liability for the minimum amount of bonuses by the end of the year in which the employees render services and, thus, the bonus payments are deductible for that year, even though paid in the next year.

In late 2012, the IRS Chief Counsel Office opined that, if it is possible for any portion of the bonus pool to be forfeited after the current tax year, the entire bonus pool could only be deducted in the year it is paid. In CCA 201246029, the IRS concluded that taxpayer/employer's liability arising from bonus compensation is taken into account in the year the bonuses are paid because taxpayer's employees must still be employed to receive their bonuses and because forfeited amounts revert back to taxpayer.

.05 Code Sec. 409A

Code Sec. 409A imposes onerous requirements on deferred compensation. However, a deferral of compensation does not occur if, absent an election to otherwise defer the payment to a later period, at all times the terms of the plan require payment by, and an amount is actually or constructively received by the employee by, the later of (i) the date that is 2 1/2 months from the end of the employee's first taxable year in which the amount is no longer subject to a substantial risk of forfeiture, or (ii) the date that is 2 1/2 months from the end of the company's first taxable year in which the amount is no longer subject to a substantial risk of forfeiture.[16]

A payment that otherwise qualifies as a short-term deferral under Code Sec. 409A, but is made after the applicable 2 1/2 month period may continue to qualify as a short-term deferral if:

---

[16] Treas. Reg. § 1.409A-1(b)(4)(ii).

- the taxpayer establishes that it was administratively impracticable to make the payment by the end of the applicable 2 1/2 month period and, as of the date upon which the legally binding right to the compensation arose, such impracticability was unforeseeable, or the taxpayer establishes that making the payment by the end of the applicable 2 1/2 month period would have jeopardized the ability of the company to continue as a going concern, and

- the payment is made as soon as administratively practicable or as soon as the payment would no longer have such effect.[17]

Example 1: On November 1, 2018, ABC Corporation awards a bonus to Employee A such that A has a legally binding right to the payment as of November 1, 2018. Under ABC's bonus plan, the bonus will be determined based on services performed during the period from January 1, 2019 through December 31, 2020. The bonus is scheduled to be paid as a lump sum payment on February 15, 2021. Under the bonus plan, A will forfeit the bonus unless he continues performing services through the scheduled payment date (February 15, 2021). Provided that at all times before the scheduled payment date A is required to continue to perform services to retain the right to the bonus, and the bonus is paid on or before March 15, 2021, the bonus plan will not be considered to have provided for a deferral of compensation.[18]

Example 2: On November 1, 2018, ABC Corporation awards a bonus to Employee B such that B has a legally binding right to the payment as of November 1, 2018. However, under the bonus plan, B will forfeit the bonus unless she continues performing services through December 31, 2020. Under the bonus plan, the bonus is scheduled to be paid as a lump sum payment on July 1, 2021. By specifying a payment date after the applicable 2 1/2 month period, the bonus plan provides for a deferred payment. The bonus plan provides for a deferral of compensation under Code Sec. 409A, and will not qualify as a short-term deferral regardless of whether the bonus is paid or made available on or before March 15, 2021.[19]

¶1535 Structuring Incentive Compensation

The aim of an effective incentive compensation structure should be to give executives an incentive to achieve specific quantifiable goals. The goals may be fixed, such as a specific percent of return on investment ("ROI") or variable, based on objective benchmarks, such as an ROI that compares favorably to other companies in the industry. This structure places the burden of strategic thinking firmly in the hand of the board of directors, the compensation committee, and the CEO.

The challenge for any company is deciding how to structure its annual and/or long-term incentive compensation plans to best attract, retain, and motivate

---

[17] Treas. Reg. § 1.409A-1(b)(4)(ii).

[18] Treas. Reg. § 1.409A-1(b)(4)(iii), example 4.

[19] Treas. Reg. § 1.409A-1(b)(4)(iii), example 5.

executive employees.[20] There are many varieties of incentive programs. For example, an executive may receive incentive compensation in traditional forms like cash, benefits, or bonuses. Other basic executive benefits may include supplemental life and disability insurance,[21] supplemental medical reimbursement plans, and perquisites. Perquisites are benefits given to executives that can take the form of property, like cars or computers; services, like parking privileges, physicals, club memberships, and financial advice; or cash, such as money to cover moving expenses. Supplemental retirement benefits may be part of an incentive package as well. However, while the nature of incentives themselves are important to executives, even more important to the company should be the way in which the incentives are awarded.

.01 Selecting the Company's Critical Objectives

The incentive plan for a start-up venture may look much different than that for a conglomerate with five different business units. A company that is aggressively trying to grow may want to reward increase in market share (or a proxy thereof). If a company is in a cyclical industry, optimizing profits during each phase of the cycle may be important, and it also may be important to measure profit performance relative to peers, since all peers will be subject to the same cycle. As a general rule, the company should ask itself a variety of questions in designing its incentive compensation program, including some of the following:

- What are the company's critical objectives? Put another way, how should the company measure success?
- Over what time period should the company measure results?
- How complex will this be to measure?
- Does the measure fit with the company's culture?
- Does the measure capture the company's business strategy?
- Is the measure consistent with industry dynamics?
- Is the measure appropriate for the company at this stage of development?

Performance measures generally are lumped into three categories:

1. Stock price or market based measures, such as stock appreciation or total stockholder return. These measures provide a direct linkage to stockholders, but are subject to all the influences of the stock market, which are out of the control of the executives.

2. Financial Measures, ranging from revenue growth to profitability and margin to capital efficiency: Growth (Revenue); Profitability (EPS, Margin, income); Capital Efficiency (EVA, ROE, ROIC).

3. Operational measures, which focus on productivity, quality, customer satisfaction, diversity goals, employee safety, merger integration, *etc.*

---

[20] *See* ¶ 10,190 for a sample incentive compensation matrix.

[21] Janet Den Uyl & Patricia Kopacz, *Executive Benefits in a Pay-for-Performance Environment*, EMPLOYEE BENEFITS J., Sept. 2002, at 15. An employer may purchase a life insurance policy for the executive's benefit, split the costs and benefits of the life insurance plan with the executive, or pay death benefits out of its own assets.

The most common financial criterion used by public companies seems to be earnings per share or net income. The next most common criterion seems to be revenue, then operating income.

.02 Setting Sights on Long-Term Goals

In today's post-Enron world, investors and employees want more than a CEO who can drive up short-term stock price.[22] They want an executive whose goal is to help their company succeed in the long run. To accomplish this, an employer must find and retain executives who are committed to the company and who will strive to increase its long-term growth. When stock options largely comprise the compensation paid to an executive, he or she may be tempted to turn the options into quick cash rather than make the company's long-term goals top priority. Executives paid largely in stock options may have greater incentive to bring about short-term jumps in stock price and less incentive to stay with their companies long-term.

Further, if stock prices drop, the executive might consider the options valueless, giving him or her little incentive to remain with the company. In addition, when the stock market is falling, options become a less-effective incentive because, once the shares are valued below the option exercise price, the executive has little incentive to curb losses.[23] When stock prices make options less valuable, one approach employers take is to change the price of the stock options, or grant the executive more of them. Both of these approaches may ultimately have the effect of diluting the stockholders' stock, and such tactics do not reward the executive for superior performance, or encourage good decision-making. In fact, this structure may promote excess risk-taking on the part of the executive.

Individuals want the companies in which they invest to continue boosting performance, even when the stock market is stagnant or falling. Rewarding executives for reaching long-term goals may encourage activities that are expensive in the short-term but pay off in the long-run, such as advertising campaigns, research and development, or replenishing physical assets.[24] In short, long-term rewards will encourage creativity and company growth.

The new revolution in executive compensation will likely be the promotion of long-term success via long-term rewards. However, just as companies have not fared well by sacrificing long-term goals in the name of short-term profits, long-term objectives must be balanced by short and medium-term targets. Therefore, companies ideally should link executive compensation to short, medium, and long-term achievements. An employer may give large bonuses every few years, rewarding an executive who meets goals consistently.

---

[22] Executives have been compared to baseball's free agents, as companies compete to entice the best candidates, and executives jump from "team to team," looking for the best compensation package. Daniel Altman, *How to Tie Pay to Goals, Instead of the Stock Price*, N.Y. TIMES, Sept. 8, 2002, at C4.

[23] *See* Michael Casey, *Stock Options Didn't Work; What Will?*, WALL ST. J., Aug. 26, 2002, at A2.

[24] *See, e.g.*, James A. Knight, *Making the Jump From Short-Term to Long-Term Performance Measures*, J. OF STRATEGIC PERFORMANCE MEASUREMENT, Feb./Mar. 1998, at 18.

.03 Options for Structuring Incentive Compensation

There are many ways that a company can structure incentive compensation to promote loyalty and longevity. For instance, an employer may consider granting stock with restrictions on its future sale, instead of options. Alternatively, an employer may offer stock, cash, or other rewards in a way that ties them to explicit accomplishments. Another option is to index compensation to take into account both the company's performance and the stock's performance. In this way, the executive is not punished merely by virtue of a poor economy beyond his or her control.

An employer may also award deferred stock grants, which have value even if the stock price falls. Alternatively, the employer could make periodic contributions to an annuity fund for the benefit of employees, thereby rewarding loyalty and longevity.[25] A company could also choose to offer an executive restricted stock grants, which would give him or her incentive to preserve stock price, even if the stock value is dropping, because the executive's shares will decline in worth along with the stock price. These stock grants should vest over time, so that the executive will be encouraged to make choices that will enhance the company's long-term success.[26] Similarly, both phantom stock and performance cash are options for employers that want to tie compensation to performance.

When a company offers stock options, there may be ways to better tie ownership to company goals. For example, some consultants are espousing a method that would require the executives to hold shares of the company and, in some cases, to hold the shares on favorable terms.[27] In addition, the options could vest periodically and be based on performance. An employer may choose to have overlapping vesting periods to encourage longevity. In this way, by the time some of the executive's equity or nonequity incentive compensation vests, he or she will already be partially through the next vesting period.[28]

A company may use a supplemental deferred compensation arrangement to compensate executives.[29] Such arrangements are important to executives where nonequity compensation is concerned because nonequity compensation is generally taxable when received. These arrangements can be advantageous because they allow executives to defer more income than the amount allowed under qualified plans.[30] While advantageous from a tax standpoint, supplemental deferred compensation arrangements have left executives feeling uncertain, as many companies have recently entered bankruptcy very publicly. The reason for this uncertainty is that, when a company enters bankruptcy, funds in nonqualified deferred compensation plans are available to pay the company's creditors.

---

[25] *See* Gary Beckett, *OMC Offers Annuity Plan for Dealers*, SOUNDINGS TRADE ONLY: THE BOATING NEWSPAPER, Sept. 1995.

[26] Pat Dorsey, *Pay Executives to Invest, Not Gamble*.

[27] Michael Casey, *Stock Options Didn't Work; What Will?*, WALL ST. J., Aug. 26, 2002, at A2.

[28] *See* Richard E. Wood, *Equity Compensation in Troubled Times*, at http://www.fed.org.

[29] *See* Chapter 17 (¶ 1701 *et seq.*) for a detailed discussion of deferred compensation.

[30] It should be noted that distributions from nonqualified plans cannot be rolled over into an IRA. In addition, participants cannot borrow money from nonqualified plans.

There are other deferred compensation alternatives as well. For example, a supplemental executive retirement plan (a "SERP") provides added retirement benefits to executives. In addition, 401(k) mirror plans allow executives to defer amounts in excess of the 401(k) limits and employers to provide matching contributions.

.04 A Tailored Approach

The company should base an executive's incentive compensation on performance goals on factors other than how much short-term profit he or she can generate. However, the factors upon which a company bases its executives' compensation must vary to fit each company's unique line of business, strategies, and goals. Some companies may choose to base incentive compensation on operating income or cultivation of client relationships, while others may decide to base compensation on creativity and initiative. Still other employers may emphasize improved customer service or quicker response time.

The company can even tailor an executive's compensation package to his or her personal likes. For example, one executive might prefer a comfortable retirement where another would prefer a more autonomous role in some aspects of company operations. Additionally, as noted above, the company may design performance award plans to be exempt from the Code Sec. 162(m) limit for employer deductions of compensation to certain employees.

.05 Incentive Bonuses for Specific Events

As discussed more fully under the Change in Control (see ¶215) and Mergers and Acquisitions Chapters (see ¶2515), many companies provide nonequity based incentive compensation for the successful completion of a transaction. For example, America West Holdings approved an incentive plan for top executives involved in its merger with US Airways. It granted the CEO 500,000 shares of restricted stock vesting one-fourth on each of the first, second, third, and fourth anniversaries of the merger. Companies offer merger bonuses like this to encourage executive stewardship in integrating mergers, and as a form of "combat pay" for the extra work involved in a merger or acquisition.

¶1545 Securities Law Reporting Requirements

A company must file a Form 8-K within four days of certain executive compensation and employment events. Public companies must disclose the execution, amendment, or termination of management contracts and compensation plans involving directors or named executive officers on Form 8-K. Such contracts and plans are reportable because they are deemed to be material agreements not made in the ordinary course of business, even if the amount involved would not otherwise be considered material to the company. In addition, companies must disclose contracts or plans involving any other executive officer, unless the amount or significance of the contract is immaterial.

The adoption of a cash bonus plan by the board of directors, under which named executive officers are eligible to participate, requires disclosure pursuant to Item 1.01 of Form 8-K, even if no specific performance criteria, performance goals or bonus opportunities have been communicated to plan participants.[31] The same position applies to the adoption of a cash bonus plan in which other executive officers are eligible to participate, unless the plan is immaterial in amount or significance within the meaning of Item 601(b)(10)(iii)(A) of Regulation S-K. However, if the company adopts the plan subject to obtaining stockholder approval, the receipt of the stockholder approval triggers the obligation to file a Form 8-K pursuant to Item 1.01. The company must comply with Item 5.02, if it applies.[32]

After a company has disclosed its adoption of a cash bonus plan on a Form 8-K, when the board of directors sets specific performance goals and business criteria for one or more participants, this action requires additional disclosure pursuant to Form 8-K.[33] If the Form 8-K reporting the plan's adoption did not disclose the specific performance goals and business criteria for the performance period (such as EBITDA, return on equity or other applicable measure), the company must file a subsequent Form 8-K to disclose these measures when the board of directors sets them. However, the SEC notes that the company is not required to provide disclosure of target levels with respect to specific quantitative or qualitative performance related-factors, or factors or criteria involving confidential commercial or business information, the disclosure of which would have an adverse effect on the registrant.

Finally, the SEC indicates that the company's actual payment of a cash award pursuant to a cash bonus plan for which it previously filed 8-K disclosure generally does not require further disclosure on Form 8-K. If the company pays out a cash award upon determining that the performance criteria have been satisfied, then a Form 8-K reporting such a payment would not be required. However, a company would be required to disclose the actual payment of a cash bonus on Form 8-K if the company exercised discretion to pay the bonus even though the specified performance criteria were not satisfied.[34]

¶1555 Litigation Over Incentive Plan Payments

As with every other area of executive compensation in this treatise, numerous cases have involved employees' disputes over whether an employer should have made an annual or long-term incentive bonus payment. Generally, the courts seek to uphold the plain wording of the incentive plan or arrangement. However, the plain meaning is not always easy to determine.

.01 Reducing Promised Bonuses

Street v. Siemens Med. Solutions Health Servs. Corp.[35] is an interesting case. In *Street*, a state court permitted 1,200 employees whose bonuses were reduced by a total of $12 to $15 million to pursue a nationwide class action against their employer. The employees argued that Siemens had no basis in any contract language for the reduction in response to declining profit margins.

---

[31] FAQs Q&A 12, November 23, 2004.

[32] FAQs Q&A 12, November 23, 2004.

[33] FAQs Q&A 13, November 23, 2004.

[34] FAQs Q&A 14, November 23, 2004.

[35] *Street v. Siemens Med. Solutions Health Servs. Corp.*, 2004 Pa. D&C LEXIS 87 (Pa. Ct. Common Pleas 2004).

To give workers financial incentives to generate increased revenue and profit, Siemens had provided commissions and bonuses in addition to their salaries for employees who met specific quotas or targets, according to the court. The bonuses were paid by the end of March for the previous calendar year. If Siemens had paid out the full amount budgeted for bonuses, it would have recorded a decline in profits in 1998 compared to the prior year. Siemens therefore, decided on a 30 percent across-the-board downward adjustment of incentive compensation payments. Each employee received a statement showing the amount of his or her commission for 1998, calculated according to the formula in the incentive compensation plan, and the amount of the 30 percent reduction as it applied to him or her. Siemens claimed it had the right to make the cuts, based on a clause present in all but about five percent of the incentive compensation plans stating: "This plan and the associated targets/quotas may be adjusted, changed, or terminated at any time, to compensate for changes in sales, support, or marketing emphasis."

In *Jensen v. International Business Machines Corporation*, the Fourth Circuit Court of Appeals observed that ordinarily an employer can only modify its offer of a unilateral contract "until the offer's conditions are satisfied." However, the court held that IBM had effectively reserved to itself the right to modify its incentive pay plan "up until actual payment has been made."[36] IBM adopted a 2001 Software Sales Incentive Plan for its software sales force. Mr. Jensen closed a sale to the IRS valued at $24 million, for which he anticipated a sales award under the Incentive Plan of approximately $2.6 million. However, IBM advised him that it would only pay an award of $500,000.

In affirming a district court's grant of summary judgment in favor of IBM, the court primarily relied on the following paragraph from the incentive plan document, which the court said "manifested its clear intent to preclude the formation of a contract:"

> Right to Modify or Cancel: While IBM's intent is to pay employees covered by this program according to its provisions, this program does not constitute a promise by IBM to make any distributions under it. IBM reserves the right to adjust the program terms or to cancel or otherwise modify the program at any time during the program period, or up until actual payment has been made under the program. Modification or cancellation may be applicable to all persons covered by the program, or to any subset as defined by management. Even though you may be given progress reports regarding plan achievement during the year, no one becomes entitled to any payment in advance of his or her receipt of the payment.

The court also cited this paragraph from the explanatory brochure (which contained the formula that Mr. Jensen used to estimate his award):

> Disclaimer: This example is provided for illustration purposes only. Actual sales incentive payments will be different than the numbers displayed here. In cases of conflict between what is shown in this booklet and local documentation, local plan documentation prevails.

---

[36] *Jensen v. International Business Machines Corporation*, (4th Cir. 2006) No. 05-1611.

The court observed that the incentive plan document contained language that would have alerted Mr. Jensen to the "Large Opportunities Clause" limiting the amount of award under certain circumstances.

.02 Increasing Promised Bonuses

In *Delta Star, Inc. v. Patton et al*,[37] a Delaware corporation brought an action against its former president and board chairman for breach of fiduciary duty and corporate waste. The court found that the former president had failed to uphold his fiduciary duty as a director to protect the interests of the corporation and act in the best interests of its stockholders, and to act independently and without self-interest. For this reason, the court held that the "business judgment" rule that normally affords great discretion to directors' business decisions did not apply, and the former president had the burden of establishing the "complete fairness" of the bonus payments under the plan.

In reviewing the bonuses the former president had paid to himself and other senior managers, the court found fault with a number of his actions and with the terms of the bonus plan, as follows: i) the former president did not follow the formula for determining bonus amounts contained in the plan; (ii) the bonuses paid exceeded what would have been due had he followed the plan's formula; (iii) he did not seek advice or review of an independent outside consultant concerning the fairness or legality of the bonuses; and (iv) he did not establish an independent committee of the board or a group of disinterested ratifying stockholders to review the fairness of the bonuses.

The court also found fault with the operation and terms of the bonus plan, itself, in that: (i) the plan did not contain predetermined targets or performance goals to be considered in determining bonus amounts; and (ii) the board or directors had never formally adopted the bonus plan or its procedures. The court found that the former president was liable for committing corporate waste by awarding himself bonuses that bore no reasonable relationship to his services and to his contributions to the financial performance of the corporation, and ordered him to return the excess payments to the corporation.

.03 Other Representative Cases

Companies often do not have legal counsel review their annual incentive plans. Sometimes the plan is one a one-page summary - or even a couple slides from a PowerPoint handout. However, many legal complications can arise from bonus plans. In *Gregg Appliances, Inc. v. Underwood*,[38] a group of the company's senior managers brought a class action after the company calculated their annual incentive bonus payouts by excluding nearly $40 million in life insurance proceeds it received after its executive chairman died, from its 2012 earnings before interest, taxes, depreciation, and amortization (EBITDA). The trial court had granted summary judgment to the employees and the company had appealed.

---

[37] *Delta Star, Inc. v. Patton et al*, 76 FSupp2d 617 (W.D. Pa. 1999).

[38] 57 N.E.3d 831 (IN 2016).

The company had provided eligible employees with a document labeled Total Rewards Statement ("TRS") and a letter from the company's president and CEO, which included a table showing 2011 compensation and a table showing 2012 targets. The trial court viewed the TRS as a contract between the company and the covered employees. The court found that the TRS used the term "EBITDA," and that the meaning of EBITDA was clear. The TRS made no reference to the possibility of adjustments.

The appellate court reversed the trial count and found in favor of the company. The appellate court emphasized the need to look at not just the terms of the contract, but also the intent of the parties and all circumstances surrounding the contract. The appellate court found "It is clear from the language in the TRS that the parties could not have intended life insurance proceeds would be included in EBITDA for purposes of determining a performance-based 'incentive' bonus." The court looked at the TRS transmittal letter, which referred to the company's growth and the importance of improving performance. The court also took into account the testimony of a company representative that the company previously had adjusted EBITDA to reflect accurately how the company was performing on a year-to-year basis, even when those adjustments resulted in higher bonuses.

Although the company won the case, it won only after discovery, depositions, a trial, and an appeal. A little better drafting could have saved the company from all of the legal costs, wasted time, and ill feelings that ensued.

In *Sommer v. Vanguard Group*, the Third Circuit Court of Appeals held that Vanguard Group did not violate the Family and Medical Leave Act when it reduced the annual bonus payment of a financial administrator who missed two months of work while on FMLA leave.[39] The court found that Vanguard's "partnership plan" was an "hours-based annual production requirement." Thus, Vanguard could lawfully reduce the employee's annual award.

In *Guerrero v. J.W. Hutton Inc.*, the U.S. Court of Appeals for the Eighth Circuit held that an employee who was fired one business day before she qualified for a bonus failed to satisfy the timing requirements for the bonus outlined in her employment contract.[40] The company had a bonus program available to full-time employees who were with the company at the end of each fiscal year quarter. The bonus was contingent on working within the company's "standard work ethic" and on remaining employed through the last day of the quarter. The court found that the employment contract governing Ms. Guerrero's bonus was "unambiguous" when it said "[a]n employee must be employed through the last working day of the quarter to be eligible for the bonus."

---

[39] *Sommer v. Vanguard Group*, 461 F.3d 397 (3d Cir., 2006). Amazingly, this case went to trial despite the fact that the company only reduced the employee's bonus by $1,788.23.

[40] *Guerrero v. J.W. Hutton Inc.*, 458 F.3d 830 (8th Cir., 2006).

¶1565 Supplemental Wage Withholding

The American Jobs Creation Act of 2004 first imposed on employers a new mandatory income tax withholding obligation at the highest rate of income tax in effect under the Code (currently 37%) to the extent an employee's total supplemental wages from an employer (and other businesses under common control with the employer) exceed $1,000,000 during the calendar year. The rate for purposes of optional flat rate withholding on other supplemental wages (*i.e.*, the supplemental wages not subject to the mandatory flat tax rate withholding at the highest rate of tax) remain at 25%.

The TCJA reduced individuals' tax rates, repealed the personal exemption, and increased the standard deduction for individuals. These changes required most employers to change their tax withholding procedures for 2018. The IRS published Notice 1036, which updated the income-tax withholding tables for 2018, reflecting changes made by the TCJA.

Before 2018, the law required an employer that made supplemental wage payments (*e.g.*, equity award vesting, annual bonus payments, *etc.*) to an employee in excess of $1 million during a calendar year to withhold on the amount above $1 million (or on the entire payment) at a rate equal to the highest individual income tax bracket in effect for the year. In 2017, this flat rate was 39.6%. The TCJA lowered the top marginal tax rate to 37%, effective January 1, 2018. Most employers had to reduce withholding on these individuals to account for this change.

For supplemental wage payments to an employee for less than $1 million in a calendar year, employers may withhold at the supplemental flat rate, which was set at 25% before 2018. IRS guidance under the TCJA reduced that rate to 22%. The employer can choose to use the supplemental rate or the W-4 method, although the employee often makes a request. Because of the increase to the standard deduction and the change to the tax rates, if an employer chooses to use the W-4 method, it should use the new tax tables provided in Notice 1036.

The regulations define supplemental wages as wages that are not regular wages. The regulations define regular wages as amounts that are paid at a regular rate and not an overtime rate, or at a predetermined fixed amount for a current payroll period. Therefore, commissions, reported tips, bonuses and overtime normally would be supplemental wages (although the regulations permit tips and overtime pay to be treated as regular wages). The final regulations do not allow an employer to treat commissions, third-party sick pay paid by agents of the employer, or taxable fringe benefits as other than supplemental wages.

Bonuses are the most common form of supplemental wage payments for which flat tax withholding is required. However, numerous other compensation items qualify as supplemental wage payments, including:

- back pay;
- commissions;
- wages under reimbursement or expense allowance arrangements;

- nonqualified deferred compensation includable in wages;
- noncash fringe benefits;
- sick pay paid by a third party as an agent of the employer;
- amounts includable in income under Code Sec. 409A;
- income recognized upon exercise of a nonqualified stock option;
- imputed income for health coverage for a nondependent; and
- the lapse of a restriction on restricted property that had been transferred from an employer to an employee.

The final regulations eliminated the requirement from the proposed regulations that a payment could qualify as a supplemental wage only if regular wages had been paid to the employee. Under the final regulations, payments that satisfy the basic definition of supplemental wages will be treated as supplemental wages regardless of whether the employee had received any regular wages in his or her working career with the employer.

¶1575 Litigation Based on State Wage Payment Laws

Companies use incentive and deferred programs, including bonuses, as a powerful mechanism to drive performance and to meet stockholder expectations. Incentive compensation plans often provide employees with better compensation packages than they would otherwise receive, while at the same time giving employers more security in knowing that their employees have a strong incentive to continue their employment. This is a classic example of what we often refer to as "Golden Handcuffs" - attractive financial benefits that a corporate employee will lose by resigning from the company.

State wage and labor statutes provide their own distinct set of protections, opportunities, and challenges. Each statute generally defines protected "wages" and establishes procedures associated with wage payment. These statutes generally come with harsh penalty provisions that subject violators to both civil and criminal liability. They often also provide for additional damages and attorney fees.

.01 ERISA Exclusion

Some companies use ERISA as a defense to these cases. ERISA Sec. 514 completely preempts state laws insofar as they relate to an employee benefit plan. While more cases are being brought under state wage laws, many cases can be exempted from state wage laws if the employer shows that they involve an ERISA employee benefit plan.

Several cases have involved a dispute as to whether a particular plan qualifies as a top-hat plan under ERISA. In order to be an ERISA top-hat plan, the plan must be (1) unfunded and (2) for a select group of management or highly-qualified employees.[41] If a plan meets these requirements, the case may be

---

[41] See *Garratt v. Knowles*, 245 F.3d 941, 946 (7th Cir. 2001).

exclusively within the federal courts' jurisdiction, and the state wage payment law completely preempted by ERISA.[42] Challenges to deferred incentive or compensation plans that ERISA does not cover may be brought under state wage and labor laws.

Deferred or incentive compensation cases brought under state wage laws present particular problems, as the courts must analyze the specific statutory language of each individual statute. Many of these cases are dealt with in arbitration. However, there is an ever-growing body of case-law on the topic. This section will address the basic parameters of wage and labor laws in several states outlined below mainly through case law. The common theme is an attempt to define "wages" in the context of each state's statute.

.02 Courts Look at Many Factors in Determining Whether Payments Fall Under the State Wage Payment Act

Courts have considered many factors in deciding whether incentive payments fall under their wage payment act. Illinois courts have found that notice of the contingent nature of certain incentive payments as a key factor in determining whether such payments fall under the Illinois Wage Payment and Collection Act. In *Tatom v. Ameritech Corp.*, the Seventh Circuit found that an employee could not bring a valid Illinois Wage Payment and Collection Act claim under an employment agreement which "expressly disavow[ed] any notion that a bonus had been promised."[43] In *Tatom*, the provision appeared on the last page of a nine page compensation brochure, was of the same typeface as the rest of the document, and appeared under the heading "Notice." The provision stated that the brochure was a statement of the employer's intentions and did not constitute a guarantee that any particular amount of compensation would be paid. It did not create a contractual relationship or any contractually enforceable rights between [the employer] and the employee. (quoting from the plan). The Seventh Circuit found that this provision doomed the employee's contractual claim under the Illinois Wage Payment and Collection claim because it "did not give rise to a reasonable belief" that the employee would receive a bonus.[44] In *Tatom* the key factor guiding the court's decision was the notice given to the employee that the bonus was contingent and uncertain.

However, Illinois courts have held in some instances that an employee is entitled to a pro rata share of their bonus even where they have left employment before the maturity date of the bonus. In *Camillo v. Wal-Mart Stores, Inc.*, the court found that a management employee's service to employer for 11 months of employer's fiscal year entitled employee to recover, under the Illinois Wage Payment and Collection Act, a pro rata share of a bonus that was based solely on length of service and yearly profits, even though the employer discharged the employee before the date of employment specified in management benefits

---

[42] For more information on qualification as a top-hat plan under ERISA, see Winston Internal Memo "PaineWebber Partner Plus Plan: Application of ERISA."

[43] *Tatom v. Ameritech Corp*, 305 F.3d 737, at 743 (2000).
[44] *Id.* at 744.

program as a condition of the bonus.[45] The determinative factor in this case was the lack of any contingency beyond the mere service of the employee and profits of the company. Unlike *Tatum*, the bonus was not clearly contingent nor was it made clear that the bonus was discretionary and could be withheld by the employer. Another factor likely influencing the *Camillo* decision was the involuntary nature of the employee's termination. If the employee had voluntarily resigned from employment, the court may have ruled differently as it would have seemed less like the employer was acting in bad faith.

In *Michael E. Highhouse, M.D., v. Midwest Orthopedic Institute, P.C.*, the Indiana Supreme Court held that a bonus calculated on the basis of both the employee's production and also the expenses of the overall business was not a "wage" governed by the Indiana Wage Payment Statute.[46] The Indiana Wage Payment Statute defines "wage" as all amounts at which the labor or service rendered is recompensed, whether the amount is fixed or ascertained on a time, task, piece, or commission basis, or in any other method of calculating such amount.[47] Under the Indiana Wage Payment Statute, a "bonus" is a wage if it is compensation for time worked and is not linked to a contingency such as the financial success of the company. A bonus whose calculation depends on expenses of the overall operations is not a "wage" under this interpretation, as its value rests on a factor beyond the control of the employee. If an employer links a bonus to anything beyond the performance of the employee, such as overall operations, the courts are unlikely to classify it as a "wage" for purposes of the Indiana Wage Payment Statute. In Indiana, using criteria outside of the employee's own labor or production for determining bonuses will generally remove said bonuses or incentive compensation from under the restrictions of the state wage laws.

The Maryland Wage Payment and Collection Act (MWPCA)[48] requires employers, upon the termination of an employee's employment, to pay that employee all wages due for work that the employee performed before the date of termination of employment. The MWPCA defines "wage" as all compensation that is due to an employee for employment and includes any bonus, commission, fringe benefit, or any other remuneration promised for service.[49] If termination payments are dependent upon conditions other than the employee's efforts, the MWPCA is inapplicable. For example, in *Stevenson v. Branch Banking and Trust Corporation*, the court held that the MWPCA was inapplicable because the employee's termination compensation was payment for her agreement not to compete, rather than for work performed.[50] Where the agreement does not condition the employee's entitlement to the bonus or compensation on conditions beyond work performed, the MWPCA will apply.[51]

---

[45] *Camillo v. Wal-Mart Stores, Inc.*, 221 Ill.App.3d 614, 582 N.E.2d 729 (1991).

[46] See *Michael E. Highhouse, M.D., v. Midwest Orthopedic Institute, P.C.*, 807 N.E.2d 737 (2004).

[47] Ind. Code § 22-2-0-1.

[48] Md. Code Ann., Lab. & Empl. § 3-501 et seq. (2005).

[49] Md. Code Ann., Lab. & Empl. § 3-501(c).

[50] *Stevenson v. Branch Banking and Trust Corporation*, 150 Md. App. 620, 646 (2004).

[51] See *Provident Bank of Maryland T/A Provident Bank v. David J. McCarthy*, 383 F.Supp.2d 858, 860, (2005).

In Maryland, a promise for compensation without specific conditions beyond mere performance by the employee can result in the implication of the MWPCA. To avoid such a result, the employer must use specific language conditioning bonuses or incentive payments on something beyond more performance during the employment period.

The language of "promise" is also very important in determining whether or not stock options or bonuses will be considered wages for purposes of the MWPCA. Once a bonus, commission, or fringe benefit has been *promised* as part of compensation for service, the employee is entitled to enforce the payment as wages.[52] The Maryland Court of Appeals in *Whiting-Turner Contracting Company v. Fitzpatrick*, found that "§ 3-501(c)(2)(iv) serves two functions: it makes clear both that the listed forms of remuneration are simply examples, by the use of the phrase 'any other remuneration,' and that the 'other remuneration' that may be included in—in order to be considered—wages must have been 'promised for service.'"[53] The court went on to explain, "reading the statute as including a bonus as wages only when it has been promised as part of the compensation for employment is logical and makes good common sense."[54]

State wage statutes are often poorly-drafted and present various problems for employers and employees attempting to explore the legal ramifications of their status. There is no "one-size-fits-all" approach to state wage and labor laws. It is necessary to look at each state statute in which an employer operates to ensure they are not in violation. Key language for employers to utilize is conditional language that makes it clear that any deferred bonuses, stock options or other incentive compensation is contingent upon conditions beyond the mere employment of the employee. The incentive compensation could be contingent on either the satisfaction of requirements beyond the termination of the employment (such as with a non-compete agreement) or at the discretion of the employer. Employers should avoid language of entitlement or promise as much as possible. To reduce the risk of possibly triggering state wage laws, the employer's plan should make it very clear that there are conditions that need to be met, which are beyond the sole control of the employee. The plan should make the employee aware of any and all conditions that he or she needs to meet before the incentive compensation becomes payable. The plan or employment agreements should emphasize the contingent nature of any bonus, stock options, or other incentive compensation between employer and employee. One means of doing this is to state clearly what is and is not included in the definition of wages in the employment agreement.

¶ 1585 Incentive Plans Can Become Subject to ERISA

Most companies want to ensure that their cash and stock incentive plans do not become subject to the vesting and other requirements of ERISA. Many incentive or bonus plans make payments or deliver stock within 2 1/2 months after the end of the year the participant became vested, in order comply with the

---

[52] See *Whiting-Turner Contracting Company v. Fitzpatrick*, 366 Md. 295, 304-05 (2001).

[53] *Whiting-Turner*, 366 Md. 295, 672.
[54] *Id.* at 672.

short-term deferral exception of Code Sec. 409A. However, some incentive plans provide for accumulations, multi-year periods, and mandatory deferrals.

In *Miller v. Olsen*,[55] the company had established an incentive plan known as the Equity Growth Plan ("EGP"). Under the EGP, future payouts were not based on the value of the company's equity, but on the appreciation in the value of a single property owned and managed by the company. The former employee alleged that he believed that the EGP was a retirement plan, based on statements allegedly made to him by the company's owner. The court found that, despite not being a true equity incentive plan, the EGP did not rise to the level of an ERISA pension plan because (1) its primary purpose was not to provide deferred compensation, (2) its express terms did not contemplate an ongoing administrative scheme, and (3) its express terms did not contemplate a method of funding. Therefore, the court did not need to consider ERISA's exemption for bonus plans. Many other companies have not been so lucky.

Federal court decisions have produced different results based on the facts of the particular case. The case of *Tolbert v. RBC Capital Markets Corporation* has gone up and down between the federal district courts and the Fifth Circuit since 2013, and was only partially decided in 2016. In *Tolbert*, the company maintained a form of plan common among financial certain institutions seeking to retain employees. Under the company's Wealth Accumulation Plan ("WAP"), participants were required to defer a portion of their compensation and the company made matching contributions to the WAP. Participants' accounts were to be distributed when the participant became vested, but participants had the option to defer distribution until a later in-service distribution date or termination of employment. Three plaintiffs who forfeited their WAP benefits upon termination of employment sued to recover those benefits by claiming that the WAP was a pension plan subject to ERISA's vesting requirements.

In *Tolbert*, the company argued that the plan was not subject to ERISA because it was not a pension benefit plan. The Fifth Circuit disagreed, because the WAP permitted participants to defer distributions to termination of employment or beyond, and remanded the case back to the district court to determine if the WAP qualified for the "top hat" plan or another exception from ERISA. In 2016, the district court issued a decision denying summary judgment in favor of either party, possibly sending the case to trial.

In *Bingham v. FIML Natural Resources LLC*,[56] a federal district court found that if even a portion of the total benefits payable under a "bonus" plan is "systematically deferred" until termination of covered employment, the entire previous plan could be governed by ERISA. Under the incentive compensation plan offered in Bingham, participants were awarded points representing ownership interests in two separate pools of assets. Critically for the outcome of the case, payments for certain award points were withheld until the participant separated from the company (except in the event of a change in control). Because of this,

---

[55] 62 EBC 1845 (D. Or. 2016).   [56] 56 EBC 2232 (D. Colo. June 18, 2013).

the court found the deferrals met the threshold for being systematic, deeming the plan subject to all of the provisions of ERISA.

ERISA contains a separate exception for "bonus" plans:

2510.3-2(c) *Bonus program.* For purposes of title I of the Act and this chapter, the terms "employee pension benefit plan" and "pension plan" shall not include payments made by an employer to some or all of its employees as bonuses for work performed, *unless such payments are systematically deferred to the termination of covered employment or beyond,* or so as to provide retirement income to employees. [emphasis added]

Regulations under ERISA provide that an incentive plan generally will be considered a "bonus program" under regulations and exempt from ERISA if it does not expressly condition payment upon termination of employment or retirement, and it does not in fact result in the systematic distribution of bonus payments upon termination or retirement. Whether an arrangement gives rise to the "systematic" deferral of payment to termination or beyond depends on the facts and circumstances of the arrangement. Some of the relevant circumstances for the determination are:

- Whether arrangement's design results in a high percentage of bonus payouts being made at or near recipients' retirement age;
- Whether the employer communicates the plan to employees as an arrangement intended to provide retirement or deferred income;
- Whether the arrangement allows for payments of unvested amounts upon employment termination;
- The length of the payout period; and
- Whether the bonus payments, by operation of the plan, are made to another type of retirement account such as an IRA.

Chapter 16

QUALIFIED RETIREMENT PLANS

¶1601 Introduction—Qualified Retirement Plans

The qualified retirement plan may not be the most exciting or exotic form of executive compensation, but no employer or pay package should be without one. The reason is simple: qualified retirement plans are the last, best tax-favored form of compensation available. In addition to tax benefits, the assets and benefits accrued and held under a qualified retirement plan are virtually completely protected from both the creditors of the employee/participants and creditors of the employer/plan sponsor (see ¶1665 for more detail on anti-alienation protections of qualified retirement plans). The only downside of a qualified retirement plan is that the Internal Revenue Code limits the amount of benefit that employers can provide.

.01 Qualification Requirements

In order to be "qualified" for favorable tax treatment, a pension, profit sharing, ESOP, 401(k) or other retirement plan must meet the requirements of the Code. These requirements are discussed in ¶1615.

.02 Favorable Tax Treatment

Unlike nearly all other forms of executive compensation, an employer can receive a tax deduction for its contributions toward qualified retirement plan benefits before the employee recognizes income on such benefits. An employer's contributions to its qualified retirement plan are immediately deductible when paid over to the plan's trust. The employee on whose behalf the employer made such contributions will not be taxed on the contributions, even if the employee is fully vested in his or her plan benefit, until the plan benefit is actually paid to the employee (usually after retirement or other employment termination). Neither the employer nor the employee will be taxed currently on the investment earnings of the plan and trust (see ¶1625 for more detail on tax-favored treatment of qualified retirement plans).

.03 Source of Law and Regulations

The law governing employee retirement plans is principally contained in two sources: the Internal Revenue Code of 1986, as amended, (the "Code")[1] and the Employee Retirement Income Security Act of 1974, as amended, ("ERISA").[2] The provisions of the Code and ERISA are overlapping in many respects. The Internal Revenue Service ("IRS") is responsible for interpreting, administering, and enforcing the Code. The U.S. Department of Labor ("DOL") is primarily

---

[1] 26 U.S.C. §§ 1-9206.

[2] P.L. 93-406, 29 U.S.C. § 1001, et seq.

responsible for interpreting, administering, and enforcing ERISA, with the Pension Benefit Guaranty Corporation ("PBGC") retaining responsibility for some provisions.

ERISA contains rules that: (1) impose fiduciary duties on plan administrators and trustees; (2) require reporting of plan information to the DOL; (3) require disclosures to plan participants; and (4) create remedies for violations of the foregoing. ERISA applies to all "employee benefit plans," as defined broadly in ERISA Section 3(3). The principal exception to this rule is governmental benefit plans, which are regulated primarily by state law, rather than ERISA.

Other laws that may affect employee benefit plans include the Age Discrimination in Employment Act ("ADEA"), the Uniformed Service Employment and Reemployment Rights Act ("USERRA"), the Family and Medical Leave Act ("FMLA"), the Americans with Disabilities Act ("ADA"), and the federal securities laws. ERISA expressly *preempts* any state law insofar as it relates to pension or welfare benefit plans. However, certain state laws governing insurance, banking and securities may be applied to pension or welfare benefit plans to the extent such plans enter into one of those areas (*i.e.*, if a pension plan were to purchase a life insurance contract as a means of funding benefits).

.04 Pension Benefit Plans

Employee benefit plans can generally be divided into the following three groups, both practically and under applicable law:

- employee *pension* benefit plans;
- employee *welfare* benefit plans;[3] and
- compensation and payroll practices (not governed by ERISA).

"Employee pension benefit plans," as defined in Section 3(2) of ERISA, generally includes all plans qualified under Section 401(a) of the Code, but also includes other plans that provide retirement or tax deferral benefits that do not qualify for special tax treatment under Code Sec. 401, such as nonqualified plans (see Chapter 17). Qualified plans, in turn, generally can be divided into two categories: defined benefit plans and defined contribution plans.

.05 Defined Benefit Plans

Defined benefit plans guarantee a specific or determinable benefit to participants at a normal retirement age and require the sponsoring employer to contribute over a period of years whatever amounts are necessary to fund those benefits. For example, under a defined benefit pension plan that provided a monthly benefit payable at age 65 equal to $30 multiplied by the participant's number of years of service, a participant who had worked for 20 years at retirement would be entitled to a benefit equal to $600 per month for life. Under defined benefit plans, the responsibility of funding and risk of investment loss is

---

[3] See Chapter 19 (¶1901 et seq.) for a detailed discussion of welfare benefit plans.

solely on the employer (see ¶1635 for more detail on defined benefit pension plans).

.06 Defined Contribution or Individual Account Plans

Defined contribution plans only promise to distribute at retirement (or other termination of employment) the dollar amount that accumulates in a participant's account over the years. Defined contribution plans leave the risk of investment loss squarely on the participant, although many such plans permit participants to elect how their accounts are invested. Forms of defined contribution plans include money purchase plans, target benefit plans, profit sharing plans, cash or deferred 401(k) plans, and stock bonus plans or ESOPs (see ¶1645 for more detail on defined contribution plans).

A 401(k) plan allows a participant to elect pre-tax compensation reduction contributions. The amount a participant elects to contribute to a 401(k) plan will not be deemed taxable compensation to him or her for income tax purposes.

> **Example::** Executive D's employer, ABC Corporation, maintains a 401(k) plan. Executive D's base salary for 2019 is $200,000. In December 2018, D elects to make a 401(k) salary reduction contribution of 5% of her salary for the year. ABC will pay the $10,000 directly to D's account in the 401(k) plan, and D's IRS Form W-2 for the 2019 year will show taxable earnings of $190,000.

.07 Limitations on Qualified Plans

The Code contains several provisions affecting employee benefit plans, including the following:

- Requirements that retirement plans must follow in order to preserve their tax-qualified status;[4]
- Provisions permitting employees to make pre-tax contributions to a retirement plan;[5]
- Provisions permitting employer and employee contributions to accumulate tax-free in a tax-exempt trust;[6]
- Nondiscrimination requirements relating to eligibility, participation, contributions and benefits under plans;[7] and
- Provisions relating to vesting, distribution, and forms of benefit.[8]

Benefits under a qualified plan may not discriminate in favor of officers, stockholders or highly compensated employees. Generally, qualified plans allocate benefits to employee-participants as a flat percentage of their pay, to a maximum of $275,000 for 2018.[9] Qualified plans must adhere to minimum standards for employee participation, eligibility, vesting, limits on annual contri-

---

[4] Code Sec. 401(a).
[5] Code Sec. 401(k).
[6] Code Sec. 501(a).
[7] Code Sec. 401(a)(4), Code Sec. 401(k)(3), Code Sec. 401(m) and Code Sec. 410(b).

[8] Code Sec. 401(a)(9), Code Sec. 411 and Code Sec. 417.
[9] The limit is subject to indexing annually for cost-of-living adjustments.

butions, rules on plan asset investments, participant allocations, voting rights, benefits distribution, treatment of stock dividends and payment of plan administrative expenses (see ¶ 1655 for more detail on the limitations on qualified plans).

.08 ERISA's Anti-Alienation Provisions Protect Retirement Plan Benefits in Bankruptcy and Nearly All Other Circumstances

ERISA and the Code provide that neither the participant nor the employer can assign or alienate pension benefits, except under very limited circumstances. This means that a participant could not pledge his or her plan benefits as security for a loan (except a loan from the plan) or otherwise be forced to turn over his or her benefits to creditors (including the employer), even in bankruptcy (see ¶ 1665).

.09 Bankruptcy of the Plan Sponsor

Under virtually all circumstances, ERISA and the Code completely protect the assets of a qualified retirement plan from the reach of bankruptcy and other creditors of the plan sponsor. Clearly, the assets of the plan are separate from the assets of the employer (see ¶ 1675).

.10 State Taxation of Qualified Retirement Plan Benefits

In response to efforts by certain states to tax the retirement income of any individual who had ever resided in the state, Congress passed Section 114 of Title 4 of the United States Code, which prohibits states from imposing an income tax on certain types of retirement income for nonresidents (see ¶ 1695).

¶ 1615 Qualification Requirements

In order to be "qualified" for the favorable tax treatment discussed in ¶ 1601, a pension or profit sharing plan must meet the requirements of the Code. The most significant of the qualification requirements are those of:

- Nondiscrimination in the eligibility and coverage of employees;
- Nondiscrimination in contributions and benefit accruals;
- Minimum vesting; and
- Minimum distribution requirements.

.01 Nondiscrimination

Code Sec. 410 prohibits a pension benefit from discriminating in favor of highly compensated employees in terms of (1) eligibility to participate in the plan, and (2) benefits earned or contributed under the plan. Code Sec. 401(a)(4) prohibits a pension benefit from discriminating in favor of highly compensated employees as to the benefits, rights and features under the plan.

Because of the strict nondiscrimination rules applicable to qualified retirement plans, disputes that are specific to an executive seldom arise. However, in *Brockett v. Utica Boilers Inc.*,[10] the court found that a company had incorrectly

---

[10] *Brockett v. Utica Boilers Inc.*, 328 FSupp2d 324 (N.D.N.Y. 2004).

categorized an executive as a regular employee when it should have characterized him as a senior management employee. Thus, the executive was entitled to the increased profit-sharing plan contributions he would have received had he been properly categorized. The Utica Boilers plan provided that the company would make contributions at three different rates, depending on a plan participant's classification. The first category was entitled "executive management employees" and participants in this category would receive yearly employer contributions of $30,000. The second category, known as "senior management employees," would receive yearly contributions in the amount of 15 percent of their annual compensation. All other regular employees were lumped in the third category and were to receive contributions in the amount of seven percent of their annual compensation.

.02 Vesting

ERISA Section 203 and Code Sec. 411 require that pension benefit plan participants become "vested" in their benefits under certain minimum schedules. A participant's vested percentage means the percentage of his or her benefit that would be nonforfeitable in the event the participant's employment terminated. Defined contribution pension plan benefits must vest no less quickly than under one of the following schedules:

Years of Service	Vested Percentage
Less than 3 years	0%
3 or more years	100%

Years of Service	Vested Percentage
Less than 2 years	0%
2 years	20%
3 years	40%
4 years	60%
5 years	80%
6 or more years	100%

Defined benefit pension plan benefits must vest no less quickly than under one of the following schedules:

Years of Service	Vested Percentage
Less than 5 years	0%
5 or more years	100%

Years of Service	Vested Percentage
Less than 3 years	0%
3 years	20%
4 years	40%
5 years	60%
6 years	80%
7 or more years	100%

Finally, a pension plan must fully vest participants in their own contributions, including 401(k) contributions, if any, at all times.[11]

.03 Plan Distributions

Many pension plans provide for distribution of benefits within a short time after a participant terminates employment. However, ERISA and the Code generally do not require plan distributions until the 60th day after the close of the plan year in which the participant attains age 65 years or the normal retirement age specified under the plan.[12] Additionally, the Code prohibits a plan from distributing a former employee's benefits to him or her without the former employee's written consent, before the plan's retirement age if the present value of the former employee's account or benefit exceeds $5,000.

ERISA, the Code and the plan's terms will determine the form of distribution from the plan. ERISA and the Code require that the normal form of payment under a defined benefit pension plan is a life annuity (or joint and survivor annuity for a married participant) commencing at normal retirement age. Under some defined benefit pension plans, this is the only form of payment permitted, although some defined benefit pension plans permit participants to elect a lump sum distribution. Defined benefit pension plans cannot permit distributions to a participant while he or she remains employed by the employer sponsoring the plan, unless the participant has attained normal retirement age. Most defined contribution plans provide for distributions of a participant's account in a lump sum cash amount. A pension plan must permit a participant to roll over a qualifying lump sum distribution directly to another qualified pension plan or individual retirement account.

In general, distributions made before age $59\frac{1}{2}$ are subject to a 10% excise penalty for premature distributions in addition to the ordinary income tax due. Participants may elect to "roll over" all, or part, of their benefits, thereby deferring taxation on the distribution and avoiding the 10% excise penalty. The participant may defer income tax at the time of distribution if the employer stock and/or cash received are transferred within 60 days of receipt to an individual retirement account ("IRA"), or to another qualified employee trust.

In the case of a lump sum distribution, a beneficiary will be taxed on the employer stock distributed to him based upon the original cost of the stock to the plan (or its market value at the time of distribution, if lower). The amount of the distribution subject to federal income tax will not include any unrealized appreciation of the employer's stock while held by the plan.

.04 Deductibility Issues

Code Sec. 404 governs the deductibility of retirement plan contributions. Generally, where the plan year and tax year of the employer coincide, employer contributions to a defined benefit or defined contribution plan that are made by the time for filing the employer's tax return, including extensions, are deductible for that tax year. The Code may require an employer to make quarterly contribu-

---

[11] Code Sec. 411(a)(1).   [12] Code Sec. 401(a)(14).

tions to its defined benefit pension plans. Deductible contributions to a defined contribution plan cannot exceed 25% of the total compensation of plan participants. The deductible contribution limit as to a defined benefit pension plan is not so simply stated as it is based on amortizing the actuarially determined cost of the plan over a period of between 10 and 30 years.

.05 Plan Termination

Upon the termination or partial termination of a qualified pension benefit plan, the accrued benefits or account balances of all plan participants must become fully vested and nonforfeitable.[13] A partial termination of a pension plan could result if a significant percentage (*e.g.*, 40%) of the plan participants are terminated from employment in a single plan year.

An employer could freeze benefit accruals under a pension plan without terminating the plan. However, in order to freeze benefit accruals or terminate a defined benefit or money purchase pension plan, affected participants must be notified at least 45 days prior to the cessation of benefits accruals.[14]

The PBGC insures defined benefit pension plans. This means that if the employer becomes insolvent before contributing sufficient amounts to fund accrued benefits under the plan, the PBGC will step in and pay participants' pension benefits up to certain levels. The plan sponsor pays premiums to the PBGC based on a flat rate of $74 per participant or a variable rate of $38 per $1,000 of unfunded vested benefits (for 2018) per year for this coverage.

.06 Fiduciary Provisions

ERISA Section 3(21) would deem persons with discretionary authority with respect to a benefit plan or control over plan assets to be fiduciaries. ERISA Section 404 requires that a benefit plan fiduciary discharge its duties to the plan:

- Solely in the interest of participants;
- With the care, skill, prudence and diligence of a prudent person, expert in such matters;
- By diversifying investments so as to avoid the risk of large losses; and
- In accordance with the terms of the plan documents.

ERISA imposes personal liability on fiduciaries.

.07 Reporting and Disclosure Requirements

ERISA requires that the sponsor or administrator of any pension and/or welfare benefit plan report certain information to the IRS and DOL, and disclose certain information to all plan participants. The plan administrator under such a plan must file, at a minimum, annual reports (on IRS Form 5500) with the IRS and DOL.

Participants in employee pension or welfare benefit plans must receive "disclosure documents" from the plan administrator, and participants (including

---

[13] Code Sec. 411(d)(3).   [14] ERISA Sec. 204(h).

certain former participants and beneficiaries) may request additional documents from the plan administrator. Foremost among the disclosure documents is the summary plan description ("SPD") prepared with respect to the plan.[15] The SPD is required to be written in a language that the average participant should understand (including a foreign language in certain cases). The plan administrator must furnish an SPD to the plan participant within 120 days after a plan becomes effective or the participant becomes eligible. The plan administrator must furnish an updated SPD or a "summary of material modifications" (SMM) to participants following substantive changes in the plan.

The plan administrator also must distribute a "summary annual report" to participants after each plan year, which includes the value of plan assets and liabilities.[16] Plan participants are entitled to receive a statement of their accrued plan benefits or account balances upon request, but not more often than once every 12 months.

Finally, a plan participant or beneficiary may request copies of the plan and trust documents (including any funding arrangements thereunder) that comprise the pension or welfare benefit plan. The plan administrator may impose a reasonable charge on the participant or beneficiary requesting these documents for reproduction and mailing, but not in excess of $.25 per page.

Potentially severe penalties apply to the employer if it fails to satisfy the reporting and disclosure requirements. The DOL imposes a penalty of $2,140 per day (in 2018) (with no maximum) for the failure to timely file annual report Form 5500.

.08 Claims Procedures

Every employee pension or welfare benefit plan must contain a claims procedure[17] that the plan administrator discloses to participants and follows. When a plan administrator denies a claim for benefits under the plan, the plan administrator must notify the claimant of the reasons for the denial and explain the appeals procedure. A federal court generally will prohibit, in accordance with ERISA, a plan participant from filing a lawsuit alleging ERISA violations until the participant has exhausted his or her administrative remedies under the plan's claims procedures, except where the participant can demonstrate that following the claim's procedures would be fruitless.

The DOL has promulgated extensive regulations on benefit plan claims procedures. Among other things, these regulations greatly increase the claimants' rights to information, increase the potential liability of plan fiduciaries, and dramatically reduce the time periods within which plan administrators must respond to claims for benefits under group health plans. For example, the plan administrator of a group health benefit plan must advise a claimant of its determination as to an "urgent" care claim for benefits as soon as practicable, but in no event later than 72 hours from the filing of the claim.

---

[15] ERISA Sec. 104.
[16] ERISA Sec. 104.
[17] ERISA Sec. 503.

.09 Remedies

A plan participant or beneficiary who has exhausted his or her remedies under the plan's claims and appeals procedures may utilize the civil enforcement provisions under ERISA. Section 502 of ERISA provides that a participant or beneficiary may bring a civil action to enforce the participant's rights under the terms of the plan, to recover benefits due the participant under the plan or to enjoin an action that violates the terms of the plan and applicable law. Participants may bring civil actions to enforce rights or recover benefits in either state or federal court. However, if a participant brings an action in state court, the defendant may remove the action to federal court. Other civil actions must be brought in the federal district courts.

ERISA Section 510 prohibits an employer from taking any actions that are intended to result in the loss of pension or welfare benefits. ERISA Section 510 does not, of course, prohibit an employer from terminating an employee at any time. However, it would prohibit an employer from terminating an employee solely to prevent him or her from becoming entitled to vested pension benefits, or filing claims under a group health plan.

As noted earlier, ERISA expressly preempts any state law insofar as it relates to pension or welfare benefit plans. Therefore, state law claims and remedies generally will not be available to participants making claims in connection with employee benefits.

¶1625 Favorable Tax Treatment and Other Benefits of Qualified Plans

Despite the limitations on benefits that an executive can earn or accrue under a qualified retirement plan, the favorable tax treatment the Code provides for such plans makes them an essential part of every executive compensation program. Unlike nearly all other forms of executive compensation described in this book, an employer can receive a tax deduction for its contributions toward qualified retirement plan benefits before the employee recognizes income on such benefits. The employer's contributions to its qualified retirement plan are immediately deductible when paid over to the plan's trust (and may be deductible for the previous year), and the employee on whose behalf the employer made such contributions will not be taxed on the contributions until the plan actually pays such benefit to the employee. The Code provides the following specific tax preferences to qualified retirement plans:

1. Code Sec. 404 provides that employer contributions to the qualified plan are fully and immediately deductible (subject to certain limits).[18]

Example 1: ABC Corporation established and maintains a qualified retirement plan and trust known as the ABC Corporation Savings and Profit Sharing Plan (the "Plan") for the benefit of its employees. On December 31, 2018, the last day of ABC's fiscal year, ABC contributes $5 million to the

---

[18] Code Sec. 404(a) generally allows an employer to contribute and deduct an amount of up to 25% of the total compensation of all employees participating in the plan.

Plan, which equals approximately 5 percent of the compensation of all employees participating in the Plan. ABC Corporation can deduct the $5 million contribution for the 2018 fiscal year.

ABC Corporation's plan allows eligible employees to make periodic, pre-tax (401(k)) salary reduction contributions to the Plan. In accordance with federal law, ABC withheld salary reduction contributions each pay period and forwarded them to the Plan's trust immediately. The total amount of employees' pre-tax contributions for 2018 was $6 million, which was equal to approximately 6 percent of the compensation of all employees participating in the Plan. ABC Corporation can deduct the $6 million contribution for the 2018 fiscal year.

In August 2019, just before filing its federal tax return, on extension, ABC contributes an additional $7 million to the retirement plan, to be allocated to the plan accounts of all participants employed by ABC on the last day of the 2018 fiscal year. ABC Corporation can deduct the additional $7 million contribution for the 2018 fiscal year.

2. Code Sec. 401(k) allows employees to make pre-tax salary reduction contributions to a qualified retirement plan

> **Example 2:** Executive D is an employee of ABC Corporation and eligible to participate in the Plan. Executive D's base salary for 2018 is $200,000. In December 2017, D (who is 55 years old) elects to make a 401(k) salary reduction contribution of 10 percent of her salary for the year. ABC will pay the $20,000 (an $18,500 regular contribution plus a $1,500 catch-up contribution) directly to D's account in the 401(k) Plan, and D's IRS Form W-2 for the 2018 year will show taxable earnings of $180,000.

3. A 401(k) plan may permit employees who make elective contributions to the plan to designate some or all of those contributions as "designated Roth contributions."[19] (Unlike Roth IRAs, there is no income limit on participants who can make designated Roth contributions to a 401(k) plan.) Designated Roth contributions are withheld from an employee's pay on an after-tax basis, as opposed to a before-tax basis like 401(k) contributions. However, many believe that Roth contributions are better for highly compensated employees. This is because, unlike 401(k) contributions, Roth contributions and the investment earnings thereon, are distributed to the employee tax-free following his or her employment termination. Additionally, a Roth 401(k) account may be rolled over to a Roth IRA, where the required minimum distribution rules would not apply.

A 401(k) plan with a Roth contribution feature can allow most plan participants to make an "In-Plan Roth Rollover" of all of a portion of their pre-tax accounts. By an In-Plan Roth Rollover, an individual participating in an employer-sponsored 401(k), profit sharing or stock bonus plan (including a former employee), regardless of compensation level, could convert all or a portion of his or her pre-tax 401(k) deferrals, employer matching contributions, employer profit sharing contribution and the earning on all such contribution to an after-tax account under the plan. (It is called a "Rollover" but the funds never leave the plan.)

4. Employees are not taxed on employer contributions made or benefits accrued on their behalf, even when the employee fully vests in those amounts.[20]

---

[19] Code Sec. 402A.   [20] Code Sec. 402 and Code Sec. 411.

Example 3: In Examples 1 and 2 above, ABC Corporation's contributions to its qualified retirement plan for 2018 resulted in an allocation to Executive D's account of $20,000, and D contributed $20,000 to the plan on a pre-tax salary reduction basis. The $40,000 added to D's account for 2018 will not be taxable to D until the plan distributes to her that amount, and any investment earnings.

5. Employer and employee contributions grow tax-free in a tax-exempt trust Code Sec. 501(c).

Example 4: Neither ABC Corporation nor its employees make any further contributions to the Plan after 2018. However, ABC continues the Plan, and the $18 million ABC contributed for 2018 grows to $28 million by 2022. Executive D's $40,000 account grows to $65,000 during that period. The Plan's investment earnings from 2018 through 2022 are not taxable to ABC or Executive D. (However, when the Plan eventually distributes D's account to her, the investment earnings on her account will be taxable as ordinary income.)

6. Favorable tax treatment is available to an employee at time of distribution, such as the ability to roll over his or her qualified plan distribution to an IRA or another qualified plan.[21]

Example 5: Executive D retires from ABC Corporation in 2018, and elects to receive a lump sum cash distribution of her $65,000 account balance in 2019. If Executive D keeps the money or uses it for a trip around the world, the full $65,000 will be taxable to her as ordinary income in 2019. (If D is younger than 59-1/2 when she receives the distributions, it could be subject to an additional 10 percent early distribution excise tax.) However, if D elects to roll over the full $65,000 directly to an individual retirement account (IRA), no amount will be taxable to her until she begins taking distributions from the IRA.

7. Company stock distributed to a participant as part of his or her qualified plan account balance may be subject to favorable taxation as net unrealized appreciation (NUA).[22] Most public companies in America offer company stock as an investment fund option under their profit sharing or 401(k) plan, and ESOPs are 100 percent invested in company stock. Most participants elect to indefinitely postpone taxation of their accumulated retirement benefits by rolling over their full account balance to an IRA when they retire or otherwise leave employment. Rollover is often the best distribution choice for tax reasons. However, the downside of a rollover is that those retirement/rollover accounts will eventually be withdrawn and taxed as ordinary income.

Executives with significant accumulations of long-held company stock in their retirement accounts need to evaluate the tax benefit of electing NUA on that stock. To receive NUA treatment, the executive elects an in-kind lump sum distribution of his or her company stock (generally depositing it in a brokerage account). The executive's basis in the stock is immediately taxable as ordinary income. (The executive's basis in the company stock is the market price on the date it was added to his account.) In exchange for this immediately ordinary income tax hit, the executive will not pay tax again until he or

---

[21] Code Sec. 402. [22] Code Sec. 402(e)(4)

she eventually sells the stock, at which time the full appreciation on the stock above the basis would be taxable at lower long-term capital gains rates.[23]

8. Qualified plan benefits are not subject to claims of the participant's creditors (see ¶1665).

9. Qualified plan benefits are not subject to claims of the company's creditors (see ¶1675).

10. In calculating whether an executive received excess parachute payments under Code Sec. 280G, payments to or from a tax-qualified plan, including a retirement plan described in Code Sec. 401(a), an annuity plan described in Code Sec. 403(a), a simplified employee pension plan described in Code Sec. 408(k) or a simple retirement account described in Code Sec. 408(p) are not counted.[24]

11. An executive's qualified plan benefits are not subject to Code Sec. 162(m)'s limit on deductible compensation.

12. Section 16b-3 under Section 16 of the Securities Exchange Act of 1934 (the "Exchange Act") gives favorable treatment to company stock held in a 401(k) or other qualified plan. Intraplan transfers are generally exempt from 16b-3 short swing profits. All non-discretionary transactions also are exempt. For purposes of determining whether a discretionary transaction (such as an investment switch into or out of the company stock fund) is exempt, the law only looks to other discretionary transaction elections within six months. The existence of open market purchases or sales is irrelevant for this purpose (see ¶1685).

13. Company stock held in a qualified plan account can be counted toward an executive's satisfaction of stock ownership guidelines applicable to the officers and directors of a public company (if the guidelines so provide).

14. The Pension Benefit Guaranty Corporation provides insurance protection for accrued benefits under a defined benefit pension plan.

15. Code Sec. 1042 provides that individuals/business owners who sell their shares to an ESOP covering all or nearly all employees of the business will not recognize gain on the sale of shares to the ESOP if: (1) the stock has been held by the shareholder for at least 3 years; (2) immediately after the sale, the ESOP owns at least 30% of the total value of all shares of the corporation's stock; and (3) the selling shareholder purchases "qualified replacement securities." As with all qualified plans, the corporation then makes fully deductible annual contributions to the ESOP, a portion of the shares are allocated among all participants each year, based on their annual compensation, and the participants are not taxed on the allocations to their accounts until they ultimately take a distribution.

16. Section 404(k) provides a deduction for a C corporation's dividends paid on or reinvested in employer securities held in an ESOP, as long as the plan gives participants the choice between having the dividends reinvested or receiving them in cash. (Dividends generally are not deductible.) The plan may include a default provision providing for the reinvestment of the dividends if the participant does not make an affirmative election.

17. A qualified plan better positions a company's employees to retire - as Social Security alone is not enough. Many companies like to incentivize their employees to retire after a certain age. If a company has a qualified plan, the chances are that it will have fewer employees who are unable to retire only because they don't have enough funds. Companies with defined benefit pension plans also have the ability to use early retirement provisions and incentives opportunistically to incentivize retirement.

---

[23] For an excellent overview of NUA and the situations best suited for it, see http://www.financial-planning.com/pubs/fp/20050401038.html.

[24] Code Sec. 280G(b)(4)(B); Proposed Reg. §1.280G-1, Q&A-8.

18. Employers and employees avoid Social Security and Medicare tax on benefits accrued under qualified plans (other than 401(k) deferrals), and distributions are not subject to Social Security or Medicare tax.

¶1635 Defined Benefit Pension Plans

A defined benefit pension plan is a form of qualified retirement plan. Defined benefit plans dominated the retirement plan landscape for decades until the 1980s when the trend among employer/plan sponsors shifted sharply toward providing retirement benefits through defined contribution or individual account plans. However, many older and larger companies continue to maintain defined benefit pension plans, and nearly all union members' retirement benefits are provided through defined benefit pension plans.

.01 Defined Benefit Plan Characteristics

There are a number of characteristics of a defined benefit plan that distinguish it from a defined contribution plan.

A defined benefit plan provides a fixed amount of annual or monthly benefit to each eligible employee at the employee's retirement, based (generally) on the employee's years of service with the employer and, either (1) the employee's final average earnings or (2) a specified dollar amount.

> **Example 1:** ABC Corporation established and maintains a qualified defined benefit plan and trust known as the ABC Corporation Pension Plan (the "Plan") for the benefit of its eligible salaried employees. The Plan provides for annual payments to a participant beginning at age 65 and continuing for the participant's life, equal to 1.5 percent of the participant's final average earnings, multiplied by the participant's number of years of service at retirement. Executive D retired in 2018 with 30 years of service for ABC and final average earnings of $200,000. The Plan will pay D an annual benefit at age 65 equal to $90,000.

> **Example 2:** ABC Corporation also maintains a defined benefit plan for its eligible hourly employees. The Hourly Plan provides for monthly payments to a participant beginning at age 65 and continuing for the participant's life, equal to $30.00, multiplied by the participant's number of years of service at retirement. Hourly employee H retired in 2018 with 30 years of service for ABC. The Plan will pay H $900 per month at age 65.

The ordinary form of benefit under a defined benefit pension plan is a joint and survivor annuity for a married participant and a single life annuity for a participant who is not married when the plan begins distributions to him or her.[25] Under a joint and survivor annuity form of benefit, the plan would pay the retired participant an actuarially reduced amount (to take into account the expected longer payment period) for the duration of his or her life. If the participant's spouse is living at the participant's death, the plan would continue payments, generally in a lesser amount, for the duration of the surviving spouse's life.

---

[25] Code Sec. 417.

Example 3: In Example 2, if Executive D is not married when the Plan is to begin distributions to her in 2019, the Plan will pay her an annual benefit equal to $90,000 for the remainder of her life. When D dies, the Plan will make no further payments. If D had been married when the Plan was to begin distributions to her, the Plan's actuary would calculate the actuarial equivalent joint and survivor amount, which might result in D receiving an annual benefit equal to $70,000 for the duration of her life, and, if D's spouse is living at D's death, the Plan would pay D's surviving spouse $35,000 for the remainder of his life.

The sponsor (and other contributing employers) must fund the benefits promised under the defined benefit pension plan with annual (or more frequent) tax-deductible contributions to a tax-exempt trust.[26]

Example 4: In addition to Executive D, the ABC Corporation Pension Plan in Example 2 provides benefits for 200 other eligible salaried employees. Each plan year, the Plan's actuaries will look at the number of participants, their salaries, their estimated salary increases, their ages, their estimated retirement ages, their years of service and estimate service at retirement, the assets in the Plan and trust, the investment return on assets for the most recent year and the projected return on investments for future years and determine the minimum contribution that ABC must make, and the maximum amount of deductible contribution that ABC may make, to the Plan for that year.

The risk of investment loss is solely on the plan sponsor. Unlike a defined contribution plan, where a participant gets whatever amount is in his or her account at retirement (or termination), if the assets of a defined benefit pension plan decline in value, the employer must contribute additional amounts necessary to provide the promised benefits.[27]

.02 Alternative Defined Benefit Plan Designs

The primary reason for defined benefit plans' decline in popularity was the fact that most employees in the modern workforce no longer work for the same employer for the duration of their careers. Thus, the promise of a pension beginning at age 65 was not a motivating factor for those employees. Employers and clever professionals responded with innovative plan design alternatives that sought to incorporate many of the characteristics of individual account plans.

The most common alternative defined benefit design is the cash balance pension plan. The key features of a cash balance plan that distinguish it from a regular defined benefit pension plan are that the cash balance plan maintains a hypothetical individual account for each participant and allows for that account to be distributed to the participant in a lump sum.

---

[26] Code Sec. 404(a) and Code Sec. 412.   [27] Code Sec. 412.

.03 Executive Compensation Linked to Pension Plan Funding

Code Sec. 430(c)(7) (ERISA Section 303(c)), provides that an employer's required pension contribution using these funding rules will be increased in any year by the amount of "excess employee compensation" it pays in that year, plus the amount of any extraordinary dividends and redemptions.[28]

Code Sec. 430(c)(7) defines "excess employee compensation" as the aggregate amount includible in income for any employee for any plan year over $1 million. Sec. 430(c)(7) also includes assets set aside or reserved (directly or indirectly) during the year in a trust (or other arrangement as determined by the Secretary of the Treasury), or transferred to such a trust or other arrangement, by a plan sponsor for purposes of paying deferred compensation of an employee.

Code Sec. 430(c)(7) applies to compensation for services performed by the employee for the employer after February 28, 2010. Notably, Code Sec. 430(c)(7) excludes from the definition of "excess employee compensation:"

1. Amounts includible in income as a result of the grant, after February 28, 2010, of employer stock options, restricted stock or certain other stock-based compensation with at least a five-year vesting schedule.

2. Remuneration payable on a commission basis solely on account of income directly generated by performance of the individual to whom such remuneration is payable, and

3. Any nonqualified deferred compensation, restricted stock, stock options, or stock appreciation rights payable or granted under a written binding contract that was in effect on March 1, 2010, and which is not modified in any material respect before such remuneration is paid.

.04 SERP Shift

Before the financial crisis of 2007, some companies had undertaken a so-called SERP Shift (also known as a SERP Swap or QSERP). This strategy almost disappeared after the crisis as few pension plans had surplus funds available. However, the SERP Shift is a strategy that companies might consider in their efforts to help mitigate the loss of the deduction for performance-based compensation under Code Sec. 162(m).

Code Sec. 162(m) prohibits a publicly traded company from taking a tax deduction for compensation in excess of $1 million paid to certain executive officers. Prior to 2018, Code Sec. 162(m) included an exception to this deductibility limit for performance-based compensation. However, the Tax Cuts and Jobs Act of 2017 ("TCJA") eliminated the performance-based compensation exception, which means that nearly every public company in America is looking for any means to deduct more of the compensation it pays to senior executives.

The SERP Shift is one possible strategy to help mitigate the loss of the compensation deduction under Code Sec. 162(m). The possibility of providing

---

[28] Added by the Preservation of Access to Care for Medicare Beneficiaries and Pension Relief Act of 2010.

additional tax deductible benefits to executives under a pension plan is a strategy that may not work for most companies, but definitely will work for some public companies. And it is preferable to providing additional benefits under a non-qualified deferred compensation plan. Having an active qualified defined benefit pension plan in place already is helpful, but not essential.

"SERP Shift" is a generic term used to describe a variety of plan design and funding strategies that shift accrued or future benefits away from a non-qualified retirement plan – where contributions are not immediately deductible, cannot accumulate tax-free, are available to creditors, and cannot be rolled over – to a qualified retirement plan – where contributions are immediately deductible, can accumulate tax-free, are not available to creditors, and can be rolled over (and that is only a partial list of the advantages). What make this strategy viable is that some plan sponsors have additional room with the Code's non-discrimination in benefits test. That is, there is space for additional benefits to accrue for highly compensated employees without a violation of the Code. Many individuals and employers with "cross-tested" retirement plans understand and use this space. The employer/plan sponsor can amend its qualified plan to slightly increase benefits for certain highly compensated employees (and also relieve itself of an obligation to provide non-qualified benefits to such employees).

Shifting accrued or future benefits from a non-qualified plan to a qualified plan is a win-win for the company and the affected employees, as it creates:

- contribution deductibility and tax-free accumulation for the company, and
- benefit protection and the 19 or so other advantages of a qualified plan for the executives and other highly compensated employees.

¶1645 Defined Contribution—Individual Account Plans

Federal pension law does not require an employer to bind itself to annual contributions under most defined contribution plans. However, certain defined contribution profit sharing plans do bind the employer to a contribution formula, and many thrift and 401(k) cash or deferred plans provide for an employer matching contribution based on participants' contributions to the plan. For example, a profit sharing plan might provide that the employer will contribute 10% of its profits each year, and allocate such contribution among all participants, *pro rata*, according to the compensation paid to each for the year. A more typical contribution formula under a profit sharing plan would provide that each year the employer will contribute to the plan an amount determined solely in the discretion of its board of directors, and allocate such contribution among all participants, *pro rata*, according to their compensation.

.01 401(k) Plan

A 401(k) plan permits eligible employees to make pre-tax contributions to a qualified retirement plan. Such contributions would accumulate in a tax-exempt trust. The company may elect to make matching contributions.

A 401(k) plan could permit investment in the company's common stock. As a result, 401(k) plan participants could make payroll deductions and invest in company stock. The payroll deductions would be excludable from the employee's gross income. The employee would be taxed on the stock when the employee withdraws it from the plan at retirement. Therefore, there would be a deferral of tax on the investment in the company stock, like under an employee stock purchase plan ("ESPP"), with an additional benefit that the payroll deduction is excludable from gross income.

A 401(k) plan is a tax-qualified profit sharing or stock bonus plan that contains a cash-or-deferred arrangement. Under a 401(k) plan, a participant may make an election to have the employer contribute to the plan on the employee's behalf or pay an equivalent amount to the employee in cash. The amount contributed to the plan on behalf of the employee is an elective contribution. Generally, elective contributions are not taxed until the employee receives a distribution from the plan. Additionally, the participant's account can accumulate tax-free earnings on elective contributions until the plan distributes the participant's account.

There are advantages and disadvantages in establishing a 401(k) plan (or a 401(k) plan that invests in its company stock). One advantage in establishing a 401(k) plan is that contributions accumulate tax-free. Upon distribution, the actual amount of tax paid may be lower than the amount of tax the employee would pay today. However, the implementation and operation expenses can be high. In addition, 401(k) plans tend to involve more communication efforts than are associated with other employee benefit plans. Furthermore, the aggregate amount of employees' investment in employer stock under 401(k) plans may be too small to purchase a significant share of the company's stock. Finally, plan participants may choose not to invest in the company's stock.

A participant who is age 50 or over in a plan year is permitted to make additional 401(k) elective deferrals up to a specific dollar limit under a plan that otherwise permits elective deferrals, so-called "catch-up contributions." An employer is not required to provide for catch-up contributions in any of its plans. However, this provision should be extremely beneficial to older employees, especially highly compensated employees age 50 and older whose contributions have been restricted by Internal Revenue Code limits. This is because the Code does not count catch-up contributions for purposes of the average deferral percentage test ("ADP") or other limits.

The applicable dollar limit for catch-up contributions is $6,000 (in 2018), provided that, the catch-up contribution limit is adjusted for cost-of-living in $500 increments. To be eligible to make a catch-up 401(k) contribution, a participant must be age 50 or older. Any individual who will attain age 50 before the end of a calendar year is deemed to attain age 50 as of January 1st of that year.

Regulations provide that a plan may treat elective deferrals made by participants age 50 and older as catch-up contributions if they exceed any one of three applicable limits for the year. These three limits are: (1) the Code Sec. 402(g) limits on elective deferrals (*e.g.*, $18,500 in 2018), (2) any employer-provided limits, and (3) the ADP limits (a/k/a, "the 2 percentage point difference test").

However, the regulations do not require a participant to make elective deferrals in excess of an otherwise applicable limit before making a catch-up contribution. Thus, a plan could, for example, allow a participant who is over age 50 to make elective deferrals in an amount projected to exceed the otherwise applicable limit by $6,000 (in 2018) at any time during the year.

An employer's plan may even provide that the plan's generally applicable matching contribution formula applies to catch-up 401(k) contributions. However, the matching contributions (including the matching contributions on the catch-up contributions) must satisfy the Code average contribution percentage ("ACP") test.

If an employer provides for catch-up contributions in any of its plans, all plans of the employer, including plans maintained by members of its controlled group that provide 401(k) elective deferrals, must offer the catch-up contribution option. However, the "universal availability" rule does not require plans that do not otherwise provide for elective deferrals to provide for catch-up contributions.

Catch-up contributions for the current plan year are not taken into account for purposes of either the top-heavy minimum contribution or the minimum coverage rules. However, catch-up contributions made to the plan in prior years will be taken into account in determining whether a plan is top heavy, as well as for purposes of the average benefit test to the extent where prior year contributions are taken into account.

While an optional feature of a 401(k) plan, it is likely that employees who have attained or nearly attained age 50 will find the catch-up contribution feature of great interest. Further, the IRS has drafted the regulations with a view towards facilitating the adoption of this feature, by seeking to minimize the disruptions to existing recordkeeping systems.

.02 Employee Stock Ownership Plans

An employee stock ownership plan ("ESOP") is a tax-deferred employee stock bonus plan that is "qualified" under the Code and ERISA. An ESOP is the only qualified retirement plan designed to invest primarily in employer stock, and may borrow the funds necessary to purchase this stock. Stock purchased by the ESOP is held in trust and allocated to employees' accounts. The ESOP will distribute employees' accounts to them after their retirement or other termination of employment.

Companies design ESOPs to benefit the company and its stockholders, in addition to providing deferred compensation to eligible employees. There are two basic forms of ESOPs. The simplest form is the nonleveraged ESOP, whereby company contributions are paid annually into the ESOP trust. The second form is the leveraged ESOP, in which the ESOP borrows funds to initiate the plan, and uses company contributions in subsequent years to provide the ESOP trust with funds to repay the loan principal and interest.

A company can set up an ESOP at any time. The company could contribute authorized but unissued stock to the ESOP, or it could purchase outstanding stock from existing stockholders. Unlike profit sharing plans, the ESOP may borrow funds in order to purchase employer securities. With a leveraged ESOP, the employer generally will make tax-deductible cash contributions to the ESOP, thereby allowing the plan to amortize the loan principal and interest. Both *principal and interest payments* are tax-deductible to the corporation.

Under a nonleveraged ESOP, the employer may fund the ESOP with tax-deductible contributions up to a limit of 25% of the organization's payroll. Under a leveraged ESOP, tax-deductible contributions may be made up to 25% of payroll to repay the loan principal, plus an unlimited deduction for payment of loan interest. In addition, the company dividend payments made on stock held in the ESOP are tax-deductible whether the ESOP uses them to repay loan principal or distributes them to plan participants.

An ESOP has a special debt financing exemption from the general "prohibited transaction" rules under ERISA and the Code. The ESOP as a legal entity can borrow money from an unaffiliated lender and sign a promissory note to repay the money. The ESOP then can use these funds to purchase shares of company stock. The sale of newly issued stock creates a pool of unrestricted capital for the company. Subsequently, the company will pay the ESOP enough money annually to enable the ESOP to make its loan repayments. All of these payments (principal and interest) made by the company are entirely tax-deductible as payments to a qualified employee benefit plan. Accordingly, if a corporation is in the 34% tax bracket, the U.S. government is subsidizing 34% of the loan. Through this technique of ESOP financing, the company extends credit to the ESOP for acquiring corporation stock for the benefit of employees, while the company is able to finance its capital requirements with pre-tax dollars.

When a participant terminates without being 100% vested in his plan account, the ESOP plan will specify how to allocate these forfeited funds. Generally, the ESOP will reallocate these forfeitures to the remaining participant accounts based on pay, pay and service, or equally to all plan participants. An employer may adopt a different formula for allocation of forfeitures than for allocation of regular contributions, if there is no discrimination in favor of the highly compensated employees.

For nonleveraged ESOPs, the maximum tax-deductible contribution to an individual's account, including forfeitures, may not exceed the lesser of 25% of the participant's pay for the year, or $55,000 (for 2018). For leveraged ESOPs, forfeitures and loan interest are excluded from the limits noted above, provided that no more than one-third of the total employer contributions used in a plan year to repay the ESOP loan is allocated to officers, large shareholders and/or highly compensated employees.

Under the "put option" requirement, the employer or the ESOP is required to repurchase the stock distributed to the employee within a specific period. This requirement is, in effect, where the stock of the corporation is not readily tradable on an established securities market, giving the employee the right to have his stock in the corporation repurchased under a fair valuation formula.

In addition to employer paid contributions, the plan may provide for employee contributions. The plan may permit employee 401(k) "before-tax" contributions or employee after-tax contributions to their individual accounts. Depending on the goals of the corporation in setting up the ESOP, use of employee contributions to help fund the ESOP may be advantageous to the company and the employees.

As with all employee programs, time and care must be taken to communicate properly and effectively the mechanics and benefits of this program. This should not only be done to meet the ERISA requirements for summary plan descriptions and annual reporting, but more importantly, to maximize the employee relations benefits. ESOPs provide employees with a stock investment in their employer and the more productive and efficient they are, the more profitable their investment will become. Installing an ESOP and sharing stock ownership with employees can build unity among employees, management and outside stockholders.

.03 Money Purchase Pension Plan

A money purchase pension plan is the only form of defined contribution plan under which the Code requires that: (1) the employer bind itself to a fixed annual contribution, and (2) the normal form of benefit is an annuity rather than a lump sum. The typical money purchase plan requires the employer to make a fixed contribution of a specified percentage of each participant's compensation.

> **Example:** ABC Corporation maintains a money purchase pension plan. The Plan requires ABC to contribute to the Plan on behalf of each eligible participant, 10 percent of the participant's compensation for the year. If Executive D's compensation for 2018 was $200,000, ABC would be required to contribute to the Plan $20,000 on D's behalf.

¶1655 Limitations on Qualified Plan Benefits

The Code imposes strict limitations on the benefits and contributions that can be earned under tax qualified plans. Four of these limitations have a significant impact on the retirement benefits of higher compensated employees.

.01 Code Sec. 401(a)(17)

Code Sec. 401(a)(17), added by the Tax Reform Act of 1986, imposed a cap of $200,000, indexed for cost-of-living, on the amount of any participant's compensation that could be counted under a qualified retirement plan for contribution and benefit purposes, effective for plan years beginning in 1989.[29] The Revenue Reconciliation Act of 1993 ("RRA") reduced this limit, which by then had risen to $235,800 due to cost-of-living increases, to $150,000, effective for plan years

---

[29] Code Sec. 416 had originally imposed an includible compensation cap of $200,000 on so-called "top heavy plans" beginning in 1984.

beginning in 1994. The Economic Growth and Tax Relief Reconciliation Act of 2001 ("EGTRRA") increased this limit, which by then had risen to $170,000 due to cost-of-living increases, to $200,000, which has been indexed for cost-of-living increases to $275,000 in 2018.

One drafting trap that appears over and over in the case law relates to the definition of compensation. In *Karras v. First Colony Life Insurance Co. Pension Plan*, the court ruled that a pension plan administrator did not act arbitrarily and capriciously when it refused to include a plan participant's stock options as "compensation" when calculating his pension benefits.[30]

.02 Code Sec. 415

Code Sec. 415 has long imposed limitations on the maximum amount of contributions and/or benefits that can be made or accrued on behalf of any participant under a qualified plan. Code Sec. 415(c)(1) sets the maximum "annual addition" for individual account plans at the lesser of $55,000 (for 2018, indexed for cost-of-living increases) or 100% of the participant's annual compensation.[31] Code Sec. 415(b)(1) sets the maximum annual benefit that can be accrued and payable under a defined benefit pension plan in any year after retirement, at the lesser of $220,000 (for 2018, indexed for cost-of-living increases), or 100% of the participant's average annual compensation for his highest three years.[32]

.03 Code Sec. 402(g)

Code Sec. 402(g) limits the maximum amount of elective deferral, *e.g.*, 401(k) contributions, that any individual can make in any calendar year. The limit is $18,500 in 2018, to be increased for inflation in $500 increments thereafter.

.04 Code Sec. 410(b)

Code Sec. 410(b) does not impose any direct dollar limitations on the benefits or contributions of qualified plan participants. Rather, this section prohibits discrimination in favor of "highly compensated employees"[33] in plan eligibility or benefits. Thus, for example, a pension plan generally could not accrue benefits equal to 3% of the average annual compensation times the number of years of service for executive employees while accruing benefits equal to 2% of the average annual compensation times the number of years of service for other employees.

Other Code limits that indirectly reduce the retirement benefits that a qualified plan can provide to executives include the deductibility limits under Code Sec. 404, the minimum coverage requirements of Code Sec. 401(a)(26) and the prohibition against discrimination in plan options, rights and features under

---

[30] *Karras v. First Colony Life Insurance Co. Pension Plan*, 37 EBC 2142 (W.D.Va. 2006).

[31] Before EGTRRA, this limit was the lesser of $30,000 or 25% of the participant's annual compensation.

[32] Code Sec. 415(b)(1).

[33] Code Sec. 414(q)(1) defines a highly compensated employee generally as any employee who (a) was a five percent owner of the employer at any time during the year or the preceding year, or (b) had compensation from the employer in excess of $120,000 (for 2018, indexed for cost-of-living).

Code Sec. 401(a)(4). However, none of these limits have the impact of the four described above.

For sample qualified retirement plan provisions, see ¶ 10,220.

¶1665 Protection of Retirement Plan Benefits in Bankruptcy

ERISA and the Code provide that neither the participant nor the employer can assign or alienate pension benefits, except under very limited circumstances.[34] This means that a participant could not pledge his or her plan benefits as security for a loan (except a loan from the plan) or otherwise be forced to turn over his or her benefits to creditors (including the employer), even in bankruptcy. The only three exceptions to this protection are that (1) the IRS has special rights to levy against a participant's vested retirement plan benefits,[35] (2) a plan participant who is also a fiduciary of the plan could be forced to forfeit his or her benefits if a court found the participant to have breached his or her fiduciary duty to the plan,[36] and (3) a court may issue a qualified domestic relations order ("QDRO") that requires the plan sponsor to turn over part or all of a participant's benefits to the participant's former spouse or dependents.[37] (See Chapter 24, Executive Compensation in Bankruptcy, for more details.)

The qualified, tax-exempt trust established in connection with the retirement plan is an entity completely separate from the employer. Under no circumstances are the assets of the qualified trust available to the employer's creditors.

> **Example:** ABC Corporation established and maintains a qualified retirement plan and trust for the benefit of its employees. Both ABC and its employees make annual (or more frequent) contributions to the plan, including Executive D. ABC Corporation begins having financial difficulties in early 2018. Despite a desperate need for cash, ABC cannot access the assets of the plan and trust.
>
> ABC files for bankruptcy in 2019. Neither the secured nor the unsecured creditors of ABC can access the assets of the plan and trust.
>
> Executive D also files for personal bankruptcy in 2019. D's creditors cannot access D's accrued benefits under the plan and trust, even if D is fully vested and has a right to withdraw the benefits.

.01 Bankruptcy of a Plan Participant

Section 541 of the Bankruptcy Code[38] provides that a debtor's estate will include "all legal or equitable interests of the debtor in property as of the commencement of the estate," wherever located and by whomever held. The Bankruptcy Code functions to sweep all of a debtor's property into his or her bankruptcy estate at the commencement of bankruptcy proceedings, and then provide a few limited exemptions.

---

[34] ERISA Section 206(d); Code Sec. 401(a)(13).

[35] Reg. § 1.401(a)-13.

[36] ERISA Section 206(d)(4); Code Sec. 401(a)(13)(C).

[37] Code Sec. 414(p).

[38] 11 U.S.C. § 101, et seq.

Section 522 of the Bankruptcy Code contains the general exemption rules applicable to debtors. Section 522(d) provides that a debtor may choose to exempt property from his or her bankruptcy estate under either the federal exemption system or the exemption system found in the state of the debtor's domicile. The federal and state exemption systems vary somewhat (state systems often give a debtor some additional exemptions), but generally, are similar.

The federal exemption system, and most state exemption systems, allow a debtor to exempt property interests including, among other things, payments under profit sharing pension plans or similar plans *to the extent reasonably necessary for the support of the debtor or the debtor's dependents*. The debtor can use this exemption to protect either accumulated retirement benefits or ongoing retirement payments from bankruptcy creditors.

The principal exemption that protects retirement funds from bankruptcy creditors is Section 541(c)(2) of the Bankruptcy Code. This exemption provides that a "restriction on the transfer of a beneficial interest of the debtor in a trust that is *enforceable under applicable nonbankruptcy law is enforceable in a case under this title*." Whether ERISA's anti-alienation provision was "applicable nonbankruptcy law" was the source of much controversy in the 1980s. The U.S. Supreme Court finally settled inconsistent holdings among U.S. Courts of Appeals as to the breadth of the "applicable nonbankruptcy law" exclusion in the 1992 case of *Patterson v. Shumate*.[39]

In *Patterson*, the Supreme Court held that ERISA qualified as "applicable nonbankruptcy law" for purposes of Section 541(c)(2) of the Bankruptcy Code. Accordingly, the Court held that ERISA's anti-alienation provision was an "enforceable restriction on transfer" sufficient to keep ERISA plan benefits out of a debtor's bankruptcy estate. Thus, after *Patterson*, creditors do not have access to assets held on behalf of the debtor in a retirement plan subject to ERISA.

.02 What Plans Are Protected by ERISA?

Clearly, most qualified retirement plans of any kind fit within ERISA's definition of "pension plan." These would include defined benefit and defined contribution plans, as well as 401(k) plans and ESOPs. Some bankruptcy courts have held that a plan is "qualified" under ERISA only if it (1) includes a nonalienation provision, (2) has qualified for tax benefits, and (3) is governed by ERISA.[40] Other courts have instead merely required that a plan be governed under ERISA and contain a nonalienation clause enforceable under ERISA.[41]

.03 Keogh/Self-Employed Plans

The courts have split on whether the assets of a tax-qualified retirement plan maintained by a self-employed person are exempt from creditors in case of a self-employed person's bankruptcy. ERISA defines an "employee benefit plan" as a

---

[39] *Patterson v. Shumate*, 504 US 753 (1992).

[40] *U.S. v. Sawaf*, 96-1 USTC ¶50,063, 74 F3d 119 (6th Cir. 1996); *In re Hall*, 151 B.R. 412 (Bankr. W.D. Mich. 1993); *In re Sirois*, 144 B.R. 12 (Bankr. D. Mass.

1992); *In re Foy*, 164 B.R. 595 (Bankr. S.D. Ohio 1994); *In re Witwer*, 148 B.R. 930 (Bankr. C.D. Calif. 1992).

[41] *In re Hanes*, 162 B.R. 733 (Bankr. E.D. Va. 1994).

plan that an employer maintains for its "employees." Based on this definition, some courts have held that ERISA does not protect a Keogh plan benefiting only the self-employed person (or only the self-employed person and his or her spouse).[42]

.04 What Plans Are Not Protected by ERISA?

ERISA Section 206(d)(1) and *Patterson* would not automatically protect assets accumulated by or on behalf of an individual under the following plans or retirement vehicles:

- Individual retirement accounts or annuities;[43]
- Tax-sheltered annuities (Section 403(b) plans);
- Section 457 plans;
- Government plans;
- Church plans;
- Welfare benefit plans; and
- Excess benefit plans.

However, such plans and programs still may be excludable from creditors if: (1) the employer can make the plan subject to ERISA; (2) the plan or program is only an unfunded promise to pay future amounts; (3) the assets of the plan held on behalf of the debtor are necessary for the support of the debtor and his or her dependents; or (4) the assets of the plan or program are exempt from creditors under the state law of the debtor's domicile. The presence or absence of language in the plan, or in the Internal Revenue Code section authorizing the plan, prohibiting alienation or assignment also may determine whether the courts will exclude a plan that ERISA does not cover from a debtor's bankruptcy estate.[44]

.05 Assets Subject to Withdrawal

The courts have interpreted the *Patterson* decision to exclude a debtor's retirement plan assets from the debtor's bankruptcy estate even though the debtor has control over the funds and may withdraw them at any time.[45] Thus, a bankruptcy trustee cannot force a bankrupt participant to request a loan, withdrawal, or distribution of his or her retirement plan funds.

Although assets in ERISA qualified plans are fully protected, once the plan distributes or the participant withdraws those assets, they may be included in the debtor's bankruptcy estate. This is true whether the debtor borrowed the money

---

[42] 11 U.S.C. §522(d)(10)(E). One court has held that single pension and husband and wife pensions are outside the scope of Patterson. *In re Hall*, 151 B.R. 412 (Bankr. W.D. Mich. 1993).

[43] In *Rousey v. Jacoway*, the U.S. Supreme Court ruled unanimously that funds in an individual retirement account might be exempted from the reach of creditors in bankruptcy (*Rousey v. Jacoway*, U.S., No. 03-1407, 4/4/05). IRAs "confer a right to receive payment on account of age and they are similar

plans or contracts to those enumerated in §522(d)(10)(E)" of the Bankruptcy Code, which exempts certain assets from the debtor's bankruptcy estate.

[44] For example, Code Sec. 457(b)(6) provides that all compensation deferrals, investments and investment income shall be treated as property of the employer, not property of the employee. Code Sec. 457.

[45] *Barkley v. Conner*, 73 F3d 259 (9th Cir. 1996).

from the plan and is making repayment, or simply elects to begin distributions.[46] Many bankruptcy courts have held that the bankruptcy trustee may attach qualified plan assets as soon as the plan distributes them to the debtor. These cases indicate that only assets actually and rightfully held in an ERISA plan (and not future contributions or repayments) will be excluded from a debtor's bankruptcy estate.

At least one nonbankruptcy court has held that a bankruptcy court may not attach distributions received during retirement. The court in *U.S. v. Smith*[47] held that ERISA safeguards a pensioner's stream of income, even when the plan pays out the funds during retirement.

.06 Nonqualified Retirement Plans

Although excess benefit plans are exempted from ERISA coverage by ERISA Section 4(b), not all nonqualified retirement plans are excess plans. Since many nonqualified plans clearly fit within ERISA's definition of a "pension plan," some courts have extended the protection of *Patterson* and ERISA Section 206(d) to such plans. Since most nonqualified plans represent only an unfunded promise to pay monies in the future, it is questionable whether a bankruptcy trustee could recover such amounts before their distribution to the participant. However, at least one court has permitted a bankruptcy creditor to attach a participant's nonqualified deferred compensation account, even though the account was only an accounting entry.[48]

.07 State Exemption Statutes

Before *Patterson*, many states had amended their exemption statutes to provide additional protection to debtors' retirement benefits.[49] Often these statutes expressly exempted plans and other retirement funds that otherwise would fall outside the protection of ERISA, such as IRAs, state and local government retirement plans, and other plans qualified under the Internal Revenue Code (*e.g.*, Keogh plans and church plans).

---

[46] *In re Harshberger*, 66 F3d 775 (6th Cir. 1995); *In re Scott*, 142 B.R. 126 (Bankr. E.D. Va. 1992); *Guidry v. Sheet Metal Workers' Nat'l Pension Fund*, 39 F3d 1078 (10th Cir. 1994); *North Jersey Welfare Fund v. Colville*, 16 F3d 52 (3d Cir. 1994); *Tenneco Inc. v. First Virginia Bank*, 698 F2d 688 (7th Cir. 1993).

[47] *U.S. v. Smith*, 47 F3d 681 (4th Cir. 1995).

[48] *Westinghouse Credit Corporation v. J. Reiter Sales, Inc.*, 443 N.W. 2d 837 (Minn. 1989).

[49] See, e.g., ILCS 5/12-1006 (drafted by the author): (a) A debtor's interest in or right, whether vested or not to the assets held in or to receive pensions, annuities, benefits, distributions, refunds of contributions, or other payments under a retirement plan is exempt from judgment, attachment, execution, distress for rent, and seizure for the satisfaction of debts if the plan (i) is intended in good faith to qualify as a retirement plan under applicable provisions of the Internal Revenue Code of 1986, as now or hereafter amended, or (ii) is a public employee pension plan created under the Illinois Pension Code, as now or hereafter amended; (b) "Retirement plan" includes the following: (i) a stock bonus, pension profit sharing, annuity, or similar plan or arrangement, including a retirement plan self-employed individuals or a simplified employee pension plan; (ii) a government or church retirement plan or contract; (iii) an individual retirement annuity or individual retirement account; and (iv) a public employee pension plan created under the Illinois Pension Code, as now or hereafter amended; (c) a retirement plan that is (i) intended in good faith to qualify as a retirement plan under the applicable provisions of the Internal Revenue Code of 1986, as now or hereafter amended, or (ii) a public employee pension plan created under the Illinois Pension Code, as now or hereafter amended, is conclusively presumed to be a spendthrift trust under the law of Illinois.

.08 ERISA Welfare Benefits

The anti-alienation protection of ERISA Section 206(d)(1) refers only to "pension plans." For that reason, courts have declined to extend the anti-alienation protection to welfare benefits. In *Mackey v. Lanier Collection Agency & Service, Inc.*,[50] the U.S. Supreme Court held that ERISA does not bar the garnishment of welfare benefits (in this case, accrued vacation pay).

.09 Misconduct of the Plan Participant

The bizarre saga of Mr. Curtis Guidry illustrates most of the relevant points concerning ERISA's anti-alienation provision as it applies to participant misconduct. Mr. Guidry pleaded guilty to embezzling funds from the Sheet Metal Workers International Union Local 9. The union obtained a judgment against Guidry and argued that his pension benefits accrued under the Sheet Metal Workers National Pension Fund should be forfeited. The union argued, in the alternative, that the court should impose a "constructive trust" in the union's favor on Guidry's pension benefits, until Guidry satisfied the judgment. The federal district court, following the holdings in a few other cases, held that ERISA Section 203, and Code Sec. 411, prohibited the forfeiture of a participant's benefits after the participant had satisfied the age or service requirements of those sections. However, the district court agreed with the union that imposing a constructive trust on Guidry's benefits was an appropriate equitable remedy.

In *Guidry v. Sheet Metal Workers*, the U.S. Supreme Court held that the ERISA prohibition on the assignment or alienation of pension benefits was *not subject to an equitable exception*—for either employee malfeasance or for criminal misconduct.[51] The Supreme Court held that ERISA Section 206(d) reflects a considered congressional policy choice, a decision to safeguard a stream of income for pensioners even if that decision prevents others from securing relief for the wrongs done to them by the pensioner. The result: ERISA's anti-alienation provisions, in conjunction with its vesting and nonforfeiture provisions, prevent a plan sponsor from seizing a participant's benefits to satisfy a claim based on the participant's theft or misconduct.

Yet Guidry and the union were not through testing the limits of ERISA's anti-alienation provision. After losing at the Supreme Court, the union pension fund began paying Guidry's current and back pension distributions. At the same time, however, the union sought to garnish Guidry's bank account into which they had made the pension payments. With respect to current monthly payments, the pension fund and the union local arranged that a representative of the pension fund would make out a deposit slip to Guidry's account. The union local would then seek to garnish the funds immediately after the deposit. The parties went back to court. This time the entire bench of the Tenth Circuit Court of Appeals held that "ERISA section 206(d)(1) protects ERISA-qualified pension benefits from a garnishment only until paid to and received by plan participants

---

[50] *Mackey v. Lanier Collection Agency & Service, Inc.*, 486 US 825 (1988).

[51] *Guidry v. Sheet Metal Workers National Pension Fund*, 493 US 365 (1990).

and beneficiaries."[52] We should note that Mr. Shumate suffered a similar fate when plan distributions began to him following his Supreme Court triumph: "once the line of actual receipt is crossed, ERISA no longer protects funds originating in a private pension plan."[53]

Some courts have interpreted the Supreme Court's decision in *Guidry* narrowly, approving the denial of benefits in certain cases. For example, courts have held that an employee may forfeit his rights to benefits where he violates a fiduciary duty to the plan[54] or engages in fraud in the inducement regarding contributions to the plan.[55] Another court has upheld the right of a plan to deny an employee the right to receive the benefits in stock of the employer, rather than cash, due to the employee's misconduct.[56]

In *United States v. Novak*, and *United States v. DeCay*, the U.S. Courts of Appeals for the Ninth Circuit and the Fifth Circuit, respectively, each held that the federal government can garnish the pension benefits of an individual who pleaded guilty to charges of conspiracy to transport stolen goods.[57] The courts found that Congress, in enacting the federal Mandatory Victims Restitution Act of 1996, created a statutory exception to ERISA's anti-alienation provision.

> "We determine that Congress, by requiring the entry of restitution orders in certain criminal cases (18 U.S.C. § 3663A(a)(1)), by making those restitution orders liens in favor of the United States (18 U.S.C. § 3613(c)), and by authorizing the enforcement of those orders against all property not exempt from the reach of the United States for the payment of taxes (see 19 U.S.C. § 3613(a)), has created a statutory exemption to ERISA's anti-alienation provision," Judge Consuelo M. Callahan said in writing for the majority in *Novak*.

.10 Costs of Incarceration

Before the go-go, ethics free 1990's, I would not have included reference in my Executive Compensation book to a case like *State Treasurer v. Sprague*.[58] However, with so many former executives incarcerated since that time, it now seems relevant.[59] In *State Treasurer v. Sprague* the court held that ERISA does not preempt an action by Michigan's state treasurer to recover from a state prisoner's pension benefits the costs of his incarceration. The court found that the trea-

---

[52] *Guidry v. Sheet Metal Workers National Pension Fund*, 39 F3d 1078, 1083 (10th Cir. 1994).

[53] *NCNB Financial Services v. Shumate*, 829 F.Supp. 178, 180 (W.D. Va. 1993).

[54] See *Coar v. Kazimir*, 990 F2d 1413, 1415 (3d Cir. 1993) (where an employee breaches a fiduciary duty with respect to a plan, Section 206(d) will not bar a recovery against plan assets held for that beneficiary) and *Reich v. Davidson Lumber Sales, Inc.*, 154 B.R. 324 (Bankr. D. Utah 1993) (same holding, noting that the purposes of Section 206(d) as determined by the Supreme Court in *Guidry*, to protect the income stream of pensioners and their dependents, would be frustrated by preventing a plan from having recourse against the plan assets of a fiduciary who has violated his duty to the plan).

[55] See *Nash v. Trustees of Boston University*, 946 F2d 960 (1st Cir. 1991) (where an employee is guilty of

fraud in the inducement relating to the entering of an early retirement agreement, the traditional contract defense of fraud in the inducement will warrant avoidance or rescission of the bargain).

[56] *Woolsey v. Marion Laboratories, Inc.*, 934 F2d 1452 (10th Cir. 1991) (approving refusal of administrator of profit sharing plan to pay an employee his benefits in the form of company stock after considering the possible detriment to future beneficiaries that could result from awarding stock to this individual).

[57] *United States v. Novak*, 37 EBC 1172 (9th Cir. 2006). *U.S. v. DeCay*, 49 EBC 2530 (5th Cir. 2010).

[58] *State Treasurer v. Sprague*, E.D. Mich., No. 06-10130-BC, 7/14/06).

[59] See Messrs. Kozlowski, Lay, Fastow, Rigas, Stanford, et.al.

surer's action brought under the State Correctional Facility Reimbursement Act (SCFRA) did not "arise under" ERISA and, thus, was not completely preempted.

However, in *DaimlerChrysler Corp. v. Cox*, the Sixth Circuit Court of Appeals held that ERISA's anti-alienation provision protects benefits from attachment by a state correctional facility to reimburse for the costs of caring for the pensioner/prisoner.[60]

.11 Qualified Domestic Relations Orders

Section 206 of ERISA and Code Sec. 401(a)(13) contain two exceptions to the anti-alienation rule. The first exception is for a voluntary, revocable assignment of not more than 10 percent of any benefit payment. The second exception is for distributions to a person other than the participant (an "alternate payee") according to the terms of a qualified domestic relations order ("QDRO").

ERISA and the Code define a domestic relations order as a judgment, decree, or order, including approval of a property settlement agreement, relating to the provision of child support, alimony payments, or marital property rights to a spouse, former spouse, child, or other dependent of a plan participant that is entered pursuant to a state domestic relations law. A QDRO is an order that creates or recognizes the existence of an alternate payee's right to, or assigns to an alternate payee the right to, receive all or part of a participant's benefits under a plan. In addition, to be a QDRO, the domestic relations order must satisfy certain requirements relating to identification of: (1) the participant and the alternate payee; (2) the plan to which the order applies; (3) the amount of benefits payable; and (4) the number of payments or period to which the order applies.

A QDRO may not require a plan to provide a type or form of benefit, or any option, not provided under the plan. A QDRO may not provide for the payment of increased benefits to the alternate payee. Also, the QDRO may not require payment of a benefit to an alternate payee if that benefit is already subject to payment to another alternate payee under a prior QDRO. The prohibition against requiring a plan to pay a type or form of benefit not otherwise available will not prohibit the payment of benefits to an alternate payee while the plan sponsor still employs the participant.

For income tax purposes, the IRS treats an alternate payee who is the spouse or former spouse of the participant as the distributee with respect to the benefits paid under the QDRO. The IRS permits the alternate payee to roll over those amounts to an individual retirement account.[61] The alternate payee will not, however, be entitled to roll over the distribution to another qualified plan, or to elect lump-sum or capital gains tax treatment on the distribution. Further, the alternate payee's distribution will not be considered when determining whether the participant is entitled to lump-sum or capital gains treatment on a later distribution from the plan.

---

[60] *DaimlerChrysler Corp. v. Cox*, 447 F. 3d 967, 37 EBC 2429 (6th 2006), On June 18, 2007, the U.S. Supreme Court denied certiorari (U.S. No. 06-237, cert. denied 6/18/07), letting the 6th Circuit's deci-

sion stand, 2006 U.S. App. Lexis 12599 (6th Cir. 2006).

[61] Reg. § 1.402(c)-2, Q & A 12.

.12 Tax Liens and Other Exceptions to ERISA's Anti-Alienation Rule

The regulations under Code Sec. 401(a)(13) also contain exceptions to the anti-alienation rule for (i) enforcement of a federal tax levy made pursuant to Code Sec. 6331,[62] and (ii) "the collection by the United States on a judgment resulting from an unpaid tax assessment."[63]

In IRS Letter Ruling 200342007,[64] the IRS considered whether the federal government could levy against qualified plan benefits pursuant to the Federal Debt Collection Procedures Act of 1977 (FDCPA).[65] The FDCPA authorizes the government to collect, among other things, criminal fines and penalties.[66] The IRS considered whether the federal government could levy against the pension account of an individual plan participant who was both sentenced to imprisonment and assessed a fine.

For guidance, the IRS looked to a case holding that the federal government may collect criminal fines from a pension plan without disqualifying the plan. In a case involving essentially the same facts as the ruling request, a participant in the Ford Motor Company Retirement Trust was convicted in federal court and ordered to pay restitution.[67] The federal government filed an Application for a Writ of Continuing Garnishment under the FDCPA and a Magistrate Judge ruled that the government was entitled to garnish the participant's interest in the Ford Trust. The court held that under the FDCPA, a fine is a lien in favor of the government, and that the liability is treated as if it were a liability for an assessed tax. Thus, the court held that collection of the ordered restitution falls implicitly within the exception listed in Reg. § 1.401(a)-13(b)(2)(ii) for "collection by the United States on a judgment resulting from an unpaid tax assessment."

Thus, consistent with the holdings and the rationales of earlier court decisions, the IRS expressed its opinion that the general anti-alienation rule of Code Sec. 401(a)(13) does not preclude a court's garnishing the account balance of a fined participant in a qualified pension plan in order to collect a fine imposed in a federal criminal action. Therefore, the company's honoring of a Court Order of Garnishment pursuant to which it was ordered to pay amounts from the plan participant account to the United States would not result in the failure of the plan to meet the requirements of Code Sec. 401(a)(13).

¶1675 Bankruptcy of the Plan Sponsor

Under virtually all circumstances, ERISA completely protects the assets of a qualified retirement plan from the reach of bankruptcy and other creditors of the plan sponsor. Clearly, the assets of the plan are separate from the assets of the employer. Courts have even held that creditors could not force a bankrupt employer (or its bankruptcy trustee) to terminate an over-funded defined benefit pension plan to make the excess assets available to the creditors.[68]

---

[62] Reg. § 1.401(a)-13(b)(2)(i).
[63] Reg. § 1.401(a)-13(b)(2)(ii).
[64] IRS Letter Ruling 200342007, July 23, 2003.
[65] 28 U.S.C. § § 3001-3308.

[66] 28 U.S.C. § 3002(3).
[67] *United States v. Tyson*, 265 FSupp2d 788 (E.D. Mich. 2003).
[68] *In the Matter of Esco Manufacturing Co.*, 33 F. 3d 509 (5th Cir. 1994).

.01 Voidable Transfer Rules

The Bankruptcy Code permits the appointed bankruptcy trustee, acting on behalf of all creditors, to recover payments made to any creditor within 90 days of the bankruptcy filing. If a contribution, or "transfer," is made between 90 days and one year before the bankruptcy filing, it may be recovered only if it was made "for the benefit of a creditor that at the time of the transfer was an insider."[69] Thus, the creditors of a bankrupt plan sponsor should not be able to recover funds contributed by the sponsor to a retirement plan more than 90 days prior to the bankruptcy filing. The U.S. Supreme Court has upheld the decision of a bankruptcy trustee to terminate the overfunded pension plan of a bankrupt employer and use the $5 million asset reversion to pay creditors in *Beck v. PACE Int'l Union*.[70]

.02 Government Contractors

The bankruptcy of Bicoastal Corporation (also known as Singer) led to a long-running dispute over whether the U.S. government had an equitable interest in an over-funded pension plan and could prevent the employer from utilizing that over-funding by merging the plan into an under-funded plan.[71] The courts found that the government would be able to recover the over-funding amount, based on the fact that the over-funding apparently had been created largely by amounts paid to Bicoastal pursuant to government contracts, but for the fact that the bankruptcy filing had occurred prior to the effective date of the statute authorizing recovery.[72] The trustee of the Bicoastal pension plan, which had resisted the merger on the grounds that it may have constituted a prohibited transaction benefiting the corporation, was ordered to transfer assets to the merged plan.[73]

¶1685 Securities Law Rules Applicable to Company Stock Held in the Plan

Most publicly traded companies offer company stock as an investment option in their qualified plans. When a qualified plan holds stock of its publicly traded sponsor, certain requirements of the Securities Act of 1933 (the "Securities Act") and the Exchange Act apply.

.01 Trading Restrictions on Qualified Plan Transactions

Section 16 of the Exchange Act ("Section 16") requires a company's directors and executive officers (each an "officer") to disgorge any profits made on purchases and sales of company stock within six months of each other (so-called "short-swing profits"). Section 16 does not require a showing of nefarious intent.

---

[69] 11 U.S.C. §547(b) and 11 U.S.C. §550. These sections were amended by the Bankruptcy Reform Act of 1994. Prior to that time, some courts had held that a contribution/transfer within one year could be recovered if it indirectly benefited an insider. See *Levit v. Ingersoll Rand Financial Corporation*, 874 F2d 1186 (7th Cir. 1989).

[70] 551 U.S. 96, 127 S.Ct. 2310 (2007).

[71] *In re Bicoastal Corporation*, 124 B.R. 593 (Bankr. M.D. Fla. 1991); *In re Bicoastal Corporation*, 136 B.R. 290 (Bankr. M.D. Fla. 1992).

[72] Federal Acquisition Regulations §31.205-6(j)(4).

[73] *Bicoastal Corporation v. The Northern Trust Company*, 146 B.R. 486 (Bankr. M.D. Fla. 1992).

It simply matches any purchases or sales of company stock by an officer with any opposite way transactions occurring within six months.

To facilitate the enforcement of Section 16(b), Section 16(a) requires that each officer file certain reports (Forms 3 and 4) regarding his holdings of, and transactions involving, the company stock. Rule 16b-3, however, is designed to allow an officer to receive stock-based compensation without incurring liability for short-swing profits under Section 16(b). Many but not all of the transactions that are exempt from the short-swing profits recovery rules of Section 16(b) by reason of Rule 16b-3 are also exempt from the reporting obligations of Section 16(a).

Rule 16b-3 provides certain favorable exemptions for officers' purchases and sales of company stock within a qualified retirement plan (typically, the company's 401(k) plan).

Exchange Act Rule 16b-3(c) expressly provides that employee deferrals into a company stock fund under a "tax-conditioned plan" (*i.e.*, a qualified plan such as a 401(k) plan, an excess benefit plan, or a stock purchase plan) are exempt from both Section 16(a) reporting and Section 16(b) liability. The SEC adopted Rule 16b-3(c) because it believed that tax-conditioned plans generally provide adequate safeguards against speculative abuse. This is a blanket exemption (except for its exclusion of "discretionary transactions") that relies on the requirements imposed by certain provisions of the Code and ERISA to protect against abuse. Discretionary transactions are volitional intra-plan transfers of company stock or a cash distribution funded by a volitional disposition (such as a loan) of company stock under a qualified plan or an excess benefit plan. Non-discretionary transactions are generally regular deferral contributions withheld by the employer and forwarded to the excess benefit plan each payroll period (or quarterly, in the case of retainer payment), according to the employee's pre-existing election.

Ongoing acquisitions of company stock made under the qualified 401(k) plan with payroll deductions or company matching contributions are exempt from Section 16(b) and are not required to be reported as line items on Form 4 under Section 16(a). Instead, when an officer is otherwise required to file a Form 4, the officer must update the end-of-period holdings column to add any of the company shares he or she has acquired under the plan since the last form filed.

The Section 16 rules characterize intra-plan transfers into and out of the company stock fund and in-service withdrawals or loans funded by dispositions of company stock under the plan as "discretionary transactions." All discretionary transactions are reportable under Section 16(a). A discretionary transaction is exempt from Section 16(b) only if it is effected pursuant to an election made by an officer at least six months after the date of his or her most recent election to effect an opposite-way discretionary transaction under *any* company employee benefit plan.

A non-exempt discretionary transaction does not in and of itself create Section 16(b) liability. However, a non-exempt discretionary transaction could be matched with an opposite-way non-exempt transaction, such as a non-exempt discretionary transaction under any other company benefit plan or an open market transaction, made within six months of the non-exempt discretionary transaction to create short-swing liability under Section 16(b).

.02 Separate Rules Apply for Nonqualified Plans

The qualified plan exemptions described above are not applicable to the company's non-qualified benefit plans. As a general rule, the conditions that Rule 16b-3 requires to exempt non-qualified plan transactions from Section 16 are more onerous than those that apply to qualified plans. Moreover, transactions involving the company stock under the non-qualified plans can impact the availability of exemptions for transactions under the qualified 401(k) plan. Therefore, transactions under all benefit plans, particularly those involving intra-plan transfers into and out of the company stock funds, should be monitored and coordinated carefully. Finally, because the rules are extremely complex and, frequently, not intuitive, we strongly suggest that each proposed transaction by a company insider be evaluated individually well before the transaction is effected.

.03 Registration Requirement

When a publicly traded company offers company stock as an investment option for employees' own contributions under a 401(k) plan, the company must register that offering of shares under the Securities Act on Form S-8.

.04 Prospectus Requirement

A qualified plan that offers company stock as an investment must provide plan participants with certain information in the form of a 10(a) prospectus. Additionally, a qualified plan must provide plan participants with a form of SPD, which meets the specific requirements set forth in ERISA. However, companies should not incorporate by reference any of the company's SEC filings. The 10(a) prospectus - or "Statement of General Information" - should be a separate document that incorporates the SPD by reference.

Several court cases have found the potential for a breach of fiduciary duty if the incorporated by reference documents are not accurate (thus converting a financial restatement issue or SEC violation into a potential ERISA fiduciary breach). Typically, these cases involve a misstatement in the company's financial reporting to the SEC. The potential penalties and market consequences of this are bad enough. However, because the ERISA documents incorporate the SEC filings by reference, the plaintiffs' lawyers are also able to sue the plan's fiduciaries for a breach of fiduciary duty under ERISA.

This is a subtle difference, but it better protects the plan fiduciaries. The separate 10(a) prospectus will refer to the SPD (the SPD will still include the legend on the inside cover page). (A third document constituting the required 10(a) prospectus would be one with charts showing the three years of annual returns for each investment fund offered.)

¶1685.02

.05 ERISA and the Federal Securities Laws

Everyone knows that ERISA governs 401(k) plans and ERISA requires plans and plan administrators to provide plan participants with a form of SPD, which meets the specific requirements set forth in ERISA. Everyone also knows that the federal securities law requires extensive information filings by public companies. Some federal courts have found a potential breach of ERISA fiduciary duty where a company's SPD incorporated by reference certain SEC filings by the company, which filings were *alleged* to be inaccurate.

A 401(k) plan that offers company stock as an investment option also must provide plan participants with certain information in the form of a 10(a) prospectus and "Statement of General Information." The 10(a) prospectus should be a separate document that incorporates the SPD by reference. Some companies have mistakenly reversed this step and instead incorporated the company's SEC filings by reference into the SPD.

This is a subtle difference, but getting it wrong can increase the potential liability risk to the 401(k) plan fiduciaries. The separate 10(a) prospectus should refer to the SPD. Only the separate 10(a) prospectus should reference the necessary SEC filings. The SPD should indicate that it is part of a 10(a) prospectus (usually with a legend on the inside cover page), but not reference the SEC filings.

¶1695 State Taxation of Qualified Retirement Plan Benefits

Section 114 of Title 4 of the United States Code prohibits states from imposing an income tax on certain types of retirement income for nonresidents.[74] The types of pension covered by Section 114 include payments from:

- A qualified trust under Code Sec. 401(a);
- A simplified employee pension plan as defined in Code Sec. 408(k);
- An annuity plan described in Code Sec. 403(b);
- An individual retirement plan described in Code Sec. 7701(a)(37);
- An eligible deferred compensation plan as defined in Code Sec. 457;
- A governmental plan as defined in Code Sec. 414(d); and
- Employee contribution trusts described in Code Sec. 501(c)(18).

This statute became necessary when some of the more rapacious tax states attempted to tax the retirement benefits of anyone who had ever lived in the state. For example, section 601(e) of the New York State Tax Law imposes a personal income tax on a nonresident's taxable income that is derived from New York sources. The New York legislature never did adopt a parallel law conforming to Section 114. However, memoranda from the New York State Department of Taxation and Finance indicate that income from the retirement plans described in the statute cannot be taxed for nonresidents.[75]

---

[74] Passed as Public Law 104-95.

[75] See TSB-A-96(6)I (December 24, 1996) (holding that New York may not tax the lump-sum payment from a 457 plan to a Florida resident); TSB-M-02(9)I (October 17, 2002) (holding that distributions from a

The prohibition on state income tax applies whenever the individual is a nonresident. For example, if the individual was a resident of New York when ten annual installment payments began, and moved to Florida after the first three payments were made, the next seven payments would not be subject to New York income tax.

---

457 plan to nonresidents are not included in New York source income).

Chapter 17
NONQUALIFIED RETIREMENT AND DEFERRED COMPENSATION PLANS

¶1701 Overview—Nonqualified Retirement and Deferred Compensation Plans

A nonqualified retirement or deferred compensation plan is simply a benefit plan that does not meet the "qualification requirements" of Internal Revenue Code Section 401(a). A nonqualified plan must be unfunded and maintained for a select group of management and highly compensated employees. A nonqualified plan must be set forth in a written legal plan document, which should be adopted by the employer's board of directors. The plan document should specify the categories of employees eligible to participate in the plan and the benefits or contributions provided for under the plan.

The repeal of the performance-based compensation exception to the Code Sec. 162(m) $1 million cap on deductible compensation by the Tax Cuts and Jobs Act of 2017 ("TCJA"), is expected to further increase the attractiveness and use of nonqualified plans in 2019 and beyond.

.01 The Problem with Qualified Plans

Tax qualified plans historically have been the source of retirement income for most employees. However, the Code imposes significant limitations on the benefits and contribution that can be earned under tax qualified plans. These and other Code limitations can endanger the accumulation of sufficient funds for the executives' retirement, and may cause executives and/or other highly compensated employees to request additional retirement benefits from nonqualified plans (see ¶1715 for a detailed discussion of the limits).

.02 FICA/Medicare Taxation of Nonqualified Plan Benefits

A negative development in the Revenue Reconciliation Act of 1993 was the elimination of the cap on wages subject to the Medicare portion of Social Security taxes. The full Medicare tax on employers and employees also applies to amounts earned under a nonqualified retirement or deferred compensation plan (see ¶1735).

.03 Application of ERISA

Although a plan document would be required, the reporting and disclosure requirements of the Employee Retirement Income Security Act of 1974, as amended ("ERISA"), and the Internal Revenue Code would not apply, as long as the nonqualified plan is available only to a "select group of management and other highly compensated employees." Only a one-time, single-page notification would need to be furnished to the U.S. Department of Labor ("DOL") within 120 days of the adoption of the nonqualified plan. A nonqualified plan is not subject to the participation, vesting, funding and fiduciary obligation provisions of Title I of ERISA (see ¶1740 for a detailed discussion of the ERISA requirements).

.04 Types of Nonqualified Plans

The main advantage of a nonqualified plan over a qualified retirement plan is that, because the Internal Revenue Code's qualification requirements do not apply, an employer has enormous flexibility in drafting the eligibility, benefit and other provisions of the nonqualified plan (see ¶1745).

.05 Other Nonqualified Plan Design Issues

Generally, employers design nonqualified retirement plans to allow executives and other highly compensated employees to receive benefits and defer compensation in excess of the Code limits applicable under qualified retirement plans. Thus, an employer will generally design its nonqualified plan to look like the qualified plan that it is intended to supplement.

> **Example:** ABC Corporation's qualified defined benefit pension plan provides an annual pension benefit equal to a participant's number of years of service with ABC, multiplied by 2% of the participant's final average compensation. Executive D has 25 years of service and final average compensation equal to $500,000 at retirement from ABC. Executive D would appear to have accrued a lifetime annual pension benefit of $250,000 per year under the pension plan's benefit formula (25 × 2% × $500,000). However, the Code limits the annual amount of compensation that a qualified plan may take into account for benefit accrual purposes to $275,000 (for 2018). Thus, Executive D's retirement benefit under the qualified plan would be only $137,500 per year (25 × 2% × $275,000).
>
> ABC Corporation may decide to adopt a nonqualified pension plan that pays Executive D (and other affected executives) the difference between what he or she would have received under the regular plan benefit formula, *e.g.*, $250,000 per year, and the annual benefit Executive D actually receives under the qualified plan due to Internal Revenue Code limits. In this example, Executive D would receive annual benefit payments of $137,500 from the qualified plan and $112,500 from the nonqualified plan.

A garden-variety nonqualified deferred compensation plan permits participants to defer all or part of their annual compensation or bonus. Some deferred compensation plans are linked to the employer's 401(k) plan and designed to permit deferrals in excess of the limitations of Code Sec. 401(k)(3) (the two percentage point difference limitation) and the Code Sec. 402(g) calendar year limitation ($18,500 in 2018). Some nonqualified deferred compensation plans even provide for supplemental employer matching and/or profit sharing contributions based on the amounts an executive would have contributed to or received under the qualified defined contribution or 401(k) plan but for the Code limitation (see ¶1755 for a detailed discussion of nonqualified plan design).

.06 Tax Treatment of Nonqualified Plans

Because a nonqualified plan does not satisfy the "qualification" requirements of the Code, contributions and benefits under a nonqualified plan do not "qualify" for the very favorable tax treatment available to employers and employees under qualified plans. Thus, the employer is not entitled to a deduction for benefits accrued or contributions made on behalf of nonqualified plan participants until a participant recognizes taxable income from the plan (generally only when benefits are paid to the participant). The employer will be entitled to a deduction equal to the amount includable in a participant's gross income, in the year such amount is includable in income. The employer cannot accumulate contributions or benefits in a tax-exempt trust, in the manner of a qualified plan trust. However, employee participants may be able to make before-tax contributions to a nonqualified plan much as they do to a qualified 401(k) plan (see ¶ 1725).

.07 "Funding" Nonqualified Plan Benefits

Although a nonqualified plan must remain nothing more than an unfunded promise to pay benefits, to avoid current taxation under the doctrine of constructive receipt, many companies "informally" fund their nonqualified plans. The IRS has approved the use of so-called "rabbi trusts" to informally fund companies' nonqualified plan benefit promises. An employer may maintain separate accounts for its nonqualified plan participants under a rabbi trust, but the assets of the rabbi trust must remain subject to the claims of the employer's general creditors if the employer becomes insolvent. The participants would hold the status of general, unsecured creditors with respect to their accounts under a rabbi trust. Code Sec. 409A imposes restrictions on funding nonqualified benefits (see ¶ 1765 for a detailed discussion of funding issues).

.08 Securities Law Issues

If the nonqualified plan participants are offered an opportunity to defer a portion of their compensation and to invest those deferrals in an employer stock fund, the participants' interests in the plan would be considered securities and the employer would be required to register those interests, along with the shares of employer stock available under the plan, on a Form S-8 Registration Statement under the Securities Act of 1933. In addition to filing a Form S-8 Registration Statement, an effective registration requires that the employer deliver to each participant documents and information that constitute a Section 10(a) prospectus (see ¶ 1775).

.09 Code Sec. 409A

The most significant development in the executive compensation world in the new millennium was the addition of Code Sec. 409A.[1] Code Sec. 409A imposed a series of requirements on deferred compensation plans and arrange-

---

[1] Added by the American Jobs Creation Act of 2004, P.L. 108-357, signed into law by President Bush on October 22, 2004.

ments. A plan or arrangement that provides for the deferral of compensation but does not satisfy the requirements of Code Sec. 409A would be immediately taxable as ordinary income (see ¶ 1785 for a detailed discussion of Code Sec. 409A issues).

.10 Top-Hat Plan Litigation

Over the years, nonqualified or "top-hat" plans have been the subject of a variety of litigation issues. See ¶ 2035 for a detailed discussion of these issues.

¶1715 The Problem with Qualified Plans

The Code imposes strict limitations on the benefits and contributions that employees can earn under tax qualified plans. Four of these limitations significantly impact the retirement benefits of higher compensated employees.

.01 Code Sec. 401(a)(17)

Code Sec. 401(a)(17), added by the Tax Reform Act of 1986, imposed a cap of $200,000 on the amount of any participant's compensation that could be counted under a qualified retirement plan for contribution and benefit purposes, effective for plan years beginning in 1989.[2] The Revenue Reconciliation Act of 1993 ("RRA") reduced this limit, which by then had risen to $235,800 due to cost-of-living increases, to $150,000, effective for plan years beginning in 1994. The Economic Growth and Tax Relief Reconciliation Act of 2001 ("EGTRRA") increased this limit, which by then had risen to $170,000 due to cost-of-living increases, to $200,000, effective for plan years beginning in 2002 (indexed upward for cost-of-living increases to $275,000 in 2018).

.02 Code Sec. 415

Code Sec. 415 has long imposed limitations on the maximum amount of contributions and/or benefits that can be made or accrued on behalf of any participant under a qualified plan. Code Sec. 415(c)(1) sets the maximum "annual addition" for individual account plans at the lesser of $55,000 (in 2018) or 100% of the participant's annual compensation (to be indexed for cost-of-living increases). Code Sec. 415(b)(1) sets the maximum annual benefit that can be accrued and payable under a defined benefit pension plan in any year after retirement at the lesser of $220,000 (for 2018) or 100% of the participant's average annual compensation for his or her highest three years.[3]

.03 Code Sec. 402(g)

Code Sec. 402(g) limits the maximum amount of elective deferral, *e.g.*, 401(k) contributions, that any individual can make in any calendar year. The limit is $18,500 in 2018.

---

[2] Code Sec. 416 had originally imposed an includible compensation cap of $200,000 on so-called "top heavy plans" beginning in 1984.

[3] Code Sec. 415(b)(1). Before EGTRRA, this limit was the lesser of $135,000, or 100% of the participant's average compensation for his or her high three years.

.04 Code Sec. 410(b)

Code Sec. 410(b) does not impose any direct dollar limitations on the benefits or contributions of qualified plan participants. Rather, this section prohibits discrimination in favor of "highly compensated employees"[4] in plan eligibility or benefits. Thus, for example, a pension plan generally could not accrue benefits equal to 3% of average annual compensation times years of service for executive employees while accruing benefits equal to 2% of average annual compensation times years of service for other employees.

Other Code limits that indirectly reduce the retirement benefits that a qualified plan can provide to executives include the deductibility limits under Code Sec. 404, the minimum coverage requirements of Code Sec. 401(a)(26) and the prohibition against discrimination in plan options, rights and features under Code Sec. 401(a)(4). However, none of these limits has the impact of the four described above.

.05 Impact of the Code Limits on Qualified Retirement Plans

The following examples illustrate the impact of the Code limits on various common qualified plan designs in a sample plan for an individual, Executive B, earning $500,000.

Example 1: Defined Contribution Plan. Assume a defined contribution plan that provides an employer contribution to all employees equal to 10.0% of their annual compensation. Under this formula, Executive B would expect to receive an annual contribution to his or her account equal to $50,000. But that does not happen.

Year	Code Sec. 401(a)(17) Compensation Cap	Contribution Made for Executive B
1993	$235,800	$23,580
1994	$150,000	$15,000
2007	$225,000	$22,500
2018	$275,000	$27,500

In Example 1, absent the Code Sec. 401(a)(17) cap, Executive B would receive annual contributions equal to $50,000. Thus, under the 2018 limits, Executive B will receive $22,500 less each year in contribution than the regular benefit formula would dictate. While the situation has improved for executives since the Clinton era, the Code's compensation cap still prevents executives from receiving the same contribution as everyone else under the plan.

Example 2: Defined Benefit Plan. Assume a defined benefit plan that provides an annual benefit, commencing at normal retirement age, of 2% of final average earnings multiplied by years of service, and assume Executive B has 25 years of service with the employer.

---

[4] Code Sec. 414(q)(1) defines a highly compensated employee generally as any employee who (a) was a five percent owner of the employer at any time during the year or the preceding year, or (b) had compensation from the employer in excess of $120,000 (for 2018, indexed for cost-of-living increases).

Year	Code Sec. 401(a)(17) Compensation Cap	Annual Pension Accrued at Retirement
1993	$235,800	$90,000[*]
1994	$150,000	$75,000
2007	$225,000	$112,500
2018	$275,000	$137,500

The Code Sec. 415 limit would apply to reduce the maximum annual benefit even below that which Executive B could have accrued under the Code Sec. 401(a)(17) cap.

In Example 2, absent the Code Sec. 401(a)(17) cap, Executive B would receive a retirement benefit equal to $250,000 per year for life. Under the 2018 limits, Executive B will receive $137,500 per year in annual retirement benefits less than the regular benefit formula would dictate.

Example 3: 401(k) Plan. The Code Sec. 401(a)(17) cap also makes it harder for a 401(k) plan to pass the average deferral percentage ("ADP") test and, thus, more likely that Executive B will have some of his or her elective deferral contributions returned. The ADP test provides that the ADP of highly compensated employees ("HCEs"), taken as a group, cannot exceed the ADP of all nonhighly compensated employees ("NHCEs") in the plan, by more than two percentage points (*e.g.*, if the ADP of NHCEs was 2%, the ADP for all HCEs could not exceed 4%). If the ADP of HCEs is based only on earnings of only $150,000 or $275,000, the ADP figure for the HCEs will be artificially increased, and the test much harder to pass. In this example, assume that Executive B elects to defer the maximum annual amount permitted by Code Sec. 402(g). (Note that, absent the Code Sec. 402(g) limit, Executive B would have been able to reduce his or her taxable earnings by $50,000 each year and contribute that amount toward his or her retirement.)

Year	Code Sec. 401(a)(17) Cap	Maximum Annual Deferral Contribution (Code Sec. 402(g))	Resulting Deferral Percentage
1993	$235,800	$8,994	3.8%
1994	$150,000	$9,240	6.2%
2007	$225,000	$15,500	6.8%
2018	$275,000	$18,500	6.7%

In Example 3, absent the Code Sec. 401(a)(17) cap, Executive B's ADP would have been 3.7%, a modest figure that most likely would have allowed the 401(k) plan to pass the ADP test and Executive B to enjoy the full contribution permitted by the Code Sec. 402(g) limit. However, the compensation cap causes Executive B's ADP to be artificially increased by three percentage points, which will make it much more difficult for the 401(k) plan to pass the overall ADP test.

¶1715.05

.06 Making Whole the Affected Executives

If the employer wishes to provide retirement benefits for its executives in the same amounts as it provides to every other employee covered under its qualified retirement plan, theoretically it has three alternatives. Under one alternative, the employer could amend the benefit formula under its existing retirement plan to increase the contribution percentage or benefit formula. However, in light of the nondiscrimination requirements of Code Sec. 410(b) and Code Sec. 401(a)(4), any increase would have to apply to all participants, or at least a nondiscriminatory group, not just the executives or highly compensated employees affected by the compensation cap. This alternative would be very expensive for the employer.

For example, if the employer in Example 1 above wanted to ensure that Executive B received the $50,000 annual contribution to which he would have been entitled absent the Code Sec. 401(a)(17) cap, the employer would have to increase the contribution percentage for all employees from 10% to 18%. Executive B would receive an additional $22,500 per year in employer contributions, but the other employees would receive an even greater percentage of their pay, the employer's total compensation costs would jump significantly, and the problem would still not be solved.

A second alternative would be for the employer to adopt another qualified retirement plan under which it provides additional contributions or benefits. Unfortunately, the nondiscrimination requirements of Code Sec. 410(b) and Code Sec. 401(a)(4) would again prevent the employer from achieving the desired result. This alternative, too, would most likely be prohibitively expensive for the employer.

The employer's third alternative is to adopt a nonqualified retirement plan that makes whole the executive and other highly compensated employees for the contributions or benefits that they could not receive under the employer's qualified plan because of the Code limits. Not surprisingly, the nonqualified plan alternative is the one adopted by the vast majority of employers.

> **Example 4:** The employer in Example 1 above could adopt a nonqualified plan under which it contributed an amount equal to the difference between the $50,000 annual contribution Executive B would have received absent the Code Sec. 401(a)(17) cap, and the amount of employer contribution Executive B actually received under the qualified plan. Under this alternative, the employer would make Executive B whole, and increase its compensation cost by only $22,500 per year (not counting the administrative expense of maintaining the nonqualified plan).

¶1725 Tax Treatment of Nonqualified Plans

Nonqualified plans have never enjoyed the favorable tax treatment available to qualified plans. For more than 50 years prior to the American Jobs Creation Act of 2004, the tax rules applicable to nonqualified plans had been developed gradually, but not uniformly, by a series of court decisions and IRS rulings. This section identifies and summarizes the tax issues applicable to nonqualified plans.

However, Code Sec. 409A(c) expressly provides that no inference on earlier income inclusion or requirement of later inclusion is to be drawn:[5]

> Nothing in this section shall be construed to prevent the inclusion of amounts in gross income under any other provision of this chapter or any other rule of law earlier than the time provided in this section. Any amount included in gross income under this section shall not be required to be included in gross income under any other provision of this chapter or any other rule of law later than the time provided in this section.

.01 Comparison to Qualified Plans

As described in Chapter 16 (¶1601 *et seq.*), qualified retirement plans enjoy the following significant tax preferences:

1. Employer contributions to the qualified plan are fully and immediately deductible (subject to certain limits under Code Sec. 404).

2. Employees are not taxed on employer contributions made or benefits accrued on their behalf, even when the employees become fully vested in those amounts.

3. Employees are permitted to make pre-tax contributions to the plan pursuant to Code Sec. 401(k).

4. Employer and employee contributions grow tax-free in a tax-exempt trust (Code Sec. 501(a)).

5. Favorable tax treatment is available to an employee at time of distribution, such as the ability to roll over[6] his or her qualified plan distribution into an IRA or another eligible retirement plan.[7]

6. In calculating whether an executive received excess parachute payments under Code Sec. 280G, payments to or from a tax-qualified plan, including a retirement plan described in Code Sec. 401(a), an annuity plan described in Code Sec. 403(a), a simplified employee pension plan described in Code Sec. 408(k) or a simple retirement account described in Code Sec. 408(p) are not counted.[8]

7. Contributions to and benefits under a qualified plan are not subject to the $1 million deductibility limit of Code Sec. 162(m).

Under a nonqualified plan, the employer's obligation to pay benefits must remain no more than an unfunded promise to pay, in order to avoid current taxation to the employee. The employer cannot make currently deductible contributions to, nor can employee benefits accumulate in, a tax-exempt trust. An employee cannot further defer taxation on a distribution from a nonqualified plan by rolling over that distribution. Contributions and benefits that become vested under a nonqualified plan are subject to Medicare tax. For a nonqualified deferred compensation plan, the employer will only receive a deduction, if at all,

---

[5] Code Sec. 409A(c).

[6] Code Sec. 401(a)(31); Code Sec. 402(c)(4).

[7] Code Sec. 402(c)(8)(B).

[8] Code Sec. 280G(b)(4)(B); Proposed Reg. § 1.280G-1, Q&A-8.

when the amount attributable to the employer contribution is includible[9] in the gross income of the plan participant;[10] which year is dependent upon the terms of the plan.

Nonqualified plans are also subject to different income tax withholding rules. Annuities and other periodic distributions from a tax-qualified plan, as well as certain nonperiodic distributions that are not eligible to be rolled over, are subject to optional withholding, while lump sum and certain installment distributions that are eligible to be rolled over are subject to a mandatory 20% withholding.[11] In contrast, distributions from nonqualified plans are subject to general rules of wage withholding.[12]

.02 Nonqualified Plans Before Code Sec. 409A

Before 2005, compensation deferred under, and employer contributions to, a nonqualified plan or program, and the earnings on such deferrals and contributions, were not subject to current federal income taxation unless a participant was in "constructive receipt" of the relevant amounts or received a measurable "economic benefit" from the arrangement. In most "unfunded" nonqualified arrangements, this is easily accomplished if: (1) the agreement to defer the receipt of compensation is entered into before the services are rendered, and (2) the employer's promise to contribute or provide benefits is not secured in any way.

If the plan were to be funded by a rabbi trust (discussed at ¶1765 below), investment earnings on the rabbi trust funds would be taxable to the employer that is the grantor of the trust. The employer would not receive a federal income tax deduction for its contribution of the deferred compensation amounts to the rabbi trust until the participant receives the funds as taxable income (generally at retirement or termination of employment). The employer's deduction coincides with the employee's recognition of taxable income.

Before 2005, the U.S. Congress had restricted the IRS's ability to regulate nonqualified deferred compensation plans. In 1977, the IRS announced that it had suspended the issuance of rulings dealing with the income tax treatment of certain elective nonqualified deferred compensation pending its review of the area. In 1978, it issued proposed regulations that would effectively have disallowed nonqualified deferred compensation arrangements if the amounts involved were deferred at the taxpayer's individual option. In response, Congress enacted Section 132 of the Revenue Act of 1978, which provided that:

> the taxable year of inclusion in gross income of any amount covered by a private deferred compensation plan should be determined in accordance with the principles set forth in regulations, rulings, and judicial decisions that were in effect on February 1, 1978.

However, according to the General Explanation of the Revenue Act of 1978:

---

[9] The deduction is allowed when benefits or contributions are "includible" in income, not when they are actually "included." Reg. § 1.404(a)-12(b)(1).

[10] Code Sec. 404(a)(5). In the case of a plan in which more than one employee participates, the

deduction is allowable only if separate accounts are maintained for each employee.

[11] Code Sec. 3405(a) through Code Sec. 3405(c).

[12] Temporary Reg. § 35.3405-1T, Q&A 18.

The Act is not intended to restrict judicial interpretation of the law relating to the proper tax treatment of deferred compensation or interfere with judicial determination of what principles of law apply in determining the timing of income inclusion.

.03 Special Rules for Tax-Exempt Employers

The Internal Revenue Code imposes additional limitations and requirements on deferred compensation programs of tax-exempt employers (see Chapter 26 [¶ 2601 *et seq.*] for a detailed discussion of executive compensation for tax-exempt employers). State and local governments and tax-exempt associates are allowed to offer deferred compensation plans subject to the limitations of Code Sec. 457. To avoid "abuses" by these entities, the maximum benefit that these plans can pay is capped.

.04 Constructive Receipt

The general principles of the constructive receipt doctrine are undisputed. The Code provides that the amount of any item of gross income shall be included in gross income for the taxable year in which received by the taxpayer unless, under the method of accounting used in computing taxable income, such amount is to be properly accounted for in a different period.[13] The receipt of gross income may be actual or constructive.[14] Elaborating on this rule, the regulations provide that income is constructively received by a taxpayer in the taxable year in which such income is (1) credited to the taxpayer's account, (2) set apart for the taxpayer, or (3) otherwise made available so that the taxpayer could have drawn upon it during the taxable year if notice of intention to withdraw had been given.[15] Expressed somewhat differently, the essence of constructive receipt is the unfettered control over income prior to the date of actual receipt.[16] Under this doctrine, a taxpayer may not deliberately turn his or her back on income otherwise available.[17] Thus, if an employee delays cashing (or picking up) his or her December 31 paycheck until January of the following year, the employee nonetheless receives taxable income on December 31 of the earlier year.[18]

Income is not constructively received if the taxpayer's control of its receipt is subject to substantial limitations or restrictions. In a series of revenue rulings, the IRS has elaborated upon the meaning of "substantial limitations or restrictions." In Rev. Rul. 80-300,[19] the IRS ruled that an individual's right to exercise a stock appreciation right ("SAR") at any time did not result in constructive receipt of the spread, because by exercising the SAR the employee forfeited the upside potential. In Rev. Rul. 80-157,[20] the IRS concluded that the penalties imposed on the taxpayer in connection with a six-month CD before its maturity constituted sufficient restrictions to preclude imposing the constructive receipt doctrine. In

---

[13] Code Sec. 451(a). The discussion in this section is limited to taxpayers who are on the cash method of accounting.

[14] Reg. § 1.446-1(c)(1)(i).

[15] Reg. § 1.451-2(a).

[16] *Hornung v. Comm'r*, 47 TC 428, 431, CCH Dec. 28,318 (1967).

[17] *CE Gullitt*, 31 BTA 1067 (1930); Rev. Rul. 60-31, 1960-1 CB 174; *Ames v. Comm'r*, 112 TC 304, CCH Dec. 53,397 (1999).

[18] Rev. Rul. 68-126, 1968-1 CB 194.

[19] Rev. Rul. 80-300, 1980-2 CB 165.

[20] Rev. Rul. 80-157, 1980-1 CB 186.

Rev. Rul. 68-482,[21] the IRS held that an employee would not be in constructive receipt of the cash surrender value of an annuity contract even though the employee had the right to surrender the contract at will, since the acquisition of another contract would entail additional loading charges. Courts have long indicated that the doctrine of constructive receipt is to be applied sparingly.[22]

In general, for purposes of the constructive receipt doctrine, the date specified by a contract is controlling, and the payment is not constructively received before then, even if the obligor would have agreed at the outset to an earlier contract date or would have paid before the due date on request.[23] For example, in *Basila v. Comm'r*,[24] the taxpayer entered into an employment contract under which his bonus would be determined in October and payable in January of the following year. Before October, the taxpayer requested and received an advance payment of a portion of his bonus and included it as income. The IRS said that the taxpayer was in constructive receipt of the balance of the bonus. The Tax Court, however, disagreed, and held that a taxpayer was not in constructive receipt of the balance of the bonus because the entire amount of the bonus was not unconditionally subject to his demand. The court noted, and the IRS conceded, "a taxpayer does not constructively receive income under a contract until the obligor becomes liable to pay it, even though the obligor is willing and able to make the payment before the date provided therein." The Tax Court also indicated that "when money is not due to be paid under the contract granting taxpayer the income, the terms of the contract are to be given effect in the absence of some supervening reason," such as the taxpayer's control over the payor corporation, which was not present in this case.

Basila was followed in *Joseph Metcalfe v. Comm'r*.[25] In that case, a division manager entered into a nonqualified deferred compensation plan that his employer offered to key employees. Although the IRS contended that the taxpayer had an unrestricted right to withdraw the deferred amounts because he could immediately rescind the agreement to participate in the plan, the Tax Court held that the taxpayer was not in constructive receipt. The Tax Court looked at the terms of the plan to determine "whether the deferred amount was made available to petitioner so that he could have drawn upon it during the taxable year if notice of intention to withdraw had been given." The court noted that the taxpayer could not rescind the agreement unless the employer consented. If the employer did not consent to rescind, the provision that the installment was not payable until the year following termination was controlling. In either situation the employee did not, by nature of the language of the contract, have unfettered control over the money, *i.e.*, the contractual language imposed a substantial limitation upon the employee's right to receive the income.

---

[21] Rev. Rul. 68-482, 1968-2 CB 186.

[22] *Dial v. Comm'r*, 24 TC 117, CCH Dec. 20,983 (1955), Acq. 1955-2 CB 5; *Hines v. Comm'r*, 38 BTA 1061, CCH Dec. 10,486 (1938), Acq. 1939-1 CB 17; *Young Door Co.*, 40 TC 890, CCH Dec. 26,283 (1963); *Lehruth v. Comm'r*, 2001-190 TC Summary Opinion.

[23] Bittker & Lottken, *Federal Taxation of Income, Estates, and Gifts*, Volume 4, ¶ 105.3.3.

[24] *Basila v. Comm'r*, 36 TC 111, CCH Dec. 24,788 (1961).

[25] *Joseph Metcalfe v. Comm'r*, 43 TCM 1393, CCH Dec. 39,029(M) (1982).

Basila was also followed in *Young Door Co. v. Comm'r*,[26] in which the Tax Court held that commissions owed to a controlling shareholder under a director's resolution requiring payment 90 days after the close of the taxable year were not constructively received before that date, even though the shareholders were willing to accelerate that date. The Tax Court concluded that, where the official corporate record limits the right to receive income to a fixed date, the income is subject to a substantial restriction, in the same manner that the contractual language in *Basila* constituted a substantial limitation on the taxpayer's rights.[27]

More recent statements of the Tax Court with respect to the constructive receipt doctrine reaffirm these principles. In *Martin v. Comm'r*,[28] the Tax Court stated "under the constructive receipt doctrine, a taxpayer recognizes income when the taxpayer has an unqualified, vested right to receive immediate payment."[29] Similarly, in *Richard A. Childs v. Comm'r*,[30] the Tax Court stated:

> Generally, there must be an amount that is immediately due and owing that the obligor is ready, willing and able to pay. The amount owed must either be credited to the taxpayer or set aside for the taxpayer so that the taxpayer has an unrestricted right to receive it immediately and the taxpayer, being aware of the facts, declines to accept the payments.

Under the approach taken by the Tax Court, a taxpayer could also avoid constructive receipt, even though the taxpayer and his employer have already entered into a deferral agreement and, before the payment date, entered into another agreement further extending the payment date. In *Veit v. Comm'r*,[31] the employee was employed under an employment contract entitling him to a bonus in 1941 based upon the employer's 1940 net profits. The 1940 net profits would be calculated in 1941 whereupon the bonus would be due and payable. In November 1940, the parties entered into an agreement to defer payment of the bonus until 1942. The Tax Court held that the employee was not in constructive receipt of income in 1941 and that the deferral agreement represented a *bona fide* arm's-length business transaction that should be protected. Although the parties executed the agreement after the employee had already performed a majority of the services, the parties had executed the agreement before the date on which the loan payment was due or, in fact, was definitely ascertainable. In *Veit v. Comm'r*,[32] commonly referred to as *Veit II*, a revised deferral agreement was executed on December 26, 1941, only six days before the deferral payment was due, providing that the deferral payments subject to the prior agreement approved in *Veit I* would be further deferred over a five-year period. Thus, under *Veit II*, even if the

---

[26] *Young Door Co. v. Comm'r*, 40 TC 890, CCH Dec. 26,283 (1963).

[27] *See also Crimmins v. U.S.*, 81-2 USTC ¶9576, 655 F2d 135 (8th Cir. 1981): *Schniers v. Comm'r*, 69 TC 511, CCH Dec. 34,800 (1977); *Snider's Estate*, 31 TC 1064, CCH Dec. 23,475 (1959).

[28] *Martin v. Comm'r*, 96 TC 814, 823, CCH Dec. 47,414 (1991).

[29] *See also Palmer v. Comm'r*, 80 TCM 101, CCH Dec. 53,968(M), 2000 TC Memo. 2000-228; *Ross v. Comm'r*, 48-2 USTC ¶9341, 169 F2d. 483, 490 (1st Cir. 1948); *Martin v. Comm'r*, 96 TC 814, 823, CCH Dec.

47,414 (1991); *Amend v. Comm'r*, 13 TC 178, 185, CCH Dec. 17,122 (1949); *Lehruth v. Comm'r*, T.C. Summary Opinion 2001-190.

[30] *Richard A. Childs v. Comm'r*, 103 TC 634, CCH Dec. 50,239 (1994).

[31] *Veit v. Comm'r*, 8 TC 809, CCH Dec. 15,718 (1947), Acq. 1947-2 CB 4, ("Veit I"). *See also Kimbell v. Comm'r*, 41 B.T.A. 940, CCH Dec. 11,077 (1940); *Palmer v. Comm'r*, 80 TCM 101, TC Memo. 2000-228, CCH Dec. 53,968(M) (2000).

[32] *Veit v. Comm'r*, 8 TCM 919 (1949), CCH Dec. 17,240(M).

amounts to be deferred are clearly ascertainable on the date on which the deferral agreement is effective, there will be no constructive receipt of income. So long as the taxpayer could not withdraw the funds or otherwise exercise control over them, the fact that the amount of the bonus was ascertainable is immaterial. Similarly, in *Oates v. Comm'r*,[33] an agent entered into a new agreement with an insurance employer several days before retirement. The new arrangement provided that the agent would receive his renewal commissions over a certain number of years, while the original agreement had provided for payments as the premiums came due. Relying on *Veit*, the Tax Court determined that the parties entered into the agreement before the payments were due, and refused to impose constructive receipt.

In like manner, in *Goldsmith v. U.S.*,[34] the Court of Claims ruled that the taxpayer did not constructively receive income deferred under an agreement merely representing an unfunded, unsecured promise to pay on behalf of the employer. Further, it was immaterial that the deferral payment was made after the original salary payments were fixed by an earlier employment agreement. According to the court, the parties may amend existing employment agreements to defer the payment date so long as they make the amendment before the taxpayer may receive the deferred amounts. In summary, the Tax Court seems clearly to accept the rationale that a cash basis taxpayer can effectively defer income if he makes an agreement to defer before the time the income is due for payment if the agreement is real and not a tax avoidance scheme.

It is true that "income that is subject to a person's unfettered command and that he is free to enjoy at his own option may be taxed to him as his income, whether he sees fit to enjoy it or not."[35] Similarly, "a taxpayer may not deliberately turn his back upon income and thus select the year for which he will report it."[36] However, cases such as *Zeltzerman* and *Willits* may be distinguished by careful structuring. In *Zeltzerman v. Comm'r*, the Tax Court held that the taxpayer constructively received income since no binding agreement existed between him and his employer limiting or restricting the taxpayer's right to receive or request immediate payment of his current salary. In *Zeltzerman* the taxpayer had requested that his employer purchase an annuity contract on his behalf in lieu of paying him his current salary. In substance, the court ruled that the employer merely acted as an agent of the taxpayer in purchasing the annuity contract. According to the Tax Court, the effect was the same as if the taxpayer had received his salary and bought the annuities himself. In *Willits v. Comm'r*, the Tax Court held that a trustee of a terminating trust constructively received the trustee's commissions he sought to defer since the sole reason for the deferral was the avoidance of tax. The Tax Court emphasized, however, that the commission income had already been earned and, in fact, paid by the trust prior to the

---

[33] *Oates v. Comm'r*, 18 TC 570, CCH Dec. 19,049 (1952), *Aff'd* 207 F2d 711 (7th Cir. 1953).

[34] *Goldsmith v. U.S.*, 78-2 USTC ¶9804, 586 F2d 810 (Ct. Cl 1978).

[35] *Zeltzerman v. Comm'r*, 34 TC 73, 85, CCH Dec. 24,139 (1960), *Aff'd per curiam* 283 F2d 514 (1st Cir.

1960), cited in *Charles S. Nicholson v. Comm'r*, 65 TCM 2478, CCH Dec. 49,007(M) (1993).

[36] *Willits v. Comm'r*, 50 TC 602, 612, CCH Dec. 29,059 (1968), cited in *Jay H. Kelley v. Comm'r*, 62 TCM 136, CCH Dec. 47,471(M) (1991).

execution of the deferral agreement. Moreover, the deferral of receipt was pursuant to an arrangement with the other trustees, not the obligor trust and, thus, was wholly unrelated to any contractual agreement with the trust.

In this respect, the courts recognize that the determination whether the constructive receipt doctrine applies is a factual one, and one of these factors is the ability of a taxpayer to manipulate the system.[37] Those cases in which the constructive receipt doctrine is invoked often involve a taxpayer who was a significant shareholder, partner or other insider.[38] Similarly, in a footnote in *Martin*, the court explained:

> For example, it might be appropriate to consider whether any participant had any ownership interest or control over the corporate entity and its Shadow Stock Plan. If some form of ownership or control existed, it might be appropriate to more closely scrutinize the terms and arrangements of the plan.

The leading recent case in the constructive receipt area, which involved the application of the constructive receipt doctrine to a nonqualified plan, is *Martin v. Comm'r*.[39] In *Martin*, the corporation had instituted a nonqualified deferred compensation plan, allowing key management employees to receive profit sharing units representing shares of the corporation's common stock. Under this plan, upon termination of employment, each employee's benefits would be payable in ten equal annual installments.

In May 1981, the corporation changed its plan to a "shadow" (or "phantom") stock plan. Under the new plan, the corporation would pay an employee a single sum upon termination unless the employees elected to receive payment in annual installments. If the employee were to choose the annual installment option, interest would accrue on the unpaid balance. After an employee chose either to receive his benefits in one lump sum or equal installments, the plan's administrative rules dictated that the employee could not then change the mode of payment unless the change was requested at least one year in advance, up until termination or retirement. Both taxpayers in *Martin* chose, in 1981, to receive payments in ten equal annual installments. That same year each taxpayer's employment with the corporation was terminated.

The IRS asserted a deficiency against the taxpayers, claiming that both had constructively received all of their benefits under the plan in the year employment was terminated. The IRS maintained that application of the constructive receipt doctrine was appropriate because both taxpayers had the right to receive payment in a single lump sum, and had demonstrated their unfettered control over receipt of the benefits by choosing to defer the benefits over a ten-year period. The Tax Court disagreed, holding that the taxpayers' election to take the benefits in ten annual installments did not warrant application of the constructive receipt doctrine.

---

[37] *Palmer v. Comm'r*, 80 TCM 101, TC Memo. 2000-228, CCH Dec. 53,968(M) (2000); *Martin v. Comm'r*, 96 TC 814, 823, CCH Dec. 47,414 (1991).

[38] *See, e.g., Brander v. Comm'r*, 3 BTA 231, CCH Dec. 1095 (1925) (taxpayer was president and owner); *Cooney v. Comm'r*, 18 TC 883, CCH Dec. 19,154 (1952) (sole stockholders); *Benes v. Comm'r*, 42 TC 358, CCH Dec. 26,794 (1964) (sole owner and company president); *Congleton v. Comm'r*, 38 TCM 584, CCH Dec. 35,990(M) (1979).

[39] *Martin v. Comm'r*, 96 TC 814, 823, CCH Dec. 47,414 (1991).

In addressing the problem of constructive receipt in the context of nonqualified deferred compensation plans, the Tax Court used a five-factor test based upon regulations and case law. The factors are:

1. whether the participant's right to receive income is subject to substantial limitations or restrictions;

2. whether the plan is funded;

3. whether the participant's rights under, and interest in, the plan is secured;

4. whether the election can only be made before the amounts became due and/or ascertainable; and

5. whether interest was payable on installment payments and when interest, if any, accrued.

In theory, a plan provision that allowed an employer to decide, in its own discretion, the time or form of payment would be a substantial restriction on an employee's right to receive payments, but the IRS will not issue a favorable ruling regarding such a provision because the employer would be free to exercise its discretion consistently in accordance with the wishes of the employee.[40]

Usually the deferral period is for a number of years but occasionally taxpayers will attempt to defer the receipt of income only until the next year. This issue arose in 1987, with the reduction in tax rates pursuant to the Tax Reform Act of 1986. In response, the IRS issued Announcement 87-38, which stated that short-term deferrals of 1986 income would be closely scrutinized in order to determine if it was constructively received in 1986. The IRS stated that a deferral agreement would be disregarded and the amounts thereunder constructively received unless (1) the deferral was pursuant to an arm's-length agreement that had a business purpose, or (2) the taxpayer's right to receive the income was subject to substantial limitations. With respect to the *bona fides* of the arrangement, the IRS indicated that an arrangement may not pass muster if the employer makes alternate funds available to the employee, either through direct loans or loans under tax-qualified plans. The IRS also indicated that the period of deferral was an important factor in determining whether there is a substantial limitation on a taxpayer's right to receive income, with a deferral of number of months to take advantage of a lower tax rate not constituting a substantial limitation on a taxpayer. Consequently, the minimum permissible period of deferral would appear to be two years.[41]

---

[40] In IRS Letter Ruling 8326151 (March 31, 1983), the IRS ruled that restricted stock would be subject to a substantial limitation despite provisions allowing early retirement without forfeiture if the consent of the employer was obtained. In the facts of that ruling, however, the consent would be given only if retirement was not detrimental to the employer, and in fact, the employer had denied distribution to certain employees. Under those facts, the IRS could not maintain the position that the employer was merely rubberstamping the participant's request for a distribution, so that the theoretical restriction of obtaining employer consent was illusory.

[41] *See* IRS Letter Ruling 9211037 (Dec. 17, 1991); Reg. § 1.83-3(c)(4), example 1.

.05 Economic Benefit Doctrine

The "economic benefit doctrine" is related to, but conceptually distinct from, the constructive receipt doctrine. It identifies when income has actually been received other than by direct cash payment. A leading case in the area is *Cowden v. Comm'r*,[42] in which the court set forth the following summary of the doctrine:

> We are convinced that if a promise to pay of a solvent obligor is unconditional and assignable, not subject to set-offs, and is of a kind that is frequently transferred to lenders or investors at a discount not substantially greater than the generally prevailing premium for the use of money, such promise is the equivalent of cash and taxable in like manner as cash would have been taxable had it been received by the taxpayer rather than the obligator.

The economic benefit issue arises in programs under which individuals, particularly directors, are allowed to direct the companies with whom they are affiliated to make charitable contributions on their behalf. The IRS and the courts have concluded that the economic benefit is inapplicable in the context, because the "satisfaction of one's charitable intentions" is not "a benefit equivalent to the realization of taxable income."[43] In a leading case, *Goldsmith v. U.S.*,[44] the Court of Claims held that the employer's promise to provide death, disability, and accidental death and dismemberment benefits to an employee under a nonqualified deferred compensation plan conferred a present economic benefit upon the employee equal to the cost of commercial coverage offered by a commercial insurer.

The economic benefit doctrine was substantially codified in 1969 with the addition of Code Sec. 83 and Code Sec. 402(b). With respect to contributions to a nonexempt trust,[45] they are includible in gross income of the employee in accordance with Code Sec. 83, which section addresses the transfer of property in connection with the performance of services, except that the value of the employee's interest in the trust is substituted for the fair market value of the property. With respect to distributions, the participant will include them in income in the taxable year under Code Sec. 72.[46] However, both of these rules are subject to an exception which in most instances will supplant these general rules, *i.e.*, if one of the reasons that a plan is not exempt under Code Sec. 401(a) is the failure to satisfy the minimum participation requirements of Code Sec. 401(a)(26)[47] or the minimum coverage rules of Code Sec. 410(b),[48] then, in lieu of

---

[42] *Cowden v. Comm'r*, 61-1 USTC ¶9382, 289 F2d 20 (5th Cir. 1961).

[43] GCM 37282, Sept. 30, 1977; *See also* Rev. Rul. 67-137, 1967-1 CB 63; Rev. Rul. 79-9, 1979-1 CB 125; IRS Letter Ruling 8211127 (Dec. 22, 1981); *Knott v. Comm'r*, 67 TC 681, CCH Dec. 34,219 (1977).

[44] *Goldsmith v. U.S.*, 78-2 USTC ¶9804, 586 F2d 810 (1978).

[45] Code Sec. 402(b)(1).

[46] Code Sec. 402(b)(2).

[47] Code Sec. 401(a)(26) applies only to defined benefit pension plans. It requires that a plan benefit the lesser of (i) 50 employees of the employer (determined on a controlled group basis) or (ii) the greater

of 40 percent of all employees of the employer or two employees (or if there is only one employee, such employee). This section can be applied on a separate line of business basis under Code Sec. 414(r), but that rule will rarely be applicable in the context of nonqualified plans.

[48] To satisfy the minimum coverage tests of Code Sec. 410(b), a plan must satisfy either the ratio percentage test or the average benefit percentage test. The ratio percentage test requires that the percentage of nonhighly compensated employees benefiting under the plan is at least 70 percent of the percentage or highly compensated employees benefiting under the plan. The average benefit percentage test requires the plan to benefit employees

the rules described above, a highly compensated employee[49] includes in income an amount equal to the vested accrued benefit of such employee as of the close of the trust's taxable year, other than the employee's investment in the contract under Code Sec. 72. When initially enacted, it was unclear whether Code Sec. 402(b)(2)(A) was intended to apply only to those plans that were intended to be tax-qualified plans but were subsequently disqualified, or also to nonqualified deferred compensation plans that were never intended to satisfy the minimum coverage and minimum participation requirements for tax-qualified plans. However, in a series of private letter rulings issued in 1992 to "secular trusts,"[50] the IRS indicated that it applied to arrangements that were never intended to be tax-qualified.

Under Code Sec. 83, a service provider who receives property is subject to taxation when the transferred property first becomes not subject to a substantial risk of forfeiture or is freely transferable.[51] For purposes of Code Sec. 83, property includes all real and personal property, other than either money or an unfunded and unsecured promise to pay money in the future. The term also includes a beneficial interest in assets (including money) that are transferred or set aside from the class of creditors of the transferor, *e.g.*, in a trust or escrow account.[52] Property is regarded as freely transferable if the person performing the services or receiving the property can sell, assign, or pledge his interest in the property to any person other than the transferor of such property and if the transferee is not required to give up the property in the event a substantial risk of forfeiture materializes.[53]

Whether a substantial risk of forfeiture has occurred depends upon the particular facts and circumstances. The most common illustration of a substantial risk of forfeiture is the conditioning of the transfer of property upon the future performance of service, but the regulations also recognize "the occurrence of a condition related to the purpose of the transfer," as may occur in an incentive arrangement. In either of the cases, the possibility of forfeiture in the event the condition is not satisfied must be substantial. A provision that an employee will forfeit the property transferred to him if he or she is terminated for cause or the commission of a crime will not constitute a substantial risk of forfeiture. Generally, a covenant not to compete will not be regarded as constituting a substantial risk of forfeiture unless the particular facts and circumstances indicate to the

---

(Footnote Continued)

qualifying as a reasonable, nondiscriminatory classification and the average benefit percentage for employees who are not highly compensated being at least 70 percent of the average benefit percentage for highly compensated employees.

[49] A highly compensated employee is an employee who was a 5% owner at any time during the year, or preceding year, or who had compensation from the employer in excess of $90,000 for the preceding year. Compensation has the same meaning as it does for purposes of Code Sec. 415(c)(3) and the employer may elect to make a top-paid group election, limiting the roster of highly compensated employees to the group consisting of the top 20 percent of employees (on a controlled group basis) when ranked on the basis of compensation during such year. Code Sec. 414(q).

[50] IRS Letter Ruling 9206009 (Nov. 11, 1991), IRS Letter Ruling 9212024 (Dec. 20, 1991), IRS Letter Ruling 9212019 (Dec. 20, 1991), and IRS Letter Ruling 9207010 (Nov. 12, 1991).

[51] Code Sec. 83(e).

[52] Reg. § 1.83-3(e).

[53] Reg. § 1.83-3(d). However, the designation of a beneficiary to receive the property upon the death of a service provider is not a transfer.

contrary. In a similar vein, rights in property transferred to a retiring employee subject to the sole requirement that it be returned unless he or she renders consulting services upon the request of the former employer will not be satisfactory unless he or she is in fact required to perform substantial services.

As was true in the constructive receipt context, close scrutiny is paid when the person to whom the property is transferred owns a significant amount of the total combined voting power or value of all classes of stock of the service recipient. The regulations cite the following factors as relevant:

- the employee's relationship to other stockholders and the extent of their control, potential control, and possible loss of control of the corporation;
- the position of the employee in the corporation and the extent to which he or she is subordinate to other employees;
- the employee's relationship to the officers and directors of the corporation;
- the person or persons who must approve the employee's discharge; and
- the past actions of the employer in enforcing the restrictions.[54]

The IRS Chief Counsel has expressed the view that even the option of getting paid by direct deposit may cause constructive receipt.[55] In general, the IRS considers an annuity payment to be gross income in the taxable year in which it is received, unless the taxpayer's method of accounting requires that he or she account for the payment in a different period.[56] Most individual taxpayers use the cash receipts and disbursements method of accounting. Under this method of accounting, taxpayers must generally include items of gross income in the year they actually or constructively received them.[57]

A taxpayer "constructively receives" income when a payer makes it available so that the taxpayer can draw upon it at any time, or so that the taxpayer could have drawn upon it during the taxable year if he or she had given notice of intention to withdraw.[58] However, income is not constructively received if the taxpayer's control of its receipt is subject to a substantial restriction or limitation. Generally, the IRS consider checks income to a cash method taxpayer in the year he or she receives them unless constructively received in an earlier year.[59] The fact that a check is issued in one year and received in another does not make the check taxable in the year issued.[60] Checks sent through the mail are typically taken into income in the year the taxpayer actually receives them, unless the amounts are made available to the taxpayer in the earlier year.[61] In other words, unless the taxpayer had access to or control over the check in the first year, no constructive receipt of the check occurred in the first year and the taxpayer

---

[54] Reg. § 1.83-3(c).

[55] Information Letter from the Office of Chief Counsel, Department of The Treasury, Internal Revenue Service. Number: INFO 2006-0005, January 30, 2006.

[56] Code Sec. 451(a).

[57] Treas. Reg. §§ 1.451-1 and 1.451-2.

[58] Treas. Reg. § 1.451-2(a).

[59] See *Lavery v. Commissioner*, 158 F.2d 859 (7th Cir. 1946).

[60] See *McEuen v. Commissioner*, 196 F.2d 127, 130 (5th Cir. 1952).

[61] See Avery v. Commissioner, 292 U.S. 210 (1934); Rev. Rul. 76-3, 1976-1 C.B. 114; Rev. Rul. 73-99, 1973-1 C.B. 412.

should recognize the income in the second year when he or she actually received the check. However, if a taxpayer has the option of receiving payments by direct deposit instead of by checks sent through the mail, there may be constructive receipt of a payment on the earlier date that the direct deposit would have been made, according to the IRS.

.06 State Taxation of Nonqualified Plan Benefits

Section 114 of Title 4 of the United States Code prohibits states from imposing an income tax on certain types of retirement income for nonresidents.[62] The types of pension covered by the Section 114 include payments from:

- A qualified trust under Code Sec. 401(a);
- A simplified employee pension plan as defined in Code Sec. 408(k);
- An annuity plan described in Code Sec. 403(a);
- An annuity plan described in Code Sec. 403(b);
- An individual retirement plan described in Code Sec. 7701(a)(37);
- An eligible deferred compensation plan as defined in Code Sec. 457;
- A governmental plan as defined in Code Sec. 414(d);
- Employee contribution trusts described in Code Sec. 501(c)(18); and
- A nonqualified plan described in Code Sec. 3121(v)(2)(C) if the payments are made (i) in a series of substantially equal periodic payments for a period of not less than 10 years, or (ii) after termination of employment under a plan maintained solely for the purpose of providing retirement benefits in excess of the limitations imposed by Code Secs. 401(a)(17), 401(k), 401(m), 402(g), 403(b), 408(k), or 415, including payments to a retired partner under a plan in effect immediately before retirement begins.

This statute became necessary when some of the more rapacious tax states attempted to tax the retirement benefits of anyone who had ever lived in the state. For example, Section 601(e) of the New York State Tax Law imposed a personal income tax on a nonresident's taxable income that is derived from New York sources. The prohibition on state income tax applies whenever the individual is a nonresident. For example, if the individual was a resident of New York when ten annual installment payments began, and moved to Florida after the first three payments were made, the next seven payments would not be subject to New York income tax.[63]

The most common nonqualified deferred compensation plans covered by Code Sec. 3121(v) include excess plans and deferred bonus plans. Generally, payments from Code Sec. 3121(v) plans are covered only if there are *substantially equal periodic payments made at least annually* for the recipient's life or life expec-

---

[62] Passed as Public Law 104-95.

[63] States may still tax payments to non-residents from other types of employment-related compensa-

tion plans not described in Code Sec. 3121(v), including, for example, stock options, stock appreciation rights, restricted stock, severance, sick leave, compensatory time and vacation pay.

tancy (or the joint lives or joint life expectancy of the recipient and the recipient's designated beneficiary), or for a period of at least 10 years. However, this periodic payment rule does not apply if the payments are made from a Sec. 3121(v) plan that is maintained solely to provide benefits in excess of the limitations under Internal Revenue Code Secs. 401(a)(17), 401(k), 401(m), 402(g), 403(b), 408(k) or 415. The law would cover lump sum payments from these types of excess plans. The exception to the periodic payment rule for Code Sec. 3121(v) plans apparently applies only to plans maintained **solely** to make up benefits limited by the listed Internal Revenue Code sections. Presumably a plan that is more than such an excess plan could be subject to the periodic payment rules. Employers may need to restructure or bifurcate their nonqualified plans to create "pure" excess plans that would be eligible for the periodic payment exception.

¶1735 FICA/Medicare Taxation of Nonqualified Plan Benefits

Before 1994, the maximum amount of an employee's annual earnings that were subject to the Medicare tax was $135,000. Beginning in 1994, the earnings cap was eliminated and employers and employees each became subject to an additional 1.45% tax on all earnings. This increase would have been burdensome enough if it only applied to cash compensation. However, the full Medicare tax on employers and employees also applies to amounts earned under a nonqualified retirement or deferred compensation plan.

Code Sec. 3121(v)(2)(A) provides that an employer must withhold Federal Insurance Contributions Act ("FICA") tax on behalf of an employee on any amount deferred under a "nonqualified deferred compensation plan." The amounts are taken into account as wages for FICA purposes when the services are performed or when there is no substantial risk of forfeiture of the amounts, whichever is later. The effect of this "special timing rule" is that the employer may be required to withhold FICA on certain benefit amounts *before* the benefits are payable under the plan. The nonduplication rule of Code Sec. 3121(v)(2)(B) prevents double taxation by providing that once an amount is taken into account as FICA wages, neither that amount, nor any income attributable to that amount, is treated as FICA wages.

> **Example 1:** Executive D defers $40,000 of her compensation into the nonqualified plan set up by ABC Corporation (to make up for the fact that D's 401(k) contributions will be limited by the Code Sec. 401(a)(17) compensation limit and/or the ADP test). ABC would owe Medicare taxes of $580.00 on that contribution, and Executive D would owe Medicare taxes of $580.00 on that contribution, which ABC would be required to withhold from D's other earnings. ABC would be required to forward the $1,160.00 to the Social Security Administration according to the regular withholding rules.

> When Executive D takes payment of that $40,000 in ten years' time, together with investment income on that amount, neither the original $40,000, nor the investment income will be then subject to FICA tax.

As a practical matter, the executives who participated in nonqualified deferred compensation plans invariably earned more than the Social Security wage base, so employers and counsel generally could assume that the maximum FICA tax would be paid on behalf of these executives, even without taking into account their nonqualified deferred compensation. However, since the repeal of the wage cap for the Medicare hospital insurance portion of FICA taxation,[64] every dollar of what would otherwise be FICA wages has been subject to the 2.9% Medicare tax.[65]

.01 Regulatory Guidance on FICA Taxation

Regulations under Code Sec. 3121(v)(2) describe exactly who must pay the tax, how it is to be paid, and when. The regulations repeat the general timing rule for treating amounts deferred under a nonqualified deferred compensation plan as "wages" for purposes of withholding and depositing FICA tax. The regulations clarify that if the employer fails to take into account any deferred amount that it should have taken into account under Code Sec. 3121(v), it may be subject to interest and penalties.[66] In addition, the nonduplication rule will not apply to any amount that the employer should have, but did not, take into account for FICA purposes. Thus, if the employer withholds later, it loses its best FICA minimizer, and must withhold from investment income on amounts deferred.[67]

Code Sec. 3121(v)(2) only applies to amounts deferred under a "nonqualified deferred compensation plan."[68] The regulations define a nonqualified deferred compensation plan as "any plan or other arrangement . . . that is established . . . by an employer for one or more of its employees, and that provides for the deferral of compensation."[69] Under applicable case law, even a one-person arrangement can be a "plan."[70] However, the regulations provide a list of several types of nonqualified plans that will *not* be considered to provide for the deferral of compensation under Code Sec. 3121(v)(2):

- *Certain Stock-Based Arrangements.* The grant of stock options, stock appreciation rights and other stock value rights is not subject to Code Sec. 3121(v)(2). Currently, FICA tax is not imposed on these stock arrangements until the time of exercise.

- *Restricted Property.* Property received by an employee from an employer does not necessarily provide for the deferral of compensation simply because the property is not includible in income under Code Sec. 83.

- *Welfare Benefits.* Generally, certain welfare benefits, including vacation benefits, sick leave, compensatory time, disability pay, severance pay and

---

[64] Omnibus Budget Reconciliation Act of 1993, Pub. L. 103-66, § 13207(a)(1).

[65] The tax rate of the Medicare hospital insurance portion of FICA tax is 1.45% for the employer and 1.45% for the employee. Therefore, taking into account both the employer and the employee's tax, the rate equals 2.9%.

[66] Reg. § 31.3121(v)(2)-1.

[67] If the employer withholds late, it is reporting late, too. This means the executive would have to pay more Medicare hospital insurance tax than he or she would have if the employer had taken the wages into account at the correct time.

[68] Reg. § 31.3121(v)(2)-1(b).

[69] Reg. § 31.3121(v)(2)-1(b)(1).

[70] *See, e.g., Williams v. Wright,* 927 F2d 1540 (11th Cir. 1991).

death benefits do not result from the deferral of compensation under Code Sec. 3121(v)(2), even if they constitute "wages" under Code Sec. 3121(a).

- *Benefits for Termination of Employment.* Benefits provided in connection with termination of employment do not provide for the deferral of compensation under Code Sec. 3121(v)(2). Benefits established after an employee's termination of employment, as well as certain benefits established within 12 months before an employee's termination of employment are considered termination pay and are not subject to the special timing rule of Code Sec. 3121(v)(2). This exception can be quite useful when an executive and an employer agree to part ways. However, cost-of-living adjustments to benefit payments under a nonqualified deferred compensation plan are not considered termination pay, even if the employee does not receive a legally binding right to receive the adjustments until after termination of employment.

.02 "Amount Deferred"

Once the employer has determined that it is maintaining a plan subject to Code Sec. 3121(v)(2), it must withhold Medicare hospital insurance tax from, and report as Medicare wages, the "amount deferred." Determining the amount deferred depends first on whether the plan is an account balance plan or a nonaccount balance plan. An account balance plan is a nonqualified deferred compensation plan under which a principal amount is credited to an individual account for an employee, income on that amount is credited or debited to the account, and benefits payable are based solely on the account balance—in other words, a defined contribution plan.[71] For purposes of Code Sec. 3121(v)(2), the amount deferred under an account balance plan generally is based on the amount of principal credited to the account.[72] If benefits are provided to an employee under a nonaccount balance plan (*i.e.*, a defined benefit plan), the amount deferred equals the present value of the additional future payment or payments to which the employee has obtained a legally binding right during that period—the executive's accrual for the period.[73]

Deferred amounts should be taken into account as they are allocated to the employee's account.[74] In an account balance plan, it should be easy to comply with this rule. If the executive actually makes compensation deferrals, the deferrals can be treated as FICA compensation each payroll period. If the employer makes a matching contribution once a year, or in a nonaccount balance plan under which accruals may be calculated no more than once a year, the regulations allow the employer to treat all amounts deferred on behalf of an employee as paid on the last day of the calendar year. However, if the employer

---

[71] Reg. §31.3121(v)(2)-1(c)(1)(ii).

[72] Reg. §31.3121(v)(2)-1(c)(1)(i). Plans that provide optional forms of benefit may be treated as account balance plans if under the plan, at the time the amount is deferred, the alternative forms of payment will be actuarially equivalent to the ac-

count balance based on an interest rate that will be "reasonable" at the time the optional form is elected. Reg. §31.3121(v)(2)-1(c)(1)(iii)(C).

[73] Reg. §31.3121(v)(2)-1(c)(2).

[74] Reg. §31.3121(v)(2)-1(d).

takes advantage of this rule of administrative convenience, it must also take into account any income attributable to the amounts deferred as of the date on which the amounts are taken into account. Any income on the amounts after the calendar year would escape FICA taxation and withholding.[75]

.03 Income and Reasonable Rate of Interest

As is mentioned in ¶1735.02, the "income" on amounts deferred escapes FICA taxation. For this reason, the final regulations place a limit on the amount of income that may be credited to amounts deferred. If an account balance plan credits income based on a reasonable rate of interest, or a rate of return that does not exceed the rate of return on a predetermined actual investment specified under the plan, FICA tax will not be imposed on that income.[76] A predetermined actual investment may be used as the basis for the rate of return under this section regardless of whether any assets set aside by the employer to pay plan benefits are actually invested in the investment, and regardless of whether the investment is generally available to the public.[77]

If income credited under an account balance plan is not based on the rate of return of a predetermined actual investment, the employer must determine whether the interest rate is reasonable, both at the time the amount deferred is required to be taken into account as FICA wages, and annually thereafter. However, if a fixed rate of interest is specified for a period not to exceed five years, and the rate was reasonable when determined, it will be considered reasonable, even if during the fixed period it becomes unreasonable.[78] If account balance plan income is based neither on a predetermined actual investment under the plan, nor on a reasonable interest rate, any income credited in excess of the mid-term applicable federal rate ("AFR") must be taken into account as an additional amount deferred in the year the income is credited.[79]

In a nonaccount balance plan, the assumptions used to discount a future payment or payment stream to present value are the notional equivalent of income under an account balance plan. For this reason, the regulations require "reasonable" actuarial assumptions and methods. The regulations specifically state that present value cannot be determined by discounting for the special risks associated with most nonqualified deferred compensation plans, including the risks posed by the unfunded nature of the plan.[80]

.04 Timing of Inclusion

The amount determined to be deferred under a nonqualified deferred compensation plan must be taken into account as of the later of the date the services creating the right to the amount deferred are performed, or the date on which the right to the amount deferred is no longer subject to a substantial risk of forfeiture.[81] Under an account balance plan, this typically means deferrals are taken

---

[75] Reg. § 31.3121(v)(2)-1(d)(1).

[76] Reg. § 31.3121(v)(2)-1(d)(2)(i)(A).

[77] Reg. § 31.3121(v)(2)-1(d)(2)(i)(B).

[78] Reg. § 31.3121(v)(2)-1(d)(2)(i)(C)(2).

[79] Reg. § 31.3121(v)(2)-1(d)(2)(iii)(A).

[80] Reg. § 31.3121(v)(2)-1(c)(2)(ii).

[81] Reg. § 31.3121(v)(2)-1(e)(1).

into account each payroll period as they are directed into the plan. Other types of contributions will typically be taken into account as of the end of the year, with any income credited to them during the year. If the contributions are not vested, the employer will wait until the contributions vest (fully or partially) and include investment income on the contributions through the date they are taken into account.

A special rule for nonaccount balance plans permits the employer to delay taking the amounts deferred into account for FICA purposes until the amount is "reasonably ascertainable."[82] An amount deferred under a nonaccount balance plan is not "reasonably ascertainable" as long as it is necessary to use any assumptions other than interest, mortality, and cost-of-living assumptions to value the benefit. In practice, this means a defined benefit excess plan often provides a benefit that does not need to be taken into account until the employee retires. These plans typically require assumptions about when the executive will retire, what his or her final pay will be, and so forth.[83] The employer may, however, at its option, include these amounts at an earlier date, with a true-up at the date when the amount deferred becomes reasonably ascertainable.[84]

.05 Withholding Rules

An employer may choose to use one of two alternative methods—the "estimated method" or the "lag method"—for purposes of withholding and depositing FICA tax.[85] The estimated method is a way to treat amounts deferred as FICA wages early. It requires the employer to make a reasonable estimate of the amount deferred on the date on which the amount is taken into account, and consider that estimated amount as wages for FICA tax purposes.[86] If the employer underestimates the amount deferred, the employer may treat the shortfall as wages paid as of the estimate date, or any date not later than three months after the estimate date.[87] If the employer overestimates the amount deferred, the employer may claim a refund or credit.[88] An employer might choose to use the estimated method if benefits data for employees is readily available in the current year. In addition, it may be less of an administrative burden on an employer to process the tax withholding on behalf of employees in the current year.

Under the lag method, the employer may treat an amount deferred, plus income on that amount, as wages paid by the employer and received by the employee, on any date that is not later than three months after the date the amount is required to be taken into account.[89] The amount deferred must be increased by income through the date on which the wages are treated as paid, at

---

[82] Reg. § 31.3121(v)(2)-1(e)(4)(i).

[83] Reg. § 31.3121(v)(2)-1(e)(7), Examples 4 through 7.

[84] Reg. § 31.3121(v)(2)-1(e)(4)(ii). The true-up is equal to the present value of the difference in benefits, taken into account as of the date on which the amount deferred becomes reasonably ascertainable.

[85] Reg. § 31.3121(v)(2)-1(f)(1). The employer is *not*, however, required to use the same method for different employees or amounts deferred.

[86] Reg. § 31.3121(v)(2)-1(f)(2)(i).

[87] Reg. § 31.3121(v)(2)-1(f)(2)(ii).

[88] Reg. § 31.3121(v)(2)-1(f)(2)(iii).

[89] Reg. § 31.3121(v)(2)-1(f)(3).

a fixed rate that is not less than the AFR.[90] An employer might choose to use the lag method if it would not have the data necessary to determine the amount deferred until the first quarter of the year after it is otherwise required to be taken into account.

.06 Defined Benefit Excess Plan

Under a nonaccount balance, or defined benefit type plan, the employer must take into account each year for FICA purposes the present value of each year's accrual, to the extent vested. In addition, if all or a portion of the benefit vests in a particular year, the employer must take into account the present value of the amount that vests during that year for FICA purposes, even if the benefit was accrued in a previous year.

> **Example 2:** ABC Corporation maintains a nonqualified defined benefit excess plan for its eligible employees that mirrors its qualified defined benefit plan. Both the qualified plan and the nonqualified plan have five-year cliff vesting schedules. Assume that Executive D's benefits vest in 2018. For 2018, the present value of D's benefit will be subject to withholding and depositing of FICA tax. In 2019, only the present value of D's additional accrual, if any, during 2019 will be subject to FICA tax.

In this example, ABC has three choices regarding withholding and depositing of FICA tax on behalf of D for 2019:

1. Treat the year's accrual as accruing ratably each pay period and withhold and report each pay period a portion of its estimate of what the year's accrual will be.

2. Take the full year's accrual into account as of the end of 2019 (or, if the calculation will not be finished until early 2020, ABC could use the lag method to take 2019's accrual into account).

3. Treat the benefit as "not reasonably ascertainable" under Reg. § 31.3121(v)(2)-(1)(e)(4), and withhold and deposit tax on the benefit only when D actually retires. ABC might take this last approach, for instance, if the plan is a final average pay plan. Under such a plan, the benefit would not be reasonably ascertainable because ABC would have to make an assumption about D's future pay.

Although the third approach is attractive from an administrative viewpoint, it could result in considerably more FICA tax being paid. The total increase in the benefit over time would be subject to FICA tax, and the tax may be required to be withheld and deposited at a time when the employee may not have other compensation that reaches the OASDI wage limit (*i.e.*, post-retirement). Therefore, the benefit might end up being subject to both the Social Security and Medicare hospital insurance portions of FICA, resulting in a much higher tax.

---

[90] Reg. § 31.3121(v)(2)-1(f)(3).

.07 Defined Contribution Excess Plan

Under the typical account balance nonqualified deferred compensation type of plan, it is easy to take the executive's deferrals into account for FICA tax purposes. The employer simply considers the deferrals to be wages for FICA purposes as they are deferred, the same way the employer counts salary deferrals under the underlying qualified plan.

With respect to the employer match under the nonqualified plan, the employer could consider the matching contribution amount as FICA wages either: (1) for each payroll period, or (2) only at the end of the calendar year. Under the year-end alternative, the employer would consider as FICA wages the full amount of match allocated during the calendar year, plus any income (but not less any losses). If the year-end plan accounting is not finished in time to include accurate numbers in the final payroll run for the year, an employer can either estimate the amount, and true it up when the year-end accounting has been completed, or use the lag method described in ¶ 1735.05.

If the nonqualified plan includes an employer contribution other than the match and salary deferrals (i.e., an employer "profit sharing," "discretionary," or "nondiscretionary" contribution), the FICA tax withholding options are essentially the same as those for matching contributions, except that nearly all employers use the year-end or the lag method.

¶1740 Application of ERISA

ERISA applies to employee benefit plans,[91] which may be one of two types—an employee welfare benefit plan[92] or an employee pension benefit plan,[93] the latter of which is the subject of this chapter. A pension benefit plan, by its express terms or as a result of surrounding circumstances, either (1) provides retirement income to employees, or (2) results in a deferral of income by employees for periods extending to the termination of covered employment or beyond, without regard to the method of calculating the contributions made to the plan, the method of calculating the benefits under the plan or the method of distributing benefits from the plan.

.01 Not an ERISA Pension Plan

Congress recognized that certain termination payments, e.g., severance payments, could be characterized as either pension payments or welfare payments, and gave the Secretary of Labor authority to promulgate regulations addressing the issue.[94] In this regard, the DOL has issued regulations establishing a safe harbor for when a severance plan will not be treated as an ERISA pension plan.[95] The three conditions are:

---

[91] ERISA Section 3(3).

[92] ERISA Section 3(1).

[93] ERISA Section 3(2). In addition, to the extent that a pension plan provides for disability benefits, it may be a separate employee welfare benefit plan.

Romlach v. Nestle, USA Inc., 211 F3d 190 (2d Cir. 2000).

[94] ERISA Section 3(2)(B).

[95] 29 C.F.R. § 2510.3-2(b).

1. Payments under the plan are not contingent directly or indirectly upon the employee's retiring;

2. The total amount of severance payments does not exceed twice the employee's annual compensation during the plan year immediately preceding termination of service; and

3. All payments to the employee are completed either (a) in the case of a termination of employment in connection with a "limited program of termination," within the later of 24 months after the termination of the employee's service or 24 months after the employee attains normal retirement age, or (b) in the case of all other employees, within 24 months after termination of the employee's service.

.02 ERISA Pension Plan

Nearly all nonqualified retirement and deferred compensation plans expressly provide retirement income to employees, or result in a deferral of income by employees for periods extending to the termination of covered employment or beyond, and thus are "pension benefit plans" under ERISA. Some bonus and incentive plans by their surrounding circumstances result in a deferral of income to the termination of employment or beyond, and thus become "pension benefit plans" under ERISA also.

In general, any pension benefit plan that is subject to ERISA must comply with the following requirements:

- reporting and disclosure under Part 1 of Title I of ERISA;

- participation and vesting under Part 2 of Title I;

- minimum funding under Part 3 of Title I;

- fiduciary responsibilities under Part 4 of Title I; and

- civil and criminal enforcement under Part 5 of Title I.

Because nonqualified plans are not designed to comply with any of ERISA's requirements, it is imperative that the nonqualified plan fit within either the "top-hat plan"[96] or "excess benefit plan" exemptions under ERISA. Both exemptions apply to the participation, vesting, minimum funding and benefit accruals,[97] as well as the fiduciary requirements of ERISA.[98] While top-hat plans are

---

[96] ERISA Section 201(2), 301(3), and 401(a)(1).

[97] See DOL Advisory Opinion 85-24A (top-hat plans remain subject to the reporting and disclosure requirements of Part 1 of Title I of ERISA and the enforcement provisions of Part 5 of Title I which would include the DOL claims procedures); See FAQ 12; Reliable Home Health Care, Inc. v. Union Central INS. Co., 295 F3d 505 (5th Cir. 2002); Barrowclough v. Kidder, Peabody, 752 F2d 923 (3d Cir. 1985). The rationale for the exclusion of top-hat plans from many of the requirements of ERISA is the Congressional view that highly compensated executives did not need the same level of protection as the average employee. See Fasco Industries, Inc. v. Mach, 843

F.Supp. 1252 (N.D. Ill. 1994); Cafaro v. PPG Industries, Inc., 203 F.3d 816 (3d Cir. 1999).

[98] See E.L. Carlyle, Debtor, 242 B.R. 881 (E.D. Va. 1999), holding that an employer has no fiduciary obligation to make a payment to an employee under a top-hat plan; Campbell v. Computer Task Group, Inc., 2001 U.S. Dist. LEXIS 9960 (S.D.N.Y. 2001) (indicating that top-hat plans are clearly exempt from the fiduciary obligations of Title I.) Also while of limited interest for our purposes, because they are not subject to ERISA's fiduciary requirements, "top-hat agreements can be partially or exclusively oral." Senior Exec. Benefit Plan Participants v. New Valley Corp., 89 F3d 143 (3d Cir. 1996); but cf Hein v.

not exempt from ERISA's reporting and disclosure requirements, these require-ments are satisfied by a simplified one-time filing.[99]

ERISA describes two types of nonqualified plans: "excess benefit plans" and "top-hat plans." ERISA Section 3(36) defines "excess benefit plan" as:

> a plan maintained by an employer solely for the purpose of providing benefits for certain employees in excess of the limitations on contributions and benefits imposed by section 415 of the Internal Revenue Code . . . .

ERISA Regulations § 2530.104-25 describes a "top-hat plan" as an unfunded plan that is "primarily for the purpose of providing deferred compensation to a select group of management or highly compensated employees." Practitioners also use labels such as Supplemental Executive Retirement Plan or "SERP," Floor SERP, Deferral Compensation Plan, Mirror Plan, and Salary Continuation Plan to describe various types of nonqualified plans.

ERISA contains a separate exception for "bonus" plans:

> **2510.3-2(c)** *Bonus program.* For purposes of title I of the Act and this chapter, the terms "employee pension benefit plan" and "pension plan" shall not include payments made by an employer to some or all of its employees as bonuses for work performed, *unless such payments are systematically deferred to the termination of covered employment or beyond,* or so as to provide retirement income to employees. [Emphasis added]

Regulations under ERISA provide that an incentive plan generally will be considered a "bonus program" under regulations and exempt from ERISA if it does not expressly condition payment upon termination of employment or retirement, and it does not in fact result in the systematic distribution of bonus payments upon termination or retirement. Whether an arrangement gives rise to the "systematic" deferral of payment to termination or beyond depends on the facts and circumstances of the arrangement. Some of the relevant circumstances for the determination are:

- Whether arrangement's design results in a high percentage of bonus payouts being made at or near recipients' retirement age;

- Whether the employer communicates the plan to employees as an ar-rangement intended to provide retirement or deferred income;

- Whether the arrangement allows for payments of unvested amounts upon employment termination;

- The length of the payout period; and

- Whether the bonus payments, by operation of the plan, are made to another type of retirement account such as an IRA.

(Footnote Continued)

Techamerica Group, Inc., 17 F3d 1278 (10th Cir. 1994) (suggesting that a top-hat plan must be written).

[99] ERISA Regulation § 2530.104-23. However, ab-sent compliance with the short form notice, a top-hat plan is subject to all of ERISA's reporting and disclosure requirements.

.03 Top-Hat Plans

Even though the top-hat definition has been included in ERISA without modification since its enactment, the DOL provided little guidance.[100] DOL Adv. Op. Ltr. 90-14A stated that the term "primarily" as under in the definition of top-hat plan in the ERISA regulations, "refers to the purpose of the plan and not the participant composition of the plan." Consequently, some cases have found that a top-hat plan could include some employees outside of the top-hat group.

Unfunded. In the view of the DOL, any determination of the "unfunded" status of an excess benefit plan or top-hat plan requires an examination of the surrounding facts and circumstances, including the status of the plan under non-ERISA law. Further, in the DOL's view, great weight should be given to the tax consequences of such arrangement.[101] That opinion was cited with approval by the Court of Appeals for the Fifth Circuit, which indicated that a court should also identify whether a policy was funded by a res separate from the general assets of the employer. In that case, the court concluded that an arrangement informally funded by an insurance policy was unfunded because:

- the participant did not own the policy;
- the participant's only right under the policy was the right to designate beneficiaries;
- the participant did not contribute to the plan; and
- the participant did not incur any tax liability in connection with the employer's payment of premiums because of a tax gross-up provision.[102]

With respect to securing the employer's promise to pay through the purchase of life insurance by the employer, the DOL has indicated[103] that the arrangement will be considered unfunded if the following criteria are satisfied:

- the insurance proceeds are payable to the employer, as named beneficiary;
- the employer has all of the rights of ownership under the policies, which would be subject to the claims of the employer's creditors;
- neither the plan nor any participant or beneficiary have any preferred claims against the policies or any beneficial ownership interest in such policies;
- there is no representation to any participant or beneficiary that the policies will be used only to provide plan benefits, or that they in any way represent security for the payment of benefits;

---

[100] The DOL opened a top-hat plan regulation project in early 1989, but was withdrawn in April 1992. *Barrowclough v. Kidder, Peabody*, 752 F2d 923 (3d Cir. 1985).

[101] DOL Advisory Opinion 92-13A. *See also Miller v. Heller*, 915 F.Supp. 651, 659 (S.D.N.Y. 1996), indicating that a plan is more likely than not to be regarded as unfunded if the beneficiaries do not incur tax liability during the year that contributions to the plan are made.

[102] *Reliable Home Health Care, Inc. v. Union Central Insurance Company*, 295 F3d 505 (5th Cir. 2002); see also *Demery v. Extebank Deferred Compensation Plan*, 216 F3d 283 (2d Cir. 2000).

[103] Opinion 81-11A.

- plan beneficiaries are not limited or governed in any way by the amount of insurance proceeds received by the employer; and
- the plan neither requires nor allows employee contributions.

There have been various verbal formulations of the unfunded requirement. One court stated that "an unfunded plan is one in which only the employer provides the necessary funding for the benefits,"[104] a second court stated that an unfunded plan is one in which "every dollar provided in benefits is a dollar spent by . . . the employer"[105] while a third stated that a plan is unfunded where benefits are paid "solely from the general assets of the employer."[106] In one troubling early ERISA case, which has not subsequently been cited, a district court indicated that if an employer makes arrangements of any kind to provide a particular source of funds for paying its deferred compensation obligations, then notwithstanding the general language about creditor's rights, a claim may be made that the arrangements do not reflect the real intentions of the parties and accordingly the plan is funded.[107]

In the proposed plan asset regulations in 1979, the Department of Labor took the position that (1) if the property in question was that of the employer sponsoring the plan and the employer represented to the plan participants or beneficiaries that the property will be used only to provide plan benefits, or (2) if the property constitutes an identified portion of less than the whole of the assets of the employer and which under the terms of the plan constitutes the sole source of contributions to such plan by such employer, the property is deemed a plan asset and the plan will therefore be considered to be funded. However, when the plan asset regulations were reproposed in 1985, the DOL specifically withdrew those portions of the 1979 proposal, which addressed the issue of when the sponsor's assets would be considered plan assets. In the preamble to the 1985 regulations, the DOL set forth a general proposition to the effect that in most instances plan fiduciaries should be able to identify plan assets based upon ordinary common law property rights and the terms of any contract to which the plan sponsor is a party.

Initially, there was a concern that the DOL regulations with respect to employee contributions[108] as plan assets had the effect of effectively eliminating the top-hat exemption. However, in a 1990 advisory opinion,[109] the DOL clarified that *bona fide* nonqualified deferred compensation plans were not ineligible for the top-hat plan exemption merely because they included voluntary compensation deferrals.

A concern with participant direction of investments is that the ability to direct investments could result in the plan being considered funded under ERISA, with adverse federal income tax consequences. One approach is to

---

[104] *Crumley v. Stonhard, Inc.*, 920 F.Supp. 589 (D.N.J. 1996).

[105] *Miller v. Eichleay Engineering*, 886 F2d 30, 33-34 (3d Cir. 1989).

[106] *Gallione v. Flaherty*, 70 F3d 724, 725 (2d Cir. 1995).

[107] *Butcher & Singer v. EP Johnson & EC Ernst, Inc.*, 1979 U.S. Dist. LEXIS 10973 (E.D. Pa. 1979).

[108] 29 C.F.R. § 2510.3-102.

[109] DOL Advisory Opinion 90-19A.

provide that the investment vehicle selected is merely a menu of rates of return that the participant may select, *i.e.*, a participant's benefit under the plan would be based upon the benefit selected, with the employer under no obligation to place the money in the designated fund.

While it is clear that an employer secular trust could be a funded arrangement for purposes of Title I of ERISA, the result is less clear if the grantor is the employee or the employee is regarded as the grantor (see ¶1765 for more information on secular trusts). The better result would appear to be that such a trust is outside of Title I of ERISA. ERISA Sec. 4(a) provides that Title I of ERISA applies only to employee benefit plans established or maintained by an employer, an employee organization, or both, and a beneficiary of a secular trust would be neither.

Primarily. The DOL has defined "primarily" to modify the types of benefits that can be provided and not to modify the classification of employees. Thus, according to the DOL, an employer can provide certain nonretirement benefits in a top-hat plan but cannot include employees who are not part of a "select group of management or highly compensated employees." While not all courts have followed the position of the DOL in this area,[110] those cases have not focused on the issue of the degree of deference (if any) that should be paid to an advisory opinion of the DOL.

> **Planning Note:** In the absence of a bright line test for a top-hat employee, it is important that the plan document address this contingency. One approach is establishing two tiers of top-hat plans, one for those individuals who under any reasonable definition would be treated as top-hat employees, and a second, smaller plan for marginal top-hat employees. In this manner, the risk of a tainted plan is minimized. Alternatively, the top-hat plan could contain an exit scenario in the event the DOL or a court were to determine that one or more of the participants did not constitute top-hat employees. The most conservative response would be to make a distribution to the affected employee, which in almost all instances will have adverse federal income tax consequences. A less onerous response would be to preclude any additional contributions to the plan by the affected employee, but allow the employee's benefits to remain in the plan. A third alternative would be a plan-to-plan transfer to a separate plan that substantially mirrors the top-hat plan but limits the length of deferral so that the plan would fall outside the scope of ERISA.

Employer. While ERISA contains a definition of "employer,"[111] it is not informative and does not include the controlled group rules of Title II of ERISA.[112] These sections apply for purposes of various sections of the Code[113] but not automatically to Title I of ERISA.[114] The issue that arises is whether an

---

[110] *See Demery v. Extebank Deferred Compensation Plan*, 216 F3d 283 (2d Cir. 2000).

[111] ERISA Section 3(5).

[112] Code Sec. 414(b), Code Sec. 414(c), Code Sec. 414(m), and Code Sec. 414(o).

[113] Code Sec. 414(a).

[114] Compare ERISA Section 3(40) (controlled group rules apply for purposes of determining the existence *vel non* of a MEWA) and ERISA Section 4001(a)(3)).

individual who would be a top-hat person at a subsidiary level is necessarily a top-hat person within the larger controlled group, particularly if the determination is made under the DOL test. There is no clear guidance on this issue.

Highly Compensated Employee. In the Code Sec. 414(q) regulations and the preamble thereto, the IRS set forth its understanding that the meaning for purposes of the Code is not determinative for purposes of Title I of ERISA, except when incorporated by reference, such as in ERISA Sec. 408(b)(1)(B).[115]

Select Group of Management or Highly Compensated Employees. Since the statutory language is disjunctive—management or highly compensated—it seems clear that an employee need be either highly compensated or management, not necessarily both, although clearly in many organizations the two categories overlap.

With respect to the meaning of "select," note the potentially troubling case of *Carrabba v. Randalls Food Market, Inc.*[116] In that case, after acknowledging it could not articulate the meaning of the phrase "select group," the court stated that all that it could do in this regard was to "express the conclusion that it cannot find from the evidence that the participant of the MSP was a select group out of the broader group of management employees or the broader group of highly compensated employees." Expressed somewhat differently, if a plan covered all of its management and highly compensated employees, the plan would not be a select group of management, *e.g.*, the determination whether a group is select is not made on the basis of the work force as a whole, but rather vis-à-vis management. While the case may be correctly decided on an alternative basis, this rationale appears aberrational.

The DOL has expressed the view that in providing top-hat plans relief from the broad remedial provisions of ERISA, Congress recognized that certain individuals by virtue of their position or compensation level have the ability to affect or substantially influence the negotiations of the design and operation of their deferred compensation plan, taking into consideration any attendant risks, and therefore are not in need of the protections of ERISA.[117] In contrast, courts have looked to the relationship between the employees covered under the arrange-

---

[115] Among the suggestions that have been made are (i) the Code Sec. 401(a)(17) limitations; (ii) the Code Sec. 415(b) dollar limitation; (iii) three times the FICA wage basis; and (iv) the top 2% of the most highly paid employees.

[116] *Carrabba v. Randalls Food Market, Inc.*, 38 F.Supp.2d 468 (N.D. Texas 1999), *aff'd* 252 F3d 721 (5th Cir. 2001).

[117] DOL Advisory Opinion 90-14A, 92-13A.

ment and the workforce as a whole.[118] Some courts have expressly acknowledged that both of these elements must be present.[119]

In performing this analysis, it is important to remember that a top-hat plan is not a third category of plan under ERISA. Therefore, even though a plan is restricted to executives, it does not necessarily follow that it is a top-hat plan.[120] Consequently, it was unnecessary to determine if an incentive plan would be a top-hat plan for ERISA purposes, because it was not an ERISA plan.[121] Similarly, stock option plans have consistently been held not to be ERISA pension plans.[122] Note that even if a stock option plan provides for a deferral feature so that an individual is not taxed when he or she exercises his or her deferral election under a stock option plan, this feature in and of itself probably does not cause the arrangement to be a deferred compensation plan for purposes of ERISA, unless it transforms the plan into one whose payments are systematically deferred to the termination of employment or whose purpose is to provide retirement income.[123]

.04 One-Person Plans

There is a divergence of views on the issue of whether one-person nonqualified deferred compensation arrangements are subject to ERISA. In a 1985 Information Letter, the DOL expressly stated that ERISA coverage is "not affected by the fact that the arrangement is limited to covering a single employee, is negotiated between the employer and the employee, or is not intended by the employer sponsor to be an employee benefit plan for purposes of ERISA coverage" and in a 1999 amicus brief stated the position that a contract between an employer and an employee could be an employee benefit plan under ERISA.[124]

---

[118] *Barrowclough v. Kidder, Peabody,* 752 F2d 923 (3d Cir. 1985) (plan covering executives earning more than $75,000 is a top-hat plan); *Loffland Bros. Co. v. C.A. Overstreet,* 758 P.2d 813 (Okla. 1988) (plan benefiting forty employees classified as executive and management personnel out of 4738 employees is a top-hat plan); *Pane v. RCA Corp.,* 868 F2d 631 (3d Cir. 1989) (61 management employees out of 80,000 employees was a top-hat plan); *Flandreau v. Signade Supply Co.,* 1990 US Dist. LEXIS 409 (N.D. Ill. 1990) (21 elected officers with salaries ranging from $83,877 to over $500,000 was a top-hat plan); *Belka v. Rowe Furniture,* 571 F.Supp.1249 (D.Md. 1983) (plan covering 4.6% of workforce was a top-hat plan); *Demery v. Extebank Deferred Compensation Plan,* 216 F3d 283 (2d Cir. 2000) (15.34% of workforce constituted a top-hat plan, although acknowledging that this percentage approached the outer limits); *Duggan v. Hobbs,* 99 F3d 307 (9th Cir. 1996) (one employee out of 23 or 4.35%, constituted a top-hat plan); *Darden v. Nationwide Mutual Insurance Company,* 717 F.Supp. 388 (E.D.N.C. 1989), *aff'd* 922 F2d 203 (4th Cir. 1991); *rev'd on other grounds* 503 U.S. 318 (1992) (18.7% of workforce too high to constitute a top-hat plan); *Starr v. JCI Data Processing,* 757 F.Supp. 390 (D.N.J. 1991) (not a top-hat plan when covered employees' salaries ranged from $12,000 to $336,000, and depending on category, covered between 25% and 37.5% of the workforce).

[119] *Senior Exec. Benefit Plan Participants v. New Valley Corp.,* 89 F3d 143 (3d Cir. 1996) (noting that top-hat plans are a "rare species" and further observing that the term "select group" "has both quantitative and qualitative restrictions). In number, the plan must cover relatively few employees. In character, the plan must cover only high level employees" and *Duggan v. Hobbs,* 99 F.3d 307, 313, (9th Cir. 1996) stating that the "select group" requirement includes more than a mere statistical analysis.

[120] *Long v. Excel Corp.,* 2000 U.S. Dist. LEXIS 15479 (N.D. Tex. 2000).

[121] DOL Advisory Opinion 98-02 A; *Emmenegger v. Bull Moose Tube Co.,* 197 F3d 929 (8th Cir. 1999).

[122] *Long v. Excel Corp.,* 2000 U.S. Dist. LEXIS 15479 (N.D. Tex. 2000); *Kaelin v. Tenseco, Inc.,* 28 F.Supp.2d 478, 484-86 (N.D. Ill. 1998); *Goodrich v. CML Fiberoptics, Inc.,* 990 F.Supp. 48, 49-50 (D. Mass. 1998); *Johnson v. TCOM Sup, Inc.,* 1989 U.S. Dist. LEXIS 15723 (D.D.C. 1989); and *Lafian v. Electronic Data Systems Corp.,* 856 F.Supp. 339, 349 (E.D. Mich. 1994).

[123] *Hahn v. National Westminster Bank, N.A.,* 99 F.Supp.2d 275, 276 (E.D.N.Y. 2000); *Oatway v. American International Group, Inc.,* 2002 U.S. Dist. LEXIS 1771 (D. Del. 2002).

[124] *Cvelbar v. CBI Illinois, Inc.,* 106 F3d 1368 (7th Cir. 1997). This represented a change from the posi-

Courts have not consistently agreed with the DOL view.[125] For the courts that are skeptical of the application of ERISA to one-person arrangements, the language from *Healy v. Rich Products Corp. Products Corp.* is instructive:

> The mere denomination of a contract or agreement as a "plan" does not necessarily make it subject to ERISA. Agreements between an employee and employer that fail to pass certain characteristics have been found to be not so subject. Agreements that are individually negotiated with a single employee rather than made available to a class of employees, agreements that designate no separate res for the funding of the benefits, agreement that contain no procedures for determining or administering benefit amounts and agreements that are terminable at will have been found to be employment or service contracts not subject to ERISA.[126]

Part of the concern in this area is a general reluctance to convert any employment contract into a pension plan. The difficulty is that because ERISA's definition of pension plan is so broad, initially a contract that provides for some type of deferred compensation will also establish a de facto pension plan, whether or not the parties intended to do so.[127]

In some instances, courts will conclude that while a contract between an employee and an employer can be an employee benefit plan governed by ERISA, under the particular facts[128] there was no ERISA plan.[129] For example, to qualify as a plan under *Donovan v. Dillingham*, a reasonable person must be able to ascertain from the surrounding circumstances (1) the intended benefit, (2) the beneficiaries of the arrangement, (3) the source of financing, and (4) procedures for determining benefits.[130] Thus, in *Bulls v. Norton Community Hospital, Inc.* the court concluded that there was no ERISA plan where "no specific details as to amounts, dates, or administration of the plan were discussed."[131] In other instances, no plan will be found to exist because there is no "ongoing administrative scheme."[132] Thus, in *Belanger v. Wyman-Gordon*, the court stated that "so long

---

(Footnote Continued)

tion set forth in some early DOL opinions. *See* DOL Opinion 76-79 and 76-110.

[125] Cases holding that there can be one person plans include *Duggan v. Hobbs*, 99 F3d 307, 312 (9th Cir. 1996); *Musmeci v. Schwegmann Giant Supermarkets*, 159 F.Supp.2d 329 (E.D. La. 2001); *Nelson v. Jones & Brown, Inc.*, 2001 U.S. Dist. LEXIS 15449 (W.D. Pa 2001); *Williams v. Wright*, 927 F2d 1540, 1545 (11th Cir. 1991), noting that the plain language of ERISA doesn't exclude one person plans. Among the cases holding that a one person arrangement is not an ERISA plan are *Jervis v. Elerding*, 504 F.Supp. 606, 608 (C.D. Cal. 1980); *Fraver v. North Carolina Farm Bureau Mutual Insurance Company*, 801 F2d 675 (4th Cir. 1986), cert. den. 480 US 919 (1987); *McQueen v. Salida Coca-Cola Bottling Co.*, 652 F.Supp. 1471 (D. Col. 1987); *Lackey v. Whitehall Co.*, 704 F.Supp 201 (D. Kansas 1988); *O'Hallaren v. Maine Cook & Stewards Union*, 730 P.2d 616 (Ore. App. 1986); *Motel 6, Inc. v. Superior Court*, 241 Cal. Rptr. 528 (Cal. Ct. App. 2d Dist. 1987); *Hettiger v. Doctors Hospital, Inc.*, 1991 U.S. Dist. LEXIS 7284 (E.D. Mich. 1991), holding that the failure to hold funds in trust precludes the find-

ing of an ERISA plan; and *Cerra v. Hitachi Zosen Cleering Inc. et al.*, 1990 U.S. Dist. LEXIS 7317 (N.D. Ill 1990), finding no ERISA plan despite the presence of the four elements discussed in *Donovan v. Dillingham Inc.* 688 F2d 1367 (11th Cir. 1982).

[126] *Healy v. Rich Products Corp. Products Corp.*, 1991 U.S. Dist. LEXIS 5925 (W.D.N.Y. 1991).

[127] *Modzelewski v. Resolution Trust Corp.*, 14 F3d 1374, 1377 (9th Cir. 1994).

[128] In *Belanger v. Wyman Gordon Co.*, 71 F3d 451, 453 (1st Cir. 1995), the court held that the existence *vel non* of an ERISA plan is primarily a question of fact.

[129] *Graham v. Balcor Corp.*, 1998 U.S. App. LEXIS 12655 (9th Cir. 1998); *Gunter v. Novopharm USA, Inc.*, 2001 U.S. Dist. LEXIS 2117 (N.D. Ill. 2001).

[130] *Donovan v. Dillingham*, 688 F2d 1367 (11th Cir. 1982).

[131] *Bulls v. Norton Community Hospital, Inc.*, 76 F.Supp.2d 710 (W.D. Va. 1999).

[132] *Fort Halifax Packing Co., Inc. v. Coyne*, 482 US 1 (1987).

as the proffered benefit does not involve employer obligations materially beyond those reflected in *Fort Halifax* . . . the benefit will not amount to a plan under the ERISA statute."[133]

Notwithstanding this divergence of authority, an individual who has entered into an agreement that a court might otherwise be reluctant to characterize as an ERISA plan may be able to maintain the position that multiple individual agreements together constitute one pension plan, particularly if these arrangements are substantially identical.[134]

.05 Excess Benefit Plan

On some occasions, a court will blur the distinction between an excess plan and a top-hat plan.[135] ERISA Sec. 3(36) defines an excess benefit plan[136] as:

> a plan maintained by an employer solely[137] for the purpose of providing benefits for certain employees in excess of the limitations on contribution and benefits imposed by [Code] Section 415. To the extent that a separable part of a plan (as determined by the Secretary of Labor)[138] maintained by the employer is maintained for such purpose, that part will be treated as a separate plan which is an excess benefit plan.[139]

Because the limitations set forth in Code Sec. 415 are not fixed, at least one court has held that an employee benefit plan cannot serve the purpose of providing benefits in excess of Code Sec. 415 without expressly referring either to Code Sec. 415 or its substantive provisions.[140]

In one case, a particular provision of a plan providing benefits in excess of both Code Sec. 415 and Code Sec. 401(a)(17) was read solely to apply to benefits in excess of the Code Sec. 415 limits, because in the particular case the application

---

[133] *Belanger v. Wyman-Gordon*, 71 F3d 451, 453 (1st Cir. 1995).

[134] *See, e.g., Pane v. RCA Corp.*, 868 F2d 631 (3d Cir. 1989); *Purser v. Enron*, 1988 U.S. Dist. LEXIS 15516 (W.D. Pa. 1988); *Collins v. Ralston Purina Co.*, 147 F3d 592 (7th Cir. 1998); *Fraver v. North Carolina Farm Bureau Mutual Ins. Co.*, 643 F.Supp. 633 (E.D.N.C. 1985) *but see Lackey v. Whitehall Corp.*, 704 F.Supp 201 (D. Kan. 1988), holding that individual identical deferred compensation arrangements do not constitute an ERISA pension plan.

[135] *See Hampers v. W.R. Grace & Co.*, 202 F3d 44, n3 (1st Cir. 2000) stating that an excess benefit plan is colloquially referred to as a top-hat plan, then observing (incorrectly) that a top-hat plan is exempt from ERISA's reporting and disclosure and civil and criminal enforcement provisions.

[136] Note that this definition is narrower than the meaning of the identical phrase under the Section 16 rules, *i.e.*, a nonqualified employee benefit plan operated in conjunction with a qualified plan that provides only the benefits or contributions that would be provided under the Code but for any Code imposed benefit or contribution limits.

[137] The "solely" language is not a legislative oversight; rather before the Tax Reform Act of 1986, the only pension law limits on the amount of allowable benefits and contributions were contained in Section 415 of the Code. *See Gamble v. Group Hospitalization a Medical Services, Inc.*, 38 F3d 126, 130-131 (4th Cir. 1994). A plan that provides benefits in excess of both the Code Sec. 401(a)(17) limit and Code Sec. 415 limit, while sometimes referred to as an excess plan, is technically not an excess benefit plan. *Catacosinos v. Applied Digital Data Systems*, 592 F.Supp. 49 (E.D.N.Y. 1984).

[138] The DOL has not yet promulgated regulations under this section. However, the IRS has issued favorable determination letters to plans that included an excess benefit component within a tax-qualified plan.

[139] The fact that benefits in excess of these permitted under Code Sec. 415 were funded from a different source than other benefits under the plan, although tending to show separateness, was not, standing alone, determinative for purposes of the severability exception under ERISA 3(36). *Farr v. U.S. West, Inc.*, 815 F.Supp. 1360 (D. Ore. 1992) *rev'd on other grounds* 58 F3d 1361 (9th Cir. 1993).

[140] *Northwestern Mutual Life v. Resolution Trust Company*, 848 F.Supp. 1515 (N.D. Ala. 1994).

of the Code Sec. 401(a)(17) limit on pensionable earnings was not relevant.[141] However, in another case,[142] the Court of Appeals for the Seventh Circuit stated that the test for an excess benefit plan turns upon the purposes of the plan in general rather than on the specific way it applies to a participant. In its view, even if a plan with other purposes only has the effect on a participant of avoiding the Code Sec. 415 limits, that does not mean that it was the sole purpose for which the employer maintained the plan, and that is the decisive consideration.

Planning Note: Some companies establish excess benefit arrangements simply by corporate resolution, and occasionally it is a component of a tax-qualified plan.[143] More frequently, the employer would establish the excess plan as a stand-alone plan. If an excess plan is a component of a plan that takes into account other Code limitations, such as Code Sec. 401(a)(17), at least for recordkeeping purposes separate accounts should be maintained if the employer wishes to obtain the benefits of a true excess benefit plan.

Planning Note: Generally, an excess benefit plan will compensate the executive in full for the difference between the benefit he or she would have received under the tax-qualified plan with respect to all of the limitations imposed under the Code other than Code Sec. 415 and the actual benefit he or she receives under the tax-qualified plan. However, this need not be the case. The excess plan may impose a dollar or percentage limit on the excess payments.

.06 ERISA Compliance

As noted above, excess benefit plans are fully exempt from all provisions of ERISA. The ERISA provisions that apply to top-hat pension plans are:

1. The plan administrator must file with the DOL the statement including name and address of the employer, employer identification number, declaration that the employer maintains one or more top-hat plans, the number of top-hat plans, and the number of participants in each plan.

2. If the DOL requests, the plan administrator must provide the DOL with annual reports, a summary plan description, and any SMMs that the plan administrator would have had to prepare but for the exemption from the general reporting and disclosure requirements.

3. Part 5 of Title I of ERISA, including:

    a. criminal penalty provision;

    b. civil enforcement provision;

    c. claims procedures;

---

[141] *Petkus v. Chicago Rawhide Mfg. Co.*, 763 F.Supp. 357 (N.D. Ill. 1991).

[142] *Olander v. Bucyrus Erie*, 187 F3d 599, 604 (7th Cir. 1999). *See also Garratt v. Knowles*, 245 F3d 941 (7th Cir. 2001).

[143] *See* IRS Letter Ruling 200151056 (Sept. 25, 2001) operation of an excess benefit plan did not disqualify tax-qualified multiemployer plan, where assets of excess benefit plan could not be used to provide qualified plan benefits, qualified plan benefits could not be used to provide excess benefit plan benefits, and the amount of benefits payable under the excess plan did not affect the benefits paid under the multiemployer plan.

    d. interference with rights protected under Act;

    e. coercive interference;

    f. preemption; and

    g. the provisions regarding the powers and duties of the various federal agencies charged with enforcing ERISA.

¶1745 Types of Nonqualified Plans

The main advantage of a nonqualified plan over a qualified retirement plan is that, because the Internal Revenue Code's qualification requirements do not apply, an employer has enormous flexibility in drafting the eligibility, benefit and other provisions of the nonqualified plan. In designing a nonqualified plan, counsel needs to ask the employer: What are you trying to accomplish? For example, the employer may be seeking to:

- make whole participants for benefits lost under a defined benefit plan, an ESOP, or a profit sharing plan;
- permit higher paid employees to make greater pre-tax contributions;
- make up for retirement benefits lost by an incoming executive; or
- provide a signing bonus, with strings attached.

.01 Defined Benefit or Individual Account

Because most nonqualified retirement plans are designed to allow executives and other highly compensated employees to receive benefits and defer compensation in excess of the Code limits applicable under qualified retirement plans, an employer will generally design its nonqualified plan to look like the qualified plan that it is intended to supplement.

    Example 1: The employer in Example 3 in ¶1715 might adopt a nonqualified mirror 401(k) plan to permit Executive D (and other, similarly affected employees) to make pre-tax elective deferral contribution in excess of $18,500. In Example 2 in ¶1715, the employer might adopt a SERP to make Executive B whole for annual pension benefits cut back by the compensation cap.

.02 Supplemental Executive Retirement Plan ("SERP")

Practitioners generally use the term "SERP" to refer to a defined benefit type nonqualified plan that is designed to provide retirement benefit amounts for executive employees above and beyond that which can be provided under a qualified plan. Although SERPs often provide benefits that are specifically linked to the employer's qualified defined benefit plan, some SERPs simply provide retirement benefits based on the executive's final salary. This latter form of SERP is also sometimes referred to as a "salary continuation plan."

.03 Floor SERP

Practitioners generally use the term "Floor SERP" to describe a type of nonqualified defined benefit pension plan that promises the participant a fixed annual benefit at retirement, but reduced by any benefits the participant actually receives under the employer's qualified retirement plans. Generally, a Floor SERP would be used when recruiting an older executive who may not be expected to work enough years with the new employer to accrue a significant benefit under the employer's qualified plans.

> **Example 2:** A client recruited and hired an executive who was age 58. The client maintained a profit sharing and 401(k) plan. It contributed 3% of the participants' compensation to the profit sharing plan each year and made matching contributions equal to 50% of the first 6% of the participant's pre-tax elective deferrals. The client only expected the executive to work for it for five years, and the executive would not be able to accrue sufficient retirement benefits under the client's plan (even if he worked until age 65). The parties' goal was to provide a retirement benefit equal to 40% of his final earnings. A nonqualified Floor SERP was designed for the executive which would pay him 8% of his final average pay times his years of service with the client, reduced by the projected annual annuity benefit that could be provided by the amount accumulated in the executive's account under the qualified plan.

.04 Excess Benefit Plans

An excess benefit plan is a nonqualified plan maintained by an employer solely for the purpose of providing benefits for certain employees in excess of the limitations on contributions and benefits imposed on qualified retirement plans by Code Sec. 415.[144] A nonqualified plan providing benefits in excess of the Code Sec. 401(a)(17) compensation cap would *not* be an ERISA excess benefit plan. Indeed, the dramatic impact of the compensation cap has greatly reduced the need for excess benefit plans, as fewer qualified plans bump up against the Code Sec. 415 limits.

As noted above, an excess benefit plan is the only type of nonqualified plan explicitly defined in ERISA. The amount of the benefit is the excess of the amount the employee would have received under the qualified plan, if not for the Code Sec. 415 limitations, over the amount the employee actually received. An excess benefit plan supplements the tax-qualified plan to make whole benefits to executive and other higher compensated employees.

> **Example 3:** Executive D has worked for ABC Corporation for 30 years and has final average compensation of $500,000. ABC's pension plan provides an annual benefit equal to 3% times a participant's years of service. The total unrestricted benefit produced by that formula would be $450,000 per year. Applying only the Code Sec. 401(a)(17) compensation cap would produce an annual benefit of $247,500. However, in this example, the Code Sec. 415 limit applicable to 2018 would limit Executive D's annual pension amount from the qualified plan to just $220,000. A true excess benefit plan maintained by ABC would pay D an annual pension equal to $27,500 ($247,500 - $220,000). If ABC's nonqualified retirement plan instead provided

---

[144] ERISA Section 3(36).

Executive D with an annual pension benefit of $230,000 ($450,000 - $220,000), the plan might not be a true excess benefit plan under ERISA.

Which Code Sec. 415 limitation should be utilized depends upon which type of qualified plan the employer has established (*e.g.*, a defined benefit plan, a defined contribution plan or both). The "excess benefit plan" exemption under ERISA Sec. 4(b)(5) is broader than the so-called "top-hat" exemption applicable to the other nonqualified plans. Excess benefit plans are fully exempt from all provisions of ERISA.

.05 Mirror Plans

One type of nonqualified plan that has been approved by the IRS in a series of private letter rulings is a "mirror" 401(k) plan.[145] These plans typically permit both salary deferral and employer matching contributions and generally mirror the tax-qualified 401(k) plan. Mechanically, a participant will make an irrevocable salary deferral election under the nonqualified plan. The salary deferral and matching contributions generally will be contributed to a rabbi trust. At the close of the 401(k) plan year (but no later than January 31), the employer will run the actual deferral percentage and actual contribution percentage tests to determine the maximum salary deferrals for each highly compensated employee. (Presumably, if the employee will have attained age 50 by the close of the plan year, the maximum salary deferral for each highly compensated employee will also include his or her catch-up contribution.) The nonqualified plan will then transfer to the 401(k) plan the lesser of (1) the maximum permitted deferral contribution or (2) the actual salary deferral contribution of each highly compensated employee pursuant to their prior election. In this regard, many investment fund and/or prototype plan providers make available to nonqualified plans a product that mirrors the qualified plan product that they make available, including the same fund choices that they have for their qualified accounts.

While these arrangements ensure that participants will maximize their pre-tax deferrals in the tax-qualified 401(k) plan, these arrangements offer considerably less flexibility than the tax-qualified 401(k) plan with respect to elections. To avoid constructive receipt, the election to defer compensation must be made before the start of the year in which the employee will render services, and cannot be changed during the year.

.06 Nonqualified Plan for Directors

Most companies maintain a nonqualified plan permitting nonemployee members of the board of directors to defer the receipt of retainer, annual meeting and/or other fees until a future date. The benefit of such deferrals is that the director defers taxation of these fees until the date the fees are withdrawn from the plan. Amounts deferred are usually placed in an interest bearing account or rabbi trust by the employer, or used to purchase an annuity contract. Distributions cannot be made until the director ceases to be a member of the board. Upon

---

[145] *See* IRS Letter Ruling 9807027 (Nov. 17, 1997), IRS Letter Ruling 9807010 (Nov. 10, 1997), IRS Letter Ruling 9752018 (Sept. 23, 1997), IRS Letter Ruling 9752017 (Sept. 23, 1997), and IRS Letter Ruling 9530038 (May 5, 1995).

retirement from the board, deferred fees and accumulated interest are paid to the director over a number of years. Usually the period over which the fees and interest are paid does not exceed 10 years. Upon the death of the director, any balance of deferred fees and accumulated interest remaining in the account are paid to the director's estate or his or her designated beneficiary, in full, on the first day of the calendar year following the year in which the director dies.

Some employers maintain a nonqualified retirement plan for nonemployee members of the board of directors. These plans were much more popular and prevalent before 2000, when adverse publicity and attention from institutional investors caused many companies to terminate their plans.

.07 "QSERP" and "Stay-for-Pay" Plans

Both "QSERP" and "stay-for-pay" are ways in which creative employers and actuaries can use the Code Sec. 401(a)(4) general nondiscrimination test to support special pension plan designs. A Qualified Supplemental Executive Retirement Plan (QSERP) is an amendment of a qualified defined benefit pension plan to include benefits for executives that otherwise would need to be paid under a nonqualified plan (e.g., due to the Code Sec. 401(a)(17) pay limits).

> **Example 4:** ABC Corporation maintains a qualified pension plan that provides a benefit of 2% of pay times years of service. Executive D's pay is $500,000. If D has 10 years of service, her qualified benefit is $55,000 (2% × 10 × $275,000), and her nonqualified pension is $45,000 (2% × 10 × $225,000). Although this is a "safe harbor" plan design, ABC can still run a "general test" and determine if there is a margin that could be used to support additional benefits for the highly compensated employees ("HCEs"). Using the "accrued to date" approach to the general test, ABC may be able to include half of Executive D's nonqualified pension under the qualified plan, and still pass the test. If so, ABC would amend the qualified plan to add a $10,000 accrued pension for Executive D. As described above, the benefits of this are as follows:
>
> - saves ABC and Executive D FICA taxes;
> - gives D the possibility of rollover treatment;
> - earns ABC an immediate deduction;
> - eliminates an unfunded obligation for ABC; and
> - better protects Executive D's benefits (e.g., from bankruptcy or change in control) in a qualified plan.

The "stay-for-pay" design uses a nontypical pension accrual formula for a selected group of employees, in order to deliver a bonus-like benefit at a specific time.

> **Example 5:** ABC Corporation establishes a freestanding, qualified defined benefit pension plan covering only information technology employees, and specifying a normal retirement age of "five years from April 1, 2018." The new plan provides a special benefit that is a lump sum payment equal to 50% of each covered employee's annual compensation, provided the covered

IT employee remains employed with ABC until at least March 31, 2022. The formula must meet the accrual rules and comply with Code Sec. 415(b) limits, and the plan must satisfy the Code Sec. 412 funding requirements. ABC can pay this "stay bonus" completely from the plan's assets.

.08 Special Purpose Nonqualified Plans

The flexibility of nonqualified plans also permits employers to make special, one-time only contributions to selected individuals for specific purposes.

> **Example 6:** In 1992, IBM looked outside of its current management for a new CEO to restructure the company. When it settled on Louis Gerstner from RJR Nabisco, a sticking point in negotiations was that Mr. Gerstner would be forfeiting significant amounts of pension and other benefits by leaving RJR before retirement. IBM chose to create a one-man nonqualified retirement plan that made whole Mr. Gerstner for the generous RJR benefits he forfeited when he came to IBM.

¶1755 Other Nonqualified Plan Design Issues

Again, because the Internal Revenue Code's qualification requirements do not apply, an employer has enormous flexibility in drafting the eligibility, benefit and other provisions of the nonqualified plan. Among the only legal requirements limiting nonqualified plans are (1) the need to prevent the constructive receipt of income, and (2) the need to satisfy either the excess benefit or the top-hat plan exemptions from ERISA.

.01 Strict IRS Requirements

In order to obtain a favorable IRS private letter ruling on nonqualified deferred compensation before Code Sec. 409A, the following conditions must be satisfied:[146]

- Deferrals must be elected before the beginning of the year of deferral, which for a cash basis, calendar year employee is the calendar year. However, there are two important exceptions to this rule. Both the year in which the plan is established or the year in which an employee first becomes eligible to participate, a 30-day period from the date of the event applies;
- The events entitling a participant to payment, the timing of payment after the event has occurred, and the method of payment must all be elected at the time of the initial election;
- Hardship distributions from the plan may be allowed in the event of "unforeseeable emergencies." The plan must define such emergencies as "unanticipated events beyond the control of the participant that would result in severe financial hardship if the early withdrawal were not permitted"; and

---

[146] Rev. Proc. 92-65, IRB 1992-33, 16. The 2002-2003 Business Plan of the IRS lists reconsideration of its position on constructive receipt with respect to nonqualified plans. Although it has been on its business plan in recent years, in the post Enron and Worldcom climate it may receive a higher priority.

- Benefits may not be anticipated, assigned, pledged or otherwise encumbered by the participant and any of his creditors.

> **Planning Note:** Because few employers apply for a private letter ruling as to their nonqualified plan, and the IRS has been unsuccessful in enforcing many of its theories of constructive receipt in court, most employers feel comfortable going beyond the limits of Rev. Proc. 92-65. Indeed, much of the law of nonqualified plan design has evolved through informal conversations among practitioners and the IRS, rather than the formal ruling process.

Note that Code Sec. 409A has codified each of the foregoing design requirements.

.02 Eligibility and Participation

For ERISA compliance reasons, an employer can offer participation in a nonqualified retirement or deferred compensation plan only to a selected group of highly compensated employees. The employer may pick and choose which employees to cover under the plan (unlike a qualified plan, which cannot discriminate in favor of highly compensated employees). As long as participation in the plan is limited to "a select group of management or highly compensated employees," the participation, vesting and reporting and disclosure rules of ERISA will not apply.

The DOL has suggested that "other highly compensated employees" in this context means something different than the definition of "highly compensated" under Internal Revenue Code Sec. 414(q), *i.e.*, a higher threshold of compensation. However, because the DOL has not published regulations or guidelines of any sort as to this matter, there is some flexibility in defining the "highly compensated" group.

> **Planning Note:** With respect to participation, an excess benefit plan can be structured in two ways. The plan can be drafted so that eligibility is automatic, *e.g.*, by title, or so that the employer's board of directors or a committee has the discretion to designate eligible employees.

.03 Contributions and Benefits

A defined-benefit-based nonqualified plan should set forth in the plan document the plan's benefit formula. An individual account-like plan should set forth the formula for any employer contributions and the maximum amount subject to deferral and contribution by employees. The employer should communicate the contribution and benefit formulas to the employee-participants.

> **Example 1:** ABC Corporation has designed a benefit formula to make whole executives whose pension benefits are cut back by the Code limits, as follows:

There shall be payable hereunder with respect to each Participant a benefit or benefits equal to the difference between the benefit or benefits that the Participant, spouse or beneficiary would have received under the Pension Plan *but for the limitations imposed under the Code*, and the benefit or benefits to which the Participant, spouse or beneficiary are entitled under the Pension Plan.

.04 Period of Deferral—Distributions

A nonqualified plan generally provides distribution options that parallel the distribution options available under the qualified plan it mirrors. Most nonqualified plans permit the participant to choose both the form and timing of the distribution of his or her benefits. The plan would permit the participant to elect between a lump-sum distribution or installments. The plan would also permit the participant to elect whether to receive his or her benefits upon retirement, employment termination, or at some fixed date in the future. Some plans simply provide that the participant's benefits or account will be distributed to the participant upon his or her termination of employment for any reason.

> **Planning Note:** Nonqualified plan participants may feel more secure if the plan also were to provide that benefits under the plan would be fully vested and distributed in full, in cash, upon the sale of the stock or assets of the employer or its dissolution.

One important plan design issue that employers face is whether to permit employees to extend their compensation deferral elections. A number of court decisions issued several years ago concluded that taxpayers could elect to extend deferral elections at least once without being in "constructive receipt" of income. Code Sec. 409A(4)(C) imposes strict limitations on distribution election changes.

> **Planning Note:** The most aggressive, or state-of-the-art (depending upon your viewpoint), form of nonqualified deferred compensation plan distribution feature developed before Code Sec. 409A was one that allowed the participants to make an irrevocable election at any time to begin receiving distribution six or twelve months from the date of the election. Although far from conforming to the IRS guidelines in Rev. Proc. 92-65, practitioners found support for this feature in the numerous court decisions against the IRS in the area of constructive receipt.

.05 Hardship Distributions

It has been the IRS's position not to issue rulings if the employer may exercise discretion as to either the time or manner of payments to nonqualified plan participants. However, even before Code Sec. 409A, IRS rulings permitted the accelerated payment of deferred income where there is financial hardship[147] or employer approval is required, provided that such approval is not automatic. IRS ruling guidelines indicate that a plan that permits such early withdrawals must, by terms set forth in the plan, limit such withdrawals to "unforeseeable emergencies."[148] The plan must define an "unforeseeable emergency" as an unanticipated emergency that is caused by an event beyond the control of the participant and that would result in severe financial hardship to the individual if

---

[147] *See, e.g.,* IRS Letter Ruling 8732005 (April 29, 1987), IRS Letter Ruling 8733008 (May 13, 1987), IRS Letter Ruling 8733038 (May 20, 1987) and IRS Letter Ruling 8746023 (Aug. 14, 1987).

[148] Rev. Proc. 92-65, IRB 1992-33, 16.

early withdrawal were not permitted. The plan must further provide that any early withdrawal approved by the employer is limited to the amount necessary to meet the emergency. For these purposes, a plan that contains language similar to that described in regulations that apply to tax-exempt organization deferred compensation plans may be used.[149] Code Sec. 409A codified the rules of early distribution for an unforeseeable emergency in Section 409A(a)(2)(A)(vi).

> **Planning Note:** If a plan contains a hardship withdrawal provision, such provision probably should mirror the regulations, and the employer should carefully follow the plan provisions. If the employer were to make deferred amounts available to a large number of employees prior to the end of the applicable elected deferral period, the IRS could view this as triggering constructive receipt of taxable income as to all plan participants.

.06 Early Distributions

Before Code Sec. 409A, many nonqualified plans permitted participants to elect a distribution date that is (or may be) before their termination of employment. Even the strictest IRS standards would not prevent the election of an "in-service distribution" so long as the election was made before the time the deferred compensation was earned.

> **Example 2:** ABC Corporation drafts its deferred compensation plan to permit participants to elect to receive a distribution of all or part of their account at a fixed date or dates in the future. In 2003, Executive A elects (1) to defer 100% of her bonus into the plan, and (2) to receive four substantially equal distributions from her account in August 2009, 2010, 2011 and 2012, the years when her oldest son will be in college.

Some nonqualified plans permit a participant to elect an accelerated distribution at any time, subject to a penalty or "haircut." This provision would allow a participant who feared for the financial stability of the employer to withdraw his or her benefits before the date the participant had previously elected. The legal rationale for a "haircut" provision is that the haircut constitutes a sufficient risk of forfeiture to prevent the participant from being in constructive receipt of their benefits.

> **Planning Note:** A haircut-withdrawal provision is a good design feature to help protect plan participants against the loss of their benefit due to the employer's insolvency. However, a practitioner should warn the client that these provisions are squarely in the crosshairs of many in Congress due to the perceived abuse by Enron executives. As Enron spiraled downward to imminent bankruptcy, an insiders committee permitted favored executives to withdraw the full amount of their nonqualified benefits, less the haircut amount. Aggrieved creditors are, of course, suing to recover these distributions.

---

[149] Reg. § 1.457-2(h)(4).

Code Sec. 409A prohibits early distributions (other than for an unforeseeable emergency). However, these rules still may be relevant for plans that qualify for "grandfathered" status under Code Sec. 409A.

.07 Defining "Compensation"

A design issue that occasionally arises in a tax-qualified plan is whether it is permissible to include deferred compensation in the definition of "earnings" used to calculate employer contributions. Code Sec. 414(s) provides the rules for defining compensation for qualified plan purposes, including the nondiscrimination provisions applicable to qualified plans.[150] However, regulations under Code Sec. 414(s) provide that, even though a Code Sec. 414(s) definition of compensation must be used in determining whether the contributions or benefits under a plan are nondiscriminatory, "except as otherwise specified, the plan is not required to use a definition of compensation that satisfies Sec. 414(s) in calculating the amount of contributions or benefits actually provided under the plan."[151] Therefore, it would appear that the inclusion of deferred compensation in pensionable earnings is permissible. The difficulty with this approach is that it becomes more difficult to satisfy the nondiscrimination requirements with respect to contributions or benefits.

Example 3: If Participant D earns $300,000 in 2018, but defers $100,000 into a nonqualified deferred compensation plan that year, should ABC Corporation's qualified profit sharing plan allocate employer contributions to D based on 2018 compensation of $275,000 (the Code Sec. 401(a)(17) limit) or $200,000? If ABC's qualified plan defines "compensation" to include amounts deferred into a nonqualified plan, this definition will not be a "safe-harbor" definition and would need to be tested for discrimination. If discrimination testing revealed that the qualified plan's definition of compensation resulted in greater contributions to highly compensated employees, the definition could be discriminatory and the plan could be disqualified.

Planning Note: To avoid complexity in nondiscrimination testing, consider limiting the amount of nonqualified plan deferral to an amount that will not reduce the participant's W-2 compensation below the Code Sec. 401(a)(17) limit for the year. In the above example, therefore, the maximum amount that the participant could have deferred would have been $25,000, rather than $100,000.

.08 Investments and Interest Crediting

An employer has a great deal of flexibility in determining the timing and amount of interest earnings credited to deferrals and employer contributions, if any, under the plan. Some plans credit earnings at a fixed rate. Others credit earnings at a fluctuating rate tied to easily referenced sources such as U.S. Treasury Bills or published bank rates. Some nonqualified plans permit election among several hypothetical investment funds, which are based on the investment funds made available in the underlying qualified plan. One advantage of a

---

[150] Reg. § 1.414(s)-1(a)(1).   [151] Reg. § 1.414(s)-1(a)(2).

rabbi trust in this regard is that the investments can be made to ensure the guaranteed rate is achieved (or possibly exceeded).

The employer must choose the method of crediting interest or other earnings on the deferred amount. However, a plan could permit the participants to select the investment vehicle. The employer also could decide that the plan should provide for all or a portion of the deferred amount to be credited to a stock account whose value is related to the common stock of the employer. Typically, deferred amounts would be converted into stock units having a value equal to the common stock of the company.

> **Planning Note:** Employers need to consider whether to permit participants to direct the investment of their nonqualified plan accounts among investment funds that essentially mirror those offered under the qualified plans. That is, should the nonqualified plan permit participants to elect investment switches on any business day of the year, under the same terms and conditions that apply to the qualified plans? The concern is that the IRS could take the view that this level of control by a nonqualified plan participant creates an issue of economic benefit or constructive receipt and, thus, the possibility of taxation to the participants.

The IRS has never directly addressed this issue in any rulings, regulations or other writing. However, IRS representatives have stated several times at practitioners' forums, such as ABA meetings, that they do not believe that giving nonqualified plan participants investment discretion/direction over their "phantom accounts," whether in a rabbi trust or not, creates a taxable event under the doctrines of economic benefit or constructive receipt. Moreover, the IRS has issued several private letter rulings approving companies' nonqualified plans where participants' ability to direct investment of their accounts was a distinctive feature of the plans.[152]

> **Planning Note:** To put the employer in the best possible position with respect to the foregoing analysis, the nonqualified plan document could contain language clarifying that, while the participant may specify how he or she would like his or her accounts invested, the ultimate decision on investments remains with the plan administrator.

.09 Plan Administration

All employee benefit plans should specify the entity that will be responsible for plan administration. Many employers appoint a committee of interested individuals (or designate an existing committee) as the plan administrator to ensure that someone is clearly and unambiguously responsible for plan administration issues.

The two most critical functions of the nonqualified plan administrator would be ensuring compliance with the legal requirements (IRS, DOL and SEC) and handling claims for benefits. With respect to benefit claims, the plan should

---

[152] *See* IRS Letter Ruling 9807004 (Oct. 16, 1997) and IRS Letter Ruling 9815039 (Jan. 7, 1998).

explicitly give the plan administrator the power and authority to interpret and apply the plan's terms.

Example 4: ABC Corporation's Nonqualified Retirement Plan could provide as follows:

The Committee shall administer the Plan in accordance with its terms and shall have all powers necessary to carry out the provisions of the Plan. The Committee shall interpret the Plan and shall determine all questions arising in the administration, interpretation, and application of the Plan, including but not limited to, questions of eligibility and the status and rights of employees, Participants and other persons.

Planning Note: In the plan document and any board resolutions creating or appointing a committee, always provide for the employer to indemnify, defend and hold harmless the committee members and any other employees serving a plan administrative function.

.10 Restrictive Covenants

Because nonqualified plans are not subject to ERISA's vesting requirement, they can include noncompete provisions and other restrictive covenants that would not be enforceable under ERISA's vesting rules.[153] As discussed in ¶475, the courts have upheld explicit benefit forfeiture provisions in nonqualified plans in a number of cases.

.11 Deferral of Stock Option Gains

Before Code Sec. 409A, a nonqualified plan could permit an employee-participant who has been granted nonqualified stock options to elect to defer any income or gain that would otherwise be recognized upon the exercise of such options (if the terms of the employer's stock option plan also permitted such deferrals). An employee (or director) holding stock options might wish to take advantage of this feature if the options were nearing the deadline for exercise, yet the employee did not want to recognize income on the option exercise gain. To utilize this feature, the employee-participant must already own shares of employer stock outright, so that he or she may use the attestation method of exercise.

Example 5: Participant D holds an option to purchase 10,000 shares of ABC Corporation stock at $10 a share. The option is to expire in 12 months. D files a written election with ABC, as permitted by ABC's nonqualified plan and its stock option plan, to exercise the options on the date that is six months from the election. On that date, ABC's stock price is $25 per share. D exercises the option through attestation, using 4,000 shares of ABC stock she already owns. D receives no further shares of stock and recognizes no taxable income, but her account under the nonqualified plan is credited with $150,000, or 6,000 stock units.

---

[153] *See, e.g., Carson v. Local 1588 International Long-shoremen's Assn.,* 769 F.Supp. 141 (S.D.N.Y. 1991); *Loffland Bros. Co. v. C.A. Overstreet,* 758 P.2d 813 (Okla 1988); *Bajour v. The Pep Boys,* 2001 U.S. Dist. LEXIS 9090 (E.D. PA 2001).

In order to use the attestation method of exercise, the participant must present a notarized statement to the employer that he or she owns the required shares. The previously owned shares are not affected by this transaction. Diversification into other investment options under the plan may not be permitted to preserve favorable accounting treatment.

.12 Change in Control Provisions

Some nonqualified plans will include protection for a participant in the event of a change in control. These protections generally are of two types: (1) improved benefits or (2) accelerated funding or payout. Benefit improvements triggered upon a change in control may include full vesting; the addition of age and years of service for purposes of vesting, benefit accrual, and benefit entitlement; eligibility for an early retirement subsidy; eliminating or reducing the early retirement adjustment; and permitting a benefit in the form of a lump sum. Accelerating funding, *e.g.*, through a rabbi trust, is more common than accelerating payout, because the latter would trigger immediate taxation. Code Sec. 409A lists a change in control as one of the six events on which a distribution of plan benefits can be made.

> **Planning Note:** Counsel should draft the plan so that the change in control event does not cause an automatic and inadvertent distribution upon "termination of employment," particularly in the case of an asset sale. In this regard, counsel may wish to include a "same-desk" rule type of exception in the plan. The plan should also consider the possibility of transferring assets and liabilities from the deferred compensation plan of the target company to the deferred compensation plan of the acquirer.

.13 Automatic Distribution Trigger

As discussed below, a rabbi trust can protect the executive's nonqualified plan benefits against all contingencies except the company's bankruptcy. (Indeed, this one risk of forfeiture is essential to prevent the executive from being in constructive receipt of such benefits.) However, executives and companies are always searching for a means to make the nonqualified plan benefits just a bit more secure. Before Code Sec. 409A, one of the plan design features designed to provide added security for executives' nonqualified plan benefits was to provide for an automatic distribution of all benefits under the plan upon the company's failure to satisfy one or more objective financial conditions specified in the plan.

The IRS had acquiesced in an automatic financial trigger in at least one private letter ruling. In IRS Letter Ruling 9508014, the IRS's description of the nonqualified plan included the following statement: "The Plan automatically terminates if the Company's net worth falls below $10,000,000."[154] Without comment on the automatic trigger provision, the IRS held that a participant would not recognize income on amounts credited to a deposit account, or any interest credited to, or appreciation in the value of, the deposit account, until the

---

[154] IRS Letter Ruling 9508014 (Nov. 22, 1994).

participant actually receives such amounts in accordance with the terms of the plan.

Code Sec. 409A(b)(2) eliminated an employer's ability to include a financial trigger in its nonqualified plan or trust.

.14 Other Plan Design Features

Some nonqualified plans will specifically attempt to include qualified domestic relations orders under Code Sec. 414(p) within a plan's general anti-assignment clause and, even if not excluded, administrators of tax-qualified plans may take the position that their procedures do not apply to nonqualified deferred compensation plans. However, there is at least one case to the contrary.[155] One practical approach that is used by some companies, particularly where the nonqualified plan is an excess benefit plan or an excess plan designed to provide benefits that cannot be provided under the plan because of any limitations on benefits and contributions, is to calculate the amount of the assigned benefit from both the qualified and nonqualified plan, but pay the assets solely from the tax-qualified plan. With respect to qualified domestic relations orders, the IRS held in a 2002 revenue ruling[156] that, if pursuant to a qualified domestic relations order, an individual's benefit under a nonqualified deferral compensation plan were transferred to the individual's former spouse, the former spouse, rather than the individual who earned the benefit, would be taxable on the amount transferred. Prior to the publication of this ruling, many practitioners believed that the employee rather than his or her spouse would be taxed in these circumstances, under traditional assignment of income principles, which require that income be taxed to the owner thereof, rather than the recipient. However, the IRS concluded that application of assignment of income principles in this context was inconsistent with the principles of Code Sec. 1041, dealing with the transfer of property incident to a divorce.

Another design issue that arises is the flexibility that an employer should retain to modify or terminate the excess benefit plan. Some plans will provide that an employer can discontinue benefits until the employee has terminated employment, and some provide that the arrangement can be discontinued even after the employee is in pay status. However, most plans provide for protection of the executives covered by the nonqualified plan by prohibiting any amendment that would reduce benefits below that earned or accrued immediately prior to the amendment.

Loans. While some nonqualified plans provide for loans, the IRS will not issue favorable rulings on such arrangements, and it is not recommended. Such loans could not be secured by the participant's interest in the plan without running afoul of the economic benefit doctrine.[157]

---

[155] *Bass v. Mid-American Co. Inc.*, 1995 U.S. Dist. LEXIS 15719 (N.E. Ill. 1995).

[156] Rev. Rul. 2002-1, IRB 2002-2, 268.

[157] Ability to pledge property as collateral for a loan would cause such property to be transferable. Reg. § 1.83-3(d).

Payments to participant's creditors. There is conflicting authority[158] as to whether a participant's interest in a nonqualified deferred compensation plan constitutes a portion of his or her estate, which can be assigned to a trustee in bankruptcy.

¶1765 "Funding" Nonqualified Plan Benefits

A fundamental requirement, and major disadvantage, of a nonqualified retirement or deferred compensation plan is that it remain an "unfunded, unsecured promise to pay money in the future." In simple terms, in the event of the employer's insolvency, a participant would be a general creditor of the employer as to any benefits accrued or compensation deferred under the plan. Thus, the challenge to practitioners is: Discover how to pre-fund the employer's promise of deferred compensation or supplemental retirement benefits when a qualified tax-exempt trust is not available.

Before Code Sec. 409A, Code Sec. 402(b) governed the taxation of employee trusts other than qualified plan trusts under Code Sec. 501(a). Under Code Sec. 402(b), contributions to trusts not exempt from taxation are included in an employee's gross income in the first taxable year in which there is no longer a substantial risk of forfeiture or the employee may transfer the amounts. Additionally, if the trust is discriminatory - which a rabbi trust always is - the Code also requires the employee to include any increases in the benefit in his/her income each year.

The use of offshore trusts to fund deferred compensation will generally trigger tax at vesting.[159] However, the final regulations continue to allow employers to use rabbi trusts, including so-called "springing rabbi trusts," except that a springing trust (rabbi or secular) that is based on the employer's financial health would trigger tax at vesting under Code Sec. 409A(b)(2).

.01 Rabbi Trusts

Many nonqualified plans are "informally" funded through the use of a rabbi trust, so-named because the first IRS ruling dealing with such a trust involved a congregation and its rabbi.[160] A rabbi trust is the most effective and well-known method of "securing" deferred compensation from employer changes in management or control. A significant difference between a rabbi trust and a qualified trust is that the assets of a rabbi trust are subject to the reach of the employer's creditors in the event of the employer's insolvency. Because the assets are subject to the reach of the employer's creditors, such assets are "subject to a substantial risk of forfeiture" and thus, the employee/beneficiary is not deemed to be in constructive receipt of such assets. The principal advantage of a properly drafted rabbi trust from the employee's perspective is that the promise of deferred compensation or additional pension benefits to the employee is funded in a

---

[158] *Compare In re Hanes,* 1994 U.S. Bankr. LEXIS 33 (E.D. Va. 1994) (interest includible in estate) with *Traina v. Sewell,* 1998 U.S. Dist. LEXIS 20486 (E.D. La.

1998) (debtor's interest in a nonqualified retirement plan is excludible from his estate.

[159] Code Sec. 409A(b).

[160] IRS Letter Ruling 8113107 (Dec. 31, 1980).

manner that is beyond the reach of the employer and other parties, in all circumstances except the employer's insolvency, without causing taxation to the employee.

While a rabbi trust does not provide protection against the risk of the insolvency of the employer/plan sponsor,[161] it does provide various protections against new management who may be unwilling to pay the participant's benefit. First, there is an independent trustee. Second, while there are no funding rules applicable to a rabbi trust and the practice of the grantor of the trust varies (some funding the obligation upfront, while others fund it over time), a common provision is accelerated funding upon a change in control, or upon demand by the trustee if the plan sponsor does not make payments as they come due. In addition, to allow the trustee effectively to protect the interests of plan participants, a rabbi trust could provide for establishing a fund for future administrative, trustee, and legal fees. Finally, a rabbi trust allows the employer to accumulate an asset to offset its growing liability for nonqualified plan benefits.

Whether the plan is "secured" through a rabbi trust may ultimately turn on the resolution of a number of business and employee relations issues. If an employer establishes a trust and retains an independent trustee, the plan would have more of the "look and feel" of a qualified plan and trust. Participants would receive account statements from a bank trustee, and the bank trustee would hold and invest real assets.

The IRS has published a model rabbi trust and procedures for obtaining a favorable advance ruling.[162] Many employers that establish a rabbi trust will closely follow the IRS model trust. The major features of the model rabbi trust are as follows:

- Plan participants and beneficiaries can have no preferential claim on the assets of the trust;

- Any rights under the plan and trust are unsecured contractual rights against the employer;

- The employer must notify the trustee if the plan becomes insolvent. Upon receiving such notice, the trustee will suspend payments from the trust. Pending an investigation by the trustee, the trustee must also suspend benefit payments if the trustee receives a written allegation that the employer is insolvent;

---

[161] As the Court of Appeals for the Fourth Circuit stated in *Goodman v. Resolution Trust Company*, 7 F3d 1123, 1129 (4th Cir. 1993): "Unfortunately, the recipients of grantor or rabbi trusts are unsecured creditors, who took the risk of being subject to the claims of general creditors for the benefit of favorable tax treatment - a gamble which failed to pay off in this case." *See also* Mertens, *Law of Federal Income Taxation* 25 B. 212 (1988) ("In reality, the recipient receives

only the company's unsecured promise to pay benefits and has no rights against any assets other than the rights of a general unsecured creditor of the Company").

[162] Rev. Proc. 92-64, IRS 1992-33, 11. The DOL has expressed the view that the use of a rabbi trust in connection with a top-hat or excess benefit plan will not cause those plans to be regarded as funded for purposes of Title I of ERISA.

- The plan sponsor must certify that the creditor's rights provisions of the trust are enforceable under state law if it wishes to obtain a favorable ruling with respect to the plan;

- The trust may be either revocable or irrevocable, or it can be a springing trust, which begins as a revocable trust and becomes irrevocable upon the occurrence of certain events—the receipt of a favorable ruling from the Internal Revenue Service, approval of the employer's board of directors, or a change in control of the plan sponsor;

- Springing funding (discussed further below) is permissible in two circumstances: the occurrence of a change of control, or a conversion of the trust from revocable to irrevocable;

- The trustee must be an independent third party that may be granted trustee powers under applicable state law. A private letter ruling cannot be obtained if an individual is designated as trustee. The model rabbi trust also contains a number of alternative provisions dealing with the resignation and removal of a trustee, which are designed to prove protection to the trust in the event of a change of control;

- The trustee must be given some investment authority over plan assets, the purpose of which is to ensure that the arrangement qualifies as a trust for federal income tax purposes;

- The trust can provide for investment in employer securities,[163] so long as such investment is permissible under state law. However, if stock or other employer securities are permissible plan investments, the trust must either be revocable or the sponsor must have the authority to substitute assets of fair market value for the trust assets; and

- Generally, all rights associated with trust assets must be exercised by the trustee or his designee, although optional language allows a plan sponsor to exercise voting rights and receive dividends.

.02 Tax Treatment of Rabbi Trusts

As noted above, because an employee's benefits and/or accounts under a rabbi trust are subject to the creditors' claims in the event of the employer's insolvency, the IRS treats those amount as subject to a substantial risk of forfeiture and, therefore, not constructively received. This is true even if the employee is fully vested in his or her benefit, and even if the trust is irrevocable. Executives can make pre-tax salary reduction contributions that are held and invested under a rabbi trust. Executives are not taxed until their nonqualified plan benefits are ultimately distributed. The tax treatment of executive's benefits under a rabbi trust are nearly as favorable as under a qualified retirement plan.[164]

---

[163] With respect to investments in company stock under a nonqualified deferred compensation plan, under an amendment to Section 16(a) of the Securities Exchange Act adopted by the SEC effective August 29, 2002, a Form 4 will be required to be filed within two business days of the transaction, if a director or officer makes a deferral under a non-

qualified deferred compensation plan, if the deferrals are credited to an investment account whose value is derived from the value of the sponsoring company's stock. This could occur if the plan involved phantom stock units.

[164] Nonqualified plan benefits cannot be rolled over.

It is a different story for the employer. Assets of a rabbi trust are deemed assets of the employer for purposes of taxation (and solvency). The employer's contributions to the rabbi trust are not deductible—at least until such amounts are eventually distributed and taxed to the executive participants. Moreover, interest earnings or appreciation on investments of the rabbi trust are taxable income to the employer.

One method that some employers have utilized to minimize the tax impact of their rabbi trust is to invest the trusts' assets in cash value life insurance. Under this funding method, generally, the employer is the owner and sole beneficiary of the policies and pays all premiums on such policies. The employer may withdraw or borrow against the cash value to pay promised benefits to employees. If the employee dies, the employer receives the proceeds tax-free, which may be used to pay a death benefit under the plan. (See ¶1815 for a discussion of the tax treatment of life insurance policies.)

.03 Code Sec. 409A Restrictions on Funding

Code Sec. 409A(b) imposes restrictions on the funding of nonqualified plan benefits. Code Sec. 409A treats any assets set aside (directly or indirectly) in a trust (or other arrangement) for purposes of paying deferred compensation under a nonqualified deferred compensation plan, as property transferred in connection with the performance of services, taxable under Code Sec. 83, whether or not such assets are available to satisfy claims of general creditors. Only a risk of forfeiture under Code Sec. 409A is sufficient to prevent taxation. Code Sec. 409A provides an exception for assets located in a foreign jurisdiction if substantially all of the services to which the nonqualified deferred compensation relates are performed in such jurisdiction.[165]

Code Sec. 409A also provides that there is a taxable transfer of property within the meaning of Code Sec. 83 with respect to such compensation as of the earlier of (A) the date on which a nonqualified plan first provides that assets will become restricted to the provision of benefits under the plan in connection with a change in the employer's financial health, or (B) the date on which assets are so restricted, whether or not such assets are available to satisfy claims of general creditors.

Additionally, for each taxable year that assets treated as transferred under the offshore trust or the financial health rule remain set aside in a trust or other arrangement, any increase in value in, or earnings with respect to, such assets shall be treated as an additional transfer of property under this subsection (to the extent not previously included in income). If amounts are required to be included in gross income by reason of the offshore trust or the financial health rule for a taxable year, Code Sec. 409A(b) provides for an increase in the tax imposed for such taxable year by 20% of the amounts required to be included in gross income, plus interest.[166]

---

[165] Code Se. 409A(b)(1).

[166] Code Sec. 409A(b)(4)(B). The interest determined under Code Sec. 409A(b)(4)(B) for any taxable year is the amount of interest at the underpayment rate plus 1 percentage point on the underpayments that would have occurred had the

The final regulations under Code Sec. 409A do not address the application of Code Sec. 409A(b), prohibiting the use of offshore trusts and financial health triggers. The regulations state that taxpayers may continue to rely upon Notice 2006-33 until further guidance is issued.[167]

However, the regulation provide that the establishment of or contributions to a trust or other arrangement from which benefits under the plan are to be paid would not be a material modification of the plan, which would eliminate the plan's ability to rely on the grandfather exception, provided that the contribution to the trust or other arrangement would not otherwise cause an amount to be includible in the service provider's gross income.[168]

.04 Insuring the Employer's Obligation to Pay

The IRS began permitting an employee/beneficiary of a nonqualified retirement plan to purchase an insurance policy on the employer's obligation to pay in 1993.[169] The IRS held that the purchase of insurance would not trigger constructive receipt or economic benefit to the participant, except that, if the employer reimbursed the participant for the premium, such reimbursement would be taxable income.

.05 Secular Trust

A secular trust is an irrevocable trust that is used to fund a nonqualified deferred compensation arrangement.[170] It is intended to produce tax consequences the opposite of a rabbi trust. These trusts accelerate the taxable event because the employee generally is taxed immediately upon the employee's contribution to the trust, and the employer receives an immediate deduction. The regulations under Code Sec. 409A provide that a right to compensation income that is required to be included in income under Code Sec. 402(b)(4)(A) is not a deferral of compensation subject to Code Sec. 409A.[171]

A typical secular trust includes the following characteristics:

- The company contributes to the trust each year on behalf of each participant in its deferred compensation plan.

- The trust is not a qualified trust under Code Sec. 401(a) and is not exempt from taxation under Code Sec. 501(a).

- The trust's assets are not subject to the claims of the company's creditors.

(Footnote Continued)

amounts so required to be included in gross income by this section been includible in gross income for the taxable year in which first deferred or, if later, the first taxable year in which such amounts are not subject to a substantial risk of forfeiture.

[167] Notice 2006-33, 2006-15 IRB 754 provides transition guidance related to the application of Code Sec. 409A(b) to certain outstanding arrangements.

[168] Treas. Reg. § 1.409A-6(a)(4)(i)(A).

[169] IRS Letter Ruling 9344038 (Aug. 2, 1993).

[170] The "secular trust" name derives from a wordplay on the more common rabbi trust. See also "rastafarian trust" which is an offshore rabbi trust and "rabbicular trust" which is essentially a rabbi trust that converts to a secular trust upon a change in control.

[171] Treas. Reg. § 1.409A-1(b)(6).

- Participants or their beneficiaries are entitled to receive their vested interest in the assets of the trust, net of applicable withholding and other taxes, on death, disability, or termination of employment.

- The trust is required to distribute to each participant each year an amount that the trustee reasonably estimates will be equal to the amount of federal, state, and local income and employment taxes payable by the participant with respect to the increase in the participant's vested accrued benefit in the trust during such year. The trust is permitted to make the distribution in part as a distribution of cash to the participant, and in part in the form of applicable employment tax withholding under federal, state, or local law. The company and the trust file income tax returns on a calendar year basis.

- The trust's assets could revert to the company only after all liabilities to participants and beneficiaries under the plan have been satisfied.

The initial designers of the secular trust envisioned the employer would be the grantor with specific federal income tax consequences.[172] The employer would have been taxed on the trust income under the grantor trust rules, but the income would also be treated as an additional contribution to the trust when allocated to participants' trust accounts and, as such, would be immediately includible in the income of the employee and deductible for the employer. The net result was that the trust income would be taxable to the employee, but neither the trust nor the employer would actually pay federal income tax on the trust income.

The IRS analyzes the tax treatment of a secular trust in a multi-step approach, as follows:

- Code Sec. 61(a)(1) provides that gross income means all income from whatever source derived, including compensation for services.

- Code Sec. 451 states that the amount of any item of gross income shall be included in gross income for the taxable year in which received by the taxpayer, unless, under the method of accounting used in computing taxable income, such amount is to be properly accounted for as of a different period.

- Reg. §1.451-2(a) states that income, although not actually reduced to a taxpayer's possession, is constructively received in the taxable year during which it is credited to the taxpayer's account, set apart, or otherwise made available so that the taxpayer may draw upon it at any time, or so that the taxpayer could have drawn upon it during the taxable year if notice of intention to withdraw had been given. However, the taxpayer does not constructively receive income if the taxpayer's control of its receipt is subject to substantial limitations or restrictions.

---

[172] *See* Code Sec. 671, Code Sec. 672, Code Sec. 673, Code Sec. 674, Code Sec. 675, Code Sec. 676 and Code Sec. 677.

- Under a secular trust, there are no substantial limitations or restrictions on a participant's right to receive a direct payment of compensation. Because a participant does not forego a valuable right by electing a direct payment to the secular trust, the amounts the company pays to a secular trust on behalf of a participant are considered to have been made available to the participant immediately prior to their transfer to the participant's trust by the company. Thus, a participant's control of the receipt of the direct payment is not subject to substantial limitations or restrictions.

- Accordingly, a participant covered by a secular trust is in constructive receipt of any contributions the company makes to the trust.

- Code Sec. 83(a) provides that the excess (if any) of the fair market value of property transferred in connection with the performance of services over the amount (if any) paid for the property is includible in the gross income of the person who performed the services for the first taxable year in which the property becomes transferable or is not subject to a substantial risk of forfeiture.

- Reg. § 1.83-3(e) provides that, for purposes of Code Sec. 83, the term "property" includes real or personal property other than money or an unfunded and unsecured promise to pay money or property in the future. Property also includes a beneficial interest in assets (including money) transferred or set aside from claims of the transferor's creditors, for example, in a trust or escrow account. However, to the extent a transfer to a trust is subject to Code Sec. 402(b), Code Sec. 83 applies to such a transfer only as provided for in Code Sec. 402(b).[173]

- Code Sec. 402(b)(1) provides, in general, that contributions to a nonexempt employees' trust made by a company are includible in the gross income of the employee in accordance with Code Sec. 83, with the value of the employee's interest in the trust substituted for the fair market value of the property for purposes of applying Code Sec. 83. Code Sec. 402(b)(4) provides rules that apply to highly compensated participants in certain nonexempt employees' trusts.

In order to limit the tax on the trust's investment earnings in a secular trust or the employee's investment earnings in a rabbi trust, an employer could invest in tax-exempt obligations. More commonly, however, employers will use life insurance contracts to fund their rabbi trusts. Other employers simply track the investment options under the tax-qualified plan, while others will fund the obligation with employer stock.

In two early secular trust rulings, the IRS denied deductions to employers for contributions before the recipient reached pay status because the Code Sec. 404(a)(5) separate accounts requirement had not been satisfied. In one of the rulings, the requirement was not satisfied because the employer had the right to receive funds back from the secular trust;[174] in the other ruling, it was not satisfied because the employer had the right to allocate earnings among the

---

[173] *See* Reg. § 1.83-8(a).

[174] IRS Letter Ruling 9207010 (Nov. 12, 1991).

different employees' accounts.[175] This separate account requirement does not mandate the establishment of separate trusts. So long as separate accounts are maintained for each employee to which employer contributions and earnings (or losses) are allocated, the employer deduction will be preserved.[176] The amount of the deduction is generally the entire amount (including actual or hypothetical interest when paid to the employee) although the rule does not apply to certain secular trusts. In this regard, in *Albertson's Inc. v. Comm'r*,[177] the court ultimately sustained the position of the IRS that interest credited to the account of a participant under a nonqualified deferred compensation plan is subject to the Code Sec. 404(a)(5) deduction timing rules, rather than the more favorable rules (from the employer's perspective) for interest deductions under Code Sec. 163.

However, in a series of private letter rulings issued in 1992, the IRS indicated that the treatment of the employer as the owner of the trust would be "fundamentally inconsistent" with the income inclusion rule of Code Sec. 402(b) and the deduction timing rules of Code Sec. 404(a)(5).[178] Consequently, the arrangement caused double taxation. All of the income earned by the trusts was held to be taxable currently to the trust and taxable again to the employees, either when distributed to them if they were nonhighly compensated employees under Code Sec. 402(b)(1) and Code Sec. 72, or when allocated to their accounts in the case of highly compensated employees as defined under Code Sec. 414(q) and Code Sec. 402(b).

There are at least two ways in which double taxation could be avoided. First, the employer could establish a simple trust under which all of the trust income would be paid out annually to the employee, with the trust receiving a deduction. The difficulty with this approach is that it undercuts one of the objectives of the arrangement, *i.e.*, the deferral of income. The second approach is an employee grantor trust, rather than an employer grantor trust. This arrangement assumes that the employee will be treated as the grantor of the entire trust. However, the funds for the trust must be given to the employee, who must have the choice whether or not to contribute them to the fund.[179] Thus, in two 1988 private letter rulings, executives signed individual trust documents or trust joinder agreements, and funds that would otherwise have been paid directly to the employees were deposited in the trust at their discretion. The IRS treated these employees as owners for purposes of the grantor trust rules, and taxable on all trust income.[180] A variation of this approach is the recontribution of prior distribution to the trust by the employee.[181]

---

[175] IRS Letter Ruling 9206009 (Nov. 11, 1991).

[176] Reg. § 1.404(a)-12(b)(3).

[177] *Albertson's Inc. v. Comm'r*, 94-2 USTC ¶ 50,619, 42 F3d 537 (9th Cir. 1994) *aff'g and rev'g* 94-1 USTC ¶ 50,016, 38 F3d 1046 (9th Cir. 1994) *cert. den.* 116 S. Ct. 51 (1995).

[178] IRS Letter Ruling 9206009 (Nov. 11, 1991); IRS Letter Ruling (Nov. 12, 1991).

[179] The ability to choose is the rationale for treating the amounts deposited as employee contributions under Reg. § 1.402(b)-1(h)(6) under the "assignment of income" doctrine.

[180] IRS Letter Ruling 8841023 (July 9, 1988); IRS Letter Ruling 8843021 (July 29, 1988).

[181] IRS Letter Ruling 9212019 (Dec. 20, 1991); IRS Letter Ruling 9212024 (Dec. 20, 1991). The IRS ruled that if participant contributions to the trust account exceed the amount of the employer contribution, then the employee is treated as the grantor of the portion of the trust allocable to the excess. If the affected employee makes repayments to the trust,

In July 2007, the IRS published Rev. Rul. 2007-48, with a significant update on secular (and rabbi) trusts in the era of Code Sec. 409A.[182] In Rev. Rul. 2007-48, the IRS discussed the federal tax consequences to the employees, the company, and the trust in a situation where a company contributes to a nonexempt employees' trust on behalf of highly compensated employees. Rev. Rul. 2007-48 also discusses the tax consequences of the vesting of an employee's interest in the trust, and distributions from the trust.

Income Tax Treatment of the Participant: Rev. Rul. 2007-48 clarifies that the company's contributions to a nonexempt employees' trust are included in the employee's gross income in accordance with Code Sec. 83, except that the value of the employee's interest in the trust is substituted for the property's fair market value.[183] Company contributions to a nonexempt employees' trust are included as compensation in the employee's gross income for the taxable year in which the contribution is made, but only to the extent that the employee's interest in the contribution is substantially vested.[184]

Because the trust is a nonexempt employees' trust whose assets are derived solely from company contributions, the entire trust is treated as a nonexempt employees' trust subject to the provisions of Code Sec. 402(b). Code Sec. 402(b)(2) provides that the amount actually distributed or made available to an employee by a nonexempt employees' trust is taxable in the taxable year in which distributed or made available to the employee.

Rev. Rul. 2007-48 also notes that, if one of the reasons a trust is not exempt from tax under Code Sec. 402(b) is the failure of the plan of which it is a part to meet the qualified plan requirements of Code Sec. 401(a)(26) or Code Sec. 410(b), then a highly compensated employee (as defined in Code Sec. 414(q)) shall, in lieu of the amount determined under Code Sec. 402(b)(1) or (2), include in gross income for the taxable year with or within which the taxable year of the trust ends an amount equal to the vested accrued benefit of the employee as of the close of the taxable year of the trust.[185]

Code Sec. 409A generally provides that unless certain requirements are met, amounts deferred under a nonqualified deferred compensation plan for all taxable years are currently includible in gross income to the extent not subject to a substantial risk of forfeiture. A right to compensation income that will be required to be included in income under Code Sec. 402(b)(4) is not a deferral of compensation for purposes of Code Sec. 409A.[186] Because the plan does not meet the requirements of Code Sec. 410(b) and the participant is a highly compensated employee, Code Sec. 402(b)(4)(A) determines the tax consequences to the participant of the participant's interest in the trust.

Income Tax Treatment of the Company: Code Sec. 404(a) provides the general deduction timing rules applicable to any plan or arrangement for the deferral of

---

(Footnote Continued)

they will qualify as miscellaneous itemized deductions under Code Sec. 67.

[182] Rev. Rul. 2007-48, I.R.B. 2007-30, July 23, 2007.

[183] Code Sec. 402(b)(1).

[184] Treas. Reg. § 1.402(b)1(a)(1).

[185] Code Sec. 402(b)(4)(A).

[186] Treas. Reg. § 1.409A-1(b)(6)(i).

compensation, regardless of the Code section under which the amounts might otherwise be deductible. Contributions paid by the company to or under a nonqualified deferred compensation plan or arrangement are deductible in the taxable year in which amounts attributable to the contributions are includible in the gross income of the employees participating in the plan or arrangement, provided that the contributions otherwise meet the requirements for deductibility.[187] In the case of a nonqualified plan in which more than one employee participates, contributions are deductible only if separate accounts are maintained for each employee.

In the case of a funded nonqualified plan under which more than one employee participates, no deduction is allowable under Code Sec. 404(a)(5) for any contribution unless separate accounts are maintained for each employee to which company contributions under the plan are allocated, along with any income earned thereon.[188] The requirement of separate accounts does not require that a separate trust be maintained for each employee.

Income Tax Treatment of the Trust: Code Sec. 641(a) provides that the tax imposed by Code Sec. 1(e) applies to the taxable income of any kind of property held in trust. Code Sec. 661(a) provides that in computing the taxable income of an estate or trust a deduction is allowed for distributions to beneficiaries equal to the sum of the amount of income for the taxable year that is required to be distributed currently and any other amounts properly paid or credited or required to be distributed for the taxable year. However, the total amount deductible under Code Sec. 661(a) cannot exceed the distributable net income as computed under the provisions of Code Sec. 643(a).

Code Sec. 663(c) provides that for the sole purpose of determining the amount of distributable net income in the application of Code Sec. 661, in the case of a single trust having more than one beneficiary, substantially separate and independent shares of different beneficiaries in the trust are treated as separate trusts. A nonexempt employees' trust is allowed a deduction under Code Sec. 661(a) for distributions to a retired employee under a deferred compensation plan.[189] Where the separate share rule of Code Sec. 663 applies to the trust, the trust's deduction under Code Sec. 661(a) is limited to the distributee's separate share of the trust's distributable net income. The taxation of the distributions is not governed by the provisions of Code Sec. 662.

Income and Deductions: When the company contributes to a nonexempt employees' trust on behalf of highly compensated employee/participants, each participant includes in gross income as compensation under Code Sec. 402(b)(4)(A) the participant's vested accrued benefit as of the end of the taxable year of the trust ending with or within the taxable year of the participant. Provided that the separate account rule of Code Sec. 404(a)(5) is satisfied, the company is entitled to deduct a contribution made to the trust on behalf of a participant in the taxable year in which amounts attributable to the contribution

---

[187] Code Sec. 404(a)(5).
[188] Treas. Reg. § 1.404(a)-12(b)(3).

[189] Rev. Rul. 74-299, 1974-1 C.B. 154.

are includible in the participant's income, to the extent the contribution otherwise meets the requirements for deductibility. The trust is taxed as a trust under Code Sec. 641. Because the separate share rule of Code Sec. 663(c) applies to the trust, the trust is entitled to deduct distributions made to a participant to the extent the distributions do not exceed the distributable net income allocable to the participant's separate share of the trust.

FICA and FUTA: If the company's contribution to a nonexempt employees' trust on behalf of a highly compensated employee is vested at the time of contribution, then the amount of the contribution is subject to FICA and FUTA taxes at the time of contribution. The company is liable for the payment of FICA and FUTA taxes. If the contribution is not vested at the time of contribution, then the amount of the contribution and the earnings thereon are subject to FICA and FUTA taxation at the time of vesting. With respect to contributions and earnings thereon that become vested after the date of contribution, the nonexempt employees' trust is considered the company for withholding tax purposes with respect to such amounts as they become vested.[190]

Income Tax Withholding: For federal income tax withholding purposes, wages are determined in the same way gross income is determined under Code Sec. 402(b)(4)(A). The employee's wages are in the amount of the employee's vested accrued benefit on the last day of the taxable year of the nonexempt employees' trust and are treated as paid for federal income tax withholding purposes on that same date. The nonexempt employees' trust is the company,[191] regardless of whether contributions made for the benefit of the employee are vested at the time of contribution. Thus, the employees' trust is responsible for all federal income tax withholding with respect to such wages paid to the employee. Distributions of benefits from the nonexempt employees' trust to the employee or for the employee's benefit are included in determining the vested accrued benefit of the employee at the end of the trust's taxable year, which is subject to federal income tax withholding at the end of the trust's taxable year.

.06 Airline Financial Woes Lead to a Surge in Secular Trust Popularity

The September 11, 2001, terrorist attacks adversely affected many sectors of the U.S. economy. However, "9/11" and its aftermath caused unprecedented operational and financial challenges for the airline industry. Several major carriers, including United Airlines, the world's largest, filed for bankruptcy protection in 2002.

In October 2002, American Airlines, Inc. established a secular trust to secure and preserve the retirement benefits promised under its Supplemental Executive Retirement Program for Officers. In addition, in the fall of 2002, Delta Air Lines, Inc. established and funded secular trusts for the benefit of its senior management employees. According to Delta's proxy statement for the 2003 shareholders'

---

[190] Code Sec. 3401(d)(1).

[191] Within the meaning of Code Sec. 3401(d)(1).

meeting, the Personnel & Compensation Committee of Delta's board of directors concluded that:

> [I]ts first priority must be to maintain a highly qualified management team capable of responding effectively to the extraordinary challenges facing Delta and the airline industry. Moreover, the Committee recognized that these challenges would likely continue for some time. This would make it difficult to retain key members of management who could be recruited by companies in other industries offering opportunities involving less risk and greater compensation. Therefore, in order to strengthen Delta's ability to retain the existing management team, the Committee took the actions discussed below.

Based on this judgment, Delta took two specific steps to retain management employees. Delta established a special retention program and funded its existing nonqualified plan. Recognizing that the benefits under its nonqualified retirement plan would be completely lost if the company were to file for bankruptcy, Delta approved the funding of employee grantor trusts to secure the nonqualified retirement benefits of 33 management personnel, according to the proxy statement. Amounts held in these individual trusts would offset the amounts that would otherwise be payable to these executives under Delta's nonqualified retirement plans as well as certain other agreements with the executives.

The funding of these trusts occurs over three years, with Delta funding 60% of the present value (as of December 31, 2001) of the executive's after-tax age 62 nonqualified retirement benefit (based on pay and service earned as of December 31, 2001) in 2002. Delta announced its intention to make further funding contributions to the employee grantor trusts in 2003 and 2004 for participants who remain active employees of Delta. After the 2003 contribution, the amount in each employee's trust will equal 80% of the present value (as of December 31, 2002) of the after-tax age 62 nonqualified retirement benefit (based on pay and service earned as of December 31, 2002). The 2004 contribution would bring the amount in the executive's trust up to 100% of the present value (as of December 31, 2003) of the after-tax age 62 nonqualified retirement benefit (based on pay and service earned as of December 31, 2003). Delta would accelerate the 2003 and 2004 contributions if it experienced a change in control.

Additionally, Delta contributed amounts necessary to pay all taxes resulting from the funding contribution. Delta designed the contributions to provide the same after-tax benefit at retirement to covered executives as the prior unfunded approach provided. Delta also amended the nonqualified retirement plan to provide that benefits will be payable as a lump sum at the time of retirement. However no lump sum would be payable before January 1, 2004, in order to further encourage retention. If an executive leaves Delta before January 1, 2004, Delta would not make additional contributions to his or her trust. If an executive leaves (whether before or after January 1, 2004) prior to his or her normal retirement date and, without the consent of Delta's Personnel & Compensation Committee, goes to work for certain competitors, he or she must repay Delta liquidated damages approximately equal to the contributions made to the executive's trust, including taxes withheld.

¶1765.06

In 2002, Delta deposited $4,542,295 into an individual trust for, and withheld $3,699,938 in taxes on behalf of, its chief executive officer. The total amounts deposited into individual trusts for, and taxes withheld on behalf of, all 33 covered executives were $14,021,447 and $11,543,509, respectively.

Because of the adverse tax consequences to executives, Delta felt it necessary to contribute (or pay) nearly as much in taxes on behalf of the executives as it did to fund the retirement benefits. Adverse tax consequences are the main reason companies do not create secular trusts. However, because of the risk of bankruptcy, Delta apparently determined that the cost was necessary to provide security for the payment of already earned retirement benefits under the nonqualified retirement plan.

.07 Company Stock in a Rabbi Trust

The IRS has revoked prior rulings that permitted rabbi trusts in which subsidiaries participate to hold parent company stock without adverse tax consequences.[192] As long as trust assets are subject to subsidiary creditors' claims (which they must be to avoid constructive receipt), some of the company stock will be considered owned by the subsidiary. The IRS has suggested that, to the extent that the subsidiary owns the stock, the IRS would impose taxes on dividends on the parent company stock, and on gains from the disposition of the stock. For dividends, the filing of a consolidated return may eliminate the gain and no adverse tax consequences should result. However, if a subsidiary's participant were to receive parent company stock in a distribution from the plan, the subsidiary may be taxed on any gain the stock has experienced above its basis as a trust asset. This tax on the gains would offset some or all of the deduction received for the compensation paid to the participant.

.08 Springing Rabbi Trust

A "springing" rabbi trust is one that remains unfunded (that is, without assets) until a triggering event specified in the nonqualified plan or trust document, such as a change in control. Effective on the triggering event, the employer must contribute an amount sufficient to fully fund the benefits under the plan. In DOL Advisory Opinion 91-16A, the DOL concluded that the springing provision of a plan would not cause it to be considered funded for purposes of ERISA.

¶1775 Securities Law Issues

If the nonqualified plan participants are offered an opportunity to defer a portion of their compensation and to invest those deferrals in an employer stock fund, the participants' interests in the plan would be considered securities and the employer would be required to register those interests, along with the shares of employer stock available under the plan, on a Form S-8 Registration Statement under the Securities Act of 1933 (the "Securities Act"), as amended. In addition to filing a Form S-8 Registration Statement, an effective registration requires that the

---

[192] IRS Letter Ruling 9609010, November 20, 1995.

¶1765.07

employer deliver to each participant documents and information that constitute a Section 10(a) prospectus.

.01 Prospectus

The nonqualified plan's prospectus consists of the summary plan description ("SPD") and the statement of general information. For example, the following should appear on the front page of the SPD:

> This Summary Plan Description constitutes part of a prospectus covering securities that have been registered under the Securities Act of 1933. It covers ABC Corporation common stock offered through the ABC Corporation Nonqualified Retirement Plan. Because you are able to invest your compensation deferral contributions in ABC Corporation common stock, Securities and Exchange Commission regulations require that ABC give you this prospectus.

.02 Updating the Plan Prospectus

The information in the prospectus must be kept current, whether by supplements or restatements. In the absence of any material changes to the plan, the prospectus should be updated every *16 months*, unless it is unreasonably expensive or burdensome to do so. If a material change has been made to the plan, the prospectus should be updated, or a supplement distributed, as soon as practicable.

.03 Short-Swing Profits Penalties

Elections to invest in company stock under a nonqualified plan may be subject to Rule 16b-3. An exemption is available, allowing intra-plan transfers to be compared only among themselves, under Section 16b-3(c) for "excess benefit plans" only. The Section 16b-3(c) definition of "excess benefit plans" appears to be slightly broader than ERISA's definition. It includes plans that are operated in conjunction with a qualified plan and provide only the benefits and contributions permitted under the qualified plan but for the benefit or contribution limitations set forth in the Code. Even if the nonqualified plan qualified for the excess benefit plan exemption, transfers into or out of a company stock fund under the plan, and withdrawals (so-called "discretionary transactions") will be compared against opposite way transactions under the nonqualified plan or any other plan (*e.g.*, the company's 401(k) plan) within the preceding six months.

.04 Reporting

Section 16 insiders are required to file a Form 4 under the Section 16 reporting rules when they defer fees in the form of company stock. The SEC has released Final Rule: Ownership Reports and Trading by Officers, Directors and Principal Security Holders, File No. S7-31-02, in which the Commission states, "transactions pursuant to nonqualified deferred compensation plans or other dividend or interest reinvestment plan transactions (such as acquisitions pursuant to voluntary contributions of additional funds) will be reportable on Form 4 within two business days after the date of execution. However, to the extent that such a transaction satisfies the affirmative defense conditions of Rule 10b5-1(c), the date of execution for Form 4 reporting purposes may be calculated on the modified basis." Under the limited extension provided by Rule 10b5-1(c), the two business day deadline is counted from a "deemed" transaction date, which is the earlier of (i) the date the insider receives notice that the transaction was executed, or (ii) the third business day after the date the transaction is executed. Consequently, the latest a Form 4 can be timely filed for these transactions is on the fifth business day after the transaction. The extended time period for these transactions is not available if the insider has selected the date for transaction execution. While this exception does allow for extended filing, it is important to note that the filing is still required.

Included in the transactions that now require accelerated reporting on Form 4 are routine deferrals of officer compensation under a nonqualified deferred compensation plan where the deferrals are credited to an investment account whose value is derived from the value of the company's stock. Typically, such an investment account would involve phantom stock units (including the use of the stock's performance as the index for crediting investment returns to the deferrals). As a result, the crediting of phantom stock units with respect to contributions to a nonqualified deferred compensation plan by directors or officers is now reportable on Form 4 within two business days of each date compensation withheld is credited to the company stock investment account (generally, at the end of each pay period). Previously, a full year's worth of these recurring acquisitions could be aggregated and reported as single item on a year-end Form 5 report.

.05 Proxy Statement Disclosure

SERPs and deferred compensation plans were among the many areas of executive compensation for which significantly greater disclosure is required under the SEC's 2006 executive compensation disclosure rules. Even before the effective date of the SEC's 2006 executive compensation disclosure rules, some companies had begun to disclose more information on their SERPs. For example, in its 2005 proxy statement, Abercrombie & Fitch disclosed that its CEO would receive $1.5 million per year if he retired in 2008.

The Exxon SERP provides for retirement payments that are a percentage of final average compensation time years of service. For purposes of calculating compensation, the Exxon SERP counts "earnings-bonus units" which Exxon awards along with cash to executives for their annual bonuses. These units are future cash payments based on an increase in Exxon's per share earnings.

¶1785 Code Sec. 409A

Code Sec. 409A imposes requirements in four main areas:

- Rules on deferral elections;
- Rules on distributions and distribution elections;
- Prohibitions on the acceleration of distributions; and
- Limits related to funding nonqualified benefits.

¶1775.05

.01 Application of Code Sec. 409A

Code Sec. 409A addresses the taxation of "nonqualified deferred compensation," including rules regarding payouts, funding methods and the timing of deferral elections. "Deferred compensation" means compensation (i) to which a service provider has a legally binding right during a taxable year (*i.e.*, it is "earned and vested"); (ii) that has not been previously taxed; and (iii) that is payable pursuant to the applicable plan in a later year.[193] (Proposed regulations under Code Sec. 409A clarify that a service provider may be an entity as well as an individual.) The failure to comply with Code Sec. 409A results in immediate income on deferrals, an excise tax of 20% and other penalties.

For most companies, the final Code Sec. 409A regulations create three categories of compensation and benefits about which to worry, with different (albeit, overlapping) issues applicable to each. The provisions of the regulations can be separated into rules applicable to, and amendments required of:

1. Deferred compensation and supplemental retirement benefits, generally provided under nonqualified plans (sometimes provided under employment or other agreements),

2. Severance benefits, generally provided under employment or change in control agreements and severance plans (see Chapter 14), and

3. Equity-based compensation, generally provided under stock incentive plans and awards (see Chapters 6, 7 and 8).

Code Sec. 409A in effect, created a class of qualified plans; one could call them "lesser qualified plans." These plans qualify for somewhat favorable tax treatment (although not as favorable as true qualified plans). To provide the desired tax treatment they need to meet the requirements of (or "qualify" under) Code Sec. 409A.

Code Sec. 409A applies to group benefit plans and to individual agreements (*e.g.*, employment contracts). It applies to both elective and nonelective arrangements. Code Sec. 409A applies to deferred compensation payable to individuals (including common law employees, nonemployee directors, and independent contractors), personal service corporations and noncorporate entities that are similar to personal service corporations. Examples of arrangements covered by Code Sec. 409A include elective and nonelective salary, bonus or fee deferrals, supplemental retirement plans (SERPs), certain equity-based compensation arrangements (*e.g.*, stock options/SARs, unless specifically exempted), and some severance arrangements.

Code Sec 409A and the regulations thereunder explicitly exclude benefits under qualified retirement plans from the definition of deferred compensation.[194] Other arrangements not covered by Code Sec. 409A include:

- Compensation paid in the same taxable year as it vests;

---

[193] Treas. Reg. § 1.409A-1(b).

[194] Code Sec. 409A(d)(1)(A). Treas. Reg. § 1.409A-1(a)(2).

- Compensation paid within 2¹/₂ months after the end of that year (*e.g.*, bonuses paid shortly following the year in which earned);
- Restricted stock;
- Tax-qualified retirement plans (such as 401(k) plans);
- Incentive stock options;
- Nonincentive options if (i) exercise price is no less than FMV at time of grant and (ii) no ability exists to defer past exercise;
- Options granted under a Code Sec. 423 employee stock purchase plan;
- Certain stock appreciation rights;
- Tax sheltered annuities (Code Sec. 403(b) plans);
- Health and welfare plans;
- Certain deferred compensation plans maintained by governmental agencies and tax-exempt organizations (457(b) plans); and
- Partnership interests (until further guidance is issued, generally treated the same as stock; the grant of a profits interest in a partnership in connection with the performance of services is not subject to Code Sec. 409A).

.02 Final Regulations — Subjects Addressed

The final regulations are an extensive discussion of the issues that can arise under Code Sec. 409A.[195] The subjects discussed include the following:

1. Initial Deferral Elections

    Performance-based Compensation

2. Short-Term Deferrals

3. Distribution Elections

    Change of Distribution Elections

4. Key Employee Distributions (and definition)

5. Employment and Change in Control Agreements and Severance Plans

6. Equity-Based Compensation

    (a) Stock Options/SARs

    (b) Private Company valuation issues

    (c) Restricted Stock and RSUs

7. Plan Termination

8. Tandem Plans and Linked Elections

9. Documentary Compliance

10. Code Sec. 457 Plans

11. Partnerships and Investment Funds

---

[195] The Treasury and IRS issued 397 pages of final regulations under Code Sec. 409A on April 10, 2007.

12. Foreign deferred compensation arrangements

13. Miscellaneous

    (a) Small Amounts

    (b) Hardship Withdrawals

    (c) Plan Aggregation

    (d) Funding

    (e) Code Sec. 162(m)

    (f) Penalties

.03 Deferral Elections

An individual employee or participant must make an irrevocable election to defer compensation before the end of the tax year preceding the year in which the individual performs the services to which the compensation relates.[196] An election to defer an amount also must include an election as to both the timing and form of the payment.[197] A plan may provide that a participant's deferral election remains in effect until he or she terminates or modifies it.[198]

> ABC Corporation sponsors a plan under which Employee A may elect to defer a percentage of Employee A's salary. Employee A has participated in the plan in prior years. To satisfy the requirements of this section with respect to salary earned in calendar year 2019, if Employee A elects to defer any amount of such salary, she must make the deferral election (including an election as to the time and form of payment) no later than December 31, 2018.[199]

If a participant has a legally binding right to a payment in a subsequent year that is subject to a condition requiring the participant to continue to provide services for a period of at least 12 months from the date the participant obtains the legally binding right to avoid forfeiture of the payment, the participant must make an election to defer such compensation on or before the 30th day after the participant obtains the legally binding right to the compensation, provided that the election is made at least 12 months in advance of the earliest date at which the forfeiture condition could lapse.[200]

> **Example:** On March 1, 2019, ABC Corporation grants Employee E a $10,000 bonus, payable on March 1, 2021 (with reasonable interest), provided that Employee E continues performing services as an employee of ABC through March 1, 2021. (The amount does not qualify as performance-based compensation, and Employee E already participates in another account balance nonqualified deferred compensation plan.) Employee E may make an initial deferral election on or before March 31, 2019 (within 30 days after obtaining a legally binding right), because at least 12 months of additional

---

[196] Code Sec. 409A(a)(4)(B), Treas. Reg. § 1.409A-2(a).

[197] Treas. Reg. § 1.409A-2(a).

[198] Treas. Reg. § 1.409A-2(a).

[199] Treas. Reg. § 1.409A-2(b)(9), Example 1.

[200] Treas. Reg. § 1.409A-2(a)(5).

services are required after the date of election for the risk of forfeiture to lapse.[201]

First Year of Eligibility

The final regulations continue the exception to the general rule regarding *initial* deferral elections.[202] In the first year in which an individual becomes eligible to participate in a plan, the individual may make an initial deferral election within 30 days after the date he or she becomes eligible to participate in such plan, with respect to compensation paid for services the individual is to perform after the election.

For compensation that is earned based upon a specified performance period (*e.g.*, an annual bonus), where a deferral election is made in the first year of eligibility (within 30 days after the date he or she becomes eligible to participate in such plan) but after the beginning of the performance period, the election may apply only to the compensation paid for services performed after the election. No more than an amount equal to the total amount of the compensation for the performance period multiplied by the ratio of the number of days remaining in the performance period after the election over the total number of days in the performance period may be deferred.[203]

Performance-Based Compensation

With respect to performance-based compensation, an employee may make his or her election to defer as late as the date that is six months before the end of the performance period, provided that an employee cannot elect to defer performance-based compensation after such compensation has become readily ascertainable.[204]

The final regulations define performance-based compensation as compensation the amount of which, or the entitlement to which, is contingent on the satisfaction of preestablished organizational or individual performance criteria relating to a performance period of at least 12 consecutive months.[205] The regulations consider organizational or individual performance criteria preestablished if the employer establishes them in writing by not later than 90 days after the commencement of the period of service to which the criteria relates (provided that the outcome is substantially uncertain at the time the criteria are established). Unlike the exception for performance-based compensation that existed under Code Sec. 162(m) before 2018, performance-based compensation under Code Sec. 409A may include (i) payments based on performance criteria that are not approved by a board compensation committee or stockholders, and (ii) compensation based on subjective performance criteria.

No Election Provided

The regulations under Code Sec. 409A provide rules for situations where an employer provides for a mandatory compensation deferral or automatic retire-

---

[201] Treas. Reg. § 1.409A-2(b)(9), Example 5.
[202] Treas. Reg. § 1.409A-2(a)(7).
[203] Treas. Reg. § 1.409A-2(a)(7)
[204] Treas. Reg. § 1.409A-2(a)(8).
[205] Treas. Reg. § 1.409A-1(e).

ment benefit, *e.g.*, with no election by the employee/participant.[206] A plan that provides for a deferral of compensation for services performed during an employee's taxable year that does not give the employee an opportunity to elect the time or form of payment of such compensation must designate the time and form of payment by no later than the later of the time the employee first has a legally binding right to the compensation or, if later, the time the employee would be required under Code Sec. 409A to make such an election if the employer had given the employee an opportunity to make such an election.

> ABC Corporation has a taxable year ending September 30. On July 1, 2019, ABC enters into a legally binding obligation to pay Employee B a $10,000 bonus. The amount is not subject to a substantial risk of forfeiture and does not qualify as performance-based compensation as described in § 1.409A-1(e). ABC does not provide Employee B an election as to the time and form of payment. Unless the amount is to be paid in accordance with the short-term deferral rule of § 1.409A-1(b)(4), ABC must specify the time and form of payment on or before July 1, 2019 to satisfy the requirements of this section.[207]

In situations where an employer provides for an automatic retirement benefit, such as under an excess benefit plan, the regulations under Code Sec. 409A provide that the employee/participant is treated as initially eligible to participate in the plan as of the first day of the participant's taxable year immediately following the first year the participant accrues a benefit under the plan. Thus, any election made within 30 days following such date is treated as applying to benefits accrued under such plan for services performed before the election.[208]

.04 Distribution Events and Elections

A Code Sec. 409A-compliant nonqualified plan may permit distributions only upon certain dates or events:[209]

1. Fixed date or dates
2. Separation from service
3. Death
4. Disability
5. Unforeseeable emergency
6. Change in control of a corporation

As noted above, a participant generally must designate the time and form of distribution at the same time as he or she makes the election to defer.

The regulations under Code Sec. 409A set forth several rules governing the payment date that a plan or participant election may specify.[210]

- The plan or election must provide that the date of the event is the payment date, or specify another payment date that is objectively determinable and nondiscretionary at the time the event occurs.

---

[206] Treas. Reg. § 1.409A-2(a)(2).
[207] Treas. Reg. § 1.409A-2(b)(9), Example 2.
[208] Treas. Reg. § 1.409A-2(a)(7)(iii).

[209] Code Sec. 409A(a)(2), Treas. Reg. § 1.409A-3(a).
[210] Treas. Reg. § 1.409A-3(b).

- The plan may provide that a payment upon one of the listed events (not including unforeseeable emergency) will be made in accordance with a schedule that is objectively determinable and nondiscretionary based on the date the event occurs (and that would qualify as a fixed schedule if the payment event were instead a fixed date).

- The schedule must be fixed at the time the permissible payment event is designated.

- A plan or election may provide that a payment, including a payment that is part of a fixed schedule, is to be made during a designated taxable year of the employee, which is objectively determinable and nondiscretionary at the time the payment event occurs. For example, a participant's election may provide for three substantially equal payments payable during the first three taxable years following the taxable year in which the participant separates from service.

- A plan or election may provide that a payment is to be made during a designated period that is objectively determinable and nondiscretionary at the time the payment event occurs, but only if (i) the designated period both begins and ends within one calendar year or (ii) the designated period is not more than 90 days and the employee does not have a right to designate the year of the payment.

- Where a plan or participant election provides for a period of more than one day following a payment event during which a payment may be made, such as within 90 days following the date of the event, the payment date for purposes of the subsequent deferral rules (described below) is treated as the first possible date upon which a payment could be made under the terms of the plan.

- A plan may provide for payment upon the earliest or latest of more than one event or time, provided that each event or time is one of those listed above.

- Generally, a plan may designate only one time and form of payment upon the occurrence of each permitted distribution event (described above).[211] For example, a plan or participant election could not provide for one payment date or schedule of payments if a specified event occurs on a Monday, but another payment date or schedule of payments if the event occurs on any other day of the week.

- A plan that provides for a payment upon death, disability, or change in control may allow for an alternative payment schedule if the event occurs on or before one (but not more than one) specified date, provided that the addition or deletion of such a different time and form of payment applicable to an existing deferral would be subject to the subsequent deferral election and accelerated payment rules (described below). For example, a plan may provide that a participant will receive a lump sum payment of the participant's entire benefit under the plan on the first day of the

---

[211] Treas. Reg. § 1.409A-3(c).

¶1785.04

month following a change in control event that occurs before he attains age 55, but will receive five substantially equal annual payments commencing on the first day of the month following a change in control event that occurs on or after he attains age 55.

- In the case of a plan or participant election that specifies payment upon a separation from service, the participant may designate a different time and form of payment with respect to a separation from service under each of the following conditions:[212]

  1. A separation from service during a limited period not to exceed two years following a change in control event.

  2. A separation from service before or after a specified date (for example, the attainment of a specified age), or a separation from service before or after a combination of a specified date, such as attaining a specified age, and a specified period of service determined under a predetermined, nondiscretionary, objective formula or pursuant to the method for crediting service under the employer's qualified plan.

  3. A separation from service not described in (1) or (2) above.

The following examples should help illustrate the application of the distribution election timing rules:

Employee A provides services as an employee of ABC Corporation (and is not a specified employee). Employee A participates in a nonqualified deferred compensation plan providing for a lump sum payment payable on or before December 31 of the calendar year in which A separates from service. The plan provides for a payment upon a separation from service in compliance with Code Sec. 409A.[213]

Employee B provides services as an employee of ABC Corporation (and is not a specified employee). Employee B participates in a nonqualified deferred compensation plan providing for a lump sum payment payable on or before the 90th day immediately following the date upon which B separates from service. ABC retains the sole discretion to determine when, during the 90-day period, it will make the payment. Although the plan does not specify a period during one calendar year in which it will make the payment, the plan provides for a payment upon a separation from service in compliance with Code Sec. 409A because the period over which the plan may make the payment is not longer than 90 days.[214]

Employee C is an employee of ABC Corporation (and not a specified employee). C participates in a nonqualified deferred compensation plan providing for a lump sum payment payable on or before the 180th day following the date upon which C separates from service. ABC retains the sole discretion to determine when, during the 180-day period, it will make the payment. Because the plan does not specify a period during one calendar year in which it will make the payment, and because the period over which the plan may make the payment is longer than 90 days, the plan does not provide for a payment upon a separation from service that complies with Code Sec. 409A.[215]

---

[212] Treas. Reg. § 1.409A-3(c).
[213] Treas. Reg. § 1.409A-3(i)(1)(vi), Example 1.

[214] Treas. Reg. § 1.409A-3(i)(1)(vi), Example 2.
[215] Treas. Reg. § 1.409A-3(i)(1)(vi), Example 3.

Employee D elects (i) an immediate lump sum payment of her account if her separation from service occurs on or before age 55, and (ii) five equal annual payments if her separation from service occurs after age 55. Employee E elects to receive (i) a lump sum payment of his account on the first day of the month following a change in control event that occurs before he attains age 55, and (ii) five substantially equal annual payments commencing on the first day of the month following a change in control that occurs on or after he attains age 55. Each of these elections satisfy Code Sec. 409A.

Separation from Service

A "separation from service" means the participant dies, retires, or otherwise has a termination of employment with the employer.[216] The IRS specifically designed the regulations to prevent employees and employers from affecting the timing of the employee's plan distribution by manipulating the time of the employee's employment termination. Under the regulations, whether a termination of employment has occurred is determined based on whether the facts and circumstances indicate that the employer and employee reasonably anticipated that no further services would be performed after a certain date or that the level of bona fide services the employee would perform after such date (whether as an employee or as an independent contractor) would permanently decrease to no more than 20% of the average level of bona fide services performed (whether as an employee or an independent contractor) over the immediately preceding 36-month period (or the full period of services to the employer if the employee has been providing services to the employer less than 36 months).[217] The regulations indicate that the facts and circumstances to be considered in making this determination include, but are not limited to, whether the employee continues to be treated as an employee for other purposes (such as continuation of salary and participation in employee benefit programs), whether similarly situated service providers have been treated consistently, and whether the employee is permitted, and realistically available, to perform services for other service recipients in the same line of business.

The regulations presume that an employee has:

- incurred a separation from service where the level of bona fide services performed by the employee decreases to a level equal to 20% or less of the average level of services performed by the employee during the immediately preceding 36-month period; and

- not incurred a separation from service where the level of bona fide services performed by the employee continues at a level that is 50% or more of the average level of service performed by the employee during the immediately preceding 36-month period.

The regulations also adopt permissive use of the rule generally referred to as the "same desk" rule, allowing the parties to an asset purchase agreement to decide whether employees of the selling corporation that continue in the same

---

[216] Treas. Reg. § 1.409A-1(h).   [217] Treas. Reg. § 1.409A-1(h)(1)(ii).

position with the purchaser of the assets will be treated as separating from service.[218]

The regulations give buyers and sellers in asset transactions the discretion to treat employees as separating from service. In a typical asset transaction, employees formally terminate employment with the seller and immediately recommence employment with the buyer. However, the employees often experience no change in their location, duties, or terms of employment. Proposed regulations that the IRS issued in 2016 clarify and make explicit that a stock purchase transaction that is treated as a deemed asset sale under Code Sec. 338 is not a sale or other disposition of assets for purposes of this rule under Code Sec. 409A, because in a deemed asset sale under Code Sec. 338, employees do not experience a termination of employment, formal or otherwise.

The regulations provide that an employee who changes his or her status to that of an independent contractor would not be deemed to have incurred a separation from service unless the level of services reasonably anticipated to be provided by the individual after the change would be insubstantial. The proposed regulations clarify that an employee who ceases providing services as an employee and begins providing services as an independent contractor (including as a director) is treated as having a separation from service if, at the time of the change in employment status, the level of services reasonably anticipated to be provided after the change would result in a separation from service under the rules applicable to employees.

Payments upon Death

Code Sec. 409A provides that a payment is treated as made upon the employee's death if the payment is made on a date within the same taxable year of the employee's death or by March 15 of the following year. In a nod to practical realities, the proposed regulations expanded this provision to allow a payment to be made no later than December 31 of the calendar year following the year of the employee's death. An employer need not specifically amend its plan to incorporate this rule.

The payment rule for amounts payable upon the death of an employee also applies in the case of the death of a beneficiary who had become entitled to a payment due to the employee's death. A deferred compensation plan may include the death, disability and unforeseeable emergency of a beneficiary who has become entitled to a payment due to an employee's death as a potentially earlier alternative payment event for amounts previously deferred. A schedule of payments that has already commenced prior to a beneficiary's death, disability or unforeseeable emergency may be accelerated upon the beneficiary's death, disability or unforeseeable emergency.

.05 Subsequent Deferral Elections

One of the most significant changes Code Sec. 409A makes to nonqualified deferred compensation plans is that a participant may change his or her election

---

[218] Treas. Reg. § 1.409A-1(h)(4).

as to the timing or form of a payment (a "subsequent deferral election"), only if:[219]

- The plan requires that such election not take effect until at least 12 months after the date on which the subsequent deferral election is made.

- In the case of an election related to a payment other than on account of disability, death, or unforeseeable emergency, the plan requires that the payment with respect to which the subsequent election is made be deferred for a period of not less than five years from the date such payment otherwise would have been paid (or in the case of annuity or installment payments treated as a single payment, five years from the date the first amount was scheduled to be paid).

Additionally, any subsequent deferral election related to a payment at a specified date or pursuant to a fixed schedule must be made, if at all, not less than 12 months before the date the payment is scheduled to be paid.[220]

The application of the restrictions on subsequent deferral elections may be best explained through a series of examples:

> Employee A has elected a lump sum payment at age 65. He wishes to make a subsequent deferral election so that the deferred amount will be payable upon the later of his attainment of a specified age or separation from service. Provided that Employee A makes such election on or before his 64th birthday [12 months before], he may modify the plan so he will receive a lump sum payment upon the later of age 70 or separation from service [five-year postponement].

> Employee B has elected a lump sum payment at age 65. She wishes to make a subsequent deferral election so that the deferred amount will be payable in installments. If she makes such election on or before her 64th birthday [12 months before], Employee B may modify the plan so she will receive installment payments at age 70 [five-year postponement].

> Employee C has elected to be paid in a lump sum payment at the earlier of age 65 or separation from service. She wishes to make a subsequent deferral election, deferring payment to a later date. Provided that Employee C continues in employment and makes the election by her 64th birthday [12 months before], C may elect to receive a lump sum payment at the earlier of age 70 or separation from service [five-year postponement].[221]

> Employee D has elected a lump sum payment at separation from service. She wishes to make a subsequent deferral election, to make the payment payable upon the later of her separation from service or her attainment of age 65. If Employee D makes such election on or before the date one year before a separation from service, she may elect to receive a lump sum payment upon the later of her attainment of age 65 or the date five years following her separation from service.

Annuities

The regulations treat the entitlement to a life annuity as the entitlement to a single payment.[222] Thus, in the case of a life annuity, the participant must make

---

[219] Treas. Reg. § 1.409A-2(b)(1).
[220] Treas. Reg. § 1.409A-2(b)(1)(iii).
[221] Treas. Reg. § 1.409A-2(b)(9), Example 15.
[222] Treas. Reg. § 1.409A-2(b)(2)(ii).

any subsequent deferral election at least 12 months before the date the first amount was scheduled to be paid. The regulations clarify that a change in the form of a payment before any annuity payment has been made under the plan, from one type of life annuity to another type of life annuity with the same scheduled date for the first annuity payment, or a change in the designated beneficiary, is not considered a change in the time and form of a payment, provided that the annuities are actuarially equivalent applying reasonable actuarial methods and assumptions.[223] A joint and survivor annuity will not fail to be treated as actuarially equivalent to a single life annuity due solely to the value of a subsidized survivor annuity benefit, provided that (i) the annual lifetime annuity benefit available to the employee under the joint and survivor annuity is not greater than the annual lifetime annuity benefit available to the employee under the single life annuity alternative, and (ii) the annual survivor annuity benefit is not greater than the annual lifetime annuity benefit available to the employee under the joint and survivor annuity.[224]

> Employee E participates in a nonqualified deferred compensation plan that permits Employee E to elect before E's separation from service whether to be paid in the form of a single life annuity beginning on the first day of the month following E's separation from service, or an annuity beginning on the first day of the month following E's separation from service under which annuity payments continue for E's lifetime but not less than 10 years. The two types of annuities are actuarially equivalent at all times applying reasonable actuarial methods and assumptions. For purposes of this section, the two types of annuities are treated as a single form of payment. Accordingly, the election provided under the plan is not treated as providing a subsequent deferral election or accelerated payment, and an election by E under the plan between the two annuity options made before the first scheduled payment date for an annuity payment is not treated as a subsequent deferral election or an acceleration of a payment.[225]

Installment Payments

With respect to installment payments, the regulations generally treat the entitlement to installments as the entitlement to a single payment, similar to the treatment of annuities.[226] Thus, in the case of installments, the participant must make any subsequent deferral election at least 12 months before the date the first installment was scheduled to be paid. However, the regulations specify that a plan may treat (consistently and at all times) the right to the series of installment payments as a right to a series of separate payments.

The regulations define installment payments as an entitlement to the payment of a series of substantially equal periodic amounts to be paid over a predetermined period of years, except to the extent any increase (or decrease) in the amount reflects reasonable earnings (or losses) through the date the amount is paid. The regulations go on to clarify that a series of installment payments over a predetermined period and a series of installment payments over a shorter or longer period, or a series of installment payments over the same predetermined

---

[223] Treas. Reg. § 1.409A-2(b)(2)(ii)(A).
[224] Treas. Reg. § 1.409A-2(b)(2)(ii)(C).
[225] Treas. Reg. § 1.409A-2(b)(9), Example 21.
[226] Treas. Reg. § 1.409A-2(b)(2)(iii).

period but with a different commencement date, are different times and forms of payment.[227] Thus, any change in the predetermined period or the commencement date is a change in the time and form of payment.

> Employee F has elected payment in a series of five equal annual installments, which are not designated as a series of five separate payments. The first amount is scheduled to be paid on January 1, 2021. F wishes to receive the entire amount paid as a lump sum payment. If she makes the election on or before January 1, 2020, she may elect to receive a lump sum payment on a specified date on or after January 1, 2026.

> Employee G has elected payment in a series of five equal annual amounts, each designated as a separate payment. The first payment is scheduled to be made on January 1, 2021. If she makes the election on or before January 1, 2020, she may elect for the first payment scheduled to be made on January 1, 2021, to be made on January 1, 2026 instead. If she makes that election, but does not elect to defer the remaining payments, the remaining payments continue to be due upon January 1 of the four consecutive calendar years commencing on January 1, 2022.[228]

Short-Term Deferrals

The most important and widely-used exception from Code Sec. 409A is the "short-term deferral" exception, also known as the "pay-when-vested" exception.[229] Under this exception, if compensation is to be paid immediately upon vesting, then it generally is not subject to Code Sec. 409A. The short-term deferral rule also provides that a deferral of compensation does not occur for purposes of Code Sec. 409A with respect to any payment that the employee receives on or before the March 15 following the end of the year in which the employee's right to the payment is no longer subject to a substantial risk of forfeiture. The 2016 proposed regulations modified the short-term deferral rule to permit a delay in payments to avoid violating federal securities laws or other applicable law.

.06 Tandem Plans and Linked Elections

Many employers maintain nonqualified deferred compensation plans - either individual account plans or defined benefit-type plans -where amounts deferred under the nonqualified plan are linked to the benefits under a qualified plan. The IRS designed the regulations to prevent employees and employers from affecting the amount of the employee's benefits or deferral contributions under the nonqualified plan by manipulating the form or timing of benefits or deferrals under the qualified plan.[230] For example, where amounts deferred under a nonqualified deferred compensation plan are linked to the benefits under a qualified plan, the participants' election changes under the qualified plan may affect the amounts deferred under the nonqualified plan in a manner forbidden by Code Sec. 409A.

The regulations provide that a participant's action or inaction under a qualified plan with respect to elective deferrals and other employee pre-tax contributions, including an adjustment to a deferral election under such qualified

---

[227] Treas. Reg. § 1.409A-2(b)(2)(iii).

[228] Treas. Reg. § 1.409A-2(b)(9), Example 18.

[229] Treas. Reg. § 1.409A-1(b)(4).

[230] Treas. Reg. §§ 1.409A-2(a) and 1.409A-3(j).

plan, will not constitute a prohibited change in election under the nonqualified plan, provided that for any given taxable year, the participant's action or inaction does not result in an increase in the amounts deferred under all nonqualified deferred compensation plans in which he or she participates in excess of the $18,500 limit (or the $24,500 limit for catch-up contributions) (for 2018) under Code Sec. 402(g) for the taxable year in which such action or inaction occurs.[231]

Similarly, the regulations provide that a participant's action or inaction under a qualified plan with respect to pre-tax or after-tax contributions that affects the amounts that are credited under a nonqualified plan as matching amounts, will not constitute a prohibited change in election under the nonqualified plan, provided that the total of such matching (or other contingent amounts), never exceeds 100% of the matching (or contingent) amounts that would be provided under the employer's qualified plan absent any plan-based restrictions that reflect limits on qualified plan contributions under the Internal Revenue Code.[232]

The regulations provide a similar, limited exception for changes under defined benefit-type nonqualified plans. This exception may be best illustrated by an example from the regulations:

> Employee M participates in a qualified retirement plan that is a defined benefit plan that offers a subsidized early retirement benefit to employees who have attained age 55 and completed 30 years of service. Employee M, who has attained age 55 and completed 30 years of service, also participates in a nonqualified deferred compensation plan, under which the benefit payable is calculated under a formula, with that benefit then reduced by any benefit that Employee M has accrued under the qualified retirement plan. In 2019, Employee M fails to elect the subsidized early retirement benefit under the qualified retirement plan, with the effect that the amounts payable under the nonqualified deferred compensation plan are increased by an amount equal to the reduction in the benefit payable under the qualified plan. In 2020, ABC Corporation amends the qualified retirement plan to increase benefits under the plan, resulting in a decrease in the amounts payable under the nonqualified deferred compensation plan equal to the increase in the benefit payable under the qualified plan. Neither of these actions constitutes a deferral election or an acceleration of a payment under the nonqualified deferred compensation plan.[233]

The regulations also make clear that increases or decreases in benefits or deferrals under the nonqualified plan that result directly from changes in benefit limitations applicable to the qualified plan under the Internal Revenue Code do not constitute a forbidden change in the deferral election under the nonqualified deferred compensation plan, where the nonqualified deferred compensation plan provides that the amount deferred under the plan is determined under the formula for determining benefits under the employer's qualified plan, but applied without regard to one or more limitations applicable to the qualified plan under the Code.[234]

---

[231] Treas. Reg. §§ 1.409A-2(a)(iii).
[232] Treas. Reg. §§ 1.409A-2(a)(iv).

[233] Treas. Reg. § 1.409A-2(b)(9), Example 14.
[234] Treas. Reg. §§ 1.409A-2(a).

.07 Small Amount Cash-Outs

As an exception to Code Sec. 409A's prohibition on the acceleration of nonqualified plan payouts, the final regulations provide that an employer may exercise the discretion to cash out a participant's entire amount deferred under a nonqualified plan at any time that the participant's amount deferred under the plan is less than the Code Sec. 402(g)(1)(B) limit for that year ($18,500 for 2018).[235] The plan does not need to be amended to provide this discretion to the employer (but experienced legal counsel may suggest it). The plan aggregation rules apply, so an employer may not use this rule to cash out an amount under one arrangement but not another arrangement where the two arrangements would be treated as one plan. The regulations do not require that a participant have separated from service for the employer to cash out the amount deferred.

A nonqualified plan also may specify a mandatory cash-out amount that exceeds the Code Sec. 402(g) limit, as long as the amount is prescribed in advance. The employer need not aggregate other deferred compensation plans when determining whether the benefit meets the threshold. Thus, an employer's plan - whether an individual account plan or a defined benefit-type plan - could impose a cash-out amount for actuarial equivalents that are under an amount the plan specifies. For example, a plan could provide that, notwithstanding the participant's distribution elections, any account balance (or the present value of any accrued benefit) that is less than $50,000 at the time of the participant's separation from service will be paid out immediately upon the separation from service.

The regulations also permit a nonqualified plan to provide for an immediate payment of all remaining installments payments if the present value of the deferred amount to be paid in the remaining installment payments falls below a predetermined amount, provided that such feature including the predetermined amount, is established by no later than the time and form of payment is otherwise required to be established, and provided further that any change in such feature including the predetermined amount is a change in the time and form of payment.[236]

.08 Substantial Risk of Forfeiture

One of the most important concepts in Code Sec. 409A is that of substantial risk of forfeiture.[237] The negative tax consequences of Code Sec. 409A do not apply while an amount remains subject to a substantial risk of forfeiture. There are certain ways to correct Code Sec. 409A violations, which are available only while an amount remains subject to a substantial risk of forfeiture. Additionally, the short-term deferral exception under Code Sec. 409A, generally turns on the definition of substantial risk of forfeiture. So long as a payment occurs once (or soon after) the substantial risk of forfeiture lapses, it is generally exempt from the onerous rules of Code Sec. 409A.

---

[235] Treas. Reg. § 1.409A-3(j)(4)(v).
[236] Treas. Reg. § 1.409A-2(b)(2)(iii).

[237] Treas. Reg. § 1.409A-1(d).

Code Sec. 409A generally prohibits parties from extending a substantial risk of forfeiture, as the IRS rightly assumes that an employee would not agree to extend a vesting condition unless the purpose was to delay recognition of tax. However, the addition or extension of a substantial risk of forfeiture would be honored if the present value of the amount subject to the additional substantial risk of forfeiture is materially greater than the present value of the amount the service provider otherwise could have elected to receive absent such risk of forfeiture.

In Chief Counsel Advice 201645012 (the "2016 CCA"), the IRS agreed that a 25% increase qualified as a materially greater amount and, thus, deferred salary was subject to a substantial risk of forfeiture. In the 2016 CCA, an employee made an election in November 2014 to defer a portion of 2015 salary. The salary would be paid on January 1, 2018, but only if the employee continued to provide substantial services through December 31, 2017. In connection with the salary deferral, the employee received a matching contribution that increased the present value of the salary by 25%. The question posed in the 2016 CCA was whether the prospect of an additional 25% would allow the deferred salary to be subject to a "substantial risk of forfeiture" for purposes of Code Sec. 409A through December 31, 2017. The IRS agreed that it would.

Practitioners have debated what level of additional compensation would be sufficient to satisfy the "materially greater" threshold. The 2016 CCA suggests that any amount that is at least 25% in excess is sufficient. Previously, practitioners had been comfortable with figures in the 5-10% range. Now, any increases less than 25% raise additional risk and should be discussed with counsel. The 2016 CCA may not be used or cited as precedent, but still gives good insight as to how the IRS might respond to similar facts and circumstances.

.09 Stock Rights Exception

One of the most important exceptions to the harsh rules of Code Sec. 409A is the so-called "stock rights exception."[238] Under the stock rights exception, a stock option or stock appreciation right will be exempt from Code Sec. 409A if (i) the award is employer common stock, (ii) the exercise price of the option or SAR is no less than the fair market value of the stock on the grant date, (iii) the award contains no deferral feature, and (iv) there is no mandatory repurchase obligation or a permanent put or call right that is based on a measure other than the fair market value. The stock rights exception allows an individual to exercise a stock option or SAR at any time (as is customary) rather than restricting exercise only to permissible Code Sec. 409A distribution events.

Under Code Sec. 409A, the term "employer stock" means common stock of the employer for which the employee provides direct services on the date of grant (and certain controlling affiliates above the employer). The proposed regulations clarify that stock awards made to a prospective employee still may qualify as employer stock for purposes of the stock rights exception, if the

---

[238] Treas. Reg. § 1.409A-1(b)(5).

prospective employee is reasonably anticipated to begin providing services within 12 months after the grant date and if the person actually begins providing services during that 12-month period (or the award lapses if services do not commence by the deadline). This allows exempt stock options to be granted as part of the negotiations that precede the employee's commencement of employment.

Employers occasionally reduce or eliminate the amount that an employee receives under a stock right arrangement if the employee is terminated for cause or violates a noncompetition or nondisclosure agreement. The proposed regulations clarify that a stock award that otherwise qualifies for the stock rights exception will not fail to so qualify solely because the amount payable under the stock right is based on a measure that is less than fair market value due to the employee's termination for cause or upon the occurrence of another condition within the employee's control, such as a violation of a restrictive covenant.

Code Sec. 409A provides special rules for payments of so-called "transaction-based compensation," which is a payment made to an employee as a result of the acquisition or merger of his or her employer and the purchase of stock or stock rights held by the employee. Under the regulations, transaction-based compensation may be treated as paid at a designated date or pursuant to a payment schedule that complies with the requirements of Code Sec. 409A if it is paid on the same schedule and under the same terms and conditions as apply to payments to shareholders generally with respect to stock of the seller in the change in control. Additionally, transaction-based compensation will not fail to meet the requirements of the initial or subsequent deferral election rules under Code Sec. 409A if it is paid not later than five years after the change in control event. The proposed regulations confirm that the special payment rules for transaction-based compensation apply to an incentive stock option (ISO) or a stock right that did not otherwise provide for deferred compensation before the purchase or agreement to purchase the stock right. The proposed regulations still do not address a menacing issue that arises in many transactions, which is whether stock right spread that remains unvested at the time of a transaction can be converted into an unvested restricted stock unit or other unvested amount. Many practitioners believe that these approaches are consistent with both the intended economics of the stock right and the spirit of Code Sec. 409A.

.10 Plan Terminations

The Code Sec. 409A regulations also were designed to prevent employers from accelerating the timing of plan distributions through a plan termination. The regulations provide three circumstances under which an employer may terminate a deferred compensation plan subject to Code Sec. 409A without causing a prohibited acceleration of benefits:[239]

1. At any time, provided that:[240]

---

[239] Treas. Reg. § 1.409A-3(j)(4)(ix).   [240] Treas. Reg. § 1.409A-3(j)(4)(ix)(C).

¶1785.10

(a) The employer terminates all arrangements of the same type (account balance plans, nonaccount balance plans, separation pay plans or other arrangements) with respect to all participants;

(b) The plan makes no payments, other than those otherwise payable under the terms of the plan absent a termination, within 12 months of the termination;

(c) The plan makes all payments within 24 months of the termination;

(d) The employer does not adopt a new plan of the same type for three years following the termination date; and

(e) The termination and liquidation does not occur proximate to a downturn in the employer's financial health.

2. A plan may provide that it terminates automatically upon a corporate dissolution taxed under Code Sec. 331, or with the approval of a bankruptcy court.[241]

3. The employer may take all necessary action to terminate and liquidate the plan within the 30 days preceding or the 12 months following a change in control event.[242] Such action must be irrevocable. All other arrangements that would be classified with the plan as a single plan must be terminated and liquidated, so that all participants receive all amounts of compensation deferred under the terminated and liquidated plans within 12 months of the date the employer takes such irrevocable action to terminate and liquidate the plans. For this purpose, the entities comprising the "employer" are determined immediately following the change in control event, but the rule only applies with respect to participants for whom a change in control has occurred. Where the change in control event consists of an asset purchase, the applicable employer with discretion to terminate and liquidate the plan is deemed to be the entity retaining the deferred compensation liability after the transaction.

The 2016 proposed regulations clarified that the acceleration of a payment under the change in control / plan termination exception is permitted only if the employer terminates and liquidates all plans of the same category that it sponsors, and not merely all plans of the same category in which a particular employee actually participates. The proposed regulations also clarified that for a period of three years following the termination and liquidation of a plan, neither the buyer nor the seller can adopt a new plan of the same category as the terminated and liquidated plan, regardless of which employees participate in such plan. Because the IRS characterized these provisions as a clarification, not a change, they apply retroactively to the date of the initial issuance of the 2008 final regulations.

.11 Acceleration or Delay of Distributions

Code Sec. 409A prohibits an employer, employee, or plan from accelerating the distribution or payment date of amounts that are deferred compensation,

---

[241] Treas. Reg. § 1.409A-3(j)(4)(ix)(A).   [242] Treas. Reg. § 1.409A-3(j)(4)(ix)(B).

except in limited circumstances.[243] The final regulations under Code Sec. 409A list certain events upon which the payment of deferred compensation may be accelerated or delayed. Under Notice 2005-1, such circumstances include: (i) if necessary to fulfil a domestic relations order, (ii) as necessary to comply with conflict of interest rules applicable to certain federal government employees, (iii) payments under government and church plans, as necessary to pay taxes on undistributed amounts, (iv) certain payments of less than $10,000, and (v) payment of employment taxes imposed on unpaid deferred compensation under Code Sec. 3121(v).

Code Sec. 409A prohibits the acceleration of plan distributions. Before Code Sec. 409A, many nonqualified plans allowed participants to accelerate payment by accepting a lesser amount, rather than waiting for the scheduled payment date. These provisions were referred to as "haircut" provisions, and typically imposed a 10% haircut on accelerated distributions. Code Sec. 409A expressly prohibits "Financial Health Triggers." Deferred compensation will become taxable at vesting if a plan provides that assets are set aside for benefits upon a change in the employer's financial health, or if assets in fact become restricted to the payment of benefits following such a change. Early taxation can occur even if assets remain subject to claims of the employer's general creditors (*i.e.*, even if the assets are in a "rabbi trust.") These rules prevent the use of so-called "springing rabbi trusts" and "springing secular trusts," which become effective/are first funded on a change in employer's financial health.

.12 Code Sec. 162(m)

Code Sec. 162(m) prohibits a publicly held company from deducting more than $1 million of compensation paid to certain covered employees in any tax year. The final regulations under Code Sec. 409A permit a delay in payment necessary to avoid the application of the deduction limitation under Code Sec. 162(m), provided that all payments that could be delayed for this reason must be delayed, and the payment must be made in the earlier of:[244]

(a) the employee's first taxable year in which the employer reasonably anticipates, or reasonably should anticipate, that if it makes such payment during such year such payment will not fail to be deductible because of Code Sec. 162(m) or,

(b) the period beginning on the day the employee separates from service and ending on the later of the last day of that calendar taxable year or the 15th day of the third month following the separation from service.

Note: where the payment has been delayed until the service provider's separation from service, the six-month delay requirement for specified employees may apply.

A plan or agreement is not required to provide explicitly for such a delay. However, we suggest that employers consider drafting into every deferred

---

[243] Treas. Reg. § 1.409A-3(j).   [244] Treas. Reg. § .409A-2(b)(7)(i).

compensation plan and employment agreement an automatic deferral of amounts that would be subject to Code Sec. 162(m) limits.

Prior to 2018, most public companies utilized the performance-based compensation exception to the $1 million cap on deductible compensation under Code Sec. 162(m). The TCJA, signed into law by President Trump in December 2017, repealed the performance-based compensation exception. This change is expected to further increase the attractiveness and use of nonqualified plans in 2019 and beyond (for a more detailed discussion of this issue, see ¶ 2225).

The TCJA amendments will make any distribution of non-qualified plan benefits to a participant who is or ever was a covered employee under Code Sec. 162(m) subject to the $1 million deductibility cap, even if the distribution is made after the participant's death, disability, retirement or other termination of employment. However, the account or benefit of a covered employee under a non-qualified plan as of November 2, 2017 (and in some cases additional accruals and contributions after that date, could be grandfathered and not subject to the $1 million cap.

> **Example:** Under a deferred compensation plan, an employee who was not a covered employee in 2015 elected to defer the entire amount [$200,000] of her 2016 annual bonus. The bonus, plus earnings based on a predetermined actual investment, will be paid in a lump sum at her separation from service. In 2018, she is promoted to CEO. In 2020, she separates from service and receives $225,000 (the deferred $200,000 bonus plus $25,000 in earnings). The full $225,000 payment is grandfathered and not subject to the Code Sec. 162(m) deduction limit.

Most non-qualified plans provide that the company may, at any time, in its discretion, amend the plan to either stop or reduce the amount of future credits to participants' account balances or benefit accruals, but such amendment may not deprive participants of any amount or benefit accrued before the date of the amendment. This commonplace reservation of rights in the company has a significant adverse effect on the amount of benefit that will be grandfathered.

.13 "Plan" and Plan Aggregation

Code Sec. 409A and the regulations thereunder provide that all plans of a similar type maintained by an employer must be aggregated for purposes of testing compliance with Code Sec. 409A.[245] Plan aggregation is a very important concept under the Code Sec. 409A regulations because a Code Sec. 409A violation "taints" all arrangements within that type of plan. The final regulations provide some relief for an employer that makes a mistake and triggers Code Sec. 409A penalties in that it creates nine separate types of plans:[246]

1. Elective account balance
2. Non-elective account balance
3. Non-account balance

---

[245] Code Sec. 409A(d)(6), Treas. Reg. § 1.409A-1(c)(2).

[246] Treas. Reg. § 1.409A-1(c)(2)(i).

    4. Stock rights

    5. Separation pay plans

    6. In-kind benefits or /reimbursements

    7. Split-dollar arrangements

    8. Foreign plans

    9. Other

.14 Specified Employees

Code Sec. 409A provides that distributions to a "specified employee" may not be made before the date that is six months after the date of the employee's separation from service or, if earlier, the date of the employee's death (the "six-month delay rule").[247] The six-month delay rule applies to payments under deferred compensation and other nonqualified plans, but also payments under employment and change in control agreements and severance plans. The final regulations provide that the employer must write into the plan or agreement the six-month delay rule.[248]

Code Sec. 409A and the final regulations provide that the term "specified employee" means an employee who, as of the date of his or her separation from service, is a key employee of an employer whose stock is publicly traded on an established securities market or otherwise. An employee is a "key employee" if the employee meets the requirements of Code Sec. 416(i)(1)(A)(i), (ii), or (iii) (the top-heavy plan rules) at any time during the 12-month period ending on a "specified employee identification date" (generally, December 31). If an employee is a key employee as of a specified employee identification date, the employee is treated as a key employee for purposes of Code Sec. 409A for the entire 12-month period beginning on the specified employee effective date (or for a different 12-month period beginning within three months of that date).

Code Sec. 416(i)(1)(A) provides that the term "key employee" means an employee who, at any time during the plan year, is —

    (i) an officer of the employer having an annual compensation greater than $175,000 (for 2018, adjusted for cost-of-living increases),

    (ii) a 5-percent owner of the employer, or

    (iii) a 1-percent owner of the employer having an annual compensation from the employer of more than $150,000.

Code Sec. 416(i)(A) also provides that no more than 50 employees (or, if lesser, the greater of 3 or 10 percent of the employees) are treated as officers. The definition of compensation under Treas. Reg. § 1.415(c)-2(a) applies, unless the plan, agreement or employer specifies another definition.

The final regulations provide that, like the six-month delay rule, a plan or agreement must specify the method for determining key employees and for

---

[247] Code Sec. 409A(a)(2)(B)(i), Treas. Reg. § 1.409-1(i).

[248] Treas. Reg. 1.409A-1(c)(3)(v).

applying the six-month delay rule.[249] To meet the six-month delay requirement, a plan or agreement may provide that:

- Any payment pursuant to a separation of service due within the six-month period is delayed until the end of the six-month period, or
- Each scheduled payment that becomes payable pursuant to a separation from service is delayed six months, or
- A combination thereof.

The plan may provide the key employee an election as to the manner in which the six-month delay is applied, provided that such election is subject to otherwise applicable deferral election rules.

.15 Unforeseeable Emergency

Code Sec. 409A allows a plan to permit distributions to participants in case of an unforeseeable emergency.[250] The term "unforeseeable emergency" means a severe financial hardship to the participant resulting from an illness or accident of the participant, the participant's spouse, or a dependent of the participant,[251] loss of the participant's property due to casualty, or other similar extraordinary and unforeseeable circumstances arising as a result of events beyond the control of the participant.[252] However, the amounts a plan may distribute with respect to an emergency may not exceed the amounts necessary to satisfy such emergency plus amounts necessary to pay taxes reasonably anticipated as a result of the distribution, after taking into account the extent to which such hardship is or may be relieved through reimbursement or compensation by insurance or otherwise or by liquidation of the participant's assets (to the extent the liquidation of such assets would not itself cause severe financial hardship).

.16 Separation Pay Exception

Code Sec. 409A provides that separation pay plans that provide for payment only upon an involuntary separation from service do not constitute deferred compensation to the extent that they meet certain requirements.[253] To qualify for the so-called "separation pay exception," the separation pay may not exceed two times the lesser of (a) the employee's annualized compensation based upon the annual rate of pay for the calendar year preceding the year in which the employee separates from service, or (b) the limit under Code Sec. 401(a)(17) for the year in which the employee separates from service. The proposed regulations clarify that this exception is available for employees whose employment begins and ends in the same taxable year. In that circumstance, the proposed regulations provide that, if the employee had no compensation from the employer in the taxable year preceding the year in which the employee separated from service, the employee's annualized compensation for the year in which the employee separates from service may be used for purposes of the separation pay exception.

---

[249] Treas. Reg. § 1.409A-1(i)(8).

[250] Code Sec. 409A(a)(2).

[251] As defined in section Code Sec. 152(a).

[252] Code Sec. 409A(a)(2)(B)(ii).

[253] Treas. Reg. § 1.409A-1(b)(9)(i).

.17 Prohibited Substitutions and Reductions

Code Sec. 409A prohibits a delay of the payment of deferred compensation amounts beyond the time or event set forth in the plan document or elected by the employee/individual.[254] Some practitioners had argued that the certain grants or transfers could satisfy the payment requirement even if they did not trigger income tax. For example, it had been argued that a distribution required by a nonqualified deferred compensation plan could be made to a participant in the form of restricted stock, which would thereafter vest and be taxable according to a vesting schedule. The proposed regulations clarified that an employer or plan cannot use unvested property (such as restricted shares) to satisfy a distribution obligation or deadline under a deferred compensation plan. Specifically, the proposed regulations clarified that the following grants or transfers, which do not result in income tax to the individual, do not satisfy the payment requirement:

(1) The grant of a stock option that does not have a readily ascertainable fair market value;

(2) The grant of restricted stock or transfer of other property that is substantially nonvested; or

(3) A contribution to a rabbi trust (unless and until the amount is includible in income under Code Sec. 402(b)).

The IRS has stated that these provisions are not changes to the current requirements under Code Sec. 409A, only clarifications. Therefore, these provisions apply retroactively to the original 2008 effective date of the final regulations. That is, any of the above transfers could violate Code Sec. 409A.

The regulations under Code Sec. 409A also generally prohibit the reduction in or offset of an employee's right to deferred compensation in satisfaction of the employee's debt. However, the regulations provide an exception if the debt is incurred in the ordinary course of the service relationship, the entire offset in any taxable year does not exceed $5,000, and the offset is taken at the same time and in the same amount as the debt otherwise would have been due from the employee. The 2016 proposed regulations expanded this exception and remove the $5,000 limit for certain offsets, in order to allow a plan to comply with federal laws regarding debt collection. Generally, this exception would only apply to debt collection by the federal government at governmental entities providing nonqualified deferred compensation.

.18 Employment-Related Legal Fees

The regulations under Code Sec. 409A provide that an arrangement does not provide for a deferral of compensation to the extent that it provides for amounts to be paid as settlements or awards resolving bona fide legal claims based on wrongful termination, employment discrimination, the Fair Labor Standards Act, or workers' compensation statutes, including claims under applicable federal,

---

[254] Treas. Reg. § 1.409A-1(b)(5)(v).

¶1785.17

state, local, or foreign laws, or for reimbursements or payments of reasonable attorneys' fees or other reasonable expenses incurred by an employee or former employee related to such bona fide legal claims.[255] The 2016 proposed regulations provide that an arrangement does not provide for a deferral of compensation simply because it provides for the payment or reimbursement of an employee or former employee's reasonable attorneys' fees and expenses incurred to enforce a claim by the employee against the employer with respect to the employment relationship.

.19 Documentary Compliance

Plans and agreements must be made compliant with Code Sec. 409A on or before December 31, 2007.[256] However, these amendments are required only to bring the document into compliance effective January 1, 2008, and are not required to reflect any amendments made or actions taken under the transition rules. For example, if a plan contains a haircut provision, the employer need not remove that provision retroactively for periods before January 1, 2008, where the employer has operated the plan in compliance with the applicable transition guidance (that is, the plan made no payment pursuant to the haircut provision after 2004).

Code Sec. 409A requires that the written plan document include certain "material terms"[257] including the following:

- Who is covered;
- The amount (or method or formula for determining amount) of deferred compensation;
- Initial and subsequent deferral election provisions (if applicable), which must be set forth on or before the date the applicable election is irrevocable;
- The time and form of payment;
- If installment payments are to be treated as separate payments, the plan document must so specify.

Regarding so-called "savings clauses," the final regulations clarify that plan terms must be compliant with Code Sec. 409A; savings clauses alone are not sufficient. (However, savings clauses still may be advisable because they could be helpful in contract interpretation and enforcement.)

.20 Penalties

If at any time during a taxable year a nonqualified deferred compensation plan fails to meet the requirements of Code Sec. 409A, or is not operated in accordance with such requirements, all compensation deferred under the plan for the taxable year and all preceding taxable years shall be includible in the gross income of affected participants for the taxable year to the extent not subject to a substantial risk of forfeiture and not previously included in gross income.[258]

---

[255] Treas. Reg. § 1.409A-1(b)(11).
[256] Treas. Reg. Preamble, Section XIII, B.

[257] Treas. Reg. § 1.409A-1(c)(3)(i).
[258] Code Sec. 409A(a)(1)(A)(i).

Taxation will only apply with respect to all compensation deferred under the plan for participants with respect to whom the failure relates.[259]

Additionally, if compensation is required to be included in gross income under Code Sec. 409A for a taxable year, the tax imposed will be increased by an amount equal to 20% of the compensation that is required to be included in gross income, plus interest. The amount of interest is determined at the underpayment rate plus 1 percentage point on the underpayments that would have occurred had the deferred compensation been includible in gross income for the taxable year in which first deferred or, if later, the first taxable year in which such deferred compensation is not subject to a substantial risk of forfeiture.[260]

The final regulations provide no further guidance on the calculation and timing of amounts required to be included in income under Code Sec. 409A.

.21 Income Tax Reporting and Withholding

Employers must report amounts deferred by or on behalf of a person under arrangements subject to Code Sec. 409A on Form W-2 (or Form 1099-MISC if the person is not an employee) for the tax year in which the deferral occurs, even if the deferrals are not yet includible in income. Employers must withhold taxes on any amounts includible in income because of Code Sec. 409A.

.22 Effective Date and Grandfather Protection

Code Sec. 409A is generally applicable to amounts deferred in 2005 and subsequent years. Compensation deferred before 2005 (and subsequent related earnings) is not subject to Code Sec. 409A if the compensation is earned and vested on December 31, 2004, unless the arrangement under which the deferral was made is "materially modified" after October 3, 2004. Notice 2005-1 provides a right to an amount is "earned and vested" only if the amount is not subject to either a substantial risk of forfeiture (as defined in Reg. § 1.83-3(c)) or a requirement to perform further services. A material modification includes any enhancement or inclusion of a new benefit to an existing plan. Plan administrators may exercise discretion as to time and form of payment under an existing plan without such exercise being considered a material modification if the plan, by its terms, allowed such discretion before October 3, 2004.

---

[259] Code Sec. 409A(a)(1)(A)(ii).   [260] Code Sec. 409A(a)(1)(B).

Chapter 18
SPLIT-DOLLAR AND OTHER LIFE INSURANCE ARRANGEMENTS

¶1801 Overview—Executive Life Insurance Arrangements

Life insurance coverage is one of the ubiquitous forms of employee benefit. There are at least four reasons for this. The first reason is that the Internal Revenue Code offers very favorable tax treatment to life insurance proceeds payable to a beneficiary.[1] The second reason is that, whether they know it or not, executives and other employees need life insurance more than any other benefit (with the exception of long-term disability insurance). The third reason is that the internal cash build up on a life insurance contract is not taxable, thus enabling employers and executives to use life insurance for education or retirement funding and other purposes not related to providing death benefits. Finally, the life insurance industry has made it very easy for employers to provide this benefit to its executives and other employees, by creating products with flexibility and a dazzling assortment of features (see ¶1815). (See also ¶1945 for a general discussion of life insurance as an executive benefit.)

A split-dollar life insurance arrangement is one under which an employer assists an employee or selected employees in acquiring whole life insurance policies or protection (including regular whole life, universal life and variable life). The term "split-dollar" derives from the original concept of these arrangements, which was that the employer and the employee would split the annual premium cost of, and other rights under, the life insurance policy.

Although split-dollar insurance arrangements can be entered into for reasons other than compensation (*e.g.*, estate planning) and between parties other than employer and employee (*e.g.*, parent and child), this chapter will focus on compensatory arrangements between employers and employees. Corporations sometimes enter into split-dollar arrangements with outside members of their boards of directors, but the taxation and other rules described herein would apply to those arrangements in much the same manner as arrangements between employer and employee.

Finally, life insurance is one of the most common methods used to fund nonqualified plan promises (see ¶1745 for a discussion of life insurance as a funding mechanism).

---

[1] Code Sec. 101.

.01 Tax Treatment

The IRS first blessed the concept of split-dollar life insurance arrangements between employers and employees in 1955.[2] Between 1955 and 2002, the tax treatment of split-dollar life insurance arrangements was generally as follows:

- The employer would not receive a deduction for its annual premium payments.

- The employee would be taxed on the economic benefit conferred by the life insurance coverage, determined by the Table 2001 rate or, more typically, the insurer's lower alternative annual term rate for standard risks unless the employee contributed to the cost of the coverage.

- The employee's beneficiary would receive the death benefit proceeds of the policy free from federal income tax, pursuant to Code Sec. 101.

In 2002, the world of split-dollar life insurance changed completely. In Notice 2002-8 and final regulations issued in 2003, the IRS announced that split-dollar life insurance arrangements will be taxed under one of two mutually exclusive regimes: the economic benefit regime and the loan regime (see ¶1815 for a detailed discussion of the tax treatment of split-dollar arrangements).[3]

.02 Split-Dollar Arrangements

Split-dollar life insurance arrangements generally come in two varieties, depending on who owns the insurance policy. Under a collateral assignment split-dollar arrangement, the employee owns the policy and assigns his or her rights to a portion of the death benefit proceeds and/or cash surrender value to the employer. Under an endorsement split-dollar arrangement, the employer owns the policy and endorses over to the employee a portion of its rights to the death benefit proceeds and/or cash surrender value (see ¶1825 for a detailed discussion of collateral assignment and endorsement method split-dollar arrangements).

.03 Notice 2002-59

Under Notice 2002-59, the IRS concluded that a party participating in a split-dollar life insurance arrangement may use the premium rates in Table 2001[4] or the insurer's lower published premium rates for taxing the value of current life insurance protection only when, and to the extent, such protection is conferred as an economic benefit by one party upon another party. Such benefits must be determined without regard to consideration or premiums paid by the other party. Consequently, if one party has any right to current life insurance protection, the parties can rely upon neither the premium rates in Table 2001 nor the insurer's lower published premium rates to value such party's current life insurance protection for establishing the value of any policy benefit to which the other party may be entitled (see ¶1835).

---

[2] Rev. Rul. 55-713, 1955-2 CB 23.

[3] See also CCH-ANNO, 2005 FED 5508.24, Compensation Paid Other Than in Cash: Insurance Provided by Employer: Split-dollar life insurance.

[4] Set forth in IRS Notice 2001-10.

.04 Sarbanes-Oxley Act

The Sarbanes-Oxley Act of 2002 ("SOX") prohibited publicly traded companies from making personal loans to directors or executive officers. While neither Sarbanes-Oxley nor its legislative history refers to split-dollar life insurance arrangements, because Notice 2002-8 and the regulations clearly outline the treatment of collateral assignment split-dollar arrangements as deemed loans to the covered employees, most practitioners have advised their public company clients not to enter into or continue collateral assignment split-dollar arrangements (see ¶1845 for a detailed discussion of the effect of Sarbanes-Oxley on split-dollar arrangements).

.05 SERP Swap or Executive Roth Program

Some employers have amended their nonqualified retirement plans to allow participants to forfeit or trade a portion of their plan benefits in exchange for employer-paid life insurance. The rationale for the trade is that nonqualified retirement benefits will be taxable to the employee or the employee's beneficiary as ordinary income when paid. However, if the employer instead uses the amount owed to the employee to purchase a life insurance policy, the proceeds of that policy will be paid to the employee's beneficiary free from federal income tax (see ¶1855).

.06 COLI Limits

Code Sec. 101(j) imposes restrictions on corporate-owned life insurance ("COLI"). Under a COLI arrangement, the company purchases insurance on the life of one or more employees. The company ordinarily owns the policy, pays the premiums, and is the sole beneficiary of the policy. Companies purchase COLI to fund executive benefits because the earnings on the COLI policy's cash value build-up are tax deferred, while the final death benefit is not subject to federal income taxation (see ¶1865).

.07 Code Sec. 409A

Code Sec. 409A(a)[5] generally provides that unless certain requirements are met, amounts deferred under a nonqualified deferred compensation plan for all taxable years are currently includible in gross income to the extent not subject to a substantial risk of forfeiture and not previously included in gross income. IRS Notice 2007-34 provides guidance regarding the application of Code Sec. 409A to split-dollar life insurance arrangements (see ¶1875).

¶1815 Taxation of Life Insurance

The reason that life insurance is, and always has been, one of the most popular forms of executive compensation is simple. The Internal Revenue Code confers very favorable tax treatment on life insurance.

---

[5] Added by Section 885 of the American Jobs Creation Act of 2004, P.L. 108-357, 118 Stat. 1418.

.01 Taxation of the Internal Cash Build Up of the Life Insurance Policies

Under Code Sections 72(a) and (e), amounts payable under a life insurance contract that meets the definition of Code Sec. 7702 and the requirements of Code Sec. 72(e) will not be taxed until received (or deemed to be received) by the insured or a beneficiary. Any increase in the policy value, such as the internal build-up of the cash surrender value, of a life insurance policy that satisfies the definition of "life insurance contract" under Code Sec. 7702, and meets the requirements of Code Sec. 72(e), will not be taxed to the policy's owner. Most insurance policies obligate the insurance company to monitor the premium payments and other features of the policy to comply with Code Sec. 7702.

.02 Taxation of the Death Proceeds Payable from the Life Insurance Policies

In general, the death benefit proceeds payable from a life insurance policy by reason of the death of the insured are excludable from the designated beneficiary's gross income pursuant to Code Sec. 101(a). This is generally true regardless of who the owner of the policy is or who paid the premiums on the policy. Certain transfers of the policy for consideration would adversely affect this tax treatment and result in the death benefit becoming taxable.

In general, the death benefit proceeds payable will be included in the covered employee's gross estate if the employee possesses any incidents of ownership in the policy, or the policy is payable to the covered employee's estate.[6] However, the covered employee may transfer to or establish ownership of the policy in an irrevocable life insurance trust (ILIT), to keep the policy out of the employee's estate. In this event, the employee would have no incidents of ownership in the policy and the policy would not be payable to the employee's estate. If a split-dollar life insurance policy is owned by an ILIT, the employee, through the ILIT will execute a collateral assignment back to the employer.

.03 Taxation of Lifetime Distributions and Loans from Life Insurance Policies

For so long as the life insurance policy remains in force, a loan taken by the policyholder from a life insurance policy is not includible in the policyholder's income because it is generally treated as indebtedness under Code Sec. 72(e), not as a distribution, unless the policy is classified as a modified endowment contract (MEC). With respect to withdrawals, if the policy is not a MEC, the amount of an individual's withdrawal from the policy generally will be treated first as a non-taxable recovery of premium payments and then as income from the policy. Thus, a withdrawal from a policy that is not a MEC will not be includible in income except to the extent it exceeds the investment in the policy (that is, the contributions to the ERP policy by the individual executive and the corporation) immediately before the withdrawal.

---

[6] Code Sec. 2042.

A MEC is a life insurance policy that meets the requirements of Code Sec. 7702 generally, but fails the "seven-pay test" of Code Sec. 7702A. The "seven-pay test" compares actual paid premiums in the policy's first seven years against a pre-determined premium amount defined in Code Sec. 7702A. A policy would be classified as a MEC if premiums were paid more rapidly than allowed by the "seven-pay test." A policy also could be classified as a MEC if it is received in exchange for another policy that is a MEC. Finally, even if the policy initially is not a MEC, it could become a MEC, in certain circumstances. These circumstances would include a material change of the policy (within the meaning of the Code), and a withdrawal or reduction in the death benefit during the first seven policy years following the last material change. Most policies are designed to avoid being characterized as MECs.

If the loan is still outstanding at the time of the policyholder's death, the death proceeds generally are reduced by the amount of the outstanding loan. If a policy lapses or if the policyholder withdraws all of the policy's value when a loan is outstanding, the amount of the loan outstanding would be treated as withdrawal proceeds for purposes of determining whether any amounts are includible in the policyholder's income. It is also possible that some or all of the loan proceeds may be includible in a policyholder's income where the interest rate credited to the so-called loan account under the policy equals the interest rate charged to the policyholder for the loan.

.04 Advantages of Using Life Insurance to Fund Nonqualified Plans and Other Compensation Promises

Generally, the most tax-efficient means of funding nonqualified plans and other deferred compensation promises is through institutionally priced and tailored company-owned life insurance policies ("COLI"). Investing grantor trust funds in mutual funds with a mutual fund provider is neither tax-efficient nor cost-efficient for the company. The majority of U.S. companies use COLI to fund their deferred compensation, non-qualified SERP and top hat plan benefits.

Compared to funding with mutual funds - or no funding at all - COLI has the following distinct advantages:

- Company and employee contributions used to pay life insurance premiums, and the earnings on the policies, will accumulate tax-free. Any investment earnings on mutual funds result in taxable income to the company.
- The yield (or return) on life insurance policies is guaranteed. There is virtually no risk of loss if the company uses one of the top-two highest rated life insurance companies, which has the best credit rating and, not coincidentally, the highest current and historic investment return. Mutual fund investments can produce both earning and losses. Even conservative and fixed income investments pose a risk of loss.
- Both annually (current) and over time (historical), life insurance policies from the top-rated companies have produced a competitive rate of return,

which is further enhanced by the fact that the return is not reduced by income taxes.

- After a period of years, the company can stop contributing to pay premiums on the policies and instead use the internal cash value from some or all of the policies to make premium payments (on a tax-free basis).

- As plan benefits become due, the company can withdraw cash value from some or all of the policies on a tax-free basis.

- If any plan participants die prematurely, *e.g.*, before complete payout of their benefits, the company would receive the death benefit proceeds from the policies tax-free, resulting in a windfall to the company. Only a fraction of those proceeds would be needed to provide the participant's accrued benefit. (In fact, even if participants survive to age eighty or beyond, the eventual death benefit proceeds will be paid to the company tax-free.)

- The tax advantages described above result in a significant long-term profit and loss (P&L) improvement (approximate 90% NPV improvement, on average) compared to current mutual fund investment strategy, even under conservative assumptions.

- Funding levels and/or policy face amounts could be altered in future years without surrender charges, penalties, etc.

- Generally superior accounting treatment relative to taxable mutual fund investments.

- Institutionally priced and structured policies provide immediate cash value (unlike the ordinary life insurance policies that you or I might purchase) to the company's balance sheet and generally do not require employees to take a physical.

¶1825 Split-Dollar Life Insurance Arrangements

In regulations finalized in 2003,[7] the IRS published for the first time a formal definition of split-dollar life insurance arrangements:

> *In general*, a split-dollar life insurance arrangement is any arrangement between an owner and a non-owner of a life insurance contract that satisfies the following criteria—
>
> (i) Either party to the arrangement pays, directly or indirectly, all or any portion of the premiums on the life insurance contract, including a payment by means of a loan to the other party that is secured by the life insurance contract;
>
> (ii) At least one of the parties to the arrangement paying premiums is entitled to recover (either conditionally or unconditionally) all or any portion of those premiums and such recovery is to be made from, or is secured by, the proceeds of the life insurance contract; and

---

[7] 68 FR 54344, Sept. 17, 2003; Treas. Reg. § 1.61-22(j) (the "2003 regulations").

      (iii) The arrangement is not part of a group-term life insurance plan described in Code Sec. 79 (unless the group-term plan provides permanent benefits to employees).[8]

The regulations contain a special rule for arrangements entered into in connection with the performance of services. Under this rule, a split-dollar life insurance arrangement is any arrangement (whether or not described in the general rule) between an owner and a nonowner of a life insurance contract under which the employer or service recipient pays, directly or indirectly, all or any portion of the premiums, and the employee or service provider designates the beneficiary of all or any portion of the death benefit (or the beneficiary is a person whom the employee or service provider would reasonably be expected to name as beneficiary).[9]

The IRS and practitioners generally divide split-dollar life insurance arrangements into two types, based on who owns the life insurance policy.

.01 Types of Split-Dollar Arrangements

Practitioners and the IRS generally classify split-dollar arrangements according to how the arrangements divide the ownership and other policy rights. The most significant distinction among split-dollar arrangements is: who is the owner of the insurance policy? Generally, the method of taxation applicable to the arrangement will be determined by the answer to this question.

Under a collateral assignment split-dollar arrangement, the employee (or a trust designated by the employee) is the formal owner of the policy. The employee (or trust) assigns his or her rights to a portion of the death benefit proceeds and/or cash surrender value to the employer, to secure the employer's economic rights in the policy.

Under an endorsement split-dollar arrangement, the employer owns the policy and endorses over to the employee a portion of its rights to the death benefit proceeds and/or cash surrender value. Before 2003, collateral assignment split-dollar arrangements were the most popular. By discouraging collateral assignment arrangements, the dramatic developments in 2002 and 2003 enhanced the desirability of endorsement split-dollar arrangements in 2004 and beyond.

Another way to classify split-dollar arrangements is by the division of the policy benefit rights under the arrangement. Under an equity split-dollar arrangement, which generally is a form of collateral assignment arrangement, the employer only recovers the sum of the premium payments it made to the policy over the years, possibly with interest, but not the full cash surrender value. The employee is the owner of the cash surrender value in excess of premiums paid by the employer or "equity" in the policy. Under an equity split-dollar arrangement, the employee receives not just life insurance coverage, but also the entire economic benefit of the investment return on the employer's contributions. Upon termination of the arrangement (or "roll out") during the employee's lifetime, or

---

[8] Reg. § 1.61-22(b)(1).

[9] Reg. § 1.61-22(b)(2).

upon the employee's death, an equity split-dollar arrangement returns to the employer only the amount the employer contributed to the policy over the years.

Split-dollar arrangements also can be classified by the division of payment obligations between the employer and the employee. Traditionally, split-dollar arrangements were contributory, requiring the employee to pay a portion of the annual policy premium. Typically, these arrangements would link the employee's contribution, if any, to the Table 2001 rates or the insurer's alternative annual rate for standard risks, the amount necessary to avoid any imputed taxable income to the employee. In most arrangements, the employers pay the full amount of the insurance premium.

.02 Taxation of Split-Dollar Arrangements Before 2002

The IRS first approved a form of split-dollar arrangement in Rev. Rul. 55-713, which, interestingly, held that the appropriate tax treatment of such an arrangement was as a tax-free loan from the employer to the employee.[10] The IRS revised its position on the tax treatment of split-dollar arrangements in Rev. Rul. 64-328,[11] under which it held that both endorsement and collateral assignment method split-dollar arrangements should be taxable under the economic benefit doctrine. Rev. Rul. 64-328 announced that the taxable "economic benefit" conferred on the covered employee is determined by reference to the so-called "P.S. 58 cost,"[12] multiplied by the dollar amount of the life insurance. The taxable economic benefit is reduced by the amount of the employee's contribution toward the annual premium payment. In Rev. Rul. 66-110,[13] the IRS modified its position generally to provide that, where the insurer has published one-year term life insurance rates available to all standard risks that are lower than the P.S. 58 rates, these lower rates may be used to compute the taxable economic benefit provided to a covered employee under a split-dollar arrangement.

IRS Revenue Ruling 2003-105 clarified that, in the case of any split-dollar life insurance arrangement entered into on or before September 17, 2003, taxpayers may continue to rely on these revenue rulings to the extent described in Notice 2002-8, but only if the arrangement is not materially modified after September 17, 2003.

These revenue rulings essentially governed split-dollar arrangements for more than three decades, so that between 1964 and 2002, the tax treatment of split-dollar life insurance arrangements was generally as follows:

- The employer would not receive a deduction for its annual premium payments.
- The employee would be taxed on the economic benefit conferred by the life insurance coverage, determined by (1) the insurer's generally available published one-year term rates, or (2) the Table 2001 rates, unless the employee contributed to the cost of the coverage. Notice 2001-10 repealed

---

[10] Rev. Rul. 55-713, 1955-2 CB 23.

[11] Rev. Rul. 64-328, 1964-2 CB 11.

[12] P.S. 58 cost was based on tables contained in Rev. Rul. 55-747, 1955-2 CB 228. It was supplanted by Table 2001 rates in IRS Notice 2001-10.

[13] Rev. Rul. 66-110, 1966-1 CB 12.

the P.S. 58 rates for measuring the current value of life insurance protection for federal income tax purposes.

- The employee's designated beneficiary would receive the death benefit proceeds of the policy (less the employer's premium contributions) free from federal income tax, pursuant to Code Sec. 101.

- The employer, too, would receive its portion of the policy's death benefit proceeds free from federal income tax, pursuant to Code Sec. 101.

The so-called Table 2001 rates, published by IRS, usually are substantially higher than an insurance carrier's published one-year term rates.

> **Example 1:** Assume ABC Corporation established a $1,000,000 endorsement method split-dollar life insurance policy on the life of Executive D, age 45. Assume the annual premium cost for the policy is $2,000. If ABC paid the entire annual premium each year, D would have imputed income equal to the value of the life insurance coverage provided by the policy. ABC would determine this value by reference to the Table 2001 rate, or the insurer's generally available published one-year term rates. Using the Table 2001 rate, D's imputed income would have been approximately $1,530.00. However, a typical insurance carrier's one-year term rate for the same cover would be only about $725. At age 65, the difference in rates for $1 million in coverage could be $11,900 under the Table 2001 rate, compared to $2,800 under a typical insurance carrier's one-year term rate.

.03 Notice 2002-8 and the 2003 Regulations

While the IRS frequently expressed interest and concern over the evolution and growing prevalence of split-dollar life insurance arrangements,[14] until 2002 the IRS was unwilling or unable to translate its concerns into a change in the law. In January 2002, the IRS issued guidance ostensibly intended to clarify the federal income tax treatment of split-dollar life insurance, but in reality completely rewriting the tax treatment understood to apply to split-dollar life insurance arrangements since 1964.[15] In Notice 2002-8, the proposed regulations that followed in July 2002,[16] and the 2003 regulations, the IRS revoked most of its pre-2002 guidance.

The IRS now provides for the taxation of split-dollar life insurance under one of two "mutually exclusive regimes," the economic benefit regime and the loan regime, depending on whether the employer or the employee is the owner of the life insurance policy. The 2003 regulations require both the owner and the nonowner of a split-dollar life insurance policy arrangement to account for all amounts under the policy under either the economic benefit regime or the loan regime fully and consistently.

---

[14] See, for example, IRS Letter Ruling 9604001 (Sept. 8, 1995), seeking to characterize certain collateral assignment split-dollar arrangements as a taxable transfer of property under Code Sec. 83.

[15] Notice 2001-10, 2001-1 CB 459.

[16] July 9, 2002, Notice of Proposed Rulemaking, 67 FR 45414 (the "2002 proposed regulations").

The general rule under the 2003 regulations is that the value of the economic benefits provided to the nonowner under the arrangement for a taxable year equals the sum of:

1. The cost of any current life insurance protection provided to the nonowner;

2. The amount of the policy cash value to which the nonowner has current access (to the extent that such amount was not actually taken into account for a prior taxable year); and

3. The value of any other economic benefits provided to the nonowner, to the extent not actually taken into account in a prior taxable year.

The 2003 regulations provide that a nonowner has "current access" to any portion of a policy cash value that is (1) directly or indirectly accessible by the nonowner, (2) inaccessible to the owner, or (3) inaccessible to the owner's general creditors. According to the preamble to the regulations, "access" is to be construed broadly, and includes any direct or indirect right under the arrangement of the nonowner to obtain, use, or realize potential economic value from the policy cash value.

The 2003 regulations created limited "grandfathering" for split-dollar arrangements entered into on or before September 17, 2003.

.04 Economic Benefit Tax Regime

Under the economic benefit regime, the IRS treats the owner of the life insurance policy as providing economic benefits to the nonowner of the policy. Endorsement split-dollar arrangements generally will be taxed under the economic benefit regime. The 2003 regulations also provide a special rule that expressly applies the economic benefit regime to any split-dollar life insurance arrangement if the parties enter into the arrangement in connection with the performance of services, and the employee or service provider is not the owner of the life insurance policy.[17]

The owner and the nonowner must account for those economic benefits fully and consistently. The IRS treats the value of the economic benefits, reduced by any consideration paid by the nonowner to the owner, as transferred from the owner to the nonowner.[18] Where the relationship between the owner and the nonowner is that of employer and employee, the transfer will generally constitute a payment of compensation.

The 2003 regulations provide that, under a nonequity split-dollar life insurance arrangement, the IRS will treat the owner of the policy as providing current life insurance protection (including paid-up additions) to the nonowner. The amount of the current life insurance protection provided to the nonowner for a taxable year equals the excess of the average death benefit of the life insurance contract over the total amount payable to the owner under the split-dollar life insurance arrangement.[19] The total amount payable to the owner is increased by

---

[17] Reg. § 1.61-22(b)(3)(ii)(A).
[18] Reg. § 1.61-22(d)(1).
[19] Reg. § 1.61-22(d)(3).

the amount of any outstanding policy loan. The cost of the current life insurance protection provided to the nonowner in any year equals the amount of the current life insurance protection provided to the nonowner multiplied by the life insurance premium factor in Table 2001, or permitted in IRS guidance.

Example 2: Assume that ABC Corporation is the owner of a $1,000,000 life insurance policy that is part of a split-dollar life insurance arrangement with Executive D. Under the arrangement, ABC pays all of the $10,000 annual premiums and is entitled to receive the greater of its premiums or the cash surrender value of the contract when the arrangement terminates or D dies. Assume that through year 10 of the arrangement, ABC has paid $100,000 of premiums and that in year 10, the cost of term insurance for D is $1.00 for $1,000 of insurance and the cash surrender value of the contract is $200,000. Under the regulations, in year 10, D must include in compensation income $800 ($1,000,000 - $200,000, or $800,000 payable to ABC, multiplied by .001 (D's premium rate factor)). If, however, D paid $300 of the premium in year 10, D would include $500 in compensation income.

In a typical equity split-dollar arrangement, the covered employee has current access to all portions of the cash value in excess of the amount payable to the employer/owner. In addition, in many instances, the employee will also be regarded as having current access to a portion of the cash value payable to the owner if, for example, that portion of the cash value is for any reason not accessible to the employer or the employer's general creditors. Further, the policy cash value is determined without regard to surrender charges or other similar charges or reductions, and generally is determined on the last day of an employee's taxable year.

With respect to the value of "other economic benefits" provided to the nonowner, the IRS construes this term broadly to include any benefit, right or feature of the life insurance policy (other than current life insurance protection and policy cash value) provided to the nonowner.

The 2003 regulations apply to split-dollar life insurance arrangements entered into on or after September 17, 2003, as well as to split-dollar life insurance arrangements entered into before that date if material modifications to the arrangement or the policy are made after that date.

Example 3: In 2013, ABC Corporation and Executive D enter into an equity split-dollar life insurance arrangement under which ABC pays all of the premiums on a life insurance policy with a death benefit of $1,500,000, until the termination of the arrangement or D's death. The arrangement also provides that upon termination of the arrangement or D's death, ABC is entitled to receive the lesser of the aggregate premiums paid or the cash value of the policy, and D is entitled to receive all remaining amounts. Under the terms of the arrangement and applicable state law, the policy's cash value is fully accessible by ABC and ABC's creditors, but D has the right to borrow or withdraw the portion of the policy's cash value exceeding the amount payable to ABC. As of December 31, 2014, ABC has paid $60,000 of premiums on the life insurance policy and the policy's cash value is

$55,000. As of December 31, 2015, the policy's cash value equals $140,000 and ABC has paid aggregate premiums of $120,000 on the life insurance policy. As of December 31, 2016, ABC has paid $180,000 of the premiums and the policy's cash value is $240,000.

Because D has the right to borrow or withdraw the portion of the policy's cash value exceeding the amount payable to ABC, D has current access to such portions of the policy's cash value for each year that the arrangement is in effect. In addition, because ABC pays all of the premiums on the life insurance policy, ABC provides to D all of the economic benefits that D receives under the arrangement. Therefore, D must include in gross income the value of all economic benefits under the arrangement.

For 2014, D has "access to" $0 of the policy's cash value (excess of $55,000 of the policy's cash value determined as of December 31, 2014 over $55,000 payable to ABC). For 2014, D is also provided current life insurance protection of $1,445,000 ($1,500,000 minus $55,000 payable to ABC). Thus, D must include in gross income for 2014 the cost of $1,445,000 of current life insurance protection.

For 2015, D has "access to" $20,000 of policy cash value ($140,000 policy cash value determined as of December 31, 2015 minus $120,000 payable to ABC). D is also provided current life insurance protection of $1,360,000 ($1,500,000 minus the sum of $120,000 payable to ABC and the aggregate of $20,000 of the policy's cash value that D actually includes in income on D's 2014 and 2015 income tax returns). Thus, D must include in gross income for 2015 the sum of $20,000 of the policy's cash value and the cost of $1,360,000 of current life insurance protection.

For 2016, D is provided $40,000 of the policy's cash value ($240,000 policy cash value determined as of December 31, 2016 minus the sum of $180,000 payable to ABC and $20,000 of aggregate policy cash value that D actually included in gross income on D's 2014 and 2015 federal income tax returns). For 2016, D is also provided current life insurance protection of $1,260,000 ($1,500,000 minus the sum of $180,000 payable to ABC and $60,000 of aggregate policy cash value that D actually includes in gross income on D's 2014, 2015, and 2016 federal income tax returns). Thus, D must include in gross income for 2016 the sum of $40,000 of the policy's cash value and the cost of $1,260,000 of current life insurance protection.

.05 Loan Regime

Under the loan regime, the IRS treats the nonowner of the life insurance contract as loaning premium payments to the owner of the contract.[20] The loan regime generally will govern the taxation of collateral assignment split-dollar arrangements. The regulations define a split-dollar loan as one that meets the following three conditions:

---

[20] Reg. § 1.7872-15.

1. The payment is made either directly or indirectly by the nonowner to the owner (including a premium payment made by the nonowner directly to the insurance company);

2. The payment is a loan under general principles of federal tax law or a reasonable person would expect the payment to be repaid in full to the nonowner (with or without interest); and

3. The repayment is to be made from, or is secured by, either the policy's death benefit proceeds or its cash surrender value.[21]

The regulations treat the owner of the policy and the nonowner, respectively, as the borrower and the lender.

The regulations characterize split-dollar loans that do not provide for interest payments by the borrower-employee (which is most of them) as "below-market loans." If a split-dollar loan is a below-market loan then, for tax purposes, the IRS will recharacterize the loan as a loan with interest at the applicable federal rate ("AFR"), coupled with an imputed transfer by the lender to the borrower. If the lender were the borrower's employer, the IRS generally would characterize the imputed transfer as a compensation payment. The IRS then would impute an additional transfer of a like amount from the borrower to the lender, which the IRS would characterize as a nondeductible interest payment.

The timing and amount of the imputed transfers between the lender and borrower of the loan will depend upon whether the loan is a demand loan or a term loan. The regulations define a "split-dollar demand loan" as a split-dollar loan that is payable in full at any time on the demand of the lender.[22] In a split-dollar demand loan, the borrower-employee will recognize taxable income each year on the foregone interest. The amount of the foregone interest is the difference between what would have accrued at the blended AFR for the year and the interest that actually accrues during the year.[23]

The regulations define a "split-dollar term loan" as any split-dollar loan other than a split-dollar demand loan.[24] Under the regulations, a split-dollar term loan would be taxable just once, at the time the employer makes the loan, based on the present value of the foregone interest.

The regulations contain special rules for split-dollar term loans that are either (1) payable on the death of the employee, or (2) conditioned on the future performance of substantial services by the employee. These split-dollar term loans are taxable to the borrower-employee annually, like demand split-dollar loans.[25]

.06 Grandfathered Split-Dollar Arrangements

As noted above, in 2002 and 2003, the IRS completely rewrote the law applicable to split-dollar life insurance arrangements. Notice 2002-8 and the

---

[21] Reg. § 1.7872-15(a)(2)(i).
[22] Reg. § 1.7872-15(b)(2).
[23] Reg. § 1.7872-15(e)(3)(iii).

[24] Reg. § 1.7872-15(b)(3).
[25] Reg. § 1.7872-15(e)(5).

regulations have combined to create at least three categories of split-dollar arrangements, subject to potentially different tax treatment:

1. Those entered into before the January 28, 2002 issuance of Notice 2002-8;

2. Those entered into on or after January 28, 2002 and before September 17, 2003 (the effective date of the 2003 regulations); and

3. Those entered into on or after September 17, 2003 (the effective date of the 2003 regulations).

Notice 2002-8 addressed the treatment of split-dollar life insurance arrangements entered into before the date of the publication of the 2003 regulations, creating several "safe harbors."

- The IRS will not treat an employer as having made a transfer of a portion of the cash surrender value of a life insurance contact to an employee for purposes of Code Sec. 83 solely because the interest or other earnings credited to the cash surrender value exceed the portion thereof payable to the employee.

- In cases where the IRS treats the value of current life insurance protection as an economic benefit the employer provides to the employee, the IRS will not treat the arrangement as having been terminated (and thus subject to taxation under Code Sec. 83) without regard to the sponsor's remaining economic interest in the contract so long as the parties continue to treat and report the value of the current life insurance protection as an economic benefit to the employee.

- Parties may treat the premiums or other payments as loans, and the IRS will not challenge reasonable efforts to comply with Code Sec. 7872, or Code Sec. 1271, Code Sec. 1272, Code Sec. 1273, Code Sec. 1274 and Code Sec. 1275 (dealing with original issue discount).

- With respect to a split-dollar arrangement entered into before January 28, 2002, under which a sponsor has made premium or other payments and has received, or is expected to receive full payment of its premiums, the IRS will not treat the termination of the arrangement as a taxable transfer under Code Sec. 83 if either: (1) the arrangement is terminated before January 1, 2004, or (2) for all periods beginning on or after January 1, 2004, all payments from the employer since the inception of the agreement (reduced by repayments) are treated as loans for federal income tax purposes.

The 2003 regulations are effective only with respect to split-dollar arrangements entered into or substantially modified on or after the September 17, 2003 publication date. The 2003 regulations provide that, if an arrangement entered into on or before September 17, 2003 is materially modified after September 17, 2003, the arrangement is treated as a new arrangement entered into on the date of the modification.[26] The 2003 regulations provide the following "non-exclusive" list of changes that are not material modifications for this purpose:[27]

---

[26] Reg. § 1.61-22(j)(2)(i).   [27] Reg. § 1.61-22(j)(2)(ii).

(A) A change solely in the mode of premium payment (for example, a change from monthly to quarterly premiums);

(B) A change solely in the beneficiary of the life insurance contract, unless the beneficiary is a party to the arrangement;

(C) A change solely in the interest rate payable under the life insurance contract on a policy loan;

(D) A change solely necessary to preserve the status of the life insurance contract under Code Sec. 7702;

(E) A change solely to the ministerial provisions of the life insurance contract (for example, a change in the address to send payment);

(F) A change made solely under the terms of any agreement (other than the life insurance contract) that is a part of the split-dollar life insurance arrangement if the change is non-discretionary by the parties and is made pursuant to a binding commitment (whether set forth in the agreement or otherwise) in effect on or before September 17, 2003;

(G) A change solely in the owner of the life insurance contract as a result of a transaction to which Code Sec. 381(a) applies and in which substantially all of the former owner's assets are transferred to the new owner of the policy;

(H) A change to the policy solely if such change is required by a court or a state insurance commissioner as a result of the insolvency of the insurance company that issued the policy; or

(I) A change solely in the insurance company that administers the policy as a result of an assumption reinsurance transaction between the issuing insurance company and the new insurance company to which the owner and the non-owner were not a party.

.07 Taxation at Death

Often, a covered employee will transfer to or establish ownership of the split-dollar insurance policy in an irrevocable life insurance trust (ILIT), to keep the policy out of the employee's estate. In this event, the employee would have no incidents of ownership in the policy and the policy would not be payable to the employee's estate. The employee, through the ILIT, will execute a collateral assignment back to the employer.

¶1835 Notice 2002-59

In August 2002, the IRS responded to press reports[28] indicating the spread of split-dollar life insurance arrangements under which one party holding a right to current life insurance protection uses inappropriately high current term life insurance rates or prepayment of premiums or other techniques to confer policy benefits other than current life insurance benefits on another party. These ar-

---

[28] David Cay Johnson, I.R.S. Loophole Allows Wealthy to Avoid Taxes, New York Times, July 28, 2002 at 1.

rangements are generally not compensatory arrangements between employers and employees.

Under Notice 2002-8, the general rule is that taxpayers may value current life insurance protection by using either the premium rates in Table 2001 or the insurer's lower published premium rates that are available to all standard risks for initial issue one-year term life. The IRS indicated its belief that some parties were using split-dollar life insurance arrangements with inappropriately high current term life insurance rates or prepayment of premiums to confer policy benefits other than current life insurance benefits on another party. For example, in a reverse split-dollar life insurance arrangement in which an employee owns the policy and endorses the employer's interest in the policy's death benefit to the employer, the use of the higher rates would significantly overstate the value of the policy benefits to the employer. This overstatement would result in the employee's share of the premiums being significantly lower than the employee's actual share of the policy benefits.

In response, under Notice 2002-59, the IRS concluded that a party participating in a split-dollar life insurance arrangement may use the premium rates in Table 2001 or the insurer's lower published premium rates for taxing the value of current life insurance protection only when, and to the extent, such protection is conferred as an economic benefit by one party upon another party. Such benefits must be determined without regard to consideration or premiums paid by the other party. Consequently, if one party has any right to current life insurance protection, the parties can rely upon neither the premium rates in Table 2001 nor the insurer's lower published premium rates to value such party's current life insurance protection for establishing the value of any policy benefit to which the other party may be entitled.

¶1845 Sarbanes-Oxley Act

Section 402 of the Sarbanes-Oxley Act added Section 13(k) to the Securities Exchange Act of 1934 (the "1934 Act"), which prohibits publicly traded companies from directly (including through a subsidiary) extending or maintaining credit, arranging for the extension of credit, or renewing an existing extension of credit, in the form of a personal loan, to or for any director or executive officer of the company.

(k) PROHIBITION ON PERSONAL LOANS TO EXECUTIVES—

(1) IN GENERAL—It shall be unlawful for any issuer (as defined in section 2 of the Sarbanes-Oxley Act of 2002), directly or indirectly, including through any subsidiary, to extend or maintain credit, to arrange for the extension of credit, or to renew an extension of credit, in the form of a personal loan to or for any director or executive officer (or equivalent thereof) of that issuer. An extension of credit maintained by the issuer on the date of enactment of this subsection shall not be subject to the provisions of this subsection, provided that there is no material modification to any term of any such extension of credit or any renewal of any such extension of credit on or after that date of enactment.

Section 13(k) does not expressly prohibit or even refer to split-dollar life insurance arrangements. However, because the IRS treats collateral assignment split-dollar arrangements as loans (as discussed in ¶1835), it affected roughly one-half of the split-dollar life insurance arrangements then in existence. Most practitioners believe that Section 13(k) prohibits split-dollar life insurance arrangements where the executive (or a trust) owns the policy, which the IRS would tax under the loan regime.

.01 Companies Affected by Section 13(k)

Section 13(k) prohibits public companies from making loans to their senior executives and board members. Section 13(k) defines "issuer" to include any company that:

- Has a class of securities listed on a national securities exchange in the United States;
- Otherwise has securities registered under Section 12 of the 1934 Act;
- Is required to file reports under Section 15(d) of the 1934 Act; and/or
- Has a registration statement pending under the U.S. Securities Act of 1933.

Section 13(k) does not distinguish between U.S. and non-U.S. companies. Its prohibition on loans to officers and directors applies to a "lender" that is a non-U.S. company, director or executive officer located outside the U.S. or loans made outside the U.S. The prohibition on loans to executives and directors does not apply to private companies.

.02 Individuals Affected by Section 13(k)

Section 13(k) prohibits a company from making loans to a "director or executive officer (or equivalent thereof)," but does not define that term. However, Rule 3b-7 of the 1934 Act defines "executive officer" of a registrant as:

> its president, any vice president of the registrant in charge of a principal business unit, division or function (such as sales, administration or finance), any other officer who performs a policy making function, or any other person who performs similar policy making functions for the registrant. Executive officers of subsidiaries may be deemed executive officers of the registrant if they perform such policy-making functions for the registrant.

Rule 3b-7 suggests that Section 13(k) applies only to directors of the issuer, not directors of any subsidiary. To date, the best interpretation of who is an executive officer of a company includes anyone who is an executive officer within the meaning of Rule 3b-7 of the 1934 Act. This includes:

- The company president;
- Any company vice president in charge of a principal business unit, division, or function;
- Any other officer of the company who performs a policy-making function;
- Any other person who performs similar policy-making functions for the company; or

- An executive officer of a subsidiary of the company, if he or she performs policy-making functions for the company.

When read together with Notice 2002-8, and the 2003 regulations analyzing equity split-dollar arrangements as a loan from the employer to the employee to purchase life insurance, Section 13(k) would prohibit a publicly traded company from entering into a collateral assignment split-dollar arrangement with a director or executive officer.

¶1855 SERP Swap and Executive Roth Program

Some employers have amended their nonqualified retirement plans to allow participants to forfeit or trade a portion of their plan benefits in exchange for employer-paid life insurance (see Chapter 17 [¶1701 *et seq.*] for a detailed discussion of nonqualified retirement plans). The rationale for the trade is that nonqualified retirement benefits will be taxable to the employee or the employee's beneficiary as ordinary income when paid. However, if the employer instead uses the amount owed to the employee to purchase a life insurance policy, the proceeds of that policy will be paid to the employee's beneficiary free from federal income tax.

.01 SERP Swap

An employer has many options regarding its approach to offering this benefit. First, the employer could allow participants to forego only *future* contributions to the plan in exchange for the employer's funding of a life insurance contract. This is the most conservative approach, and would be least likely to result in adverse tax consequences for the participant.

Second, the employer could allow participants to forego a portion of their existing plan account balance in exchange for payments to a life insurance contract over time.

> **Example:** Executive D elects to forfeit $100,000 of her accounts in the ABC Corporation Deferred Compensation Plan in exchange for a payment of $20,000 each year for five years to an insurance contract. ABC could either make the annual $20,000 payments from its assets or arrange to pay them from the rabbi trust.

Though paying the premiums from the rabbi trust would add another layer to the transaction, it should not adversely affect the tax effects of the transaction. Due to the lack of guidance in this area, however, payments directly by the employer would be the more conservative approach of these two options.

Finally, the employer could allow participants to forego a portion of their existing plan account balance in exchange for a *lump sum payment* to a life insurance contract. For example, a participant could forgo $100,000 of his or her plan accounts in exchange for a payment of $100,000 to a life insurance contract. This approach could result in adverse tax consequences for the participant, depending upon his or her individual situation and the amount of the payment. As in the second option mentioned above, either the employer could pay this sum from its assets or it could arrange to pay them from the rabbi trust. Paying it from the rabbi trust would be a less conservative approach.

.02 Flexibility for Participants

If an executive already has the life insurance contract and life insurance trust for which he or she wishes to utilize this arrangement, the employer (or the trust) would simply be making payments to the insurance company in satisfaction of the executive's existing obligation to pay premiums. Other participants who use this benefit may be in a different position. The employer needs to consider whether it wishes to place any restrictions on the use of this benefit in the nonqualified plan. These restrictions could include a limit on the accounts from which participants can forfeit benefits or a maximum dollar amount per year, or in total, that the participant could forfeit. As an alternative, the plan administrator could establish its own guidelines for these arrangements.

.03 Taxation Issues

The so-called SERP (supplemental executive retirement plan) swap transaction raises a couple of tax issues. First, under the tax regime implemented by the 2003 regulations, if the executive (or the executive's trust) is the owner of the policy and the value of the policy's equity build-up, the IRS generally will tax the policy under the loan regime; under which the IRS treats the nonowner of the life insurance contract as loaning premium payments to the owner of the contract. Second, there is also the possibility that the IRS could take the position that the SERP swap causes constructive receipt and, thus, taxation of the funds to the participant. The IRS is not expected to take this position because the participant and the employer are exchanging one nontaxable vehicle for another.

.04 Executive Roth Program

An Executive Roth Program (ERP) is designed to pay out to executives the unfunded and unsecured benefits held under a defined benefit supplemental executive retirement plan (SERP) and allow those executives to reinvest the after-tax benefits in special life insurance policies that will "loan" to the executives the amount lost to income taxes. Future earnings accumulate tax-free and death benefits would be paid tax-free. The executives also could borrow or tax withdrawals from the life insurance policies on a tax-free basis.

A company with an existing SERP would amend the SERP to provide for the distribution of the existing (currently accrued) vested benefits for all participants in one or more lump sum cash payments. The company also would amend the SERP to provide that, going forward, the company automatically will pay out in cash to each participant in the SERP in each future year, an amount equal to the lump sum present value of all benefits that accrue or vest under the SERP in that future year.

Example: ABC Corporation maintains a SERP providing benefits to its highly compensated executives. Under the existing SERP, benefits would be paid out annually, for the duration of the executive's life, beginning when the executive retires. The SERP benefits are based on the executives' average final compensation and years of service with ABC. Each executive is vested in his or her SERP benefit after five years of service with ABC.

In 2011, ABC amends the SERP to provide for the distribution of all executives' currently accrued, vested benefits in a single lump sum cash payment. Following the 2012 payout, the SERP will cease to provide benefits for service before 2012. ABC also amends the SERP to provide that, beginning in 2012, and in all future years until an executive terminates employment, ABC will pay the executive a cash amount equal to the lump sum present value of the annual benefit that accrues under the SERP formula in that future year, as of January 15 in the following year.

As of December 31, 2011, Executive D has accrued a vested benefit under the SERP with a present value of $1 million. In July 2012, ABC pays D a lump sum cash payment of $1 million. Executive D directs ABC to make the lump sum payments directly to a LLC, of which D is a member, where the manager uses the payment to make premium payments on a life insurance policy on D's life.

On January 15, 2013, ABC pays D a cash amount equal to $100,000, which is the lump sum present value of the annual benefits that D would have accrued under the old SERP formula for the 2012 plan year. At D's direction, ABC makes the payment directly to the LLC, where the manager uses the payment to make premium payments on a life insurance policy on D's life.

¶1865 Insurable Interest

Code Sec. 101(j) imposes restrictions on corporate-owned life insurance ("COLI").[29] The COLI provisions apply to policies issued after August 17, 2006 (with an exception for insurance contracts covered under Code Sec. 1035, relating to certain exchanges of insurance policies). IRS Notice 2009-48 provides additional guidance concerning the application of Code Sec. 101(j) and the reporting obligations of employers that purchase COLI.

Under a COLI arrangement, the company purchases insurance on the life of one or more employees. The company ordinarily owns the policy, pays the premiums, and is the sole beneficiary of the policy. Companies purchase COLI to fund executive benefits because the earnings on the COLI policy's cash value build-up are tax deferred, while the final death benefit is not subject to federal income taxation (see ¶1815).

Code Sec. 101(j) limits an employer's tax deduction unless the employer meets certain conditions. Code Sec. 101(j) (i) limits the employees that an employer may purchase life insurance on, and (ii) imposes recordkeeping and reporting requirements on employers with COLI.[30] Unless the employer/policyholder meets the notice and consent requirements and limits coverage to the group of employees listed below, the amount excluded from the employer's income as a death benefit cannot exceed the amount of the premiums paid by the employer on the policy.

---

[29] Amending Code Secs. 101 and 6039H.   [30] Code Sec. 101(j)(1).

.01 Who Can the Employer Insure?

Under Code Sec. 101(j), the employer only receives the tax advantages of life insurance if:[31]

- The company employed the insured employee within 12 months of his or her death;
- The insured employee is a "highly compensated employee" within the meaning of Code Sec. 414(q) or Code Sec. 105(h); or
- The life insurance benefits are paid to the family of the insured employee, a trust established for the benefit of a family member, or used to purchase an equity interest in the company (e.g., pursuant to a buy-sell arrangement).

.02 Notice and Consent

An employer will retain the tax advantages of the life insurance only if, before the policy's effective date, the employer notifies the employee in writing:

- that the employer is the beneficiary of death benefits, and
- of the life insurance coverage and the maximum face amount for which the employee could be insured.[32]

In addition, the employee must give written consent to being insured and to the coverage continuing beyond his or her termination of employment. Finally, the employer must report on the number of employees insured at year-end, the number of covered employees, and the total amount of insurance in force.

.03 Reporting Requirement

Employers must report certain company-owned life insurance (COLI) contracts on Form 8925, under Code Sec. 6039I. For each tax year ending after 2007, every policyholder owning one or more "employer-owned life insurance contracts" issued after August 17, 2006, must attach Form 8925 to its income tax return. For this purpose, "employer-owned life insurance contract" is defined in Code Sec. 101(j) and generally is a policy:

- Owned by a person engaged in a trade or business and under which that person (or certain related persons) is the direct or indirect beneficiary; and
- Covering the life of a U.S. citizen or resident who is an employee of the applicable policyholder on the date of contract issuance. "Employee" includes an officer, director, or highly compensated employee under Code section 414(q).

Form 8925 reports, among other things, the number of employees covered by such company-owned life insurance contracts and whether each employee provided advance written consent to be insured and for the coverage to continue after termination of employment. (Where those consents are obtained, the Code Sec. 101(j) limitation on the exclusion of death proceeds from the policyholder's

---

[31] Code Sec. 101(j)(2)(A) and (B).

[32] Code Sec. 101(j)(4).

taxable income is inapplicable in certain circumstances, based on the status of the insured or the payment of death proceeds to heirs of the insured.)

¶1875 Code Sec. 409A

Code Sec. 409A generally provides that unless certain requirements are met, amounts deferred under a nonqualified deferred compensation plan for all taxable years are currently includible in gross income to the extent not subject to a substantial risk of forfeiture and not previously included in gross income. Code Sec. 409A also provides rules under which deferrals of compensation will not result in such immediate and additional tax liability, including rules about the timing of initial elections to defer compensation, payments of deferred compensation, and changes to the time or form of a scheduled payment of previously deferred amounts.

In the preamble to the 2002 proposed regulations, the IRS stated its view that a nonowner's interest in a split-dollar life insurance policy is less like that of an employee covered under a nonqualified deferred compensation plan and more like that of an employee who obtains an interest in a specific asset of the employer (such as where the employer makes an outright purchase of a life insurance contract for the benefit of the employee). The 2003 regulations expanded on the IRS's ownership interest theory by explaining that, in its view, for equity split-dollar arrangements, the owner of the life insurance policy pays policy premiums, thereby establishing a pool of assets with respect to which the nonowner has certain rights, such as the rights of withdrawal, borrowing, surrender, or assignment.

IRS Notice 2007-34 provides guidance regarding the application of Code Sec. 409A to split-dollar life insurance arrangements.[33] Because certain types of split-dollar life insurance arrangements provide for deferred compensation as defined under Code Sec. 409A, the requirements of Code Sec. 409A apply to such arrangements. As noted above, Notice 2002-8 and the 2003 regulations provide for the taxation of split dollar life insurance arrangements under one of two mutually exclusive regimes, according to how the arrangements divide the ownership and other policy rights:

- The economic benefit regime, which generally applies to collateral assignment split dollar arrangements, under which the employee owns the policy and assigns his or her rights to a portion of the death benefit proceeds and/or cash surrender value to the employer.[34]

- The loan regime, which generally applies to endorsement split dollar arrangements, under which the employer owns the policy and endorses over to the employee a portion of its rights to the death benefit proceeds and/or cash surrender value.[35]

If the split dollar arrangement qualified for grandfather protection under the 2003 regulations, it would not be subject to Code Sec. 409A (unless materially

---

[33] Notice 2007-34, I.R.B. 2007-17, April 23, 2007.
[34] Reg. § 1.61-22.
[35] Reg. § 1.7872-15.

modified). As noted above, the 2003 regulations provide that, for purposes of the general effective date provision, if an arrangement entered into on or before September 17, 2003 is materially modified after that date, the arrangement would be treated as a new arrangement entered into on the date of the modification and, thus, subject to Code Sec. 409A.[36] As discussed above, the 2003 regulations provide a non-exclusive list of changes that are not material modifications for this purpose.[37]

Split dollar life insurance arrangements pursuant to which payments are treated as loans generally will not give rise to deferrals of compensation within the meaning of Code Sec. 409A. However, in certain situations, such as where amounts on a split-dollar loan are waived, cancelled, or forgiven, split-dollar loan arrangements could give rise to deferrals of compensation for purposes of Code Sec. 409A.

Notice 2002-8 provides that, in cases where the value of current life insurance protection is treated as an economic benefit provided by a sponsor to a benefited person under a split dollar life insurance arrangement, the IRS will not treat the arrangement as having been terminated for so long as the parties to the arrangement continue to treat and report the value of the life insurance protection as an economic benefit provided to the benefited person. In such cases, provided that all other requirements of Notice 2002-8 are satisfied, the IRS will not treat the right to the economic benefit of current life insurance protection (within the meaning of Notice 2002-8) as deferred compensation for purposes of Code Sec. 409A.

.01 Arrangements Exempt from Code Sec. 409A

Split-dollar life insurance arrangements that provide only death benefits to or for the benefit of the employee/service provider are excluded from coverage under Code Sec. 409A under the exception for death benefit plans contained in the 2003 regulations under Code Sec. 409A.[38] Thus, collateral assignment split dollar arrangements, taxable under the economic benefit regime, generally are not subject to Code Sec. 409A. However, an arrangement could be subject to Code Sec. 409A if the employee had a legally binding right during a taxable year, which could be payable in a later year, *e.g.*, current access to the policy cash value[39] or other economic benefits described in the 2003 regulations.[40]

Similarly, arrangements that provide a legally binding right to amounts that are included in income in accordance with the exception for short-term deferrals under § 1.409A-1(b)(4) also do not provide for deferred compensation subject to Code Sec. 409A to the extent so included.

Finally, Code Sec. 409A would not apply to amounts deferred in taxable years beginning before January 1, 2005 (unless the arrangement under which the

---

[36] Reg. § 1.61-22(j)(2)(i).

[37] Reg. § 1.61-22(j)(2)(ii)

[38] Reg. § 1.409A-1(a)(5) provides that the term death benefit plan refers to a plan providing death benefits as defined in Reg.

§ 31.3121(v)(2)-1(b)(4)(iv)(C), through insurance or otherwise.

[39] Within the meaning of Reg. § 1.61-22(d)(4)(ii).

[40] As described in Reg. § 1.61-22(d)(2)(ii) or § 1.61-22(d)(2)(iii).

amount deferred was made is materially modified after October 3, 2004). An amount is considered deferred before January 1, 2005 and, therefore, grandfathered from application of Code Sec. 409A if, before January 1, 2005, the service provider had a legally binding right to be paid the amount, and the right to the amount was earned and vested.[41] Earnings on Code Sec. 409A grandfathered benefits under a split-dollar life insurance arrangement include any increase in the policy cash value, or an increase in any portion of the policy cash value, which is attributable to the Code Sec. 409A grandfathered benefits. For this purpose, earnings on Code Sec. 409A grandfathered benefits do not include any increase in the policy cash value attributable to continued services performed, compensation earned, or premium payments or other contributions made on or after January 1, 2005.

.02 Certain Modifications Allowed to Comply with Code Sec. 409A

Notice 2007-34 also provides that certain modifications of split-dollar life insurance arrangements necessary to comply with, or avoid application of, Code Sec. 409A will not be treated as a material modification.[42]

---

[41] Reg. § 1.409A-6(b).   [42] For purposes of Reg. § 1.61-22(j).

Chapter 19

HEALTH AND WELFARE BENEFIT PLANS

¶1901 Introduction—Health and Welfare Benefit Plans

Health and welfare benefits are not generally a major issue in negotiating and drafting executive compensation arrangements. As a rule, the executive simply wants to know that the employer will provide him or her (and family members) with immediate coverage under all available plans. The significant exceptions to the rule, where welfare benefits become a matter of serious negotiation, generally involve one or more of the following:

- Life insurance;
- Long-term care insurance;
- Executive physicals or supplemental coverage;
- Medical benefits extending beyond the executive's retirement;
- Health or disability benefits, where the executive or a family member has a significant preexisting condition; and/or
- Severance benefits.

.01 Life Insurance

Nearly every employer in the United States provides life insurance coverage to its executive employees. Most employers provide a certain level of coverage to all employees under a group term life insurance plan. An employer can provide up to $50,000 of group term life insurance coverage to its employees without any tax to them. Any employer-provided life insurance above that amount would generally result in imputed income to the covered employees. Many employers provide or make available additional coverage to, at a minimum, executive employees, under a supplemental life insurance plan (see ¶1945 for a more detailed discussion of life insurance benefits).

> **Planning Note:** The exclusion from income for the first $50,000 of coverage is available to executive (and other employees) even if the employer provides much greater levels of coverage to executives, as long as the employer provides that level of coverage on a nondiscriminatory basis.

> **Example:** If ABC Corporation provides group term life insurance coverage without charge to all eligible employees equal to 100% of their base salary or earnings up to $50,000, and supplemental life insurance coverage to executives equal to 100% of their earnings without limit, only the life

insurance coverage above $50,000 should create imputed income tax to the executives.

.02 Retiree Medical Benefits

Retiree medical benefits used to be a part of the compensation and benefits packages of most large and mid-sized employers (see ¶ 1955 for a more detailed discussion of retiree medical benefits). However, a combination of factors led many employers to eliminate or reduce their retiree medical coverage, including:

- The cost of providing medical benefits to retirees, which rose even more dramatically than the cost of providing coverage to employees;

- Financial Accounting Statement 106, which required employers to reflect the projected future liability of their retiree medical obligations on their financial statements; and

- A shrinking and aging workforce in which fewer active employees supported more retirees.

.03 Disability Insurance

Most employers also provide some form of disability insurance coverage to employees: short-term disability for illnesses and injuries that keep the employee from work for a period of weeks or months, and long-term disability coverage for disabilities that are permanent and total. Short-term disability payments ordinarily are taxable as ordinary income. Whether a disabled former employee is taxed on long-term disability payments made from an employer-sponsored plan depends on whether the employee contributed to the plan coverage or recognized income for the value of the employer-paid coverage. If the now-disabled employee had paid all or part of the premiums for the coverage on an after-tax basis, or recognized income for the value of employer-paid coverage, the employee should be able to receive payments due to long-term disability tax-free (see ¶ 1945 for a more detailed discussion of disability insurance benefits).

.04 Medical and Health Benefits

Group health plan coverage is the most prevalent benefit provided by employers to their employees (see ¶ 1925). Employers only offer 401(k) plans as frequently. The Affordable Care Act ("ACA" or "ObamaCare") requiring employers to offer affordable health coverage only increased the ubiquity of employer group health plan coverage. Although the Internal Revenue Code did not regulate health and welfare benefits nearly as much as qualified retirement plans, several important provisions of the Code do apply to health plans and benefits:

- Employer contributions to, or payments of, health benefits are fully and immediately deductible;[1]

- Employees are not taxed on benefits or payments made on their behalf;[2]

---

[1] Code Sec. 106.   [2] Code Sec. 105.

¶ 1901.02

- Employees are permitted to make pre-tax contributions to a "cafeteria plan;"[3]
- Contributions toward future health benefits can accumulate tax-free, to a limited extent, in a tax-exempt trust;[4]
- Employers must offer group health plan coverage that meets certain standards, including the market reforms under ERISA and the ACA;[5] and
- Large employers must offer full-time employees the opportunity to enroll in minimum essential coverage in an employer group health plan that is affordable.[6]

An employer may also provide its executives with certain additional health benefits, such as executive physicals and reimbursement of out-of-pocket medical expenses (see ¶1935).

.05 Severance Benefits

A plan, policy, or arrangement providing for severance payments could be deemed either a pension benefit plan or a welfare benefit plan under ERISA.[7] Under regulations promulgated by the DOL, a severance plan will be treated as a welfare benefit plan, not an ERISA pension plan, unless:[8]

1. Payments under the plan are contingent directly or indirectly upon the employee's retiring;

2. The total amount of severance payments exceeds twice the employee's annual compensation during the plan year immediately preceding termination of service; or

3. All payments to the employee are not completed either (a) in the case of a termination of employment in connection with a "limited program of termination," within the latter of 24 months after the termination of the employee's service or 24 months after the employee attains normal retirement age, or (b) in the case of all other employees, within 24 months after termination of the employee's service.

Chapter 14 (¶1401 *et seq.*) discusses severance benefits in detail and, therefore, this chapter will not discuss them further.

.06 Sources of Law and Regulation

The law governing employee welfare benefit plans is principally contained in two sources—the Internal Revenue Code of 1986, as amended, (the "Code")[9] and the Employee Retirement Income Security Act of 1974, as amended, ("ERISA") (see ¶1915).[10] The provisions of the Code and ERISA overlap in many respects. The Internal Revenue Service ("IRS") is responsible for interpreting, administering, and enforcing the Code. The U.S. Department of Labor ("DOL") is primarily responsible for interpreting, administering, and enforcing ERISA.

---

[3] Code Sec. 125.
[4] Code Sec. 501(c)(9).
[5] Code Sec. 4980D.
[6] Code Sec. 4980H.

[7] Reg. § 2510.3-2(b)(1); Reg. § 2510.3-1(a)(2).
[8] Reg. § 2510.3-2(b)(1).
[9] 26 U.S.C. §§ 1-9206.
[10] 29 U.S.C. § 1001 et seq.

.07 Flexible Benefit—"Cafeteria" Plans

A flexible benefit plan, referred to as a "cafeteria plan" is an employee benefit plan that permits an employee to pay health or other eligible plan contributions on a pre-tax basis, and/or to choose his or her benefit coverage from among several benefits. An employer or its counsel must design a flexible benefit plan in accordance with the tax provisions of Code Sec. 125 (see ¶ 1965). The Code and the IRS also allow employers and executives to establish health savings accounts ("HSAs") and/or health reimbursement accounts ("HRAs"). The advantage of HSAs and HRAs is that the executive may be able to carry over his or her account balance beyond retirement.

.08 Code Sec. 409A

Code Sec. 409A[11] does not apply to certain welfare benefit plans, including bona fide vacation leave, sick leave, compensatory time, disability pay, and death benefit plans. Where an employer with a self-insured group health plan provides for continued coverage beyond retirement or other termination (other than pursuant to COBRA), that coverage may violate the nondiscrimination rules of Code Sec. 105(h) and, thus, might be subject to Code Sec. 409A (see ¶ 1975).

.09 Proxy Statement Disclosure

SEC proxy disclosure rules do not require a public company to disclose welfare benefits that the company provides to its executives under substantially the same terms as apply to other employees. SEC disclosure rules would require a public company to disclose in its annual proxy statement any supplemental health, life, or disability benefits that the company provides to its executives. However, the expansion of the SEC's proxy statement disclosure rules in 2007 had the interesting effect of causing more companies to consider providing supplemental health, life, and disability benefits to their executives (see ¶ 1985).

.10 Corporate Owned Life Insurance

Corporate owned life insurance ("COLI") had become a vehicle for funding a variety of corporate obligations on a tax-favored basis. Congress took note of this fact and imposed significant restrictions on employers' use of COLI in the Pension Protection Act of 2006 ("PPA") (see ¶ 1995).

¶1915 Application of ERISA

ERISA applies broadly to any employer-sponsored plan that is an "employee welfare benefit plan," defined as follows:

> The terms "employee welfare benefit plan" and "welfare plan" mean any plan, fund, or program which was heretofore or is hereafter established or maintained by an employer or by an employee organization, or by both, to the extent that such plan, fund, or program was established or is maintained for the purpose of providing for its participants or their beneficiaries, through the purchase of insurance or otherwise, (A) medical, surgical, or hospital care or

---

[11] Added by the American Jobs Creation Act of 2004 (P.L. 108-357).

¶1901.07

benefits, or benefits in the event of sickness, accident, disability, death or unemployment ....[12]

Thus, the term "employee welfare benefit plan," as defined in ERISA Section 3(1), includes plans that provide benefits such as medical care, dental care, disability coverage, death benefits, vacation pay, unemployment benefits, severance pay, and educational and dependent care. Virtually every health or medical plan maintained or contributed to by an employer in the U.S. is subject to ERISA.[13] The only meaningful exceptions to ERISA's coverage are for group health plans that are "government plans"[14] or "church plans"[15] (government plans and church plans are, however, subject to state or other federal laws mandating coverage).

Since the inception of ERISA, welfare benefit plans and pension benefit plans have been subject to nearly the same reporting and disclosure requirements under both ERISA and the Code. Specifically, ERISA's (1) written plan document,[16] (2) summary plan description,[17] and (3) annual reporting[18] requirements apply to both welfare and pension benefit plans.

Planning Note: Because the IRS has long regulated welfare benefit plans much less heavily than qualified retirement plans, some employers have paid them less attention. This is a mistake. With health care costs skyrocketing and governmental regulation increasing each year, a poorly drafted welfare benefit plan can create just as much liability as a poorly drafted retirement plan.

An employer can provide welfare benefits either by purchasing insurance or self-insuring its welfare benefit plans. Larger employers usually self-insure their group health plans, while maintaining a separate stop-loss policy to protect against large claims, thereby avoiding intrusive state law requirements. Employers with numbers of employees that are too small to allow for adequate risk spreading generally purchase group health insurance policies. Nearly all employers provide life and disability insurance benefits through the purchase of insurance.

.01 ERISA Preemption of State Laws

ERISA Section 514 expressly provides that its provisions "shall supersede any and all state laws insofar as they may now or hereafter relate to any

---

[12] ERISA § 3(1).

[13] ERISA is intended to be broad. ERISA expressly provides that its provisions "shall apply to any employee benefit plan if it is established or maintained-(1) by any employer engaged in commerce or in any industry or activity affecting commerce ...." 29 U.S.C. § 1003(a).

[14] ERISA Section 3(32) defines a government plan as "a plan established or maintained for its employees by the Government of the United States, by the government of any State or political subdivision thereof, or by any agency or instrumentality of any of the foregoing."

[15] ERISA Section 3(33) defines a "church plan" as "a plan established and maintained . . . for its employees (or their beneficiaries) by a church or by a convention or association of churches which is exempt from tax under section 501 of [The Internal Revenue Code of 1986]."

[16] ERISA § 402. For Educational Assistance Programs, the "written plan" requirement is in the text of Code Sec. 127.

[17] ERISA § § 101 and 102.

[18] ERISA § 104.

employee benefit plan."[19] The U.S. Supreme Court has interpreted ERISA's preemption of state law provision very broadly.[20]

ERISA's preemption provision includes a "savings clause" that provides an exemption for state laws that regulate insurance.[21] However, the Supreme Court has interpreted this exception to ERISA preemption narrowly to only exempt state laws that are specifically directed to the insurance industry or to insurance policies sold within the state.[22] Thus, group health insurance policies sold to an employer must contain the benefit provisions and coverage mandated by state law in the respective states where the employer has employees. ERISA Section 514 also contains a provision that prevents employers' health benefit plans from being "deemed to be an insurance company . . . or engaged in the business of insurance . . . for purposes of any law of any State purporting to regulate insurance companies."[23]

Courts have found state laws preempted by ERISA if such laws in any way "relate to" an employee benefit plan that is not an insured plan.[24] Thus, any state law that purports to mandate benefits or coverage under employers' medical benefit plans would not apply to an employer maintaining a self-insured plan.[25]

> **Planning Note:** Most employers prefer to self-insure their health benefit plans to avoid the extensive and varying state law coverage mandates. Some states also impose premium and other taxes on insured plans, which they cannot impose on self-insured plans.

.02 ERISA's Protection Against Retaliatory Termination

ERISA Section 203 expressly provides vesting requirements for pension plans, but not health and welfare benefit plans. Generally, this means that an employer could amend or terminate its health benefit plan at any time, effective even as to the ongoing conditions of covered participants.[26] However, the termination of an employee to avoid reimbursing such employee's medical expenses could be a violation of ERISA Section 510. ERISA Section 510 reads, in relevant part, as follows:

> It shall be unlawful for any person to discharge, fine, suspend, expel, discipline, or discriminate against a participant or beneficiary for exercising any right to which he is entitled under the provisions of an employee benefit plan,

---

[19] ERISA § 514(a).

[20] *Pilot Life Ins. Co. v. Dedeaux*, 481 US 41, 56 (1987); see also *Shaw v. Delta Air Lines, Inc.*, 463 US 85, 98 (1983).

[21] ERISA § 514(b)(2)(a) ("[N]othing in this title shall be construed to exempt or relieve any person from any law of any State which regulates insurance, banking, or securities.")

[22] *Pilot Life Ins. Co. v. Dedeaux*, 481 US 41, 56 (1987).

[23] ERISA § 514(b)(2)(B).

[24] See *Metropolitan Life Ins. Co. v. Massachusetts*, 471 US 724, 739 (1985); see also *Russo v. Boland*, 431 N.E.2d 1294, 1298 (Ill. App. Ct. 1982).

[25] *FMC Corp. v. Holliday*, 498 US 52, 72 (1990). Indeed, one of the main reasons for operating a self-insured plan is to avoid the restrictions and costly mandates of state law.

[26] See *McGann v. H & H Music Co.*, 946 F2d 401, 403 (5th Cir. 1991). In this widely publicized case, the employer amended its health benefit plan to impose a $5,000 limit on reimbursement of claims related to AIDS, after Mr. McGann had begun submitting claims for AIDS-related medical expenses.

this title, ... or for the purpose of interfering with the attainment of any right to which such participant may become entitled under the plan, this title . . . .[27]

The summary plan description for the welfare benefit plan must disclose the employer's funding method and the involvement of any insurance company. In contrast to pension benefits, welfare benefits are not subject to the vesting requirements and employers nearly always fund them on a pay-as-you-go basis from the employer's general assets. However, the reporting, disclosure and fiduciary duty rules under ERISA apply to welfare benefit plans.

¶1925 Group Health Plans

Although employer-provided group health benefits are not particularly exotic, exciting, or costly, they are a critical part of the executive's compensation package. Without good health coverage for the executive and his or her spouse and dependents, most executives would be unwilling or unable to perform the duties for which they are hired.

.01 Insured Medical Benefit Plans vs. Self-Insured Plans

The vast majority of employers with over 500 employees do not provide group health benefits through the purchase of insurance or an insurance policy. These employers are "self-insured." That is, they pay employees' medical benefit claims from general corporate assets or a dedicated trust fund. Although the employer may utilize an insurance company to process claims, the insurance company is providing administrative service only, not "insurance."

It can be difficult to determine whether an employer's medical benefit plan is insured or self-insured. Many employers use an insurance company to administer their self-insured plans, under what is referred to as an administrative services only ("ASO") contract.[28] Courts have uniformly held that an ASO arrangement does not cause an employer's plan to be insured.[29]

Most self-insured employers also maintain a "stop-loss" insurance policy on their medical benefit plans.[30] The vast majority of courts have held that a stop-loss policy does not cause an employer's plan to be insured, as long as there is sufficient risk borne by the employer—that is, as long as the insurance truly is stop-loss or excess claims insurance.[31]

Finally, some employers' medical benefit plans are operated under a so-called "minimum premium contract" with an insurance company.[32] Most courts

---

[27] ERISA §510.

[28] Insurance companies still seem to be the recognized experts on administering medical benefit plans and paying claims. Thus, most self-insured employers continue to utilize an insurance company for administration of their medical benefit plans.

[29] See Ins. Board v. Muir, 819 F2d 408, 412-13 (3d Cir. 1987); see also Powell v. Chesapeake & Potomac Telephone Co., 780 F2d 419, 423-24 (4th Cir. 1985).

[30] Stop-loss insurance is designed to protect the self-insured employer from unacceptable losses due to catastrophic claims. Typically, an employer's

stop-loss policy will pay individual and group claims in excess of certain predetermined maximums.

[31] See United Food & Commercial Workers v. Pacyga, 801 F2d 1157, 1161 (9th Cir. 1986); see also Thompson v. Talquin Bldg. Prods. Co., 928 F2d 649, 653 (4th Cir. 1991).

[32] A "minimum premium arrangement" is somewhat a combination of an ASO arrangement and stop-loss insurance coverage. The employer pays a minimal premium amount, but is obligated to make additional payments, up to a specified limit, as its employees submit claims.

have held that a minimum premium arrangement does not create an insured plan as long as such arrangement shifts the risk of loss to the employer by requiring continuing premium contributions as employees submit claims.[33]

Planning Note: An employer that negotiates a special health benefit for an executive must take care to ensure that it reflects the negotiated exception in the insurance plan document or stop-loss policy. Most employers' stop-loss policies promise to pay benefit claims *"payable under the terms of the plan"* and in excess of a specified amount.

Example 1: If ABC Corporation promises Executive D that it will extend coverage to his nondependent adult child, who otherwise would not be eligible for coverage under the plain term of the plan, the stop-loss insurer will likely resist covering claims for that child if he ever incurs significant claims.

Thus, different sets of laws apply to employers' medical benefit plans that are insured and those that are self-insured. Each of the fifty states has adopted an expansive and detailed list of coverages, benefits, and provisions that must be contained in policies covering individuals employed within its borders. State laws mandating specific coverages apply to employers' plans that are insured, but not to employers' self-insured plans. Only ERISA governs the benefits under an employer's self-insured plan.

.02 Eligibility for Coverage

The ACA requires a large employer to provide health and welfare plan benefits to its full-time employees and their child dependents. Employers are required to offer affordable minimum essential coverage to employees and dependents, but an offer of coverage is not required for spouses of employees. Dependent children up to age 26 must be offered coverage.

Large employers are those employers with more than 50 full-time equivalent employees on average during the year. A full-time employee is any employee who is regularly scheduled to work 30 or more hours a week or 120 or more hours a month. The employer must calculate its non-full-time employees into full-time equivalents, for example so that two 15-hour a week employees equal one full-time employee. If two employers are under common control or members of the same group of companies, then the employee count aggregates the employees of all employers in the group or common control.[34] There are a multitude of exceptions and rules.

For variable-hour employees or employees where total working hours during the year are uncertain, the employer may use the monthly measurement method or the look-back measurement method to determine if the employee is full-time. The monthly measurement method is made on an ongoing basis and provides more coverage flexibility from month to month. The look-back mea-

---

[33] *See United Food & Commercial Workers v. Pacyga,* 801 F2d 1157, 1161 (9th Cir. 1986); see also *Thompson v. Talquin Bldg. Prods. Co.,* 928 F2d 649, 653 (4th Cir. 1991).

[34] Control is defined by Code Sec. 414(b), (c), (m), and (o).

surement method allows a long measurement period, during which the employee may be excluded from health coverage, but limits flexibility during the ensuing stability period. If an employee is measured as full-time during a look-back period, then the employee must be eligible for a health coverage offer for a stability period that is at least as long as the look-back period.

Other than the ACA, the principal limit on an employer's right to cover only the individuals that it wants covered is the nondiscrimination requirements applicable to self-insured health plans under Code Sec. 105(h).[35] The Code provides that an amount received by an employee through employer-provided accident and health insurance is not included in the employee's gross income.[36] However, Code Sec. 105(h)(4) also provides that the exclusion from income will not apply to "excess reimbursements" made to highly compensated individuals ("HCIs") from a self-insured group health benefit plan that discriminates in favor of the HCIs with respect to either (1) eligibility to participate in the plan or (2) benefits provided under the plan.[37]

Regulations under Code Sec. 105(h) provide that plan benefits are nondiscriminatory if "all benefits provided for participants who are highly compensated individuals are provided for all other participants."[38] When a self-insured medical plan fails this "nondiscrimination in benefits" test, HCIs must include in their ordinary income the employer-provided part of the "excess reimbursement." The excess reimbursement is the dollar amount reimbursed to an HCI with regard to any discriminatory benefits.

The ACA expanded the nondiscrimination provisions of Section 105(h) to non-grandfathered fully insured plans. The penalty for violating the requirements for a fully insured program is borne by the employer, not the executive.

.03 HIPAA

The Health Insurance Portability and Accountability Act of 1996 ("HIPAA") added Part 7 to Title I of ERISA, and amended the Code to prohibit certain plan provisions and require other provisions. (Part 7 was to be further amended by the ACA, see ¶1925.06.) HIPAA prohibits a group health plan from discriminating against employees or dependents because of their health conditions, *e.g.*, by refusing coverage or charging higher premiums. HIPAA also prevents group health plans from applying preexisting condition exclusions to a covered person, except in limited circumstances. Finally, HIPAA requires group health plans to offer special enrollment opportunities to employees and/or their dependents in cases of marriage, birth, adoption or change of employment status.

In accordance with HIPAA, group health plans can impose a preexisting condition exclusion only under three circumstances:[39]

1. The preexisting condition was treated in the six months before the effective date of coverage;

---

[35] Code Sec. 105(h).
[36] Code Sec. 105(b).
[37] Code Sec. 105(h)(4).

[38] Code Sec. 105(h).
[39] ERISA §701(a)(1)-(3).

2. The preexisting condition exclusion lasts only until the individual has been covered under the plan for a continuous period of six months; and

3. The exclusion period is reduced by the individual's period of "previous creditable coverage."

HIPAA broadly defines "creditable coverage" to include coverage under any group health plan, including a government or church plan, health insurance, Medicare or Medicaid, military-sponsored health care, and state-provided health care, including risk-pools. HIPAA also requires an employer to provide an employee who was covered by its group health plan when he or she left employment with a notice of creditable coverage, which the employee may use to verify his or her prior coverage for future employers. (See also ¶1925.06 for a discussion of the ACA coverage improvements.)

.04 COBRA

The Consolidated Omnibus Budget Reconciliation Act of 1985 ("COBRA") added Section 4980B to the Code.[40] COBRA provides that a group health plan must offer each "qualified beneficiary" who would lose coverage under the plan as a result of a "qualifying event" the right to elect, within the "election period," "continuation coverage" under the plan. "Qualified beneficiary" means, with respect to a covered employee under a group health plan, any other individual who, on the day before the qualifying event for that employee, is a beneficiary under the plan (1) as the spouse of the covered employee, or (2) as the dependent child of the employee including a child born to or placed for adoption with the covered employee during the period of continuation coverage. "Covered employee" means an individual who is (or was) provided coverage under a group health plan by virtue of the performance of services for the employer maintaining the plan (including self-employed individuals). "Qualifying event" means, with respect to any covered employee, any of the following events which would result in a qualified beneficiary's loss of coverage:[41]

1. The death of the covered employee;

2. The termination (other than by reason of such employee's gross misconduct) or reduction of hours, of the covered employee's employment;

3. The divorce or legal separation of the covered employee from the employee's spouse;

4. The covered employee becoming entitled to Social Security retirement benefits; or

5. A covered employee's dependent child ceasing to be a dependent child under the generally applicable requirements of the plan.

The "election period" begins not later than the date on which coverage terminates under the plan because of a qualifying event, and ends not earlier than sixty days after the date the employer or plan administrator notifies the qualified beneficiary of his or her continuation rights.

---

[40] Code Sec. 4980B.　　　　　　　　[41] ERISA § 603(1)-(5).

Group health plans subject to COBRA must provide two forms of COBRA notices. First, the plan administrator must provide each participant with an "initial" notice of COBRA continuation rights at the time the participant first becomes eligible for coverage or benefits under the plan. Second, the plan administrator must provide each qualified beneficiary a notice of continuation rights upon the occurrence of a qualifying event. In the event of a qualifying event that is a divorce or loss of dependent status, COBRA provides that the qualified beneficiary must notify the plan administrator of the event before the plan administrator is required to provide the notice of continuation rights. The eligible employee or former spouse must then elect whether to purchase COBRA continuation coverage within sixty days.

Employers frequently negotiate with incoming or departing executives over COBRA coverage. COBRA issues for incoming executives usually relate to one of the following:

- The incoming executive is eligible for COBRA from his or her previous employer and the new employer agrees to reimburse the executive for the cost of COBRA premiums.

- The incoming executive is negotiating the terms of his or her employment agreement, including severance, and COBRA is an issue.

Example 2: ABC Corporation hires Executive D. Because one of D's family members has a serious health condition, ABC finds it desirable to let D's previous employer cover the large and ongoing expenses. D agrees because the family member is in the middle of a course of treatment that a switch in health care coverage could adversely affect. ABC's reimbursements are taxable to Executive D as ordinary income, so ABC also agrees to make a tax gross up payment to D.

COBRA agreements for retiring or terminating executives usually take one of the following forms:

- The employer agrees to continue the executive's coverage at regular employee rates. The agreement specifies whether the required COBRA coverage period runs concurrently (at the same time, so that no additional COBRA period results at the end of the agreed period) or consecutively (the executive may be entitled to an additional 18 or 36 months of COBRA coverage after the employer-paid period).

- The executive will be entitled to and elect COBRA continuation coverage. The employer will reimburse the executive for some or all of the cost of such coverage. An employer and executive might agree to this where the employer could not simply continue the executive as a covered employee following termination, *e.g.*, because the insurer would not allow it.

Planning Note: Health insurance is a very significant issue for most executives, whether they know it or not. The largest severance package in the world could be eaten up by one year's worth of catastrophic health claims of the executive and/or the executive's family. Moreover, many executives are approaching retirement age, when it can be nearly impossible to find affordable private health insurance.

Drafting Tip: An employment or separation agreement under which the employer promises to subsidize COBRA continuation coverage also should provide that:

- The employer's obligation to reimburse the former employee for COBRA premiums will cease on the date the employee becomes eligible for coverage under another group health plan offered by a new employer.

- This provision shall be construed to extend the period of time over which COBRA continuation coverage shall be provided to the former employee or dependents beyond that mandated by law.

- In the event that the premium payments or reimbursements by the employer, by reason of change in the applicable law, may result in tax or other penalties on the employer, this provision will terminate and the employee and the employer will negotiate for a substitute provision that would not result in such tax or other penalties.

As a matter of historical interest, the American Recovery and Reinvestment Act (ARRA), signed into law by President Bush in 2009, included COBRA provisions for the benefit of both employees and employers. Under ARRA, individuals who were eligible for COBRA due to an involuntary termination of employment during the period *from September 1, 2008 through May 31, 2010,* were generally eligible to receive a COBRA subsidy for up to nine months, under which they were only required to pay 35% of the COBRA premium. The employer subsidized the other 65% of the premium, which the employer then could recoup by claiming a credit against its required payroll taxes. The COBRA subsidy was nontaxable to the assistance-eligible individual. However, the subsidy was subject to phase-outs and recapture for individuals above certain income thresholds.

Under the law, for a period of up to nine months, the employer could only require these "assistance eligible individuals" to pay 35% of their applicable COBRA premiums. The employer would pay the remaining 65% percent of the premium, which the government then reimbursed to the employer through a reduction in the employer's federal payroll tax obligations. Importantly, the COBRA subsidy phased out for the "rich" who earned between $125,000 - $145,000 (for single filers) or between $250,000-$290,000 (for joint filers) in the year they received the subsidy. Any individual who received the subsidy during the year, whose income exceeded the limits, was required to repay the subsidy.

An employer that already subsidized COBRA coverage to some employees under a severance benefit plan or other negotiated severance could shift the cost of this subsidy to the government. An employer that did not provide a subsidy for COBRA coverage had an opportunity to do something very positive for its employees/former employees without increasing its costs. The government subsidy worked in conjunction with an employer's promise to subsidize under a severance agreement as follows:

The government is subsidizing 65% of the "applicable premium." For this purpose, the applicable premium is the amount the employer is actually charging the employee (up to 102%). If the employer has agreed to subsidize all or a portion of the applicable premium for a given month under a severance agreement, that portion is not eligible to be reported to the government as eligible for the subsidy.

COBRA rules may require the employer to provide additional notices at the end of the COBRA period.

.05 Long-Term Care Insurance

Code Sec. 7702B governs the treatment of qualified long-term care insurance. Under Code Sec. 7702B, employer contributions to provide long-term care insurance are deductible and any benefits paid out to an employee or former employee are not taxable income. Code Sec. 7702B treats a "qualified long-term care insurance contract" as an accident and health insurance contract. Code Sec. 7702B also provides that amounts (other than policyholder dividends, as defined in Code Sec. 808, or premium refunds) received under a qualified long-term care insurance contract shall be treated as amounts received for personal injuries and sickness and shall be treated as reimbursement for expenses actually incurred for medical care (as defined in Code Sec. 213(d)).

Code Sec. 7702B(b) defines "qualified long-term care insurance contract" as an insurance contract that:

A. only provides coverage of qualified long-term care services;

B. does not pay or reimburse expenses incurred for services or items that are reimbursable under Medicare;

C. is guaranteed to be renewable;

D. does not provide for a cash surrender value or other money that can be borrowed or pledged as collateral for a loan;

E. provides that any premium refunds, policyholder dividends or similar amounts, are applied as a reduction in future premiums or to increase future benefits; and

F. such contract satisfies the consumer protection requirements of Code Sec. 7702B(g).

Example 3: For example, an Executive Employment Agreement could provide as follows: Each calendar year during the Term the Company will pay premiums in an annual amount of $20,000 to provide Executive and his spouse with long-term care insurance pursuant to a qualified long-term care insurance contract (as defined in Code Sec. 7702B, with a guaranteed renewal period for life and containing such other terms and conditions as are mutually acceptable to Executive and the Company. To the extent permitted by the Long-Term Care Policy, Executive may pay additional (or after the Term, the entire) premium for the Policy as may be required to provide such continued, additional or enhanced benefits, rights or features as Executive determines in his sole discretion.

Long-term care insurance may not be the most exciting benefit available to executives — certainly not as exciting as a corporate jet. However, it could be very useful as portfolio protection - against the asset depleting costs of health care - and it will not raise shareholders' anger like a corporate jet. In the real world, those of us who have to negotiate givebacks from the CEO (and other executives) may need to bring something else with us to the table. In our experience, shareholders, the media and Congress are much less agitated by a welfare benefit than a trip to Augusta National Golf Club for the *Masters*.

.06 Affordable Care Act

The ACA amended Part 7 of ERISA to apply a number of market reforms to improve employer-sponsored group health plan coverage.[42] The ACA market reforms and coverage improvements are enforceable against employer group health plans both by the DOL and the IRS.[43] The ACA coverage improvements include, among other reforms:[44]

- Prohibition of pre-existing condition exclusions;
- Prohibiting discrimination against participants and beneficiaries based on a health factor;
- Prohibition on waiting periods the exceed 90 days;
- Prohibition on annual and lifetime dollar limits;
- Rules limiting rescissions;
- Coverage of preventive health services;
- Eligibility of children until at least age 26;
- Summary of benefits and coverage; and
- Claims, appeals and review rules.

These requirements apply to all employer-sponsored group health coverage, so executives can expect health coverage to include all of the above coverage improvements. The coverage improvements also apply to non-ERISA employers through the Code and through the Public Health Service Act ("PHSA"), as well.

.07 Continuing the Group Health Plan Coverage for Terminated Executives

Ordinarily, Code Sec. 105 provides that employer-provided health plan coverage is not taxable to a covered employee (or the employee's family). However, to qualify for the ability to provide tax-free coverage, a self-insured medical plan (as opposed to a fully insured plan) must (A) not discriminate in favor of highly compensated individuals as to eligibility to participate; and (B) provide benefits that do not discriminate in favor of participants who are highly compensated individuals. Additionally, a self-insured medical plan does not

---

[42] ACA Sections 1001 and 1201.
[43] Code Sec. 4980D.
[44] ERISA Sec. 715.

meet the nondiscrimination requirements unless all benefits provided for participants who are highly compensated individuals are provided for all other participants. For purposes of Code Sec. 105(h), the term "highly compensated individual" means an individual who is (A) one of the five highest paid officers, (B) a 10% or more shareholder, or (C) among the highest paid 25% of all employees.

Nearly all employers provide group medical coverage through some form of self-insured plan. Amounts paid to a highly compensated individual under a self-insured medical plan that does not satisfy the non-discrimination requirements are deemed excess reimbursements to the highly compensated individual and taxable.

A trap that some overlook exists for an employer that provides continuing, subsidized coverage under its self-insured medical plan to executives who retire or otherwise terminate employment, but not to other employees. The former executives receiving this continuing subsidized coverage could be at risk for the IRS treating that coverage as taxable ordinary income.

The ACA would subject an employer to daily penalty taxes if it offers post-termination health benefits to executives only (*i.e.*, on a discriminatory basis). Code Sec. 4980D imposes an excise tax on a failure to meet the requirements of Chapter 100 of the Code, which includes Code Sec. 9815 and the requirements of Part A of Title XXVII of the Public Health Service Act. This part includes several health care reform mandates including no lifetime or annual limits, prohibition on rescissions, coverage of preventive health services, extension of dependent coverage, summary of benefits and coverage, health outcome reporting, external appeals, primary care provider selection, emergency services requirements, *and* prohibition on discrimination in favor of highly compensated individuals. The excise tax applies to insured plans and not to self-insured plans.

As of July 2018, companies and compensation professionals are waiting for regulations on fully-insured discriminatory health plans. Until our government provides us with guidance, employers should tread carefully. What many employers are currently doing is providing a fully taxable, additional cash payment to the employee that he or she can use to pay for COBRA continuation coverage.

¶1935 Executive Supplemental Health Benefit Plans

An employer may provide its executives with additional health benefits, such as executive physicals and reimbursement of out-of-pocket medical expenses. Many employers require their executives to obtain annual physicals. Employers view executive physicals as a benefit to both the executive and the employer. The annual physical is "medical care" within the meaning of Code Sec. 213(d), and is, therefore, excludable from the executive's income. Usually, when a medical plan is self-insured, plan services are subject to the nondiscrimination requirements of Code Sec. 105(h). However, even under a self-insured plan, reimbursing executives for routine medical examinations will not create a discrimination issue because medical diagnostic procedures are not considered part of the plan for purposes of Code Sec. 105(h) and, therefore, are not subject to the nondiscrimination requirements.[45] Such diagnostic procedures must be performed at a facility that provides no services (directly or indirectly) other than medical, and ancillary, services.[46]

Some employers reimburse their executives for out-of-pocket medical expenses, such as deductibles and co-payments. These arrangements can be tax-deductible to the company and tax-free to the employee when structured properly. For example, employees and dependents participating in such arrangements must be covered under an employer-sponsored health plan. In addition, such reimbursements must be made pursuant to an insurance contract. This requirement exists because of the nondiscrimination requirements of Code Sec. 105(h), which requires that self-insured plans meet certain nondiscrimination tests. Therefore, if the employer offers reimbursement plans only to executives and their dependents, it must do so pursuant to an insurance policy. If they do not, the plans will fail the nondiscrimination requirements of Code Sec. 105(h) and result in taxable income to the employee.

Under the ACA, insured group health plans are subject to the requirements of Code Sec. 105(h)(2), which prohibits discrimination in favor of highly compensated individuals, for plan years beginning on or after September 23, 2010. This change does not apply to "grandfathered plans" that were in effect on March 23, 2010, and have not been modified so as to lose grandfathered status after that date. The ACA legislation amended Code Sec. 105(h)(2) so that it applies to all health benefit plans (except for "grandfathered" plans - plans in effect on March 23, 2010 and not changed after that date) for plan years beginning on or after September 23, 2010. The penalty for a discriminatory insured plan is assessed against the employer. The penalty is $100.00 per employee discriminated against. The penalty will not be assessed until regulations are provided.

¶1945 Other Types of Welfare Benefit Plans

Health benefit plans are an integral part of the executive's compensation package, as they provide necessary care to the executive and his or her family during the executive's employment. However, life insurance and disability plans are important to the executive as well because these plans help to insure that his or her family will have its needs met if he or she can no longer work. This section will explore these plans, and their tax implications, in more depth.

.01 Life Insurance Plans

Life insurance coverage is one of the ubiquitous forms of employee benefit. There are at least four reasons for this. The first reason for this is that the Internal Revenue Code offers very favorable tax treatment to life insurance proceeds payable to a beneficiary (see ¶1815 for a more complete description of the favorable tax treatment of life insurance policies).[47] The second reason is that, whether they know it or not, executives and other employees need life insurance more than any other benefit (with the exception of long-term disability insur-

---

[45] Reg. § 1.105-11(g).
[46] Reg. § 1.105-11(g).

[47] Code Sec. 101.

ance). The third reason is that the internal cash build up on a life insurance contract is not taxable, thus enabling employers and executives to use life insurance for education or retirement funding and other purposes not related to providing death benefits. Finally, the life insurance industry has made it very easy for employers to provide this benefit to its executives and other employees, by creating products with flexibility and a dazzling assortment of features. (See also ¶ 1801 for a discussion of life insurance as an executive benefit.)

Under Code Sec. 79(a), the cost of employer-provided group term life insurance is included in an employee's gross income only to the extent it exceeds both the cost of $50,000 of life insurance and the amount the employee paid toward the purchase of the insurance. However, if the insurance is provided on a basis that discriminates in favor of key employees with respect to either coverage or benefits, no key employee may exclude the cost of the first $50,000 of insurance (although he or she still enjoys the exclusion for the amount he or she paid toward the cost of the insurance).[48]

> **Planning Note:** An employer that negotiates a special insurance benefit for an executive must take care to ensure that the negotiated exception is reflected in the insurance plan document or agreed to by the insurer. Most employers' group insurance policies provide coverage only to *"regular full-time employees."*
>
> **Example 5:** If ABC Corporation promises Executive D that it will continue her life insurance coverage for 36 months following her retirement, ABC had better consult with its insurer and/or negotiate a policy rider to ensure such coverage.

Insurance is "group term life insurance," available for exclusion from income if it meets the following four general requirements:[49]

1. The life insurance plan provides a general death benefit excludible from gross income under Code Sec. 101(a). Employer-provided accidental death and disability policies and travel accident insurance are not Code Sec. 79 plans.

2. The plan provides life insurance to a group of employees. Regulations provide that a "group of employees" is either all employees of the employer or some of the employees, if membership in the group is determined based on age, marital status, or employment-related factors. These factors may include compensation, years of service, union membership, or job duties.[50]

3. The life insurance is carried directly or indirectly by the employer. Insurance is carried "directly or indirectly" by the employer if the employer pays (directly or through another person) any part of the cost of the insurance, or if the employer arranges for payment by its employees of the cost of the life insurance and charges at least one employee

---

[48] Code Sec. 79(d).
[49] Reg. § 1.79-1(a).
[50] Reg. § 1.79-0(b).

less than his or her Table I cost for the insurance, and at least one other employee more than his or her Table I cost.[51] Table I is a uniform premium table computed on the basis of five-year age brackets, found in Reg. § 1.79-3(d)(2), for insurance provided after December 31, 1988. The Table I premium is used to determine the amount of employer-provided group term life insurance in excess of $50,000 included in the gross income of employees benefiting from a nondiscriminatory plan.

4. The employer's plan provides life insurance to employees in amounts computed under a formula that precludes individual selection. The formula must be based on factors such as age, years of service, compensation, or position.

An employer must test a plan that covers both current and retired employees (for example, a retired executive) for nondiscrimination purposes in such a way that it tests each of these groups of employees separately. However, if the plan fails with respect to either group, all key employees in each group must pay a penalty as to coverage and benefits.[52] When testing a group of former employees, the employer need consider only those who terminated service with the employer on or after the earliest termination date of any former employee covered by the plan. In addition, if the only former employees that the plan may cover are retired employees, the employer must only consider retired employees when applying the coverage tests. Finally, the employer may make "reasonable mortality assumptions regarding former employees who are not covered under the plan, but must be considered in applying coverage tests."[53]

.02 Disability Insurance

Arguably, long-term disability protection is even more important than life insurance. If the executive employee dies, his or her family members can use the life insurance proceeds to replace the employee's income and maintain their lifestyle. However, if the executive employee becomes permanently and totally disabled, the family not only needs funds to replace the employee's income, but also to care for a disabled family member.

Most employers provide some form of disability insurance coverage to employees. Employers intend that short-term disability benefits provide income replacement for a temporary period of days, weeks, or months during which the employee's illness or injury keeps the employee from working. Short-term disability payments are taxable as ordinary income, except in the highly unusual situation where the employee has paid the premiums for the coverage on an after-tax basis, or recognized income for the value of employer-paid coverage.

Long-term disability provides coverage for disabilities that are permanent and total. Some employers will offer an employee the choice between fully-employer-paid long-term disability insurance coverage—which would result in any disability benefits ultimately paid to the employees being fully taxable as

---

[51] Reg. § 1.79-0.

[52] Code Sec. 79(d)(8); Temporary Reg. § 1.79-4T.

[53] Temporary Reg. § 1.79-4T.

ordinary income—and the opportunity to pay either all or part of the disability insurance premiums on an after-tax basis, or recognize current income for the value of employer-paid coverage—which would result in the employee being entitled to receive long-term disability payments tax-free. Most employees select the first alternative.

> **Example 6:** Executive D's base salary is $500,000. ABC Corporation provides D with long-term disability insurance coverage that will replace 50% of her salary in the event D becomes disabled. ABC also makes available to D, and D elects to purchase, supplemental disability insurance coverage equal to 10% of base salary on an employee-pay-all basis.
>
> As a result of a horrific auto accident, D becomes totally and permanently disabled. ABC's insurance company begins paying D $250,000 per year in disability insurance benefits, which is taxable to D as ordinary income, and $50,000 in disability insurance benefits, which is tax-free to D.

.03 Definition of Compensation

Life and long-term disability insurance benefits are usually based on compensation, as defined in the applicable plan or insurance contract. Therefore, as in other areas of executive compensation and benefits, employers and their counsel must take care in defining covered compensation for purposes of determining benefits under life and disability benefit plans.

In *McAfee v. Metro. Life Ins. Co.*, a federal district court in California found that Metropolitan Life Insurance Inc., the plan administrator for the long-term disability plan of PeopleSoft Inc., violated the terms of the plan and ERISA by failing to include stock options in its calculation of disability benefits for a covered executive.[54]

The disability plan provided that if McAfee became disabled, he would receive monthly benefits depending on the amount of his pre-disability earnings, which included performance bonuses. Following a disabling injury, MetLife began paying McAfee disability benefits, but did not take into consideration the PeopleSoft stock options when calculating his benefits. The court sided with McAfee, holding that his stock option performance bonuses should be considered "income" in the calculation of his disability benefits under the plan. The court based its decision, in part, on the fact that the plan used the term "pre-disability earnings" rather than "salary."

.04 Supplemental Unemployment Benefits

Supplemental Unemployment Benefits (SUB) plans are "employee welfare benefit plans" under ERISA Sec. 3(1). Code Sec. 501(c)(17)(E) and the regulations under it recognize that supplemental unemployment benefit plans can be tax-exempt under either Code Sec. 501(c)(9) or Sec. 501(c)(17).

---

[54] *McAfee v. Metro. Life Ins. Co.*, E.D. Cal., No. S-05-0227 WBS KJM (May 24, 2006).

Under a properly designed SUB plan, an employer may pay its employees severance and/or unemployment benefits free of Federal Unemployment Tax Act ("FUTA"), Federal Insurance Contributions Act ("FICA") and possibly state unemployment ("SUI") taxes. Similarly, payments received by the employee under a SUB plan are not subject to FICA withholding, so the employee's cash flow is greater during his or her time of unemployment. However, SUB plan payments are subject to federal income tax withholding and, in general, state income tax withholding.

In order for severance payments to be excluded from the definition of "wages" for federal FICA and FUTA tax purposes, an employer must establish a valid SUB plan that meets certain federal requirements. In addition, the SUB plan must be linked to state unemployment benefits (with limited exceptions) and, as stated above, the severance payments must not be made in a lump sum. Some of the major requirements are as follows:

- Benefits are paid only to unemployed former employees who are laid off by the employer (*e.g.*, an involuntary separation from service).
- Amount of weekly benefits payable is based upon state unemployment benefits and the amount of straight-time pay.
- The employee receives benefits weekly or according to the frequency of their pay when employed, so benefits *cannot be payable in a lump sum*.

    Example 7: ABC Corporation will be terminating 200 employees in connection with a reduction in force and will pay each of them severance of $13,000 each. Using a SUB Plan, each employee receiving severance of $13,000 will save $1,000 in FICA taxes and ABC will save $100,000 in FICA taxes (assuming a FICA rate of 7.65%).

Additionally, in general, a Code Sec. 501(c)(17) trust must not discriminate in favor of highly compensated employees ("HCEs").[55] Benefits based on a uniform relationship to total compensation are not considered discriminatory. Accordingly, benefits provided for HCEs may be greater than those provided for lower paid employees if the benefits are determined by reference to their compensation. However, a SUB plan would not qualify if the benefits paid to the highly compensated employees bear a larger ratio to their compensation than the benefits paid to the lower paid employees bear to the latter's compensation. Code Sec. 501(c)(17) does not address how "compensation" is calculated. However, this section does define an HCE in accordance with Code Sec. 414(q), which in turn, uses the definition of "compensation" provided in Code Sec. 415(c).

¶1955 Retiree Medical Benefits

Medical coverage that continues after the executive's retirement or other termination of employment is a valued benefit. For an executive who retires or otherwise terminates employment before age 65, continuing coverage for the executive and his or her spouse and dependents can be critical, as the executive would have great difficulty finding individual coverage during middle age. In

---

[55] See Code Sec. 501(c)(17)(A)(ii), (iii).

addition, continuing employer-provided coverage is desirable for the executive who retires after age 65, as a supplement to Medicare.

Apart from the cost, the primary issue for employers that wish to provide retiree medical benefits to former executives is the potential for discrimination under the employer's self-insured medical plan. The nondiscrimination requirements described in ¶1925 apply. The nondiscrimination testing applicable to active employees' benefits generally disregard retirees. However, benefits for retired HCIs are excludible from gross income only if they are the same as the company's benefits for other retired participants.[56]

Financial Accounting Statement 106 requires employers to reflect the projected future liability of their retiree medical obligations on their financial statements.

.01 Funding Retiree Medical Benefits

As an exception to the typical pay-as-you-go structure of welfare benefit plans, employers may establish a tax-exempt trust under Code Sec. 501(c)(9). These trusts are referred to as "VEBAs," which stands for "voluntary employees' beneficiary associations." An employer can use a VEBA to pay medical, life, severance and long-term disability benefits. A VEBA is a tax-exempt trust, just like a trust under a qualified pension plan, which uses accumulations and contributions to pre-fund welfare benefits.

The employer can pay into the VEBA and deduct for the tax year the amount necessary to pay claims for that year. The employer can make deductible pre-funding contributions only by paying into the VEBA by the end of one tax year, and deducting for that year, an amount equal to thirty-five percent of that year's claims. However, the VEBA will not pay out that amount until the following year. Additionally, funding amounts held in a VEBA do accumulate tax-free over the course of the year.

> **Planning Note:** Many executives retire before age 65 (because they can afford to retire). Medicare eligibility does not begin until age 65. As noted above, individuals over age 60 but below age 65 can find it nearly impossible to purchase private health insurance at any price. In addition, Medicare only covers part of most older Americans' medical expenses. Therefore, retiree medical coverage is a very significant issue for older executives, whether they know it or not.

In Private Letter Ruling 200914018, the IRS ruled that an employee would not be in constructive receipt of income due solely to the availability of a one-time irrevocable election to waive retiree health benefits in exchange for an increase in the rate of pay for future services to the employer.[57]

---

[56] Reg. § 1.105-11(c)(3)(iii).

[57] Private Letter Ruling 200914018, December 19, 2008.

¶1965 Flexible Benefit—"Cafeteria" Plans

A flexible benefit plan, referred to as a "cafeteria plan" in Code Sec. 125, is an employee benefit plan that permits an employee to pay health or other plan contributions on a pre-tax basis, and/or to choose his or her benefit coverage from among several benefits. An employer or its counsel must design a flexible benefit plan in accordance with the tax provisions of Code Sec. 125. These plans require that all participants are employees and state that participants may choose (1) among two or more benefits consisting of cash and qualified benefits or (2) among two or more qualified benefits. Qualified benefits include (a) group term life insurance up to the amount ($50,000) normally excludable from taxable income; (b) accident and health insurance; (c) group legal services; (d) dependent care assistance; or (e) cash-or-deferred arrangements.

There are various tax advantages of a flexible benefit plan. Employees contribute to a flexible benefit plan on a pre-tax basis. As a result, the amount of the contribution reduces both the employer's payroll and the employee's taxable income. Similarly, the employer's FICA and FUTA contributions decrease. In addition, the employee is able to spend his or her benefits dollars and not pay taxes on them.

A flexible benefit plan must meet various nondiscrimination requirements. First, each of the qualified benefits must meet specific nondiscrimination requirements when tested alone. Secondly, Code Sec. 125 imposes rules on the plan. A flexible benefit plan may allocate no more than twenty-five percent of the total contribution under a dependent care reimbursement plan or a group legal services plan to anyone who owns five percent or more of the employer. In addition, the plan cannot permit the average benefit provided to non-HCIs to be less than fifty-five percent of the average benefit provided to HCIs.

Flexible benefit plans may not discriminate in favor of HCIs regarding eligibility to participate. In addition, the plan may provide no more than twenty-five percent of the total nontaxable benefits to key employees. The employer and its counsel should address the nondiscrimination rules at various intervals, such as the plan design stage or participation and selection stage. The nondiscrimination rules that the employer should address at the plan design stage relate to provisions such as eligibility and contributions. Upon the completion of all enrollment forms, the employer should consider the rules that cover participation and selection. Usually, the administrator will test each part of the plan to be sure it complies with all of the nondiscrimination rules.

There are various advantages in establishing a flexible benefit plan. As the name implies, flexible benefit plans offer executives and employees greater flexibility to select and pay for the types of benefits they need. As a result, flexible benefit plans may raise employee morale. Flexible benefit plans also help retain top-level management, improve the company's image, and increase the employees' awareness of the cost of medical care.

Any employer can design its flexible benefit plan to accomplish the employer's own objectives. If a company wants to offer an improved benefits package but still needs to control costs, the flexible benefit plan can be designed so that it provides a similar level of benefits as the employer's traditional plan while giving employees the option to purchase additional benefits through pre-tax salary reductions.

> **Planning Note:** Although the tax savings from a flexible benefit plan are small, the employer should not overlook them. To satisfy the Code's nondiscrimination rules, the employer will need to offer the flexible benefit plan to all employees, not just executives, but the savings to the employer in FICA contributions should make this worthwhile.

.01 Health Reimbursement Arrangements

In 2002, the IRS blessed a new form of plan—an employer-provided health reimbursement arrangement or "HRA." The simple principle behind HRAs is that plan participants will become better and more cost-efficient consumers of health care services if they benefit directly from the cost savings. As described with approval in Notice 2002-45 and Revenue Ruling 2002-41, an HRA has the following characteristics:

- The HRA is paid for solely by the employer and not provided pursuant to a salary reduction election or otherwise under a Code Sec. 125 plan.

- The HRA provides reimbursements up to maximum dollar amounts for a coverage period. Any unused portion of the maximum dollar amount at the end of a coverage period is carried forward to increase the employee's maximum reimbursement amount in later coverage periods.

- The HRA reimburses the employee for medical care expenses incurred by him or her, his or her spouse, and his or her dependents. These expenses, which the employee must substantiate, include premiums paid for accident or health coverage.

- An HRA may continue to reimburse former employees or retired employees for medical care expenses incurred after termination of employment, even if the employee does not elect COBRA continuation coverage.

- An HRA may not reimburse a medical care expense that is attributable to a deduction taken for any prior taxable year, incurred before the date the HRA was in existence or incurred before the employee was first enrolled under the HRA.

- The IRS does not make available the tax benefits of an HRA to self-employed individuals (partners, for example).

- The HRA is subject to COBRA.

- To the extent it is self-insured, the HRA is subject to the Code's nondiscrimination requirements for self-insured health plans.

- An HRA that is also a flexible spending arrangement ("FSA") may not reimburse expenses for qualified long-term care services (the HRA would be an FSA if the maximum reimbursement available to a participant is less than five times the value of coverage under the HRA).

The Internal Revenue Code provides that coverage and reimbursements of the medical care expenses of an employee or former employee, or a spouse or dependent of an employee, former employee or deceased employee, are excludible from the employee's gross income. However, this tax benefit would not be available if any person has the right to receive cash or any other benefit (taxable or nontaxable) under the HRA other than reimbursement of medical care expenses. If the employer or HRA violates this rule, the favorable income tax treatment of the reimbursements is lost for all employees, even with respect to those amounts paid to reimburse medical care expenses. For example, if the arrangement provided for a death benefit without regard to medical care expenses, or if it provided severance benefits only to employees who terminated employment with amounts remaining in a purported HRA at the time of termination, none of the reimbursements made to any participant for any reason in the current tax year would be excludible from gross income.

To qualify as an HRA, an employer contribution may not be attributable to an employee's salary reduction or otherwise provided under a Code Sec. 125 flexible benefit plan. However, an employer may provide an HRA in conjunction with a flexible benefit plan, so long as the HRA does not interact with the flexible benefit plan in a way that permits employees to use salary reductions, directly or indirectly, to fund the HRA. Further, if the amount credited to a reimbursement arrangement is directly or indirectly based upon the amount forfeited under a health FSA under Code Sec. 125, the arrangement will be treated as funded by a salary reduction and therefore not as an HRA. The IRS Notice provides several examples of arrangements intended to be HRAs that the IRS will not treat as such because the employer or employees fund them through, or based on, a salary reduction arrangement.

The IRS emphasizes that the two arrangements—HRAs and Code Sec. 125 flexible benefit plans—must be separate and distinct, because of the far greater flexibility of HRAs. The following restrictions on Code Sec. 125 plans do *not* apply to HRAs, making HRAs even more attractive:

- The "use it or lose it" rule (the rule that prohibits employees from carrying over unused amounts in their accounts from one year to another);
- The mandatory twelve-month period of coverage;
- The requirement that the maximum amount of coverage be available at all times during the coverage period; and
- The requirement that the medical expenses reimbursed must have been incurred during the period of coverage (although they cannot have been incurred *before* the date the HRA came into existence or before the date an employee first became enrolled in the HRA).

The notice also contains rules coordinating benefits under a Code Sec. 125 health FSA and an HRA. As a rule, a health FSA may not reimburse a medical care expense if the expense has been reimbursed or is reimbursable under any other accident or health plan. Therefore, if an employer provides coverage under both an HRA and a health FSA for the same medical care expense, the employee must exhaust amounts available under the HRA before the FSA can make reimbursements. However, it should be a very simple matter to draft around this requirement.

The IRS has interpreted the ACA market reforms as limiting employer HRAs.[58] The IRS position is that an HRA is a group health plan and therefore must satisfy the ACA market reforms. The ACA rules against annual and lifetime dollar limits and requiring preventive coverage without cost-sharing are violated by a standalone HRA, according to IRS interpretation. The amount of money offered through an HRA is a dollar limit, the IRS argues, and since the HRA does not provide for no-cost preventive coverage it requires impermissible cost-sharing. The IRS suggests that an HRA would satisfy the ACA rules if it is integrated with a group health plan that satisfies them. For employers, this means that HRAs must require participants to be enrolled in a group health plan, though for ACA purposes the HRA participant could be enrolled in a group health plan not offered by the employer, for example the spouse's employer's group health plan.

.02 Health Savings Accounts

The Medicare Prescription Drug, Improvement and Modernization Act of 2003, which President George W. Bush signed into law on December 8, 2003, added Code Sec. 223.[59] For tax years beginning after December 31, 2003, Code Sec. 223 allows "eligible individuals" to establish health savings accounts (HSAs) to pay for their current or future medical expenses. Contributions to HSAs are excluded from taxable income, whether made by the employer or by the individual. Like HRAs, the advantage of an HSA is that the executive may be able to carry over his or her account balance beyond retirement or other termination of employment.

HSAs are free of several of the restrictions associated with health FSAs, including the "use-it-or-lose it" requirement. Account funds are owned by the individual, so they may be invested by the owner and may be moved to another account with a new employer. Employers may offer HSAs through their existing cafeteria plan; or eligible employees can establish an HSA without the employer's involvement. An HSA is generally exempt from tax unless it has ceased to be an HSA. Earnings on amounts in an HSA are not includable in the individual's gross income while held in the HSA.

An "eligible individual" can establish an HSA. An "eligible individual" is any individual, during a particular month, who: (1) is covered under a high-deductible health plan (HDHP) on the first day of that month; (2) is not also covered by any other health plan that is not an HDHP (with certain exceptions for plans providing certain limited types of coverage); (3) is not entitled to benefits under Medicare (generally, has not yet reached age 65); and (4) may not be claimed as a dependent on another person's tax return.[60] To qualify as a high deductible plan,

---

[58] IRS Notices 2013-54 and 2015-17.
[59] P.L. 108-173, Sec. 1201.

[60] Notice 2004-2, December 22, 2003.

the annual deductible must be at least $1,350 for individual coverage and at least $2,700 for family coverage (2018 limits annually adjusted for inflation). However, there does not have to be a deductible for preventive care, and ACA rules on preventive coverage prevent cost-sharing even in HDHPs. In addition to the minimum deductible requirement, however, Code Sec. 223 imposes a maximum on the total deductible and other annual out-of-pocket expenses required under the plan (other than for premiums). Such amounts in 2018 cannot exceed $6,650 for self-only coverage; and $13,300 for family coverage.

Contributions made by an eligible individual or by a family member, subject to the contribution limits, are deductible by the eligible individual in determining adjusted gross income (*i.e.*, "above-the-line"). The contributions are deductible whether or not the eligible individual itemizes deductions. However, the individual cannot also deduct the contributions as medical expense deductions under Code Sec. 213.

Amounts contributed to an HSA on behalf of an eligible individual are excluded from taxable income, whether contributed by the employee through a cafeteria plan, by the employer, or by an individual outside of the employment context. The contribution limit in 2018 is $3,450 for individuals with single coverage and $6,900 for individuals with family coverage. The amounts are annually adjusted for inflation. Individuals age 55 or older can contribute an extra $1,000 in catch-up contributions. If the contributions are made through a cafeteria plan by an employee or by an employer, then the income is also deductible for purposes of FICA. Contributions to an HSA not made through a cafeteria plan are deductible for income tax purposes but not for FICA purposes.

An HSA beneficiary can receive distributions from an HSA at any time. Distributions from an HSA used exclusively to pay for qualified medical expenses of the account beneficiary, his or her spouse, or dependents are excludable from the account beneficiary's gross income. In general, amounts in an HSA can be used for qualified medical expenses and will be excludable from gross income even if the individual is not currently eligible for contributions to the HSA. However, any amount of the distribution not used exclusively to pay for qualified medical expenses of the account beneficiary, spouse or dependents is includable in gross income of the account beneficiary and is subject to an additional 10 percent tax on the amount includable, except in the case of distributions made after the account beneficiary's death, disability, or attaining age 65. "Qualified medical expenses" are expenses paid by the account beneficiary, his or her spouse or dependents for medical care as defined in Code Sec. 213(d) (including nonprescription drugs as described in Rev. Rul. 2003-102), but only to the extent the expenses are not covered by insurance or otherwise. The qualified medical expenses must be incurred only after the HSA has been established.

Generally, health insurance premiums are not "qualified medical expenses" except for the following: qualified long-term care insurance, COBRA health care continuation coverage, and health care coverage while an individual is receiving unemployment compensation. In addition, for individuals over age 65, premiums for Medicare Part A or B, Medicare HMO, and the employee share of premiums for employer-sponsored health insurance, including premiums for employer-sponsored retiree health insurance can be paid from an HSA. Premiums for Medigap policies are not qualified medical expenses.

If the account beneficiary is no longer an eligible individual, distributions used exclusively to pay for qualified medical expenses continue to be excludable from the account beneficiary's gross income. When the account beneficiary dies, any balance remaining in the HSA becomes the property of the individual named in the HSA instrument as the beneficiary of the account. If the account beneficiary's surviving spouse is the named beneficiary of the HSA, the HSA becomes the HSA of the surviving spouse. The surviving spouse is subject to income tax only to the extent distributions from the HSA are not used for qualified medical expenses. If, by reason of the death of the account beneficiary, the HSA passes to a person other than the account beneficiary's surviving spouse, the HSA ceases to be an HSA as of the date of the account beneficiary's death, and the person is required to include in gross income the fair market value of the HSA assets as of the date of death. For such a person (except the decedent's estate), the includable amount is reduced by any payments from the HSA made for the decedent's qualified medical expenses, if paid within one year after death.[61]

¶1975 Code Sec. 409A

Amazingly, even welfare benefits can become subject to Code Sec. 409A where the employer continues such benefits beyond the employee's termination of employment.

.01 Continuation of Welfare Benefits May be Subject to Code Sec. 409A

Code Sec. 409A(d)(1)(B) contains a list of welfare benefits that are specifically excluded from coverage under Code Sec. 409A, including bona fide vacation leave, sick leave, compensatory time, disability pay and death benefit plans. The regulations expand on this exclusion:

> (5) *Certain welfare benefits.* The term *nonqualified deferred compensation plan* does not include any bona fide vacation leave, sick leave, compensatory time, disability pay, or death benefit plan. For these purposes, the term "disability pay" has the same meaning as provided in § 31.3121(v)(2)-1(b)(4)(iv)(C) of this chapter, and the term *death benefit plan* refers to a plan providing death benefits as defined in § 31.3121(v)(2)-1(b)(4)(iv)(C) of this chapter, provided that for purposes of this paragraph, such disability pay and death benefits may be provided through insurance and the lifetime benefits payable under the plan are not treated as including the value of any taxable term life insurance coverage or taxable disability insurance coverage provided under the plan. The term *nonqualified deferred compensation plan* also does not include any Archer Medical Savings Account as described in section 220, any Health Savings Account as described in section 223, or any other medical reimbursement arrangement, including a health reimbursement arrangement, that satisfies the requirements of section 105 and section 106 such that the benefits or

---

[61] Notice 2004-2, December 22, 2003.

reimbursements provided under such arrangement are not includible in income.[62]

Thus, employer-provided group health benefits generally would not be subject to Code Sec. 409A as long as they are not taxable under Code Sec. 105(h). However, where an employer with a self-insured group health plan provides for continued coverage beyond retirement or other termination (other than pursuant to COBRA), that coverage may violate the nondiscrimination rules of Code Sec. 105(h) and, thus, might be subject to Code Sec. 409A.

The regulations under Code Sec. 409A clarify that, to the extent a separation pay plan (including a plan providing payments due to a voluntary separation from service) entitles an employee to reimbursement by the employer of payments of medical expenses incurred and paid by the employer but not reimbursed by a person other than the employer and allowable as a deduction under Code Sec. 213,[63] such plan does not provide for a deferral of compensation to the extent such rights apply during the period of time during which the employee would be entitled to continuation coverage under a group health plan of the employer under Code Sec. 4980B (COBRA) if the employee elected such coverage and paid the applicable premiums.[64] However, this provision would seem to subject health benefits the employer provides for longer than 18 months to Code Sec. 409A.

.02 Disability Under Code Sec. 409A

Disability of the participant is one of the six events upon which a nonqualified deferred compensation plan may allow for distribution or payment of benefits. However, the regulations under Code Sec. 409A provide a specific definition of disability that applies for this purpose.

Under the regulations, an employee is considered disabled if the employee meets one of the following requirements:[65]

(A) The employee is unable to engage in any substantial gainful activity by reason of any medically determinable physical or mental impairment that can be expected to result in death or can be expected to last for a continuous period of not less than 12 months.

(B) The employee is, by reason of any medically determinable physical or mental impairment that can be expected to result in death or can be expected to last for a continuous period of not less than 12 months, receiving income replacement benefits for a period of not less than three months under an accident and health plan covering employees of the employer.

The regulations also state that a plan may provide that an employee will be deemed disabled if determined: (i) to be totally disabled by the Social Security

---

[62] Treas. Reg. § 1.409A-1(a)(5).

[63] Disregarding the requirement of Code Sec. 213(a) that the deduction is available only to the

extent that such expenses exceed 7.5% of adjusted gross income.

[64] Treas. Reg. § 1.409A-1(b)(9)(v)(B).

[65] Treas. Reg. § 1-409A-3(i)(4).

Administration or Railroad Retirement Board, or (ii) to be disabled in accordance with a disability insurance program, provided that the definition of disability applied under such disability insurance program complies with the requirements of the definition above.

The regulations clarify that a plan may provide for a payment upon any disability, and need not provide for a payment upon all disabilities, provided that any disability upon which a payment may be made under the plan complies with the definition above.

Finally, the regulations indicate that a plan may provide for or permit a cancellation of an employee's deferral election where such cancellation occurs by the later of the end of the taxable year of the employee or the 15th day of the third month following the date the employee incurs a disability.[66] The regulations provide that, for purposes of this rule, a disability refers to any medically determinable physical or mental impairment resulting in the employee's inability to perform the duties of his or her position or any substantially similar position, where such impairment can be expected to result in death or can be expected to last for a continuous period of not less than six months.

¶1985 Proxy Statement Disclosure

SEC proxy disclosure rules do not require a public company to disclose welfare benefits that the company provides to its executives under substantially the same terms as apply to other employees. SEC disclosure rules require a public company to disclose in its annual proxy statement any supplemental health, life, or disability benefits that the company provides to its executives.

.01 Ordinary Coverage

Under Item 402(a) of Regulation SK (6)(ii) a company may omit information regarding group life, health, hospitalization, or medical reimbursement plans that do not discriminate in scope, terms or operation, in favor of executive officers or directors of the registrant and that are available generally to all salaried employees.[67] The Compliance and Disclosure Interpretations (C&DIs) explain this as follows:

Question 117.07

Question: Item 402(a)(6)(ii) provides that "registrants may omit information regarding group life, health, hospitalization, or medical reimbursement plans that do not discriminate in scope, terms or operation, in favor of executive officers or directors of the registrant and that are available generally to all salaried employees." Does this provision also apply to a disability plan that satisfies these nondiscrimination conditions?

Answer: Yes. To the extent that the disability plan provides benefits not related to termination of employment, a registrant may rely on Item 402(a)(6)(ii) to omit information regarding the disability plan. To the extent that the disability plan provides benefits related to termination of employment, a registrant may rely on Instruction 5 to Item 402(j) to omit information regarding the disability plan. [July 8, 2011]

---

[66] Treas. Reg. § 1.409A-3(j)(xii).   [67] Item 402(a)(6)(ii).

Similarly, Instruction 5 to Item 402(j), applicable to the "Potential Payments Upon Termination or Change-in-Control" reporting requirement, provides that a company need not provide information with respect to contracts, agreements, plans, or arrangements to the extent they are available generally to all salaried employees and do not discriminate in scope, terms, or operation, in favor of executive officers of the company.

A trend that developed somewhat unexpectedly as a result of compensation committees' focus on executive compensation reporting in the 2007 proxy statement was a re-examination of executive perquisites that protect the executive from the worst-case scenario, such as death, disability, or critical illness, at only a modest cost to the company. Many companies have implemented generous SERPs and change in control agreements, but overlooked simple, yet potentially important perquisites such as supplemental life insurance, supplemental disability insurance, long-term care insurance, and critical illness protection.

The rationale for re-examining these perquisites is simple: the committee can make a compelling case for providing them, and they do not antagonize shareholders. (For example, many executive contracts do not pay severance for employment termination due to disability and most company-sponsored long-term disability plans cap benefits at a small fraction of executives' annual pay.)

In negotiating and drafting employment agreements, executive compensation counsel should take care to protect their executive clients from what would be the "worst-case scenario" for most executives (and their families): a sudden death or disability.

.02 Payments Triggered by Death or Disability

Many companies' equity incentive plans or award agreements provide for full or partially accelerated vesting upon an executive's termination of employment due to death or disability. Some employment agreements also provide for payments or benefits on death or disability. However, from time to time, we come across a proxy statement that fails to reflect these amounts in the Payments on Termination or Change in Control disclosure. Companies usually justify this omission by arguing that, Instruction 5 to Item 402(j), quoted above, provides that a company need not provide information with respect to contracts, agreements, plans, or arrangements to the extent they are available generally to all salaried employees and do not discriminate in scope, terms, or operation, in favor of executive officers of the company. However, C&DI Question 126.02 states that the Instruction 5 standard that the "scope" of arrangements not discriminate in favor of executive officers would not be satisfied where the awards to executives are in amounts greater than those provided to all salaried employees - which is nearly always the case.

Question 126.02

Question: A company's employee stock option plan provides for full and immediate vesting of all outstanding unvested awards upon a change-in-control of the company and this provision is included in each option recipient's award agreement (whether the recipient is an executive officer or an employee). Instruction 5 to Item 402(j) provides that a company need not provide information with respect to contracts, agreements, plans, or arrangements to the extent they are available generally to all salaried employees and do not discriminate in scope, terms, or operation, in favor of executive officers of the company. Can the company rely on Instruction 5 to omit disclosure of these awards when quantifying the estimated payments and benefits that would be provided to named executive officers upon a change-in-control?

Answer: No. The Instruction 5 standard that the "scope" of arrangements not discriminate in favor of executive officers would not be satisfied where the option awards to executives are in amounts greater than those provided to all salaried employees. [Aug. 8, 2007]

This is in contrast to ordinary group term life and long-term disability insurance, which is not reported, as noted above.

¶1995 Corporate Owned Life Insurance

Many companies use corporate owned life insurance ("COLI") as a vehicle for funding a variety of corporate obligations on a tax-favored basis, with the death benefits of the COLI policies going to the company, not the employees. Some critics have derided COLI as "janitors' insurance" based on the implication that companies purchased COLI on the lives of all employees, even the janitors, for the tax benefits and death benefit it could produce.

Code Sec. 101(j)(4) sets forth the notice and consent requirements that an employer must meet in order to claim an exemption from gross income for the life insurance policy proceeds payable from a corporate owned life insurance policy on the death of an employee:

> (4) The notice and consent requirements are met if, before the issuance of the contract, the employee:
>
> (A) is notified in writing that the applicable policyholder intends to insure the employee's life and the maximum face amount for which the employee could be insured at the time the contract was issued,
>
> (B) provides written consent to being insured under the contract and that such coverage may continue after the insured terminates employment, and
>
> (C) is informed in writing that an applicable policyholder will be a beneficiary of any proceeds payable upon the death of the employee.

Code Sec. 101(j)(3)(A) defines "employer-owned life insurance contract" as a life insurance contract that: (1) is owned by a person engaged in a trade or business and that person (or a related person) is a beneficiary under the contract; and (2) covers the life of the individual who is an employee of the trade or business of the applicable policyholder on the date the contract was issued. Code Sec. 101(j) limits employer-owned life insurance contracts qualifying for tax benefits to insured individuals that were employees at any time during the 12-month period preceding death, highly compensated employees, highly compensated individuals, and directors.[68]

---

[68] Pub. L. No. 109-280 at §863(2)(A)(i-ii); see Code Sec. 414(q) defining "highly compensated employee;" Code Sec. 105(h)(5) defining "highly compensated individual."

An employer that owns life insurance on employees under a contract issued after August 17, 2006, is required to report on a yearly basis of the existence of the policies and that consent was obtained. Code Sec. 6039I(a) requires policyholders to file a yearly return showing "that the applicable policyholder has a valid consent for each insured employee (or, if all such consents are not obtained, the number of insured employees from whom such consent was not obtained.)". In addition, the return must include the number of employees of the policyholder at the end of the year; the number of employees insured under employer-owned life insurance contracts at the end of the year; the total amount of insurance in force at the end of the year in such contracts; and the name, address and taxpayer identification number of the policyholder and type of business of the policyholder.[69] The employer/policyholder is also required to maintain all records necessary for determining whether the requirements of Code Secs. 6039I and 101(j) are met.[70]

Section 863 of the Pension Protection Act, which added Code Sec. 101(j) only applies to life insurance contracts issued after August 17, 2006.[71] The exception is contracts issued after August 17, 2006, pursuant to an exchange detailed in Code Sec. 1035. Also of significance is that a life insurance policy that experiences certain material increases in death benefit or other material changes is treated as a new contract. The exception is in the case of a master contract, when new covered lives are added, only the new covered lives are treated as a new contract.[72]

To comply with Code Sec. 101(j) and qualify for the exemption from income, an employer must give notice to and receive the consent of an employee in order to insure the employee's life. Such notice must contain the maximum face amount for which the employee could be insured at the time the (life insurance) contract was issued. Notice must also inform the employee that the life insurance coverage may continue after the employee's termination of employment.[73] Thus, possible model employment agreement language could be:

> *Insurance.* The Company shall have the right to take out life, health, accident, "key-man" or other insurance covering Executive, in the name of the Company and at the Company's expense in any amount deemed appropriate by the Company. Executive hereby agrees to consent to the Company obtaining such insurance, and agrees to assist the Company in obtaining such insurance, including, without limitation, submitting to any required examinations and providing information and data required by insurance companies. Executive shall have no interest in any such policies obtained by the Company. The maximum face value for which the Executive could be insured at the time of issuance is $. Executive understands that such life insurance coverage may continue after termination of employment.

---

[69] Code Sec. 6039I(1-4).
[70] Code Sec. 6039I(b).
[71] Pub. L. No. 109-280 at § 863(d).

[72] Pub. L. No. 109-280 at § 863(d).
[73] Code Sec. 101(j)(4)(B).

Chapter 20
EXECUTIVE COMPENSATION LITIGATION

¶2001 Overview—Executive Compensation Litigation

Executive compensation often involves big money, big egos and high stakes. These factors often lead to litigation when someone's expectations are not met. Just as Chapter 17 (¶1701 *et seq.*) noted that nonqualified retirement plans (so-called "top-hat plans") have been the subject of a variety of litigation issues, executive compensation disputes generally lead to litigation, whether or not the arrangement was a top-hat plan.

Although many disputes and court cases involve a series of interlocking issues, the major executive compensation issues over which companies and executives have litigated include:

- The granting, vesting, exercise, and/or expiration of stock awards;
- Employment agreement provisions;
- Top-hat plans;
- Employment termination benefits; and
- Promises and misleading statements.

.01 Litigation Over Stock Awards

The 1990's saw an explosion in the amount of litigation over stock option and other stock-based awards. Employers awarded stock to more executive (and nonexecutive) employees than ever before. With stock awards in the hands of more employees and highly volatile stock prices, an increase in litigation over stock awards was inevitable (see ¶2015 for a detailed discussion of the types of litigation over stock awards).

.02 Litigation Over Employment Agreement Provisions and Other Compensation

Although employers and executives have been entering into employment agreements since the dawn of the republic, both the number and the percentage of executive (and nonexecutive) employees with written agreements have increased dramatically in the last decade. As sure as morning follows the night, more executives with more contracts means more litigation (see ¶2025 for a detailed discussion of the types of litigation over employment agreement provisions and other compensation).

.03 Litigation Over Top-Hat Plans

Nonqualified retirement plans are essentially unilateral contracts to provide benefits to specified employees. So-called "top-hat plans" are subject to some of the same provisions of ERISA that apply to qualified retirement plans, but exempted from many other requirements. This unique status frequently leads to litigation (see ¶ 2035).

.04 Litigation Over Employment Termination

An employment termination can be a life-changing event complete with all the emotional issues attendant to such an event. When change in control and employment agreements are added to the mix, employers and executives can find plenty of issues to litigate (see ¶ 2045 for a detailed discussion of the types of litigation over employment termination).

.05 Litigation Over Promises and Misleading Statements

As in all areas of the law, there has been significant litigation involving executive compensation and (allegedly) broken promises and miscommunications (see ¶ 2055).

.06 Litigation Over SEC Disclosures

Plaintiffs' lawyers have had very little success challenging decisions of companies' boards of directors on executive compensation issues. However, as the proxy statement disclosure rules have grown more complicated, plaintiffs' lawyers have grown adept at finding mistakes or omissions in reporting (see ¶ 2065). See also ¶ 595 for a discussion of litigation over non-employee directors' compensation.

.07 Litigation Over Non-Employee Director Compensation

Since 2012, we have seen a surge in complaints and litigation over the cash and stock compensation that boards of directors choose to pay themselves. See also ¶ 595 for a discussion of litigation over non-employee directors' compensation.

¶2015 Litigation Over Stock Awards

The use of stock-based compensation among both public and private companies skyrocketed during the 1990s. Additionally, the internet/technology bubble of the 1990s led to more stock awards and more instant millionaires (at least on paper) than at any time in history. With an unprecedented number of new public companies and stock compensation in the marketplace, lawsuits over stock awards were certain to follow. The volatile mix of quick riches and unsophisticated and inexperienced executives and advisors led not only to corporate and accounting scandals but also to a veritable explosion of litigation over stock compensation.

.01 Forfeiture of Nonvested Options Under Noncompete Clause

Litigation over non-compete provisions and other restrictive covenants is not always within the purview of executive compensation professionals. However, as companies continue to search for an effective way to protect their trade secrets, knowledge and goodwill, placing restrictive covenants in executive compensation and stock award agreements has become one of the more effective tools.

Although many companies—most notably, IBM—had long incorporated forfeiture provisions into their stock award agreements, these provisions, also sometimes referred to as "claw back" provisions, became very popular in the 1990's (see ¶475 for a discussion of restrictive covenants in stock option agreements).

> **Example::** ABC Corporation grants 10,000 stock options to Executive D. The options vest ratably over three years. However, the form of Stock Option Agreement between ABC and D contains a noncompete and other restrictive covenants. The Stock Option Agreement provides further that:
>
> *Remedy for Breach.* The Participant agrees that in the event of a breach or threatened breach of any of the covenants contained in this Section, in addition to any other penalties or restrictions that may apply under any employment agreement, state law, or otherwise, the Participant shall forfeit:
>
> > (i) any and all Options granted or transferred to her under the Plan and this Agreement, including vested Options; and
> >
> > (ii) the profit the Participant has realized on the exercise of any Options, which is the difference between the Exercise Price of the Options and the applicable Fair Market Value of the Shares (the Participant may be required to repay such difference to the Company);
>
> The forfeiture for competition provisions of this Section shall continue to apply, in accordance with their terms, after the noncompete provisions of any employment or other agreement between the Company and the Participant have lapsed.

A number of cases have upheld provisions forfeiting both vested and nonvested stock options. In *Tatom v. Ameritech Corp.*,[1] the Court of Appeals for the Seventh Circuit affirmed a district court decision that an employer acted properly when it forfeited the employee's options under a forfeiture-for-competition clause. The grantee argued that Illinois law disfavored noncompete provisions in employment contracts. In response, the court noted a distinction in the case law between provisions that prevent an employee from working for a competitor and those that call for a forfeiture of certain benefits should he choose to do so. Further, in the court's view, the forfeiture provision was reasonable. A stock option, unlike other types of regular and bonus compensation, gives an employee the right to acquire an ownership interest in a company. In theory, that interest gives the employee a long-term stake in the company and supplies him or her with an incentive to contribute to the company's performance. Consequently, "a provision calling for the forfeiture of such options in the event that a

---

[1] *Tatom v. Ameritech Corp.*, 305 F3d 737 (7th Cir. 2002). *See also, IBM v. Bajorek*, 191 F3d 1033 (9th Cir. 1999); *International Business Machines Corp. v. Martson*, 37 F.Supp. 2d 613 (S.D. N.Y. 1999).

holder goes to work for a competitor . . . serves to help the option holder's interests align with the company's."[2]

"Employee Choice Doctrine": Under the so-called "employee choice doctrine," courts are more likely to enforce a non-compete (or other restrictive covenant) where the terms of an employment, severance, stock award or other compensation plan or agreement provide that the employee or former employee will forfeit certain items of compensation if he or she goes to work for a competitor, rather than simply prohibiting the former employee from working for a competitor.

Some court decisions considering whether to enforce restrictive covenants, particularly non-compete provisions, begin their opinions by observing that the law of the governing state strongly disfavors the enforcement of restrictive covenants as a matter of public policy because enforcement could prevent the individual (often a citizen of that state) from earning a living in his or her chosen profession. However, many award agreements with restrictive covenants provide for a forfeiture of the awards as the company's exclusive remedy in the event of a breach by the employee. The employee choice doctrine essentially holds that a restrictive covenant in a stock award or other compensation agreement does not violate (or even implicate) the state's public policy against non-compete provisions if the remedy set forth in agreement for violating the non-compete provision is merely the forfeiture of the outstanding award. Thus, the employee has the choice between (i) adhering to the covenants and keeping the valuable award or (ii) earning a living in his or her chosen profession at a competitor, but forfeiting the award.

In *IBM v. Naganayagam*,[3] the widely respected federal district court in the Southern District of New York, easily upheld the company's ability to force a former employee to forfeit and repay amounts recognized on stock awards that had vested before he accepted employment with and began to work for a competitor.

What Constitutes "Consideration" for an Agreement to a Restrictive Covenant? In order to create a binding contract, an employer must provide some type or form of "consideration" to the employee. An argument made by some former employees seeking to escape from a non-compete or other restrictive covenant in or related to a stock award agreement is that, because the stock award may be forfeited before vesting, it is insufficient consideration to support the restrictive covenant – particularly when the employee has actually left the company before vesting and realized no gain from the award.

In *Newell Rubbermaid Inc. v. Storm*,[4] a Delaware Chancery Court found that an RSU award with a vesting schedule constituted sufficient consideration. In that case, the former employee had been awarded RSUs, with a three year vesting schedule, using an award agreement with a non-compete and other restrictive covenants. The court held that the award of options was sufficient

---

[2] *Tatom v. Ameritech Corp.*, 305 F3d 737 (7th Cir. 2002).

[3] 2017 WL 5633165 (S.D.N.Y. 2017).

[4] 2014 WL 1266827 (Del. Ch. 2014).

consideration to support the non-compete provisions, despite the fact that the executive had terminated employment and forfeited the RSUs.

In *Stericycle, Inc. v. Simota*,[5] a federal district court in Illinois considered whether a stock option with a three-year cliff vesting schedule constituted sufficient consideration to support a restrictive covenant. The court noted that, "Generally, Illinois courts do not examine the adequacy of consideration; they merely verify its existence." However, the court continued, when analyzing post-employment restrictive covenants, a court should depart from the traditional rule based on a recognition that "a promise of continued employment may be an illusory benefit where the employment is at-will." To address this issue, and avoid the need to investigate the employer's intentions, Illinois courts require that at-will employment must continue for a "substantial period" after an employee signs a restrictive covenant, in order to be sufficient.

The court quoted extensively from the Delaware Chancery Court's opinion in *Newell*, emphasizing that, in support of its holding, the *Newell* court discussed how there was little chance that the company would fire the employee shortly after she signed the restrictive covenant, pointing to evidence showing that the RSUs were awarded as an incentive for her to remain with the company.

> Looking again at the totality of the circumstances, the Court concludes that the stock options served as adequate consideration for the Covenant Agreement. The Court agrees with *Newell* that options have actual value even though payout may be deferred for a period of time. Presumably Simota thought so as well, as the agreement he signed states that he was "voluntarily willing" to enter into the restrictive covenants in exchange for the options.

The court observed that, as in *Newell*, there was no allegation in this case that the company was likely to terminate the employee shortly after he signed the agreement. "Rather, it is reasonable to infer from the complaint that [the company] had an incentive to retain Simota following its acquisition of Double Barrel in light of his experience managing Double Barrel's Las Vegas office and developing customers in the southern Nevada area."

The court also found it significant that the former employee had resigned voluntarily in order to take a position with a competing company, which weighed against his argument that the options' vesting schedule prevented them from constituting adequate consideration. The court stated that if the employee were permitted to void the consideration by simply resigning, he would be turning the "judicially-crafted requirement for adequate consideration that is meant to shield employees into a sword that can potentially harm employers' legitimate business interests."

In *Simota*, the court began its opinion by noting that Illinois courts require that consideration based on at-will employment must continue for a "substantial period" after an employee signs a restrictive covenant, in order to be sufficient. This fact, together with the court's emphasis on the voluntary nature of the employee's decision to resign, indicates that unvested stock awards may not

---

[5] No. 16 C 4782, (N.D. Illinois 2017).

constitute adequate consideration for a non-compete or other restrictive covenant in all situations. In the 2014 *Newell* case, the employee also had left voluntarily, but the Chancery Court's decision did not emphasize that issue.

A court might be unwilling to enforce a non-compete or other restrictive covenant in a situation where the company had terminated the employee without cause shortly after its initial award of stock options or another form of stock to the employee. However, it seems that most courts would find an unvested stock award to be adequate consideration in situations where the employee terminated employment voluntarily, where the "former employee caused the options to expire through his own action and that was not the company's fault."

Similarly, in *IBM v. Naganayagam*, the court stated "Additionally, Defendant himself testified during his deposition that . . . his supervisor at IBM, expressed a desire to match CSC's offer and keep Defendant at IBM. IBM's willingness-even eagerness-to continue employing Defendant is clear." Since the former employee was clearly afforded the choice of continuing to receive awards by refraining from competing with the company, or forfeiting the monetary value of awards by competing with the company, recession of his awards was permitted under the employee choice doctrine.

Companies' Ability to Clawback Vested and Paid Out Awards: Another important issue in litigation over non-competes and other restrictive covenants in stock award agreements is the extent to which a company can enforce the restrictive covenant by "clawing back" or requiring the former employee to repay gains recognized on awards that already have vested or been paid out. It is easy for a company to cancel or forfeit unvested options. However, it is more difficult to recover stock that already has been transferred to a former employee and, potentially, even harder to recover the cash proceeds the employee may have received upon a sale of the transferred stock.

In our experience, at some point during the conversation with a client on the use of restrictive covenants in stock award agreements, two questions usually arise. First, should we provide that our remedy for violation of the non-compete or other covenant is to seek an injunction against the former employee to prevent him or her from working for the competitor, or only for the forfeiture of the stock awards? There is not a clear answer to this question and different companies have followed different approaches. However, as discussed above, we do know that most courts will enforce award forfeiture provisions under the employee choice doctrine. This relative certainty of enforcement is an advantage.

But, a potential disadvantage of drafting to provide only for forfeiture is that this provision does not create a retention incentive to the employee (or a disincentive to work for a competitor) until and unless the awards are vested and have some value. For new hires and companies with lower stock grant practices (or declining stock prices), the mere forfeiture of awards may not appear to be a significant disincentive.

The second question clients ask is, as a practical matter, will we be able to make the former employee forfeit an award that already has been vested or paid out? The history of court decisions suggest that the answer to this second question is: yes.

Courts have enforced *well-drafted* forfeiture / clawback provisions in stock award agreements - even as to awards that vested (and may have been sold by the former employee). The recent federal court case of *IBM v. Naganayagam* (also mentioned above), allowed the company to recover the monetary value of RSU awards that had vested and paid out to the former employee.

The court observed that the company had clearly provided in its stock plan and all applicable stock award agreements that "IBM may cancel, modify, rescind, suspend, withhold or otherwise limit or restrict [the] Award[s] in accordance with the terms of the Plan, including, without limitation, canceling or rescinding this Award if [the Participant] render[s] services for a competitor prior to, or during the Rescission Period." The rescission period was 12 months.

These precedents appear to be relevant to companies' ability to enforce compensation clawback provisions against amounts (compensation) that have been paid to the employee and taxed. As with non-compete provisions, the key may be how well counsel drafted the clawback provisions of your plan and agreements. Courts have been willing to enforce clear provisions.

.02 Expiration of Stock Options

It seems that the federal courts decide at least one new case each month involving an employee's claims that the employer never gave, or gave incorrect, information on the expiration date of vested stock options following employment termination. In many of these cases, of course, there is animosity between the employer and the employee over the employment termination. When the employer then advises the former employee that he/she cannot exercise his/her vested stock options because the exercise period has expired, litigation ensues. Employers following best practices almost always win these cases. However, we still counsel our clients to avoid the litigation entirely, by taking care to communicate accurately with departing employees as to the expiration of their stock options. (This also is a good time to remind the former employee of the non-compete or other restrictive covenants applicable under the option agreement.)

In *Rawat v. Navistar International*[6] a federal district court held that two former employees could continue with their claim alleging that the company breached a stock-option "contract" by permitting the options to expire during a mandated blackout period. The blackout period began in April 2006, due to an accounting restatement, and was not lifted until June 2008. Only "accredited investors" were allowed to exercise their options during the blackout period. As a result of the blackout period, the two employees (and 54 others) could not exercise any of their remaining vested stock options after leaving employment in 2007, and the options expired. (The other 54 affected former employees accepted the company's cash make-whole offer and did not join the lawsuit.) The court primarily focused on the issue of whether releases signed by the two employees when they

---

[6] (N.D. Ill., No. 1:08-cv-04305, 2012).

left employment foreclosed them from bringing this lawsuit. The court found that the releases did not apply to the options, because the releases only covered claims that arose on or before the employees signed them and the employees each signed the releases before the options expired.

In *Porkert v. Chevron Corp.*[7], the Fourth Circuit held that vested stock options properly expired according to plan terms. The former employee, now plaintiff, claimed that pursuant to his hiring negotiations, he could exercise stock options for up to ten years from the date he received them. However, the plaintiff could not produce any documents containing these terms and he testified that he never read the employment agreement.

The company's stock plan documents provided vested options may be exercised within three months from the date of termination (but in no case later than ten years from the date of grant). The plaintiff argued that the phrase "may be exercised" in the plan language was permissive rather than mandatory and, thus, the clause should be construed so that he may, but was not required, to exercise his options three months after his retirement. The court rejected the plaintiff's arguments and found in favor of the company.

In *Sheils v. Pfizer, Inc.*[8], a former employee claimed that he was entitled to additional time to exercise stock options upon termination of employment because he did not receive adequate information about the new process for exercising options. The unique fact in this case was that, between the time of the former employee's termination of employment and the expiration of his options, the company had changed from in-house administration of its stock option plan to an outside stock plan administrator. Additionally, although the stock option agreement required the employee to exercise his options in writing, it did not indicate more specifically how the employee was to do so. In particular, the agreement did not indicate what information the employee should include in his exercise notice or to whom the employee should give notice.

Nonetheless, the court held that the employee did not exercise his options in the limited period of time set forth in the option agreement, and that the company could strictly enforce this timeframe. The stock option agreements explicitly set forth manner and time requirements for the exercise of options. The agreements required that all employees exercise their options by giving written notice to the company, and required that a terminated employee exercise his or her options within three months after the date on which his or her employment terminated.

The employee received a mailing from the company a few weeks before his employment was terminated, advising him of the switch to the outside administrator. The company also provided the employee with separation documents upon his termination of employment reminding him that his stock options were subject to the terms and conditions of the stock option agreements. The separation documents also included a phone number for the outside administrator that

---

[7] (4th Cir., No. 10-1384, 2012).

[8] *Sheils v. Pfizer, Inc.*, 2005 WL 2404536 (3rd Cir. 2005).

terminated employees could call if they had questions regarding their stock options. That phone number was the same number provided to employees in the kit.

The company did well by providing multiple forms of communication concerning the change in stock plan administrator (and therefore the change in the process for exercising options). It sent an initial mailing to employees, informing them that there would be a subsequent, more detailed, mailing to follow. In addition, the company provided an appropriate contact telephone number for the new stock plan administrator in the employee's separation documents. The company might have improved its position further if it had in place a clear protocol with the new stock plan administrator requiring that it address the option exercise requirements with participants even before those participants had established an account with the administrator for implementing any decision to exercise.

Similarly, in *Preece v. Physicians Surgical Care Inc.*,[9] the U.S. District Court for the Southern District of Texas held that a former employee cannot proceed in his claim that his employer and its successor breached stock option contracts by denying his request to exercise options after the options had expired.

In *In re Cendant Corp. Securities Litigation*,[10] the U.S. Court of Appeals for the Third Circuit held that an employer did not breach a contract with an employee who participated in two stock option plans by not allowing the employee to exercise her options during a blackout period or by extending the exercise term once the blackout period ended. The court said the plans gave the employer the discretion to do what was necessary to comply with securities law, and the authority to restrict the sale or disposition of the shares of common stock acquired upon the exercise of an option. In addition, the appeals court said the employer's acts of imposing the blackout was practically indistinguishable from what it was unequivocally authorized to do and the extension of the exercise term was reasonably construed as a modified option term.

Planning Note: Companies should: (1) Address option expiration issues and blackout period in the plan or award agreement. Even Code Sec. 409A allows an option period to be extended during a blackout period. (2) Clearly communicate the expiration and other terms of equity awards with terminating employees. (3) Take extra care in drafting the plan and agreement terms governing employment termination, vesting, forfeiture and expiration.

A significant number of cases have considered whether an employer has a duty to notify an optionee that his or her right to exercise vested options is about to expire. Most courts have held that the employer does *not* owe a fiduciary duty to the participant (or beneficiaries) to notify them of their right to exercise options.[11] However, in an unusual fact pattern, a Massachusetts court held that

---

[9] *Preece v. Physicians Surgical Care Inc.*, S.D. Tex., No. H-06-0715 (May 26, 2006).

[10] *In re Cendant Corp. Securities Litigation*, 37 EBC 2816 (3d Cir. 2006).

[11] *Estate of McLoone v. Intel Corp.*, 2001 U.S. App. LEXIS 578 (9th Cir. 2001) (stock option plan not an ERISA plan, hence no fiduciary duty under ERISA); *Becher v. Tyco International, Ltd.*, 2001 U.S. App. LEXIS 25194 (2d Cir. 2001) (no fiduciary relationship

an employer's failure to notify an employee of his or her termination of employment, as a result of which the employee failed to exercise his or her options within the timeframe provided in his or her option agreement, constituted a breach of his or her option agreement.[12]

> **Planning Note:** Although the vast majority of court cases have held that an employer does not have a duty to inform employees and/or former employees of the imminent expiration of their stock options, employers that wish to avoid disputes may adopt a system of notification as a form of "best practice."

In *Dinger v. Allfirst Financial*,[13] Mr. Dinger was terminated when Dauphin Deposit Corporation merged with First Maryland Bancorp (and changed its name to AllFirst Financial). All of his options became fully vested upon the merger. After the stockholders had approved the merger but before it was completed, Dinger asked Dauphin's in-house counsel how long he had to exercise his options. Counsel explained that he would have 90 days, which was true for employees that were terminated in past nonmerger situations. Dinger exercised most of his options shortly after the merger when the market price was $51.50, ostensibly in reliance on this advice. After Dinger had exercised most of his options, he learned that a vice president at First Maryland had distributed a memo to employees explaining that, based on "careful legal and accounting review," the company could offer a more "generous interpretation" of the post-termination exercise period: All stock plan participants had three years after any severance agreement period to exercise the options granted under the 1995 plan. Dinger exercised the remainder of his options a couple years later when the market price rose to over $92 per share.

Despite the absence of any obvious harm, Dinger sued the company, alleging that Dauphin, through its in-house counsel, made negligent misrepresentations and breached fiduciary duties. The plaintiff claimed that if in-house counsel had not given incorrect information on the post-termination exercise rules, he would have held the pre-1997 options longer. The court decided that in-house counsel did not act in bad faith and did not knowingly provide the executive with false information, but merely offered his interpretation of the plan language and past practices. The subsequent memo explaining the longer exercise period did not prove that in-house counsel knowingly gave a wrong interpretation.

.03 Sale of the Company or a Subsidiary

Stock incentive plans, and the agreements under them, are contracts. As with other contracts, stock incentive plans and agreements require precise drafting. Some recent cases have addressed the issue of whether the sale of a subsidiary constitutes a termination of employment, affecting a grantee's exercise

---

(Footnote Continued)

exists between company and its option holder employees); *Powers v. British Vita, PLC*, 969 F.Supp. 4 (S.D.N.Y. 1997); *McLaughlin v. Cendant Corp.*, 76 F.Supp. 2d 539, 550 (D. N.J. 1999).

[12] *Pollen v. Aware, Inc.*, 53 Mass App Ct 823, 762 N.E.2d 900 (Mass. App. Ct. 2002).

[13] *Dinger v. Allfirst Financial*, 2003 U.S. App. LEXIS 22392 (3rd Cir. 2003).

rights. For example, in *Monsanto Co. v. Boustany*,[14] the Supreme Court of Texas held that the sale of a subsidiary of Monsanto resulted in a "termination of employment" within the meaning of the Monsanto incentive plan for employees to whom Monsanto had granted nonqualified stock options, even though they continued in the employ of the subsidiary after the sale. The option agreements provided that employees who held nonqualified stock options ceased to be employees of the subsidiary when Monsanto ceased to own 50% or more of the subsidiary's stock. Therefore, the employees were subject to the exercise deadlines specified in the plan and option agreements upon termination of employment. Similarly, in *Morschbach v. Household International*,[15] an optionee was employed by a subsidiary of Beneficial, which was sold. The agreements clearly stated that once the optionee ceased to be employed by Beneficial or its subsidiaries, he lost his right to purchase any unvested options. Further, a change-in-control provision in his employment agreement, which provided for vesting of options upon the merger of Beneficial (which occurred a few months after the sale of the subsidiary by which he was employed), was unavailing because he was no longer an employee of a subsidiary of Beneficial at the time of the merger. That is, even though he worked for the same bank, it was owned by a different company.[16]

In *Moses v. Corning Inc.*,[17] the executive's stock option agreements provided that the options would terminate when he ceased working for Corning or when CPF ceased to be a Corning subsidiary. In December 1996, CPF was spun off from Corning and became Quest Diagnostics, an independent company. Shortly before the spin-off, Corning sent two letters to employees notifying them that their stock options would not terminate after the spin-off, but the options would be forfeited if their positions with Quest Diagnostics were terminated for any reason. Moses's employment with CPF/Quest Diagnostics terminated in May 1997. When Moses attempted to exercise his stock options nearly two years later, Corning denied his request, and Moses sued. The court noted that the stock option agreements unambiguously stated that the options would be terminated if CPF ceased to be a Corning subsidiary. The court noted that while Corning sent employees such as Moses a letter informing them that their options would not terminate once CPF was spun off into Quest Diagnostics, the agreements clearly provided that upon termination of employees' employment with any Corning subsidiary, the stock options would be terminated.

.04 Damages

A number of cases have considered the proper measure of damages resulting from an employer's failure to deliver stock options to an employee as

---

[14] *Monsanto Co. v. Boustany*, 73 SW 3d 225 (Tex. 2002).

[15] *Morschbach v. Household International*, 2002 U.S. Dist. LEXIS 1874 (D. Del. 2002).

[16] *Cf. Thompson v. General Electric Co.*, 2002 U.S. Dist. LEXIS 5316 (S.D. N.Y 2002) (employee required to receive a distribution from a top-hat plan upon termination of employment, after employee was

transferred to a company that acquired a subsidiary); *Cogan v. Phoenix Life Insurance Co.*, 2002 U.S. Dist. LEXIS 5846 (D. Mich. 2002) (no authority for the proposition that sale of subsidiary by an employer means as a matter of law that employment was terminated).

[17] *Moses v. Corning Inc.*, 2004 U.S. App. LEXIS 14807 (3rd Cir. 2004).

promised. At least where an option is in the money, a number of courts have measured an optionee's damages in reference to their value at the time of breach. The date of breach was the date the plaintiff attempted to exercise the options, but the company did not honor the request.[18] The proper date for the calculation of damages becomes more complex if there is an anticipatory repudiation by the employer.[19] In *Miga v. Jensen*,[20] a divided court held that the correct measure of damages is the difference between the exercise price for the stock and the fair market value of the stock. For the majority, the analysis was straightforward. A failure to deliver stock when promised is no different from a failure to deliver other marketable goods, and therefore the damages for a failure to deliver stock "are measured precisely as they were 150 years ago, the difference between the value of goods bargained for and the contract price at the time set for delivery." The dissent disagreed, arguing that the majority's approach encouraged provisions to breach stock option agreements in a rising market, and the appropriate measure of damages should more closely approximate the value of the benefit lost, *i.e.*, "the stock's highest intermediate value between the date of breach and a reasonable period in which the injured party could have entered the market and replaced the stock."[21]

A wrinkle on the basic fact pattern occurred in *Scully v. US Wats, Inc.*[22] In that case, the grantor of the option breached an agreement when it wrongfully terminated the grantee and prevented him from exercising an option. Affirming a district court decision, the Court of Appeals for the Third Circuit held that it was reasonable to determine the value of the stock options as of the date the grantee was entitled to exercise them, even though under the terms of the agreement the stock could not have been sold for one year. The court also approved of the district court's method of valuation. The defendant argued that the company should have applied a 30% marketability discount to reflect the lack of marketability. While the court acknowledged there was some validity to the argument that the hypothetical value of similarly restricted stock would have reflected a marketability discount, the approach taken by the district court in rejecting it was not unreasonable because measuring the plaintiff's loss at the date of breach did not reflect the plaintiff's economic loss. In contrast, in *Pollen v. Aware, Inc.*,[23] the court based the award of damages on the IPO price of the employer stock rather than the price on the date the company breached the option agreement, because "there was no public market for the stock on the date of the breach."

---

[18] See *Ertugrul v. Octel Communications Corp.*, 1996 U.S. Dist. LEXIS 22580 (N.D. Calif. 1996); *Hermanowski v. Acton Corp.*, 729 F2d 921 (2d Cir. 1984) (*per curiam*); *Colorado Management Corp. v. American Founders Life Ins. Co.*, 148 Colo. 519, 367 P2d 335, 337 (1961); *Finnell v. Bromberg*, 79 Nev. 211, 381 P2d 221, 227 (1963).

[19] See *Holm v. CalEnergy Co.*, 2000 U.S. App. LEXIS 17941 (9th Cir. 2000) (unpublished opinion); *Lucente v. IBM*, 146 F. Supp. 2d 298 (S.D. N.Y 2001), reversed and remanded, 310 F3d 243 (2d Cir. 2002).

[20] *Miga v. Jensen*, 96 SW3d 207 (Tex. 2002).

[21] In *Lucente v. IBM*, 310 F3d 243 (2d Cir. 2002), the Court of Appeals for the Second Circuit applying New York law held that the "highest intermediate value" is not the proper measure of damages in a breach of contract action.

[22] *Scully v. US Wats, Inc.*, 238 F3d 497 (3d Cir. 2001).

[23] *Pollen v. Aware, Inc.*, 53 Mass App Ct 823, 762 N.E. 2d 900 (Mass App Ct 2002).

In *Boyce v. Soundview Tech. Group*,[24] the U.S. Court of Appeals for the Second Circuit held that a former employee who proved that Soundview breached its agreement to allow him to exercise stock options was entitled to a new trial on the issue of damages. A jury in the Southern District of New York had awarded Mr. Boyce $400,000 in damages. However, the Second Circuit held that the trial judge mistakenly imposed a "bright line" ruling that barred evidence about events after the breach of contract occurred; such evidence might have convinced the jury that the stock options had a higher value.

.05 Procedural Issues

As with any other agreement, despite counsel's best efforts to resolve the outcome of every possible issue in the four corners of a compensation plan or agreement, some unforeseen issues arise. Well-drafted change in control agreements provide that the calculation of whether or not payments under the agreement trigger an excise tax (and, thus, either a cutback in payments or a gross up payment) will be performed by a public accounting firm (see ¶ 10,030 for a Checklist of Provisions Common in Change in Control Agreements). In *Manzon v. Stant Corp.*,[25] the executive's change in control agreement required an independent auditor to calculate the severance pay and tax counsel to examine the calculation. Despite the fact that the company had engaged Deloitte & Touche to perform the calculations, the court found that the company had failed to comply with the agreement, because it had not submitted the calculations to tax counsel for examination.

Occasionally companies depart from the formal terms of their written stock plan, producing unfortunate results, as illustrated by *Mauldin v. WorldCom, Inc.*[26] In that case, a plan contained a provision that, in the event of a change in control, an optionee who was involuntarily terminated or constructively terminated could request that the compensation committee accelerate the vesting of unvested options. Further, the plan allowed the compensation committee to delegate authority to determine whether vesting should be accelerated. The plaintiff petitioned the committee for vesting acceleration, on the grounds that the company had constructively terminated him. The Senior Vice President of Human Resources investigated the claim and denied the request. The Court of Appeals for the Tenth Circuit, reversing a lower court decision, found after examining the minutes of the compensation committee, that it had never, either implicitly or explicitly, delegated authority to the Senior Vice President, or ratified the decision previously made by an unauthorized agent, or specifically denied the request by the plaintiff.

Planning Note: Public company boards of directors have enough duties and responsibilities to worry about without administering benefit plans. However, if the board wishes to effectively delegate authority and responsi-

---

[24] *Boyce v. Soundview Tech. Group*, 2d Cir., No. 05-1685-cv (September 29, 2006).

[25] *Manzon v. Stant Corp.*, 202 F.Supp.2d 851 (S.D. Ind. 2002).

[26] *Mauldin v. WorldCom, Inc.*, 263 F3d 1205 (10th Cir. 2001).

bility (and the attendant liability) it should do so by a carefully drafted written resolution.

In *Ostler v. Codman Research Group*,[27] the court considered whether, under Delaware law, management could extend an optionee's period for exercising an option without board approval. Delaware General Corporate Law Section 157 provides that the term of options shall be determined, if not by the certificate of incorporation itself, by the board of directors. The court noted Delaware cases have read Section 157 to require board approval for fundamental actions such as the creation of options, a substantial reduction in exercise price, and swapping new options for old ones, and noted that "corporate law remains fairly fussy about the actual authority of officers when their actions affect stock options," although it also noted that courts have applied the doctrines of apparent authority and estoppel to protect those who have relied on corporate officials later found to have lacked actual authority.

¶2025 Litigation Over Employment Agreement Provisions and Other Compensation

Litigation over employment agreements is nearly as old as the Magna Carta. However, the meaning of certain terms, plan drafting and a few other issues seem to be fertile sources of litigation in any era.

.01 Contract Principles

Option plans and agreements evidencing them are contracts, and a number of cases turn upon basic contract principles. *Sugerman v. MCY Music World, Inc.*,[28] is a good illustration of such a case. Under a letter agreement in the event that a certain event occurred, "the Company would like to put you on the company stock option plan, which is in development at this point in time. As soon as the plan is properly in place, we would be happy to address the relevant documents to you immediately." The plaintiff claimed that he was entitled to stock options pursuant to this language, but the district court disagreed, finding that the language was merely precatory and reflected no actual promise or commitment. The letter agreement contained none of the basic terms of an option agreement—the number of options, the exercise price, the schedule for exercise or the expiration date—and was thus legally unenforceable.

Similarly, in *Cochran v. Quest Software*,[29] the employee challenged a unilateral reduction in the number of stock options the company had awarded him, but the court granted summary judgment for the defendant. The court acknowledged that the stock option agreement did not specifically give the employer the discretion to cancel existing option awards unilaterally. However, according to the court, the modification was effectively a mutual modification, *i.e.*, the employee's continued employment was valid consideration for the reduction in the

---

[27] *Ostler v. Codman Research Group*, 241 F3d 91 (1st Cir. 2001).

[28] *Sugerman v. MCY Music World, Inc.*, 158 F.Supp. 2d 316 (S.D. N.Y. 2001).

[29] *Cochran v. Quest Software*, 2002 U.S. Dist. LEXIS 16204 (D. Mass. 2002).

number of options. While the company did not expressly present the reduction to the employee in this matter, legally it had the right to terminate him.

Kreiss v. McCown DeLeeuwm & Co.[30] provides a further variation. In that case, partners executed a term sheet providing that a new company would grant the plaintiff a stated number of stock options. However, the option agreement executed by the parties granted fewer options than promised in the term sheet. The plaintiff alleged in the alternative that failure to award options in accordance with a term sheet constituted breach of contract, or that he was entitled to the shares on an unjust enrichment theory because he had performed his obligations under the term sheet. The district court, applying New York law, disagreed on both counts. With respect to the action on the contract, the court noted that under New York law, a subsequent contract regarding the same subject matter supersedes a prior contract. Therefore, the option agreement superseded the term sheet. Second, with respect to the action for unjust enrichment, under New York law the existence of a valid written contract precluded recovery under a *quantum meruit* or unjust enrichment theory.[31] In *Sanders v. Wang, et al.*,[32] the court held that where a stock compensation plan contains a clear, unambiguous limitation on the total number of shares authorized, the board of directors may not exceed that limit based upon a general provision that does nothing more than grant them authority to administer the plan. The plan was unusual in that it did not contain a standard anti-dilution provision, so that the plan did not permit the committee to adjust the number of shares granted to account for stock splits or any other recapitalization transaction. Even if a company grants a committee broad authority to interpret a plan, such power does not empower the committee to alter the terms of the plan.

> **Planning Note:** Employment and stock award agreements are important legal documents. Not only should employers avoid letting their accountants, consultants and other advisors draft these documents, but they should even seek expert review among the legal community.

Walden v. Affiliated Computer Services, Inc.[33] also involved the issue of valid consent. A company's board of directors amended a plan and agreement retroactively to provide for vesting upon a change of control of the company rather than one of its stockholders. The amended agreement modified the vesting schedule to allow for immediate exercise of vested options in lieu of a five-year waiting period from the date the company awarded the options. The court held that plaintiffs could not establish, as a matter of law, that the amendments were void for lack of consideration because the amended vesting schedule provided employees with some benefits by giving them an opportunity to exercise options immediately without having to wait five years.

---

[30] *Kreiss v. McCown DeLeeuwm & Co,* 37 F.Supp. 2d 294 (S.D.N.Y. 1999).

[31] *Quantum meruit* means "as much as he deserves."

[32] *Sanders v. Wang, et al.,* 1999 Del. Ch. LEXIS 203 (Del. Ch. 1999).

[33] *Walden v. Affiliated Computer Services, Inc.,* 2002 Tex. App. LEXIS 6396 (Tex. App. Ct. 2002).

In *Snyder v. Time Warner, Inc.*,[34] a federal district court held that a company's actions in allowing a former employee to exercise options to purchase shares under a stock option agreement (here, resulting from a computer error), even though the options had allegedly expired, created a mutual departure from the terms of the contract, which would have necessitated notice to return to the original contract terms.

In *Simpson v. Mead Corp.*,[35] the U.S. Court of Appeals for the Sixth Circuit held that Mead Corp. did not act arbitrarily when it denied early retirement benefits under its top-hat plan to an executive who was fired by the company at the age of 51. The company's top-hat plan allowed for early retirement benefits to commence when a plan participant reached age 55 if the company gave "written consent" to the participant's early retirement. In this case, Mead did not give "written consent" to Mr. Simpson's early retirement. Mr. Simpson had requested early retirement several times. Eventually the company terminated his employment.

.02 Fee-Shifting Provisions

An issue in some plans and agreements is: who is responsible for the cost of litigation in case of a dispute? The answer often determines whether the case goes to trial (and a reported decision for all to see) in the first place. However, at least one recent case focused on litigation over a fee-shifting provision. In *Krumme v. Westpoint Stevens, Inc.*,[36] the nonprevailing plaintiff was denied payment of his attorney's fees where a fee-shifting provision provided that the employer would pay for reasonable attorney's fees for nonfrivolous disputes regardless of the prevailing party. The court held that the fee-shifting provision had not been triggered because the dispute arose before the triggering event (a change in control).

> **Comment:** Many employment agreement cases are won or lost before the parties even start shouting. If the executive (or former executive) has the right to force the company to advance his or her legal fees without risk of repayment, the executive (and his or her counsel) has every incentive to litigate and little incentive to settle. It takes a brave company to fight even spurious claims in the face of such a fee-shifting provision.
>
> On the other hand, without some prospect that he or she may recover fees, many former executives would not have the financial wherewithal to battle a large public company and its seemingly unlimited resources. Therefore, some employment agreements will attempt to balance the parties' interests with something like the following:
>
> > All reasonable costs and expenses (including fees and disbursements of counsel) incurred by the Executive in seeking to interpret this Agreement or enforce rights pursuant to this Agreement shall be paid on behalf of or

---

[34] *Snyder v. Time Warner, Inc.*, 179 F.Supp. 2d 1374 (N.D. Ga. 2001).

[35] *Simpson v. Mead Corp.*, 6th Cir., No. 05-3707, unpublished (June 27, 2006).

[36] *Krumme v. Westpoint Stevens, Inc.*, 238 F3d 133, 139-41 (2d Cir. 2000).

reimbursed to the Executive promptly by the Company, if the Executive is successful in asserting such rights.

.03 Compensation, Retirement and Other Defined Terms

The application or interpretation of defined terms is another common source of litigation over compensation plans and agreements. A single plan or agreement likely will include dozen of defined terms. When these definitions are incorrect, ambiguous, or absent, litigation often ensues.

Such provisions are generally evaluated under federal common law.[37] Commonly litigated contract interpretation issues include the meaning of a certain term,[38] whether a provision is ambiguous,[39] and the scope of a provision.[40]

Retirement. From time to time we see companies tripped up by conflicting definitions of the term "retirement" among their qualified retirement plans, nonqualified retirement plans, stock incentive plans and other benefit plans. Stock plans often distinguish an executive's retirement from other circumstances of employment termination for purposes of whether unvested stock awards become vested and/or the period after termination within which vested options may be exercised.

The case of *Jones v. Bank of America*,[41] illustrates some of the problems that can arise in this situation. Upon termination of employment due to "retirement," the stock incentive plan at Bank of America ("BOA") gave an employee the full remaining term of the stock option (*i.e.*, until the 10-year expiration date) to exercise vested options. However, the BOA stock plan gave employees terminated for other reasons only 90 days to exercise any vested options. (Employees terminated due to death or disability were allowed 12 months to exercise.)

The BOA stock plan defined "retirement" as a termination of employment after the employee has: (i) attained at least age 50; (ii) completed a minimum of fifteen years of "vesting service"; and (iii) attained a combined age and years of "vesting service" equal to at least 75. Mr. Jones had accumulated service at a company that had a "Rule of 70" before BOA acquired it, and BOA carried that service forward to its pension plan. One year after Mr. Jones lost his job in a reduction in force, he tried to exercise options, which BOA personnel had allegedly led him to believe would be exercisable for the remainder of their term, due to his eligibility for retirement under the pension plan. However, BOA now

---

[37] *Aramony v. United Way of America*, 254 F3d 403, 411-12 (2d Cir. 2001); *Healy v. Rich Products*, 981 F2d 68, 72 (2d Cir. 1992).

[38] *Healy v. Rich Products*, 981 F2d 68, 72 (2d Cir. 1992) (determining the definition of "vested" as used in a top-hat plan); *Goldstein v. Johnson & Johnson*, 241 F3d 433 (3d Cir. 2001) (determining the meaning of "covered compensation"); *Matter of Rexene Corp.*, 154 B.R. 430, 433-34 (Bankr. D. Del. 1993) (defining the word "retirement" with reference to a separate qualified plan).

[39] *Aramony v. United Way of America*, 254 F3d 403, 411-12 (2d Cir. 2001) (finding the terms of a plan

relating to replacement of lost benefits to be unambiguous); *Matter of Rexene Corp.*, 154 B.R. 430, 433-34 (Bankr. D. Del. 1993) (determining that the plan unambiguously specified how a "period of service" was to be calculated).

[40] *In re E.L. Carlyle*, 242 B.R. 881, 891-94 (Bankr. E.D. Va. 1999) (finding that an employer was allowed to set-off against top-hat benefit payments because the anti-alienation provision did not clearly prohibit set-off).

[41] *Jones v. Bank of America*, 311 FSupp2d 828 (D.C. Ariz. 2003).

informed him that his options had expired because he had not terminated due to retirement as defined in BOA's stock plan. Thus, his termination came under "all other terminations," with the 90-day exercise-or-canceled rule.

The court took a strict interpretation of the stock plan. The stock plan's definition of "retirement" was clear. The court found that Jones's treatment as "retired" for purposes of the pension plan did not make his termination a retirement under the stock plan. Jones clearly did not meet the conditions for "retirement" under the stock plan.

In *Willis Re, Inc. v. Hearn*,[42] a chief executive officer announced his "retirement" from his long-time employer – and went to work for a competitor. The company sought repayment from the former CEO of a portion of a $1.75 million incentive awards made to him during the three years before his retirement. According to the former CEO, the governing award agreement allowed him to retain the award if he retired.

The CEO had signed a series of award agreements making "AIP Awards" to him of $1,750,000 each for 2012, 2013, and 2014, subject to:

> If your employment with Willis ends prior to December 31, [2015] [2016] [2017] for any reason other than your incapacity to work due to your permanent disability (as "disability" or a substantially similar term is defined within an applicable Willis long term disability plan/policy), death, your redundancy (as redundancy is determined by Willis in accordance with its usual human resource administration practices) or your retirement, you will be obligated to repay to Willis a pro-rata portion of the net amount . . . of the Willis Retention Award (the "Repayment Obligation").

To define "retirement" the award agreements referred to (i) "your employment agreement" or (ii) "a written retirement policy applicable to you as a Willis employee," (iii) "by reference to the ending of your employment at such mandatory age as may apply in the applicable employment jurisdiction" or (iv) "as may be determined by Willis in its absolute discretion." The pension plan provided for retirement benefits, including an "Early Retirement Benefit" for a participant who retires on his "Early Retirement Date," which the plan defined as the first day of any month following the date the participant attains age 55 and has completed at least 10 years of service.

In May 2015, when he was 59 years old and employed by the company for 21 years, the CEO announced his "decision to retire from Willis Re Inc., effective May 15, 2015 to explore other options and pursue other interests." The company agreed that the CEO was eligible for an "Early Retirement Benefit" under the pension plan, but argued that the pension plan was not a "written retirement policy" under the AIP Award letters. Instead, the company claimed that the AIP Awards allowed it to define "retirement" in its absolute discretion, and that it had determined that the CEO did not retire.

Rather than construing the ambiguous contract terms against the drafter of the agreement, as most courts would do, the court instead announced that it

---

[42] 200 F. Supp. 3d 540 (E.D. Pa. 2016).

would not assume the contract's language "was chosen carelessly" or "that the parties were ignorant of the meaning of the language employed."

> The words used in subsection (ii) are "written retirement policy," not "Pension Plan." If these sophisticated parties negotiated incentive payments for a chief executive officer intended the term "written retirement policy" to be defined as eligibility for benefits under the Pension Plan, they were free to include it. The parties could have done so in the same way the parties expressly defined "disability" in the phrase "incapacity to work due to your permanent disability" as the definition "within an applicable Willis long term disability plan/policy" and "redundancy" as "determined by Willis in accordance with its usual human resource administration practices." The parties could have referred to the Pension Plan in subsection (ii), but did not do so.

The court held that the company was entitled to define "retirement under the AIP Awards in its absolute discretion" and upheld the company's decision that the CEO did not retire. Because the CEO left to work for a competitor, it seems like the case should have been an easy one. The court observed that the CEO had acknowledged his obligation to "comply with certain terms and conditions applicable to time after his retirement from Willis, including an obligation not to compete with Willis for a period of [12] months beginning May 15, 2015." However, apparently those provisions also were not clear.

In *Healy v. MCI Worldcom Network Serv. Inc.*,[43] the language in an executive's separation agreement contradicted the terms of the stock option agreement. The separation agreement provided that the stock options vested when the executive was terminated. The stock option agreement stated that the options vested a year after the executive, who was disabled, began receiving short-term disability benefits. A federal court in California rejected the language in the option agreement and held that the executive's stock options vested when he was terminated without cause. The court awarded the executive damages and prejudgment interest dating back to the termination date.

Compensation. Several cases seem to arise each year involving a dispute over whether certain components of an executive's remuneration should be counted as "compensation" for purposes of determining benefits under a plan or agreement. Often, the stakes are high, as the remuneration at issue is a single, extraordinary or significant payment.

The recurring scenario that seems to result in a reported federal court decision at least once every few months, is a participant claiming that his/her employer's plan should have counted some extraordinary payment or remuneration in determining his/her accrued benefit amount. For example, in *Adams v. Louisiana-Pacific Corp.*,[44] the U.S. Court of Appeals for the Fourth Circuit ruled that a supplemental executive retirement plan's administrative committee did not abuse its discretion when it excluded from the calculation of a plan participant's benefits over $1 million in stock options he cashed out in prior years.

---

[43] *Healy v. MCI Worldcom Network Serv. Inc.*, E.D. Cal., No. S-02-1575 LKK/DAD (January 6, 2006).

[44] *Adams v. Louisiana-Pacific Corp.*, 37 EBC 2107 (4th Cir. 2006).

In *Scipio v. United Bankshares Inc.*,[45] the court ruled that an executive retirement plan administrator acted reasonably in not considering stock options exercised by a company's senior executive as "earnings," and thereby excluding them from the calculation of his retirement benefits. The court said the administrator's interpretation of the term "earnings" to exclude the stock option gain "was the product of a reasoned and principled decision-making process based upon adequate materials and inquiry."

In *O'Neill v. Retirement Plan for Salaried Employees of RKO General, Inc.*,[46] the Court of Appeals for the Second Circuit held that a retirement plan administrator did not act arbitrarily and capriciously in excluding payments received under a stock incentive plan from pensionable earnings under a tax-qualified plan, even though such payments would have been required to be included as compensation for certain purposes under Code Sec. 414(s). Similarly, in *Olander v. Bucyrus-Erie Co.*,[47] the court upheld a committee determination that a payment by the company to an employee to buy out stock options was not compensation for purposes of a SERP.

In *Craig v. Pillsbury Non-Qualified Pension Plan*,[48] the U.S. Court of Appeals for the Eighth Circuit ruled that the administrator of a top-hat plan sponsored by Pillsbury Co. abused its discretion when it excluded from the calculation of a plan participant's benefits two retention bonuses he received in 2001 while working for a subsidiary of Pillsbury. The court decided that the plain language of the plan, as well as the SPD, required all bonuses to be included in the calculation of final average compensation.

Undefined Terms in an Annual Incentive Bonus Plan. Companies often do not have legal counsel review their bonus plans. Sometimes the plan is one a one-page summary – or even a couple slides from a PowerPoint handout. However, many legal complications can arise from bonus plans. In *Gregg Appliances, Inc. v. Underwood*,[49] a group of the company's senior managers brought a class action after the company calculated their annual bonus payouts by excluding nearly $40 million in life insurance proceeds it received, from its 2012 earnings before interest, taxes, depreciation, and amortization (EBITDA). The trial court had granted summary judgment to the employees and the company had appealed.

The company had provided eligible employees with a document labeled Total Rewards Statement ("TRS") and a letter from the company's president and CEO, which included a table showing 2011 compensation and a table showing 2012 targets. The trial court viewed the TRS as a contract between the company and the covered employees. The court found that the TRS used the term "EBITDA," and that the meaning of EBITDA was clear. The TRS made no reference to the possibility of adjustments.

---

[45] *Scipio v. United Bankshares Inc.*, 2004 US App LEXIS 26680 (4th Cir. 2004).

[46] *O'Neill v. Retirement Plan for Salaried Employees of RKO General, Inc.*, 37 F3d 55 (2d Cir. 1994).

[47] *Olander v. Bucyrus-Erie Co.*, 187 F3d 599 (7th Cir 1999).

[48] *Craig v. Pillsbury Non-Qualified Pension Plan*, 8th Cir., No. 05-2211 (August 14, 2006).

[49] 57 NE 3d 831, Ind: Court of Appeals, 2016.

The appellate court reversed the trial count and found in favor of the company. The appellate court emphasized the need to look at not just the terms of the contract, but also the intent of the parties and all circumstances surrounding the contract. The appellate court found: "It is clear from the language in the TRS that the parties could not have intended life insurance proceeds would be included in EBITDA for purposes of determining a performance-based 'incentive' bonus." The court looked at the TRS transmittal letter, which referred to the company's growth and the importance of improving performance. The court also took into account the testimony of a company representative that the company previously had adjusted EBITDA to reflect accurately how the company was performing on a year-to-year basis, even when those adjustments resulted in higher bonuses.

The company won the case. However, it won only after discovery, depositions, a trial, and an appeal. A little better drafting could have saved the company from all of the legal costs, wasted time, and ill feelings that ensued.

.04 Release of Claims

When an executive and an employer sign a separation agreement and release of claims, it should end the relationship between the parties, resolve all issues between the parties, and eliminate the possibility of any future disputes (except for situations where one party flatly violates the agreement). However, litigation between employers and former employees arises after the execution of a separation agreement and release more often than it should.

In *Buster v. Mechanics Bank*[50], a federal district court in California ruled in favor of the former executive seeking to recover vested SERP benefits that the company claimed he had released. The release read, in relevant part, as follows:

> [T]his Agreement extends to and fully releases the Bank and any and all Releasees from all claims of every nature and kind, known or unknown, suspected or unsuspected, vested or contingent, past or present, arising from or attributable to the Bank or any Releasee including but not limited to claims arising under . . . the Employee Retirement Income Security Act . . . any other civil rights law, attorney fee law, or Executive benefits law, and any other law or tort. The only exceptions to this release are claims for workers' compensation, claims for unemployment compensation, and claims for indemnification.

The court essentially held that a company cannot trick a former employee into signing away rights to compensation and benefits to which he is indisputably entitled. However, this is a lawsuit that never should have been necessary. A release this broad should never have gotten past the executive's counsel. A release should set forth the claims and potential claims being released, but it should also list the claims not released, such as right to vested benefits. If there is any question at all as to what the vested benefits are (or other questions, such as the amount of unpaid bonus, *etc.*), the release or the separation agreement should address them unambiguously. Executive compensation counsel must concern itself with more than just the dollars involved in an agreement.

[50] (N.D. Cal., 2016).

.05 Importance of a Forum Selection Clause

Including a forum selection clause in employment and other agreements can help protect a company against aggrieved or miscreant employees. In some cases, a forum-selection clause is a matter of convenience. The company is located in a city and would prefer to arbitrate or litigate any disputes or claims in that city. In other situations, the forum-selection clause and governing law provisions can be critical to the company's ability to enforce the terms of the agreement.

A case from 2010 involving a junior sports agent working in Minneapolis for Cleveland-based IMG Worldwide illustrates this second situation. The agent, who was part of IMG's team representing several top college and professional coaches, defected to Hollywood agency CAA (allegedly taking some 7,000 confidential files), and moved to California, where he sued IMG in federal district court to void the clause in his contract barring him for two years from soliciting IMG clients he had represented. He argued that as a resident of California—with a new apartment lease to prove it—he was entitled to the state's protections against such covenants.

Although CAA was not named in the litigation, a CAA lawyer initially said that California law did not allow employers to prevent their former employees from making a living in whatever industries they choose. There might have been some truth to IMG's allegations as to theft, because before the case was litigated, CAA "cut its ties" with the agent. The parties eventually reached a settlement under which the agent agreed to abide by the terms of his contract, which prevented him from soliciting IMG clients for one year.

In *Slater v. ESG International, Inc.*,[51] the Eleventh Circuit Court of Appeals upheld the forum selection clause in an employment agreement against a former employee's attempt to sue in her state of residence. The former employee/plaintiff claimed that the company could not enforce the forum selection clause in her employment agreement because the clause:

- Was not mandatory by its terms,
- Did not apply to her claims, since they were statutory-based, and not based on the employment agreement, and/or
- Should not be enforced for public policy reasons.

Ms. Slater had signed an employment agreement with the company upon commencement of her employment, which set the terms and conditions of her employment. The agreement stated that Slater was an at-will employee and included the following forum-selection clause: *"The parties agree that all claims or causes of action relating to or arising from this Agreement shall be brought in a court in the City of Richmond, Virginia."* The agreement also included a choice of law provision designating Virginia law as controlling and stated that the agreement "constitutes the sole and entire agreement" between Slater and the company.

---

[51] No. 09-13794, March 8, 2011.

The selection of Richmond, Virginia as the forum for disputes under the agreement became an issue after the company staffed her at its facility in Crystal River, Florida. Later, the company terminated Ms. Slater's employment either (i) for performance concerns and excessive absenteeism, after her supervisor accused Slater of making an error in a physical examination of a crane operator, according to the company, or (ii) because she informed her supervisor that she was pregnant, according to Ms. Slater. The court's decision does not explore the substance or merits of the claims, because Ms. Slater sued the company in the Middle District of Florida, and the company filed a motion to dismiss for improper venue based on the forum-selection clause in the employment agreement.

The Eleventh Circuit reviewed the district court's construction of the forum selection clause *de novo*, meaning without regard to the district court's decision or the parties interpretation, rather than under the more deferential abuse of discretion standard.

Mandatory vs. Permissive: Regarding the plaintiff's claim that the contractual forum selection clause was not mandatory, the court observed that the use of the term *"shall"* is one of requirement, and held that claims within the scope of the forum-selection clause must be brought in a court in Richmond, Virginia. (The court first explained that: "If no other contract principles point to a particular meaning, the court will prefer the reasonable interpretation that operates more strongly against the party who drafted the document." – highlighting another one of our design and drafting strategies.)

Scope of the Forum-Selection Clause: Regarding the issue of whether the plaintiff's statutory-based claims fell with the scope of the forum-selection clause, the court concluded that the parties intended the contract for employment to govern the entirety of the employment relationship between them and, thus, the plaintiff's claims fell squarely within the scope of the forum-selection clause. The clause is expressly applicable to "all claims or causes of action relating to or arising from [the employment agreement]."

Public Policy: Finally, the court cited prior case law holding unambiguously that mandatory forum-selection clauses are "presumptively valid and enforceable" absent a "strong showing that enforcement would be unfair or unreasonable under the circumstances."

> "A forum-selection clause will be invalidated when: (1) its formation was induced by fraud or overreaching; (2) the plaintiff would be deprived of its day in court because of inconvenience or unfairness; (3) the chosen law would deprive the plaintiff of a remedy; or (4) enforcement of the clause would contravene public policy."

The court found nothing preventing – or having prevented – Ms. Slater from filing her lawsuit in Richmond, Virginia. (Her counsel apparently did not allege that there was fraud or overreaching in the employment agreement.)

.06 Status as ERISA Plans

A number of courts, as well as the U.S. Department of Labor (DOL), have addressed the issue of whether a stock incentive plan is an employee benefit plan within the meaning of ERISA Section 3(3). The courts and the DOL have uniformly held that stock incentive plans are not subject to ERISA.[52] Courts have also held that a phantom stock plan is not a pension plan within the meaning of ERISA.[53] If a stock incentive plan was found to be an ERISA plan, ERISA Section 514 would preempt certain state law causes of action.

Of course, even if a court held a stock incentive plan to be an ERISA pension plan, in many instances it would qualify as a top-hat plan, exempting it from various provisions of ERISA (discussed more fully in ¶ 2035). For example, in *Lucente v. International Business Machines Corporation*,[54] the court noted that even if a stock option plan were an ERISA plan, an issue that it would not address because the plaintiff did not raise it before the district court, the plaintiff's claim that ERISA's vesting provisions were violated would be unavailing because a top-hat plan is not subject to ERISA's vesting rules.

.07 Implied Covenant of Good Faith and Fair Dealing

Wilson v. Career Education Corp. (N.D. Ill 2015), considered a company's ability to terminate its annual bonus plan in a manner that would lead to lower bonuses to some employees. On remand from the Seventh Circuit, the district court found that, although the plan created an enforceable contract, the company had reserved to itself "the unambiguous right to terminate the plan and refuse to pay bonuses." However, the interesting aspect of this case is that a majority of the Seventh Circuit found a potential violation of the "implied covenant of good faith and fair dealing," in the company's decision to terminate the plan and the federal trial court only narrowly decided that the company's decision had not violated that implied covenant.

The concept of implied covenant of good faith and fair dealing seems to be coming up more often in executive compensation litigation. The *Wilson* court described it this way:

> While "the element of good faith dealing implied in a contract is not an enforceable legal duty to be nice or to behave decently in a general way. . . . [a]vowedly opportunistic conduct has been treated differently."

* * *

---

[52] *Oatway v. American International Group, Inc.*, 2002 U.S. Dist. LEXIS 1771 (D. Del. 2002); *Long v. Excel Telecommunications Corp.*, 2000 U.S. Dist. LEXIS 15479 (N.D. Tex. 2000); *Hahn v. National Westminster Bank, N.A.*, 99 F.Supp. 2d 275 (E.D. N.Y. 2000); *Goodrich v. CML Fiberoptics, Inc.*, 990 F.Supp. 48 (D. Mass. 1998); *Butzberger v. Halliburton Co.*, 2001 U.S. Dist. LEXIS 21666 (N.D. Tex. 2001); *Musachia v. Medtronics USA, Inc.*, 2001 U.S. Dist. LEXIS 15984 (ND Ill. 2001); *Raskin v. Cynet*, 131 F.Supp.2d 906 (S.D. Texas 2001);

Johnson v. TCOM Systems, Inc., 1989 U.S. Dist. LEXIS 15723 (D. D.C. 1989); *Kaelin v. Tenneco, Inc.* 28 F.Supp. 2d 478 (N.D. Ill. 1998); *Courtney v. Satellite Glass Co.*, 811 F.Supp. 1466 (D. Kan. 1992); *Estate of McLoone v. Intel Corp.*, 2001 U.S. App. LEXIS 13475 (9th Cir. 2001).

[53] *Emmenegger v. Bull Moose Tube Co.*, 197 F3d 929 (8th Cir. 1999).

[54] *Lucente v. International Business Machines Corporation*, 310 F3d 243 (2d Cir. 2002).

"Wilson alleges, CEC simply kept for itself more than $5 million it should have paid to its admissions representatives. That looks like the 'avowedly opportunistic conduct' that we recognized as actionable. (Citations omitted)

In the court's view, what won the day for the company was the fact that it had terminated the incentive bonus plan in response to Department of Education regulations prohibiting incentive compensation of the type provided under the company's bonus plan, which were proposed in June 2010, and finalized in October 2010. The final regulations were effective July 1, 2011. The company terminated the bonus plan effective February 28, 2011, and increased salaries for the affected employees effective March 1, 2011. The court allowed that the plaintiff and some other employees might have received more compensation if the company had terminated the bonus plan a few months later than it did, but found that (i) not all employees would have been better off with a later termination, (ii) the company had more than ample administrative reasons to terminate it in February, and (iii) the company certainly did not violate the implied covenant of good faith and fair dealing by the February termination.

The court's decision provides an interesting analysis of the issue and one that compensation professionals should consult in the future if similar circumstances arise.

Another federal court case alleging a breach of the implied contract between employee and employer, and breach of the implied covenant of good faith and fair dealing was *Timian v. Johnson & Johnson*.[55] In January 2006, Ms. Timian commenced employment with the company as a patent attorney, providing legal services to one of its subsidiaries, Ortho-Clinical Diagnostics, Inc. ("OCD"). The company had awarded restricted stock units to Timian under its long-term incentive plan ("LTIP") for several years. The RSUs had a vesting period of three years, which required Timian to be employed by the company on the third anniversary of the vesting date in order to receive the value of the RSUs.

In early 2013, the company began discussions to sell OCD. The patent attorneys supporting OCD, including Timian, were included as assets to the sale and were not allowed to look for work within the company or any of its other subsidiaries. The patent attorneys were forced to either leave the company's employment or become an employee of OCD after the sale. In January 2014, the company announced its formal intention to sell OCD. In February 2014, the company awarded RSUs to Timian based on her 2013 work performance. On June 29, 2014, the company's sale of OCD became final, Timian's employment with the company was terminated, and she became an employee of OCD. Upon the sale of OCD, the company terminated the RSUs granted to Timian in 2012, 2013, and 2014, on the basis that these RSUs had not vested prior to the termination of her employment. Timian lost the full value of the RSUs awarded in 2012, 2013, and 2014, and sued the company for a breach of the LTIP, breach of the implied contract between employee and employer, and breach of the implied covenant of good faith and fair dealing.

---

[55] No. 6:15-cv-06125, United States District Court, W.D. New York.

The federal court ruled against Timian on each of her claims. The claims for breach of the implied contract between employee and employer, and breach of the implied covenant of good faith and fair dealing, were based on a notion that some rules apply to the relationships among parties, even though they are not written into a contract or agreement. Courts sometimes find a breach of these implied covenants in cases of egregious conduct. However, in this case, the terms of the LTIP addressed situations like the one at issue and were clear on the outcome.

The court found that the language of the LTIP was clear. There could be no legal dispute that Timian's employment with the company had terminated, even though she continued to sit at the same desk and performed the same job functions on the day after the sale of OCD as she did on the day before the sale. The LTIP did not provide for accelerated vesting of Timian's RSUs. The provisions of the LTIP on change in control simply did not apply to the sale of a division of the company.

The court's decision in *Timian v. Johnson & Johnson* is consistent with that of nearly every other federal court that has considered a similar issue. Some companies' LTIPs would provide for accelerated vesting for an employee terminated solely because of a sale of a division of the company. However, this LTIP did not. Executive compensation professionals should take care in considering all of the terms of a stock plan or employment or other agreements, because the courts will uphold those terms for better or worse.

In *Feldman, et al v. National Westminister Bank, N.A.*,[56] which facially involved the construction of a non-ERISA phantom stock appreciation plan, the court resolved the case based on the following clause:

> Neither Bancorp, nor Affiliate, any member of the Board of Directors or the Committee . . . shall be liable for any action or determination made in good faith with respect to the Plan, any Valuation, or any Phantom Stock Award granted hereunder.

The court noted that, as a matter of common law, good faith is not a defense to a breach of contract claim. However, under Delaware law, parties are free, through the terms of the contract itself, to limit or eliminate liability for breach of the contract. While such disclaimers are strictly construed, they cannot be construed contrary to the plain and ordinary meaning of the words. Applying these principles, the court found that the above quoted language would excuse a good faith breach of the plan's terms. Although the court did not agree with the committee's interpretation of the plan, it nonetheless believed the interpretation was well within the discretion the plan afforded it, to construe the plan and make all other determinations and take all other actions deemed necessary or advisable for the proper administration of the plan.

Another stock compensation case explored the meaning of good faith, but with a different result. In *Scribner v. WorldCom*,[57] a federal appellate court held

---

[56] *Feldman v. National Westminster Bank, N.A.*, 303 A.2d 271 (2003).

[57] *Scribner v. WorldCom*, 249 F3d 902 (9th Cir. 2001).

that the company's termination of an employee to facilitate the sale of the division in which he worked, rather than for poor performance, could not be construed as a termination for cause. Even though the committee had a broad grant of discretion to interpret the plan, it nevertheless had a duty to act in good faith. However, that term had a specific meaning. It did not impose upon the plaintiff an obligation to show that the committee acted with affirmation malice towards him, or even that it knew its decisions were inappropriate when it made them. Rather, the court could find the committee to have breached the contractual duty by disregarding the optionee's justified expectation under the contract. As the court stated:

> Good faith limits the authority of a party retaining discretion to interpret contract terms; it does not provide a blank check for that party to define terms however it chooses.[58]

.08 Benefit Claims and Appeals Procedures

In *Beggins v. CBRE Capital Markets of Texas L.P.*,[59] the former executive claimed that he had been wrongfully denied nonqualified pension benefits under the company's severance pay policy when the company fired him for refusing to sign a retention agreement. The court rejected both parties' motions for summary judgment because it was unclear whether the former executive had exhausted his administrative remedies by properly submitting his claim.

A case out of the influential federal district court for the Southern District of New York suggests that companies should consider adding a benefit claims and appeals procedure to any plan that could be subject to ERISA. In *Quigley v. Citigroup Supplemental Plan*,[60] the court held that 47 former employees must exhaust their administrative remedies before they can pursue their action/litigation alleging that their employer had short-paid their benefits under a supplemental executive retirement plan.

The supplemental plan document and summary plan description ("SPD") included comprehensive administrative claim procedures requiring participants to (i) file initial claims with a plan administrative committee, (ii) appeal any adverse benefit determinations to the committee, and (iii) exhaust their administrative remedies before seeking judicial relief. There are two reasons a company should want to make plan participants go through the claim procedures before filing a lawsuit. First, claim procedures are much less expensive than litigation. Second, most courts will apply a favorable standard of review to a plan administrator's decision reached as part of the claims process. That is, the court will only overturn the plan administrator's decision if it was arbitrary and capricious. Companies should make sure that any plans they maintain that are (even arguably) subject to ERISA have claims procedures (and the so-called *Firestone* language).

---

[58] *Scribner v. WorldCom*, 249 F3d 902, 910 (9th Cir. 2001).

[59] No. H-17-1541, S.D. TX., June 26, 2018.
[60] 51 EBC 1065 (S.D.N.Y. 2011).

.09 Changes in Control

A significant amount of litigation involving terminated executives involves change in control provisions (see Chapter 2 [¶ 201 *et seq.*] for a detailed discussion of change in control agreement drafting and issues). As the prevalence and value of change in control plans and agreements increased, so did the litigation over payments required by such agreements.

A change in control of the company is a critical, and often "trigger," event in most executive compensation arrangements. Participants in a top-hat plan may receive additional or an immediate payout of benefits upon a change in control. But a change in control also can be a risk for top hat plan participants (see ¶ 1765 for a discussion of the risks and how to minimize them).

One common issue regarding change in control provisions is whether a change in control has occurred. For example, in *Bedrosian v. Tenet Healthcare Corp.*, the size of the board of directors shrank from 21 to 10 in two years.[61] The employee alleged that this was a "change in control" as defined in the plan provisions. The court held there was no change in control since the provisions did not require that a majority of directors at the beginning of a two-year period remain on the board of directors at the end.[62] Additionally, in *Threadgill v. Prudential Securities Group, Inc.*, a change in control had not occurred where a stock purchase agreement was executed, but was conditioned on the occurrence of future events.[63]

In *Fasco Industries, Inc. v. Mack*, the issue was not whether a change in control had occurred, but whether the employee was entitled to the benefits under the plan after a change in control.[64] The administrator alleged that the officers increased the benefits that they were to receive under the plan in anticipation of a change in control.[65]

In *Feinberg v. RM Acquisition LLC*,[66] the plaintiffs were participants in the Rand McNally & Company Supplemental Pension Plan (the "SERP Plan"). The SERP Plan provided benefits in the form of an annuity at the time they reached retirement age. However, once renowned Rand McNally had filed for bankruptcy protection in 2003, apparently after failing to adapt quickly enough to the changing world of GPS, MapQuest, *etc.* Often, a company's bankruptcy wipes out all promises and benefits under a nonqualified plan. But, for reasons not discussed in either of the federal court opinions, Rand McNally's obligations under the SERP Plan were not cancelled in the bankruptcy process. In December 2007, Rand McNally entered into an asset purchase agreement with RM Acquisition, LLC. The agreement included a clause stating that RM would not be obligated or responsible for certain specified pre-existing liabilities belonging to

---

[61] *Bedrosian v. Tenet Healthcare Corp.*, 2000 U.S. App. LEXIS 2840, *5-6 (9th Cir. 2000).

[62] *Bedrosian v. Tenet Healthcare Corp.*, 2000 U.S. App. LEXIS 2840, *5-6 (9th Cir. 2000).

[63] *Threadgill v. Prudential Securities Group, Inc.*, 145 F3d 286, 296 (5th Cir. 1998).

[64] *Fasco Industries, Inc. v. Mack*, 843 F.Supp. 1252, 1254 (N.D. Ill. 1994).

[65] *Fasco Industries, Inc. v. Mack*, 843 F.Supp. 1252, 1254 (N.D. Ill. 1994).

[66] 629 F. 3d 671 (7th Cir. 2011).

Rand McNally, and the SERP Plan was an excluded liability under the agreement.

When one company acquires another by purchasing all of its outstanding stock, the buyer steps into the shoes of the seller and automatically assumes all of its liabilities—including SERP and other non-qualified plan obligations. However, when a company purchases just the assets of another company, as happened in this case, the buyer assumes only those obligations and liabilities (*e.g.*, non-qualified plans) that it explicitly agreed to acquire. Since RM Acquisition purchased only Rand McNally's assets and certain specified obligations, and the purchase price paid to Rand McNally was equal to its outstanding secured debt obligations, the obligation to pay SERP benefits was left to the empty shell of the former Rand McNally. Plaintiffs were informed that and that the benefits were terminated and they sued.

Plaintiff's argued that RM Acquisition (i) remained liable under the SERP Plan as the successor of Rand McNally, and (ii) interfered with the plaintiffs' rights under ERISA Sec. 510 by attempting to evade its existing and future liability under the plan. (Plaintiffs did not pursue Rand McNally in the litigation.)

First the federal district court and then the Seventh Circuit rejected these claims. The courts held that the plaintiffs could not make a case for successor liability because RM did not:

- assume the top-hat plan's liabilities,
- "connive" with Rand McNally to deprive plan participants of their benefits, or
- appear to be a mere continuation of Rand McNally under another name.

Instead, the court held that the asset purchase agreement specifically excluded the top hat plan as one of the liabilities RM Acquisition would assume, leaving plan participants with only the empty shell corporation of Rand McNally from whom to pursue their benefits. A buyer of assets, with exceptions that were inapplicable in the case, does not have an obligation to assume a seller's liabilities.

For similar reasons, the courts also rejected the plaintiffs' ERISA Sec. 510 claim ("interference with protected rights") against RM, despite the fact that the asset sale excluded the SERP Plan liabilities and left Rand McNally with insufficient assets to pay benefits under the SERP Plan.

> RM wasn't trying to interfere with any rights that the plaintiffs may have had under the top hat plan. RM had nothing to do with the plan. Suppose you bought a $250 lawnmower from a hardware store and the owner of the store told you the store owed a contractor $100 for fixing a hole in the roof and asked would you like to assume that debt and you said no, and later the owner defaulted on his debt to the contractor. Could the contractor sue you for interfering with his right to collect the debt? That would be ridiculous. Feinberg's argument seems less ridiculous only because the defendant bought the store's entire assets. But the principle is the same, and brings us back to Feinberg's claim against RM under ERISA's section 502. A buyer of assets has,

with exceptions inapplicable to this case, no obligation to assume the seller's liabilities.

Change is not always good.

Planning Note: Like employment termination, a change in control is a highly charged transaction. Generally, the only time anyone will look at the terms of a change in control agreement is when large sums of money are on the line. Clarity is critical in these important legal documents.

¶2035 Litigation Over Top-Hat Plans

Nonqualified or "top-hat" plans have been the subject of a variety of litigation issues over the years, including the following:

1. The ERISA requirements to qualify as a top-hat plan;
2. Top-hat plans as unilateral contracts;
3. Enforceability of amendments;
4. The effect of forfeiture provisions;
5. The standard of review for plan administrator decisions;
6. Vesting;
7. Preemption of state claims;
8. Interpretation of plan provisions;
9. Fiduciary duty claims;
10. Change in control benefits;
11. Interference with an employee's right to receive plan benefits;
12. Priority of claims in bankruptcy; and
13. Tax reporting.

.01 Qualification Under ERISA as a Top-Hat Plan

Top-hat plan litigation often includes a dispute as to whether a particular plan qualifies as a top-hat plan under ERISA. In order to be an ERISA top-hat plan, the plan must be (1) unfunded and (2) for a select group of management or highly compensated employees.[67] Often, a company or an employee may argue that a plan satisfies these requirements in order to gain federal jurisdiction.[68] Alternatively, a party may argue that the plan does not satisfy these requirements in order to have a case dismissed for lack of jurisdiction.[69]

In the event that a benefits plan fails to qualify as a top-hat plan, it is either a non-ERISA plan or an ERISA plan that is subject to the vesting, funding, trusteeship, and reporting provisions. Since non-top-hat ERISA plans must in-

---

[67] 29 U.S.C. § 1051(2).

[68] In *Garratt v. Knowles*, 245 F3d 941, 943 (7th Cir. 2001) the defendant-company removed the case to federal court arguing that the relevant plan was a top-hat plan and thus governed by ERISA. The court agreed that it was a top-hat plan and thus exclusively within the federal courts' jurisdiction.

[69] In *Emmenegger v. Bull Moose Tube Co.*, 197 F3d 929, 934 (8th Cir. 1999), the company argued against federal jurisdiction in efforts to have the case dismissed. The court found that the plan at issue was not an ERISA top-hat plan and dismissed the plaintiff's ERISA claims for lack of federal jurisdiction.

clude all employees, an employer may be exposed to greater liability when a plan fails as a top-hat plan.[70] Employees or former employees often dispute that a plan satisfies the top-hat qualifications in order to receive the benefits afforded by the ERISA requirements that top-hat plans are not required to satisfy. For example, in an early case, *Carrabba v. Randalls Food Markets, Inc.*, the defendant-company argued that the plan was a top-hat plan and thus not subject to the vesting, funding, trusteeship, and reporting provisions of ERISA.[71] The court held that the plan failed as a top-hat plan because the participants were not a select group of individuals, even though the company intended it to be a top-hat plan and "operated on a good faith belief that it so qualified."[72] Likewise, in *Demery v. Extebank Deferred Compensation Plan (B)*, the employees argued that they were entitled to certain benefits under ERISA while the employer argued that the plan was a top-hat plan and thus not subject to the requirements of ERISA. The court held in favor of the employer.[73]

In *Guiragoss v. Khoury*,[74] the U.S. District Court for the Eastern District of Virginia ruled that a deferred compensation plan is not a top-hat plan exempt from the ERISA's substantive provisions because participation in the plan was offered to a nonhighly compensated employee. The court found that the employees who participated in the plan were neither management nor highly compensated employees. The court said that a participant who was a sales clerk was "the type of employee that ERISA's substantive provisions are intended to protect." Thus, the court found the plan was not a top-hat plan exempt from ERISA's fiduciary, funding, vesting, and participation requirements.

Another case in which aggrieved participants claimed that the plan failed to satisfy the top-hat plan exemption from ERISA and, thus, all of ERISA's requirements should apply, was *Accardi v. IT Corp.*[75] In *Accardi*, the Third Circuit rejected the employees' contention that certain features of the plan obligated the employer to fund a trust—outside the reach of creditors—and thus the plan was a funded plan subject to ERISA's substantive provisions and protections. Because IT Corp. had filed for Chapter 11 bankruptcy protection, a ruling the other way might have allowed employee/participants to avoid waiting in line for recovery of their deferred compensation plan benefits along with IT's other general creditors.

Alternatively, employees argue for top-hat plan qualification in order to benefit from certain ERISA provisions that apply to top-hat plans but not to non-

---

[70] *Three Cases Explore Boundaries of the ERISA Exception for Top Hat Plans*, 9 ERISA LITIG. REP. No.2, 9 (2001); *Carrabba v. Randalls Food Market, Inc.*, 145 F.Supp.2d 763, 772 (N.D. Tex. 2000).

[71] *Carrabba v. Randalls Food Markets, Inc.*, 38 F.Supp.2d 468, 470 (N.D. Tex. 1999), *aff'd*, 252 F3d 721 (5th Cir. 2001).

[72] *Carrabba v. Randalls Food Markets, Inc.*, 38 F.Supp.2d 468, 470 (N.D. Tex. 1999), *aff'd*, 252 F3d 721 (5th Cir. 2001).

[73] *Demery v. Extebank Deferred Compensation Plan (B)*, 216 F3d 283, 285 (2d Cir. 2000). *See also Gallione*

v. Flaherty, 70 F3d 724 (2d Cir. 1995); *Virta v. DeSantis Enterprises, Inc.*, 1996 U.S. Dist. LEXIS 17110 (N.D.N.Y. 1996); *Hollingshead v. Burford Equip. Co.*, 747 F.Supp. 1421 (M.D. Ala. 1990); *Starr v. JCI Data Processing, Inc.*, 757 F.Supp. 390, 393-94 (D.N.J. 1991), *vacated in part*, 767 F.Supp. 633 (D.N.J. 1991); *Duggan v. Hobbs*, 99 F3d 307, 309-10 (9th Cir. 1996); *Leonard v. Sunnyglen Corp. (In re Battram)*, 214 B.R. 621, 624-26 (C.D. Cal. 1997).

[74] E.D. Va., No. 1:06cv187 (August 10, 2006).

[75] In re IT Group Inc., (3d Cir., No. 05-2191, May 25, 2006.

ERISA plans. For example, in *Long v. Excel Telecommunications Corp.*, a discharged employee sued his employer under ERISA Sec. 510, which prohibits interfering with the attainment of benefits to which an employee is entitled.[76] The employee argued that ERISA Sec. 510 applied because the plan was a top-hat plan. The court held that the plan was not an ERISA plan, and thus not subject to the requirements of Sec. 510.[77]

Many incentive or bonus plans make payments or deliver stock within $2\frac{1}{2}$ months after the end of the year the participant became vested, in order comply with the short-term deferral exception of Code Sec. 409A. However, some incentive plans provide for accumulations, multi-year periods, and mandatory deferrals. These plans may unwittingly become subject to ERISA's requirements and/or fail to qualify for the top hat plan exemption. In *Miller v. Olsen*, 62 EBC 1845 (D. Or. 2016), the company had established an incentive plan known as the Equity Growth Plan ("EGP"). Under the EGP, future payouts were not based on the value of the company's stock, but on the appreciation in the value of a single property owned and managed by the company. The former employee alleged that he believed that the EGP was a retirement plan, based on statements allegedly made to him by the company's owner. The court found that, despite not being a true stock incentive plan, the EGP did not rise to the level of an ERISA pension plan because (1) its primary purpose was not to provide deferred compensation, (2) its express terms did not contemplate an ongoing administrative scheme, and (3) its express terms did not contemplate a method of funding. Therefore, the court did not need to consider ERISA's exemption for bonus plans. Many other companies have not been so lucky.

Federal court decisions have produced different results based on the facts of the particular case. The case of *Tolbert v. RBC Capital Markets Corporation* has gone up and down between the federal district courts and the Fifth Circuit since 2013, and was only partially decided in 2016. In *Tolbert*, the company maintained a form of plan common among certain financial institutions seeking to retain employees. Under the company's Wealth Accumulation Plan ("WAP"), participants were required to defer a portion of their compensation and the company made matching contributions to the WAP. Participants' accounts were to be distributed when the participant became vested, but participants had the option to defer distribution until a later in-service distribution date or termination of employment. Three plaintiffs who forfeited their WAP benefits upon termination of employment sued to recover those benefits by claiming that the WAP was a pension plan subject to ERISA's vesting requirements.

The company argued that the plan was not subject to ERISA because it was not a pension benefit plan. The Fifth Circuit disagreed, because the WAP permitted participants to defer distributions to termination of employment or beyond, and remanded the case back to the district court to determine if the WAP qualified for the "top hat" plan or another exception from ERISA. In 2016, the

---

[76] *Long v. Excel Telecommunications Corp.*, 2000 U.S. Dist. LEXIS 15479 (N.D. Tex. 2000).

[77] *Long v. Excel Telecommunications Corp.*, 2000 U.S. Dist. LEXIS 15479 (N.D. Tex. 2000).

district court issued a decision denying summary judgment in favor of either party, possibly sending the case to trial.

In *Bingham v. FIML Natural Resources LLC*[78], a federal district court found that if even a portion of the total benefits payable under a "bonus" plan is "systematically deferred" until termination of covered employment, the entire previous plan could be governed by ERISA. Under the incentive compensation plan offered in Bingham, participants were awarded points representing ownership interests in two separate pools of assets. Critically for the outcome of the case, payments for certain award points were withheld until the participant separated from the company (except in the event of a change in control). Because of this, the court found the deferrals met the threshold for being systematic, deeming the plan subject to all of the provisions of ERISA.

In a 2016 unpublished opinion, *Bond v. Marriott International, Inc.*, the Fourth Circuit Court of Appeals dismissed as untimely, plaintiffs' lawsuit alleging that they should have been vested in certain accrued benefits under Marriott's deferred compensation plan. That alone is not big news. Nonetheless, this decision is newsworthy because of what *the court did not do.*

Plaintiffs had filed this lawsuit alleging that the company's deferred stock incentive plan violated the vesting requirements of ERISA. The key issue was whether the deferred plan qualified as a top hat plan exempt from ERISA's requirements. Plaintiffs argued that the plan was not a top hat plan, because it covered too many employees and, thus, failed the requirement that a top hat plan be maintained, "primarily for the purpose of providing deferred compensation for a select group of management or highly compensated employees." If the plan was not a top hat plan, plaintiffs' argued, then it would be subject to ERISA's vesting requirements, and many of the former employees would be entitled to some benefit.

We watched this case closely for two reasons. First, the plaintiffs' lawyers had attempted to qualify the suit as a class action, brought on behalf of all plan participants - ever. Class actions are more difficult and costly to defend. In 2015, the federal district court had refused to grant class action status due to participants' diverse claims. The case then became more prominent because the U.S. Department of Labor ("DOL") filed a lengthy and strident amicus brief with the Fourth Circuit in support of plaintiffs, arguing among other things, that to qualify for the top hat exemption, the plan must be maintained "exclusively" for the purpose of providing deferred compensation for a group of management or highly compensated employees. According to the DOL, participation in the plan by just one individual who was neither management nor highly compensated, would cause the plan to fail to qualify as a top hat plan.

The DOL argued that, in providing relief for "top hat" plans from the broad remedial provisions of ERISA, Congress recognized that certain individuals, by virtue of their position or compensation level, have the ability to affect or substantially influence, through negotiation or otherwise, the design and opera-

---

[78] 56 EBC 2232 (D. Colo. June 18, 2013).

tion of their deferred compensation plan, taking into consideration any risks attendant thereto, and, therefore, would not need the substantive rights and protections of Title I. The DOL made the following arguments as to the language of the ERISA regulations, "primarily for the purpose of providing deferred compensation for a select group of management or highly compensated employees:"

- This language "does not mean that the 'select group' may be primarily composed of management or highly compensated individuals."

- This language does not mean that "a top hat plan can have a secondary purpose that is inconsistent with the primary purpose, such as a secondary purpose of covering individuals who are outside the 'select group' set by statute."

- The language means that the plan must be maintained "only" for a select group of management or highly compensated employees.

Technically, the Fourth Circuit did not reject the DOL position; it just decided the case on other grounds. However, the fact that the court could have accepted the DOL's interpretation and chose not to do so should be encouraging to employers and executive compensation professionals.

Sikora v. UPMC[79], reflects the understanding of most compensation professionals and contains one of the most thorough discussions of the definition of top-hat plan and the law in every federal circuit. Those seeking to be familiar with the regulatory and case law that has grown up around this issue should consider reading the *Sikora* case.

In *Sikora*, the court declared that it must consider both quantitative and qualitative factors to determine whether the deferred compensation plan is primarily maintained for the purpose of providing deferred compensation for a select group of management or highly compensated employees. The Third Circuit has boiled this down into a pretty simple formula: "the plan must cover relatively few employees . . . [and] the plan must cover only high level employees." The court rejected the plaintiff's attempt to argue that "bargaining power," an element once referenced in a DOL Opinion Letter in 1990, was a critical element of employees considered part of a top hat group. The court found that the Opinion Letter was "not entitled to deference." Finally, the court found that the requirement that a plan be maintained "primarily for the purpose of providing deferred compensation for a select group of management or highly compensated employees" is disjunctive, that is, high level employees can be either management or highly compensated employees. In the end, the court concluded that "The infinitesimally small number of participants in this Plan means, by any measure (UPMC's or Sikora's), it was primarily maintained for a 'select group.'"

When a plan fails to qualify as a top-hat plan, as in *Carrabba*, the damages awarded may be significant since all participants in the plan, not just those that

---

[79] 876 F.3d 110 (3d Cir. 2017).

would not qualify if it had been a top-hat plan, are entitled to damages. Second, the employees may be treated as 100% vested upon termination of the plan even though not required by ERISA. Third, a trend has developed in awarding prejudgment interest and attorney's fees to employees, which can be significant.

.02 Top-Hat Plans as Unilateral Contracts

Recently, courts have begun to apply unilateral contracts principles to top-hat plans to determine whether an employee is entitled to plan benefits and whether certain amendments are effective.[80] Under such principles, a top-hat plan is a "unilateral contract which creates a vested right in those employees who accept the offer it contains by continuing in the employment for the requisite number of years."[81] For example, in *Kemmerer v. ICI Americas Inc.*, the court held, based on unilateral contract principles, that the employer could not amend the payout scheme because the participants had accepted the contract through performance.[82] Thus, whether the employee has "accepted" under unilateral contract principles often determines whether subsequent amendments are valid or whether the employee's rights have vested.

.03 Amendments to Top-Hat Plans

Litigation involving top-hat plans often includes issues regarding the effectiveness of amendments to the plan. Employees frequently dispute the effectiveness of amendments that alter the benefits the employee will receive under a plan.[83] If the amendment is made after the employee's benefits have vested under unilateral contract principles, a court may find the amendment to be invalid.[84]

In *Hoffman v. Textron*,[85] the company had amended its deferred compensation plan to provide that, in the event of a participant's death, benefits would be paid in a lump sum. The former executive had elected to have any death benefits paid in annual installments and, despite no obvious damage to him, he sued, alleging that his family had relied upon the installment plan in their retirement and tax planning, and there could be "significant tax consequences associated with the lump-sum option, because most of it would presumably be taxed at the highest marginal income-tax rate." The federal court refused to dismiss the lawsuit's claim that the company was equitably estopped from making this amendment, even though the triggering event of the executive's death had not yet occurred.

Alternatively, an employee may argue that an amendment or modification was made to a plan in order to receive benefits.[86] For example, in *Moore v. Acme*

---

[80] *In Re New Valley Corp.*, 89 F3d 143, 150 (3d Cir. 1996); *Moore v. Acme Corrugated Box Co.*, 1998 U.S. Dist. LEXIS 9897, *39 (E.D. Penn. 1998).

[81] *Kemmerer v. ICI Americas Inc.*,70 F3d 281, 287 (3d Cir. 1995).

[82] *Kemmerer v. ICI Americas Inc.*, 70 F3d 281, 287 (3d Cir. 1995).

[83] For example, in *Garratt v. Knowles*, 245 F3d 941, 944 (7th Cir. 2001) an employee brought a cause of action because the employer amended the benefits

plan to expressly exclude success bonuses from the benefits calculation reducing the employee's benefits from $3,200,000 to $1,349,000.

[84] *Kemmerer v. ICI Americas Inc.*, 70 F3d 281, 287 (3d Cir. 1995); *Koenig v. Waste Management, Inc.*, 76 F.Supp.2d 908, 914 (N.D. Ill. 1999).

[85] Civil Action No. 17-11849-FDS, (D. Mass. July 9, 2018).

[86] *See Moore v. Acme Corrugated Box Co.*, 1998 U.S. Dist. LEXIS 9897, *40 (E.D. Penn. 1998); *Bedrosian v.*

Corrugated Box Co., the employee argued that the plan had been modified when the employer orally agreed to amend the plan "to provide for the full retirement benefit regardless of the employee's retirement date."[87] Whether such an amendment is valid will generally depend on the plan provisions, which the court will interpret in accordance with general contract principles.[88]

In *Paneccasio v. Unisource Worldwide Inc.*,[89] a federal district court held that IKON Office Solutions Inc. did not act arbitrarily when it terminated a top-hat plan because of unfavorable interest rates. Importantly, Mr. Paneccasio did not lose any cash. He was paid a lump-sum benefit of $75,419 as a result of the plan termination, instead of the $15,000 per year for 10 years that he would have started receiving once he reached age 65. Nonetheless, he sued. The deciding factor for the court, seemed to be that the plan gave IKON's board of directors the discretion to terminate the plan whenever "proposed or pending tax law changes or other events cause, or are likely in the future to cause, the Plan to have an adverse financial impact."

Similarly, in *Starr v. MGM Mirage*,[90] the U.S. District Court for the District of Nevada held that a participant in a terminated top-hat plan that was sponsored by Mandalay Resort Group cannot pursue a state law fiduciary breach claim against Mandalay and its associated companies alleging they breached their duties by paying him a lump-sum distribution instead of an annuity payment. Mr. Starr did not lose any money. While the plan was in effect, Mr. Starr elected to receive his benefits in the form of an annuity in the amount of $181,560 per year for the sooner of 20 years or his lifetime, which would be paid upon his retirement after the age of 55. When the plan was terminated, Mandalay tendered Starr a check for $1.47 million, allegedly representing the full payment of benefits owed to Starr. The court also rejected the plaintiff's contention that because ERISA exempts fiduciary responsibility from its requirements for top-hat plan administrators, he was entitled to bring a state law cause of action for breach of fiduciary duty.

However, in another case apparently involving the same plan termination, *Parlanti v. MGM Mirage*,[91] a Nevada federal court allowed a former casino worker to continue with his claim that a company that purchased his employer violated ERISA when it terminated its SERP and distributed his benefits in a lump sum. This court found, among other things, that there was insufficient evidence to establish whether the SERP was a top-hat plan that would be exempt from ERISA's fiduciary duty standards. The court thus said it would allow the worker

---

(Footnote Continued)

Tenet Healthcare Corp., 2000 U.S. App. LEXIS 2840, *5 (9th Cir. 2000); *Pereira v. Cogan*, 200 F.Supp.2d 367, 372 (S.D.N.Y. 2002).

[87] *Moore v. Acme Corrugated Box Co.*, 1998 U.S. Dist. LEXIS 9897, *40 (E.D. Penn. 1998).

[88] *Moore v. Acme Corrugated Box Co.*, 1998 U.S. Dist. LEXIS 9897, *40 (E.D. Penn. 1998); *Pereira v. Cogan*, 200 F.Supp.2d 367, 377 (S.D.N.Y. 2002);

Krumme v. Westpoint Stevens, Inc., 238 F3d 133, 138 (2d Cir. 2000).

[89] D. Conn., No. 3:01 CV 2065 (CFD) July 26, 2006.

[90] D. Nev., No. 2:06-cv-00616-RLH-RJJ (November 7, 2006).

[91] D. Nev., No. 2:05-CV-01259-ECR (RJJ), March 20, 2007.

to continue with his claim that MGM Mirage breached its ERISA fiduciary duties by terminating the SERP.

In *Wegmann v. Young Adult Inst., Inc.*, the federal district court for the Southern District of New York rejected a former employee's claim that her employer had amended its deferred compensation plan to make women ineligible. When the plaintiff began her employment with the non-for-profit YAI in 1986, the entity had in place a "Supplemental Pension Plan for Certain Management Employees," which provided deferred compensation benefits to employees who satisfied the plan's eligibility requirements, specifically, "Each Management Employee who shall complete 15 years of service" at YAI. However, in 2008, YAI amended the eligibility requirements of the plan such that only five senior employees — all of whom were male — were expressly deemed the sole participants in the plan. When plaintiff resigned from YAI and was denied benefits under the plan, she sued alleging that this amendment had the dual effect of (i) excluding all females from participation, and (ii) divesting her of benefits to which she was entitled.

The court dismissed plaintiff's ERISA claim because she had failed to allege that she was in fact a management employee eligible under the plan. Regarding the plan amendment, the court observed that ERISA Sec. 510 was designed to protect the employment relationship that gives rise to an individual's pension or benefit rights. This means that a fundamental prerequisite to an ERISA Sec. 510 action is an allegation that the employer-employee relationship, and not merely the pension plan, was changed in some discriminatory or wrongful way. "Plaintiff's allegation that the Plan was amended to deny her benefits on the basis of her sex does not set forth the sort of interference with an employment relationship typically required for claims under § 510."

In *Hoak v. Ledford*,[92] the federal district court held that the termination of a nonqualified plan, revocation of the rabbi trust, and a lump sum payout was flawed because it eliminated the third-party claims administrator, thus impermissibly reducing the rights of participants.

In *Moore v. Raytheon Corp.*, a federal court held that Raytheon did not violate ERISA when its merger of a qualified and a nonqualified pension plan resulted in Mr. Moore owing his ex-wife additional plan benefits under a qualified domestic relations order ("QDRO").[93] Mr. Moore participated in two qualified retirement plans and two nonqualified plans. After Raytheon acquired his employer, it combined the two nonqualified plans into the two qualified plans, a process sometimes referred to as a SERP Shift or SERP Swap. However, Mr. Moore was subject to a QDRO, which assigned his ex-wife a significant fractional interest in one of the qualified plans, but not any interest in the nonqualified plans. Thus, the plan combinations had two adverse effects on Mr. Moore. First, his ex-wife would arguably become entitled to monies derived from the nonqualified plan. Second, the qualified plans would pay out a smaller amount of benefits over a

---

[92] 1:15-cv-03983 (N.D. Ga.9/27/16). [93] 314 F. Supp. 2d 658 (N.D. Texas, 2004).

longer period of time. The court dismissed all of Mr. Moore's claims on summary judgment.

.04 Forfeiture Provisions

Another area of frequent litigation regarding top-hat plans involves the interpretation and effect of provisions that require employees to forfeit their benefits if they engage in a competitive business activity or other specified behavior.[94] Top-hat plans are excluded from the nonforfeitability requirement that applies to other ERISA plans, and thus forfeiture provisions are generally valid.[95] In addition, forfeiture provisions are more likely to be enforced because they do not prevent an employee from working in a particular field, unlike covenants not to compete.[96] However, an employee may argue that his/her behavior is not within the scope of the forfeiture provision in order to avoid its application. For example, in *Aramony v. United Way Replacement Benefit Plan*, the employee, who had been convicted of fraud, was entitled to his benefits since the plan did not clearly contain a felony forfeiture provision.[97]

Similarly, in *Berg v. BCS Financial Corporation*,[98] the court allowed a company to forfeit an executive's benefits under a supplemental retirement plan where the executive had falsified the minutes of a board meeting company to increase the benefits that would be payable to him. In *Miniace v. Pacific Maritime Association*,[99] the court allowed a company to forfeit an executive's right to severance benefits where the executive had caused an amendment of his executive compensation package without the approval of the company's board.

In *Foley v. American Electric Power*,[100] the court held that a former energy trader forfeited a $2 million accrued benefit under the company's nonqualified pension plan when he was fired for falsely reporting energy transactions. What made this case highly unusual is that the nonqualified plan did not even contain an explicit forfeiture provision. The court held that, because the plan was exempt from ERISA, ordinary contract principles applied. Because the contract did not contain a provision prohibiting set-off against the participant's benefits, the company was entitled to set-off against his benefit the amount of losses it incurred in connection with the employee's misconduct.

.05 Standard of Review for Plan Administrator's Decisions

According to the Supreme Court, the proper standard of review for administrator decisions made with regard to ERISA plans is *de novo*, unless the plan gives discretion to the administrator, in which case the standard is abuse of discretion.[101] Most courts have applied this standard to administrator decisions made

---

[94] *Bigda v. Fischbach Corp.*, 898 F.Supp. 1004, 1016 (S.D.N.Y. 1995); *Spitz v. Berlin Industries, Inc.*, 1994 U.S. Dist. LEXIS 6277, *6 (N.D. Ill. 1994).

[95] *Bigda v. Fischbach Corp.*, 898 F.Supp. 1004, 1016 (S.D.N.Y. 1995); *Bryan v. The Pep Boys*, 2001 U.S. Dist. LEXIS 9090, *12 (E.D. Penn. 2001).

[96] *Spitz v. Berlin Industries, Inc.*, 1994 U.S. Dist. LEXIS 6277, *7-8 (N.D. Ill. 1994).

[97] *Aramony v. United Way Replacement Benefits*, 191 F3d 140, 149-50 (2d Cir. 1999).

[98] *Berg v. BCS Financial Corporation*, N.D. Ill. 2006.

[99] *Miniace v. Pacific Maritime Association*, N.D. Cal. 2006.

[100] *Foley v. American Electric Power*, (S.D. Ohio 2006).

[101] *Firestone Tire & Rubber Co. v. Bruch*, 489 US 101, 115 (1989).

with regard to top-hat plans.[102] However, other courts have strayed from the standard set forth in *Firestone Tire*. For example, in *Goldstein v. Johnson & Johnson*, the court viewed top-hat plans differently than other ERISA plans and applied a stricter standard stating that "neither party's interpretation is entitled to any more 'deference' than the other party's."[103] However, the court agreed that an administrator's decision may still receive deference depending on the language in the contract, and subject to the implied duty of good faith and fair dealing.[104] Additionally, in *Emmenegger v. Bull Moose Tube Co.*, the district court, before being overturned on jurisdictional grounds, applied a less deferential standard due to a conflict of interests and procedural irregularity on the part of the administrator.[105] Thus, although the Supreme Court has set a clear standard of review for ERISA plans generally, the proper standard for top-hat plans remains somewhat unclear. The Third and Eighth circuits found that top-hat plans are unilateral contracts that should be interpreted according to ordinary contract principles and without any deference to the plan administrator that denied benefits.[106]

By contrast, the Seventh and Ninth circuits have afforded judicial deference to decisions made by top-hat plan administrators (see, *Comrie v. IPSCO, Inc.*,[107] *Olander v. Bucyrus-Erie Co.*,[108] and *Sznewajs v. U.S. Bancorp Amended & Restated Supp. Benefits Plan*[109]). In *Niebauer v. Crane & Co.*,[110] the U.S. Court of Appeals for the First Circuit approved a company's decision to deny severance benefits to its former chief technology officer, and clarified the standard of review applicable to "top-hat" plans that provide benefits for highly paid executives. The First Circuit declined to take a clear position on this split, instead reasoning that "it is a distinction without a difference where, as here, the plan grants the administrator discretion to interpret the plan." Because the plan in question—sponsored by paper manufacturer Crane & Co. Inc.—gave the plan administrator discretion to review benefit claims, the First Circuit found that the administrator's decision was entitled to judicial deference under either competing standard.

.06 Vesting in Top-Hat Plans

Top-hat plans are generally exempt from the vesting requirements of ERISA.[111] However, a top-hat plan may have its own vesting provision or courts may find that benefits have vested upon the occurrence of certain events, such as retirement, under unilateral contract principles.[112] Thus, when litigation involves vesting under a top-hat plan, it is generally resolved with reference to federal

---

[102] *Spitz v. Berlin Industries, Inc.*, 1994 U.S. Dist. LEXIS 6277, *12-13 (N.D. Ill. 1994); *Threadgill v. Prudential Securities Group, Inc.*, 145 F3d 286, 292 (5th Cir. 1998); *Olander v. Bucyrus-Erie Co.*, 187 F3d 599, 606 (7th Cir. 1999); *Schikore v. Bankamerica Supp. Ret. Plan*, 1999 U.S. Dist. LEXIS 14578, *11 (N.D. Cal 1999).

[103] *Goldstein v. Johnson & Johnson*, 251 F3d 433, 436 (3d Cir. 2001).

[104] *Goldstein v. Johnson & Johnson*, 251 F3d 433, 436 (3d Cir. 2001).

[105] *Emmenegger v. Bull Moose Tube Co.*, 13 F.Supp.2d 980, 996-97 (E.D. Mo. 1998).

[106] *Goldstein v. Johnson & Johnson*; *Craig v. Pillsbury Non-Qualified Pension Plan*, 458 F.3d 748, 38 EBC 1974 (8th Cir. 2006).

[107] 636 F.3d 839, 50 EBC 2473 (7th Cir. 2011).

[108] 187 F.3d 599, 23 EBC 1369 (7th Cir. 1999).

[109] 572 F.3d 727, 733 (9th Cir. 2009).

[110] 783 F. 3d 914 (1st Cir. 2015).

[111] 29 U.S.C. § 1051.

[112] *Healy v. Rich Prods. Corp.*, 981 F2d 68, 71 (2d Cir. 1992); *Carr v. 1st Nationwide Bank*, 816 F.Supp. 1476, 1488-91 (N.D. Cal. 1993).

common law regarding contract interpretation.[113] Once the employee's benefits have vested, the employer may not be able to amend or terminate the plan.[114] Finally, an employer's failure to meet the disclosure requirements of ERISA will not cause an employee to be automatically vested.[115]

.07 Preemption Issues

A highly litigated area of the law is whether state claims, such as contract claims or fraud claims, are preempted by ERISA. ERISA supersedes a state claim "if (1) the state law claim addresses an area of exclusive federal concern, such as the right to receive benefits under the terms of an ERISA plan; and (2) the claim directly affects the relationship between the traditional ERISA entities—the employer, the plan, and its fiduciaries, and the participants and beneficiaries."[116] Courts frequently find that state claims related to top-hat plans are preempted by ERISA, even though top-hat plans are not subject to all of the substantive provisions of ERISA.[117] For example, in *Reliable Home Health Care*, the employer sued a company that had created its top-hat plan for breaching fiduciary duties and fraud. The court held that the fraud claims were preempted by ERISA since the claim involved the funding and implementation of the plan.[118]

.08 Breach of Fiduciary Duty

Although top-hat plans are not subject to the fiduciary requirements under ERISA,[119] employees often bring complaints alleging that the employer or plan administrator breached a fiduciary duty. Since top-hot plans are explicitly exempt from such requirements, the employer usually defeats these claims.[120] For example, in *Campbell v. Computer Task Group, Inc.*, the employer, plan, and plan administrators were not liable for denying benefits to an employee who transferred to another company since the plan was a top-hat plan and not subject to ERISA fiduciary requirements.[121] Moreover, the court held that there were no ERISA common law fiduciary requirements.[122] Thus, fiduciary duty claims that relate to top-hat plans often fail.

---

[113] *Healy v. Rich Prods. Corp.*, 1994 U.S. Dist. LEXIS 6306, *3-4 (W.D.N.Y. 1994); *Carr v. 1st Nationwide Bank*, 816 F.Supp. 1476, 1493 (N.D. Cal. 1993).

[114] *Kemmerer v. ICI Americas, Inc.*, 70 F3d 281, 287 (3d Cir. 1995); *Black v. Bresee's Oneonta Dept. Store, Inc. Security Plan*, 919 F.Supp. 597, 602-03 (N.D.N.Y. 1996); *compare Gallione v. Flaherty*, 70 F3d 724, 729 (2d Cir. 1995) (top-hat plan could be eliminated prior to employee's retirement).

[115] *Hein v. TechAmerica Group, Inc.*, 17 F3d 1278, 1280 (10th Cir. 1994).

[116] *Reliable Home Health Care, Inc. v. Union Central Ins. Co.*, 295 F3d 505 (5th Cir. 2002).

[117] *Reliable Home Health Care, Inc. v. Union Central Ins. Co.*, 295 F3d 505 (5th Cir. 2002); *see also Hampers v. W.R. Grace & Co., Inc.*, 202 F3d 44, 49-54 (1st Cir. 2000); *Cogan v. Phoenix Life Ins. Co.*, 2002 U.S. Dist.

LEXIS 5846, *4-5 (D. Maine 2002); *Bigda v. Fischbach Corp.*, 898 F.Supp. 1004, 1014-16 (S.D.N.Y. 1995).

[118] *Reliable Home Health Care, Inc. v. Union Central Ins. Co.*, 295 F3d 505 (5th Cir. 2002).

[119] 29 U.S.C. § 1101(a)(1).

[120] *Garratt v. Knowles*, 245 F3d 941, 949 (7th Cir. 2001); *In re E.L. Carlyle*, 242 B.R. 881, 889-90 (Bankr. E.D. Va. 1999); *Duggan v. Hobbs*, 99 F3d 307, 313 (9th Cir. 1996); *Reliable Home Health Care, Inc. v. Union Central Ins. Co.*, 295 F3d 505 (5th Cir. 2002); *Moore v. Acme Corrugated Box Co.*, 1998 U.S. Dist. LEXIS 9897 (E.D. Penn. 1998).

[121] *Campbell v. Computer Task Group, Inc.*, 2001 U.S. Dist. LEXIS 9960, *8-14 (S.D.N.Y. 2001).

[122] *Campbell v. Computer Task Group, Inc.*, 2001 U.S. Dist. LEXIS 9960, *8-14 (S.D.N.Y. 2001).

.09 Interference with an Employee's Right to Receive Plan Benefits

Sec. 510 of ERISA provides that an employer may not discharge an employee "for the purpose of interfering with the attainment of any right to which such participant may become entitled under the plan."[123] Employers frequently are sued for dismissing employees allegedly in order to avoid paying top-hat benefits in violation of ERISA Sec. 510.[124] However, the employer must interfere with rights that exist under the current plan rather than possible future rights. For example, in *Moore v. Acme Corrugated Box Co.*, an employee sued his employer for terminating him prior to increasing employees' benefits rights under the plan.[125] The court held this was not in violation of ERISA Sec. 510 since it did not interfere with the employee's current rights under the plan.[126]

.10 Priority in Bankruptcy

In times of economic downturn, litigation tends to increase regarding what level of priority top-hat claims are afforded in the bankruptcy process. For example, in *Kucin v. Devan*, employees argued for administrative expense priority for benefits that had vested before bankruptcy. The court held that they were pre-petition claims and thus received general unsecured priority.[127]

In *Bolton v. Actuant Corporation & Wachovia Bank, N.A.*,[128] the court held that plaintiffs cannot bring a declaratory judgment action against a former corporate owner that may be liable to fund a deferred compensation plan because the current corporate owner, while experiencing financial difficulties, is not yet insolvent and, thus, there is no controversy yet.

In *Sposato v. First Mariner Bank*,[129] a federal district court allowed the creditor (First Mariner Bank) of a former executive (Mr. Sposato) to garnish the non-qualified retirement (top-hat) plan (the Cecil Bank Supplemental Executive Retirement Plan) benefits of the former executive even though the company (Cecil Bank) was not in bankruptcy. The court based its decision on two key findings: (i) ERISA's anti-alienation provisions did not apply to non-qualified plans such as the Cecil Bank SERP, and (ii) ERISA does not preempt Maryland garnishment law. There is conflicting authority as to whether a non-qualified plan participant's interest in the plan is subject to claims of the participant's creditors or constitutes a portion of the participant's bankruptcy estate. Contrary to the *Sposato* case, some courts have found that ERISA's anti-alienation provisions apply to qualified and non-qualified plans alike or that the unfunded promise to pay benefits in the future in insufficiently certain to allow for garnishment. Of course, once distributions or payments from a non-qualified plan have begun, they become just like any other asset of the recipient/participant.

---

[123] 29 U.S.C. § 1140.

[124] *Emmenegger v. Bull Moose Tube Co.*, 13 F.Supp.2d 980, 999-1001 (E.D. Mo. 1998); *Long v. Excel Telecomms. Corp.*, 2000 U.S. Dist. LEXIS 15479, *13-15 (N.D. Tex. 2000).

[125] *Moore v. Acme Corrugated Box Co.*, 1998 U.S. Dist. LEXIS 9897, *36-39 (E.D. Penn. 1998).

[126] *Moore v. Acme Corrugated Box Co.*, 1998 U.S. Dist. LEXIS 9897, *36-39 (E.D. Penn. 1998).

[127] *Kucin v. Devan*, 251 B.R. 269, 272 (D. Md. 2000); see also *Resolution Trust v. MacKenzie*, 60 F3d 972, 977 (2d Cir. 1995).

[128] *Bolton v. Actuant Corporation & Wachovia Bank, N.A.*, 2004 US Dist. LEXIS 15192 (C.D. Cal. 2004).

[129] 2013 WL 1308582 (D. Md. March 29, 2013).

One strategy that could have helped prevented Mr. Sposato from losing his non-qualified benefits in this manner was to fund the non-qualified plan with a rabbi trust. The assets of a well-drafted rabbi trust would be accessible only to pay benefits to the participant or to the company's general creditors, in the event of the company's insolvency. Another strategy that could have helped prevent Mr. Sposato from losing his benefits would have been to ensure that the company's qualified plan was absolutely maxed out in terms of the benefits that it could legally provide to Mr. Sposato. Qualified plans are always better than non-qualified plans, including in terms of protection against creditors.

.11 Tax Withholding and Reporting

Contributions (employer and employee) to, and benefits accrued under, a non-qualified plan are subject to Federal Insurance Contributions Act ("FICA") taxes (both capped Social Security taxes and uncapped Medicare taxes) when vested (the "special timing rule"). The employer and the employee each pay a portion of the FICA taxes due. As a practical matter, this rule benefits employees, as all non-qualified (or "top-hat") plan participants earn in excess of the FICA wage base ($128,400 in 2018) and, thus, technically pay no Social Security taxes on non-qualified plan benefits or contributions. If FICA tax is withheld when non-qualified plan benefits or contributions become vested, then no FICA tax is due when the benefits are eventually paid (the "non-duplication rule").

In *Davidson v. Henkel Corporation*, a former employee who was receiving distributions from the company's non-qualified deferred compensation plan sued the company (and the plan) when the company began withholding required FICA tax payments from his distributions - including for payments it had failed to previously withhold. The plaintiff alleged that because the company failed to properly withhold taxes when he retired pursuant to the Code's special timing rule, he lost the benefit of the Code's non-duplication rule and, thus, had a greater tax burden. In denying the company's motion to dismiss the lawsuit for the failure to state a claim, the court stated:

> Plaintiff has alleged that the Plan Administrator discussed and provided Plaintiff with calculations of his benefits and tax liabilities at the time he was deciding whether to retire . . . . He further alleges that Defendants were aware or should have been aware of the devastating tax consequences if Plaintiff's FICA taxes were not withheld pursuant to the special timing rule and that Plaintiff relied to his detriment upon Defendants' erroneous representations. Lastly, Plaintiff has alleged special circumstances warranting the application of estoppel by setting forth facts detailing Defendants grossly negligent management of the Plan, negotiated resolution with the IRS without prior notice to Plaintiff and subsequent reduction to Plaintiff's benefits. Accordingly, the Court concludes that Plaintiff has stated claims in Count I and III of his Complaint and these claims are not subject to dismissal.

The court found that Henkel violated no law or regulation by waiting until distribution to withhold FICA taxes. FICA tax regulations provide the special timing rule and the non-duplication rule, but do not require that employers use them, which the court acknowledged. What lost the case for Henkel was the following language in the plan:

Taxes. For each Plan Year in which a Deferral is being withheld or a Match is credited to a Participant's Account, the company shall ratably withhold from that portion of the Participant's compensation that is not being deferred the Participant's share of all applicable Federal, state or local taxes. If necessary, the Committee may reduce a Participant's Deferral in order to comply with this Section.

The court concluded that the plan required the employer to withholding FICA tax at the time an employee deferral contribution was withheld or an employer matching was credited to an employee's account. If Henkel had done so, following the special timing rule, no FICA taxes would have been due on payments from the plan because of the non-duplication rule and employee/participants would have enjoyed more favorable tax consequences. The court granted summary judgment to plaintiffs on their claim that the employer "committed a FICA error in violation of the Plan."

Future plaintiffs could argue that *Henkel* creates an obligation on employers to cause the best possible tax consequences to plan participants and, thus, could be a template for future lawsuits against employers by executives hit with Code Sec. 409A penalties. However, most non-qualified plans and other compensation agreements do not include the language that doomed Henkel and its plan. The lessons for employers from *Henkel* are (1) to have plans and agreements drafted by experts and (2) follow best practices in plan administration (*e.g.*, advantageous withholding).

Ultimately, a federal judge approved a $3.3 million settlement, which included attorneys' fees and expenses, between Henkel and a class of its retirees. A very sweet deal indeed. Always a good idea to verify that you are correctly reporting FICA and others taxes on non-qualified plan deferrals and accruals.

¶2045 Litigation Over Employment Termination

Most executive compensation litigation does not occur absent an employment termination. However, many cases focus on issues that are unique to the termination.

.01 Voluntary Resignation, Involuntary Resignation, and Good Reason

Most employment, severance, and change in control agreements provide for severance benefits if the company terminates the executive without cause or the executive terminates his or her employment for good reason. Some stock award agreements provide for accelerated vesting in this circumstance. As a result of Code Sec. 409A, the definition of good reason has become relatively standardized. Importantly, "good reason" describes circumstances that are much different from a "constructive termination." In general, a constructive termination only occurs when an employer makes an employee's working conditions so intolerable, a reasonable person would feel compelled to resign.[130]

---

[130] *Simpson v. Borg-Warner Automotive, Inc.,* 196 F3d 873, 877 (7th Cir. 1999); *Rabinovitz v. Pena,* 89 F3d 482, 489 (7th Cir. 1996).

In *Zaharko v. San Juan Regional Medical Center Executive 457(f) Retirement Plan*,[131] The employer argued that two executives were not entitled to retirement benefits because they had effectively quit, rather than involuntarily terminated, by refusing to agree to a new compensation plan that would reduce their severance pay and make them at-will employees. The court held that the executives may proceed with their claim (this was not a final decision), because the retirement plan administrator appeared to have a conflict of interest, it had not considered all of the facts and circumstances before making its denial decision, and there may have been other senior management employees—that were either fired or quit—who were automatically given retirement benefits.

Many cases in this area involve a former employee's claim for severance benefits despite his or her apparent voluntary termination of employment. While the analysis is based on the facts of each case, companies have prevailed in most of these cases. as courts have looked to extrinsic evidence to determine the parties' intent in forming the severance or change in control agreement. Whether a constructive discharge has occurred generally requires an objective rather than a subjective inquiry.[132]

An optionee grantee or other executive relying on a constructive discharge provision must establish working conditions that are "even more egregious than the high standard for hostile work environment because, in the ordinary case, an employee is expected to remain employed while seeking redress."[133] Applying these standards, in *Stensrud v. Metlife Investors Insurance Co.*,[134] a federal district court found for the defendant. The plaintiff was unable to establish that he was "relegated to performing insignificant tasks unrelated to his experience and abilities." Rather, the plaintiff retained his same salary and title, and continued to perform some but not all of his duties. In addition, the court found that the plaintiff made no effort to endure the change in responsibilities. He began a job search before the individuals who were to share some of his former duties were even hired, and tendered his resignation approximately five weeks after meeting with these individuals, without knowing what his future with the company would be.

However, while the plaintiff's burden may be substantial, unless a plan expressly so provides—and this is not the customary case—there is no requirement that the plaintiff also establish a nexus between these events that were the predicate for a constructive discharge and the employee's decision to sever the employment relationship. Thus, in *Kerkhof v. MCI WorldCom, Inc.*,[135] the court

---

[131] No. 1:17-cv-00489-WJ-JHR, (D. NM, June 29, 2018).

[132] *EEOC v. Massey Yardley Chrysler Plymouth, Inc.*, 117 F3d 1244, 1250-51 (11th Cir. 1997) (noting that a showing of employer willfulness is not required to establish a constructive discharge); *Pittman v. Hatiesburg Mun. Separate Sch. District*, 644 F2d 1071, 1077 (5th Cir. 1981) (stating that to establish a constructive discharge, an employee does not need to prove that the employer subjectively intended to force the employee to resign); *Borgue v. Powell Electric Mfg.*

Co., 617 F2d 61, 65 (5th Cir. 1980) (holding that the conditions endured, rather than the employer's state of mind, are relevant to the constructive discharge inquiry).

[133] *Tutman v. WBBM-TV, Inc.*, 209 F3d 1044, 1050 (7th Cir. 2000); *Drake v. Minnesota Mining & Mfg. Co.*, 134 F3d 878, 886 (7th Cir. 1998).

[134] *Stensrud v. Metlife Investors Insurance Co.*, 2002 U.S. Dist. LEXIS 13238 (N.D. Ill. 2002).

[135] *Kerkhof v. MCI WorldCom, Inc.*, 282 F3d 44 (1st Cir. 2002).

held that an optionee, to obtain the benefit of a constructive discharge, needed only to establish that the company materially reduced her compensation or responsibilities. She was also not required to establish that her termination was subjectively motivated. The defendant wanted to establish that the grantee would have terminated employment in any event; its position was that she had been talking about moving to Maine and therefore would have terminated employment with the defendant in any event.

In *Collins v. Ralston Purina Co.*,[136] a former employee claimed that the company effectively terminated his employment (1) upon sale of company; (2) when his job responsibilities were reduced; or (3) upon the acquirer's attempt to transfer him to another region. The court found the language of Mr. Collins' retention agreement to be ambiguous as to whether compensation and benefits were payable upon the sale of the company, or only upon the actual termination of employment. Upon an examination of extrinsic evidence, however, the court concluded that neither the company nor Collins intended that the mere sale of the company would trigger a payout. The court further held that, although Collins anticipated his reassignment to a less attractive position in another region, he voluntarily left employment with the company before the time the acquirer actually made the reassignment, and thus, he was not entitled to payments under the agreement.

In *Epps v. NCNB Texas National Bank*,[137] the agreement provided for payment if the employee "should cease to be employed by the bank for any reason other than termination for cause or voluntary termination." Mr. Epps claimed that he was effectively terminated from his job because the duties that he was initially hired to perform were no longer needed. The court found that nothing in the agreement provided for payment upon a change in the employee's job duties. Therefore, when the employee left the bank to accept another job, he voluntarily terminated his employment. The court also rejected the employee's argument that the change in job responsibilities constituted a constructive discharge, finding that the employee had not met Texas' strict, objective standard of constructive discharge in this case. Under Texas law, a constructive discharge only occurs when an employer makes conditions so intolerable that an employee reasonably feels compelled to resign.

In *Grun v. Pneumo Abex Corp.*,[138] the agreement stated that benefits would be payable if, following a change in control, the company relocated its principal

---

[136] *Collins v. Ralston Purina Co.*, 147 F3d 592 (7th Cir. 1998). Similarly, in *Televantos v. Lyondell Chemical Company*, 2002 U.S. App. LEXIS 3700 (3d Cir. 2002) (unpublished), the company apparently offered the employee employment in the same position in another location to which the company was moving, and advised him that he would be entitled to change in control severance if he declined the offer. The court held the employee was not entitled to payment where he resigned and took another job before the date of the relocation. *See also, Shipner v. Eastern Air Lines, Inc.*, 868 F2d 401 (11th Cir. 1989),

where the former employee claimed that the termination of his status as an officer of the company following a takeover constituted "termination following change in control." The court agreed with the company that the phrase "termination of your employment" was clear and unambiguous and meant a complete termination of the employment relationship with company.

[137] *Epps v. NCNB Texas National Bank*, 838 F.Supp. 296 (N.D. Tex. 1993).

[138] *Grun v. Pneumo Abex Corp.*, 808 F.Supp. 632 (N.D. Ill. 1992).

executive offices or the employee's place of employment. Mr. Grun claimed although his work location was unaffected, the agreement required payments to him because the company moved its principal executive office after the change in control. Again, despite the language of the agreement, the court found that, because the intended purpose of the agreement was to induce Grun to remain employed by the company following a change in control, and the relocation "had minimal, if any, effect on Grun's work-related activities," a payment of benefits upon relocation of the company's principal office only would not achieve the purpose of the agreement.

In *Godfrey v. Eastman Kodak Co.*,[139] the relevant provision of the agreement stated that one "good reason" for resignation was "a significant diminution of . . . your status, duties or responsibilities in effect on the date of this Agreement." Mr. Godfrey claimed that the company had reduced or altered his business responsibilities, constituting "good reason" for resignation under his golden parachute agreement. However, he admitted that the company had not reduced his duties from those he enjoyed on the date of agreement, but as he rose to a higher level in the company, the company had diminished his duties. The court found that the language of the agreement was unambiguous. The court held that Mr. Godfrey was not entitled to terminate employment for "good reason" because the reduction in responsibilities occurred at a higher level than the one at which the employee worked on the date of the agreement, and he did not terminate employment for "good reason" in accordance with the agreement.

Finally, in *Barnes v. Bradley County Memorial Hospital*,[140] the U.S. Court of Appeals for the Sixth Circuit held that an executive's resignation immediately before being fired is still a voluntary resignation, which does not require severance payments under his employment agreement.

.02 Wrongful Termination

Authority is split on the permissibility of discharging an employee specifically to prevent him from exercising stock options. In *Fleming v. Parametic Technology Corp.*,[141] the Court of Appeals for the Ninth Circuit found in favor of a grantee who alleged that his employer fired him to prevent him from exercising stock options. The court concluded that "where an employee has earned a right to a benefit, which is contingent upon his being employed at some later date, the employer cannot terminate him for the very purpose of depriving him of that benefit." In *Greene v. Safeway Stores, Inc.*,[142] the Court of Appeals for the Tenth Circuit awarded a division manager in excess of four million dollars in a stock option suit brought under the Age Discrimination in Employment Act ("ADEA"). The court concluded that the difference between the value of his stock options at the time he was forced to exercise them because of his discharge and at the time he would otherwise have exercised them was contingent compensation that he would have received had the company not wrongfully terminated him.

---

[139] *Godfrey v. Eastman Kodak Co.*, 1991 U.S. Dist. LEXIS 4803 (S.D. N.Y. 1991).

[140] *Barnes v. Bradley County Memorial Hospital*, 2006 WL 20551 (6th Cir. unpub. 2006).

[141] *Fleming v. Parametic Technology Corp.*, 1999 U.S. App. LEXIS 14864 (9th Cir 1999).

[142] *Greene v. Safeway Stores, Inc.*, 210 F3d 1237 (10th Cir. 2000).

However, in *Benard v. Netegrity, Inc.*,[143] a district court in New York dismissed an action by an employee who claimed that he was fired to prevent his vesting under two stock option agreements, holding that New York law does not recognize a cause of action for wrongful termination or bad faith discharge by an at-will employee.

.03 Termination for Cause

Most compensation plans and agreements provide for a forfeitures or clawback if the executive is terminated for "cause." The courts will carefully review the definition of "cause" in the plan or agreement and the facts and circumstances of the executive's termination.

In *Peck v. Selex Systems Integration, Inc.*,[144] the company argued that a former executive was not entitled to deferred compensation benefits because, by declining a transfer to a different position in the company he had effectively refused to perform the "material duties and obligations" of his position, which constituted "cause" under the deferred compensation plan. The court rejected this argument, finding that the executive's refusal to transfer to a different position in the company could not reasonably be considered cause for termination.

Some cases have considered the meaning of termination for cause under state law. For example, in *Hammond v. T.J. Litle & Company*,[145] the Court of Appeals for the First Circuit held that an employee who was terminated because of "relationship issues" with management over the terms of the employer's stock compensation plan and not for reasons relating to his job performance was not required to sell his shares back to the employer under a provision that took effect only if the employee was terminated for cause. Applying Massachusetts law, the court held that an employee may be terminated without cause, but when other rights and duties depend upon whether the employee is terminated for cause, the employer's stated reason for the termination is determinative. Similarly, in *Scribner v. WorldCom*,[146] applying Washington law, the Court of Appeals for the Ninth Circuit held that termination of an employee to facilitate the sale of the division in which he worked, rather than for poor performance, could not be construed as a termination for cause.

In *Anderson v. U.S. Bancorp*,[147] the U.S. Court of Appeals for the Eighth Circuit held that an employer's severance plan committee did not abuse its discretion when it determined that a former employee was ineligible for benefits because he was fired for "cause" after an investigation discovered he had accessed his supervisor's unrestricted files on a shared computer drive. The severance plan provided that employees terminated for "cause" would not receive severance pay under the Plan. "Cause" was defined in relevant part as follows:

---

[143] *Benard v. Netegrity, Inc.*, 2000 U.S. Dist. LEXIS 17299 (S.D. N.Y. 2000).

[144] No. 17-7138 (D.C. Cir. July 17, 2018).

[145] *Hammond v. T.J. Litle & Company*, 82 F3d 1166 (1st Cir. 1996).

[146] *Scribner v. WorldCom*, 249 F3d 902 (9th Cir. 2001).

[147] *Anderson v. U.S. Bancorp*, 8th Cir., No. 06-3216 (April 24, 2007).

[G]ross and willful misconduct during the course of employment ... including, but not limited to, theft, assault, battery, malicious destruction of property, arson, sabotage, embezzlement, harassment, acts or omissions which violate the Employer's rules or policies (such as breaches of confidentiality), or other conduct which demonstrates a willful or reckless disregard of the interests of the Employer or its Affiliates ... Circumstances constituting Cause shall be determined in the sole discretion of [U.S. Bancorp].

Employees who were terminated without cause within twenty-four months of the merger were eligible for severance payments of up to the equivalent of 104 weeks of salary.

The court decided that it was reasonable for the company to determine that Mr. Anderson had violated the company's code of conduct when he accessed his supervisor's computer files without a legitimate business purpose, even though the files were not restricted.

In *Leedy v. Vis.align LLC*,[148] the Superior Court of Pennsylvania held that an executive's employment contract allowing him to be discharged "for cause" as determined "in the judgment of" officials of Vis.align LLC gave a state court jury no "legally sufficient basis" for finding that the executive was fired without cause. The opinion noted that Mr. Leedy's employment agreement allowed Vis.align the "contractual right to assess and pass judgment on" Leedy's actions and performance, leaving the employee with "a contract that cannot be construed in his favor."

In *Wal-Mart Stores Inc. v. Coughlin*,[149] the Arkansas Supreme Court held that Wal-Mart can pursue state law claims that a former company executive wrongfully hid his misconduct from the company and fraudulently obtained millions of dollars in retirement benefits from the company. The court found that Wal-Mart sufficiently pleaded that former Executive Vice President and Chairman Thomas M. Coughlin had a fiduciary duty to disclose material facts to the company and raised genuine issues of fact precluding dismissal of the company's claim that Coughlin fraudulently obtained retirement benefits by concealing his misconduct.

The definition of "cause" is a critical fact because many instances of employee misconduct are not discovered until after the employee has voluntarily resigned from the company, *e.g.*, when another employee starts reviewing the books. In *Marsh Supermarkets, Inc. v. Marsh*,[150] the company terminated the employment of its CEO, Mr. Marsh, and begun making severance and retirement plan payments to him under the terms of his employment agreement. However, the company stopped payments and benefits to Mr. Marsh when it discovered a pattern of highly irregular expense reimbursements to him (according to an earlier jury verdict in favor of the company on this point). Thus, the company argued that Mr. Marsh had: "snookered [it] into terminating [his] employment without cause and then paying him over $2 million in Salary Continuation

---

[148] *Leedy v. Vis.align LLC*, Pa. Super. Ct., No. 1805 EDA 2005 (September 12, 2006).

[149] *Wal-Mart Stores Inc. v. Coughlin*, Ark., No. 06-315 (April 12, 2007).

[150] 56 EBC 2965 (SD IN 2013).

Benefits when, by any reasonable analysis of facts now proven, Mr. Marsh should have been terminated for cause and would have been but for his fraud."

In turn, Mr. Marsh countersued the company for $2,171,261.48 as equitable relief under ERISA Sec. 502(a)(3) and other breach of contract claims. Both parties asked the court for an award of attorneys' fees and costs under ERISA Sec. 502(g)(1).

The company terminated Mr. Marsh "without cause," and then sought to recharacterize the termination as "for cause" after discovering the fraud. Despite the jury verdict in favor the company on the question of fraud by Mr. Marsh, the court found in favor of Mr. Marsh on the ERISA and contract claims. The court based its decision on the unambiguous wording of the employment agreement, which provided for payments and benefits to Mr. Marsh if the company terminated his employment "without cause," which it inarguably did. The employment agreement included no clawback provisions, no exception for "fraud," and no provision for after-discovered cause.

The parties had previously agreed that part of Mr. Marsh's employment agreement was subject to ERISA, presumably as an ERISA severance benefit plan. This appears to have been a major mistake by the company for several reasons. First, the court found that the provisions of the employment agreement that were subject to ERISA were segregable from the others. Second, with respect to the provisions subject to ERISA, the court found that ERISA compelled it to confine its inquiry to "the face of written plan documents." The court observed that the written plan documents (the employment agreement) provided: "Each and every payment made hereunder by the Company shall be final, and the Company shall not seek to recover all or any part of such payment from [Mr. Marsh] or from whosoever may be entitled thereto, for any reasons whatsoever."

Finally, the company's agreement that part of the employment was subject to ERISA opened the door for the court to order the reimbursement of the legal fees of the prevailing party – Mr. Marsh - as ERISA permits.

The bottom line for the company was that, despite a jury verdict finding that Mr. Marsh had breached his employment agreement and committed fraud against the company, the court ordered the company to pay $2,171,261.48 to Mr. Marsh and held that Mr. Marsh was entitled to recover attorneys' fees and costs as incurred in litigating the ERISA claims.

> **Planning Note:** Companies should consider adding language to covers the situation of an "after-discovered" case, such as the following: "In addition, a Participant's Service shall be deemed to have terminated for Cause if, after the Participant's Service has terminated, facts and circumstances are discovered that would have justified a termination for Cause."

¶2055 Litigation Over Promises and Miscommunications

As in all areas of the law, there has been significant litigation involving executive compensation and (allegedly) broken promises and miscommunications.

.01 Miscommunications as to the Company

In *Bors v. Duberstein*,[151] the controlling stockholders and the CEO convinced an executive to exchange her shares of phantom stock, for which she then was entitled to a cash payment, for shares of restricted stock. The restricted stock became worthless when the company filed for bankruptcy. The executive sued, arguing that by failing to disclose to her important facts about the poor financial prospects of the company, various stockholders and officers committed "fraud by omission." The court dismissed the executive's complaint because it concluded that the stockholders and officers owed the executive no duty to speak under Illinois law. The court's holding was primarily based on two findings. First, the defendants' statements referred to future events, and statements that relate to contingent events, expectations or probabilities, rather than to present facts, will not support a claim of fraud under Illinois law.

Second, the court found that the stockholders and officers had no duty to speak because the executive's restricted stock agreement specifically disclaimed any such duty, providing that neither the company nor its directors and officers had "any duty or obligation to disclose to [the executive] any material information regarding the business of [the company] or affecting the value of the stock." Thus, the court found, the executive was not justified in relying on oral statements made prior to her signing the restricted stock agreement.

In contrast, in *Byczek v. Boelter Companies, Inc.*,[152] a 2003 decision from the same court, the plaintiff was able to bring a cognizable fraud claim by alleging a scheme to fraudulently misstate and conceal the net worth of his company. The court found this was a cognizable claim because it involved misrepresentations and omissions of current financial conditions, not predictions of future performance.

In *Houston v. Aramark Corp.*,[153] the executive had alleged the plan's administrator breached its fiduciary duty under ERISA and common law by not telling him the company was going public, thus doubling its stock price, when he decided to sell his shares upon his retirement. The court held that the stock option plan was not governed by ERISA. The court also affirmed the district court's dismissal of Houston's common law breach of fiduciary duty claims. Houston waived away Aramark's duty to disclose future events that would impact the value of Houston's shares by signing a stockholder's agreement that said Aramark was not obligated to inform him of such events, the court said.

In *Syverson v. FirePond Inc.*,[154] the court found that two option holders who could not sell or exercise their options while they watched the company's stock price rise from $3 to $100 a share, only to fall to less than $1 a share, have no fraud claim against the company for convincing them to sign a lock-up agreement in anticipation of the company's public offering.

---

[151] *Bors v. Duberstein*, 2004 U.S. Dist. LEXIS 1358 (N.D. Ill. 2004).

[152] *Byczek v. Boelter Companies, Inc.*, 264 FSupp2d 720 (N.D. Ill. 2003).

[153] *Houston v. Aramark Corp.*, 2004 U.S. App. LEXIS 20642 (3rd Cir. 2004).

[154] *Syverson v. FirePond Inc.*, 2004 U.S. App. LEXIS 22035 (8th Cir. 2004).

The option holders sued FirePond Inc., Robertson Stephens, and others alleging federal securities fraud, and claims under state law for negligent misrepresentation, breach of fiduciary duty, and breach of contract. The option holders claimed that they were told the IPO would not go forward without lock-ups from all share and option holders, although this was not true and some investors were allowed to sell early when the price was high.

The court rejected the option holders' arguments that the company coerced them into signing the lock-up agreements by allegedly misrepresenting that a lucrative initial public offering would not go forward unless all stock and option holders signed. "The facts as alleged reflect a business decision [of the option holders], which hindsight shows imprudent, that was entered into after normal bargaining."

The court affirmed the dismissal of the state-law fraud and negligent misrepresentation claims, finding that the option holders could not have reasonably relied on any of the alleged misrepresentations because they were contradicted by the express terms of the lock-up agreement. The option holders also alleged that both FirePond and Robertson Stephens owed them a duty to inform them that not all stockholders and options holders were required to sign lock-ups. However, the court said the option holders each signed the standard lock-up agreement, which contained an express provision that allowed the underwriter to waive "any provision . . . without notice to any third party."

.02 Inconsistencies Between Stock Award Communications and Award Agreements

In *Vespremi v. Tesla Motors, Inc.*, a California Court of Appeals allowed a lawsuit by a former employee over allegedly vested stock options to continue. The former employee, who had been terminated *after only 7 months of employment*, sued the company alleging that it had denied him his contractual right to exercise vested portion of his stock options. The company claimed that none of his stock options had yet vested.

The source of confusion was some loose language in the employment agreement with the company, which promised to grant him an option to purchase 10,000 shares of stock that vested over 48 months "commencing with his first day of employment." The award agreement made clear that one quarter of the option shares would vest on the first anniversary of the award date (not immediately upon the award date). However, the court refused to grant the company's motion for summary judgment because of that pesky language in the employment agreement, which, "when viewed in the light most favorable to the plaintiff," offered some support for his claim.

Many similar cases have held that the offer letter failed to create a binding contract because the terms were not complete and "lacks essential terms, such as exercise price, term of the option and the post-termination exercise period, rendering it judicially unenforceable." And, in any event, the ambiguous contractual promise was displaced by the unambiguous written plan document and award agreement. Unfortunately for the company, it failed to raise these arguments in its summary judgment motion.

Importantly, this decision only allowed the case to continue - it was not a decision on the merits. Most executive compensation professionals in the country would agree that the plaintiff should not have been allowed to exercise a portion of the options, and that is probably how the case ultimately will be decided. However, the case has already been through a trial court and an appellate court and discovery and depositions have been undertaken, which means the company has incurred significant legal costs. And all because of a few loose words (and an error by its lawyers).

In *McElrath v. Uber Technologies Inc.*, a federal district court ruled that an employee will not be compelled to arbitrate his claim that the company promised him incentive stock options, but actually granted him non-qualified stock options. According to the court's opinion, the plaintiff was being recruited by Uber and another technology company, but accepted the offer from Uber, "Relying primarily on Uber's offer to provide Plaintiff with 20,000 Incentive Stock Options ('ISO')".

> Plaintiff subsequently entered into an Employment Agreement with Uber. Among other things, the Agreement promised Plaintiff 20,000 ISOs "to the maximum extent allowed by the tax code" and that an ISO-qualifying exercise schedule would apply, specifically: "[t]he Option shall vest and become exercisable at the rate of 25% of the total number of option shares after the first 12 months of continuous service and the remaining option shares shall become vested and exercisable in equal monthly installments over the next three years of continuous service."

However, when the plaintiff (and others) received a Notice of Stock Option Grant labeled "Incentive Stock Option," approximately two months later, the Notice contained a different and accelerated exercisability schedule, "allowing the grantee to exercise all the options after six months, regardless of the vesting schedule." From the court's opinion, one could not discern whether this provision was intended to allow the employee to exercise the options early and receive the stock, which would still be subject to the vesting schedule, which would not be uncommon for technology companies (so-called West Coast Options).

Further, when the company adopted an online stock administration system one year later, the plaintiff (and others) was informed that most of his options were being treated as non-qualified stock options, not ISOs (of the 20,000 options, the company treated 14,000 as NSOs and only 6,000 as ISOs). When the plaintiff attempted to exercise the options, he was informed he must immediately pay taxes on the transaction, as is typical of NSOs.

.03 Inconsistency Between Plan Drafting and Operation

In *Fox v. CDx Holdings*, a group of employees holding stock options sued the company following a merger-spinoff transaction in which their options were cancelled without payment. The Delaware Chancery Court held that the company had violated the terms of its stock incentive plan by determining the options to be valueless. The court awarded the class members damages in excess of $16 million.

The optionees held approximately 2.9% of the company's fully diluted equity. The terms of the stock plan were exactly as one would expect, providing that each holder was entitled to receive for each share covered by an option the amount by which the fair market value of the share exceeded the exercise price. The plan defined fair market value as an amount determined by the company's board of directors. Under the terms of the stock plan, "[a]ll decisions made by the Administrator pursuant to the provisions of the Plan shall be final and binding on the Company and the Participants, unless such decisions are determined to be arbitrary and capricious."

The optionees alleged, and the court agreed, that (i) the company breached the plan because members of management, rather than the board, determined how much the option holders would receive, and (ii) regardless of who made the determination, the per share value attributed to the company was not a good faith determination and resulted from an arbitrary and capricious process.

The evidence at trial established that the board did not make the determinations it was supposed to make. The company's CFO made the determinations, then received perfunctory signoff from the principal stockholder. The evidence at trial further established that the number the CFO picked for the company was not a good faith determination of fair market value. It was the figure generated by an accounting firm serving as the company's tax advisor, using an intercompany tax transfer analysis that was designed to ensure that the merger-spinoff would result in zero corporate-level tax. The CFO told the accounting firm where to come out, and he supplied it with reduced projections to support the valuation he wanted. The accounting firm's conclusion that the company had a value of $65 million conflicted with the CFO's subjective belief from earlier in the year that one part of the company alone was worth between $150 and $300 million. Additionally, the value set by the CFO and his tax advisor was lower than the values that a different accounting firm had generated for the same businesses in a series of valuation reports prepared during 2011.

The acquirer insisted on a second opinion from the accounting firm that had performed the previous valuations. The CFO met with the firm serving as the company's tax advisor and the firm that had performed the previous valuations before the latter firm started work. The firm that had performed the previous valuations "then proceeded to prepare a valuation that largely—and admittedly!—copied" the analysis of the firm serving as the company's tax advisor. Not surprisingly, the second valuation came in just below the first. The court found that the valuation was not determined in good faith, and the process was arbitrary and capricious.

Some lessons from *Fox v. CDx Holdings*, are as follows: The company should have either designed and drafted the plan and award agreement to be more flexible as to valuation or followed the valuation process set forth in the plan. Plan provisions stating that the decisions of the board, company, or administrator "shall be final and binding" do not protect decisions that are arbitrary and capricious.

.04 Other (Allegedly) Broken Promises

In *Cochran v. Quest Software, Inc.*,[155] the court held that a company can rescind unvested options without initially terminating a poor performer. Brian Cochran was offered 60,000 options at hire by Quest Software. Although the options became very valuable, Cochran apparently did not live up to the company's expectations. According to the court, Cochran's supervisor expressed disappointment in his performance and told him that the company might recall some of his stock options. Shortly thereafter, before any of the options vested, the plan administrator informed Cochran that the unvested portion of his options would be reduced by nearly one-third. Cochran signed a form acknowledging this change. Cochran then was laid off. He exercised the vested portion of his options and sued.

Cochran also argued that the company "unlawfully canceled a portion of the unvested stock options." The court rejected this claim, using a three part test to determine whether the company had properly cancelled the options. First, the court observed that the company changed the number of options granted before any of the options had vested. Second, the employee acknowledged and consented to the reductions. The court indicated that a company may not cancel unvested options unilaterally; valid consensual modification is needed by both company and employee. Finally the employee must receive "legally sufficient consideration in exchange for accepting this reduction in future benefits." The court found that the "employer's forbearance from ending the employment relationship, coupled with the employee's continued performance, can satisfy the consideration requirement."

.05 Alleged Misstatements in Mergers, Acquisitions and Spin-Offs

In *Nauman v. Abbott Laboratories*,[156] the U.S. District Court for the Northern District of Illinois ruled that Hospira Inc. - a company that was spun off from Abbott Laboratories - could not be held liable for misrepresentations that Abbott allegedly made to its employees about their retirement and health benefits. This holding was based primarily on the fact that Hospira was not in existence at the time of the alleged misrepresentations and thus was not a fiduciary. However, a separate lawsuit alleging that Abbott violated ERISA Sec. 510 by transferring certain employees to Hospira to prevent them from obtaining retirement benefits, was allowed to proceed.

In *Adams v. Lockheed Martin Energy Systems Inc.*,[157] the U.S. Court of Appeals for the Sixth Circuit ruled that Lockheed Martin Energy Systems Inc. did not breach its fiduciary duties by allegedly misleading employees about their ability to roll over their Code Sec. 401(k) plan account balances after they were out-

---

[155] *Cochran v. Quest Software, Inc.*, 328 F3d 1 (1st Cir. 2003).

[156] *Nauman v. Abbott Laboratories*, N.D. Ill., No. 04 C 7199 (August 14, 2006).

[157] *Adams v. Lockheed Martin Energy Systems, Inc.*, 6th Cir., No. 04-6204, unpublished (August 21, 2006).

sourced to another company. The court had little trouble concluding that Lockheed was not acting as an ERISA fiduciary when it made comments to the employees about their ability to rollover their 401(k) balances into the new company's plan.

In *Prior v. Innovative Communications Corp.*,[158] the U.S. Court of Appeals for the Third Circuit held that a new company created when two business owners split up their business did not assume liability for the former co-chief executive officers' unfunded top-hat plan benefits. Following the split-up, one of the former co-CEOs alleged that the other company assumed all the old company's liabilities, including his supplemental pension. The court was forced to look at extrinsic evidence, since the employee benefits agreement ("EBA") created as part of the split-up was ambiguous regarding liability for nonqualified supplemental pension benefits. The court said the structure of the split-up deal, shown through a memo and a principal terms agreement, said that the liability for supplemental benefits to the former co-CEOs would be to their respective companies after the split-up.

In *Deich-Keibler v. Bank One*,[159] the U.S. Court of Appeals for the Seventh Circuit held that Bank One did not interfere with two employees' potential right to severance benefits, in violation of ERISA Sec. 510, when it sold its division to another firm that offered the employees jobs that they declined, thus making them ineligible for severance benefits. The court concluded that the employees could have shown a violation of ERISA Sec. 510 only if they had could provide evidence that Bank One intended to discriminate against their division because of some characteristic of the severance plan.

In *Aretakis v. General Signal Inc.*,[160] the U.S. District Court for the District of Massachusetts held that an employer did not breach its employment and compensation agreement with an executive by failing to give the executive stock in an anticipated spin-off that had been promised as an inducement for the executive to take the position. In the court's opinion, the discussions between the employer's president and the executive before the executive accepted the position were far too indefinite to form a legally binding oral contract guaranteeing the executive stock in the anticipated spin-off. The court also rejected the executive's promissory estoppel and fraud claims because the executive's reliance on the president's promise of stock was unreasonable.

In *Antolik v. Saks Inc.*,[161] the U.S. Court of Appeals for the Eighth Circuit held that former employees of Saks were not entitled to severance pay under the terms of a letter they received, which promised them benefits in the event of a "change of control." The court found that the letter was not an SPD but instead was simply an explanation of why the plan was being implemented. The court found that Saks issued the letter to its employees to quell the employees' concerns that Saks would be acquired by another company. The letter stated,

---

[158] *Prior v. Innovative Communications Corp.*, 3d Cir., No. 05-2044, unpublished (October 20, 2006).

[159] *Deich-Keibler v. Bank One*, 7th Cir., No. 06-3802 unpublished (June 26, 2007).

[160] *Aretakis v. General Signal Inc.*, D. Mass., No. 05-10257-DPW (June 7, 2006).

[161] *Antolik v. Saks Inc.*, 8th Cir., No. 06-1046 (September 14, 2006).

among other things, that Saks was "not for sale" and that, in the event there was a "change of control or sale of a major business unit," employees would receive severance pay equal to 26 weeks of salary. The letter did not define the term "change of control." Change of control was defined in the severance pay plan's formal documents as "the acquisition of voting control or majority ownership of Saks securities, or a shift in the controlling majority of its Board of Directors."

¶2065 Litigation Over SEC Disclosures

Reporting and disclosure on executive compensation dominates the annual proxy statement. Nearly all of what companies disclose is required by a specific rule in the federal securities laws (*see* Chapter 31 for more detail on these requirements). Because stockholders will ostensibly base their proxy voting decisions on these disclosures, and because the disclosures are required by law, plaintiffs' lawyers often allege that the disclosures were inaccurate or insufficient. And sometimes the plaintiffs' lawyers are right.

.01 Actions and Awards Not Authorized by the Plan

One recurring scenario involves a board or compensation committee granting stock awards to executives, which are not authorized by the stock plan document.

In *Halpert ex rel. AsiaInfo-Linkage, Inc. v. Zhang*,[162] the Delaware District Court allowed a stockholder lawsuit over stock option awards in excess of the plan limits to proceed. In 2011, the board of AsiaInfo-Linkage Inc. adopted and stockholders approved a stock incentive plan. Later that year, the compensation committee of the board granted 750,000 stock options to Mr. Zhang, the president and chief executive officer of AsiaInfo, and 110,000 stock options to Guoxiang Liu, executive vice president of the company. "Stockholders" sued, alleging that these stock option grants exceeded the limits set forth in the stock incentive plan, which provided that "no individual may be granted within any one fiscal year of [AsiaInfo] one or more Awards intended to qualify as Performance-Based Compensation which in the aggregate are for more than (a) 100,000 shares . . . [or] up to 200,000 shares . . . to newly hired or newly promoted individuals."

The multimillion dollar question in this case was whether the stock options were intended to qualify as performance-based compensation. As many readers know, not everyone considers stock options to be performance-based compensation. However, the court looked at the terms of the stock incentive plan, which defined "performance-based compensation" as that which satisfies Code Sec. 162(m). As readers also know, stock options nearly always qualify as performance-based compensation under Code Sec. 162(m).

The court cited another most famous case in the area of excess stock awards, *Sanders v. Wang*[163] (eventually settled for $230 million), and found that the facts of

---

[162] 966 F. Supp. 2d 406 - Dist. Court, D. Delaware 2013; motion denied, 47 F.Supp.3d 214 (2014); Litigation rendered moot by the merger of Asiainfo-Linkage, Civil Action No. 12-1339-SLR-SRF (D. Del. Apr. 1, 2015).

[163] Civ. No. 16640, 1999 WL 1044880, (Del.Ch. Nov. 8, 1999).

the case raised "a reasonable doubt that the stock option grants were a valid exercise of business judgment," thus allowing the litigation to go forward without a "demand" on the directors. This was not a final decision in favor of plaintiffs. However, it allowed the case to continue to the next (costly) stage and did not bode well for the future result. The parties eventually settled.

In *Louisiana Municipal Police Employees Retirement System, et al. v. Melvyn E. Bergstein, et al. and Simon Property Group, Inc.*,[164] the Delaware Chancery Court ruled against Simon Properties Group, Inc., refusing to dismiss plaintiffs' claims that the Simon Properties' directors had exceeded their authority under the company's stock incentive plan. The court's decision came down to a relatively narrow issue of whether the company's amendment of its stock incentive plan to allow a different type of stock award required stockholder approval. However, the transcript of the bench ruling includes several hints of the possibility of a shift in Delaware courts' attitudes toward executive compensation lawsuits.

Many lawsuits over the years have been based on the premise that the company had announced and emphasized a "pay-for-performance" philosophy, but the actual compensation or awards were inconsistent with that philosophy. None had succeeded. Indeed, the court acknowledged that the company's total shareholder return was up almost 600% in the last ten years vs. an increase of 172 % for the Morgan Stanley REIT index and only 58% for the S&P. Since the date of the award alone, the company's market cap had gone from $33 billion to $57 billion.

In *Simon Properties*, the plaintiffs added a claim that the company's directors had exceeded their authority under the company's stock incentive plan by granting time-based restricted stock units pursuant to an amendment of the plan – because the amendment did not receive stockholder approval as (allegedly) required by the New York Stock Exchange ("NYSE") rules. Surprisingly, the court agreed, despite an email from the NYSE to the company's counsel in which an NYSE lawyer agreed with counsel's interpretation that the amendment did not require stockholder approval. The case was rendered moot when the company cancelled the earlier awards, amended the plan, and made a similar award. Although the plaintiffs sued again, the Delaware Supreme Court rejected their claims.

.02 Section 162(m) Disclosures

Code Sec. 162(m) prohibits a publicly held company from deducting more than $1 million of compensation paid to certain covered employees in any tax year. However, Code Sec. 162(m) included an exception to the $1 million cap for qualified performance-based compensation. Among the many requirements necessary to qualify for the performance-based compensation exception was that the material terms of any performance goals be disclosed to and subsequently approved by the company's stockholders before the compensation is paid. Thus,

---

[164] Delaware Supreme Court, No. 199, 2015, (Appeal from Court of Chancery, C.A. No. 10249-VCL).

the proxy statements of most public companies include a discussion of Code Sec. 162(m).

However, another reason that companies discuss Code Sec. 162(m) is Item 402(b)(2)(xii) of Regulation S-K, which lists, as an example of material information to be disclosed under the Compensation Discussion and Analysis, "The impact of the accounting and tax treatments of the particular form of compensation." Most companies include this disclosure under the heading: "Federal Tax and Accounting Consequences"

The Tax Cuts and Jobs Act of 2017 ("TCJA"), signed into law by President Trump in December 2017, repealed the performance-based compensation exception. But rather than reducing companies' discussion of compensation deductibility, this change is likely to increase companies' discussion of it. When a significant portion of a company's executive compensation is not deductible, many companies will come under increasing pressure to justify their decisions to incur non-deductible expenses.

In *Freedman v. Adams*,[165] plaintiffs had filed a stockholder derivative complaint alleging that the board's decision to pay certain executive bonuses without adopting a plan that could make those bonuses tax deductible constituted corporate waste. The trial court held that the complaint failed to allege, with particularity, that the board's decision not to implement a so-called Code Sec. 162(m) plan was a decision that no reasonable person would have made. The Delaware Supreme Court agreed.

> The board believed that a Section 162(m) plan would constrain the compensation committee in its determination of appropriate bonuses. The decision to sacrifice some tax savings in order to retain flexibility in compensation decisions is a classic exercise of business judgment. Even if the decision was a poor one for the reasons alleged by Freedman, it was not unconscionable or irrational.

In *Hoch v. Alexander*[166], the federal district court in Delaware issued a memorandum opinion allowing plaintiff's claims against Qualcomm and its directors to go forward. In its 2011 proxy statement, Qualcomm sought stockholders' approval of an amendment of its Long Term Incentive Plan ("LTIP"), which included an increase in the share reserve by 65,000,000 shares. As required by SEC rules, the proxy statement included standard, albeit, imperfect language, regarding the deductibility of certain stock-based compensation under the heading "Federal Income Tax Information."

The lawsuit alleged that the representations made in the proxy statement about the availability of tax deductions were materially false or misleading: "Because the defendants would still pay performance-based compensation under the 2006 LTIP as unamended, regardless of stockholder approval, no vote of the stockholders would make such payments deductible . . . Therefore, contrary to the representations and omissions in the Proxy Statement, awards under the 2006

---

[165] 58 A. 3d 414 - Del: Supreme Court 2013.
[166] Civil Action No. 11-217-RGA, United States District Court, D. Delaware, July 2, 2013; Civil Action No. 11-217, United States District Court, D. Delaware, July 1, 2011.

LTIP as amended will not be tax-deductible even if the stockholders approve it." In a July 2011 ruling that surprised most executive compensation professionals, the court denied the defendants' motion to dismiss plaintiffs' claims and allowed the suit to continue.

In 2013, a Delaware federal court again refused to dismiss the plaintiffs' claims and allowed the suit to continue. The court gave two primary reasons for its decision:

1. The issue of whether the Qualcomm board implicitly ratified the allegedly defective actions relating to board approval and slating matters for a vote is not properly decided at the motion to dismiss stage.

2. "Defendants have not shown the compensation is deductible," under Code Section 162(m).

This second basis for the court's decision was shocking, as Qualcomm and the IRS had entered into an Issue Resolution Agreement, pursuant to which the IRS concurred with Qualcomm that the 2011 LTIP approved by stockholders *was compliant with Code Section 162(m)*.

.03 Stockholder Say on Pay Disclosures

In the fall of 2012, a single plaintiffs' firm filed dozens of lawsuits in different states alleging that companies' disclosures as to say on pay were insufficient to all stockholders to make an informed vote. Nearly all of these lawsuits were eventually dismissed, but a few made it into a court or settled.

In *Mancuso v. The Clorox Company*,[167] the Superior Court of Alameda County California denied a motion for preliminary injunction of The Clorox Company's annual stockholders' meeting on the basis that (i) plaintiffs had failed to establish that allowing the votes to go forward at the meeting posed any risk of interim, much less irreparable harm, and (ii) the parties' agreement that the stockholder actions could be voided by court order, proxies resolicited with full disclosure, and a new vote taken, if plaintiffs were to ultimately prevail at trial. However, the court did not dismiss the case. Plaintiffs had sued Clorox and its directors in October 2012, shortly before its stockholders' meeting scheduled for November 2012. The lawsuit alleged that the proxy statement filed by Clorox omitted material information regarding a request that Clorox stockholders approve an amendment to Clorox's 2005 Stock Incentive Plan that would add 2.9 million shares to the 4.2 million shares remaining available for issuance under the plan.

The court's decision examined in detail each of the seven specific disclosure deficiencies alleged by plaintiffs based on the argument, evidence and expert testimony submitted by the parties. The court concluded that, while each of the items allegedly missing from Clorox's proxy statement disclosure may have been helpful to investors, much of the information was available at other locations in the proxy (or other recent SEC filings) and none of the disclosure items was material or required.

---

[167] No. RG12-651653 (Cal. Super. Ct. Alameda Cnty, 2013).

The court's decision in *Clorox* initially gave us heartburn. First, if every court facing such a lawsuit were to conclude that it had to determine whether the allegedly omitted disclosure information was "material," it would be difficult for companies to have these claims dismissed at a preliminary, motion to dismiss stage. Thus, even if companies ultimately were to prevail in these lawsuits over disclosure, the companies would have spent significant amounts of time and legal fees over executive compensation disclosure matters that, out the outset, seemed trivial. Additionally, most executive compensation and litigation professionals assumed that if we could avoid a preliminary injunction of the stockholders meeting, the threat would be over. The possibility that this litigation can live on after the stockholder meeting, possibly reversing the results of that meeting, increases the costs and the risks to companies. However, the *Clorox* case was the farthest that any of the disclosure cases have made it in court.

.04 Other Errors

In June 2014, Cheniere Energy, Inc. issued a press release and filed a Form 8-K announcing that it had postponed its scheduled 2014 Annual Meeting of Stockholders due to a lawsuit filed against Cheniere's officers and directors. The lawsuit, *Jones v. Souki, et al.*,[168] alleged inaccuracies and deficiencies in the Cheniere Stock Plan and the proxy statement disclosures concerning the stock plan.

A substantial majority of Cheniere stockholders had approved the Cheniere Energy, Inc. 2011 Incentive Plan (the "2011 Plan") with a share reserve of 10 million shares at the company's 2011 annual stockholders meeting. By December 31, 2012, the share reserve was almost completely depleted. Yet, on that date, the compensation committee approved an aggregate grant of 17.4 million shares of restricted stock under the 2011 Plan, including 6 million restricted shares to the CEO and 3,840,000 restricted shares to the other five executives named in the lawsuit. Since there were almost no shares left in the 2011 Plan share reserve to cover these grants, it was necessary for Cheniere to request stockholder approval of an increase to the share reserve under the terms of the 2011 Plan. Pursuant to a special meeting proxy statement filed in December 2012, Cheniere called a Special Meeting of Stockholders on February 1, 2013 ("Special Meeting"), at which it asked stockholders to approve an additional 25 million shares for the 2011 Plan share reserve.

In its 2014 proxy statement filed in May, Cheniere asked stockholders to approve an additional 30 million shares for the 2011 Plan share reserve. However, after postponing the 2014 meeting, Cheniere announced a new annual meeting date of September 11, 2014 in a Notice of Postponed Annual Meeting of Stockholders and 2014 Proxy Statement filed July 25, 2014. The proxy statement for this meeting did not include a proposal for additional shares for the 2011 Plan share reserve, explaining:

---

[168] Converted to *In re Cheniere Energy, Inc. Stockholders Litigation*, C.A. No. 9710-VCL (Del. Ch. May 29, 2014).

Are these proxy materials different from the proxy materials I already received?

Yes, although you may have received proxy materials dated April 28, 2014, these proxy materials are different in a few important ways, including:

- The date of the Meeting has changed to September 11, 2014.
- Two of the proposals in the previously sent proxy materials have been withdrawn, as described below.
- The record date for determination of stockholders eligible to vote in the Meeting has changed to July 23, 2014.

Proposals relating to the 2014-2018 Long-Term Incentive Compensation Program (the "2014-2018 LTIP") and the Cheniere Energy, Inc. 2011 Incentive Plan were included in the previously sent proxy materials. The Board in consultation with the Compensation Committee has subsequently withdrawn these proposals. After receiving feedback from stockholders and consulting with management, the Board determined that this is not the appropriate time to ask the stockholders to approve a new pool of shares. The Company will reassess its strategy in this context given the need to attract, retain and motivate employees with the talent and experience to effectively execute the Company's strategic business plan.

The Form 8-K Cheniere filed after the February 1, 2013 Special Meeting disclosed the stockholder vote on the approval of additional shares for the 2011 Plan as follows:

Votes For	77,011,739
Votes Against	57,907,345
Abstentions	36,252,581

This was an unusually high number of abstentions for a stock plan proposal. If abstentions were either counted as "yes" votes or not counted, the additional shares were approved by a majority of stockholders. However, if abstentions were counted as "no" votes, the additional shares were not approved by a majority. (There were no broker non-votes because it was a special meeting that did not have any routine proposals on the agenda on which brokers could vote.)

At the time of the Special Meeting, when stockholders voted to approve the addition of 25 million shares to the 2011 Plan reserve, Cheniere's bylaws had closely tracked the Delaware law default rule (8 Del. C. § 216), which suggests that in determining whether a stockholder proposal has passed in a circumstance where the vote is required of a majority of the shares present and entitled to vote on the subject matter, abstentions are to be treated as shares present and entitled to vote on the subject matter. Applying that standard, an abstention would be counted as a "no" vote.

In April 2014, Cheniere's Board restated its bylaws, allowing it not to count abstentions as "no" votes. Plaintiffs alleged that not only was this bylaw ineffective as to the 2013 vote to approve shares, but this bylaw was created for an improper purpose – to disenfranchise stockholders by making it far easier for Cheniere to gain approval of unpopular items such as increases to the 2011 Plan share reserve.

In addition to seeking to enjoin the upcoming June 12, 2014 stockholder vote to increase the authorized share reserve under the 2011 Plan by 30 million shares, the complaint sought three forms of relief. The plaintiffs' primary claim was that the resolution to permit awards under the 2011 Plan did not receive the required majority stockholder vote. Plaintiffs argued that Cheniere had improperly failed to count abstentions as "no" votes at the 2013 Special Meeting, as Delaware law requires. If Cheniere had properly counted the abstentions, the complaint alleged, the proposal to increase the 2011 Plan share reserve by 25 million shares would not have passed with a majority vote. Thus, the subsequent granting of restricted stock awards under the 2011 Plan was an unauthorized act by the board, which exceeded its authority under its own bylaws and was *ultra vires*.

Ultimately, Cheniere cancelled the awards and started from scratch. Among the lessons to be learned from this case for companies, boards, and counsel might be (i) to double check the precise method specified in the company's bylaws for counting votes and (ii) to the take greater care in determining the number of shares for which the company seeks stockholder approval, so that the company does not need to ask stockholders to approve additional shares for the plan reserve in two of the first three years after it first adopts the plan.

.05 What the Plaintiffs' Firms Usually Want

The plaintiffs' firms that file most of these disclosure lawsuits, like those that file lawsuits over the disclosure in virtually every merger or acquisition situation, do not necessarily expect to win their cases at trial. What these firms hope for is to survive the company's initial motions for summary judgment. This they can do by filing a lawsuit early, without following the requirement that a stockholder first must file a "demand" with the board, demanding that the board investigate the alleged transaction or disclosure. Generally, plaintiffs can only avoid the demand requirement by showing that demand would be futile, *e.g.*, because the board members themselves have an interest in the transaction being challenged.

Alternatively, plaintiffs could comply with the demand requirement and then file a lawsuit alleging that the board breached its fiduciary duty, committed corporate waste, or failed in some other way. The business judgment rule contained in the corporate statutes of Delaware and most other states protects any decision of a board of directors that is made by disinterested directors in good faith. Again, when the company files its motion to dismiss the often frivolous lawsuit, the plaintiffs generally will attempt to show that the board members were not disinterested because they somehow had an interest in the transaction being challenged.

If the plaintiffs can overcome the motion for summary judgment by either of these two strategies, they may feel that they already have "won." The reason is that, when litigation continues beyond a motion for summary judgment, the costs to the company in terms of legal fees and time lost to discovery, depositions, and other matters, quickly begin to mount, and the company often settles the lawsuit with some modest governance actions and a hefty payment to the plaintiffs' lawyers.

¶2065.05

In *Raul v. Astoria Financial Corporation*,[169] a plaintiffs firm sent a demand letter to the Astoria board ten days after Astoria filed its 2012 proxy statement, asserting that, "[i]n violation of Securities and Exchange Commission ('SEC') regulation disclosure standards and the Astoria Board's duty of candor," the Astoria board "concealed material and required information concerning the Company's executive compensation policies and practices in the 2012 Proxy Statement" by failing to disclose *"whether, and if so, how, the Astoria Board considered the results of the 2011 say-on-pay vote,"* and "how frequently it has decided to hold future say-on-pay votes." [Emphasis in original] That same month, Astoria filed with the SEC, pursuant to Item 5.07(d), an amendment on Form 8-K/A, which disclosed that, in light of the stockholder advisory vote at the 2011 Annual Meeting on the frequency of stockholder votes on approval of the compensation of the company's named executive officers, the company intended to hold a say-on-pay vote every year. Astoria also mailed a letter to its stockholders, which, among other things, clarified whether and how the company considered the results of the stockholder advisory vote on the approval of the compensation.

The plaintiffs firm then demanded attorneys' fees and, when Astoria refused, filed suit "seeking an equitable assessment of attorneys' fees," and alleging that the plaintiff's efforts to remedy the disclosure violations identified in its demand conferred upon Astoria a benefit justifying an award of fees.

Under the corporate benefit doctrine in Delaware, a plaintiff may receive attorneys' fees where (i) the underlying cause of action was meritorious when filed; (ii) the action producing benefit to the company was taken by the defendants before a judicial resolution was achieved; and (iii) the resulting corporate benefit was causally related to the lawsuit. The court declined to award attorneys' fees to plaintiff under the corporate benefit doctrine:

> Our law provides that if the actions of the board of directors were such that, at the time a demand was made, a suit based on those actions would have survived a motion to dismiss, and a material corporate benefit resulted, the attorneys' fees incurred by the stockholder may be recovered despite the fact that no suit was ever filed. If, on the other hand, the stockholder has simply done the company a good turn by bringing to the attention of the board an action that it ultimately decides to take, she is not entitled to coerced payment of her attorneys' fees by the stockholders at large. Finding that the demand at issue here falls into the latter category, I decline to shift fees onto the corporation and its stockholders.

The decision in *Raul v. Astoria Financial Corporation* was reassuring to companies facing the decision of whether to file a supplement to the proxy statement to address disclosure issues raised by a plaintiffs' firm, which are not material, but which could be clarified with some additional disclosure.

---

[169] C.A. No. 9169-VCG (Del. Ch. June 20, 2014) (Glasscock, V.C.).

Chapter 21
ROLE OF STOCKHOLDERS AND BOARD OF DIRECTORS IN EXECUTIVE COMPENSATION

¶2101 Overview—Role of Stockholders and Board of Directors in Executive Compensation

One of the primary responsibilities of a company's board of directors is selecting the chief executive officer ("CEO") and setting his or her compensation. The board's compensation committee is responsible for setting the compensation of other executive officers. Recent securities law requirements have greatly enhanced the complexity and visibility of the compensation committee in the executive compensation process in public companies.

The role of stockholders in the executive compensation process is critical, but more limited. Stockholders of public companies have the right to approve (or reject) most forms of equity-based compensation paid to executive officers. In recent years, stockholders have been asserting themselves and their opinions like never before.

.01 Boards of Directors' Responsibility and Potential Liability

It is a fundamental principle of corporate law that the board of directors is responsible for selecting and compensating the company's chief executive officer. Together with this responsibility for setting compensation is potential liability to stockholders for wasting corporate assets. The board also has the responsibility to monitor the performance of the chief executive officer. As executive compensation packages soared, stockholder litigation over those packages also increased. The extravagant severance amounts paid to executive officers who failed were particularly likely to draw criticism and legal challenge (see ¶2115 for a detailed discussion of the board's liability for compensation decisions and ¶2125 for a discussion on director liability for excessive executive compensation).

.02 Stockholders' Role in Executive Compensation

Even before the Dodd-Frank Wall Street Reform and Consumer Protection Act (the "Dodd-Frank Act"),[1] a variety of legal and regulatory considerations required stockholder approval of equity-based compensation and other forms of executive compensation. Code Sec. 422 requires stockholder approval of a plan that will award incentive stock options (see ¶2135 for a detailed discussion of the stockholder approval requirements). Public companies seek stockholder approval of stock awards to protect the awards from Section 16(b) of the Securities

---

[1] Pub. L. No. 111-203.

Exchange Act of 1934 (the "Exchange Act") and satisfy the stock exchange listing requirements of the New York Stock Exchange ("NYSE") and the Nasdaq Stock Market ("Nasdaq") (see ¶2145 for a detailed discussion of the stock exchange requirements).

.03 Disclosures to Stockholders

The Securities and Exchange Commission ("SEC") Regulation S-K sets forth extensive rules on executive compensation and related person disclosure (see ¶2155).

.04 Executive Compensation in ESOP-Owned Companies

ERISA expressly contemplates that corporate directors and officers will serve as plan fiduciaries, and provides that actions taken by directors and officers in their corporate capacity are not subject to review under ERISA (see ¶2165).

.05 Special Focus on CEO Compensation

Boards of directors, the courts and judiciary, plaintiffs' class action lawyers, the IRS, the SEC, institutional investors, the press, and the U.S. Congress are all focusing on corporate governance as applied to CEO compensation. The Congress and the IRS have affected some minor changes. However, the major developments - the ones that have most significantly changed the responsibility and potential liability for directors - have come from the SEC, the judiciary and the plaintiffs' lawyers (see ¶2175).

.06 Institutional Stockholders and Proxy Advisory Firms

In the 2010s, institutional investors and proxy advisory firms began to more strongly assert themselves to influence companies' corporate governance and other policies, including executive compensation. Institutional Shareholder Services Inc. ("ISS") and Glass Lewis are the most active and prominent proxy advisory firms. ISS, in particular, publishes extensive and detailed guidelines on its policy and governance preferences. Based on these preference, ISS will recommend that its clients – mostly large institutional investors – vote "For," "Against," or "Withhold" on the various proposals that each company must put to a vote of its stockholders each year (see ¶2185).

¶2115 Board of Directors' Responsibility

A company's board of directors is responsible for overseeing the compensation of the company's top executives. Both the NYSE and Nasdaq stock markets require companies listed on their exchange to maintain a compensation committee. While responsibilities of compensation committees vary among companies, the primary responsibility of a board compensation committee is to recommend, oversee, and approve the company's compensation policy and process. Compensation committees generally determine or approve compensation arrangements for senior management and executives of the company, as well as (generally) the board of directors itself. Often, companies link this role with the functions of performance review, management development, and CEO succession.

¶2101.03

Every state corporation statute authorizes the creation and use of board committees, although most state statutes impose limitations on the authority that the board may delegate to a committee. (For example, Delaware, and most other states would prohibit the board from delegating the power to execute and adopt a merger agreement to a committee.)

.01 Statutory Reasons for Director Approval

Both the federal securities laws and the Internal Revenue Code offer special protection to executive compensation plans and agreements approved by a board compensation committee. However, in each case, to earn this protection, the compensation committee must be made up of independent or outside directors. Prior to 2018, stockholder approved performance-based compensation was an exception to the $1 million deductibility limits of Code Sec. 162(m). To qualify for the exemption, the performance goals had to be determined by a compensation committee of the board of directors of the corporation, which is comprised solely of two or more outside directors.[2] The legislation known as the Tax Cuts and Jobs Act of 2017 ("TCJA"), signed into law by President Trump in December 2017, eliminated this exception.

This is a different requirement than the "disinterested director" requirements of Securities and Exchange Commission Rule 16b-3. Section 16(b) of the Exchange Act prohibits senior officers and directors from retaining any profits realized from a short-swing purchase and sale of company stock within a six-month period. Companies can obtain protection from Rule 16b-3 for the award and exercise of stock incentive plan grants by obtaining stockholder approval of the entire stock incentive plan (which most do, for reasons described in ¶2135) or approval of the particular transaction by the board of directors or a committee composed of "nonemployee directors."[3]

.02 Public vs. Private Companies

The federal securities laws do not apply to private companies but the actions of the SEC and its requirements can point out traps and help illustrate best practices. The fact that a company is private does not mean that the Delaware courts will hold the directors to a lower threshold. Recent decisions in the Delaware courts have applied to the boards of directors, individual directors, and management of any Delaware corporation with stockholders. Because courts are finding that private company directors have duties similar to those of public companies, it is important for private companies to understand the duties and responsibilities (and potential liabilities) that courts are imposing on public company boards of directors.

As a practical matter, while strict director independence requirements apply to public company boards of directors, no such rules apply to private companies. In fact, many private company boards are composed of solely of owners and family members. Particularly in the case of private companies, whether a director

---

[2] Code Sec. 162(m)(4)(C)(i).

[3] 17 C.F.R. § 240.16b-3.

is disinterested and independent depends on the facts and circumstances of each situation.

The sources of lawsuits against organizations vary. While stockholders make up the vast majority of the sources of litigation against directors and officers of public companies, nearly half of the lawsuits against private companies are from employees.[4]

.03 Independence of Compensation Committees

Section 952 of the Dodd-Frank Wall Street Reform and Consumer Protection Act ("Dodd-Frank") added Section 10C to the Exchange Act, which requires the SEC to promulgate rules that direct the NYSE, Nasdaq, and other national securities exchanges and associations to prohibit the listing of any equity security of a company that does not have an independent compensation committee. In determining the definition of the term "independence," the national securities exchanges and associations must consider relevant factors to be determined by the SEC, including: (A) the source of compensation of a member of the company's board of directors, including any consulting, advisory, or other compensatory fee paid by the company to such member; and (B) whether a member of the company's board of directors is affiliated with the company, or a subsidiary or affiliate of the company.

At the time the Dodd-Frank Act became law, most public companies already satisfied the independent compensation committee requirement of Section 952, due to their compliance with the outside director requirements of Code Sec. 162(m), which was necessary to qualify for the performance-based compensation exception to the deductibility limits of Code Sec. 162(m). However, the TCJA eliminated the performance-based compensation exemption under Code Sec. 162(m). The rules maintained by the NYSE and Nasdaq are now more critical. (See ¶3135 Compensation Committee Independence, for a more detailed discussion of this issue.)

¶2125 Director Liability for Excessive Compensation

Historically, judges were reluctant to intrude on a board of directors' business judgment in setting compensation because these decisions were so subjective. Accordingly, for decades, the courts had broadly interpreted the corporate waste standard and plaintiffs had been discouraged from bringing lawsuits that alleged excessive compensation. However, based on recent case law developments and surprisingly candid statements from the Delaware judiciary, it appears that judges now may be willing — even eager — to wade in these waters. The *Cendant* case and others indicated that the plaintiffs' bar is emboldened to bring excessive compensation cases.

---

[4] See Tillinghast D&O Insurance Survey (reporting a 10-year average through 2004). Fifty-seven percent of the lawsuits against public company officers and directors were brought by stockholders, followed by 23% brought by employees. Alternatively, lawsuits brought by stockholders of private companies accounted for 31% of the litigation, while 48% of the suits were brought by the employees.

If a court were to find that directors permitted a CEO to receive several million dollars in excessive compensation by failing to meet minimal standards of due care or not considering all material information, the court might find that the board abrogated its duties to the company and failed to act in good faith. This could mean that each director would have to pay out of his or her own pocket — without being reimbursed by the company or the D&O insurance carrier—several million dollars each.

Delaware law requires that its corporations indemnify current or former officers and directors who are "successful on the merits or otherwise" in defense of legal actions against them for service on the board. However, Delaware law prohibits a company from indemnifying an officer or director if he acted in bad faith or in a manner that the director did not reasonably believe was in the best interests of the company.

Take note of the widely reported settlement with the former WorldCom directors, under which the directors had agreed to pay $18 million of their own money to settle claims that they were negligent in discharging their fiduciary duties. There was a lot more going on at WorldCom than careless compensation practices, but the undisclosed loans to the CEO were among the focal points. Directors at Cendant, Disney and other companies have faced similar claims. On the heels of the announcement of the WorldCom directors' settlement, came the announcement that Enron directors had agreed to pay $13 million personally as part of a settlement. (The WorldCom settlement initially was rejected by the court, whereas the Enron settlement was approved.)

Additionally, in 2007, five former outside directors of bankrupt Just for Feet, Inc. paid out a combined $41.5 million of their own money to settle allegations that they breached their fiduciary duties to stockholders, easily surpassing the out-of-pocket settlements paid by former outside directors of Enron and WorldCom. The original securities class action complaint charged the defendants with violations of the federal securities laws by, among other things, misrepresenting and/or omitting material information concerning the company's net earnings. The complaint further charged that these misrepresentations were the result of the combined defendants actions in, among other things, creating false billings for advertising and fixed asset costs to its vendors, understating its cost of sales through acquisition accounting, capitalizing inventory costs that should have been recorded as expenses, overstating inventory by failing to account for missing or obsolete inventory, and creating fictitious postings to both the inventory and expense accounts. Although executive compensation was not an issue in this case, director readers should be aware this development.

Within the ambit of power granted to the board of directors is the authority and wide discretion to make decisions on executive compensation.[5] There is,

---

[5] See e.g., 8 Del.C. § 122(5) (holding that a corporation may appoint "such officers and agents as the business of the corporation requires and to pay or otherwise provide for them suitable compensation."); 8 Del.C. § 122(15) (holding that a corporation may "[p]ay pensions and establish and carry out pension, profit sharing, stock option, stock purchase, stock bonus, retirement, benefit, incentive and compensation plans . . . for any or all of its directors, officers, and employees").

however, an outer limit to this discretion, a point at which a compensation package is so disproportionate to services rendered as to be unconscionable and constitute waste.[6] When stockholders believe the board of directors has crossed this line they often bring derivative actions against the board of directors alleging breach of fiduciary duty and corporate waste. Delaware, recognizing the potential burden these suits could impose, has developed two main protections for the board of directors: the demand requirement and the business judgment rule. These two protections, in all but the rarest of cases, serve to protect the board from liability for their compensation decisions.

.01 Demand Requirement

The demand requirement protects most executive compensation decisions before a court even reaches a fiduciary duty issue. Delaware Chancery Rule 23.1 provides that before bringing a derivative action, plaintiff stockholders must exhaust their intra-corporate remedies by demanding that the board take corrective action before suing. If the board refuses to take corrective action or if the plaintiff does not make demand, the plaintiff must meet the requirements of the demand futility test in order to sue. The test, laid out in *Aronson v. Lewis*, asks "whether, under the particularized facts alleged, a reasonable doubt is created that: (1) the directors are disinterested and independent or (2) the challenged transaction was otherwise the product of a valid exercise of business judgment."[7]

In the Disney case (discussed below), as in most derivative cases, the plaintiff stockholders failed to make a demand on the board and alleged demand futility.[8] The court, however, refused to excuse demand, holding that the plaintiffs failed to plead with the requisite specificity that the board was interested or that the decision was not a valid exercise of the board's business judgment.

.02 Business Judgment Rule

The business judgment rule is a director's best protection against liability. Unless, "the board or the relevant committee that awarded the compensation lacked independence (*e.g.*, was dominated or controlled by the individual receiving the compensation), . . . or . . . lacked good faith (*i.e.*, lacked an actual intention to advance corporate welfare) in making the award," the business judgment rule will protect the board's decisions on executive compensation issues.[9]

For a Delaware court to uphold the validity of a compensation plan, the plan must meet two requirements. First, the plan must involve an identifiable benefit to the company. To that end, the plan must contain conditions upon which the company can reasonably expect to obtain some benefit (the "Benefit Prong"). To constitute benefit, the company need only receive some consideration. Such benefit may even be intangible and not subject to valuation. Second, the value of

---

[6] See *Saxe v. Brady*, 184 A2d 602, 610 (Del. Ch. 1962).

[7] *Aronson v. Lewis*, 473 A2d 805, 814 (Del. 1984).

[8] *Brehm v. Eisner*, 746 A2d 244, 254-55 (Del. 2000).

[9] *Gagliardi v. TriFoods Intl., Inc.*, 683 A2d 1049 (Del. Ch. 1996).

the package must bear a reasonable relationship to the value of the benefit passing to the company (the "Value Prong").[10]

Directors must be particularly cautious when approving their own compensation. In *Tate & Lyle PLC v. Staley Continental, Inc.*,[11] the court held that the directors acted improperly in approving a company-wide compensation program on the eve of a takeover attempt, because part of the program would benefit the directors. After Tate & Lyle filed an intention to accumulate shares of Staley, the Staley board of directors approved an Outside Directors Retirement Plan, which would benefit the outside directors upon a change in control, and a Funding Trust, which would set aside company funds in a grantor trust to pay benefits under a variety of compensation plans, including the Outside Directors Retirement Plan. Portions of the court's strongly worded opinion are worth quoting in full:

> The most troublesome plan is the Outside Directors Retirement Plan. This plan specifically benefits non-management directors upon a change of control and the non-management directors, who comprised the Compensation Committee, proposed this plan to the full Board for approval. This indicates a reasonable likelihood that the plan is not protected by the business judgment rule as it will, upon a change in control, immediately benefit the same directors who proposed its adoption. The use of the Funding Trust to fund the largesse to the non-management directors also on its face seems to serve no valid business purpose. *Saxe v. Brady*, Del. Ch. 184 A2d 602 (1962). Directors have no right to expect to continue to be paid after the term of office for which they are elected by the stockholders expires. The adoption of a Funding Trust to protect such provisions seriously taints the entire propriety of the Funding Trust.

.03 Compensation Committee

The use of independent and disinterested persons to evaluate a compensation plan is helpful in upholding a compensation plan. Further, if the plan involves the granting of stock options as compensation, the conditions for vesting and exercise of options should support the business purpose of the plan. In *Byrne v. Lord*,[12] for example, the court held invalid a stock option plan that gave current and future board members options to purchase 4.6 million shares of stock when the company, at the time, had only 6 million shares of stock outstanding. The court found that the plan failed to meet the Benefit Prong because it failed to contain safeguards or circumstances to ensure the company received the benefit they bargained for, retaining key personnel. In so holding, the court noted that the company's position would have been stronger if the directors had looked to an independent compensation committee to evaluate the plan or if the stockholders had ratified the plan (see ¶10,300 for a sample compensation committee charter).

---

[10] *Beard v. Elster*, 160 A2d 731, 737 (Del. Supr. 1960); see also *Kerbs v. Cal. Eastern Airways*, 91 A2d 62 (Del. Supr. 1952).

[11] *Tate & Lyle PLC v. Staley Continental, Inc.*, 1988 Del. Ch. LEXIS 61 (Del. Ch. 1988).

[12] *Byrne v. Lord*, 1995 Del. Ch. LEXIS 131 (Del. Ch. 1995).

The compensation committee and the board of directors should evaluate the terms, cost, and likely outcomes of the CEO compensation arrangements to protect themselves from potential liability, and for the good of: (i) the members/stockholders, (ii) the company's public image, and (iii) the CEOs themselves. The CEO, too, has a fiduciary obligation to review his compensation. See *In re Walt Disney* (described below). Additionally, by participating in the process of setting reasonable compensation, the CEO will gain a greater assurance that he or she will actually receive the compensation he or she expects.

.04 Director Independence

The Sarbanes Oxley Act of 2002 ("SOX") added director independence requirements, particularly for the audit committee. However, what we see more often in challenges/litigation over executive compensation decisions is not an allegation that the director(s) failed to satisfy the independence requirements of SOX or the SROs, but that other, generally personal, relationships affected the director's independence. See *Beam v. Martha Stewart Living*,[13] holding that social relationships, without more, among directors are not sufficient to rebut the presumption of independence of pre-suit demand issues.

In a Form 8-K filed by Applied Materials, Inc. in March 2006, the company reported a board member's resignation from the audit committee for failing to meet the independence criteria that all audit committee members must meet under Nasdaq Marketplace Rule 4350(d)(2) (independence requirements). Under Nasdaq Marketplace Rule 4200(a)(15)(B), a director is not considered independent if he or she "accepted any payments from the company . . . in excess of $60,000 during any period of twelve consecutive months within the three years preceding the determination of independence," other than specified payments such as "compensation for board or board committee service." In the case of Applied Materials, Mr. Liu served as a consultant to the board for approximately three months prior to his appointment as a director.

.05 *Disney* Case: Round One

One way to illustrate directors' potential liability for excessive executive compensation is by using the story of Michael Ovitz and the Walt Disney Corporation as a lens through which to view the principles of this area of the law. Through four separate court decisions over ten years, the Disney case addressed the tough question of how much is too much, and in so doing, likely sets the outer boundary of permissible executive compensation.

In *Brehm v. Eisner*[14] (*Disney I*), Disney stockholders brought a derivative suit against the Disney board of directors alleging breach of fiduciary duty and corporate waste for approving a large severance package for former Disney president, Michael S. Ovitz, and for later approving a no-fault termination of that agreement. The Court of Chancery dismissed the claim, holding that demand on the board was not futile, and the plaintiff stockholders appealed.[15]

---

[13] 845 A.2d 1040, 1050 (Del. 2004).

[14] *Brehm v. Eisner*, 746 A2d 244 (Del. 2000).

[15] *Brehm v. Eisner*, 746 A2d 244, 248 (Del. 2000).

¶2125.04

In October of 1995, The Walt Disney Company hired Michael S. Ovitz, a prominent Hollywood talent broker, as its president. Ovitz was a long-time friend of Disney Chairman and CEO Michael Eisner. Despite at the time being a highly sought-after executive, Ovitz had no previous experience managing a diversified public company.[16]

The employment agreement was negotiated solely by Eisner, although the Disney board subsequently approved the agreement. The five-year contract provided a base salary of one million dollars per year, a discretionary bonus, and options to purchase five million shares of Disney common stock. The agreement provided that if Disney granted Ovitz a no-fault termination, three million of the options would vest immediately. The contract further provided that if Ovitz left Disney on such a basis, he would be entitled to the present value of his remaining salary, a $10 million severance payment, and $7.5 million for each year remaining on his employment contract.

Soon after Ovitz began working at Disney, problems surfaced. Before a year had passed, Ovitz began to look for new employment and sent Eisner a letter indicating his dissatisfaction with the position. Shortly thereafter, Ovitz and Eisner agreed to Ovitz's departure on a no-fault basis and the board subsequently approved the agreement. As a result, Ovitz left Disney with roughly $140 million ($39 million in cash, $101 million in options) in severance payments.[17]

The sheer size of the severance payment to Ovitz coupled with his poor performance was tantamount to an invitation for a derivative action. The action, similar to most all actions for excessive executive compensation, alleged breach of fiduciary duty of care and corporate waste.

.06 Breach of Fiduciary Duty

An executive compensation decision, like most business decisions, is protected from claims of breach of fiduciary duty by the business judgment rule. The business judgment rule "is a presumption that in making a business decision the directors of a company acted on an informed basis, in good faith and in the honest belief that the action taken was in the best interests of the company."[18]

On the procedural due care issue, the Disney complaint initially alleged that the Disney board breached its duty of care by failing to inform itself properly about the total costs and incentives of the Ovitz employment contract and severance package.[19] More precisely, the plaintiffs alleged that the contract gave Ovitz an incentive to leave the company through a no-fault agreement as soon as possible because doing so would be more lucrative for him than staying. The board rebutted this argument by noting that they sought the counsel of a corporate compensation expert, Graef Crystal, when formulating Ovitz's compensation package. Crystal, however, subsequently admitted that he never considered the cost to Disney if it were to terminate Ovitz without cause before the natural expiration of the contract.

---

[16] *Brehm v. Eisner*, 746 A2d 244, 249-50 (Del. 2000).

[17] *Brehm v. Eisner*, 746 A2d 244, 251-53 (Del. 2000).

[18] *Smith v. Van Gorkom*, 488 A2d 858, 872 (Del. 1985).

[19] *Brehm v. Eisner*, 746 A2d 244, 251 (Del. 2000).

The court rejected the plaintiffs' argument, noting that even if *ex post* Crystal regretted not calculating the value of the severance package, the essence of the business judgment rule is that a court will not apply 20/20 hindsight to second-guess a board's decision. Additionally, the court held that Section 141(e) of the Delaware general corporation law fully protected the Disney board from liability in that they reasonably relied in good faith on a qualified expert.[20]

.07 Corporate Waste

Corporate waste occurs only when a company exchanges assets for consideration so insignificant that no reasonable person would be willing to make such an exchange.[21] In other words, "[i]f it can be said that ordinary business [persons] might differ on the sufficiency of the terms, then the court must validate the transaction."[22] As such, claims for corporate waste are almost never successful.[23]

The Supreme Court of Delaware, in *Lewis v. Vogelstein*, summarized the state of the corporate waste doctrine, saying:

> The judicial standard for determination of corporate waste is well developed. Roughly, a waste entails an exchange of corporate assets for consideration so disproportionately small as to lie beyond the range at which any reasonable person might be willing to trade. Most often, the claim is associated with a transfer of corporate assets that serves no corporate purpose; or for which no consideration is received. Such a transfer is in effect a gift. If, however, any substantial consideration is received by the corporation, and if there is good faith judgment that in the circumstances the transaction is worthwhile, there should be no finding of waste, even if the fact finder would conclude *ex post* that the transaction was unreasonably risky.[24]

In the Disney case, the stockholders alleged that the Disney board committed waste in two respects. First, they alleged that agreeing to an employment contract with such a lucrative severance package amounted to corporate waste. Second, they alleged that terminating the Ovitz employment agreement on a no-fault basis, when they should have terminated it for cause, also amounted to waste. The court disagreed. While recognizing that there are "outer limits . . . where directors irrationally squander or give away corporate assets," the court held that was not the case here. In so finding, the court noted "the size and structure of executive compensation are inherently matters of judgment [for the Board]."

Despite finding that the actions of the board "were hardly paradigms of good corporate governance practices," and that "the sheer size of the payout to Ovitz . . . pushes the envelope of judicial respect for the business judgment of directors in making compensation decisions," the court nonetheless found that the plaintiffs failed to set forth particularized facts excusing pre-suit demand.[25] In the end, the court found that the "decision is for the stockholders to make in voting for the directors, urging other stockholders to reform or oust the board, or

---

[20] *Brehm v. Eisner*, 746 A2d 244, 261 (Del. 2000); 8 Del.C. § 141(e).

[21] See *Lewis v. Vogelstein*, 699 A.2d 327, 336 (Del. Ch. 1997).

[22] *Saxe v. Brady*, 184 A2d 602, 610 (Del. Ch. 1962).

[23] *Steiner v. Meyerson*, 1995 Del. Ch. LEXIS 95 (Del. Ch. 1995).

[24] *Lewis v. Vogelstein*, 699 A.2d 327, 336 (Del. Ch. 1997).

[25] *Brehm v. Eisner*, 746 A2d 244, 249 (Del. 2000).

in making individual buy-sell decisions involving Disney securities."[26] Additionally, the court was "fearful of invit[ing] courts to become super-directors, measuring matters of degree in business decision making and executive compensation."[27]

.08 *Disney* Case: Round Two

In May 2003, the Delaware Chancery Court issued its decision in *In re The Walt Disney Company Litigation*[28] (Disney II); which could be read as a 180-degree reversal of the 1998 decision in Brehm v. Eisner.

- In 1998, a Delaware court upholds the business judgment of a disinterested and independent board of directors, which paid $140 million in severance to Ovitz.

- In 2003, a Delaware court finds that Disney's directors may be personally liable for failing to: (1) exercise any business judgment, and (2) make any good faith attempt to fulfill their fiduciary duties to Disney and its stockholders.

What changed? According to the court, it heard new information obtained by plaintiffs through discovery about the nature of the Disney board's involvement in the decision to hire and, eventually, to terminate Ovitz. However, it also appeared that the Delaware courts had noticed the cumulative effects of the Enron/WorldCom/Tyco/Andersen scandals on the country. Indeed, the Chief Justice of the Delaware Supreme Court, Norman Veasey, stated publicly in 2002 that, "if directors claim to be independent by saying, for example, that they based decisions on some performance measure and don't do so, . . . the courts in some circumstances could treat their behavior as a breach of the fiduciary duty of good faith."

The facts described in *Disney II*[29] read like a "how-not-to-guide" to corporate governance in the realm of executive compensation. Among the damning facts the court lists in the opinion are the following:

1. Eisner unilaterally hired Ovitz, sending an offer letter before the board or compensation committee had ever discussed hiring Ovitz;

2. An executive compensation expert the board used from time to time had informed one of the board members—who also happened to be Eisner's personal attorney—in writing, that a large signing bonus is hazardous because the full cost is borne immediately and completely even if the executive fails to serve the full term of employment;

3. An internal Disney document prepared at Eisner's request warned that the number of stock options Eisner proposed to award to Ovitz was "far beyond the normal standards of both Disney and corporate America and would receive significant public criticism";

---

[26] *Brehm v. Eisner*, 746 A2d 244, 256 (Del. 2000).
[27] *Brehm v. Eisner*, 746 A2d 244, 266 (Del. 2000).

[28] *In re The Walt Disney Company Litigation*, 825 A2d 275 (Del. 2003).
[29] *In re The Walt Disney Company Litigation*, 825 A2d 275 (Del. 2003).

4. When Eisner first informed some of the board members they "protested" (including the board member who was Eisner's personal attorney);

5. Neither the compensation expert's letter nor the internal documents were shared with the compensation committee or the full board;

6. Disney prepared a draft employment agreement and sent it to Ovitz but did not give it to the compensation committee or the board;

7. After all this, the board compensation committee met for less than one hour to consider Ovitz's employment and two other issues;

8. According to the compensation committee's meeting minutes, it spent the least amount of time during the meeting discussing Ovitz's hiring;

9. The compensation committee spent the most time during its short meeting discussing the payment of $250,000 to Eisner's personal attorney "for his role in securing Ovitz's employment";

10. At their meeting, the compensation committee members had only an incomplete "rough" summary of the employment agreement already sent to Ovitz;

11. At their meeting, the compensation committee did not have "a spreadsheet or similar type of analytical document showing the potential payout to Ovitz throughout the contract, or the possible cost of his severance package upon a non-fault termination";

12. The committee did not have or request any information as to how the draft agreement compared with similar agreements throughout the entertainment industry, or information regarding other similarly situated executives in the same industry;

13. The compensation committee "lacked the benefit of an expert to guide them through the process";

14. The compensation committee approved the general terms and conditions of the employment agreement contained in the summary, but did not condition their approval on being able to review the final agreement;

15. At the full board meeting later that day, the committee did not make any recommendations or report to the board concerning its resolution to hire Ovitz. The board did not ask any questions about Ovitz's salary, stock options, or possible termination;

16. The board did not consider the consequences of a termination and the various payout scenarios that existed;

17. The board and the compensation committee left the final negotiation of Ovitz's employment agreement to Eisner, "Ovitz's close friend for over twenty-five years";

18. Neither the board nor the compensation committee was kept apprised of the negotiations between Disney and Ovitz, which continued for two months;

19. The final version of the employment agreement differed substantially from the summary presented to the compensation committee. The final agreement paid severance benefits for an employment termination "even if he acted negligently or was unable to perform his duties, as long as his behavior did not reach the high level of gross negligence or malfeasance." The final agreement did not contain a non-compete clause;

20. The final agreement was, in the words of the compensation consultant Disney used for Eisner but not for Ovitz, "more valuable to Ovitz the sooner he left Disney." The agreement provided for severance payments of approximately $140 million;

21. Ovitz's agreement provided for in-the-money stock options. (However, Ovitz did not countersign the stock option agreement until nearly one year later, when he was already discussing his plans to leave Disney);

22. Ovitz admitted the "he did not know his job" and "studiously avoided attempts to be educated";

23. Ovitz and Eisner worked together "as close personal friends to have Ovitz receive a non-fault termination" and they reached a written agreement to allow Ovitz to collect all $140 million;

24. Neither Eisner nor Ovitz, who had then been appointed to the board, consulted with or sought the approval of the board or compensation committee for the final agreement or the non-fault termination payments. At no time did the board ever approve or even discuss the agreement or the payments to Ovitz, or any alternatives to the giant payments; and

25. Disney's by-laws required board approval of Ovitz's non-fault termination, yet the board was not asked to approve the termination.

Courts that take the time and effort to compose a list such as this usually do so for a reason: to create a roadmap for better practices in the future.

.09 *Disney* Case Round Three: Delaware Court Holds its Nose but Rules in Favor of the Disney Directors

In August 2005, the Delaware Chancery Court issued its long-awaited decision *In re The Walt Disney Company Derivative Litigation (Disney III)*.[30] Although the court starkly expressed its disapproval of nearly every aspect of the Disney directors' actions, it eventually found in favor of all of the directors on all counts. If you have time for only a one-paragraph summary, it is:

> "For the future, many lessons of what not to do can be learned from defendants' conduct here. Nevertheless, I conclude that the only reasonable application of the law to the facts as I have found them, is that the defendants did not act in bad faith, and were at most ordinarily negligent, in connection with the hiring of Ovitz and the approval of the [original employment agreement]. In

---

[30] *In re The Walt Disney Company Derivative Litigation*, Del. C.A. No. 15452, Chandler, 35 EBC 1705 (Del. Ch. August 9, 2005).

accordance with the business judgment rule (because, as it turns out, business judgment *was* exercised), ordinary negligence is insufficient to constitute a violation of the fiduciary duty of care."

If you wonder what I mean by "Holds its Nose," consider the following:

"Despite all of the legitimate criticisms that may be leveled at Mr. Eisner, especially for having enthroned himself as the omnipotent and infallible monarch of his personal Magic Kingdom . . . "

Some commentators characterized the *Disney III* decision as a setback for those persons and entities pushing for better corporate governance practices in the area of executive compensation. This is not accurate, except in the limited sense that a board (or compensation committee) that is bent on ignoring good governance and best practices might be able to look to the *Disney III* decision for some cover.

Moreover, accepting this characterization could be very dangerous for directors and their counsel, who instead should be alert to the distinct possibility that the *Disney* cases, the attention surrounding them, and the best practices that have developed since the Disney board's actions in 1996, have acted as a catalyst for setting new standards. As we have seen in the development of case law in many other areas over the years, yesterday's "ordinary negligence" can develop into tomorrow's "bad faith." That is, courts could hold the board actions of today and in the future to a higher standard, based on the lessons directors should have learned from *Disney*.

Finally, even though the Delaware Chancery Court found the directors not liable, keep in mind that the financial costs of this trial certainly approach and may have exceeded the limits of the directors and officers liability insurance policy. Of course, the cost of this matter in time and bad publicity is incalculable.

The Delaware courts often take great pains to provide guidance to companies and other potential litigants as to how to improve governance procedures in the future (note the 25 specific items in the Delaware Chancery Court's 2003 decision (*Disney II*) described above). This decision is another good example of that tendency, a fact that the court acknowledges in it opinion:

Are there many aspects of Ovitz's hiring that reflect the absence of ideal corporate governance? Certainly, and I hope that this case will serve to inform stockholders, directors and officers of how the Company's fiduciaries underperformed. As I stated earlier, however, the standards used to measure the conduct of fiduciaries under Delaware law are not the same standards used in determining good corporate governance. (p. 161)

Director Independence (or the Lack Thereof) at The Walt Disney Company

The *Disney III* decision makes the following observations about the board's independence:

This dichotomy places the Court in a somewhat awkward position. By virtue of his Machiavellian (and imperial) nature as CEO, and his control over Ovitz's hiring in particular, Eisner to a large extent is responsible for the failings in process that infected and handicapped the board's decision-making abilities. Eisner stacked his (and I intentionally write "his" as opposed to "the Company's") board of directors with friends and other acquaintances who, though not necessarily beholden to him in a legal sense, were certainly more willing to accede to his wishes and support him unconditionally than truly independent directors. On the other hand, I do not believe that the evidence, considered fairly, demonstrates that Eisner actively took steps to defeat or short-circuit a decision-making process that would otherwise have occurred.

Nevertheless, the board's collective kowtowing in regard to Ovitz's hiring is also due to Eisner's desire to surround himself with yes men. *See* 3845:20-3847:3 (Gold) (testifying that he believes that Bowers, Poitier, Stern, Watson and Mitchell are not competent as board members). As examples of Eisner's success at surrounding himself with non-employee directors who would have sycophantic tendencies: Russell was Eisner's personal attorney, Tr. 2650:10-2651:7; Mitchell was hand-selected by Eisner to serve on the board, Tr. 5627:18-5628:2, and now serves as chairman, a position which provides Mitchell with substantial remuneration worth about $500,000 annually, Tr. 5629:9-24, Reveta Bowers is an administrator of a private school in West Hollywood, California, Tr. 5901:11-5903:9, that was attended by three of Eisner's children, Tr. 5944:24-5945:8; and to which Eisner and entities related to the Company have made substantial contributions, Tr. 5945-9-5947-16; O'Donovan was president of Georgetown University from 1989 to 2001, Tr. 6710:7-6711:15, (Eisner served on Georgetown University's board of directors from 1985 to 1991, Tr. 6712:16-24) where Eisner's son attended college until 1992, Tr 6712:16-6713:3, and to which Eisner made a $1 million donation in 1996 at O'Donovan's request, Tr. 6713:4-16.

Corporate Waste

Regarding plaintiffs' claim the payments to Ovitz were so excessive as to constitute corporate "waste," the *Disney III* court observed, "the standard for waste is a very high one that is difficult to meet." The court concluded that:

> As a result, terminating Ovitz and paying the [no fault termination] did not constitute waste because he could not be terminated for cause and because many of the defendants gave credible testimony that the Company would be better off without Ovitz, meaning that it would be impossible for me to conclude that the termination and receipt of NFT benefits resulted in "an exchange that is so one sided that no business person of ordinary, sound judgment could conclude that the company has received adequate considera- tion, or a situation where the defendants have irrationally squander[ed] or give[n] away corporate assets. In other words, defendants did not commit waste.

CEO's Fiduciary Duties

Among the many reasons we traditionally cite for following good govern- ance practices in setting CEO compensation is that the CEO (usually) is also a member of the board subject to potential liability for excessive compensation. In absolving Michael Ovitz from potential personal liability for the Disney board's decision to pay him $140 million in severance for one undistinguished year of service, the *Disney III* court had this to say about Ovitz's fiduciary responsibilities:

> Ovitz did not breach his fiduciary duty of loyalty by receiving the [no fault termination] payment because he played no part in the decisions: (1) to be terminated and (2) that the termination would not be for cause under the [original employment agreement]. Ovitz did possess fiduciary duties as a director and officer while these decisions were made, but by not improperly

interjecting himself into the corporation's decision making process nor manipulating that process, he did not breach the fiduciary duties he possessed in that unique circumstance. Furthermore, Ovitz did not "engage" in a transaction with the corporation—rather, the corporation imposed an unwanted transaction upon him.

Once Ovitz was terminated without cause (as a result of decisions made entirely without input or influence from Ovitz), he was contractually entitled without any negotiation or action on his part, to receive the benefits provided by the [original employment agreement] for a termination without cause, benefits for which he negotiated at arms-length *before* becoming a fiduciary. No reasonably prudent fiduciary in Ovitz's position would have unilaterally determined to call a board meeting to force the corporation's chief executive officer to reconsider his termination and the terms thereof, with that reconsideration for the benefit of shareholders and potentially to Ovitz' detriment.

In-House Counsel

Like Dante Alighieri's *The Inferno*, the *Disney III* opinion spares no one in its criticism of the process by which Ovitz was hired and fired (the various parties are just assigned to different circles of Hell). Regarding the role of Disney's in-house counsel, Sanford Litvack, the court tartly observed the following:

I do not intend to imply by these conclusions that Litvack was an infallible source of legal knowledge. Nevertheless, Litvack's less astute moments as a legal counsel do not impugn his good faith or preparedness in reaching his conclusions with respect to whether Ovitz could have been terminated for cause and whether board action was necessary to effectuate Ovitz's termination, as I have independently analyzed the record and conclude that Litvack's decisions as to those questions were correct. First, Litvack's silence at the December 10, 1996 EPPC meeting, when Russell informed the committee that Ovitz's bonus was contractually required, was unquestionably curious, and some might even call it irresponsible. His excuse that he did not want to embarrass Russell in front of the committee is, in a word, pathetic. Litvack should have exercised better judgment than to allow Russell to convince the committee that a $7.5 million bonus was contractually required. Luckily for Litvack, no harm was done because in the end Ovitz's bonus was rescinded.

However, the court concluded that Mr. Litvack gave the "proper advice and reached the proper conclusions when it was necessary," and he "was adequately informed in his decisions, and he acted in good faith for what he believed were the best interests of the Company." Again, although the court properly absolves this defendant of liability, it takes great pains to provide guidance to companies and other potential litigants as to how to improve governance procedures in the future.

.10 Final Round in the *Disney* Case: Delaware Supreme Court Upholds the Ruling for the Disney Directors

In June 2006, the Delaware Supreme Court unanimously affirmed the ruling by the Delaware Court of Chancery that the members of Walt Disney Co.'s board of directors did not breach their fiduciary duties in the Michael Ovitz employment and severance matter.[31] Although somewhat anticlimactic, the decision

---

[31] *In re Walt Disney Co. Derivative Litigation*, Del., No. 411, 2005 (June 8, 2006).

solidly supported Disney directors and strongly reaffirmed the business judgment rule. The court went so far as to indicate that directors' failure to inform themselves of material facts does not constitute bad faith.

Challenging a board decision is still difficult. The business judgment rule still stands as a very high hurdle to finding liability. However, directors and their counsel should be careful to learn the right lessons from the *Disney* cases. The board actions of today and in the future could be held to a higher standard, based on the lessons directors should have learned from *Disney I-IV*. The source for the warning is none other than Chancellor Chandler's Introduction to his opinion, which states:

> "Recognizing the protean nature of ideal corporate governance practices, particularly over an era that has included the Enron and WorldCom debacles, and the resulting legislative focus on corporate governance, it is perhaps worth pointing out that the actions (and the failures to act) of the Disney board that gave rise to this lawsuit took place ten years ago, and that applying 21st century notions of best practices in analyzing whether those decisions were actionable would be misplaced."

The best reading of this statement seems to be that applying "21st century notions of best practices" to the facts of this case might have produced a different result, *e.g.*, a decision against the directors. Thus, directors should learn two equally important lessons from the *Disney* case. First, the courts will not punish directors for taking reasonable risks. To do so would risk pushing American business innovation offshore. The second lesson, however, is that process counts. Appearances count. Most well-intentioned directors will see the *Disney* cases as a stern reminder that executive compensation decisions carry with them the potential for liability.

.11 Courts Take a Harder Line Since *Disney*

In 2016, the Delaware Court of Chancery issued an opinion on a Section 220 books and records demand made against Yahoo! In *Amalgamated Bank v. YA-HOO!*,[32] the facts were almost as damning as in *Disney*, as even the court itself observed:

> Mark Twain is often credited (perhaps erroneously) with observing that history may not repeat itself, but it often rhymes. The credible basis for concern about wrongdoing at Yahoo evokes the *Disney* case, with the details updated for a twenty-first century, New Economy company. Like the current scenario, *Disney* involved a CEO hiring a number-two executive for munificent compensation, poor performance by the number-two executive, and a no-fault termination after approximately a year on the job that conferred dynastic wealth on the executive under circumstances where a for-cause termination could have been justified. Certainly there are factual distinctions, but the assonance is there.

While the decision only involved the disclosure of books and records, and did not face the question of whether the Yahoo! directors breached their fiduciary duties, the Vice Chancellor observed:

---

[32] (Del.Chan.Ct., February 2, 2016.)

Based on the current record, the Yahoo directors were more involved in the hiring than the Disney directors were, but the facts still bear a close resemblance to the allegations in Disney III. The directors' involvement appears to have been tangential and episodic, and they seem to have accepted Mayer's statements uncritically. A board cannot mindlessly swallow information, particularly in the area of executive compensation: _While there may be instances in which a board may act with deference to corporate officers' judgments, executive compensation is not one of those instances. The board must exercise its own business judgment in approving an executive compensation transaction. . . . Directors who choose not to ask questions take the risk that they may have to provide explanations later, or at least produce explanatory books and records as part of a Section 220 investigation.

Until 2018, no court had decided in favor of plaintiffs alleging that the payment of executive compensation was a breach of fiduciary duty for a waste of corporate assets. The reason is that [in the face of the business judgment rule] corporate waste is very difficult to prove. In *Feuer v. Redstone*,[33] the Delaware Chancery Court allowed plaintiffs to continue with their stockholder derivative claims against the board of CBS Corporation.

This court has commented many times on the difficulty of pleading a viable claim for waste against a corporate director under our law. But the particularized allegations of the complaint here depict an extreme factual scenario—one sufficiently severe so as to excuse plaintiff from having to make a demand on the CBS board of directors to press claims concerning certain (but not all) of the challenged payments, and to permit plaintiff to take discovery so that an evidentiary record may be developed before the court adjudicates whether those payments were made in accordance with the directors' fiduciary duties.

In 2016, stockholders of Viacom had filed a class action securities derivative suit in the Delaware Chancery Court against certain officers and directors of Viacom alleging that those individuals breached their fiduciary duties (among other causes of action) regarding the $13 million of compensation Viacom paid to its founder and then Chairman (Sumner Redstone) from July 2014 to May 2016. The lawsuit alleged that the board members approved these payments despite the fact that they knew that Redstone was incapacitated and incapable of doing his job.

Throughout the relevant period, the compensation committee was responsible for setting the level of Redstone's compensation as CBS's Chairman of the Board. This is reflected in the compensation committee's charter, which provides that the compensation committee shall:

Review and approve corporate goals and objectives relevant to the compensation of the Chairman of the Board and the Chief Executive Officer. Together with the Nominating and Governance Committee, evaluate annually the performances of the Chairman and the Chief Executive Officer in light of these goals and objectives and report the results of the evaluations to the non-management directors. *The Committee shall set the compensation levels of the Chairman and the Chief Executive Officer taking into account the evaluations.* [Emphasis in original]

---

[33] C.A. No. 12575-CB (Del.Chan., April 19, 2018).

The compensation committee approved a set of goals for Redstone for 2014 that included being "a sounding-board/counselor to [the] CEO on issues of strategic importance," ensuring that "strategic plans are up-to-date" and "being executed on," providing "effective communications with [the] Board," and assisting "the Board in maintaining best governance practices." Not long after these goals were set, beginning in the spring of 2014, Redstone suffered from "a precipitous decline in his physical health" according to a complaint in an elder abuse lawsuit filed on Redstone's behalf in 2016 (the "Elder Abuse Complaint").

Additionally, Redstone's employment agreement expressly required him to "be actively engaged" in performing certain specified duties. The court devoted two full pages of its opinion to listing facts and information "demonstrating that it should have been abundantly clear to the members of the Board—from their attendance at Board meetings, press publicity, and other interactions with the Company—that far from being 'actively engaged' in the CBS's affairs, Redstone was providing no meaningful services to the Company beginning at some point in the latter part of 2014 or in 2015." During and after that period, CBS paid Mr. Redstone more than $13 million, most of it in performance bonuses.

Note that this is far from a complete victory for plaintiffs. The decision only allows the plaintiffs to continue to trial with their lawsuit. But no allegations of compensation being corporate waste have made it this far in more than 30 years.

.12 Stockholder Ratification

Stockholder approval of executive compensation, whether or not required under the securities law or the tax code may allow a company to gain Rule 12(b)(6) dismissal of claims of breach of the duty of loyalty.[34] Courts have found that a board of directors may immunize itself from litigation involving violations of the duty of care or loyalty by having the stockholders ratify any questionable transaction.[35] While stockholder ratification is a wise practice, neither Delaware law, the Model Business Corporation Act, nor SEC Rule 16b-3 require that stockholders ratify a stock option plan.[36] In comparison, the New York Business Corporation Law Section 505(d) "requires that any issuance of options be approved by a majority vote to the stockholders."[37]

Even though stockholder ratification can usually cure breaches of fiduciary duty, it cannot cure all actions of corporate waste. In *Steiner v. Meyerson*, the court noted that "[s]tockholders' ratification of voidable acts of directors is effective for all purposes unless the action of the directors constituted a gift of corporate assets to themselves or was *ultra vires*, illegal, or fraudulent."[38]

---

[34] See e.g., *Steiner v. Meyerson*, 1995 Del. Ch. LEXIS 95 (Del. Ch. 1995).

[35] *Lewis v. Vogelstein*, 699 A2d 327, 336 (Del. Ch. 1997).

[36] Richard H. Wagner & Catherine G. Wagner, Recent Developments in Executive, Director, and Employee Stock Compensation Plans: New Concerns for Corporate Directors, 3 Stan. J.L. Bus. & Fin. 5, 12-14 (1997).

[37] N.Y. Bus. Corp. Law § 505(d).

[38] *Steiner v. Meyerson*, 1995 Del. Ch. LEXIS 95 (Del. Ch. 1995).

.13 Executive Compensation for Past Performance

Generally, retroactive compensation is prohibited. However, compensation may be granted for past services where an implied contract was shown, or where the amount awarded is not unreasonable in view of the services rendered.[39] In *Zupnick v. Goizueta*, the court held that Coca-Cola's action in granting its CEO, Roberto Goizueta, one million stock options based "on the substantial performance of the Company . . . and remarkable increase in market value of the Company during this period (nearly $69 billion)" was a valid exercise of the board's business judgment.[40] The court determined that reasonable, disinterested directors properly concluded that the CEO's past services resulted in such an extraordinary benefit to the company, that, as a matter of law, the situation fell into the recognized exception to the common law rule that usually prohibits retroactive executive compensation.

Similarly, in *Lewis v. Akers*,[41] the IBM board of directors voted to pay the CEO, John F. Akers, $925,000 in recognition of his years of service to the company and $2.5 million as part of a retirement incentive program, as well as to accelerate the vesting of his stock options. There, the court held that the trial court properly dismissed the complaint for failure to state a cause of action because the plaintiffs did not allege with the required particularity that the compensation granted to Akers lacked a legitimate business purpose or was the product of fraud, bad faith or a conflict of interest.[42]

.14 Reliance on a Compensation Expert

Delaware Corporate Law expressly enables the board of directors to rely on outside experts when making business decisions and provides them shelter from liability when they do so. 8 *Del.C.* § 141(e) reads:

> A member of the board of directors . . . shall in the performance of such member's duties be fully protected in relying in good faith upon . . . information, opinions, reports or statements presented to the corporation by . . . any other person as to matters the member reasonably believes are within such other person's professional or expert competence and who has been selected with reasonable care by or on behalf of the corporation.[43]

In *Brehm* (Disney I), the court held that when a company has been advised by an expert, a derivative action challenging the transaction is ripe for summary judgment unless the complaint alleges particularized facts (not conclusions) that:

- The directors did not in fact rely on the expert;

- Their reliance was not in good faith;

- They did not reasonably believe that the expert's advice was within the expert's professional competence;

---

[39] *Zupnick v. Goizueta*, 698 A2d 384 (Del. Ch. 1997).

[40] *Zupnick v. Goizueta*, 698 A2d 384, 385 (Del. Ch. 1997).

[41] *Lewis v. Akers*, 227 A.D.2d 595, 644 N.Y.S.2d 279 (N.Y.A.D. 1996).

[42] *Lewis v. Akers*, 227 A.D.2d 595, 596, 644 N.Y.S.2d 279 (N.Y.A.D. 1996).

[43] 8 Del.C. § 141(e).

- The expert was not selected with reasonable care by or on behalf of the company, and the faulty selection process was attributable to the directors;
- The subject matter that was material and reasonably available was so obvious that the board's failure to consider it was grossly negligent regardless of the expert's advice or lack of advice; or
- That the decision of the board was so unconscionable as to constitute waste or fraud.[44]

Thus, even if a plaintiff can evade the pleading challenges of the demand requirement and the business judgment rule, if the board has relied in good faith on a compensation expert, their cause of action will almost certainly be doomed by Section 141(e).

Interestingly, although the compensation consultant used by the Disney board characterized his own role as nothing more than a "high-priced calculator" (*Disney III*), the court gave the board significant credit for having sought and considered an independent expert opinion.

> "Regarding the consultant's role, the Court also notes that although Crystal testified that he viewed his role as nothing more than a 'high-priced calculator,' nothing in the record suggests the compensation committee placed such a restriction on Crystal's work or analysis of the [original employment agreement] . . . . In the parts of the record just cited, Crystal laments that the compensation committee did not follow his recommendations. I believe it is important to understand that the compensation committee relied in good faith on Crystal's report and analysis even though they chose not to follow Crystal's recommendations to the letter. The role of experts under §141(e) is to assist the board's decision making—not supplant it. An interpretation of §141(e) that would require boards to follow the advice of experts (substantially? completely? in part?) before being able to claim reliance on those experts would be in conflict with the mandate in §141(a) that the company is to be managed "by or under the direction of a board of directors."

Directors, officers, and their advisers need to get beyond the astonishing dollar signs ($140 million in severance) and judicial flair ("Mr. Eisner, . . . having enthroned himself as the omnipotent and infallible monarch of his personal Magic Kingdom . . . ") and absorb the critical lessons from the Disney case. One of these lessons is that the courts still favor the use of independent experts.

.15 Avoiding Traps When Negotiating Compensation Arrangements

A compensation committee should review and understand, with the help of someone from the company's executive compensation group, a compensation consultant, and/or outside counsel, each element of the CEO's compensation. The committee also should analyze how various scenarios (*i.e.*, change in control, termination without cause, termination for cause) would affect that compensation. The "tally sheet" approach for the review and reporting of the CEO's compensation is a good one.

---

[44] *Brehm v. Eisner*, 746 A2d 244, 262 (Del. 2000).

Regarding annual incentive compensation, the committee must ensure that it understands and approves (i) the precise metrics/objectives used in the formula, (ii) why these objectives are appropriate, and (iii) how achievement of the objectives will lead (or have led) directly to the amount paid.

Among the most common traps in negotiating and drafting CEO compensation agreements are the following:

- Insufficient analysis of surveys and peer group information (compensation and performance data), and internal factors.

- Failure to price out value to executive, and cost to company, of long-term incentives, severance, SERP benefits, etc., under likely and possible scenarios (including termination due to poor performance).

- Ignoring the potential effects of provisions that base severance or retirement payouts on other compensation (*e.g.*, ripple impact of above-target bonuses).

- Inattention to items often poorly disclosed in proxy statements under current rules (cumulative deferred compensation, SERPs, perquisites).

- Defining "cause" too narrowly; "good reason" too broadly.

- Agreements should provide for little or no payments to executives in the event of a termination for "cause." (See, Ovitz, Cendant, Gemstar/TV Guide, Computer Associates, Aramony.)

- How to address internal investigation scenarios (failure to cooperate, impact of suspension). Other misconduct that may or may not be criminal.

- Address how to handle restatements of earnings, *etc.*, previously certified by the CEO and CFO in terms of impact of same on previously awarded annual bonuses and other incentives paid to the CEO, CFO and other senior executives directly involved.

- Golden parachute agreement issues: single trigger parachutes, size of multiples, scope of compensation included in multiples, cost of gross-ups, triggering of protection even if deal collapses.

.16 Corporate Law of Other States

Delaware is the most popular state of incorporation for both public and private companies. Sixty percent of the Fortune 500 companies are incorporated in Delaware. Moreover, most states have patterned their corporate law on Delaware law.

However, this section looks at another popular state of incorporation: Maryland. Maryland law imposes certain duties on the directors of a Maryland corporation. Section 2-405.1(a) of the Maryland General Corporate Law (MGCL) provides that a director shall perform his or her duties:

- In good faith;

- In a manner he reasonably believes to be in the best interests of the company; and

¶2125.16

- With the care that an ordinarily prudent person in a like position would use under similar circumstances.[45]

The failure by a director to satisfy any one of these statutory standards would constitute a breach of the director's fiduciary duties.

Good faith as applied to a director pursuant to MGCL §2-405.1(a)(1) is the absence of any desire to obtain a personal benefit or a benefit for some person other than the company.[46] "Good faith is generally synonymous with adherence to what is referred to in other states as the duty of loyalty or the duty of fair dealing."[47] The obligation of good faith includes a duty of candor with the stockholders to reveal to them all facts about important matters involving the company. This duty arises in order to provide stockholders with sufficient information, among other things, to decide how to vote in the election of directors and whether to continue to hold their shares or sell them.[48]

The "reasonable belief" requirement under MGCL §2-405.1(a)(2) means that there must be some rational basis for a director's action, that the director must have knowledge of that basis when taking such action and that the director must base his performance upon that knowledge.[49] Moreover, directors are required to act in a manner they reasonably believe to be "in the best interests of the corporation," rather than the best interests of any particular stockholder or group of stockholders.[50]

Finally, MGCL §2-405.1(a)(3) requires a director to act with the same care that an "ordinarily prudent person" would use in a "like position under similar circumstances." The principal focus of §2-405.1(a)(3) regarding directors executing their duties as a reasonably prudent person is on "the process by which the decision is made, not the wisdom of the decision or the results."[51] The process by which a director makes his decision will vary with the significance, complexity and other aspects of the decision. However, as a rule, board members should have available to them all information material to the decision and should have some opportunity to ask questions of management and to meet and evaluate the matter with other directors and management.

MGCL §2-405.2 allows a Maryland corporation to limit the recovery of damages from officers or directors for certain breaches of fiduciary duty. Experienced legal counsel will draft the Articles of Incorporation to provide the maximum protection to directors and officers permitted under Maryland law.

Example: ABC Corporation's outside counsel drafts ABC's Articles of Incorporation to provide that:

---

[45] MGCL §2-405.1(a).

[46] See *Yost v. Early*, 589 A2d 1291, 1298 (Md. App. 1991).

[47] James J. Hanks, Jr., Maryland Corporation Law §6.6(b) (Aspen 2001).

[48] James J. Hanks, Jr., Maryland Corporation Law §6.6(b) (Aspen 2001).

[49] *Martin Marietta Corp. v. Bendix Corp.*, 549 F. Supp. 623, 633-34 (D. Md. 1982).

[50] *Werbowsky v. Collomb*, 766 A2d 123, 133 (Md. App. 2001).

[51] Hanks, Maryland Corporation Law §6.6(b) (Aspen 2001).

Directors and Officers, when acting in their capacities as Directors or Officers, shall not be liable for money damages to the Corporation or its Stockholders except to the extent (i) it is proven that the Director or Officer actually received an improper benefit or profit in money, property, or services, for the amount of the benefit or profit in money, property, or services actually received, or (ii) that a judgment or other final adjudication adverse to the Director or Officer is entered in a proceeding based on a finding in the proceeding that the Director's or Officer's action, or failure to act, was the result of active and deliberate dishonesty and was material to the cause of action adjudicated in the proceeding.

¶2135 Stockholder Approval Requirements

When companies grant their officers and directors equity compensation, the company must obtain stockholder approval under certain circumstances. Specifically, there are four main reasons that companies seek stockholder approval of such stock issuances:

- To satisfy the stock exchange listing requirements of the NYSE and the Nasdaq;
- To receive protection from Section 16(b) of the Exchange Act;
- To comply with Code Sec. 422 for incentive stock option plans; and
- Prior to the TCJA changes, to receive protection from Code Sec. 162(m).

.01 Protection from Section 16(b) of the Securities Exchange Act of 1934

Companies seek stockholder approval of equity compensation plans in order to protect themselves from Section 16(b) of the Exchange Act.[52] Section 16(b) prohibits senior officers and directors from retaining any profits realized from a short-swing sale of company stock within a period of six months. The purpose of that law is to deter insiders, including officers and directors, from trading company securities when they possessed material information that was not available to other investors.

However, the 1996 Securities and Exchange Commission Rule 16b-3 provides an exemption to Section 16(b).[53] Rule 16b-3 exempts "any transaction involving a grant, award, or other acquisition from the issuer," except certain discretionary transactions, if certain approval requirements are satisfied.[54] Specifically, Rule 16b-3 exempts a transaction if the stockholders approve it.[55] Stockholder approval must be obtained pursuant to Section 14 of the Exchange Act, by either the majority of the stockholders present, represented, or entitled to vote at a meeting or by the written consent of a majority of the stockholders entitled to vote, provided that the transaction is approved before the next annual meeting.[56] However, stockholder approval is effective only if the stockholders approve each

---

[52] 15 U.S.C. §78p(b).

[53] 17 C.F.R. §240.16b-1 et seq.

[54] 17 C.F.R. §240.16b-3(d).

[55] 17 C.F.R. §240.16b-3(d)(2).

[56] 17 C.F.R. §240.16b-3(d)(2).

award individually, although approval of an entire plan will suffice if the awards are granted under a discretionary formula plan. Nonetheless, it is worth noting that equity compensation plans can still be exempt from Section 16(b) even without stockholder approval, provided either a reporting person holds the equity securities for at least six months after the grant date or the transaction is approved by the board of directors of a committee composed of "non-employee directors."[57] Therefore, stockholder approval is simply one way to receive protection from Section 16(b).

.02 Protection from Code Sec. 162(m)

Prior to 2018, companies sought stockholder approval for certain equity compensation awards made to directors and officers in order to qualify for the performance-based compensation exception to Code Sec. 162(m).[58] In order to qualify for the exception, a company had to disclose and obtain stockholder approval of the material terms of the performance goals under the plan.[59] If the company were to later amend any of the performance goals under the plan, the rule would require the company to resubmit the plan for stockholder approval.

.03 Compliance with Code Sec. 422 for Incentive Stock Options

Companies also seek stockholder approval of equity compensation plans in order to comply with Code Sec. 422 in implementing an incentive stock option plan ("ISO"), which consequently enables them to receive favorable treatment of those ISOs.[60] An ISO, as defined in Code Sec. 422, is an option to purchase stock, which a company grants to an employee in connection with his or her employment by the company.[61] However, before a stock option can qualify as an ISO under Code Sec. 422, a company is required to obtain its stockholders' approval of the plan granting ISOs within 12 months before or after the board of directors has adopted the plan.[62] The board of directors could grant an ISO before stockholders approve the plan, if no exercises under the plan are permitted until it is actually approved by the stockholders.

.04 Elimination of Discretionary Voting by Brokers on Executive Compensation Proposals

Section 957 of the Dodd-Frank Act amended Section 6(b) of the Exchange Act to require that national securities exchanges prohibit brokers from voting shares they do not beneficially own in connection with:

- the election of directors,
- executive compensation, and
- any other significant matter, as determined by the SEC,

unless the beneficial owner of the security has instructed the broker to vote the proxy in accordance with the voting instructions of the beneficial owner.

---

[57] See 17 C.F.R. §240.16b-3(d)(1), 17 C.F.R. §240.16b-3(d)(3).
[58] Code Sec. 162(m).
[59] Code Sec. 162(m)(4)(C).
[60] Code Sec. 422.
[61] Code Sec. 422(b).
[62] Code Sec. 422(b)(1).

Previously, the approval of equity plans were "non-routine matters" upon which brokers were not permitted to vote uninstructed shares. In 2009, the NYSE amended its Rule 452 to eliminate broker voting of uninstructed shares in uncontested director elections.

Inasmuch as every public company has some portion of its outstanding equity securities held in "street name" on behalf of their beneficial owners, this provision affected all public companies. The most immediate effect of this provision was the elimination of broker voting of uninstructed shares in the votes required by Section 951 of the Dodd-Frank Act, including:

- the advisory vote on executive compensation (Say on Pay),
- the vote on the frequency of the advisory vote, and
- the advisory vote on golden parachutes.

Stockholder votes on these matters join the approval of equity plans as non-routine matters upon which brokers are not permitted to vote uninstructed shares. It remains to be seen what other executive compensation matters the SEC will determine to be "any other significant matter" for which broker voting of uninstructed shares is prohibited.

Section 957 was effective on enactment, so any exchange rules inconsistent with its requirements are no longer applicable. Companies should step-up their efforts to reach-out to stockholders to explain their compensation programs and encourage them to vote their proxies.

¶2145 Stock Exchange Listing Requirements

Another reason for seeking stockholder approval for stock issuances to officers and directors is to comply with the stock exchange listing requirements of the NYSE and Nasdaq. While both exchanges have similar requirements, they do differ in some important respects.

.01 NYSE and Nasdaq Stockholder Approval Requirements

Both the NYSE and Nasdaq have long required member companies to obtain stockholder approval for stock options and other equity compensation in which officers and directors may acquire company stock.[63]

Equity Compensation Plans. The rules require domestic-listed companies to obtain stockholder approval for all equity compensation plans and any material revisions to such plans, with very limited exceptions. An equity compensation plan is a plan or arrangement that provides for the delivery of equity securities as compensation for services to any employee, director or other service provider. The rules, however, specifically note that compensatory grants that are not made under a "plan" (i.e., individual awards or stand-alone option agreements) are still subject to stockholder approval. Under the rules, the following are not "equity compensation plans" and hence not subject to the stockholder approval requirement:

---

[63] See Section 312.03(a) of the NYSE Listed Company Manual.

- Arrangements under which employees receive cash payments based on the value of shares, rather than actual shares (*e.g.*, cash-settled phantom stock);

- Arrangements that are made available to stockholders generally (such as a typical dividend reinvestment plan); and

- Arrangements that merely provide a convenient way for employees, directors or other service providers to purchase stock at fair market value.[64]

Exemptions. The rules provide exemptions from the stockholder approval requirement for the following types of arrangements:

- Plans intended to qualify under Code Sec. 401(a) or Code Sec. 423;

- "Parallel excess plans"—a narrowly defined category of excess benefit plans;[65]

- Equity grants made as a material inducement to a person's becoming an employee of the issuer or any of its subsidiaries;[66]

- The rollover of options and other equity awards in connection with a merger or acquisition; and

- Post-acquisition grants, to those who are not employees of the acquiring company at the time of acquisition, of shares remaining under a target company plan that had been approved by the target's stockholders.[67]

The rules require that listed companies notify the NYSE or Nasdaq in writing when using one of these exemptions. A grant, adoption, or revision of a plan that would require stockholder approval but for the availability of one of these exemptions must be approved by the company's independent compensation committee or a majority of all of the company's independent directors.

Nasdaq Rule 4350(i)(1)(A) requires that a Nasdaq listed company seek stockholder approval when it establishes or materially amends a stock option or purchase plan or other arrangement pursuant to which stock may be acquired by officers, directors, employees or consultants.[68] This includes any sale of securities at a discount to the market value to an officer, director, employee, or consultant, even if part of a larger financing transaction. There is no exception for *de minimis* issuances under Rule 4350(i)(1)(A). The rule requires stockholder approval when-

---

[64] The rules clarify that a plan can fall into this category regardless of whether (a) shares are delivered immediately or on a deferred basis, and (b) the payments for the shares are made directly or by foregoing compensation otherwise due (*i.e.*, via payroll deductions).

[65] The exemption in the rules is even narrower than the "parallel nonqualified plan" concept originally proposed, as it requires that no participant in the plan receive employer equity contributions under the plan in excess of 25% of the participant's cash compensation.

[66] The rules clarify that the exemption covers grants to new employees in connection with a

merger or acquisition. In addition, the rules add the requirement that listed companies issue an explanatory press release promptly following the grant of any inducement award in reliance on the exemption.

[67] Use of such share reserves in connection with the transaction will be counted by the NYSE in determining whether the transaction must receive stockholder approval as an issuance of 20% or more of the company's outstanding common stock.

[68] http://www.nasdaq.com/about/FAQsCorpGov.stm#cg12.

ever the company establishes or materially amends a stock option or purchase plan or other arrangement pursuant to which stock may be acquired by officers, directors, employees, or consultants. Additionally, the fact that shares will be issued from the company's treasury or repurchased shares has no impact on the analysis of whether stockholder approval is required under the rule. Such shares are subject to the rule.

A company may adopt an equity plan or arrangement, and grant options (but not shares of stock) under the plan, before obtaining stockholder approval, provided that: (i) no options can be exercised prior to obtaining stockholder approval and (ii) the plan can be unwound, and the outstanding options cancelled, if stockholder approval is not obtained. However, a company may not grant restricted stock awards subject to obtaining subsequent stockholder approval.

Generally, stockholder approval is not required of plans or arrangements that are in place at the time of a company's listing on Nasdaq. Stockholder approval is required, however, for any material amendment to such plans after listing. In addition, if the plan contains an evergreen provision, the plan cannot have a term in excess of ten years unless stockholder approval is obtained every ten years as set forth in IM-4350-5.

Formula and evergreen plans cannot have a term in excess of ten years unless stockholder approval is obtained every ten years. Plans that do not contain a formula and do not impose a limit on the number of shares available for grant would require stockholder approval of each grant under the plan. The Nasdaq rules define a formula plan as a plan that provides for automatic grants pursuant to a formula. Examples include restricted stock grants based on a certain dollar amount and/or matching stock contributions based on the amount of compensation a participant elects to defer. The Nasdaq rules define an evergreen plan as a plan that contains a formula for the automatic increase in the number of shares available under the plan.

Material Revisions. The rules offer a nonexclusive list of those revisions that the NYSE will deem "material" and therefore cannot be effected without stockholder approval. For example, stockholder approval is required for any action that:

- Materially increases the number of shares available under the plan (except those made solely to reflect a reorganization, stock split, merger, spin-off, or similar transaction). An automatic increase in the number of shares available under a plan pursuant to an "evergreen" formula is not considered a modification under the rules so long as the plan term does not exceed ten years;

- Expands the types of awards available under the plan;

- Materially expands the class of persons eligible to participate in the plan;

- Materially extends the term of the plan;

¶2145.01

- Materially changes the method of determining the strike price of options under the plan;[69] or

- Deletes or limits a prohibition on option repricing (or actually reprices options issued under a plan that does not expressly permit repricing, even if the plan itself is not revised).

The rules also note that an amendment will not be considered a material revision if it curtails, rather than expands, the scope of the plan.

Under the Nasdaq rules, a "material" amendment includes, but is not limited to, the following:[70]

- any material increase in the number of shares to be issued under the plan (other than to reflect a reorganization, stock split, merger, spin-off or similar transaction);

- any material increase in benefits to participants, including any material change to: (i) permit a repricing (or decrease in exercise price) of outstanding options, (ii) reduce the price at which shares or options to purchase shares may be offered, or (iii) extend the duration of a plan;

- any material expansion of the class of participants eligible to participate in the plan; and

- any expansion in the types of options or awards provided under the plan.

While general authority to amend a plan would not obviate the need for stockholder approval, if a plan permits a specific action without further stockholder approval, then no such approval would generally be required. In that regard, absent specific authorization in the plan, a repricing, or a similar action, would not be permitted without stockholder approval.

Planning Note: Counsel should design any stock incentive plans so that it may change the terms of grants without having to amend the plan in a manner that may require stockholder approval. Counsel should seek to be over inclusive when describing the class of eligible plan participants (for example, by not limiting eligibility to key employees), the powers of the compensation committee under the plan, and the types of awards granted under the plan.

.02 NYSE Corporate Governance Rules

The NYSE maintains SEC-approved corporate governance standards for listed companies.[71] The standards give more weight to independent directors, who must comprise a majority of the company's board. Additionally, the NYSE rules include a definition of independence, requiring an independent director to have no material relationship with the listed company as an executive director, officer, or stockholder.

---

[69] The NYSE commented that a "change in the method of determining fair market value; from the closing price on the date of grant to the average of the high and low price on the date of grant" will not be considered material.

[70] As set forth in IM-4350-5.

[71] SEC Release No. 34-48745.

The rules provide that the audit committee will have the sole authority to hire and fire independent auditors and to approve any significant nonauditing relationship with the independent auditors. Moreover, the role of the audit committee would be contained in a written charter and the committee would be responsible for reviewing a report by the independent auditor describing the firm's internal quality control procedures and any material issues raised by the most recent internal audit. Finally, and perhaps most importantly, the audit committee would be required to meet separately at least every quarter with management, internal auditors, and the company's independent auditors.

In conjunction with the stockholder-approval issue, the NYSE rules address numerous other compensation-related issues. The rules require that listed companies maintain a compensation committee composed solely of independent directors. The compensation committee would also be required to have a formal written charter that addresses its purpose, duties, and responsibilities. Those duties and responsibilities must include implementing goals and objectives applicable to CEO compensation, evaluating a CEO's performance, and determining actual CEO payouts based upon performance. Moreover, the charter would also be expected to address committee member qualifications, the process for appointing and removing members, and provisions for the use of an outside compensation expert. Under these rules, listed companies will be required to adopt governance standards that historically have been only "best practice" recommendations.

¶2155 Disclosure to Stockholders

The SEC requires its registrants to comply with myriad disclosure rules in the SEC Form DEF 14A, Notice of Annual Shareholders Meeting and Definitive Proxy Statement, and also when granting equity compensation plans and equity securities available for future issuances. In August 2006, the SEC published final rules on Executive Compensation and Related Person Disclosure, the most sweeping and comprehensive revision of its disclosure rules since 1992.

The SEC requires public companies to disclose substantial information on stock plans in an Equity Compensation Plan Information table included in the company's annual reports on Form 10-K and 10-KSB, as well as in the proxy statements in years when they are submitting a compensation plan for stockholder approval. The table must disclose, separately for approved and nonapproved plans, (1) the number of securities to be issued upon exercise of outstanding options, warrants, and rights, (2) the weighted-average exercise price of outstanding (compensatory) options, warrants and rights, and (3) the number of securities remaining available for future issuance under all of the issuer's equity compensation plans. Thus, investors can simply look at a company's table in order to assess the impact that equity compensation plans may have on their own investments.

.01 Risk Assessment under the SEC's Executive Compensation Disclosure and Governance Rules

In December 2009, the SEC issued rules requiring each public company to assess whether its executive compensation plans encourage risk taking. The rules require a company to address its compensation policies and practices for all employees, including non-executive officers, if the compensation policies and practices create risks that are reasonably likely to have a material adverse effect on the company. This "reasonably likely" disclosure threshold parallels the Management Discussion and Analysis requirement, which requires risk-oriented disclosure of known trends and uncertainties that are material to the business. (Smaller reporting companies are not required to provide the risk assessment disclosure.)

The SEC believes that by focusing on risks that are "reasonably likely to have a material adverse effect" on the company, the rules are likely to elicit disclosure about incentives in the company's compensation policies that would be most relevant to investors, rather than burdening them with voluminous disclosure of potentially insignificant and unnecessarily speculative information. The rules also allow companies to consider mitigating or offsetting steps or controls designed to limit risks of certain compensation arrangements. If a company has compensation policies and practices for different groups that mitigate or balance incentives, it could consider these in deciding whether risks arising from the policies are reasonably likely to have a material adverse effect on the company as a whole.

The required risk assessment disclosure should be made in a separate paragraph, outside of the Compensation Discussion and Analysis ("CD&A"), since it would be potentially confusing to expand the CD&A beyond the named executive officers to include disclosure of the company's broader compensation policies for employees. Note also that a separate provision of the final rule requires a discussion of the board's role in risk oversight (see below).

The rule contains the "non-exclusive list" of situations where compensation programs may have the potential to raise material risks to companies, and examples of the types of issues that would be appropriate for a company to address, including compensation policies and practices:

- At a business unit of the company that carries a significant portion of the company's risk profile;
- At a business unit with compensation structured significantly differently than other units within the company;
- At a business unit that is significantly more profitable than others within the company;
- At a business unit where the compensation expense is a significant percentage of the unit's revenues; and
- That vary significantly from the overall risk and reward structure of the company, such as when bonuses are awarded upon accomplishment of a

task, while the income and risk to the company from the task extend over a significantly longer period of time.

The SEC's rules only require disclosure if the compensation policies create risks that are reasonably likely to have a material adverse effect on the company, and do not require a company to make an affirmative statement that it has determined that the risks arising from its compensation policies and practices are not reasonably likely to have a material adverse effect on the company. However, when the SEC gives examples of issues that could be important, the company should address those issues in its proxy statement, or it may receive a comment letter from the SEC staff.

Similarly, the SEC adopted illustrative examples of issues that would potentially be appropriate for a company to address, including:

- The general design philosophy of the company's compensation policies and practices for employees whose behavior would be most affected by the incentives established by the policies and practices, as such policies and practices that relate to or affect risk taking by those employees on behalf of the company, and the manner of their implementation;

- The company's risk assessment or incentive considerations, if any, in structuring its compensation policies and practices or in awarding and paying compensation;

- How the company's compensation policies and practices relate to the realization of risks resulting from the actions of employees in both the short term and the long term, such as through policies requiring clawbacks or imposing holding periods;

- The company's policies regarding adjustments to its compensation policies and practices to address changes in its risk profile;

- Material adjustments the company has made to its compensation policies and practices as a result of changes in its risk profile; and

- The extent to which the company monitors its compensation policies and practices to determine whether its risk management objectives are being met with respect to incentivizing its employees.

The SEC's rules also require companies to describe the board's role in the oversight of risk in the corporate governance disclosures section of the proxy statement. The SEC believes that risk oversight is a key competence of the board, and that additional disclosures would improve investor and stockholder understanding of the role of the board in the company's risk management practices. Companies face a variety of risks, including credit risk, liquidity risk, and operational risk. Disclosure about the board's involvement in the oversight of the risk management process should provide important information to investors about how a company perceives the role of its board and the relationship between the board and senior management in managing the material risks facing the company. This disclosure requirement gives companies the flexibility to describe how the board administers its risk oversight function, such as through the whole board, or through a separate risk committee or the audit committee, for example. Where relevant, companies should address whether the individuals who supervise the day-to-day risk management responsibilities report directly to the board as a whole or to a board committee or how the board or committee otherwise receives information from such individuals.

The SEC also requires each registered investment fund to provide disclosure about the board's role in risk oversight. Inasmuch as funds face a number of risks, including investment risk, compliance, and valuation, the SEC believes that additional disclosures would improve investor understanding of the role of the board in the fund's risk management practices.

.02 Enhanced Director and Nominee Disclosure

The SEC requires companies to disclose for each director and any nominee for director the particular experience, qualifications, attributes or skills that led the board to conclude that the person should serve as a director for the company. (The same disclosure, with respect to any nominee for director put forward by another proponent, would be required in the proxy soliciting materials of that proponent.) Companies must make this disclosure annually because the composition of the entire board is important information for voting decisions.

The rules do not require companies to disclose the specific experience, qualifications or skills that qualify a person to serve as a committee member. However, the rules provide that if the board chose an individual to be a director because of a particular qualification, attribute or experience related to service on a specific committee, such as the audit or compensation committee, then it should disclose this fact as part of the individual's qualifications to serve on the board.

The rules also require disclosure of any directorships at public companies or registered investment companies held by each director and nominee at any time during the past five years. The SEC believes that this disclosure will allow investors to better evaluate the relevance of a director's or nominee's past board experience, as well as professional or financial relationships that might pose potential conflicts of interest.

The rules require disclosure of legal proceedings involving directors, director nominees and executive officers within the past ten years, "as a means of providing investors with more extensive information regarding an individual's competence and character." The SEC believes that certain legal proceedings can reflect on an individual's competence and integrity to serve as a director, and that this disclosure provides investors with valuable information for assessing the competence, character and overall suitability of a director, nominee or executive officer.

Finally, the SEC's rules require companies to disclose whether, and if so, how, a nominating committee considers diversity in identifying nominees for director.[72] If the nominating committee (or the board) has a policy with regard to the consideration of diversity in identifying director nominees, the company

---

[72] Item 407(c) of Regulation S-K.

must disclose how this policy is implemented, as well as how the nominating committee (or the board) assesses the effectiveness of its policy. For purposes of this disclosure requirement, the SEC allows companies to define diversity in ways that they consider appropriate. The rules do not define diversity.

.03 Disclosures Regarding Compensation Consultants

The SEC's rules require disclosure about the fees paid to compensation consultants (and their affiliates) when the consultants played a role in determining or recommending the amount or form of executive and director compensation, and also provided additional services to the company.[73] In addition to the requirement under the current rule to describe the role of the compensation consultant in determining or recommending the amount or form of executive and director compensation, the rules require fee disclosure related to the retention of a compensation consultant under the following circumstances:

- If the board or compensation committee has engaged its own consultant to provide advice or recommendations on the amount or form of executive and director compensation, the final rule requires fee and related disclosure if the consultant (or any affiliate) provides other non-executive compensation consulting services to the company, provided the fees for the non-executive compensation consulting services exceed $120,000 during the company's fiscal year.

- The final rule also requires disclosure of whether the decision to engage the compensation consultant (or its affiliates) for non-executive compensation consulting services was made or recommended by management, and whether the board has approved these non-executive compensation consulting services provided by the compensation consultant.

- If the board has not engaged its own consultant, the final rule requires fee disclosures if there is a consultant (including affiliates) providing executive compensation consulting services and non-executive compensation consulting services to the company, only if the fees for the non-executive compensation consulting services exceed $120,000 during the company's fiscal year.

- If the board has its own consultant, the company need not provide fee and related disclosure for consultants that work with management (whether for only executive compensation consulting services or for both executive compensation consulting and other non-executive compensation consulting services).

- Services involving only broad-based non-discriminatory plans or the provision of information, such as surveys, which is not customized for the company, or is customized based on parameters that are not developed by the consultant, are not treated as executive compensation consulting services for purposes of the final rule.

---

[73] Item 407 of Regulation S-K.

The SEC apparently believes that these disclosure requirements provide investors with information that will enable them to better assess the potential conflicts a compensation consultant may have in recommending executive compensation, and the compensation decisions made by the board.

Dodd-Frank Act Section 952 added Section 10C to the Exchange Act, "Independence of Compensation Consultants and Other Compensation Committee Advisers," which provides that the compensation committee, in its sole discretion, may obtain the advice of independent compensation consultants, legal counsel and other advisers. If it does, the committee may only select a compensation consultant, legal counsel or other adviser after taking into consideration factors identified by the SEC, including, at least, the following:

A. The provision of other services to the company by the firm that employs the compensation consultant, legal counsel, or other adviser;

B. The amount of fees received from the company by the firm that employs the compensation consultant, legal counsel, or other adviser, as a percentage of the total revenue of that firm;

C. The policies and procedures of the firm that employs the compensation consultant, legal counsel, or other adviser, which are designed to prevent conflicts of interest;

D. Any business or personal relationship of the compensation consultant, legal counsel, or other adviser with a member of the compensation committee; and

E. Any stock of the company owned by the compensation consultant, legal counsel, or other adviser.

Dodd-Frank Act Section 952 requires companies to disclose in its annual proxy statement whether the compensation committee retained or obtained the advice of an independent compensation consultant and whether the consultant's work raised any conflict of interest issues (and, if so, the nature of the conflict and how the conflict is being addressed). Section 952 does not require disclosure on those issues with respect to legal counsel or other advisers. However, companies and compensation committees should discuss these issues in proxy statements to address stockholders' heightened disclosure expectations.

.04 Disclosure of Hedging by Employees and Directors

Section 955 of the Dodd-Frank Act, "Disclosure of Hedging by Employees and Directors," added subsection 14(j) to the Exchange Act, which requires the SEC to require companies to disclose in their annual proxy statement whether the company permits any employee or director to purchase financial instruments that are designed to hedge or offset any decrease in the market value of equity securities (1) granted to the employee or director by the company as part of the compensation; or (2) held, directly or indirectly, by the employee or director. The obvious aim of this provision is to encourage companies to adopt policies that prohibit hedging transactions. Investors want executives to own large amounts of company stock [not hedged] so they will manage for long-term gains, not just a short-term pop with devastating long-term effect. Section 955 does not require any company to adopt such a policy, but we expect that most will do so.

.05 Disclosure of Pay Versus Performance

Section 953(a) of the Dodd-Frank Act, "Disclosure of Pay Versus Performance," added Section 14(i) to the Exchange Act, which requires each public company to disclose in its annual proxy statement "information that shows the relationship between executive compensation actually paid and the financial performance of the issuer." Section 953 is one of the least clear provisions of Dodd-Frank, with numerous open questions that the SEC will need to answer in its rulemaking. Additionally, like most of the provisions the Dodd-Frank Act, Section 953(a) was not immediately effective. Section 953(a) directs the SEC to adopt rules implementing this disclosure requirement, but does not give it a deadline for doing so.

.06 Pay Ratio Disclosure

Section 953(b) of the Dodd-Frank Act, "Executive Compensation Disclosures" required the SEC to amend the proxy statement disclosure rules to require each public company to disclose the ratio of the median of the annual total compensation of all employees of the company, except the CEO (including employees outside the US) to the annual total compensation of the CEO. This is a political disclosure, not an economic one, intended to give unions and certain media folks a tool to bash corporate America. In August 2015, the SEC issued final rules under Section 953(b), adding Item 402(u) to Regulation S-K, effective for the first fiscal year of the company beginning on or after January 1, 2017. (See ¶3175 CEO Pay Ratio Disclosure, for a detailed discussion of these rules.)

.07 Enhanced Disclosure and Reporting of Compensation Arrangements

Section 956 of the Dodd Frank-Act, "Enhanced Compensation Structure Reporting," would apply only to financial institutions with assets of $1 billion or more. It required the federal regulators to jointly prescribe regulations or guidelines that require each covered financial institution to disclose to the appropriate federal regulator the structures of all incentive-based compensation arrangements offered by the institution, sufficient to determine whether the compensation structure (A) provides an executive officer, employee, director, or principal stockholder of the covered financial institution with excessive compensation, fees, or benefits; or (B) could lead to material financial loss to the covered financial institution. The regulations must **prohibit** any such incentive-based payment arrangement or features. This provision would not require a financial institution that does not have an incentive-based payment arrangement to make any disclosures, or the reporting of the actual compensation of particular individuals.

In 2011, the Office of the Comptroller of the Currency, FDIC, Office of Thrift Supervision, SEC, Board of Governors of the Federal Reserve System, National Credit Union Administration, and Federal Housing Finance Agency (collectively, the "Agencies") jointly issued proposed rules pursuant to Section 956 of the Dodd-Frank Act. The proposed rules would require the reporting of incentive-based compensation arrangements by a covered financial institution (one that has total consolidated assets of $1 billion or more). Numerous entities and organizations submitted comments to the Agencies requesting clarification and revisions to the proposed rules, and the SEC eventually announced that it did not plan to adopt rules (jointly with other agencies) regarding disclosure of, and prohibitions of certain executive compensation structures and arrangements until some future date.

The proposed rules also would have required each covered financial institution to develop and maintain policies and procedures applicable to any incentive-based compensation arrangement, or any feature of any such arrangement, which are approved by the board of directors (or a committee thereof), and reasonably designed to ensure and monitor compliance with the anti-risk requirements. Finally, the proposed rules would have required each covered financial institution to submit a report annually to, and in the format directed by, its appropriate regulator or supervisor, which:

- describes the structure of the covered financial institution's incentive-based compensation arrangements for covered persons, and

- is sufficient to allow an assessment of whether the compensation structure or features of those arrangements provide or are likely to provide covered persons with excessive compensation, fees, or benefits to covered persons or could lead to material financial loss to the covered financial institution.

.08 Reporting of Cash Compensation and Stock Awards in the Summary Compensation and Other Tables

The SEC imposes strict and detailed requirements on public companies for tabular executive compensation disclosure and a CD&A in proxy statements, including a Summary Compensation Table ("SCT"), Director Compensation Table ("DCT") and the Grants of Plan-Based Awards Table. (Chapter 12 discusses these reporting requirements in detail.)

¶2165 Executive Compensation in ESOP-Owned Companies

ERISA expressly contemplates that corporate directors and officers will serve as plan fiduciaries, and provides that actions taken by directors and officers in their corporate capacity are not subject to review under ERISA. Specifically, ERISA Section 408(c)(3) states that "[n]othing in section 406 shall be construed to prohibit any fiduciary from serving as a fiduciary in addition to being an officer, employee, agent, or other representative of a party in interest."

ERISA Section 408(c)(3) permits a fiduciary with respect to a plan to serve as a director or officer of a company that is a party in interest to such plan.[74] With respect to such a "dual capacity" individual, who serves as both a corporate

---

[74] See, *e.g.*, *Donovan v. Bierwirth*, 680 F2d 263, at 271 (2d Cir.) cert. denied, 459 US 1069 (1982); *Eckelkamp v. Beste*, 201 F.Supp. 2d 1012 (E.D. Mo. 2002).

representative and a plan fiduciary, ERISA's fiduciary standards of conduct do *not* apply when such person acts in his or her corporate capacity.[75]

> The fiduciary obligations imposed by ERISA are implicated only where an employer acts in a fiduciary capacity. Thus, we must examine the conduct at issue to determine whether it constitutes "management" or "administration" of the plan, giving rise to a fiduciary concern, or merely a "business decision" that has an effect on an ERISA plan not subject to fiduciary standards . . . . The fact that an action taken by an employer to implement a business decision may ultimately affect the security of employees' welfare [or pension] benefits does not automatically render the action subject to ERISA's fiduciary duties . . . . Instead, only discretionary acts of *plan* management or administration, or those acts designed to carry out the very purposes of the *plan*, are subject to ERISA's fiduciary duties.[76]

ERISA does not prohibit a company from acting in its own interests when the company is not administering an employee benefit plan.[77] Moreover, business decisions made by a company are not subject to review under ERISA's fiduciary standards, regardless of the collateral impact of such business decisions upon employee benefit plans.[78] As noted by the Eighth Circuit in *Martin v. Feilen*,[79] "[v]irtually all of an employer's significant business decisions affect the value of its stock, and therefore the benefits that . . . plan participants will receive. However, ERISA's fiduciary duties under [Section 404(a)] attach only to transactions that involve investing the [plan's] assets or administering the *plan*."[80]

Courts have recognized that corporate directors and officers have duties to a company that are separate and apart from their duties as fiduciaries to employee benefit plans,[81] and that actions undertaken in a corporate capacity are not subject to ERISA's fiduciary standards. For example, the decision to establish, amend, or terminate an employee benefit plan is generally a settlor function that is not subject to review under ERISA,[82] even if by terminating such plan, the

---

[75] *Lockheed Corp. v. Spink*, 517 US 882 (1996); *Curtiss-Wright Corp. v. Schoonenjongen*, 514 US 73 (1995); *Hozier v. Midwest Fasteners, Inc.*, 908 F2d 1155 (3d Cir. 1990); *Johnson v. Georgia-Pacific Corp.*, 19 F3d 1184 (7th Cir. 1994).

[76] *Hunter v. Caliber System, Inc.*, 220 F3d 702, 718 (6th Cir. 2000) (emphasis added) (internal citations omitted).

[77] *Hunter v. Caliber System, Inc.*, 220 F3d 702, 718 (6th Cir. 2000). See also, *Hickman v. Tosco Corp.*, 840 F2d 564, 566 (8th Cir. 1988); *Adams v. LTV Steel Mining Company*, 936 F2d 368, 370 (8th Cir.1991); *Sabell v. U.S. West Management Pension Plan*, 1992 U.S. Dist. LEXIS 22470 (D. Colo. 1992).

[78] *Dzinglski v. Weirton Steel Corp.*, 875 F2d 1075, 1079-80 (4th Cir.), cert. denied, 493 US 919 (1989); *Canale v. Yergen*, 782 F.Supp. 963, 967 (D. N.J. 1992) ("A claim that alleges nothing more than mismanagement of entities in which the administrator serves as an officer or director is . . . not actionable under ERISA, even if the plan has an interest in the entity").

[79] *Martin v. Feilen*, 965 F2d 660, 665-666 (8th Cir. 1992).

[80] *Martin v. Feilen*, 965 F2d 660, 665-666 (8th Cir. 1992) (emphasis added). Even with respect to plan investment or plan administration decisions, however, ERISA does not require fiduciaries to maximize pecuniary benefits for a plan, or for particular classes of plan participants. *Foltz v. U. S. News & World Report, Inc.*, 865 F2d 364, 373 (D.C. Cir. 1989).

[81] *Foltz v. U.S. News & World Report, Inc.*, 663 F.Supp. 1494 (D. D.C 1987), aff'd, 865 F2d 364 (D.C. Cir. 1989).

[82] See, e.g., *Lockheed Corp. v. Spink*, 517 US 882, 890 (1996) (an employer's decision to amend a retirement plan is not a fiduciary act, but is instead analogous to the settlor of a trust); *Curtiss-Wright Corp. v. Schoonenjongen*, 514 US 73, 78 (1995) ("[e]mployers or other plan sponsors are generally free under ERISA, for any reason at any time, to adopt, modify, or terminate employee welfare plans"); *Averhart v. U.S. West Management Pension Plan*, 46 F3d 1480 (10th Cir. 1994) (plan amendment excluding certain classes of employees from enhanced benefits is not subject to ERISA's fiduciary standards); *Belade v. ITT Corp.*, 909 F2d 736 (2d Cir. 1990) (same); *Hozier v. Midwest Fasteners*, 908 F2d 1155 (3d Cir. 1990) (amending a plan is a settlor

company will recapture the plan's surplus assets.[83] Inasmuch as " . . . the ERISA scheme envisions that employers will act in a dual capacity as both fiduciary to [a] plan and as employer[,] ERISA does not prohibit an employer from acting in accordance with its interests as an employer when not administering the plan or its assets."[84]

> Clearly then, for persons having dual roles, the threshold requirement for fiduciary status under ERISA is discretionary authority or control regarding the management of the plan or its assets. However, this definition is not all encompassing. *A court must still inquire as to whether a person is a fiduciary with respect to the particular transaction or conduct at issue.*[85]

In the case of *Eckelkamp v. Beste*,[86] an employee stock ownership plan ("ESOP") that was the sole stockholder of a closely held corporation alleged that certain management employees, who also served as the ESOP's trustees, violated ERISA's fiduciary duties by paying themselves excessive salaries. The ESOP alleged that this resulted in an under-valuation of the company's stock, and the underpayment of dividends to the ESOP. In granting summary judgment for the defendant trustees of the plan, the court held that matters of compensation are within the purview of corporate management or a board of directors, and that in establishing compensation levels, management or directors are making business decisions that are not subject to review under ERISA's fiduciary standards, *even if such decisions negatively impact employee benefit plans.* Specifically, the court held that:

> Setting compensation levels is a business decision or judgment made in connection with the on-going operation of a business. An employer's discretion in determining salaries is a business judgment that does not involve the administration of an ERISA plan or the investment of an ERISA plan's assets. *Such a decision may ultimately affect a plan indirectly but it does not implicate fiduciary concerns regarding plan administration or plan assets. Business decisions can still be made for business reasons, notwithstanding their collateral effect on prospective, contingent employee benefits* . . . . Under ERISA, an individual acts in a fiduciary capacity only to the extent that s/he exercises discretionary control or responsibility over plan administration or plan assets. The discretion required to invoke ERISA's fiduciary obligations must relate to fiduciary functions such as plan management or plan administration. A business decision regarding salaries does not meet this requirement . . . . Thus, the defendants [who served as trustees with respect to the ESOP] were not acting in their fiduciary capacities when compensation levels were determined for themselves and other employees of [the company].[87]

(Footnote Continued)

function); *Johnson v. Georgia Pacific Corp.*, 19 F3d 1184 (7th Cir. 1994) (increase in plan's benefits to ward off hostile takeover is a settlor function, not reviewable under ERISA).

[83] *Champ v. American Pub. Health Assn.*, 1987 U.S. Dist. LEXIS 14203 (D. D.C.), aff'd, 851 F2d 1500 (D.C. Cir. 1988) (decision to terminate a plan and recapture the plan's assets is a business decision).

[84] *Hickman v. Tosco Corp.*, 840 F2d 564, 566 (8th Cir. 1988) (quoting *Phillips v. Amoco Oil Co.*, 799 F2d

1464, 1471 (11th Cir. 1986), cert. denied, 481 US 1016 (1987)).

[85] *Eckelkamp v. Beste*, 201 F.Supp. 2d 1012, 1022 (E.D. Mo. 2002) (emphasis added) (citing, *inter alia*, *Maniace v. Commerce Bank of Kansas City, N.A.*, 40 F3d 264, 267 (8th Cir. 1994); *Coleman v. Nationwide Life Ins. Co.*, 969 F2d 54, 61 (4th Cir. 1992)).

[86] *Eckelkamp v. Beste*, 201 F.Supp. 2d 1012, 1022 (E.D. Mo. 2002).

[87] *Eckelkamp v. Beste*, 201 F.Supp. 2d 1012, 1023 (E.D. Mo. 2002) (emphasis added).

The court's decision in *Eckelkamp* is consistent with decisions reached by other courts concerning ERISA challenges to compensation paid to management employees who also served as fiduciaries to employee benefit plans.[88]

¶2175 Special Focus on CEO Compensation

Directors and companies must understand the duties and responsibilities (and potential liabilities) that courts are imposing on board members. Boards of directors, the courts and judiciary, plaintiffs' class action lawyers, the IRS, the SEC, institutional investors, the press, and the U.S. Congress are all focusing on corporate governance as applied to CEO compensation. The Congress and the IRS have effected some minor changes. However, the major developments—the ones that have most significantly changed the responsibility and potential liability for directors—have come from the SEC, the judiciary and the plaintiffs' lawyers.

Boards of directors have been taking increased notice of and responsibility for succession planning, stock ownership guidelines, and internal pay equity issues in recent years.

.01 Should the Compensation Committee Explore Existing Arrangements?

There are a few reasons why the compensation committee may need to undertake the difficult task of reevaluating the CEO's existing compensation package. The compensation committee and the board of directors should evaluate the terms, cost and likely outcomes of the CEO's and other officers' compensation arrangements to protect themselves from potential liability, and for the good of: (i) the stockholders, (ii) the company's public image, and (iii) the CEO himself. The CEO, too, has a fiduciary obligation to review his compensation. (See *In Re The Walt Disney Company Derivative Litigation* and *Integrated Health Systems* (Elkins).) Additionally, by participating in the process of setting reasonable compensation, the CEO will gain a greater assurance that he will actually receive the compensation he expects.

Reason Number 1: To protect the board members themselves from liability. If a court were to find that directors permitted a CEO to receive millions of dollars in excessive compensation (i) by failing to meet minimal standards of due care, (ii) by not considering information such as the aggregate costs of a pay package, including severance, a court might find that the board abrogated its duties to the company and failed to act in good faith. This could mean that each director

---

[88] See, *e.g.*, *Local Union 2134, United Mine Workers of America v. Powhatan Fuel, Inc.*, 828 F2d 710 (11th Cir. 1987) (holding that the defendant did not breach ERISA's fiduciary duties by paying salaries and business expenses before paying insurance premiums required to maintain the employer's ERISA-covered plan, since the payment of salaries was a business decision exempt from ERISA's fiduciary standards); *Gelles v. Skrotsky*, 983 F.Supp. 1398 (M.D. Fla. 1997) (corporate directors and officers did not violate ERISA by paying significantly increased salaries to members of a management group, since the decision to do so was a business judgment not subject to ERISA's fiduciary standards); *Ches v. Archer*, 827 F.Supp. 159 (W.D. N.Y. 1993) (an employer's decision to pay operating expenses and salaries rather than to pay contributions to a retirement plan sponsored by the company did not violate ERISA's fiduciary or prohibited transaction provisions, even though the employer served as trustee of the plan).

would have to pay several million dollars out of his or her own pocket - without being reimbursed by the company or the D&O insurance carrier. In addition, even if you win the case - like the Walt Disney directors have, so far, the cost to your time and reputation is incalculable. To some extent, it is all about process. Even just having this conversation with the CEO buys the board some protection under the business judgment rule.

Reason Number 2: To protect the company and its stockholders. There are two parts to this protection. First, the money the committee can save the company and its stockholders by reducing payments. That can be significant, but the real savings we are talking about, the second part, comes from avoiding an embarrassing fiasco or fight that plays out in the press and/or the courtroom over excessive pay.

Reason Number 3: To protect the CEO himself or herself by providing a greater certainty that the CEO actually will receive the full amount of compensation and benefits for which he or she has bargained. There are several cases where a bitter and costly battle ensued after termination over the compensation to be paid and further examples occur weekly. Some of these occur because directors now - at the time of termination - realize the enormous amount that is due to the CEO and feel compelled to act. It is a tough love message, but the committee needs to ask the CEO: "Wouldn't you rather have a few less dollars that you are certain to receive - than set both of us up for a costly fight and a lot of bad publicity?"

Do not think it is too late; it is always better late than never. Former SEC Chief Breeden's report in the Hollinger affair states exactly that: the board should be judged by its entire record, including prompt efforts to clean up a mess once it is discovered.

.02 Strategies for Fixing Packages and Agreements

The following are some concrete strategies designed to make this difficult task go as smoothly as possible - and some obvious places to look for improvements. (Not all of the strategies will be applicable to any given company or CEO.)

1. Do the tally sheet. After the CEO has sat through the tally sheet presentation together with the board - you just might find that he or she has a holy cow moment and volunteers to relinquish some items without the difficulties of negotiation.

2. Look for ways to better link pay to performance. Again, if you can get the CEO's buy-in to the principle of true pay-for-performance, that should help set the stage for a more constructive discussion than if you come into the meeting demanding cut-backs.

3. Get independent help. Get the support of an independent consultant and your own lawyer. With luck, the process can be a cooperative one. If not, the board should be ready to call on experienced legal counsel "to wear the black hat."

4. Annual pay decisions (base, bonus, long-term incentives) are usually easier to address than existing contractual commitments. Look there first.

5. Future equity awards are always easier to fix than past ones. These are the easy and painless fixes.

6. Look for excessive perquisites. Perceptions DO matter. How many articles have appeared in the press ripping into a CEO and its board about some perk? However, you never see an article criticizing the CEO or board for paying the CEO $10,000 more in salary.

7. Look for items that do not have an immediate economic impact. Fixing and adding "for cause" provisions in employment and all other compensation agreements is a no-brainer, including "after discovered cause." Also consider fixing and adding "clawbacks" of compensation for cause terminations. You might want to extend a "clawback" of compensation to cover expressly a situation where there is a restatement of earnings. You might want to double-check those indemnification agreements for the officers to ensure you are not indemnifying even in the event of bad acts.

8. Look for the compounding effects of the intertwined compensation programs. NYSE CEO Richard Grasso's SERP started out looking like most every other SERP. However, the compensation components that were added over time had a dramatic multiplying effect on the payments required under the SERP, with results we all know too well. Eliminating some of these "multipliers" also can be a relatively pain-free step for the board and the CEO.

9. Look for changed circumstances. For example, when a company brought in the CEO over seven years ago, it had to lure him or her away from a nice, high paying, secure job at a good company - where he or she had in-the money equity awards - and get the CEO to move cross country to take over the company. Generous compensation and severance protection was necessary at the time. Now that the CEO has been at the company for seven years, those factors do not apply. The company may be able to ratchet down some of those protections.

10. Look at how external factors, like a run up in the stock price, that have affected the CEO's compensation and employment contract. Have circumstances changed due to stock market values, or the CEO's tenure or success with the company?

11. Look for and eliminate holdover provisions from the go-go, ethics free 90's.

12. Look for over-reliance on compensation surveys and situations where pay is based on peer groups that really do not match up with the company.

13. Look for and emphasize the actual amount of accumulated wealth, realized and unrealized - or "carried interest" as some refer to it - resulting from previous equity grants.

14. Look for bargaining chips or trade-offs. The CEO wants something more - or the committee proposes to give something more - let's bargain.

¶ 2175.02

15. Look for provisions that create the wrong incentive - such as a retention plan or agreement that actually pays better for an early departure.

16. Make a list of all the prominent CEOs who have set an example by voluntarily reducing their salary or bonus or equity award - and well-known companies that have taken action - and maybe even a list of some CEOs who were forced to accept a reduction by a court or the SEC.

CEO turnover is increasing. Most CEOs understand that they do not hold all of the cards anymore — that the board may fire them. The key here is to prepare, prepare, prepare. The committee should expect resistance when it appears at the meeting and suggests a rollback.

.03 Succession Planning

Boards of directors have recognized that succession planning is one of the most important functions they play in securing the company's future. Effective succession planning essentially has two parts: planning for the sudden departure or loss of the CEO, and planning for the gradual transition of authority from a retiring CEO to his or her successor.

Almost as important as the undertaking of succession planning is the desirability of including a discussion of succession planning efforts in the company's annual proxy statement. Among the factors ISS looks for in its review is a "Confirmation of a formal CEO and key executive officers succession plan."

Many boards place this responsibility with the compensation committee, but certainly not all. The board could add succession planning to the responsibilities listed in the compensation committee (or other committee) charter. Although boards and board committees may not be eager to add another item to their already significant responsibilities, most boards are eager to learn of and adopt best practices.

In one of the only cases to consider this issue, *Zucker v. Andreessen,*[89] the Delaware Court of Chancery dismissed claims against Hewlett-Packard Company and its board alleging that the lack of a long-term CEO succession plan was a breach of the directors' duty of care. This case arose out of the HP board's decision to terminate then-CEO, Mark Hurd, after allegations of an improper relationship with an HP contractor. Plaintiffs claimed that Hurd's unexpected termination harmed the company by effectively leaving HP leaderless, "a harm that would not have occurred if the defendants had anticipated that risk and adopted a formal succession plan in advance." Plaintiffs could not cite any Delaware precedent for the proposition that failure to adopt a long-term succession plan amounts to a breach of duty, but requested that the court take the opportunity "to establish for the first time, as a specific application of the duty of care, a rule requiring directors to adopt succession plans." This, the court declined to do. Plaintiffs' also challenged the amounts paid to Hurd under his severance agreement as "corporate waste." The court dismissed both claims due

---

[89] 2012 WL 2366448 (Del. Ch. June 21, 2012).

to the plaintiffs' failure to file a presuit demand for corrective action on the board.

It is difficult to measure or ensure a CEO's effectiveness at succession planning. Measures can include, for example, holding a specified number of discussions with candidates, interviewing a specified number of candidates, or introducing a candidate to the board. In 2005, Clorox awarded its CEO a bonus based on criteria that included succession planning. In 2005, Viacom announced that succession planning was a factor in determining whether the CEO's bonus should be adjusted. Harley-Davidson awarded CEO Jeffrey Bluestein $2 million for among other things, "excellent performance in 2004 and his successful completion of his goals and objectives including certain financial objectives and executive succession planning." In December 2004, Harley Davidson had announced that Bluestein would retire and be replaced by James Ziemer, effective April 30, 2005.

.04 Stock Ownership Guidelines

Nearly all boards of directors have adopted stock ownership guidelines applicable to senior executives and, generally, the directors themselves. Item 402(b)(2) of Regulation S-K suggests certain issues that would be appropriate for the company to address in the CD&A, including:

> (xiii) The Company's equity or other security ownership requirements or guidelines (specifying applicable amounts and forms of ownership), and any Company policies regarding hedging the economic risk of such ownership. The CD&A should discuss shares pledged by NEOs, directors and director nominees, as well as owned shares.

If all directors and executive officers exceed the guidelines, a company should consider adding a chart showing the requirement and the actual holdings of each.

ISS suggests a minimum stock ownership for executives of three times base pay, but generally requires ownership levels in the range of six times pay, in order to give maximum credit.

.05 Internal Pay Equity

As better corporate governance and compensation practices began to take root, many companies also have explored or implemented internal pay equity policies and procedures. To accomplish this, the compensation committee generally tasks its HR department to provide internal pay equity audits. The theory is that, when compensation committee members have before them a chart that shows graphically how the CEO's total compensation has gotten out of line with other employees, including other levels of executives, it will become clearer and easier for a board to say: "enough is enough."[90] Companies like DuPont and Intel have been using an internal pay equity approach for years.

---

[90] Jesse Brill, Founder and Editor of TheCorporateCounsel.net.

¶2185 Stockholder Proposals and Proxy Advisory Firms

Among the proposals that each company must put to a vote of its stockholders each year are the election or re-election of members of the board of directors, ratification of appointment of the company's independent auditors for the upcoming fiscal year, and a general resolution to transact any other business that may properly come before the annual meeting or any adjournment thereof.

In the 2010s, institutional investors and proxy advisory firms began to more strongly assert themselves to influence companies' corporate governance and other policies, including executive compensation. ISS and Glass Lewis are the most active and prominent proxy advisory firms. ISS, in particular, published extensive and detailed guidelines on its policy and governance preferences. Based on these preference, ISS will recommend that its clients – mostly large institutional investors – vote "For," "Against," or "Withhold" on the various proposals that each company must put to a vote of its stockholders each year. Regardless of whether companies and boards of directors agree with the policy and governance preferences of ISS, and many strongly disagree, they know that many large stockholders will follow their recommendations.

.01 Stockholder Proposals on Executive Compensation

SEC rules give certain stockholders the right to submit proposals on which stockholders may vote. Companies had seen a surge in stockholder proposals in many areas, but not in the area of executive compensation. The most common stockholder proposals in 2013 were requests that the corporation/target adopt one or more of the following:

- A stock retention policy,
- Pro-rata vesting of equity awards (rather than acceleration) upon a change in control, and
- A compensation clawback policy (or a stricter clawback policy).

When stockholders and their advisors first gained the right to vote "For" or "Against" companies' shareholder Say on Pay resolutions in 2011, stockholder proposals on executive compensation matters decreased significantly.

However, perhaps not surprisingly in these politicized times, stockholder proposals have been directed at other issues recently. Through May 31, 2017, 330 stockholder proposals had gone to a vote. The most common proposals have involved climate change, environmental issues and sustainability. Together with proposals requiring reports on lobbying payments and policies, political contributions, holy land principles, and gender diversity and equality proposals, these "political" proposals accounted for nearly one-half of the proposals so far. Proposals on executive compensation failed even to make the top ten.

The most common stockholder proposals on executive compensation issues have been requests for adoption of a stock retention policy, adoption (or improvement) of a compensation clawback policy, and pro-rata vesting of equity awards, rather than acceleration, upon a change in control. Few of the stockholder proposals on executive compensation matters succeeded in garnishing a majority vote. However, quite a few proposals were withdrawn only after the targeted company agreed to make changes.

.02 ISS

ISS is a provider of proxy voting and corporate governance services. It analyzes proxies and issues research and vote recommendations to institutional investors. The underlying premise of ISS is that good corporate governance ultimately results in increased stockholder value. ISS is currently considered the most influential of the proxy advisory firms and can often be a "swing vote" factor in the success of a vote on an equity plan. However, ISS subscribers are not rigid in their adherence to ISS voting guidelines. Many are willing to listen, discuss incentive plan issues with issuers, and potentially vote contrary to ISS recommendations.

In order for a company to get a "For" vote recommendation from ISS on Shareholder Say on Pay or a stock plan or increase in the authorized share pool under a stock plan, a company's executive compensation package and/or stock plan design must pass a variety of tests. Each year ISS issues its U.S. Corporate Governance Policy Guidelines. These guidelines cover a variety of topics including board composition, corporate responsibility, guidelines on stock plan design, and guidelines on best pay practices. ISS updates its policies applicable to stockholder meetings every year.

ISS maintains a list of "problematic pay practices," which may warrant recommendations of "Against" or "Withhold" votes. The list of the practices that carry greatest weight in this consideration and may result in negative recommendations is as follows:[91]

- Repricing or replacing of underwater stock options/SARS without prior shareholder approval (including cash buyouts and voluntary surrender of underwater options);

- Extraordinary perquisites or tax gross-ups, including any gross-up related to a secular trust or restricted stock vesting, or lifetime perquisites;

- New or extended agreements that provide for:

  - Excessive change in control payments (generally exceeding three times base salary and average/target/most recent bonus);

  - Change in control severance payments without involuntary job loss or substantial diminution of duties ("single" or "modified single" triggers);

  - Change in control payments with excise tax gross-ups (including "modified" gross-ups);

  - Multi-year guaranteed awards that are not at risk due to rigorous performance conditions;

---

[91] United States Proxy Voting Guidelines, Benchmark Policy Recommendations, Effective for Meetings on or after February 1, 2018, Published January 4, 2018.

- Liberal change in control definition combined with any single-trigger change in control benefits;
- Insufficient executive compensation disclosure by externally-managed issuers (EMIs) such that a reasonable assessment of pay programs and practices applicable to the EMI's executives is not possible;
- Incentives that may motivate excessive risk-taking, including:
  - Multi-year guaranteed awards;
  - A single or common performance metric used for short-and long-term incentives;
  - Lucrative severance packages;
  - High pay opportunities relative to industry peers;
  - Disproportionate supplemental pensions; or
  - Mega equity grants that provide overly large upside opportunity.

  Factors that potentially mitigate the impact of risky incentives include rigorous claw-back provisions, robust stock ownership/holding guidelines, and limitations on accelerated vesting triggers.
- Options backdating; and
- Any other provision or practice deemed to be egregious and present a significant risk to investors.

.03 Glass Lewis

For the 2018 proxy season, Glass Lewis listed 14 separate circumstances under which it will recommend a vote against all or some members of the compensation committee, including:

- Where the committee failed to address stockholder concerns following majority stockholder rejection of the Say on Pay proposal in the previous year,
- Where the company failed to align pay with performance, but the company is not providing for a say on pay vote at the annual meeting,
- Where the company entered into excessive employment agreements and/or severance agreements,
- When performance goals were lowered because employees failed or were unlikely to meet original goals,
- When performance-based compensation was paid despite goals not being attained,
- If excessive employee perquisites and benefits were allowed,
- When the company repriced options or completed a "self-tender offer" without stockholder approval within the past two years,
- When vesting of in-the-money options is accelerated,
- When option exercise prices were spring-loaded or otherwise timed around the release of material information, and

- If the committee failed to implement a stockholder proposal regarding a compensation-related issue, which had received the majority vote.

.04 ISS Equity Plan Scorecards

ISS makes voting recommendations on equity-based compensation plans on a case-by-case basis using its equity plan scorecard ("EPSC") approach, with three pillars, (i) plan cost, (ii) plan features, and (iii) equity grant practices, where positive factors may counterbalance negative factors and vice versa, as evaluated. ISS generally recommends a vote against the plan proposal if the combination of the EPSC factors indicates that the plan is not, overall, in stockholders' interests, **or** if certain egregious factors apply.

For companies that are subject to the S&P 500 scoring model, an EPSC score of 55 or higher (out of a total 100 possible points) generally will result in a positive recommendation for the proposal (absent any overriding factors). For all other EPSC models, the passing score is 53. ISS considers three categories of factors under each EPSC model (referred to as "pillars"). EPSC factors are not equally weighted. Each factor is assigned a maximum number of potential points, which may vary by model. The FAQs include a chart summarizing the scoring basis for each factor.

Pillar	Model	Maximum Pillar Score	Comments
Plan Cost	S&P 500	45	All models include the same Plan Cost factors.
	Russell 3000		
	Non-Russell 3000		
	IPO/Bankruptcy	60	
Plan Features	S&P 500	20	All models include the same Plan Features factors.
	Russell 3000		
	Non-Russell 3000	30	
	IPO/Bankruptcy	40	
Grant Practices	S&P 500	35	The Non-Russell 3000 model includes only Burn Rate and Duration factors. The IPO/Bankruptcy model does not include any Grant Practices factors.
	Russell 3000		
	Non-Russell 3000	25	
	IPO/Bankruptcy	0	

Plan Cost Pillar

ISS will continue to evaluate the total potential plan cost of the company's equity plans relative to industry/market cap peers, based on its proprietary shareholder value transfer ("SVT") measure, in relation to the company's peers. However, under EPSC, ISS will calculate SVT for both:

(a) New shares requested, plus shares remaining for future grants, plus outstanding unvested/unexercised grants, and

(b) Only on new shares requested plus shares remaining for future grants.

¶2185.04

The second measure reduces the impact of grant overhang on the overall cost evaluation, recognizing that high grant overhang is a sunk cost that the company has already expensed.

Additionally, under this dual cost measurement approach, ISS will no longer factor overhang carve-outs or burn rate commitments into its vote recommendations option. ISS will consider the company's burn rate as part of the EPSC evaluation, based on a range relative to its peers. We have confirmed that ISS will run its analysis of the plan's/company's SVT relative to peers, even though a company is not seeking approval of additional shares.

Under the EPSC, ISS will calibrate burn rate benchmarks separately for the equity plans of companies in four groups: (1) S&P 500, (2) Russell 3000 (excluding S&P 500), (3) Non-Russell 3000; and (4) Recent IPO/Bankruptcy Emergent companies. ISS still would use the relevant GICS industry classification within each index group.

Plan Features Pillar

ISS will continue to review a few key plan features under the EPSC. The presence of some of these features would result in negative recommendations, regardless of other factors, including the authority to reprice stock options without seeking stockholder approval. Other features the ISS also calls out for special scrutiny include:

- Single-triggered award vesting upon a change in control, which is automatic, even when other options (*e.g.*, conversion or assumption of existing grants) are available;

- Broad discretionary vesting authority that may result in "pay for failure" or other scenarios contrary to a pay-for-performance philosophy;

- Liberal share recycling on various award types (previously, ISS included liberal share counting in its SVT calculations); and

- Absence of a minimum required vesting period (at least one year) for grants made under the plan.

Company Grant Practices Pillar

The third category of factors that ISS will consider under the EPSC is the company's historical grant practices for equity awards. Again, the scorecard proposal specifies a few key elements for ISS consideration:

- The company's three-year average burn rate relative to its industry and index peers – this measure of average grant "flow" provides an additional check on plan cost per SVT. The EPSC compares a company's burn rate relative to its index and industry (GICS groupings for S&P 500, Russell 3000 (ex-S&P 500), and non-Russell 3000 companies);

- Vesting schedule(s) that incentivize long-term retention under the CEO's most recent equity grants during the prior three years;

- The plan's estimated duration, based on the sum of shares remaining available and the new shares requested, divided by the three-year annual average of burn rate shares;
- The proportion of the CEO's most recent equity grants/awards subject to performance conditions;
- Whether the company maintains a claw-back policy; and
- Whether the company has established post exercise/vesting share-holding requirements.

Certain factors will result in a negative recommendation on an equity plan proposal, regardless of the score from all other EPSC factors. The following egregious features will result in an "Against" recommendation, regardless of other EPSC factors.

- A liberal change-of-control definition (including, for example, stockholder approval of a merger or other transaction rather than its consummation) that could result in vesting of awards by any trigger other than a full double trigger;
- If the plan would permit repricing or cash buyout of underwater options or SARs without stockholder approval (either by expressly permitting it – for NYSE and Nasdaq listed companies – or by not prohibiting it when the company has a history of repricing – for non-listed companies);
- If the plan is a vehicle for problematic pay practices or a pay-for-performance disconnect; or
- If any other plan features or company practices are deemed detrimental to stockholder interests; such features may include, on a case-by-case basis, tax gross-ups related to plan awards or a provision for reload options.

Chapter 22
DEDUCTIBILITY OF EXECUTIVE COMPENSATION

¶2201 Introduction—Deductibility of Executive Compensation

This chapter discusses limitations on the deductibility of executive compensation, primarily the $1 million limit set forth in Code Sec. 162(m), for covered employees of publicly held corporations.

.01 Code Sec. 162(m) —Covered Employees and the $1 Million Deductibility Limit

Code Sec. 162(m), which became effective in 1994, prohibits a publicly held company from deducting more than $1 million of compensation paid to certain covered employees in any tax year.[1] The Tax Cuts and Jobs Act of 2017 ("TCJA"), signed into law by President Trump in December 2017, expanded the definition of "covered employee" and eliminated the most significant exception to the deductibility limit of Code Sec. 162(m) (see ¶2215 for a more detailed discussion of the $1 million compensation cap and the definition of covered employee).

.02 Grandfathered Protection for Certain Plans and Agreements

Until the grandfathering protection applicable to payments provided under a written binding contract that was in effect on November 2, 2017, and not modified in any material respect on or after that date, companies will want to continue to comply with many of the provisions of Code Sec. 162(m) relating to the performance-based compensation exception (see ¶2225 for a more detailed discussion of the grandfathered protection for certain plans and agreements).

.03 Strategies for Mitigating the Lost Code Sec. 162(m) Deduction

Companies' options for preserving the deductibility of executive compensation amounts not grandfathered are limited. However, we have come up with a few design strategies that public companies should consider (see ¶2235 for a more detailed discussion of strategies for mitigating the lost Code Sec. 162(m) deduction).

.04 Provisions No Longer Relevant After the Tax Cuts and Jobs Act of 2017

Until 2018, Code Sec. 162(m) contained a significant exception for so-called "performance-based compensation." For the past 24 years, executive compensation lawyers, compensation committees, and other executive compensation pro-

---

[1] President Clinton signed into law the Omnibus Budget Reconciliation Act of 1993 on August 10, 1993.

fessionals spent countless hours each year working to preserve the deductibility of compensation under the exception for performance-based compensation. The TCJA eliminated the performance-based compensation exception, rendering such design considerations moot (see ¶2245 for a more detailed discussion of the provisions no longer relevant after the TCJA).

.05 Supplemental Wage Withholding and Code Sec. 409A

The American Jobs Creation Action of 2004 first provided for mandatory income tax withholding at the highest rate of income tax in effect under the Code (currently 35%) to the extent an employee's total supplemental wages from an employer (and other businesses under common control with the employer) exceed $1,000,000 during the calendar year. The TCJA revised the withholding rates.

The American Jobs Creation Act also added Section 409A to the Internal Revenue Code. Code Sec. 409A applies to employment and change in control agreements and separation pay plans in addition to the deferred compensation plans that it initially was drafted to cover. Code Sec. 409A and the regulations contain a few special rules affecting Code Sec. 162(m) (see ¶2255) for a more detailed discussion of Code Sec. 409A and the supplemental wage withholding rules).

.06 Deduction Timing Rules for Annual Bonus Payments

Many bonus plans provide that the company will pay bonuses attributable to Year 1, early in Year 2, *but only to participants who are employed on the date of payment.* This provision could create a deduction-timing trap for the unwary. Generally, an employer is permitted to deduct in its Year 1 tax year, bonuses that it pays within the first 2½ months of Year 2 (for example, for a calendar-year employer, payment by March 15, 2019, for a 2018 deduction). However, that grace period only applies if "all events" fixing the obligation have occurred by the end of Year 1 (see ¶2265 for a more detailed discussion of the deduction timing rules for annual bonus payments).

.07 Code Sec. 162(m)(6) Applicable to Covered Health Insurance Providers

The Patient Protection and Affordable Care Act ("ACA"),[2] added Code Sec. 162(m)(6), which limits to $500,000 the allowable deduction for the "aggregate applicable individual remuneration" and "deferred deduction remuneration" attributable to services performed by an "applicable individual" for a "covered health insurance provider" in a "disqualified taxable year" beginning after December 31, 2012 (see ¶2275).

---

[2] Public Law 111-148, 124 Stat. 119, 868 (2010).

¶2201.05

¶2215 Covered Employees and the Deductibility Limit of Code Sec. 162(m)

Since 1994, Code Sec. 162(m) has prevented publicly held corporations from deducting more than $1 million per year for compensation paid to a covered employee (generally, the CEO and the next three or four highest compensated officers). Numerous exceptions provide planning opportunities. Code Sec. 162(m)(1) begins as follows:

> In the case of any publicly held corporation, no deduction shall be allowed under this chapter for applicable employee remuneration with respect to any covered employee to the extent that the amount of such remuneration for the tax year with respect to such employee exceeds $1,000,000.

.01 Limit Applies Only to Publicly Held Corporations

Before 2018, the $1 million deduction limit of Code Sec. 162(m) applied only to "publicly held corporations," which Sec. 162(m)(2) defined as a corporation that has a class of common equity securities that is *required* to be registered under Section 12 of the Securities Exchange Act of 1934 (the "Exchange Act") as of the last day of the corporation's tax year.[3]

> **Example 1:** ABC Corporation is a calendar year taxpayer that does not have any securities traded on a national securities exchange. During its 2018 fiscal year, ABC satisfies the asset and shareholder tests of Section 12(g) of the Exchange Act for the first time. As a result, ABC is required to file a registration statement for its applicable class of equity securities by April 30, 2018. Since ABC Corporation did not have to register the securities by December 31, 2017, ABC is not a publicly held corporation for purposes of its 2017 taxes.[4] However, ABC will be a publicly held corporation—and the $1 million deduction limit will apply—for 2017, assuming that ABC's class of equity securities is still subject to registration under Section 12 of the Exchange Act as of December 31, 2017.

If a publicly held corporation is part of an affiliated group of corporations, as defined under Code Sec. 1504 (but without regard to Code Sec. 1504(b)), then, for purposes of the $1 million deduction limit, all of the corporations in the affiliated group are essentially treated as one publicly held corporation. The compensation paid to a "covered employee" (as defined in ¶2215.02) by the member of the affiliated group that is a publicly held corporation would be combined with the compensation paid to the covered employee by the nonpublicly held corporate affiliates of the publicly held corporation. If the aggregate compensation paid to the covered employee by all of the members of the affiliated group is more than $1 million, then the amount that is disallowed for deduction purposes must be prorated among the payor corporations in proportion to the amount of compensation paid to the covered employee by each payor corporation in the tax year. However, if the affiliated group includes a subsidiary that is itself a publicly held corporation, then the Code essentially treats the publicly held subsidiary and its

---

[3] Reg. § 1.162-27(c)(1)(i).   [4] See Reg. § 1.162-27(c)(6), Example (3).

subsidiaries as a second publicly held corporation that is subject to a separate $1 million deduction limit.[5]

The TCJA amended Code Sec. 162(m)(2) to expand the definition of "publicly held corporation" to include any company that is required to file reports under Exchange Act Sec. 15(d) (generally, Forms 10-K, 10-Q, 8-K). For example, a company that has publicly traded debt (but not publicly traded stock) would be required to file these reports. These companies became subject to the $1 million deduction limit Code Sec. 162(m) in 2018.

.02 Covered Employees Whose Compensation Is Subject to the Limit

The $1 million deduction limit applies to the compensation paid by a publicly held corporation to its "covered employees." According to Code Sec. 162(m)(3), as amended by the TCJA, a covered employee is any employee of a company who is:

- The principal executive officer ("PEO" or "CEO") or principal financial officer ("PFO" or "CFO") of the company (or an individual acting in such a capacity) at any time during the company's taxable year, or

- The company is required to report to stockholders on its proxy statement by reason of such employee being among the three highest compensated officers for the company's taxable year (other than the CEO or CFO), including any employee who would have been among the three highest compensated officers for the year if the company had been required to report such employee's total compensation for the year, or

- Was a covered employee of the taxpayer (or any predecessor) for any preceding taxable year beginning after December 31, 2016.

Before 2018, the term "covered employee" for purposes of Code Sec. 162(m) did not include a company's principal financial officer. IRS Notice 2007-49[6] provided that the IRS will interpret the term "covered employee" for purposes of Code Sec. 162(m) to mean any employee of the company if, as of the close of the taxable year, such employee is the principal executive officer of the company or an individual acting in such a capacity, or if the total compensation of such employee for that taxable year is required to be reported to shareholders under the Exchange Act by reason of such employee being among the three highest compensated officers for the taxable year (other than the principal executive officer or the principal financial officer). Private Letter Ruling 200945009[7] further clarified that the IRS really did intend to exclude CFOs from Code Sec. 162(m) if they are not in the highest compensated group *and* employed on the last day of the year.

.03 No End-of-Year Employment Requirement

Before 2018, the IRS had issued a number of private letter rulings that discuss whether certain individuals are covered employees. Although the IRS

---

[5] Reg. § 1.162-27(c)(1)(ii).

[6] Notice 2007-49, I.R.B. 2007-25, June 18, 2007.

[7] Private Letter Ruling 200945009, July 31, 2009.

had promulgated final regulations, the letter rulings have focused on the preamble to the proposed regulations for Code Sec. 162(m). This preamble indicated that an individual will *not* be treated as a covered employee if the individual is not employed as an executive officer on the last day of the corporation's tax year *or* if the individual does not appear on the "summary compensation table" under the SEC's executive compensation disclosure rules, as set forth in Item 402 of Regulation S-K, 17 C.F.R. § 229.402, under the Exchange Act (the proxy statement).

For example, the IRS ruled in IRS Letter Ruling 200216001[8] that individuals who resign from their positions as officers before the last day of the tax year are not covered employees, despite the fact that they may be listed on the summary compensation table as the CEO or one of the highest compensated officers with respect to the tax year during which they resigned as officers. The IRS also indicated in IRS Letter Ruling 200216001 and in other private letter rulings that individuals who cease to serve as officers may continue to serve as consultants or non-officer employees without affecting the analysis under Code Sec. 162(m).[9]

In accordance with the TCJA amendments, Notice 2018-68 provides that there is no requirement that an employee must have served as an executive officer at the end of the taxable year to be considered a covered employee. If an employee (other than the CEO or CFO) is among the three most highly compensated executive officers for the taxable year, the employee will be a covered employee regardless of whether he or she is serving in such position at the end of the taxable year. Similarly, any individual who serves as the company's CEO or CFO is a covered employee for that year (and beyond), regardless of employment status at year end. This means that multiple CEOs and CFOs may be covered employees for a single year.

Example: For 2018, Employee A served as the sole CEO of a publicly held company and Employees B and C both served as the CFO of the company at different times during the year. Employees D, E, and F were, respectively, the first, second, and third most highly compensated executive officers of the company for 2018 (other than the CEO and CFO), but all three retired before the end of 2018. Employees G, H, and I were, respectively, the company's fourth, fifth, and sixth highest compensated executive officers (other than the CEO and CFO) for 2018, and all three were serving at the end of 2018. In April 2019, the company filed its annual proxy statement and disclosed the compensation of Employee A for serving as the CEO, Employees B and C for serving as the CFO, and Employees G, H, and I pursuant to Item 402(a)(3)(iii) of Regulation S-K. The company also disclosed the compensation of Employees D and E pursuant to Item 402(a)(3)(iv).

- Because Employee A served as the CEO during 2018, Employee A is a covered employee for 2018. Because Employees B and C each served as the CFO during 2018, Employees B and C are covered employees for 2018.

---

[8] IRS Letter Ruling 200216001 (Oct. 17, 2001).   [9] See, for example, IRS Letter Ruling 200219015 (Feb. 5, 2002).

- Even though the SEC rules require the company to disclose the compensation of Employees D, E, G, H, and I for 2018, the company's covered employees for 2018 under Code Sec. 162(m) are Employees D, E, and F, because they are the three highest compensated executive officers other than the CEO and CFO for 2018, even though they were not employed on the last day of the year.

The Notice partially severs the link between the definition of "covered employee" under Code Sec. 162(m) and the definition of "named executive officer" under the Exchange Act. The Notice provides that an executive officer of a publicly held company can be a covered employee under Code Sec. 162(m) even when disclosure of his or her compensation is not required under SEC's executive compensation reporting rules. For example, the executive officers of a company whose securities are delisted or that undergoes a transaction resulting in the non-application of the proxy statement filing requirement, which may not be required to disclose executive officer compensation for that year, will not be exempt from being "covered employees." The Notice also suggests that executive officers of smaller reporting companies and emerging growth companies may be considered covered employees notwithstanding that the company is not required to report their compensation in its proxy statement.

.04 Once a Covered Employee, Always a Covered Employee

The TCJA amended Code Sec. 162(m)'s definition of covered employee to include any employee of the taxpayer who is, or ever was, a covered employee. Under prior law, covered employee status discontinued once the individual no longer met the definition. Following the TCJA, being a covered employee is now a permanent status, during both the time an employee is employed by the company or any successor at any time thereafter.

In fact, an individual's status as a covered employee does not stop, even at the employee's death. Under "new" Code Sec. 162(m), payments made to a beneficiary of a covered employee are considered as made to the covered employee and subject to the $1 million deduction limitation.

> **Example:** A CEO retired in 2021, with vested stock options that were granted in 2018, and a nonqualified deferred compensation plan account of $5,000,000, payable in equal installments over five years. The former CEO dies in 2022, before exercising any of the vested options and after receiving one installment payment from his plan account. In 2023, the beneficiaries of the former CEO exercise the vested options for a $1,500,000 gain and the deferred compensation plan distributed $4,000,000 (the deferred compensation plan provides that a participant's accounts will be paid out in full upon the participant's death). If the former CEO receives no other payments from the company in 2023, $1,000,000 of the $5,500,000 "payout" made on behalf of the former CEO will be deductible and the remaining $4,500,000 will not be deductible by the company.

The TCJA amended Code Sec. 162(m)(3) to expand the definition of "covered employee" to include any individual who was a covered employee of the company taking the compensation deduction or any predecessor of it, for any preceding taxable year beginning after December 31, 2016. This is referred to as the "once a covered employee, always a covered employee" rule.

Example: For 2019, Executive E's base salary, annual incentive, and stock awards (reported at their fair value for that year) placed her among the three most highly compensated executive officers of the company for 2019, other than the CEO and the CFO, requiring ABC Corporation to list her in the Summary Compensation Table ("SCT") of its annual proxy statement for the 2019 fiscal year. That was the only year for which Executive E was required to be shown. ABC had not been required to report Executive E in the SCT for any prior or subsequent fiscal year. That was the only year for which E was required to be shown in the SCT. Under this new rule, the following payments would be subject to the $1 million deductibility limit:

- All salary, bonus, and other compensation provided to E (*e.g.*, upon the vesting of a restricted stock award) by ABC in 2019 and any fiscal year of ABC thereafter.
- Severance payments made by ABC to E upon her termination of employment with ABC in 2021.
- Ordinary income recognized by E in 2023, two years after her termination of employment with ABC in 2021, upon the exercise of stock options awarded by ABC in 2019.
- Payments made from ABC's nonqualified retirement plan to D's surviving spouse upon D's death in 2025.

.05 Compensation Subject to $1 Million Deduction Limit

The $1 million deduction limit under Code Sec. 162(m) pertains only to "applicable employee remuneration." Except for certain types of compensation that Code Sec. 162(m) specifically excludes, "applicable employee remuneration" encompasses all compensation for services that is deductible (before applying the limit under Code Sec. 162(m)) for the tax year that an individual is a covered employee. The focus is on the tax year during which the company would otherwise take the deduction for the compensation, not on the tax year during which the covered employee provided the services.[10]

Example: Publicly held ABC Corporation granted Executive E a nonqualified stock option in 2017 for services rendered in 2017, when E was not a covered employee. In 2019, E became a covered employee and also exercised the option and received a compensatory benefit of $100,000. The $100,000 would normally be deductible in 2019 and, therefore, is applicable employee remuneration for 2019, even though ABC granted the option for services performed in 2017.

Code Sec. 162(m)'s definition of applicable employee remuneration does *not* include the following types of compensation:

---

[10] Code Sec. 162(m)(4)(A).

- Commissions (excluded only if they are based solely on income generated by the individual performance of the executive);
- Performance-based compensation (excluded only if the compensation committee and shareholders approve the compensation and if certain other requirements are met);
- Qualified plan contributions referred to in Code Sec. 3121(a)(5)(A) through Code Sec. 3121(a)(5)(D), including:

  –salary reduction contributions to a 401(k) plan;

  –other contributions to plans qualified under Code Sec. 401(a);

  –payments under or to annuity plans described in Code Sec. 403(a);

  –payments under simplified employee pension plans as defined in Code Sec. 408(k)(1), other than contributions made under a salary reduction agreement;

  –payments under or to annuity contracts described in Code Sec. 403(b), other than under a salary reduction agreement;

- Any benefit provided to or on behalf of an executive if at the time the benefit is provided, it is reasonable to believe that the executive will be able to exclude the benefit from gross income (for example, employer-provided health benefits and fringe benefits excludable from taxation under Code Sec. 132); and
- Certain remuneration paid under a written binding contract that was in effect on February 17, 1993.[11]

¶2225 Grandfathered Protection For Certain Plans and Agreements

In August 2018, the IRS released Notice 2018-68, its much-anticipated guidance on the circumstances under which certain compensation amounts and payments promised or awarded by a company on or before November 2, 2017, but paid in 2018 or later, could be grandfathered and not subject to the compensation deductibility limits of Code Sec. 162(m). Companies will want to take whatever steps are necessary to preserve the grandfathering protection for payments, plans, and agreements that qualify for it.

.01 Compensation Under a Written Binding Contract in Effect on November 2, 2017

Most public companies have entered into employment agreements with their senior executive officers. Some companies may have entered into change in control agreements or severance agreements instead of or in addition to the employment agreements. As noted above, the interpretation of amounts paid under a written binding contract under the TCJA's transition rule is unexpectedly harsh. The grandfather rule allows deductibility for applicable employee remuneration paid to a covered employee under a written binding contract in

---

[11] Code Sec. 162(m)(4).

effect on November 2, 2017, which is not materially modified after that date. The Notice provides helpful examples of payments that may or may not be grandfathered, depending on the particular facts.

Enforceability Under Applicable Law. A contract must obligate the company under applicable law (*e.g.,* state contract law) to pay compensation if the employee performs the requisite services and otherwise satisfies the conditions set forth in the agreement, such that the employee can seek to enforce the payment obligation. The Notice does not limit "applicable law" for this purpose solely to state law. The obligation will be considered binding solely to the extent of the amount stated in the contract. Any payment in excess of the amount the company is legally obligated to pay (other than due to the application of a reasonable interest rate or investment returns), would not be grandfathered.

The legal determination of whether an arrangement is a written binding contract and how long the contract remains in effect is crucial to the grandfather rule. Counsel should assist public company clients in determining whether their November 2, 2017, compensation arrangements, including both individual agreements and broader based plans, qualify as written binding contracts. This analysis would require identification of the applicable state and local law, as well as federal statutory and common law.

"Renewal" of a Legally Binding Contract. Importantly, a legally binding written contract that is considered "renewed" after November 2, 2017, is outside the grandfather rule. The Notice makes clear that a renewal can occur actively or passively and covers a range of fact patterns.

Example: A CFO is a party to a three-year employment agreement providing an annual salary of $2,000,000, beginning on January 1, 2018, and the terms of the agreement provide for automatic extensions after the three-year term for additional one-year periods, unless the corporation exercises its option to terminate the agreement within 30 days before the end of the three-year (or subsequent) term:

- The CFO's annual salary of $2,000,000 for the 2018, 2019, and 2020 taxable years (before the end of the three-year terms/renewal) would *not* be subject to the Code Sec. 162(m) deduction limit.

- However, the employment agreement would be treated as renewed on January 1, 2021, and Code Sec. 162(m) would apply to any payments made under it on or after that date.

- Termination of the employment agreement does not require the termination of the CFO's employment relationship with the company.

Note that the $2,000,000 only need be promised. It did not have to be performance-based compensation because the CFO was not a covered employee under prior law.

However, there are three exceptions where renewals do not cause the contract to fall outside the grandfather rule:

- If the company is legally obligated by the contract at the sole discretion of the employee;
- If the contract may only be terminated by the employee no longer being employed; or
- If upon termination or cancelation of the contract the employment relationship continues but is no longer covered by the contract.

In the situation where a covered employee continues employment beyond the duration of the contract, compensation after the contract expires will not be grandfathered, but compensation paid pursuant to the contract could remain grandfathered.

Contractual Promise of Future Participation. While the legally binding written contract must have been in effect as of November 2, 2017, the employee did not have to be eligible to participate in the arrangement or plan as of that date. However, the covered employee must have been employed by the company, or otherwise had a legally binding right to later participation in the arrangement, as of November 2, 2017.

> **Example:** In January 2015, an individual who is not a covered-employee executes a deferred compensation agreement providing for a payment of $3,000,000 if he continues to provide services through December 31, 2017. In October 2017, however, he terminates employment with that company and executes a *new* employment agreement with a *new* company as CFO. The employment agreement provides that, in April 2018, the CFO will participate in the nonqualified deferred compensation plan available to all executives of the company and that his benefit accrued on that date will be $3,000,000. On April 1, 2021, the CFO receives a payment of $4,500,000, which is the entire benefit accrued under the plan.
>
> - The CFO is a covered employee solely as a result of the TCJA's amendment to Code Sec. 162(m)(3). Even though he was not eligible to participate in the nonqualified deferred compensation plan on November 2, 2017, he was employed on November 2, 2017, and had the right to participate in the plan under a written binding contract as of that date.
> - $3,000,000 of the $4,500,000 payment made in April 2021 is deductible and $1,500,000 is not.

.02 Contracts that Give the Company Discretion to Reduce Amounts

Many November 2, 2017, arrangements provided significant discretion for companies to adjust executive compensation in light of changing circumstances or include unlimited "negative discretion" which taken to the extreme, would allow the company to reduce the payment amount to zero, even when performance and service requirements were met. To the extent that an executive's compensation is legally binding and enforceable, the grandfather rule may apply to protect the company's deduction. However, to the extent that compensation is subject to employer discretion, the grandfather rule is far less likely to apply unless such amounts are legally enforceable under state or other applicable law.

¶2225.02

Example: In February 2017, a company establishes a bonus plan under which the CEO will receive a cash bonus of $1,500,000 if a specified performance goal is satisfied. The compensation committee retains the right, even if the performance goal is met, to reduce the bonus payment to not less than $400,000 if, in its judgment, other subjective factors warrant a reduction. In 2018, the compensation committee reduces the award to $500,000. In this example, only $400,000 of the $500,000 payment is deductible, but the failure of the compensation committee to exercise negative discretion to reduce the award to $400,000, instead of $500,000, does not result in a material modification of the contract.

.03 Material Modification

The grandfather rule permits a deduction for compensation paid to covered employees under a written binding contract in effect as of November 2, 2017, unless the contract is *materially modified* after that date. A legally binding contract that is materially modified is treated as a new contract as of the date of the modification. Compensation actually paid pursuant to the contract's terms prior to the material modification would remain grandfathered and subject to "old" Code Sec. 162(m). Compensation paid after the date of the modification would not be grandfathered.

The Notice defines a material modification as one that *increases the amount of compensation* payable to the employee. If the contract is modified to accelerate the payment of compensation, a material modification will not have occurred where the payment amount is reasonably discounted for the time value of money. If the contract is modified to defer payment of the compensation, an increase in the payment amount would not be a material modification if it is based on either a reasonable rate of interest or the performance of predetermined investments.

Paying additional or increased compensation under a grandfathered contract, or adopting a supplemental contract that provides for increased or additional compensation would be a material modification if the additional compensation is paid on the basis of substantially the same elements or conditions as the compensation that is otherwise paid under the written binding contract. This determination is based on the facts and circumstances surrounding the additional payment or supplemental contract. However, if the additional payment or supplemental contract is no greater than a reasonable cost-of-living adjustment, it would not be a material modification.

Example: In January 2017, a CFO signs a five-year employment agreement providing for a salary of $1,800,000 per year. In 2018, the CFO became a covered employee solely as a result of the TCJA's amendment to Code Sec. 162(m)(3). In 2019, the company increases the CFO's compensation with a supplemental payment of $40,000. On January 1, 2020, the company increases the CFO's salary to $2,400,000.

- The $1,800,000 salary is paid under a written binding contract signed when the CFO was not subject to Code Sec. 162(m) and, therefore, is grandfathered unless the change in her compensation in either 2019 or 2020 is a material modification.

- The $40,000 supplemental payment in 2019 does not constitute a material modification of the written binding contract because the $40,000 payment is less than or equal to a reasonable cost-of-living increase from 2017. The $40,000 supplemental payment is, however, subject to the deduction limitation of Code Sec. 162(m).

- The $560,000 salary increase to $2,400,000 in 2020 is a material modification of the written binding contract because the additional compensation is paid on the basis of substantially the same elements or conditions as the compensation that is otherwise paid pursuant to the written binding contract, and it is greater than a reasonable, annual cost-of-living increase.

Because the written binding contract is materially modified as of January 1, 2020, all compensation paid to the CFO in 2020 and thereafter will be subject to the $1 million deduction limit.

If the CFO had received a restricted stock grant instead of a salary increase, there would *not* have been a material modification of the written binding contract (although the restricted stock grant would be subject to the deduction limitation). The additional compensation paid under the grant is based on the stock price and the CFO's continued service, not paid on the basis of substantially the same elements and conditions as the CFO's salary.

The presence of a material modification is a fact-driven question and requires employers to exercise caution up until the point that all payments have been made under any November 2, 2017 arrangement. Affected companies should be extremely careful about modifying arrangements that might still be grandfathered, including modifications to employment agreements and amendments to executive compensation plans. Companies with grandfathered written binding contracts also should be careful when implementing any new arrangements that might be a supplemental contract based on the same criteria as the prior contract, which would be a material modification.

.04 Amounts Designed to be Performance-Based Compensation

For employees who were covered employees even before the adoption of the TCJA, amounts paid in 2018 and after could still be deductible if the amounts or awards would have qualified as performance-based compensation under old Code Sec. 162(m).

> **Example:** In January 2017, the CEO signs a four-year employment agreement with an annual salary of $1,000,000. Pursuant to the employment agreement, in January 2017, the company grants the CEO nonqualified stock options to purchase 1,000 shares of stock, SARs on 1,000 shares, and 1,000 shares of restricted stock. The restricted stock, options and SARs vest in January 2019. After vesting, the CEO can exercise the options and SARs at any time through January 2027. In January 2021, the CEO exercises the options and SARs.

- Because the stock options and SARs were designed to satisfy the performance-based compensation requirements and would have been deductible but for the elimination of the exception for qualified performance-based compensation by the TCJA, the compensation attributable to the options and the SARs upon their exercise in 2021 will be grandfathered and deductible.

- However, the company will not be entitled to a deduction for the compensation attributable to the vesting of the restricted stock in 2019.

If the employment agreement had provided that the stock options, SARs, and restricted stock would be granted in January 2018, there would be no written binding contract as of November 2, 2017, and the options and SARS also would have been subject to the Code Sec. 162(m) deduction limit.

.05 Nonqualified Deferred Compensation

Many companies maintain a nonqualified deferred compensation plan and/or a supplemental executive retirement plan (SERP). Generally, these plans are designed to make up for benefits or contributions that could not be provided under the company's qualified retirement plan due to Code limits. Under a nonqualified deferred compensation plan or SERP, distribution of a participant's account balance or accrued benefit usually does not occur until after the participant has terminated employment. Therefore, under Code Sec. 162(m) prior to the TCJA amendments, distributions would be fully deductible.

The TCJA amendments will make any distribution of nonqualified plan benefits to a participant who is *or ever was* a covered employee under Code Sec. 162(m) subject to the $1 million deductibility cap, even if the distribution is made after the participant's death, disability, retirement or other termination of employment. However, the account or benefit of a covered employee under a nonqualified plan as of November 2, 2017 (and in some cases additional accruals and contributions after that date) could be grandfathered and not subject to the $1 million cap.

Example: Under a deferred compensation plan, an employee who was not a covered employee in 2015 elected to defer the entire amount [$200,000] of her 2016 annual bonus. The bonus, plus earnings based on a predetermined actual investment, will be paid in a lump sum at her separation from service. In 2018, she is promoted to CEO. In 2020, she separates from service and receives $225,000 (the deferred $200,000 bonus plus $25,000 in earnings). The full $225,000 payment is grandfathered and not subject to the Code Sec. 162(m) deduction limit.

Ability to Amend or Terminate. Most nonqualified plans provide that the company may, at any time, in its discretion, amend the plan to either stop or reduce the amount of future credits to participants' account balances or benefit accruals, but such amendment may not deprive participants of any amount or benefit accrued before the date of the amendment. This commonplace reservation of rights in the company has a significant adverse effect on the amount of benefit that will be grandfathered.

Example: In January 2016, a company and its CFO enter into a nonqualified deferred compensation arrangement. Under the terms of the plan, the company will pay the CFO's account balance in April 2019, but only if he continues to serve as the CFO through December 31, 2018. Pursuant to the terms of the plan, the company credits $100,000 to CFO's account annually for three years, beginning on December 31, 2016 (and credits earnings on the account). However, the plan provides that the company may, at any time, amend the plan to either stop or reduce the amount of future credits to the account balance in its discretion. In April 2019, the company distributes the CFO's $350,000 (including earnings) account balance.

- The plan only constitutes a written binding contract to pay the $100,000 credited to his account balance on December 31, 2016, because the arrangement would have allowed the company to halt contributions in 2017, prior to crediting of the second $100,000. The remaining $250,000 is subject to the Code Sec. 162(m) deduction limit when distributed in 2019.

- If the plan credited earnings quarterly, the participant's $110,000 account balance under the plan as of November 2, 2017, would be grandfathered and $240,000 of the $350,000 payment would subject to the Code Sec. 162(m) deduction limit.

Note that, if this employee had been the CEO instead of the CFO, the entire $350,000 payment would be subject to the Code Sec. 162(m) deduction limit because it was paid while he was still employed. The grandfathering rules only protect compensation that would have been deductible under Code Sec. 162(m) in the year promised, but for 2017 TCJA amendments. That is zero for a CEO (other than performance-based compensation), but unlimited for a CFO.

.06 Steps to Preserve Grandfathering Status

It is important to preserve the grandfathering protection applicable to payments provided under to a written binding contract that was in effect on November 2, 2017, and not modified in any material respect on or after that date.

A company should inventory all compensation plans, policies, and agreements that could be grandfathered, including employment, change in control, severance, and equity award agreements; and nonqualified, short- and long-term incentive plans, and severance plans. The company should list employees covered under any plan or agreement as of November 2, 2017. And the company should not just apply this process to its current NEOs. The TCJA dramatically expanded the universe of employees and former employees who are or can become subject to the deductibility cap and the period of time for which they are subject to it. An employee who is well below the NEO threshold in 2017, also may have accrued benefits or an account balance under a nonqualified plan of the company, which are paid out five, 10, or even 20 years later, after the employee has become a covered employee.

Example: Company awards nonqualified stock options vesting after three years of service to a middle management employee in 2016. By 2020, the employee has worked her way up to named executive officer reported in the proxy. In 2024, she exercises the options. If the company took care to preserve the grandfather status of the 2016 options, it will be entitled to the entire deduction in 2024, despite the fact that the employee is then a covered employee.

Any company not already doing so should track any and all covered employees each year from and after 2017, maintain a historical record, and retain that information until all payments have been made to the employee, former employee, and the beneficiaries of the former employee. Compensation committees and tax departments may need to periodically review the list to make sure the record is being updated and that its consequences are incorporated into compensation decisions and tax reporting.

The company will likely need to seek legal advice on the extent to which each plan and agreement creates a legally binding obligation for the company to pay a specific amount of compensation, including for use by auditors to calculate the deferred tax asset on the company's balance sheet. For how long will the grandfather protection be available to these amounts?

Importantly, companies should not make any changes or amendments or provide for any compensation increases without carefully considering whether such changes could constitute a material modification of a grandfathered plan or agreement.

¶2235 Strategies for Mitigating the Lost Code Sec. 162(m) Deduction

In 2018, companies' focus shifted to mitigating the effect of the loss of a significant deduction for the compensation paid to covered employees, including by exploring other strategies for compensating executives in a manner that preserves deductibility. Companies' options for preserving the deductibility or executive compensation amount not grandfathered are limited. However, we have come up with a few that public companies should consider.

.01 Use of Nonqualified Deferred Plans to Mitigate Lost Deduction Under Code Sec. 162(m)

Nonqualified plans offer one of the best opportunities to limit the impact of new Code Sec. 162(m). Because distribution of a covered employee's nonqualified plan benefit usually occurs after employment termination and can be spread out over a period of time, companies may be able to control the distribution amount in any taxable year, so that, when combined with any other payments to the former employee in that year, the distributions are less than $1 million and, thus, fully deductible. After a covered employee's retirement or other termination of employment, the company still will be able to pay and deduct up to $1 million in benefits each year.

For active executive employees at many companies, $1 million per year may be only a fraction of salary, bonus, and long-term incentive. However, the payments made by many, if not most, companies to former covered employees after retirement or termination will be less than $1 million and, therefore, fully deductible. Even in situations where the annual distribution amount, when combined with other deductible payments, cannot be reduced below $1 million, at least the company will be able to postpone the outflow of cash (with no corresponding deduction) for several years. Cash flow is important to most companies.

Example: As of November 12, 2017, Executive E has an account balance under the nonqualified deferred compensation plan of ABC Corporation of $10 million. If ABC contributed an additional $5 million to A's account over the five-year period ending in 2022 when E retired, ABC could pay out the full $15 million account balance to E in five equal annual installments of $3 million each, after her retirement and, if ABC was making no other payments to E, ABC should be able to deduct each of the annual installment payments in full.

The same deferral and spreading approach could be used to help preserve the deductibility of a portion of a company's annual bonus or stock awards.

Example: In 2019, ABC Corporation intends to award RSUs to Executive E, which would vest in 2021, with a value of $3 million. If ABC made one-half of the award in RSUs that are automatically deferred on vesting, and distributed the shares of stock underlying the RSUs in five installments beginning after E has terminated employment, ABC should be able to deduct each of the annual installment payments in full.

Generally, investors, proxy advisory firms, and regulators (*e.g.*, bank regulators, where applicable) will welcome any plan or program that defers the delivery of stock to executives, as it clearly binds executives to the company's long-term performance

A company that currently maintains a nonqualified plan under which all or a portion of executives' account balances and accrued benefits could be grandfathered, should consider adopting a new plan, effective as of January 2018 or 2019. This way, any future plan design changes should not require a material modification of the existing, grandfathered plan. Of course, companies should be careful to allow the type of continued accruals and contributions that the Notice allows, *e.g.*, for an employee who the company was obligated to add to the plan by contract on or before November 2, 2017, under the existing plan.

.02 Automatic of Voluntary Deferral of RSUs or Annual Bonus

Companies may consider providing for the automatic deferral of certain compensation amounts, such as RSU awards and all or a portion of the short-term incentive bonus. Essentially, the deferred amounts then would become nonqualified deferred compensation and future annual installment payouts could be limited to $1 million per year or less. Many companies have used automatic of voluntary deferral as a part of their compensation programs in the past. Often these companies offered a "kicker" to compensate employees for additional risk of unsecured deferral. For example, in June 2019, a company might offer executives and other employees the choice to receive their 2020 incentive bonus in cash or in deferred RSUs with a fair value equal to 125% of the indicated cash amount.

Future gain or loss on the deferred amounts could be based solely on the company's stock price, particularly in the case of deferred RSUs. The company could place company stock in a rabbi trust to fund the promised deferral.

.03 Code Sec. 409A

Two different sections of the regulations under Code Sec. 409A provide an exception to the prohibition on delaying or deferring payments and allow a company to decide to defer the payment of compensation to an executive, without an election in advance, if the compensation is not deductible under Code Sec. 162(m). In each case, however, the deferred payment must be made as soon as reasonably practicable following the first date on which the company antici- pates that its deduction with respect to such payment will no longer be limited by the application of Code Sec. 162(m). The new "once a covered employee, always a covered employee" rule will complicate some companies' ability to utilize these exceptions, but should not eliminate them.

The exception for further deferral of payments that otherwise would qualify for the short-term deferral exception, also seems to require an element of surprise on the part of the company. This exception requires that the company establish that "as of the date the legally binding right to the payment arose, a reasonable person would not have anticipated the application of section 162(m) at the time of the payment." Therefore, this exception may only be useful for future pay- ments that were promised before November 2, 2017, but not grandfathered. However, every little bit helps.

.04 Incentive Stock Options

One action available to many companies is to award qualifying incentive stock options under Code Sec. 422 ("ISOs"). Generally, ISOs do not result in a tax deduction for the company. However, if a company will not be able to deduct the compensation because of Code Sec. 162(m), why not provide favorable tax consequences for the employee/recipients? Of course, the many requirements that Code Sec. 422 applies to ISOs, including the limit on award date value of $100,000 vesting in any future tax year, will reduce their utility to many employ- ers. And the difference between the market value and the exercise price of an ISO at exercise is subject to the alternative minimum tax ("AMT"). Nonetheless, awarding ISOs it is something to consider.

.05 Scrutinize the Executive Officer Setting and Named Executive Officer Selecting Processes

As discussed above, Notice 2018-68 partially severs the link between the definition of "covered employee" under Code Sec. 162(m) and the definition of "named executive officer" under the Exchange Act. However, the most common scenario under which an individual will become a covered employee is to be reported as a named executive officer of a publicly held company in its proxy statement.

In light of the new once a covered employee, always a covered employee rule, the company should attempt to limit the number of individuals designated who become named executive officers under the proxy statement rules[12] at some point in their career. This will not always be possible, but in some cases, where two executive officers have nearly the same total annual compensation and one of them has not previously been reported as a named executive officer, the company could slightly increase the compensation of the executive who previously had been a named executive officer to limit the number of individuals who become covered employees. Most companies simply let the chips fall where they may in the named executive officer process. However, now that covered employee status is permanent under the once a covered employee, always a covered employee rule, it may make sense to minimize the number of different employees who became named executive officers from year to year.

Additionally, there is no requirement that a public company have five named executive officers. If an employee is not an "executive officer," the employee cannot become a named executive officer. SEC rules[13] define the term executive officer to mean the company's president, any vice president in charge of a principal business unit, division or function (such as sales, administration or finance), any other officer who performs a policy making function or any other person who performs similar policy making functions for the company. Executive officers of subsidiaries may be deemed executive officers of the company if they perform such policy making functions for the company. In our experience, most company have tended to err on the side of overinclusion of individuals as executive officers. Companies may want to reconsider this approach.

.06 Qualified Plan SERP-Shift

Another possibility that could be available to some companies is something we used to call a "QSERP" or "SERP-Swap." The SERP-shift was a highly tax-efficient method for providing deductible and secure compensation for executive employees under a tax-qualified 401(k) or pension plan. The possibility of providing additional tax deductible benefits to executives under a pension plan is a strategy that may not work for most companies, but definitely will work for some public companies. And it is always preferable to providing additional benefits under a nonqualified deferred compensation plan. Having a pension plan in place already is helpful, but not essential.

.07 Coordinated Covered Employees' Exercises of Nonqualified Options

With the cooperation of covered employees, a company could attempt to keep the amount of gain any such employee realizes upon exercise of his or her stock options in any year, when combined with any other payments to the employee in that year, to $1 million or less. This may help preserve deductibility in some cases.

---

[12] Item 402(a)(3) of Regulation S-K.   [13] § 240.3b-7

¶2235.06

.08 New Code Sec. 199A

The TCJA tightened the screws on Code Sec. 162(m), but created a new Code Sec. 199A, providing a generous 20% deduction for individual taxpayers to exclude pass-through trade or business income (*i.e.*, from a sole proprietorship, partnership, LLC, S corporation) referred to as "qualified business income" or "QBI." One might think that this new provision is only for the small entrepreneurial companies for which is was designed, with no application for executives at public companies or large pass-through companies. But one would be wrong! A public company might look among its subsidiaries and find a qualifying trade or business that throws off predictable income, and that could be housed in an LLC or other pass-through entity, or is already in a pass-through, which generates "QBI" as defined in Code Sec. 199A, Then the company could award partnership interests to a few senior executives. This approach could deliver compensation that potentially avoids the deductibility cap of Code Sec. 162(m) – because that income never flows up to the public parent. Additionally, any such compensation would be taxable to the executive at a reduced rate of only 20%, due to the Code Sec. 199A deduction.

¶2245 Provisions No Longer Relevant After the Tax Cuts and Jobs Act of 2017

In light of the repeal the performance-based compensation exception and other changes made to Code Sec. 162(m) by the TCJA, the following requirements no longer will apply:

- The requirement that the compensation committee establish performance goals in advance,

- The requirement that the performance goals be based solely on objective factors,

- The requirement that the compensation committee has no ability or discretion to increase payout above those dictated by the pre-established performance goals,

- *The requirement that the compensation committee be comprised solely of two or more outside directors,*

- The requirement that the compensation committee certify that performance goals were achieved, before payment is made, and

- The requirement that the material terms of any performance goals be disclosed to and subsequently approved by the company's stockholders before the compensation is paid.

Until the grandfathering protection applicable to payments provided under to a written binding contract that was in effect on November 2, 2017, and not modified in any material respect on or after that date, companies will want to continue to comply with many of the provisions of Code Sec. 162(m) relating to the performance-based compensation exception.

.01 Qualified Performance-Based Compensation under Old Law

Before 2018, the exemption for qualified performance-based compensation provided most of the planning opportunities under Code Sec. 162(m). Nearly every public company in the country had a portion of its executives' compensation qualified as performance-based compensation. Until the grandfathering protection applicable to payments provided under to a written binding contract that was in effect on November 2, 2017, and not modified in any material respect on or after that date, companies will want to continue to comply with many of the provisions of Code Sec. 162(m) relating to the performance-based compensation exception.

To qualify as performance-based compensation the company and the compensation paid had to satisfy a number of requirements. These requirements were as follows:

- The compensation is paid *solely* because the executive has attained one or more *pre-established, objective* performance goals;

- A compensation committee comprised solely of two or more outside directors establishes the performance goals;

- The material terms of the performance goals must be disclosed to and subsequently approved by the corporation's shareholders before the compensation is paid; and

- The compensation committee must certify in writing, before payment of the compensation, that the performance goals and any other material terms were in fact satisfied.[14]

To consider a performance goal "pre-established" under Code Sec. 162(m), the compensation committee must put it in writing no later than the 90th day of the period of service to which the performance goal relates. However, if the period of service is shorter than 360 days, then the goal cannot be set after 25% of the period of service has elapsed. In addition, the outcome must be substantially uncertain at the time the compensation committee sets the goal.[15] There is little formal guidance regarding the meaning of "substantially uncertain." However, the regulations indicate that a bonus based on profits will generally be substantially uncertain, even if the company has a history of profitability, while a bonus based on total sales will generally not be substantially uncertain because the company is virtually certain to have at least some sales.[16]

A pre-established performance goal must be objective both in terms of determining whether the goal is met and in terms of determining the amount of compensation payable to the executive if the goal is met. The objectivity requirement is generally satisfied if a third party, having knowledge of the relevant performance results, could determine whether the goal is met and could calculate the amount the company must pay to the executive.[17]

---

[14] Reg. § 1.162-27(e).
[15] Reg. § 1.162-27(e)(2)(i).

[16] Reg. § 1.162-27(e)(2)(vii), Example 2 and Example 3.
[17] Reg. § 1.162-27(e)(2).

The compensation formula, or standard, must preclude discretion to *increase* the compensation payable upon attainment of the performance goal. On the other hand, the company may retain discretion with regard to *reducing* the amount of compensation payable to the executive. As a result, a compensation committee can retain significant discretion by establishing an extremely high ceiling on compensation and then "reducing" the compensation to a level it later determines to be appropriate. The compensation committee can also base the compensation formula on a percentage of salary and retain discretion to increase the executive's salary, but only if the objective compensation formula sets forth, at the time the performance goal is established, a maximum dollar amount that can be paid upon attainment of the performance goal.[18]

Before 2018, Code Sec. 162(m) treats compensation as paid on a commission basis (and, therefore, excluded from the $1 million deduction calculation) if facts and circumstances indicate that the company paid the compensation *solely* on account of income generated *directly* by the individual performance of the executive to whom the compensation is paid. The executive's use of support services, such as secretarial or research services, in order to generate income does not prevent the executive's related compensation from being treated as commissions. Otherwise, the test for determining "commissions" is strict: if compensation paid to an executive is based on broader performance standards than the executive's individual performance (*e.g.*, a performance standard based on the income produced by a business unit of the corporation), then the compensation will not be treated as commissions for purposes of Code Sec. 162(m).[19] Compensation that the Code does not treat as "commissions" can still be exempt from the $1 million deduction limit if it qualifies as performance-based compensation. Most senior executives are not paid on a commission basis. However, the IRS has ruled that the equity fee paid to a senior executive of a publicly traded executive search firm, for work for a client, meets the exception in Code Sec. 162(m)(4)(B) for remuneration paid on a commission basis.[20]

.02 Compensation Committee Consisting Solely of Outside Directors

In order to qualify as performance-based compensation, such compensation must be awarded or approved by a compensation committee that consists solely of two or more outside directors. Until the grandfathering protection applicable to payments provided under to a written binding contract that was in effect on November 2, 2017, and not modified in any material respect on or after that date, companies may need to continue to comply with the outside director provisions of Code Sec. 162(m).

For purposes of the performance-based compensation exception, a director is an outside director if the director:

- Is not a current employee of the corporation;

---

[18] Reg. § 1.162-27(e)(2)(iii)(A).
[19] Reg. § 1.162-27(d).

[20] P.L.R. 200541033, June 30, 2005.

- Is not a former employee of the corporation who, during the tax year at issue, receives compensation for prior services other than benefits under a tax-qualified retirement plan;

- Has not been an officer of the corporation; and

- Does not receive remuneration from the corporation, either directly or indirectly, in any capacity other than as a director.[21]

This test could be one of the more vexing issues under Code Sec. 162(m) for compensation committees and their counsel. The IRS has ruled that a former director of an acquired corporation qualifies as an "outside director" of the acquiring corporation for purposes of Regulations § 1.162-27(e)(3).[22] In the case of an affiliated group, the outside directors of the publicly held member are treated as the outside directors of all the members of the affiliated group.[23]

Most public companies request that non-employee directors complete annually a questionnaire designed to verify that they are "outside" directors for purposes of Code Sec. 162(m) (and that they satisfy the independence requirements of the NYSE and Nasdaq). Among the questions asked to determine "outside director" status for Code Sec. 162(m) purposes are the following:

1. During the previous taxable year of the Company ended December 31, 2016, did the Company or an affiliate of the Company make a payment to an entity in which you have a 5% to 50% interest at least equal to the lesser of $60,000 and 5% of the gross revenue of that entity or make a payment for legal, accounting, investment banking or management consulting services to an entity by which you are employed or self-employed in an amount equal to the lesser of $60,000 and 5% of the gross revenue of that entity.

2. Are you employed, other than as a director, by an entity (or any such entity's affiliates) that received or contemplated receiving in any taxable year payments or other consideration from the Company?

The company cannot pay remuneration to the director for any other service. If the director is employed or self-employed (other than as a director) by any entity, the company **can** pay *de minimis* remuneration, directly or indirectly, to that entity during the company's preceding taxable year, but no more.

If the director has a beneficial ownership interest of greater than 50 percent in any entity, the company cannot pay any remuneration, directly or indirectly, to that entity during the company's preceding taxable year. If the director has a beneficial ownership interest in any entity of at least 5 percent but not more than 50 percent, the company **can** pay *de minimis* remuneration, directly or indirectly, to that entity during the company's preceding taxable year, but no more.

For this purpose, remuneration that was paid by the publicly held corporation in its preceding taxable year to an entity is *de minimis* if payments to the entity did not exceed 5 percent of the gross revenue of the entity for its taxable

---

[21] Reg. § 1.162-27(e)(3)(i).   [23] Reg. § 1.162-27(e)(3)(viii).
[22] P.L.R. 200423012.

year ending with or within that preceding taxable year of the publicly held corporation, *except that*, remuneration in excess of $60,000 is not *de minimis* if the remuneration is paid to an entity in which (i) the director has an ownership interest of at least 5%, or (ii) the director is employed or self-employed (other than as a director) and the remuneration is paid for personal services.

Remuneration from a publicly held corporation is considered "for personal services" if (i) the remuneration is paid to an entity for personal or professional services performed for the publicly held corporation (and not for services that are incidental to the purchase of goods or to the purchase of services that are not personal services); *and*, (ii) the director performs significant services (whether or not as an employee) for the corporation, division, or similar organization within the entity that actually provides the personal or professional services to the publicly held corporation, or more than 50 percent of the entity's gross revenues (for the entity's preceding taxable year) are derived from the corporation, subsidiary, or similar organization within the entity, which actually provides personal or professional services to the publicly held corporation.

Also for this purpose, "personal or professional services" includes legal, accounting, investment banking, and management consulting services.

.03 Disclosure to and Approval by Shareholders

The final requirement for compensation to qualify as performance-based compensation was that the company must disclose the material terms of the performance goal to its shareholders, and the shareholders must subsequently approve the compensation by a majority of the votes cast on the issue in a separate vote.[24] Because of this requirement, most public companies sought shareholder approval of their stock and other incentive plans at least every five years.

Despite the elimination of the performance-based compensation exception, a public company will still need to seek shareholder approval of its stock incentive plans because of stock exchanges requirements. However, in 2018 and after, after the elimination of the performance-based compensation exception, companies are likely to only seek shareholder approval when they are adopting a new plan or amending an existing plan (including an amendment to increase the number of shares authorized for issuance).

Until 2018, to qualify for the performance-based compensation exception, a public company had to disclose to shareholders the material terms of its incentive plan, which included:

- The employees who are eligible to receive compensation (particular individuals do not have to be identified by name; instead, a general description of the class of eligible employees by title or class is sufficient);
- A description of the business criteria on which the performance goal is based (the specific targets that are specified under the performance goal do not have to be identified; instead, a general description of the type of

---

[24] Code Sec. 162(m)(4)(C)(ii).

the business criteria being used for the performance goal is sufficient); and

- Either the maximum dollar amount of compensation that could be paid to any employee or the formula used to calculate the amount of compensation to be paid to the employee if the performance goal is attained (the maximum dollar amount must still be disclosed if compensation is based, in whole or in part, on a percentage of salary or base pay).[25]

The company did not need to disclose a material term of a performance goal to shareholders if the compensation committee determines that the information is confidential commercial or business information, the disclosure of which would have an adverse effect on the corporation. Even if the compensation committee makes such a determination, the company still must make certain disclosures to shareholders regarding the performance goal. The company must disclose the specific executives eligible for the performance-based compensation and the maximum amount of compensation. In addition, the disclosure to shareholders must state the compensation committee's belief that material terms of the performance goal are not being disclosed because the information is confidential commercial or business information and that its disclosure would have an adverse effect on the corporation.[26]

Item 402(b)(2)(xii) of Regulation S-K lists, as an example of material information to be disclosed under Compensation Discussion and Analysis of the annual proxy statement, "The impact of the accounting and tax treatments of the particular form of compensation."

Before the elimination of the performance-based compensation exception, companies usually addressed this requirement under the heading: "Federal Tax and Accounting Consequences," with general, non-committal language such as the following:

Code Sec. 162(m) limits the Company's ability to deduct compensation paid in any given year to our CEO and the three other most highly compensated officers other than the chief financial officer (the "Covered Employees") in excess of $1 million. Performance-based compensation may be structured to be exempt from this restriction. The Compensation Committee may grant awards under the Stock Plan, including annual incentive awards, which are intended to meet the performance-based compensation exception under Code Sec. 162(m). However, we reserve the right to design compensation plans and grant awards that recognize a full range of performance and other criteria important to our success regardless of the federal tax deductibility of compensation paid under those plans. Each member of the Compensation Committee satisfies the independence requirements of the NYSE (including the enhanced independence requirements for Compensation Committee members) and is an "outside director" as defined in Code Sec. 162(m).

Rather than reducing companies' discussion of compensation deductibility, the elimination of the performance-based compensation exception is likely to increase companies' discussion of the federal tax consequences. For many companies, a significant portion of executives' compensation will no longer be

---

[25] Reg. § 1.162-27(e)(4).   [26] Reg. § 1.162-27(e)(4)(iii).

deductible. Companies may come under pressure to justify their executive compensation decisions when a significant portion of that compensation is not deductible.

In *Freedman v. Adams*,[27] plaintiffs had filed a stockholder derivative complaint alleging that the board's decision to pay certain executive bonuses without adopting a plan that could make those bonuses tax deductible constituted corporate waste. The trial court held that the complaint failed to allege, with particularity, that the board's decision not to implement a special Code Sec. 162(m) plan was a decision that no reasonable person would have made. The Delaware Supreme Court agreed.

> The board believed that a Section 162(m) plan would constrain the compensation committee in its determination of appropriate bonuses. The decision to sacrifice some tax savings in order to retain flexibility in compensation decisions is a classic exercise of business judgment. Even if the decision was a poor one for the reasons alleged by Freedman, it was not unconscionable or irrational.

Additionally, some cases found a potential violation of federal securities laws where the corporation did not fully disclose the material terms of an executive's incentive compensation program. In *Shaev v. Datascope Corp.*,[28] the court held that the material terms of the company's incentive plan and the performance goals on which the chief executive's compensation was based were "material" within the meaning of Code Sec. 162(m)(4)(C)(ii), even though the specific business criteria, discussed in Reg. § 1.162-27(e)(4), were not. Thus, Datascope's failure to disclose those terms could be a material omission under SEC Rule 14a-9. This case illustrates that more may be at stake in the disclosure of executive compensation than the mere deductibility.

In *Hoch v. Alexander*[29], the Federal District Court in Delaware issued a memorandum opinion allowing plaintiffs' claims against Qualcomm and its directors to go forward. In its 2011 proxy statement, Qualcomm sought stockholders' approval of an amendment of its Long Term Incentive Plan ("LTIP"), which included an increase in the share reserve by 65,000,000 shares. As required by SEC rules, the proxy statement included standard, albeit, imperfect language, regarding the deductibility of certain stock-based compensation under the heading "Federal Income Tax Information."

The lawsuit alleged that the representations made in the proxy statement about the availability of tax deductions were materially false or misleading: "Because the defendants would still pay performance-based compensation under the 2018 LTIP as unamended, regardless of stockholder approval, no vote of the stockholders would make such payments deductible . . . Therefore, contrary to the representations and omissions in the Proxy Statement, awards under the 2018 LTIP as amended will not be tax-deductible even if the stockholders approve it." In a July 2011 ruling that surprised most executive compensation professionals,

---

[27] 58 A. 3d 414, Del. Supreme Court 2013.

[28] *Shaev v. Datascoper*, 2003 U.S. App. LEXIS 3272 (3d Cir. 2003).

[29] Civil Action No. 11-217-RGA, United States District Court, D. Delaware, July 2, 2013.; Civil Action No. 11-217, United States District Court, D. Delaware, July 1, 2011.

the court denied the defendants' motion to dismiss plaintiffs' claims and allowed the suit to continue.

In 2013, a Delaware federal court again refused to dismiss the plaintiffs' claims and allowed the suit to continue. The court gave two primary reasons for its decision:

1. The issue of whether the Qualcomm board implicitly ratified the allegedly defective actions relating to board approval and slating matters for a vote is not properly decided at the motion to dismiss stage.

2. "Defendants have not shown the compensation is deductible," under Code Sec. 162(m).

This second basis for the court's decision was shocking, as Qualcomm and the IRS had entered into an Issue Resolution Agreement, pursuant to which the IRS concurred with Qualcomm that the 2011 LTIP approved by stockholders *was compliant with Code Sec. 162(m)*.

Once the company has disclosed the material terms of a performance goal to the shareholders and they have approved them, no additional disclosure or approval is required unless the compensation committee changes the material terms of the performance goal. However, if the compensation committee retains the authority to change the targets of a performance goal after shareholders approve the goal, material terms of the performance goal must be disclosed to and reapproved by shareholders no later than the first shareholder meeting that occurs in the fifth year following the year in which shareholders previously approved the performance goal.[30]

For purposes of the shareholder disclosure and approval requirements, the shareholders of the publicly held member of the affiliated group are treated as the shareholders of the entire affiliated group.[31]

Except as otherwise specifically provided in the Treasury Regulations, the standards for adequate disclosure that apply under the Exchange Act also apply to the disclosure of the material terms of a performance goal under Code Sec. 162(m).[32]

.04 Stock Options and Stock Appreciation Rights as Performance-Based Compensation

Prior to 2018, Code Sec. 162(m) and the regulations treat stock options and stock appreciation rights more favorably than other types of performance-based compensation. In order to qualify as performance-based compensation, the stock option or a stock appreciation right must satisfy the following requirements:

- The compensation committee must make the grant or award;
- The plan under which the company grants the option or right must state the maximum number of shares with respect to which the company may grant options or rights during a specified period to any employee;

---

[30] Reg. § 1.162-27(e)(4)(vi).   [32] Reg. § 1.162-27(e)(4)(v).
[31] Reg. § 1.162-27(e)(4)(vii).

- The terms of the option or right must provide that the amount of compensation that the employee could receive is based solely on an increase in the value of the stock after the date of the grant or award; and

- The shareholder approval and disclosure requirements discussed above must be satisfied.

If the amount of compensation is not based solely on an increase in the value of the stock after the date of the grant or award, then none of the compensation attributable to the grant or award is qualified performance-based compensation. The only exception to this rule is that the grant or award will qualify as performance-based compensation if the grant or award is made on account of, or if the vesting or exercisability of the grant or award is contingent on, the attainment of a performance goal that satisfies the performance goal requirements.[33]

> **Example:** ABC Corporation grants Executive E an option to purchase 10,000 shares of ABC stock. On the date of grant, the fair market value of the stock is $100 per share, but the stock options' exercise price is $99 per share. E exercises the option to purchase all 10,000 shares three years later, when the fair market value is $150. Although nearly all of D's compensatory benefit stems from the increase in the value of the stock, none of the compensation attributable to the stock option will be qualified performance-based compensation. However, if the stock option plan precluded E from exercising the option granted to her unless ABC experienced a 10% increase in earnings per share, all of the compensation attributable to the stock option could be qualified performance-based compensation and excluded from the $1 million deduction limit.

Another caveat is that compensation attributable to stock options does not constitute qualified performance-based compensation to the extent that the number of shares for which options are granted under an approved plan exceeds the maximum number of shares for which options may be granted under the plan. This can occur, for example, if the company reduces the exercise price of an option after it grants the option, since the reduction is a cancellation of the option and a grant of a new option. The canceled option continues to count against the maximum number of shares for which the company may grant options under the plan, and the new option counts against the maximum number.[34]

However, a grant or award of stock-based compensation may be changed to reflect either a change in corporate capitalization, such as a stock split or dividend, or a corporate transaction, such as a merger, consolidation, spin-off, taxable or tax-free reorganization, or any partial or complete liquidation by a corporation. A modification for one of the reasons will not prevent the stock-based compensation from satisfying the performance goal requirements and thereby becoming exempt from the $1 million deduction limit.[35]

---

[33] Reg. § 1.162-27(e)(2)(vi)(A).
[34] Reg. § 1.162-27(e)(2)(vi)(B).
[35] Reg. § 1.162-27(e)(2)(iii)(C).

.05 Coordination with the Golden Parachute Rules

The $1 million deduction limit is reduced (but not below zero) by the amount of compensation paid to an executive that the golden parachute rules set forth in Code Sec. 280G disallow.

> **Example:** In 2016, ABC Corporation paid $1,500,000 to Executive E, who was a covered employee for the tax year. None of the compensation paid to D was exempt from the $1 million deduction limit, as commissions, perform-ance-based compensation or otherwise. Therefore, ABC could not deduct $500,000 of D's compensation due to Code Sec. 162(m). In addition, $600,000 of the $1,500,000 ABC paid to D was non-deductible because it was an excess parachute payment, as defined in Code Sec. 280G(b)(1). As a result, the $1 million compensation deduction limit under Code Sec. 162(m) is reduced to $400,000, which is the amount that ABC can deduct from the $1,500,000 in compensation that it paid to D.[36]

.06 Companies That Become Publicly Held Corporations

When a company initially becomes a publicly held corporation, the $1 million deduction limit does not apply to any remuneration paid pursuant to a compensation plan or agreement that existed during the period in which the corporation was not publicly held. However, if the corporation became publicly held in connection with an initial public offering ("IPO"), then the exemption applies only to the extent that the prospectus accompanying the IPO disclosed information concerning the preexisting plans or agreements in a manner that satisfied all securities laws then in effect. The company may rely upon this exemption until the earliest of:

- The expiration of the plan or agreement;
- The material modification of the plan or agreement;
- The issuance of all company stock and other compensation that can be allocated under the preexisting plan;
- The first meeting of shareholders, at which directors are to be elected, that occurs after the close of the third calendar year following the calendar year in which the IPO occurred; or
- If no IPO occurred, the first calendar year following the calendar year in which the corporation became publicly held.

If a company grants an executive an award or right after it becomes publicly held but on or before any of the events listed above, any compensation received pursuant to the exercise of the related stock option or stock appreciation right, or the substantial vesting of restricted property, will be exempt from the $1 million deduction limit if the grant was under a plan or agreement that existed prior to the corporation becoming publicly held. If the corporation became publicly held in connection with an IPO, the exemption applies only if the prospectus con-tained sufficient disclosures.[37]

---

[36] Reg. § 1.162-27(g).   [37] Reg. § 1.162-27(f).

Special rules also apply to subsidiaries in affiliated groups that become separate publicly held corporations.

¶2255 Supplemental Wage Withholding and Code Sec. 409

The American Jobs Creation Action of 2004 provided for mandatory income tax withholding at the highest rate of income tax in effect under the Code (currently 35%) to the extent an employee's total supplemental wages from an employer (and other businesses under common control with the employer) exceed $1,000,000 during the calendar year. The rate for optional flat rate withholding on other supplemental wages (i.e., the supplemental wages not subject to the mandatory flat tax rate withholding at the highest rate of tax) remains at 25%.

.01 Supplemental Wage Withholding

The regulations define supplemental wages as wages that are not regular wages. Regular wages are amounts that are paid at a regular rate and not an overtime rate, or at a predetermined fixed amount for a current payroll period. Therefore, commissions, reported tips, bonuses and overtime would normally be supplemental wages (although the regulations permit tips and overtime pay to be treated as regular wages).

The regulations include a list of items that are supplemental wage payments:

- bonuses;
- back pay;
- commissions;
- wages under reimbursement or expense allowance arrangements;
- nonqualified deferred compensation includable in wages;
- noncash fringe benefits;
- sick pay paid by a third party as an agent of the employer;
- amounts includable in income under Code Sec. 409A;
- income recognized upon exercise of a nonqualified stock option;
- imputed income for health coverage for a nondependent; and
- the lapse of a restriction on restricted property that had been transferred from an employer to an employee.

.02 Code Sec. 409A

Under a special rule in the regulations, a payment that otherwise qualifies as a short-term deferral under Code Sec. 409A but that is made after the applicable 2 1/2-month period, may continue to qualify as a short-term deferral if:

(i) the executive employee establishes that the employer reasonably anticipated that Code Sec. 162(m) would prevent the employer from receiving a deduction for such payment,

(ii) as of the date the legally binding right to the payment arose, a reasonable person would not have anticipated the application of Code Sec. 162(m) at the time of the payment, and

(iii) the payment is made as soon as reasonably practicable following the first date on which the employer anticipates that the employer's deduction with respect to such payment would no longer be restricted due to Code Sec. 162(m)'s application.[38]

Another special rule in the regulations provides that an employer may delay a payment to the extent that it reasonably anticipates that if the employer made the payment as scheduled, Code Sec. 162(m) would prevent the employer from deducting the payment. In this situation, the employer must make the payment either during (i) the executive's first taxable year in which the employer reasonably anticipates that the deduction of such payment will not be barred by application of Code Sec. 162(m) or (ii) the period beginning with the date of the executive's separation from service and ending on the later of the last day of the taxable year of the employer in which the executive separates from service or the 15th day of the third month following the executive's separation from service.[39] Additionally, where any scheduled payment to a specific executive in an employer's taxable year is delayed in accordance with this exception, the delay in payment will be treated as a subsequent deferral election unless all scheduled payments to that executive that could be delayed in accordance with this exception are also delayed. Where the payment is delayed to a date on or after the executive's separation from service, the payment will be considered a payment upon a separation from service for purposes of the rules of Code Sec. 409A and, in the case of a specified employee, the six-month delay rule may apply.

¶2265 Deduction Timing Rules for Annual Bonus Payments

Many bonus plans provide that bonuses attributable to Year 1 will be paid early in Year 2, *but only to participants who are employed on the date of payment*. This provision could create a deduction-timing trap for the unwary. Generally, an employer is permitted to deduct in its Year 1 tax year, bonuses that it pays within the first 2½ months of Year 2 (for example, for a calendar-year employer, payment by March 15, 2018, for a 2019 deduction). *However, that grace period only applies if "all events" fixing the obligation have occurred by the end of Year 1.*

Under Code Sec. 461 and the regulations, an accrual-basis taxpayer generally can deduct expenses that meet the "all-events test." The all-events test has three requirements: (i) all events have occurred that determine the fact of the liability, (ii) the amount of the liability can be determined with reasonable accuracy, and (iii) the "economic performance" has occurred (*e.g.*, the employee's performance that triggered the bonus payout).

To the extent Year 1 bonus payments are contingent upon future service in Year 2 (*i.e.*, an employee must work until the payment date), the all events test may not be satisfied and the deduction cannot be taken until the Year 2 tax year.

For plans that pay awards within 2½ months of the employer's year end, the plan terms determine whether the employer can deduct the awards for the year just ended or in the payment year. To satisfy the all-events test, *the award*

---

[38] Treas. Reg. § 1.409A-1(b)(4)(ii).   [39] Treas. Reg. § 1.409A-2(b)(7)(i).

amounts and the obligation to pay must be fixed by year end. A plan based entirely on financial performance should meet the requirement that bonus amounts be fixed as of year end, because the information needed for calculating the bonus is available at year end (even if the numbers still need to be audited).

The requirement that participants' rights to bonuses be vested (that is, the obligation to pay the bonuses be fixed) as of year end can be met in one of two ways. An individual participant's right to a bonus may be vested at year end. That is, even if the person quits early in the following year, before the bonus is actually paid to him or her, the person would be entitled to the bonus. Alternatively, an employer could meet the all-events test by creating a fixed-dollar bonus pool and provide for it to be allocated among and paid to employees who satisfy the plan's terms as of the payment date. If the employer has to pay out the bonus pool even if only one employee ultimately meets the requirements—the all-events test should be satisfied.

Some employers require employees to remain employed until the date the annual bonus is paid in order to receive it. This can be problematic. First, for companies that seek to take the deduction in a prior tax year for bonuses paid within $2^{1}/_2$ months of the subsequent year, requiring employment beyond the last day of the bonus year could cause the plan to fail the "all-events" test for deductibility in the prior year.

In December 2009, the IRS released a Chief Counsel Advice Memorandum that seemed to tighten the deduction of annual bonus rules further.[40] The CCA concluded that the bonus arrangement did *not* satisfy the "all events test" for deductibility in year 1 because services were required of the employees in year 2. Under the facts described in the CCA, an employer/taxpayer paid bonuses to its non-executive employees under a plan that required employees to be employed by the taxpayer on the date that bonuses are paid in order to receive that compensation. Under the terms of the bonus plan, any amounts not paid to employees by virtue of their leaving the company would revert back to the employer.

The IRS Chief Counsel stated that a liability for bonus compensation paid under such a plan is not a fixed liability in the year of the related service. Liabilities meet the all-events test only to the extent that they are firmly established and not contingent. Where, as in these facts, employees cannot receive bonuses unless they are employed on the date of payment, the liability for that bonus compensation is subject to a contingency. Therefore, the liability does not become fixed until the contingency is satisfied—that is, when the employee is still employed on the date of payment and receives the bonus compensation.

The employer argued that it had a fixed and determinable liability at the end of year 1 for 90% of the amount accrued for financial statement purposes for the bonus plan for year 1 and that, as a result, it is entitled to take that amount into account in year 1 under Code Secs. 404(a) and 461. The employer argued that the

---

[40] Chief Counsel Advice 200949040, December 4, 2009.

combination of its bonus plan and its obligation to contribute to charity any amounts not paid to employees was sufficient to fix its liability. The CCA flatly rejected this argument.

The CCA did not address the situation where the employer/taxpayer fixes the precise amount of bonus (or bonus pool) that it will pay in year 2 before the close of year 1, and pays 100% of that amount to the group of employees who are still employed on the payment date. For example, where the employer's board of directors adopts a resolution before the close of year 1 specifying a bonus pool of $x,xxx,xxxx, payable in year 2, and the full amount of that pool will be paid to employees. This still appears to work under Code Sec. 461.

¶2275 Limits on Deductibility for Health Insurance Companies

To punish executives in the private sector health insurance market, Section 9014 of ACA modified Code Section 162(m) to impose limits on the compensation of certain employees of any "aggregate group" of employers that includes a covered health insurance provider ("CHIP"). Code Sec. 162(m)(6) prohibits any member of a CHIP from deducting the compensation paid to certain "applicable individuals" in excess of $500,000. In September 2014, the IRS issued final regulations under Code Sec. 162(m)(6).[41]

Unlike the rest of Code Sec. 162(m), this $500,000 limitation applies to both privately held and public traded companies. As noted above, the TCJA repealed the performance-based compensation exception for publicly traded corporations. Code Sec. 162(m)(6) never contained an exception for performance-based compensation.

> **Example 1:** Assume that Corporations A, B, C and D are part of the same controlled group (and, thus, treated as a single employer under Sec. 162(m)(6)). Corporations A, B and C do not receive any "health insurance premiums" for the 2018 taxable year, and Corporation D receives health insurance premiums for the 2018 taxable year in an amount equal to 4% of the combined gross revenues of A, B, C and D. All officers, directors, and employees of Corporations A, B, C and D would be treated as "applicable individuals" of a CHIP for the 2018 taxable year, and any deferred compensation attributable to services performed in the 2018 taxable year, which otherwise would be deductible in future taxable years, would be subject to the $500,000 deduction limitation.

> **Example 2:** Under the same facts, except that Corporation D receives health insurance premiums for the 2018 taxable year in an amount that is less than 2% of the combined gross revenues of A, B, C and D. Corporations A, B, C and D would not be treated as a CHIP for the 2018 taxable year, and any deferred compensation attributable to services performed in the 2018 taxable year, which otherwise would be deductible in future tax years, would not be subject to the $500,000 deduction limitation.

---

[41] 26 C.F.R. § 1.162-31.

.01 Defining the CHIP

For purposes of Code Sec. 162(m)(6), the aggregate group includes parent-subsidiary controlled groups, affiliated service groups and non-corporate entities under common control. Generally, a brother-sister controlled group would not an aggregate group. All compensation from all employers in the aggregate group would be aggregated for this purpose. If one entity in an aggregate group is a CHIP, the $500,000 limit applies to all compensation paid to any applicable individual of any entity in that aggregate group.[42]

.02 Other Defined Terms

A "disqualified taxable year" for any employer is any taxable year beginning after 2009, for which the employer is a CHIP. Any health insurance issuer would be a CHIP for a year if no less than 25% of its gross premiums are from providing health insurance coverage that is "minimum essential coverage" (as defined in the ACA). An "applicable individual," with respect to any CHIP for any "disqualified taxable year," is any individual (i) who is an officer, director, or employee in such taxable year, or (ii) who provides services for or on behalf of such covered health insurance provider during such taxable year. The term "applicable individual" does not include an independent contractor providing substantial services to multiple unrelated customers.

.03 Affected Compensation

Code Sec. 162(m)(6) limits the allowable deduction to $500,000 for "applicable individual remuneration" *and* "deferred deduction remuneration" attributable to services performed by applicable individuals at a CHIP.

- "Applicable individual remuneration" for any disqualified taxable year is the aggregate amount otherwise allowable as a deduction for such taxable year, *e.g.*, salary and some annual bonuses, for remuneration for services performed by such individual (whether or not during the taxable year), but does not include any deferred deduction remuneration with respect to services performed during the disqualified taxable year.

- "Deferred deduction remuneration" is compensation for services that an applicable individual performs during a disqualified taxable year but that is not deductible until a later taxable year (*e.g.*, nonqualified deferred compensation; equity compensation).

In the case of deferred deduction remuneration attributable to services performed in a disqualified taxable year, the unused portion of the $500,000 limit (if any) for the taxable year in which the services to which the deferred deduction remuneration is attributable were performed is carried forward to the taxable year or years in which such compensation is otherwise deductible, and applied in calculating the allowable deduction with respect to such amount.

---

[42] Treas. Reg. Sec. 1.162-31(b)(4)(v) provides an exception for *de minimis* premiums. If the premiums for minimum essential coverage received by all members of the aggregate group are less than 2 percent of the gross revenue of the aggregate group for the tax year, the aggregate group would not be subject to the deduction limit.

The final regulations describe various methods for carrying forward deferred deduction remuneration for different types of plans. Generally, stock options, SARs, restricted stock, restricted stock units, and other stock-based compensation must be attributed on a daily pro rata basis to service performed by the applicable individual from the grant date until the date the compensation is paid and becomes taxable (*e.g.*, the exercise of the option or vesting of restricted stock). However, for stock options and SARs the regulations allow an employer to attributes the compensation over the period from grant until vesting, which would better align the tax allocation with the financial accounting expense accrual.

For account balance plans, the regulations describe two permitted allocation methods.[43] Under the account balance ratio method an employer would allocate the deductible amount to each year the individual provided services, based on the ratio of the increase in the account balance for that year over the total increases in the account balance for all years in which the individual provided services. Under the principal additions method an employer would attribute earnings to the tax year in which the individual's account is credited with the principal amount.

The regulations also describe two permitted allocation methods for allocating deferred deduction remuneration for nonaccount balance plans, *e.g.*, a SERP. Under the present value ratio method, the deduction is attributed to each of taxable years based on the ratio of the increase in the present value of the individual's benefit for the year to the sum of all such increases for all taxable years in which the individual was a service provider. Under the formula benefit ratio method, the employer would allocate the deferred deduction remuneration to each year of service in which there was an increase in the individual's accrued benefit.

Code Sec. 162(m)(6) applies to deferred deduction remuneration attributable to services performed in a disqualified taxable year beginning after December 31, 2009, which otherwise would be deductible in a taxable year beginning after December 31, 2012.

In January 2011, IRS issued Notice 2011-02, providing guidance on the application of Code Sec. 162(m)(6). Code Sec. 162(m)(6) generally applies to remuneration attributable to services performed in a "disqualified taxable year" beginning after December 31, 2012, which is otherwise deductible in such taxable year. However, Code Sec. 162(m)(6) applies to *deferred deduction remuneration attributable to services performed in a disqualified taxable year beginning after December 31, 2009*, which otherwise would be deductible in a taxable year beginning after December 31, 2012.

---

[43] Treas. Reg. § 1.162-31(d)(1).

Chapter 23
EXECUTIVE COMPENSATION ISSUES FOR MULTINATIONAL EMPLOYERS

¶2301 Introduction—Executive Compensation Issues for Multinational Employers

With increasing frequency, employers incorporated or based in the United States employ U.S. citizens or local residents as executives outside the U.S. Similarly, foreign employers employ U.S. citizens both within and outside the U.S. This chapter will identify and summarize the significant tax and other regulations affecting these employment relationships. This includes issues arising in income tax liability, pension and retirement benefits, equity compensation, Social Security contributions and benefits, employee health and welfare benefit plans, and employment discrimination. This chapter will not address the significant social and cultural differences or immersion problems that may affect employees on international assignment.

Multi-national corporations that attempt worldwide consistency among their compensation programs have found that there is no one-size-fits-all, and instead are customizing compensation and benefit packages to meet the needs of the individual markets. Employing inpatriate or expatriate executives for international assignment invokes countless nation-specific issues. It would be nearly impossible to categorize all forms of the intricacies of each country or region where an employer may station international workers. For example, every country will have varying degrees of regulatory sophistication, tax and law enforcement abilities, foreign exchange controls, or adequate housing options. Any such differences from the home country could have an effect on the employee benefits and executive compensation package that would be appropriate.

.01 Taxation Issues

Employers' stock option awards in the U.S. have favorable tax consequences to the recipient employees. However, this is not the case in many other countries. Some countries will treat the mere grant of a stock option or other award as a taxable event to the recipient employee. For estate tax purposes, shares of stock and stock options issued by U.S. corporations are deemed to be situated in the U.S. and, therefore, subject to estate tax, even if the decedent/holder was a noncitizen or nonresident at his or her time of death (see ¶2315).

.02 Retirement Plan Issues

Non-U.S. citizens who work for employers in the U.S. frequently wish to receive benefits under the U.S. employer's retirement plans. ERISA and the Internal Revenue Code generally permit non-U.S. citizens to accrue benefits based on their U.S. earned income (see Chapter 17 [¶1701 et seq.] for a detailed description of nonqualified retirement plans and Chapter 16 [¶ 1601 *et seq.*] for a detailed description of qualified retirement plans). Tax treaties between the U.S. and other nations govern the portability and taxation of retirement benefits accrued by an executive working in one country and paid to the executive when he or she is living in a different country.

However, non-U.S. citizens who work for employers in the U.S. on a temporary basis often do so pursuant to a "secondment agreement." That is, while working in the U.S., the employer treats the individual for all purposes, including retirement benefits, as continuing employment with the foreign company. U.S. citizens working abroad generally want to remain covered under the U.S. companies' benefit plans (see ¶ 2325 for a detailed discussion of pension and retirement plan issues).

.03 Stock Plan Issues

Most U.S. corporations that compensate their U.S. executives with stock options, restricted stock and other equity-based awards wish to provide similar awards to their executive employees outside of the U.S. (see Chapter 6 [¶ 601 *et seq.*] for a detailed description of stock incentive plans). The non-U.S. executives often demand such awards. While U.S. multinational companies making stock awards to non-U.S. citizens in foreign countries is widespread, the legal issues relating to such awards are extremely complex. Experienced U.S. legal counsel will seek the advice of a foreign counsel expert in the following matters:

- Exchange control laws;
- Severance benefit issues;
- Discrimination issues;
- Data privacy and restrictions on the transfer of employee data;
- Restrictions on amending plans or halting awards;
- Communications issues;
- Taxation and deductibility issues; and
- Registration and other governmental filing requirements.

(See ¶ 2335 and ¶ 2345 for a detailed discussion of stock plan issues.)

.04 Health and Welfare Benefit Plan Issues

Because of the immediacy of most health plan coverage matters, most executive employees receive such coverage in the country of their employment (see Chapter 19 [¶ 1901 *et seq.*] for a detailed description of health and welfare benefit plans). The exception is for (1) U.S. citizens who work for employers outside of the U.S., and (2) citizens of any nation who work in a country that is not a "first-world" nation, and generally seek the right to return home for significant medical care. An executive's relocation to another country generally does not affect his or her life and disability insurance coverage (see ¶ 2365 for a detailed discussion of welfare benefit plan issues).

.05 Social Security

The U.S. Social Security system applies to any person who performs services for wages in the United States for an employer.[1] American expatriates are not subject to Social Security for employment abroad unless the employer qualifies as an "American employer." Most European countries provide their citizens with very generous Social Security-like benefits, which increase European executives' desire for secondment (see ¶2355 for a detailed discussion of Social Security issues).

.06 Employment Discrimination

Employers of expatriate or inpatriate employees also face the risk of conflicting with local employment discrimination laws because of a compensation arrangement. This can occur where an expatriate executive is directly employed by a foreign subsidiary but compensated according to the norms of his or her home country. For example, under Brazilian labor law, an employer cannot have different salaries and other benefits for similarly situated employees (see ¶2375 for a detailed discussion of employment discrimination issues).

.07 Code Sec. 409A

Code Sec. 409A[2] applies to any plan, program, or agreement providing for deferred compensation. The Code Sec. 409A regulations address several special categories of multinational individuals and plans that may be subject to special rules, including U.S. citizens working outside the U.S. and participating in a foreign plan, non-U.S. citizens working in the U.S. and participating in a foreign plan, and nonresident aliens participating in a U.S.-based plan (see ¶2385).

.08 OFAC Compliance and Other Issues

Multination companies and companies that employ non-U.S. citizens also may need to consider so-called "OFAC" compliance. The U.S. Treasury Department's Office of Foreign Assets Control ("OFAC") currently oversees more than two dozen different sanction programs, currently including countries such as Cuba, Iran, Libya, North Korea, Syria, Russia and many other less obvious countries, and also individuals involved in drug trafficking, terrorism, and other crimes. The list changes from time to time (see ¶2395).

¶2315 Tax Issues for Employee and Employer

Federal income taxes present a myriad of complexities when employees work abroad. Generally, an American expatriate working for a foreign corporation does not have to pay U.S. income tax on income earned abroad.[3] However, the expatriate is subject to the income tax of the host country.

---

[1] *See* Code Sec. 3121(a) (defining "wages" for purposes of Social Security).

[2] Added by the American Jobs Creation Act of 2004, P.L. 108-357, signed into law by President George W. Bush on October 22, 2004.

[3] Code Sec. 114(a) ("Gross income does not include extraterritorial income").

In the case of a foreign national who is transferred to a U.S. employer and becomes a U.S. resident, the inpatriate employee is subject to U.S. federal income taxes on his worldwide income as a U.S. resident. The inpatriate employee also could be subject to the income taxes of the employee's country of citizenship.

.01 Expatriation

By "expatriate" we refer to relocating one's domicile outside the U.S. temporarily — not forever foreswearing allegiance to another country — which is "true expatriation," covered by Code Sec. 877. Expatriation is also sometimes used interchangeably to mean both (i) the act of relinquishing legal status as a U.S. national and (ii) the act of abandoning U.S. domicile.[4] However, the two are very different.

The U.S. international tax regime for individuals is based on nationality status rather than domicile, unlike the tax regimes for most countries, which tax based on residence rather than nationality. The act of abandoning U.S. domicile, *e.g.*, in the case of a transfer of employment overseas, might be more appropriately referred to as emigration.

The United States is one of the few major industrialized nations to tax its citizens regardless of where they work or reside. The U.S. international tax system, like most countries, distinguishes between individuals generally subject to its taxing jurisdiction, who are taxed on their world-wide income by reason of their affiliation with the U.S ("residence-based taxation") and foreign individuals who are not subject to the general taxing jurisdiction of the U.S. and are taxed only on income derived from U.S. sources ("source-based taxation").

The U.S. asserts its general jurisdiction to tax individuals more expansively than almost any other country in two respects. (One could debate whether this is necessary because of the fact that the U.S. has the cleverest tax lawyers or because it has the most rapacious taxing authorities.) First, the U.S. taxes its citizens and green card holders on their worldwide income, whether or not they are actually domiciled or resident in the U.S. This expansive reach has led some to refer to the U.S. system as "nationality-based."[5] With a few exceptions, every other nation asserts its jurisdiction to tax individuals under a residency-based regime, only if they are actually resident in the nation.

Second, the U.S. also defines its international income tax base more broadly than most countries. U.S. citizens and green card holders are subject to net income tax on their worldwide income, wherever earned or paid. However, the U.S. then offers a foreign tax credit for the income tax imposed by other countries on the income earned in those countries.[6] U.S. citizens working and living abroad are also permitted to exclude employer-reimbursed housing costs over a base amount.

---

[4] Every election year, a few dim-witted Hollywood celebrities threaten to leave the country if their candidate does not win. Sadly, none of them made good on their threat.

[5] See, Andrew Walker, "The Tax Regime for Individual Expatriates: Whom to Impress," Tax Lawyer, Vol. 58, No. 2, p. 555.

[6] Code Secs. 901-904.

However, since this tax credit is limited, it allows foreign nations to tax the income of U.S. citizens working there, while preserving the U.S. government's right to any income above the credited amount.

By asserting this expansive taxing authority, the U.S. tax system creates an incentive for true "expatriation." Cognizant of this fact, the U.S. Congress has made it progressively harder over the years for U.S. citizens to expatriate. In the American Jobs Creation Act of 2004 (P.L. 108-357), Congress voted to crack down on U.S. citizens who relinquish their citizenship for tax avoidance purposes. The American Jobs Creation Act amended Code Sec. 877 to impose an alternative tax on the worldwide income of a U.S. citizen or green card holder who renounces his or her citizenship and relocates to a different country. Additionally, the law sets out objective rules for determining if tax avoidance motivated the move offshore. If these individuals return to the U.S. for more than 30 days, they will be treated as citizens for federal tax purposes and be taxed on their worldwide income. They also will be required to file annual returns if they are subject to the alternative tax regime.

.02 Tax Equalization

Most employers of expatriates have adopted a policy of tax equalization, or tax reimbursement, for their expatriate workers. Under a tax equalization scheme, the employer sums all U.S. taxes the employee would have been subject to had she worked in the U.S. and the actual amount of foreign taxes owed. Then, the employer subtracts a hypothetical U.S., state, and local tax from that sum and pays the balance to the employee.

A tax equalization agreement is an agreement or program that provides payments intended to compensate the employee for some or all of the excess of the taxes actually imposed by a foreign jurisdiction on the compensation paid by the employer to the employee over the taxes that would be imposed if the compensation were subject solely to United States federal, state, and local income tax, or some or all of the excess of the United States federal, state, and local income tax actually imposed on the compensation paid by the employer to the employee over the taxes that would be imposed if the compensation were subject solely to taxes in the foreign jurisdiction.

Formula for Employer's Tax Reimbursement Cost:

Actual U.S. and State and Local Taxes

+ Actual Foreign Tax

Hypothetical U.S. and State and Local Taxes

= Employer's Tax Reimbursement Cost

Thus, the expatriate realizes the same net income as if he or she worked domestically.[7] If the expatriate is required to file U.S. income taxes, Code Sec. 911 provides a foreign earned income ("FEI") exclusion from the calculation of the taxpayer's gross income.[8] For foreign earned income received in 2018 or thereafter, the expatriate may exclude up to $103,900 of foreign earned income.[9]

Tax exposure of inpatriate employees depends upon the person's residency for tax purposes. Under Code Sec. 7701(b), a person is a U.S. resident alien if the individual (1) is a lawful, permanent resident at any time during the calendar year; (2) meets the "substantial presence test";[10] or (3) elects to be treated as a resident.[11] If the inpatriate is neither a U.S. citizen nor a resident alien under Code Sec. 7701(b)(1)(A), then the Internal Revenue Code will treat such individual as a nonresident alien ("NRA").[12] The Code provides an exception for inpatriates who were present in the U.S. for less than one-half of the current calendar year (fewer than 183 days), can establish a "tax home" in another country, and have "a closer connection to such foreign country than to the United States."[13] The determination of a "tax home" for purposes of this exception is the same as under Code Sec. 162(a)(2).[14]

A separate tax regime for U.S. earned income applies to an inpatriate who remains an NRA under the criteria set forth under Code Sec. 7701(b)(1)(B). First, income from sources within the U.S. that are not connected with a U.S. trade or business including wages, salaries, and other compensation, is subject to federal income taxation at a flat 30% rate.[15] Capital gains income that is not "effectively connected with the conduct of a trade or business within the United States" is also taxed at a flat 30% rate.[16] Except for casualty or theft losses under Code Sec. 165(c), charitable contributions under Code Sec. 170, and the Code Sec. 151 personal exemption, there are no allowable deductions to reduce the burden of the 30% tax.[17] Income of an NRA engaged in trade or business within the U.S. is taxable as provided under the graduated tax scheme under Section 1 or the alternative minimum tax imposed under Code Sec. 55.[18]

---

[7] This ignores the actual purchasing power of the net income in U.S. dollars abroad, which rises and falls.

[8] Code Sec. 911(a) ("At the election of a qualified individual . . . there shall be excluded from the gross income of such individual, and exempt from taxation under this subtitle, for any tax year . . . the foreign earned income of such individual.")

[9] Code Sec. 911(b)(2)(D).

[10] A person meets the substantial presence test if he was present in the U.S. on at least 31 days during the calendar year *and* was present in the U.S. for at least 183 days during the current year and the preceding two calendar years (discounted by an applicable multiplier). *See* Code Sec. 7701(b)(3) (setting forth the requirements of the substantial presence test and providing a table for the applicable multiplier for presence in prior calendar years).

[11] Code Sec. 7701(b)(1)(A).

[12] Code Sec. 7701(b)(1)(B); *see* Reg. §1.872-1 (as amended in 1974) (defining inclusions and exclusions for gross income of NRAs).

[13] Code Sec. 7701(b)(3)(B).

[14] Code Sec. 7701(b)(3)(B)(ii). *See* Code Sec. 911(d)(3) (defining "tax home"); *see also* Code Sec. 162(a)(2) (deduction for ordinary and necessary traveling expenses in the course of carrying on any trade or business).

[15] Code Sec. 871(a)(1).

[16] Code Sec. 871(a)(2).

[17] Code Sec. 873. *See also* Code Sec. 165(c), Code Sec. 170 and Code Sec. 151 (detailing deductions that would be deductible from the 30% tax).

[18] Code Sec. 871(b)(1); *see also* Code Sec. 1 ("Tax Imposed"); Code Sec. 55 ("Alternative Minimum Tax" imposed).

An inpatriate employee also may be subject to state income taxes if he or she meets the residency criteria under applicable state tax laws. State residency is not necessarily determined in the same manner as federal residency. In other words, an inpatriate may be treated as a resident alien for federal tax purposes, but as a nonresident for state tax purposes, and vice versa. Most states determine residency using the concept of domicile.[19]

Foreign tax authorities have been known to enforce their laws vigorously much like the U.S. Internal Revenue Service. In one widely publicized case, Japanese tax authorities from the National Tax Administration leveled income tax surcharges on some 180 expatriates of Credit Suisse First Boston, Macquarie Securities, Dresdner Kleinwort Wasserstein, and other foreign securities companies.[20] These foreign employers apparently were treating performance bonuses and commissions earned by expatriate workers as retirement income subject to much lower tax rates. The NTA determined that such characterization constituted tax evasion.

.03 Tax Increase Prevention and Reconciliation Act

The ironically titled Tax Increase Prevention and Reconciliation Act ("TIPRA"), signed into law in May 2006, revised Code. Sec. 911, which limits taxation of U.S. citizens working abroad. Specifically, TIPRA (i) taxes U.S. citizens working overseas at higher marginal rates, and (ii) subjects any employer-paid housing allowance to higher tax rates. Therefore, many expatriates paid more U.S. income tax in 2006 and after.

TIPRA changes the way marginal tax rates apply to foreign income that is not excluded from U.S. income tax, so that the first dollar earned above the exclusion amount (set at $103,900 for 2018) is taxed at a higher rate—the rate that would have applied if there had been no exclusion.

> For example: ABC Corporation sends Executive D to manage its location in France. D earns $100,000 for 2006. D would have $82,400 of excluded income and $17,600 of taxable income, taxed at rates that apply to the taxable income range of $82,400-$100,000 (25 percent or 28 percent), instead of the $0-$20,000 range (10 percent or 15 percent) applicable previously.

TIPRA also placed a cap on the amount of housing allowance U.S. residents living abroad can receive tax-free from their employer. TIPRA limits the exclusion of housing reimbursements by overseas employees to 30% of the maximum foreign compensation exclusion, less the base amount that is set as the government-estimated cost for housing in the United States (set at $14,456 for 2018). As limited, the maximum housing exclusion for 2018 amounts to $14,546 (30% × $103,900 − 16% × $103,900).

However, TIPRA authorized the Treasury Department to issue regulations or other guidance to adjust the maximum limitation on housing expenses for

---

[19] *See, e.g.*, 35 ILCS 5/1501(a)(20)(A) (defining resident as a person present or domiciled in the state); N.Y. Tax Law Section 605(b)(1) (defining resident individual as one who is domiciled in the state, with some exceptions).

[20] As reported in the Bureau of National Affairs Pension & Benefits Daily, October 6, 2004.

areas with high housing costs. In response, the IRS issued guidance that established the complete list of adjusted housing expense limitations for specified cities and countries for the tax year.[21] These limitations, less the base U.S. housing cost of $16,624 (for 2018), constitute the maximum housing exclusion amount that a taxpayer living in these locations may claim. The IRS will re-issue the guidelines each year.[22]

.04 Deferred Compensation and Equity Compensation

Taxation of income earned by expatriates and inpatriates largely revolves around application of the Internal Revenue Code's "source rules." Generally, the Code considers compensation for labor or personal services performed in the United States as U.S.-source income.[23] Deferred compensation for the inpatriate employee will be subject to U.S. tax in proportion to the inpatriate's service in the U.S.[24] In contrast, to the extent that the deferred compensation relates to service performed outside the United States, it will not be subject to U.S. federal income taxes.[25]

The IRS taxes deferred compensation for services performed in the United States by authority of Code Sec. 871(b). In a private letter ruling, the IRS considered the amount of tax for restricted stock compensation with regard to an inpatriate employee.[26] The employees at issue were non-U.S. citizens performing services in the U.S. who were awarded stock compensation before returning to their home country. The employees' stock vested either upon retirement or upon five years from the date of award. Because the stock was subject to a substantial risk of forfeiture until it vested, the stock was not taxable as compensation under Code Sec. 83 until it became vested and transferable.[27] The individual performed some services within the U.S. during the vesting period, but was an NRA at the time the stock became vested and transferable. The IRS decided that a portion of the stock's value was compensation for service performed in the United States, and subject to 30% U.S. income tax. To calculate the amount of U.S.-source income subject to the tax, the IRS advised the taxpayer to use the following formula:

---

[21] http://www.irs.gov/pub/irs-pdf/i2555.pdf.

[22] Notice 2007-25, 2007-12 I.R.B. 760.

[23] There are three exceptions to this general rule: (1) Labor or services performed by an NRA present in the U.S. for a period or periods not exceeding a total of 90 days during the tax year; (2) if the compensation is less than $3,000 in the aggregate, it is deemed not to be U.S.-source income [known as the "de minimis" rule]; and (3) if the compensation is for labor or services performed as an employee of a NRA, foreign corporation or partnership that is *not* engaged in trade or business with the United States. Code Sec. 861(a)(3).

[24] Harold Adrion, *Compensating the International Executive Using Stock Options*, TAX NOTES INTERNATIONAL, March 27, 2000, at 1481.

[25] Harold Adrion, *Compensating the International Executive Using Stock Options*, TAX NOTES INTERNATIONAL, March 27, 2000, at 1481.; *see also* Code Sec. 911(a) (excluding foreign earned income from calculation of gross income).

[26] IRS Letter Ruling 8711107 (Dec. 17, 1986).

[27] *See* Code Sec. 83(a) (property transferred in connection with performance of services is not included in the taxpayer's gross income until "the rights of the person having the beneficial interest in such property are transferable or are not subject to a substantial risk of forfeiture . . . ").

Fair Mkt. Value of Stock at Time of Vesting	−	Amount Paid for Stock, if any	×	No. of Days Worked in U.S. During Vesting Period
				Total No. of Days Worked During Vesting Period

U.S. tax law would include the amount yielded by this formula in gross income and tax it according to the 30% rate imposed on a nonresident alien's income.

If the inpatriate employee had been a resident on the date of substantial vesting, however, the employee would be taxed on all of the income as if he or she was a U.S. citizen. Similarly, under the "source rules," if an expatriate employee earns equity compensation for services performed abroad, that income is excludable as FEI.[28]

.05 U.S. Estate and Gift Taxes Applicable to NRAs

A citizen or resident of the United States for estate and gift tax purposes is generally liable for U.S. estate and gift taxes on transfers of all property, whether such property is located within or outside the U.S. For NRAs, that is, non-U.S. citizens *not* domiciled in the U.S., transfers of property at death or during lifetime could be subject to U.S. estate or gift taxes at the same graduated marginal rates applicable to transfers by U.S. citizens and residents. However, this is only true with respect to certain property that is physically situated or deemed to be situated in the U.S. ("U.S. situs property").[29] Lifetime transfers of intangible property (such as stock or stock options) by an NRA are exempt from U.S. gift tax. This is true even if the property is U.S. situs property (for example, U.S. shares or stock options), and whether gifts are made outright to the donee or in trust.

U.S. real estate is property situated in the U.S. for estate and gift tax purposes, as is tangible personal property physically located in the U.S. In general, equity securities (including stock options, restricted stock and mutual fund shares) issued by U.S. corporations are deemed to be situated in the U.S., and, therefore, are subject to estate tax if owned by an NRA at death. Therefore, stock options and restricted stock granted by U.S. corporations are subject to U.S. estate tax when owned by an NRA, unless a tax treaty provides otherwise or the NRA's U.S. situs assets are $60,000 or less. U.S. estate tax rates are high compared to inheritance tax rates in most other countries.

An NRA can eliminate a significant amount or, in most cases, all of his or her U.S. estate and gift tax exposure by holding U.S. situs assets in a company incorporated outside of the U.S. because, in such cases, the nondomiciled noncitizen directly owns only non-U.S. property (that is, the non-U.S. company shares). The NRA may hold the shares of this offshore company in a trust. An NRA could establish a holding company outside the U.S. precisely for the

---

[28] Code Sec. 911(a).

[29] Arthur Winter, Winter & Associates Client Memorandum, January 31, 2000.

purpose of holding U.S. assets. If the holding company observes essential corporate formalities, U.S. tax authorities should not attack this arrangement as a sham.[30]

¶2325 Pension and Retirement Benefits

Non-U.S. citizens who work for employers in the U.S. frequently wish to receive benefits under the U.S. employer's retirement plans. ERISA and the Internal Revenue Code generally permit non-U.S. citizens to accrue benefits based on their U.S. earned income (see Chapter 17 [¶ 1701 *et seq.*] for a detailed description of nonqualified retirement plans and Chapter 16 [¶ 1601 *et seq.*] for a detailed description of qualified retirement plans). Similarly, U.S. employers often wish to continue the qualified retirement plan coverage of expatriate employees they send to work overseas.

.01 Covering U.S. Citizen - Expatriate Employees Under U.S. Qualified Plans

Whether the U.S. employer can cover the employee under its U.S. qualified plan may depend largely on whether the employee is transferred to an affiliate that is in the same controlled group under Code Sec. 414 as the U.S. employer, an affiliate that is not within the same controlled group, or to a branch of the U.S. employer that is not a separate affiliate.

If an expatriate employee is transferred to a foreign branch of the U.S. employer, the employee is employed by the same entity and therefore, the expatriate employee's coverage in U.S. tax-qualified plans may be continued. Similarly, in the case of an employee transferred to a foreign affiliate that is in the same controlled group, the expatriate employee's coverage under the U.S. qualified plan may be continued because Code Sec. 414(b) and Code Sec. 414(c) treat all members of a controlled group as a single employer for most plan qualification purposes.[31] Code Sec. 407 also provides that employees of a U.S. parent corporation's domestic subsidiary may be treated as employees of the U.S. parent for purposes of covering such employees under the U.S. parent's tax-qualified plans if, among other things, the U.S. parent owns at least 80 percent of the domestic subsidiary and substantially all of its income is foreign source.

If a U.S. employee is transferred to a foreign affiliate that is not in the same controlled group as the U.S. employer, the continued coverage of the U.S. employee under the U.S. employer's tax-qualified plan while employed by the foreign affiliate can be problematic. However, the employer may be able cover the expatriate employee under one of the following methods:[32]

1. Using the special rules of Code Sec. 406, which allows an employee of a "foreign affiliate" of a U.S. employer to be treated as an employee of the U.S. employer for purposes of the qualified plan rules if (a) the U.S.

---

[30] Arthur Winter, Winter & Associates Client Memorandum, January 31, 2000.

[31] Code Sec. 414(b) and Code Sec. 414(c); IRS Letter Ruling 200205050 (November 8, 2001) and IRS Letter Ruling 8228116 (April 19, 1982).

[32] Edward E. Bintz, "Cross-Border Employee Transfers Affect Pension, Stock Option, Other Benefits Plans," Bureau of National Affairs Daily Tax Reporter, June 29, 2004.

employer enters into an agreement to provide Social Security coverage with respect to the employees of the foreign subsidiary who are U.S. citizens or residents under Code Sec. 3121(l),[33] (b) the plan expressly provides for contributions or benefits for U.S. citizens or residents who are employees of foreign affiliates of the U.S. employer to which a Code Sec. 3121 agreement applies, and (c) no contributions are made to a funded deferred compensation plan (whether or not qualified under Code Sec. 401(a)) by any other person with respect to the remuneration paid to the employee by the foreign affiliate.[34]

2. Causing the foreign affiliate to adopt the U.S. qualified plan so that the plan becomes a "multiple employer plan," which will be required to satisfy many of the qualification requirements separately with respect to the foreign affiliate's controlled group.[35]

3. Continue the expatriate employee as an employee of the U.S. employer and treat him or her as a "leased" employee of the foreign affiliate. The foreign affiliate would pay a fee to the U.S. employer to cover the employee's compensation and benefits. This is the expatriate equivalent of the secondment arrangement often used by non-U.S. employers that send inpatriate employees to the U.S.

4. Provide the employee with "imputed" service and compensation credit under the U.S. employer's plan.[36] Code Sec. 401(a)(4) and Code Sec. 414(s) would permit an employee who is transferred by a U.S. employer to a foreign branch or affiliate to receive service and compensation credit under the U.S. employer's tax-qualified plan in respect of employment with the foreign affiliate in situations where the plan does not otherwise directly cover such service or compensation.[37] For a defined benefit plan, both imputed compensation and service may be credited. However, for a defined contribution plan, generally only imputed service may be credited. Moreover, (a) the provisions under which imputed compensation and/or service is credited must apply to all similarly situated employees, (b) there must be a legitimate business purpose, based on all of the facts and circumstances, for providing the imputed compensation and/or service, and (c) the plan provisions under which imputed compensation and/or service is credited must not by operation or design discriminate significantly in favor of highly compensated employees, based on all of the facts and circumstances.[38]

Code Sec. 406(b) addresses the application of nondiscrimination requirements with respect to American expatriates performing services for foreign affiliates of American employers under 3121(l) arrangements. In essence, the

---

[33] See ¶ 2355 (explaining agreements under Code Section 3121(l)).

[34] Code Sec. 406(a).

[35] Code Sec. 413.

[36] Edward E. Bintz, "Cross-Border Employee Transfers Affect Pension, Stock Option, Other Benefits Plans," Bureau of National Affairs Daily Tax Reporter, June 29, 2004.

[37] See Reg. § 1.401(a)(4)-11(d) and Reg. § 1.414(s)-1(f).

[38] See Reg. § 1.401(a)(4)-11(d) and Reg. § 1.414(s)-1(f).

provision requires that if the expatriate is a highly compensated employee ("HCE") within the meaning of Code Sec. 414(q), the Code will treat him or her as such for testing purposes.[39] Code Sec. 406(b)(2) attributes the total amount of compensation for the expatriate paid by the foreign affiliate to the American employer.[40]

.02 Covering Non-U.S. Citizen Under U.S. Qualified Plans

Because the transferring employee will be employed by the U.S. employer that sponsors the plan, he or she will, in many cases, automatically be covered by the plan, or can be so covered by means of a simple plan amendment if coverage is desired. As a result, there is no need to have an affiliate adopt the plan, establish a leased employee arrangement, or provide imputed service and compensation credit with respect to the employee's U.S. employment. The coverage of a foreign national in a U.S. employer's tax-qualified plan does not affect the ability to exclude nonresident aliens who have no U.S. source income for purposes of nondiscrimination testing under Code Sec. 410.

Non-U.S. citizens who work for employers in the U.S. on a temporary basis often do so pursuant to a "secondment agreement." That is, while working in the U.S., the employer treats the individual for all purposes, including retirement benefits, as continuing employment with the foreign company. U.S. citizens working abroad generally want to remain covered under the U.S. companies' benefit plans.

An inpatriate employee residing in the U.S. is subject to U.S. federal income taxes on his or her worldwide income as a U.S. resident and is potentially subject to income taxes under his or her home country's tax laws. Pursuant to Code Sec. 401(a), benefits and contributions under a U.S. qualified plan are not taxable income to a U.S. resident, including an inpatriate. However, benefits and contributions under a U.S. qualified plan could be taxable under the income tax laws of the employee's home country.

The tax treatment of distributions from U.S.-based deferred compensation and pension benefit plans depends upon whether the recipient of the distribution is a resident of a country with which the United States has an income tax treaty.[41] In the absence of a tax treaty, the rules of taxation and withholding on income of NRAs, discussed in ¶2315, will apply.[42] The rate of taxation imposed on inpatriate workers turns upon whether the income is "effectively connected with the conduct of a trade or business within the United States."[43] As discussed above, the Internal Revenue Code will apply a 30% tax on an inpatriate's income that is not effectively connected with the conduct of a trade or business in the U.S.[44] Income that is effectively connected is subject to the graduated income tax rates

---

[39] Code Sec. 406(b)(1)(A); *see* Code Sec. 414(q) (defining HCEs as those who are five-percent owners, had compensation from the employer in excess of $120,000 (for 2018), or are members of the "top-paid group of employees" as defined therein).

[40] Code Sec. 406(b)(2).

[41] IRS Letter Ruling 9041041 (July 13, 1990).

[42] IRS Letter Ruling 9041041 (July. 13, 1990); *see* Code Sec. 894(a)(1) ("The provisions of this title shall be applied to any taxpayer with due regard to any treaty obligation of the United States which applies to such taxpayer.")

[43] Code Sec. 871.

[44] Code Sec. 871(a).

under Code Sec. 1 or the alternative minimum tax.[45] A number of U.S. income tax treaties provide benefits accrued by an employee under a pension plan that is "established and recognized" under the laws of one of the "contracting states" while the employee is employed in the other contracting state are excludible from the employee's income (subject to various conditions).[46]

A frequent issue with regard to pension benefits is whether an NRA who previously performed services in the U.S. must pay U.S. income tax when he or she receives a pension distribution, and, if so, which tax rate is imposed on the distributions. The IRS has considered this question with regard to plans qualified under Code Sec. 401(k). In 1989, the IRS considered whether German citizens who worked in the United States for an American employer would be taxed on 401(k) distributions while they are NRAs residing in Germany.[47] Code Sec. 864(c)(6) provides that deferred payments to an NRA attributable to the performance of services in another tax year will be treated as such income would be treated if it had been received in that prior year.[48] For the inpatriate, a current distribution of pension benefits earned for performing services in the U.S. in past years will be taxed as if the distribution had been made while the inpatriate was performing services in the United States. Distributions not connected with United States business are subject to the 30% tax. That portion of the distributions that are effectively connected, or would have been considered effectively connected in the year the services were performed, will be subject to Code Sec. 1 or the alternative minimum tax.[49] Accordingly, the IRS was of the opinion that a German expatriate's distributions, except for earnings and accretions, would be U.S.-source income effectively connected with a trade or business within the U.S.[50] Therefore, the German citizen-taxpayer would be subject to U.S. taxes under Code Sec. 871(b).[51]

A nonresident alien may participate in a Code Sec. 401(a) qualified pension plan only if the NRA receives earned income within the meaning of Code Sec. 911(d)(2) from the employer, which constitutes income from sources within the U.S.[52]

A foreign retirement plan will be designed to comply with local country law. Therefore, unless a treaty prescribes other treatment, the foreign pension plan generally will be treated as a nonqualified deferred compensation plan for U.S.

---

[45] Code Sec. 871(b).

[46] See United States Model Income Tax Convention of Sept. 20, 1996 (Article 18).

[47] IRS Letter Ruling 8904035 (Oct. 31, 1988).

[48] Code Sec. 864(c)(6) provides: "For purposes of this title, in the case of any income or gain of a nonresident alien individual or a foreign corporation which—(A) is taken into account for any tax year, but (B) is attributable to the sale or exchange of property or the performance of services (or any other transaction) in any other tax year, the determination of whether such income or gain is taxable under section 871(b) or 882 (as the case may be) shall be made as if such income or gain were taken into account in such other tax year and without

regard to the requirement that the taxpayer be engaged in a trade or business within the United States during the tax year referred to in subparagraph (A)."

[49] IRS Letter Ruling 9041041 (July 13, 1990); IRS Letter Ruling 8904035 (Oct. 31, 1988).

[50] IRS Letter Ruling 9041041 (July 13, 1990); IRS Letter Ruling 8904035 (Oct. 31, 1988).

[51] Provided, however, that an income tax treaty does not require otherwise.

[52] Code Sec. 410(b)(3)(C); see Code Sec. 911(d)(2) (defining earned income as wages, salaries, professional fees and other amounts received as compensation).

federal income tax purposes, and covered employees will be subject to U.S. federal income taxes with respect to benefit accruals in accordance with the rules applicable to participation in nonqualified deferred compensation plans.[53] Whether an employee recognizes income with respect to the accrual of vested benefits under a nonqualified deferred compensation plan generally depends upon whether the accrued benefit is treated as "unfunded" and "unsecured" for federal income tax purposes. Because a foreign pension plan is generally treated as a nonqualified plan for U.S. tax purposes, it may not be desirable from a tax perspective for either (a) an expatriate U.S. employee to participate in a funded foreign pension plan while on a foreign assignment or (b) an inpatriate foreign national to continue to participate in a funded foreign pension plan. However, such participation may be feasible from a tax perspective if accruals under the plan are exempted from U.S. federal income taxes by a treaty. In contrast to a funded foreign pension plan, an expatriate or inpatriate employee can generally participate in an unfunded foreign pension plan without adverse U.S. federal income tax consequences under the tax principles described above.

Nonqualified plan benefits or contributions also could be subject to taxation under the income tax laws of the employee's country of citizenship. The tax consequences of a distribution to an inpatriate employee who receives a distribution from a U.S. employer's nonqualified deferred compensation plan generally will depend on whether the recipient is a resident of a country with which the U.S. has an income tax treaty. If a treaty applies and the distribution qualifies as a "pension," it generally would be taxable only in the country in which the employee is resident. However, the IRS has indicated that the phrase "pension and other similar remuneration," as used in the model tax treaty, is intended to refer to qualified plans.[54]

Since overseas assignments often come with relocation bonuses and other supplemental pay, the employer needs to take care to define what types of compensation count in pension and other benefit calculations.

¶2335 Equity Compensation Outside the U.S.

U.S. stock plans have gone global (at the risk of sounding trite). However, a multinational company based in the U.S. or elsewhere must evaluate the myriad of different legal rules and restrictions applicable in each country where the company employs executives to whom it will make awards. Just as it will retain experienced legal counsel to navigate the interlocking requirements applicable to stock incentive plans and award agreements in the U.S., a company making awards to employees outside the U.S. should consult with a foreign counsel expert in compensation matters before making such awards. According to a survey by Towers Perrin, U.S. multinational companies are reducing their long-

---

[53] Edward E. Bintz, "Cross-Border Employee Transfers Affect Pension, Stock Option, Other Benefits Plans," Bureau of National Affairs Daily Tax Reporter, June 29, 2004.

[54] See Treasury Department Technical Explanation of the United States Model Income Tax Convention, (Sept. 20, 1996).

term incentive programs for executives by significantly decreasing the size of the equity awards paid to executives outside the U.S.[55]

Planning Note: Because of the many (and varied) provisions that may need to be added to the plan or an award agreement to comply with local/non-U.S. laws, counsel should consider drafting the plan to expressly permit the company's board or compensation committee to make such additions. For example:

10.1 *Awards to Foreign Nationals and Employees Outside the United States.* To the extent the Company's Board deems it necessary, appropriate or desirable to comply with foreign law or practice and to further the purposes of this Plan, the Board may, without amending the Plan, (i) establish rules applicable to Awards granted to Participants who are foreign nationals, are employed outside the United States, or both, including rules that differ from those set forth in this Plan, and (ii) grant Awards to such Participants in accordance with those rules.

.01 Exchange Control Laws

Many foreign countries have exchange control laws that restrict, or require reporting of, the use of foreign currency—such as U.S. dollars—for transactions in that country.

Some local laws require that both the employee's remittance of funds (*e.g.,* in a cash purchase option exercise) or receipt of funds (*e.g.,* upon sale of the stock acquired) be in local currency. Other countries' laws require that local employees exercise options and/or buy foreign shares only through a local broker. Finally, some countries (*e.g.,* for a time, Brazil) do not permit their citizens or residents to make investments outside the country. Where this is the case, the option agreements of affected employees should provide for cashless exercise only, with a proviso: "unless the [country name] creates a regulation permitting nationals or residents of [country name] to make investments outside the country."

Planning Note: Counsel should draft stock incentive plans and award agreements to authorize expressly the company to discontinue the plan as to any specified country if the company cannot grant stock options to an employee residing in that country due to exchange control laws or any other reason.

.02 Severance Benefit Issues

Many foreign countries require employers to pay severance benefits to a terminated employee. Some of these countries require the employer to take into account any compensation benefits received by the employee under any benefit plan, including a stock option or other stock award plan, when calculating the severance payments due the employee.

---

[55] *2007 Global Long-Term Incentive Policies,* Towers Perrin, 2007.

Planning Note: Legal counsel should always draft the award agreements and all other communications to employees outside the U.S. to make it clear that the stock options or other awards are special remuneration granted in connection with a special offering of securities. For example, in Spain, award agreements and communications could state that: *"options are special remunerations in kind granted in connection with the offering, not suitable to be settled nor consolidated."*

Additionally, some countries will not permit a forfeiture of vested option or stock rights for competition or cause. For example, in Germany, vested rights become part of an employee's assets, and once an option has vested, the company, even in the event of a termination for cause, can never take it away.

.03 Restrictions on Amending Plans or Halting Awards

Some foreign countries, such as Argentina and Mexico, do not allow employers to reduce compensation or withdraw or amend unilaterally an employee benefit plan. Sometimes these laws contain an exception allowing the company to withdraw benefits granted unilaterally to employees if the plan document expressly incorporates the company's power to amend or terminate the plan.

.04 Communications Issues

U.S. companies granting options or other equity awards in foreign countries generally need to be concerned about two categories of issues when preparing and circulating communications, including award notices or agreements, to employees in foreign countries:

1. Drafting the communications to protect the employer from additional liability for compensation or severance. As discussed elsewhere in this chapter, communications should make it clear that the stock award is not part of periodic remuneration. Communications should indicate there are requirements for the employees to whom the company grants options, and that eligibility to participate is at the discretion of the company. For example, Spanish law may treat options as a contractual entitlement if the plan, award agreements and communications do not make clear the company's board awards options in its sole discretion.

2. Just as U.S. securities laws impose certain requirements on securities offerings in the U.S., including option grants and other equity awards, many foreign countries impose restrictions on "publicity or advertising" related to the grant of options or other awards.

Planning Note: Legal counsel should always draft the award agreements and all other communications to employees outside the U.S. to make it clear that the stock options or other awards are special remuneration granted in connection with a special offering of securities.

Finally, some countries require that a company notify local union leaders (or their equivalent) of its intention to make compensation awards to employees in that country. For example, Belgian law could require any employer with a

"Labor Union Delegation" or a "Works Council" to inform such delegation or council of the plan.

.05 Taxation and Deductibility Issues

An employer's award of stock options in the U.S. has very favorable tax consequences to the recipient employee. However, this is not the case in many other countries. Some countries will treat the mere grant of a stock option or other award as a taxable event to the recipient employee. Some other countries will assess tax on the vesting of a stock option or other award. The employer's desire to motivate and reward its foreign employees may be lost if the stock award has negative tax consequences to the employees.

Example: ABC Corporation awards stock options to its executives worldwide. Executive D in Singapore is thrilled, because, as in the U.S., Singapore tax will be charged only on the gain, if any, D realizes when she actually exercises the option. At exercise, D's taxable gain will be the fair market value of the shares at the time of exercise less the exercise price D paid. However, Executive E in Norway is not so happy, since Norway treats both the acquisition of the option and potential gain on sale as taxable events.

A U.S. employer must evaluate, on a country-by-country basis, whether other forms of equity-based compensation, such as stock appreciation rights or phantom stock, would better achieve its goal of rewarding foreign executives with stock ownership (see Chapter 9 [¶ 901 et seq.] for a detailed discussion of phantom stock and SARs).

.06 Registration and Other Governmental Filing Requirements

Many foreign countries require a U.S. (or other foreign) corporation to comply with local securities law registration requirements for any awards it makes to residents of their country, just as U.S. law requires a foreign corporation to comply with securities law registration requirements for any awards it makes to U.S. residents. For example, depending on the type of employees being offered options, a corporation offering stock options to employees in Australia may have to register the prospectus with the Australian Securities Commission ("ASC") before any offer (or within seven days after it makes the offer). If the corporation or plan were awarding stock options only to Australian management employees meeting the definition of "executive officers" under Australian law, the plan would generally be exempt from the registration requirement. For stock awards in Canada, an employer was required to pay Cdn. $100 to the Ontario Securities Commission ("OSC") on the date it commenced a purchase plan or arrangement, and on each anniversary of that date if securities were distributed in Ontario during the preceding 12 months under the plan or arrangement.

.07 Governing Law

In some cases, the company may be able to defeat the application of foreign laws through a clear choice of law provision. In *Oracle Corp. v. Falotti,*[56] a California federal court upheld a stock option plan committee's decision to apply California law to deny unvested options to a former employee who sought to have Swiss law (where he was employed) apply.

However, in most cases, this will not work if the aggrieved executive brings an action in his or her home country. Additionally, some countries expressly forbid a choice of law other than local. For example, German laws operating for the benefit of employees would prevail over any foreign law that is less protective.

¶2345 Issues for Foreign Corporations Making Equity Awards in the U.S.

Any offering or sale of securities to U.S. employees will require registration under the Securities Act of 1933 (the "1933 Act"), *unless* the offering qualifies for an exemption from registration. Any award of stock options or restricted stock, and even an election made by an employee to authorize payroll deductions under a Code Sec. 423/employee stock purchase plan, would be an offer of securities for purposes of the 1933 Act. Accordingly, an award or offer by a foreign corporation to its U.S. employees would violate the 1933 Act's prohibition on the offer or sale of unregistered securities *unless* (1) the foreign corporation files a registration statement covering the award or plan, or (2) an exemption applies (see Chapter 12 [¶1201 *et seq.*] for a detailed discussion of federal securities law issues relating to compensation plans).

Registration of option or other awards on the short Form S-8, although simple, is only available to companies that have already become reporting companies under the Securities Exchange Act of 1934 (the "1934 Act"). Thus, privately held companies and/or unregistered foreign corporations need to qualify for an exemption from registration. The 1933 Act Rule 701 exemption is available for offers and sales under a "written compensatory benefit plan," such as an employee stock option or purchase plan.

.01 Rule 701

Rule 701 restricts the amount of securities that an issuer can sell in reliance on the rule. The aggregate sales price of securities sold in reliance on Rule 701 during any consecutive 12-month period must not exceed the greatest of the following:

1. $1,000,000;
2. 15% of the issuer's total assets; or
3. 15% of the outstanding amount of the class of securities being offered and sold in reliance on this section.

---

[56] *Oracle Corp. v. Falotti,* 187 F.Supp. 2d 1184 (N.D. Calif. 2001).

For purposes of determining the "aggregate sales price," an option is valued based on its exercise price. The SEC considers options to be sold on the date of option grant, not on the date of exercise. Certain disclosures are required (before the date of the exercise) if the securities sold in a 12-month period exceed $5 million. However, Rule 701 is not available to a company that is registered under the 1934 Act.

To satisfy Rule 701's disclosure requirements, an issuer must give each stock plan participant a copy of the plan. In addition, if the amount of the grants during any 12-month period exceeds $5 million U.S. dollars, the heightened disclosure requirements apply.[57] If the company were to issue $5 million U.S. dollars or more in options, it would be required to give the following documents to plan participants (in addition to a copy of the plan):

- A description of the risk factors associated with investing under the plan;
- Financial statements (in a specified format, and reconciled to GAAP); and
- A summary of material plan terms.

.02 Foreign Private Issuer Exemption

Section 12(g) of the 1934 Act requires every issuer meeting the jurisdictional requirements of the 1934 Act and having total assets of more than $10 million and a class of equity securities held of record by 500 or more persons to register such securities. Rule 12g3-2(a) under the 1934 Act requires every foreign private issuer with 300 shareholders as of a year-end to register.

> **Planning Note:** Companies granting stock options or other equity awards (and their counsel) must recognize that a proposed stock plan or awards could easily cause the company to have 300 or more stockholders after an offering period, thus *forcing it to register and become a "reporting company"* under Section 12(g).

Rule 12g3-2(b) provides an exemption to full registration if the foreign issuer submits the requisite documents. Registering with the SEC under Rule 12g3-2(b) is generally not difficult for a publicly held foreign corporation. It includes making an undertaking to submit (not file) to the SEC (in English) anything the corporation distributes to its stockholders pursuant to the rules of a stock exchange on which its stock is listed or which it is required to file or make public by law in its home country (or the country where the stock is listed). A company complying with Rule 12g3-2(b) is exempt from the 1934 Act registration and can use 1933 Act Rule 701.

.03 Large Foreign Issuers

If the foreign issuer does *not* qualify for an exemption from the registration requirements of the 1933 Act, it could be required to file a Form F-1 registration statement with the SEC. (As a foreign private issuer, the company would file

---

[57] The SEC feels that additional disclosure protections are necessary when issuers use Rule 701 to sell large quantities of shares. Thus, it added a height- ened disclosure requirement when an issuer sells $5 million U.S. dollars or more under Rule 701 in a 12-month period.

Form F-1 rather than Form S-1.) The Form F-1 requirements are very similar to the Form S-1 requirements, and involve broad disclosure regarding a variety of issues. Among other things, the foreign issuer would be required to provide a detailed prospectus, as well as descriptions of risk factors, use of proceeds, and the method for determining the offering price. The foreign issuer would also need to provide detailed financial schedules and other information. In addition, the Form F-1 requires filing the information required in Part I of Form 20-F. Part I of Form 20-F requires disclosure of selected financial data for five years and audited financial statements prepared in U.S. GAAP accordance (or accompanied by a reconciliation to U.S. GAAP).

If the foreign issuer files a Form F-1 under the 1933 Act, it would lose its ability to rely on Rule 12g3-2(b) for an exemption from the requirements of the 1934 Act. Filing a Form F-1 registration statement would trigger the reporting requirements of Section 15(d) of the 1934 Act. Rule 12g3-2(d) states that the Rule 12g3-2(b) exemption is not available to a foreign private issuer that has a reporting obligation under Section 15(d) of the 1934 Act. Section 15(d) imposes reporting requirements on issuers who register a class of securities under the 1933 Act. If the foreign issuer were to become subject to Section 12(g) of the 1934 Act as a result of losing the Rule 12g3-2(b) exemption, it would be required to file Forms 20-F and 6-K on an annual basis.

If the foreign issuer intends to rely on Rule 12g3-2(b), it must provide the SEC with any information that is "material to an investment decision" and that the issuer released or filed since the beginning of its last fiscal year, if the information falls into any of the following categories:

- It was made public or is required to make public pursuant to applicable foreign securities law;
- It was filed or is required to be filed with a stock exchange on which its securities are traded, if the information is made public by the exchange; or
- The foreign issuer distributed it or is required to distribute it to its security holders.

Additionally, the foreign issuer must provide the SEC with a significant number of other documents relating to its financial condition; acquisitions and dispositions; changes in management or control; transactions with interested parties, such as directors or officers; and changes in business conditions.

.04 Alternatives for Foreign Issuers

Thus, most foreign corporations that want to make stock option or other equity awards in the U.S. generally have three choices in connection with such plan or awards:

1. Register with the SEC under Rule 12g3-2(a) of the 1934 Act as a foreign private issuer with 300 shareholders as of year-end, and use Form S-8 to offer its shares under the plan.

2. Limit participation in the plan to less than 300 purchasers and avoid 1934 Act registration.

3. Claim an exemption from registration under the 1934 Act by making the undertaking and submissions required under 1934 Act Rule 12g3-2(b). In that case the company will not be registered under the 1934 Act and can avail itself of 1933 Act Rule 701.

¶2355 Social Security

The U.S. Social Security system applies to any person who performs services for wages in the United States for an employer.[58] American expatriates are not subject to Social Security for employment abroad unless the employer qualifies as an "American employer."[59] An employer qualifies as an American employer if the employer is:

- The United States government or any instrumentality thereof;
- An individual who is a resident of the United States;
- A partnership, if at least two-thirds of the partners are residents of the United States; or
- A corporation organized under the laws of the United States or of any state.[60]

If the expatriate employee is an American citizen whose employer is a corporation incorporated in the United States, then the expatriate employee will participate in the U.S. Social Security system just as if he or she had worked domestically. American citizens who perform services for foreign affiliates or subsidiaries of American employers may, but are not required to, be covered by U.S. Social Security by contract, a so-called "3121(l) arrangement," as long as the foreign affiliate is at least 10% owned by the American employer.[61] A Section 3121(l) agreement may also determine an expatriate employee's ability to participate in qualified pension plans.[62] The majority of U.S.-based corporations that send workers overseas continue to contribute to Social Security for those employees.

With regard to inpatriate employees, the Code requires contribution to U.S. Social Security by the employer and the employee for individuals employed in the United States. Section 3121(b)(A) states: ". . . the term 'employment' means any service, of whatever nature, performed . . . by an employee for the person employing him, *irrespective of the citizenship or residence of either* . . . within the United States . . . ."[63] To avoid the possibility of dual coverage and double taxation (*i.e.*, the employee being covered under his or her home country and the U.S. Social Security system), the U.S. and several countries have enacted "totalization agreements."[64] Totalization agreements essentially allow an inpatriate

---

[58] *See* Code Sec. 3121(a) (defining "wages" for purposes of Social Security).

[59] Code Sec. 3121(b).

[60] Code Sec. 3121(h).

[61] Code Sec. 3121(l).

[62] *See* ¶2325 (discussing whether an American expatriate working for a foreign affiliate of an American employer may participate in the American employer's qualified plan).

[63] Code Sec. 3121(b) (emphasis added).

[64] Code Sec. 3111(c) (authorizing employment tax relief for taxes under totalization agreements); *see* Social Security Act, 42 U.S.C. § 433 (authorizing the President to enter into totalization agreements between the U.S. and foreign social security systems); *see also* Rev. Rul. 92-9, 1992-1 CB 344 (listing coun-

employee to contribute and receive benefits from a single system, as opposed to mandated participation in multiple systems. In the absence of a totalization agreement, the taxpayer bears the burden of demonstrating that the foreign tax credit under Code Sec. 901 is applicable in an enforcement action.[65] Code Sec. 901 allows a U.S. income tax credit for certain taxes of foreign countries.[66]

¶2365 Health and Welfare Benefits

A critical function of the benefit package of every expatriate employee is to protect the employee against the risks of medical and other emergencies while the employee is on an overseas assignment. The quality and availability of health care in many countries is inferior to that of the United States. The medical benefit package of an expatriate employee (and his or her family) often will include not just the reimbursement of expenses, but also arrangements for emergency evacuation to the U.S. or another country with a higher quality of medical care.

The U.S. Department of Labor has advised that plans of foreign employers are not exempt from ERISA regulation if they are established and maintained in the United States. In ERISA Op. Letter 93-10A (March 22, 1993), the DOL considered a request for advice from the unofficial representative of the people of Taiwan. The employer sought to provide accident, dental, medical, and surgical benefits to its employees residing in the United States, including Taiwanese nationals, American nationals, and individuals maintaining citizenship of both Taiwan and the U.S. The DOL concluded that because the proposed welfare plan was to be "established or maintained by an employer . . . for the purpose of providing for its participants or their beneficiaries," it met the requisites of an ERISA welfare plan. Moreover, the plan's coverage of inpatriate employees did not exempt the plan from ERISA coverage under Section 4 of ERISA. In fact, a welfare benefit plan established or maintained in the U.S. presumptively covers inpatriate employees, regardless of their citizenship or the employers' nation of origin. The statutory language suggests no distinction in coverage. Any distinction between participants must comply with ERISA provisions and all exclusions must be explicit in the plan documents.

¶2375 Title VII and Employment Discrimination

Another issue confronting employers of expatriate or inpatriate employees is the prospect of running afoul of local employment discrimination laws as a result of a compensation arrangement.[67] Where a foreign-based multinational corporation operates a branch or subsidiary in the U.S. and an inpatriate executive manages the U.S. operation, possible employment discrimination issues arise where the inpatriate employees receive different compensation than similarly

---

(Footnote Continued)

tries with whom the U.S. has entered totalization agreements); Reg § 31.3101-1.

[65] See *Wada v. Comm'r*, 69 TCM 2793, CCH Dec. 50,672(M), T.C. Memo. 1995-241 (1995) (holding that the taxpayer failed to establish that payments to Japanese social security meet the requirements of income tax regulations under Code Sec. 901).

[66] Code Sec. 901.

[67] This book focuses on Executive Compensation, not employment discrimination, so this chapter will not discuss the thicket of discrimination issues that has grown around U.S. employment law. Many other countries have equally complex discrimination laws.

situated local executives. However, it appears that such dual compensation schemes would not violate Title VII, provided that the compensation structure is consistently applied to all inpatriate employees regardless of their place of origin, nationality, and gender.

Historically, corporations had "no legal existence out of the boundaries of the sovereignty by which [they were] created."[68] However, as commerce became increasingly international, nations entered treaties with trade partners to recognize each other's corporations and grant them rights and privileges of operation within their borders. After World War II, the United States entered a series of Friendship, Commerce and Navigation Treaties ("FCN Treaties") that granted U.S. corporations the right to conduct business abroad and, reciprocally, allowed foreign corporations the right to operate in the U.S. A standard provision in these treaties permits companies incorporated in the foreign nation to engage the accountants, consultants, executive personnel, attorneys and other specialists of their choice.[69]

Despite the bold and sweeping language contained in some FCN Treaties, whenever a multinational corporation or other business entity draws distinctions among employees based on nation of origin or citizenship, it risks, at the least, the appearance of favoritism that could provide, in some cases, the basis for a claim of unlawful employment discrimination. Immediate parties to an FCN Treaty, however, are immune from allegations of Title VII violations because the treaties authorize the engagement of personnel of their choice. For instance, suppose a French corporation with a branch office in New York sends a French executive to the United States for an indefinite period. Must the employer pay its expatriate the salary of a similarly situated American executive, or can the employer base the salary on the take-home pay of the executive in France? Must the employer pass any income tax savings on to the employee? Perhaps, fortunately for employers, citizenship is not a protected class under employment discrimination law.[70] Thus, an employer, even if subject to Title VII, could apparently treat employees differently based on citizenship.[71] Moreover, the FCN Treaties authorize foreign companies to employ the executive personnel of their choice, which should protect parties directly affected under such a treaty from Title VII complaints.[72] The FCN Treaties grant reciprocal benefits, that is, American companies operating abroad are immune from any local law that would

---

[68] *Sumitomo Shoji America v. Avagliano*, 457 US 176, 186 (1982) (quoting *Bank of Augusta v. Earle*, 38 US 519, 588 (1839)).

[69] *Sumitomo Shoji America v. Avagliano*, 457 US 176, 181 (1982); *see also Fortino v. Quasar Co.*, 950 F2d 389, 392 (7th Cir. 1991) (explaining that the treaty between Japan and the United States authorizes companies from either country to employ the "executive personnel" of their choice).

[70] *See Fortino v. Quasar Co.*, 950 F2d 389, 391-93 (7th Cir. 1991) (noting that Title VII prohibits discrimination on the basis of national origin, but not on the basis of citizenship).

[71] However, to the extent national origin is correlated with citizenship, the line between lawful employment preference and unlawful discrimination may be ambiguous.

[72] *See Sumitomo Shoji America v. Avagliano*, 457 US 176, 184 (1982) (holding that subsidiaries incorporated in the United States, even if wholly owned by a Japanese company, do not enjoy the treaty protection that the Japanese parent would have under the treaty).

require the employment of local nationals to executive posts when an American citizen is preferable.[73]

Thus, a business entity incorporated in a foreign state that is a signatory to an FCN Treaty with the U.S. is protected from employment discrimination claims, and a U.S. corporation operating abroad is free to select its own executives without restriction under local law. However, wholly owned subsidiaries of foreign companies, incorporated in the U.S., may not enjoy immunity under the treaties,[74] and subsidiaries of U.S. corporations, if incorporated in the nation of operation, will not be protected from the discrimination laws of the host country. Finally, Title VII does not have extraterritorial reach. Employers incorporated in the United States are not subject to Title VII for discriminatory conduct outside the U.S. against either host-country nationals or American expatriates.[75]

¶2385 Code Sec. 409A

The American Jobs Creation Act of 2004[76] added Code Sec. 409A to the Internal Revenue Code. Code Sec. 409A applies to any plan, program, or agreement providing for deferred compensation. The Code Sec. 409A regulations address several special categories of multinational individuals and plans that may be subject to special rules, including the following:

- U.S. citizens working outside the U.S. and participating in a foreign plan.
- Non-U.S. citizens working in the U.S. and participating in a foreign plan.
- Nonresident aliens participating in a U.S.-based plan.

The Code Sec. 409A regulations provide a variety of exceptions for deferred compensation arrangements maintained by non-U.S. companies in which U.S. citizens or residents participate. Given the complexity of Code Sec. 409A, most foreign plans would not satisfy all of its requirements. Thus, qualifying for one of the exemptions provided under the Code Sec. 409A regulations may be essential.

.01 Participation Addressed by Treaty

The regulations provide an exception from Code Sec. 409A for any scheme, trust, arrangement, or plan to the extent contributions made by or on behalf of an individual to such scheme, trust, arrangement, or plan, or credited allocations, accrued benefits, earnings, or other amounts constituting income, of such individual are excludable by such individual for federal income tax purposes pursuant to any bilateral income tax convention to which the United States is a party.[77]

---

[73] *See Fortino v. Quasar Co.*, 950 F2d 389, 393-94 (7th Cir. 1991) (stating that the rights granted by the Japan-U.S. FCN Treaty are reciprocal).

[74] *Compare Fortino v. Quasar Co.*, 950 F2d 389, 393-94 (7th Cir. 1991) (holding that an American subsidiary of a Japanese corporation can invoke the treaty powers of its parent) *with Kirmse v. Hotel Nikko of San Francisco*, 59 Cal. Rptr. 2d 96 (Calif. Ct. App. 1996) (holding that a domestic subsidiary of a foreign corporation cannot invoke its parent's FCN treaty rights as a defense to a Title VII claim).

[75] In *Boureslan v. Aramco, Arabian American Oil Co.*, 892 F2d 1271, 1272 (5th Cir. 1990), the Fifth Circuit, *en banc*, held that an American expatriate could not pursue a Title VII claim for discrimination by his employer that took place while he was working abroad in Saudi Arabia. The court applied the presumption that, absent a clear expression to the contrary by Congress, American law does not have extraterritorial effect.

[76] P.L. 108-357, signed by President George W. Bush on October 22, 2004.

[77] Treas. Reg. § 1.409A-1(a)(3)(i).

Some tax treaties classify nonqualified deferred compensation as "pension income" taxable only in the jurisdiction of the taxpayer's residence. This exception would be useful where the individual is considered, for treaty purposes, a resident of the foreign country both while he or she is accruing the deferred compensation and when it is distributed. Note that many treaties limit "pension income" to that provided under tax-qualified plans, which may limit the applicability of this exception. The following example from Deloitte Consulting's *Washington Bulletin* may be helpful:[78]

> The U.S.-Australia income tax treaty provides that "pensions and other similar remuneration paid to an individual who is a resident of one of the Contracting States in consideration of past employment shall be taxable only in that State" (Article 18(1)). It defines "pensions and other similar remuneration" broadly as "periodic payments made by reason of retirement or death, in consideration for services rendered" (Article 18(4)). Mr. A is an American citizen who works in Australia, meets the treaty's criteria for classification as a resident of Australia, and accrues benefits under an unfunded pension plan. If he retires in Australia, the treaty will safeguard his pension distributions from IRC § 409A. Unhappily, if he moves back to the United States or, for that matter, relocates to any country that does not have a similar treaty with the U.S., he will lose the treaty protection. Since treaties change and the future of one's residence is unpredictable, it will rarely be prudent to rely on a particular treaty for long-term planning.

.02 Broad-Based Foreign Retirement Plan

Code Sec. 409A does not apply to benefits accrued under a "broad-based" foreign retirement plan in which substantially all participants are nonresident aliens. Code Sec. 409A defines the term "broad-based foreign retirement plan" to mean a scheme, trust, arrangement, or plan (regardless of whether sponsored by a U.S. person) that is written and that, in the case of an employer-maintained plan, satisfies the following conditions:[79]

(A) The plan is nondiscriminatory in that it covers (together with other comparable plans) a wide range of employees, substantially all of whom are nonresident aliens, resident aliens, or bona fide residents of a possession, including rank and file employees.

(B) The plan (or together with other comparable plans) actually provides significant benefits for a substantial majority of such covered employees.

(C) The benefits the plan provides to such covered employees are nondiscriminatory.

(D) The plan contains provisions or is the subject of tax law provisions or other legal restrictions that generally discourage employees from using plan benefits for purposes other than retirement or restrict access to plan benefits before separation from service, including, for example, restricting in-service distributions except in events similar to an unfore-

---

[78] See the May 21, 2007 issue of *Deloitte's Washington Bulletin,* http://benefitslink.com/articles/ washbull070521.html. for an excellent summary of these provisions.

[79] Treas. Reg. § 1.409A-1(a)(3)(v).

seeable emergency, hardship, or for educational purposes or the purchase of a primary residence.

.03 Plans Subject to a Totalization Agreement and Similar Plans

Code Sec. 409A does not apply to any Social Security system of a jurisdiction to the extent that benefits provided under or contributions made to the system are subject to an agreement entered into under Social Security Act Section 233 with any foreign jurisdiction.[80] Code Sec. 409A also does not apply to a Social Security system of a foreign jurisdiction to the extent that benefits are provided under or contributions are made to a government-mandated plan as part of that foreign jurisdiction's social security system.

.04 Participation by Nonresident Aliens, Certain Resident Aliens, and Bona Fide Residents of Possessions

The regulations also provide that Code Sec. 409A will not apply to any individual who is a nonresident alien, a resident alien,[81] or a bona fide resident of a possession[82] covered by a broad-based foreign retirement plan (as described above).[83]

.05 Employees Working in the U.S. and Participating in a Foreign Plan

Code Sec. 409A generally will apply to U.S.-based employees of foreign companies. Foreign companies that maintain a plan that covers U.S.-based employees should be particularly cognizant of Code Sec. 409A's prohibition on funding benefits through an offshore trust.

The Code Sec. 409A regulations provide an exception for a nonresident alien's U.S. source deferred compensation to the extent that it does not exceed the Code Sec. 402(g) limit on elective deferrals ($18,500 in 2018). However, the plan providing the deferred compensation must have a "substantial number of participants," and substantially all of them must be either nonresident aliens or individuals who are classified as resident aliens but are not green card holders.

.06 Participation by U.S. Citizens and Lawful Permanent Residents

Code Sec. 409A does not apply to a U.S. citizen's or permanent resident's deferrals of foreign earned income as long as the total of his current and deferred compensation does not exceed the Code Sec. 911(b) exclusion.[84]

.07 Tax Equalization Payments

Code Sec. 409A excludes tax equalization arrangements to the extent they provide for payments intended to compensate the employee for the excess foreign taxes imposed on compensation over the taxes that would have been

---

[80] Treas. Reg. § 1.409A-1(a)(3)(iv).

[81] A resident alien who is classified as a resident alien solely under Code Sec. 7701(b)(1)(A)(ii), and not Code Sec. 7701(b)(1)(A)(i).

[82] A bona fide resident of a possession within the meaning of Code Sec. 937(a).

[83] Treas. Reg. § 1.409A-1(a)(3)(ii).

[84] Generally, this exception is useful only for relatively low-paid employees.

imposed under U.S. federal income tax.[85] Under this exception, the employer must make payment by the end of the second taxable year of the employee following the latest of (i) the deadline for filing a U.S. tax return or (ii) the deadline for filing foreign tax returns, in each case reflecting the compensation for which the employer provided the tax equalization payment. The exception will not apply to the extent that the tax equalization payment may not exceed the amount necessary to compensate the employee for the additional foreign taxes the employee pays.

¶2395 Other Issues

Multination companies and companies that employ non-U.S. citizens also may need to consider so-called "OFAC" compliance. The U.S. Treasury Department's Office of Foreign Assets Control ("OFAC") currently oversees more than two dozen different sanction programs, currently including countries such as Cuba, Iran, Libya, North Korea, Syria, Russia and many other less obvious countries, and also individuals involved in drug trafficking, terrorism, and other crimes. The list changes from time to time.

.01 OFAC Compliance

In August 2017, President Trump signed the Countering America's Adversaries Through Sanctions Act (the "Sanctions Bill"), which codified many of the sanctions programs that had previously been established by the Obama Administration through executive order, added additional restrictions on interactions with individuals who are subject to sanctions or reside in a sanctioned location, and directed the Trump Administration to issue new sanctions against Iran and North Korea.

OFAC imposes civil and criminal penalties on U.S. entities that engage in transactions or otherwise have interactions with individuals, commercial enterprises, or governments that are on the list or reside in a country on the list. From an executive compensation perspective, a multinational company could run afoul of the OFAC rules by providing compensation or benefits under an employment or other agreement, a deferred compensation plan, or its stock or other incentive plan.

Multinational companies that could possibly have employees from a sanctioned country in any of these plans could be violating OFAC rules. To assist in compliance efforts, these companies should consider adding compliance language into their stock and other plan vendor agreements, to the extent the vendor is making payments. Banks and financial institutions have direct, independent obligations under OFAC, so this is more important when dealing with a non-bank vendor.

---

[85] 1.409A-1(a)(8)(iii).

.02 Sample Employment Agreement Provisions

Employers typically prepare an employment or other agreement including special provisions applicable to expatriate employees. Among the provisions that such an agreement might include are the following:

> *Payment of Salary*: Your base salary will be administered in accordance with Corporate salary guidelines for U.S. based salaried employees and will be used for the purposes of determining any differentials or allowances described in this letter. Differentials and allowances will be adjusted to reflect the impact of any salary increases that occur. Hypothetical U.S. taxes will be deducted and the company will be responsible for other taxes as explained in the tax equalization policy as attached.

> *Tax Return Preparation*: Despite the fact that you will be living and working outside the United States, you will be required to file U.S. income tax returns annually during your assignment. Due to the length of your assignment to [The People's Republic of China], you may also be required to file People's Republic of China income tax returns. Compliance with filing requirements in both the U.S. and assignment location are your personal responsibility, but the preparation of your returns will be provided by the Company through an income tax consultant designated by the Company. For purposes of this provision, filing years include, at least, the year you begin your assignment, the year your assignment is terminated, and the year(s) on assignment.

> It is your responsibility to provide all necessary information and documents to the tax consultant on a timely basis to avoid late filings. Taxes, interest, or penalties incurred as a result of your failure to file a timely and accurate return or to take other appropriate action will be your personal responsibility.

> *Tax Equalization*: During the term of your international assignment, your remuneration will be administered in accordance with the Company's Tax Equalization Policy. Your signature on this letter of understanding is an affirmation that you have reviewed the Company's Tax Equalization Policy and agree to all its provisions.

.03 Public Company Proxy Statement Disclosure

SEC disclosure rules apply only slightly differently for executives who are resident or employed outside the U.S. Item 402(a) of Regulation S-K includes the following exclusion for cash compensation relating to overseas assignments performed by executive officers (other than the CEO or CFO):

> 3. *Exclusion of executive officer due to overseas compensation*. It may be appropriate in limited circumstances for a registrant not to include in the disclosure required by this Item an individual, other than its PEO or PFO, who is one of the registrant's most highly compensated executive officers due to the payment of amounts of cash compensation relating to overseas assignments attributed predominantly to such assignments.[86]

The rules also require reporting companies to show all amounts reported in the Summary Compensation Table in U.S. dollars. The SEC's position is that the conversion of compensation amounts to U.S. dollars for reporting purposes should take place at the time the payment is made.

---

[86] Instructions to Item 402(a)(3), Section 3.

.04 Data Privacy and Restrictions on the Transfer of Employee Data

A close analysis of data privacy laws is beyond the scope of this treatise. However, many countries, including most European nations, have much stricter requirements on sharing data or information on employees. An employer that outsources its stock award or benefit plan administration functions or otherwise uses a third-party administrator to administer any aspect of its plan must be cognizant of these requirements.

In May 2018, General Data Protection Regulation (GDPR) became effective in the European Union ("EU"). GDPR applies to any business that is collecting personal data from an individual located in the EU, and includes substantial fines for non-compliance. Multinational companies and their advisers should make themselves aware of data privacy laws in the EU and elsewhere. Privacy and data security issues affect every aspect of an organization's information management life cycle, including executive compensation.

Companies may need to develop and assess their privacy compliance and risk management programs and policies with respect to compensation and benefit plans and transactions, including assessing privacy/cyber risks. Companies also may need to provide employee training, respond to government inquiries and investigations and, when necessary, litigate to protect the company's assets and rights.

.05 Code Section 457A

Code Sec. 457A imposes more restrictive income timing rules on nonqualified deferred compensation from "tax indifferent" or "nonqualified entities" (such as certain foreign corporations in "tax haven" jurisdictions), effectively prohibiting deferrals by U.S. taxpayers employed by such entities. Under Code Sec. 457A, "deferred amounts" under a "nonqualified deferred compensation plan" of "a non-qualified entity" are includible in the gross income of a U.S.-taxpayer (executive or partner) as soon as there is no "substantial risk of forfeiture." Code Sec. 457A originally targeted offshore hedge fund compensation. However, it was poorly drafted and applies well beyond its intended target. Code Sec. 457A applies to all deferred compensation attributable to services performed after December 31, 2008, with no grandfathering provisions for pre-2009 deferrals.

Code Sec. 457A defines "nonqualified entity" as any:

- Foreign corporation, unless substantially all of its income is effectively connected with a trade or business in the U.S., or is subject to a comprehensive foreign income tax; and

- Partnership, unless substantially all of its income is allocated to persons other than: (i) foreign persons with respect to whom such income is not subject to a comprehensive foreign income tax, and (ii) organizations that are exempt from U.S. tax.

Nonqualified entities are typically foreign companies in "tax-indifferent" jurisdictions (colloquially, tax havens) or domestic partnerships and other pass-through entities that are owned more than 20% by tax-exempt entities. Code Sec. 457A most commonly applies to hedge funds and U.S. citizens working outside the U.S. for a non-U.S. employer in a tax-indifferent jurisdiction.

Code Sec. 457A defines "nonqualified deferred compensation plan" the same as Code Sec. 409A, with two important differences:

- A plan that provides compensation based on the appreciation in value of a specified number of equity units of a service recipient is included in the definition of a nonqualified deferred compensation plan.

- Compensation that is paid within 12 months after the close of the taxable year in which the right to payment is no longer subject to a substantial risk of forfeiture is excluded from the definition of nonqualified deferred compensation plan (as compared to 2 1/2 months, under the short-term deferred rule of Sec. 409A).

Finally, Code Sec. 457A tests for a "substantial risk of forfeiture" using essentially the same rules that currently apply to deferred compensation for state and local governments and other tax-exempt entities under Code Sec. 457(f). A substantial risk of forfeiture exists as to compensation only if the right to the compensation is "conditioned upon the future performance of substantial services." Thus, vested deferred compensation would be taxable immediately. Generally, other conditions related to the transfer of the compensation (*e.g.,* the attainment of a prescribed level of earnings or equity value, *etc.*) that would constitute a substantial risk of forfeiture under Code Secs. 83 or 409A generally will not constitute such under Code Sec. 457A.

Code Sec. 457A also provides that if the amount of the compensation to be included in income is "not determinable" at the time it is to be included in income, then the amount is included in income when it is later determinable – and a penalty tax applies equal to 20% of the amount of the compensation, plus interest (at the underpayment rate under Code Sec. 6621 plus 1%) on the underpayments. The date of underpayment is the date that taxation under Code Sec. 457A should have occurred had the compensation been included income in the year deferred or, if later, the first year the compensation was not subject to a substantial risk of forfeiture.

Code Sec. 457A provides two exceptions. Under the "Gain on Investment Assets Exception," if compensation is determined solely by reference to the amount of gain *recognized on the disposition of an investment asset*, it will be treated as subject to a substantial risk of forfeiture until the date of disposition.

- An investment asset is any single asset (other than an investment fund or similar entity) that is acquired directly by an investment fund or similar entity, with respect to which the entity does **not** participate in the active management and substantially all of the gain on the disposition is allocated to investors in the entity.

- The short-term deferral exception does not apply to deferred compensation treated as subject to a substantial risk of forfeiture under this "investment gain" exception.

Under the "Effectively Connected Income Exception," Code Sec. 457A will **not** apply to compensation from a foreign corporation with income taxable under Code Sec. 882 (*i.e.*, tax on income of foreign corporations connected with United States business), which, had it been paid in cash on the date it ceased to be subject to a substantial risk of forfeiture, would have been deductible by the foreign corporation against such income.

IRS Revenue Ruling 2014-18 clarified that stock options and stock-settled stock appreciation rights ("SS-SARs") will not be considered nonqualified deferred compensation for purposes of Code Sec. 457A, provided the awards are settled in stock and designed to satisfy Code Sec. 409A's "stock right" exemption. However, unlike Code Sec. 409A, Code Sec. 457A still applies to stock appreciation rights that are or may be settled in cash. Revenue Ruling 2014-18 applies retroactively.

Chapter 24
EXECUTIVE COMPENSATION IN BANKRUPTCY

¶2401 Overview—Executive Compensation in Bankruptcy

This chapter focuses primarily on bankruptcies filed under the Chapter 11 reorganization provisions of the federal bankruptcy law.[1] Liquidation under Chapter 7 of the federal bankruptcy law presents few executive compensation issues. Generally, there are two scenarios for a successful Chapter 11 filing. One scenario is that all or substantially all of the company's/debtor's assets are administered (possibly including a sale of some or all of the assets) through the Chapter 11 reorganization proceeding and the company comes out of the process with, generally, fewer liabilities and different owners. A second scenario is that a new owner acquires all or substantially all of the company's/debtor's assets as part of the proceeding, in a so-called "Section 363 sale," with the new owner paying cash (or other securities) to be distributed among creditors and assuming few, if any of the debtor-company's liabilities.

This chapter focuses on the two primary compensation issues that arise in the context of a bankruptcy. First, the chapter discusses the affect of a bankruptcy on the company's existing compensation and benefit programs. Most promises of executive compensation are only as good as the company making the promise. When times are good, companies pay their executives loads of cash and promise other benefits and rewards in the future. However, when an executive's employer goes bankrupt, the value of the executive's stock awards, nonqualified retirement benefits, long-term incentive payments and severance benefits may go with it.

The second key compensation issue that arises after a company's bankruptcy filing is the need to balance the interests of the company's/debtor's creditors in maximizing their recovery against the company's need to recruit and retain executive talent, and compensate them, in order to maximize that recovery. Balancing these interests is seldom simple or without controversy.

.01 Caps on Claims Arising from Termination of Employee Contracts

The Bankruptcy Code[2] gives a company/debtor the right to terminate most outstanding contracts, including employment agreements. The Bankruptcy Code also generally limits the maximum allowable claim to an employee under a terminated employment contract to one-year's future compensation plus past due compensation. The courts have upheld this cap in numerous cases (see ¶2415).

[1] Beverly Helm, Esq. provided substantial assistance in writing and reviewing this Chapter.

[2] 11 U.S.C. § 101, et. seq.

.02 Severance, Retention and Incentive Payments by Companies in Bankruptcy

A company that is in financial difficulty, inevitably headed for bankruptcy, or in bankruptcy, generally needs to make special compensation arrangements to retain its key employees. The value of a company/debtor's business cannot be preserved and maximized for the creditors' benefit without the employees critical to the operation of that business. However, anyone who reads the newspapers knows that a bankrupt company's payments to current or departing executives are often one of the most contentious issues in the bankruptcy case (see ¶ 2425).

.03 Retirement and Other Benefit Plans of Bankrupt Companies

A qualified retirement plan is a separate entity whose assets are protected from the creditors of the company/plan sponsor. However, a nonqualified retirement or deferred compensation plan must remain an unfunded promise to pay benefits in the future to avoid immediate taxation of the covered executives. If the nonqualified plan sponsor files for bankruptcy, the status of covered executives is the same as that of other general, unsecured creditors to whom the company owes money. The one contingency against which a rabbi trust cannot protect the covered executives is the company's insolvency. For this reason, some companies, including Delta Air Lines, Inc., have resorted to creating funded secular trusts for key executives, which are immediately taxable to the executives but unavailable to the company's creditors (see ¶ 2435).

.04 Preferential and Fraudulent Transfers

The Bankruptcy Code gives a trustee the power to set aside and recover transfers made prior to a bankruptcy filing. The avoidance powers limit a company's/debtor's ability to play favorites among creditors and to prevent a company from transferring assets out of the reach of creditors before filing for bankruptcy. The Bankruptcy Code gives a trustee the power to avoid both preferential and fraudulent transfers (see ¶ 2445).

.05 Personal Bankruptcy of an Executive

Adding one more item to the long list of good things about qualified retirement plans, ERISA and the Internal Revenue Code explicitly provide that participants' accounts and benefits under the plan are always beyond the reach of the company's creditors. A participant's accounts and benefits under the plan are also beyond the reach of the participant's creditors (see ¶ 2455).

Partially vested, unexercised stock options are a significant asset of some individuals who file for bankruptcy protection. In other cases, after a filing for bankruptcy protection, a company's/debtor's stock options may have fully vested or the individual may have actually exercised the options and realized significant gains. All or part of the stock options' value may be assets of the company's bankruptcy estate.

¶2401.02

¶2415 Cap on Claims Arising from Termination of Employee Contracts

Section 365 of the Bankruptcy Code gives the bankrupt company/debtor the power to reject contracts. Section 502 of the Bankruptcy Code controls the allowance and disallowance of claims. Under Section 502(a), a claim or interest evidenced by a proof of claim filed pursuant to Section 501 of the Bankruptcy Code "is deemed allowed, unless a party in interest . . . objects." If a party objects to a claim, under Section 502(b) "the court, after notice and a hearing, shall determine the amount of such claim in lawful currency of the United States as of the date of the filing of the petition." The different subsections of Section 502(b) set forth certain types of claims that the bankruptcy court must disallow or limit in amount (*i.e.*, "cap").

Section 502(b)(7) of the Bankruptcy Code caps "the maximum allowable claim to an employee under a terminated employee contract." In general, Section 502(b)(7) limits an employee's damage claim to one-year's future compensation plus past due compensation.[3] Section 502(b)(7) specifically provides that the bankruptcy court should allow an objected-to claim, except to the extent that:

> (7) if such claim is the claim of an employee for damages resulting from the termination of an employment contract, such claim exceeds —
>
> a. the compensation provided by such contract, without acceleration, for one year following the earlier of —
>
>> (i) the date of the filing of the petition; or
>>
>> (ii) the date on which the employer directed the employee to terminate, or such employee terminated, performance under such contract; plus
>
> b. any unpaid compensation due under such contract, without acceleration, on the earlier of such dates.[4]

Litigation relating to Section 502(b)(7) generally arises from employees asserting claims against their bankrupt employers and attempting to avoid the Section 502(b)(7) cap on such claims. Illustrative of such cases is the Delaware bankruptcy court's decision in *In re Continental Airlines, Inc., et al.*[5] In the *Continental* case, Eastern Airlines had ratified a collective bargaining agreement ("CBA") providing that upon a merger of Eastern with another airline, the Eastern pilots would be integrated with the other airline's pilots so as to preserve the Eastern pilots' seniority. After Continental acquired Eastern, the Eastern pilots' union sought enforcement of the CBA. Continental subsequently filed for bankruptcy. As part of the bankruptcy process, instead of granting specific performance of the CBA, the bankruptcy court allowed Continental to reject the CBA, which in turn gave rise to a pre-petition claim for money damages. The Eastern pilots sought a declaration by the bankruptcy court that their claim for money damages under the CBA was not subject to the Section 502(b)(7) cap.[6]

---

[3] Accord *Halper v. Halper*, 164 F3d 830, 834 n. 3 (3d Cir. 1999); *In re Worldwide Direct, Inc.*, 268 B.R. 69, 71 n. 2 (Bankr. D. Del. 2001).

[4] 11 U.S.C. §502(b)(7).

[5] *In re Continental Airlines, Inc. et al.*, 257 B.R. 658 (Bankr. D. Del. 2000).

[6] *In re Continental Airlines, Inc. et al.*, 257 B.R. 658, 661 (Bankr. D. Del. 2000).

According to the bankruptcy court, the CBA was an "employment contract" as Section 502(b)(7) uses that term. Because the CBA at issue provided for the "employment relationship itself," Section 502(b)(7) applied and the court capped the Eastern pilots' claims.[7]

The bankruptcy court also ruled against the Eastern pilots' argument that they had never become "employees" of Continental under Section 502(b)(7). The bankruptcy court, however, noted that Section 502(b)(7) does not state that it applies only where the company/debtor actually employs the claimant. Rather, according to the bankruptcy court, Section 502(b)(7) applies to claims of an employee for damages resulting from termination of an *employment contract*.[8] Noting that "it is the nature of the claim that is the relevant question under Section 502(b)(7)," the bankruptcy court found that the Eastern pilots' claims "are fundamentally claims of employees for breach of an employment contract." The bankruptcy court further asserted that "it would be absurd to conclude that their claims derive from the termination of that contract, but that they are not employees simply because the contract was breached one day prior to the beginning of work under that contract."[9] The *Continental* case illustrates that a bankruptcy court will construe the terms "employee" and "employment contract" to reflect the nature of the underlying claim and effectuate the purposes of Section 502(b)(7).

In different factual contexts, other courts have faced additional Section 502(b)(7) issues. In *Folsom v. Prospect Hill Resources, Inc. (In re Prospect Hill Resources, Inc.)*,[10] the appellate court found that a retired corporate officer's vested retirement benefits were not capped by Section 502(b)(7). In its holding, the Eleventh Circuit reasoned that Section 502(b)(7) refers to claims by employees, not retired workers. Moreover, retirement benefits provide a form of compensation, not "damages resulting from the termination of an employment contract."[11] Section 502(b)(7) limits severance benefits arising from termination of an employment contract.[12] Severance pay differs from retirement benefits in that severance benefits tend to measure damages from termination and fall within the statutory language of Section 502(b)(7): "the severance pay was designed to compensate [the employee] for the loss he would suffer upon being terminated."

In *Hall v. Goforth*,[13] the court found that, while a claim by a former employee against a Chapter 11 company/debtor, as employer, was limited by Section 502(b)(7), there was no limitation on the liability of the company that was jointly liable on the wrongful termination judgment, but was not the former employee's employer.

---

[7] But see *In re Gee & Missler Servs., Inc.*, 62 B.R. 841 (Bankr. E.D. Mich. 1986) (finding that CBA did not constitute an employment contract under Section 502(b)(7)).

[8] *In re Gee & Missler Servs., Inc.*, 62 B.R. 841 (Bankr. E.D. Mich. 1986) (citing *Hall v. Goforth (In re Goforth)*, 179 F3d 390, 393 (5th Cir. 1999)).

[9] *In re Continental Airlines, Inc. et al.*, 257 B.R. 658, 661 (Bankr. D. Del. 2000).

[10] *Folsom v. Prospect Hill Resources, Inc. (In re Prospect Hill Resources, Inc.)*, 837 F2d 453, 454 (11th Cir. 1988).

[11] 11 U.S.C. § 502(b)(7).

[12] *In re Rexene Corp.*, 183 B.R. 369, 372 (Bankr. D. Del. 1995).

[13] *Hall v. Goforth*, 179 F3d 390, 394–95 (5th Cir. 1999).

Planning Note: The result in *Goforth* suggests that an executive of a financially troubled company may want to obtain a guaranty, letter of credit or other third party credit enhancement for his or her promised benefits.

In another case, *Anthony v. Interform Corp.*,[14] the Third Circuit found that Section 502(b)(7) limits the recovery of a pre-petition judgment creditor in a Chapter 11 bankruptcy "when the creditor's claim arose from the wrongful termination of an employment contract that had been breached over two years before the bankruptcy petition was filed." In the *Anthony* case, after giving him a two-year extension of his contractual term of employment, Interform terminated Mr. Anthony midway through the additional two-year term. Mr. Anthony received an arbitration award of approximately $650,000. However, when he attempted to execute upon the judgment, Interform filed for bankruptcy.

The Third Circuit upheld the lower courts' decisions, holding that Section 502(b)(7) caps employment contract termination claims regardless of whether "(1) the claim has been reduced to judgment; (2) there is any connection between the employee's termination and a debtor's financial problems; and (3) a number of years has passed between the employee's termination and a debtor's filing of the bankruptcy petition."[15]

Payments due under a change in control agreement were held to be claims for breach of the employment agreement and subject to the cap on claims under Section 502(b)(7). In *In re Verasun Energy Corp.*,[16] change in control agreements executed on the eve of a merger guaranteed executives a cash payment of at least twice their annual salary if they remained with the company through a forthcoming merger, or upon an executive's termination without cause within two years. Less than a year later the company filed for bankruptcy, terminated the executives' employment. However, the company refused to pay claims under the change in control agreements, contending that payments due were damages arising from the employment contracts and subject to the 502(b)(7) cap of one year of salary. The executives contended that each change in control agreement was a "stand alone change in control agreement," with payments due for services already rendered, and not subject to the cap. The court found the change in control agreement changed the terms of the employment contracts given to the executives at the time of hire, by requiring a release, and guaranteeing the continuation of their existing work duties, location, and fringe benefits.

The change in control agreements left certain terms undefined and required reference to the employment agreement. The agreements ensured that executives would perform obligations due under their employment agreements and "see the merger through." It reduced the executives' uncertainty about future work responsibilities and compensation in light of the forthcoming merger. The change in control agreements also guaranteed continuation of existing work duties and

---

[14] *Anthony v. Interform Corp.*, 96 F3d 692, 693 (3d Cir. 1996).

[15] *Anthony v. Interform Corp.*, 96 F3d 692, 697 (3d Cir. 1996); see *Bitters v. Networks Elec. Corp. (In re*

Networks Elec. Corp.), 195 B.R. 92 (B.A.P. 9th Cir. 1996).

[16] 467 B.R. 757, 765 (Bankr. D. Del. 2012).

location, provided for a payment of two to three times salary and target bonus, and vested all outstanding equity awards.

The court found the change in control agreements did *not* stand alone. It is axiomatic under general principles of contract law that an employment contract may be modified by a later agreement. The change in control agreements defined the payments due as severance pay, in lieu of salary. The court held that the change in control agreements were integrated with the employment agreements and that plaintiffs' claims were claims for breach of the employment agreement. Consequently, the claims were subject to the cap on claims under Bankruptcy Code Section 502(b)(7).

From a policy perspective, Section 502(b)(7) seeks "to strike a balance between creditors with long-term employment contracts resulting in large unsecured claims and other unsecured creditors, all of whom seek payment of their claim from a pool of assets which is often too meager."[17] Section 502(b)(7) reflects a policy that former employees should mitigate their damages by imposing a cap of one-year's salary. This cap preserves the company's/debtor's assets for other creditors.

¶2425 Severance, Retention and Incentive Payments by Companies in Bankruptcy

A company that is in financial difficulty, inevitably headed for bankruptcy, or in bankruptcy, generally needs to make special compensation arrangements to retain its key employees. Bankrupt companies' payments to current or departing executives have become one of the more contentious issues in many bankruptcy cases. The Bankruptcy Abuse Prevention and Consumer Protection Act of 2005 ("BAPCPA") and subsequent court cases have made the words "severance" and "retention" taboo for companies/debtors seeking to provide additional compensation to executives or other employees. Courts may approve a post-bankruptcy filing compensation program that the company characterizes as providing "incentive compensation" to executives or other employees, but generally will not approve any program providing "severance" or "retention" payments.

Whether the courts will permit a company in bankruptcy proceedings to make severance payments to terminated employees also may depend on when the company established the severance plan, *e.g.*, before or after the bankruptcy filing. The Bankruptcy Code allows a company/debtor to seek court approval to adopt a severance plan for employees it terminates after filing for bankruptcy protection. However, the courts may not permit a bankrupt company to pay severance to employees under a plan established before the filing. In some situations, the trustee or the creditors' committee may even seek to recover severance and retention bonuses paid pre-petition as fraudulent transfers (*See*, for example, *In re K-Mart Corp.*).[18]

---

[17] *In re Continental Airlines, Inc. et al.*, 257 B.R. 658, 665 (Bankr. D. Del. 2000).

[18] *See In re Kmart Corp.*, No. 02-B02474 (Bankr. N. D. Ill. January 22, 2002).

.01 Rationale for Severance, Retention and Incentive Plans at a Bankrupt Company

Generally, the courts authorized companies to implement severance, retention and/or incentive plans because key employees were an essential component of a company's continued operation and successful reorganization. For example, in *In re America West Airlines, Inc.*, the bankruptcy court approved a success bonus to certain officers and employees as within the company's sound business judgment.[19] Similarly, in *In re Interco Inc.*, the court authorized a company to assume pre-petition severance contracts and approved a performance-based retention program to ensure critical employees remained with the debtor.[20]

Companies typically request the courts' authority to (1) continue their current incentive programs for their current employees, and (2) adopt or enhance a form of incentive program for current employees and new hires. The company argued that the value of its business could not be preserved and maximized for the creditors' benefit without the employees critical to the operation of that business.

Many companies in bankruptcy argue that key employees are among their most valuable assets. These employees possessed unique skills, knowledge, and experience that are vital to the business enterprise and, in many cases, impracticable to replicate. The continued employment, dedication, and motivation of the key employees was essential to the preservation and prosperity of the company/debtor and the success of the entire reorganization effort. Moreover, many of a company's key employees undertake significant additional duties as a result of a Chapter 11 filing. Finally, companies frequently found it necessary to enhance their current incentive programs because the substantial fall in the company's stock price prior to the bankruptcy filing caused a decline in the income and net worth of many key employees, negating the effectiveness of the company's existing stock-based retention plans.

Before filing its bankruptcy petition date, a company's management, with the assistance of counsel, would likely develop an employee retention program ("ERP"). The company would design the ERP to provide a financial incentive for continued employment and to assure its employees that the company would reward them for dedicated service during the company's reorganization. The ERP addressed (1) the company's anticipated needs during the reorganization process and (2) the employment relationship of the debtor with a specified number of current employees and planned hires deemed critical to the performance of a debtor's business. Generally, the majority of the ERP costs were consistent with the amount of annual incentive compensation that the company paid in prior years. The company's filing would estimate the cost of the ERP for the current and following fiscal years.

Companies also often sought the bankruptcy courts' approval to enhance their current severance programs. For example, if a company originally paid two

---

[19] *In re America West Airlines, Inc.*, 171 B.R. 674, 678 (Bankr. D. Ariz. 1994).

[20] *In re Interco Inc.*, 128 B.R. 229, 234 (Bankr. E.D. Mo. 1991).

weeks base salary plus one week for every full or partial year of service for a maximum of 12 months, the enhanced program might provide for up to 18 months' salary continuation for highly critical employees.

.02 Argument Against Severance, Retention and Incentive Plans at a Bankrupt Company

As noted above, previously "bankruptcy courts [would] approve KERPs if the Debtor has used proper business judgment in formulating the program and the court finds the program to be fair and reasonable."[21] However, approval by a bankruptcy court of retention bonuses was not always the end of the saga. For example, a few years ago, Polaroid, which had obtained bankruptcy court approval of payments of at least $5 million in retention bonuses to top executives, withdrew its plan after receiving intense criticism from its employees and retirees.

Retention bonuses have come under intense scrutiny as bankrupt companies have paid high-ranking executives large sums of money to stay a short time while many other employees are facing lower salaries, loss of retirement and health benefits, and termination without severance. Some disagree with the choice to pay bonuses worth millions of dollars to a few key employees while the company is laying off other employees who find themselves without health or pension benefits. Others found it difficult to justify paying large sums of money to the employees whose mismanagement may have been responsible for the company's downfall.

Retention bonuses were not always successful in retaining employees. Those who the company paid often stayed for a short time, then left anyway, keeping the money. Others stayed on, but pursued other occupations, such as looking for their next job. Some companies paid retention bonuses regardless of company performance and allowed employees to keep the bonus even if they were fired. While retention bonuses, when a company paid them sensibly, were an effective way of facilitating the preservation of a struggling company, they were injurious to companies when paid unnecessarily to employees who would have stayed without the bonus or to employees who left despite receiving a bonus.

Despite the controversy, companies/debtors continued to assert that in many cases it was better to pay to keep key employees in the company, inasmuch as paying them for their experience and knowledge of the business was less costly than hiring and training new employees who were unfamiliar with the nuances of the business. As a result of the BAPCPA and subsequent court cases, companies/debtors design their post-bankruptcy filing compensation programs to provide additional "incentive compensation" to executives or other employees for achieving certain goals and favorable results. Companies/debtors no longer propose to provide additional compensation to executives merely for remaining with the company.

---

[21] *In re Aerovox, Inc.*, 269 B.R. 74, 80 (Bankr. D. Mass. 2001).

.03 Limitations on Retention, Severance and Incentive Packages: The BAPCPA

The BAPCPA was the largest overhaul of the Bankruptcy Code since its inception in 1978. The BAPCPA limited retention bonuses for key employees and restricted severance payments and nonroutine executive compensation. As a result of the BAPCPA and subsequent court cases, the words "severance" and "retention" have become taboo for companies/debtors seeking to provide additional compensation to executives or other employees.

The BAPCPA amended Section 503(c) of the Bankruptcy Code. Section 503(c) limits retention and severance transfers and payments to insiders[22] made by the company/debtor. Specifically, Section 503(c) provides, subject to certain exceptions:

> [T]here shall neither be allowed, nor paid (1) a transfer made to, or an obligation incurred for the benefit of, an insider of the debtor for the purpose of inducing such person to remain with the debtor's business . . . (2) a severance payment to an insider of the debtor . . . or (3) other transfers or obligations that are outside the ordinary course of business and not justified by the facts and circumstances of the case, including transfers made to, or obligations incurred for the benefit of, officers, managers, or consultants hired after the date of the filing of the petition.[23]

> Section 503(c) "s[eeks] to eradicate the notion that executives [are] entitled to bonuses simply for staying with a company through the bankruptcy process."[24] To that extent, the provisions of Section 503(c) impose significant obstacles to obtaining court approval of key employee retention plans ("KERPs") and severance packages.[25] As such, debtor companies have attempted to circumvent the compensation limitations of Section 503(c) by defining post-bankruptcy petition compensation plans and severance packages as incentivizing "Produce Value for Pay" plans which are subject to the more liberal "business judgment lens of section 363" of the Bankruptcy Code.[26]

Planning Note: The adoption of a severance plan must now be disclosed to the SEC by filing a Form 8-K within four days of adoption of the plan. Because this disclosure may generate interest in the company as a takeover target, development of a strategy in light of this is an important consideration.

.04 Courts' Interpretations of BAPCPA

Early cases addressing the categorization of compensation plans have provided conflicting interpretations of Section 503(c). In *In re Dana Corporation* ("*Dana I*"), the Dana Corporation ("Dana") filed a motion seeking court approval of extensive executive compensation packages under Section 363 of the Bankruptcy Code.[27] In addition to receiving a base salary, executives were eligible for

---

[22] Officers and directors are defined as corporate insiders. 11 U.S.C. § 101(31) (2007).

[23] 11 U.S.C. § 503(c) (2007).

[24] Karen Lee ("Kitt") Turner & Ronald S. Gellert, Dana Hits a Roadblock: Why Post-BAPCPA Laws May Impose Stricter KERP Standards 4 (2006).

[25] Id.

[26] Id; *In re Dana Corporation*, 351 B.R. 96, 98 (Bankr. S.D.N.Y. 2006) [hereinafter *Dana I*].

[27] *Dana I*, 351 B.R. at 98.

an Annual Incentive Bonus conditioned on obtaining short-term financial goals.[28] Michael Burns, the President and Chief Executive Officer, was entitled to a Completion Bonus containing a fixed and variable component and a conditional Non-Compete Package.[29] Burns was also eligible to participate in the Senior Executive Retirement Program.[30] The Creditor's Committee objected to the compensation packages, based on Section 503(c) of BAPCPA.[31] The Bankruptcy Court of the Southern District of New York found that the Completion Bonus was a poorly disguised retention bonus conditioned only upon the completion of the Chapter 11 Bankruptcy Case.[32] According to the court, the Completion Bonus "walk[ed], talk[ed] and [was] a retention bonus."[33] Further, the court opined that the Annual Incentive Bonuses were akin to a retention bonus because the financial thresholds were artificially low, which rendered the bonus a virtual guarantee.[34] As such, both the Completion Bonus and the Annual Incentive Bonus were subject to Section 503(c)(1).[35] Finally, the court concluded that the Non-Compete Package constituted a severance payment subject to Section 503(c)(2), despite Dana's efforts to characterize it as "payments in exchange for non-compete agreements."[36] The court based this holding on the Second Circuit's determination that severance payments are any "amounts due whenever termination of employment occurs."[37] In conclusion, the court surmised that incentivizing "Produce Value for Pay" plans containing components that arguably have a retentive effect did not preclude the court from evaluating the Plan under the business judgment lens of Section 363.[38]

The same court evaluated a subsequent motion for approval of a post-petition compensation package on behalf of Dana Corporation in *In re Dana Corporation ("Dana II")*.[39] In its opinion authorizing the revamped executive compensation plan in part, the court affirmed the holistic approach of viewing compensation plans under the business judgment lens of Section 363 articulated in *Dana I* and outlined several characteristics of an incentivizing "Produce Value for Pay" plan subject to the liberal business judgment presumption.[40] First, the court held that the proposed pension benefits, which were essentially the executives' entire retirement package, was not a severance payment and was not primarily retentive in nature.[41] As such, the proposed pension benefits were not governed by Section 503(c)(2).[42] The court based its conclusion on several defining characteristics including (i) the future vestment of the pension plan benefits; (ii) the actual pension benefits were based on various interim accruing factors in the nature of a true pension plan; (iii) the assumption of the pension benefits was not conditioned upon a specified employment period; (iv) the pension plan was comparable to pension plans forgone by the executives; (v) the post-petition

---

[28] Id. at 99.
[29] Id. at 99–100.
[30] Id. at 100.
[31] Id. at 98.
[32] Id. at 102.
[33] Id.
[34] Id.
[35] Id.

[36] Id.
[37] Id.
[38] Id. at 103.
[39] *In re Dana Corporation*, 358 B.R. 567 (Bankr. S.D.N.Y. 2006).
[40] Id.
[41] Id. at 577.
[42] Id.

pension plan was assumed as part of the employee agreement, replacing more lucrative provisions; and (v) the payment of the pension benefits was conditioned upon the continuance of "Dana's salaried and bargained unit defined benefit pension plans."[43]

Dana's compensation plan also contained a Pre-Emergence Claim for Burns.[44] Under the Pre-Emergence Claim, Burns was eligible for a general unsecured recovery if he was "involuntarily terminated without cause or resigned for good reason" prior to the conclusion of the Chapter 11 case.[45] The provision prohibited Burns from accepting an employment position with one of Dana's competitors, disclosing Dana's confidential information, or soliciting Dana's employees for a period of six months.[46] Based on the plain language of the statute, the court held that the Pre-Emergence Claim, a general unsecured claim, was not governed by the limitations of Section 503(c) because "on its face [section 503(c)] only limits the allowance and payment of administrative claims."[47] The Dana compensation plan also included a similarly conditioned Post-Emergence Claim for Burns.[48] Although the court declined to approve the provision at this early stage of the case, the court noted Dana's contention that the Post Emergence Claim was not a severance payment under Section 503(c) because the provision was conditioned upon continued compliance with the agreement, not on Burn's termination or resignation from Dana.[49]

The court also examined Dana's proposed 2006 Annual Incentive Plan (the "AIP").[50] The AIP was similar to a 2005 pre-petition short-term incentive program.[51] In addition, compensation plans at Dana had included a short-term incentive component for the past 50 years.[52] To this extent, Dana asserted that implementation of the AIP was not conditioned upon court approval because it was a transaction in the ordinary course of business.[53] The court noted, "the Bankruptcy Code [was] designed to allow a debtor-in-possession the flexibility to engage in ordinary transactions without unneeded oversight by the creditors or the court, while at the same time giving creditors an opportunity to contest those transactions that are not ordinary."[54] Under this doctrine, the court reasoned that Section 503(c)(1) did not govern the AIP.[55]

Finally, the court evaluated a long-term performance based incentive plan (the "LTIP") included in Dana's proposed compensation plan.[56] Senior executives would be eligible for the LTIP if Dana reached specified EBITDAR (Earnings Before Interest Taxes Depreciation Amortization and Rent) benchmarks.[57] In contrast to the artificially low financial thresholds previously proposed in *Dana I*, the company argued that the current LTIP "require[d] management to stretch in

---

[43] Id. at 577–78.
[44] Id. at 573.
[45] Id.
[46] Id.
[47] Id. at 578.
[48] Id. at 573.
[49] Id. at 578.
[50] Id. at 579–580.

[51] Id. at 579.
[52] Id. at 580 n. 18.
[53] Id. at 579–580.
[54] Id.
[55] Id. at 581.
[56] Id.
[57] Id. at 574.

order to achieve superior operating results."[58] The court concurred, finding that the EBITDAR benchmarks clearly weren't "lay ups"[59] As such, the LTIP was an incentivizing "Produce Value for Pay" plan, not a KERP subject to Section 503(c)(1) of BAPCPA.[60]

In summation, having found Section 503(c) inapplicable to the provisions of Dana's post-petition compensation plan, the court returned to the holistic approach to determine whether Dana's compensation plan was reasonable and cost effective under the business judgment lens of Section 363 of the Bankruptcy Code.[61] The court found that "the record [was] not sufficiently transparent to support an affirmative finding" due to the potentially overly generous bonuses under the AIP and LTIP provisions in 2007.[62] The court indicated that it would be inclined to approve Dana's compensation plan if Dana amended it to impose reasonable ceilings on LTIP payments.[63]

The United States Bankruptcy Court in the District of Delaware similarly analyzed a post-petition compensation plan in *In re Global Home Product, LLC*.[64] The same court however, prescribed a different scheme of analysis for post-petition compensations plans in *In re Nellson Nutraceutical, Inc. ("Nellson")* just two months later.[65] Specifically, the court in *Nellson* focused on the *Dana II* court's holding that the AIP was not governed by Section 503(c)(1) because the payment was a transaction in the ordinary course of business.[66] The *Nellson* Court determined that the plain language of the statute indicated that this interpretation was erroneous.[67] According to the *Nellson* court, "nothing in Section 503(c)(1) of the Bankruptcy Code limit[ed] its applicability to transactions or payments made outside the ordinary course of business."[68] The *Nellson* court also found that the language of Section 503(c)(3) indicated that section 503(c)(1) applied to transfers made to insiders in the ordinary course of business under the principle of *noscitur a sociisi*.[69] Accordingly, the *Nellson* court determined that transfers in the ordinary course of business, like Dana's AIP, must be analyzed under Section 503(c)(1) to determine if they are primarily retentive in nature.[70] These early interpretations indicate that provisions of BAPCPA are unclear and its true limitations are yet to be determined.

Since BAPCPA, courts have continued to restrict the bonuses to executives of companies in bankruptcy based on the objections of creditors and unions. For example, unions' and creditors' challenges to the fairness of proposed executive bonus programs compelled courts to reduce the bonus packages in the initial stages of the Delphi and the Tribune bankruptcies in 2010. In the Delphi bank-

---

[58] Id. at 581 (internal citations omitted).

[59] Id. at 583.

[60] Id.

[61] Id.

[62] Id.

[63] Id. at 584.

[64] *In re Global Home Products*, LLC, No. 06-10340(KG), 2007 WL 689747 (Bankr. D. Del. Mar. 6, 2007).

[65] *In re Nellson Nutraceutical, Inc.*, Nos. 06-10072 (CSS), 1222, 2007 WL 1502169 (Bankr. D. Del. May 25, 2007).

[66] Id. at *6.

[67] Id.

[68] Id.

[69] The words of a statute are to be construed in light of their context.

[70] Id.

ruptcy, the Bankruptcy Court ordered the company to reduce bonuses by 80% from the amount proposed.

The Tribune Company sought bankruptcy protection in December 2008, due to difficulties retiring its ESOP debt in the face of declining advertising revenue. The incentive bonus plan that Tribune management proposed was comprised of a transition management incentive program (TMIP), a key operators bonus (KOB), and management incentive program (MIP). The company sought to provide $10.6 million to 21 members of the core management team, $1.3 million for 50 employees under the TMIP, and $9.3 million in "pay for performance" bonuses to 23 employees under the KOB plan. The only party objecting to the proposed MIP was the union, which questioned its fairness.

The Delaware Bankruptcy Court Judge denied authority to the Tribune management to pay bonuses to the top executives and the top two portions of the program.[71] He approved only the management incentive plan for 720 mid to upper level managers, at a cost of $45.6 million, specifically noting the lack of objections from any representative of the Committee of Secured Creditors (other than the Guild) or any senior lender.

A question the courts have not resolved is whether BAPCPA applies to transactions in the ordinary course of business. Section 503(c)(3) states that it is applicable to "transfers or obligations that are outside the ordinary course of business." Section 503(c)(1) restricts payments to insiders, and does not state whether it applies only to transfers outside the ordinary course of business. *Dana II* held that it does not. In *Nellson*, the Bankruptcy Court for the District of Delaware held that BAPCPA does apply to transactions in the ordinary course of business.[72] It remains to be seen whether payments to insiders in the ordinary course of business can escape the restrictions in Section 503(c)(1). Many courts have followed *Dana II*, including Bankruptcy courts in New York, Delaware and Maryland.[73] The Borders Group bankruptcy also followed *Dana II*.[74]

Often, the issue is decided based on whether the court views the proposed program as providing incentive compensation (which is "good") or retention payments (which are "bad"). In *Global Home Products*, the Delaware Bankruptcy court found a sales plan was incentivizing rather than retentive. The court considered first that compensation is generally governed by a business judgment standard, and that, historically, courts have considered a company's reasonable use of incentive and performance bonuses to be a proper form of business judgment. The court noted that BAPCPA set up standards for challenging "stay" bonuses. Because the court found that the plans before it were not primarily designed to retain personnel, like a KERP, or provide severance pay, it found them to be outside the scope of Section 503(c). The court interpreted Section

---

[71] *In re Tribune Co., Bankr. D. Del., No. 08-131-41,* March 23, 2010.

[72] See *Dana II,* 358 B.RE. 567 at p.575 and *Nellson,* 369 B.R. 787.

[73] See *Global Home Products, LLC, supra,* and *In re Mattress Discounters Corp.,* 2008 Bankr. LEXIS 4547 (B 4547 (Bankr. D. Md. Oct. 10, 2008).

[74] *In re Borders Group, Inc.,* 2011 Bankr. LEXIS 1537, 54 Bankr. Ct. Dec. (LRP) 167, 9 Bankr. S.D.N.Y. 2011).

503(c) to limit KERPs, severance payments, and other payments to insiders. The court then reviewed the structure of the proposed compensation plan, its development process, and the reasonableness of the plan in relation to results sought, costs, the fairness and reasonableness of its scope, and the due diligence issue. It found due diligence was established, since all requirements were met but for the one requirement of independent counsel, which the court deemed not to be a problem.

The plan before the court in *In re Mattress Discounters Corp.*, was a severance plan for eligible nonunion employees restated from prior years. Mattress Discounters was a retailer. Under its reorganization strategy, it closed all stores in the New England area. The company sought court approval of the prepetition severance plan, with modifications. The plan was for employees in the New England area as well as the Mid Atlantic area where the company continued to operate. The company's rationale for including the New England area employees in the plan was that this would provide a comfort level for remaining employees. The company argued that the severance plan was outside the ordinary course of business and, thus, the business judgment test applied under Section 363. The Maryland Bankruptcy Court did not discuss the applicability of Section 503(c). However, the court cited *Dana II* in its analysis of the business judgment test. It held that the company had offered no business justification for adopting the plan for New England employees since most of them had been terminated or retained by the purchaser. The court acknowledged the company's goal of providing a comfort level to employees as benevolent, but found the goal, as manifest in the severance plan, not to be a "sound business judgment," in light of the company's extreme financial difficulties.

Two other bankruptcy court decisions in the Third Circuit have followed *Nellson*.[75] The *Nellson* court disagreed with *Dana II*, by finding the Section 503(c) limits applicable both inside and outside of the ordinary course of business. However, the *Nellson* court did follow the framework for analysis set forth in *Dana II*. The distinction between the two cases, at this point, appears to be an issue not raised before either court. Courts continue to follow the analytical framework established in *Dana II*, considering the:

- purpose of Section 503(c) (to address abuses of the bankruptcy system),
- restrictions of Section 503(c) when payments are outside the ordinary course of business, and
- business judgment test for payments not governed by Section 503(c), which are not motivated by retention and not severance payments.

.05 Severance Plans Established Before Bankruptcy Filing

The courts disagree on the priority of employees' severance pay claims arising from the post-petition termination of employees covered by a pre-petition severance pay program. The minority view, held by the Second Circuit, is that

---

[75] *In re Goody's Family Clothing, Inc.*, 392 B.R. 604, 617 (Bankr. D. Del. 2008) and *In re N.J. Mobile Dental Practice, P.A.*, 200 Bankr. LEXIS 1184 (Bankr. D.N.J. 2008).

such severance claims are post-petition administrative claims.[76] As noted by the Court of Appeals for the Tenth Circuit in *In re Amarex*, the conflict between the circuits "revolves largely around the definition of severance pay."[77] The Second Circuit agreed that to the extent severance pay represents compensation for the employee's past services, it is not an administrative expense entitled to priority.[78] The portion attributable to the employee's past services is prorated such that only the amount earned during the 90 days immediately preceding the filing of the bankruptcy petition is entitled to priority.

In *In re Campo Associates*,[79] the court noted the split in authority between the Second Circuit and the First, Third and Ninth Circuits. It observed, however, that these latter three courts "did not consider the issue of whether severance pay, offered to employees as an incentive to continue working with a financially troubled company, should be given priority status." In upholding the decision of the bankruptcy court, which had adopted the reasoning of the Second Circuit and allowed payments under a severance plan adopted pre-petition, the court concluded:

> There are important policy reasons for permitting severance pay agreements to have administrative expense priority status, especially when a financially troubled company offers such an agreement to employees as an incentive not to leave. Companies faced with financial problems and/or impending bankruptcy must have the authority to enter into enforceable severance agreements with key employees. If severance pay is denied priority status, this incentive will be lessened.[80]

The majority view bifurcates severance pay claims relating to post-petition terminations into two categories.[81] These cases distinguish between:

1. Severance payment at termination in lieu of notice, which the majority view gives an administrative expense priority; and

2. Severance payment made at termination based on length of employment, which the majority view gives no additional priority other than that allowed under Bankruptcy Code Section 507(a)(3).

The rationale for providing administrative priority to severance pay in lieu of notice is that such payments are made in consideration of a quick departure from the company after the petition date, and the payment is made post-petition.[82] In contrast, severance pay at termination based upon length of em-

---

[76] *Matter of Unishops, Inc.*, 553 F2d 305 (2d Cir. 1977); *In re W.T. Grant*, 620 F2d 319 (2d Cir. 1980), cert. denied, 446 U.S. 983 (1980); *In re Golden Distributors, Ltd., et al.*, 152 B.R. 35 (S.D. N.Y. 1992); *In re Finley Kumble Wagner Hein Underberg Manley Myerson & Casey*, 160 B.R. 882, 810 (Bankr. S.D. N.Y. 1993) (when termination occurs post-petition, severance pay is automatically classified as an administrative response regardless of the benefit to the estate), cited by *Supplee v. Bethlehem Steel Corp.*, 2006 U.S. Dist. LEXIS 8029 (S. D. N. Y., March 1, 2006).

[77] *In re Amarex*, 853 F2d 1526, 1530 (10th Cir. 1988).

[78] *Trustees of Amalgamated Insurance Fund v. McFarlin's*, 789 F2d 98 104 (2d Cir. 1986).

[79] *In re Campo Associates*, 247 B.R. 646 (E.D. La. 1998).

[80] *In re Campo Associates*, 247 B.R. 646, 651 (E.D. La. 1998).

[81] *In re Public Ledger*, 161 F2d 762, 771–73 (3d Cir. 1947); *In re Roth American, Inc.*, 975 F2d 949, 957 (3d Cir. 1992).

[82] See also *In re Mammoth Mart*, 536 F2d 950, 955 (1st Cir. 1976), explaining the rationale of *In re Public Ledger*, 161 F2d 762 (3d Cir. 1947); and *In re Jeannette Corp.*, 118 B.R. 327, 330 (Bankr. W.D. Pa. 1990) ("if the right to severance pay is based upon failure to

ployment is given in consideration of work performed both pre- and post-petition, and thus not all such pay is entitled to treatment as an administrative expense.[83]

The case of *Mason v. Official Comm. of Unsecured Creditors (In re FBI Distribution Corp.)*,[84] is typical. A subsidiary of Filene's Basement, Inc. ("FBI") hired a new president and chief merchandising officer at a time when the company was already in some financial difficulty. The president's employment agreement provided for three years severance. When FBI filed for bankruptcy under Chapter 11, it allegedly promised the president that it would continue to honor the terms of her agreement. However, FBI never applied to the bankruptcy court for approval or continuation of the agreement. The president eventually terminated employment while FBI was still in bankruptcy, and FBI's trustee rejected her employment agreement. The court found that FBI was justified in rejecting the executory contract and that the former president's claims for severance pay under the noncourt-approved agreement were not entitled to administrative priority.

In re Russell Cave Co., Inc.[85] is another typical case. It held that severance pay claims, as well as any other administrative expense claims, are entitled to administrative priority only to the extent that the employees earned them after the company filed its bankruptcy petition. In order to calculate any administrative expenses allowable under this rationale, courts have used a multiplier fraction, which has the number of days of employment after the petition date as the numerator, and 365 as the denominator.[86]

The *In re Russell Cave Co., Inc.* court also rejected the employee's position that any termination payments received within the 90-day pre-petition period meant that he earned the severance pay on the date of his termination, rather than over the entire period of the employee's tenure with the company. The court followed the majority interpretation of Section 507(a)(3), which holds that only those benefits actually earned during the 90-day period immediately preceding the filing of a petition are entitled to priority. In making this determination, the same type of pro ration through use of a multiplier fraction occurs. Finally, a court may reduce the amount of severance benefits entitled to Section 507(a)(3) priority after this allocation by any wages and other benefits the company paid to the employee pursuant to a first day order approving the pre-petition severance agreement or authorizing a new retention plan.

(Footnote Continued)

give notice and not based on length of service, it is 'earned' when termination occurs and the full amount thereof is entitled to the priority treatment statutorily prescribed for such a period").

[83] *In re Health Maintenance Foundation*, 680 F2d 619, 621 (9th Cir. 1982); *In re Allegheny Int'l, Inc.*, 118 B.R. 276, 280 (Bankr. W.D. Pa. 1990); *In re World Sales, Inc.*, 183 B.R. 872 (9th Cir. B.A.P.1995); *In re Wean, Inc.*, 171 B.R. 528, 532 (Bankr. W. D. Pa. 1994); *In re Harnischfeger Industries, Inc.*, 270 B.R. 188 (C.D. Del. 2001); *Rawson Food Services, Inc. v. Creditor's*

Committee, 67 B.R. 351 (M.D. Fla. 1986); *In re Yarn Liquidation, Inc.*, 217 B.R. 544 (Bankr. E.D. Tenn. 1997).

[84] *Mason v. Official Comm. of Unsecured Creditors (In re FBI Distrib. Corp.)*, 330 F3d 36 (1st Cir. 2003).

[85] *In re Russell Cave Co., Inc.*, 248 B.R. 301 (Bankr. E D. Ky. 2000).

[86] See *e.g.*, *In re Yarn Liquidation, Inc.*, 217 B.R. 544, 548 (Bankr. E.D. Tenn. 1997). The *Yarn* court also suggested dividing the total number of post petition work days by 260 (52 weeks of five work days).

The court in *Mammoth Mart* articulated the rationale for denying severance benefits as an administrative priority under Section 503(b)(1) as follows:

> An expense is administrative only and if it arises out of a transaction between the creditor and the bankruptcy trustee or debtor in possession and only to the extent that the consideration supporting the claimant's right to payment was both supplied to and beneficial to the debtor in possession in the operation of the business.[87]

In *Former Employees of Builders Square Retail Stores v. Hechinger Investment Company of Delaware*,[88] the Court of Appeals for the Third Circuit considered the post-petition treatment of so-called "stay-on" and retention bonuses under a pre-petition retention plan. Under that program, to be able to receive the applicable bonus, an employee had to remain with the company until the company closed the employee's store or released the employee. Employees who remained with the company until their store released them or closed, only to see their payments halted upon the bankruptcy filing, argued that they had earned the benefits post-petition. The Court of Appeals disagreed, noting that the relevant time under Section 503(b)(1)(A) of the Bankruptcy Code was when the services were "rendered," not when they were scheduled for payment. According to the court, it was also irrelevant that the services the employees performed before the company filed for bankruptcy continued to benefit the company after it filed. Similarly, in *In re Cincinnati Cordage and Paper Co.*,[89] employees sought administrative expense claim priority for certain severance benefits. The bankruptcy court acknowledged that the employees' services were beneficial to the orderly liquidation of a company's assets. However, because the severance benefits arose from pre-petition executive employment agreements, they did not qualify as an administrative expense claim.

In *Matson v. Alarcon*, the Fourth Circuit interpreted the Section 507(a)(4) requirement that priority treatment be given to claims earned within 180 days of filing the petition,[90] and found that employees earn the full amount of severance pay on the date they terminated employment and, thus, became entitled to receive severance under the terms of the severance plan. The severance pay in this case was for 125 employees terminated within the 180-day period prior to filing the petition. Upon an employee's termination, the employee became a participant in the severance plan. The court noted triggering events allowing employees to receive severance pay are within a company's control, as is the decision to terminate the employment relationship. The severance plan's stated purpose was to assist employees upon termination, providing compensation for injury and loss resulting from the termination of employment. The court rejected the trustee's argument that an employee earned severance pay over the course of

---

[87] *In re Mammoth Mart*, 536 F2d 950, 955 (1st Cir. 1976). This two-pronged test was cited with approval in *In re Commercial Financial Services*, 246 F3d 1291, 1295 (10th Cir. 2001). See also *Matter of Jartran, Inc.*, 732 F2d 584 (7th Cir. 1984), holding that to achieve priority under Code Section 503(b)(1) the right to payment must arise from a transaction with the debtor and must have benefited the debtor.

[88] *Former Employees of Builders Square Retail Stores v. Hechinger Investment Company of Delaware*, 298 F3d 219 (3d Cir. 2002).

[89] *In re Cincinnati Cordage and Paper Co.*, 271 B.R. 264 (Bankr. S.D. Ohio 2001).

[90] *Matson v. Alarcon*, No. 10-2352, (4th Cir. 2011).

his or her full term of employment, in exchange for service rendered, reasoning that such an approach would result in employees "earning" severance pay prior to the time the severance plan was adopted.

The courts draw a distinction between pre-petition programs and programs established after filing the bankruptcy petition. Courts generally will evaluate pre-petition programs under both:

- Section 363(b) of the Bankruptcy Code, involving a determination of whether the use of estate assets assists in a debtor's reorganization; and

- The doctrine of necessity, which "recognizes the existence of the judicial power to authorize a debtor in a reorganization case to pay pre-petition claims where such payment is essential to the continued operation of the debtor."[91]

Planning Note: Employment agreements, severance plans and other benefit promises entered into or made before a bankruptcy filing may be unenforceable after the filing if the company/debtor does not specifically seek and receive bankruptcy court approval of their continuation.

Importantly, in *AARS Brook LLC v. Jalbert*, the First Circuit found that the cost of litigating the claim was an important factor to consider in determining whether a claim should be settled.[92] The court upheld a bankruptcy court's approval of a settlement between the bankrupt company's trustee and the company's president based on finding the cost of litigation exceeded the settlement amount. The president's employment agreement provided he was entitled to 12 months' salary and benefits if terminated without cause. He elected to reduce his salary when the company experienced financial difficulty. Two months later the company filed a bankruptcy petition under Chapter 11, and converted to a Chapter 7 liquidation several months thereafter. The court held the president earned the right to severance before the bankruptcy petition was filed and did not provide consideration after filing of the petition. The appeals court noted acrimony of the proceedings indicated litigation was certain and the expense of litigation of the claim was certain to exceed the $147,000 claim.

.06 Recent Cases

Courts continue to uphold compensation plans for executives in situations where the plans are properly structured as an incentive plan, and rely on precedent established in *Global Home Products*[93] and *Dana II*[94]. Structuring plans to benefit executives who are not insiders, or to be in the ordinary course of business, are other strategies to circumvent the stringent requirements of Section 503(c) of the Bankruptcy Code. As established in *Dana II*, the statutory limits on

---

[91] *In re Ionosphere Clubs, Inc.*, 98 B.R. 174, 176 (Bankr. S.D. N.Y. 1989). But see *Capital Factors, Inc. v. K Mart Corp.*, 291 B.R. 818 (N.D. Ill. 2003). In *Capital Factors*, the court rejected the argument that bankruptcy courts have the power to authorize payment of pre-petition claims based on the doctrine of necessity. The court found that Congress' failure to codify the doctrine of necessity in the Bankruptcy

Code and the court's lack of equitable power to authorize pre-petition payment of unsecured claims precluded using the doctrine of necessity to prioritize the payment of such claims.

[92] *AARS Brook LLC v. Jalbert (In re ServiSense.com Inc.)*, No. 03-2512, (1st Cir. 2004).

[93] Supra, note 73.

[94] Supra, note 72.

compensating insiders under "pay to stay" plans, where the primary purpose of the plan is to retain employees, does not foreclose a corporation in bankruptcy from reasonably compensating employees.

A Southern District of New York Bankruptcy court stated that court approval of Key Employee Incentive Plans, or KEIPs, has "become commonplace in large bankruptcy cases", in *In re Velo Holdings, Inc.*[95] In *Velo Holdings*, the court made a specific finding of fact that the KEIP encouraged executives to increase their pre-bankruptcy job responsibilities to address issues unique to the bankruptcy proceeding. Implicit in this finding is that proponents of an incentive plan must establish for the record that the KEIP requires an increase in responsibilities to meet the target. Once the addition to job responsibilities was established, this overcame the hurdle that the incentive plan required net operating cash flow targets that were based on the budget. The court approved the plan because more services were required of the executives.

Another example of a case where a bankruptcy court approved a performance plan is *In re Borders Group.*[96] In *Borders*, the court approved a proposed KEIP to benefit insiders that required them to confirm an ongoing business plan or consummate a sale of the business as a going concern under 11 U.S.C Section 363, and meet financial targets for annual cost reductions, and distributions to unsecured creditors. Both financial goals and a qualifying transaction that continued the business were required.

If a court finds an incentive plan is "justified under the facts and circumstances", the plan will also avoid the limits of Bankruptcy Code Section 503(c). For incentive plans, the threshold question on review of a plan is whether it is a true incentive plan, or a disguised retention plan. Section 503(c) limits govern retention plans applicable to insiders. If a company sets productivity and performance goals, and connects the compensation to achievement of the goals, generally the court will approve the plan if it is justified under the facts and circumstances, and it is an incentive plan not subject to 503(c)[97].

On the other hand, where a payment under a plan is based upon actions occurring prior to filing the bankruptcy petition, a court may not find the plan to be primarily incentivizing. *In re Residential Capital LLC*[98] is a case where 50% of the incentive award was tied to a budget metric that appeared to have been established by asset sale negotiations prior to filing of the bankruptcy petition. The court held the difficulty of achieving the metrics was not sufficiently established.

Section 503(c) only applies to payments to employees outside of the ordinary course of business, unless justified by the facts and circumstances of the case. Payments in the ordinary course of business are subject to a different standard, the business judgment standard of Section 363. To determine whether a transac-

---

[95] *In re Velo Holdings, Inc.*, 472 B.R. 201 (Bankr. S.D.N.Y. 2012).

[96] *In re Borders Group*, 453 BR 459, 471-472 (Bankr. S.D.N.Y. 2011).

[97] 472 B.R. 201 at 209.

[98] *In re Residential Capital LLC*, 478 B.R. 154 (Bankr. S.D. N.Y. 2013).

tion is in the ordinary course of business, many courts apply both a "horizontal" test and a "vertical" test. The horizontal test determines whether the transaction is unusual, or reasonably common, in the industry. The vertical test examines whether the transaction is one that creditors would reasonably expect. If the incentives and targets are the same as those used in previous years, the court may find they were in the ordinary course of business.

The court in *In re Velo* considered factors established in *Dana II*, in determining whether a compensation plan met the business judgment test. It noted that *Global Home* used the business judgment standard of Section 363, and applied the factors from *Dana II* to find the business judgement standard test was met.

.07 Severance and Retention Plans Established After Bankruptcy Filing Pre-BAPCPA

Before the enactment of the BAPCPA, Bankruptcy Code Section 503(b)(1)(A) gave a priority for the actual, necessary costs and expenses of preserving the bankrupt company's estate, including salaries, wages and commissions awarded after the bankruptcy filing (referred to as "post-petition" expenses). Courts generally gave an administrative priority to employees' claims for severance pay where the company/debtor established its severance plan after its bankruptcy filing. Because such plans used assets of the company's estate for purposes outside the ordinary course of business (assets that otherwise would be available to pay creditors) the company would seek court approval of the plan in accordance with Bankruptcy Code Section 363(b). In *Bagus v. Clark*,[99] the court denied administrative expense priority status to employees' severance pay claims because the company in Chapter 11 had adopted the severance plan without the court's approval.

The legal standard for approving key employee retention plans was well established: "Bankruptcy courts [would] approve key employee retention programs ('KERP') if the debtor has used proper business judgment in formulating the program and the court finds the program to be fair and reasonable."[100] Most companies asserted that the programs they proposed satisfy both of these requirements and, therefore, the bankruptcy court should approve the programs.

Section 363(b) of the Bankruptcy Code provides in relevant part that "the trustee, after notice and a hearing, may use, sell, or lease, other than in the ordinary course of business, property of the estate." A court can authorize a company to use property of the estate pursuant to Section 363(b)(1) of the Bankruptcy Code when such use is an exercise of a company's sound business judgment and when the company proposes the use in good faith.[101]

---

[99] *Bagus v. Clark*, 5 F3d 455 (10th Cir. 1993).

[100] *In re Aerovox, Inc.*, 269 B.R. 74, 80 (Bankr. D. Mass. 2001). See also In re Interco, Inc., 128 B.R. 229, 234 (Bankr. E.D. Mo. 1991).

[101] See, *e.g.*, *In re Delaware & Hudson R.R. Co.*, 124 B.R. 169, 176 (D. Del. 1991) (adopting the "sound business purpose" test to evaluate motions brought pursuant to Section 363(b)); See also *Stephen Indus., Inc. v. McClung*, 789 F2d 386, 390 (6th Cir. 1986) (adopting the "sound business purpose" standard for sales proposed pursuant to Section 363(b)); *In re Abbotts Dairies of Pennsylvania, Inc.*, 788 F2d 143 (3d Cir. 1986).

Companies (and courts) had to justify post-petition employment retention and bonus programs as an appropriate use of estate assets under Bankruptcy Code Section 363(b). The courts evaluated these programs under the "business judgment test," which required a showing that the use of the assets of the company will assist in a company's reorganization.[102] In *Montgomery Ward Holding Corp., et al.*,[103] the court applied this test, citing the need to stabilize employee turnover rates, boost employee morale, and retain key employees as the basis for offering the program.

In *In re Aerovox, Inc.*,[104] the bankruptcy court approved a bonus plan and severance package for four key employees because these programs would help retain the critical employees during the course of the bankruptcy case. The court stated, "bankruptcy courts will approve KERPs if the Debtor has used proper business judgment in formulating the program and the court finds the program to be fair and reasonable."[105] The court also indicated that the determination "whether to approve a plan depends upon the facts and circumstances of the specific case."

The company/debtor had the burden of establishing that a valid business purpose existed for the use of estate property in a manner that was not in the ordinary course of business.[106] Once the company had articulated a valid business purpose, however, a presumption arose that a company made its decision on an informed basis, in good faith and in the honest belief the action was in the best interest of the company.[107]

¶2435 Retirement and Other Benefit Plans of Bankrupt Companies

Retirement and other benefit plans can be among a company's/debtor's largest liabilities at the time of a bankruptcy filing. Some companies have used the bankruptcy process to rid themselves of burdensome pension and retiree medical benefit liabilities. Most benefit plans can be rescinded or revised in the bankruptcy process. However, qualified retirement plans enjoy certain additional protections.

.01 Qualified Retirement Plans

Under virtually all circumstances, ERISA completely protects the assets of a qualified retirement plan from the reach of bankruptcy and other creditors of the plan sponsor. Clearly, the assets of the plan are separate from the assets of the company.[108] Courts have even held that creditors could not force a bankrupt company (or its bankruptcy trustee) to terminate an over-funded defined benefit

---

[102] *In re Lionel Corp.*, 722 F2d 1063, 1071 (2d Cir. 1983).

[103] *Montgomery Ward Holding Corp., et al.*, 242 B.R. 147, 153 (D. Del. 1999).

[104] *In re Aerovox, Inc.*, 269 B.R. 74 (Bankr. D. Mass. 2001).

[105] *In re Aerovox, Inc.*, 269 B.R. 74, 80 (Bankr. D. Mass. 2001).

[106] See *In re Lionel Corp.*, 722 F2d 1063, 1070–71 (2d Cir. 1983).

[107] See *In re Integrated Resources, Inc.*, 147 B.R. 650, 656 (Bankr. S.D. N.Y. 1992).

[108] ERISA § 403, 29 U.S.C. § 1103; Code Sec. 401(a).

pension plan to make the excess assets available to the creditors.[109] If the pension plan is overfunded, the company may not want to terminate it, since that would allow creditors to recover the excess assets. Many companies prefer to keep excess assets for use when they come out of bankruptcy.

Some pension plans' terms provide that upon bankruptcy or insolvency the plan will automatically terminate. This could be a problem for a company that wants to file for reorganization under Chapter 11, but wants to continue its retirement plan. As part of pre-bankruptcy planning, companies should carefully review the terms of their plans so that they are aware of any automatic termination provisions. If plans contain those provisions, the company could easily amend them to eliminate the automatic termination provisions before commencing a Chapter 11 proceeding.

If the company is filing for liquidation under Chapter 7 of the Bankruptcy Code, then it will be terminating its employees and its retirement plan. Employees must fully vest in their benefits under the plan at the time of the plan termination.

One concern that may arise when a bankruptcy filing is impending is the continuation of contributions to a qualified plan. Many companies may try to reduce their costs and may choose to suspend or stop contributions. As previously stated, this may raise numerous issues. The Pension Benefit Guaranty Corporation ("PBGC") guarantees benefits under defined benefit plans. As part of this federal insurance scheme, ERISA and the PBGC regulate defined benefit plans more heavily, particularly when the plan sponsor files for bankruptcy or chooses to terminate its defined benefit plan.

Some companies may choose to terminate (or allow the plan to terminate if provided by its terms) when they file for bankruptcy. If the company has fully funded its defined benefit pension plan, the company can terminate the plan in a standard termination.[110] However, if a company has not fully funded the plan, the insolvent company can file for a "distress" termination of its defined benefit plan, the effect of which is to turn over the plan to the PBGC. The PBGC then has a right to a specified percentage of the company's assets. However, in enforcing this right, the PBGC generally would have to take its place in line after the company's secured creditors.

If the company does not seek termination, the bankruptcy court will decide whether the plan sponsor-debtor should continue making regular funding contributions during the bankruptcy case. The courts that have considered the issue have treated employee benefit plans as executory contracts, capable of being assumed or rejected under Section 365.[111] Several courts have held that an executory contract remains enforceable until assumed or rejected.[112] Thus, the executory contract will "ride through" the bankruptcy process and be binding on

[109] *In the Matter of Esco Manufacturing Co.*, 33 F3d 509 (5th Cir. 1994).

[110] See ERISA § 4041, 29 U.S.C. § 1341.

[111] *Morse v. Adams*, 1987 U.S. Dist. LEXIS 15425 at *4 (E.D. Mich. 1987).

[112] *Century Indem. Co. v. NGC Settlement Trust (In the matter of Nat'l Gypsum Co.)*, 208 F3d 498, 508 (5th Cir. 2000).

the company, even after discharge.[113] The argument against continuing to fund a plan in bankruptcy is that such contributions represent payment on account of pre-petition labor and therefore constitute impermissible payments on account of pre-petition liabilities.

BAPCPA added Section 706(a)(11) to the Bankruptcy Code, which provides that the bankruptcy trustee steps into the role of plan administrator when the company maintains plans subject to ERISA at the time it files for bankruptcy protection. Section 704(a) also provides that a bankruptcy trustee that acted as an ERISA fiduciary is discharged from any potential fiduciary liability once the trustee has discharged all of its duties.

However, courts will continue to protect participants' ERISA rights against fiduciaries after a bankruptcy filing. In *Vengurlekar v. HSBC*, plan participants sued a bank and management company that assumed management of a company in bankruptcy for an alleged breach of fiduciary duty, for allegedly failing to deposit funds the companies withheld from employees' paychecks to the 401(k) plan.[114] The plan delinquencies were alleged to be $900,000. The district court refused to dismiss the claim, despite the lack of a clearly identified plan document. The court ultimately ruled that the bank and the management company were not fiduciaries because there was insufficient proof that they exercised discretionary control over the management or disposition of the 401(k) plan assets. Interestingly, in its opinion, the court specifically stated that participants' claims were neither insubstantial nor frivolous.

In *In re NSCO Inc.*, a bankruptcy court in Massachusetts refused to keep a case open for six years to wait for the ERISA statute of limitations to expire.[115] The court noted that the case could be reopened if a DOL audit showed evidence of breach of a fiduciary duty.

If the company maintains the plan pursuant to collective bargaining, the union may force the company to continue the plan (if the PBGC does not seize it). Section 1113 of the Bankruptcy Code allows a bankrupt company to terminate its contracts, including collective bargaining agreements (following negotiation with the union). For many companies, going forward without the union is not an alternative.[116]

In 2006, the Third Circuit Court of Appeals affirmed a federal district court holding that a pension plan amendment made just prior to the plan sponsor's bankruptcy that increased benefits for some 400 plan participants was a fraudulent transfer and, thus, was void.[117] According to the court, the two executives who proposed the amendment had their benefits increased by 200 percent and 470 percent, respectively. Under Section 548 of the Bankruptcy Code, a transfer is

---

[113] *Century Indem. Co. v. NGC Settlement Trust (In the matter of Nat'l Gypsum Co.)*, 208 F3d 498, 504 (5th Cir. 2000).

[114] *Vengurlekar v. HSBC Bank*, 2004 U.S. Dist. LEXIS 6838, 33 E.B.C. 1638 (S.D.N.Y. 2004).

[115] *In re NSCO Inc.*, Bankr. D. Mass., No. 08-43-494A.

[116] Collective bargaining agreements are considered executory contracts and, while rejected or modified under Section 1113, they are assumed under Section 365. *Mass. Air Conditioning & Heating Corp. v. McCoy*, 196 B.R. 659, 663 (D. Mass. 1996).

[117] *Pension Transfer Corp. v. Beneficiaries Under the Third Amendment to Fruehauf Trailer Corp. Retirement Plan No. 003*, 3rd Cir., No. 05-1374, April 12, 2006.

considered fraudulent and is voidable if the bankruptcy trustee can establish that: (1) the debtor had an interest in the property; (2) the interest was transferred within one year of the filing of the bankruptcy petition; (3) the company was insolvent at the time of the transfer or became insolvent as a result thereof; and (4) the company received less than a reasonably equivalent value in exchange for such transfer. The court said there was no dispute that the company made the transfer within one year of the company's filing its bankruptcy petition on Oct. 7, 1996 or that the company was insolvent at the time it made the transfer.

The court found that the company had an interest in the pension plan assets and the amendment. "Even assuming there was no surplus in the Plan at the time of the transfer in September 1996, under [the Employee Retirement Income Security Act] and section 9.4 of the Plan, Fruehauf, as the Plan's sponsor, was entitled to any surplus upon termination of the Plan." The court found that the company had made a "transfer" of assets under the plan because, in adopting the amendment, the company made an irrevocable election to allocate a portion of the plan's surplus to the benefit increases called for under the amendment. Finally, the court found that the amendment had value because, among other things, future services, such as those likely received from a plan that would encourage employee retention, constitute "value" within the meaning of Section 548. The court did find that the amendment provided the company with value reasonably equivalent to its cost because of the retention value.

In *Burden v. Seafort*,[118] the U.S. Bankruptcy Appellate Panel for the Sixth Circuit ruled, on an issue of first impression under BAPCPA, holding that Chapter 13 individuals/debtors who are not contributing to their 401(k) plans at the time they file for bankruptcy cannot start contributing to their plans until after their creditors have been paid off. BAPCPA allows for Chapter 13 filers to exclude from their bankruptcy repayment plans any contributions they are making to qualified retirement plans. The court held that while the BAPCPA allows for Chapter 13 filers to continue making contributions to their retirement plans while repaying their debts, it only allows for the contributions to continue if the individual was making contributions at the time he or she filed for bankruptcy. The panel recognized that the purpose of BAPCPA was to allow individuals to continue to save for retirement, but held that income that becomes available after filing a petition and repaying a plan loan is "protected disposable income" that an individual must use to pay creditors.

.02 Northwest Airlines Corp. Pension Plan

In *Cress v. Wilson*,[119] the plaintiffs claimed that the board of directors and certain officers of Northwest Airlines Corp. were liable for a breach of ERISA fiduciary duty for "allowing the underfunding" of the Northwest Airlines Pension Plan. A breach of fiduciary duty under ERISA can result in personal liability.

The federal district court for the Southern District of New York rejected the directors' and officers' motion to dismiss plaintiffs' claims, despite the fact that:

---

[118] *Burden v. Seafort*, 2010 WL 3564709 (Bktcy. CA6 2010).

[119] *Cress v. Wilson*, S.D.N.Y., No.06 Civ. 2717 (June 7, 2007).

1. The pension plan was not underfunded on a legal basis;

2. The pension plan did not hold Northwestern stock;

3. No plan participant's benefit was reduced, because Northwest did not terminate the plan; and

4. The directors and officers were acting in a settlor capacity, not as fiduciaries.

Under these facts and the law as it exists today, the plaintiffs' claims seemed implausible, at best. However, the history of ERISA includes many cases where a single federal court issued a decision that goes way beyond any possible reading of the previous decisions — thus, opening the door for numerous copycat lawsuits. This decision does not find liability, but rather only allows the plaintiffs to proceed to trial with their claims. However, it is another warning to executives and board members that imperfections in retirement plan documents is an area that can lead to liability.

.03 Nonqualified Plans in Bankruptcy

Many companies establish nonqualified retirement plans to help key management personnel save or accrue more retirement money. Nonqualified retirement plans are normally unfunded, so that executives that participate in them are not subject to current taxation on benefits vested under them. A company can set up a "rabbi" trust to fund a nonqualified plan. The IRS will not treat the plan as funded (with trust assets currently taxable to executives) if the assets of the trust are subject to the claims of the company's general creditors, should the company become insolvent.[120] In other words, if the company's business fails, the plan's participants simply become unsecured creditors of the company with no special priority claims.

Although ERISA Section 4(b) exempts excess benefit plans from ERISA coverage, most nonqualified retirement plans are not excess plans. Since many nonqualified plans clearly fit within ERISA's definition of a "pension plan," some courts have extended the protection of *Patterson v. Shumate* and ERISA Section 206(d) to such plans (see ¶2455.01). Since most nonqualified plans represent only an unfunded promise to pay monies in the future, it is questionable whether a bankruptcy trustee could recover such amounts before their distribution to the participant. However, at least one court has permitted a bankruptcy creditor to attach a participant's nonqualified deferred compensation account, even though such account was only an accounting entry.[121]

Litigation often involves what level of priority the bankruptcy process affords to top hat plan claims. For example, in *Kucin v. Devan*,[122] employees argued for administrative expense priority for benefits that had vested before bankruptcy. The court held that they were pre-petition claims and thus received general unsecured priority.

---

[120] See IRS Letter Ruling 8113107, Dec. 31, 1980; DOL Op. Ltr. 90-14A, May 8, 1990.

[121] *Westinghouse Credit Corporation v. J. Reiter Sales, Inc.*, 443 N.W. 2d 837 (Ct. App. Minn. 1989).

[122] *Kucin v. Devan*, 251 B.R. 269 (D. Md. 2000).

With respect to nonqualified plan benefits payable to an executive in a company facing the possibility of bankruptcy, the executive could negotiate for the company to purchase an annuity for the executive's benefit, rather than hope the nonqualified plan promises survive the bankruptcy. The annuity would be immediately taxable to the executive, but would be certain of payment. Creditors might challenge the annuity purchase as a preferential payment. As discussed above, payments made during the 90-day period immediately before a bankruptcy filing may be deemed "preferential" and subject to recapture by the bankruptcy trustee if the payments cause the recipient to recover more than he, she or it would have recovered in the bankruptcy proceeding. For payments made to "insiders" this look back period before the bankruptcy filing is 12 months. However, the executive and the company may decide that the risk of recovery is worth taking for two very practical reasons. First, having a paid-up annuity contract in hand, the executive is in a better position to ride out the bankruptcy than the executive would be if he or she had to hope that the company was successful in getting the bankruptcy court to approve, and the creditors not to object, an order to continue paying or accruing nonqualified plan benefits during and after the proceeding. Second, as a practical matter, creditors often do not pursue preferential payments in Chapter 11 cases unless the payments are egregious. If the creditors decide to pursue preferential payments, they will bear the burden of proving and recovering the payments.

The district court overseeing the reorganization of Enron Corp. authorized efforts to seek the return of $53 million in controversial deferred compensation payments set aside for 126 executives on the eve of the company's December 2001 bankruptcy filing.[123] Any bonus money reclaimed would go into the bankruptcy estate toward partial settlement of the $66 billion in claims pending against the company, according to the bankruptcy trustee.

Efforts to Protect Nonqualified Plan Benefits. Some companies in some bankruptcy filings have a much better chance of paying out nonqualified plan benefits after bankruptcy than others. Among the factors that tip the scales in favor of or against greater protection of nonqualified plan/rabbi trust payouts are the following:

- What did other general unsecured creditors recover in the bankruptcy?

- Can/Does the company's bankruptcy plan of reorganization classify the employee/plan creditors separately from other unsecured creditors (*e.g.*, trade creditors or lease rejection creditors)?

- Does the company's rabbi trust include so-called "Moglia language" (from the 2003 Seventh Circuit case of *Bank of America v. Moglia*)?

- Were the assets of the rabbi trust owned by the company that filed for bankruptcy, or by a parent, subsidiary or other affiliate that did not participate in the bankruptcy filing? Were subtrusts maintained?

---

[123] *In re: Enron Corp.*, Bankr. S.D.N.Y., No. 01-16034, agreement September 22, 2003.

The 2003 Seventh Circuit case of *Bank of America v. Moglia*,[124] was different from any previous case on rabbi trusts in its distinction between secured and unsecured creditors. Companies can provide significantly better protection for the rabbi trust assets - that is, a greater likelihood that the assets will be used to pay executive's benefits in all cases, even insolvency - by including the *Moglia* language in their rabbi trust.

There are situations where a company's/debtor's nonqualified plan promises funded by a rabbi trust could survive the company's bankruptcy. One scenario involves companies that voluntarily file for bankruptcy reorganization due to an external liability threat, which may or may not materialize. This scenario unfortunately has occurred in several situations of potential mass tort liability (*e.g.*, any company that ever touched asbestos). In these cases, the company is fundamentally sound, but it needs to create a separate liability trust for the circling vultures of the tort bar. During and after the bankruptcy filing, the company maintains business as usual and it needs to retain all of its employees through and after the bankruptcy proceeding.

One example of this scenario was the Armstrong World Industries Form 10-K filing for the fiscal year ended December 31, 2006.[125] Armstrong World Industries, Inc. filed a voluntary petition for relief under Chapter 11 of the U.S. Bankruptcy Code in order to use the court-supervised reorganization process to achieve a resolution of AWI's asbestos-related liability. In October 2006, AWI emerged from Chapter 11. As of December 31, 2006, the CEO retained a nonqualified benefit plan accrual of $3.6 million, including a benefit formula giving him two years of service credit for every one year of actual service toward the calculation of his pension benefits under the plan and an additional five years of service credit in from the board of directors in 2005.

Another example is not one attributable to potential mass tort liability. In April 2001, PG&E filed a voluntary petition for relief under the provisions of Chapter 11 of the U.S. Bankruptcy Code (the factors that caused PG&E to take this action are discussed in the MD&A from the PG&E Form 10-K filing for the fiscal year ended December 31, 2003).[126] In December 2003, PG&E settled all relevant disputes with a "Plan of Reorganization" that paid allowed creditor claims in full, plus applicable interest, and emerged from Chapter 11 as an investment grade entity. Form 10-K described the pension plan result:

> "PG&E Corporation and the Utility provide retirement benefits to some of the executive officers named in the Summary Compensation Table. The benefit formula for eligible executive officers is 1.7 percent of the average of the three highest combined salary and annual Short-Term Incentive Plan payments during the last ten years of service multiplied by years of credited service. During 2002 and 2003, annuities were purchased to replace a significant portion of the unfunded retirement benefits for certain officers whose entire accrued benefit could not be provided under the Retirement Plan due to tax

---

[124] *Bank of America v. Moglia*, 330 F.3d 942 (7th Cir. 2003).

[125] http://www.sec.gov/Archives/edgar/data/7431/000119312507070590/d10k.htm#tx85057_19.

[126] http://www.sec.gov/Archives/edgar/data/1004980/000095014904000430/f95893ae10vk.htm.

code limits. The annuities will not change the amount or timing of the after-tax benefits that would have been provided upon retirement under the Supplemental Executive Retirement Plan (SERP) or similar arrangements. In connection with the annuities, tax restoration payments were made such that the annuitization was tax-neutral to the executive officer."

Plan Amendments to Protect Nonqualified Plan Benefits. Because non-qualified plan benefits are nothing more than promises to pay, subject to the same treatment as the claims of the company's other general creditors, these benefits typically evaporate in bankruptcy. Therefore, companies and executives often work to preserve the benefits at the last minute. *In Liquidating Trustee of the Amcast Unsecured Creditor Liquidating Trust v. Baker (In re Amcast Industrial Corp.)*,[127] the U.S. Bankruptcy Court for the Southern District of Ohio allowed the liquidating trustee for the bankrupt company to continue with its claim that the company's former officers and directors breached their fiduciary duties to the company by making modifications to the structure and payment of executives' retirement benefits on the eve of the company's bankruptcy.

Generally, no fiduciary duty applies to a plan sponsor's decision to amend an ERISA-qualified plan. However, the court found that a "possible exception" exists in cases involving sham transactions or unlawful transfers to parties in interests. Specifically, the company took the following actions:

- Implemented a so-called "Q-SERP" transfer, where benefits owed under a nonqualified retirement benefit plan are shifted to the qualified retirement plan (as noted above, qualified retirement plan assets are exempt from the reach of creditors), and

- Transferred an annuity contract held by a rabbi trust to a covered executive, thus placing its asset beyond the reach of the company's creditors.

However, the court also held that the bankruptcy trustee could not pursue a claim that Amcast's officers and directors breached their fiduciary duties to creditors by restructuring the retirement benefits at a time when Amcast was close to insolvency - but not yet insolvent. The court found that under Ohio law, officers and directors owe no fiduciary duty to creditors.

Amendments to Reduce Nonqualified Plan Benefits. In 2008, as part of the bankruptcy process and as a condition of its bankruptcy and its subsequent purchase by the United States Treasury, General Motors was required to amend its nonqualified plan, the Executive Retirement Plan (ERP) to reduce certain vested retirement benefits of current retirees, including two-thirds of ERP benefits exceeding $100,000, as part of the sale of assets of General Motors Corporation to General Motors LLC.

[F]or executive retirees who have a combined tax-qualified SRP plus nonqual-ified benefit under this Plan in excess of $100,000 per annum on a life annuity basis, the amount of benefits under this Plan over the combined $100,000 per annum threshold shall be reduced by 2/3rds.

---

[127] *In re Amcast Industrial Corp.*, Bankr. S.D. Ohio, No. 04-40504 (March 12, 2007).

The retirees/participants in the ERP sued to have the plan amendment interpreted more favorably to them. The court found that the language of the amendment was clear and rejected the retirees' challenge in *Tate v. General Motors LLC*.[128] The retiree-participants' claim was "a reach" and the court's decision was not surprising. However, the good news is that the plan participants retained any nonqualified benefit at all following the bankruptcy. Many nonqualified plan participants lose all of their benefits in bankruptcy. Although a loss for the GM retirees, *Tate* highlights a situation where nonqualified plan benefits were reduced in bankruptcy, but not entirely lost.

A Memorandum from the Office of Chief Counsel[129] concluded that certain former employees could not recover FICA taxes that were withheld on their nonqualified plan benefit accruals after the former employees forfeited the benefits due to the company's bankruptcy. Although compensation generally is subject to FICA tax when it is actually or constructively paid, a special rule applies to nonqualified plan benefits and other deferred compensation. Code Sec. 3121(v)(2)(A) provides that any amount deferred under a nonqualified deferred compensation plan must be taken into account as wages for FICA purposes as of the later of (i) when the services are performed or (ii) when the benefits or compensation becomes vested and the amount ascertainable.

In CCA 200823001, the former employees had lost their vested accrued benefits because of the company's bankruptcy. Not surprisingly, a large number of the retired employees filed claims for a refund of a portion of the employee's FICA taxes previously paid on the nonqualified deferred compensation benefits. The claim refund amount is based on the difference between the FICA taxes paid on the retired employee's original accrued deferred plan benefit and the FICA taxes that would have been assessed on the actual deferred compensation benefit received by the retiree.

Seeming to concede that the purpose of Code Sec. 3121(v)(2)(A) was punitive, at least in part, the IRS concluded that:

> "because the intent of section 3121(v)(2) is to impose FICA taxation on amounts deferred under a nonqualified deferred compensation arrangement when the amounts become vested in the employee . . . , the fact that the employee later receives less than the amount originally deferred (or ultimately receives nothing at all) as a result of an employer's bankruptcy does not give rise to a right to a refund of the FICA taxes paid on amounts deferred."

Participants Lose Benefits After Sale of Company. A case decided by the U.S. Court of Appeals for the Seventh Circuit in January 2011, produced an unhappy result for former executives of once-renowned mapmaker Rand McNally & Co. In *Feinberg v. RM Acquisition LLC*,[130] the plaintiffs were participants in the Rand McNally & Company Supplemental Pension Plan (the "SERP Plan"). The SERP Plan provided benefits in the form of an annuity at the time they reached retirement age and was utilized as a tax-advantaged means of providing deferred compensation.

---

[128] (56 EBC 1363, 6th Cir. 2013).
[129] CCA 200823001, May 6, 2008.

[130] 629 F.3d 671, 50 EBC 1682 (7th Cir. 2011).

Rand McNally had filed for bankruptcy protection in 2003, apparently after failing to adapt quickly enough to the changing world of GPS, MapQuest, etc. Interestingly, for reasons not discussed in either of the federal court opinions, Rand McNally's obligations under the SERP Plan were not cancelled in the bankruptcy process. In December 2007, Rand McNally entered into an asset purchase agreement with RM Acquisition, LLC. The agreement included a clause stating that RM would not be obligated or responsible for certain specified pre-existing liabilities belonging to Rand McNally. The SERP Plan was an excluded liability under the agreement.

When one company acquires another by purchasing all of its outstanding stock, the buyer steps into the shoes of the seller and automatically assumes all of its liabilities—including SERP and other nonqualified plan obligations. However, when a company purchases just the assets of another company, as happened in this case, the buyer assumes only those obligations and liabilities (*e.g.*, nonqualified plans) that it explicitly agreed to acquire. Since RM Acquisition purchased only Rand McNally's assets and certain specified obligations, and the purchase price paid to Rand McNally was equal to its outstanding secured debt obligations, the obligation to pay SERP benefits was left to the empty shell of the former Rand McNally. Plaintiffs were informed that and that the benefits were terminated.

Plaintiffs gamely argued that RM Acquisition (i) remained liable under the SERP as the successor of Rand McNally, and (ii) interfered with the plaintiffs' rights under ERISA Sec. 510 by attempting to evade its existing and future liability under the plan. (Plaintiffs did not pursue Rand McNally in the litigation because it was an empty shell.)

First the federal district court and then the Seventh Circuit rejected these claims. The courts held that the plaintiffs could not make a case for successor liability because RM did not:

- assume the top-hat plan's liabilities,
- "connive" with Rand McNally to deprive plan participants of their benefits, or
- appear to be a mere continuation of Rand McNally under another name.

Instead, the court held that the asset purchase agreement specifically excluded the top hat plan as one of the liabilities RM Acquisition would assume, leaving plan participants with only the empty shell corporation of Rand McNally from whom to pursue their benefits. A buyer of assets, with exceptions that were inapplicable in the case, does not have an obligation to assume a seller's liabilities.

For similar reasons, the courts also rejected the plaintiffs' ERISA Section 510 claim ("interference with protected rights") against RM, despite the fact that the asset sale excluded the SERP Plan liabilities and left Rand McNally with insufficient assets to pay benefits under the SERP Plan.

> RM wasn't trying to interfere with any rights that the plaintiffs may have had under the top hat plan. RM had nothing to do with the plan. Suppose you

bought a $250 lawnmower from a hardware store and the owner of the store told you the store owed a contractor $100 for fixing a hole in the roof and asked would you like to assume that debt and you said no, and later the owner defaulted on his debt to the contractor. Could the contractor sue you for interfering with his right to collect the debt? That would be ridiculous. Feinberg's argument seems less ridiculous only because the defendant bought the store's entire assets. But the principle is the same, and brings us back to Feinberg's claim against RM under ERISA's section 502. A buyer of assets has, with exceptions inapplicable to this case, no obligation to assume the seller's liabilities.

The Seventh Circuit allowed that Rand McNally may have committed a fraud by paying off most or all of its obligations and debts, other than the SERP, citing *Lessard v. Applied Risk Management*,[131] "However, courts make exceptions for corporate mergers fraudulently executed to avoid the predecessor's liabilities, . . . , or for transactions where the purchaser has specified which liabilities it intends to assume." However, that claim had not been made.

How can SERP and nonqualified plan participants attempt to protect themselves against the loss of benefits in these circumstances? There is no foolproof solution. However, employee participants might take some or all of the following actions:

- Ensure or encourage the company/plan sponsor to place the plan funds in an irrevocable rabbi trust, apart from the company's general assets. Assets in a rabbi trust remain subject to the claims of the company's general creditors in the event of its insolvency. However, the assets are protected from all other uses, including from the reach of a new employer who might renege on the contractual promise to pay benefits.

- Draft the rabbi trust to include the so-called *Moglia* language.

- Draft the SERP and nonqualified plan to include strong "successor" language "and a requirement that no merger, sale or other transaction, including a sale of assets, may occur without the acquiring or surviving company agreeing to assume the plan.

One court rejected a company's agreement with an acquirer to cancel the company's nonqualified plan benefits. The Sixth Circuit's decision in *Lee Gardner v. Heartland Industrial Partners*,[132] may give nonqualified deferred compensation plan participants a new tool in their toolbox for challenging the attempts their employers (or an acquirer of their employers) to terminate the plan without paying benefits to them.

The private equity investment firm Heartland Industrial Partners owned Metaldyne. Heartland had contracted to sell Metaldyne to another private equity firm. However, when the prospective buyer learned of the Metaldyne SERP and its $13 million benefit obligation, the buyer threatened to back out of the transaction. According to the court's opinion, two principals of Heartland who

---

[131] 307 F.3d 1020, 9th Cir. 2002, in turn citing *Chaveriat v. Williams Pipe Line Co.*, 11 F.3d 1420, 1425 (7th Cir. 1993).

[132] 715 F.3d 609, 55 EBC 2018 (6th Cir. 2013).

were the chairman and a member of the Metaldyne board apparently persuaded the Metaldyne board "simply to declare the SERP invalid."

After the sale closed, Metaldyne informed the participants that it had invalidated the plan. The participants filed multiple lawsuits against Heartland and the two Metaldyne board members who were Heartland principals, including this one in Michigan state court. This lawsuit alleged tortious interference with contractual relations against Heartland and its two principals who served on the Metaldyne board for their role in forcing Metaldyne "simply to declare the SERP invalid." Defendants sought to remove the lawsuit to federal court, arguing that ERISA completely preempted the participants' state law claims. (The vast majority of SERP and other nonqualified deferred compensation plan documents would prohibit an employer from terminating the plan without paying benefits accrued to date. It is unclear how the termination of the SERP could even be legal under the plan document, but the court's decision did not discuss this issue.)

In point of fact, the court did not decide the merits of the participants' claim that Heartland and two of its principals had tortuously interfered with the plaintiff/participants' contractual relationship. It only decided that the claim was not preempted by ERISA and, therefore, the participants could continue with their state court claims at trial.

Court Allows Creditor to Garnish Nonqualified Plan Benefits. The case of *Sposato v. First Mariner Bank*,[133] contains a few important lessons for executives, companies and their counsel. In *Sposato*, a federal district court allowed the creditor (First Mariner Bank) of a former executive (Mr. Sposato) to garnish the nonqualified retirement (top-hat) plan (the Cecil Bank Supplemental Executive Retirement Plan) benefits of the former executive even though the company (Cecil Bank) was not in bankruptcy.

The court based its decision on two key findings: (i) ERISA's anti-alienation provisions did not apply to nonqualified plans such as the Cecil Bank SERP, and (ii) ERISA does not preempt Maryland garnishment law. There is conflicting authority as to whether a nonqualified plan participant's interest in the plan is subject to claims of the participant's creditors or constitutes a portion of the participant's bankruptcy estate. Contrary to the *Sposato* case, some courts have found that ERISA's anti-alienation provisions apply to qualified and nonqualified plans alike or that the unfunded promise to pay benefits in the future is insufficiently certain to allow for garnishment. Of course, once distributions or payments from a nonqualified plan have begun, they become just like any other asset of the recipient/participant.

Planning Note: One strategy that could have helped prevent Mr. Sposato from losing his nonqualified benefits in this manner was to fund the nonqualified plan with a rabbi trust. The assets of a well-drafted rabbi trust

---

[133] 2013 BL 83891 (D. Md. March, 2013) and 2013 BL 207955 (D. Md. August, 2013).

would be accessible only to pay benefits to the participant or to the company's general creditors, in the event of the company's insolvency.

Another strategy that could have helped prevent Mr. Sposato from losing his benefits would have been to ensure that the company's qualified plan was absolutely maxed out in terms of the benefits that it could legally provide to Mr. Sposato. Qualified plans are always better than nonqualified plans, including in terms of protection against creditors.

.04 Delta Air Lines Retention Program

The September 11, 2001 terrorist attacks adversely affected many sectors of the U.S. economy. However, "9/11" and its aftermath caused unprecedented operational and financial challenges for the airline industry. Several major carriers, including United Airlines, the world's largest, filed for bankruptcy protection in 2002.

In May 2003, many former executives of United Airlines received a letter informing them that their nonqualified plan benefits were gone:

> As you know, UAL Corporation and its affiliates (collectively the "Company") filed for Chapter 11 bankruptcy protection December 9, 2002. As part of its plan to emerge from bankruptcy, the Company has made and will continue to make many difficult cost-cutting decisions. These decisions are especially difficult when they impact the benefits of individuals who provided loyal and dedicated service to the Company. However, after thoughtful consideration, the Company has decided that future nonqualified pension payments will not be paid to you under the United Air Lines, Inc. Supplemental Benefit Plan (the "Nonqualified Plan"), regardless of whether such future payments are payable pursuant to the terms of the Nonqualified Plan or special agreement.

According to the Delta Air Lines, Inc. proxy statement for the 2003 shareholders' meeting, the Personnel & Compensation Committee of Delta's board of directors concluded that:

> [I]ts first priority must be to maintain a highly qualified management team capable of responding effectively to the extraordinary challenges facing Delta and the airline industry. Moreover, the Committee recognized that these challenges would likely continue for some time. This would make it difficult to retain key members of management who could be recruited by companies in other industries offering opportunities involving less risk and greater compensation. Therefore, in order to strengthen Delta's ability to retain the existing management team, the Committee took the actions discussed below.

Based on this judgment, Delta took two specific steps to retain management employees. Delta established a special retention program and funded its existing nonqualified plan.

Retention Program. Each participant in Delta's 2002 retention program received a contingent cash retention award tied to his or her then current base salary. Subject to remaining employed by Delta throughout 2003 and 2004, respectively, a participant would receive 33% of his or her award in January 2004 and the remaining 67% in January 2005. If Delta's EBITDAR Margin for the two-year period ending December 31, 2003 were at or above the median of a designated airline peer group, Delta would accelerate the second payment to early 2004 for participants who remain employed by Delta throughout 2003. According to the proxy statement, Delta selected the EBITDAR Margin as an appropriate measure in this context because it is an indicator of an airline's efficiency in generating cash flow from revenues, and is widely used to compare the performance of different companies.

Funding Delta's Nonqualified Retirement Plan. Like nearly all mid- to large-sized companies, Delta maintained nonqualified retirement plans to supplement the retirement benefits it provided under its qualified retirement plan.[134] Unlike a qualified plan, benefits under a nonqualified plan would be completely lost if the company filed for bankruptcy. Therefore, according to the proxy statement, Delta approved the funding of employee grantor trusts to secure the nonqualified retirement benefits of 33 management personnel. Amounts held in these individual trusts would offset the amounts that would otherwise be payable to these executives under Delta's nonqualified retirement plans as well as certain other agreements with the executives.

The funding of these trusts would occur over three years, with 60% of the present value (as of December 31, 2001) of the executive's after-tax age 62 nonqualified retirement benefit (based on pay and service earned as of December 31, 2001) being funded in 2002. Delta announced its intention to make further funding contributions to the employee grantor trusts in 2003 and 2004 for participants who remained active employees of Delta. After the 2003 contribution, the amount in each employee's trust would equal 80% of the present value (as of December 31, 2002) of the after-tax age 62 nonqualified retirement benefit (based on pay and service earned as of December 31, 2002). The 2004 contribution would bring the amount in the executive's trust up to 100% of the present value (as of December 31, 2003) of the after-tax age 62 nonqualified retirement benefit (based on pay and service earned as of December 31, 2003). Delta would accelerate the 2003 and 2004 contributions if it experienced a change in control.

Delta's contributions also would include amounts necessary to pay all taxes resulting from the contribution. Delta designed the contributions to provide the same after-tax benefit at retirement to covered executives as the prior unfunded approach provided. Apparently, Delta did not increase any participants' benefits under the nonqualified plan.

Delta also amended the nonqualified retirement plan to provide that benefits would be payable as a lump sum at the time of retirement. However, no lump sum would be payable before January 1, 2004, in order to further encourage retention. If an executive left Delta before January 1, 2004, Delta would not make additional contributions to his or her trust. If an executive left (whether before or after January 1, 2004) prior to his or her normal retirement date and, without the consent of Delta's Personnel & Compensation Committee, goes to work for certain competitors, he or she would be required to repay Delta liquidated

---

[134] See Chapter 17 (¶1701 et seq.) for a detailed discussion of why companies establish nonqualified retirement plans.

damages approximately equal to the contributions made to the executive's trust, including taxes withheld.

In 2002, Delta deposited the $4,542,295 into an individual trust for, and withheld $3,699,938 in taxes on behalf of, its CEO. The total amounts deposited into individual trusts for, and taxes withheld on behalf of, all 33 covered executives were $14,021,447 and $11,543,509, respectively.

The typical trust for executive compensation, deferrals and retirement benefits is a "rabbi trust," which protects the executives' benefits from all events except a bankruptcy.[135] The trusts Delta established were so-called "secular trusts."[136] The two key differences between a rabbi trust and a secular trust are that: (1) amounts in a secular trust are not forfeitable in the event of the company/settlor's bankruptcy and, because of that, (2) amounts in the secular trust are immediately taxable to the executives.

Because of the adverse tax consequences to executives, Delta felt it necessary to contribute (or pay) nearly as much in taxes on behalf of the executives as it did to fund the retirement benefits. Ordinarily companies do not create secular trusts because of these adverse tax consequences. However, because of the risk of bankruptcy, Delta apparently determined that the cost was necessary to provide security for the payment of already earned retirement benefits under the non-qualified retirement plan.

Turns out that Delta and its executives were justified in their concern over the airline's future ability to pay retirement benefits. Delta filed for Chapter 11 bankruptcy protection in September 2005, citing high labor costs and record-breaking jet fuel prices as factors in its filing. At the time of the filing, Delta had $20.5 billion in debt, $10 billion of which accumulated since January 2001.

.05 Health Care Plans—COBRA Continuation Coverage

Business failures will also affect health care benefits provided to employees. If the company implements a reduction in force, terminated employees will lose their health coverage because of their employment termination. Employees, as well as their dependents and spouses, who lose coverage because of employment termination, are entitled to continue their health coverage for a period of time under the Consolidated Omnibus Budget Reconciliation Act of 1985 ("COBRA"). Generally, COBRA continuation coverage is available for up to 18 months following the termination of employment. However, certain circumstances extend the 18-month period. Note that the COBRA continuation rules apply to all "group health plans," as defined in the COBRA statute. The definition of group health plan is broad, and generally includes medical, dental and vision plans, as well as health care flexible spending accounts.

Companies need to be intimately familiar with COBRA's notice, election and continuation requirements. Companies also need to be familiar with state contin-

---

[135] See ¶1765 for a detailed discussion of Rabbi Trusts.

[136] A name made up to distinguish them from rabbi trusts. See ¶1765 for a detailed discussion of Secular Trusts.

uation laws. Generally, the federal law is more comprehensive, and compliance with federal law will satisfy state law requirements. However, some states provide more generous rules regarding notification and continuation coverage. A company that maintains an insured health plan will need to comply with both sets of rules.[137]

For example, Section 367.2 of the Illinois Insurance Code requires insured group health plans to provide special spousal continuation coverage. Specifically, that Section provides that if an employee's spouse has reached age 55 at the time of the employee's retirement, the spouse may be entitled to continue his or her health insurance coverage until he or she is eligible for Medicare.

Companies that maintain self-funded group health plans will not need to comply with state continuation laws, as self-funded plans are not subject to state law under ERISA's preemption provisions.[138]

Bankruptcy itself can cause the requirement for continuation coverage. Filing for bankruptcy under Chapter 11 is a COBRA qualifying event for retirees, their dependents and spouses who are covered under the company's group health plan. Retirees and surviving spouses of deceased retirees may elect to continue health coverage for the duration of their lives; spouses and dependents of retirees may elect to continue health coverage for the duration of the retiree's life, plus an additional 36 months.[139] Note, current employees (and their family members) of a company that files for bankruptcy may not have any right to continuation coverage after the company terminates all of its group health plans (if it does).[140]

.06 Health Care—Retiree Medical Benefits

Business failures generally result in the end of (and sometimes are triggered by) health care benefits the company was providing to retirees. Additionally, if the company implements a reduction in force, terminated employees will lose their health coverage because of their employment termination. In 2003, bankrupt Bethlehem Steel Corporation sought and received bankruptcy court approval to terminate health and life insurance benefits for approximately 95,000 retired workers, pursuant to the Bankruptcy Code.[141]

In 1986, Congress enacted the Retiree Benefits Bankruptcy Protection Act (RBBPA), Public Law No.100-334; after 89,000 retirees lost their health care benefits in the LTV bankruptcy (see below). This law made two changes designed to protect retirees. It added Section 1114 to the Bankruptcy Code, which provides that a "debtor in possession, or the trustee, if one has been appointed . . . shall timely pay and shall not modify any retiree benefits, except that:

---

[137] ERISA § 514(b)(2)(A), 29 U.S.C. § 1144(b)(2)(A).

[138] See ERISA § 514, 29 U.S.C. § 1144; Metropolitan Life Insurance Co. v. Massachusetts, 471 US 724 (1985).

[139] Code Sec. 4980B(f)(2)(B)(i)(III); Code Sec. 4980B(f)(3)(F).

[140] See Code Sec. 4980B(f)(2)(B)(iv).

[141] Bethlehem Steel Corporation Press Releases, February 7, 2003 and March 5, 2003.

- A court, on motion of the trustee or authorized representative, and after notice and a hearing, may order modification of such payments, but only after following the complicated procedures of Section 1114, or
- The trustee and the authorized representative of the recipients of the retiree benefits may agree to modification of such payments, after which the trustee must continue to pay the modified benefits.[142]

The company or trust first must present any proposed modifications to a representative of the retirees, together with financial information. If the parties cannot reach a consensus, the court may approve modifications to benefits, but only if the retirees' representative did not have good cause to refuse to accept the proposal, and the court finds the modification is "clearly favored by a balance of the equities".

Section 1114 defines the term "retiree benefits" to include payments to any entity or person to provide for or reimburse payments for retired employees or dependents for medical benefits under any plan, fund or program.[143]

The RBBPA also amended Section 1129 of the Bankruptcy Code to require that any reorganization plan must continue all retiree benefits "for the duration of the period the debtor has obligated itself to provide such benefits.[144]

Most courts have read Sections 1114 and 1129 to only to require payment of retiree benefits that the debtor is legally obligated to pay under a plan or collective bargaining agreement, and not to require the continuation of benefits that the debtor/company could have legally terminated outside of bankruptcy. For example, in the seminal case of *LTV Steel Co. v. U.S. Mineworkers*[145], the Second Circuit Court of Appeals held that the Section 1114 requirements were no longer applicable to benefits under a wage agreement after it expired while the debtor was in a Chapter 11 bankruptcy. LTV retirees were granted health benefits for life under a collective bargaining agreement that expired after the company ceased operations and was in Chapter 11. The agreement did not mention what would happen to benefits if the agreement expired without any subsequent replacement agreement. The court found the obligation to provide benefits ended when the plan expired.

However, more recently, the Third Circuit did not follow *LTV*, and strictly interpreted Bankruptcy Code Section 1114 to impose its procedural protections for retirees to *all* retiree benefits. This was the holding in the *Visteon*[146] case. The court considered that Section 1114 does contain a specific exclusion of some benefits - for individuals earning more than $250,000 - and does not state benefits terminable at will are excluded from its requirements. It did not discuss the fact that the statue applies specifically only to benefits the employer is obligated to pay.

---

[142] Bankruptcy Code Section 1114(e).
[143] Bankruptcy Code Section 1114(a).
[144] Bankruptcy Code Section 1129(a)(13).

[145] *LTV Steel Corp. v. United Mineworkers of America (In re Chateaugay Corp.)*, 945 F. 2d 1205 (2d Cir. 1991).
[146] *IUE-CW v. Visteon Corp. (In re Visteon)*, 612 F. 3d 210, 17 237 (3d Cir. 2010).

The *Visteon* court also considered that one of the purposes of BAPCPA of 2005 was to add protections for retirees by limiting the ability of a debtor to modify retiree benefits during the 180 day period prior to bankruptcy. The American Bankruptcy Institute Commission to Study the Reform of Chapter 11 recommends following the *Visteon* interpretation, in order to give retirees a seat at the table during bankruptcy.[147]

Another case in the Third Circuit held that a forced retirement one month prior to bankruptcy could not be used to circumvent requirements of Section 1114.[148] In *General Datacom. Indus., Inc. v. Acara*, the company had terminated employees eligible for retirement, without cause, in the month preceding the company's filing in Chapter 11. But for the termination of their employment, the employees could have retired and been afforded the protections under the section.

Where an asset purchase agreement operated as an amendment to the benefit plan, the Fifth Circuit ruled in *Evans v. Sterling Chemicals, Inc.*[149] that benefits required under the asset purchase agreement were covered by the protections of Section 1114. This is important to consider in the due diligence process for transactions. Benefits promised in agreements, but not in the four corners of the actual plan document, could be protected under Section 1114. The court looked back to the agreement obligating the company to provide benefits. All contractual obligations to provide benefits should be reflected in plan documents, to track them through various transactions and ensure that any reservation of the right to amend covers all benefits under the plan.

In the case of *In re Patriot Coal*, a bankruptcy court made it more difficult for a company to shed obligations for retired employees in a spin off.[150] Peabody Holding, Patriot Coal and Heritage Coal Co. were originally subsidiaries of Peabody Energy Corporation. Heritage Coal agreed with United Mine Workers of America, (UMWA), to provide health benefits for certain designated "assumed retirees," comparable to benefits negotiated with the Bituminous Coal Operators' Association for a number of workers employed by the parties, under a "me too" agreement." In a later transaction Peabody Energy spun off Patriot Coal, and several other subsidiaries. Patriot Coal became the parent of Heritage Coal and other subsidiaries.

Five years later Patriot Coal, Heritage Coal and other subsidiaries filed for bankruptcy. Patriot Coal filed a motion to reject the collective bargaining agreement (CBA) and modify retiree benefits pursuant to Sections 1113 and 1114 of the Bankruptcy Code. The Bankruptcy Court for the Eastern District of Missouri granted the motion. The requested order would modify retiree benefits, other than those of assumed retirees, by transferring them to a Voluntary Employees'

---

[147] American Bankruptcy Institute, *Commission to Study Reform of Chapter 11*, 23 ABI L. Rev. 1(2015) (see also commission.abi.org/full-report).

[148] *General Datacom. Indus., Inc. v. Acara*, (In re General Datacom. Indus.) 407 F. 3d 616 (3d Cir. 2005).

[149] *Evans v. Sterling Chemicals, Inc.*, 660 F. 3d 862 (5th Cir. 2011)

[150] *In re Patriot Coal Corp.*, 497 B.R. 36 (B.A.P. 8th Cir., 2013)

Benefit Association (VEBA). The liabilities Heritage Coal assumed under its "me too" agreement, remained with Heritage Coal, and Peabody remained obligated to fund them. The Bankruptcy Court framed the issue as whether the obligation to pay benefits was with Heritage, and funded by Peabody, or whether the obligation belonged to Peabody, with Heritage acting as its agent.

The Bankruptcy Court determined that the latter was the case. It held that rejection of the CBA under which retiree health benefits were provided eliminated the contractual liability to provide benefits.[151] However, Patriot Coal and Heritage also sought a declaratory ruling that Peabody Holdings obligations for healthcare benefits of the assumed retirees were not affected by this modification of benefits under Section 1114, which was not granted, so they appealed.

Implementation of the order would have left Peabody obligated to fund benefits exceeding those the union was obligated to provide, that remained a contractual obligation of Heritage. Patriot Coal and Heritage appealed, contending that the Section 1114 order did not modify the assumed retiree benefits. Peabody Holding contended that the Bankruptcy Court holding was correct, that liabilities for assumed retirees should remain with Heritage. It also contended that it only agreed to be liable for paying Patriot's contractual obligation to provide healthcare benefits, not any statutory obligation.

The Bankruptcy Appellate Panel of the Eight Circuit reviewed the case *de novo*, and reversed the Bankruptcy Court's ruling that only Heritage was liable for the assumed retiree benefits. The panel ruled that rejection of the CBA under which retiree health benefits were provided eliminated the contractual liability to provide benefits, but did not eliminate the statutory obligation to provide benefits, at least until the procedure under Section 1114 of the Bankruptcy Code was followed. The panel rejected Peabody Holding's contention that it was only liable for the assumed retiree benefits that Heritage was *contractually obligated* to provide.

It should be noted that neither the benefit plan nor the bargaining agreement in this case contained any reservation of the right to amend benefits in the plan or the agreement. The result was that Peabody Energy was responsible for health care benefits of retirees it spun off in transaction years earlier, and was required to follow the procedure in Section 1114 to modify or terminate the benefits. As part of a settlement, Patriot Coal was allowed to terminate its retiree health benefits plan and replace it with a VEBA, to allow retirees to maintain some of their health care benefits. The VEBA was guaranteed funding of $15 million and royalty of 20 cents per ton from coal produced. The company also promised to transfer 35 percent ownership to the VEBA, which theoretically could be sold to raise funds.

Patriot Coal exited bankruptcy as a private entity. The cost of the retiree benefits combined with market forces, led Patriot Coal to file a second bank-

---

[151] *In re Patriot Coal*, 493 B.R. 65 (Bankr. E.D. Mo. 2013). The case was reopened in 539 B.R. 812 (Bankr. E.D. Mo. 2015).

ruptcy only two years later and seek to sell the business.[152] In addition, Peabody Energy, the world's largest private sector coal miner, together with 97 of its affiliated companies, followed suit with its own bankruptcy.

Several legislative proposals have been made to ensure health care coverage for miners in danger of losing their benefits due to the Patriot Coal bankruptcy. A Miners' Protection Act was proposed in 2016, and again in 2017. A portion of the Miners Protection Act of 2016 was passed as part of a 2017 government funding bill. It provided about ten years of government funding of health care benefits for retired miners who lost benefits due to the coal bankruptcies, and was expected to save the health care benefits of about 22,500 miners; 12,150 of whom were retirees from Patriot Coal.

.07 VEBAs

One strategy some companies have adopted in response to the difficulty of using a spin off to transfer liability for retiree medical benefits is to create and fund a VEBA trust to assume responsibility for retiree health benefits. Funding of the VEBA will subsidize at least a portion of the retiree health benefits, and avoid the expense of multiple corporate transactions.

VEBAs were used to facilitate bankruptcy settlements of Dana Corporation, AK Steel, Delphi Corporation, a subsidiary of General Motors (GM), and later by GM itself. Delphi filed for bankruptcy in 2005. The same year, GM also reduced its own retiree health benefits. Delphi sold substantially all of its assets, and sought satisfaction of the contribution obligation. The union proposed a class of retirees, who then filed suit, in what is known as *Henri I*.[153]

In *Henri I*, the parties reached a settlement in 2006, which provided for a Defined Contribution VEBA (DC VEBA). In June of 2007 the financial support obligation for the VEBA was defined in a Memorandum of Understanding (MOU), as a deferred onetime contribution to the VEBA of $450 million, contingent upon Delphi owning and operating four particular sites employing union workers. The union and a class of Delphi and GM retirees sued again and *Henry II*[154] led to the 2008 Retiree Settlement Agreement (RSA), and establishment of a new VEBA trust, which assumed GM's responsibility for retiree medical benefits.

The UAW sued, in the Bankruptcy Court that approved the asset sale. The court found it had jurisdiction, but abstained from action, as the issue regarding New GM was not mentioned in the bankruptcy case of Old GM.[155] The Bankruptcy Court determined that the pertinent settlement agreement specified what obligations New GM assumed and did not mention the VEBA obligation as one of them, so the court granted summary judgment for New GM. The UAW appealed, and the case went to the Sixth Circuit Court of Appeals.

---

[152] *In re Patriot Coal*, No. 15-32450, filed July 15, 2015 (Bankr. E.D. Va.).

[153] *Int'l Union, UAW v. General Motors Corp.*, (Henri I), No. 05-73991, (E.D. Mich. filed 2005).

[154] *Int'l Union, UAW et al v. General Motors Corp.*, (Henry II), No, 07-14074, (E.D. Mich., filed Sept. 7, 2007).

[155] *In re Motors Liquidation Co.*, 457 B.R. 276, 289-90 (Bankr. S.D.N.Y. 2011).

After reviewing settlement agreements in an effort to determine whether the intent of the parties was for New GM to assume the obligation, the Sixth Circuit Court of Appeals seemed reluctant to allow silence to control the issue of whether the obligation was extinguished, particularly in light of its magnitude. The court concluded that New GM did assume the VEBA obligation, because it explicitly assumed the CBA, and defined the CBA to include "any contract understanding or mutually recognized past practice between old GM and the UAW." However, the court found other language in the agreement that extinguished the obligation. Section 2 of the agreement stated that the new plan and VEBA were exclusively responsible for providing all retiree medical benefits of the New GM plan or any other New GM entity or benefit plan for retirees arising from any agreements between New GM and the UAW, and that all other obligations were forever terminated. Section 5B stated that the new VEBA had sole responsibility for providing retiree medical benefits and was the exclusive source of funds, and neither New GM, the New GM plan, the existing internal VEBA, nor any other person, entity or benefit plan shall have any responsibility or liability for retiree medical benefits. Finally, Section 5D of the agreement required the Approval Order to provide that all obligations of New GM and the New GM Plan in any way related to retiree medical benefits and all provisions of applicable collective bargaining agreements, contracts, letters, and understandings in any way related to retiree medical benefits are terminated, or otherwise amended to be consistent with the retiree settlement agreement and its fundamental understanding that all New GM obligations regarding retiree medical benefits are terminated.[155]

More recently, in *M & G Polymers*[156] the United States Supreme Court ruled that any CBA providing retiree medical benefits should be construed under principles of ordinary contract law, without considering any inferences which favored retirees. The *Polymers* court held that a CBA with a three-year term, or durational clause, indicates a three-year commitment for benefits, absent a clear statement otherwise. For thirty years before the *Polymers* decision, the Sixth Circuit had applied the so-called "*Yardman* inference," which was favorable to retirees. After *Polymers*, the Sixth Circuit reversed its earlier decision in *Gallo v. Moen*[157], and held a clause reserving the right to amend retiree benefits will be honored, unless the collective bargaining agreement promised unalterable benefits. Where no such promise was made, employees were not entitled to vested health benefits. Most cases on this issue are now decided in favor of companies, unless the plan documents are ambiguous and extrinsic evidence becomes admissible.[158]

---

[156] *M & G Polymers USA, LLC v. Tackett*, 135 S. Ct. 926, 190 L. Ed 2d 809, 202 LRRM 3201 (2015).

[157] *Gallo v. Moen*, 813 F. 3d 265 (6th Cir., 2016) reversing 716 F. 2d (6th Cir., 1983)

[158] See, *e.g. Sloan v. Borg Warner, Inc.*, No. 09-10918 (E.D. Mich., Dec. 5, 2016); *Kepner v. Weyerhaeuser Co.*, No. 6:16-011050-AA (D. Or., Oct. 10, 2016), 2016 U.S. Dist. LEXIS 140996; *Grove v. Johnson Controls*, 776 F. Supp. 3d 455 (2016).

.08 Directors and Officers Liability Insurance

Bankruptcy courts in some jurisdictions have found that D&O coverage is an asset of the bankruptcy estate, thereby potentially subordinating directors' and officers' claims to those of other creditors. Suggestions made by some compensation professionals include: (i) separate policy limits for the individuals; (ii) negotiate a clause in the policy requiring the insurer to pay the individuals first for unindemnified claims; or (iii) carry separate Side A coverage for the officers and directors.[159]

Lawsuits filed against directors and officers usually cause executives to seek to utilize insurance proceeds for costs of defense or settlement, and occasionally result in the executive, the company, or both, filing bankruptcy. When a company files for bankruptcy, trustees may seek to include insurance policy proceeds payable to directors and officers as an asset of the bankruptcy estate, and request a court order preventing its use for the executive's claims.

In re World Health Alternatives, Inc., a Delaware Bankruptcy Court decision,[160] is a typical case involving this issue. The company, a temporary staffing service for hospitals and healthcare providers, purchased a Management Liability and Company Reimbursement (D&O) policy. One month later reports surfaced of possible irregularities of management, which led to the filing of class action lawsuits, alleging securities law violations. A shareholder derivative action also was filed. The class actions and derivative action were consolidated.

World Health filed for bankruptcy protection under Chapter 11, and the case was later converted to Chapter 7. The D&O policy lapsed and was not renewed. The parties reached an agreement to settle the consolidated action, which provided for payment of $1.7 million from the policy, in addition to funds from individual defendants. The trustee in bankruptcy intervened in the lawsuit, and filed a complaint alleging breach of fiduciary duty, unjust enrichment, self-dealing and fraudulent transfer. Use of the insurance proceeds to fund the settlement agreement for officers and directors would exhaust the proceeds, and no funds would remain available for litigation commenced by the trustee on behalf of creditors. The trustee attempted to obtain a court order prohibiting use of insurance proceeds on behalf of directors and officers to fund the proposed settlement agreement.

The policy was a "wasting policy," in that it insured directors and officers for costs incurred, but payment of such costs reduced the policy's limits. Thus, defense costs paid reduced the amount available for settlement. The policy also contained a typical "Insured v. Insured" endorsement, and excluded from coverage any action brought on behalf of the company against its directors and payable to the directors and officers, not the estate.

---

[159] See "Negotiating D&O Policies: Key Terms And Conditions," Carolyn Rosenberg, Duane Sigelko, Kit Chaskin, Neil Posner, and Venus Mc-

Ghee, Review of Securities & Commodities Regulation - Vol. 37, No. 4, pp. 31–43.

[160] In re World Health Alternatives, Inc., 369 B.R. 805 (Bankr. D. Del. 2007).

The court analyzed the policy, then attempted to reconcile differing rulings by other courts. The policy provided three types of coverage. Coverage A insured directors and officers against damages and litigation defense costs they were legally obligated to pay in connection with claims against them in their capacity as directors and officers. Coverage B provided reimbursement to the company for indemnification it may make to directors and officers. Coverage C directly insured the company for certain securities claims against it. The Priority of Payments endorsement specifically provided for payment of damages and defense costs to directors and officers under Coverage A before any payment would be made to the company.

The *World Heath* court reviewed and relied on a prior Delaware bankruptcy court decision dealing with whether proceeds from a liability insurance policy were property of the Chapter 7 estate, *In re Allied Digital Technologies Corp.*[161] In that case, the trustee had sued directors and officers directly. In *Allied Digital*, the court ruled that the proceeds were not property of the estate, because the policy provided direct coverage to directors and officers for claims and defense costs, and indemnification to the debtor for amounts paid to directors and officers. As in *World Health*, the trustee and individual executive defendants sought payment from the same wasting liability policy. The *Allied Digital* court summarized the applicable law, and stated that when insurance policies provide direct coverage to directors and officers, the proceeds of the insurance policy are not property of the bankruptcy estate because the proceeds are payable to the directors and officers, not the estate.[162]

Because the insurance proceeds of *World Health* were payable directly to directors and officers, the court held such proceeds were not part of the bankruptcy estate. The policy insured officers and directors, and the company had no coverage unless a claim was made against it for which it sought to be repaid, or indemnified. No claims had been made against the company. Therefore the trustee was not entitled to preference over the directors and officers. Other impediments the trustee faced were the "Insured v. Insured" exclusion, and the failure to bring suit before the policy lapsed. The policy also provided for priority of payments; payments were required to be made first to Coverage A, insuring directors and officers against damages and litigation defense costs. The request for an injunction against use of proceeds to fund the settlement of litigation against directors and officers was therefore denied, and the insurance could be used to fund the settlement. The court acknowledged that the purpose of the policy was to protect the directors and officers.

In contrast to the results in *World Health* and *Allied Digital*, when a liability insurance policy provides direct coverage to the company or an individual that files bankruptcy, the proceeds of the policy generally will be found to be

[161] 306 B.R. 505 (Bankr. D. Del. 2004).

[162] Courts continue to follow this rule. See *In re Laminate Kingdom LLC*, 2008 Bankr. LEXIS (Bankr. Fla. 2008), 15375 Memorial Corp., 382 B.R. 652, 2008 (Bankr. D. Del. 2008).

property of the bankruptcy estate.[163] Exceptions to this rule are not unheard of, as courts have allowed directors to utilize insurance proceeds for defense costs, even though coverage under the policy includes indemnification to the company. For example, the Bankruptcy Appellate Panel for the Ninth Circuit allowed a director access to his liability insurance for legal fees and expenses based on a showing of clear, immediate and ongoing expenses. The sole director was also the majority shareholder. The bankruptcy trustee opposed such use of estate assets, anticipating a request for indemnification under the policy. The court found the concern speculative when no claim for indemnification had yet occurred. It was not inclined to be concerned with exhausting policy limits since multiple parties were not involved trying to access the proceeds, just one officer and one trustee.[164]

If a policy covers both executives and the company, where the company files bankruptcy the proceeds will be property of the estate if depletion of the proceeds would have an adverse effect on the estate. Where the policy provides coverage for indemnification, but the indemnification has not yet occurred, or is speculative, the proceeds are not property of the estate, as discussed above.[165]

Therefore, in individual cases coverage for directors and officers will depend on whether claims are filed against the company, and policy provisions on priority of payment of claims.

If the insurance carrier that issued the D&O policy were to file for bankruptcy, its assets should be beyond the reach of federal bankruptcy. Insurance companies are regulated by state law rather than the Bankruptcy Code. Intercompany transactions are also regulated by state law, which should insulate assets of the subsidiary from its parent, should the parent corporation attempt to draw on assets of a subsidiary. State laws vary, but most are patterned on The Model Act adopted by the National Association of Insurance Commissioners.

¶2445 Preferential and Fraudulent Transfers

The Bankruptcy Code gives a trustee the power to set aside and recover transfers made by a company prior to its bankruptcy filing. If, for example, a trustee believes that the company/debtor paid a bonus to defraud creditors or made a severance payment to satisfy a pre-petition debt, the Code allows the trustee to recover, or "avoid," that payment.[166] The avoidance powers limit a company's ability to play favorites among creditors and to prevent a company from transferring assets out of the reach of creditors before filing for bankruptcy.

Bankruptcy Code Section 547[167] gives a trustee the power to avoid preferential transfers and Section 548[168] governs the recovery of fraudulent transfers. Section 544 gives a trustee the rights and powers of a lien creditor and the ability

---

[163] *In re W.R. Grace & Co.*, 475 B.R. 34 (Bankr. D. Del. 2012) citing cases in the First, Second, Third and Fourth Circuit Courts of Appeal.

[164] 423 B.R. 537 at 544 (citations omitted).

[165] 369 B.R. at 809, citing *Allied Digital Technologies, Corp.* 306 B.R. 505, at 510-11 (Bankr. D. Del. 2004).

[166] The Bankruptcy Code grants the same power to debtors-in-possession. See 11 U.S.C. § 1107(a).

[167] 11 U.S.C. § 547.

[168] 11 U.S.C. § 548.

to use other laws as necessary to avoid transfers by the company.[169] Some courts limit the use of avoidance actions to trustees and debtors-in-possession, while others will allow interested parties to bring an avoidance action.[170] In most cases, the trustee brings the action to recover transfers.

Some executive employment agreements provide for special payments upon the company's insolvency. These provisions could be subject to challenge as voidable preferences under Section 547 of the Bankruptcy Code, if received within the 90-day period prior to filing bankruptcy, or one year, if the executive is an insider. The agreement would be deemed an executory contract subject to assumption or rejection by the bankruptcy trustee under Section 365 of the Code. Bankruptcy Court approval is also required to assume or reject the contract, and courts generally defer to the trustee's judgment, particularly when a contract requires payments that appear to be "generous." For example, the Maryland bankruptcy court rejected a contract requiring payment of salary for two years following an employees' termination in *In re Constant Care Community Health Center, Inc.*[171] See also *Burnham Lambert, Inc.* (In re Drexel Burnham Lambert, Inc.).[172]

Some executive employment agreements provide for the forgiveness of debt upon the company's insolvency. Debt owed by an executive to the company is often forgiven on termination of employment without justifiable cause under the agreements. Any such agreement must be analyzed in light of current case law to determine if it is subject to challenge as a preferential transfer.

Bankruptcy trustees are charged with the responsibility of recovering funds transferred and minimizing payments that do not benefit the bankruptcy estate. Even large payments for the benefit of employees who are not executives are sometimes challenged, when a trustee challenges payments by a company to fulfill obligations to pay benefit claims under its health and welfare benefit plans of the corporation. *Golden v. Guardian* (In re Lenox Healthcare, Inc.).[173]

.01 Preferential Transfers

To maintain equality among creditors of an insolvent company, the Bankruptcy Code prohibits transfers deemed "preferential." Section 547(b) of the Bankruptcy Code defines a preferential payment as any transfer from the company made (1) to or for the benefit of a creditor; (2) for an antecedent debt owed

---

[169] 11 U.S.C. § 544.

[170] See *Commodore Int'l Ltd. v. Gould (In re Commodore Int'l, Ltd.)*, 262 F3d 96 (2d Cir. 2001) (recognizing creditors' rights to avoid preferential transfers when trustee unjustifiably failed to sue for recovery); *Glinka v. Fed. Plastics Mfg., Ltd. (In re Housecraft Indus. USA, Inc.)*, 310 F3d 64, 70 (2d Cir. 2002) (creditors have standing to bring Section 548 claims when it is in the best interest of the estate). But see *Official Comm. of Asbestos Prop. Damage Claimants of W.R. Grace & Co. v. Sealed Air Corp. (In re W.R. Grace and Co.)*, 285 B.R. 148, 156 (Bankr. D. Del. 2002), relying on *Official Comm. of Unsecured Creditors of Cybergenics Corp. v. Chinery*, 304 F3d 316 (3d Cir.

2002) vac'd, reh'g granted, 310 F3d 785 (3d Cir. 2002) (agreeing that the plain language of Bankruptcy Code Section 544 and the Supreme Court's analysis in *Hartford Underwriters Insurance Company v. Union Planters Bank, N.A.*, 530 U.S. 1 (2000) (finding that Bankruptcy Code Section 506(c) did allow an administrative claimant to seek payment of a claim) allowed only a trustee or debtor-in-possession to bring avoidance actions).

[171] 99 B.R. 697, 702 (Bankr. D. Md., 1989).

[172] 138 B.R. 687 (Bankr. S.D.N.Y. 1992).

[173] 343 B.R. 96, 38 EBC 1505, (Bankr. D. Del., June 1, 2006).

by the company before the transfer was made; (3) while the company was insolvent; and (4) having a preferential effect, meaning the transferee must end up with more than it would have had the case been a Chapter 7 liquidation.[174] The general rule is that any preferential transfer may be avoided if it was made within 90 days of the initial filing date. However, transfers made to a creditor who is an insider may be avoided for up to one year before the bankruptcy filing.[175]

A transfer is preferential only if it is a payment made for an antecedent debt; that is, a debt incurred before the transfer is made. Courts have been strict in requiring that the debt be incurred *prior* to payment before finding that the transfer was preferential. In *Southmark Corp. v. Marley (In re Southmark Corp.)*,[176] Southmark sought to recover a pre-petition severance payment of $400,000 given to an employee the day that employee was terminated. Southmark argued that the $400,000 severance bonus was payment for an antecedent debt that had been incurred under a previous employment contract. The court disagreed and found that Southmark incurred the debt at the same time it terminated the employee, and thus Southmark made the payment to satisfy a simultaneous debt, not an antecedent debt. The *Southmark* case also indicates that a pre-petition severance payment might not be considered a preferential transfer if the payment is made in full upon the employee's termination.[177]

The bankruptcy trustee may recover any transfer that a court finds to be preferential, if that transfer was made during the 90 days preceding the company's/debtor's initial filing of a bankruptcy petition. The filing date is the date that the company (or its creditors, in the case of an involuntary filing) originally files its petition for bankruptcy, even if the company subsequently amends the petition. The effective date of a transfer is the date the creditor/transferee acquires the rights to the property transferred.[178] The 90-day window is calculated by counting backward from the date the petition was filed as opposed to counting forward from the transfer date.[179] The transfer also must have been made while the company was insolvent. However, the Bankruptcy Code includes, and the courts apply, a rebuttable presumption that the company was insolvent during the 90 days preceding the bankruptcy filing.[180]

> **Planning Note:** The preferential transfer rules often trap executives who "try to do the right thing" by declining salary, bonus or other payment in the wind down to bankruptcy. The courts generally do not "give credit" for these selfless acts.

---

[174] See *Lawson v. Ford Motor Co. (In re Roblin Indus.)*, 78 F3d 30, 34 (2d Cir. 1996).

[175] 11 U.S.C. § 547(b)(4)(B).

[176] *Southmark Corp. v. Marley (In re Southmark Corp.)*, 62 F3d 104 (5th Cir. 1995), cert. denied, 516 US 1093 (1996).

[177] See also *G. Survivor Creditor Corp. v. Harari (In re G. Survivor Corp.)*, 217 B.R. 433, 440–41 (Bankr.

S.D. N.Y. 1998); *White v. Bradford (In re Tax Reduction Inst.)*, 148 B.R. 63, 79–80 (Bankr. D. D.C. 1992).

[178] 11 U.S.C. § 547(e)(3).

[179] *Locke v. MBNA America (In re Greene)*, 223 B.R. 548 (N.D. Calif. 1998).

[180] 11 U.S.C. 547(f); *Official Comm. Of Unsecured Creditors ex rel. R.M.L. Inc. v. Conceria Sabrina, S.P.A (In re R.M.L., Inc.)*, 195 B.R. 602, 611 (Bankr. M.D. Pa. 1996).

The bankruptcy trustee may recover transfers occurring between 90 days and one year from the date of the bankruptcy filing as "preferential" if the company made such payments to an insider of the company. Bankruptcy Code Section 101(31)(B) defines the term "insider." For companies, insiders are directors, officers, or persons in control of the company, as well as any partnership in which the company is a general partner and any general partners of the company. Also included are any affiliates or relatives of the aforementioned persons. Moreover, the definitions delineated in Section 101(31) are not exclusive, and courts will find an insider to be "any entity or person with a sufficiently close relationship with the company that his conduct is made subject to closer scrutiny than those dealing at arm's length with the debtor."[181]

Finally, Section 547(b)(5) provides that, for a payment to be considered preferential, the company must have paid the creditor more than it would have received from the company/debtor in a Chapter 7 liquidation. Thus, pre-petition transfers to fully secured creditors are not preferential because the secured creditor receives no more than it would have received in a liquidation. If the creditor is partially secured or unsecured, then the court will determine whether the creditor would have received less than a 100% payout from the company's Chapter 7 estate.[182]

.02 Fraudulent Transfers

A bankruptcy trustee also may recover transfers that are made with the intent to defraud creditors, as well as transfers made in exchange for less than reasonable consideration. "Fraudulent transfers" are covered by Bankruptcy Code Section 548. The Bankruptcy Code considers transfers made in exchange for nominal consideration to be fraudulent if the company (1) was insolvent at the time of the transfer or made insolvent by the transfer; (2) was left with an unreasonably small amount of capital; or (3) anticipated at the time of the transfer that it would incur debts beyond its ability to pay them as they matured. If the transfer was made to defraud creditors, the trustee does not need to show the company's insolvency at the time of the transfer or any failure to receive something of reasonable equivalent value in exchange for the transfer.

Under Section 548, a trustee may only avoid fraudulent transfers made within a year before the bankruptcy filing. If the transfer occurred more than a year prior, the trustee may have recourse under state fraudulent transfer law, which often provides for recovery of transfers made more than a year before filing for bankruptcy.[183]

A fraudulent conveyance is not a preferential transfer and can be distinguished from a preferential transfer in several ways. Preferential transfers are based solely in the Bankruptcy Code, while fraudulent conveyances are not.

---

[181] *In re Acme-Dunham, Inc.*, 50 B.R. 734, 739 (D. Me. 1985).

[182] *Committee of Creditors Holding Unsecured Claims v. Koch Oil Company (In re Powerine Oil Co.)*, 59 F3d 969, 972 (9th Cir. 1995).

[183] See *Mancuso v. Champion (In re Dondi Financial Corp.)*, 119 B.R. 106 (Bankr. N.D. Tex. 1990).

Preferential transfers lead to a decrease in both assets and liabilities as creditors are paid off on a selective basis. Fraudulent transfers are rarely transfers to creditors but an effort to hide assets from creditors; thus, assets decrease while liabilities remain unchanged. One final distinguishing element of preferential transfers is the requirement that the payment be made to satisfy an antecedent debt. Thus, a transfer may be preferential but not fraudulent if the payment is for an antecedent debt and the value of that payment is reasonably equivalent to the value of what the company received in exchange for that payment. A transfer may be fraudulent but not preferential if it is not payment for an antecedent debt and the value paid exceeds the value received.

.03 Other Avoidance Powers

Section 544 of the Bankruptcy Code allows a bankruptcy trustee to exercise all the rights and powers of a lien creditor and, as a result, gives a trustee the ability to enforce fraudulent transfer claims available to lien creditors under state laws and other federal laws. One benefit of this authorization is the ability to recover under state fraudulent transfer laws, which often extend the period during which trustees can recover pre-petition payments beyond the period allowed by Section 548.[184]

If the United States is a creditor in the bankruptcy case through debts such as taxes due or other claims, a trustee may be able to use the powers under Section 544 to rely on the fraudulent transfer provision of the Federal Debt Collective Procedures Act,[185] which permits claimants to recover fraudulent transfers made beyond the one-year period allowed in Section 548.[186]

¶2455 Bankruptcy of the Executive

Just as old-line, seemingly successful companies sometimes end up seeking bankruptcy protection, so too do seemingly wealthy executives. Some types of compensation and benefits are treated more favorably in personal bankruptcy than others. For example, the Internal Revenue Code and ERISA provide nearly ironclad protection for executives' qualified retirement plan benefits.

.01 Qualified Retirement Plan Benefits

Sections 206(d)(1) of ERISA and Code Sec. 401(a)(13) require that every retirement plan provide that "benefits provided under the plan may not be assigned or alienated." The anti-alienation provisions of ERISA and the Code protect retirement benefits in the event of the bankruptcy of a plan participant or the plan sponsor.

---

[184] See, e.g., Mancuso v. Champion (In re Dondi Financial Corp.), 119 B.R. 106 (Bankr. N.D. Tex. 1990) (Texas Fraudulent Conveyance Act allows for recovery of transfers occurring up to four years prior to filing for bankruptcy); Daly v. Deptula (In re Carrozella & Richardson), 286 B.R. 480, 483 (D. Conn. 2002) (Connecticut Uniform Fraudulent Transfer Act allows for recovery of transfers occurring up to four years prior to filing for bankruptcy); Hoult v. Hoult, 2003 U.S. Dist. LEXIS 10212 (D. Mass. June 18, 2003)

(limitations under Massachusetts Uniform Fraudulent Transfer Act based on the statute of limitations applicable to the underlying claim).

[185] 28 U.S.C. § 3304.

[186] 28 U.S.C. § 3306(b). The six-year statute of limitations allows a transfer to be avoided within six years of the date the transfer was made and, if more than six years elapsed before the transfer could have reasonably been discovered, the claimant has two years to file a claim for relief.

Section 541 of the Bankruptcy Code provides that a debtor's estate will include "all legal or equitable interests of the debtor in property as of the commencement of the estate," wherever located and by whomever held. The Bankruptcy Code functions to sweep all of a debtor's property into his or her bankruptcy estate at the commencement of bankruptcy proceedings, and then provides a few limited exemptions.

Section 522 of the Bankruptcy Code contains the general exemption rules applicable to individual debtors. Section 522 of the Bankruptcy Code allows a debtor to exempt funds in deferred compensation plans under Code Sec. 457, plans of tax-exempt organizations under Code Sec. Section 501(a) and governmental plans under Code Sec. 414. The BAPCPA added an exemption from the bankruptcy estate for eligible rollovers distributions and direct transfers from qualified plans.

Section 522(d) provides that a debtor may choose to exempt property from his or her bankruptcy estate under either the federal exemption system or the exemption system found in the state of a debtor's domicile. The federal and state exemption systems vary somewhat (state systems often give a debtor some additional exemptions), but, generally, are similar with respect to the treatment of qualified retirement plan benefits.

The federal exemption system, and most state exemption systems, allow an individual debtor to exempt property interests including, among other things, payments under profit sharing pension plans or similar plans *to the extent reasonably necessary for the support of the debtor or a debtor's dependents*. The debtor can use this exemption to protect either accumulated retirement benefits or ongoing retirement payments from bankruptcy creditors.

The principal exemption that protects retirement funds from bankruptcy creditors is Section 541(c)(2) of the Bankruptcy Code. This exemption provides that a "restriction on the transfer of a beneficial interest of the debtor in a trust that is *enforceable under applicable nonbankruptcy law is enforceable in a case under this title.*" Whether ERISA's anti-alienation provision was "applicable nonbankruptcy law" was the source of much controversy in the 1980s. The U.S. Supreme Court finally settled inconsistent holdings among U.S. Courts of Appeals as to the breadth of the "applicable nonbankruptcy law" exclusion in the 1992 case of *Patterson v. Shumate.*[187]

In *Patterson*, the Supreme Court held that ERISA qualified as "applicable nonbankruptcy law" for purposes of Section 541(c)(2) of the Bankruptcy Code. Accordingly, the Court held that ERISA's anti-alienation provision was an "enforceable restriction on transfer" sufficient to keep ERISA plan benefits out of a debtor's bankruptcy estate. Thus, after *Patterson*, creditors do not have access to assets held on behalf of the debtor in a retirement plan subject to ERISA.

Tax Exempt Status. Plans with determination letters confirming their tax-exempt in effect at the time the petition is filed are presumed exempt. If a plan

---

[187] *Patterson v. Shumate*, 504 US 753 (1992).

does not have such a determination letter in effect when the bankruptcy is filed, the plan sponsor must prove the qualified status of the plan.[188] There must be no prior determination by the IRS or a court that the plan is not tax-qualified. Adopters of prototype plans that rely on an opinion letter for the master plan may, in certain instances, rely on the opinion letter for the prototype plan, provided the plan is adopted after issuance of the opinion letter.[189]

Plans must be operated in substantial compliance with current requirements of the Internal Revenue Code in order to be exempt. However, IRS Announcement 2015-19 stated the IRS's curtailment of the determination letter process. The intent is to make such letters available only on the creation of a plan, or termination of a plan. Effective January 1, 2017, the IRS eliminated the five-year cycles available for individually designed plans.

Any noncompliance with Internal Revenue Code requirements creates a risk of precluding availability of the exemption. The First Circuit Court of Appeals held an IRA containing assets tainted by a rollover from a qualified plan where the debtor engaged in prohibited transactions was not excluded from the bankruptcy estate in *In re Daniels*.[190] This is consistent with the IRS's position that once an IRA holder deals with IRA assets in a prohibited transaction, the IRA is deemed to be distributed and is no longer considered an IRA.[191] The penalty for prohibited transactions in a qualified plan is imposition of an excise tax, and generally does not disqualify the plan, unless there are multiple prohibited transactions.

Owner Only Plans - ERISA Plans and Non ERISA Plans. Retirement plans established by sole owners of companies, partnerships, or other business entities may be exempt from inclusion in the bankruptcy estate if there is at least one plan participant who is not an owner or a member of the owner's family. In 2004, the Supreme Court ruled *Raymond B. Yates, M.D., P.C. Profit Sharing Plan v. Hendon*,[192] that a self-employed owner of a professional corporation could be a participant in an ERISA plan as a working owner, if there was at least one other common law employee, other than a spouse, participating in the plan.

Yates presented the not uncommon factual scenario of unpaid loans to a qualified 401(k) or profit sharing plan. Dr. Yates borrowed funds from his qualified plan, under a loan with a five-year term. He made no payments during the term of the loan, and defaulted. He then renewed the loan for an additional five-year term, and again made no payments. Ten years after the date of the original loan, and after he sold his home, Dr. Yates repaid the plan loan. Creditors filed an involuntary petition in bankruptcy three months after the loan repayment. The profit sharing plan contained a provision prohibiting assignments other than loans. Dr. Yates claimed the plan assets were exempt, based upon the anti-alienation provision in the plan required under ERISA. The Bankruptcy Court granted summary judgment in favor of the trustee, and held that

---

[188] Bankruptcy Code Section 522(b)(4), as amended by BAPCPA.

[189] Rev. Proc. 2015-36.

[190] 736 F. 3d 70 (1st Cir. 2013).

[191] See IRS FAQs at www.irs.gov and Publications 590-A and B.

[192] 541 U.S. 1 (2004).

under ERISA, Dr. Yates could not participate in the plan as an employee. It noted that under the ERISA definition of employee benefit plan,[193] an individual and his spouse are deemed not to be employees, in a plan where the self-employed are the only participants. Dr. Yates was precluded from using ERISA to enforce the anti-alienation provision of the plan.

Dr. Yates appealed, and both the District Court and Court of Appeals affirmed. The Supreme Court granted certiorari, and reviewed the case. On review it considered that at all times Yates had had at least one non-family participant in the plan, and a DOL Advisory Opinion Letter indicated that *an employee benefit plan* would not include a plan where an owner and his or her spouse were the only participants, but *could include* a plan that covered one or more employees in addition to the owner and his or her spouse. The Supreme Court reversed the lower court and remanded the case for consideration of whether the loan repayments, after defaults, close to bankruptcy, become plan assets and constituted a preferential transfer.

Where an owner is the sole plan participant, and there are no non-family participants, the plan is not an ERISA plan. Nevertheless, it may be possible to exempt plan assets. Bankruptcy Code Section 522(3)(c) applies to "any retirement funds in an account exempt from tax under Section 401, 403, 408, 408A, 414, 457 or 501(a) of the Internal Revenue Code of 1986." The text of the statute requires compliance with the Internal Revenue Code; it does not state that plans must comply with ERISA. An Eleventh Circuit Case has ruled that Section 522 requires only that a plan be qualified under the Internal Revenue Code, not under ERISA.[194] *Baker v. Tardiff* allowed an exemption of retirement plan assets under Florida law, where the statute specifically stated plans need not be subject to ERISA to be exempt.

In *Rogers v. RES-GA Dawson, LLC,*[195] a plan provided benefits only to Mr. Rogers, the sole owner of the business. The plan was not covered by ERISA. Mr. Rogers sought to exempt plan assets under Section 541(c)(2) of the Bankruptcy Code, based on a restriction on the transfer of his beneficial interest in the plan and trust. He contended the trust restriction was enforceable under applicable non-bankruptcy law, and therefore its assets were exempt under *Patterson v. Shumate*. The court analyzed whether the plan was a definite written program communicated to employees under Code Sec. 401. The bankruptcy trustee contended the plan was not qualified because plan assets were used to purchase real estate and a boat used by Mr. Rogers. The trustee also contended that Mr. Rogers created and used a checking account under the plan, which he used to pay for personal living expenses, which was a prohibited transaction. The trustee contended these transactions were violations of the restriction on alienation, exclusive benefit rule and Code requirements for distributions.

---

[193] DOL Reg. Sec. 2510.3-3(b).

[194] *Baker v. Tardiff,* (In re Baker) 590 F. 3d 1261, (11th Cir. 2009),

[195] (In re Rogers), 538 B.R. 158 (Bankr. N.D. Georgia, 2015).

Mr. Rogers contended that the real estate and boat were plan investments. There was an opinion letter for the prototype plan, and Mr. Rogers contended this established favorable tax status of his plan, in order to exempt its assets. However, the opinion letter on qualification of the plan was for a different type of prototype plan, and was issued *after* the date the plan was adopted, so it could not be used to establish that the plan was exempt when adopted. The court determined the record did not contain sufficient evidence to determine whether the expenditures met plan requirements for distributions and loans, and denied both parties' requests for summary judgment. The case settled before a final decision was issued.

Qualified Plan Contributions. Funds withheld from employee-participants' wages for any employee welfare or pension plan under Title I of ERISA, or any governmental plan under Code Sec. 414(d), deferred compensation plan under Code Sec. 457, tax deferred annuity under Code Sec. 403(b), or any health insurance plan regulated by state law, are excluded from the bankruptcy estate, pursuant to Bankruptcy Code Section 541(b)(7). This would apply to employee contributions that the company has withheld from the employee's wages but has not yet contributed to the appropriate benefit plan. The DOL takes the position that funds withheld from participants' wages but not contributed to the plan are ERISA plan assets under regulations at 29 C.F.R. Section 2510.3-102. There is no similar regulation for employer contributions. Unpaid employer contributions are generally not plan assets.

An individual with control over corporate finances who uses available funds to pay bills or taxes but fails to make plan contributions who is a plan fiduciary may be found personally responsible for failure to make the contributions due. If a court imposes personal liability on the fiduciary, any debt due to such failure will not be dischargeable in a bankruptcy filing. In *Bos v. Board of Trustees*,[196] the court found language in a plan document did not make an unpaid contribution a plan asset, so the expenditure of available funds for other purposes was not defalcation and could be discharged in bankruptcy The Sixth Circuit and the Tenth Circuit have also refused to find unpaid contributions to a plan to constitute a plan asset.[197]

Employers unable to make plan contributions required by a plan document or union agreement are forewarned that some jurisdictions may entertain litigation claiming individual trustees or owners are personally responsible to make plan contributions, and are fiduciaries to the plan, with personal liability that would not be dischargeable in bankruptcy. Some courts have held that employer contributions that are due and not paid may be considered plan assets, if characterized as such by the plan documents. *See e.g. ITPE Pension Fund.*[198] The Second Circuit adopted a similar approach in *In re Halpin.*[199]

---

[196] 795 F. 3d. 10056 (9th Cir. 2015).

[197] *Board of Trustees of Ohio Carpenters Pension Fund v. Bucci,* (In re Bucci,) 493 F. 3d 635 (6th Cir. 2007),

Navarre v. Luna (In re Luna), 406 F. 3d 1192 (19th Cir. 2005).

[198] 334 F. 3d 1011, 1013-14, (11th Cir. 2003).

[199] 566 F. 3d 286, 290 (2d Cir. 2009).

Elective 401(k) Deferrals. Participant' elective deferrals to a 401(k) plan may continue after filing of the bankruptcy petition, unless the plan is amended to preclude same. If elective deferrals continue after a bankruptcy filing, there will be an issue of whether increases in deferrals are allowable exclusions from the estate. A bankruptcy court in Wisconsin ruled that a debtor in a Chapter 7 bankruptcy could continue contributions to a Section 457 governmental plan.[200]

Plan Loans. Outstanding loans from retirement plans are not dischargeable in bankruptcy. Section 1322(f) to the Bankruptcy Code clarifies the prior case law by providing that participants may continue to repay plan loans after filing of the bankruptcy in a Chapter 13 filing. Thus, plan sponsors may continue to withhold funds from participants to repay outstanding loan arrangements in a Chapter 13 case. The issue of whether plan loans are an exempt asset in bankruptcy is of fundamental importance to both debtors and plan sponsors. IRS Revenue Rulings[201] require plan loans to be structured in a certain manner with the intent of creating a true debtor/creditor relationship. Paradoxically, cases under the Bankruptcy Code generally hold that retirement plan loans do not create a debt.

The BAPCPA shifted the emphasis of the Bankruptcy Code from providing a fresh start, to forcing repayment to creditors, to the extent possible. Courts must use a means test or mathematical formula, to determine whether a debtor's financial circumstances create a presumption that the individual has the financial ability to repay debts without a Chapter 7 bankruptcy or liquidation. If assets, liabilities and expenses under the formula create a presumption of means to repay, then there is a presumption of abuse. This presumption is rebuttable on a showing of special circumstances, or if the totality of the circumstances demonstrate abuse of Chapter 7 under Section 707(b)(3).

The Ninth Circuit Court of Appeals considered plan loan issues in *In re Egebjerg*.[202] In *Egebjerg* the court ruled that a debtor's repayment of a 401(k) plan loan was not a secured debt or a "necessary expense" that could be deducted in order to compute his monthly income for purposes of the means test in a Chapter 7 bankruptcy. This decision was consistent with the majority of courts, which hold that a debtor's obligation to repay a loan from his or her retirement account is not a "debt" under the Bankruptcy Code, because the plan has no right to sue for the amount. The loan is an offset against future benefits.[203]

The significance of these holdings is that a participant-employee generally will not be able to continue making loan repayments to his or her qualified plan account following a bankruptcy filing. There is a financial penalty for failure to repay plan loans, as IRS considers the funds "borrowed" from the plan, and not repaid according to terms of the loan, as a deemed distribution. The Code imposes income tax and a penalty on the borrower.

---

[200] See *In re Mravik*, 399 B.R, 202 (Bankr. E.D. WI. 2008).

[201] See Rev. Rul. 67-288, 71-437, 81-1127. See also *Medina v. Com'r*, 112 T. C. 51 (1999) (excise tax on prohibited transactions was imposed on a loan to a husband and wife from a plan maintained by the husband's corporation).

[202] 574 F. 3d. 1045, 1049-50 (9th Cir. 2009).

[203] The court cited *In re Villare*, 648 F. 2d 810 (2d Cir. 1981) and a list of other cases to support its ruling.

However, individuals with unpaid plan loans may have other bases to exclude the loans from the estate. The means test of Bankruptcy Code Section 707(b)(2)(A)(ii) permits debtors to deduct payments on secured debt, and "actual monthly expenses for the categories specified as Other Necessary Expenses issued by the Internal Revenue Service." The Internal Revenue Manual ("IRM") lists 15 categories of expenses that may be considered necessary, and states that the list is not exhaustive. This argument was not successful for the debtor in *Egebjerg*.[204] The court determined that repayment of the loan at issue did not fit in any of the IRM's listed categories. Some bankruptcy courts consider the IRM list as exhaustive, based on the language of Section 707 limiting the deductions to "categories specified." The *Egebjerg* court did not resolve the debate, but found the qualified plan loan is not a necessary expense.

Mr. Egebjerg also contended that the repayment was an involuntary deduction from wages, and necessary for his long-term health and welfare. These were conclusory arguments not supported by specific facts on asset levels needed to support any particular lifestyle at a certain age, at a definite future point in time. The court rejected both arguments, finding the loan was not a condition of the debtor's employment and the debtor did not prove that repayment of the loan was necessary for his long term health and welfare

The court also found the loan repayment obligation was not in itself a special circumstance to rebut any presumption of abuse. The debtor's explanation for the loan was that it was "to pay off bills," with the hopes of forestalling bankruptcy. All individuals have bills, and that argument alone does not establish the reason for the bills. The court followed the majority of courts that have addressed this issue.[205] The court quoted *Smith, supra*, with approval, stating the fact that the debtor now wishes to pay back the loan "is not a life altering circumstance of the kind referenced in the statute. It is simply the consequence of a prior financial decision."

The Bankruptcy Code allows Chapter 13 debtors to deduct 401(k) loan repayments from disposable income. This was intended to encourage debtors to utilize Chapter 13 for bankruptcy, rather than Chapter 7. An individual's payments on a plan loan are not considered disposable income in a Chapter 13 filing. This is not the case in a Chapter 7 filing. In circumstances where a loan is repaid prior to the expiration of the Chapter 13 plan, courts may require the amounts previously used to repay the loan to become available as disposable income to be redirected to unsecured creditors.

Interestingly, if a debtor has funds that are available immediately prior to bankruptcy, he or she may be able repay the loan prior to filing bankruptcy and convert the funds to exempt property. In *Dunbar and Dunbar v. CNH Retirement Savings Plan*,[206] the debtor borrowed funds from his 401(k) plan, made several payments, and then repaid the loan in its entirety. The trustee contested the

---

[204] 574 F 3d 1045, 1050 citing IRM 5.15.1.10(1).

[205] Citing *In re Smith*, 388 B.R. 885, 888 (Bankr. C.D. Ill. 2008), *In re Mowris*, 384 B.R. 235, 240 (Bankr. W.D. Mo. 2008) and *In re Turner*, 376 B.R. 370, 378 (Bankr. D. N.H., 2007).

[206] 313 B. R. 430 (Bankr. C.D. Ill., 2004).

repayment, arguing that the transfer of personal assets to the retirement plan was a fraudulent transfer. However, a Bankruptcy Court in Illinois ruled this was not a fraudulent transfer, on the basis that the transfer of funds from a savings account resulted in a similar amount of funds in the plan participant's account. The court used a balance sheet approach, and noted the statute did not require the net value of the debtor's estate for available distribution to creditors to be the same. The debtor moved funds from one account to the other, and received equivalent value, notwithstanding the shift to an exempt asset.

Qualified Plan Benefits Subject to Withdrawal. The courts have interpreted the *Patterson* decision to exclude a debtor's retirement plan assets from a debtor's bankruptcy estate even though the debtor has control over the funds and may withdraw them at any time.[207] Thus, a bankruptcy trustee cannot force a bankrupt participant to request a loan, withdrawal, or distribution of his or her retirement plan funds.

Although assets in ERISA-qualified plans are fully protected, once the plan distributes or the participant withdraws those assets, they may be included in a debtor's bankruptcy estate. This is true whether the debtor borrowed the money from the plan and is making repayment, or simply elects to begin distributions.[208] Many bankruptcy courts have held that the bankruptcy trustee may attach qualified plan assets as soon as the plan distributes them to the debtor. These cases indicate that ERISA only excludes assets actually and rightfully held in an ERISA plan—and not future contributions or repayments—from a debtor's bankruptcy estate.

At least one nonbankruptcy court has held that a bankruptcy court may not attach distributions received during retirement. The court in *U.S. v. Smith*[209] held that ERISA safeguards a pensioner's stream of income, even when the plan pays out the funds during retirement.

.02 What Plans Does ERISA Protect?

Clearly, most qualified retirement plans of any kind fit within ERISA's definition of "pension plan." These would include defined benefit and defined contribution plans, as well as 401(k) plans and ESOPs. Some bankruptcy courts have held that a plan is "qualified" under ERISA only if it (1) includes a nonalienation provision; (2) has qualified for tax benefits; and (3) is governed by ERISA.[210] Other courts have instead merely required that a plan be governed under ERISA and contain a nonalienation clause enforceable under ERISA.[211]

The courts have split on whether the assets of a tax-qualified retirement plan maintained by a self-employed person are exempt from creditors in case of a self-employed person's bankruptcy. ERISA defines an "employee benefit plan" as a

---

[207] *Barkley v. Conner*, 73 F3d 258 (9th Cir. 1996).

[208] *In re Harshbarger*, 66 F3d 775 (6th Cir. 1995); *Guidry v. Sheet Metal Workers' Nat'l Pension Fund*, 39 F3d 1078 (10th Cir. 1994); *Trucking Employees of North Jersey Welfare Fund v. Colville*, 16 F3d 52 (3d Cir. 1994); *Tenneco Inc. v. First Virginia Bank*, 698 F2d 688 (4th Cir. 1983).

[209] *U.S. v. Smith*, 47 F3d 681 (4th Cir. 1995).

[210] *U.S. v. Sawaf*, 74 F3d 119 (6th Cir. 1996); *In re Hall*, 151 B.R. 412 (Bankr. W.D. Mich. 1993); *In re Sirois*, 144 B.R. 12 (Bankr. D. Mass. 1992); *Gilbert v. Foy (In re Foy)*, 164 B.R. 595 (Bankr. S.D. Ohio 1994); *In re Witwer*, 148 B.R. 930 (Bankr. C.D. Calif. 1992).

[211] *In re Hanes*, 162 B.R. 733 (Bankr. E.D. Va. 1994).

plan that an employer maintains for its "employees." Based on this definition, some courts have held that ERISA does not protect a Keogh plan benefiting only the self-employed person (or only the self-employed person and his or her spouse).[212]

.03 What Plans Are Not Protected by ERISA?

ERISA Section 206(d)(1) and *Patterson* would not automatically protect assets accumulated by or on behalf of an individual under the following plans or retirement vehicles:

- Individual retirement accounts or annuities;
- Tax-sheltered annuities (Section 403(b) plans);
- Section 457 plans;
- Government plans;
- Church plans;
- Welfare benefit plans; and/or
- Excess benefit plans.

However, such plans and programs still may be excludable from creditors if the debtor can demonstrate one of the following facts:

1. The employer has made the plan subject to ERISA;
2. The plan or program is only an unfunded promise to pay future amounts;
3. The assets of the plan held on behalf of the debtor are necessary for the support of the debtor and his or her dependents; or
4. The assets of the plan or program are exempt from creditors under the state law of a debtor's domicile.

The presence or absence of language in the plan, or in the Internal Revenue Code Section authorizing the plan, prohibiting alienation or assignment also may determine whether the courts will exclude a non-ERISA plan from a debtor's bankruptcy estate.[213]

.04 Individual Retirement Accounts

In *Rousey v. Jacoway*[214], the U.S. Supreme Court extended to IRAs the same protection from bankruptcy creditors that *Patterson* had provided to ERISA plans. In *Rousey*, the court held that Bankruptcy Code Section 522(d)(10)(E) protected the debtors' IRA from the claims of their creditors. Section 522(d)(10)(E) protects a debtor's right to receive

> (E) a payment under a stock bonus, pension, profit sharing, annuity, or similar plan or contract on account of illness, disability, death, age, or length of

---

[212] 11 U.S.C. § 522(d)(10)(E). One court has held that single pension and husband and wife pensions are outside the scope of *Patterson. In re Hall*, 151 B.R. 412 (Bankr. W.D. Mich. 1993).

[213] For example, Code Sec. 457(b)(6) provides that all compensation deferrals, investments and investment income shall be treated as property of the employer, not property of the employee.

[214] *Rousey v. Jacoway*, 541 U.S. 320 (2005).

service, to the extent reasonably necessary for the support of the debtor and any dependent of the debtor, unless—

  (i) such plan or contract was established by or under the auspices of an insider that employed the debtor at the time the debtor's rights under such plan or contract arose;

  (ii) such payment is on account of age or length of service; and

  (iii) such plan or contract does not qualify under section 401(a), 403(a), 403(b), or 408 of the Internal Revenue Code of 1986.

The court found IRAs to be "similar plans or contracts within the meaning of Section 522(d)(10)(e)." The Court also found that the 10% penalty imposed for distributions from an IRA prior to age 59-1/2 is a "substantial barrier" to early withdrawal and, thus, provides "a right to payment on account of age."

Bankruptcy Code Section 522 also expressly exempts IRA assets from the bankruptcy estate, whether the debtor elects to use the federal or state exemptions. Both traditional and Roth IRAs are excluded, up to a $1 million limit. This limit is adjusted every three years for changes in the Consumer Price Index, under Bankruptcy Code Section 104. The adjustment was increased to $171,650 in 2010, to $1,245,475 in 2013, and to $1,283,025 in 2016.

The limit may be even higher, where an IRA contains a rollover distribution from a qualified plan, as rollover amounts from qualified plans are excluded when computing the IRA limit. In some states the state exemptions for IRAs may exceed the $1 million amount cap, as adjusted for inflation. State laws vary on whether IRA assets are protected from creditors, and how much protection is afforded.

Assets in a SEP or SIMPLE may also be excluded in greater amounts than the IRA limit. SEPS or SIMPLE IRAS are particular variations on the IRA theme, and the dollar limit on the exclusion available for IRAs does not apply to IRAs included in a Simplified Employee Pension, or SEP, or to SIMPLE IRAs, pursuant to Bankruptcy Code Section 522(n). Under a SEP an employer allocates deductible contributions among IRAs for participating employees. An employer may use Form 5305-SEP or an IRS-approved prototype SEP agreement, or a prototype of a sponsoring organization acting as trustee or custodian, to adopt the plan. Traditionally employers have the option of requesting a private letter ruling on the SEP as an individually designed plan.

The IRA exclusion will not apply to custodial accounts, as they are not trusts. They are treated as a trust for purposes of Code Sec. 408(h), but this "treatment as a trust" does not make the IRA a trust, so as to qualify for the Bankruptcy Code 541(c)(2) exclusion. This exclusion is for restrictions on the transfer of a beneficial interest in a *trust* that are enforceable under applicable non-bankruptcy law.

The IRA exclusion also will not apply to inherited IRAs. The U.S. Supreme Court, in *Clark v. Rameker*,[215] held that, after the death of an IRA owner, assets in an inherited IRA for a non-spouse beneficiary no longer constitute retirement

---

[215] 134 S.Ct. 2242 (2014).

funds for bankruptcy purposes. Consequently, the IRA assets are not protected from creditors' claims when a non-spouse beneficiary files for bankruptcy. The debtor in *Clark* was the beneficiary of her deceased mother's IRA worth approximately $300,000. Where a spouse inherits an IRA after the death of their spouse, such a spousal IRA is subject to different tax rules. Inheritance of a spousal IRA may not be covered under the ruling in *Clark*, as the tax rules are somewhat different for surviving spouses. *Clark* does not directly impact any state law protection afforded IRAs. Several states have adopted laws exempting inherited IRAs by statute, and the dollar limits on excludable assets may be higher under such statutes.

A bankruptcy court held that the exemption for IRAs does not apply to custodial accounts, and such accounts are not excluded from the bankruptcy estate under the Bankruptcy Code.[216]

.05 Bankruptcy of an Executive Holding Stock Awards

Partially vested, unexercised stock options are a significant asset of some individuals who file for bankruptcy protection. In other cases, after filing for bankruptcy protection, a debtor's stock options may have fully vested or the individual may have actually exercised the options and realized significant gains. All or part of the options' value may be assets of the debtor's bankruptcy estate.

Generally, the courts have characterized stock options as assets, rather than wages, for purposes of determining the extent to which the options should be included in the bankruptcy estate. One court explained the relevant test as follows:

> Employee stock options given to general employees and not tied to their individual performances are characterized as assets. Stock options given to executive in lieu of or in addition to salary and determined by their individual performance are characterized as income.[217]

However, in *Larson*,[218] the court found that stock options granted to a sole director to compensate him for his involvement with the company were wages. The court noted that "decisions made as a director have a direct bearing on the success or failure of the company which would ultimately affect the total amount of compensation received upon option exercise."

Several cases have considered the affect of an individual's personal bankruptcy on his or her outstanding stock options. In *Stoebner v. Wick*,[219] the Court of Appeals for the Eighth Circuit considered whether a debtor's bankruptcy estate was entitled to the value of a debtor's stock option proceeds, even though the options had not fully vested when the debtor filed for bankruptcy. The court observed that the Bankruptcy Code excludes from the estate earnings based on a debtor's work performance after he or she files for bankruptcy protection. In this case, two-thirds of the stock option's vesting period occurred after a debtor's

---

[216] *Walsh v. Benson*, U.S. Dist. LEXIS 2760, 56 Collier Bankr. Cas. 869, 2006.

[217] *In re Lawton*, 261 B.R. 774 (Bankr. M.D. Fla. 2001).

[218] *Larson v. Cameron*, 147 B.R. 39, 41 (Bankr. D. N.D. 1992).

[219] *Stoebner v. Wick*, 276 F3d 412 (8th Cir. 2002).

bankruptcy petition. The court reasoned that, since one-third of the vesting period was attributable to the debtor's work before filing bankruptcy, the trustee in bankruptcy was entitled to one-third of the proceeds of the stock options.

In *Allen v. Levey*,[220] the bankruptcy court held that a stock option agreement is an interest in property that becomes property of the estate at the commencement of the bankruptcy filing. However, the court held that Mr. Allen's interest in the stock options was only contingent, because Allen could not exercise the options unless he remained in employment, and it therefore became relevant whether the contingency actually occurred. In *Allen*, because the debtor remained employed, and all of the options became exercisable, the court held that the options were included in the bankruptcy estate. However, like *Stoebner v. Wick*, the court allocated to the bankruptcy estate only the percentage of the total option proceeds that was attributable to a debtor's pre-petition work.[221]

In *DeNadai v. Preferred Capital Markets, Inc.*,[222] the court rejected a debtor's contention that options that had not vested as of the bankruptcy filing date were post-petition earnings and excluded from his estate. Following a debtor's bankruptcy filing, his stock options became fully vested due to the change in control of his or her employer. The court allocated a percentage of the stock option proceeds to the bankruptcy estate based on a debtor's pre-petition services.

However, the court in *In re Dibiase*[223] reached a different result, holding that the entire stock option belonged to the bankruptcy estate. The *In re Dibiase* court expressed its view that the *Allen* court had confused conditions precedent with conditions subsequent:

> The debtor does not earn the right to use the Option in this case at all. It was granted the Option at the outset. The debtor can forfeit some or all of the benefit of the Option by quitting (or lose the benefit by being fired), but absent the occurrence of these events, the Option has its full value on the day it is granted. As of the filing, the debtor was employed, and thus owned the Option. There were no conditions precedent to its ownership, though there were qualifications on how and when the Option could be used. The Option in *Allen* did not have to be earned. Neither does the Option in this case.[224]

In *Parks v. Dittmar*, the U.S. Court of Appeals for the Tenth Circuit held that stock appreciation rights (SARs) distributed to Boeing Co. employees are part of those employees' bankruptcy estates, even though the SARs payments did not occur until after the employees filed for bankruptcy.[225] In reversing the decision of the U.S. Bankruptcy Appellate Panel for the Tenth Circuit, the appeals court found that Boeing and its successor, Spirit AeroSystems Inc., had a contractual obligation to make the SARs payments to the employees once an initial public offering occurred. Since the obligation to make the SARs payments to the eight

---

[220] *Allen v. Levey*, 226 B.R. 857 (Bankr. N.D. Ill. 1998).

[221] *Allen v. Levey* was followed in *In re Lawton*, 261 B.R. 774 (Bankr. M.D. Fla. 2001) and *Larson v. Cameron*, 147 B.R. 39 (Bankr. D. N.D. 1992).

[222] *DeNadai v. Preferred Capital Markets, Inc.*, 272 B.R. 21 (D. Mass. 2001).

[223] *In re Dibiase*, 270 B.R. 673 (Bankr. W.D. Tex. 2001).

[224] *In re Dibiase*, 270 B.R. 673 (Bankr. W.D. Tex. 2001).

[225] *Parks v. Dittmar*, 49 EBC 2521 (10th Cir. 2010).

workers existed before those workers filed for bankruptcy, the SARs were "sufficiently rooted in the pre-bankruptcy past" and were part of the workers' bankruptcy estates, even though the SARs were not paid out until after they filed for bankruptcy.

The "Sufficiently Rooted" Test. The majority of courts continue to analyze whether payments to executives in bankruptcy are "sufficiently rooted in the pre-bankruptcy past" under the framework of set forth in the *Dittmar* case. This is the test originating prior to the 1978 Bankruptcy Code, in the Supreme Court decision of *Segal v. Rochelle*.[226] Recent cases have applied *Dittmar's* analysis to include assets in mineral leases transferred prior to filing bankruptcy and profit sharing benefits under collective bargaining agreements in the bankruptcy estate.

In the Fifth Circuit a Texas bankruptcy court found a mineral lease the debtor transferred prior to filing the bankruptcy petition, in a transfer requiring approvals not obtained, was included in the bankruptcy estate, in *In re Vallecito Gas LLC*[227]. The lease was on land owned by the Navajo Nation, and the transferee entity disclaimed its interest in the lease. The transfer was invalid, as it required the approval of the Navaho Nation and the United States Secretary of the Interior through the Bureau of Indian Affairs, neither of which was obtained.

The Illinois bankruptcy court determined an executive was eligible for collectively bargained profit sharing benefits when he filed his petition for bankruptcy, in *In re Powell*.[228] A portion of the benefit was derived from post-petition services, and excluded from the estate. Section 541(a)(6) of the Bankruptcy Code excludes a debtor's earnings for services performed after the petition is filed from the estate, so the court allocated the portion of the benefit derived from pre-petition services to the estate.

It is important not to neglect consideration of stock rights when filing for bankruptcy, despite the fact that any payment is only a possibility in the future. The general rule is that contingent interests are includable in the estate, unless the plan reserves discretion on whether to make the payment.

A minority of courts have held that Bankruptcy Code Section 541 determines whether an interest is included in the estate, and rejected the "sufficiently rooted in pre-bankruptcy" test. These courts are of the opinion that the "sufficiently rooted" test was extinguished by the 1978 Bankruptcy Code. Cases with this view, such as *In re Burgess*, have involved payments authorized by legislation enacted after the individual filed for bankruptcy. The individual had no legal or equitable right to any payment without legislation that was passed after the filing for bankruptcy. In *Burgess*, crop disaster relief payments were made after the bankruptcy petition was filed, pursuant to legislation enacted after the bankruptcy was filed. The *Burgess* court noted that the "sufficiently rooted" test

---

[226] See *In re Powell*, 511 B.R. 107, 111-112, (Ill. Bankr. 2014) where the court found a profit sharing benefit under a pre-petition CBA payable post-petition was included in the estate. The court stated the term property is construed generously under the Bankruptcy Code, citing *Segal v. Rochelle*, 382 U.S. 375, 380, 86 S. Ct. 511, 515, 15 L. Ed. 2d 428, 432 (1966), and may include future, contingent, speculative and derivative interests (citations omitted).

[227] 461 B.R. 358 (Bankr. Court, N.D. Tex., 2011).

[228] *In re Powell*, 611 B. R. at 112.

established in the *Segal* case involved a net operating loss (NOL) paid after bankruptcy, for losses incurred prior to bankruptcy, where payment was pursuant to Code Sec. 172, which was in existence at the time the bankruptcy petition was filed. Thus, a claim for tax refund existed at the time the bankruptcy petition was filed, if provisions of Code Sec. 172 were met.

The *Burgess* court relied on *Drewes v. Vote*[229], an earlier Eighth Circuit case involving disaster relief payments, with similar facts. As in *Drewes*, a farmer, incurred a crop loss before filing bankruptcy, but had no legal claim to any disaster relief at the time he filed his petition; other than a "mere hope" that his losses might generate revenue. The reasoning of the *Burgess* court was succinctly stated with the following comment " . . . we have found no case in which a pure loss with no attendant potential benefit was included as property of the estate."[230]

The Absolute Priority Rule. When a company issues stock or stock options in the reorganized company to incumbent management holders of equity in the pre-bankruptcy enterprise, care must be taken to avoid violation the Absolute Priority Rule (APR). Creditors use this rule to oppose granting equity interests in the reorganized business to former shareholders.

The Absolute Priority Rule was judicially enacted prior to the 1978 Bankruptcy Code, and its genesis is based on the concept that fairness and equity require creditors be paid before the stockholders could retain equity.[231] In bankruptcy a stockholder's interest in property is subordinate to the rights of creditors. The purpose of the rule is to ensure creditors are paid ahead of equity, and it is a form of creditor protection to restrict corporate owners from depleting a failing business. The rule is designed to prevent reorganization plans proposed by a debtor from giving management an unfair advantage.

Bankruptcy Code Section 1129 allows the confirmation of a reorganization plan without the consent of each class of creditors, known as a cram down, provided it meets criteria for being "fair and equitable." This "fair and equitable" standard is what leaves room for a potential exception to the rule, known as the new value corollary.

When a shareholder contributes new value in order to retain or obtain an interest in the post bankruptcy enterprise, the new value exception to the APR may be utilized. A reorganizing company must demonstrate that stock options in the reorganized enterprise were not issued on account of the prior shareholdings, and are in return for providing new equity or an incentive to provide future services. The Supreme Court's decision in *Bank of America Nat'l Trust and Savings Assoc. v. 203 North La Salle St Partnership*[232] acknowledged the new value exception exists in certain circumstances, provided that the offer of equity must not be exclusively to former shareholders. There must be some offer to others, and an opportunity to propose a competing plan. The plan also must meet a market test,

---

[229] 276 F. 3d 1024 (8th Cir. 2002). *See also, In re Bracewell*, 322 F. 3d 46, 473 (7th Cir. 2002).

[230] 438 F. 3d at 503, quoting from *Drewes v. Vote*, 322 F. 3d 468, 473 (7th Cir. 2002).

[231] *Northern Pacific R. Co. v. Boyd*, 228 U.S. 482, 508 (1913).

[232] 526 US 434, 441 (1999).

to establish that compensation is within what is generally standard in the industry.

The American Bankruptcy Institute Commission to Study the Reform of Chapter 11 has recommended that the mechanism to allow the new value exception to the APR be codified in the Bankruptcy Code, to facilitate adoption of reorganization plans and minimize litigation. This recommendation would require new value in an amount proportionate to the equity retained or received, by pre-petition equity security holders, and a reasonable market test.[233]

> **Planning Note:** Corporations would be well advised to compile data establishing that option incentives offered to former shareholders are no more favorable than the market rate for similar services, to sustain their burden of proof in any challenge by a dissenting creditor. Consideration could be given to offering managers as well as shareholders an opportunity for stock options or other equity

If the company is owned primarily by one principal owner, or is closely held, continued equity participation of former equity owners may be required for the business to continue. Creditors must be convinced that continued participation is in their best interest, and payment of some consideration will be required, to avoid providing ammunition for any objections.

The APR for Sole Proprietorships. Many executives operate businesses as a sole proprietor, and will be impacted by a particular subset of changes under BAPCPA. After BAPCPA, individual debtors are now allowed to retain earnings from services performed after commencement of the case. Section 1129 now states, to be fair and equitable a proposed plan must provide:

> the holder of any claim that is junior to the claim of a dissenting class will not receive or retain any property on account of their junior claim, except that in a case where a debtor is an individual, the debtor may retain property included in the estate under section 1115 . . .

Section 1115, added by BAPCPA, provides

> (a) In a case in which the debtor is an individual, property of the estate includes, in addition to the property specified in section 541—

> (1) All property of the kind specified in section 541 that a debtor acquires after commencement of the case . . . ; and

> (2) Earnings from services performed by the debtor after the commencement of the case . . . .

Bankruptcy courts have reached different conclusions on the issue of whether Section 1115 includes property specified in Section 541. The text of the statute is susceptible to two different, but plausible, interpretations. A minority of courts have ruled that Section 1115 repeals the absolute priority rule, since it expressly allows the debtor to retain earnings after commencement of the case, in addition to all property of the estate under Section 541 of the Bankruptcy Code.[234]

---

[233] See the Final Report and Recommendations released December 8, 2014 at 23 Am. Bankr. Inst. L. Rev. 4 (2015), an abridged and edited version of the American Bankruptcy Institute Commission to Study the Reform of Chapter 11. The Final Report and Recommendations are more fully set forth at commission.abi.org.

[234] See *In re Maharaj*, 681 F. 3d, (4th Cir. 2012).

The majority view, adopted by the Fourth, Fifth and Tenth Circuits, is that the BAPCPA amendments have the effect of allowing individual debtors to retain property and earnings acquired after commencement of the case, as stated in Section 1115. Under this view the absolute priority rule continues to apply to individual debtors, and courts refuse to find an implied repeal of such a long standing principle as the absolute priority rule. This precludes the individual debtor from retaining any property over the objection of a creditor, unless it is exempt property. The absolute priority rule often makes it impossible for individual debtors operating a sole proprietorship or pass through business entity to continue their business after bankruptcy.

An example of the impact of the APR on individual debtors filing bankruptcy is found in *In re Stephens*,[235] decided by the Tenth Circuit Court of Appeals. Mr. and Mrs. Stephens operated a Quick Mart, formed as a limited liability company (LLC). The LLC owned multiple convenience stores, which supplied gasoline and other products. The LLC fell behind on payments, due to the rising price of gas and a diminishing customer base, and became liable to a supplier for $1.8 million. The individual owners mortgaged various tracts of real estate, including a house, and farmlands, to secure the debt. After a period of time the individuals filed for bankruptcy under Chapter 11, showing former operation as an LLC.

A plan was proposed to pay a lump sum to the secured creditor, retain possession and control of business property, and pay the creditor supplier a monthly payment for five years. A major creditor objected to the plan, and contended it violated the APR. The bankruptcy court found *the plain language of BAPCPA abrogated the APR for individual debtors* and approved the plan. The major creditor appealed to the Tenth Circuit Court of Appeals. The Tenth Circuit Court of Appeals noted that courts have reached differing results on this issue.[236] The BAPCPA amendments to Chapter 11 will continue to cause delay and expense for individual debtors, until this issue is clarified.

.06 Loans from the Company

If a company grants loans to executives to purchase company stock, financial difficulties of the company create a perfect storm of problems for the company and the executive. An example of these problems is found in the bankruptcy of Conseco. The company arranged for and guaranteed loans to executives from various banks to use to purchase its stock while it was in a period of rapid growth. Seven years later the company filed bankruptcy.

The executives whose employment was terminated experienced a decline in value of their equity investment in the company, and retained a continuing obligation to repay the loans. Many were heavily invested in the stock that was tanking, and could not repay the loans. The company proposal to forgive debts from its former officers drew objections from some creditors, the Securities and Exchange Commission, and the trustee in bankruptcy. The unpaid loan balances

---

[235] 704 F. 3d 1279 (10th Cir. 2013).   [236] 704 F. 3d at 1284.

created an obstacle to emerging from bankruptcy. The company filed suit against its former officers and directors who ceased payments on loans after their employment was terminated, when it believed they had the ability to repay.

Some executives tried to offset the financial risk of the lack of diversification of their investments, and arranged for split dollar insurance from the company. However, the company was unable to honor its obligation to pay the premiums after bankruptcy, and the bankruptcy court allowed Conseco to terminate the split dollar arrangement.[237]

The Sarbanes-Oxley Act now prohibits publicly traded companies from providing personal loans to officers and directors. This generally has greatly restricted loan programs to officers and directors of publicly held companies for the purpose of acquiring stock. However, such loans continue to be available for executives of privately held firms. From **a planning perspective**, it is important to contact securities counsel prior to structuring any arrangements involving loans to executives to purchase stock or options in the company, to avoid violations.

.07 State Exemption Statutes

Before *Patterson*, many states had amended their exemption statutes to provide additional protection to debtors' retirement benefits.[238] Often these statutes expressly exempted plans and other retirement funds that otherwise would fall outside the protection of ERISA, such as IRAs, state and local government retirement plans, and other plans qualified under the Internal Revenue Code (*e.g.*, Keogh plans and church plans).

When an executive files bankruptcy and chooses the state exemption scheme, a significant portion of distributions from a non-qualified plan are generally exempt from garnishment under state law. A typical case involving an interest in a nonqualified plan is found in the Fourth Circuit case of *In re Gnat*.[239]

---

[237] In re *Conseco, Inc.*, 2005 U.S. Dist. LEXIS 24584 (N.D. Ill. Oct. 18, 2005), affirmed by *Dick v. Conseco*, 458 F. 3d 573 (7th Cir. 2006).

[238] See, *e.g.*, ILCS 5/12-1006: (a) A debtor's interest in or right, whether vested or not to the assets held in or to receive pensions, annuities, benefits, distributions, refunds of contributions, or other payments under a retirement plan is exempt from judgment, attachment, execution, distress for rent, and seizure for the satisfaction of debts if the plan (i) is intended in good faith to qualify as a retirement plan under applicable provisions of the Internal Revenue Code of 1986, as now or hereafter amended, or (ii) is a public employee pension plan created under the Illinois Pension Code, as now or hereafter amended; (b) "Retirement plan" includes the following: (i) a stock bonus, pension profit sharing, annuity, or similar plan or arrangement, including a retirement plan self-employed individuals or a simplified employee pension plan; (ii) a government or church retirement plan or contract; (iii) an individual retirement annuity or individual retirement account; and (iv) a public employee pension plan created under the Illinois Pension Code, as now or hereafter amended; (c) a retirement plan that is (i) intended in good faith to qualify as a retirement plan under the applicable provisions of the Internal Revenue Code of 1986, as now or hereafter amended, or (ii) a public employee pension plan created under the Illinois Pension Code, as now or hereafter amended, is conclusively presumed to be a spendthrift trust under the law of Illinois.

[239] *In re Gnadt*, 2015 Bankr. LEXIS 1552, Case No. 11-10378-BFK, E.D. Va. An option may be subject to Code Sec. 409A if it is not exempt. Options that qualify as Incentive Stock Options, or "ISOs", under Code Sec. 422, are exempt. Options created under an Employee Stock Purchase Plan ("ESPP"), pursuant to Code Sec. 423, and options with an exercise price equal to or exceeding fair market value at the time of the grant are also exempt from requirements under Code Sec. 409A for timing of distribution and related tax penalties.

Part of an executive's compensation package included a balance in a nonqualified deferred compensation plan. The plan stated benefits were not assignable. The executive filed for bankruptcy under a voluntary Chapter 11. His employer subsequently terminated his employment, and paid him under the plan. The trustee then motioned to convert the case to a Chapter 7 liquidation, on the basis that proposed payments under the plan were not feasible after the loss of employment.

The court included the plan benefits in the bankruptcy estate, as they stemmed from events occurring prior to the filing of bankruptcy, and were sufficiently rooted in the pre-bankruptcy past. The payments did not depend on performance of any future services.

The executive took the position that payments under the nonqualified plan were exempt from garnishment under Virginia law, as wages, bonuses or commissions. The court agreed, which protected seventy-five percent (75%) of the payments from garnishment. Most states have laws which exempt retirement plans from garnishment or inclusion in the bankruptcy estate, and laws of each individual state differ.

The executive contended that the remaining twenty-five percent (25%) portion of the payments were also excluded, as subject to a restriction on transfer under Bankruptcy Code Section 541(c)(2) and *Patterson v. Shumate*.[240] Section 541(c)(2) excludes a beneficial interest in a trust, subject to a restriction on transfer, under applicable non-bankruptcy law, from the bankruptcy estate.

The court viewed the nonqualified plan interest as a contingent interest, not a trust. It also found the anti-alienation provision was not enforceable, as it was not contained in Code Sec. 409A or its regulations. The court notes that courts have consistently held that contingent interests are included as property of the bankruptcy estate where they are 'sufficiently rooted in the (debtor's) pre-bankruptcy past, citing the *Segal* case.

In one California case an executive contended that stock options were a retirement plan under state law, and therefore excluded from the estate in a Chapter 7 bankruptcy. After reviewing the plan and its promotional materials, the court concluded the stock option plan was not intended as a source of retirement income, and did not exclude the options from the estate.[241]

---

[240] See *Patterson v. Shumate*, 504 U.S. 753, 112 S. Ct. 2242, 119 L. Ed. 2d 519 (1992).

[241] *Segovia v. Shoenmann*, (In re Segovia), No. 08-3075 (N.D. Cal., 2009).

Chapter 25
EXECUTIVE COMPENSATION IN MERGERS AND ACQUISITIONS

¶2501 Overview—Executive Compensation in Mergers and Acquisitions

Often the most rigorous test of whether a company (and its counsel) properly designed its executive compensation plans and arrangements comes during a sale, purchase, or merger transaction. The seller or target, the prospective buyer, and the executives (and counsel for each) will be examining, evaluating, or testing the compensation plan and arrangements. Additionally, outside parties, such as institutional investors, investment bankers and the market, will all be examining or testing the compensation plans and arrangements.

.01 Goals of Executive Compensation in a Merger or Acquisition Situation

The parties each will inquire as to whether the seller's compensation plans and arrangements:

- Allow the seller to retain the executives through the closing (or abandonment) of the transaction?
- Allow the buyer to retain the executives after the transaction?
- Properly motivate the executives to assist in the transaction and a smooth transition?
- Encourage the seller's executives to work for the highest sale price?
- Make it likely the executives will immediately send out their resumes and/or resist the transaction every step of the way?
- Contain terms and provisions so onerous as to impede the transaction or frighten off prospective buyers?
- Protect the executives from employment termination by the buyer?
- Create tax or securities law barriers that inhibit the transaction?
- Create adverse tax results for the buyer, the seller, or the executives?

For a detailed discussion of designing compensation plans and arrangements to achieve these goals, see ¶2515.

The various interested parties are likely to scrutinize the meaning of each phrase or provision of each plan and arrangement. If the terms and provisions are not clear, or do not produce the desired result, the parties may end up in court, where a judge will scrutinize their meaning. In short, counsel's skill in design and drafting will meet its sternest test.

.02 Tackling Executive Compensation in a Merger or Acquisition

Several critical steps occur in the process of preparing for, evaluating, and concluding a successful transaction. The first step always should be preparing for the transaction. The seller (and its counsel) will want to evaluate its current executive compensation plans and arrangements to determine whether they will accomplish the seller's goals. The company and its counsel should address any gaps or ambiguities before embarking on the transaction. For a detailed discussion of evaluating and designing compensation plans and arrangements prior to a transaction, see ¶ 2515.

> **Example:** ABC Corporation informs its outside executive compensation counsel that it is exploring a sale transaction. Counsel immediately asks the following questions in the following order:
>
> 1. Is ABC the buyer or the seller?
> 2. Is the transaction a sale of stock or assets?
> 3. Who is the target or acquirer?
> 4. How far along is the negotiation and due diligence of the transaction?

.03 Understanding the Transaction

Most transactions can be characterized as either a "sale of assets" or a "sale of stock." Both parties need to approach the transaction in a significantly different way depending upon whether it is a sale of assets or a sale of stock. When one company buys 100% of the stock (or other equity) of another company, the buyer steps into the shoes of the seller and automatically takes on all of the seller's liabilities. When a company buys all or substantially all of the assets of another company, the buyer only takes on the assets and liabilities that it agrees to take on in the acquisition agreement.

.04 Differing Goals of Buyer and Seller

Whether the company will be the buyer or the seller in a prospective transaction can make all the difference in the world in setting its goals. The common denominator among all sellers is that they seek a higher price for their stock or assets. Many sellers also seek to protect their employees and the benefits of their employees. A careful seller seeks to end all of its responsibility and liability for former employees and their benefit plans. Finally, a company selling less than all of its stock or its assets seeks to avoid an adverse impact on its remaining employees and benefit plans.[1]

In juxtaposition to sellers, the buyer generally seeks a lower price for the stock or assets it acquires. However, because the buyer must continue to run the business going forward, it also must avoid hidden liabilities and an adverse impact on its existing/ongoing employee benefit plans and arrangements. Most buyers need to retain key employees of the seller. Many buyers also seek to

---

[1] Combining these goals and summarizing them, one of my partners once described the seller's primary goal as: getting the buyer's money into its pocket and keeping it there.

provide for a smooth transition to the new company for executives and employees of the old company.

.05 Due Diligence

A critical part of every transaction is the discovery, investigation, and review of the other party's executive compensation plans and arrangements. Due diligence is particularly important for the buyer, since it will be assuming part or all of the seller's compensation plan liabilities. The buyer and the seller have slightly different goals in due diligence. In the case of a hostile takeover attempt of a public company, the buyer's opportunity for due diligence may be limited. For a detailed discussion of due diligence, see ¶ 2525.

.06 Negotiating Employee Benefit Representations, Warranties and Covenants

Once the parties have discovered and evaluated all of the compensation plans and liabilities, they must negotiate the treatment of the plans and liabilities and draft the terms of the purchase agreement accordingly. As noted above, if the terms and provisions are not clear, or do not produce the desired result, the parties may end up in court, where a judge will scrutinize their meaning. In short, counsel's skill in design and drafting will meet a stern test. For a detailed discussion of representations and warranties and covenants in a transaction, see ¶ 2535.

.07 Stock Award Issues

The treatment of stock option, restricted stock, and other stock-based awards in a transaction is critical to executives. Among the more important issues that frequently arise are:

- Whether outstanding unvested awards will fully vest upon the change in control;
- Whether the buyer will assume outstanding awards or substitute new awards;
- How awards of seller's stock will be converted to awards of buyer's stock; and/or
- What will be the tax and accounting effects of the transaction on outstanding awards?

For a detailed discussion of critical stock award issues that arise in a transaction, see ¶ 2545 and ¶ 2555.

.08 Code Sec. 409A

Code Sec. 409A sets forth some of the most complicated rules and restrictions affecting executive compensation.[2] Therefore, upon the scrutiny applied in

---

[2] Added by the American Jobs Creation Act of 2004 (P.L. 108-357), signed by President Bush on October 22, 2004.

the due diligence process, compliance issues frequently arise under Code Sec. 409A (see ¶2565).

¶2515 Executive Compensation Issues in a Transaction

The goals and objectives of the parties to a transaction vary in many ways, large and small, obvious and subtle. In some respects, the parties' goals are the same. In some friendly transactions, the parties work together to ensure that everyone's goals are met. However, the designer of a company's compensation plans and arrangements should never assume that it will have the luxury of revising and adjusting them at the eleventh hour of an acquisition. Rather, the designer should endeavor to protect its executives (or clients) from all possible contingencies.

Some executives and their counsel focus strictly on the current salary, bonus, and other compensation aspects of the employment agreement. True, most executives want an agreement that pays them big money. However, careful executives (and counsel) also want to be certain that the agreement and compensation plans protect the executives at the time of this life-changing, career-threatening event.

.01 Retaining the Company's Executives During a Transaction

In most cases, both the buyer and the seller will want to ensure that the seller retains its executives through the closing of the transaction. Additionally, every company must recognize that a significant percentage of proposed transactions never close, and plan for that possibility. Therefore, one objective of every executive compensation and benefit plan or arrangement should be to motivate the executive to cooperate in the event of a proposed transaction. Neither buyer nor seller will be served if the seller's executives feel compelled to send out their resumes immediately upon the first hint of a possible transaction. Similarly, neither buyer nor seller is served if the seller's executives are motivated to resist a transaction every step of the way, *e.g.*, because they fear the loss of their jobs.

In some industries during periods of consolidation, for example, banking and financial services in the 1990s, a merger or takeover was possible at any time. No executive with the slightest bargaining leverage would accept or stay in a position without change in control protection.

In industries where change in control agreements are not the norm, the company and its executives may wait until a sale becomes a distinct possibility before entering into agreements. One important factor that parties consider in preparing for a transaction is whether the buyer is likely to be a "strategic" buyer or a "financial" buyer. A strategic buyer is one that already has operations in the same or a similar business as the seller. Therefore, the strategic buyer is less likely to retain seller's current management to operate the business. On the other hand, a financial buyer generally has capital to invest, but not operational experience in the seller's industry. Financial buyers are more interested in retaining current management. Sometimes a financial buyer's primary interest in an acquisition is to acquire the existing, skilled management team.

Companies contemplating a sale generally follow either of two approaches with respect to executive retention and motivation, depending on the industry, type of executive and other circumstances. The two approaches generally followed are:

1. *Change in control agreement.* The change in control agreement allows the executive to remain focused on operating the business or even facilitating the sale, confident that, if he or she loses employment due to the sale, the change in control agreement will provide income and benefits throughout the executive's search for a new position.

2. *Retention bonus plan.* Companies that do not have change in control agreements in place for key executives will often adopt a retention bonus plan before putting the company on the market or beginning of sale or merger discussions. Companies generally structure retention bonus agreements so that the executive must remain employed until the transaction closes, or for a specified period thereafter, to receive the bonus.

Example 1: ABC Corporation has received purchase inquiries from several other companies in its industry, a fact the senior executives know. To avoid possible defections and ensure that the executives focus on operating the business, ABC implements a retention bonus plan that would pay each executive 100 percent of his or her annual base salary on the closing date of any transaction.

.02 Change in Control Agreements

Change in control agreements between companies and executives, the so-called "golden parachute agreements," have become a ubiquitous part of the executive compensation scene. Congress added the golden parachute provisions to the Internal Revenue Code in 1984. Code Sec. 280G prohibits a corporation from taking a deduction for any excess parachute payments.[3] An "excess parachute payment" is an amount equal to the excess of the aggregate present value of all parachute payments paid to a disqualified individual ("DI") over the DI's base amount.[4]

The types of benefits and compensation that companies pay, vest or accelerate upon a change in control, by the terms of the companies' change in control agreements, employment agreements and other benefit plans, is limited only by the companies' imagination (see Chapter 2 [¶201 *et seq.*] for a detailed discussion of all aspects of change in control agreements).

Experienced counsel will define "change in control" differently depending on whether the company is privately held or publicly traded and, if public, how widely the company's stock is held. Counsel also may need to refer to the definition given under Code Sec. 409A.

Planning Note: Experienced legal counsel for a private company will draft the definition of change in control to ensure that transfers by the controlling stockholder or family that are incidental to estate planning or to

---

[3] Code Sec. 280G(a).

[4] Code Sec. 280G(b)(1).

other family members do not trigger a change in control. For example, privately held ABC Corporation might define change in control as follows:

"Change of Control" shall mean a transaction or series of transactions (including by way of merger, consolidation, sale of stock, recapitalization or otherwise) the result of which is that James Q. Owner and any members of his immediate family no longer own, directly or indirectly, an equity interest in the Company that represents at least fifty percent (50%) of the Company's outstanding voting common shares, or at least fifty percent (50%) of the equity interest of an entity that is a successor to the Company or owns substantially all of the Company's voting common shares.

Experienced counsel also will make certain that the definition of change in control is consistent among all of the company's executive compensation and employee benefit plans and programs, including:

- Change in control agreements;
- Stock incentive plans;
- Employment agreements;
- Qualified retirement plans;
- Severance plans; and
- Nonqualified deferred compensation and/or retirement plans.

Experienced counsel will also discuss with the company whether to draft the definition of change in control to provide expressly that a transaction where the executive is part of a purchasing group will not trigger the executive's change in control benefits. To allow an executive to receive benefits in this situation would be akin to letting the executive have his cake and eat it too.

Example 2: ABC Corporation's counsel drafts the change in control definition in ABC's stock incentive plan, employment agreements, and severance plan to provide as follows:

In no event will a Change in Control be deemed to have occurred, with respect to the Executive, if the Executive is part of a purchasing group that consummates the Change in Control transaction. The Executive will be deemed "part of a purchasing group" for purposes of the preceding sentence if the Executive is an equity participant in the purchasing company or group (except: (i) passive ownership of less than two percent (2%) of the stock of the purchasing company; or (ii) ownership of equity participation in the purchasing company or group that is otherwise not significant, as determined prior to the Change in Control by a majority of the nonemployee continuing Directors).

Finally, companies should consider whether the definition of change in control in their plans and agreements will draw criticism from the proxy advisory firms, such as Institutional Shareholder Services Inc. ("ISS"). ISS may object to a "liberal change in control definition" that triggers accelerated vesting of stock awards. According to ISS, a liberal change in control definition is one that triggers vesting upon: (i) stockholder approval of a transaction, rather than its consummation; (ii) an unapproved change in less than a majority of the board; (iii) acquisition of a low percentage of outstanding common stock (15% or less); (iv) announcement or commencement of a tender or exchange offer; (v) definition so broad as be triggered by ordinary course events (such as death or retirement situations); or (vi) any other trigger that could result in compensation without the occurrence of an actual change in control of the company. A definition that is triggered by the addition of new directors that were not nominated by the incumbent board (*i.e.*, in a proxy contest) would not be considered liberal.

Exchange Act Section 14A, added by the Dodd-Frank Wall Street Reform and Consumer Protection Act ("Dodd-Frank") Section 951, provides for "Shareholder Approval of 'Golden Parachute' Compensation." Referred to as "Shareholder Say on Parachute Payments," this provision requires that in any proxy or consent solicitation material for a meeting of stockholders at which stockholders are asked to approve an acquisition, merger, consolidation, or proposed sale or other disposition of all or substantially all the assets of the company, the party soliciting the proxy or consent must disclose any agreements or understandings that the party soliciting the proxy or consent has with any named executive officers of the company (or of the acquiring company) concerning any type of compensation (whether present, deferred, or contingent) that is based on or otherwise relates to the acquisition, merger, consolidation, sale, or other disposition of all or substantially all of the assets of the company and the aggregate total of all such compensation that may (and the conditions upon which it may) be paid or become payable to or on behalf of such executive officer.

However, a Shareholder Say on Parachute Payments vote is not binding on the company or the company's board of directors and, according to Section 951(c), may not be construed as (1) overruling their decision, (2) creating or implying any addition or change to their fiduciary duties, or (3) restricting or limiting stockholders' ability to make proposals for inclusion in proxy materials related to executive compensation.

.03 Allow the Buyer to Retain Key Executives After the Transaction

To the buyer, the difference between retaining an executive until closing and retaining the executive for a period of six to twelve months, or more, after closing may be critical. Retaining executives through the closing of the transaction is important to the seller and, often, to the executives. However, plans and arrangements that retain executives for some transition period following the closing, and, in some cases even permanently, are for the benefit of the buyer.

One key to designing a successful retention bonus program is to obtain the desired level of retention while limiting the cost of the program. In general, this result is best achieved by limiting the number of participants in the program to those individuals who are considered crucial to the ongoing success of the company or the successful completion of the desired corporate transaction (which can include post-merger integration), and providing these individuals with meaningful benefits. Allocation of a limited retention budget among a smaller group of employees identified as critical often accomplishes the company's retention objectives better than spreading the same budget over broader groups of employees. Accordingly, most companies provide significant retention and integration incentive opportunities to key employees, rather than covering large numbers of employees with marginal incentives.

The retention period needs to cover the entire period of uncertainty. If the retention period is not long enough, there is a risk that a company will incur retention expenses without accomplishing the intended retention objectives. The size of the bonus amount generally depends on the employee's current pay, the importance of the employee to the organization in the short and/or long term, the likelihood the employee may leave, and potential replacement costs. The greater the employee's pay, the more benefits that will be required to create a meaningful retention incentive. Some companies incorporate performance objectives that increase the maximum payout to up to double the levels of programs that are based on continued employment only (in order to offset the risk of failing to meet the performance goals). Retention programs are most effective when they offer both pure retention dollars (a guaranteed payment) and a leveraged integration payment to key employees.

> **Example 3:** ABC Corporation has begun sale discussions with a financial buyer. At the urging of the prospective buyer, ABC establishes a retention bonus arrangement for key executives. The arrangement provides for lump sum cash payments on the six-month anniversary of the closing of the transaction, payable to executives who remain employed with ABC and any successor until that date. The six-month period ensures that the buyer will have the services of key executives at least through a transition period, and gives the buyer six months to negotiate longer lasting employment agreements with the executives.

.04 Encourage the Executives to Work for the Highest Sale Price

Privately held companies often establish a plan or arrangement to share a portion of the proceeds of a sale to ensure that senior executives are highly motivated to prepare the business to sell at the highest possible price. This type of agreement would be especially useful where the likely buyers are "strategic" buyers, in the same industry as the seller, meaning that the executives most likely will not retain their positions after the sale.

A sale incentive agreement is essentially a form of a retention bonus arrangement under which the amount of the payment is linked solely to the purchase price. Moreover, the agreements most often provide that the executive will receive payment in the same form and at the same time as the selling stockholders, to reflect the fact that many private company sales have earn-out features to ensure the stockholders' cooperation in the transition period.

> **Example 4:** Family-owned ABC Corporation has decided to put itself up for sale. An independent valuation places the value of ABC at between $50 to $60 million. To avoid possible defections and ensure that the top three executives (none of whom is a family member) are highly motivated to

operate the business and negotiate the transaction to achieve the highest price, ABC implements a sale incentive plan that provides for 10% of the proceeds of the sale above $50 million to be shared by the top three executives.

.05 Terms and Provisions That Impede a Transaction

Companies need to protect their executives and encourage them to remain employed during the time of a possible transaction. However, most companies do not want these protective provisions to be so onerous that they impede the negotiation of a transaction or frighten off prospective buyers. Sophisticated buyers expect to see some form of change in control agreement providing severance payments to the seller's executive employees. These buyers have seen them before, and they know how to build the likely severance payments into the cost of the transaction.

However, certain provisions of change in control agreements can go beyond protecting executives to become a significant deterrent to a transaction. Specifically, buyers hate to find any of the following three provisions in a target's executive compensation plans or agreements:

1. A lapse of noncompete, nonsolicit and other restrictive covenants in the event of employment termination following a change in control. A lapse of these provisions makes it substantially more likely that (a) the executive may be able to leave employment and damage the business of the newly acquired company, and (b) golden parachute excise taxes and gross-up payments will apply to the severance benefits provided to executives under the change in control agreements (because restrictive covenants can reduce the value of other golden parachute payments).

2. So-called single trigger provisions in the change in control agreements with key executives. A single trigger provision allows the covered executive to leave employment with the acquiring company after a change in control for any reason (or no reason) and receive payments. Buyers feel that this type of provision, which does not require any adverse compensation or employment effect on the executive to trigger payments, substantially reduces their ability to retain key executives who may be vital to ongoing operations. Single trigger provisions also eliminate a buyer's ability to avoid severance payments by retaining an executive in the same (or better) position as he or she had before the change in control.

3. A full gross-up payment to all executives for any golden parachute excise taxes. Change in control agreements commonly provide gross-up payments to the most senior executive officers. Buyers may swallow hard and accept a gross-up provision for the chief executive officer, but gross-up payments much below that level will repulse prospective buyers.

   - First, the buyer makes the severance payments to the former executive;

- Second, the buyer reimburses the executive for excise taxes;
- Third, the buyer reimburses the executive for the additional excise taxes on the initial gross-up payment; and
- Finally, the buyer loses its deduction for both severance and gross-up payments above one times the executive's base amount.[5]

Many nonqualified deferred compensation plans provide for automatic full vesting and distribution upon a change in control. In addition to the cash flow problems this could create for the buyer or seller, the affected employee may face unwanted tax liability. The parties may negotiate to prepare plan documents, election forms, and communications that enable sellers' employees to defer benefits under the deferral plans beyond the change in control, subject to Code Sec. 409A.

.06 Protect the Executives from Employment Termination by the Buyer

The preceding sections describe change in control and retention plans designed to protect and retain executives. However, once a seller and its counsel have succeeded in retaining key executives to serve the buyer during a transition period, a critical design point they must not overlook is the need to protect the executives from termination by the buyer during that period. The seller and its counsel can accomplish this by adding to the requirement in the change in control or retention plan or arrangement that the executive remain in the service of the buyer for a specified period following change in control, the proviso that, if the buyer terminates the executive before the end of the period without cause, or if the executive terminates for good reason, the plan or arrangement will immediately provide payments and benefits to the executive.

> **Example 5:** In Example 4 above, ABC Corporation established a retention bonus arrangement for key executives. The arrangement provides for lump sum cash payments on the six-month anniversary of the closing of the transaction, payable to executives who remain employed with ABC and any successor until that date. To protect the executives, the arrangement also provides for an immediate cash payment to a covered executive if, before the end of the six-month transition period, (1) the buyer terminates his or her employment, without cause, or (2) the executive terminates employment for "good reason."

.07 Create Adverse Tax or Securities Law Results

In designing and drafting executive compensation plans and arrangements to protect the seller and its executives, the seller and its counsel also should avoid creating tax or security law barriers that inhibit the transaction or create adverse tax results for the buyer, the seller, or the executives. Sellers create executive compensation barriers to a transaction by drafting compensation plans, employ-

---

[5] *See* ¶275 for a detailed discussion of golden parachute excise taxes.

ment agreements and change in control agreements to provide, pay or trigger any of the following automatically upon a change in control:

1. Significant, nondeductible severance liabilities, such as under a change in control agreement with a tax gross-up provision.

2. Large funding responsibilities, such as a requirement in a qualified or nonqualified retirement plan that all accrued benefits become vested and fully funded immediately upon a change in control.

3. Eliminating noncompetes and other restrictive covenants, which not only reduces the buyer's ability to retain the executives it wants, but also increases the likelihood that golden parachute penalty taxes will apply.

4. Eliminating any incentive for executives to stay beyond the change in control, such as by making all benefits and payments fully and immediately vested and payable on the change in control.

Sellers commonly draft some or all of the foregoing provisions into their executive compensation plans, employment agreements and change in control agreements. However, the seller must understand that each of these provisions will reduce the value of the business to the buyer and, therefore, the price the buyer is willing to pay.

¶2525 Due Diligence

A critical part of every transaction is the discovery, investigation, and review of the other party's executive compensation plans and arrangements. Due diligence is particularly important for the buyer, since it will be assuming part or all of the seller's compensation plan liabilities. Due diligence also helps determine: (1) the employee benefits and compensation costs of the transaction, (2) how to handle the plans on a going-forward basis, and (3) whether the price or structure of the deal needs to be altered to accommodate executive compensation issues and liabilities.

> **Example 1:** A publicly traded Canadian corporation ("CC") acquired all of the stock of a public traded U.S. corporation ("USC") operating in the same business. After the acquisition, many of the USC executives began pulling their golden parachute agreements. This seemed to catch CC by surprise and enrage it. CC took out its anger on both USC's outside counsel (the author) who had drafted the airtight parachute agreements and rabbi trust, and on outside counsel who had represented CC in the acquisition. One outside counsel served its client very well. The other served its client not so well.

.01 Sale of Stock or Assets

Most transactions can be characterized as either a "sale of assets" or a "sale of stock." (For due diligence and liability purposes, a merger transaction is the same as a sale of stock.) Both parties need to approach the transaction in a significantly different way depending upon whether it is a sale of assets or a sale of stock. When a company buys most or all of the stock (or other equity) of another company, the buyer steps into the shoes of the seller and automatically assumes complete responsibility and liability for the seller's plans and agreements—and the liabilities attendant to such plans and agreements.

When a company buys all, or substantially all, of the assets of another company, the buyer does not assume the liabilities for the seller's plans and agreements, unless the acquisition agreement expressly provides for such assumption. The buyer only takes on the assets and liabilities that it agrees to take on in the acquisition agreement.

> **Example 2:** ABC Corporation acquires all of the outstanding stock of Little Corp. On the effective time of the transaction, ABC automatically becomes responsible for Little Corp.'s qualified and nonqualified retirement plans, employment agreements and any executive compensation arrangements. No assumption agreement is necessary. If ABC had negotiated with Little to acquire only its assets, ABC and Little might have separately negotiated over whether ABC would also assume Little's qualified and nonqualified retirement plans, employment agreements, and executive compensation arrangements. If ABC agreed to assume one or more of Little's plans or arrangements, ABC and Little most likely would have prepared and executed additional documentation to expressly reflect the assumption of the plan or arrangement by ABC.

.02 Seller's Due Diligence

The buyer and the seller have different goals in due diligence. As discussed in ¶2525.01, the seller first needs to be aware of every compensation plan and arrangement it maintains. When compiling the list, the seller should pay particular attention to plans or agreements that have special provisions triggered by a change in control. The seller needs to understand the impact of a change in control—and different types of possible changes in control—on all of its compensation plans and arrangements. However, the seller also should consider whether other plans and arrangements should have special provisions triggered by a change in control. As part of this process, the seller should consider whether to adopt or amend change in control or retention agreements.

.03 Buyer's Due Diligence

The primary objective to a buyer's due diligence is to identify all of the seller's existing benefit plans and compensation arrangements. Among the sources of plan document information for due diligence purposes are the following:

- Copies of the plans or agreements, and any related documents and/or summaries obtained from the seller;
- If the company is public, its filings with the U.S. Securities and Exchange Commission ("SEC"), such as its annual reports and proxy statements;
- The company's audited financial statements;
- Collective bargaining agreements;
- Employee handbooks; and

- Board resolutions.

However, even in the 21st century, buyers may find it difficult or impractical to identify and find all of a seller's compensation plans, programs, and arrangements in some cases. Some of the circumstances that may make it difficult or impractical to identify and find all of a seller's compensation plans, programs, and arrangements, include the following:

- The selling company has grown very quickly in the last few years;
- The selling company is privately held;
- The selling company is small and/or unsophisticated;
- The acquisition is hostile and the selling company, even if publicly traded, is not sharing any information;
- The deal is a small one and the buyer instructs counsel not to dig deep; and
- The buyer is acquiring assets only, and not assuming any plans or plan liabilities.

> **Planning Note:** Where any or all of the foregoing circumstances prevent the buyer's counsel from conducting a thorough due diligence investigation (except for a hostile takeover situation), an aggressive set of covenants, representations, and warranties can help to limit the buyer's potential exposure to unknown liabilities.

Different types of compensation plans and arrangements raise different issues and, therefore, require different review. However, certain questions apply to all plans and arrangements, including:

1. Does the plan have any provisions triggered by a change in control and, if so, what exactly would be the effect of those provisions? In addition to obvious golden parachute agreements, the buyer must determine what types of extra or accelerated payments the transaction will trigger. Sometimes, a change in control will trigger payments under the seller's severance plan, even though no one loses his or her job. Sometimes an acquisition will trigger an early retirement window.

2. What is the funded status of all plans and compensation arrangements? Federal pension law requires a company to fund its qualified retirement plans according to certain standards. Whether a qualified retirement plan is over funded, fully funded, or underfunded will make a difference to the buyer's future liability.[6]

Companies often informally fund their nonqualified retirement plan through a rabbi trust. If the seller informally funds its nonqualified retirement plan through a rabbi trust, the buyer may be able to acquire an asset to offset the liability for such benefits.[7]

---

[6] *See* Chapter 16 [¶1601 *et seq.*] for a detailed discussion of qualified retirement plans.

[7] *See* Chapter 17 [¶1701 *et seq.*] for a detailed discussion of nonqualified retirement plans.

Executive compensation plans often present the ultimate underfunding issue because many are deigned to be, or are intentionally, not funded at all. This can mean the company/buyer will face big payments when its key employees (or principals) retire, which may happen sooner, because of the acquisition.

> 3. If the buyer does not have plans comparable to the seller's, the buyer may have to establish new plans or employment agreements to preserve the compensation.

Finally, the buyer's due diligence must be vigilant to ensure that the seller is not able to enhance its executive compensation plans and arrangements during the period pending a transaction.

.04 Eliciting Critical Information in the Representations and Warranties

One method of due diligence is to require the parties to list certain critical information in the body of the purchase or merger agreement. This is particularly appropriate for information such as the number of shares authorized, issued, or outstanding under a company's equity incentive plan. For example, one section under the representations and warranties section of the agreement could read as follows:

> *Capitalization.* The Company represents and warrants to Parent that the authorized capital stock of the Company consists of [],000,000 shares of Company Common Stock. As of June 1, 2018, (i) [] shares of Company Common Stock were reserved for issuance upon exercise of Company Stock Options issued and outstanding; (ii) [] shares of Company Common Stock were reserved for issuance under the Company's 401(k) Retirement Savings Plan; (iii) [] shares of Company Common Stock were reserved for issuance under the Company's Employee Stock Purchase Plan; and (iv) [] shares of Company Common Stock were reserved for issuance under the Company's Directors' Deferral Plan.

For information that is important, but not as critical as the target company's capitalization, the purchase or merger agreement could require the parties to list the information in schedules attached to the agreement. For example, another section under the representations and warranties section of the agreement could read as follows:

> *Employee Benefit Plans; ERISA.* The Company Disclosure Schedule includes a complete list of each employee benefit plan, program or policy providing benefits to any current or former employee, officer or director of the Company or any of its subsidiaries or any beneficiary or dependent thereof that is sponsored or maintained by the Company or any of its subsidiaries or to which the Company or any of its subsidiaries contributes or is obligated to contribute (other than those programs or policies that do not provide material benefits), including without limitation any employee welfare benefit plan within the meaning of Section 3(1) of ERISA, any employee pension benefit plan within the meaning of Section 3(2) of ERISA (whether or not such plan is subject to ERISA, and including any "multiemployer plan" within the meaning of Section 4001(a)(3) of ERISA and any material bonus, incentive, deferred compensation, vacation, stock purchase, stock option, stock based, severance, employment, change of control or fringe benefit agreement, plan, program or policy (collectively, the "*Company Employee Benefit Plans*").

Contrary to the devious instincts of some sellers, 11th hour disclosures by a seller are never good. There is some thinking that certain negative issues should be sprung on the buyer only after the buyer is too committed to the deal to walk away. However, most buyers' negotiators would tell you that it gives the buyer a final, huge, opening to renegotiate the price or restructure the deal the way it wishes it would have done in the first place.

¶2535 Negotiating Representations, Warranties and Covenants

Once the parties have discovered and evaluated all of the compensation plans and liabilities, they must negotiate the treatment of the plans and liabilities and draft the terms of the purchase agreement accordingly. If the terms and provisions are not clear, or do not produce the desired result, the parties may end up in court, where a judge will scrutinize their meaning. In short, counsel's skill in design and drafting will meet a stern test. Representations, warranties, and covenants usually govern a few common issues, including:

- Compliance with applicable securities (and other) laws;
- Vesting of any outstanding, unvested stock awards;
- Acquirer's obligations to continue executives' employment and compensation arrangements;
- Assumption, substitution or cash-out of outstanding awards;
- Conversion formula for outstanding awards;
- Registration of assumed stock incentive plan; and
- Seller's ability to amend, modify or enter into new arrangements with executives during the period prior to closing the transaction.

.01 Compliance with Applicable Securities Laws

The acquirer will want the seller to represent and warrant that the seller has complied with all applicable federal and state securities laws in connection with its executive compensation plans and arrangements. Acquirer's counsel should review the Form S-8 filed by the seller with respect to these plans. The parties might negotiate a provision into the acquisition agreement similar to the following:

> The Company has filed with the SEC all required reports, schedules, forms, statements, financial statements and the notes thereto and other documents (including exhibits and all other information incorporated therein) required under the Securities Act of 1933 as amended (the "Securities Act") and the Securities Exchange Act of 1934 as amended (the "Exchange Act") (the "Company SEC Documents"). As of their respective dates, the Company's SEC Documents complied in all material respects with the requirements of the Securities Act or the Exchange Act, as the case may be, and the rules and regulations of the SEC promulgated thereunder applicable to such Company SEC Documents and none of the Company SEC Documents at the time they were filed (other than with respect to the transactions contemplated by this Agreement) contained any untrue statement of a material fact or omitted to state a material fact required to be stated therein or necessary in order to make the statements therein, in light of the circumstances under which they were

made, not misleading. The financial statements of the Company included in the Company SEC Documents comply as to form and substance, as of their respective dates of filing with the SEC, in all material respects with applicable accounting requirements and the published rules and regulations of the SEC with respect thereto, have been prepared in accordance with GAAP (except, in the case of unaudited statements, as permitted by Form 10-Q of the SEC) applied on a consistent basis during the periods involved (except as may be indicated in the notes thereto) and fairly present in all material respects the consolidated financial position of the Company and its consolidated Subsidiaries as of the dates thereof and the consolidated results of their operations, stockholders' equity and cash flows for the periods then ended (subject, in the case of unaudited statements, to normal recurring year-end audit adjustments) and are consistent in all material respects with the books and records of the Company and its consolidated Subsidiaries.

.02 Vesting of Outstanding, Unvested Awards

If the terms of any plan or agreement do not expressly provide for full and immediate vesting of options and awards, the parties may negotiate over this issue. For example, the parties might negotiate a provision into the acquisition agreement similar to the following:

> Prior to the Effective Time, the Company's Board of Directors shall adopt by resolution an amendment to the Company Stock Incentive Plan, which amendment shall be approved by Parent (such approval to not be unreasonably withheld), to provide that one-half of the stock award that are unvested prior to the Effective Time and held by any person employed by or providing services to the Company at the Effective Time shall become fully vested as of the Effective Time, and the other one-half of such award shall become vested over the 12-month period immediately following the Effective Time in equal amounts on a monthly basis.

.03 Seller's Executives

If the employment or other agreements do not expressly provide for the retention of the selling company's executives, the parties may negotiate over this issue. For example, the parties might negotiate a provision similar to the following:

> Each of Executive D, Executive E, Executive F, Executive G, and Executive H has executed and delivered an employment agreement, in substantially the form attached hereto as Exhibit X.

.04 Assumption, Substitution, or Cash-Out of Outstanding Awards

The parties will generally negotiate for the acquirer to assume the selling company's plan and any of the outstanding awards under the plan, or for the acquirer to substitute new awards under its existing plan for the outstanding awards under the selling company's plan. The parties might negotiate a provision similar to the following:

> Prior to the Effective Time, the Company and Parent shall take such action as may be necessary to cause each unexpired and unexercised option to purchase shares of Company Stock (each, a "Company Option") under the 2018 Stock Incentive Plan (the "Company Stock Plan"), to be exercisable solely for such number of shares of Parent Stock as is equal to the number of shares of Company Stock that could have been purchased under such Company Option

immediately prior to the Effective Time multiplied by the Stock Exchange Ratio (rounded down to the nearest whole number of shares of Parent Stock), at a price per share of Parent Stock equal to the per-share option exercise price specified in the Company Option divided by the Stock Exchange Ratio (rounded up to the nearest whole cent). Such Company Option shall otherwise be subject to the same terms and conditions (including provisions regarding vesting and the acceleration thereof) as in effect at the Effective Time. At the Effective Time, (1) all references to the Company in the Company Stock Plan and in the related stock option agreements shall be deemed to refer to Parent and (2) Parent shall assume all of the Company's obligations with respect to Company Options as so amended.

ISS has adopted certain exceptions to its share counting and other stock plan rules, which apply to substitute awards in a merger or acquisition.

.05 Registration of Assumed Stock Plan

As discussed below, by assuming the selling company's stock incentive plan and outstanding awards, the acquirer can avoid using up the stockholder-approved allocations under its own stock plan. However, the acquirer would need to register its assumption of the selling company's plan with the SEC. Accordingly, the parties might negotiate a provision similar to the following:

Not later than fifteen (15) calendar days after the Effective Time, Parent shall provide for registration of shares of Parent Stock subject to the Company Options and Restricted Stock by filing with the SEC a registration statement on Form S-8 (or any successor form) with respect to such shares of Parent Stock. Such registration shall be kept effective (and the current status of the prospectus required thereby shall be maintained in accordance with the relevant requirements of the Securities Act and the Exchange Act) at least for so long as such Company Options, and Restricted Stock remain outstanding.

.06 Changes Prior to Closing

As emphasized in ¶2525, the acquirer needs to be certain that it understands what it is acquiring. As part of any initial letter of intent and the negotiated acquisition agreements, the acquirer could insist on provisions that clearly prohibit the seller from enhancing or changing its executive compensation plans and agreements before the closing. Accordingly, the parties might negotiate a provision similar to the following:

Except for the execution and delivery of this Agreement and the transactions to take place pursuant hereto on the Closing Date, since the Audited Financial Statement Date there has not been any event or development that, individually or in the aggregate, would result in a Material Adverse Change with respect to the Company or any of its Subsidiaries. Without limiting the foregoing, except as disclosed in Clause of the Disclosure Schedule, or as permitted pursuant to Clause of the Agreement, there has not occurred between the Audited Financial Statement Date and the date hereof:

(x) Any material increase in the salary, wages or other compensation of any officer, employee or consultant of the Company or any of its Subsidiaries whose annual salary is, or after giving effect to such change would be, US dollars or more; (y) any establishment or material modification of (A) targets, goals, pools or similar provisions in respect of any fiscal year under any Benefit Plan, employment contract or other employee compensation arrangement or (B) salary ranges, increase guidelines or similar provisions in respect of any Benefit Plan, employment contract or other employee compensation arrangement; or (z) any adoption, entering into, amendment, modification or termination (partial or complete) of any Benefit Plan except to the extent required by applicable Law and, in the cases of clauses (x), (y) and (z), except in the ordinary course of business and consistent with past practices, provided that employee stock option programs may not be modified or increased.

.07 Whether A Merger Agreement Can Amend the Terms of an Employee Benefit Plan

ERISA requires that an employee benefit plan contain an amendment procedure that specifies how the plan may be modified. Any subsequent amendment of the plan must comply with the plan's amendment procedure. However, a few cases have found that a merger agreement may affect the amendment of a separate benefit plan or agreement.

In *Halliburton Co. v. Graves*,[8] the Fifth Circuit held that a provision in a merger agreement could amend a welfare plan, even if not labeled as a plan amendment. In 1998, Dresser Industries, Inc. merged into a wholly owned subsidiary of Halliburton Company. The Dresser Plan (Plan) provided that the company may amend the welfare benefit plan by a written instrument signed by the vice president of human resources. The terms of the merger agreement stated that Halliburton could amend the Plan so long as Halliburton made modifications to the plans of its own similarly situated active employees. After the merger, Halliburton attempted to make modifications to the Plan without making changes to its similarly situated active employees' plans.

The court looked to the original Plan and then applied corporate law principles, finding that officers may act on behalf of the company when that action is approved by the board of directors. In this case, Dresser's CEO and chairman of the board of directors signed the merger agreement. The board of directors also approved the merger. The court found that this action was more than sufficient to constitute an action by the company to amend the Plan. The court reached this position even though the vice president of human resources never signed the merger agreement. The actions taken by Dresser's CEO and board of directors complied with the amendment procedures set forth in the Plan and, thus, effectively amended the Plan. Therefore, Halliburton had to make changes to its similarly situated active employees' plans when amending the Plan.

Significantly, there was no language included in the merger agreement limiting the benefit continuation covenant to a specified time period. The court also found that there was no provision in the merger agreement expressly stating that the merger agreement was not intended to modify or amend a particular plan. The court went on to state that it would not express any views as to the effect of such language.

---

[8] *Halliburton Co. v. Graves*, 463 F.3d 360 (5th Cir. 2006).

In *Franklin v. First Union Corp.*,[9] the District Court for the Eastern District of Virginia held that a board resolution that approved a merger agreement amended a defined benefit pension plan. The defendant merged with Signet Banking Corporation and both parties agreed to merge their employee benefit plans. Signet provided its employees with an employee benefit plan in which employees could make investments to provide for their retirement. The Signet Plan also authorized the company, through the action of the board of directors, to amend it. Both sides approved the merger agreement. When approving the merger, Signet's Board of Directors adopted a resolution that approved all amendments contemplated by the merger. Amendment 1997-2, approved four months after the merger, was an amendment contemplated by the merger that allowed the defendant to transfer the plan's assets outside the plan. The plaintiffs were former employees who brought suit for breach of fiduciary duty. They alleged that the plan was not properly amended. The court disagreed and noted that both sides had approved the merger agreement and all amendments to carry out the agreement. Applying principles of corporate law, the court found that Signet's Board of Directors had the authority to amend the plan by means of a board resolution.

In *Beck v. Dillard*,[10] the District Court for the Eastern District of Louisiana held that a merger agreement amended a severance plan. The plaintiff's employer entered into a merger agreement with the defendant. The plaintiff's employer informed him that he was being laid off and was entitled to severance pay. The plaintiff's employer then offered the plaintiff a job, which he refused. In the merger agreement, the plaintiff's employer and the defendant modified the plaintiff's employer's preexisting severance plan. They agreed that there would be no severance pay for employees who refused continuing employment. Under these terms, the defendant refused to give the plaintiff severance pay. The court found that the merger agreement amended the severance plan. The plaintiff's employer and the defendant had the power to amend the severance plan unilaterally and thus did not violate ERISA.

See also *Ljubisaveljevic v. Nat'l City Corp.*,[11] holding that a merger agreement did not create an independent ERISA plan for severance benefits because it failed to set forth the specific intended benefits and the procedures for receiving such benefits and *Courtney v. Am. Airlines*,[12] in which AirCal's employee welfare benefit plan provided that a merger would terminate the plan and thus the plan terminated when AirCal entered into a merger agreement with the defendant.

The following federal district court cases found that a purchase agreement did not modify a benefit plan or agreement:

---

[9] *Franklin v. First Union Corp.*, 84 F. Supp. 2d 270 (E.D. Va. 2000).

[10] *Beck v. Dillard*, No. 89-5174, 1991 U.S. Dist. LEXIS 5958 (E.D. La. May 1, 1991).

[11] *Ljubisaveljevic v. Nat'l City Corp.*, C-1-05-202, 2007 U.S. Dist. LEXIS 39126 (W.D. Oh. May 30, 2007).

[12] *Courtney v. Am. Airlines*, 40 F. Supp. 2d 389 (N.D. TX. 1999).

- *Moline Machinery Ltd. v. The Pillsbury Co.:*[13] purchase agreement did not modify the plaintiff or the defendant's ERISA plan because the agreement merely referenced the plans and there was no showing that the agreement altered either of the plans.

- *Dwyer v. Galen Hosp., Inc.:*[14] purchase agreement did not modify a severance plan because the agreement never stated that it modified the plan, and purchase agreements are informal written documents that cannot legally operate to amend a plan document.

- *In Re Fairchild Indus., Inc.:*[15] purchase agreement did not amend an employee stock option plan because the purchase agreement was an informal document and contained a clause excluding third party rights.

¶2545 Stock Compensation Issues in a Change in Control

The treatment of stock compensation awards in a transaction is generally an issue of extreme interest to executives. Among the more important issues that frequently arise are:

- Whether outstanding unvested awards will become fully vested upon the change in control;

- Whether the buyer will assume outstanding awards or substitute new awards;

- How awards of the seller's stock will be converted to awards of the buyer's stock; and

- What will be the tax and accounting effects of the transaction on outstanding awards?

.01 Stock Plan Vesting

Generally, the terms of the seller's stock incentive plan will determine whether outstanding unvested awards will become fully or partially vested upon the change in control. If the plan is silent, it will be up to the seller's board of directors to determine whether to vest all outstanding awards. The seller may negotiate with buyer over whether to vest outstanding awards fully or partially.

For more than two decades, most stock plans and award agreements provided for full or partially accelerated vesting of outstanding stock awards in the event of a change in control. This trend began to reverse itself in the 2010s, as investors and proxy advisory firms pressured companies to eliminate such provisions. For example, under its Equity Plan Scorecard, for change in control vesting, ISS will award points only if the equity plan contains both of the following provisions:

- for performance-based awards, acceleration is limited to (A) actual performance achieved, (B) prorate of target based on the elapsed proportion

---

[13] *Moline Machinery Ltd. v. The Pillsbury Co.*, 259 F. Supp. 2d 892 (D. Minn. 2003).

[14] *Dwyer v. Galen Hosp., Inc.*, No. 94 C 544, 1996 U.S. Dist. LEXIS 2921 (N.D. Ill. March 11, 1996).

[15] *In Re Fairchild Indus., Inc.*, 768 F. Supp. 1528 (N.D. Fla. 1990).

of the performance period, (C) a combination of both actual and pro-rata, or (D) the performance awards are forfeited or terminated upon a change in control; and

- for time-based awards, acceleration cannot be automatic single-trigger or discretionary. Where there are no performance-based awards, points will be based solely on the treatment of time-based awards.

If the plan is silent as to treatment of awards upon a change in control, the treatment will be considered discretionary.

If a plan would permit accelerated vesting of performance awards upon a change in control (either automatically upon the change in control, at the board's discretion, or only if they are not assumed), ISS will consider whether the amount of the performance award that would be payable/vested is (a) at target level, (b) above target level, (c) prorated based on actual performance as of the change in control date and/or the time elapsed in the performance period as of the change in control date, or (d) based on board discretion.

Some stock incentive plans, executive employment agreements, and change in control severance plans give the board of directors discretionary authority to cause an acceleration of vesting or trigger of payouts, or an override right (that is, the right to determine that a change in control, as the plan or agreement defines it, did not occur). Such provisions are not recommended because they potentially put the board of directors in a position of deciding whether to benefit executives and other employees or receive the highest price for stockholders. Despite talk about a corporation's "responsibility to other stakeholders" in some enlightened circles, two hundred years of corporate law are clear: the board of directors' sole responsibility and loyalty must be to the corporation's stockholders.

Example 1: MegaCorp has made an offer to purchase all of the outstanding stock of ABC Corporation for $25.00 per share. ABC's stock incentive and change in control severance plans give the board of directors the sole authority to trigger an acceleration of vesting and eligibility for severance upon a change in control. MegaCorp has learned of these provisions through due diligence and advises ABC's board of directors that it will lowers its offer price to $24.00 per share if they vote to trigger accelerated vesting and severance. ABC's directors have two clear choices:

1. Vote to trigger accelerated vesting and severance and face a stockholders' lawsuit; or

2. Vote to accept MegaCorp's $25.00 per share offer and disappoint executives and other employees by not triggering accelerated vesting and severance.

In addition, less than full vesting of stock awards is generally recommended on a change in control to balance the desires of each party to the transaction:

- The selling company's desire for the highest purchase price;

- The purchasing company's desire to be able to retain key employees following the acquisition; and

- The desire of the executives at the acquired company for protection from a loss of employment and benefits following a change in control.

As another alternative to full vesting of awards upon a change in control, experienced legal counsel will draft some plans and agreements to provide that if the company is the surviving entity and any adjustments necessary to preserve the value of the participant's outstanding stock options have been made, or the company's successor at the time of the change in control irrevocably assumes the company's obligations under the plan or replaces the participant's outstanding stock options with stock options of equal or greater value and having terms and conditions no less favorable to the participant than those applicable to the participant's stock options immediately prior to the change in control, then the options or their replacements shall fully vest and become immediately exercisable only if the company terminates the participant's employment without cause, or the participant terminates employment with good reason within two years after the change in control.

.02 Assumption of Awards or Substitution?

Parties to a purchase transaction generally negotiate whether the buyer will assume outstanding awards or substitute new awards. Assumption means that the acquirer assumes the rights and obligations of the selling company under the stock incentive plan and stock award agreements. In an assumption situation, the number of shares subject to the award changes, but the same option or award agreements continue to govern the executives' awards. The parties adjust the exercise price and/or number of shares under the award to reflect the difference in value of the acquirer as compared to the seller. The parties make this adjustment based on the exchange ratio specified in the purchase agreement. Generally, the parties make no other changes to the stock plan or award agreement, except that the acquirer is now the plan sponsor and "the company" under the plan, and things stay the same for the executive employee.

In a substitution situation, the acquirer grants new options under its plan to replace the options and other awards under the selling company's plan. The acquirer issues new options to purchase the acquiring company's stock. The acquirer cancels the selling company's plan and awards. The primary difference from the assumption situation is that the terms of the acquiring company's plan and agreements will then control. Similar to an assumption, the new award agreements would specify a different number of shares and/or a different exercise price, based on the exchange ratio in the purchase agreement.

.03 Why Select Assumption of Awards over Substitution?

Assumption of the buyer's awards could be preferable where the acquirer's stock incentive plan is low on authorized shares or the acquirer is otherwise experiencing overhang problems. In the assumption situation, the acquirer takes over the authorized shares under the seller's plan. Thus, the acquiring company's existing authorized shares are not used up for the option or stock awards to the seller's employees, and the acquirer does not need to go back to stockholders for approval of more shares. Parties also generally find an assumption to be simpler than a substitution. If the acquirer negotiates a substitution, it may need to register the new awards on Form S-8 as a new plan. Finally, assumption greatly reduces the risk of an inadvertent modification of the options, which could have negative results under accounting, tax, or federal securities laws.

Additionally, some companies' stock incentive plans would not permit a substitution. For example, many companies' stock plans provide that the exercise price of an option cannot be below the market value of the underlying stock on the date of grant. If an acquirer grants substitute options, the substitute options will start with an exercise price below current market.

> **Planning Note:** Experienced legal counsel will sometimes draft stock option plans to permit the company to grant substitute options with an exercise price below current market value in the event of an acquisition and substitution. Institutional stockholders may object if this exception is any broader, so be careful.

Substitution could be preferable where the selling company's stock incentive plan contains terms that are unacceptable to the acquirer. However, if the terms of the acquirer's stock incentive plan are much more restrictive than the selling company's plan, the acquirer may want to do assumption instead of substitution because it does not want to start off the new relationship on a sour note.[16] Another possible argument for substitution would be if the acquiring company wants all its outstanding options to have the same terms and conditions for administrative ease.

.04 Adjusting Outstanding Award for a Transaction

All well-drafted stock incentive plans provide that, if the company's shares are changed into or exchanged for a different number or kind of shares of stock or other securities of the company or of another corporation (whether because of merger, consolidation, recapitalization, reclassification, split, reverse split, combination of shares, or otherwise) or if the number of shares is increased through the payment of a stock dividend, then the board or compensation committee will substitute for or add to each share previously appropriated, later subject to, or which may become subject to, an award, the number and kind of shares of stock or other securities into which each outstanding share was changed, for which each such share was exchanged, or to which each such share is entitled, as the case may be. Stock incentive plans also generally permit the board or compensation committee to amend outstanding awards as to price and other terms, to the extent necessary to reflect the events described above.

For example, when a company pays a dividend, particularly a large special dividend, its stock value declines by this amount after the ex-dividend date. For stockholders, this decline is offset by the cash they receive. However, dividends are not paid to holders of stock options and may not be paid to holders of RSUs (dividends generally are paid to restricted stock holders). With more companies

---

[16] This consideration is more important when the labor market is tight and retention is at a premium.

paying dividends because of the lower tax rate on "qualified dividends," companies may want to consider whether this places options and RSUs at a disadvantage, and how to adjust for it. For example, before paying its $33 million special dividend in 2004, Microsoft amended its stock incentive plan to allow the board to adjust existing options, RSUs and performance awards for special dividends (defined as any dividend other than a normal cash dividend), using the same formula it would use for other capital events such as stock splits or reorganizations. Microsoft sought the plan amendment at the same time it announced its intention to pay the special dividend.

In *Shaev v. Claflin*,[17] involving 3Com Corp.'s spin-off of its Palm Inc. subsidiary to the public, the court found that the 3Com board of directors did not breach its fiduciary duties in adjusting 3Com stock options after the spin-off to reflect a sharp drop in the company's stock price. After the spin-off of Palm, 3Com's stock price dropped from $64.56 per share to $13.37 per share. As a consequence, the stock options held by 3Com employees and directors also decreased in value. To preserve the value of the options, the board adjusted the stock options so that each 3Com option holder received 4.8 3Com stock options for each option held prior to the Palm distribution.

The strike suit lawyers sued, as they always do, alleging corporate waste and breach of fiduciary duty. However, the court found that in making the stock option adjustments, the 3Com directors acted in accordance with stock option plans approved by the stockholders, and that the adjustments did not amount to corporate waste. The 3Com plan contained provisions authorizing the board to adjust the number and exercise price of outstanding options under certain circumstances. Even though neither option plan expressly provided for an adjustment in the event of a spin-off of a subsidiary, a catch-all provision in the adjustment clause allowed the board, in the exercise of its business judgment, to decide whether there was a change in the capital structure of 3Com that was "like" or "similar" to a stock dividend, stock split, recapitalization, or reclassification.

.05 ISOs

When a company acquires and assumes a stock incentive plan, federal tax and securities laws could treat the plan as a nonstockholder-approved plan for some purposes if the company makes new awards under that plan. The acquiring company may not be able to award incentive stock options ("ISOs") under the assumed plan. If the acquirer is treated as granting new options, and those options are in the money, the options could be disqualified from ISO treatment.[18] There seems to be no direct IRS authority on the issue at this time. In a situation where the acquirer's stockholders approved the acquisition transaction (and the acquirer's assumption of the seller's option plan was described in the acquisition

---

[17] *Shaev v. Claflin*, 2004 Cal. App. Unpub. LEXIS 5840 (Cal. Ct. App. 2004). Shaev's name appears frequently as a plaintiff in strike suits.

[18] *See* Chapter 6 for a detailed discussion of the tax favored treatment of ISOs.

agreement), the IRS has held that such approval satisfied the ISO stockholder approval requirement.

However, in the situation of either an assumption or a substitution, Code Sec. 424 permits the ISO to continue as such if the parties comply with its requirements. Code Sec. 424 and the regulations thereunder provide that the status of an ISO will not be adversely affected by a substitution of a new option for the ISO, or an assumption of such ISO, by a corporation in conjunction with any corporate merger, consolidation, acquisition of property or stock, separation, reorganization, or liquidation, as long as:

1. The excess of the aggregate fair market value of the shares subject to the ISO immediately after the substitution or assumption over the aggregate option price of such shares is not more than the excess of the aggregate fair market value of all shares subject to the ISO immediately before such substitution or assumption over the aggregate option price of such shares; and

2. The new ISO or the assumption of the old ISO does not give the employee additional benefits that he or she did not have under the old ISO.[19]

Code Sec. 424(a) generally provides that no taxable event would occur upon a substitution of a new option for the old option, or an assumption of the old option, by an acquiring corporation, (or a parent or subsidiary of such corporation), by reason of a corporate merger, consolidation, acquisition of property or stock, separation, reorganization, or liquidation, as long as the parties do not increase (1) the aggregate difference of spread of selling company options, (2) the ratio of the exercise price to the fair market value of the option, measured on an option-by-option basis, or (3) the optionee's rights and benefits under the options. The same rules should apply in a transaction where a public company spins-off a subsidiary to its stockholders or sells the subsidiary's shares to the public.

In short, if the parties convert the option for the seller's stock to an option for the acquirer's stock, with no increase in value or benefit to the employee, the option can maintain its ISO status.

As a practical matter, the acceleration of ISO vesting in a change in control could cause the ISOs to exceed the $100,000 limit on ISOs that vest in any year.

.06 Cash-Out of Options

Some parties will negotiate the cash-out of unexercised options as part of a transaction. Payments should be deductible as compensation, rather than capitalized as part of the transaction. The company for which the optionee performed services, which generally is the selling company, should get the deduction for the cash-out payments. However, the acquiring company would have the withholding obligation and information-reporting obligation for the payments, since it

---

[19] Reg. § 1.425-1(a)(1)(i).

controls the payment (although the company that received the services could handle this if it is intact).[20]

.07 Cancellation of Options

Before pooling of interest accounting was eliminated as a goal for most transactions, any provision in an executive compensation plan arrangement that gave the board or compensation committee discretion to accelerate vesting or make any other decision at the time of a change in control was bad. Even after pooling of interest accounting was eliminated, provisions granting the board or compensation committee discretion in matters of executive compensation are often disfavored. The reasoning is that the board of a selling corporation would be forced to make a decision between favoring the employees and risking a lower purchase price for (and lawsuit from) stockholders, and favoring the stockholders and risking disappointment among the employees.

However, there are some circumstances under which the discretionary provisions are helpful. For example, the following provision in a company's stock option plan could reserve valuable discretion to the compensation committee of the company's board of directors:

> The Committee shall have the discretion to provide in applicable Award Agreements that, in the event of a "Change in Control" of the Company, the following provisions will apply:
>
> (1) Each outstanding Option will immediately become exercisable in full.
>
> (2) In the event of a Change in Control that is a merger or a consolidation in which the Company is not the surviving corporation or which results in the acquisition of substantially all of the Company's outstanding Stock by a single person or entity or by a group of persons or entities acting in concert, or in the event of a sale or transfer of all or substantially all of the Company's assets (a "Covered Transaction"), the Committee shall have the discretion to provide for the termination of all outstanding Options as of the effective date of the Covered Transaction; provided, that, if the Covered Transaction follows a Change in Control or would give rise to a Change in Control, no Option will be so terminated (without the consent of the Participant) prior to the expiration of 20 days following the later of (i) the date on which the Award became fully exercisable and (ii) the date on which the Participant received written notice of the Covered Transaction.

The key language is in paragraph (2) above. Among the scenarios under which this discretion is particularly useful to all parties are the following (keep in mind that most option agreements do not permit the company to terminate the option if it is not exercised):

1. ABC Corporation buys XYZ Corporation. XYZ is a tech company with millions of outstanding options. Most are underwater. ABC does not want the dilution that will come by acquiring so many outstanding

---

[20] Code Sec. 280G imposes an excise tax on disqualified individuals who receive a payment that is contingent on a change in control, such as the value of accelerated option vesting.

options and advises XYZ that: "We will assume the outstanding options for your top ten employees (by substituting options to purchase ABC stock). We will not assume the other 900,000+ options."

2. A sale of assets occurs when some or all of the outstanding options are underwater. Obviously, no optionee will want to exercise the options. However, absent some affirmative action, the legal contract formed by the option agreement does not go away. Most likely, there is never any liability or issue, but clients do not feel good about these undying options floating around for the next 10 years.

Under each of these scenarios, the language cited in the example would give the compensation committee the ability and right to eliminate all outstanding options, after first giving the optionees a fair chance to exercise their options.

Litigation brought by former executives of MediaOne Group, Inc. and U. S. West, Inc. against AT&T Corp. and AT&T Wireless Services, Inc. illustrates how this problem arises in the real world.[21] Plaintiffs originally received stock options from MediaOne or U. S. West. The options were exchanged for AT&T options when MediaOne was acquired by AT&T, and when AT&T Wireless was split off from AT&T in 2001, the options were adjusted. According to the lawsuit, in February 2004, Wireless revealed that it would, in effect, unilaterally cancel plaintiffs' out-of-the-money options when it merged with Cingular Wireless Corporation. In addition to canceling out-of-the-money options as part of the Cingular merger, the lawsuit alleged that Wireless would be cashing out plaintiffs' in-the-money options at a discount. This second claim was based on the fact that Wireless was paying the spread between the merger price and the exercise price for the options, rather than paying plaintiff's calculated Black-Scholes value for the options. The lawsuit alleged that AT&T "expressly promised to preserve the value of the options," including in connection with future mergers or changes in control, in connection with its acquisition of MediaOne, based on language in the applicable stock option plan, which provided that, in the event of "any consolidation, combination, recapitalization, split-off, spin-off, combination of shares, exchange of shares or other like change in capital structure, the number of kind of shares or interests subject to an Award and the per share price or value thereof shall be appropriately adjusted at the time of such event, provided that each Participant's economic position with respect to the Award shall not, as a result of such adjustment, be worse than it had been immediately prior to such event."

.08 Accounting Issues

Before repeal of pooling of interest accounting, it was imperative that a selling company not modify options before the transaction. Now, companies can make pre-merger changes without worrying about an additional accounting charge.

---

[21] *Lillis v. AT&T Corp.*, Delaware Court of Chancery, Filed September 24, 2004.

For example, where the selling company's options are far out of the money, the parties may agree to have the selling company reprice the options on the eve of the transaction, which would greatly benefit the seller's employees without adversely affecting the acquirer's ability to assume the options and avoid over-hang issues. The repricing will still trigger variable accounting for the seller, but only for a moment in time before the transaction.

.09 Securities Law Issues

In a significant acquisition by a public company, the acquirer often will file with the SEC a Form S-4 to register shares of the acquirer's common stock issuable in the merger. The shares registered should cover shares of the acquirer's common stock that both (i) will be issued to the target's stockholders in exchange for their outstanding common stock at the closing of the merger and (ii) may be issued upon the exercise of the converted options. Then, prior to the time that the converted options become exercisable, the acquirer would register the common stock issuable upon the exercise of the options on Form S-8. The primary advantage of this method is avoidance of the need to pay a separate registration fee for the shares registered on Form S-8. The S-8 registration would be effective upon filing with the SEC.

Once the S-8 registration is made, the acquirer would be in a position to satisfy the prospectus requirements related to offerings of securities registered on Form S-8.[22] SEC rules require the acquirer to deliver to each option holder the information required by Part I of Form S-8.[23] This information, together with the documents incorporated by reference in the S-8 registration, constitutes a pro-spectus (the "10(a) prospectus") that meets the requirements of Section 10(a) of the Securities Act.

The SEC has provided relief for the potential Section 16b violation that could occur where an executive of the seller company, who is an "insider" for Section 16 purposes, is then deemed to have received options upon the acquirer's assumption or substitution of its options or awards for those of the seller. Under a no-action letter issued by the SEC,[24] the seller's insiders could avoid Section 16 liability for short swing profits if the selling company's board of directors approves the disposition of the seller's stock by insiders before the date of the transaction. Section 16 would treat the sale as a "disposition to the company," which is an exempt transaction and would not be matched against open market transactions within the preceding six months. If one of the selling company's employees could be a Section 16 insider of the acquirer, the acquirer's board would need to vote on and approve the acquirer's assumption or substitution of his or her selling company awards so that the acquisition of acquirer stock would not be treated as a matchable transaction.

Planning Note: When in doubt, the companies' boards of directors should vote on and approve any purchases and the assumption or substitu-

---

[22] Such requirements are set forth in Rule 428 of Regulation C (17 CFR 230.428).

[23] Rule 428(b)(1).

[24] Skadden, Arps, Slate, Meagher & Flom LLP, January 12, 1999.

tion for any selling company employee who could conceivably be a Section 16 insider of the acquirer.

Example 2: ABC Corporation hires Executive D as its new chief executive officer on September 5, 2018. On her date of hire, D purchases 100,000 shares of ABC stock at $25.00 per share in the open market to show her confidence in and commitment to ABC. On December 15, 2018, MegaCorp acquires all of the outstanding stock of ABC (including, of course, the stock recently purchased by D) for $40.00 per share.

.10 Tender Offer Issue

To ensure fairness in the market, Rule 14d-10, known as the "all-holders, best-price" rule, promulgated under the Securities Exchange Act of 1934,[25] provides that: "No bidder shall make a tender offer unless . . . [t]he consideration paid to any security holder pursuant to the tender offer is the highest consideration paid to any other security holder during such tender offer." That is, all stockholders tendering shares during a tender offer must receive the same consideration. The tender offer best-price rule was adopted to assure fair and equal treatment of all security holders of the class of securities that are the subject of a tender offer by requiring that the consideration paid to any security holder is the highest paid to any other security holder in the tender offer.[26] (References to the "tender offer best-price rule" or the "best-price rule" are intended to refer to both Exchange Act Rule 13e-4(f)(8)(ii) and Exchange Act Rule 14d-10(a)(2).)

Compensation agreements and payments to executives of a target company can raise issues in the context of a tender offer. Some courts have held that certain executive compensation payments in connection with a tender offer constitute disparate treatment of stockholders in violation of Rule 14d-10. Generally speaking, executive compensation arrangements that were in existence prior to the commencement of the tender offer do not create issues. However, where special payments are made to one or more executives that could be perceived as inducements for them to go along with the deal, a court may find a violation of Rule 14d-10.[27]

The best-price rule was the basis for baseless litigation until 2006, with plaintiffs claiming that the bidder violated the best-price rule by entering into new agreements, or adopting the target company's existing agreements, with executive who also are stockholders of the target.[28] The agreements or arrangements with stockholders that most frequently are the subject of best-price rule litigation have involved employment compensation, severance or other employee benefit arrangements with employees or directors of the subject company.

---

[25] 17 C.F.R. § 240.14d-10.

[26] See Amendments to Tender Offer Rules: All-Holders and Best-Price, Release No. 34-23421 (July 11, 1986) [51 FR 25873] (the "Rule 14d-10 Adopting Release").

[27] *Epstein v. MCA, Inc.*, 50 F3d 644 (9th Cir. 1995).

[28] See, *e.g., Epstein v. MCA*, 50 F.3d 644 (9th Cir. 1995), rev'd on other grounds sub nom. *Matsushita Electrical Industrial Co. v. Epstein*, 516 U.S. 367 (1996); *Lerro v. Quaker Oats*, 84 F.3d 239 (7th Cir. 1996); *Walker v. Shield Acquisition Corp.*, 145 F. Supp.2d 1360 (N.D. GA 2001).

The SEC clarified the "best price" tender offer rule in 2006 by exempting employment compensation, severance and employee benefit arrangements that meet specified criteria and creating a safe harbor for such arrangements that are approved by independent directors under procedures set forth in the amendments.[29]

Employment compensation, severance and other employee benefit arrangements would be exempt if the amount payable: (i) is being paid or granted for past services performed or future services to be performed or refrained from performing, and (ii) is not calculated based on the number of securities tendered. The SEC created a safe harbor for compensatory arrangements, that are approved by the compensation committee or another committee of the board, comprised solely of independent directors, of either the target company or, for any such arrangement to which the acquirer is a party, the acquirer.

.11 Stock Exchange Requirements

With certain exceptions, both the New York Stock Exchange ("NYSE") and Nasdaq rules require member companies to obtain stockholder approval of any plan under which shares may be issued to executive officers or directors. However, as long as the acquirer makes no material amendment to the terms of the seller's plan, the stock exchanges would not require approval of the acquirer's stockholders for either the assumption of the outstanding options or the future grant of acquirer options under the plan. The stock exchange rules are evolving. Therefore, an acquiring company should contact its NYSE or Nasdaq representative to be sure that the representative agrees with the foregoing analysis (and so that it can make a note of a specific conversation for its files).

Section 303A.08 of the NYSE's Listed Company Manual, "Shareholder Approval of Equity Compensation Plans," provides that: "Shareholders must be given the opportunity to vote on all equity-compensation plans and material revisions thereto, with limited exemptions explained below." Section 303A.08 provides two exceptions from the shareholder approval requirements in the context of corporate mergers and acquisitions.[30]

- Shareholder approval will not be required to convert, replace, or adjust outstanding options or other equity-compensation awards to reflect the transaction.

- Shares available under certain plans acquired in corporate acquisitions and mergers may be used for certain post-transaction grants without further shareholder approval. This exemption applies to situations where a party that is not a listed company following the transaction has shares available for grant under pre-existing plans that were previously approved by shareholders. A plan adopted in contemplation of the merger

---

[29] Release Nos. 34-54684; IC-27542; November 1, 2006.

[30] Both the NYSE and the Nasdaq provide an exception from the shareholder approval requirements in the context of corporate mergers and acquisitions.

or acquisition transaction would not be considered "pre-existing" for purposes of this exemption.

The NYSE rules provide that an acquirer may use the shares available under a pre-existing (acquirer) plan for post-transaction grants of options and other awards with respect to equity of the acquirer, either under the pre-existing plan or another plan, without further shareholder approval, so long as:

- the number of shares available for grants is appropriately adjusted to reflect the transaction;

- the time during which those shares are available is not extended beyond the period when they would have been available under the pre-existing plan, absent the transaction; and

- the options and other awards are not granted to individuals who were employed, immediately before the transaction, by the post-transaction listed company or entities that were its subsidiaries immediately before the transaction.

The NYSE would count any shares reserved for listing in connection with a transaction pursuant to either of these exemptions in determining whether the transaction involved the issuance of 20% or more of the company's outstanding common stock and, thus, required shareholder approval under the Listed Company Manual.[31]

Whether shareholder approval of an acquired company's stock plan would be required in connection with the acquisition would depend on the applicable stock exchange rules and state law. Generally, if a company wants to have additional shares in the plan to make subsequent grants, it should get shareholder approval and just add the shares to its own plan. The NYSE rules allow a company to make future grants under the acquired company's old plan if the acquired company was public and got shareholder approval of the shares reserved under that plan. For Nasdaq companies, there is an M&A exception, so that the acquirer doesn't need to obtain shareholder approval to assume the target's plan; however, the acquirer cannot use the target company's plan share reserve for grants to its own employees unless it obtains shareholder approval.

.12 Public Company Assumption of Acquired Private Company's Stock Plan

When a public company acquires a private company with a stock incentive plan and outstanding stock awards, an issue that frequently arises is whether the acquirer can assume the seller's plan and continue to make awards under the plan without seeking stockholder approval of the plan by the acquirer's stockholders. A public company generally seeks stockholder approval of its stock incentive plan for several reasons, including stock exchange requirements (as discussed above) and the rules related to ISOs under Code Sec. 422.

---

[31] Section 312.03(c).

.13 Code Sec. 162(m)

Code Sec. 162(m) provides that a publicly held corporation may not claim a deduction for "applicable remuneration" over $1 million in the case of certain employees. Prior to 2018, Code Sec. 162(m) included an exception to the deduction limit for performance-based compensation. The legislation known as the Tax Cuts and Jobs Act of 2017 ("TCJA") signed into law by President Trump in December 2017, eliminated that exception.

¶2555 Conversion of Outstanding Awards

In either an assumption or a substitution situation, the mechanism for converting selling company stock options and restricted stock awards into acquirer options and awards is critical. The goal in nearly every transaction is to put the target company executives in the exact same place *vis-à-vis* the acquiring company as they were with respect to the target, that is, to preserve any increase in the value of the awards before the transaction. Moreover, the parties must provide for a conversion that does not confer additional rights or benefits on the optionee in order to preserve ISO treatment and, until 2018, the exclusion from Code Sec. 162(m).

Most companies would determine the conversion ratio as follows:

> First, divide the purchase price by the share price of acquirer's stock on the day before close (or potentially an average of acquirer's share price over a few days). This will indicate the number of acquirer shares necessary to purchase target. Next, divide this number by the number of fully diluted common shares of target at close. This will give us a conversion ratio. The ratio indicates the number of acquirer shares a holder of target shares will receive upon close. The following example below demonstrates this calculation:
>
> Purchase price: $430,000,000
>
> Fully diluted target shares: 29,351,976
>
> Acquirer share price: $145.00

$$\frac{\$430,000,000}{\$145.00} = 2,965,517 \qquad \frac{2,965,517}{29,351,976} = .10103 \text{ (conversion ratio)}$$

Next, apply this conversion ratio to outstanding stock options and restricted shares to convert them into acquirer shares upon close. In the case of a restricted share, multiply the number of outstanding target shares by the conversion ratio. To convert an outstanding stock option, divide the exercise price by the conversion ratio and multiply the number of outstanding stock options by the conversion ratio. Any vesting restrictions on the options or shares remain intact.

Example: ABC Corporation acquires 100% of the outstanding stock of XYZ Corp. for a negotiated price of $430 million. XYZ's stock incentive plan provides that unvested XYZ stock options and restricted shares are vested 50% upon close and 50% ratably over the 12 months immediately following the transaction. All outstanding XYZ awards will be converted to ABC awards. On the closing date of the transaction, XYZ Corp. has exactly 29,351,976 fully diluted shares outstanding (including outstanding awards).

Step 1: Calculating the Conversion Ratio: Using the purchase price of $430 million, an acquirer share price of $145.00, and fully diluted shares for target of 29,351,976, a conversion ratio of .10103 is determined as shown below.

Purchase price: $430,000,000

Fully diluted target shares: 29,351,976

Acquirer share price: $145.00

$$\frac{\dfrac{\$430,000,000}{\$145.00} = 2,965,517}{29,351,976} = \frac{2,965,517}{29,351,976} = .10103 \text{ (conversion ratio)}$$

Step 2: Convert the Shares: Apply the .10103 conversion ratio to the outstanding stock options and restricted shares to convert them into ABC shares upon close. In the case of a restricted share, multiply the number of outstanding target shares by the conversion ratio. To convert an outstanding stock option, divide the exercise price by the conversion ratio and multiply the number of outstanding stock options by the conversion ratio.

By dividing the $430 million purchase price by the number of fully diluted target shares, XYZ's value per share is determined to be $14.65.

Step 3: Convert the awards to ABC shares: The table below displays the pre- and post-conversion awards and values. The conversion should leave XYZ's employees holding the same "intrinsic" value after the conversion as before the conversion.

	Number of Shares	Value of Shares
XYZ Options—Pre-conversion ($.273 ex. price)	653,000	$9,388,038
XYZ Restricted Shares—Pre-conversion	7,858,130	$115,119,879
Pre-Conversion Total (XYZ shares)	**8,511,130**	**$124,507,917**
XYZ Options—Post-conversion ($2.70 ex. price)	65,974	$9,388,038
XYZ Restricted Shares—Post-conversion	793,390	$115,119,879
Post-Conversion Total (ABC shares)	**859,904**	**$124,507,917**

.01 When Conversion Is Not Available

In some transactions, the parties will not be able or willing to convert the target company's options and/or restricted stock awards into options and awards for the acquirer's stock. Two common situations where this occurs are (1) when a private company acquires a public company and (2) when the acquirer pays cash instead of stock for the target. In these transactions, the parties may need to negotiate the cash-out of the target company's options and/or restricted stock awards. From the executives' standpoint, the most desirable approach would be for the acquirer to treat all awards as fully vested and pay each executive cash equal to the transaction purchase price, for restricted stock, and the spread between the option exercise price and the transaction purchase price, for options. However, the parties in some transactions will negotiate for a termination of underwater options and all unvested awards.

The parties would need to examine the plan documents and any employment agreements to determine whether vesting and/or cash-out is automatic or a subject of negotiation for the parties. Additionally, the plan documents or employment agreements may require the optionee's consent to a cash-out or other action that may alter or impair the optionee's rights.

Finally, when the acquirer is not assuming the seller's stock incentive plans, the parties (particularly the buyer) need to ensure that such plans are terminated. Most stock incentive plans do not provide for termination upon change in control. However, most plans provide that the company may amend or terminate the plan at any time (subject to the rule on actions that alter or impair participants' rights). The parties should draft into the merger or acquisition agreement specific provisions requiring termination or other disposition of the plan as of the effective date of the transaction.

.02 Earn-Outs

Converting selling company options to acquiring company options will be complicated when there is an earn-out or other contingent payment. The IRS has approved situations where a company gave the optionees the right to receive the same amount of shares that they would have received if they had been a stockholder at the time of the transaction, by implementing a formula that allowed them to participate in the earn-out as if they had exercised the options and become stockholders. Alternatively, a company may be able to calculate the exercise price for the number of shares by determining the present value of the contingent shares or the right to receive future payments, and use that value to convert the selling company options to acquiring company options.[32] The IRS has indicated in its proposed regulations that the company does not have to establish the exchange ratios before the merger to get the protection of Code Sec. 424.[33]

Another issue for ISOs is when transaction consideration is part cash and part stock. This may prevent a conversion under Code Sec. 424. Parties want to provide that optionees have the right to acquire cash only, or allow optionees to exercise and receive stock immediately before the transaction.

.03 Fractional Shares

Applying the exchange ratios and converting the selling company options and awards into options to purchase acquiring company stock in a merger or acquisition transaction can create fractional shares. Most companies do not want to grant options or other awards for fractional shares.[34] The IRS has approved

---

[32] Presentation at National Association of Stock Plan Professionals Conference 2002, Las Vegas, Nevada.

[33] Proposed Reg. § 1.424-1(a)(5)(iii).

[34] One exception is Citigroup, which granted options over fractional shares in its 1996 acquisition of

several methods of dealing with fractional shares, including giving the optionee cash in lieu of shares at the time of exercise (or credit the amount toward what the company would withhold for income tax purposes).[35]

¶2565 Code Sec. 409A

Code Sec. 409A sets forth some of the most complicated rules and restrictions affecting executive compensation. Therefore, upon the scrutiny applied in the due diligence process, compliance issues frequently arise under Code Sec. 409A.

For most companies, Code Sec. 409A and the regulations thereunder create three categories of compensation and benefits about which to worry, with different (albeit, overlapping) issues applicable to each. The provisions of the regulations can be separated into rules applicable to, and amendments required of:

1. Deferred compensation and supplemental retirement benefits, generally provided under nonqualified plans (sometimes provided under employment or other agreements),

2. Severance benefits, generally provided under employment or change in control agreements and severance plans (see Chapter 14), and

3. Equity-based compensation, generally provided under stock incentive plans and awards (see Chapters 6, 7 and 8).

The regulation under Code Sec. 409A contain a variety of special rules for payment, distributions and benefits payable following a change in control event described in the regulations.

.01 Change in Control Events

The regulation under Code Sec. 409A describe three types of change in control events: (1) change in the ownership of a corporation;[36] (2) change in the effective control of a corporation;[37] and (3) change in the ownership of a substantial portion of a corporation's assets.[38] The definitions in the Code Sec. 409A regulations are similar to those used by most corporations in their employment and change in control agreements and equity compensation plans. However, the definitions are not identical and other definitions or events "shalt" not qualify.[39]

A change in the ownership of a corporation occurs on the date that any one person, or more than one person acting as a group, acquires ownership of stock of the corporation that, together with stock held by such person or group, constitutes more than 50% of the total fair market value or total voting power of

---

(Footnote Continued)

Travelers. *See* Citigroup presentation at National Association of Stock Plan Professionals Conference 2002, Las Vegas, Nevada.

[35] IRS Letter Ruling 8635038 (June 3, 1986).

[36] Treas. Reg. § 1.409A-3(i)(5)(v).

[37] Treas. Reg. § 1.409A-3(i)(5)(vi).

[38] Treas. Reg. § 1.409A-3(i)(5)(vii).

[39] ".. then shalt thou count to three, no more, no less. Three shall be the number thou shalt count, and the number of the counting shall be three. Four shalt thou not count, neither count thou two, excepting that thou then proceed to three. Five is right out." *Book of Armaments* (Chapter 2, verses 9-21), *Monty Python and the Holy Grail*, Sony Pictures.

the stock of such corporation.[40] However, if any one person, or more than one person acting as a group, is considered to own more than 50% of the total fair market value or total voting power of the stock of a corporation, the regulations do not consider the acquisition of additional stock by the same person or persons to cause a change in the ownership of the corporation. An increase in the percentage of stock owned by any one person, or persons acting as a group, as a result of a transaction in which the corporation acquires its stock in exchange for property will be treated as an acquisition of stock for purposes of this section. This definition applies only when there is a transfer of stock of a corporation (or issuance of stock of a corporation) and stock in such corporation remains outstanding after the transaction.

For purposes of the change in the ownership of a corporation and change in the effective control of a corporation definitions, persons will be considered to be acting as a group if they are owners of a corporation that enters into a merger, consolidation, purchase or acquisition of stock, or similar business transaction with the corporation. If a person, including an entity, owns stock in both corporations that enter into a merger, consolidation, purchase or acquisition of stock, or similar transaction, the regulations consider that stockholder to be acting as a group with other stockholders only with respect to the ownership in the corporation before the transaction giving rise to the change and not with respect to the ownership interest in the other corporation. Persons will not be considered to be acting as a group solely because they purchase or own stock of the same corporation at the same time, or as a result of the same public offering.

A change in the effective control of a corporation occurs only on either of the following dates:

(1) The date any one person, or more than one person acting as a group acquires (or has acquired during the 12-month period ending on the date of the most recent acquisition by such person or persons) owner-ship of stock of the corporation possessing 30% or more of the total voting power of the stock of such corporation.[41]

(2) The date a majority of members of the corporation's board of directors is replaced during any 12-month period by directors whose appoint-ment or election is not endorsed by a majority of the members of the corporation's board of directors before the date of the appointment or election.

A change in the ownership of a substantial portion of a corporation's assets occurs on the date that any one person, or more than one person acting as a group, acquires (or has acquired during the 12-month period ending on the date of the most recent acquisition by such person or persons) assets from the corporation that have a total gross fair market value equal to or more than 40% of

---

[40] A plan or agreement may provide that amounts payable upon a change in the ownership of a corpo-ration will be paid only if the conditions in the preceding sentence are satisfied but substituting a percentage specified in the plan that is higher than 50%, but only if the provision is set forth in the plan or agreement. Treas. Reg. § 1.409A-3(i)(5)(v)(A).

[41] The plan or agreement may specify a percent-age higher than 30%. Treas. Reg. § 1.409A-3(i)(5)(v)(A)(1).

the total gross fair market value of all of the corporation's assets immediately before such acquisition or acquisitions. For this purpose, gross fair market value means the value of the assets of the corporation, or the value of the assets being disposed of, determined without regard to any liabilities associated with such assets.

A change in effective control may occur in a transaction in which one of the two corporations involved in the transaction has a change in control event. For example, assume ABC Corporation transfers more than 40% of the total gross fair market value of its assets to XYZ Corporation in exchange for 35% of XYZ's stock. Under Code Sec. 409A, ABC has undergone a change in ownership of a substantial portion of its assets and XYZ has a change in effective control.

If any one person, or more than one person acting as a group, is considered to effectively control a corporation, the acquisition of additional control of the corporation by the same person or persons is not considered to cause a change in the effective control of the corporation (or to cause a change in the ownership of the corporation).

.02 Earn-Outs and Other Delayed Payments

The regulations under Code Sec. 409A provide special rules for certain delayed payments pursuant to a change in control event.[42] The regulations provide that payments of compensation related to a change in control event that occur because an employer purchases its stock held by the employee or because the employer or a third party purchases a stock right held by an employee, or that are calculated by reference to the value of stock of the employer (collectively, "transaction-based compensation"), may be treated as paid at a designated date or pursuant to a payment schedule that complies with the requirements of Code Sec. 409A if the transaction-based compensation is paid on the same schedule and under the same terms and conditions as apply to payments to stockholders generally with respect to stock of the employer pursuant to a change in the ownership of a corporation or as apply to payments to the employer pursuant to a change in the ownership of a substantial portion of a corporation's assets. The regulations provide that, to the extent that the transaction-based compensation is paid not later than five years after the change in control event, the payment of such compensation will not violate the initial or subsequent deferral election rules of Code Sec. 409A solely as a result of such transaction-based compensation being paid pursuant to such schedule and terms and conditions. The regulations also provide for transaction-based compensation that is subject to conditions that constitute a substantial risk of forfeiture.[43]

.03 Employer Stock Rules

Code Sec. 409A does not apply to stock awards that satisfy certain requirements, including (i) the award must be based on the stock of the recipient's

---

[42] Treas. Reg. § 1.409A-3(i)(5)(iv).

[43] Or to payments to the employer pursuant to a change in the ownership of a substantial portion of a corporation's assets. Treas. Reg. § 1.409A-3(i)(5)(iv)(B).

employer, and (ii) the award may not be modified. However, the regulations provide exceptions for substitutions and assumptions of employer stock by reason of a corporate transaction.[44]

.04 Different Form or Time of Distribution Following a Change in Control Event

Under Code Sec. 409A and the regulations, a plan or agreement may designate only one time and form of payment for each of the permitted distribution events. For example, a plan or agreement that provides for payment upon a separation from service could provide for two years of salary continuation for a termination by the company without cause and a lump sum payment equal to two times the employee's annual salary for termination within two years after a change in control event. However, the plan or agreement can only provide for this different form and timing of payment if the definition of change in control complies with the one in the Code Sec. 409A regulations (which is described above).[45]

.05 Plan Termination Following a Change in Control Event

Code Sec. 409A and the regulations also provide special rules permitting the termination of a nonqualified deferred compensation plan and acceleration of benefits following a change in control event.[46] A plan may provide for the acceleration of the time and form of a payment, or a payment under such plan may be made, where the acceleration of the payment is made pursuant to a termination and liquidation of the plan under one of three scenarios specified in the regulations. One of the scenarios under which an employer may terminate a plan and accelerate distributions is the employer's termination and liquidation of the plan pursuant to irrevocable action taken by the employer within the 30 days preceding or the 12 months following a change in control event.[47] Under this exception, the employer also must terminate all other plans and agreements that it sponsored and distribute all amounts of compensation deferred under the terminated plans and agreements within 12 months of the date the employer irrevocably takes all necessary action to terminate the plans and agreements. The regulations also provide that where the change in control event results from an asset purchase transaction, the employer with the discretion to liquidate and terminate the plan and agreements is the employer that is primarily liable immediately after the transaction for the payment of the deferred compensation.

In June 2016, the Department of the Treasury and the Internal Revenue Service issued proposed amendments to the final regulations under Code Sec. 409A. The proposed regulations clarify that the acceleration of a payment under this exception is permitted only if the employer terminates and liquidates all plans of the same category that it sponsors, and not merely all plans of the same category in which a particular employee actually participates. The proposed regulations also clarify that for a period of three years following the termination

[44] Treas. Reg. § 1.409A-1(b)(5)(iii)(E)(4) and (v)(D).
[45] Treas. Reg. § 1.409A-3(c).
[46] Treas. Reg. § 1.409A-3(j)(4)(ix).
[47] Treas. Reg. § 1.409A-3(j)(4)(ix)(B).

and liquidation of a plan, neither the buyer nor the seller can adopt a new plan of the same category as the terminated and liquidated plan, regardless of which employees participate in such plan. Although this guidance was published as proposed regulations, the IRS characterized this provision as a clarification, not a change, so it applies retroactively to the date of the initial issuance of the 2007 final regulations.

.06 Transaction-Based Compensation

The regulations under Code Sec. 409A provide special rules for payments of so-called "transaction-based compensation," which is a payment made to an employee as a result of the acquisition or merger of his or her employer and the purchase of stock or stock rights held by the employee. Under the regulations, transaction-based compensation may be treated as paid at a designated date or pursuant to a payment schedule that complies with the requirements of Code Sec. 409A if it is paid on the same schedule and under the same terms and conditions as apply to payments to stockholders generally with respect to stock of the seller in the change in control. Additionally, transaction-based compensation will not fail to meet the requirements of the initial or subsequent deferral election rules under Code Sec. 409A if it is paid not later than five years after the change in control event. The final regulations failed, however, to discuss whether stock right gain (or "spread") could similarly be distributed over that same schedule.

The proposed regulations issued by the IRS in 2016 confirm that the special payment rules for transaction-based compensation apply to an ISO or a stock right that did not otherwise provide for deferred compensation before the purchase or agreement to purchase the stock right. Note, however, that the new proposed regulations did not address a menacing issue that arises in some transactions, which is whether stock right spread that remains unvested at the time of a transaction can be converted into an unvested restricted stock unit or other unvested amount. Many practitioners believe that these approaches are consistent with both the intended economics of the stock right and the spirit of Code Sec. 409A.

Chapter 26
EXECUTIVE COMPENSATION FOR TAX-EXEMPT ENTITIES

¶2601 Overview—Executive Compensation for Tax-Exempt Entities

Tax-exempt entities face unique issues when compensating executive employees. Although not all tax-exempt entities are small, struggling charitable organizations, certainly the compensation packages of executives at tax-exempt entities often feature dollar amounts with one less "zero" at the end. However, a number of critical legal distinctions and requirements apply as well. Specifically, in exchange for their tax-exempt status, these entities must comply with two additional Internal Revenue Code sections that limit the type and amount of compensation they can pay to directors, executives and other employees.

.01 Types of Tax-Exempt Entities

The tax-exempt entities that face executive compensation issues usually are not the small, struggling charitable or civic organizations. Generally, only the large, national charities and not-for-profit organizations have both the interest and wherewithal to create significant compensation packages for executive employees. These organizations, such as the Red Cross and the United Way, control enormous budgets and face huge logistical issues, which require top-drawer executive talent to manage. Many of the nation's largest hospitals and health systems are also tax-exempt entities.

.02 Deferred Compensation

In contrast to the deferred compensation programs maintained by private sector employers discussed in Chapter 17 [¶1701 *et seq.*], Code Sec. 457 governs the nonqualified deferred compensation plans provided by a state, political subdivision of a state, any agency or instrumentality of a state or political subdivision of a state, and any other organization (other than a governmental unit) exempt from federal income taxes.[1] Code Sec. 457 applies to both employees and independent contractors performing services for state and local governments and tax-exempt organizations. For example, a physician who contracts with a tax-exempt hospital as an independent contractor would be eligible to defer compensation under Code Sec. 457. Code Sec. 409A also applies to some Code Sec. 457 Plans (see ¶2615 for a detailed discussion of deferred compensation issues for tax-exempt entities).

---

[1] Code Sec. 457(e).

.03 Excess Benefit Transactions

Neither a public charity nor a private foundation can provide more than reasonable compensation. Reasonable compensation is determined with respect to the market value of the services performed and depends upon the circumstances of the case. In general, reasonable compensation is measured with reference to the amount that would ordinarily be paid for comparable services by comparable enterprises under comparable circumstances.

The Internal Revenue Code has long contained restrictions on "private inurement" for the directors, officers, and employees of tax-exempt entities. If the private inurement rules are broken, the organization can lose its tax-exempt status. Because the penalty for violating the private inurement rules was so harsh, Congress sought to enact new laws that would allow lesser penalties for lesser violations. This effort resulted in the passage of Code Sec. 4958, part of the Taxpayer Bill of Rights II. Code Sec. 4958 applies to so-called "excess benefit transactions" by 501(c)(3) and 501(c)(4) organizations, and places specific restrictions on transactions with "disqualified parties." A disqualified party is any person in a position to exercise substantial influence over the affairs of an organization any time during the five-year period ending on the date of the transaction. While organizations are subject to penalties under the private inurement doctrine, individuals are subject to penalties under Code Sec. 4958. To avoid Code Sec. 4958 penalties, tax-exempt organizations must tailor all transactions with disqualified persons to meet Code Sec. 4958's presumption of reasonableness (see ¶2635).

.04 Code Sec. 409A

Code Sec. 409A applies to any plan, program, or agreement providing for deferred compensation.[2] Under Code Sec. 409A, the term nonqualified deferred compensation plan does not include any eligible deferred compensation plan within the meaning of Code Sec. 457(b).[3] However, the rules of Code Sec. 409A apply to nonqualified deferred compensation plans under Code Sec. 457(f) in addition to any requirements already applicable to such plans under Code Sec. 457(f) (see ¶2645).[4]

.05 Code Sec. 4960 Excise Tax on Excess Compensation and Excess Parachute Payments

The legislation knowns as the Tax Cuts and Jobs Act of 2017 ("TCJA"), signed into law by President Trump in December 2017, added a new Code Sec. 4960, which imposes a 21% excise tax on excessive executive compensation and excessive separation payments paid by certain tax-exempt organizations to their covered employees (see ¶2665).

---

[2] Added by the American Jobs Creation Act of 2004, P.L. 108-357.

[3] Notice 2005-1, Q&A 3(b).

[4] Notice 2005-1, Q&A 6.

¶2615 Deferred Compensation

Employees or independent contractors who defer compensation under Code Sec. 457 are considered participants of Code Sec. 457 plans. State and local governmental employers can fund their Code Sec. 457 plans for employees and can offer catch-up contributions after age 50. Code Sec. 457(b) governs eligible plans, while Code Sec. 457(f) covers ineligible plans. A plan cannot be both eligible and ineligible. Deferred compensation under an eligible Code Sec. 457 plan is not taxed until the plan actually pays or makes it available to the participant.

.01 Annual Deferrals

The regulations define an annual deferral as all amounts contributed or deferred under an eligible plan, whether by voluntary salary reduction contribution or by other employer contribution, and all earnings thereon.[5] This definition includes both elective and nonelective contributions. Agreements to defer compensation will be valid if made before the first day of the month in which the compensation is paid or made available.[6] There is no requirement that the agreement itself exist before the beginning of the services giving rise to the compensation. However, the parties must finalize any agreement to defer compensation in the first month of employment, before the plan participant begins work.[7] Plans must be in writing, include all material terms, and comply with regulatory requirements.[8] Code Sec. 457(g) also requires the employer to put all deferred amounts in a trust, custodial account, or annuity contract for the exclusive benefit of the participants and their beneficiaries.[9] Taxation of deferrals under eligible Code Sec. 457 plans does not occur until the participant actually receives the distribution.

.02 Deferral Limitations

Under Code Sec. 457(b), the maximum amount of compensation that an employee can defer is the lesser of (1) a specific dollar amount for the year, or (2) 100% of a participant's "includible compensation."[10] Includible compensation is the participant's compensation for service performed for the employer that is currently includible in gross income. Thus, it may be possible for a participant to defer 100% of compensation. The maximum annual deferral is the same as that under 401(k) plans: $18,500 for 2018 and adjusted thereafter for cost of living.[11]

.03 Catch-Up Contributions

Code Sec. 457(e) allows for an age 50 catch-up contribution (the "Age 50 Catch-up"), akin to that available to 401(k) plan participants,[12] and a special Code Sec. 457 catch-up contribution (the "Special Catch-up").[13] These catch-up provisions are optional: plans are not required to include them. The Age 50 Catch-up

---

[5] Reg. §1.457-2(b).

[6] Reg. §1.457-4(b).

[7] Reg. §1.457-4(b).

[8] Reg. §1.457-3(a).

[9] Reg. §1.457-8.

[10] Reg. §1.457-4(c)(1).

[11] Reg. §1.457-4(c)(1)(i)(A).

[12] Code Sec. 457(e)(18).

[13] Reg. §1.457-4(c)(2).

allows an increased deferral limit if the plan participant reaches age 50 by the end of the year. The additional amount allowed by the Age 50 Catch-up is $6,000 for 2018 and after, to be adjusted for cost of living increases.[14]

The Special Catch-up applies only to the last three years before the participant attains normal retirement age.[15] Eligible Code Sec. 457 plans must either designate a retirement age or have the participant designate an age. The age chosen must be between the age at which the participant has the right to receive immediate retirement benefits without actuarial reduction and 70 1/2.[16]

The Special Catch-up contribution limit is two times the maximum deferral amount in effect. For example, the total limit in 2018 is $37,000 ($18,500 x 2). This catch-up contribution is only available, however, to the extent the participant has not deferred the maximum amount in previous years. The difference between the maximum deferral and the amount actually deferred in previous years is the underutilized amount.[17] For example, if the deferral limitation is $37,000 and the participant has deferred $30,000, the underutilized amount would be $7,000. A participant may use the Special Catch-up provision only once per plan. If the participant has another separate plan and meets the requirements for a Special Catch-up contribution independently on that plan, the participant may use the Special Catch-up again. If the Age 50 Catch-up amount is greater than the Special Catch-up amount, the participant may use the Age 50 Catch-up within the last three years before retirement age.[18]

In order to illustrate the interaction between the different deferral limitations, the regulations offer the following hypothetical:

> Participant F, who will turn 61 on April 1, 2018, becomes eligible to participate in an eligible plan on January 1, 2018. The plan provides a normal retirement age of 65. The plan provides limitations on annual deferrals up to the maximum permitted under the proposed regulations. What is F's maximum deferral for 2018?[19]

> F's base deferral limit is $18,500. In addition to the base amount, F is also eligible for the Age 50 Catch-up. The additional contribution allowed under the Age 50 Catch-up is $6,000 for 2018. F is not eligible for the Special Catch-up because he is not within three years of retirement. Therefore, the maximum amount F may defer in 2018 is $24,500.

.04 Coordination Limit

The Code Sec. 457(c) deferral limitations apply to a participant's total deferrals, regardless of the number of different plans involved.

.05 Sick and Vacation Pay Deferrals

The regulations modify Code Sec. 457(b)(4) to allow a participant to defer accumulated sick pay, vacation pay and back pay. The IRS would only permit

---

[14] Reg. § 1.457-4(c)(2).

[15] Reg. § 1.457-4(c)(3).

[16] Reg. § 1.457-4(c)(3)(v). The regulations provide an alternate range for the retirement age of police and firefighters. Under the regulations, the earliest

normal retirement age allowed for qualified police and firefighters is 40 and the latest is 70 1/2.

[17] Reg. § 1.457-4(c)(3)(ii).

[18] Reg. § 1.457-4(c)(2)(ii).

[19] Reg. § 1.457-4(c)(3)(vi) Example 1.

such deferrals if the parties reach an agreement providing for deferral before the start of the month in which the employer is to pay or otherwise make available the amounts to the participant.

.06 Excess Deferrals

If a plan permits a participant to defer an amount greater than the plan's applicable ceiling in a given year, the plan may lose eligibility under Code Sec. 457(b). The regulations deal with this problem by allowing a governmental plan to maintain eligibility as long as the excess funds deferred are distributed to the participant as soon as administratively possible.[20] If the plan does not distribute the excess funds as soon as administratively possible, the plan loses eligibility. The rule for excess deferrals under tax-exempt plans is stricter. If an excess deferral occurs under a plan maintained by a tax-exempt employer, the plan will become ineligible.

.07 Minimum Distribution Requirements

Amounts held under a plan are not taxed until distributed. This applies to all participants in eligible governmental plans. Code Sec. 401(a)(9) applies to minimum distributions under Section 457 plans. Code Sec. 401(a)(9) provides a uniform table to determine the minimum distribution allowed during the lifetime of employees, including those who are participants in eligible deferred compensation plans. The exception to this rule applies when a participant's spouse is the sole beneficiary of the plan and the spouse is more than 10 years younger than the participant. In such a case, the plan may use the participant and spouse's joint and last survivor expectancy to determine the value of the required minimum lifetime distribution.

.08 Loans

Code Sec. 457(g) does not address the topic of participants obtaining loans from eligible governmental plans, but the legislative history of the Small Business Job Protection Act of 1996 suggests that it allows such loans. Allowing loans from eligible plans would make these plans much more attractive to prospective participants. Under the regulations, whether a loan is valid is subject to a facts and circumstances analysis. The relevant factors under this analysis include whether the loan has a fixed repayment schedule and reasonable interest rate, and whether there are repayment safeguards to which a prudent lender would adhere. The purpose of this analysis is to ensure that the eligible plan holds assets for the exclusive benefit of the plan participants.

.09 Plan Terminations

In order for an employer to terminate a plan, the employer/plan must distribute all deferred amounts to the participants as soon as administratively possible. If the plan does not distribute these amounts, the Internal Revenue Code plan will treat it as a "frozen plan." Frozen plans must comply with all of Code Sec. 457's requirements in order to maintain eligibility. If benefit accruals

---

[20] Reg. § 1.457-4(e).

cease, the Internal Revenue Code will not treat the plan as terminated as long as the plan assets remain in the plan's related trust.[21]

.10 Plan-to-Plan Transfers

An eligible governmental plan may transfer its assets to another eligible governmental plan without violating the distribution requirements of Code Sec. 457(d).[22] Similarly, a tax-exempt unfunded plan may transfer its assets to another tax-exempt plan. However, a governmental plan cannot transfer assets to a tax-exempt plan, and vice versa.

Transfers from one eligible governmental plan to another may occur only in two distinct circumstances. The first occurs when a participant terminates employment with the transferor and commences employment with the transferee governmental employer. The Code permits such a transfer only if both plans agree to the transfer and the deferred amount immediately after the transfer is equal to or greater than the deferred amount immediately before the transfer.

The other circumstances in which a plan-to-plan transfer may take place are when the activity of the participant's employer (1) is privatized or (2) ceases to be performed by a governmental entity. The plan will not terminate under these circumstances if it is transferred to another eligible governmental employer within the same state.

.11 Qualified Domestic Relations Orders ("QDROs")

Under the proposed regulations, payments made pursuant to QDROs will not cause a plan to lose eligibility. Such payments include child support, alimony, and other payments to a spouse, former spouse, or dependent. Even if the QDRO requires payments to an alternate payee before the time when the plan allows disbursements, the plan remains eligible. Any amounts paid to an alternate payee under a QDRO are taxable to the alternate payee when received. In addition, the alternate payee may roll over the payment to another plan in the same way that a participant can roll over distributions.

.12 Taxation of and Withholding on Distributions

Code Sec. 3401(a)(12)(E) provides that remuneration paid to an employee or beneficiary from a Code Sec. 457(b) plan maintained by a state or local governmental employer (a governmental Code Sec. 457(b) plan) is no longer treated as wages for purposes of income tax withholding under Code Sec. 3402(a), but is instead subject to income tax withholding under Code Sec. 3405. This change was effective for distributions made after December 31, 2001.

Distributions to an individual from a governmental Code Sec. 457(b) plan are subject to income tax withholding in accordance with the income tax withholding requirements of Code Sec. 3405 applicable to distributions from qualified plans, annuities, and IRAs. Code Sec. 3405(c) also applies to direct rollover and mandatory 20% withholding rules to governmental Code Sec. 457(b) plan distributions that qualify as eligible rollover distributions under Code Sec. 402(c)(4).

---

[21] Rev. Rul. 89-87, 1989-2 CB 81.   [22] Reg. § 1.457-10(b).

Periodic distributions from governmental Code Sec. 457(b) plans that are not eligible rollover distributions are subject to withholding under Code Sec. 3405(a) as if the distribution were wages, and nonperiodic distributions from such plans that are not eligible rollover distributions are subject to withholding under Code Sec. 3405(b) at a 10% rate. In either case (periodic or nonperiodic distributions), the recipient may elect not to have withholding apply under Code Sec. 3405(a) or (b) to a distribution that is not an eligible rollover distribution from a governmental Code Sec. 457(b) plan.

Distributions to an individual during a tax year under a governmental Code Sec. 457(b) plan are reported on Form 1099-R, "Distributions from Pensions, Annuities, Retirement or Profit-Sharing Plans, IRAs, Insurance Contracts, etc."

Distributions to a participant from a tax-exempt employer's Code Sec. 457(b) plan are wages under Code Sec. 3401(a) that are subject to income tax withholding in accordance with the income tax withholding requirements of Code Sec. 3402(a). The pension withholding rules of Code Sec. 3405 do not apply to distributions from a tax-exempt employer's Code Sec. 457(b) plan.[23] Employers or plan administrators must calculate the income tax withholding on distributions to a participant under a tax-exempt employer's Code Sec. 457(b) plan in the same manner as withholding on other types of wage payments, and report the distribution on Form W-2, "Wage and Tax Statement."

.13 Rollovers

An eligible governmental plan may accept rollovers, but only if they are kept in a separate account. The rollover value, however, does not count toward the plan ceiling for maximum annual deferrals. An individual may roll over his or her distribution from a Section 457 plan into a qualified plan, 403(b) annuity, or individual retirement account. Rollovers from Section 457 plans to other plans are subject to the trust requirements of Code Sec. 401(a).

.14 Correction Program

If the IRS notifies a state in writing that its plan does not comply with the applicable regulations, the state must bring the plan into compliance before the first day of the first plan year beginning more than 180 days after the date on which the IRS notified the state. If the plan comes into compliance on time, it will remain eligible. However, the IRS will not severely punish even plans that do not comply on time, as the amounts deferred before the determination of the plan's ineligibility will still not be includible in the participant's gross income until paid.

.15 Ineligible Plans

Code Sec. 457(f) applies solely to ineligible plans. It provides that deferred compensation under ineligible plans is included as gross income when deferred or when the participant's rights to payment of the deferred compensation cease

---

[23] Notice 2003-20, IRB 2003-19; Temporary Reg. §35.3405-1T, Q&A-23.

to be subject to a substantial risk of forfeiture.[24] The participant's rights to compensation are subject to a substantial risk of forfeiture if the plan conditions the right to compensation upon future performance by the participant. The IRS has held that an involuntary termination, other than for cause, is not a substantial risk of forfeiture.[25] One commentator has described the standard under Code Sec. 457(f)'s substantial risk of forfeiture requirement as "if you don't quit, you won't forfeit."[26]

The interaction between Code Sec. 457(f) and Code Sec. 83, which applies to the transfer of property in connection with the performance of services, has been the source of considerable confusion. The regulations attempt to clear up this confusion by stating that Code Sec. 457(f) does not apply to a transfer of property if Code Sec. 83 applies.[27] To determine whether Code Sec. 457(f) applies, one must look at the timing of the transaction. Code Sec. 457(f) does not apply if the date on which there is no substantial risk of forfeiture with respect to the compensation is on or after the date on which there is a transfer of property to which Code Sec. 83 applies. Code Sec. 457(f) applies if the date on which there is no substantial risk of forfeiture with respect to the deferred compensation precedes the date on which there is a Code Sec. 83 transfer of property. This provision marked the end of tax advantages for mutual fund option programs in tax-exempt organizations and state and local governments. Specifically, the regulations tax options when the employer grants them, even if there is a substantial risk of forfeiture.

.16 Employee's Bankruptcy

The case of *Rhiel v. OhioHealth Corp. (In re Hunter)*,[28] clarified that, as with qualified retirement plan benefits, the 403(b) plan account assets of an employee of a tax-exempt employer do not constitute property of the employee's bankruptcy estate.

.17 Conclusion

The regulations permit increased deferrals for governmental and nonprofit employees with eligible Code Sec. 457 plans. This allows participants with eligible plans to defer greater sums of money without having to pay taxes on those sums until the plan actually distributes the amounts. The benefits of Code Sec. 457 for ineligible plans are significantly less, however, because of Code Sec. 457(f)'s substantial risk of forfeiture requirement.

¶2635 Excess Benefit Transactions

Most of the Code Sec. 501(c) sections provide that the assets of an organization cannot inure to the benefit of private shareholders or individuals. If an organization pays or distributes assets to insiders in excess of the fair market

---

[24] Code Sec. 457(f)(3)(b).

[25] IRS Letter Ruling 9815039 (Jan. 7, 1998).

[26] Michael S. Goldstein, Uses of Life Insurance in Nonqualified Deferred Compensation Planning for the Profit and Not-For-Profit Entity, A.B.A. Continuing Legal Education, May 2002.

[27] Reg. § 1.457-11(d)(1).

[28] *Rhiel v. OhioHealth Corp. (in re Hunter)*, 380 B.R. 753 (Bankr. S.D. OH 2008).

value of the services rendered, the organization can lose its tax-exempt status. Moreover, insiders of public charities and of private foundations are subject to excise taxes on any overpayments they receive. Although an overpayment to an insider of a public charity could result in a revocation of tax-exempt status, Code Sec. 4958 provides an intermediate sanction that ameliorates that result in many cases. Under Code Sec. 4958, an excise tax can be imposed on the insider who received the overpayment and on certain managers who knowingly approved the overpayment.

Code Sec. 4958 was added by the Taxpayer Bill of Rights.[29] Code Sec. 4958 imposes certain excise taxes on transactions that provide excess economic benefits to disqualified persons with respect to public charities and social welfare organizations described in Code Sec. 501(c)(3) and (4), respectively. Code Sec. 4958(e) refers to these organizations collectively as "applicable tax-exempt organizations."

The payment of excessive compensation to an insider of a private foundation likewise may give rise to excise taxes under Code Sec. 4941 on both the insider and on certain managers who knowingly approved the overpayment. In addition, the foundation itself and its managers may be subject to tax on any overpayment under Code Sec. 4945. Although the private foundation rules permit the payment of reasonable and necessary compensation to foundation insiders, most other transactions between a private foundation and its insiders are prohibited outright, without regard to subjective factors such as the reasonableness of the amounts, fair market value of property involved, or whether the transaction benefits or harms the foundation.

Code Sec. 4958 established a system to stop resources of tax-exempt organizations from inuring to the benefit of private individuals. Code Sec. 4958 applies to so-called "excess benefit transactions," and places specific restrictions on transactions with "disqualified parties." This prohibition is intended to prevent insiders from using the income or assets of a charitable organization for themselves.

.01 Intermediate Sanctions

The tax-exempt status of charitable organizations under Code Sec. 501(c)(3) and Code Sec. 501(c)(4) is, in part, dependent on the inurement proscription, which forbids any part of the net earnings of the organization from inuring to the benefit of a private individual or shareholder.[30] Traditionally, the only sanction available if such an inurement occurred was total disqualification of the organization from tax-exempt status. Disqualification was a severe punishment, however, and the IRS only pursued it under extreme circumstances. Furthermore, disqualification disproportionately punished an entire organization when only one or a few individuals within the organization were abusing their positions of power for personal gain.

---

[29] Public Law 104-168 (110 Stat. 1452; July 30, 1996). Final regulations under Code Sec. 4958 were published on January 23, 2002.

[30] Code Sec. 501(a); Code Sec. 501(c)(3).

In order to address this disproportionate punishment, the IRS established "intermediate sanctions" in the form of an excise tax on excess benefit transactions.[31] Intermediate sanctions are less harsh penalties that allow the IRS to target specific transactions. Under Code Sec. 4958, intermediate sanctions will apply when a disqualified person enters into an excess benefit transaction with a tax-exempt organization.[32]

.02 Penalties

Code Sec. 4958 creates three different intermediate sanctions: the 25% initial tax, the 200% additional tax, and the 10% tax on organization managers.[33] The 25% initial tax refers to the penalty imposed on a disqualified person who engages in an excess benefit transaction.[34] The excise tax is equal to 25% of the excess benefit.

The 200% additional tax applies if the disqualified person does not "correct" the excess benefit transaction on time.[35] To avoid the 200% additional tax, the disqualified person must correct the excess benefit transaction before the earliest of (1) the date of mailing of a notice of deficiency with respect to the 25% initial tax or (2) the date on which the IRS assesses the 25% initial tax.[36] In order to "correct" the excess benefit transaction, a disqualified person must repay the tax-exempt organization not only an amount equal to the value of the excess benefit, but also any additional amount needed to compensate the organization for the lost use of the money during the period after the occurrence of the transaction and before the correction.

The third type of tax penalty is the 10% tax on organization managers.[37] An organization manager who knowingly participates in a transaction that is an excess benefit transaction will be subject to a penalty that is the lesser of 10% of the excess benefit or $10,000, with respect to each excess benefit transaction. An organization manager is an officer, director, or trustee of the organization, or anyone having similar powers as individuals in those positions.[38] An organization manager will escape this tax if his or her knowing participation was not willful and was due to reasonable cause.[39] An organization manager will not be liable for the tax if he or she relies on a reasoned, written, legal opinion from legal counsel (including in-house counsel) stating that the transaction is not an excess benefit transaction, even if the IRS or a court subsequently holds that the transaction conferred an excess benefit.[40]

.03 Disqualified Persons

The IRS can only assess intermediate sanctions in transactions dealing with disqualified persons. A disqualified person is any person in a position to have exercised substantial influence over the affairs of an organization at any time

---

[31] Code Sec. 4958. The effective date for intermediate sanctions was January 23, 2002.

[32] Code Sec. 4958(a)(1).

[33] Code Sec. 4958(a).

[34] Code Sec. 4958(a)(1); Reg. § 53.4958-1.

[35] Code Sec. 4958(b).

[36] Code Sec. 4958(f)(5); Reg. § 53.4958-7.

[37] Code Sec. 4958(a)(2); Reg. § 53.4958-1(d).

[38] Code Sec. 4958(f)(2); Reg. § 53.4958-1(d)(2).

[39] Code Sec. 4958(a)(2); Reg. § 53.4958-1(d).

[40] Reg. § 53.4958-1(d)(4)(iii).

during the five-year period ending on the date of the transaction in question.[41] The organization's president, chief executive officer, treasurer, and voting members of the organization's governing body are, per se, disqualified persons.[42] A corporation, partnership, or trust that is at least 35% owned by disqualified persons is also a disqualified person.[43] Additionally, the family members of disqualified persons are disqualified persons.[44]

Parties not explicitly categorized in Code Sec. 4958 will be subject to a facts and circumstances analysis to determine whether they have a substantial influence over the affairs of an organization.[45] Facts tending to show that a person *does not* have substantial influence include that:

- The person has taken a vow of poverty on behalf of a religious organization;

- The person is acting as an independent contractor and is not benefiting from the transaction in any way other than by having received fees for professional services; and

- Any preferential treatment the organization offered to a person based on his or her donation amount is also offered to other donors as part of a solicitation intended to attract contributions.[46]

Facts tending to show that a person *does* have substantial influence include that the person:

- Founded the organization;

- Is a substantial contributor to the organization;

- Receives compensation based on revenues of the organization that are derived from activities that the person controls;

- Has authority to control a significant portion of the organization's budget; and

- Owns a controlling interest in an entity that is a disqualified person.[47]

Illustrating this analysis, the regulations implementing Code Sec. 4958 offer the following example:

> E is the headmaster of Z, a school that is an applicable tax-exempt organization for purposes of Code Sec. 4958. E has the ultimate responsibility for supervising Z's day-to-day operations. E can hire and fire faculty and staff, change the school curriculum, and discipline students without board approval.[48]

> Under these facts, E exercises substantial influence over Z, and is therefore a disqualified person with respect to Z.

---

[41] Code Sec. 4958(f)(1); Reg. § 53.4958-3.

[42] Reg. § 53.4958-3(b).

[43] Reg. § 53.4958-3(b)(2).

[44] Code Sec. 4958(f)(1)(B); Reg. § 53.4958-3(b)(1).

[45] Reg. § 53.4958-3(e).

[46] Reg. § 53.4958-3(e)(3).

[47] Reg. § 53.4958-3(e)(2).

[48] Reg. § 53.4958-3(g), Example 4.

.04 Excess Benefits

An excess benefit is equal to the excess value of the benefit provided to the disqualified person over the value of the consideration received by the organization.[49] Amounts that are not excess benefits under Code Sec. 4958 include:

- Reasonable expenses of attending meetings of the organization's governing body (not including spouse or luxury travel expenses);

- Benefits provided to a disqualified person that would be available to members of the public in exchange for a membership fee of $75 or less;

- Benefits to a disqualified person that are only available to that person as a member of the charitable class the organization is intended to benefit; and/or

- Reasonable payment of a liability insurance policy to protect against intermediate sanctions.[50]

The Internal Revenue Code will deem compensation paid to a disqualified person to be an excess benefit transaction if the compensation is greater than the amount that a similar enterprise would ordinarily pay for similar services under similar circumstances.[51] The Code will take into account the circumstances in existence on the date the parties made the contract. In order to ensure payments will be classified as reasonable compensation, the organization should, at the time of payment, make clear in its records an intent to treat the benefit as compensation for services rendered.[52]

.05 Rebuttable Presumption Against Excess Benefits

The Internal Revenue Code and IRS will presume that a transaction with a disqualified person did not create an excess benefit if:

- The organization's governing body, or a committee of the governing body composed of individuals who do not have a conflict of interest with respect to the transaction, approved the transaction;

- The committee obtained and relied on comparability data in making its decision; and

- The committee adequately and contemporaneously documented the basis for its determination.[53]

.06 Conflict of Interest

A member of the governing body has a conflict of interest with respect to a transaction if the member:

- Is a disqualified person or is related to any disqualified person participating in or economically benefiting from the transaction;

- Is in an employment relationship subject to the direction of a disqualified person who is economically benefiting from the transaction;

---

[49] Code Sec. 4958(c)(1)(A).
[50] Reg. § 53.4958-4.
[51] Reg. § 53.4958-4(b).

[52] Code Sec. 4958(c)(1)(A).
[53] Reg. § 53.4958-6(c).

- Has a material financial interest affected by the transaction; or

- Approves a transaction providing economic benefits to any disqualified person who in turn has approved or will approve a transaction providing economic benefits to the member.[54]

.07 Comparability Data

Comparability data upon which the governing body may base its decision includes, but is not limited to:

- Compensation levels paid by similarly situated organizations for functionally comparable positions;

- The availability of similar services in the geographic area of the exempt organization;

- Independent compensation surveys compiled by independent firms;

- Actual written offers from similar institutions competing for the services of the disqualified person; and

- Independent appraisals of the value of the property the organization plans to buy from or sell to the disqualified person.[55]

Demonstrating appropriate comparability data, the regulations offer the following example:

> Z is a large university that is a tax-exempt entity for purposes of Code Sec. 4958. In determining appropriate compensation for the new president, the Board of Trustees relies only upon a national survey of compensation for university presidents. The survey, however, does not divide the data into size of university or any other criteria. Furthermore, none of the board members has expertise in higher education compensation.[56]

Under these facts, the Board of Trustees has not relied upon appropriate comparability data. The data is not specific enough and the board members lack expertise in the area. Therefore, a compensation level decided upon while relying solely on this data will not be entitled to the presumption of reasonableness.

.08 Documentation

The third requirement of a transaction that is necessary to obtain the rebuttable presumption of reasonableness is proper documentation. Proper documentation means written or electronic records of the governing body, and must include (1) the terms of the transaction, (2) the date it was approved, (3) the members who voted on it, and (4) the comparability data relied upon. These records must be prepared concurrently with the transaction, meaning that they must be prepared before the first meeting of the governing body that takes place after the transaction.[57] Furthermore, the governing body must review the prepared records within a reasonable time.

---

[54] Reg. § 53.4958-6(c)(1)(iii).
[55] Reg. § 53.4958-6(c)(2).
[56] Reg. § 53.4958-6(c)(2)(iv).
[57] Reg. § 53.4958-6(c)(3).

.09 Reporting on Form 990

Organizations must report compensation information on IRS Form 990, Schedule J for certain officers, directors, trustees, key employees, and highly compensated employees. Certain questions on the form may require changes in governance practices at some organizations. Among the questions tax-exempt organizations must answer on Schedule J are the following:

- Does the organization use a compensation committee, compensation consultant, compensation survey or study, or employment agreement to establish the compensation of its CEO/Executive Director?
- Does the organization provide first class or charter travel for the executive or companions?
- Does the organization provide tax indemnification or gross-up payments?
- Does the organization pay club dues or fees?
- Does the organization provide personal services such as a maid, chauffeur, or chef?
- Did the organization make severance or change in control payments during the year?
- Did the organization provide equity-based compensation or supplemental non-qualified retirement benefits?

Schedule J also includes a chart that requires substantial executive compensation information broken down by recipient and type of compensation received.

.10 IRS Enforcement

The Internal Revenue Service has included guidance on its web site in the form of a continuing professional education article intended for training purposes to help agents determine when compensation received by a disqualified person from a tax-exempt organization should be considered an "automatic" excess benefit transaction under Code Sec. 4958.[58] In past years, the IRS has launched special initiatives to audit tax-exempt organizations, such as public charities and private foundations, with a focus on the compensation arrangements for executives.[59]

¶2645 Code Sec. 409A

Code Sec. 409A applies to ineligible nonqualified deferred compensation plans maintained by tax-exempt and governmental employers, as well as to nonqualified deferred compensation plans maintained by taxable employers. Code Sec. 409A generally provides that, unless certain requirements are met, amounts deferred under a nonqualified deferred compensation plan for all taxable years are currently includible in gross income to the extent not subject to

---

[58] "Automatic" Excess Benefit Transactions Under IRC 4958," by Lawrence M. Brauer and Leonard J. Henzke, Jr.

[59] In June 2004, the IRS announced that it would be auditing tax-exempt organizations, with a focus

on the compensation arrangements for executives. At that time, the IRS indicated that it had already identified approximately 100 to 200 charities whose compensation arrangements exceed $1 million. Tax Exempt Compensation Initiative, announced June 22, 2004.

a substantial risk of forfeiture and not previously included in gross income. Code Sec. 409A provides that the rights of a person to compensation are subject to a substantial risk of forfeiture if such person's rights to such compensation are conditioned upon the future performance of substantial services by any individual.[60]

Section 409A does not apply to eligible deferred compensation plans under Code Sec. 457(b), or qualified governmental excess benefit arrangements described in Code Sec. 415(m).[61] However, Code Sec. 409A applies to nonqualified (ineligible) deferred compensation plans to which Code Sec. 457(f) applies, separately and in addition to the requirements applicable to such plans under Code Sec. 457(f).[62] Code Sec. 409A(c) provides that nothing in Code Sec. 409A prevents the inclusion of amounts in gross income under any other provision of the Code (*e.g.*, Code Sec. 457) or any other rule of law earlier than the time provided in Code Sec. 409A.

The IRS issued Notice 2007-62 concerning the definition of a bona fide severance pay plan under Code Sec. 457(e)(11) and the definition of substantial risk of forfeiture under Code Sec. 457(f)(1)(B).[63] Notice 2007-62 also describes the guidance that the IRS anticipates issuing under Code Sec. 409A. The notice provides that, with respect to periods before such guidance is issued, no inference should be made from the anticipated guidance described in the notice regarding either the definition of a bona severance pay plan or the determination of substantial risk of forfeiture. However, pending the issuance of further guidance, taxpayers may rely on the definition of a bona fide severance pay plan in the anticipated guidance described in the notice.

.01 Bona Fide Severance Pay Plans under Code Sec. 457(e)(11)

The IRS anticipates issuing guidance providing that an arrangement is a bona fide severance pay plan under Code Sec. 457(e)(11), and thus is not subject to the requirements of Code Sec. 457, if:

(1) the benefit is payable only upon involuntary severance from employment,

(2) the amount payable does not exceed two times the employee's annual rate of pay (taking into account only pay that does not exceed the maximum amount that may be taken into account under a qualified plan pursuant to Code Sec. 401(a)(17) for the year in which the employee has a severance from employment—$275,000 for 2018), and

(3) the plan provides that the payments must be completed by the end of the employee's second taxable year following the year in which the employee separates from service. With respect to the requirement that benefits be payable only upon involuntary severance from employment, it is anticipated that the guidance would include exceptions for

---

[60] Treas. Reg. § 409A(d)(4).

[61] Treas. Reg. § 1.409A-1(a)(2).

[62] Treas. Reg. § 1.409A-1(a)(4).

[63] Notice 2007-62, I.R.B. 2007-32, August 6, 2007.

window programs, collectively bargained separation pay plans, and certain reimbursement or in-kind benefit arrangements.[64]

.02 Substantial Risk of Forfeiture under Code Sec. 457(f)

The Code Sec. 409A regulations provide that a right to an amount of compensation is subject to a substantial risk of forfeiture if entitlement to the amount is conditioned on the performance of substantial future services or the occurrence of a condition that is related to a purpose of the compensation and the possibility of forfeiture is substantial. For this purpose, if an employee's entitlement to the amount is conditioned on the occurrence of the employee's involuntary separation from service without cause, the right is subject to a substantial risk of forfeiture if the possibility of forfeiture is substantial. An amount is not subject to a substantial risk of forfeiture merely because the right to the amount is conditioned, directly or indirectly, upon refraining from the performance of services, *e.g.*, a noncompete. Further, the addition of any risk of forfeiture after the right to the compensation arises, or any extension of a period during which compensation is subject to a risk of forfeiture (sometimes referred to as a "rolling risk of forfeiture"), is generally disregarded for purposes of determining whether such compensation is subject to a substantial risk of forfeiture under Code Sec. 409A.[65]

The final Code Sec. 409A regulations,[66] provide that an amount is not considered subject to a substantial risk of forfeiture beyond the date or time at which the recipient otherwise could have elected to receive the amount of compensation, unless the present value of the amount made subject to a risk of forfeiture is materially greater than the present value of the amount the recipient otherwise could have elected to receive absent such risk of forfeiture. Therefore, in this situation, agreement to subject the amount to a substantial risk of forfeiture indicates that the recipient of the compensation is confident that there is not a real risk of forfeiture and is only subjecting the amount to the purported risk of forfeiture as a means of avoiding taxation. Notice 2007-62 states that amounts that an individual could have elected to receive under a salary deferral election generally cannot be made subject to a substantial risk of forfeiture under the rules of Code Sec. 409A beyond the date or time the salary would otherwise have been received.

.03 Interaction of Code Secs. 409A and 457 under the Proposed Regulations

Code Sec. 409A does not apply to eligible deferred compensation plans under Code Sec. 457(b). However, Code Sec. 409A applies to nonqualified deferred compensation plans to which Code Sec. 457(f) applies, separately and in addition to the requirements applicable to such plans under Code Sec. 457(f). In

---

[64] Similar to the exceptions in Treas. Reg. §§ 1.409A-1(b)(9)(ii), (iv), and (v).

[65] Treas. Reg. § 1.409A-1(d)(1)

[66] Treas. Reg. § 1.409A-1(d)(1). This is because, absent tax considerations, a rational participant nor-

mally would not agree to subject a right to amounts that may be earned and payable as current compensation, such as salary payments, to a condition that subjects the right to the same payments to a real possibility of forfeiture.

2016, the IRS issued proposed regulations that would make changes to the 2003 final regulations under Code Sec. 457(f) and clarify certain aspects of the interaction with Code Sec. 409A. The IRS has not yet finalized these regulations. However, employers generally can rely on these proposed regulations until they are finalized.

Short-Term Deferrals. The proposed regulations incorporate the "short-term deferral" exemption concept from Code Sec. 409A. Thus, a deferral of compensation does not occur (and Code Sec. 457(f) does not apply) if the compensation is required to be paid and is actually or constructively paid on or before the 15th day of the third month following the end of the employee's or the employer's tax year (whichever is later) in which the employee's right to the payment is no longer subject to a substantial risk of forfeiture. For example, if an arrangement provides for the payment of a bonus on or before March 15 of the year following the calendar year in which the right to the bonus is no longer subject to a substantial risk of forfeiture and the bonus is paid on or before that March 15, the arrangement would not be a plan providing for a deferral of compensation to which Code Sec. 457(f) applies.

Exclusions: The proposed regulations clarify that Code Sec. 457(f) does not apply to annuity plans and contracts described in Code Sec. 403 and plans described in Code Sec. 401(a).[67] Additionally, the proposed regulations state that a deferral of compensation does not occur for purposes of Code Sec. 457(f), to the extent that a plan provides for:[68]

- The payment of expense reimbursements, medical benefits, or in-kind benefits;

- Certain indemnification rights, liability insurance, or legal settlements; or

- Taxable educational benefits for an employee under Code Sec. 127(c)(1) (but not for the education of any other person, including any spouse, child, or other family member of the employee).

Substantial Risk of Forfeiture. The proposed regulations adopt a more lenient definition of substantial risk of forfeiture than set forth under Code Sec. 409A. Generally, an amount would be subject to a substantial risk of forfeiture under the proposed regulation only if entitlement to that amount is conditioned on: the future performance of substantial services, or the occurrence of a condition that is related to a purpose of the compensation, if the possibility of forfeiture is substantial. An amount is not subject to a substantial risk of forfeiture if the facts and circumstances indicate that the forfeiture condition is unlikely to be enforced, based on, among other things, the employer's past practices, the employee's level of control or influence, and the legal enforceability of the provisions.

---

[67] Proposed Treas. Reg. § 1.457-12(b). [68] Proposed Treas. Reg. § 1.457-12(d)(4).

However, unlike Code Sec. 409A, the proposed regulations allow that noncompete provisions may constitute a substantial risk of forfeiture, if the following conditions are met:[69]

- The right to payment of the amount is expressly conditioned upon the employee refraining from the future performance of services pursuant to an enforceable written agreement.

- The employer makes reasonable ongoing efforts to verify compliance with noncompetition agreements (including the noncompetition agreement applicable to the employee).

- At the time that the enforceable written agreement becomes binding, the facts and circumstances demonstrate that the employer has a substantial and bona fide interest in preventing the employee from performing the prohibited services and that the employee has bona fide interest in, and ability to, engage in the prohibited competition.

An employer may show that it has a substantial and bona fide interest in preventing the employee from performing the prohibited services by showing significant adverse economic consequences that would likely result from the prohibited services; the employee's marketability based on specialized skills, reputation, or other factors; and the employee's interest, financial need, and ability to engage in the prohibited services.

Further, to constitute a substantial risk of forfeiture, the possibility of actual forfeiture in the event that the forfeiture condition occurs must be substantial based on the employer's relevant facts and circumstances.[70] Factors to be considered for this purpose include, but are not limited to, the extent to which the employer has enforced forfeiture conditions in the past, the level of control or influence of the employee with respect to the organization and the individual(s) who would be responsible for enforcing the forfeiture condition, and the likelihood that such provisions would be enforceable under applicable law.

Extension of the Risk of Forfeiture. The proposed regulations permit initial deferrals of current compensation to be subject to a substantial risk of forfeiture and also allow an existing risk of forfeiture to be extended only if all of the following requirements are met. First, the present value of the amount to be paid upon the lapse of the substantial risk of forfeiture (as extended, if applicable) must be materially greater than the amount the employee otherwise would be paid in the absence of the substantial risk of forfeiture (or absence of the extension). The proposed regulations provide that an amount is materially greater for this purpose only if the present value of the amount to be paid upon the lapse of the substantial risk of forfeiture, measured as of the date the amount would have otherwise been paid (or in the case of an extension of the risk of forfeiture, the date that the substantial risk of forfeiture would have lapsed without regard to the extension), is more than 125 percent of the amount the participant otherwise would have received on that date in the absence of the new or extended substantial risk of forfeiture.

---

[69] Proposed Treas. Reg. § 1.457-12(e)(1)(iv).

[70] Proposed Treas. Reg. § 1.457-12(e)(1)(v).

Second, the initial or extended substantial risk of forfeiture must be based upon the future performance of substantial services or adherence to an agreement not to compete. It may not be based solely on the occurrence of a condition related to the purpose of the transfer (for example, a performance goal for the organization), though that type of condition may be combined with a sufficient service condition.

Third, the period for which substantial future services must be performed may not be less than two years (absent an intervening event such as death, disability, or involuntary severance from employment).

Fourth, the agreement subjecting the amount to a substantial risk of forfeiture must be made in writing before the beginning of the calendar year in which any services giving rise to the compensation are performed in the case of initial deferrals of current compensation or at least 90 days before the date on which an existing substantial risk of forfeiture would have lapsed in the absence of an extension. Special rules apply to new employees. The proposed regulations do not extend these special rules for new employees to employees who are newly eligible to participate in a plan.

¶2655 Insured Security Option Plan

The Insured Security Option Plan ("ISOP") seeks to allow non-profits to provide tax advantaged retirement benefits. A not-for-profit could use an ISOP to provide tax-advantaged retirement benefits in excess of the qualified plan limits to a select group of highly compensated individuals, without creating a liability for the employer, or otherwise affecting its future financial condition.

Example: Not-for-profit hospital system ABC will pay Executive D a $100,000 bonus at 2018-year end. After paying all applicable federal and state taxes, D would have approximately $60,000 to invest. Under the ISOP, ABC reports $100,000 of ordinary income to D, withholds and pays the $40,000 in taxes and contributes the remaining $60,000 to an ISOP account it has established on D's behalf.

The real benefit to Executive D is that, pursuant to the contractual provisions of the ISOP, the insurance carrier immediately "loans" $40,000 (the amount paid in taxes) to D's ISOP account, so that D immediately has the entire $100,000 amount earning interest on the investments.

The $40,000 is a non-recourse "policy loan." However, if D and the ISOP hold the policy until maturity, D never pays back the loan. The policy loan is simply deducted from the policy's death benefit.

.01 Possible Advantages to the Employer

The ISOP's perceived advantages to the employer are as follows:

- The ISOP does not create a liability for the employer.
- The employer may limit participation to a select group.
- The insurance company handles all of the plan administration and the participants direct the investment of their funds.

- The ISOP is not subject to Code Sec. 409A.
- Amounts contributed to the ISOP are not subject to the claims of the employer's creditors.

.02 Possible Advantages to the Participant

The ISOP's perceived advantages to the participant are as follows:

- The entire amount the participant earned is put to work earning investment returns.
- If the policy is held until maturity, all investment gains and future withdrawals can be structured as tax-free to the participant.
- If the policy is held until maturity, it provides a significant death benefit to named beneficiary(ies).
- Allows the participant to self-direct his or her account, just as they would in a 403(b) or 401(k) plan.
- Is safe from the claims of the employer's creditors.

¶2665 Excise Tax on Compensation in Excess of $1,000,000 Paid by Certain Tax-Exempt Entities

The TCJA added new Code Sec. 4960, which imposes a 21% excise tax on (a) excess parachute payments, and (b) any compensation paid in a year in excess of $1,000,000 by certain tax-exempt organizations to their covered employees, effective for taxable years beginning after December 31, 2017. Under Code Sec. 4960, a "covered employee" is any employee who is one of the five highest compensated employees of the organization for the taxable year, or was a covered employee of the organization (or any predecessor) for any preceding taxable year beginning after December 31, 2016. This means that once an individual is a covered employee of a tax-exempt organization, the individual is a covered employee of that organization for all future years, even after the individual's employment terminates.

Code Sec. 4960 applies to any organization that for the taxable year is exempt from taxation under Code Sec. 501(a), is a farmers' cooperative organization described in Code Sec. 521(b)(1), has income excluded from taxation under Code Sec. 115(1), or is a political organization described in Code Sec. 527(e)(1). Code Sec. 4960, applies to all payments that constitute "wages," as defined in Code Sec. 3401(a), except for a designated Roth contribution (as defined in Code Sec. 402A(c)). Compensation paid to a licensed medical professional (including a veterinarian) which is for the performance of medical or veterinary services by such professional is not included.

Any payment in the nature of compensation to (or for the benefit of) a covered employee could be a "parachute payment" if the payment is contingent on the employee's separation from employment with the employer. A parachute payment would be an "excess parachute payment," to the extent the aggregate present value of all such payments to the employee equal or exceed an amount equal to three times the employee's "base amount." A covered employee's base amount is determined under rules similar to the rules of Code Secs. 280G(b) and (d). Additionally, payments described in Code Sec. 280G(b)(6) (*e.g.*, payments under qualified pension and 401(k) plans, 403(b) annuity plans, or Code Sec. 457(b) plans) are not counted as parachute payments. Payments made under a Code Sec. 457(f) plan could be subject to the excise tax.

Code Sec. 4960 also includes any payments to a covered employee paid by any person, organization, or governmental entity that is related to the applicable tax-exempt organization. A person or governmental entity is treated as related to an applicable tax-exempt organization if the person or governmental entity (i) controls, or is controlled by, the organization, (ii) is controlled by one or more persons that control the organization, (iii) is a supported organization (as defined in Code Sec. 509(f)(2)) during the taxable year with respect to the organization, (iv) is a supporting organization described in Code Sec. 509(a)(3) during the taxable year with respect to the organization, or (v) in the case of an organization that is a voluntary employees' beneficiary association described in Code Sec. 501(a)(9), establishes, maintains, or makes contributions to such voluntary employees' beneficiary association. Where payments from more than one employer are taken into account, each employer will be liable for a portion of the excise tax based on the ratio that the payments by that employer to the employee bears to the total payments made by all employers to the employee.

Chapter 27
EXECUTIVE COMPENSATION IN THE CONTEXT OF DIVORCE

¶2701 Overview—Executive Compensation in the Context of Divorce

Employers are increasingly utilizing alternative methods of compensation to attract and retain employees, particularly high-ranking executives. Divorce laws, however, have not fully adjusted to these changes in compensation structure. It used to be that the largest asset in divorce cases was real estate (the family home).[1] Now, however, the largest assets in divorce cases are often stock options and deferred compensation plans. Courts are struggling with the treatment of such compensation methods in the context of divorce. Moreover, tax issues arise when one former spouse transfers a deferred compensation plan or equity interest to the other former spouse incident to divorce.

Not only do stock and other forms of executive compensation make up a significant part of the divorce estate, but they also can be a potential source of embarrassment for an executive whose spouse (and unethical counsel) plays hardball with public disclosures to the press.[2]

.01 Stock Options and Other Stock Awards

Courts have struggled with how to treat stock options and other stock awards in divorce cases, particularly in determining whether unvested options are marital property subject to division and, if so, how to distribute them properly. However, courts' opinions have found and most states' law now provide that stock options and other stock awards made or earned during the marriage are marital property, subject to division (see ¶2715).

.02 Other Deferred Compensation Plans

Courts treat interests in other deferred compensation plans similarly to stock options. The goal of distributing deferred compensation plans is to apportion all compensation earned during a marriage between the former spouses, either equitably or equally (see ¶2735).

.03 Tax Issues Incident to Divorce

Prior to 2019, alimony and separate maintenance payments are deductible by the payor spouse and includible in income by the recipient spouse under Code Secs. 215(a), 61(a)(8) and 71(a). Under the Tax Cuts and Jobs Act ("TCJA"), for any divorce or separation instrument executed after December 31, 2018,

---

[1] Margaret A. Jacobs, *As Workers' Pensions Swell in Value, Ex-Spouses Demand a Share*, WALL ST. J., Mar. 17, 2000, at B1.

[2] As former General Electric CEO Jack Welch, and the rest of the world learned in 2002.

alimony and separate maintenance payments are not taxable to the payee spouse and not deductible by the payor spouse.

After determining that stock options are marital property subject to division, the tax implications of transferring the options become important to consider. At this stage, not only are both former spouses involved, but the division also will affect the employer that granted the stock options (see ¶ 2745).

.04 Securities Law Issues

With respect to securities laws, transfers of stock options pursuant to a domestic relations order are generally exempt from the reporting rules of Section 16 of the Securities Exchange Act of 1934. Rule 16a-12 provides a general exemption from reporting for both acquisitions and dispositions of securities pursuant to a domestic relations order (see ¶ 2755).

¶2715 Stock Options and Other Stock Awards

The widespread use of stock options as compensation for executive level (and increasingly, for lower level) employees has led to a greater entanglement of stock options in divorce situations. Courts struggle with how to treat stock options in divorce cases, particularly in determining whether unvested options are marital property subject to division and, if so, how to distribute them properly. Although state laws vary as to both issues, general trends are developing.

.01 Are Stock Options Marital Assets to Be Distributed upon a Dissolution of Marriage?

Courts struggle with various factors that relate to stock options and divorce. Stock options are often nontransferable and their vesting is dependent upon a spouse's continued employment. In addition, compensatory stock options generally do not have a readily ascertainable value. These circumstances make difficult the decision whether to treat stock options as marital property and, if so, how to divide such options. In fact, courts only began to consider stock options as assets in dividing the marital estate in the early 1980s. Factors considered in determining whether stock options will constitute marital property generally include the granting and vesting dates of the options, the length and dates of the marriage, and the employer's purpose in granting the options.[3]

Nearly all jurisdictions agree that stock options granted during a marriage, which vest before the dissolution of the marriage, are marital property, regardless of whether the employee exercises the options during the marriage. Courts now treat stock options as consideration for work performed during the marriage because, at the time they vest, the options become irrevocable by the employer. Courts also generally hold that stock options granted after dissolution of the marriage are not marital property. Courts are less consistent, however, in situations where (1) stock options were granted prior to a marriage that vest

---

[3] *See, e.g.,* Illinois Marriage and Dissolution of Marriage Act, 750 ILCS 5/503(b)(3).

during or after the marriage, and (2) stock options were granted during a marriage that vest after dissolution of the marriage. With regard to unvested stock options, the key issue courts often consider is the employer's primary purpose for granting the options. The two main reasons for granting stock options are to compensate for past services and to provide incentives for future services. Often, however, the purpose for granting options is unclear or may be a combination of both reasons.

Courts usually treat stock options granted during the marriage, which vest after the dissolution of the marriage, as marital property, at least in part. The general rationale is that companies grant these options in part to reward work performed during the marriage. Therefore, many courts consider the portion of the options attributable to work performed during the marriage as distributable marital property.[4] There are, however, a few jurisdictions holding that options granted during the marriage that vest after divorce are not marital property but merely contingent expectancies that are personal to the holder. These jurisdictions reason that a stock option is not marital property because the option is not an employee's irrevocable right, and it does not have value in the marketplace. Many courts also consider the issue of the employer's purpose for granting stock options when determining whether stock options granted prior to marriage that vest during the marriage are distributable marital property.[5]

.02 Examples of State Laws

In *Bornemann v. Bornemann*, the Connecticut Supreme Court held that employee stock options granted during the marriage, but exercisable after a divorce, constituted property subject to division.[6] The court opined that such options created an enforceable right in the employee-spouse that amounted to more than an expectancy. In doing so, the court analogized the options to pension benefits, which had previously been determined to be subject to distribution. The court stated that stock options, like pension benefits, are not merely expectancies because they give an enforceable contract right to their holder. Furthermore, the court noted that lawmakers intended to provide a broad range of divisible resources in the state's property division statute.

In *Stachofsky v. Stachofsky*, a Washington state court held that stock options may be included in marital dissolution property divisions.[7] The employee-spouse in this case had worked for over 20 years before his marriage, receiving several grants of stock options. The court held that stock options granted prior to the marriage that vested during the marriage were marital assets. The determining factors were that the options were granted for both present and future performance and that the options were exercised using community property. With regard to stock options vesting after the dissolution of the marriage, the court again

---

[4] See, e.g., *In re Valence*, 798 A.2d 35, 37-40 (N.H. 2002), holding modified by *In re Chamberlin*, 918 A.2d 1 (N.H. 2007).

[5] Whether the employee-spouse used separate or marital funds to exercise the options is also an important consideration when determining whether

stock options vesting during or after a marriage are distributable.

[6] *Bornemann v. Bornemann*, 245 Conn. 508 (Conn. 1998).

[7] *Stachofsky v. Stachofsky*, 951 P.2d 346 (Wash. Ct. App. 1988).

considered the employer's purpose for granting the options. The court found that these stock options were granted for past, present and future service, and held that the stock options were partially divisible.

In *Melancon v. Melancon,*[8] one spouse was granted options during his marriage with a four year vesting schedule. The marriage ended after only the first tranche of options had vested. The Louisiana court held that it was not appropriate to split only the options that vested before the marriage ended. Instead, the court held that the stock from the last three tranches (which vested after the marriage ended) must be prorated, based on the lengths of the marriage and separate employment between the stock option's grant date and vesting date.

.03 Valuation and Distribution of Stock Options

After determining that at least a portion of stock options are marital property, courts must determine their proper distribution between the spouses. In community property states, each spouse is entitled to an equal share of stock options determined to be marital assets. In non-community property states, such stocks are subject to equitable division by the courts. Determining a proper distribution in either a community or non-community property state usually involves a fact-intensive inquiry into such factors as the dissolution date of the marriage, the length of the marriage, and the granting and vesting dates of the stock options.[9]

One distribution option is to create a constructive trust. In this arrangement, actual division of the stock options is delayed until the options are exercisable. In the meantime, the options continue to be viewed as jointly owned. A variation of this option allows for continuing court jurisdiction. Here, the employee-spouse is required to notify the former spouse of any decision to exercise options vested after dissolution of the marriage. Because the constructive trust approach does not provide a clean financial break between former spouses, courts rarely choose it and instead apply other valuation and distribution alternatives.

The most common method of distribution involves the application of a "time rule formula."[10] Under this approach, courts apply a mathematical formula in an attempt to calculate ownership ratios for determining what percentage of the assets to allocate as marital property. Although this is the most frequently used approach, courts vary on the exact formula applied. The most common time rule formula is the *"Hug"* rule. The California Court of Appeals, in *In re Marriage of Hug,* applied a fraction to determine the percentage of options that were community property.[11] The complex fraction consisted of the number of months between the commencement of the spouse's employment and the date of separation of the parties, divided by the number of months between the commencement of em-

---

[8] *Melancon v. Melancon,* 928 So.2d 10 (La. Ct. App. 2005).

[9] *See, e.g.,* Illinois Marriage and Dissolution of Marriage Act, 750 ILCS 5/503(b)(3).

[10] *See, e.g.,* Raymond S. Dietrich, *Qualified Domestic Relations Orders: Strategy and Liability for the Family Law Attorney* § 16.08 (2017).

[11] *In re Marriage of Hug,* 154 Calif. App. 3d 780 (Cal. Ct. App. 1984). Noncommunity property states applying this formula use the fraction to determine the percentage of options that are marital property.

ployment and the date on which the options first became exercisable.[12] Other jurisdictions have applied the date of dissolution of the marriage as opposed to the date of separation.

One well-documented case applying a version of the *Hug* formula is the *Wendt* case[13]—notable for the amount in controversy and the position of the spouses. Gary Wendt was the CEO of GE Capital Services, a highly profitable division of General Electric. His former wife brought an unsuccessful appeal seeking to increase her share of marital property from $20 million to $35 million. The former spouse's appeal was primarily focused on the significant appreciation in Mr. Wendt's assets, stock options, and retirement and pension plans, between the couple's date of separation and the date of the divorce decree. Apart from its notoriety, the case is important in that it was the first time a Connecticut appellate court applied a "coverture formula" for distributing assets. The coverture formula applied by the court in this case subtracted the date of marital separation from the date the stock options were granted and divided this result by the date the stock options were granted, less the vesting date. Under this formula, the court partially divided the stocks between the two former spouses.[14]

.04 Other Issues Involving Stock Options

In *Lantz v. Lantz*,[15] stock option grants were divided in a divorce settlement and then later cancelled due to the employee's termination of employment. Under the terms of the divorce settlement, the employee's options and stock appreciation rights were split equally between him and his former spouse. Because the grants were non-transferable, the employee was required to hold half of the grants in constructive trust for his former spouse. Upon exercise of that portion of the grants, the employee would then have to pay over the proceeds to the former spouse. After the settlement was final, the employee terminated his employment, which began a shortened period for exercise of the options. The employee failed to exercise the options within that period and the options were cancelled. The employee's former spouse sued, claiming that by failing to exercise the options within the prescribed period, the employee had deprived her of the opportunity to realize the nearly $15,000 gain. The court agreed and held that the employee owed his former spouse nearly $15,000.

---

[12] *In re Marriage of Hug*, 154 Calif. App. 3d 780 (Cal. Ct. App. 1984); *see also*, Raymond S. Dietrich, *Qualified Domestic Relations Orders: Strategy and Liability for the Family Law Attorney* § 16.08[1] (2017).

[13] *Wendt v. Wendt*, 757 A.2d 1225 (Conn. App. Ct. 2000).

[14] Note that a later case decided by the same court, *Calo-Turner v. Turner*, 83 Conn. App. 53 (Conn. App. Ct. 2004), came out differently on similar facts. Like *Wendt*, the value of the assets, stock, etc. appreciated between the time the couple separated and

the divorce was finalized. In *Calo-Turner*, however, the same Connecticut Appellate Court held that the trial court was within its discretion to award the plaintiff the appreciated value of the employee-spouse's property. This discrepancy highlights the position taken by many states that state trial courts have a high degree of discretion regarding financial awards in dissolution actions and that no single rule/formula applies to every divorce case involving employee stock options.

[15] *Lantz v. Lantz*, No. A-1622-08T1 (N.J. Super. Ct. App. Div. 2010).

.05 Restricted Stock and Other Issues

The same tax principles that apply to the transfer of stock options in a divorce generally apply to transfers of restricted stock, restricted stock units, performance shares, and other stock awards. Unlike stock options, actual shares of stock are distributed to the employee immediately upon the vesting of restricted stock, restricted stock units, and performance shares. It is only when these awards are not yet vested that issues arise.

Unvested restricted stock, restricted stock units, and performance share awards generally are not transferable. Therefore, such awards are often taken into account in the division of assets, but not actually transferred to the non-employee/former spouse. Under the laws of many states restricted stock, stock options, and other stock awards acquired during marriage are presumed to be marital property.[16]

Under the principles of Rev. Rul. 2002-22 (discussed further below), a transfer of unvested property or property that is vested, but not taxable because it is subject to a substantial risk of forfeiture, would be taxable to the holder at the time of vesting or the lapse of restrictions. In private letter ruling 201016031,[17] the IRS specifically addressed the treatment of restricted stock transferred to a former spouse pursuant to a divorce decree in a non-community property state. The IRS ruled that, because the division of the restricted stock occurred in the context of a judicial proceeding that was formalized in a divorce decree, it was a nontaxable event under Code Sec. 1041. The income attributable to the vesting of the restricted stock was includible in the gross income of the transferee/former spouse for federal income tax consequences, and all subsequent tax consequences with respect to such stock would belong to the former spouse.

Under the TCJA, beginning in 2019, alimony and separate maintenance payments are not taxable to the payee spouse and not deductible by the payor spouse. This should not affect the division of unvested property. Code Sec. 1041 confers nonrecognition treatment on any gain that the executive might otherwise realize when the executive transfers these interests to the former spouse in the year of divorce.

¶2735 Other Deferred Compensation Plans

As with stock options and other forms of marital property, the courts allocate all deferred compensation earned during a marriage either equitably or equally between the former spouses. The IRS has promulgated special rules to cover the unique tax issues that exist in the deferred compensation area.

.01 Splitting Deferred Compensation

While it varies some by jurisdiction, courts generally treat interests in other deferred compensation plans similarly to stock options. The goal of distributing deferred compensation plans is to apportion all compensation earned during a

---

[16] See, e.g., the Illinois Marriage and Dissolution of Marriage Act, 750 ILCS 5/503.   [17] I.R.S. Priv. Ltr. Rul. 201016031 (Jan. 15, 2010).

marriage between the former spouses, either equitably or equally. Unlike Code Sec. 414(p) in the qualified plan area, to date there is little guidance on dividing and/or transferring nonqualified plan benefits, including the tax effect of it. However, the IRS has provided guidance on these issues in Rev. Rul. 2002-22.[18]

Under the facts of Rev. Rul. 2002-22, the executive's employer maintained two unfunded, nonqualified deferred compensation plans, an individual account plan and a supplemental pension (SERP). The SERP permitted lump sum distributions. The executive was fully vested in his benefits under both plans.

The IRS observed that under the applicable state law, unfunded deferred compensation rights earned by a spouse during the period of marriage are marital property subject to equitable division between the spouses in the event of divorce. Pursuant to the property settlement incorporated into their judgment of divorce, the executive transferred to his former spouse (1) the right to receive deferred compensation payments from the employer under the account balance plan based on 75% of the executive's account balance under that plan at the time of the divorce, and (2) the right to receive a single sum payment of 50% from the employer under the SERP upon the executive's termination of employment with the employer.

The IRS concluded that, under the given facts, the interests in nonqualified deferred compensation that the executive transfers to the former spouse are property within the meaning of Code Sec. 1041. Code Sec. 1041 confers nonrecognition treatment on any gain that the executive might otherwise realize when the executive transfers these interests to the former spouse in the year of divorce. Further, the assignment of income doctrine does not apply to these transfers. Therefore, the executive is not required to include in gross income any income resulting from the payment of deferred compensation to the former spouse in the year he retires and the plans make payments. The former spouse must include the amount realized from payments of deferred compensation in income in the year such payments are paid or made available to the former spouse. The IRS noted that the same conclusions would apply if the executive and the former spouse resided in a community property state and all or some of these income rights constituted community property that was divided between the executive and the former spouse as part of their divorce.

The former spouse, and not the executive, is required to include an amount in gross income when the deferred compensation is paid or made available to the former spouse.

Finally, the IRS stated that its ruling does not apply to transfers of property between spouses other than in connection with divorce. The ruling also does not apply to transfers of unfunded deferred compensation rights, or other future income rights to the extent such options or rights are unvested at the time of transfer or to the extent that the transferor's rights to such income are subject to substantial contingencies at the time of the transfer.[19]

---

[18] Rev. Rul. 2002-22, 2002-1 C.B. 849.

[19] Rev. Rul. 2002-22, 2002-1 C.B. 849 (citing *Kochansky v. Comm'r*, 92 F.3d 957 (9th Cir. 1996)).

Courts ordinarily hold that nonemployee-spouses are entitled to a portion of the employee-spouse's pension. Courts applying this rule deem pensions to be provided by an employer for work performed, at least in part, during a marriage. In general, the longer a marriage, the larger a spouse's share in a pension plan will be. Once an unvested pension is determined to be a marital asset, courts must then decide how to distribute it.

The two main methods courts use to distribute unvested pensions are the "deferred distribution" method and the "present payout" method.[20] Because the deferred distribution method postpones distribution until the pension vests, the method avoids uncertainties in the value of the benefit.[21] However, this method also has the disadvantage of not providing for a complete financial separation of the former couple.[22]

Conflicts among courts develop when the value of deferred compensation plans (such as retirement benefits) experience an unanticipated increase in value after marriage. Some courts, including those in Texas and Florida, say the nonemployee-spouse does not deserve a share of such increases. Other courts, including those in New York, New Jersey and California, have granted shares of the unexpected increased value to nonemployee-spouses.

There are a few jurisdictions, moreover, that do not treat unvested pension plans as marital assets subject to distribution. For example, the Indiana Court of Appeals held in *In re Hodowal* that a spouse's early retirement subsidy was not marital property subject to division because it was contingent on the spouse's continued employment.[23] The court stated that unvested pension benefits are not "property" as defined under the Indiana Code.[24] Since the court found that the retirement subsidy was an option contingent on future events and not a vested right, the court determined that it was separate property.[25]

.02 FICA and FUTA Taxes on the Split Deferred Compensation

The IRS followed up Rev. Rul. 2002-22 with Rev. Rul. 2004-60, giving additional guidance on the Federal Insurance Contributions Act ("FICA") and Federal Unemployment Tax Act ("FUTA") taxes and withholding applicable in the case of transfers of nonqualified deferred compensation incident to divorce.[26] In Rev. Rul. 2002-22, the IRS ruled that when interests in nonqualified deferred compensation are transferred from an employee to his or her former spouse (the nonemployee-spouse) pursuant to their divorce, the transfer does not result in a payment of wages for purposes of FICA and FUTA.

Rev. Rul. 2004-60 reaffirmed that the transfer of interests in nonqualified deferred compensation from the employee-spouse to the nonemployee-spouse

---

[20] The New Jersey Supreme Court examined both approaches in *Moore v. Moore*, 553 A.2d 20 (N.J. Sup. Ct. 1989).

[21] *Moore v. Moore*, 553 A.2d 20 (N.J. Sup. Ct. 1989).

[22] *Moore v. Moore*, 553 A.2d 20 (N.J. Sup. Ct. 1989).

[23] *In re Hodowal*, 627 N.E.2d 869 (Ind. Ct. App. 1994).

[24] *In re Hodowal*, 627 N.E.2d 869, 872 (Ind. Ct. App. 1994).

[25] *In re Hodowal*, 627 N.E.2d 869, 873 (Ind. Ct. App. 1994).

[26] Rev. Rul. 2004-60, 2004-1 C.B. 1051, revising the proposed revenue ruling set forth in Notice 2002-31, 2002-1 C.B. 908.

incident to a divorce does not result in a payment of wages for FICA and FUTA tax purposes. The nonqualified deferred compensation is subject to FICA and FUTA taxes to the same extent as if the employee-spouse had retained the rights to the compensation.

To the extent FICA and FUTA taxation apply, the wages are the wages of the employee-spouse. The employee portion of the FICA taxes is deducted from the wages as and when the wages are taken into account for FICA tax purposes. The employee portion of the FICA taxes is deducted from the payment to the nonemployee-spouse.[27]

.03 Tax Withholding on the Split Deferred Compensation

The amounts distributed to the nonemployee-spouse from the nonqualified deferred compensation plans are also subject to withholding under Code Sec. 3402. The amounts to be withheld for income tax withholding are deducted from the payments to the nonemployee-spouse. The employer may use the supplemental wage flat rate to determine the amount of income tax withholding. The nonemployee-spouse is entitled to the credit allowable for the income tax withheld at the source on these wages.[28]

The Social Security wages, Medicare wages, Social Security taxes withheld, and Medicare taxes withheld, if applicable, are reportable on Form W-2 with the name, address, and Social Security number of the employee-spouse. However, no amount is includible in Box 1 and Box 2 of the employee's Form W-2 with respect to these payments. The income with respect to the distributions from the nonqualified deferred compensation plans to the nonemployee-spouse is reportable in Box 3 as other income on Form 1099-MISC with the name, address, and Social Security number of the nonemployee-spouse. Income tax withholding with respect to these payments of wages is included in Box 4, federal income tax withheld.[29]

.04 Tax Reporting on the Split Deferred Compensation

Income tax withholding on payments to the nonemployee-spouse is included on Form 945 filed by the employee-spouse's employer. The employer reports the Social Security tax and Medicare tax on its Form 941, and reports the FUTA tax on the employer's Form 940.

.05 Code Sec. 409A

The American Jobs Creation Act added Section 409A to the Internal Revenue Code. Code Sec. 409A applies to employment and change in control agreements and separation pay plans in addition to the deferred compensation plans that it initially was drafted to cover. Code Sec. 409A and the regulations contain a few special rules affecting executive compensation in the context of divorce.

---

[27] Rev. Rul. 2004-60, 2004-1 C.B. 1051, revising the proposed revenue ruling in set forth in Notice 2002-31, 2002-1 C.B. 908.

[28] Rev. Rul. 2004-60, 2004-1 C.B. 1051.
[29] Rev. Rul. 2004-60, 2004-1 C.B. 1051.

Code Sec. 409A imposes strict limits on the deferral of compensation and the distribution of deferred amounts. Among the limits of Code Sec. 409A is a prohibition on the acceleration of the time or schedule of any payment or amount scheduled to be paid pursuant to a deferred compensation arrangement.[30] Code Sec. 409A(a)(3) explicitly provides that the Secretary of Treasury may provide exceptions to this rule by published regulations, which it has done.

The regulations under Code Sec. 409A state that a plan may provide for acceleration of the time or schedule of a payment under the plan to an individual other than the employee, or a payment under such plan may be made to an individual other than the employee, to the extent necessary to fulfill a domestic relations order (as defined in Code Sec. 414(p)(1)(B)).[31]

The regulations under Code Sec. 409A also provide an exception to the rules governing changes in the time and form of payment, which would require a five-year postponement of payments in most cases. The postponement rules do not apply to elections by individuals other than the employee, with respect to payments to a person other than the employee, to the extent such elections are reflected in, or made in accordance with, the terms of a domestic relations order (as defined in section 414(p)(1)(B)).[32]

Finally, the regulations under Code Sec. 409A provide that the six-month delay in payment rule applicable to specified employees of a public company does not apply to a payment made under a domestic relations order.[33]

¶2745 Tax Issues Incident to Divorce

Prior to 2019, alimony and separate maintenance payments are deductible by the payor spouse and includible in income by the recipient spouse under Code Secs. 215(a), 61(a)(8) and 71(a). Under the Tax Cuts and Jobs Act ("TCJA"), for any divorce or separation instrument executed after December 31, 2018, alimony and separate maintenance payments are not taxable to the payee spouse and not deductible by the payor spouse.

.01 Income Tax Consequences

Prior to the TCJA, Code Sec. 61(a)(8) required alimony money be included in the taxable income of the recipient (payee) spouse and Code Sec. 71(a) provided that gross income includes amounts received as alimony or separate maintenance payments. Code Sec. 215(a) provided that in the case of an individual, there shall be allowed as a deduction an amount equal to the alimony or separate maintenance payments paid during such individual's taxable year. Alimony or separate maintenance payments were defined to include any alimony or separate maintenance payment that is includible in the gross income of the recipient under Code Sec. 71. The treatment of child support is not changed.

The TCJA shifts the tax burden from the recipient spouse to the payor spouse. Income used for alimony payments is taxed at the rates applicable to the

---

[30] Code Sec. 409A(a)(3).
[31] Treas. Reg. § 1.409A-3(j)(4)(ii).
[32] Treas. Reg. § 1.409A-2(b)(4).
[33] Treas. Reg. § 1.409A-3(i)(2)(i).

payor spouse rather than the recipient spouse. The TCJA changes are effective for any divorce or separation instrument executed after December 31, 2018, or for any divorce or separation instrument executed on or before December 31, 2018, and modified after that date, if the modification expressly provides that the amendments made by the TCJA apply to such modification.

.02 Income Tax Consequences of Split Stock Options

After determining that stock options are marital property subject to division, the tax implications of transferring the options become important to consider. At this stage, not only are both former spouses involved, but so too is the employer that granted the stock options. An IRS revenue ruling provides guidance as to the tax consequences to former spouses and to employers.

Rev. Rul. 2002-22 held that nonstatutory stock options transferred incident to divorce are property within the meaning of Code Sec. 1041 and that this transfer is entitled to nonrecognition treatment under Code Sec. 1041.[34] Additionally, the ruling held that the "assignment of income doctrine" does not apply in cases of transfers of stock options incident to divorce. The assignment of income doctrine provides that income is generally taxed to the person who earned it and cannot be shifted by assignment. The ruling recognized that applying this doctrine to stocks divided in a marital dissolution would "thwart the purpose of allowing divorcing spouses to sever their ownership interests in property with as little tax intrusion as possible."

Under the facts of Rev. Rul. 2002-22, prior to the divorce, the executive's employer had issued nonstatutory stock options to the executive as part of his compensation. The nonstatutory stock options did not have a readily ascertainable fair market value at the time granted to the executive, and thus no amount was included in the executive's gross income with respect to those options at the time of grant.

The IRS observed that under the applicable state law, stock options earned by a spouse during the period of marriage are marital property subject to equitable division between the spouses in the event of divorce. Pursuant to the property settlement incorporated into their judgment of divorce, the executive transferred to the former spouse one-third of the nonstatutory stock options issued to the executive by the employer.

The IRS concluded that, under the given facts, the interests in nonstatutory stock options that the executive transferred to the former spouse were property within the meaning of Code Sec. 1041. Code Sec. 1041 confers nonrecognition treatment on any gain that the executive might otherwise realize when the executive transfers these interests to the former spouse in the year of divorce. Further, the assignment of income doctrine does not apply to these transfers. Therefore, the executive is not required to include in gross income any income resulting from the former spouse's exercise of the stock options in a future year.

---

[34] Rev. Rul. 2002-22, 2002-1 C.B. 849. Although the ruling applied specifically to nonstatutory stock options, it is important to note that after a transfer pursuant to divorce, the character of options change from incentive stock options to nonstatutory stock options.

When the former spouse exercises the stock options in a future year, the former spouse must include in income an amount determined under Code Sec. 83 as if the former spouse were the person who performed the services. The same conclusions would apply if the executive and the former spouse resided in a community property state and all, or some, of these income rights constituted community property that was divided between the executive and the former spouse as part of their divorce.

Finally, the IRS stated that its ruling neither applies to transfers of (1) property between spouses other than in connection with divorce nor (2) nonstatutory stock options or other future income rights to the extent such options or rights are unvested at the time of transfer or to the extent that the transferor's rights to such income are subject to substantial contingencies at the time of the transfer.[35]

.03 FICA and FUTA Taxes on the Split Options

The IRS followed up Rev. Rul. 2002-22 with Rev. Rul. 2004-60, giving additional guidance on FICA and FUTA taxes and withholding applicable in the case of transfers of nonstatutory stock options incident to divorce.[36] In Rev. Rul. 2002-22, the IRS ruled that when interests in nonstatutory stock options are transferred from an employee to his or her former spouse (the nonemployee-spouse) pursuant to their divorce, the transfer does not result in a payment of wages for purposes of the FICA and FUTA.

Rev. Rul. 2004-60 reaffirmed that the transfer of interests in nonstatutory stock options from the employee-spouse to the nonemployee-spouse incident to a divorce does not result in a payment of wages for FICA and FUTA tax purposes. The nonstatutory stock options are subject to FICA and FUTA taxes at the time of exercise by the nonemployee-spouse to the same extent as if the employee-spouse had retained the options and exercised them. To the extent FICA and FUTA taxation apply, the relevant wages are those of the employee-spouse. The employee portion of the FICA taxes is deducted from the wages as, and when, the wages are taken into account for FICA tax purposes. The employee portion of the FICA taxes is deducted from the payment to the nonemployee-spouse.

.04 Tax Withholding on the Split Options

The income recognized by the nonemployee-spouse with respect to the exercise of the nonstatutory stock options is subject to withholding under Code Sec. 3402.[37] The amounts to be withheld for income tax withholding are deducted from the payments to the nonemployee-spouse. The supplemental wage flat rate may be used to determine the amount of income tax withholding. Pursuant to Code Sec. 31, the nonemployee-spouse is entitled to the credit allowable for the income tax withheld at the source on these wages.

---

[35] Rev. Rul. 2002-22, 2002-1 C.B. 849 (citing *Kochansky v. Comm'r*, 92 F.3d 957 (9th Cir. 1996)).

[36] Rev. Rul. 2004-60, 2004-1 C.B. 1051, revising the proposed revenue ruling set forth in Notice 2002-31, 2002-1 C.B. 908.

[37] Rev. Rul. 2004-60, 2004-1 C.B. 1051.

The Social Security wages, Medicare wages, Social Security taxes withheld, and Medicare taxes withheld, if applicable, are reportable on Form W-2 with the name, address, and Social Security number of the employee-spouse. However, no amount is includible in Box 1 and Box 2 of the employee's Form W-2 with respect to these payments. The income with respect to the exercise of the nonstatutory stock options by the nonemployee-spouse is reportable in Box 3 as other income on Form 1099-MISC with the name, address, and Social Security number of the nonemployee-spouse. Income tax withholding with respect to these payments of wages is included in Box 4, federal income tax withheld.

.05 Tax Reporting on the Split Options

Income tax withholding on payments to the nonemployee-spouse is included on Form 945 filed by the employee-spouse's employer. The employer reports the Social Security tax and Medicare tax on its Form 941, and reports the FUTA tax on the employer's Form 940.[38]

.06 Split-up of Incentive Stock Options

In private letter ruling 200519011, the IRS described the tax consequences of the split-up of an incentive stock option ("ISO") in divorce.[39] The IRS held as follows:

- The split-up of the ISO did not trigger income tax to either the employee or the former spouse.

- The split-up of the ISO did not result in a disqualifying distribution or otherwise prevent the option from continuing to qualify as an ISO.

- The alternative minimum taxable income recognized on the employee's exercise of the options now owned by the former spouse would be includible in the former spouse's alternative minimum taxable income for tax purposes.

¶2755 Securities Law Issues

With respect to securities laws, transfers of stock options pursuant to a domestic relations order are generally exempt from the reporting rules of Section 16 of the Securities Exchange Act of 1934. Rule 16a-12 provides a general exemption from reporting for both the acquisition and disposition of securities pursuant to a domestic relations order.[40] According to the SEC, the domestic relations order need not be "qualified" (as defined under Code Sec. 414(p)(1)(A) or Title I of ERISA) to be exempt; the Section 16 exemption applies to "nonqualified" domestic relations orders as well.[41]

---

[38] Rev. Rul. 2004-60, 2004-1 C.B. 1051.

[39] I.R.S. Priv. Ltr. Rul. 200519011 (May 18, 2005).

[40] 17 C.F.R. § 240.16a-12.

[41] See Ownership Reports and Trading by Officers, Directors and Principal Security Holders, Ex-

change Act Release No. 37,260, Fed. Sec. L. Rep. (CCH) ¶85810 (May 31, 1996); Amer. Bar Ass'n, SEC No-Action Letter, Fed. Sec. L. Rep. (CCH) ¶77236 (Mar. 3, 1997).

Chapter 28
REPRESENTING THE BOARD IN
NEGOTIATING NEO AGREEMENTS

¶2801 Introduction—Representing the Board in Negotiating NEO Agreements

In this day and age, one of the board of director's most critical functions, typically delegated to the compensation committee, is to determine the compensation of the company's named executive officers (the "NEOs"). Of course, the most important NEO is the chief executive officer ("CEO"). No less than four major areas of the law apply to this process.

- The Internal Revenue Code

- Federal securities laws

- State law fiduciary rules

- The Employee Retirement Income Security Act ("ERISA")

The courts and judiciary, plaintiffs' class action lawyers, the IRS, the Securities and Exchange Commission ("SEC"), institutional investors, the press, other boards of directors, and the U.S. Congress are all focusing on corporate governance as applied to executive compensation.

.01 Hiring Process

To comply with the applicable laws and regulations, and satisfy the other interested constituencies, we recommend to boards of directors and compensation committees a multi-step process, consisting of separate but interrelated tasks (see ¶2815 for a more detailed discussion of the appropriate process for negotiating with and hiring a new executive officer).

.02 Fiduciary Duties and Corporate Governance

Extensive experience is necessary in each of the distinct laws that apply to the executive compensation and corporate governance process, including state law fiduciary rules and the steps necessary to obtain the protection of the business judgment rule (see ¶2825 for a more detailed discussion of fiduciary duties and corporate governance).

.03 Terminating a NEO

Terminating a named executive officer raises just as many issues and creates just as many traps as hiring a new NEO (see ¶2835 for a more detailed discussion of the issues surrounding a NEO termination).

.04 SEC Reporting

The SEC requires public companies to report promptly the hiring or termination of a named executive officer by filing Form 8-K (see ¶2845 for a more detailed discussion of the SEC reporting requirements).

.05 Dodd-Frank Act Requirements

The Dodd-Frank Wall Street Reform and Consumer Protection Act of 2010 (the "Dodd-Frank Act") included ten separate changes in the area of executive compensation. These provisions apply to all publicly traded companies (see ¶2855 for a more detailed discussion of the Dodd-Frank Act requirements).

¶2815 Process

To comply with the applicable laws and regulations, and satisfy the other interested constituencies, we recommend a multi-step process, consisting of separate but interrelated tasks:

1. Re-read the "Compensation Philosophy" adopted by the board or compensation committee and the applicable compensation committee charter. It is useful to re-read and review these two important documents, possibly during the meeting, before embarking on a major new task such as hiring a CEO (or if you are counsel to the board, beginning a new representation).

The compensation committee charter generally will set forth the precise responsibilities of the committee vis-à-vis the board. The board and compensation committee must determine whether all actions necessary or planned fall within the responsibility of the compensation committee or some other, *e.g.*, the nominating and governance committee for board appointments and/or compensation. If succession planning has been handled by the nominating committee then that committee should make a recommendation to the board.

The "Compensation Philosophy" and the compensation committee charter also may list certain governing principles that the committee should follow (or change) before it begins the negotiation of the agreement. These documents also may obligate the committee to consider certain steps it had not originally planned.

2. Design the compensation proposal. Among the specific factors the board or committee should review and consider are the following:

(a) Market forces. Who has greater negotiating strength, the company or the CEO? During the irrational period of the dot-com bubble, CEOs seemed to hold all the cards and were capable of naming their terms. Since then, real negotiation has come back to the market. However, if a company wants to hire a well-known CEO away from another company, where the CEO will leave behind large amounts of long-term awards and/or retirement benefits, the hiring company usually will have to pay the price.

(b) Comparables. The compensation committee should consider an independent compensation consultant. The committee should analyze surveys and peer group information. The committee should take care in selecting the appropriate "peers."

(c) Other, similar employment agreements of the company. Although everyone understands that the CEO makes more and gets more, the committee should start the negotiations with the terms contained in its current executives' employment agreements (or the terms the committee wishes it had in its current employment agreements). Make no mistake about it; the CEO's agreement will set the standard.

(d) The incoming CEO's current employment agreement (with his or her current employer). If the incoming CEO's current agreement is sparse, the committee may be able to use that to hold the line. If the incoming CEO's current agreement is generous, the committee may need to steel itself for difficult negotiations.

(e) Look for ways to link pay to performance. Regarding annual or long-term incentive compensation, the committee should ensure that it understands and approves (i) the precise metrics/objectives used in the formula, (ii) why these objectives are appropriate, and (iii) how achievement of the objectives will lead to a payment amount.

(f) Review the company's incentive plan(s) to (i) make sure the plan offers the award type(s) the committee wants to make to the new CEO and (ii) review whether the plan has adequate shares reserved for the award (especially since initial and inducement awards for CEOs can often be larger than normal). A plan amendment and/or a Form S-8 adding shares and a revised prospectus may be needed to make the proper incentive awards.

The board or compensation committee should review a term sheet or offer letter for preliminary approval. With this preliminary approval, when we make the offer, the CEO candidate will know that it can bind the company.

3. Utilize your outside advisors. As noted above, the board should compare the CEO's compensation package with those of peer group companies. Because this is a very specialized and high stakes matter, and because it is not fair to expect the company's general counsel to negotiate hard with the individual who will soon be his or her boss, the board should use experienced outside counsel to handle this matter.

4. Discuss, deliberate and understand every element of the compensation proposal, including:

(a) The substantive provisions.

(b) The annual cost, through the use of a tally sheet. The committee should avoid excessive perquisites and recognize that perceptions do matter.

(c) The cost of termination: The committee should use a tally sheet to analyze how various scenarios (i.e., change in control, termination without cause, termination for cause) would affect the CEO's compensation. Remember, the company will need to report this information in its proxy statement.

(d) The accounting cost of the arrangements.

5. Draft the employment agreement to protect the company. Clarify the parties' rights and obligations, and comply with all applicable laws. For example, the committee and its counsel should add clawbacks of compensation for "cause" terminations and situations in which there is a restatement of earnings.

6. Negotiate the compensation package and the terms of the employment agreement, keeping the compensation committee apprised of developments.

7. Seek the final approval of the compensation committee and ratification[1] by the board following and explanation of the agreement and its costs, and some demonstration (generally by the independent compensation consultant) that it is reasonable.

8. Prepare and adopt board and/or compensation committee resolutions appointing the new CEO and approving any compensation (including any grants or awards) in connection with the appointment. The board or committee also may need resolutions terminating the current CEO, accepting the resignation of current CEO, and approving any severance, consulting or other arrangements (including grants or awards) in connection with the termination or retirement.

9. Prepare a press release. The board or committee should supervise the preparation and filing of a press release announcing the appointment of the new CEO and, if applicable, the termination or retirement of the prior CEO.

10. File Form 8-K. The company must file SEC Form 8-K within four business days. The 8-K must describe the new CEO appointment (including an updated biography) and any material compensation or agreements entered into in connection with it (including amendments and grants or awards). If the prior CEO is retiring or being terminated, the 8-K must describe any material compensation, severance or agreements entered into in connection therewith (including amendments and grants or awards). The 8-K also generally will include the press release, if it was not filed previously.

11. Provide notice to NYSE/Nasdaq. The company must provide notice of the CEO change, including a copy of the press release (generally, at least 10 minutes prior to its release or during aftermarket hours). If there is also a change in the board of directors in connection with the appointment, then the company may need to provide interim written affirmation within five business days.

12. File Form 4. The company must file a Form 4 for any grants, vesting, *etc.* associated with the changes, and may need to file a Form 3 for a first-time reporting person.

13. File Form 10-K or Q. The company must attach any employment or other agreements with the new CEO to the next Form 10-K or Q it files. Additionally, a new CEO appointed prior to the filing of the Form 10-K would be required to sign the Form 10-K and the CEO certifications that are filed as exhibits thereto. Alternatively, the company may need to update the Form 10-K to reflect the new CEO, including signature pages, title references and change in bios.

The following time line/task list summarizes the steps discussed above that the board and/or compensation committee might take when hiring a new CEO (or other NEO).

---

[1] Treasury Regulation § 1.162-27(c)(4) provides that "A committee of directors is not treated as failing to have the authority to establish perform- ance goals merely because the goals are ratified by the board of directors."

Appointment of Candidate as CEO (D-Day):	**Compensation Committee Meeting. Committee uses tally sheet to understand and quantify all elements of the proposed compensation package and examines competitive data to benchmark the package. Committee deliberates and (presumably) approves the Employment Agreement and the compensation and awards thereunder. Board of Directors Meeting.**

- Board understands the Employment Agreement and all compensation and awards thereunder
- Board (i) appoints candidate as CEO; and (ii) elects new CEO to Board effective D +14, and contingent on his/her showing up for work on that day

Board sends two copies of Employment Agreement, signed by Board Chair (or Compensation Committee Chair), to new CEO by PDF (signed originals sent by overnight)

All parties comment on Press Release

D +1:	Candidate/New CEO meets with his/her current employer CEO and resigns
	New CEO countersigns the PDF versions (and the originals, if possible) and returns them by PDF
D +2:	Company files Form 8-K with SEC
	Company sends Press Release, after the close of business
	Company notifies key employees, customers, suppliers and other stakeholders of the change
D +14:	New CEO's start date; "Effective Date" of the Employment Agreement

- New CEO's election to Board and appointment as officer becomes fully effective (Board Resolution)
- Restricted Stock or Option Award effective
- Company pays signing bonus, if any
- New CEO to Sign required Director's Resignation

Company files Form 3 with SEC

Company files Form 8-K for Restricted Stock or Option Award and Director appointment

Company formally adds New CEO to D&O liability policy

¶2825 Fiduciary Duties and Corporate Governance

Extensive experience is necessary in each of the distinct laws that apply to the executive compensation and corporate governance process:

- The Internal Revenue Code, including key Sections 162(m) ($1 million limit on deductibility), 280G (golden parachute), and 409A (deferred compensation).

- Federal securities laws, including critical Securities Exchange Act of 1934 Section 16b (insider trading restrictions) and Rule 10b-5 (short-swing profit provisions), and the necessary 8-K and proxy statement reporting provisions.

- State law fiduciary rules, including the steps necessary to obtain the protection of the business judgment rule.

- ERISA, including qualified, non-qualified, and welfare benefit plan provisions.

The company should be certain that its counsel has experience with every type of executive compensation, including:

- Stock options, restricted stock, cash and stock, stock appreciation rights, phantom stock, and other innovative equity and equity-based compensation programs.
- Long- and short-term incentive compensation programs.
- Employee stock purchase plans under Code Sec. 423.
- Severance and retention plans and agreements, golden parachutes, and other change in control protective measures.
- Deferred compensation, SERPs, and other post-retirement compensation arrangements.

The board should be advised by inside or outside counsel with significant experience in each critical phase of the governance, drafting, negotiating, and reporting process:

- Negotiation
- Contract drafting
- Business judgment rule
- Practical impact of the federal securities law reporting requirements

The company likely will require assistance with the design and drafting of the various forms of executive compensation arrangements, including stock option plans, restricted stock plans, employee stock purchase plans, stock appreciation rights, phantom stock, and other innovative equity and equity-based compensation programs. Counsel should have extensive experience in designing and drafting all kinds of employment contracts, change in control agreements, retention agreements, and severance agreements. This experience ensures that the company receives the most advanced and up-to-date advice on the "market" for these agreements.

.01 Executive Compensation - Corporate Governance Process

One of the most critical functions of the board of directors, often delegated to the compensation committee, is to determine the compensation of the company's NEOs, with the most important being the CEO. To comply with the applicable laws and regulations, and satisfy the other interested constituencies, we guide our clients through the following multi-step process, consisting of separate but interrelated tasks.

We often suggest presenting the term sheet or offer letter to the board or committee for preliminary approval. We explain that this is not a full-fledged agreement, so the committee understands that subsequent negotiation could raise the cost. However, with this preliminary approval, when we make the offer, the CEO candidate will know that it is binding on the company. If (and when) the CEO candidate or other executive makes additional requests, we will go back to the committee with any material cost increases (or initially get its authority to negotiate the best deal).

A critical component of corporate governance, including the adoption and implementation of executive compensation plans, programs, and agreements, is simply following the appropriate procedures. We want to protect the directors, so we ensure that they follow these procedures. The "business judgment rule" mandates that the courts will not second-guess the merits of a decision of disinterested and independent directors — who after reasonable investigation — adopt a course of action that they, in good faith, honestly and reasonably believe will benefit the corporation. Under the business judgment rule, the courts will uphold almost any decision that is:

- Made by an independent board of directors acting disinterestedly;
- Decided after careful and informed deliberation; and
- Reflected in the meeting minutes.

We guide clients through the questions, deliberations, and documentation necessary to achieve the critical protection of the business judgment rule.

.02 Liabilities and Costs

It is a fundamental principle of corporate law that the board of directors is responsible for selecting and compensating the corporation's chief executive officer. Together with this responsibility for setting compensation is potential liability to stockholders for wasting corporate assets. The board also has the responsibility to monitor the performance of the CEO. As executive compensation packages soared to new heights in recent years, stockholder litigation over those packages also increased. The extravagant severance amounts paid to executive officers who failed were particularly likely to draw criticism and legal challenge.

As described below, the compensation committee or the board of directors should evaluate the terms, cost, and likely outcomes of the CEO compensation arrangements to protect all parties involved, including:

- The board members themselves. If the board or committee follows the correct procedures, it will not face personal liability. If a court were to find that directors permitted a CEO to receive millions of dollars in excessive compensation by failing to meet minimal standards of due care or by failing to consider information such as the aggregate costs of a pay package, including severance, the court might find that the board abrogated its duties to the company and failed to act in good faith. This could mean that each director would have to pay several million dollars out of his or her own pocket, without reimbursement by the company or the D&O insurance carrier. And even if they win the case (see *In re Walt Disney* and *Integrated Health Systems* [Elkins]), the cost in time and reputation is incalculable.

- The company's public image. There are two parts to this protection. The money the directors can save the company and its shareholders by reducing payments can be significant. However, the real savings come from avoiding legal issues that play out in the courtroom and the press.

- The stockholders. The company's stockholders stand to suffer the most from damage to the company's image.

- The CEO. The CEO also has a fiduciary obligation to review his or her compensation. See *In re Walt Disney* and *Integrated Health Systems*.

The courts and judiciary, plaintiffs' class action lawyers, the IRS, the SEC, institutional investors, the press, other boards of directors, and the U.S. Congress are all focusing on corporate governance as it applies to executive compensation. Congress and the IRS have effected some minor changes. However, the major developments — the ones that have significantly changed the responsibility and potential liability for directors — have come from the judiciary, the plaintiffs' lawyers, and the SEC.

Historically, judges were reluctant to intrude on a board of directors' business judgment in setting compensation because these decisions were subjective. For decades, the courts had broadly interpreted the corporate waste standard, and plaintiffs had been discouraged from bringing lawsuits that alleged excessive compensation. However, based on recent case law developments and surprisingly candid statements from the Delaware judiciary in particular, it appears that judges now may be willing — even eager — to hear these cases.

Delaware law requires that its corporations indemnify current or former officers and directors who are "successful on the merits or otherwise" in defense of legal actions against them for service on the board. However, Delaware law prohibits a corporation from indemnifying an officer or director if he or she acted in bad faith or in a manner that the director did not reasonably believe was in the best interests of the corporation.

Now that select courts are breaking down the absolute shield of the business judgment rule, the compensation committee process, like other boards of directors' functions, is becoming even more important. If the committee members carefully and thoroughly reviewed and understood all of the elements of CEO compensation, and documented (in the minutes) the process and deliberations undertaken, a court will be very unlikely to overturn the committee's judgment. Recent cases challenging compensation decisions have focused on situations in which either there was no review process and understanding of the potential compensation or the directors were not independent.

As a result, plaintiffs' lawyers have been quick to try to capitalize on recent court rulings that have weakened the once insurmountable business judgment rule. Most directors are familiar with the widely reported settlement with the former WorldCom Directors, under which the directors agreed to pay $18 million of their own money to settle claims that they were negligent in discharging their fiduciary duties. Undisclosed loans to the CEO were among the focal points of this matter. On the heels of the announcement of the WorldCom Directors' settlement was the announcement that the former Enron Corp. Directors had agreed to pay $13 million personally as part of their settlement.

¶2825.02

.03 Director Independence

The use of independent and disinterested persons to evaluate a compensation agreement or plan increases the likelihood that a court will uphold the plan. For this reason, corporations create compensation committees composed solely of independent and disinterested directors, and retain independent compensation consultants and counsel to advise them. Counsel should assist clients in determining whether any relationships between a member of the compensation committee and the CEO warrants special attention, recusal, or disclosure.

Director independence is a mechanism to ensure that a board acts in the best interests of the company and its shareholders. Courts give a great deference to the business judgment of an independent board of directors. Whether a director is disinterested and independent depends on the facts and circumstances of each situation.

Section 952 of the Dodd-Frank Act added section 10C to the Exchange Act, which requires the SEC to promulgate rules that direct the New York Stock Exchange ("NYSE"), Nasdaq, and other national securities exchanges and associations to prohibit the listing of any equity security of a company that does not have an independent compensation committee. In determining the definition of the term "independence," the national securities exchanges and associations must consider relevant factors to be determined and published by the SEC, including: (A) the source of compensation of a member of the company's board of directors, including any consulting, advisory, or other compensatory fee paid by the company to such member; and (B) whether a member of the company's board is affiliated with the company, or a subsidiary or affiliate of the company.

When the Dodd-Frank Act was signed into law, most public companies already satisfied the independent compensation committee requirement, due to their compliance with Code Sec. 162(m), which generally was more restrictive than the stock exchange rules. However, the legislation known as the Tax Cuts and Jobs Act of 2017, signed into law by President Trump on 2017, eliminated the need to comply with specific independence requirements under Code Sec. 162(m).

Beginning in 2018, the stock exchange rules and securities laws, as well as Institutional Shareholder Services Inc. ("ISS") voting guidelines, will govern the independence requirements for compensation committee membership. Both NYSE and Nasdaq rules contain general independence requirements for directors, and enhanced independence requirements for compensation committee members.

NYSE and Nasdaq Rules Concerning Independence. The NYSE and Nasdaq rules concerning independence are largely identical. The NYSE rules require listed companies to have a compensation committee composed entirely of independent directors.[2] Similarly, Nasdaq rules require that each listed company

---

[2] NYSE Rule 303A.05(a).

have a compensation committee with at least two independent directors.[3] Both exchanges require the compensation committee to have a written charter.

NYSE rules indicate that directors are generally independent only if the board of directors affirmatively determines that the director "has no material relationship with the listed company."[4] This includes a direct relationship or as a partner, shareholder, or officer of an organization that has a relationship with the company. General independence under Nasdaq rules requires a director be neither an executive officer or employee of the company.[5] The individual may also not have a relationship which the company's board of directors determines would interfere with the exercise of independent judgment in carrying out the responsibilities of a director.

Nasdaq rules specifically proscribe the holding of certain positions (executive and employee), while NYSE rules prohibit these same positions in describing that "direct relationships" are not allowed, and enumerate that a relationship as a "partner, shareholder, or officer" is also not permissible.

Enhanced Independence for Compensation Committee Members. Additional independence requirements apply to individuals serving on a compensation committee. Both NYSE and Nasdaq rules provide that the board of directors must consider all factors specifically relevant to determining whether a director has a relationship to the company that is material to that director's ability to be independent from management in connection with the duties of a compensation committee member, including, but not limited to, (i) the source of compensation of such director, including any consulting, advisory or other compensatory fee paid by the company to such director; and (ii) whether such director is affiliated with the company, a subsidiary of the company or an affiliate of a subsidiary of the company.[6]

The rules automatically preclude a finding of independence in certain scenarios, including family members and employees of the company. "Family member" includes a spouse, parent, parents-in-law, children, daughters- and sons-in law, siblings, and sisters- and brothers-in-law, as well as anyone residing in a person's home.[7] A director is not independent if the director is currently an employee of the company, or has been an employee within the last three years.[8] Both sets of rules, in commentary, indicate that acting as interim CEO does not alone disqualify a director from being independent. A director is not independent if a director's family member is currently or has been an executive officer of the company within the last three years.[9]

Additionally, under both sets of rules, a director is not independent if either the director or a family member accepted compensation from the company greater than $120,000 during any period of twelve months within the past three

---

[3] Nasdaq Rule IM-5605-5(d).

[4] NYSE Rule 303A.02(a)(i).

[5] Nasdaq Rule 5605(a)(2).

[6] NYSE Rule 303A.02(a)(ii); Nasdaq Rule 5605-5(d)(2)(A).

[7] Nasdaq Rules 5605(a)(2), IM-5605; NYSE General Commentary to Section 303A.02(b).

[8] Nasdaq Rule 5605(a)(2)(A); NYSE Rule 303A.02(b)(i).

[9] Nasdaq Rule 5605(a)(2)(C); NYSE Rule 303A.02(b)(i).

years.[10] A director is not independent if the director or a family member is currently, or has been within the past three years, employed as an executive officer of another company where any of the listed company's present executive officers serve or served on that company's compensation committee.[11]

Under both Nasdaq and NYSE rules, a director is not independent if that individual or a family member was either a partner or an employee within the past three years, if that person personally worked on the company's audit.[12] The rules apply differently for internal and external auditors.

.04 Use of Experts

Corporation law in most states expressly enables the board of directors to rely on outside experts when making business decisions and provides them shelter from liability when they do so. For example, Delaware corporate law provides as follows:

"A member of the Board of Directors ... shall in the performance of such member's duties be fully protected in relying in good faith upon ... information, opinions, reports or statements presented to the corporation by ... any other person as to matters the member reasonably believes are within such other person's professional or expert competence and who has been selected with reasonable care by or on behalf of the corporation." 8 Del.C. § 141(e)

In most cases, the courts will dismiss any lawsuit challenging a transaction or other board action in which an expert had advised the corporation, as long as the following is true:

- The directors rely on the expert; that is, they do not ignore his or her advice;
- The directors' reliance was in good faith;
- The directors reasonably believe that the expert's advice is within the expert's professional competence; and
- The directors selected the expert with reasonable care.

By bringing in experienced counsel and an independent compensation consultant, the board or committee gains additional protection for whatever decision it makes on compensation (assuming it is not directly contrary to what we recommend).

Exchange Act Section 10C, added by Dodd-Frank Act Section 952, also adds a subsection (b), "Independence of Compensation Consultants and Other Compensation Committee Advisers," which provides that:

- The compensation committee may only select a compensation consultant, legal counsel or other adviser after taking into consideration factors identified by the SEC (see below);

---

[10] Nasdaq Rule 5605(a)(2)(B); NYSE Rule 303A.02(b)(ii).

[11] Nasdaq Rule 5605(a)(2)(E); NYSE Rule 303A.02(b)(iv).

[12] Nasdaq Rule 5605(a)(2)(F); NYSE Rule 303A.02(b)(iii).

- The committee, in its sole discretion, may retain and obtain the advice of independent legal counsel and other advisers; and

- The company must provide for appropriate funding, as determined by the compensation committee, for payment of reasonable compensation to independent legal counsel or any other adviser.

The Dodd-Frank Act does *not* require a compensation committee to hire its own independent compensation consultant, legal counsel or other advisers. However, it seems to require the compensation committee to consider the possibility. Dodd-Frank requires the SEC to identify factors that affect the independence of legal counsel to a compensation committee, but specifies that these factors shall include at least—

(A) The provision of other services to the company by the firm that employs the compensation consultant, legal counsel, or other adviser;

(B) The amount of fees received from the company by the firm that employs the compensation consultant, legal counsel, or other adviser, as a percentage of the total revenue of that firm;

(C) The policies and procedures of the firm that employs the compensation consultant, legal counsel, or other adviser, which are designed to prevent conflicts of interest;

(D) Any business or personal relationship of the compensation consultant, legal counsel, or other adviser with a member of the compensation committee; and

(E) Any stock of the company owned by the compensation consultant, legal counsel, or other adviser.

Beginning with the proxy statement for annual shareholders' meetings occurring in 2011, Dodd-Frank requires disclosure of whether the compensation committee retained or obtained the advice of an independent compensation consultant and whether the consultant's work raised any conflict of interest issues (and, if so, the nature of the conflict and how the conflict is being addressed), but no disclosure on those issues with respect to legal counsel or other advisers.

Finally, Exchange Act Section 10C states that it should not be construed (i) to require the compensation committee to implement or act consistently with the advice or recommendations of the compensation consultant; or (ii) to affect the ability or obligation of a compensation committee to exercise its own judgment in fulfilment of the duties of the compensation committee.

.05 Other Executive Officers

The process described above is particularly important for the hiring and compensation of the CEO. The extent to which the board of directors or compensation committee should follow a similar process in the hiring and compensation of any other NEO depends on what the committee charter says about its responsibility. However, we suggest that the compensation committee review, discuss, and deliberate the package of any NEO and its cost, and then approve it in principle, primarily because the company will be required to discuss the package and its cost in the Compensation Discussion & Analysis ("CD&A") of the proxy statement (see ¶1201, *et. seq*, for a discussion of proxy statement reporting requirements). If the committee will be uncomfortable by this disclosure, that should be addressed sooner rather than later.

.06 Internal Candidate Who is Not Selected

In the search for a new CEO, often there is an internal candidate. Retention issues can arise if the board does not select the internal candidate. Chapter 14 discusses retention issues in detail.

.07 Private Companies

Federal securities laws do not apply to private companies, but the actions of the SEC and its requirements can point out traps and help illustrate best practices. The fact that a company is private does not mean that the Delaware courts will hold the directors to a lower threshold. Recent decisions in the Delaware courts have applied to the boards of directors, individual directors, and management of any Delaware corporation with shareholders.

Because courts are finding that private company directors have duties similar to those of public companies, it is important for private companies to understand the duties and responsibilities (and potential liabilities) that courts are imposing on public company boards of directors.

.08 Executive Employment Agreements

Generally, the company and the new CEO execute an employment agreement. No law requires an employer and an employee to set forth the terms of their relationship in a written agreement, and some companies do not use employment agreements for even their most senior executive officers. However, employers without any employment agreements are in the minority, as most employers feel it is necessary to have some form of written agreement for the employer's protection.

An employment agreement is a legal contract between the company and the CEO that sets forth the terms of the employment relationship. The employment agreement could cover as many or as few aspects of the employment relationship as the parties' desire. (We recommend that it cover as many terms as possible.) Among the terms and conditions that employment agreements commonly address are the following:

- Title;
- Duties;
- Employment Term;
- Base Salary;
- Bonus;
- Equity Compensation;
- Other Incentive Compensation;

- Retirement Plan Benefits;
- Health and Welfare Benefits;
- Perquisites;
- Severance Benefits; and
- Change in Control Provisions.

.09 Inducement Awards

When a company brings in a new CEO, it is often necessary to make a significant stock award to the new CEO on his or her date of hire. In this situation, many companies use an exception available under the stock exchanges for so-called "inducement awards."[13] Under an inducement award, stock is awarded from the company's authorized but unissued shares, but does not count against the authorized share pool under the company's stock plan. Stock is awarded from outside of the company's stock plan.

The stock exchanges each impose specific requirement on companies' inducement awards. First, the award must be made in connection with an offer of employment to a new employee, including an individual who was previously an employee or director but is re-joining the company following a bona fide period of non-employment. The award must be a material inducement to the individual accepting the job. A stand-alone award agreement must be drafted. The exception is not available to induce an individual to join the company as a non-employee director, consultant, advisor or independent contractor.

The material terms of the award must be disclosed in a press release within four days of issuance (*e.g.*, the CEO's start date, assuming the award is made on the start date). The committee or a majority of independent board members must approve the award. If the inducement grant is made to a named executive officer, a Form 8-K must be filed within four days of the grant. The company also may need to file a Form 3 within 10 calendar days of the employee becoming a Section 16 insider.

The company must disclose an inducement award in its 10-K or proxy statement. In addition to describing the inducement award in the CD&A and tables (assuming the award was made to an NEO), the company must disclose the award in the Equity Compensation Plan Information Table in a separate row titled "Equity Compensation Plan Not Approved by Stockholders." The company must disclose the number of shares subject to outstanding inducement awards; the weighted-average exercise price of outstanding inducement awards; and the number of shares remaining available for issuance under the plan. An additional narrative disclosure must be provided with the table explaining the material terms of the inducement awards and an inducement plan as it was not approved by stockholders.

---

[13] NYSE Listing Company Manual Rule 303A.08; Nasdaq Listing Rule 5635(c)(4).

The company must file a Form S-8 to register the shares underlying the inducement award. The company also must file a Listing of Additional Shares notification with the stock exchange by the earlier of five days from after the acceptance of the offer of employment or the disclosure of the material terms of the CEO's employment inducement award in a press release, for Nasdaq-listed companies.[14]

ISS and Glass Lewis, as well as many institutional investors, will include inducement grant overhang and usage in their applicable dilution and burn rate evaluations. Therefore, while use of inducement grants can help extend the life of a company's share plan, it can negatively impact a company's dilution and burn rate profiles relative to proxy advisory firm and institutional investor standards when it comes time to seek a new or amended share request. Depending on the magnitude and duration of use, inducement grants may negatively impact perceived plan "cost" (as defined by shareholder value transfer "SVT") and burn rate requirements that must be satisfied in order to obtain a positive vote recommendation from ISS and Glass Lewis on any future equity plan proposal submitted to shareholders for approval. It is important to note that grants made under an inducement exception aren't "free"— they are in essence an advance on a future share request.

¶2835 Terminating a NEO

Terminating a named executive officer raises just as many issues and creates just as many traps as hiring a new NEO.

.01 Potential Steps for ABC Board Consideration

1. On the Termination Date, a group of the independent directors should advise the executive that, after due investigation and deliberation, the independent members of the ABC Board have unanimously determined that the best course for the company is for the executive to resign his/her position as Chairman, President, and Chief Executive Officer, effective at the close of business on the Termination Date.

2. Advise the executive that the primary rationale for the board's decision is the independent directors' unanimous loss of confidence in his/her judgment and ability to lead the company.

3. The board could note that, from a termination benefit standpoint, the resignation could be deemed a "retirement" under the company plans and policies, which could provide the executive with termination benefits of accrued and unpaid base salary, incentive compensation, deferred compensation, and any other accrued cash compensation, vacation pay, and expense reimbursements.

4. Advise the executive that if he/she resigns/retires immediately as requested by the board, the independent members of the board, in the exercise of their reasonable business judgment, will allow him/her to retire effective as of a date in the near future. The independent directors

---

[14] Nasdaq Listing Rule 5635(c)(4).

should fully evaluate the reasonableness of any economic package proposed to the executive in this process.

5. Ask the General Counsel and Vice President of Human Resources jointly to prepare a set of documents relating to the executive's resignation, such as a letter reflecting the form of "Termination/Retirement and Release Agreement" reached with the board, a form of resignation letter for the executive's signature, a form of press release announcing his/her resignation, and other appropriate material. The company should provide these items to the executive when it advises the executive of the independent directors' desire that he/she resign.

6. Invite the executive to confer with counsel concerning the resignation terms offered by the board.

7. Advise the executive that the deadline to indicate to the board whether he/she will abide by the requested resignation process is no later than 5 p.m. on the Termination Date. Advise the executive that, if he/she opts not to accept the board's recommended resignation, that the board, based on its investigation and deliberations, will go forward on the Termination Date with a meeting to address whether to terminate the executive.

8. Provide the executive with notice of the board meeting.

9. In considering the executive's "Termination/Retirement and Release Agreement," the board should understand the changing attitudes toward executive compensation in the courts and in the public. Executive compensation has become a hot button issue in the courts and generally among the investor community. Recent trends suggest that the courts are more likely to overturn compensation arrangements they consider too generous or poorly structured.

10. Before taking any action with respect to the executive's employment, the independent directors should have a plan in place for interim or permanent leadership of the company.

11. In connection with this entire process, the board should avail itself of the advice of independent counsel and other professionals, as it deems necessary in the prudent discharge of its fiduciary duties.

12. Document Preparation:

    • Contacts List (showing all information for all directors, involved executives and outside counsel)

    • Draft Press Release and Form 8-K

    • Applicable Notices

    • Draft internal communication/announcement

    • Chart of compensation and benefits provided for under Employment Agreement for immediate termination vs. future date retirement

    • Talking Points and Areas of Caution for meeting with the executive

- Draft Copy of "Termination/Retirement and Release Agreement"

.02 Task List

The following is a summary of actions under two possible NEO separation scenarios:

Termination	Retirement
• Board meeting	• Board meeting
• Resolutions of Board - Termination - Appointment of new Chairman and CEO	• Resolutions of Board - Approving retirement - Appointment of new Chairman and CEO
• Notice of Termination	
• Release	• Retirement agreement and release
• Resignation from Board	• Resignation from Board
• Notify stock exchange	• Notify stock exchange
• Press release	• Press Release
• File Form 8-K	• File Form 8-K
• Notify key customers and other key business partners	• Notify key customers and other key business partners
• Notify key investors	• Notify key investors
• Notify government regulator, if applicable	• Notify government regulator, if applicable
• Notify other employees	• Notify other employees
• File Form 4 and Form 5, checking the "exit box" to indicate that the reporting person is no longer subject to Section 16	• File Form 4 and Form 5, checking the "exit box" to indicate that the reporting person is no longer subject to Section 16

When an executive ceases to be an "insider" subject to Section 16, the company should review his or her transactions for the year of termination for any that have not been reported. If the company discovers any unreported transactions, it should file a Form 4 to report the transactions at that time (rather than waiting until the end of the year, when it is more likely to forget about them). The company should be certain to include the former insider in its year-end surveys and reconciliations for Section 16 (and should consider obtaining a "no Form 5 due" statement from them).

The company also should review the former insider's transactions for the past six months for any non-exempt transactions. If the company counts out six months from the former insider's last non-exempt purchase, that will tell it how long the company needs to report future non-exempt sales. Then the company can count out six months from the former insider's last non-exempt sale to determine the last date he/she needs to report non-exempt purchases. The company should inform the former insider of these dates, so he/she is aware that non-exempt transactions are still subject to Section 16, both for reporting purposes and short-swing profits recovery purposes.

Section 16 imposes a legal obligation on the individual insider, not the company. However, most companies assist their officers and directors with this obligation by preparing and submitting the required forms on their behalf. Often, this continues to be the case during that short period where the individual has ceased to be a designated insider but is still subject to the reporting and short-swing profits recovery provisions of Section 16. (The exception might be where an insider has left on bad terms, *e.g.*, was dismissed for some sort of egregious behavior or violated a non-compete or other agreement, in which case, some companies might leave the offending insider to his/her own devices for Section 16 purposes.) If the company will continue to assist with the former insider's post-Section 16 reporting, it may want to make a note of these dates in its calendar as well.

¶2845 SEC Disclosure

A public company must file Form 8-K with the SEC for the appointment of certain new executive officers, under Item 5.02(c). A public company also must file Form 8-K with the SEC if it enters into a material contract or arrangement with certain executive officers, under Item 5.02(e).

.01 Appointment of New Executive Officers

A public company must file Form 8-K with the SEC, under Item 5.02(c), if it "appoints a new principal executive officer, president, principal financial officer, principal accounting officer, principal operating officer, or person performing similar functions." In its filing, the company must disclose the following information with respect to the newly appointed officer:

(1) the name, age, and all positions with the company held by the newly appointed officer and the date of the appointment;

(2) the term of office as officer, any previous period during which he or she has served as such, and any arrangement or understanding between the officer and any other person(s) (naming such person) pursuant to which he or she was or is to be selected as an officer;

(3) any family relationship between the executive officer and any director or executive officer;

(4) the business experience during the past five years of the executive officer, including his or her principal occupations and employment during the past five years; the name and principal business of any corporation or other organization in which such occupations and employment were carried on; and

(5) a brief description of any material plan, contract or arrangement (whether or not written) to which the covered officer is a party or in which he or she participates that is entered into or material amendment in connection with the triggering event or any grant or award to any such covered person or modification thereto, under any such plan, contract or arrangement in connection with any such event.

The Form 8-K requirement applies even if the new CEO is appointed from inside the company. For example, if a company were to promote its CFO to CEO, the Form 8-K would report that promotion and any new awards or agreements entered into in connection with the promotion.

Section B of the instructions to Form 8-K states that when the company appoints a new executive officer, "a report is to be filed or furnished within four business days after occurrence of the event." This four-day period runs from the date the company appoints the new executive officer. However, according to the SEC's Compensation Disclosure and Interpretation Question 117.05 for Form 8-K, if the company intends to make a public announcement of the appointment other than by means of a report on Form 8-K, it may delay disclosure until the date of the announcement. If the terms of a new officer's employment agreement have not been settled by the time disclosure is required, a company may state that fact in the Form 8-K filing, then file an amendment to the Form 8-K containing the required information within four business days of the date it becomes known.

Until the board of directors or a committee thereof appoints an individual as an executive officer, there is no obligation or requirement to file a Form 8-K. Discussions, expectations, and negotiations are not sufficient to trigger an 8-K filing requirement. If the company and candidate reach an understanding that, if everything goes according to plan over the next few months the company will employ the candidate under certain terms, *but nothing is signed and the board has not approved or appointed him/her,* and either party could back out at any time - and may well back out, given the length of time between "understanding" and the onset of a legal obligation - then an appointment requiring disclosure has *not* occurred and generally no Form 8-K is required.

The result could be different in the situation where a candidate actually comes to work for the company before an agreement is signed or terms fully agreed, where he/she could be deemed to have accepted his/her appointment by performing duties.

.02 Termination of Executive Officers

A public company must file Form 8-K with the SEC, under Item 5.02(b), if the company terminates its principal executive officer (CEO), president, principal financial officer (CFO), principal accounting officer, principal operating officer, or any person performing similar functions, or any named executive officer, retires, resigns or is terminated from that position. As with the "appointment" filing requirement, the company must file the Form 8-K within four business days after occurrence of the event.

Additionally, both Form 4 and Form 5 include a checkbox to indicate that the reporting person is no longer subject to Section 16, commonly referred to as the "exit box." Any time a new form is submitted after an insider is no longer subject to Section 16, whether to report newly occurring non-exempt transactions that are still reportable or to report previously unreported transactions, this box should be selected.

.03 Material Agreement with Executive Officers

A public company must file Form 8-K with the SEC, under Item 5.02(e), if it enters into a material contract or arrangement (whether or not written), as to which the company's principal executive officer (CEO), principal financial officer

(CFO), or a named executive officer (NEO) participates or is a party, or such compensatory plan, contract or arrangement is materially amended or modified, or a material grant or award under any such plan, contract or arrangement to any such person is made or materially modified. In its filing, the company must provide a brief description of the terms and conditions of the plan, contract or arrangement and the amounts payable to the officer thereunder.

¶2855 Dodd-Frank Act Requirements

The Dodd-Frank Act included ten separate changes in the area of executive compensation (eleven, for companies that are "covered financial institutions"), many of which will affect the process of negotiating with and hiring new executive officers.

1. Shareholder Say on Pay
2. Shareholder Approval of Golden Parachute Compensation
3. Director Independence
4. Independence of Compensation Consultant, Legal Counsel and Other Advisers
5. Compensation Clawback Policy
6. Disclosure Regarding Chairman and CEO Structure
7. Disclosure of Hedging by Employees and Directors
8. Disclosure of Pay Versus Performance
9. Pay Equity Disclosure
10. Elimination of Discretionary Broker Voting

The provisions apply to all publicly traded companies. Most of the provisions were not self-executing, in that they required the SEC to modify its requirements for maintaining an effective registration under the Securities Exchange Act of 1934 (the "Exchange Act") and/or required the national securities exchanges to modify their listing standards.

.01 Shareholder Say on Pay Issues

Section 951 of Dodd-Frank added a Section 14A to the Exchange Act, entitled "Shareholder Approval of Executive Compensation." Section 14A provides that, not less frequently than once every three years, a company's annual proxy statement must include a separate resolution subject to shareholder vote to approve the compensation of executives, effective for annual meetings in 2011 and after.

Final rules published by the SEC in 2010, clarified that the shareholder say on pay ("SSOP") vote only applies to the compensation of the NEOs, as disclosed in the proxy statement for that year in the CD&A, compensation tables, and any related narrative disclosure.

According to the Dodd-Frank Act, the SSOP vote will not be binding on the company or the board. A company must disclose this fact in its explanation or recommendation as to the SSOP vote in its proxy statement. Additionally, a

SSOP vote may not be construed as: (a) overruling the board's decisions on compensation, (b) creating or implying any addition or change to the board's fiduciary duties, or (c) restricting or limiting shareholders' ability to make proposals for inclusion in proxy materials related to executive compensation.

However, every public company in America should be focused on maximizing the likelihood of achieving a favorable vote on SSOP. A majority vote "Against" a company's compensation package is certain to generate adverse publicity. Additionally, ISS and other institutional shareholder advisors have stated that, with respect to any company that receives a majority vote "Against" its compensation package and fails to make significant changes to address issues that are recognized as leading to the "Against" vote, they would recommend an "Against" vote as to the company's compensation committee members and, possibly, other directors, in the next election of directors.

The SSOP vote is a single "For" or "Against" vote on the total compensation package provided to the named executive officers, as disclosed in the company's CD&A, the compensation tables, and any related material. If the overall packages of the NEOs are reasonable - even below market - but there is one blemish, such as a gross-up on perquisite payments or a single trigger golden parachute agreement, shareholders may vote "Against" the package. *There is no other way for shareholders to register disapproval.* They cannot criticize or object to that one provision or practice only.

Therefore, most compensation committees have added one more factor to their consideration of compensation for the new executive officer: How will we explain this decision, payment or policy in the proxy statement CD&A, and will it increase the risk that shareholders will vote "Against" on Say on Pay?

.02 Compensation Clawbacks

Section 954 of Dodd-Frank added Section 10D, entitled "Recovery of Erroneously Awarded Compensation Policy," to the Exchange Act. This section requires the SEC to direct the national securities exchanges to prohibit the listing of any security of an issuer that does not develop and implement a clawback policy. The time to add a clawback policy to an executive's employment and other agreements is at hire.

The policy *must* provide that, "in the event that the issuer is required to prepare an accounting restatement due to the material noncompliance of the issuer with any financial reporting requirement under the securities laws, the issuer will recover from any current or former executive officer of the issuer who received incentive-based compensation (including stock options awarded as compensation) during the 3-year period preceding the date on which the issuer is required to prepare an accounting restatement, based on the erroneous data, in excess of what would have been paid to the executive officer under the accounting restatement."

Until the SEC issues the rules required under Section 954, there will be more questions than answers as to compensation clawbacks. However, we do know the following:

Individuals Covered: A company's compensation clawback policy must apply at least to the individuals who are subject to Section 16 of the Exchange Act (usually referred to as "Section 16 officers" and including the president, any vice president in charge of a principal business unit, division or function (such as sales, administrations or finance or other officer performing a policy-making function)) and individuals who formerly were Section 16 officers.

Compensation Covered: We expect the compensation clawback policy required by Section 10D to apply to all annual and long-term incentive compensation plans and arrangements, and stock options. Whether the SEC attempts to extend the policy requirements to stock-based awards other than options remains to be seen.

Clawback Period: The clawback policy must provide for a potential recovery period of three years, measured from the date the company is "required to prepare the accounting restatement."

Triggering Event: The compensation clawback policy must be triggered in the event that the company is required to restate its financial statements as the result of material noncompliance with applicable accounting principles and the original financial statements resulted in an erroneous payment to a current or former executive officer. The policy must apply regardless of whether (i) the noncompliance was accidental or intentional and (ii) the executive was at fault.

The Dodd-Frank Act provides that companies must disclose their policy on the recovery of incentive-based compensation that is based on erroneous financial information, presumably in the proxy statement, if not before then.

Compensation clawback policies already had become a best practice for compensation committees. However, the actual design and implementation of a clawback policy is very complicated and involves the need to balance a number of legitimate competing interests. Unfortunately, the Dodd-Frank Act mandates exactly the type of compensation clawback policy that companies must adopt. One unintended consequence of this requirement is likely to be a move to higher salaries and less "at-risk" compensation. By its terms, Dodd-Frank seems to leave little room for compensation committee discretion in pursuing clawbacks.

Chapter 29
ETHICAL ISSUES, CONFLICTS AND PRIVILEGE IN EXECUTIVE COMPENSATION

¶2901 Overview—Ethical Issues, Conflicts and Privilege in Executive Compensation

Ethical issues arise in all areas of business, law and public life, including executive compensation and benefits. Additionally, anyone who reads the papers knows that business and professional people (not to mention politicians) often face potential conflicts of interest. Attorney-client privilege issues are unique to the legal world. However, attorney-client privilege issues are common in the employee benefits and executive compensation area, and nearly every area in the practice of law.

.01 Conflicts of Interest

Two types of conflicts of interest can arise in the executive compensation and benefits area: (i) ethical conflicts of interest for attorneys, and (ii) business conflicts of interest for officers, directors and other business people making decisions. In employment, change in control and other executive compensation agreements, as well as deferred compensation, equity and incentive compensation awards, all the design decisions and definitions can make a huge difference in the amount of compensation paid, and even whether compensation is paid, to the executive. When designing and drafting plans and agreements, counsel generally take their directions from directors and officers who will be the beneficiaries of the plans and agreements. However, for conflict of interest purposes, the client is the organization itself and not the officers or other client contacts through whom the organization acts. Each party owes a duty to the company. Therefore, each party must take care to separate its own self-interest from the interest of the company (see ¶2915).

.02 Ethical Issues

Executives, employees and board members must resolve the conflicts of interest issues inherent in the area of executive compensation and benefits according to common law rules and good judgment. However, inside and outside counsel advising the executives, employees and board members must adhere to strict ethical codes (see ¶2925).

.03 Attorney-Client Privilege Issues

Practitioners in the field of executive compensation face many of the same attorney-client privilege issues as those in other areas of the law. However, the executive compensation and employee benefits areas also raise some unique attorney-client privilege issues. Generally, these issues involve the question of who is the attorney's client - who has the right to assert the attorney-client privilege (See ¶ 2935).

.04 Independent Consultant and Counsel Provisions of the Dodd-Frank Act

President Obama signed into law the "Dodd-Frank Wall Street Reform and Consumer Protection Act" (the "Dodd-Frank Act") in July 2010. The Dodd-Frank Act imposed additional requirements on board compensation committees. Section 952(a) of the Dodd-Frank Act adds Sections 10C(b), (d) and (e) to the Securities Exchange Act of 1934, which provide that the compensation committee of a company's board may only select a compensation consultant, legal counsel, or other adviser to the compensation committee after taking into consideration factors identified by the SEC.

.05 Independence Requirements for the Compensation Committee

Dodd-Frank Act Section 952(a) also required the Securities and Exchange Commission ("SEC") to promulgate rules that direct the New York Stock Exchange ("NYSE"), Nasdaq, and other national securities exchanges to prohibit the listing of any equity security of a company that does not have an independent compensation committee. In June 2012, the SEC issued final rules on the independence of compensation committee members and the national securities exchanges adopted nearly identical rules in July 2013 (see ¶ 2955).

¶2915 Conflicts of Interest in Executive Compensation

Executives, employees and directors each have a right to consider their own self-interest in receiving compensation and benefits for their services. The company's board of directors serves as the primary bulwark to ensure independent compensation decisions. However, executives, employees and directors each must take care to separate their own self-interest from the interest of the company in the area of compensation.

In employment, change in control, separation, retention and other executive compensation agreements, all the design decisions and definitions can make a huge difference in the amount of compensation the company pays, and even whether the company pays compensation, to the executive. Drafting and design decisions have a substantial impact on the payment of deferred compensation, equity and incentive compensation awards.

.01 Independent Boards of Directors

Requiring that an independent board of directors make compensation decisions and awards has always been the primary mechanism for avoiding conflicts of interest in the executive compensation process. (See Chapter 21 for a detailed discussion of the responsibilities of board members.)

- The "business judgment rule" mandates that the courts will not second-guess the merits of a decision of disinterested and independent directors who, after reasonable investigation, adopt a course of action that they, in good faith, honestly and reasonably believe will benefit the corporation.

- Rule 16b-3(d) under Section 16 of the Securities Exchange Act of 1934 will exempt stock awards from short swing trading liability if the transaction is approved by the company's board of directors, or a committee of the board of directors that is composed solely of two or more non-employee directors (see ¶ 1215).

- Until 2018, Code Sec. 162(m) required that performance-based compensation be established and approved by a compensation committee consisting solely of two or more outside directors.

- The SEC's proxy statement disclosure rules have required a discussion of compensation committee interlocks and insider participation for more than two decades now. The company should be able to state that none of the members of its compensation committee has ever been an employee of the company or its subsidiaries. The company also should be able to state that none of its executive officers serves as a member of the board of directors or compensation committee of any entity that has one or more executive officers serving on the company's board or compensation committee.

- Each of the stock exchanges impose director independence requirements in their listing standards for public companies.

The SEC's executive compensation disclosure rules require a discussion of director independence in the proxy statement and an even more detailed discussion and disclosure of potential conflicts. Under these rules, the full board must assess the independence of each non-employee director, usually based on the stock exchange listing requirements and the company's own, often more stringent, director independence standards. Generally, a company's independence standards will:

- Require the board to determine that each director has no material relationship with the company other than as a director,

- Prohibit directors from having any direct or indirect financial relationship with the company,

- Restrict both commercial and not-for-profit relationships of all directors with the company,

- Prohibit directors from receiving personal loans or extensions of credit from the company,

- Require all directors to deal at arm's length with the company and its subsidiaries, and

- Require all directors to disclose any circumstance that might be perceived as a conflict of interest.

The full board generally will strictly scrutinize any past employment or affiliation of the director or the director's immediate family members with the company or its independent registered public accounting firm.

.02 Involvement of Executives in the Compensation Process

It is axiomatic that a company acts through its officers. The company's board of directors oversees the officers' actions. As noted above, the board of directors, through its compensation committee, bears a special responsibility for the compensation and benefit plans of executives.

As a practical matter, when designing and drafting compensation and benefit plans, as well as employment and award agreements, counsel generally takes direction from the company officers who will be the beneficiaries of the plans and agreements. How does the company's general counsel, CEO, or other decision-making executive resolve the conflicts inherent in drafting the terms of employment agreements or equity-based awards (or directing outside counsel to draft those terms) when he or she will be one of the recipients of the agreement or award?

The compensation committee of the board of directors will ultimately determine the compensation, agreements, benefits and awards of the company's executive officers. However, a significant amount of detail on the agreements and awards already will have been determined, designed, or drafted before a proposal ever goes to the compensation committee (or will be below the level of detail considered by the committee). Additionally, the compensation committee does not typically review and determine the compensation and agreements of officers and employees outside of the executive officer group.

At least five factors work together to help the company's general counsel and other decision-making executives resolve the conflicts inherent in drafting the terms of employment agreements, benefit plans and equity-based awards (or directing outside counsel to draft those terms) that apply to them.

First, as discussed above, the compensation committee will ultimately review, revise, and approve the compensation awards and agreements of the company's executive officers. The compensation committee has a legal obligation, indeed a fiduciary duty, to understand, evaluate, and establish appropriate compensation arrangements. Additionally, compensation committees often have their own counsel and consultants to advise them of the appropriateness of the officers' compensation arrangements.

Second, the company's officers owe a fiduciary duty to the company. Most states have both statutory and case law sources for officer fiduciary duty.[1] Below, we discuss litigation over fiduciary duty of corporate officers (including in-house legal counsel) with respect to their own compensation.

The primary common law source is the law of agency—officers being agents—and the recent *Restatement (Third) of Agency* is the most authoritative and thorough source of agency law principles. Section 8.42 of the Model Business Corporation Act, which serves as the basis for most of the state laws on officer fiduciary duty, explicitly provides that an officer, when performing in such

---

[1] Johnson, Lyman, "Having the Fiduciary Duty Talk: Model Advice for Corporate Officers (and Other Senior Agents)," The Business Attorney, Vol. 63, November 2007, p. 147.

capacity, has the duty to act in good faith, with the care that a person in a like position would reasonably exercise under similar circumstances, and *in a manner the officer reasonably believes to be in the best interests of the corporation.*[2]

The Model statute provides further that, in discharging his or her fiduciary duties to the corporation, an officer generally is entitled to rely on:

(1) the performance of properly delegated responsibilities by one or more employees of the corporation whom the officer reasonably believes to be reliable and competent in performing the responsibilities delegated; or

(2) information, opinions, reports or statements, including financial statements and other financial data, prepared or presented by one or more employees of the corporation whom the officer reasonably believes to be reliable and competent in the matters presented or by legal counsel, public accountants, or other persons retained by the corporation as to matters involving skills or expertise the officer reasonably believes are matters (i) within the particular person's professional or expert competence or (ii) as to which the particular person merits confidence.[3]

Third, in these days of nearly instant Form 8-K disclosure of compensation, awards, and agreements, the general counsel and other officers are sensitive to the fact that anyone in the world with internet access can instantly access their agreements. The media focus can be particularly harsh.

Fourth, the general counsel recognizes that the terms he or she negotiates for his or her own agreement and awards and places in the agreements and awards of the other "C-suite" executives often will serve as a template for the awards and agreements of other employees. For example, if the general counsel or CEO negotiates hard for a favorable definition of "good reason" or an extremely lax non-compete, he or she probably will face a demand for similar language from every other employee and future employee of the company. Enforcing overly generous agreements against employees in the future can cause both costs to the business and headaches to the officers. In fact, after a company's general counsel or other chief legal officer assumes that role, he or she probably cannot ever ethically negotiate his or her own compensation with the company. That may be an unwaivable conflict of interest. Each party should get its own separate counsel.

Finally, in our experience, corporate general counsels' integrity and ethical training acts as a safeguard against the general counsel acting solely in his or her own interests in these areas.

Note that, if an executive/candidate is represented by counsel, ethics rules prohibit counsel for the company from discussing this with the executive directly (so the company counsel does not "take advantage" of the executive when his or her attorney is not present), unless the executive's counsel specifically consents.

---

[2] Model Business Corporation Act Ann. (2005), §8.42(a).

[3] Model Business Corporation Act Ann. (2005), §8.42(c).

.03 Litigation Over Officers' Fiduciary Duty

A few cases have considered the fiduciary duty of a corporate officer (including the chief legal officer) with respect to the officer's own compensation agreements. In one early case, the Delaware Chancery Court in its *In re The Walt Disney Corporation Derivative Litigation* decision[4] blasted Michael Ovitz for ignoring his fiduciary duty to the company. (See also ¶2125.) In absolving Michael Ovitz from potential personal liability for the Disney board's decision to pay him $140 million in severance, the *Disney* court had this to say about Ovitz's fiduciary responsibilities:

> Ovitz did not breach his fiduciary duty of loyalty by receiving the [no fault termination] payment because he played no part in the decisions: (1) to be terminated and (2) that the termination would not be for cause under the [original employment agreement]. Ovitz did possess fiduciary duties as a director and officer while these decisions were made, but by not improperly interjecting himself into the corporation's decision making process nor manipulating that process, he did not breach the fiduciary duties he possessed in that unique circumstance. Furthermore, Ovitz did not "engage" in a transaction with the corporation—rather, the corporation imposed an unwanted transaction upon him.

> Once Ovitz was terminated without cause (as a result of decisions made entirely without input or influence from Ovitz), he was contractually entitled without any negotiation or action on his part, to receive the benefits provided by the [original employment agreement] for a termination without cause, benefits for which he negotiated at arms-length before becoming a fiduciary. No reasonably prudent fiduciary in Ovitz's position would have unilaterally determined to call a board meeting to force the corporation's chief executive officer to reconsider his termination and the terms thereof, with that reconsideration for the benefit of shareholders and potentially to Ovitz' detriment.[5]

Some cases have found that the executives' involvement in the compensation process created a conflict. In *Kelly v. Handy & Harman*,[6] the federal district court in New York City ruled that the board of directors had not formally adopted an amendment of the H&H Supplemental Executive Retirement Plan some seven years earlier and, therefore, the plaintiffs (former officers of H&H) were not entitled to increased benefits under the amendment. From the facts the court gives in its opinion, it is impossible for us to tell whether this was merely a foot fault failure to complete the corporate formalities necessary to adopt the SERP amendment or, as the defendant (an acquirer of H&H) alleged, inappropriate conduct by the plaintiff/CFO, the CEO and the general counsel in amending the SERP for their personal benefit.

Corporate officers need to be mindful of their fiduciary duties to the corporation. In making its decision, the court seemed particularly swayed by the fact that the CFO, CEO and general counsel each participated in the SERP and would benefit from the benefit enhancements under the amendment. As a practical

---

[4] *In re the Walt Disney Company Derivative Litigation*, 731 A.2d 342 (Del.Ch. 1998), 825 A.2d 275 (Del.Ch. 2003), 907 A.2d 693 (Del.Ch. 2005).

[5] 907 A.2d 693 (Del.Ch. 2005).

[6] *Kelly v. Handy & Harman*, 49 EBC 1142 (S.D.N.Y. 2010). See also *Godina v. Resinall International, Inc.*, 677 F.Supp.2d 560 (D.C. Conn. 2009).

matter, a company's senior executives nearly always direct the design and amendment of compensation plans and arrangements. However, this typical approach only passes muster if an independent board of directors ultimately reviews and approves the plans.

In *Taylor v. University of the Cumberlands*,[7] Dr. Taylor was employed as president of the University of the Cumberlands for 35 years. Following his retirement from that position, and after serving as chancellor of the University for a short time, Dr. Taylor attempted to enforce a contract (which the court and the parties refer to as the "Disputed Agreement"). The University refused to honor the terms of the Disputed Agreement which, among other benefits, provided Dr. Taylor with compensation for life following his retirement from the position of president. The University "vehemently" argued that the Disputed Agreement was never properly and fully submitted for board ratification. In depositions, several trustees claimed the board never took up the Disputed Agreement for consideration. Dr. Taylor produced meeting minutes showing that the Disputed Agreement was read to and approved by the board. But the University also disputed the authenticity of the minutes. The court decided to leave to a jury the question of material fact as to whether the board actually ratified the Disputed Agreement.

The issue before the court was whether the University had "manifested in Jim Oaks, the then-Chairman of the Board of Trustees, the authority to bind the University to the terms of the Disputed Agreement." Dr. Taylor claimed Oaks' position as chairman of the board alone was enough of a manifestation to bind the University, which would be correct in most circumstances. However, the University argued that it maintained a specific process for approving contracts, with which Dr. Taylor was familiar, and that Oaks' apparent authority to enter into contracts was not sufficient to bind it. On this issue, the court found in favor of the University.

Among the deciding factors was the fact that Dr. Taylor was intimately familiar with the University's practices and procedures due to his long-time tenure as president. "Dr. Taylor knew well the importance of procedure and the need to have bylaws amended in order to implement certain hierarchical changes." The bylaws, as amended in 2009, while Dr. Taylor was president, contained a provision that explicitly limited the chairman's ability to execute contracts. Additionally, the minutes of the executive session of the board meeting in which Dr. Taylor claimed the Disputed Agreement was approved "contains absolutely no details concerning the terms of the Disputed Agreement."

In the H&H case described above, the two facts that were not disputed were that (a) only the board of directors of H&H could amend the SERP, and (b) the board had agreed "in concept" to the amendment, but never formally adopted it. Unlike H&H case, the court's opinion in *Taylor* makes no reference to the possibility of improper conduct by the executive or board members involved.

---

[7] *Taylor v. University of the Cumberlands*, Civil No:
6:16-cv-109-GFVT (E.D. Ky. 2018).

Regardless of what the parties' intentions may have been in this case (and the H&H case), for the rest of us, the facts of, and decision in, the case contain an important lesson. Always take care to follow corporate formalities through to completion when preparing and implementing a compensation plan or agreement, or an amendment of the same. Courts generally apply a higher standard of scrutiny to executives' actions that benefit themselves.

In *Chism v. Tri-State Constr., Inc.*,[8] an appellate court in Washington state reversed a trial court's decision and found that an officer of and legal counsel to a company did not breach his fiduciary duty to the company when he arranged with the company's president, who he knew to be afflicted with early onset Alzheimer's disease, for a substantial bonus for himself. During a car ride back from a project meeting, the in-house counsel had proposed to the company's president a bonus of $500,000. Upon their return, the in-house counsel memorialized the terms of their discussion in a memo stating that (i) the president "had already indicated that he thought the proposed $500,000 bonus was fair," and (ii) the president should let him know if he recalled their conversation differently. The president signed the memo.

When the company later refused to pay the bonus and certain other compensation, the in-house counsel sued. The company counterclaimed and requested disgorgement of other compensation it had paid to the in-house counsel, asserting common law breach of fiduciary duty and violations of Washington Rules of Professional Conduct. The company asserted the same claims as defenses to enforcement of the bonus contract.

The trial court found that the company proved actionable breaches of common law fiduciary duties. However, the appellate court reversed, finding that the company had neither alleged nor established at least two of those requisite elements—causation and damages – of a fiduciary duty claim. The trial court also found that the in-house counsel had breached his fiduciary duties to the company under the Rules of Professional Conduct. Again, the appellate court reversed, finding that a lawyer-employee is not generally bound by a fiduciary duty or the requirements of the Rules of Professional Conduct when negotiating his or her own compensation with the client-employer.

Reading between the lines, the results of this case may not be as surprising as they seem. In a footnote, the appellate court commented on the company's choice of claims, observing, "this was a strategic choice stemming from the difficulty of proving damage from a lawyer's misconduct when the lawyer in question was found by the trial court to have saved the company through his efforts." Apparently, the general counsel had apparently achieved outstanding results for the company in the transactions that led to the disputed bonus.

.04 Representing Executives

Practicing in the field of executive compensation requires expertise in the areas of taxation, federal securities law, employment law, ERISA, and contracts;

---

[8] 374 P.3d 193; 193 Wash.App. 818 (2016).

skill in negotiating and drafting plans and agreements and knowledge of market conditions and accounting rules. It is not a field into which even highly intelligent but otherwise inexperienced lawyers should venture. As a result, only a limited number of lawyers have the necessary knowledge and experience to handle capably matters in this field. Therefore, those who are experienced in the field often handle matters for individual executives as well as for companies and boards of directors.

As outside counsel, the easy case is where your contact at the client tells you that the client/company is letting him go - and asks for your advice. As outside counsel to the company, you absolutely cannot advise him.

The more typical case is where your contact tells you that the client/company is putting in place new executive contracts - and she asks you to draft them. Does outside counsel have a potential conflict when drafting today's (sometimes extravagant) executive compensation awards and agreements? The answer is that, like the executive who will be receiving the award or agreement, outside counsel should be sensitive to the *potential* for conflict. It helps to restate (and remember) the obvious: outside counsel represents the company, not the executive.[9]

.05 Representing Multiple Executives

Experienced executive compensation counsel are often asked to represent "the executive group" in connection with an acquisition, merger or other transaction. Sometimes an attorney is asked to represent more than one executive in a situation where they are leaving one employer and moving to another. Usually there is one "leading" executive (often the CEO, occasionally the general counsel or the "rainmaker").

An attorney can represent multiple executives in many executive compensation matters, if he or she takes the proper precautions. As a preliminary matter, counsel must receive the acknowledgment of and waiver of the potential conflict from each of the executives. The key is to use an engagement and waiver letter that is styled as a Joint Representation Agreement and Waiver, and that each executive signs. The Agreement and Waiver should specifically refer to each of the following points:

- Executive 1, Executive 2 and Executive 3 have asked Counsel to represent you in connection with employment negotiations with ABC, Inc.

- Ideally, each one of you would be represented by separate counsel in this Matter. However, we recognize that there are considerations of cost as well as strategic advantages for each of you in being jointly represented by Counsel.

---

[9] Other interesting issues arise, such as the decision of whether to award ISOs or NSOs. The tax treatment of the company and the executive is much different for ISOs than for NSOs. The executive will not recognize taxable income on grant or exercise of the ISO. The executive will be taxed only when he or she sells the stock acquired by exercising the ISO, at capital gains rates. The company will not receive a deduction for the ISO.

- Counsel is willing to undertake such multiple representation in the Matter so long as the following terms and conditions are understood and agreed to by each of you:

  - Executive 1, Executive 2 and Executive 3 each waive any objection to, or any possible conflict in, Counsel's joint representation of Executive 1, Executive 2 and Executive 3 in the Matter.

  - Executive 1, Executive 2 and Executive 3 each consents to Counsel's joint representation of Executive 1, Executive 2 and Executive 3 in the Matter.

  - Executive 1, Executive 2 and Executive 3 acknowledge and agree that communications between Counsel and each of you concerning the Matter will be treated by Counsel as confidential and not disclosed to anyone other than each of you without your consent or as otherwise provided by law.

  - Executives 1, 2 and 3 further acknowledge and agree that whatever communications or information Counsel receives from any one or more of you concerning the Matter will be shared with each of you as Counsel deems appropriate. In particular, if Counsel receives material information about one of you from the other that Counsel believes Executive 1, Executive 2 and Executive 3 should have in order to make decisions regarding your individual interests, Counsel will give you that information. [*Optional:* However, each of you further acknowledges and agrees that not all of the information that may be disclosed in the representation of one of you will be necessary or material to Counsel's representation of the other in negotiating the Matter. For example, Counsel does not expect to share certain salary information negotiated on behalf of one of you with the other. On the other hand, certain compensation terms may be common to each of you and Counsel will therefore provide that information to each of you.]

  - Executive 1, Executive 2 and Executive 3 acknowledge and agree that there exists the possibility that a conflict of interest may arise in the course of the multiple representation by Counsel. Executive 1, Executive 2 and Executive 3 acknowledge and agree that in the event a conflict of interest arises regarding the multiple representation by Counsel, then Counsel may withdraw from the representation of the client who has created the conflict (the "conflicted client") and may continue to represent the other clients. In such event, the conflicted client understands that he/she would be responsible for obtaining his/her own legal representation and for paying the cost of that representation.

  - Executive 1, Executive 2 and Executive 3 acknowledge and agree that if Counsel withdraws as one of their attorneys, Counsel may continue to represent the other remaining clients, even if such representation is contrary to the interests of the conflicted client. In the event of a conflict of interest, the conflicted client further understands that the conflicted client's privileged communications with Counsel might no longer be protected from disclosure and adverse use.

- Executive 1, Executive 2 and Executive 3 acknowledge and agree that, in the unlikely event that any of you commences litigation against one or more of the others regarding the subject of the joint representation, you each understand that Counsel's advice to you and our prior communications with each of you during the joint representation may not be shielded from disclosure in such litigation. We are advising you of these possibilities solely to comply with our ethical requirements and are not suggesting that you may have claims against one another.

- Executive 1, Executive 2 and Executive 3 further acknowledge and agree that in the event a conflict of interest arises regarding the multiple representation by Counsel, a court may disqualify us from continuing our representation of all of you, notwithstanding the terms of this Agreement.

- Executive 1, Executive 2 and Executive 3 acknowledge and agree that, prior to entering this Agreement, they have been advised and have had the opportunity to consult with independent counsel (not Counsel) regarding the terms and conditions of this Agreement.

Does that sound severe? Well, it is designed to sound that way so that the three (or more) executives understand that counsel represents all of them as a group. There will be no secrets among the group, and counsel cannot favor any one of them individually.

.06 Attorney-Client Privilege Issue for Executive Email Communications

Because the work of executive compensation professionals often involves email communications among executives, I wanted to note a recent case on the extent to which the attorney-client privilege would apply to communications between the executive and his/her lawyer. The issue in *Stengart v. Loving Care*,[10] was whether the privilege would apply to communications from an executive's personal email account, which the executive accessed from a company computer on company time (while at work), to an outside lawyer representing her in connection with her departure from the company. This is an issue that should be important to anyone who:

- Advises executives in compensation and/or employment matters,
- Advises employers in compensation and/or employment matters, or
- Drafts company computer-use policies.

The application of the privilege to email sent from the workplace is fact-intensive. The factual analysis determines whether or not the communication was truly confidential. This is that case for both company-owned email accounts and personal email accounts accessed via company computers from the work-

---

[10] *Stengart v. Loving Care Agency, Inc.*, 990 A.2d 650, 201 N.J. 300 (N.J.S.C. 2010).

place. The leading federal case on the question, *In re Asia Global Crossing, Ltd,*[11] set forth several factors to consider:

- Does the company maintain a policy banning personal or other objectionable use?
- Does the company monitor the use of the employee's computer or email?
- Do third parties have a right of access to the computer or emails?
- Did the company notify the employee, or was the employee aware, of the use and monitoring policies?

The approach adopted by the *In re Asia Global* court and every other court we surveyed, focuses on the effect that the company policy had on the employee's *expectation of confidentiality*. A strong and clear company policy can make it impossible for an employee to claim that his/her communication was confidential. On the other hand, a policy that is unclear or does not cover a certain type of electronic communication will leave the door open for the employee to claim that his/her communication was confidential.

However, the court in *Stengart v. Loving Care* held that emails sent by an employee from her personal, web-based, password protected email account, accessed from a company-owned computer while at work, *were protected by the attorney-client privilege.* The court held this, despite the company having a computer use policy that indicated that employees had no expectation of privacy in their computer use, and that all data stored, created, or transmitted via company computer was the property of the company. The *Stengart* court may have misunderstood the role of company policy. The issue should not be whether a court will enforce company policy, but rather whether company policy had the effect of placing the employee on notice that his/her electronic communications through company computers could not be considered confidential.

DeGeer v. Gillis considered the question of whether a former executive could claim attorney-client privilege for email communications he made from an employer-issued computer using both his work address and his personal email address.[12] As other courts have done, the federal district court in Chicago focused on the employer's email, computer use and confidentiality policies in applying a five factor test to determine that the former employee did not waive the privilege as to emails sent from either address:

1. Does the employer maintain a policy banning personal use of emails?
2. Does the employer monitor the use of its computer or email?
3. Does the employer have access to the computer or emails?
4. Did the employer notify the employee about these policies?
5. How did the employer interpret its computer usage policy?

In this case, the court found the fifth factor to be decisive, concluding that: "The record unambiguously demonstrates that Huron believed that employees

---

[11] *In re Asia Global Crossing, Ltd,* 322 B.R. 247 (S.D.N.Y. 2005).   [12] 755 F.Supp.2d 909 (N.D.IL 2010).

did not waive the attorney-client privilege by communicating with counsel over their work email addresses and on Huron computers."

.07 Company Code of Ethics

Sarbanes-Oxley Act Section 406 directed the SEC to adopt rules requiring a company to disclose whether it has adopted a code of ethics for its senior financial officers, and if not, the reasons therefor.[13] A company disclosing that it has not adopted such a code must disclose this fact and explain why it has not done so. A company also will be required to promptly disclose amendments to, and waivers from, the code of ethics relating to any of those officers. In 2013, the SEC released final rules on Sarbanes-Oxley Act Section 406, adding an Item 406 to Regulation S-K and Item 10 of Form 8-K.[14]

For purposes of Item 406, "senior financial officers" include to the company's chief executive officer, chief financial officer, principal accounting officer or controller, or persons performing similar functions. The term "code of ethics" means written standards that are reasonably designed to deter wrongdoing and to promote: (1) honest and ethical conduct, including the ethical handling of actual or apparent conflicts of interest between personal and professional relationships; (2) full, fair, accurate, timely, and understandable disclosure in reports and documents that a company files with, or submits to, the Commission and in other public communications made by the company; (3) compliance with applicable governmental laws, rules and regulations; (4) the prompt internal reporting of violations of the code to an appropriate person or persons identified in the code; and (5) accountability for adherence to the code.[15]

The company also must file with the SEC a copy of its code of ethics as an exhibit to its annual report on Form 10-K and (i) post the text of the code of ethics on its website, along with its website address, and the fact that it has posted the code of ethics on its website, or (ii) undertake in its annual report filed to provide to any person without charge, upon request, a copy of its code of ethics, and include an explanation of how to make such request.

The company may incorporate its code of ethics into a broader document that addresses additional topics or applies to more persons. The company may have separate codes of ethics for different types of officers. If the company incorporates its code of ethics into a broader document or applies it to more persons, the company need only file, post or provide the portions of the broader document that constitutes a "code of ethics" and applies to it senior financial officers, as defined in the SEC's rules.

If the company amends any element of the code of ethics listed in (1) – (5) above, it must disclose that fact in the Form 10-K, briefly describe the nature of such amendment, and file a copy of the amendment as an exhibit. If the company has granted a waiver to any element listed in (1) – (5) above, or otherwise approved a material departure from a provision of its code of ethics, including an

---

[13] Release Nos. 33-8177; 34-47235; File No. S7-40-02; 17 C.F.R. Parts 228, 229 and 249 https://www.sec.gov/rules/final/33-8177.htm.

[14] § 229.406.

[15] Item 406(b) of Regulation S-K.

implicit waiver,[16] during the most recently completed fiscal year, the company must briefly describe the nature of the waiver, the name of the person to whom the waiver was granted, and the date of the waiver.

¶2925 Ethical Issues

Executives, employees and board members must resolve the business conflicts of interest issues inherent in the area of executive compensation and benefits according to common law rules, disclosures and good judgment. However, inside and outside counsel advising the executives, employees and board members must adhere to strict ethical codes regarding ethical conflicts of interest.

.01 Basic Duties Owed to Clients

In representing a client, an attorney can take on a variety of roles depending on the nature of the representation. While the attorney has general ethical obligations regardless of the role he or she plays, different considerations arise depending on the nature of the attorney's representation. An attorney generally may serve the client in the following capacities, which are not mutually exclusive:

- As an advisor, where the attorney provides the client with information about the client's legal rights and obligations;

- As an advocate, where the attorney fervently advocates the client's positions within the confines of the adversarial system;

- As a negotiator, where the attorney seeks to press the client's advantage while remaining within the bounds of honest and fair dealing; and

- As an evaluator, where the attorney undertakes an examination of the client's affairs and reports on them frankly and honestly to the client and to others.[17]

An attorney must consider a host of ethical considerations when representing clients in the executive compensation context. The American Bar Association Model Rules of Professional Conduct (the "Model Rules") provide that:

> In all professional functions [an attorney] should be competent, prompt and diligent. [An attorney] should maintain communication with a client concerning the representation. [An attorney] should keep in confidence information relating to representation of a client except so far as disclosure is required or permitted by the Rules of Professional Conduct or other law.[18]

The Model Rules establish and set forth the duties that an attorney owes each of his or her clients. Note that each state has adopted its own standards of professional conduct that may deviate from the Model Rules in important respects. Among the most important of these duties are the duties of loyalty, confidentiality, zealous representation, competence, communication and avoidance of conflicts of interest. A breach of any of these duties can subject the

---

[16] The term "implicit waiver" means the company's failure to take action within a reasonable period of time regarding a material departure from a provision of the code of ethics that has been made known to an executive officer, as defined in Rule 3b-7, of the company.

[17] ABA Model Rules Preamble [2].

[18] ABA Model Rules Preamble [4].

attorney to disciplinary hearings, the denial or disgorgement of legal fees, or in some cases (such as the failure to make mandatory disclosure) criminal proceedings.

.02 Loyalty

An attorney owes the client a duty of loyalty. The Model Rules reflect this duty by laying out strict conflicts of interest rules. An attorney may cure many, but not all, conflicts by receiving informed consent in writing from a client before a conflict arises.[19] However, before determining whether informed consent is even possible, the attorney must consider whether the interests of the client will be adequately protected if the client gives informed consent (see the discussion in ¶2915.03 above).[20] For a client to give informed consent, the client must be aware of the circumstances under which a conflict of interest could affect his or her interests. If the attorney represents multiple clients in a single matter, the information provided to all the clients must include an explanation of the implications of the common representation. This explanation should include the effects that the representation is likely to have on the attorney's duty of loyalty, client confidentiality and the attorney-client privilege,[21] and explain that if the common representation fails because the interests of each client cannot be reconciled, the attorney generally will be required to withdraw from representing all of the clients.[22] In certain circumstances, informed consent will not cure the conflict of interest. For example, an attorney can never engage in a representation that is against the law or represent two opposing sides in the same litigation.[23]

The Model Rules generally provide that a conflict can arise in the following manner:

- conflicts with other clients;
- conflicts with third parties; and
- conflicts with the attorney's own interests.

Where an attorney has a conflict of interest, the Model Rules impute the conflict to all of the members of the attorney's firm.[24] This means that, with the exception of conflicts that are personal to the attorney, each attorney associated with the representing attorney shares the conflict of interest, irrespective of his or her involvement in the matter.

An attorney generally cannot represent a client if the representation involves a concurrent conflict of interest. A concurrent conflict of interest exists if "the representation of one client will be directly adverse to another client," or "there is a significant risk that the representation of one or more clients will be materially limited by the attorney's responsibilities to another client, a former client or a third person or by a personal interest of the attorney."[25] In this regard, ethical conflicts of interest for attorneys could be separated into three categories:

---

[19] ABA Model Rule 1.7, comment [6].
[20] ABA Model Rule 1.7, comment [15].
[21] ABA Model Rule 1.7, comment [18].
[22] ABA Model Rule 1.7, comment [29].

[23] ABA Model Rule 1.7 (b)(2), (3).
[24] ABA Model Rule 1.10 (a).
[25] ABA Model Rule 1.7(a).

1. Direct adversity conflicts with other, current clients.

2. Conflicts with former clients (a different standard applies to current and former clients).

3. Material limitation conflicts, where an attorney's duties to the client are materially limited by duties to other clients, third parties, or the attorney's own interests.

However, an attorney may represent a client despite a concurrent conflict of interest, if:

- the attorney "reasonably believes that the attorney will be able to provide competent and diligent representation to each affected client;"

- the "representation is not prohibited by law;"

- the "representation does not involve the assertion of a claim by one client against another client" represented by the same attorney in the same litigation or other proceeding; and

- "each affected client gives informed consent, confirmed in writing."[26]

Therefore, the attorney, in order to navigate concurrent conflicts of interests, must clearly: (i) identify the clients; (ii) determine whether a conflict of interest exists; and (iii) determine if the representation can be undertaken.[27] This requires the attorney to adopt reasonable procedures, which may vary depending on the size of his or her firm, to determine whether a conflict of interest exists.[28]

.03 Confidentiality

An attorney owes each client a duty of confidentiality. The duty of confidentiality is set out in the Model Rules, which provide that "[a] fundamental principle in the client-[attorney] relationship is that, in the absence of the client's informed consent, the [attorney] must not reveal information relating to the representation."[29] The duty of confidentiality applies to an extensive amount of information. The duty not only applies to communications told in confidence to an attorney, but to all information relating to the representation of the client, regardless of the information's source.

The duty of confidentiality applies during and after representation and may even apply in circumstances where no attorney-client relationship is formed.[30] An attorney must guard the confidentiality of information obtained even after the representation has terminated unless the information becomes generally known.

A client may give informed consent to an attorney to reveal confidential information. Informed consent requires the attorney to explain the impact that consent will have on the use of the client's confidential information, including all the material risks associated with the disclosure of confidential information and

---

[26] ABA Model Rule 1.7(b).

[27] ABA Model Rule 1.7, comment [2].

[28] ABA Model Rule 1.7, comment [3].

[29] ABA Model Rule 1.6, comment [2].

[30] ABA Model Rule 1.18(b).

the reasonably available alternatives to the disclosure of confidential information.[31]

.04 Exceptions to the Duty of Confidentiality

The duty of confidentiality is not absolute. The Model Rules explicitly set forth certain exceptions.

Substantial injury to the organization. The Model Rules provide an exemption to the duty of confidentiality for organizational clients where an attorney believes disclosure of confidential information is necessary to prevent a substantial injury to the organization. The Model Rules provide:

> If [an attorney] for an organization knows that an officer, employee or other person associated with the organization is engaged in action, intends to act or refuses to act in a matter related to the representation that is a violation of a legal obligation to the organization, or a violation of law that reasonably might be imputed to the organization, and that is likely to result in substantial injury to the organization, then the [attorney] shall proceed as is reasonably necessary in the best interest of the organization. Unless the [attorney] reasonably believes that it is not necessary in the best interest of the organization to do so, the [attorney] shall refer the matter to higher authority in the organization, including, if warranted by the circumstances to the highest authority that can act on behalf of the organization as determined by applicable law.[32]

If, despite the attorney's best efforts, the highest authority of the organization fails to address an action or a refusal to act that is a violation of law in a "timely and appropriate manner," and the attorney "reasonably believes that the violation is reasonably certain to result in substantial injury to the organization," the attorney is authorized to disclose confidential information to the extent necessary to prevent the substantial injury to the organization.[33]

A similar duty to report "up the ladder" has been adopted by the SEC to implement Section 307 of the Sarbanes-Oxley Act.[34]

Imminent death and bodily harm. An attorney may reveal confidential information to prevent a client from committing a criminal act "that the attorney believes is likely to result in imminent death or substantial bodily harm."[35] (Note: the rules on when an attorney can disclose confidential information regarding a crime, imminent death, *etc.*, can be very different from state to state.)

Substantial injury to another. Where the attorney becomes aware that a client will engage in an act that will result in non-imminent or non-physical harm, the attorney may reveal the client's confidential information to the extent the attorney believes it is necessary to prevent the "client from committing a crime or fraud that is reasonably certain to result in substantial injury to the financial interests or property of another" only if the client has used the attorney's services in furtherance of the crime or fraud.[36] An attorney also may disclose a client's confidential information to "prevent, mitigate or rectify substantial injury to the financial interests or property of another" that has resulted from the client's

---

[31] ABA Model Rule 1.0(e).
[32] ABA Model Rule 1.13(b).
[33] ABA Model Rule 1.13(c).

[34] See infra ¶ 2925.10 below.
[35] ABA Model Rule Model Rule 1.6(b).
[36] ABA Model Rule 1.6(b)(2).

commission of a crime or fraud in furtherance of which the client has used the attorney's services.[37]

The Model Rules permit these exceptions because the use of an attorney by a client for a serious breach of the law forfeits the right of the client to the protection of the duty of confidentiality.[38]

Court order. The Model Rules provide an exemption to the duty of confidentiality to comply with other law or a court order.[39] Thus, unless the court determines that information is subject to the attorney-client privilege or the work product doctrine (discussed below), the attorney is required to reveal confidential information to comply with other law or a court order. If an attorney makes a disclosure in a judicial proceeding, the attorney must take care to ensure he or she makes the disclosure in a way that limits access to the court and others who have a need to know it.[40]

Claim or defense of the attorney. An attorney also may reveal confidential information to: (i) establish a claim or defense in a controversy between the attorney and the client; (ii) defend him or herself in a criminal or civil proceeding against the attorney based on conduct which involved the client; or (iii) respond to allegations in any proceeding concerning the attorney's representation of the client.[41]

All of the aforementioned exemptions apply only to the extent the attorney reasonably believes the disclosure of confidential information is necessary to accomplish the purpose of the exemption. Where practicable, the attorney must first attempt to persuade the client to take suitable action to obviate the attorney's need to disclose confidential information.[42]

.05 Zealous Representation

An attorney owes the client a duty of zealous representation. An attorney "should pursue a matter on behalf of a client despite opposition, obstruction or personal inconvenience" and the attorney must take "whatever lawful and ethical measures are required to vindicate a client's cause or endeavor."[43] An attorney must also act with "commitment and dedication to the interests of the client and zeal in advocacy upon the client's behalf."[44]

This duty of zealous representation has its limits. An attorney may exercise professional discretion to determine how he or she will pursue a matter. The duty of zealous representation also does not require the attorney to use offensive tactics nor does it preclude the attorney from treating all persons involved in the representation with courtesy and respect.[45]

---

[37] ABA Model Rule 1.6(b)(3).
[38] ABA Model Rule 1.6, comment [7].
[39] ABA Model Rule 1.6(b)(6).
[40] ABA Model Rule 1.6 comment [14].
[41] ABA Model Rule 1.6(b)(5), (6).

[42] ABA Model Rule 1.6, comment [14].
[43] ABA Model Rule 1.3, comment [1].
[44] ABA Model Rule 1.3, comment [1].
[45] ABA Model Rule 1.3, comment [1].

.06 Competence

An attorney is required to provide competent representation to a client. Competent representation requires the legal knowledge, skill, thoroughness and preparation reasonably necessary for the representation.[46] The requisite knowledge and skill is determined by looking at: (i) the specialized nature and the complexity of the matter the client brings before the attorney; (ii) the attorney's general experience in the field; or (iii) whether he or she can refer it to another attorney with more experience.[47]

Generally, an attorney need only be as competent as a general practitioner in any particular area.[48] Similarly, a new attorney can be just as competent as a long-time practitioner would be, provided that the attorney undertakes the requisite study.[49]

To handle competently a matter, the attorney must inquire into and analyze the factual and legal elements of a problem, using the methods that competent practitioners would generally use.[50] An attorney is also required to keep abreast of changes in the law and to engage in continuing study and education.[51] Many states encourage this by setting continuing legal education requirements.

.07 Communications

An attorney has a duty to keep a client reasonably informed about the matter in which the attorney is representing the client. The Model Rules specifically provide that an attorney must:

- "promptly inform the client of any decision or circumstance with respect to which the client's informed consent, as defined in Rule 1.0(e), is required by these Rules;"
- "reasonably consult with the client about the means by which the client's objectives are to be accomplished;"
- "keep the client reasonably informed about the status of the matter;"
- "promptly comply with reasonable requests for information;" and
- "consult with the client about any relevant limitation on the lawyer's conduct when the lawyer knows that the client expects assistance not permitted by the Rules of Professional Conduct or other law."

An attorney is also limited in the statements he or she can make to a third party. An attorney is prohibited from making false statements of material fact or law to third persons in the course of representing a client and may not fail to disclose non-confidential information to a third person when disclosure of the information is necessary to avoid a criminal or fraudulent act by the client.[52]

When representing a client on a matter, an attorney may not directly communicate with persons that the attorney knows are represented by another

---

[46] ABA Model Rule 1.1.

[47] ABA Model Rule 1.1, comment [1].

[48] ABA Model Rule 1.1, comment [1].

[49] ABA Model Rule 1.1, comment [2], [4].

[50] ABA Model Rule 1.1, comment [5].

[51] ABA Model Rule 1.1, comment [6].

[52] ABA Model Rule 4.1 (a).

attorney, unless the attorney receives the consent of the other attorney or is authorized by a court order to communicate with the person.[53] This prohibition is aimed at preventing overreaching by attorneys. In the case of a represented organization, the prohibition on engaging represented persons directly extends to persons who supervise, direct, or regularly consult with the organization's attorney or whose actions can be imputed to the organization.[54]

.08 Limitations

Ethical rules prohibit an attorney from counseling or assisting a client in conduct the attorney knows or reasonably should know is criminal or fraudulent.[55] An attorney can generally avoid assisting a client in fraudulent conduct by withdrawing from the representation, although in some circumstances the attorney may be required to give notice of their withdrawal and disaffirm any opinions, documents, affirmations, etc. In extreme circumstances, the attorney may reveal confidential information to avoid having the law consider the attorney to have assisted the client in the commission of a crime or fraud.[56]

.09 Entity Representation

An attorney representing an organization faces a multitude of questions concerning the scope and limits of effective representation. Most importantly, the attorney must determine precisely who the client is. For example, in the employee benefit context, the attorney must determine if the client is the organization, the plan, or the plan's committees. A failure to identify properly the client can result in a violation of the Model Rules and specifically, the conflict of interest rules.

The Model Rules clarify that in representing an organizational client, such as a corporation, the attorney's obligations run to the organization and not to any particular individual or group. The Model Rules provide that an attorney "employed or retained by an organization represents the organization acting through its duly authorized constituents."[57]

> [t]his does not mean, however, that constituents of an organizational client are the clients of the [attorney]. The [attorney] may not disclose to such constituents information relating to the representation except for disclosures explicitly or impliedly authorized by the organizational client in order to carry out the representation or as otherwise permitted by the duty of confidentiality.[58]

Thus, by representing the corporation, the attorney does not necessarily represent any constituent or affiliated organization, such a as a parent or subsidiary.[59] The ABA Model Rules do not prohibit attorneys from also representing officers or employees of the entity.[60]

> [An attorney] representing an organization may also represent any of its directors, officers, employees, members, shareholders or other constituents, subject to the provisions of Rule 1.7. If the organization's consent to the dual

---

[53] ABA Model Rule 4.2.
[54] ABA Model Rule 4.2, comment [7].
[55] ABA Model Rule 1.2 (d).
[56] ABA Model Rule 4.1, comment [3].

[57] ABA Model Rule 1.13.
[58] ABA Model Rule 1.13, comment [2].
[59] ABA Model Rule 1.7, comment [34].
[60] ABA Model Rule 1.13.

representation is required by Rule 1.7, the consent shall be given by an appropriate official of the organization other than the individual who is to be represented, or by the shareholders.[61]

However, when dealing with officers or employees of the organization who are not represented by counsel, the attorney may not imply that the attorney is disinterested. The attorney must take reasonable steps to avoid any misunderstanding of the arrangement.

> In dealing with an organization's directors, officers, employees, members, shareholders or other constituents, [an attorney] shall explain the identity of the client when the attorney knows or reasonably should know that the organization's interests are adverse to those of the constituents with whom the attorney is dealing.[62]

Where the organization's interests are adverse to a director, officer, or employee, the attorney should advise the director, officer, or employee of the following:

- Because of the potential for a conflict of interest, the attorney cannot represent the director, officer, or employee;

- The director, officer or employee may wish to obtain independent representation; and

- Discussions between the attorney and the director, officer or employee may not be privileged.[63]

The attorney must ensure that the director, officer or employee understands each of these points. Whether this warning (sometimes referred to as the "corporate Miranda warning") is required before engaging in a discussion with a director, officer or employee will depend on the facts and circumstances of each case.[64]

If an attorney is aware that an officer or employee of an organizational client is engaged in an activity that could result in substantial injury to the organization, the attorney must act "as is reasonably necessary in the best interests" of the organization.[65] This may include the disclosure of confidential information if the attorney produces this information to the highest authority in the organization and the highest authority refuses to act or persists in the conduct at issue.[66] If the attorney reasonably believes that the organization discharged him or her because of his or her actions, or withdraws because the highest authority fails to act, the attorney may do what is necessary to ensure the highest authority at the organization is aware of the attorney's discharge or withdrawal.[67]

Additionally, as noted above, an attorney whose fees are paid by a party other than the client (*i.e.*, a corporation paying the bill for an employee) must seek consent from the client and must consider whether the arrangement com-

---

[61] ABA Model Rule 1.13(g).   [65] ABA Model Rule 1.13 (b).

[62] ABA Model Rule 1.13 (f).   [66] ABA Model Rule 1.13 (b)

[63] ABA Model Rule 1.13, comment [10].   [67] ABA Model Rule 1.13 (e).

[64] ABA Model Rule 1.13, comment [11].

promises the attorney's duty of loyalty or independent judgment to the client before undertaking the representation.[68]

Conflicts of interest. An attorney for an organization who is also on its board of directors is required to examine and determine whether the dual role creates a conflict of interest. For example, a conflict may arise where the attorney is required to advise the organization in matters involving the actions of the directors. If there is a material risk that the dual role will compromise the attorney's independence, the attorney should refrain from serving as a director or should not act as the organization's attorney when a conflict of interest arises.[69] Similarly, the attorney-client privilege may not protect conversations among board members where the attorney is present in his or her capacity as director.[70]

Any vote on whether the company/board should retain the attorney or his or her law firm to handle legal work for the company creates an inherent tension between the roles of director and counsel. A director can make decisions that entail some risk to the company, based on the business judgment rule. Counsel to the company generally needs to advise it of all potential risks.

.10 Sarbanes-Oxley Act of 2002

In response to a wave of corporate scandals in the 1990's, Congress passed the Sarbanes-Oxley Act.[71] The Sarbanes-Oxley Act required the SEC to issue rules for minimum standards of professional conduct for attorneys appearing and practicing before the SEC to protect investors from acts of fraud, coercion or manipulation, or lying to independent public or certified accountants by officers or directors of an organization.

Attorney Rules. In 2003, the SEC adopted regulations governing the standard of professional conduct for attorney's "appearing and practicing" before the SEC.[72] An attorney appears or practices before the SEC if the attorney:

- transacts any business with the SEC, including communicating with the SEC in any form;

- represents an issuer in an SEC administrative proceeding, an SEC investigation, an SEC inquiry, an SEC informational request or an SEC subpoena;

- provides advice in respect to U.S. securities laws, or SEC rules and regulations with respect to any document that is filed or submitted to the SEC; or

- provides advice to an issuer as to whether an information, statement, opinion, or other writing is required to be filed with the SEC.[73]

---

[68] ABA Model Rule 1.7, comment [13].
[69] ABA Model Rule 1.7, comment [35].
[70] ABA Model Rule 1.7, comment [35].

[71] Signed into law President Bush in July 2002. 15 U.S.C. § 7242.
[72] 17 CFR Part 205, Release Nos. 33-8185; 34-47276; IC-25919; File No. S7-45-02.
[73] 17 C.F.R. § 205.2(a)(1).

These standards will cover nearly every attorney representing publicly traded companies in the area of executive compensation. An attorney does not "appear or practice" before the SEC if he or she provides the services described above in a context other than providing legal advice or if the attorney is a non-appearing foreign attorney.[74]

An attorney who appears or practices before the SEC is under a duty to report a material violation if the attorney "becomes aware of evidence of a material violation by the issuer or by any officer, director, employee, or agent of the issuer."[75] A material violation includes:

> A material violation of an applicable United States federal or state securities law, a material breach of fiduciary duty arising under United States federal or state law, or a similar material violation of any United States federal or state law.[76]

The attorney must report the violation to the company's chief legal officer or to the chief executive officer. The chief legal officer is required to inquire into the material violation to the extent the chief legal officer thinks an inquiry is appropriate. If the chief legal officer concludes that no material violation has occurred, is ongoing, or is about to occur, the chief legal officer is required to notify the reporting attorney and explain the basis of his or her determination.[77]

If the attorney does not feel that the chief legal officer or chief executive officer has appropriately responded to the violation, the attorney is required to report the violation to the audit committee of the organization's board of directors, another committee of the organization's board of directors that is made up of non-employees, and finally, to the organization's board of directors.[78] An appropriate response by the chief legal officer or chief executive officer is a response that leads the reporting attorney to believe reasonably that:

- no material violation, has occurred, is ongoing, or is about to occur;
- "the issuer has, as necessary, adopted appropriate remedial measures, including appropriate steps or sanctions to stop any material violations that are ongoing, to prevent any material violation that has yet to occur, and to remedy or otherwise appropriately address any material violation that has already occurred and to minimize the likelihood of its recurrence;" or
- "the issuer [of the response], with the consent of the issuer's board of directors, [an appropriate committee], or a qualified legal compliance committee, has retained or directed an attorney to review the reported evidence of a material violation" and has either (i) "substantially implemented any remedial recommendations made by such attorney after a reasonable investigation and evaluation of the reported evidence;" or (ii) the reviewing attorney has advised the company that the attorney may assert a colorable defense on behalf of the company.[79]

---

[74] 17 C.F.R. § 205.2(a)(2).
[75] 17 C.F.R. § 205.3(a).
[76] 17 C.F.R. § 205.2(i).

[77] 17 C.F.R. § 205.3(a)(2).
[78] 17 C.F.R. § 205.3(a)(3).
[79] 17 C.F.R. § 205.2 (b).

If the attorney reasonably believes that reporting to the chief legal officer and chief executive officer will be ineffective, the attorney may directly report the material violation to the audit committee, another committee, or the company's board of directors.[80]

If the attorney receives a reasonable response as described above, the attorney's obligations are discharged. However, if the attorney does not reasonably believe that an appropriate response was undertaken, he or she is required to report his or her reasons for determining that an appropriate response was not undertaken to the company's chief legal officer, the chief executive officer, and the directors to whom the attorney originally reported the material violation.[81] If the company discharges the reporting attorney, and if the attorney believes that the company discharged him or her for reporting a material violation, the attorney may notify the company's board of directors or any appropriate committee that the attorney believes the company discharged him or her for making such a report.

An attorney practicing before the SEC may reveal confidential information related to the attorney's representation of the client to the extent the attorney reasonably believes disclosure is necessary to:

- "prevent the issuer from committing a material violation that is likely to cause substantial injury to the financial interest or property of the issuer or investors;"
- "prevent the issuer, in [an SEC] investigation or administrative proceeding from committing perjury," "suborning perjury," or committing an act that is likely to perpetrate a fraud on the SEC; or
- "rectify the consequences of a material violation by the issuer that caused, or may cause, substantial injury to the financial interest or property of the issuer or investors in the furtherance of which the attorney's services were used."[82]

An attorney who violates these requirements is subject to civil penalties and remedies for the violation of the federal securities laws and is subject to disciplinary proceedings by the SEC and any local jurisdiction. However, the SEC has made clear that an attorney is not required to follow rules adopted by local jurisdictions, to the extent they conflict with the requirements set out by the SEC. "An attorney who complies in good faith with the provisions of this part shall not be subject to discipline or be otherwise liable under inconsistent standards imposed by any state or other United States jurisdiction where the attorney is admitted or practices."[83]

In February 2011, the SEC filed a complaint against R. Allen Stanford and three of his companies, alleging a fraudulent, multi-billion dollar investment scheme. The alleged "Ponzi" scheme seems to have been brought to the attention of the SEC, in part, by the "noisy withdrawal" of Stanford International Bank's

---

[80] 17 C.F.R. § 205 (b)(4).

[81] 17 C.F.R. § 205.2 (b)(8)(9).

[82] 17 C.F.R. § 205.2 (d)(2).

[83] 17 C.F.R. § 205.6(b), (c).

general counsel, Thomas Sjoblom of Proskauer Rose LLP. Court documents filed alongside the complaint include the following statement: "SIB's counsel advised the Commission he and his law firm 'disaffirm all prior oral and written representations' regarding Stanford Financial Group and its affiliates."

According to news reports, Mr. Sjoblom gave notice that his firm was no longer Stanford's counsel to the SEC on February 11. A day later, Mr. Sjoblom sent a fax to Kevin Edmundson, the assistant director in the SEC's Fort Worth office, and left a voice message for him the next evening. Finally, Mr. Sjoblom typed a note on his BlackBerry to Mr. Edmundson, on February 14, reading: "Kevin, this will advise the SEC, and confirm my voice message last evening, that I disaffirm all prior oral and written representations made by me and my associates . . . to the SEC staff regarding Stanford Financial Group and its affiliates." Mr. Sjoblom was acting under the "noisy withdrawal" provisions of Sarbanes-Oxley Act Section 307.

.11 Multiple Representations

The Model Rules governing the representations of multiple clients are designed to avoid conflicts of interest (see also, ¶ 2915.03 above).[84] In the context of employee benefit plans, conflicts can arise between multiple fiduciaries, between fiduciaries and the plan, between the sponsor and fiduciaries, or between all of the above and employees. Where there is a risk that the attorney's responsibilities to one client will materially limit the representation of one or more other clients, the attorney must reasonably believe that:

- the attorney will be able to provide competent and diligent representation to each affected client;
- the representation is not prohibited by law;
- the "representation does not involve the assertion of a claim by one client against another client" represented by the same attorney in the same litigation or other proceeding; and
- "each affected client gives informed consent, confirmed in writing."[85]

The attorney must fully explain to the clients at the outset of the representation any limitations on the scope of the representation that the common representation causes.

The Model Rules permit an attorney to represent multiple parties whose interests are generally aligned.[86] However:

> In considering whether to represent multiple clients in the same matter, [an attorney] should be mindful that if the common representation fails because the potentially adverse interests cannot be reconciled, the result can be additional cost, embarrassment and recrimination. Ordinarily, the [attorney] will be forced to withdraw from representing all of the clients if the common representation fails.[87]

---

[84] ABA Model Rule 1.7.
[85] ABA Model Rule 1.7(b).
[86] ABA Model Rule 1.7 and 1.16.
[87] ABA Model Rule 1.7, comment [29].

In some instances, the representation of multiple parties cannot be undertaken. For example, an attorney must not "undertake common representation of clients where contentious litigation or negotiations between them are imminent or contemplated." Additionally, the attorney must not undertake a representation of multiple parties if it is unlikely that the attorney will be able to remain impartial. An attorney should not undertake a common representation once the relationship between the parties has become antagonistic.[88]

A particularly important issue that arises in common representations is the limitation a common representation imposes on attorney-client confidentiality and the attorney-client privilege. The prevailing rule is that the attorney-client privilege does not attach among the parties to a common representation if litigation eventually results between the parties.[89]

One of the attorney's paramount duties is to keep a client's information confidential.[90] An attorney is also required to provide a client with the information he or she needs to make informed decisions regarding the representation.[91] These duties come into direct conflict in the multiple representation context when the attorney learns of information that the attorney should disclose to one client, but that would also be detrimental to the other client. The Model Rules provide that the "continued common representation will almost certainly be inadequate if one client asks the attorney not to disclose to the other client information relevant to the common representation."[92]

There are two points in the common representation where the attorney must address this issue.[93] The first is at the outset of the representation, as part of the process of obtaining informed consent from each party. It is generally recommended that an attorney advise the parties whether or not the attorney will share information among the parties. There is no rule that an attorney must share information among joint clients. However, if the clients do not agree to share confidential information with one another, if a conflict were to develop regarding that information, the attorney would have to withdraw from representing all of the joint clients. The second is at the time the attorney realizes that the disclosure to one client will adversely affect the interests of the other. If this occurs, the attorney must balance his or her obligations under Model Rules 1.6 (confidentiality) and 1.4 (communication). Addressing this issue, the ABA Committee on Ethics and Professional Responsibility (the "Committee") found that:

> Absent an express agreement among the [attorney] and the clients that satisfies the 'informed consent' standard of Rule 1.6(a), the Committee believes that whatever information related to the representation of the client may be harmful to the client in the hands of a client or third person, the [attorney] is prohibited by Rule 1.6 from revealing that information to any person, including the other client and the third person, unless disclosure is permitted under an exception to Rule 1.6.[94]

---

[88] ABA Model Rule1.7, comment [29].

[89] ABA Model Rule 1.7, comment [30].

[90] ABA Model Rule 1.6.

[91] ABA Model Rule 1.4(b).

[92] ABA Model Rule 1.71.7, comment [31].

[93] ABA Committee on Ethics and Professional Responsibility Formal Opinion 08-450.

[94] ABA Committee on Ethics and Professional Responsibility Formal Opinion 08-450.

The Committee then held that in the event an attorney is prohibited from revealing confidential information and the failure to reveal that information would result in a violation of Model Rule 1.4(b), the attorney is required to withdraw from representing the other client under Model Rule 1.16(a)(1). The Committee also noted that three circumstances exist under which the attorney may disclose confidential information to the other client: (i) where the attorney has informed consent; (ii) where the attorney has implied authority to act; and (iii) where an exemption applies.[95]

In certain circumstances, the parties may agree at the outset of a representation to keep certain information confidential from each other after being fully informed as to the potential consequences of such a decision.[96]

Representation of multiple parties limits the attorney's ability to represent zealously the parties. The attorney thus should make it clear to the parties that the attorney's "role is not that of a partisanship normally expected in other circumstances and, thus, that the clients may be required to assume greater responsibility for decisions than when each client is separately represented."[97]

Whenever an attorney represents multiple clients, it is imperative that the attorney fully examine and understand the potential implications of the multiple representation before undertaking the representation. When undertaking a multiple party representation, the attorney should:

- fully disclose and explain all the implications of the common representation;
- explain that neither party will be able to assert the attorney-client privilege if the parties later find themselves in litigation;
- explain whether or not confidential information will be shared among the co-clients;
- obtain the client's written consent and maintain records of all communications;
- establish ground rules for the representation;
- explain when withdrawal may become necessary;
- have the parties enter into a conflict waiver agreement, which is explained in further detail below; and
- finally, prepare a contingency plan in the event a conflict arises.

Subject to the limitations inherent in the representation of multiple parties, each party is entitled to the attorney's loyalty and diligence.

.12 Advance Waivers

The Model Rules permit the waiver of future conflicts of interests with existing or future clients within certain limits and subject to certain protections.[98] Advance waivers are only permissible if the attorney fully discloses the existence

---

[95] ABA Committee on Ethics and Professional Responsibility Formal Opinion 08-450.

[96] ABA Model Rule 1.7, comment [31].

[97] ABA Model Rule 1.7, comment [31].

[98] See D.C. Legal Ethics Comm. Op. 309 (Sept. 30, 2001).

and nature of possible conflicts and the possible adverse consequences of such conflicts (for an example, see ¶ 2915.03 above).

The Model Rules also prohibit, absent an advanced waiver, representations that involve direct adversity between two clients or that create a significant risk that the representation of one client will materially limit the attorney's representation of another client.[99] Whether an attorney may properly request a client to waive conflicts that might arise in the future is subject to the general conflict of interest requirements:

- the attorney "reasonably believes that the attorney will be able to provide competent and diligent representation to each affected client;"
- the "representation is not prohibited by law;"
- the "representation does not involve the assertion of a claim by one client against another client" represented by the same attorney in the same litigation or other proceeding;
- the client generally understands the type of advance conflict that it is waiving (for example, an advance waiver of a future litigation conflict should be explicit); and
- "each affected client gives informed consent, confirmed in writing."[100]

It is critical that the attorney thoroughly explain the potential risks associated with an advanced waiver. The Model Rules provide that:

> The effectiveness of the waiver is generally determined by the extent to which the client reasonably understands the material risks that the waiver entails. The more comprehensive the explanation of the types of future representations that might arise and the actual and reasonably foreseeable adverse consequences of those representations, the greater the likelihood that the client will have the requisite understanding. Thus, if the client agrees to consent to a particular type of conflict with which the client is already familiar, then the consent ordinarily will be effective with regard to that type of conflict.[101]

However, an overly broad consent by the client will generally not be effective "because it is not reasonably likely that the client will have understood the material risks involved."[102] Nonetheless, the experience level of the client is an important factor in determining whether an advanced waiver will be effective:

> if the client is an experienced user of the legal services involved and is reasonably informed regarding the risk that a conflict may arise, such consent is more likely to be effective, particularly if, e.g., the client is independently represented by other counsel in giving consent and the consent is limited to future conflict unrelated to the subject of the representation.[103]

The Committee released Formal Opinion 05-436(6) in May 2005. The Formal Opinion provides that Model Rule 1.7 (conflict of interest) permits advance waivers in circumstances where the conflicts that the client is waiving are indeterminable at the time the client enters into the advanced waiver. In the

---

[99] ABA Model Rule 1.7.
[100] ABA Model Rule 1.7, comment [22].
[101] ABA Model Rule 1.7, comment [22].

[102] ABA Model Rule 1.7, comment [22].
[103] ABA Model Rule 1.7, comment [22].

Formal Opinion, the Committee concluded that Model Rule 1.7 permits informed consent to future conflicts of interest in a way that is more expansive than previous versions of the rule permitted.

The Committee expressly disregarded a prior Formal Opinion that held that a client's information consent was limited to the circumstances where an attorney identified the potential party or class of parties with whom the client could have a potential conflict of interest.

The Committee interpreted Comment 22 to Model Rule 1.7 in a manner that permits a waiver, with informed consent, of virtually any potential conflict, provided, that the matters as to which the attorney seeks informed consent do not involve the same transaction or legal dispute that is the subject of the attorney's present representation of the consenting client, and the information the attorney learns from the representation of the client is not the type of information that would materially advance the position of future clients. Nonetheless, the Formal Opinion made clear that an attorney cannot use confidential information obtained from the client against the client and that an attorney must still consider whether accepting the engagement is generally permissible under the Model Rules.

¶2935 Attorney-Client Privilege and Doctrine of Work Product Immunity

Practitioners in the field of executive compensation face many of the same attorney-client privilege issues as those in other areas of the law. However, the executive compensation and employee benefits areas also raise some unique attorney-client privilege issues. Generally, these issues involve the question of who is the attorney's client - who has the right to assert the attorney-client privilege.

.01 Attorney-Client Privilege Issues

Unlike the duty of confidentiality found in the Model Rules, the attorney-client privilege is a testimonial privilege governed by the law of evidence. This privilege exists at the federal level and in the laws of all fifty states, and protects the attorney and the client from having to make involuntary disclosures of confidential information exchanged between the attorney and the client. While the attorney-client privilege does not cover as many communications as the duty of confidentiality, communications subject to the attorney-client privilege are permanently protected from disclosure. The attorney-client privilege belongs to the client, and only the client may enforce or waive the privilege. The burden of establishing all the elements of the attorney-client privilege rests on the person claiming the privilege.[104] The purpose of the attorney-client privilege is to promote full and frank communications between a client and his or her attorney.

To establish the attorney-client privilege, the following factors must be present:

---

[104] See *Martin v. Valley National Bank of Arizona,*
140 F.R.D. 291, 302 (S.D.N.Y. 1991).

- the client must seek legal advice;
- from an attorney in his or her capacity as an attorney;
- the communications must be related to the client's seeking of legal advice; and
- the communications must be made in confidence.[105]

Once the attorney-client privilege is established, the law permanently protects the communications from disclosure by the client or by the attorney, except if the client waives the protection.[106] The attorney-client privilege applies to oral and written communications between an attorney and his or her clients, materials that memorialize oral communications between the attorney and his or her client, and communications with the attorney's subordinates, such as an attorney's paralegal and support staff.

Where the client is an organization, only certain individuals are entitled to assert the attorney-client privilege. The determination of who is entitled to the protection afforded by the attorney-client privilege differs from jurisdiction to jurisdiction.

In federal civil cases, if state law governs the claim or the defense, state law also governs the question of privilege. If federal law governs the claim or defense, federal common law governs the privilege.[107] Federal common law analyzes the attorney-client privilege under certain factors set out by the United States Supreme Court in *Upjohn v. United States*.[108] The *Upjohn* Court examined the following factors to determine who was entitled to assert the attorney-client privilege:

- whether communications were made to the attorney at the behest of superiors for the purpose of obtaining legal advice;
- whether the communications contained information needed by the organization's attorney;
- whether the subject of the communications covered matters within the scope of the employee's duties for the organization;
- whether the employee was made aware that the communication was for the purpose of the corporation obtaining legal representation; and
- whether the communication was ordered to be and remained confidential.[109]

Many states follow similar approaches.[110] However, not all states follow the *Upjohn* test. The Illinois Supreme Court explicitly rejected the test in *Consolidation Coal Co. v. Bucyrus-Erie*.[111] Under the Illinois test, only members of an organization's control group are entitled to assert the attorney-client privilege. The control

---

[105] See *Fisher v. United States*, 425 U.S. 391, 403 (1976).

[106] *United States v. United Shoe Mach. Corp.*, 89 F.Supp. 357, 358-59 (D. Mass. 1950).

[107] FRE 501.

[108] *Upjohn v. United States*, 449 U.S. 390 (1980).

[109] *Upjohn v. United States*, 449 U.S. 390, 392 (1980).

[110] See e.g. *Niesig v. Team I*, 558 N.E.2d 1030, 1034 (1990).

[111] 432 N.E.2d 250 (1982).

group includes the top management of an organization and those who advise the top management of the organization.[112]

.02 Doctrine of Work Product Immunity: Distinguished from Attorney-Client Privilege

Separate and distinct from the duty of confidentiality and the attorney-client privilege, the work product doctrine protects from discovery documents or materials prepared in anticipation of litigation.[113] The law divides work product into two categories, only one of which is immune from discovery. This includes an attorney's mental impressions, conclusions, and legal theories concerning the litigation. This first category of work product is immune from discovery to the same extent as attorney-client communications. The second category includes all other work product produced in anticipation of litigation. This can be discoverable upon a showing of substantial need.[114]

Protected materials can include written statements, private memos, fact chronologies, mental impressions, personal beliefs and any information assembled by the attorney in anticipation of litigation.

In some ways, the work product doctrine is broader than the attorney-client privilege. The work product doctrine not only covers materials that the attorney has prepared, but also materials prepared by any person so long as future litigation was a real possibility. For example, the work product doctrine encompasses materials produced by an attorney's staff, materials created by the client acting on the attorney's direction, and materials produced by consultants and investigators at the behest of the attorney. Either the attorney or the client may assert the doctrine of work product immunity to protect materials prepared in anticipation of litigation from disclosure.[115]

.03 Exceptions to Attorney-Client Privilege and Work Product Doctrine

The Federal Rules of Civil Procedure contain an express exception to the work product doctrine. A party may obtain materials covered by the work product doctrine "upon a showing that the party seeking discovery has a substantial need of the materials in the preparation of the party's case and the party is unable, without undue hardship, to obtain the substantial equivalent of the materials by other means."[116]

Example 1: In determining whether an investment committee decided a matter in good faith, the work product doctrine might not protect the notes of the committee's meeting taken by the committee's attorney.

Example 2: Where a party asserts reliance on counsel as a defense in litigation. Here the client makes the advice of counsel a critical area of inquiry in the case. Where the attorney's advice is directly at issue, the client

---

[112] *Mlynarski v. Rush-Presbyterian St. Luke's Medical Center*, 213 Ill. App. 3d 427, 430 (1st Dist. 1991).

[113] FRCP §26(b)(3); Ill. S. Ct. R. §201(b)(2); NY.CPLR §3101.

[114] FRCP §26(b)(3).

[115] See *In re Grand Jury Subpoena Duces Tetum*, 112 F.3d 910, 924 (8th Cir. 1997).

[116] FRCP §26(b)(3).

cannot raise the attorney-client privilege to prevent disclosure of relevant communications or materials.

Example 3: Where communications from counsel to a client are vital to determining the fiduciary process followed as to the investment decision in question. The process followed as to an investment decision is often dispositive in ERISA cases. Where the attorney is intimately involved in the process, relevant communications and materials may not be protected.

Example 4: Where the client or attorney has already turned over the documents or communications at issue, even inadvertently, to an adverse party or its counsel.

Common representation. One important exemption to the attorney-client privilege arises where an attorney undertakes a common representation of multiple clients (for example, see ¶ 2915.03 above). Generally, the attorney-client privilege will not attach between parties that are commonly represented.[117] Therefore, the parties run the risk that subsequent litigation will eventually develop and none of their communications with the attorney will be protected. Similarly, the duty of confidentiality will be reduced, as the attorney will not be able to withhold information relevant to the common representation.

Waiver. The attorney-client privilege and work product doctrine can be waived through a variety of methods. One method is by disclosure, for example when producing documents or answering deposition questions. Waiver can also occur by disclosing the contents of the confidential information to anyone other than the attorney or the client. The attorney-client privilege and work product protection also may be waived by putting the attorney's legal advice at issue during the course of litigation. An attorney may not selectively waive the attorney-client privilege or work product protection. Generally, a waiver of privilege with respect to some communications waives the privilege as to all other communications related to the same subject matter.[118]

Attorney as negotiator. It is possible that an attorney who negotiates a contract will be deemed to be acting primarily as a business negotiator and not as a legal advisor. This may preclude the client from asserting the attorney-client privilege and work product doctrine with respect to communications related to the negotiation. Generally, an attorney is considered a business negotiator when the services provided by the attorney are divorced from any legal issues and someone other than an attorney can provide the work.[119] When utilizing attorneys to negotiate an employment contract or severance agreement, there is a possibility

---

[117] ABA Model Rule 1.7, comment [30].

[118] See e.g., *Ryan v. Gifford*, 2007 WL 4259557 (Del. Ch. Ct. 2007) (the sharing of a report prepared for a special committee of a corporation with the entire board of directors waived privilege for all communications regarding the subject matter); *SEC v. Brady*, 238 F.R.D. 429 (N.D. Tex. 2006) (the disclosure of a report of internal investigation with current auditors waived the privilege and required production of the underlying documents).

[119] Raymond L. Sweigart, Attorney-Client Privilege: Pitfalls and Pointers for Transactional Attorneys, ABA Section of Business Law, Business Law Today, Vol. 17, No. 4 March/April 2008. www.abanet.org/buslaw/ blt/2008-03-04/sweigart.shtml.

that the courts will view the attorney as acting as a negotiator and not as a legal counselor to the organization.[120]

.04 Application of Attorney-Client Privilege to Fiduciaries

The attorney-client privilege generally cannot be asserted against ERISA benefit plan participants and beneficiaries to withhold communications between an attorney advising a fiduciary as to the administration of the plan. Therefore, it is important to determine whether a fiduciary is involved and whether an act of plan administration is implicated.

ERISA defines a fiduciary as anyone who exercises discretionary control or authority over plan management or plan assets, anyone with discretionary authority or responsibility for the administration of a plan, or anyone who provides investment advice to a plan for compensation or has any authority or responsibility to do so. Plan fiduciaries include, for example, plan trustees, plan administrators, and members of a plan's investment committee.[121] Generally, corporate officers are not considered ERISA fiduciaries unless they are designated fiduciaries or are delegated administrative or investment authority over the plan.[122] Similarly, plan sponsors are not fiduciaries because the sponsoring or amending of a plan is not a fiduciary action.[123]

The federal courts have recognized a fiduciary exception to the attorney-client privilege. This exception prevents a plan fiduciary from asserting the attorney-client privilege against plan participants and beneficiaries if the communications occur in furtherance of the fiduciary's duties to the beneficiaries.[124] Courts have identified two distinct rationales for the fiduciary exception. The first rationale derives from a fiduciary's obligation to disclose to plan participants and beneficiaries all information regarding a plan's administration. Under this rationale, a fiduciary is obligated to provide complete and accurate information to plan participants and beneficiaries regarding the administration of the plan. As part of this obligation, the fiduciary is generally required to provide participants and beneficiaries, upon request, communications that the fiduciary has engaged in with an attorney related to the administration of the plan or related to a fiduciary breach.[125] The second rationale derives from the notion that a fiduciary exercises his or her authority not for him or herself, but for the benefit of plan participants. Thus, the fiduciary is not the real client, but rather the participants.[126]

---

[120] See e.g. *Georgia-Pacific Corp. v. GAF Roofing Mfg. Corp.*, No.93 Civ. 5125, 1996 U.S. Dist. LEXIS 671 (S.D.N.Y. Jan. 25, 1996) (finding that an environmental in-house counsel who served as negotiator of environmental provisions of an acquisition was not entitled to the protection of his conversations regarding the status of negotiations, the tradeoffs involved in an acquisition and the employer's options).

[121] ERISA § 3(21)(A).

[122] 29 C.F.R. § 2509.75-8, Q&A D-4 and D-5.

[123] *Lockheed Corp. v. Spink*, 517 U.S. 882, 889-90 (1996).

[124] See *Bland v. Fiatallis N. America, Inc.*, 401 F.3d 779, 787 (7th Cir. 2005); *U.S. v. Segal*, No. 02-CR-112, 2004 WL 830428 (N.D. Ill. June 8, 1981); *U.S. v. Mett*, 178 F.3d 1058, 1062-64 (9th Cir. 1999).

[125] *In re Long Island Lighting Co.*, 129 F.3d 268, 272 (2d Cir. 1997); *Bland v. Fiatalis*, 401 F.3d at 787-88 (7th Cir. 2005).

[126] *U.S. v. Mett*, 178 F.3d 1058, 1065 (9th Cir. 1999).

When an attorney advises a fiduciary about a matter dealing with the administration of an employee benefit plan, the attorney's client is not the fiduciary personally, but rather the trust's beneficiaries.[127]

Settlor functions. Generally, when a fiduciary is engaged in settlor functions, such as the establishment, amendment or termination of a plan, or the alteration or elimination of unaccrued benefits under a plan, the attorney-client privilege will apply to communications made for the purpose of advising the client on how to proceed with the settlor function.[128] The fiduciary exception does not apply because the law does not consider a plan sponsor that is engaged in settlor functions to be acting as a fiduciary of the plan. The employer's invocation of the attorney-client privilege turns on whether or not the attorney encompasses a matter where the employer owes participants a fiduciary duty.[129]

In *Beesly v. International Paper Co.*[130], participants of a 401(k) plan charged that International Paper and fiduciaries of the International Paper 401(k) plan breached fiduciary duties by failing to monitor fees paid by the 401(k) plan. The participants sought to depose the 401(k) plan's former director of investments with respect to International Paper's decision to form an administrative committee to oversee the 401(k) plan's investments. During a deposition, the director of investments revealed that the committee was created in response to a potential conflict of interest resulting from members of International Paper's board serving on the 401(k) plan's administrative committee.[131] The director then testified that her knowledge of the potential conflict of interest came from her attorney, and her attorney objected to the questioning on the ground that the information was subject to the attorney-client privilege.[132]

The 401(k) participants also sought to depose the plan administrator who was removed after International Paper's new corporate counsel reviewed the 401(k) plan's governance and decided to remove the administrator. The participant's counsel sought information concerning the scope of the corporate counsel's review. The plan administrator's attorney also objected based on the attorney-client privilege.

Following the commonly accepted principle that the exception does not apply to settlor functions, the court determined that the formation of the committee was an amendment of the plan and not an administrative function. Rejecting the fiduciaries' argument that the creation of the committee automatically was a settlor function because its formation required amendments to the plan, the court noted that this was an insufficient test as any administrative function could be memorialized in a plan amendment. Instead, the court determined that it "must look to the nature of the act."[133] Comparing the creation of the committee to a

---

[127] *Washington-Baltimore Newspaper Guild, Local 35 v. Washington Star Co.*, 543 F. Supp. 906, 909 (D.D.C. 1982).

[128] See *Bland v. Fiatallis N. America, Inc.*, 401 F.3d 779, 788 (7th Cir. 2005); *In re Long Island Lighting Co.*, 129 F.3d 268, 273 (2d Cir. 1997).

[129] *In re Long Island Lighting Co.*, 129 F.3d 268, 271 (2d Cir. 1997).

[130] *Beesley v. International Paper Co.*, 44 EBC 1038 (S.D. Ill. 2008).

[131] *Beesley v. International Paper Co.*, 44 EBC 1038 (S.D. Ill. 2008).

[132] *Beesley v. International Paper Co.*, 44 EBC 1038, 1039 (S.D. Ill. 2008)

[133] *Beesley v. International Paper Co.*, 44 EBC 1038, 1041 (S.D. Ill. 2008).

settlor function, the court determined that the creation of the committee was not an administrative function.

Similarly, the court found that questions to the plan administrator "designed to find out the nature and scope of the corporate counsel's review of plan governance structures" were protected communications and did not fall within the fiduciary exception."[134]

Legal defense of fiduciaries. Courts have also found a distinction between matters fiduciaries discuss before making a benefit determination, and matters they discuss after they have made the benefit determination and the threat of litigation has arisen. In the latter cases, communications are protected because they form part of a legal defense and not part of the administration of the plan.[135]

However, the point at which communications cease to be subject to the fiduciary exception to the attorney-client privilege is not altogether clear. Courts have noted however that "[t]he prospect of post-decisional litigation against the plan by a disappointed beneficiary . . . is an insufficient basis for gainsaying the fiduciary exception to the attorney-client privilege."[136] Rather, "the attorney-client privilege reasserts itself as to any advice that a fiduciary obtains in an effort to protect herself from civil or criminal liability."[137]

In *U.S. v. Mett,* two plan fiduciaries sought to prevent the disclosure of several legal memorandum prepared by an attorney who acted as counsel for both the plan and the fiduciaries.[138] The memoranda at issue related to criminal and civil liabilities the fiduciaries faced for having inappropriately withdrawn assets from the plans they managed. In addition, the government argued that the attorney who prepared the memoranda could also testify against the fiduciaries based on the fiduciary exception to the attorney-client privilege. Noting that a fiduciary does not completely relinquish its right to a confidential attorney-client relationship and that the privilege applies when a fiduciary retains counsel to defend themselves, the court found that the attorney-client privilege protected the memoranda and the attorney's testimony, in light of the context and content of the memoranda.[139] The court noted that the memoranda were prepared at a time that a federal investigation for fraud was underway, that employees had begun to inquire about the financial condition of the plans, and that the memoranda contained information about the liabilities faced by the fiduciaries.[140] The court further noted that in cases where the applicability of the attorney-client privilege is unclear, courts should rule in favor of protecting the application of the privilege.[141]

In *Geissal v. Moore Medical Corp.,* a welfare plan administrator and employer sought to prevent a former employee from deposing the attorneys retained by the plan to provide legal advice regarding the plan's decision to terminate the

---

[134] *Beesley v. International Paper Co.,* 44 EBC 1038, 1043 (S.D. Ill. 2008).

[135] See *Wildbur v. Arco Chemical Co.,* 974 F.2d 631, 645 (5th Cir. 1992).

[136] *Geissal v. Moore Med. Corp.,* 192 F.R.D. 620, 625 (E.D. Mo. 2000).

[137] *U.S. v. Mett,* 178 F.3d 1058, 1066 (9th Cir. 1999).

[138] *U.S. v. Mett,* 178 F.3d 1058 (9th Cir. 1999).

[139] *U.S. v. Mett,* 178 F.3d 1058, 1064 (9th Cir. 1999).

[140] *U.S. v. Mett,* 178 F.3d 1058, 1064 (9th Cir. 1999).

[141] *U.S. v. Mett,* 178 F.3d 1058, 1065 (9th Cir. 1999).

employee's coverage. The court found that "[w]hen an administrator is required to justify or to defend against a beneficiary's claims because of an act of plan administration, the administrator does not act directly in the interests of the disappointed beneficiary but in his own interests or the interest of the rest of the beneficiaries."[142] The court then found the fiduciary exception applied to a legal opinion used by the plan to determine whether the employer had a sound legal basis for terminating the employee's COBRA coverage. However, the court refused to extend the fiduciary exception to materials produced after the plan administrator received a warning that litigation would ensue if the denial of COBRA coverage was not rescinded.[143]

In *Tatum v. R.J. Reynolds Tobacco Co.*, the court, noting that the application of the fiduciary exception to the attorney-client privilege was a matter of first impression in the Fourth Circuit, found documents relating to settlor functions and communications that arose from fiduciaries' attempt to protect themselves against liability were not subject to the attorney-client privilege. The *Tatum* court specifically rejected the plaintiff's argument that all communications that took place before the fiduciaries made the benefit determination were subject to the fiduciary exception. The court noted that the rationale for the fiduciary exception "vanishes where the fiduciary is faced with a threat of litigation for its own protections against plan beneficiaries, regardless of whether the threat of litigation occurs before, during, or after the administrative claim process."[144] The court instead found that an examination of each communication, in light of the context and content, was warranted because this was "crucial if the attorney-client privilege and fiduciary exception are to coexist."[145] The court then found that the fiduciaries' hiring of outside counsel to provide legal advice with respect to the anticipated lawsuit was a reasonable response to the fiduciaries' "concern for their personal liability arising out of the [p]laintiff's threat of litigation."[146] The court examined each communication to determine its nature and denied application of the fiduciary exception to those communications that evinced concern for the fiduciaries' liability but not those that clearly included materials that were administrative in nature.

The fiduciaries also claimed that the work product doctrine protected some of the documents at issue. The *Tatum* court found that the fiduciary exception did not apply to work product materials because "the fiduciary exception is based on the 'mutuality of interests' between the fiduciary and the beneficiaries, but once there is a real anticipation of litigation, the 'mutuality is destroyed'" and "[i]t is not reasonable to indulge in the fiction that counsel, hired by management, is also constructively hired by the same party counsel is expected to defend against."[147] While concluding that the documents at issue were created after a

---

[142] *Geissal v. Moore Med. Corp.*, 192 F.R.D. 620, 624 (E.D. Mo. 2000).

[143] *Geissal v. Moore Med. Corp.*, 192 F.R.D. 620, 625 (E.D. Mo. 2000).

[144] *Tatum v. R.J. Reynolds Tobacco Co.*, M.D.N.C., No. 1:02CV373 at 22 (Feb. 15, 2008).

[145] *Tatum v. R.J. Reynolds Tobacco Co.*, M.D.N.C., No. 1:02CV373 at 23 (Feb. 15, 2008).

[146] *Tatum v. R.J. Reynolds Tobacco Co.*, M.D.N.C., No. 1:02CV373 at 25 (Feb. 15, 2008).

[147] *Tatum v. R.J. Reynolds Tobacco Co.*, M.D.N.C., No. 1:02CV373 at 25 (Feb. 15, 2008) (citing *Int'l Sys. Koenig v. Int'l Sys. & Controls Corp. Sec. Litig. (In re*

threat of litigation arose, the court noted that the fiduciaries were required to establish that the materials were produced in anticipation of litigation. The fiduciaries could do this by showing that the documents at issue contained (i) information gathered at the request of counsel in anticipation of litigation, or (ii) the attorney's mental impressions.[148]

Some courts will require the fiduciary to demonstrate that communications relate solely to non-fiduciary activities or settlor functions, or that the communications are "wholly unrelated to plan administration and have not been used in connection with [its] role as plan administrator."[149] Yet other courts will focus on identifying the intended recipients of the legal advice.[150]

Below are a few suggestions for preserving the attorney-client privilege. The attorney and client should:

- identify the nature of the advice being given (*i.e.*, does it relate to administrative matters or personal matters);
- identify specific communications by participants and beneficiaries that indicate that a potential for litigation exists;
- determine in whose interest the communications are being made (are the communications intended to assist participants or plan fiduciaries);
- maintain a separate attorney for the plan and for the plan's fiduciaries;
- segregate accounts, communications and fees; and
- arrange for fiduciaries to pay their own legal fees, where appropriate.

This area of law varies widely from jurisdiction to jurisdiction. Some circuits have not adopted the fiduciary exception in the context of ERISA; other circuits have adopted the fiduciary exception but continue to struggle to determine the point at which the fiduciary exception applies.

.05 Application of Work Product Doctrine to Fiduciaries

The work product doctrine serves a different purpose than the attorney-client privilege. The work product doctrine protects an attorney's effective preparation for trial by immunizing certain information and materials from discovery. "The purpose of the work-product protection is to safeguard the efforts of the attorney on behalf of his client by preventing an adversarial counsel from obtaining a free ride on the work of the attorney ... " "On its face then, the rule does not give the attorney the right to withhold work product from his own client."[151]

(Footnote Continued)

Int'l Sys. & Controls Corp. Sec. Litig.), 693 F.2d 1235, 1239 (5th Cir. 1982).

[148] *Tatum v. R.J. Reynolds Tobacco Co.*, M.D.N.C., No. 1:02CV373 at 33-34 (Feb. 15, 2008).

[149] See *Everett v. US AirGroup, Inc.*, 165 F.R.D. 1, 4 (D.D.C. 1995); but see *U.S. v. Mett*, 178 F.3d 1058, 1066 (9th Cir. 1999) (rejecting a construction of the fiduciary exception that the "fiduciary exception ap-

plies to all fiduciary-attorney communications unless the fiduciary can demonstrate that the advice was solely related to personal, non-fiduciary matters.").

[150] See *Wachtel v. Health Net, Inc.*, 482 F.3d 225 (3d Cir. 2007).

[151] *Martin v. Valley National Bank of Arizona*, 140 F.R.D. 291, 320 (S.D.N.Y. 1991).

However, because the work product doctrine applies to materials prepared in anticipation of litigation, some courts have declined to apply the work product doctrine to materials prepared by an attorney in anticipation of litigation with a participant or beneficiary. In *Donovan v. Fitzimmons*, the court found that the attorney-client privilege did not translate into the context of work-product immunity because "the right to assert the work-product barrier to disclosure belongs at least in part, if not solely, to the attorney and not the client."[152] Further, the court noted, that the work product doctrine applies to materials prepared in anticipation of litigation, thus the materials protected would not generally relate to the administration of an ERISA plan.[153] The court also refused to apply the fiduciary exception to the work product doctrine on the basis that the mutuality of interests between fiduciary and participant that underlies the fiduciary exception is "destroyed" when the prospect of litigation arises.[154]

.06 In-House Corporate Counsel

In Re Long Island Lighting affirmed that in-house counsel could engage in communications related to non-administrative matters without foregoing the protection of the attorney-client privilege.[155] However, as a practical matter, the communications of in-house corporate counsel are more difficult to protect under the attorney-client privilege, because the courts often view in-house corporate counsel as serving in the dual role of legal counselor and business advisor. In *Rossi v. Blue Cross and Blue Shield of Greater New York*, the court ruled that in-house counsel's claims of attorney-client privilege should be subject to stricter scrutiny due to the closeness of the ongoing, permanent relationship between counsel and the company.[156] Similarly, the distinction between fiduciary legal advice and non-fiduciary legal advice may become blurred. There is a greater risk that the attorney-client privilege will not apply to in-house counsel if they are frequently engaged in the claim administration process. This makes it less likely that a court will find their work qualifies for both the attorney-client privilege and the work-product doctrine because of the prospect of litigation.[157]

The application of the attorney-client privilege to communications by in-house corporate attorneys ultimately depends on the types of communications involved and the role the attorney is playing. As discussed above, the party who seeks to assert the attorney-client privilege must ultimately demonstrate that the elements of the privilege exist. The organization will need to demonstrate that the communication between officers or employees of the organization and the attorney were for the purpose of obtaining legal advice and that the attorney provided advice in his or her role as an attorney. To avoid waiver of the privilege, the attorney should examine the rules of his or her local jurisdiction, be cognizant of the need to assert the privilege at the proper time, be certain to

---

[152] *Donovan v. Fitzimmons*, 90 F.R.D. 583, 587-88 (N.D. Ill. 1981).

[153] *Donovan v. Fitzimmons*, 90 F.R.D. 583, 587-88 (N.D. Ill. 1981).

[154] *Donovan v. Fitzimmons*, 90 F.R.D. 583, 587-88 (N.D. Ill. 1981).

[155] 129 F.3d 268 (2d Cir. 1997).

[156] *Rossi v. Blue Cross and Blue Shield of Greater New York*, 73 N.Y.2d 588 (N.Y. 1989).

[157] See *Wildbur v. ARCO Chemical Company*, 974 F.2d 631 (6th Cir. 1992).

maintain confidentiality, and be wary of inadvertently waiving the privilege by disclosing otherwise confidential information.

.07 Plans Not Subject to ERISA

In *Marsh v. Marsh Supermarkets Inc.*,[158] the court denied a former executive of a company discovery of communications between the company and its attorneys because the court found that the fiduciary exception did not apply to top-hat plans. In *Marsh*, a terminated former employee subpoenaed the law firm of his employer's attorney requesting all documents constituting, referring or relating to any communication between Marsh supermarkets and any attorney relating to plaintiff's top-hat plan benefits.[159] Marsh supermarkets argued both the attorney-client privilege and the work product doctrine protected the materials. In rejecting the plaintiff's contention that the documents were subject to the fiduciary exception, the court found that the plan was unfunded and maintained primarily for the purpose of providing a select group of employees deferred compensation, thus falling squarely outside of the fiduciary protections afforded by ERISA.[160] Noting that the Seventh Circuit had not specifically addressed the issue, the court ruled that "since Plaintiff's plan was a top hat plan, Marsh Supermarkets was under no fiduciary duty to the Plaintiff under ERISA. The fiduciary exception therefore does not apply."[161]

.08 Recurring Issues: Attorney's Fees Paid with Plan Assets

The Department of Labor ("DOL") has explained that a determination as to whether to pay a particular expense out of plan assets "is a fiduciary act governed by ERISA's fiduciary responsibility provisions."[162] In discharging their duties, fiduciaries "must act prudently and solely in the interest of plan participants and beneficiaries, and in accordance with the documents and instruments governing the plan . . . As a general rule, reasonable expenses of administering a plan include direct expenses properly and actually incurred in the performance of a fiduciary's duty to the plan."[163] The DOL has made an important distinction between expenses incurred in the administration of a plan and expenses incurred in settlor functions.

> Expenses incurred in connection with the performance of settlor functions would not be reasonable expenses of a plan as they would be incurred for the benefit of the employer and would involve services for which an employer could reasonably be expected to bear the cost in the normal course of its business operations. However, reasonable expenses incurred in connection with the implementation of a settlor decision would generally be payable by the plan.[164]

This distinction precludes plan sponsors from paying legal fees associated with the establishment of a plan, designing a plan, amending a plan, and the

---

[158] No. 1:06-cv-1395-JDT-TAB (S.D. Ind., March 29, 2007).

[159] *Marsh v. Marsh Supermarkets Inc.*, No. 1:06-cv-1395-JDT-TAB 3 (S.D. Ind., March 29, 2007).

[160] *Marsh v. Marsh Supermarkets Inc.*, No. 1:06-cv-1395-JDT-TAB 4 (S.D. Ind., March 29, 2007); see ERISA § 401(a)(1).

[161] *Marsh v. Marsh Supermarkets Inc.*, No. 1:06-cv-1395-JDT-TAB 5 (S.D. Ind., March 29, 2007).

[162] DOL Advisory Opinion 2001-01A.

[163] DOL Advisory Opinion 2001-01A.

[164] DOL Advisory Opinion 2001-01A.

termination of a plan. This conforms with court decisions that provide that the fiduciary exception to the attorney-client privilege does not apply to communications related to settlor functions. When the DOL initiates a plan audit, it often examines the propriety of plan expenses. In addition to potential liability that may arise from paying legal expenses out of plan assets for tasks that are settlor in nature, courts may look at the source of payment for legal fees to determine who the real client of the attorney's advice is, resulting in the application of the fiduciary exception to the attorney-client privilege. If the attorneys' fees were paid from plan assets, the court is almost certain to find that the plan was the client and the fiduciary exception to the attorney-client privilege applies.

.09 Recurring Issues: Trustees

Trustees and other fiduciaries may assert the attorney-client privilege, provided all the requirements of the attorney-client privilege are met with respect to the communications at issue. To ensure the attorney-client privilege attaches to a communication, the attorney and trustee should make clear that: (i) the attorney is conducting the work for the trustee, often a bank, in its corporate capacity and not for the employer, the plan, the plan administrator, or any other fiduciary; and (ii) the trustee will be paying the attorney's fees. As with other fiduciaries, once a government agency, a participant, or a beneficiary threatens litigation, advice given to the trustee by the trustee's counsel as to that subject is privileged.[165]

For particularly sensitive matters, an engagement letter between the bank and counsel should (i) expressly direct and authorize the research or advice as to the matter, (ii) state its purpose, including giving legal advice on potential litigation and other relevant matters, (iii) specify that the bank is engaging counsel strictly to assess the trustee's responsibilities and potential liability in the event of litigation (to enable counsel to provide legal advice to the bank), and (iv) emphasize the confidential nature of the matter.

In *Electrical Workers IBEW Local No. 26 Pension Trust Fund Trustees v. Trust Fund Advisors Inc.*,[166] the federal district court in Washington, D.C. held that the attorney-client privilege between pension fund trustees and their attorney was not defeated when trustees and attorney discussed a potential lawsuit against the fund's investment manager at a meeting attended by two unpaid consultants for the fund. The court also held that the privilege was not defeated by subsequent distribution of meeting minutes to consultants.

Regarding the meeting, the defendant investment manager argued that the trustees could have no reasonable expectation that the communications were privileged because they were made in front of individuals who were not paid employees. The court rejected this argument, finding that application of attorney-client privilege is not a direct function of whether the person providing or receiving information to or from counsel is a paid employee. The court noted that

---

[165] See *Martin v. Valley National Bank*, 140 F.R.D. 291 (S.D.N.Y. 1991).

[166] *Electrical Workers IBEW Local No. 26 Pension Trust Fund Trustees v. Trust Fund Advisors Inc.*, 48 EBC 2138 (D. D.C. 2010).

the consultants had significant managerial responsibilities that would have been done by high-level corporate managers had the fund been incorporated, and the attorney considered the consultants to be representatives of the fund and considered his communications with consultants to be privileged.

Regarding the meeting minutes, the court held that the pension fund trustees had not forfeited the attorney-client and work-product privileges when they redacted certain information from meeting minutes and notes regarding the meeting at which their attorney discussed the potential lawsuit against the investment manager, which were then produced to the investment manager. The defendant investment manager argued that privileges were forfeited because the trustees disclosed non-privileged documents that dealt with the same subject matter as the disclosed documents. The court held that disclosure of non-privileged information does not justify forced disclosure of privileged information, and disclosure of privileged work-product does not extend to other privileged information merely because they pertain to the same subject matter.

.10 Recurring Issues: Predecessor or Successor Trustees

In the context of trusts, courts have held that successor trustees are holders of the attorney-client privilege because the privilege belongs to the office of the trustee, and not to any particular trustee.[167] "[A] new trustee succeeds to all rights, duties and responsibilities of his or her predecessors, including those related to dealings with an attorney retained to assist the trustee in the management of the trust."[168]

As noted above, the attorney-client privilege generally protects communications between a trustee and an attorney. However, the authority to exercise the privilege may remain with the trust, the plan and its participants and not the trustee. If a bank or other trustee resigns its trusteeship, the successor trustee may have the authority to waive, on behalf of the plan, a claim of attorney-client privilege with respect to an attorney who previously worked for the plan.

In *Martin v. Valley National Bank of Arizona*, the DOL alleged Valley National Bank, a trustee of an employee stock ownership plan, violated its fiduciary duties as trustee, based on Valley National Bank's role in arranging and approving a leveraged buyout of the plan sponsor by the plan that resulted in the plan paying more than adequate consideration for shares of the sponsor.[169] After the DOL filed suit, Valley National Bank resigned and was replaced as trustee of the ESOP. Shortly after becoming trustee, the new trustee waived all claims of attorney-client privilege on behalf of the ESOP in a bankruptcy proceeding. This waiver included materials prepared for the previous trustee by two law firms. Both the former trustee and the former trustee's attorneys asserted the attorney-client privilege.

---

[167] See *Moeller v. Superior Court*, 16 Cal. 4th 1124 (1997).

[168] *Eddy v. Fields*, 121 Cal. App. 4th 1543, 1548 (Cal. Ct. App. 2004).

[169] *Martin v. National Bank of Arizona.*, 140 F.R.D. 291, 299 (S.D.N.Y. 1991).

The court first found that National Valley Bank could not assert the attorney-client privilege because one of the law firms represented the ESOP directly. The court also found that the law firm could not decline to turn over materials prepared for National Valley Bank to the DOL at the behest of the ESOP based on the work-product doctrine because the doctrine "does not give an attorney the right to withhold work product from his own client."[170]

With respect to materials prepared by the second law firm, the court noted that the firm represented the National Valley Bank and not the ESOP and that therefore, a waiver by the successor trustee was not sufficient to justify production of the documents requested. Examining the issue under trust law, the court determined that "[i]nsofar as the trustee is consulting an attorney to assist him in providing adequate service to the trust, and hence to its beneficiaries, the trustee cannot shield those communications from the beneficiaries."[171] The court noted that as a representative for the beneficiaries of the trust, the trustee is not the real client, but rather the beneficiaries are. Thus, the court permitted the DOL to invoke the fiduciary exception to the attorney-client privilege as a person duly authorized by the beneficiaries of the trust to inspect documents related to the trust, but only with respect to discussions that did not concern the DOL investigation.[172] With respect to work-product immunity, the court determined that documents related to the DOL investigation were prepared in anticipation of litigation and alternately the fiduciary exception did not apply to these same documents because a conflict of interest had arisen between the trustee and the beneficiaries of the trust.[173]

.11 Recurring Issues: The Government's Rights

Generally, the attorney-client privilege cannot be asserted against plan participants and beneficiaries to withhold communications between attorneys and fiduciaries related to the administration of the plan. Some courts have held that a fiduciary is similarly barred from asserting the attorney-client privilege against the DOL where the DOL has filed a claim to enforce the rights of plan participants.

The DOL enforces Title I of ERISA, which includes reporting, prohibited transactions and fiduciary obligations. ERISA provides that the DOL may enforce, on behalf of participants, the following breaches via civil action: (i) breaches of fiduciary duty under Section 502(a)(2) of ERISA; (ii) violation of certain disclosure requirements under Section 502(a)(4) of ERISA; and (iii) to enjoin and obtain equitable relief for violations of Title I of ERISA. The DOL has litigated several types of violations against plan fiduciaries. These include: (i) the failure to act prudently and for the exclusive benefit of plan participants; (ii) the misuse of plan assets; (iii) failure to hold plan assets in trust; (iv) failure to follow the terms of the plan; (v) failure to select carefully service providers; and (vi) taking adverse action against participants for exercising their rights under ER-

---

[170] *Martin v. National Bank of Arizona*, 140 F.R.D. 291, 320 (S.D.N.Y. 1991).

[171] *Martin v. National Bank of Arizona*, 140 F.R.D. 291, 322 (S.D.N.Y. 1991).

[172] *Martin v. National Bank of Arizona*, 140 F.R.D. 291, 325-26 (S.D.N.Y. 1991).

[173] *Martin v. National Bank of Arizona*, 140 F.R.D. 291, 327 (S.D.N.Y. 1991).

ISA. Importantly, courts have held that the DOL may obtain independent relief despite the resolution of a private action based on the same allegations.[174]

Several courts have held that the DOL has a sufficient "identity of interests" with plan participants to allow it to override plan fiduciaries' claims of attorney-client privilege.

In *Doe v. U.S.*, the U.S. Court of Appeals for the Ninth Circuit found that a trustee of a plan was not entitled to raise the attorney-client privilege to prevent his attorney's grand jury testimony in connection with the trustee's fiduciary breaches, where the government stood in the shoes of plan beneficiaries.[175] In *Doe*, Doe, a trustee for an ERISA pension fund, was suspected of hiring an investment monitor because Doe was receiving kickbacks from the investment monitor. The government later subpoenaed the attorney advising Doe. Doe and the attorney asserted attorney-client privilege in response to the subpoena. The court noted that the Ninth Circuit has extended the fiduciary exception to the government where it is seeking to "vindicate the rights of ERISA beneficiaries."[176] The court noted that:

> Just as there is little justification for hiding trustee-attorney communications from beneficiaries investigating the plan's administration, so there is little justification for hiding the communications from public prosecutors seeking to protect those beneficiaries.[177]

In *WSOL v. Fiduciary Management Associates Inc.*, the trial court examined a claim by trustees that disclosure to the government of privileged information should not result in waiver to third parties. In examining whether waiver was appropriate, the trial court noted:

> the principles underlying the fiduciary exception to the attorney-client privilege are applicable to this case. The exception recognizes that when the government enforces the rights of fund beneficiaries under ERISA, it seeks the same end as a fund trustee—vindicating the interests of the beneficiaries—and therefore attorney communications concerning that end are not privileged as against the government. It looks to the government's relationship to the beneficiary, and not to whether the government's relationship with the trustee is hostile. If a finding that the government stands in the shoes of the beneficiary is enough to supersede privilege issues as against the government when the trustee opposes disclosure, then certainly the same result should obtain when the trustee's disclosure is voluntary.[178]

In addition, government agencies have shown an increased willingness to coerce organizations to waive the attorney-client privilege to avoid indictment or to receive lesser sentences. Prosecutors have begun to charge organizations with more serious charges if the organizations fail to cooperate by waiving the attorney-client privilege over privileged communications.[179] Cooperation could

---

[174] *Herman v. South Carolina Bank*, 140 F.3d at 1367 (11th Cir. 1998) (finding that actions by private parties do not interfere with the DOL's independent rights under ERISA).

[175] *U.S. v. Doe*, 162 F.3d 554, 557 (9th Cir. 1998).

[176] *U.S. v. Doe*, 162 F.3d 554, 557 (9th Cir. 1998) (citing U.S. v. Evans, 796 F.2d 264 (9th Cir. 1986).)

[177] *U.S. v. Doe*, 162 F.3d 554, 557 (9th Cir. 1998).

[178] *WSOL v. Fiduciary Management Associates Inc.*, 23 EBC 2583, 2587-88 (N.D.Il. 1999).

[179] See William R. McLucas, Howard Shapiro & Julie Song, The Decline of the Attorney-Client Privilege in the Corporate Setting, 96 J.L. & Crim. 2, 631 (2006) (discussing SEC and DOJ policies regarding cooperation by organizations).

result in a waiver of the privilege with respect to third party litigants.[180] However, some courts have held that disclosure to a governmental entity does not negate the attorney-client privilege where the trustees and the government share a common interest under the common legal interest doctrine, which provides that disclosure of communications to a third party who shares a common legal interest with the disclosing party concerning the subject matter of legal advice does not waive the attorney-client privilege.[181]

.12 Recurring Issues: Plan Audits

Self-correction programs make it highly desirable for plan sponsors to self-audit their benefit plans. Generally, the plan sponsor can correct administrative errors discovered on audit without paying a fine and with no IRS involvement. However, the concern with conducting an internal audit is that it may result in a roadmap for the DOL, the IRS, or plaintiff's attorneys. Therefore, it is critical for employers to understand the discoverability of documents created and the communications made during an audit.

To preserve the attorney-client privilege to the maximum extent possible, the organization should hire outside counsel to conduct the audit. It should be clear that the organization is hiring the attorney and not the plan's trustees, plan administrator, or some other fiduciary. Communications between the organization and the attorney should make clear that the organization expressly directs the audit to take place, this communication should state the purpose of the audit, specify that employees are completing materials under the direction of the organization in order to enable the attorney to provide the organization with legal advice, and emphasize the privileged and confidential nature of the communications.[182]

Importantly, the organization should be aware that the attorney-client privilege protects only communications between the organization and the attorney and does not protect underlying facts uncovered during the audit.[183]

The organization must also be careful to avoid inadvertent waiver of the attorney-client privilege. This can occur by disclosing privileged information to third parties, or by selectively revealing information that may then result in waiver as to the entire subject. Waiver may also occur if the organization uses the conduct of the audit as a defense in subsequent litigation. For example, in other contexts, courts have ruled that an organization cannot hire an attorney to conduct an audit, cite the audit as a defense and produce only select portions of the audit.[184]

The payment of expenses by a plan related to a plan audit will not necessarily waive the attorney-client privilege with respect to communications between

---

[180] See *Burden-Meeks v. Welch*, 319 F.3d 897, 899 (7th Cir. 2003).

[181] *WSOL v. Fiduciary Management Associates Inc.*, 23 EBC 2583, 2588 (N.D.Ill. 1999).

[182] See *Deel v. Bank of Am.*, 227 F.R.D. 456 (W.D. Va. 2005) (finding that the attorney-client privilege

did not protect completed questionnaires because they failed to provide that the questionnaire was for the purpose of obtaining legal advice).

[183] *Upjohn v. U.S.*, 449 U.S. 383, 396 (1981).

[184] *Wellpoint Health Networks v. Superior Court*, 59 Cal. App. 4th 110 (1997).

employees of an organization and the attorney.[185] However, a strong case can be made that the cost and expense of a plan audit is a legitimate plan expense only if the results of the audit are made available to plan participants and beneficiaries upon request. Therefore, in most circumstances it is important that the plan not pay the cost of an audit if waiver of the attorney-client privilege is an issue.

The work-product doctrine may protect audit materials if the audit was conducted in anticipation of litigation or for trial. A mere concern that past actions might result in future litigation may not be enough to treat the audit as having been made in anticipation of litigation.[186] In addition, courts will look at the main purpose of the audit. For example, in *In re Royal Ahold N.V. Securities & ERISA Litigation*, the court determined that despite the existence of an SEC investigation and several fraud and ERISA class actions, the organization was not entitled to the protection of the work-product doctrine for materials generated from an internal investigation because "the investigation would have been undertaken even without the prospect of preparing a defense to a civil suit."[187]

To ensure the protections afforded by the attorney-client privilege and the work-product doctrine remain intact to the fullest extent possible, organizations should consider:

- involving outside counsel as early as possible;
- documenting the initial outreach to outside counsel and include the potential litigation at issue and clarify that the organization is seeking legal advice;
- conducting as much of the audit verbally as possible;
- having all reviews conducted only at the discretion of counsel;
- communicating to employees the need to cooperate with counsel, that the organization is the client and not the employee, that communications with outside counsel should be kept confidential, and that the purpose of the communications are to enable the organization to obtain legal advice;
- controlling all documents produced as a result of the audit; and
- limiting the scope of the audit.

Importantly, the IRS has stated that it will oppose privilege claims where a lawyer representing a client in a tax case hired the accountants directly, although they acknowledge that some taxpayers have successfully argued in court that an accountant is working for the taxpayer's lawyer and, thus, the privilege applies to the accountant.

.13 Recurring Issues: Disclosure Outside the Privileged Group

Several courts have ruled that the disclosure of a report of internal investigation to auditors[188] or other parties outside the attorney-client relationship waived

---

[185] See *Simpson v. James*, 903 F.2d 372 (5th Cir. 1990); *Dole v. Milonas*, 889 F.2d 885, 888 (9th Cir. 1989).

[186] See *Diversified Indus., Inc. v. The Honorable James H. Meredith*, 572 F.2d 596, 603 (10th Cir. 1997).

[187] In *re Royal Ahold N.V. Securities & ERISA Litigation*, 230 F.R.D. 433 (D. Md. 2006).

[188] *SEC v. Brady*, 238 F.R.D. 429 (N.D. Tex. 2006). See also *Ryan v. Gifford*, 2007 WL 4259557 (Del. Ch. Ct. 2007), the sharing of a report prepared for a

the privilege and required production of the underlying documents. In *Hexion Specialty Chemicals, Inc. v. Huntsman Corp.*,[189] the Delaware Chancery Court allowed Hexion, the plaintiff, discovery of documents prepared by or relating to the activities of defendant Huntsman's financial advisor Merrill Lynch. The court concluded that Huntsman's investment banker could not properly be regarded as a litigation or trial consultant within the meaning of a Delaware rule of evidence that would protect from disclosure information and material prepared by such a consultant. The court also concluded that the documents prepared by Merrill Lynch did not fall within the protection of the attorney work product doctrine. Huntsman had hired Merrill Lynch to serve as its financial advisor under an October 2005, engagement letter. Acting pursuant to that engagement, Merrill Lynch advised Huntsman in connection with the negotiation and signing of a July 2007, merger agreement with Hexion. Merrill Lynch continued to serve as Huntsman's financial advisor pursuant to that engagement. After economic conditions worsened, Hexion changed its mind and filed suit to avoid the transaction in June 2008. Merrill Lynch did not form separate and distinct financial advisory and litigation consulting teams. Instead, the same Merrill Lynch group that had been performing financial advisory services for Huntsman added litigation advisory services to their duties.

Similarly, in *SEC v. Roberts*,[190] the U.S. District Court for the Northern District of California ordered McAfee Inc. to turn over interview notes and other materials gathered by an outside law firm. Ironically, in this case, it was the McAfee's former general counsel who sought the disclosure, as part of his defense against a civil action brought against him by the SEC for allegedly altering the grant date for stock options awarded to him and other executives. McAfee Inc. formed a special committee to investigate allegations of stock options backdating at the company. The special committee hired Howrey LLP, a law firm.

The court ordered Howrey to produce certain information and notes related to its investigation, including:

- all documents provided or made available to the SEC, Justice Department officials, or McAfee's board of directors;[191]

- all factual information disclosed to the government or the board in response to their questions regarding statements made by various individuals interviewed by Howrey;

- interview notes with respect to three interviewees whose credibility, culpability, and demeanor had been discussed by Howrey attorneys with third parties; and

---

(Footnote Continued)

special committee of a corporation with the entire board of directors waived privilege for all communications regarding the subject matter.

[189] *Hexion Specialty Chemicals, Inc. v. Huntsman Corp.*, 965 A. 2d 715 - (Del: Court of Chancery, 2008).

[190] *SEC v. Roberts*, 2008 WL 3925451 (N.D. Cal. Aug. 22, 2008).

[191] See also, *SEC v. Microtune Inc.*, 2009 WL 1574872 (N.D. Texas, June 4, 2009).

- Notes of meetings or communications with the government, the full board, or any McAfee board members who were not members of the special committee, subject to redaction to protect Howrey attorneys' mental impressions and conclusions.

After its investigation, Howrey made PowerPoint presentations to the McAfee board, SEC, the Department of Justice, and McAfee's former and current outside auditors. During the presentations, Howrey discussed some of its findings and answered questions about the individuals it interviewed. The court found that, to the extent Howrey orally disclosed to the government or to the board any information contained in the written material sought, the firm waived the attorney-client and work product privileges with respect to the material.

On a positive note, the court allowed McAfee to protect most of Howrey's interview notes under the attorney work product doctrine, because those notes included Howrey attorneys' mental impressions, conclusions, and opinions of the individuals interviewed. Additionally, except in a couple of cases, there was no evidence that Howrey had shared its mental impressions or conclusions with the government or with the McAfee board - which could have waived the protection.

The court also refused to compel Howrey to disclose its discussions with McAfee's outside auditors regarding what certain witnesses said during their interviews, or Howrey's characterizations of the interviewees as either "clean" or "dirty" in response to the auditors' questions. Noting that there was a split of authority on the issue, the court said it agreed with the reasoning in Merrill Lynch & Co. v. Alleghany Energy Inc.,[192] which held that information revealed to an auditor does not amount to a waiver of privilege under the common interest doctrine because auditors are not adversaries or potential adversaries. The court observed that the special committee and the outside auditors had "aligned interests" and a common goal to correct past wrongdoings at McAfee, and represented a common body—McAfee shareholders.

Finally, occasionally a company or its counsel, will share too much information with the company's public relations or crisis management firm. In this scenario, a crisis occurs, the CEO (or other senior executive) brings in the PR or crisis management firm to provide advice, and meetings occur among outside law firm, the CEO, and the PR firm. The fact that the PR firm sat in on the meetings destroys the attorney-privilege for the meeting. Similarly, a public company with SEC reporting responsibilities will sometimes send drafts of a press release, Form 8-K, or other disclosure materials to a PR or crisis management firm, which most likely would render all the documents and drafts discoverable. The law firm should directly hire the consulting firm to preserve privilege.

---

[192] *Merrill Lynch & Co. v. Alleghany Energy Inc.*, 229 F.R.D. 441 (S.D.N.Y. 2004).

.14 Exceptions for Attorneys in Business Transactions and Acting as Negotiators

In applying the attorney-client privilege, courts have decided that the privilege does not apply to communications made to or by an attorney who is transacting business that another agent who is not an attorney could have transacted.[193]

In *Montebello Rose Co. v. Agric. Labor Rel'n Bd.*, the court raised the concern that if it deemed all communications between attorneys and clients privileged, regardless of whether legal advice was involved, clients able to hire attorneys to negotiate on their behalf would have an advantage over those who use lay negotiators. Such an outcome could be inherently unfair to clients who cannot afford to hire an attorney to negotiate on their behalf.[194]

.15 Attorney Serving Solely as Negotiator

Generally, if a transactional attorney or in-house counsel serves purely as a negotiator, then the client risks losing the attorney-client privilege. In the seminal case of *Georgia-Pacific Corp. v. GAF Roofing Mfg. Corp.*, Michael Scott, an environmental attorney and in-house counsel for defendant GAF, was asked to review various documents related to GAF's proposed acquisition of Georgia-Pacific's assets, and to comment on various environmental issues raised by the acquisition. Scott did that and also served as the negotiator for various environmental provisions in a contract related to the acquisition. The deal fell apart, and Georgia-Pacific filed suit. Georgia-Pacific sought to compel Scott's testimony regarding his recommendations and other communications about the negotiations. In response to GAF's contention that the attorney-client privilege protected the communications, Georgia-Pacific argued that Scott was not acting in his legal capacity but rather as a negotiator, and thus the privilege was not applicable.[195]

The court held that the attorney-client privilege did not apply. The court reasoned that Scott was not exercising an attorney's traditional function. Rather, the court found that Scott was acting as a negotiator on behalf of management in a business capacity. The court concluded that conversations regarding the status and development of the negotiations, the trade-offs that Scott perceived Georgia-Pacific was willing to make, and GAF's options, all involved business judgments of environmental risks. The court held that such reporting of developments in negotiations was sufficiently divorced from legal advice and not protected by the attorney-client privilege.

In *MSF Holdings, Ltd. v. Fiduciary Trust Co. Int'l.*, two email communications by FTCI's senior vice president and deputy corporate counsel regarding whether to honor a letter of credit were found to fall outside the scope of the attorney-client privilege. In *MSF Holdings*, the court noted that the fact that the business decision of whether to honor the letter of credit was influenced by a considera-

---

[193] "Attorney-Client Privilege," Raymond L. Sweigart, Business Law Today, Volume 17, No. 4, March/April 2008, American Bar Association, Section of Business Law.

[194] 119 Cal. App. 3d 1 (Cal. Ct. App. 1981).

[195] No. 93 Civ. 5125, 1996 U.S. Dist. LEXIS 671 (S.D.N.Y. Jan. 25, 1996).

tion of FTCI's legal obligations complicated the analysis of whether the attorney-client privilege protected the emails. Reasoning that the attorney never alluded to a legal principle or engaged in any legal analysis, the court determined that the email communications were predominantly commercial in nature and thus not privileged. The court concluded by noting that the attorney simply did what any business executive would do in deciding whether to honor a letter of credit: she collected facts. The attorney thus primarily relied on her commercial knowledge rather than her legal expertise in making her decision.[196]

.16 Communications by Business Attorneys

In today's legal marketplace, attorneys frequently claim with some justification that they can "add value" by bringing both legal knowledge and business acumen to work for the benefit of the client. A transactional attorney's communications thus quite often serve a dual purpose, incorporating both legal and business advice. Commercial entities that engage in large and complex financial transactions are inclined to engage the services of attorneys who have the training and experience to handle sophisticated legal and business issues. However, dual-purpose communications can present special challenges for the assertion of the attorney-client privilege.

In *Note Funding v. Bobian Investment Co.*, there was a demand to Bobian Investment to produce several hundred documents related to business negotiations. Note Funding argued that many of the communications handled by Bobian's attorneys concerned business negotiations and analyses and did not involve legal advice; therefore, the privilege should not apply and the documents should be produced. After conducting an *in camera* review, the court determined that the majority of the documents sought by Note Funding were protected by the attorney-client privilege. The fact that Bobian's attorneys' advice encompassed business as well as legal considerations did not strip the documents of their privilege. The court stated that in cases where the attorney's advice rests "predominantly" on an assessment of legal issues, the privilege should be recognized. In contrast, in cases where the attorney is consulted solely for business advice based on commercial, rather than legal expertise, the attorney's communications are not protected.[197]

After reviewing each document separately, the court found that while the majority of the challenged documents included discussions of financial questions and issues of commercial strategy and tactics, they did so in a context that made it evident that the Bobian attorneys were relying predominantly on their legal expertise. The court thus concluded that the attorney-client privilege protected the documents from disclosure. However, the court did not find all of Bobian's documents protected. The court found that some documents were simply reports related to the developments of the negotiations, or mere discussions of commercial prospects and financial considerations, and thus were not covered by the

---

[196] No. 03 Civ. 1818, 2005 U.S. Dist. LEXIS 34171 (S.D.N.Y. Dec. 7, 2005).

[197] No. 93 Civ. 7427, 1995 U.S. Dist. LEXIS 16605 (S.D.N.Y. Nov. 9, 1995).

privilege. The district court held that the reports on negotiations, divorced from legal advice, were not protected.

.17 Work Product Protection

A determination that the dominant purpose of the services provided by an attorney is non-legal may also affect the attorney's ability to assert work product protection. *Watts Industries, Inc. v. Superior Court* involved a suit for rescission of the sale of a condominium because the buyers made fraudulent representations about their intentions to live in the condominium in order to close the deal. During the negotiations prior to the sale, an officer of Watts Industries had a telephone conversation with the attorney for the buyers. Watts later claimed that it agreed to sell to the buyers based on representations made by the buyers' attorney during this conversation. In discovery, Watts sought to compel the attorney's answers and notes about the contents of the phone conversation. The court held that where the attorney acts "merely as a business agent" by conveying the client's bargaining position to a contracting party, the attorney's notes of the conversation should not be protected. The court reasoned that if it recognized the privilege in this type of situation, there would be increased incentive to use attorneys as business agents, and non-attorneys and clients negotiating for themselves would be at a disadvantage because their notes about negotiations would not be protected. The court concluded that the work product protection applies to documents related to legal work performed for a client, "not to notes memorializing acts performed as a mere agent." Accordingly, the court of appeals ordered the trial court to compel production of the attorney's notes of the telephone conversation. Again, we see the important distinction drawn between legal work provided by an attorney and non-legal work that any agent could have provided.[198]

¶2945 Independent Counsel and Adviser Provisions of the Dodd-Frank Act

Section 952(a) of the Dodd-Frank Act added Sections 10C(b), (d) and (e) to the Securities Exchange Act of 1934, which provide that the compensation committee of a company's board of directors may only select a compensation consultant, legal counsel, or other adviser to the compensation committee after taking into consideration factors identified by the SEC.[199] In June 2012, the SEC issued final rules on the independence of advisers to the compensation committee. In turn, the national securities exchanges adopted nearly identical rules in July 2013.

Section 10C of the Exchange Act and the SEC's rule does not require a compensation committee to hire its own independent legal counsel (or compensation consultant). It provides that:

- The compensation committee, in its sole discretion, may retain and obtain the advice of independent legal counsel and other advisers;

---

[198] 171 Cal. Rptr. 503 (Cal. Ct. App. 1981).   [199] 17 C.F.R. §240.10C-1.

- The committee may only select a compensation consultant, legal counsel or other adviser after taking into consideration factors identified by the SEC (see below); and

- The company must provide for appropriate funding, as determined by the compensation committee, for payment of reasonable compensation to the independent legal counsel or any other adviser.[200]

The SEC's rule added one additional independence factor to the five factors set forth in Section 952, which compensation committees must consider before selecting a compensation adviser. The six independence factors are as follows:[201]

1. The provision of other services to the company by the entity that "employs" (many advisers will be partners of an entity) the compensation consultant, legal counsel, or other adviser;

2. The amount of fees received from the company by the entity that employs the compensation consultant, legal counsel, or other adviser, as a percentage of the total revenue of the entity that employs the compensation consultant, legal counsel, or other adviser;

3. The policies and procedures of the entity that employs the compensation consultant, legal counsel, or other adviser that are designed to prevent conflicts of interest;

4. Any business or personal relationship of the compensation consultant, legal counsel, or other adviser with a member of the compensation committee;

5. Any stock of the company owned by the compensation consultant, legal counsel, or other adviser; and

6. Any business or personal relationships between the executive officers of the company and the compensation adviser or the entity employing the adviser.

The compensation committee should consider the six factors in their totality, without viewing any one factor as a determinative of independence. The SEC expressly declined to adopt any materiality, numerical or other thresholds for use in applying the six factors.

The SEC considered and expressly rejected the position "that a compensation committee conferring with or soliciting advice from the company's in-house or regular outside legal counsel would not be required to consider the independence factors with respect to such counsels." The SEC also considered and expressly rejected the position "that a compensation committee should be required to consider the independence factors only when the committee itself selects a compensation adviser, but not when it receives advice from, but does not select, an adviser."

The SEC's rule states that a compensation committee may select any compensation advisers that it prefers, including ones that are not independent, after

---

[200] § 240.10C-1(b)(2).   [201] § 240.10C-1(b)(4).

considering the independence factors outlined above. The rule expressly states that the compensation committee need not consider the six independence factors before consulting with or obtaining advice from in-house counsel.

In contrast to the rules for compensation consultants, the SEC's rule does not require proxy statement disclosure of whether the compensation committee retained or obtained the advice of independent legal counsel. However, the rule suggests that the compensation committee discuss the issue in the proxy statement.

Clearly the Dodd-Frank Act does not require any compensation committee (or company) to hire independent legal counsel. However, a rule like this sends a strong message to companies that the SEC believes that retaining independent legal counsel is "best practice." Institutional shareholders, shareholder advocates, and the media may jump on this bandwagon. For several years, investor advocates and the media have focused on the independence of the consultants.

¶2955 Independence Requirements for the Compensation Committee

Exchange Act Section 10C also required the SEC to promulgate rules that direct the NYSE, Nasdaq, and other national securities exchanges to prohibit the listing of any equity security of a company that does not have an independent compensation committee. In June 2012, the SEC issued final rules on the independence of compensation committee members and the national securities exchanges adopted nearly identical rules in July 2013, which they have updated from time to time since then.

.01 General Requirements

At the time, nearly every public company in America already had a compensation committee composed solely of independent, outside directors, in accordance with Exchange Act Section 16 and Code Sec. 162(m). However, in determining the definition of the term "independence," Section 10C and the SEC's rule requires the national securities exchanges to consider two additional factors: (i) the source of compensation of a member of the board, including any consulting, advisory, or other compensatory fee paid by the company to such member; and (ii) whether a member of the board is affiliated with the company, or a subsidiary or affiliate of the company.[202]

In establishing their independence requirements, the exchanges may determine that, even though affiliated directors are not allowed to serve on audit committees, such a blanket prohibition would be inappropriate for compensation committees, and certain affiliates, such as representatives of significant shareholders, should be permitted to serve.

The SEC rule does not prescribe any standards or relationships that would automatically preclude a finding of independence for a board member. However, the SEC emphasizes that the exchanges should consider other ties between the

---

[202] § 240.10C-1(b)(1)(ii).

company and a director, in addition to share ownership, that might impair the director's judgment as a member of the compensation committee, such as a personal or business relationships between members of the compensation committee and the company's executive officers.

The SEC's rule also permits the national securities exchanges to exempt a particular relationship from the independence requirements, taking into consideration the listed company's size and other relevant factors.

Finally, the new independence rule does not apply to a "controlled company" (50% owned), a limited partnership, or a company that is in bankruptcy proceedings (subject to possible exceptions for controlled, regulated institutions).

.02 Reporting Requirements

The SEC's rules also impose reporting requirements applicable to compensation consultants (not counsel), as required by Dodd-Frank Act Section 952(c)(2). Item 407(e)(3)(iv) requires that "with regard to any compensation consultant identified in response to Item 407(e)(3)(iii) whose work has raised any conflict of interest, disclose the nature of the conflict and how the conflict is being addressed." For purposes of determining whether there is a conflict of interest that may need to be disclosed, the committee must apply the six independence factors listed above.

Item 407(e)(3)(iii) requires companies to disclose "any role of compensation consultants in determining or recommending the amount or form of executive and director compensation." With respect to the requirement in Item 407(e)(3)(iv) to disclose compensation consultant conflicts of interest, the SEC uses the "any role" disclosure trigger rather than the "obtained or retained the advice of" trigger applicable to legal counsel and other advisers. The requirement applies to any compensation consultant whose work must be disclosed pursuant to Item 407(e)(3)(iii), regardless of whether the compensation consultant was retained by management or the compensation committee or any other board committee.

The final rule does not require disclosure of potential conflicts of interest or an appearance of a conflict of interest. The SEC's rule also continues an exception to reporting for consulting work on broad-based plans and providing non-customized benchmark data.

.03 "Golden Leash" Disclosure

When an investor has the right to appoint one of its employees/partners to the board of a corporation and the investor provides a separate compensation arrangement to that director, it is referred to as a "golden leash." Nasdaq's rules added a golden leash disclosure requirement, effective for proxy statements filed on or after August 2016.[203] The rule is aimed at the potential or perceived conflicts that may arise when a third-party investment group appoints a director and maintains a separate or additional compensation arrangements for the individual, which "may lead to conflicts of interest among directors, call into

---

[203] Nasdaq Rule 5250(b)(3).

question their ability to satisfy their fiduciary duties [and] tend to promote a focus on short-term results at the expense of long-term value creation."

Rule 5250(b)(3) requires listed companies to publicly disclose the material terms of all agreements and arrangements between any director or nominee and any person or entity (other than the company) relating to compensation or other payment in connection with that person's candidacy or service as a director. The terms "compensation" and "other payment" as used in this rule are not limited to cash payments and are intended to be construed broadly.

Subject to exceptions provided in the rule, the company must make disclosure on or through its website or in the proxy or information statement. Rule 5250(b)(3) does not separately require the initial disclosure of newly entered into agreements or arrangements, provided that disclosure is made pursuant to this rule for the next shareholders' meeting at which directors are elected. In addition, for publicly disclosed agreements and arrangements that existed prior to the nominee's candidacy and thus not required to be disclosed in accordance with Rule 250(b)(3)(A)(ii) but where the director or nominee's remuneration is thereafter materially increased specifically in connection with such person's candidacy or service as a director of the company, only the difference between the new and previous level of compensation or other payment obligation needs to be disclosed.

Chapter 30
EXECUTIVE COMPENSATION IN INITIAL PUBLIC OFFERINGS

¶3001 Overview

Unique executive compensation issues arise in connection with an initial public offering ("IPO") transaction. When preparing for an IPO, companies must consider a number of changes to their existing compensation arrangements. Companies first must consider how to modify existing compensation arrangements to comply with the various requirements and shareholder expectations that apply to public companies. An IPO company also generally will have to create new arrangements, and modify those already in place, in order to comply with new requirements and to take advantage of the upcoming changes in its capitalization. Finally, an IPO company must work closely with its outside advisers throughout this process in order to navigate the various reporting and approval requirements that will apply at the time of the IPO and beyond. Typically, a company will assemble an IPO working group consisting of its outside and inside counsel, senior executives, board members and compensation consultants.

.01 Compensation Differences at Public Companies

Public companies' executive compensation plans generally are different than the executive compensation plans of private companies. This is due to many factors, including the increased liquidity and constant valuation of a public company's stock, the application of certain requirements under the Internal Revenue Code of 1986 ("Code") and various securities laws, as well as the financial reporting requirements that apply to a public company (see ¶3015).

.02 New Plans and Arrangements

A private company contemplating an IPO typically will have in place some form of equity compensation plan already, in addition to other standard employee benefit plans and arrangements, such as a 401(k) plan and group health insurance. However, given the vast difference between the capitalization of a private company and that of a public company, most companies adopt entirely new and different executive compensation plans and agreements at the time of an IPO. This is particularly true for plans and agreements that provide for equity-based compensation (see ¶3025).

.03 Corporate Actions and Controls

After the IPO, the company will become subject to the Securities Act of 1933 (the "Securities Act") and the Securities and Exchange Act of 1934 (the "Exchange Act") (see ¶3035). The securities laws impose a variety of reporting and disclosure requirements that do not apply to private companies. These requirements have a significant effect on the structure and type of compensation a public company can offer. Public disclosure also leads to unsolicited input from institutional investors and other shareholders, which can affect company compensation policies.

.04 Code Sec. 162(m) Issues

Code Sec. 162(m) only applies to publicly traded companies. Code Sec. 162(m) prohibits a publicly traded company from taking a tax deduction for compensation paid to certain executive officers that exceeds $1 million. However, the regulations under Sec. 162(m) provide a transition rule for certain compensation paid by private companies that become publicly held. This transition rule was not affected by the changes to Code Sec. 162(m) made by the Tax Cuts and Jobs Act, signed into law by President Trump in December 2017 ("TCJA") (see ¶3045).

.05 Special Rules for Emerging Growth and Smaller Reporting Companies

An IPO company may initially qualify as an emerging growth company or a smaller reporting company. The Exchange Act provides more lenient reporting rules to emerging growth companies or smaller reporting companies (see ¶3055).

.06 Other Plans and Miscellaneous Issues

Many other executive compensation issues arise in connection with an IPO, including whether to adopt an Employee Stock Purchase Plan ("ESPP"), the application of additional rules under Code Sec. 409A, what, if any, changes are needed to the company's 401(k) and/or retirement plan, employee communications regarding changes to plans and new plans, vendor selection for new equity plans, whether to adopt a directed share program ("DSP"), and issues that arise under international laws that may apply to plans of the company (see ¶3065).

¶3015 Compensation Differences at Public Companies

Public companies' executive compensation plans generally are different than executive compensation plans of private companies. This is owing to several factors, including:

- The liquidity and constant, clear valuation of public company stock make equity compensation easier and more attractive.

- Public companies are much more willing to award stock to employees than private company owners.

- A variety of Internal Revenue Code provisions apply differently (or exclusively) to public companies (*e.g.*, Code Secs. 162(m), 280G and 409A).

- Federal securities laws impose significant requirements and limitations on equity compensation and executives of public companies, including the requirement that public companies report detailed information on executive compensation in their annual proxy statements.

- The public marketplace expects to see certain types of executive compensation and agreements.

- Most companies look to their peer group companies when setting compensation, which accelerates and perpetuates the differences once a company goes public.

- The Nasdaq and New York Stock Exchange ("NYSE") each impose their own sets of rules on companies listed on that exchange.

- Because public companies report their financial results quarterly, they need to be more sensitive to non-cash accounting charges that arise from many forms of equity compensation.

.01 IPO Creates Liquidity for Equity Compensation

The liquidity and constant, clear valuation of public company stock make equity compensation easier for companies to award and administer. The liquidity of the stock also makes the awards more attractive to recipients. With private company equity compensation awards, often neither the company nor its executive employee are certain of the value of the awards. Private companies, therefore, have a more difficult time using equity as a tool to attract and retain executive talent. On the other hand, some private companies will emphasize equity awards as a valuable form of compensation because of the possibility of an IPO. When a private company is considering an IPO at some point in the future, the most attractive part of working for the company from the employees' perspective is often the potential value of equity awards. This has been particularly true in recent years for many technology start-ups.

Nevertheless, public companies are typically more willing and able to award stock to employees than private company owners. This makes it very important for an IPO company to review and properly plan its executive compensation arrangements prior to the IPO.

.02 New Requirements Apply

A variety of Internal Revenue Code provisions apply differently (or exclusively) to public companies. For example, Code Sec. 280G applies differently to a public company. A company can qualify for an exemption from Code Sec. 280G if none of the company's stock is readily tradeable on an established securities market and certain shareholder approval requirements are met.[1] While the shareholder approval requirements for this exemption can be difficult to obtain for some private companies, they are less onerous than similar requirements for public companies. An IPO company should consider revising its compensation arrangements to account for any effect Code Sec. 280G may have.[2]

Certain of Code Sec. 409A's requirements also apply differently to a public company's compensation arrangements. For example, the six-month delay requirement for payments upon an employee's separation from service only applies to certain employees of a public company. Specifically, payments of

---

[1] Code Sec. 280G(b)(5); Reg. § 1.280G-1, Q&A-6.

[2] *See* Chapter 2 (¶ 201 *et seq.*) for a detailed discussion of Code Sec. 280G.

deferred compensation to "specified employees" of a public company (generally defined as the 50 most highly paid officers, five percent owners and certain one percent owners)[3] upon the employees' separation from service must be delayed for six months following the date of such separation.[4] The identification of specified employees is based on a fixed 12-month period ending on a fixed annual "identification date."[5] The same identification date must be used for all arrangements of the company subject to Code Sec. 409A.[6] If an employee is identified as a specified employee on the identification date, the employee's status as a specified employee becomes effective as of a specified "effective date" following the identification date.[7]

In an IPO, the six-month delay rule applies to employees who would have been specified employees at the time of the IPO, as if the company's specified employee rules had been in place prior to the IPO.[8] After an IPO, the next "identification date" is presumed to be the next December 31 following the IPO, unless otherwise elected prior to the IPO.[9] Also, the next "effective date" following the IPO is presumed to be the April 1 following the presumed post-IPO identification date, unless otherwise elected prior to the IPO.[10] There are certain exceptions that may allow specified employees to avoid the six-month delay rule. However, a public company must incorporate the six-month delay rule and other provisions into its compensation arrangements if they provide for payments to any specified employees of the company once it goes public.

The rules regarding valuation of a company's stock for purposes of the exemption of certain stock options under Code Sec. 409A are also different for a publicly traded company. Regulations under Code Sec. 409A provide an exemption for stock options, as long as certain requirements are met.[11] One of these requirements is that the options be granted at fair market value at the time of grant.[12] Under Code Sec. 409A, the fair market value of a publicly traded company's stock under Code Sec. 409A may be determined using one of the following methods:

    (i) the last sale before or the first sale after the stock option grant;

    (ii) the closing price on the trading day before or the trading day of the grant;

    (iii) the mean of the high and low prices on the trading day before or the trading day of the grant;

    (iv) the average selling price during a specified period that is within 30 days before or 30 days after the applicable valuation date, provided that the program under which the stock right is granted must irrevoca-

---

[3] Reg. § 1.409A-1(i).
[4] Reg. § 1.409A-3(i)(2).
[5] Reg. § 1.409A-3(i)(3).
[6] Id.
[7] Reg. § 1.409A-3(i)(4).
[8] Reg. § 1.409A-1(i)(6)(iv).
[9] Id.

[10] Id.
[11] See generally Reg. § 1.409A-1(b)(5).
[12] Reg. § 1.409A-1(b)(5)(i)(A). The other two general requirements for the exemption are that the options (i) be tied to "service recipient" stock and (ii) do not contain any deferral feature that defers recognition of income beyond the exercise date. Id.

bly specify the commitment to grant the stock right with an exercise price set using such an average selling price before the beginning of the specified period; or

(v) any other reasonable method using actual transactions in such stock as reported by such market.[13]

These valuation methods are significantly less complicated than those for private companies. However, an IPO company may have to amend its equity compensation arrangements as a result of the change.

Federal securities laws also impose significant requirements and limitations on public company executives' equity compensation, including the requirement that public companies report detailed information on executive compensation in their annual proxy statements and obtain shareholder approval for grants of equity compensation.[14]

Finally, the Nasdaq and NYSE each impose their own sets of rules on their listed companies. The NYSE Corporate Governance Standards require each NYSE-listed company to have a compensation committee composed entirely of "independent" directors.[15] For these purposes, a director is "independent" only if the company affirmatively determines that the director has no material relationship with the company, either directly or as a partner, shareholder or officer of an organization that has a relationship with the company.[16] Companies must disclose these determinations.[17] In addition, the following rules apply to a determination of independence:

- A director who is an employee or whose immediate family member is an executive officer of the company is not independent until three years after the end of the employment relationship.[18]

- A director who receives, or whose immediate family member receives, more than $100,000 per year in direct compensation from the company, other than director and committee fees and pension or other forms of deferred compensation for prior service (provided such compensation is not contingent on continued service), is not independent until three years after he or she ceases to receive more than $100,000 per year in such compensation.[19]

- A director who is affiliated with or employed by, or whose immediate family member is affiliated with or employed in a professional capacity by, a present or former internal or external auditor of the company is not independent until three years after the end of the affiliation or the employment or auditing relationship.[20]

---

[13] Reg. § 1.409A-1(b)(5)(iv)(A).

[14] *See* Chapter 12 (¶ 1201 *et seq.*) for a detailed discussion of the application of securities laws to executive compensation.

[15] NYSE Listed Company Manual Sec. 303A.05.

[16] NYSE Listed Company Manual Sec. 303A.02(a).

[17] *Id.*

[18] NYSE Listed Company Manual Sec. 303A.02(b)(i).

[19] NYSE Listed Company Manual Sec. 303A.02(b)(ii).

[20] NYSE Listed Company Manual Sec. 303A.02(b)(iii).

- A director who is employed, or whose immediate family member is employed, as an executive officer of another company where any of the listed company's present executives serve on that company's compensation committee is not independent until three years after the end of such service or the employment relationship.[21]

- A director who is an executive officer or an employee, or whose immediate family member is an executive officer, of a company that makes payments to, or receives payments from, the listed company for property or services in an amount which, in any single fiscal year, exceeds the greater of $1 million or two percent of such other company's consolidated gross revenues, is not independent until three years after falling below such threshold.[22]

The NYSE rules also require a listed company's compensation committee to have a written charter that addresses the following:

- An annual performance evaluation of the compensation committee; and

- The committee's purpose and responsibilities, which, at a minimum, must include direct responsibility to:

  - Review and approve corporate goals and objectives relevant to CEO compensation, evaluate the CEO's performance in light of those goals and objectives, and, either as a committee or together with the other independent directors (as directed by the board), determine and approve the CEO's compensation level based on this evaluation;

  - Make recommendations to the board with respect to non-CEO compensation, incentive compensation plans and equity-based plans; and

  - Produce a compensation committee report on executive compensation as required by the SEC to be included in the company's annual proxy statement or annual report on Form 10-K filed with the SEC.[23]

Finally, the NYSE rules contain shareholder approval requirements for certain equity compensation plans of a listed company. The rules require domestic listed companies to obtain shareholder approval for all equity compensation plans and any material revisions to such plans.[24] The rules define an equity compensation plan as a plan or other arrangement that provides for the delivery of equity securities (either newly issued or treasury shares) of the listed company to any employee, director or other service provider as compensation for services.[25] Even a compensatory grant of options or other equity securities that is not made under a formal plan is, nonetheless, an equity compensation plan under the rules.[26] The following, however, are not considered equity compensation plans:

---

[21] NYSE Listed Company Manual Sec. 303A.02(b)(iv).

[22] NYSE Listed Company Manual Sec. 303A.02(b)(v).

[23] NYSE Listed Company Manual Sec. 303A.05.

[24] NYSE Listed Company Manual Sec. 303A.08.

[25] Id.

[26] Id.

- Plans that are made available to shareholders generally, such as a dividend reinvestment plan.
- Plans that merely allow employees, directors or other service providers to elect to buy shares on the open market or from the listed company for their current fair market value, regardless of whether the shares are delivered immediately or on a deferred basis, or whether the payments for the shares are made directly or by giving up compensation that is otherwise due.[27]

In general, a "material revision" of an equity compensation plan includes, but is not limited to, the following:

- A material increase in the number of shares available under the plan (other than an increase solely to reflect a reorganization, stock split, merger, spinoff or similar transaction);
- An expansion of the types of awards available under the plan;
- A material expansion of the class of employees, directors or other service providers eligible to participate in the plan;
- A material extension of the term of the plan;
- A material change to the method of determining the strike price of options under the plan; or
- The deletion or limitation of any provision prohibiting repricing of options.[28]

There are a number of exemptions from the NYSE shareholder approval requirements. Importantly, the company must notify NYSE in writing when it plans to use an exemption. The exemptions are:

- An award of options or other equity-based compensation as a material inducement to a person or persons being hired by the company or a subsidiary, or being rehired following a bona fide period of interruption of employment. Inducement awards include grants to new employees in connection with a merger or acquisition. Promptly following a grant of any inducement award relying on this exemption, the company must disclose in a press release the material terms of the award, including the recipient(s) of the award and the number of shares involved.
- In the context of a merger or acquisition, two exemptions apply:
  - Shareholder approval is not required to convert, replace or adjust outstanding options or other equity-based compensation awards to reflect the transaction; and
  - Shares available under certain plans acquired in a merger or acquisition may be used for certain post-transaction grants without further shareholder approval. This exemption applies to situations where a party that is not a listed company following the transaction has shares available for grant under pre-existing plans that were previously ap-

---

[27] Id.   [28] Id.

proved by shareholders. A plan that was adopted in contemplation of the transaction would not be considered "pre-existing" for purposes of this exemption. There are also a number of other requirements to qualify for this exemption.

- The following types of plans (and material revisions to such plans) are exempt as well:
  - Plans intended to meet the requirements of Code Sec. 401(a) (*e.g.*, ESOPs and 401(k) plans);
  - Plans intended to meet the requirements of Code Sec. 423 (*e.g.*, ESPPs); and
  - A parallel nonqualified plan such as a supplemental employee retirement plan ("SERP").[29]

Nasdaq's listing rules also require that a majority of a listed company's directors be independent.[30] The company's determination of director independence must be disclosed.[31] The compensation of the company's CEO and all other executive officers must be determined, or recommended to the board for determination, either by a majority of the independent directors or a compensation committee comprised solely of independent directors.[32] In addition, the Nasdaq rules do not allow the CEO to be present during voting or deliberations regarding the CEO's compensation.[33] Notwithstanding these requirements, if the compensation committee is comprised of at least three members, one director (who is not independent and is not a current officer or employee or a family member of an officer or employee) may be appointed to the compensation committee if the board, under "exceptional and limited circumstances," determines that such individual's membership on the committee is required by the best interests of the company and its shareholders, and the board discloses, in its next proxy statement, the nature of the relationship and the reasons for the determination.[34] A member appointed under this exception may not serve longer than two years.[35]

Under the Nasdaq rules, "independent" means a person other than an executive officer or employee of the company or any other individual having a relationship which, in the opinion of the company's board of directors, would interfere with the exercise of independent judgment in carrying out the responsibilities of a director.[36] In addition, the following persons shall not be considered independent:

- A director who is, or at any time during the past three years was, employed by the company;
- A director who accepted or who has a family member who accepted any compensation from the company in excess of $100,000 during any period of twelve consecutive months within the three years preceding the determination of independence, other than the following:

---

[29] *Id.*
[30] Nasdaq Marketplace Rule 4350(c).
[31] *Id.*
[32] *Id.*
[33] *Id.*
[34] Nasdaq Marketplace Rule 4350(c)(3)(C).
[35] *Id.*
[36] Nasdaq Marketplace Rule 4200.

- Compensation for board or board committee service;
- Compensation paid to a family member who is an employee (other than an executive officer) of the company; or
- Benefits under a tax-qualified retirement plan, or non-discretionary compensation.

- A director who is a family member of an individual who is, or at any time during the past three years was, employed by the company as an executive officer;
- A director who is, or has a family member who is, a partner in, or a controlling shareholder or an executive officer of, any organization to which the company made, or from which the company received, payments for property or services in the current or any of the past three fiscal years that exceed five percent of the recipient's consolidated gross revenues for that year, or $200,000, whichever is more, other than the following:
  - Payments arising solely from investments in the company's securities; or
  - Payments under non-discretionary charitable contribution matching programs.
- A director of the issuer who is, or has a family member who is, employed as an executive officer of another entity where at any time during the past three years any of the executive officers of the issuer serve on the compensation committee of such other entity; or
- A director who is, or has a family member who is, a current partner of the company's outside auditor, or was a partner or employee of the company's outside auditor who worked on the company's audit at any time during any of the past three years.[37]

Finally, the Nasdaq rules contain shareholder approval requirements for equity compensation plans of a listed company. The rules require listed companies to obtain shareholder approval prior to the establishment of equity compensation plans and material amendments to such plans, subject to the following exemptions:

- Warrants or rights that are offered generally and on equal terms to all security holders of the company;
- Tax qualified plans under Code Secs. 401(a) and 423, and parallel non-qualified plans;
- Issuances to a person not previously an employee or director of the company, or following a bona fide period of non-employment, as a material inducement to enter into employment with the company, provided the issuances are approved by either the issuer's compensation committee or a majority of the issuer's independent directors. Following

---

[37] Id.

such an issuance, the company must disclose the material terms of the grant, including the recipient(s) and the number of shares involved, in a press release;

- Issuances that will result in a change of control of the company;

- Certain post-transaction awards relating to a merger or acquisition, including those that are used to convert, replace or adjust outstanding options or other equity compensation awards to reflect the transaction, and those that are made with respect to shares available under certain pre-existing plans acquired in the transaction; and

- Certain grants in connection with the company's acquisition of the stock or assets of another company.[38]

Importantly, the Nasdaq rules also contain a provision allowing for a "financial viability" exemption to the shareholder approval requirements. This exemption is available upon prior written application to Nasdaq where:

- The delay in securing stockholder approval would seriously jeopardize the financial viability of the enterprise; and

- The company's reliance on the exception is expressly approved by the company's audit committee or a comparable body of the board comprised solely of independent, disinterested directors.[39]

If the company receives such an exemption, it must notify all shareholders in writing, and by public announcement through the news media no later than 10 days before the issuance of the securities.[40] The notice must disclose the terms of the transaction, the fact that the company is relying on the exemption, and that the company's audit or comparable committee has expressly approved reliance on the exemption.[41]

.03 Expectations of a Public Company

The public marketplace expects to see certain types of executive compensation arrangements and agreements. For example, the markets/investors generally expect a public company's key executives to have employment agreements. This expectation will be even more important in an IPO because potential investors will want to know that these executives have an incentive to remain employed after the company goes public. In addition, IPO investors and future shareholders will want to see equity compensation arrangements in place that directly tie company stock performance to a portion of the executives' pay.

Executives of an IPO company also will expect to see certain types of compensation arrangements in addition to those discussed above, such as change in control or golden parachute agreements. These types of arrangements may be necessary to attract executive talent in the future.

---

[38] Nasdaq Marketplace Rule 4350(i)(1).
[39] Nasdaq Marketplace Rule 4350(i)(2).
[40] Id.
[41] Id.

.04 Peer Group Benchmarking

Most companies look to their peer group companies when setting compensation. This makes an IPO company's revision of its compensation structure more important, because after the IPO, the company's compensation structure may be greatly different from that of its peers due simply to the fact that it is no longer privately held.

.05 Accounting Ramifications

Because public companies report their financial results quarterly, they need to be more sensitive to non-cash accounting charges that arise from equity compensation. Non-cash accounting charges arise upon the grant of stock options, restricted stock, stock appreciation rights, performance shares, and stock rights under an ESPP (see ¶755). Worse yet, some awards produce an accounting charge that varies with the company's stock price and, therefore, must be recalculated quarterly. After an IPO, a company will be forced to consider these charges on a more frequent basis.

¶3025 New or Amended Plans and Agreements

Most companies adopt new and different executive compensation plans and agreements at the time they first offer stock for sale to the public through an IPO.

.01 New or Amended Equity Incentive Plan

Many companies adopt a new equity incentive plan effective immediately prior to their IPO. Although many private companies also maintain equity incentive plans, the design of public company equity incentive plans is usually different due to the increased liquidity and constant valuation of company stock, the application of new sections in the tax code, and new shareholder expectations and demands.

The company or IPO working group should begin this process several months before the projected IPO date. Typically, the IPO company will adopt an omnibus equity incentive plan, permitting a broad array of awards. At some IPO companies, this will be the first equity award plan, or the first plan to make awards outside of the senior executives.

Investors hope (and expect) that the company's stock price will rise in value immediately upon the IPO. Therefore, the company's board will adopt the new plan (and have it approved by shareholders) before the IPO, and disclose the new plan to the public in its offering prospectus. Shareholder approval, which is important and necessary for a variety of tax and securities law reasons, is usually easy to obtain for a private company.

The new equity incentive plan design may be the product of, or subject to review by, an IPO working group that includes the company's executives, board members, outside counsel (who also will draft the plan), inside counsel and compensation consultants. Once the working group has settled on the plan design and approved the draft, the equity incentive plan document should be submitted to shareholders for approval.

One of the most important design decisions for the IPO company and its advisers is the number of shares authorized for awards under the new equity plan. IPO companies usually strive to authorize enough shares to make awards in the IPO and for a few years thereafter. Companies often need to fill several key positions during the period immediately following an IPO, which requires a large number of share awards and, consequently, a plan that authorizes a large number of shares for such awards.

In connection with the IPO process, in addition to preparing the plan document itself, counsel will need to:

- Prepare all documents necessary to obtain shareholder approval of the equity incentive plan;
- Prepare and file with the SEC, a Form S-8 for the plan; and
- Prepare and furnish to award recipients a statement of general information, required by the SEC for the offering of stock awards.

The company also must determine the types of awards that it will issue under the equity incentive plan, who will be eligible for such awards and whether the terms will differ among award recipients. Counsel generally will prepare model employee and director award agreements to be reviewed by the working group. The company should then determine the types and number of awards to be granted at the IPO to each employee or employee group and each director. This will require any necessary board, shareholder or working group approval. This process should begin several months before the projected IPO date.

After the company has determined the number of awards to be granted at IPO to each eligible employee or director, the company must work with counsel to prepare individual award agreements for each recipient. The company or compensation committee chair, as appropriate, will then execute the award agreements and distribute them, along with statements of general information about the award (required by the SEC), to each eligible employee or director. Each recipient must then execute his or her agreement and return it to the company. However, depending on when the awards are granted, this process does not need to be completed prior to the IPO.

.02 Awards Under Existing Stock Plan

The company or IPO working group also must also decide what to do with any existing equity incentive plan. Alternatives generally include freezing the plan, merging the plan into the new IPO plan, or amending and restating the old plan to incorporate public company plan design features and provisions. For example, the company would need to eliminate private company plan design features like put rights, call rights, and rights of first refusal.

With respect to outstanding awards under a prior plan, the company should determine the effect of the IPO on the outstanding awards. For example, the company should decide whether the awards vest upon the IPO (most do not vest).

¶3025.02

The company also should review option awards made during the preceding 12 months for so-called "cheap stock" charges. Before Code Sec. 409A, cheap stock issues arose frequently in the IPO process. A "cheap stock" issue arises where, in the SEC's determination, the company has granted options at exercise prices that were below fair market value at the time of grant. The SEC will require the company to recognize a non-cash accounting charge for such option grants. It is important to note that, although private company boards usually grant options at their best estimate of current fair market value, the SEC does not always agree, in hindsight, with board determinations of fair market value. Clearly, this can be a difficult issue for private companies, because of a lack of constant valuation through market trading. Private company boards often have the difficult task of quantifying many different variables in order to arrive at a fair market price. For a private company that is backed by venture capital, this task can be even more difficult due to the often disparate value of rights afforded to common stock and preferred stock.

An additional problem in the area of valuing private company stock lurks in the application of Code Sec. 409A to stock options granted by private companies. Regulations under Code Sec. 409A provide for an exemption for stock options granted by private companies as long as certain requirements are met.[42] One of these requirements is that the options be granted at fair market value at the time of grant.[43] The final regulations provide that the valuation method used to determine fair market value for private company stock must be "reasonable" in order for the options to qualify for the exemption. The regulations provide certain factors and actual methods that are relevant to this analysis.

First, the regulations provide a list of factors that should be considered in a valuation of private company stock, in order for the valuation method to be considered reasonable. Those factors include: (i) the value of tangible and intangible assets of the corporation, (ii) the present value of anticipated future cashflows of the company, (iii) the market value of stock or equity interests in similar corporations and other entities engaged in trades or businesses substantially similar to those engaged in by the company that is to be valued (the value of which can be readily determined through nondiscretionary, objective means such as through trading prices on an established securities market or an amount paid in an arm's length private transaction), (iv) recent arm's length transactions involving the sale or transfer of such stock or equity interest, and (v) other relevant factors such as control premiums or discounts for lack of marketability and whether the valuation method is used for other purposes that have a material economic effect on the service recipient, its stockholders, or its creditors.[44] The use of a valuation method is not reasonable if the valuation method does not take into account all available information that is material to the value of the company.[45] A previously calculated market value is not reasonable if the

---

[42] *See generally* Reg. § 1.409A-1(b)(5).

[43] Reg. § 1.409A-1(b)(5)(i)(A). The other two general requirements for the exemption are that the options: (i) be tied to "service recipient" stock and

(ii) do not contain any deferral feature that defers recognition of income beyond the exercise date. *Id.*

[44] Reg. § 1.409A-1(b)(5)(iv)(B)(1).

[45] *Id.*

calculation fails to reflect information available after the date of the calculation that may materially affect the value of the corporation or if the value was calculated more than 12 months prior to the date for which the valuation is being used.[46] The company's use of a valuation method to determine its stock value for other purposes, including purposes that are unrelated to employee compensation, is also a factor that supports the reasonableness of the valuation method.

Second, the regulations provide that using one of three methods for determining fair market value will result in a valuation that is presumed to be reasonable, unless the IRS can show that the method was "grossly unreasonable." These methods are: (i) a qualified independent appraisal as of a date no earlier than 12 months before the transaction to which the valuation is applied (such as the date of a stock option grant); (ii) a non-lapse repurchase formula; and (iii) a written "illiquid start-up" valuation.[47] Importantly, the last method is not available to companies that reasonably anticipate, at the time of the valuation, undergoing a change in control within 90 days, or a public offering within 180 days.[48]

As a consequence of potential "cheap stock" charges and tax ramifications under Code Sec. 409A, a company that is contemplating an IPO should consider retaining an independent appraiser of fair market value, especially during the period leading up to the IPO. Although these determinations do not bind the SEC in any way, they help ensure that the company has taken reasonable steps to accurately determine the value of its stock. Independent appraisals also help ensure that the IRS will consider the valuation to be reasonable under Code Sec. 409A. In particular, the company must pay attention to valuations taken during the 12 month period leading up to the IPO, because often the SEC will expect to see the stock price gradually increase to approach the anticipated IPO price. During this period, IPO companies should work closely with their auditors and counsel (and underwriters during the final IPO stages) with regard to the accounting results of proposed option grants to determine how the cheap stock and Code Sec. 409A rules will affect the IPO process.

.03 Director Compensation

Shortly before the IPO, companies generally take on new directors who will satisfy the various director independence requirements of the tax and securities laws. The company must decide on the compensation package it will provide to these new directors. The compensation provided to existing directors is usually redesigned as well.

Counsel will typically prepare an invitation letter to the new director(s), which includes a description of the proposed compensation arrangement, for review by the working group. The company then must execute the director invitation letters and any award agreement under the company's equity plans. The recipient must execute the agreement and return it to the company.

---

[46] *Id.*

[47] Reg. § 1.409A-1(b)(5)(iv)(B)(2).

[48] *Id.*

.04 Employment, Change in Control, Severance and Other Agreements

Companies generally establish new (or improved) employment, change in control, and/or severance agreements for senior executives prior to or in conjunction with an IPO. The public markets generally want to know that the IPO company has locked up its key executives with employment agreements. In addition, the executives will want the protection of severance and/or change in control agreements. Counsel will need to provide drafts of the proposed employment agreements for review by officers and directors, and there may be some negotiation.

Most employment agreements prohibit the executive from serving on the board of directors of any other publicly traded company without the board's written consent, or limit the number of boards on which the executive can serve. Most employment agreements also prohibit the executive from engaging in consulting work or any trade or business outside of the executive's employment with the company.

The parties should execute any employment, change in control, and/or severance agreements before the IPO. Change in control agreements in particular are more common among public companies than private companies, and a company often will adopt such agreements at the time of an IPO. Importantly, the terms and conditions of the new agreements must be disclosed in the registration statement and offering prospectus.

Finally, IPO companies often prepare comprehensive indemnification agreements for officers and directors to reflect the increased legal risks and liabilities facing public company officers and directors. Counsel will need to provide drafts of the proposed indemnification agreements for review by officers and directors, and there may be some negotiation.

.05 Annual Incentive (Bonus) Plan

An IPO company generally will revise its existing annual incentive or cash bonus plan, or create a new plan, to better align performance goals under the plan with the company's goals as a publicly traded corporation. Revisions also may be required to comply with the requirements of Code Sec. 162(m), which will apply once the company goes public. While some performance goals under a bonus plan may be retained, new goals are often required to better meet the expectations of the new shareholders.

Counsel typically will prepare the revised or new plan, and the company should create a related bonus schedule for the upcoming year. The company or working group will review these changes, and ultimately approve the revised or newly created plan prior to the IPO. The new plan and bonus schedules then should be distributed to covered executives and disclosed in the company's registration statement and prospectus.

As a final note, if a public company is required to restate its accounting results due to material noncompliance with financial reporting requirements as a result of misconduct, then, under the Sarbanes-Oxley Act of 2002, the company's CEO and CFO could be required to reimburse the company for any bonus or other incentive-based compensation or equity-based compensation (such as from the company's annual bonus plan) and profits from the sale of the company's securities during the 12-month period following initial publication of the financial statements that had to be restated. This may be an important consideration in an IPO company's executive compensation decisions where Sarbanes-Oxley has never before applied.

¶3035 Corporate Actions and Controls

Certain formal corporate actions are required when revising existing compensation arrangements and creating new arrangements in conjunction with an IPO. Additionally, because a company will become subject to both the Securities and Exchange Acts, a number of disclosures and shareholder approvals are required.

.01 Compensation Committee Charter

An IPO company's compensation committee charter may need to be revised in order to better describe the committee's purpose once the company goes public, and to comply with certain NYSE rules (see ¶3015.02). The company's counsel typically will prepare revisions to the compensation committee's charter and distribute them to the company or working group for comments. Once the company or working group approves a final version, the new charter should be distributed to the entire board.

.02 Board Resolutions

In addition, depending on the actions the IPO company will be taking with regard to new and existing compensation arrangements, certain board resolutions will be necessary. The following is a list of compensation plans and arrangements that the board may need to adopt or approve:

- Stock incentive plan (including number of shares reserved)
- Employee stock purchase plan (including number of shares reserved)
- Severance agreements
- Director compensation
- Bonus plan
- Target bonus levels for the executive leadership team (including target bonus level and performance goals for each covered executive)
- Stock grants to be made at IPO to individual recipients
- Amendment(s) to 401(k) plan
- Indemnity agreements
- Board and committee charters

The IPO company also should consider delegating authority to award options to employees who are not subject to Section 16 of the Exchange Act to the company's CEO or other executive. Section 16 of the Exchange Act applies to 10 percent shareholders, directors and executive officers of the company ("insiders"). Section 16 requires both (i) that insiders report their beneficial ownership of, and certain transactions involving, the company's securities and (ii) that the company recover any "short-swing" profits on company stock attributable to such insiders. The company's board of directors should retain the authority to grant options to insiders in order to preserve the exemption from the short-swing profits restrictions under Rule 16b-3 of Section 16.[49] Before the TCJA, an IPO company also would have needed to restrict the officer with delegated authority to make awards (whether it be the CEO or other officer) from making grants to persons covered by Code Sec. 162(m), as such grants must be made by a compensation committee of the board of directors in order to preserve the exemption of the option grants from the $1 million tax deduction limit. Finally, Delaware and other state laws allow the board to delegate to an officer the authority to grant options to a non-insider.[50]

.03 Securities Law Compliance and Controls

After a company goes public through an IPO, it will have to comply with federal securities laws in its administration of equity compensation arrangements.[51] However, prior to an IPO, a company must take certain actions under the securities laws.

First, the company, typically through counsel, must prepare a description of its compensation programs ("Compensation Discussion & Analysis" or "CD&A") in the Registration Statement on Form S-1. The preparation of this description will require the cooperation of the company's named executive officers and directors.[52]

The company also should work with counsel to develop securities law compliance and internal controls guidelines (including insider trading guidelines). Such compliance programs typically require all Section 16 insiders to pre-clear transactions in company stock (including the exercise of options and certain benefit plan transactions) with the office of the corporate secretary or general counsel.[53] The company also should consider conducting training sessions for company personnel prior to the IPO.

.04 Securities Law Reporting

As discussed above, IPO companies must comply with certain reporting requirements under Section 16 of the Exchange Act. First, the IPO company must file an Initial Statement of Beneficial Ownership on Form 3 for all pre-IPO insiders. Following the IPO, the company must file the same Form 3 for anyone who becomes an insider thereafter. The company should also establish procedures for the filing of any required Statement of Changes of Beneficial Owner-

---

[49] One possible way to qualify for the exemption is by having the company's board of directors or a board committee composed solely of two or more "nonemployee" directors approve the transaction in question. See Rule 16b-3(b)(3) of the Exchange Act. *See also* ¶ 1275.04.

[50] DEL. CODE tit. 8, § 157(c).

[51] *See* Chapter 12 (¶ 1201 *et seq.*) for a detailed discussion of the application of securities laws to executive compensation.

[52] *See* ¶ 1285 for a detailed discussion of CD&A.

[53] *See* ¶ 1275 for a discussion of such compliance programs.

ship of Securities on Form 4. The Form 4 must be filed after any transaction involving company securities, including transactions that are exempt from Section 16, such as equity compensation awards. Finally, the company must file a Schedule 13G for anyone who holds more than 5 percent of the outstanding shares of the company before the IPO. A Schedule 13G must generally be filed by February 14th of the year following the year of the IPO.

.05 Shareholder and Media Scrutiny

One of the inevitable results of becoming publicly traded is that the company's performance and compensation programs—and most other activities—will become subject to the scrutiny of outsiders, including the media, institutional investors and other shareholders. Institutional investors and shareholder advocates make their opinions known and often exert pressure for changes. Most public companies take into account the views of institutional investors and shareholder advocates to some extent in the design of their executive compensation programs.

¶3045 Code Sec. 162(m) Issues

After an IPO, a company will be subject to the limitations imposed by Code Sec. 162(m). Code Sec. 162(m) prohibits a publicly traded company from taking a tax deduction for compensation paid to certain executive officers that exceeds $1 million. The regulations under Sec. 162(m), provide a transition rule for certain compensation paid by private companies that become publicly held (*e.g.*, as a result of an IPO).

.01 Code Sec. 162(m) Transition Rule

The regulations under Code Sec. 162(m) provide that, in the case of a company that was not publicly held but then becomes publicly held in an IPO, spin-off or similar transaction, the $1 million deduction limit of Code Sec. 162(m) does not apply to any remuneration paid pursuant to a compensation plan or agreement that existed during the period in which the corporation was not publicly held.[54] For a company that becomes publicly held in connection with an initial public offering, this exception applies only to the extent that the prospectus accompanying the initial public offering disclosed information concerning the plans or agreements, which satisfied all applicable securities laws then in effect.[55] Importantly, a company that is a member of an affiliated group that includes a publicly held corporation is considered publicly held and therefore cannot rely on the transition rule.[56]

The newly public company can rely on the transition rule until the earliest of (i) the expiration of the plan or agreement, (ii) the material modification of the plan or agreement, (iii) the issuance of all stock and other compensation that has been allocated under the plan, or (iv) the first meeting of shareholders at which directors are to be elected that occurs after the close of the third calendar year following the calendar year in which the IPO occurs.[57] The transition rule will

---

[54] Reg. § 1.162-27(f)(1).

[55] *Id.*

[56] *Id. See also* Reg. § 1.162(c)(1)(ii).

[57] Reg. § 1.162-27(f)(2).

apply to any compensation received pursuant to the exercise of a stock option or stock appreciation right, or the substantial vesting of restricted property, if the grant occurs on or before the earliest of these events.[58]

Regulations under Code Sec. 162(m) also provide special rules for the situation where a company becomes publicly traded in a spin-off or similar transaction. Under the special rules, any remuneration paid to covered employees of the new publicly traded corporation will satisfy the exception for performance-based compensation if the following requirements under the regulations of Code Sec. 162(m) are satisfied before the spin-off or similar transaction: (i) the remuneration is based on the satisfaction of preestablished performance goals, (ii) the performance goals are established by a compensation committee comprised solely of two or more outside directors, and (iii) the material terms of the performance goal under which the remuneration is to be paid are disclosed to and subsequently approved by the company's shareholders. A final requirement is that the new publicly traded corporation's compensation committee must certify that the performance goals have been attained under the regulations of Code Sec. 162(m) (unless the performance goals were attained prior to the transaction, in which case the certification may be made before the transaction).[59]

The Code Sec. 162(m) regulations also provide relief during a transition period following the spin-off if the following requirements are satisfied with respect to the remuneration: (i) the remuneration must be based on the satisfaction of preestablished performance goals (either before or after the transaction) under the regulations of Code Sec. 162(m), (ii) the performance goals must be established by a compensation committee (either before or after the transaction) comprised solely of two or more outside directors under the regulations of Code Sec. 162(m), and (iii) the company's compensation committee must certify *after* the transaction that the performance goals have been attained under the regulations of Code Sec. 162(m). The main distinction for this "transition period" option is that shareholder approval of the proposed payments is not required either before or after the transaction. However, this "transition period" option can only be invoked for compensation paid, or stock options, stock appreciation rights, or restricted stock granted, prior to the new corporation's first regularly scheduled shareholders meeting that occurs more than 12 months after the date of the transaction. All compensation paid after such meeting must satisfy all of Code Sec. 162(m)'s requirements, including the shareholder approval requirement, in order to satisfy the exception for performance-based compensation.[60]

.02 Code Sec. 162(m) Performance-Based Compensation Exception

Prior to 2018, Code Sec. 162(m) provided an exception for compensation that was based on the company's performance.[61] The TCJA eliminated this exception.

---

[58] Reg. § 1.162-27(f)(3).
[59] Reg. § 1.162-27(f)(4)(ii).

[60] Reg. § 1.162-27(f)(4)(iii).
[61] *See* Chapter 22 (¶ 2201 *et seq.*) for a detailed discussion of Code Sec. 162(m).

¶3055 Special Rules for Emerging Growth and Smaller Reporting Companies

An IPO company may initially qualify as an emerging growth company or a smaller reporting company. The Exchange Act provides more lenient reporting rules to emerging growth companies or smaller reporting companies.

.01 Smaller Reporting Companies

The Exchange Act set forth more lenient reporting rules for smaller reporting companies ("SRC").[62] The company itself determines whether it qualifies as an SRC and, if it determines that it so qualifies, may elect to file as an SRC. The determination does not need to be cleared with the SEC or require a legal determination from the SEC. The determination of whether or not company is a smaller reporting company is made on an annual basis.[63] Under SEC rules, a smaller reporting company is one that is not an investment company, an asset-backed issuer, or a majority-owned subsidiary of a parent that is not a smaller reporting company, and that:

- had a public float of less than $250 million; or
- had annual revenues of less than $100 million and either: (A) no public float; or (B) a public float of less than $700 million.

The determination is made based on the information as to shares outstanding as reported in the Form 10-Q relating to the second fiscal quarter of the company's previous fiscal year (*e.g.*, for June 30, 2018, for calendar year companies' determination for 2019), but excluding shares held by affiliates on that date. Affiliates include directors, executive officers and shares held by other significant stockholders that may be deemed to be affiliates of the issuer (*i.e.*, they "control, are controlled by, or are under common control with" the issuer). "Control" is "the possession, direct or indirect, of the power to direct or cause the direction of the management and policies of the issuer, whether through the ownership of voting securities, by contract, or otherwise." A company must reflect its determination to take advantage of the smaller reporting company exception on the cover page of its quarterly report on Form 10-Q for the first fiscal quarter of the next year.

Item 402(l) of Regulation S-K allows a company that is an SRC to provide the scaled executive compensation disclosures set forth in Items 402(m)-(r) of Regulation S-K. An SRC need only report two years of summary compensation table information in its annual proxy statement, rather than three. Executive compensation disclosure is limited to the chief executive officer, the two most highly compensated executive officers, and up to two additional individuals no longer serving as executive officers at year end. Additionally, certain compensation disclosures are not required, including:

- Compensation discussion and analysis;
- Grants of plan-based awards table;

---

[62] Reg. § 229.10(f).   [63] Reg. § 229.10(f)(1) and (f)(2).

- Option exercises and stock vested table;
- Change in present value of pension benefits;
- CEO pay ratio;
- Compensation policies as related to risk management;
- Pension benefits table; and
- Description of retirement benefit plans.

.02 Emerging Growth Companies

The Jumpstart Our Business Startups Act, known as the JOBS Act, amended the Securities Act and the Exchange Act to create exceptions to certain of the SEC reporting rules for a company that undertakes an IPO as an emerging growth company ("EGC") after December 2011. An EGC is one that had total annual gross revenues of less than $1 billion (indexed for inflation every five years) during its most recently completed fiscal year. A company that is an EGC as of the first day of that fiscal year shall continue to be deemed an EGC until the *earliest* of (i) the last day of the fiscal year during which the company had total annual gross revenues of $1 billion or more (indexed); (ii) the last day of the company's fiscal year following the fifth anniversary of the company's IPO date; (iii) the date on which the company has, during the previous three-year period, issued more than $1 billion in non-convertible debt; or (iv) the date on which the company is deemed to be a "large accelerated filer."[64]

With regard to executive compensation disclosure, an EGC is permitted to follow the same more lenient Item 402 requirements that apply SRCs (described above). Additionally, Section 14A(e) of the Exchange Act exempt EGCs from say-on-pay, say-on-frequency votes, golden parachute compensation votes and the related disclosure provisions.

In March 2017, the SEC adopted final rules, technical amendments, and interpretations to conform several rules and forms to amendments made by the JOBS Act.[65] The final rules also effectuated inflation adjustments required under the JOBS Act, increasing the threshold to $1,070,000,000.

¶3065 Other Plans and Miscellaneous Issues

Many other executive compensation issues arise, and opportunities become available, in connection with an IPO.

.01 Employee Stock Purchase Plan

Code Sec. 423 does not prohibit a private company from maintaining an employee stock purchase plan. However, as a practical matter only public companies generally adopt ESPPs.[66]

Many companies will consider whether to adopt an ESPP in connection with the IPO. Some companies will decide to postpone adoption of an ESPP until after the IPO, because of the number and complexity of the other tasks related to the

---

[64] As defined in Section 240.12b-2.
[65] Release Nos. 33-10332; 34-80355.

[66] *See* Chapter 10 (¶1001 *et seq.*) for a detailed discussion of ESPPs.

IPO. Yet many companies decide to adopt an ESPP contemporaneous with the IPO and begin the first purchase period on the IPO effective date, because the ESPP may offer the only means by which non-executive employees can purchase stock at the IPO price and share in the hoped-for "IPO pop."

The board or working group should determine the number of shares to authorize for purchase under the ESPP. As with the stock incentive plan, counsel will typically:

- Prepare a draft of the proposed ESPP document and distribute it to the working group;
- Prepare any other documents necessary to obtain shareholder approval of the ESPP;
- Distribute the ESPP document (with any other necessary documents) to shareholders for their review and approval;
- Prepare Form S-8 for the ESPP and file it with the SEC; and
- Prepare a statement of general information for the ESPP, as required by the SEC.

.02 401(k) and Retirement Plan

In connection with an IPO, a company also may wish to revise its current 401(k) or retirement plan, or create a new plan, to allow company stock to be offered through the plan. Counsel will typically prepare the plan documents, including amendments to the plan, the trust, the summary plan description ("SPD") and the investment election documents. Counsel also should prepare the Form S-8 and a statement of general information if company stock will be offered through the plan. The statement of general information should be distributed to plan participants, as required by the SEC. These activities will have to be coordinated with the plan's other outside vendors such as administrators or recordkeepers.

.03 Employee Communications

Once the IPO company determines what changes will be made to its compensation structure, it will need to develop a strategy for communicating these changes to employees and the markets. This strategy will most often be part of the company's overall communications strategy with regard to the IPO generally. In particular, the company will need to develop and distribute informational materials to employees, as well as to the public through media outlets. The company's counsel and other outside advisers are typically active in this process.

.04 Vendor Selection (for Stock Award and ESPP Administration)

If the IPO company decides to create a new equity incentive plan and/or an ESPP, it also may need to identify and select vendors for such plans. Many public companies "outsource" the administration of their equity plans. The company should work with its outside advisers, including counsel, in this process. The process should begin with an initial phone interview with and the completion of a questionnaire by potential vendors. The company should then invite vendors for in-office visits, and follow-up interviews as necessary, to determine capabilities and ask follow-up questions. Those involved with this process will typically prepare a final report and present the report to senior management, who will often make the final decisions. Once vendors are selected, the company and its advisers should meet with the new vendors to discuss implementation of the plans in conjunction with the IPO.

.05 Directed Shares Program

An IPO company may also want to create a directed shares program ("DSP") in connection with the IPO. A DSP allows certain individuals to purchase stock as a part of the IPO, at the IPO price, and is sometimes referred to as a "friends and family" offering. The company must identify who will be eligible to participate in the DSP, and the number of shares that will be available for purchase, typically between 5 and 25 percent of the total offering. The company's counsel typically prepares the DSP materials that are distributed to participants. The participants then make their elections to purchase shares through the DSP, which is often administered by the lead underwriter to the IPO.

The participants in a DSP are often a combination of employees, directors, officers, suppliers or other business partners. The National Association of Securities Dealers ("NASD") rules, however, effectively limit who can participate in a DSP. Specifically, NASD Conduct Rule 2790 prohibits NASD members from selling "new issues" of equities to an account in which certain types of "restricted persons" have an interest.[67] A "restricted person" includes, among others, broker-dealers, owners and most employees of broker-dealers, and affiliates engaged in the investment banking or securities business. There is an exemption to the rule, however, if the recipient is also an employee or director of the issuer or a related company. Nevertheless, this rule may prevent certain individuals and entities that are related to the underwriter from participating in the DSP.

Finally, the SEC may request further information on the DSP to determine if the program complies with Section 5 of the Securities Act. Section 5 prohibits an IPO company, from the time the registration statement is filed but before it becomes effective (often referred to as the "quiet period"), from communicating in writing an offer to sell a security other than through a prospectus meeting the requirements of Section 10(a) of the Securities Act.[68] Any written communication offering to sell a security during the quiet period that does not meet 10(a)'s requirements is prohibited. The main exception to Section 5's prohibition is contained in Rule 134 of the Securities Act, which allows certain written communications to be made during the quiet period. For purposes of a DSP, Rule 134 generally allows for the communication of the necessary details during the quiet period if the communication is accompanied or preceded by a prospectus and contains a specific legend. As a result of these securities law requirements, the

---

[67] The NASD rules apply to the underwriters and generally any other broker-dealer participants in the IPO.

[68] Section 10(a) requires the prospectus to contain nearly all of the information in the registration statement.

company, through counsel and its underwriter, should pay particular attention when distributing any written communications regarding the DSP.

.06 International Plan Issues

The laws of foreign jurisdictions may have an effect on an IPO company's compensation arrangements and plans, if the arrangements and plans cover employees in such foreign jurisdictions. In these situations, a company will typically seek guidance from foreign counsel regarding the legality and feasibility of revising current arrangements and creating any new arrangements under applicable foreign law. This process should be part of the company's initial decisions regarding the modification and creation of new arrangements as it generally will require specific modifications to plan documents and agreements.

Chapter 31
EXECUTIVE COMPENSATION PROVISIONS OF THE DODD-FRANK ACT

¶3101 Overview—Executive Compensation Provisions of the Dodd-Frank Act

In July 2010, President Obama signed into law the Dodd-Frank Wall Street Reform and Consumer Protection Act (the "Dodd-Frank Act"). Subtitle E, "*Accountability and Executive Compensation*" and Subtitle G, "*Strengthening Corporate Governance*" of "Title IX—Investor Protections and Improvements to the Regulation of Securities" are only about 10 pages of the 848-page Act. However, Congress packed a lot of new law into those ten pages.

Most of the provisions are not self-executing, in that they require the SEC to modify its requirements for maintaining an effective registration under the Securities Exchange Act of 1934 (the "Exchange Act") and/or require the national securities exchanges to modify their listing standards.

The Dodd-Frank Act included at least 11 separate changes in the area of executive compensation.

1. Shareholder Say on Pay
2. Shareholder Approval of Golden Parachute Compensation
3. Independence of Compensation Committee
4. Independence of Compensation Consultant, Legal Counsel and Other Advisers
5. Policy on Recovery of Erroneously Awarded Compensation
6. Disclosure Regarding Chairman and CEO Structure
7. Disclosure of Hedging by Employees and Directors
8. Disclosure of Pay Versus Performance
9. CEO Pay Ratio Disclosure
10. Elimination of Discretionary Broker Voting
11. Enhanced Disclosure and Reporting of Compensation Arrangements

Item 11 only applies to financial institutions with assets over $1 billion. The other ten provisions apply to all publicly-traded companies. The eleven critical provisions relating to executive compensation in the Dodd-Frank Act are each discussed separately, below.

.01 Shareholder Say on Pay

Section 951 of the Dodd-Frank Act added Section 14A to the Exchange Act, entitled "Shareholder Approval of Executive Compensation," which provides that, not less frequently than once every three years, a company's annual proxy statement must include a separate resolution, subject to non-binding shareholder vote, to approve the compensation of executives, as disclosed in the company's Compensation Discussion and Analysis (CD&A), the compensation tables, and any related material. This resolution applies only to the named executive officers ("NEOs"), although the Act does not contain this explicit limitation.

Section 951 also requires that, not less frequently than once every six years, the proxy statement must include a separate resolution subject to a non-binding shareholder vote to determine whether future votes on the resolutions required under the preceding paragraph will occur every one, two, or three years (see ¶3115).

.02 Shareholder Approval of Golden Parachute Compensation

Section 14A to the Exchange Act, added by Section 951 of the Dodd-Frank Act, also added a "Shareholder Approval of 'Golden Parachute' Compensation" provision, which requires in any proxy or consent solicitation material for a meeting of shareholders *at which shareholders are asked to approve an acquisition, merger, consolidation, or proposed sale or other disposition of all or substantially all the assets of the company*, the party soliciting the proxy or consent *must disclose* any agreements or understandings that the party soliciting the proxy or consent has with any named executive officers of the company concerning any type of compensation that relates to the transaction and the aggregate total of all such compensation that may be paid or become payable to or on behalf of such executive officer (see ¶3125).

.03 Independence of Compensation Committee

Section 952 of the Dodd-Frank Act, "Compensation Committee Independence," added Section 10C to the Exchange Act, which contain two parts:

- "Independence of Compensation Committees," which requires the SEC to promulgate rules that direct the NYSE, Nasdaq, and other national securities exchanges and associations to prohibit the listing of any equity security of a company that does not have an independent compensation committee, and

- "Independence of Compensation Consultants and Other Compensation Committee Advisers," which provides that the compensation committee, in its sole discretion, may obtain the advice of independent legal counsel and other advisers. If it does, the committee may only select a compensation consultant, legal counsel or other adviser after taking into consideration factors identified by the SEC (see ¶3135).

.04 Policy on Recovery of Erroneously Awarded Compensation

Section 954 of the Dodd-Frank Act added Section 10D, entitled "Recovery of Erroneously Awarded Compensation Policy," to the Exchange Act. This section requires the SEC to direct the national securities exchanges to prohibit the listing of any security of an issuer that does not develop and implement a clawback policy (see ¶ 3145).

.05 Disclosure of Hedging by Employees and Directors

Section 955 of the Dodd-Frank Act, "Disclosure of Hedging by Employees and Directors," added a subsection 14(j) to the Exchange Act, which requires the SEC to require companies to disclose in their annual proxy statement whether the company permits any employee or director to purchase financial instruments that are designed to hedge any decrease in the market value of equity securities (1) granted to the employee or director by the company as part of the compensation; or (2) held, directly or indirectly, by the employee or director (see ¶ 3155).

.06 Disclosure of Pay Versus Performance

Section 953(a) of the Dodd-Frank Act, "Disclosure of Pay Versus Performance," added a Section 14(i) to the Exchange Act, which requires each public company to disclose in its annual proxy statement "information that shows the relationship between executive compensation actually paid and the financial performance of the issuer" (see ¶ 3165).

.07 CEO Pay Ratio Disclosure

Section 953(b) of the Dodd-Frank Act, "Executive Compensation Disclosures" requires the SEC to amend the proxy statement disclosure rules to require each public company to disclose the ratio of the median of the annual total compensation of all employees of the company, except the CEO (including employees outside the US) to the annual total compensation of the CEO. Everyone recognizes that this is a political disclosure, not an economic one, intended to give unions and certain media folks a tool to bash corporate America (see ¶ 3175).

.08 Disclosure Regarding Chairman and CEO Structures

Section 972 of the Dodd-Frank Act added Section 14B "Corporate Governance" to the Exchange Act, which requires the SEC to issue rules that require the company to disclose in its annual proxy statement the reasons why it has chosen the same or different persons to serve as chairman of the board of directors and chief executive officer (or in equivalent positions) of the company (see ¶ 3185).

.09 Elimination of Discretionary Voting by Brokers on Executive Compensation Proposals

Section 957 of the Dodd-Frank Act amended Section 6(b) of the Exchange Act to provide that national securities exchanges must prohibit brokers from voting shares they do not beneficially own in connection with the election of directors, executive compensation, and any other significant matter, as determined by the SEC, unless the beneficial owner of the security has instructed the broker to vote the proxy in accordance with the voting instructions of the beneficial owner (see ¶3115).

.10 Enhanced Disclosure and Reporting of Compensation Arrangements

Section 956 of the Dodd Frank-Act, "Enhanced Compensation Structure Reporting," applies only to financial institutions with assets of $1 billion or more. It required the federal regulators to jointly prescribe regulations or guidelines by March 22, 2011 (see ¶3195).

¶3115 Shareholder Say on Pay

Section 951 of the Dodd-Frank Act added Section 14A to the Exchange Act, entitled "Shareholder Approval of Executive Compensation," which provides that, not less frequently than once every three years, a company's annual proxy statement must include a separate, non-binding resolution subject to shareholder vote to approve the compensation of executives, as disclosed in the company's CD&A, the compensation tables, and any related material.

Section 951 of the Dodd-Frank Act also requires that, not less frequently than once every six years, the proxy statement must include a separate resolution subject to a non-binding shareholder vote to determine whether future votes on the resolutions required under the preceding paragraph will occur every one, two, or three years.

The SEC adopted final rules on Section 951, generally referred to as "Shareholder Say on Pay" and "Frequency of Shareholder Say on Pay," in January 2011, in a 3-2 vote. The SEC's rules became fully effective in March 2011. A company's proxy statement for the first annual meeting of shareholders occurring after January 21, 2011, must include both the Shareholder Say on Pay resolution and a separate Frequency of Shareholder Say on Pay resolution.

(The rule allows the SEC, by rule or order, to exempt an issuer or class of issuers (such as small issuers) from the requirement of shareholder vote as to say on pay or golden parachute pay.)

.01 Shareholder Say on Pay

Section 951 of the Dodd-Frank Act added Section 14A to the Exchange Act, entitled "Shareholder Approval of Executive Compensation," which provides that, not less frequently than once every three years, a company's annual proxy statement must include a separate resolution subject to shareholder vote to approve the compensation of executives, as disclosed in the company's CD&A, the compensation tables, and any related material.

In the rules, the SEC stated its belief that companies should have the flexibility to design the resolution language asking for shareholder approval of their executive compensation packages. However, the SEC's rules imply that the resolution must include the following language: "the shareholder advisory vote under this subsection is to approve the compensation of the registrant's named executive officers as disclosed pursuant to Item 402 of Regulation S-K."

The SEC's rules also provide the following non-exclusive example of a resolution that would satisfy the applicable requirements. (The SEC's rules do *not* provide a form of resolution for the Frequency of Shareholder Say on Pay vote.)

> "RESOLVED, that the compensation paid to the company's named executive officers, as disclosed pursuant to Item 402 of Regulation S-K, including the Compensation Discussion and Analysis, compensation tables and narrative discussion, is hereby APPROVED."

The SEC rules added an Item 24 to the proxy statement disclosure rules, which provides that a company that is required to offer any of the Shareholder Say on Pay, Frequency of Shareholder Say on Pay, or Say on Parachute Payment votes must:

- Disclose that it is providing each such vote as required pursuant to Section 14A of the Securities Exchange Act,
- Briefly explain the general effect of each vote, such as whether each vote is non-binding, and
- When applicable, disclose the current frequency of shareholder advisory votes on executive compensation and when the next such shareholder advisory vote will occur.

The Shareholder Say on Pay vote does not apply either to disclosures relating to (i) the compensation of directors required by the proxy statement, or (ii) the company's compensation policies and practices as they relate to risk management and risk-taking incentives. However, the SEC's rules state that to the extent that risk considerations are a material aspect of the company's compensation policies or decisions for NEOs, the company would be required to discuss them as part of its CD&A and, therefore, shareholders would consider such disclosure when voting on executive compensation.

.02 Frequency of Shareholder Say on Pay

Section 951 of the Dodd-Frank Act requires that, not less frequently than once every six years, a public company's proxy statement must include a separate resolution subject to a non-binding shareholder vote to determine whether future votes on the Shareholder Say on Pay resolutions will occur every one, two, or three years. The SEC's rules provide that companies must give shareholders *four choices*: whether the shareholder vote on executive compensation will occur every one, two, or three years, or to abstain from voting on the matter, similar to the following:

☐ The shareholder vote on executive compensation will occur every year.

☐ The shareholder vote on executive compensation will occur every two years.

☐ The shareholder vote on executive compensation will occur every three years.

☐ Abstain.

The SEC's rules note that companies may vote uninstructed proxy cards in accordance with management's recommendation for the frequency vote only if the company follows the existing requirements of Rule 14a-4 to (1) include a recommendation for the frequency of say-on-pay votes in the proxy statement, (2) permit abstention on the proxy card, and (3) include language in bold on the proxy card regarding how it will vote uninstructed shares. In case we needed one, this rule is a very good reason why management should make a recommendation to shareholders on this vote.

.03 Effect of Shareholder Votes

Dodd-Frank Act Section 951(c) provides that neither the Shareholder Say on Pay vote nor the Frequency of Shareholder Say on Pay vote shall be binding on the company or its board of directors, and may not be construed:

(1) as overruling a decision by the company or its board of directors;

(2) to create or imply any change to the fiduciary duties of the company or its board of directors;

(3) to create or imply any additional fiduciary duties for the company or its board of directors; or

(4) to restrict or limit the ability of shareholders to make proposals for inclusion in proxy materials related to executive compensation.

Exchange Act Rule 14a-8(i)(10) permits a company to exclude future shareholder proposals that would provide a Shareholder Say on Pay vote, seek a future Shareholder Say on Pay vote, or that relate to the Frequency of Shareholder Say on Pay. However, this exception only applies if, in the most recent shareholder vote on Frequency of Shareholder Say on Pay votes, a single frequency (*i.e.*, one, two, or three years) received the support of a majority of the votes cast (and the company adopted a policy consistent with that choice). That is, if one of the choices on Frequency of Shareholder Say on Pay receives as much as 49% of the shareholder votes, no other choice receives more than 20% of the votes cast, and the company adopts a policy that is consistent with the 49% choice, the company still would not be able to exclude subsequent shareholder proposals regarding Frequency of Shareholder Say on Pay. For purposes of *this analysis only, an abstention would not count as a vote cast.* This voting standard applies only for purposes of determining the scope of the exclusion under the note to Rule 14a-8(i)(10), and not for determining whether a particular voting frequency should be considered to have been adopted or approved by shareholder vote as a matter of state law.

.04 Smaller Reporting and Emerging Growth Companies

The SEC's rules adopted a temporary exemption for smaller reporting companies (public float of less than $75 million). These companies were not required to conduct *either* a Shareholder Say on Pay vote or a Frequency of Shareholder Say on Pay vote until the first annual or other meeting of shareholders occurring on or after January 21, 2013. The SEC expressly refused to adopt a permanent exemption for smaller companies. However, Rule 14a-21 of the Exchange Act does not require an emerging growth company (as defined in Rule

12b-2 of the Exchange Act) to submit a Shareholder Say on Pay proposal to its shareholders.

.05 Disclosing the Results of Shareholder Say on Pay Votes

A company must disclose the result of the Shareholder Say on Pay and Frequency of Shareholder Say on Pay votes on a Form 8-K within four business days after the shareholders meeting at which the votes are held. Form 8-K generally requires a company to "state the number of votes cast for, against, or withheld, as well as the number of abstentions and broker non-votes as to each such matter." The SEC's rules clarify that, with respect to the Frequency of Shareholder Say on Pay vote, the company will be required to disclose the number of votes cast for *each of* one year, two years, and three years, as well as the number of abstentions.

A company also must disclose its decision, in light of the voting results, as to how frequently the company will include future Shareholder Say on Pay votes in its proxy materials. The company must make this disclosure on Form 8-K, but due at a later date, to give the company additional time to make its decision. To comply, a company will file an amendment to its prior Form 8-K filing that disclosed the preliminary and final results of the shareholder vote on frequency. This amended Form 8-K will be due no later than 150 calendar days after the date of the end of the annual (or other) meeting in which the vote took place, but in no event later than 60 calendar days prior to the deadline for the submission of shareholder proposals for the subsequent annual meeting. Alternatively, the SEC allows a company to disclose its decision on the frequency of future Shareholder Say on Pay votes on a Form 10-Q, in lieu of a Form 8-K/A, if it files the 10-Q before the 150-day deadline. This disclosure would be in Part II, Item 5 "Other Information" of the Form 10-Q.

Under the SEC's rules, a company must disclose in its proxy statement when the next scheduled Shareholder Say on Pay vote will occur. Also in the proxy statement, in the CD&A, a company must discuss whether, and if so, how the company has considered the results of the *most recent Shareholder Say on Pay vote* in determining compensation policies and decisions, and how that consideration has affected the company's executive compensation policies and decisions (although the SEC acknowledges that Dodd-Frank Act Section 951 does not require such disclosure).

Finally, the SEC's rules added shareholder advisory votes on executive compensation, including Shareholder Say on Pay votes and the Frequency of Shareholder Say on Pay vote, to the list of items that do not trigger a preliminary filing of the proxy statement.

.06 Preparing for Shareholder Say on Pay Votes

The Shareholder Say on Pay vote is a single "For" or "Against" vote on the total compensation package provided to the named executive officers, as disclosed in the company's CD&A, the compensation tables, and any related material. If the overall packages of the NEOs are reasonable - even below market - but there is one perceived blemish, such as a gross-up on perquisite payments or a single trigger golden parachute agreement, many shareholders may vote "no" on the package. *There is no other way for shareholders to register disapproval.* They cannot criticize or object to that one provision or practice only.

Therefore, most public companies have focused on developing and implementing a strategy to maximize the likelihood of achieving a favorable vote on Shareholder Say on Pay. In the immortal words that NASA Flight Director Gene Kranz never actually uttered: "Failure is not an option." Companies and compensation committees also need to acknowledge shareholders' heightened disclosure expectations and address *both the reality and the perception* of the company's/committee's adherence to best practices in executive compensation. We suggest that companies do more than arrange a presentation or rely on the tender mercies of ISS (and other shareholder advisors). Outside legal counsel and a compensation consultant should be involved. A little bit of research and maybe a few modest adjustments could help address outsiders' perception of the company's pay packages.

Going forward, compensation committees might want to add one more factor to their consideration of each compensation issue: How will we explain this decision, payment or policy in the proxy statement CD&A, and will it increase the risk that shareholders will vote "Against" us on Shareholder Say on Pay? Again, the Shareholder Say on Pay vote is a single "yes" or "no" vote on the total compensation package provided to the named executive officers, as described in the proxy statement. One questionable action, payment, or practice could cause shareholders to vote "Against," regardless of the reasonableness of the overall packages.

Many of the rules added by the Dodd-Frank Act - or to be added by required SEC or stock exchange regulations - had already become best practices in recent years. Therefore, many public companies were implementing these policies and practices on their own.

Most companies and compensation committees have worked to improve both (i) their compensation policies and practices, and (ii) the CD&A disclosure of those policies and practices. Companies and compensation committees now generally write the CD&A and tabular disclosures for a new target audience - institutional shareholders. Previously, many of us had focused on drafting primarily to meet the SEC's disclosure requirements.

.07 Elimination of Discretionary Voting by Brokers on Executive Compensation (and other) Matters

Section 957 of the Dodd-Frank Act amends Section 6(b) of the Exchange Act to provide that national securities exchanges must prohibit brokers from voting shares they do not beneficially own in connection with:

- the election of directors,

- executive compensation, and

- any other significant matter, as determined by the SEC,

¶3115.07

unless the beneficial owner of the security has instructed the broker to vote the proxy in accordance with the voting instructions of the beneficial owner. Even before the Dodd-Frank Act, the approval of equity plans was a "non-routine matter" upon which brokers were not permitted to vote uninstructed shares and the NYSE amended its Rule 452 to eliminate broker voting of uninstructed shares in director elections.

Inasmuch as every public company has some portion of its outstanding equity securities held in "street name" on behalf of their beneficial owners, this provision affected all public companies. The most immediate effect of this provision was the elimination of broker voting of uninstructed shares in the Shareholder Say on Pay and the Frequency of Shareholder Say on Pay votes required by Section 951 of the Dodd-Frank Act. Shareholder votes on these matters joined the approval of equity plans as non-routine matters upon which brokers are not permitted to vote uninstructed shares.

It remains to be seen what other executive compensation matters the SEC will determine to be "any other significant matter" for which broker voting of uninstructed shares is prohibited. In July 2011, the SEC announced that it planned to issue rules defining "other significant matters" for purposes of exchange standards regarding broker voting of uninstructed shares at a date "still to be determined."

Section 957 was effective on enactment, so any exchange rules inconsistent with its requirements were no longer applicable and brokers were prohibited from voting uninstructed shares in their 2011 Shareholder Say on Pay votes.

.08 Institutional Investor Reporting

Finally, Dodd-Frank Act Section 951 also requires every institutional investment manager subject to Exchange Act Section 13(f) to report at least annually how it voted on any shareholder vote as to say on pay or golden parachute pay, unless such vote is otherwise required to be reported publicly by rule or regulation of the Commission.

¶3125 Shareholder Say on Parachute Payments

Exchange Act Section 14A, added by Dodd-Frank Act Section 951, also provides for "Shareholder Approval of 'Golden Parachute' Compensation." Referred to as "Shareholder Say on Parachute Payments," this provision requires that in any proxy or consent solicitation material for a meeting of shareholders *at which shareholders are asked to approve an acquisition, merger, consolidation, or proposed sale or other disposition of all or substantially all the assets of the company*, the party soliciting the proxy or consent *must disclose* any agreements or understandings that the party soliciting the proxy or consent has with any named executive officers of the company (or of the acquiring company) concerning any type of compensation (whether present, deferred, or contingent) that is based on or otherwise relates to the acquisition, merger, consolidation, sale, or other disposition of all or substantially all of the assets of the company and the aggregate total of all such compensation that may (and the conditions upon which it may) be paid or become payable to or on behalf of such executive officer.

The SEC adopted final rules on Shareholder Say on Parachute Payments in January 2011, in a 3-2 vote. The SEC's rules provided that the requirement for non-binding shareholder advisory vote on "Golden Parachute Payments" in merger transactions would be effective for proxy statements initially filed on or after April 25, 2011 (unlike the Shareholder Say on Pay and Frequency votes, which went into effect on January 21, 2011).

A Shareholder Say on Parachute Payments vote will *not* be binding on the company or the company's board of directors and, according to Section 951(c), may not be construed as (1) overruling their decision, (2) creating or implying any addition or change to their fiduciary duties, or (3) restricting or limiting shareholders' ability to make proposals for inclusion in proxy materials related to executive compensation.

.01 Format of Disclosure

The SEC's rules require disclosure of this so called "golden parachute compensation" in both tabular *and* narrative formats. The current disclosure required by Item 402(j) of Regulation S-K (Potential Payments upon Termination of Employment or Change in Control) does not satisfy the Dodd-Frank Act requirements with respect to golden parachute arrangements. The SEC's rules adopt the following table:

Name (a)	Cash ($) (b)	Equity ($) (c)	Pension/NQDC ($) (d)	Perquisites/Benefits ($) (e)	Tax Reimbursement ($) (f)	Other ($) (g)	Total ($) (h)
PEO							
PFO							
A							
B							
C							

In connection with a proxy statement soliciting shareholder approval of a merger or similar transaction (or a filing made with respect to a similar transaction), the SEC's rules generally require the company to use the "consideration per share" as the stock price for calculating dollar amounts in the table. For disclosure in a regular annual meeting proxy, the company would use the price as of the last day of the preceding fiscal year.

The SEC's rules permit companies to add additional officers or columns if they wish. The SEC's rules do not require companies to use any specific language or form of resolution for this shareholder vote.

The SEC's rules require separate footnote identification of amounts in the table attributable to "single-trigger" arrangements and amounts attributable to "double-trigger" arrangements, "so that shareholders can readily discern these amounts." The SEC's rules do not require disclosure or quantification of vested pension or nonqualified deferred compensation payouts, or previously vested equity awards. The SEC's rules do not permit companies to exclude *de minimis* perquisites and other personal benefits from this disclosure.

Item 402(t) of Regulation S-K requires the company to describe any material conditions or obligations applicable to an executive's receipt of payment, including but not limited to non-compete, non-solicitation, non-disparagement or confidentiality agreements, their duration, and provisions regarding waiver or breach. The SEC's rules also require a company to provide a description of the specific circumstances that would trigger payment, whether the payments would or could be lump sum, or annual, and their duration, by whom the payments would be provided, and any material factors regarding each agreement, similar to the narrative disclosure required with respect to termination and change in control agreements in proxy statements.

The SEC's rules clarify that a company need not provide narrative or tabular disclosure for persons who are NEOs only because they would have been among the most highly compensated executive officers but for the fact that they were not serving as an executive officer at the end of the last completed fiscal year. However, the rules also provide that where Item 402(t) disclosure is provided in a proxy statement soliciting shareholder approval of a merger or similar transaction, this instruction will be applied with respect to the NEOs for whom disclosure was required in the company's most recent filing requiring Summary Compensation Table disclosure.

.02 Which Transactions Require Disclosure and by Which Party?

In any proxy statement soliciting shareholder approval of an acquisition, merger, consolidation, sale or other disposition of all or substantially all assets of a company, the SEC's rules require disclosure for each NEO of the target company *and the acquiring company*, regarding any agreement or understanding, whether written or unwritten, between such NEO and the acquiring company or target company, concerning any type of compensation, whether present, deferred or contingent, that is based on or otherwise relates to the transaction.

Although Item 402(t) requires disclosure of golden parachute arrangements between the *acquiring company* and the NEOs of either company, if such parachute arrangements are based on or related to the subject transaction, any golden parachute arrangements between the acquiring company and the NEOs of the target company need not be subjected to the Shareholder Say on Parachute Payments vote. In this case, two tables would be required.

The SEC's rules expand the types of transactions for which Item 402(t) disclosure is required (but not a shareholder vote) to all proxy statements that are required to include disclosure of information required under Item 14 of Schedule 14A pursuant to Note A of Schedule 14A, specifically citing going-private transactions and acquiring companies that solicit proxies to approve the issuance of shares or a reverse stock split in order to conduct a merger transaction.

The SEC's rules clarify, however, that bidders in third-party tender offers (other than Rule 13e-3 going-private transactions) are *not* required to provide the golden parachute payment disclosure otherwise required, as they could have difficulty obtaining the information necessary to provide such disclosure and, in any event, the target company would be required to provide the Item 402(t) golden parachute compensation disclosure in Schedule 14D-9 filed by the tenth business day from the date the tender offer is first published, sent or given to security holders.

For foreign private issuers, the SEC's rules include exceptions to the disclosure requirement (a) where the target or subject company in a third-party tender offer or going-private transaction is a foreign private issuer, and (b) where the target or acquirer is a foreign private issuer, with respect to agreements with the senior management of foreign private issuers.

.03 Exception for Previously Disclosed and Approved Parachute Payments

The SEC's rules provide an exception for golden parachute payment disclosure and approval in a change in control transaction if the company's shareholders already have approved such agreements or understandings in a Shareholder Say on Pay vote. This exception seems to have been designed to discourage companies from adding or improving their payouts at the eleventh hour before a change in control.

The SEC's rules emphasize that the exception will be available only to the extent the same golden parachute arrangements previously subject to an annual meeting shareholder vote remain in effect, and the terms of those arrangements have not been modified subsequent to the shareholder vote. If the disclosure under Item 402(t) has been updated to change only the value of the items in the Golden Parachute Compensation Table to reflect price movements in the company's stock, no new shareholder advisory vote would be required. Changes that result only in a reduction in value of the total compensation payable would not require a new shareholder vote.

However, the addition or substitution of a named executive officer would defeat the company's ability to rely on the exception. On this point, the SEC's Division of Corporation Finance issued a Compliance and Disclosure Interpretation, which provides that, even if a company's shareholders approve a say-on-parachute payments resolution in the annual meeting proxy, if the company adds a new CEO one month later, it would need to seek shareholders' approval again in any future merger proxy. New golden parachute arrangements and any revisions to golden parachute arrangements that were subject to a prior shareholder vote will be subject to the separate merger proxy shareholder vote requirement. The SEC would view any change that would result in a Section 280G tax gross-up becoming payable as *a change in terms triggering such a separate vote*, even if such tax gross-up becomes payable only because of an increase in the company's share price.

Thus, the practicality of this exception is limited. Additionally, ISS has announced that, in cases where a company incorporates the Shareholder Say on Parachute Payments vote into its Shareholder Say on Pay vote, ISS will evaluate the Shareholder Say on Pay proposal in accordance with its usual guidelines, *"which may give higher weight to that component of the overall evaluation."* Companies with an excise tax gross-up provision and/or a three times multiplier in their change in control agreements might be better off waiting for a merger proxy to seek shareholder approval, rather than risking ISS (or other shareholder) disapproval of its entire compensation package due to these features. For some companies, the benefit of having their "golden parachute compensation" arrangements approved in advance may not be worth the additional attention and risk that shareholders might not approve them.

Additionally, making disclosure and seeking approval in a merger proxy generally is less risky because the request for shareholder approval would be non-binding in any event, and a vote to disapprove would not affect the merger transaction in any way. The risk of postponing this disclosure and request for approval until a merger proxy would seem to be that, in very close cases, shareholders might vote against the merger itself if they believe the parachute payments are excessive. However, that seems unlikely. As pointed out in a Morrow & Co. update, the announcement of a merger often results in a change in the target company's shareholder profile, with institutions selling shares and arbitrageurs and hedge funds buying. Thus, the merger proxy voting shareholder profile may be one that has a greater interest in seeing the transaction consummated and is less concerned about matters of compensation.

¶3135 Compensation Committee Independence

Section 952 of the Dodd-Frank Act, "Compensation Committee Independence," added Section 10C to the Exchange Act, which contain two parts:

- "Independence of Compensation Committees," and
- "Independence of Compensation Consultants and Other Compensation Committee Advisers."

.01 Independence of Compensation Committees

Section 952 of Dodd-Frank added Section 10C to the Exchange Act, which requires the SEC to promulgate rules that direct the NYSE, Nasdaq, and other national securities exchanges and associations to **prohibit the listing of any equity security of a company that does not have an independent compensation committee**. In determining the definition of the term "independence," the national securities exchanges and associations must consider relevant factors to be determined by the SEC. The SEC issued final rules under Section 10C in June 2012.

As directed, the SEC's rules require each national securities exchange and national securities association that lists equity securities to establish rules related to the independence of compensation committees, but sets forth certain minimum standards. Under the SEC's rules, in determining independence requirements for members of compensation committees, the securities exchanges and associations must consider the following factors:[1]

(A) The source of compensation of a member of the company's board of directors, including any consulting, advisory, or other compensatory fee paid by the company to such member; and

(B) Whether a member of the company's board of directors is affiliated with the company, or a subsidiary or affiliate of the company.

The SEC's rules exempt certain categories of listed issuers from the independence requirements, including (i) limited partnerships, (ii) companies in bankruptcy proceedings, (iii) open-end management investment companies registered under the Investment Company Act of 1940, and (iv) any foreign private issuer that discloses in its annual report the reasons that the foreign private issuer does not have an independent compensation committee. The SEC's rules also allow a national securities exchange or a national securities association to exempt particular relationships with members of the compensation committee, taking into consideration the size of an issuer and any other relevant factors from the independence requirements.

At the time the Dodd-Frank Act was signed into law, most public companies already satisfied the independent compensation committee requirement of Section 952, due to their compliance with performance-based compensation exemption under Code Sec. 162(m) and the then current stock exchange rules. However, the legislation known as the Tax Cuts and Jobs Act of 2017 ("TCJA") signed into law by President Trump in December 2017, eliminated the performance-based compensation exemption under Code Sec. 162(m), the rules adopted by the NYSE and Nasdaq will be critical.

.02 Stock Exchange Independence Requirements

As required by the SEC's rules, the NYSE and Nasdaq each established rules related to the independence of compensation committees. NYSE requires listed companies to have a compensation committee composed entirely of directors who satisfy the independence requirements specific to compensation committee membership.[2] Nasdaq requires listed companies to have a compensation committee of at least two members, each of whom qualifies as an independent director under Nasdaq's standards.[3]

Both the NYSE and Nasdaq require a listed company's board of directors to affirmatively determine the independence of any director who will serve on the compensation committee, considering all factors specifically relevant to determining whether a director has a relationship to the company, which is material to that director's ability to be independent from management in connection with

---

[1] § 240.10C-1(b)(i).

[2] NYSE Listed Company Manual Section 303A.02(a)(ii).

[3] Nasdaq Listing Standards Rule 5605(d)(2).

the duties of a compensation committee member. Each exchange calls out two factors that warrant particular attention: (i) the source of any compensation paid to the director by the listed company, including any consulting, advisory or other compensatory fees, and (ii) whether the director is affiliated with the listed company, a subsidiary of the listed company, or an affiliate of a subsidiary of the listed company.

The stock exchange listing standards also provide some examples of when they will consider a director *not* to be independent. For example, both the NYSE and Nasdaq provide that a director will not be considered independent if:

- The director is, or has been within the last three years, an employee of the company, or an immediate family member is, or has been within the last three years, an executive officer of the company. Employment as an interim Chairman or CEO or other executive officer would not disqualify a director from being considered independent following that employment.

- The director or an immediate family member has received, during any twelve-month period within the last three years, more than $120,000 in direct compensation from the company (other than director and committee fees and pension or other forms of deferred compensation for prior service; provided such compensation is not contingent in any way on continued service). Compensation received by an immediate family member for service as an employee of the company *other than an executive officer* need not be considered in determining independence under this test.

- The director is a current partner or employee of a firm that is the company's auditor, has an immediate family member who is a current partner of the auditor, has an immediate family member who is or was a current employee of the auditor and personally works on the company's audit, or has an immediate family member who was within the last three years a partner or employee of the auditor or firm and personally worked on the company's audit within that time.

- The director or an immediate family member is, or has been with the last three years, employed as an executive officer of another company where any of the company's present executive officers at the same time serves or served on that company's compensation committee.

- The director is a current employee, or an immediate family member is a current executive officer, of a company that has made payments to, or received payments from, the company for property or services in an amount which, in any of the last three fiscal years, exceeds the greater of $1 million, or 2% of such other company's consolidated gross revenues. The payments and the consolidated gross revenues to be measured are those reported in the last completed fiscal year of the other company.

Both the NYSE and Nasdaq require a listed company to certify that it satisfies and will continue to satisfy the compensation committee independence rules. Both the NYSE and the Nasdaq have posted on their websites a form that listed companies must use to certify their compliance with the revised listing standards concerning compensation committees.[4]

.03 Independence of Compensation Consultants, Legal Counsel and Other Advisers

Exchange Act Section 10C, added by Dodd-Frank Act Section 952, also included a subsection (b), "Independence of Compensation Consultants and Other Compensation Committee Advisers," which provides that:

- The compensation committee may only select a compensation consultant, legal counsel or other adviser after taking into consideration factors identified by the SEC (see below);

- The compensation committee, in its sole discretion, may retain and obtain the advice of independent legal counsel and other advisers; and

- The company must provide for appropriate funding, as determined by the compensation committee, for payment of reasonable compensation to independent legal counsel or any other adviser.

The Dodd-Frank Act does *not* require a compensation committee to hire its own independent compensation consultant, legal counsel or other advisers. However, it seems to require the compensation committee to consider the possibility.

The Dodd-Frank Act requires the SEC to identify factors that affect the independence of consultants, counsel and advisers to a compensation committee, but specifies that these factors shall include at least—

(A) The provision of other services to the company by the firm that employs the compensation consultant, legal counsel, or other adviser;

(B) The amount of fees received from the company by the firm that employs the compensation consultant, legal counsel, or other adviser, as a percentage of the total revenue of that firm;

(C) The policies and procedures of the firm that employs the compensation consultant, legal counsel, or other adviser, which are designed to prevent conflicts of interest;

(D) Any business or personal relationship of the compensation consultant, legal counsel, or other adviser with a member of the compensation committee; and

(E) Any stock of the company owned by the compensation consultant, legal counsel, or other adviser.

The SEC issued final rules under Section 10C in June 2012. In addition to the five factors that affect the independence of consultants, counsel and advisers to a compensation committee specified in the Dodd-Frank Act, the SEC's rules added a sixth: Any business or personal relationship of the compensation consultant,

---

[4] See, NYSE Listed Company Manual Sec. 303A.05.

legal counsel, other adviser or the person employing the adviser with an executive officer of the company.

As required by the SEC's rules, the NYSE and Nasdaq each established rules related to the independence of advisers to the compensation committees.[5] Exchange Act Section 10C expressly states and the stock exchanges rules repeat that the required independent adviser inquiry may not be construed (i) to require the compensation committee to implement or act consistently with the advice or recommendations of the adviser; or (ii) to affect the ability or obligation of a compensation committee to exercise its own judgment in fulfillment of the duties of the compensation committee.

¶3145 Policy on Recovery of Erroneously Awarded Compensation - Clawback

Section 954 of the Dodd-Frank Act added Section 10D, entitled "Recovery of Erroneously Awarded Compensation Policy," to the Exchange Act. Under Section 954, a company's compensation recovery policy *must* provide that:

> "in the event that the issuer is required to prepare an accounting restatement due to the material noncompliance of the issuer with any financial reporting requirement under the securities laws, the issuer will recover from any current or former executive officer of the issuer who received incentive-based compensation (including stock options awarded as compensation) during the 3-year period preceding the date on which the issuer is required to prepare an accounting restatement, based on the erroneous data, in excess of what would have been paid to the executive officer under the accounting restatement."

Like most of the provisions the Dodd-Frank Act, Section 954 was not immediately effective. This section requires the SEC to direct the national securities exchanges to prohibit the listing of any security of an issuer that does not develop and implement a clawback policy. After the SEC publishes its final rules, the stock exchanges will have a period of time to amend their listing standards before the rules become fully effective for publicly traded companies.

Once Section 954 becomes effective, companies must disclose their policy on the recovery of incentive-based compensation that is based on erroneous financial information, presumably in the proxy statement, if not before then.

.01 Individuals and Compensation Covered

Under Section 954, a company's compensation clawback policy must apply at least to the individuals who are subject to Section 16 of the Exchange Act (usually referred to as "Section 16 officers" and including the president, any vice president in charge of a principal business unit, division or function (such as sales, administrations or finance) or other officer performing a policy-making function)) and individuals who formerly were Section 16 officers.

We expect the compensation clawback policy required by Section 10D to apply to all annual and long-term incentive compensation plans and arrange-

---

[5] NYSE Listed Company Manual Section 303A.05(c); Nasdaq Listing Standards Rule 5605(d)(3)(D).

ments, and stock options. However, Section 954 is ambiguous, providing that it applies to:

- Incentive-based compensation that is based on financial information required to be reported under the securities laws, and
- Incentive-based compensation (including stock options awarded as compensation) in excess of what would have been paid but for the erroneous data in the reported financial information.

Whether the SEC attempts to extend the policy requirements to stock-based awards other than options remains to be seen.

The clawback policy must provide for a potential recovery period of three years, measured from the date the company is "required to prepare the accounting restatement." Until the SEC publishes final rules, we will not know whether that means three years from the discovery of the error, three years from the filing of the restatement (which could be much later), or something else.

.02 Triggering Event

The compensation clawback policy must be triggered in the event that the company is required to restate its financial statements as the result of material noncompliance with applicable accounting principles and the original financial statements resulted in an erroneous payment to a current or former executive officer. The policy must apply regardless of whether (i) the noncompliance was accidental or intentional, and/or (ii) the executive was at fault.

.03 Comparison to SOX Section 304

Dodd-Frank Section 954 is much broader that Section 304 of the Sarbanes-Oxley Act of 2002 ("SOX"). Section 304 only applies to the chief executive officer and the chief financial officer, requires a look-back period of one year, instead of three (the Troubled Asset Relief Program "TARP" clawback requirements apply to any payment made during the period that the financial institution is a TARP participant), and only applies if the financial restatement is a result of misconduct.

.04 Other Issues

Compensation clawback policies already have become a best practice for compensation committees. However, the actual design and implementation of a clawback policy is very complicated and involves the need to balance a number of legitimate competing interests. Unfortunately, Section 954 mandates exactly the type of compensation clawback policy that companies must adopt. One unintended consequence of this new requirement is likely to be a move to higher salaries and less "at-risk" compensation. By its terms, Dodd-Frank Act Section 954 seems to leave little room for compensation committee discretion in pursuing clawbacks.

Companies and compensation committees should consider adding compensation clawback provisions to any awards and agreements they enter into.

¶3145.02

.05 Whistleblower Bounties and Protections

Section 922 of the Dodd-Frank Act added Section 21F to the Exchange Act, "Securities Whistleblower Incentives and Protection." Section 21F requires a payment of between ten percent and thirty percent (10% - 30%) of the amount of monetary sanctions to "1 or more whistleblowers who voluntarily provided original information to the Commission that led to the successful enforcement." Previously, the SEC could only pay bounties to informants for insider trading violations. (Note that the SEC settlement with AIG was $800 million, which would have produced a bounty of *at least $80 million* to some lucky winner and his or her lawyer.)

In June 2011, the SEC issued final rules under the "Whistleblower Incentives and Protection" provisions, making the provisions fully effective on August 12, 2011. The final rules made modest changes in response to some business community concerns, but expressly declined to require whistleblowers to report violations or concerns under the company's internal policies first in order to be eligible to receive a bounty, which was the primary concern of the business community.[6] Instead of requiring whistleblowers to report violations or concerns under the company's internal program first, in order to be eligible to receive a bounty, the SEC's final rules provide "incentives" for whistleblowers to use the internal reporting program, including:

- A whistleblower's voluntary participation in an internal compliance program is a factor that can increase the amount of the award;

- A whistleblower who reports original information to the company's compliance and reporting program will get credit for all information that is provided to the SEC by the company, regardless of whether such information was included in the whistleblower's report to the company; and

- A whistleblower will be deemed to have reported information to the SEC on the date that he or she made an internal report to the company, as long as the whistleblower or the company then reports that information to the SEC within 120 days of the initial internal report.

Whistleblower incentives are relevant to executive compensation because more "whistle blowing," accurate or not, could lead to more SEC enforcement actions and more financial restatements, which could require enforcement of more companies' compensation clawback provisions under Dodd-Frank Act Section 954.

The obvious problem with the whistleblower bounties is that people make mistakes. Until now, an employee who discovered an accounting or reporting error would promptly report it to the company, which would then address it, possibly even with a financial restatement. However, the bounty provisions

---

[6] David Hirschmann, president and CEO of the U.S. Chamber's Center for Capital Markets Competitiveness, and Lisa Rickard, president of the Institute for Legal Reform, commented that: "In approving this whistleblower rule, the SEC has chosen to put trial lawyer profits ahead of effective compliance and corporate governance."

create a very powerful financial incentive to individuals to report potential accounting or securities law issues directly to the SEC, rather than internally.

¶3155 Disclosure of Hedging by Employees and Directors

Section 955 of the Dodd-Frank Act added subsection 14(j) to the Exchange Act, "Disclosure of Hedging by Employees and Directors." Section 955 requires the SEC to require companies to disclose in their annual proxy statement whether the company permits any employee or director (or any designee of such employee or director) to purchase financial instruments (including prepaid variable forward contracts, equity swaps, collars, and exchange funds) that are designed to hedge or offset any decrease in the market value of equity securities (1) granted to the employee or director by the company as part of the compensation; or (2) held, directly or indirectly, by the employee or director.

The obvious aim of this provision is to encourage companies to adopt policies that prohibit hedging transactions. Investors want executives to own large amounts of company stock [not hedged] so they will manage for long-term gains, not just a short-term pop with devastating long-term effect. Section 955 does not require any company to adopt such a policy, but we expect that most will do so.

Like most of the executive compensation provisions of the Dodd-Frank Act, Section 955 was not immediately effective. Section 955 directs the SEC to adopt rules implementing this disclosure requirement, but does not give it a deadline for doing so.

¶3165 Disclosure of Pay Versus Performance

Section 953(a) of the Dodd-Frank Act added 14(i) to the Exchange Act, "Disclosure of Pay Versus Performance." Section 953(a) requires a public company to disclose in its annual proxy statement "information that shows the relationship between executive compensation actually paid and the financial performance of the issuer." The company's "financial performance" must take into account any change in the value of the company's stock and dividends or other distributions. Section 953(a) allows, but does not require, this disclosure to include a graphic representation of the information required to be disclosed. Presumably, this would be an enhancement to the Performance Graph.

Section 953 is one of the least clear provisions of Dodd-Frank. Open questions that the SEC will need to answer in its rulemaking include:

- The definition of the new term "compensation actually paid." Does this include gains actually recognized in the year on equity awards from prior years? Does it include a bonus actually paid in the year but attributable to a prior year?

- Whether this disclosure applies to the compensation of the named executive officers only, all of those in the Section 16 group, or some other group.

- Whether this disclosure requirement applies to the same five-year period as the existing Performance Graph and, if so, how to show fluctuating annual bonuses.

Like most of the provisions the Dodd-Frank Act, Section 953(a) was not immediately effective. Section 953(a) directs the SEC to adopt rules implementing this disclosure requirement, but does not give it a deadline for doing so.

¶3175 CEO Pay Ratio Disclosure

Section 953(b) of the Dodd-Frank Act, "Executive Compensation Disclosures" required the SEC to amend the proxy statement disclosure rules to require each public company to disclose:

(A) The median of the annual total compensation of all employees of the company, except the chief executive officer (including employees outside the US);

(B) The annual total compensation of the chief executive officer (or any equivalent position) of the company; and

(C) The ratio of the amount described in subparagraph (A) to the amount described in subparagraph (B).

In August 2015, the SEC issued final rules under Section 953(b), adding Item 402(u) to Regulation S-K, effective for the first fiscal year of the company beginning on or after January 1, 2017. Thus, public companies were required to disclose their "CEO Pay Ratio." in proxy statements for fiscal years ending December 31, 2017 and after.

The disclosure requirements do not apply to smaller reporting companies, foreign private issuers, multijurisdictional filers, emerging growth companies, and registered investment companies.

There are two primary components of the new rules: calculating the ratio and disclosing the ratio in the company's proxy statement. However, within those two primary components, there are several sub-components. Since calculation necessarily comes before disclosure, we will discuss that first, with some cross-referencing, as needed.

.01 Calculating the Ratio

After briefing the board and/or compensation committee on the requirements of the final rules and organizing a team of internal professionals to comply with the rules, the company can develop an action plan for compliance. Companies need to have systems in place to collect data. To create or implement those systems will require the company to make certain decisions, as discussed below.

Alternative Methodologies for Identifying the Median Employee. The final rules allow a company to use alternative methodologies and statistical sampling to identify its median employee. Each company may select a methodology to identify its median employee based on the company's facts and circumstances, including total employee population, a statistical sampling of that population, or other reasonable methods. For example, a company could identify the median of its population or sample using any consistently applied compensation measure from compensation amounts reported in its payroll or tax records.

Cost-of-Living Adjustments. The rules explicitly allow a company to apply a *cost-of-living adjustment* to the compensation measure it uses to identify the median employee. The SEC acknowledged that differences in the underlying economic conditions of certain countries in which companies operate would have an effect on the compensation paid to employees in those jurisdictions, resulting in a statistic that does not appropriately reflect the value of the compensation paid to individuals in those countries. Therefore, the rules give companies the option to adjust for these differences.

The rules allow a company to make cost-of-living adjustments to the compensation of its employees in jurisdictions other than that in which the CEO resides. If a company uses this option to identify the median employee, and the median employee identified is an employee in a jurisdiction other than the jurisdiction in which the CEO resides, the company must use the same cost-of-living adjustment in calculating the median employee's annual total compensation (and disclose the median employee's jurisdiction).

Using cost-of-living adjustments could be useful for some multinational companies. In its discussion of the new rules, the SEC observes that India, China, Mexico, and Brazil have a cost of living below the U.S. level (the United Kingdom, Canada, Germany, Japan, France, and Australia have a cost of living similar to or above the U.S. level). However, a company that elects to calculate and disclose the pay ratio using cost-of-living adjustments still must disclose the median employee's annual total compensation and pay ratio without the adjustment. (As discussed further under "Disclosure" below.)

Determination of Total Compensation. Each company should assess its ability to calculate precisely all items of compensation or whether reasonable estimates may be appropriate for some elements. The rules confirm that companies must calculate the annual total compensation for its median employee using the same rules that apply to the CEO's compensation in the Summary Compensation Table (Item 402(c)(2)(x) of Regulation S-K). However, companies may use reasonable estimates when calculating any elements of the annual total compensation for employees other than the CEO (with disclosure).

Selecting a Testing Date. The final rules allow a company to *select a date within the last three months of its last completed fiscal year* on which to determine the employee population for purposes of identifying the median employee. The company would *not* need to count any individual who is not employed on that date. Companies that employ temporary or seasonal workers should pay particular attention to this rule.

Additionally, the rules permit the company to identify its median employee *once every three years*, unless (i) the median employee's compensation changes within those three years, or (ii) there has been a change in its employee population or employee compensation arrangements that would result in a significant change in the pay ratio disclosure. Some have suggested that a company could use triennial disclosure to game the testing and disclosure rules by frontloading the CEO's compensation package for 2016, and reducing it in 2017. However, this would seem to be a high-risk strategy, as investors and their advisors may not be too keen on such a blatant manipulation.

When a company appoints a new CEO during the year, the rules give it the option of calculating the annual total compensation for the CEO for the year by (i) separately calculating the compensation provided to each person who served as CEO during the year for the time he or she served as CEO and then combining those figures; or (ii) using the CEO serving on the testing date it selects to identify the median employee and annualizing that CEO's compensation. Again, some have suggested that a company could game this rule by frontloading or backloading the compensation of the new CEO or annualizing the compensation of the lower paid CEO.

Non-U.S. Employees. The rules also allow a company to exclude non-U.S. employees from the determination of its median employee in two circumstances:

1. Non-U.S. employees that are employed in a jurisdiction with data privacy laws that make the company unable to comply with the rule without violating those laws. The rules require a company to obtain a legal opinion on this issue. In its discussion of the new rules, the SEC observes this may be an issue for China and Mexico. However, the data privacy rules in most countries would appear to allow collection of the limited information necessary for these calculations.

2. Up to 5% of the company's non-U.S. employees, including any employees it has excluded using the data privacy exemption. Under this exception, if a company excludes *any* non-U.S. employee in a particular jurisdiction, it must exclude *all* non-U.S. employees in that jurisdiction. Companies that use low wage locations such as India, China, or the Philippines should take note.

A company should: (1) evaluate favorable testing dates and even testing years, (2) determine whether any non-U.S. employees are employed in a jurisdiction with data privacy laws that make the company unable to comply with the rule without violating those laws, (3) consider which non-U.S. employees to exclude under the 5% exclusion allowance, (4) examine the relationship with and likely status of leased employees and others the company currently treats as independent contractors, and (5) consider the feasibility (and benefit) of applying a cost-of-living adjustment in certain non-U.S. jurisdictions.

New Employees. The rules also allow a company to exclude certain new employees from its calculation. A company can exclude any employees obtained in a business combination or acquisition for the fiscal year in which the transaction becomes effective. (The company must disclose the acquired business and disclose the approximate number of employees it is omitting.) Additionally, the rule allows companies to annualize the total compensation for a permanent employee who did not work for the entire year, such as a new hire or an employee on an unpaid leave of absence. Note that the rules expressly prohibit companies from annualizing the compensation of part-time, temporary, or seasonal workers when calculating the required pay ratio.

Independent Contractors. The rules also allow a company to exclude limited categories of employees from the determination of its median employee. Individuals employed by unaffiliated third parties or independent contractors would *not* be considered employees of the company. Companies may, in the process of determining who is an "employee" for purposes of the pay ratio calculation, apply a widely recognized test under another area of law (*e.g.*, tax or employment laws) that they would otherwise use to determine whether their workers are employees. For example, for a U.S. workforce, a company could determine who is an employee for pay ratio purposes by whether or not an individual receives a Form W-2 or a Form 1099. The initial guidance provided by C&DI Q/A 128C.05 (later withdrawn) stated that a company had to include workers whose compensation it determined, regardless of any classification made under tax or employment laws.

Other Benefits Provided to Employees. The rules allow a company to include personal benefits that aggregate less than $10,000 and compensation under non-discriminatory benefit plans such as health and retirement plans in calculating the annual total compensation of the median employee as long as these items are also included in calculating the CEO's annual total compensation. Inasmuch as the value of the benefits, such as health and retirement plan coverage, provided to rank-and-file employees in the U.S. is usually much greater, as a percentage of pay, than the benefits provide to the CEO, companies should calculate this value.

.02 Disclosing the Ratio

Each company should consider how it will draft the required disclosure. Companies that expect a significant gap in the ratio or have union employees (or are targeted for organization) might want to give special consideration to this issue.

Basic Disclosure. The rules generally only require a company to disclose the ratio and "briefly" describe the methodology it used to identify the median employee. A company also must "briefly" describe any material assumptions, adjustments (including any cost-of-living adjustments, discussed below), or estimates it used to identify the median employee or to determine total compensation or any elements of total compensation (emphasizing that the company must consistently apply such assumptions and adjustments). Finally, the company must clearly identify any estimates it used.

If there is a material difference between the CEO's annual total compensation used in the pay ratio disclosure and the total compensation amounts reflected in the Summary Compensation Table, the company must explain it.

Supplemental Disclosure. The rules explicitly state that: "The required descriptions should be a brief overview; it is not necessary for the company to provide technical analyses or formulas." However, many companies have not been brief. The rules allow companies to supplement the required disclosure with a narrative discussion or additional ratios. Any additional discussion and/or ratios need to be clearly identified, not misleading, and not presented with greater prominence than the required pay ratio.

Cost-of-Living Adjustments. As noted above, a company that uses a cost-of-living adjustment to identify the median employee must disclose:

- the cost-of-living adjustments it used to identify the median employee,
- the cost-of-living adjustments it used to calculate the median employee's annual total compensation,
- the measure used as the basis for the cost-of-living adjustment,
- the median employee's jurisdiction (if the employee is in a jurisdiction other than the jurisdiction in which the CEO resides), and
- the median employee's annual total compensation and pay ratio without the cost-of-living adjustment (for which the company will need to identify the median employee without using any cost-of-living adjustments).

A company also must disclose if it changed from using the cost-of-living adjustment to not using that adjustment or vice versa.

Changes to Methodology, Assumptions, Adjustments, or Estimates. If a company changes its methodology or its material assumptions, adjustments, or estimates from those used in its pay ratio disclosure for the prior fiscal year, the company must briefly describe the change and the reasons for the change, but only if the effects of any such change are significant.

¶3185 Disclosure Regarding Chairman and CEO Structure

Section 972 of the Dodd-Frank Act added Section 14B "Corporate Governance" to the Exchange Act, which requires the SEC to issue rules that require the company to disclose in its annual proxy statement the reasons why it has chosen the same or different persons to serve as chairman of the board of directors and chief executive officer (or in equivalent positions) of the company. Obviously, the intent of this provision is to encourage companies to separate these roles and make it easier for investors to identify which companies have not separated the roles. This provision is currently effective.

¶3195 Enhanced Disclosure and Reporting of Compensation Arrangements

Section 956 of the Dodd Frank Act, "Enhanced Compensation Structure Reporting," applies only to financial institutions with assets of $1 billion or more. It required the federal regulators to jointly prescribe regulations or guidelines by March 22, 2011, which require each covered financial institution to disclose to the appropriate federal regulator the structures of all incentive-based compensation arrangements offered by the institution, sufficient to determine whether the compensation structure (A) provides an executive officer, employee, director, or principal shareholder of the covered financial institution with excessive compensation, fees, or benefits; or (B) could lead to material financial loss to the covered financial institution. The regulations must **prohibit** any such incentive-based payment arrangement or features. This provision would not require a financial institution that does not have an incentive-based payment arrangement to make any disclosures, or the reporting of the actual compensation of particular individuals. (The "appropriate Federal regulators" are the Board of Governors of the Federal Reserve System, the Office of the Comptroller of the Currency, the Board of Directors of the Federal Deposit Insurance Corporation, the Director of the Office of Thrift Supervision, the National Credit Union Administration Board, the Securities and Exchange Commission, and the Federal Housing Finance Agency.)

In March 2011, the OCC, FDIC, OTS, SEC, Board of Governors of the Federal Reserve System, National Credit Union Administration, and Federal Housing Finance Agency (collectively, the "Agencies") jointly issued proposed rules pursuant to Section 956 of the Dodd-Frank Act. Numerous entities and organizations submitted comments to the Agencies requesting clarification and revisions to the proposed rules, and in July 2011, the SEC announced that it did not plan to adopt rules (jointly with other agencies) regarding disclosure of, and prohibitions of certain executive compensation structures and arrangements until a later date.

The proposed rules would have (i) required the reporting of incentive-based compensation arrangements by a covered financial institution (one that has total consolidated assets of $1 billion or more), and (ii) prohibited incentive-based compensation arrangements that encourage inappropriate risks by covered financial institutions by providing a covered person with excessive compensation, or that could lead to material financial loss to the covered financial institution. The proposed rules also would have required each covered financial institution to develop and maintain certain policies and procedures for the adoption and monitoring of incentive-based compensation.

In June 2010, the OCC, Federal Reserve Board, FDIC and OTS, issued the 2010 Interagency Guidance on Sound Incentive Compensation Policies. Additionally, since 2009, the Federal Reserve Board has been conducting a so-called "horizontal review" of incentive compensation practices at 28 Large Complex Banking Organizations. The proposed rules were inconsistent with the 2010 Interagency Guidance as well as interpretations issued by the Federal Reserve Board under the horizontal review process.

If the proposed rules were finalized without revision, nearly every financial institution in the United States would be forced to redesign its executive compensation program.

The proposed rules were particularly unclear as to how they apply in the context of consolidated groups, where not all of the members of the group are covered financial institutions or the group includes more than one type of covered financial institution. Additionally, the proposed rules offered little guidance on the definitions of key terms such as "executive officer," "compensation," and "incentive-based compensation," or the distinction between the definitions of "compensation" and "incentive-based compensation."

¶3195

In the proposed rules, the Agencies were moving in a direction that financial institution regulators had never before gone. Historically, regulators have not attempted to dictate or influence the form or amount of compensation that an institution provided to its officers and employees, but have only required full disclosure of such compensation. Instead, the regulators have focused on principles-based regulation and required the institution to establish the appropriate levels and forms of compensation, based on the characteristics, including risk profile, of the institution. The proposed rules would have changed all that by creating overly prescriptive rules.

The proposed rules would have established a mandatory deferral requirement for the incentive-based compensation of an executive officer at a covered financial institution with total consolidated assets of $50 billion or more. Under the proposed rules, an institution must require that:

- At least 50% of the annual incentive-based compensation of each executive officer must be deferred over a period of no less than three years, with the institution allowed to release (or allow vesting of) the full deferred amount in a lump-sum at the end of the deferral period in equal increments, pro rata, for each year of the deferral period; and

- This required deferral amount must be adjusted to reflect actual losses or other measures or aspects of performance that are realized or become better known during the deferral period.

Additionally, under the proposed rules, the board of directors (or a committee thereof) of a larger covered financial institution must approve any incentive-based compensation arrangement for certain covered persons who individually have the ability to expose the institution to possible losses that are substantial in relation to the institution's size, capital, or overall risk tolerance. The board (or committee) must identify these covered persons (other than executive officers). The board of a large financial institution may not approve an incentive-based compensation arrangement for any covered person unless the board determines that the arrangement, including the method of paying compensation under the arrangement, effectively balances the financial rewards to the employee and the range and time horizon of risks associated with the employee's activities, employing appropriate methods for ensuring risk sensitivity such as: (i) deferral of payments, (ii) risk adjustment of awards, (iii) reduced sensitivity to short-term performance, or (iv) extended performance periods.

These prescriptive rules inevitably would have led to unintended consequences. For example, the proposed rules seem likely to push institutions and their officers toward more fixed compensation such as base salaries. This result would be counterproductive at a time when shareholders are demanding more performance-based compensation. Moreover, the proposed rules could create problems with existing incentive-based compensation arrangements, since institutions may be legally unable to change the terms of such arrangements.

The proposed rules also would have required each covered financial institution to develop and maintain policies and procedures applicable to any incentive-based compensation arrangement, or any feature of any such arrangement, which are approved by the board of directors (or a committee thereof), and reasonably designed to ensure and monitor compliance with the anti-risk requirements.

Finally, the proposed rules would have required each covered financial institution to submit a report annually to, and in the format directed by, its appropriate regulator or supervisor, which:

- describes the structure of the covered financial institution's incentive-based compensation arrangements for covered persons, and

- is sufficient to allow an assessment of whether the compensation structure or features of those arrangements provide or are likely to provide covered persons with excessive compensation, fees, or benefits to covered persons or could lead to material financial loss to the covered financial institution.

Practice Tools

¶10,010 SAMPLE LEGAL AGREEMENT—Executive Employment Agreement

The following is a sample employment agreement between an employer and an executive, which sets forth the legal and business terms of the employment relationship. Most employers and most executives feel it is necessary to have some form of written agreement for their mutual protection. Either a public or private company or other business entity could use this sample agreement. For a discussion of executive employment agreements, see Chapter 1 (¶101 *et seq.*).

Executive Employment Agreement

This Employment Agreement (the "Agreement") is effective as of _____, (the "Effective Date"), by and between ABC Corporation (the "Company"), and _____ (the "Executive").

WHEREAS, the Company desires to employ the Executive as its _____; and

WHEREAS, the Company and the Executive have reached agreement concerning the terms and conditions of the Executive's employment and wish to formalize that agreement;

NOW, THEREFORE, in consideration of the mutual terms, covenants and conditions stated in this Agreement, the Company and the Executive hereby agree as follows:

1. **Employment.** The Company hereby employs the Executive and the Executive hereby accepts employment with the Company as _____. During the Term (as hereinafter defined), Executive will have the title, status and duties of _____ and will report directly to the Company's _____.

2. **Term of Employment.** This Agreement shall commence on the Effective Date and shall expire on 5:00 pm E.S.T. on December 31, _____ (the "Initial Term"), unless terminated earlier pursuant to the provisions of Sections 5 or 6 hereof. The term of employment shall be renewed automatically for successive periods of one (1) year each (a "Renewal Term") after the expiration of the Initial Term, unless the Company provides the Executive, or the Executive provides the Company, with written notice to the contrary at least one hundred eighty (180) calendar days prior to the end of the Initial Term or any Renewal Term. The Initial

Term and any Renewal Terms are collectively referred to herein as the "Term." If either the Company or the Executive elect not to renew the Term of this Agreement in accordance with this Section 2 and the Executive thereafter continues in employment with Company, the Executive shall be employed on an at-will basis and the terms of such employment and any subsequent termination of employment shall be subject solely to the Company's general employment practices and policies. In the event of a "Change in Control" of the Company (as defined below) during the Term, the Term automatically will be extended until the later of (i) the second anniversary of the Change in Control, or (ii) the scheduled expiration of the then-current Term.

3. **Duties.** During the Term:

   (a) The Executive will perform duties assigned by the Company's _____, or the Company's Board of Directors (the "Board"), from time to time; provided that the Executive shall not be assigned tasks inconsistent with those of _____.

   (b) The Executive will devote the Executive's full time and best efforts, talents, knowledge and experience to serving as the Company's _____. However, the Executive may devote reasonable time to activities such as supervision of personal investments and activities involving professional, charitable, educational, religious and similar types of activities, speaking engagements and membership on other boards of directors, provided such activities do not interfere in any material way with the business of the Company; *provided that*, the Executive cannot serve on the board of directors of more than one publicly-traded company without the Board's written consent. The time involved in such activities shall not be treated as vacation time. The Executive shall be entitled to keep any amounts paid to the Executive in connection with such activities (*e.g.*, director fees and honoraria).

   (c) The Executive will perform the Executive's duties diligently and competently and shall act in conformity with Company's written and oral policies and within the limits, budgets and business plans set by the Company. The Executive will at all times during the Term strictly adhere to and obey all of the rules and regulations in effect from time to time relating to the conduct of executives of the Company. Except as provided in (b) above, the Executive shall not engage in consulting work or any trade or business for the Executive's own account or for or on behalf of any other person, firm or company that competes, conflicts or interferes with the performance of the Executive's duties hereunder in any material way.

4. **Compensation and Benefits.** During Executive's employment hereunder, Company shall provide to Executive, and Executive shall accept

from Company as full compensation for Executive's services hereunder, compensation and benefits as follows:

(a) *Base Salary.* The Company shall pay the Executive at an annual base salary ("Base Salary") of _____ thousand dollars ($_____). The Board, or such committee of the Board as is responsible for setting the compensation of senior executive officers, shall review the Executive's performance and Base Salary annually in [January] of each year, and determine whether to adjust the Executive's Base Salary on a prospective basis. The first review shall be in [January] [year]. Such adjusted annual salary then shall become the Executive's "Base Salary" for purposes of this Agreement. The Executive's annual Base Salary shall not be reduced after any increase, without the Executive's consent. The Company shall pay the Executive's Base Salary according to payroll practices in effect for all senior executive officers of the Company.

(b) *Incentive Compensation.* The Executive shall be eligible to participate in any annual performance bonus plans, long-term incentive plans, and/or equity-based compensation plans established or maintained by the Company for its senior executive officers, including, but not limited to, the Management Incentive Plan and the ABC Corporation [year] Long-Term Incentive Plan. For the Company's [year] fiscal year, the Executive shall be eligible for a target bonus under the Company's annual incentive plan equal to 40% of the Executive's Base Salary provided that all performance goals set by the Company are met. The Board (or appropriate Board committee) will determine and communicate to the Executive the Executive's annual incentive plan participation for subsequent fiscal years, no later than [March 31] of such fiscal year. The Company will pay any annual bonus to the Executive within the period ending on the 15th day of the third month following the end of the Company's fiscal year, but in no event after the close of the Company's fiscal year following the year the Annual Bonus is earned.

(c) *Executive Benefit Plans.* The Executive will be eligible to participate on substantially the same basis as the Company's other senior executive officers in any executive benefit plans offered by the Company including, without limitation, medical, dental, short-term and long-term disability, life, pension, profit sharing and nonqualified deferred compensation arrangements. The Company reserves the right to modify, suspend or discontinue any and all of the plans, practices, policies and programs at any time without recourse by the Executive, so long as Company takes such action generally with respect to other similarly situated senior executive officers.

(d) *Business Expenses.* The Company shall reimburse the Executive for all reasonable and necessary business expenses incurred in the performance of services with the Company, according to Company's policies and upon Executive's presentation of an itemized written statement and such verification as the Company may require.

(e) *Perquisites.* The Company will provide the Executive with all perquisites it provides to other senior executive officers. Such perquisites shall not be less than those provided to the Executive on the Effective Date. The Company will also reimburse the Executive for annual income tax return preparation and tax counseling up to $_____ per year.

(f) *Vacation.* The Executive will be entitled to vacation in accordance with the Company's vacation policy for senior executive officers, but in no event less than ___ weeks per calendar year. Unused vacation shall be carried over for a period not in excess of twelve (12) months.

(g) The Company shall provide the Executive with the use of an automobile chosen by the Executive with lease payments of no more than _____ dollars ($____) per month throughout the Term and pay all expenses with respect to such automobile, including without limitation, insurance, maintenance, and fuel.

(h) *Relocation Benefit.* The Company shall reimburse the reasonable expenses of the Executive and the Executive's family in relocating to the _____ metropolitan area from _____, including, without limitation: (i) moving expenses, (ii) temporary living arrangements, (iii) "home visit" expenses, (iv) real estate commissions and closing costs on the sale of the Executive's current residence, and (v) real estate commissions and closing costs on the purchase of a residence in the _____ metropolitan area. The Company shall reimburse the Executive on a "grossed up basis" in the event any tax is assessed upon the Executive with respect to such reimbursement. If the Executive is able to sell the Executive's current residence without a real estate broker, the Company and the Executive shall reasonably agree on some additional form of compensation.

5. **Payments on Termination of Employment.**

(a) *Termination of Employment for any Reason.* The following payments will be made upon the Executive's termination of employment for any reason:

    (i) Earned but unpaid Base Salary through the date of termination;

    (ii) Any annual incentive plan bonus, or other form of incentive compensation, for which the performance measurement period has ended, but which is unpaid at the time of termination;

    (iii) Any accrued but unpaid vacation;

(iv) Any amounts payable under any of the Company's executive benefit plans in accordance with the terms of those plans, except as may be required under Code Sec. 401(a)(13); and

(v) Unreimbursed business expenses incurred by the Executive on the Company's behalf.

(b) *Voluntary Termination of Employment for Other Than Good Reason.* In addition to the amounts determined under (a) above, if the Executive voluntarily terminates employment for other than Good Reason, then in addition to the amounts determined under (a) above, the Executive shall be entitled to a pro rata portion of the target bonus under the Company's annual incentive plan for the year in which such termination occurs.

(c) *Termination of Employment for Death or Disability.* In addition to the amounts determined under (a) above, if the Executive's termination of employment occurs by reason of death or Disability, the Executive (or the Executive's estate) will receive a pro rata portion of any bonus payable under the Company's annual incentive plan for the year in which such termination occurs determined based on the highest of (i) the actual annual bonus paid for the fiscal year immediately preceding such termination, (ii) the target bonus for the fiscal year in which such termination occurs, or (iii) the actual bonus attained for the fiscal year in which such termination occurs. For purposes of this Agreement, "Disability" means the Executive's long-term disability as defined under the Company's long-term disability plan, or if the Executive is not covered by a long-term disability plan sponsored by the Company, the Executive's inability to engage in any substantial gainful activity by reason of any medically-determined physical or mental impairment that can be expected to result in death or to be of long-continued and indefinite duration.

(d) *Termination by the Company Without Cause, or Voluntary Termination by the Executive for Good Reason.* If the Company terminates the Executive's employment other than for Cause, or the Executive voluntarily terminates the Executive's employment for Good Reason, in addition to the benefits payable under (a), and subject to the Executive's compliance with Sections 7 and 8, the Company will pay the following amounts and provide the following benefits:

(i) The Base Salary and annual bonus that the Company would have paid under the Agreement had the Executive's employment continued to the end of the Term. For this purpose, annual bonus will be determined as the highest of (*a*) the actual bonus paid for the fiscal year immediately preceding such termination, (*b*) the target bonus for the fiscal year in which such termination occurs, or (*c*) the actual bonus attained for the fiscal year in which such termination occurs.

¶10,010

(ii) Continued coverage under the Company's medical, dental, life, disability, pension, profit sharing and other executive benefit plans through the end of the Term, at the same cost to the Executive as in effect on the date of the Executive's termination. If the Company determines that the Executive cannot participate in any benefit plan because the Executive is not actively performing services for the Company, the Company may provide such benefits under an alternate arrangement, such as through the purchase of an individual insurance policy that provides similar benefits or, if applicable, through a nonqualified pension or profit sharing plan. To the extent that the Executive's compensation is necessary for determining the amount of any such continued coverage or benefits, such compensation (Base Salary and annual bonus) through the end of the Term shall be at the highest rate in effect during the 12-month period immediately preceding the Executive's termination of employment.

(iii) The period through the end of the Term shall continue to count for purposes of determining the Executive's age and service with the Company with respect to (*a*) eligibility, vesting and the amount of benefits under the Company's executive benefit plans, and (*b*) the vesting of any outstanding stock options, restricted stock or other equity-based compensation awards.

(iv) Outplacement services, as elected by the Executive (and with a firm elected by the Executive), not to exceed $_____ in total.

(e) *Good Reason.* For purposes of this Agreement, "Good Reason" shall mean the occurrence of any of the following by the Company, without the Executive's written consent:

(i) materially reduces Executive's base compensation;

(ii) materially diminishes Executive's authority, duties, or responsibilities;

(iii) materially diminishes the authority, duties, or responsibilities of the supervisor to whom Executive is required to report;

(iv) materially diminishes the budget over which Executive retains authority;

(v) materially changes the Geographical Employment Area at which Executive must perform the services, or assigns to Executive duties that would reasonably require such a change; or

(vi) takes or fails to take any other action that constitutes a material breach by the Company of this Agreement.

Notwithstanding the foregoing, no termination shall be deemed to be for Good Reason unless (1) Executive gives written notice to the Company of the event or condition claimed to constitute Good Reason within ninety (90) days of the first occurrence of such event or condition, (2) the Company fails to cure such event or condition within thirty (30) days of such notice, and (3) Executive gives a Notice of Termination creating a Date of Termination not later than thirty (30) days after the expiration of such cure period.

(f) *Cause.* For purposes of this Agreement, "Cause" shall mean: (i) the Executive's willful and continued failure to substantially perform the Executive's duties as an executive of the Company (other than any such failure resulting from incapacity due to physical or mental illness) after a written demand for substantial performance is delivered to the Executive by the Board, which demand specifically identifies the manner in which the Board believes that the Executive has not substantially performed the Executive's duties, and which gives the Executive at least 30 days to cure such alleged deficiencies, (ii) the Executive's willful misconduct, which is demonstrably and materially injurious to the Company, monetarily or otherwise, or (iii) the Executive's engaging in egregious misconduct involving serious moral turpitude to the extent that the Executive's creditability and reputation no longer conforms to the standard of senior executive officers of the Company. The Executive's employment shall be deemed to have terminated for Cause if, after the Executive's employment has terminated, facts and circumstances are discovered that would have justified a termination for Cause. For purposes of this Agreement, no act or failure to act on the Executive's part shall be considered "willful" unless it is done, or omitted to be done, by the Executive in bad faith or without reasonable belief that such action or omission was in the best interests of the Company or a Subsidiary. Any act or failure to act based upon authority given pursuant to a resolution duly adopted by the Board or based upon the advice of counsel for the Company shall be conclusively presumed to be done, or omitted to be done, in good faith and in the best interests of the Company.

(g) *Timing of Payments.* All payments described above shall be made in a lump sum cash payment as soon as practicable (but in no event more than 10 days) following the Executive's termination of employment. If the total amount of annual bonus is not determinable on that date, the Company shall pay the amount of bonus that is determinable and the remainder shall be paid in a lump sum cash payment within 10 days of the date that annual performance results are finalized.

6. **Change in Control.**

The Executive may become entitled to payments under this Section 6 or under Section 5, but not both.

(a) *Payments and Benefits Upon Employment Termination After a Change in Control.* If within two years after a Change in Control (as defined below), the Company terminates the Executive's employment other than for Cause, or the Executive voluntarily terminates the Executive's employment for Good Reason, the Company will provide the following payments and benefits to the Executive, in lieu of those payments and benefits provided under Sections 5(c) or (d) above, but in addition to the amounts payable under Section 5(a) above:

    (i) Three times the Executive's Base Salary as in effect on the date of the Executive's termination of employment.

    (ii) Three times the highest of (1) the average annual bonus paid for the three fiscal years immediately preceding the Executive's employment termination, (2) the target bonus for the fiscal year in which such termination of employment occurs, or (3) the actual bonus attained for the fiscal year in which such termination occurs.

    (iii) Continued coverage for a period of 36 months from the Executive's termination under the Company's medical, dental, life, disability and other welfare benefit plans, at the same cost to the Executive as in effect on the date of the Change in Control (or, if lower, as in effect at any time thereafter). If the Company determines that the Executive cannot participate in any benefit plan because the Executive is not actively performing services for the Company, the Company may provide such benefits under an alternate arrangement, such as through the purchase of an individual insurance policy that provides similar benefits. The amount of such continued coverage shall be determined, if applicable, by adding 36 additional months of age and service to the Executive's actual age and service as of the Executive's termination date and as if the Executive earned compensation during such 36-month period at the rate in effect during the 12-month period immediately preceding the Executive's termination date. The Executive's eligibility for any retiree medical or life coverage following such termination date shall also be determined by adding 36 additional months of age and service to the Executive's actual age and service as of the termination date.

    (iv) The value of continued coverage for a period of 36 months under any pension, profit sharing or other retirement plan maintained by the Company. The value of such coverage under a tax qualified plan may be provided through a non-qualified pension or profit sharing plan and shall be determined by adding 36 additional months of age and service to the Executive's actual age and service at the date of the Executive's termination of employment and as if the Executive earned compensation during such 36-month period at the rate in effect during the 12-month period immediately preceding the Executive's termination date. In the case of a defined benefit pension plan, such value shall include any early retirement subsidies to which the Executive would have become entitled under the plan and shall be determined using the actuarial factors set forth in such plan.

(v) Immediate vesting of all stock options, restricted stock and other equity-based awards.

(vi) Outplacement services, as elected by the Executive (and with a firm elected by the Executive), not to exceed $_____.

(b) *Timing of Payment.* All payments under paragraphs (a)(i), (ii) and (iv) above, and paragraph (c) below, shall be made in a lump sum cash payment as soon as practicable, but in no event more than 10 days after the Executive's termination of employment (or the date of the Change in Control, if applicable). If the total amount of bonus is not determinable on that date, the Company shall pay the amount of bonus that is determinable, and shall pay the remainder in a lump sum cash payment within 10 days of the date that annual performance results are finalized.

(c) *Best-After Tax Payment.* If a Change in Control occurs and payments are made under this Section 6, and a final determination is made by legislation, regulation, or ruling directed to the Executive or the Company, by court decision, or by independent tax counsel, that the aggregate amount of any payments made to the Executive under this Agreement and any other agreement, plan, program or policy of the Company in connection with, on account of, or as a result of, such Change in Control ("Total Payments") will be subject to an excise tax under the provisions of Code Section 4999, or any successor section thereof ("Excise Tax"), the Total Payments shall be reduced (beginning with those that are exempt from Code Section 409A) so that the maximum amount of the Total Payments (after reduction) shall be one dollar ($1.00) less than the amount that would cause the Total Payments to be subject to the Excise Tax; provided, however, that the Total Payments shall only be reduced to the extent that the after-tax value of amounts received by the Executive after application of the above reduction would exceed the after-tax value of the Total Payments received without application of such reduction. For this purpose, the after-tax value of an amount shall be determined taking into account all federal, state, and local income, employment, and excise taxes applicable to such amount. In making any determination as to whether the Total Payments would be subject to an Excise Tax, consideration shall be given to whether any portion of the Total Payments could reasonably be considered, based on the relevant facts and circumstances, to be reasonable compensation for services rendered (whether before or after the consummation of the applicable Change in Control). To the extent Total Payments must be reduced pursuant to this Section, the Company, without consulting the Executive, will reduce the Total Payments to achieve the best economic benefit, and to the extent economically equivalent, on a pro-rata basis.

(i) In the event that upon any audit by the Internal Revenue Service, or by a state or local taxing authority, of the Total Payments, a change is determined to be required in the amount of taxes paid by, or Total Payments made to, the Executive, appropriate adjustments will be made under this Agreement such that the net amount that is payable to the Executive after taking into account the provisions of Code Section 4999 will reflect the intent of the parties as expressed in this Section 6(c). the Executive shall notify the Company in writing of any claim by the Internal Revenue Service that, if successful, would require payment of an Excise Tax or an additional Excise Tax on the Total Payments (a "Claim"). Such notification shall be given as soon as practicable but no later than ten (10) business days after the Executive is informed in writing of such Claim and shall apprise the Company of the nature of such Claim and the date on which such Claim is requested to be paid. The Executive shall not pay such Claim prior to the expiration of the thirty (30) calendar day period following the date on which the Executive gives such notice to the Company (or such shorter period ending on the date that any payment of taxes with respect to such Claim is due). If the Company notifies the Executive in writing prior to the expiration of such period that it desires to contest such Claim, the Executive shall: (A) give the Company any information reasonably requested by the Company relating to such Claim, (B) take such action in connection with contesting such Claim as the Company shall reasonably request in writing from time to time, including, without limitation, accepting legal representation with respect to such Claim by an attorney reasonably selected by the Company, (C) cooperate with the Company in good faith in order to contest effectively such Claim, and (D) permit the Company to participate in any proceedings relating to such Claim; provided, however, that the Company shall bear and pay directly all costs and expenses (including additional interest and penalties) incurred in connection with such contest and shall indemnify and hold the Executive harmless for any Excise Tax, additional Excise Tax, or income tax (including interest and penalties with respect thereto) imposed as a result of such representation and payment of costs and expenses. Without limitation on the foregoing provisions of this subparagraph (c)(i), the Company, at its sole option, may pursue or forgo any and all administrative appeals, proceedings, hearings and conferences with the taxing authority in respect of such Claim and may, at its sole option, either direct the Executive to pay the tax claimed and sue for a refund or contest the Claim in any permissible manner, and the Executive agrees to prosecute such contest to a determination before any administrative tribunal, in a court of initial jurisdiction and in one (1) or more appellate courts, as the Company shall determine, provided, however, that if the Company directs the Executive to pay such Claim and sue for a refund, the Company shall advance the amount of such payment to the Executive on an interest-free basis or, if such an advance is not permissible thereunder, pay the amount of such payment to the Executive as additional compensation, and shall indemnify and hold the Executive harmless from any Excise Tax, additional Excise Tax, or income tax (including interest or penalties with respect thereto) imposed with respect to such advance or additional compensation; and further provided that any extension of the statute of limitations relating to payment of taxes for the taxable year of the Executive with respect to which such contested amount is claimed to be due is limited solely to such contested amount. The Company shall reimburse any fees and expenses provided for under this Section 6(c) on or before the last day of the Executive's taxable year following the taxable year in which the fee or expense was incurred, and in accordance with the other requirements of Code Section 409A and Treasury Regulation § 1.409A-3(i)(1)(v) (or any similar or successor provisions).

(ii) If, after the receipt by the Executive of an amount advanced or paid by the Company pursuant to paragraph (c)(i) above, the Executive becomes entitled to receive any refund with respect to such Claim, the Executive shall (subject to the Company's complying with the requirements of subparagraph (c)(i)) promptly pay to the Company the amount of such refund (together with any interest paid or credited thereon after taxes applicable thereto). If, after the receipt by the Executive of an amount advanced by the Company pursuant to paragraph (c)(i), a determination is made that the Executive shall not be entitled to any refund with respect to such Claim and the Company does not notify the Executive in writing of its intent to contest such denial of refund prior to the expiration of sixty (60) calendar days after such determination, then such advance shall be forgiven and shall not be required to be repaid.

¶10,010

(d) *Definition of Change in Control.* For purposes of the Agreement, a "Change in Control" of the Company will be deemed to occur as of the first day that any one or more of the following condition is satisfied:

(i) The "beneficial ownership" (as defined in Rule 13d-3 under the Securities Exchange Act of 1934, as amended (the "Exchange Act")) of securities representing more than thirty-five percent (35%) of the combined voting power of the then outstanding voting securities of the Company entitled to vote generally in the election of directors (the "Company Voting Securities") is accumulated, held or acquired by a Person (as defined in Section 3(a)(9) of the Exchange Act, as modified, and used in Sections 13(d) and 14(d) thereof) (other than the Company, any trustee or other fiduciary holding securities under an employee benefit plan of the Company or an affiliate thereof, any corporation owned, directly or indirectly, by the Company's stockholders in substantially the same proportions as their ownership of stock of the Company); provided, however that any acquisition from the Company or any acquisition pursuant to a transaction that complies with clauses (A), (B) and (C) of subparagraph (iii) of this paragraph will not be a Change in Control under this subparagraph (i), and provided further, that immediately prior to such accumulation, holding or acquisition, such Person was not a direct or indirect beneficial owner of 20 percent or more of the Company Voting Securities; or

(ii) Individuals who, as of the date of the Agreement, constitute the Board of Directors (the "Incumbent Board") cease for any reason to constitute at least a majority of the Board of Directors; provided, however, that any individual becoming a director subsequent to the date hereof whose election, or nomination for election by the Company's stockholders, was approved by a vote of at least a majority of the directors then comprising the Incumbent Board will be considered as though such individual were a member of the Incumbent Board, but excluding, for this purpose, any such individual whose initial assumption of office occurs as a result of an actual or threatened election contest with respect to the election or removal of directors or other actual or threatened solicitation of proxies or consents by or on behalf of a person other than the Board (including without limitation any settlement thereof); or

(iii) Consummation by the Company of a reorganization, merger or consolidation, or sale or other disposition of all or substantially all of the assets of the Company or the acquisition of assets or stock of another entity (a "Business Combination"), in each case, unless immediately following such Business Combination: (A) more than 60% of the combined voting power of then outstanding voting securities entitled to vote generally in the election of directors of (x) the corporation resulting from such Business Combination (the "Surviving Corporation"), or (y) if applicable, a corporation that as a result of such transaction owns the Company or all or substantially all of the Company's assets either directly or through one or more subsidiaries (the "Parent Corporation"), is represented, directly or indirectly by Company Voting Securities outstanding immediately prior to such Business Combination (or, if applicable, is represented by shares into which such Company Voting Securities were converted pursuant to such Business Combination), and such voting power among the holders thereof is in substantially the same proportions as their ownership, immediately prior to such Business Combination, of the Company Voting Securities, (B) no Person (excluding any employee benefit plan (or related trust) of the Company or such corporation resulting from such Business Combination) beneficially owns, directly or indirectly, 20% or more of the combined voting power of the then outstanding voting securities eligible to elect directors of the Parent Corporation (or, if there is no Parent Corporation, the Surviving Corporation) except to the extent that such ownership of the Company existed prior to the Business Combination and (C) at least a majority of the members of the board of directors of the Parent Corporation (or, if there is no Parent Corporation, the Surviving Corporation) were members of the Incumbent Board at the time of the execution of the initial agreement, or of the action of the Board, providing for such Business Combination; or

(iv) Approval by the Company's stockholders of a complete liquidation or dissolution of the Company.

However, in no event will a Change in Control be deemed to have occurred, with respect to the Executive, if the Executive is part of a purchasing group that consummates the Change in Control transaction. The Executive will be deemed "part of a purchasing group" for purposes of the preceding sentence if the Executive is an equity participant in the purchasing company or group (except: (1) passive ownership of less than two percent (2%) of the stock of the purchasing company; or (2) ownership of equity participation in the purchasing company or group that is otherwise not significant, as determined prior to the Change in Control by a majority of the nonemployee continuing Directors).

7. **Restrictive Covenants.**

    (a) *Definitions.* For purposes of this Agreement, the following terms will be defined as follows:

        (i) "Confidential Information" shall mean the Company's trade secrets and all other information unique to the Company and not readily available to the public, including developments, designs, improvements, inventions, formulas, compilations, methods, strategies, forecasts, software programs, processes, know-how, data, research, operating methods and techniques, and all business plans, strategies, costs, profits, customers, vendors, markets, sales, products, key personnel, pricing policies, marketing, sales or other financial or business information, and any modifications or enhancements of any of the foregoing.

        (ii) The term "Business Conducted by the Company or any of its Affiliates" shall mean all businesses conducted by the Company or any of its Affiliates as of the Effective Date, of whatever kind, within or outside of the United States.

        (iii) The term "Affiliates" shall mean (1) any entity that directly or indirectly, is controlled by the Company, and (2) any entity in which the Company has a significant equity interest.

    (b) *Inventions or Developments.* The Executive agrees that the Executive will promptly and fully disclose to the Company all discoveries, improvements, inventions, formulas, ideas, processes, designs, techniques, know-how, data and computer programs (whether or not patentable, copyrightable or susceptible to any other form of protection), made, conceived, reduced to practice or developed by the Executive, either alone or jointly with others, during the Executive's employment with the Company (collectively, the "Inventions or Developments"). All Inventions and Developments shall be the sole property of the Company, including all patents, copyrights, intellectual property or other rights related thereto and Executive assigns to the Company all rights (if any) that the Executive may have or acquire in such Inventions or Developments.

Notwithstanding the foregoing, any right of the Company or assignment by the Executive as provided in this paragraph shall not apply to any Inventions or Developments for which no equipment, supplies, facility or trade secret information of the Company or its Affiliates were used and which were developed entirely on the Executive's own time, unless: (i) the Inventions or Developments relate to the Business Conducted by the Company or any of its Affiliates or the actual or demonstrably anticipated research or development of the Company or any of its Affiliates; or (ii) the Inventions or Developments result from any work performed by the Executive for the Company or any of its Affiliates.

(c) *Nondisclosure of Confidential Information or Inventions or Developments.* The Executive acknowledges that the Executive has had and will have access to Confidential Information or Inventions or Developments of the Company and/or its Affiliates and agrees that the Executive shall not, at any time, directly or indirectly use, divulge, furnish or make accessible to any person any Confidential Information or Inventions or Developments, but instead shall keep all such matters strictly and absolutely confidential.

(d) *No Diversion of Business Opportunities and Prospects.* The Executive agrees that during the Executive's employment with the Company: (i) the Executive shall not directly or indirectly engage in any employment, consulting or other business activity that is competitive with the Business Conducted by the Company or any of its Affiliates; (ii) the Executive shall promptly disclose to the Company all business opportunities that are presented to the Executive in the Executive's capacity as an employee of the Company or which is of a similar nature to the Business Conducted by the Company or any of its Affiliates or which the Company or its Affiliates have expressed an interest in engaging in the future; and (iii) the Executive shall not usurp or take advantage of any such business opportunity without first offering such opportunity to the Company.

(e) *Actions Upon Termination.* Upon the Executive's employment termination for whatever reason, the Executive shall neither take or copy nor allow a third party to take or copy, and shall deliver to the Company all property of the Company, including, but not limited to, all Confidential Information or Inventions or Developments, regardless of the medium (*i.e.*, hard copy, computer disk, CD ROM) on which the information is contained.

(f) *Noncompetition.* The Executive agrees that so long as the Executive is employed by the Company and for a period of two (2) years thereafter (the "Period"), the Executive shall not, without the prior written consent of the Company, participate or engage in, directly or indirectly (as an owner, partner, employee, officer, director, independent contractor, consultant, advisor or in any other capacity calling for the rendition of services, advice, or acts of management, operation or control), any business that, during the Period, is competitive with the Business Conducted by the Company or any of its Affiliates within the United States (hereinafter, the "Geographic Area").

(g) *Nonsolicitation of Employees.* The Executive agrees that, during the Period, the Executive shall not, without the prior written consent of the Company, directly or indirectly solicit any current employee of the Company or any of its Affiliates, or any individual who becomes an employee during the Period, to leave such employment and join or become affiliated with any business that is, during the

¶10,010

Period, competitive with the Business Conducted by the Company or any of its Affiliates within the Geographic Area.

(h) *Nonsolicitation of Suppliers or Customers.* The Executive agrees that, during the Period, the Executive shall not, without the prior written consent of the Company, directly or indirectly solicit, seek to divert or dissuade from continuing to do business with or entering into business with the Company or any of its Affiliates, any supplier, customer, or other person or entity that had a business relationship with or with which the Company was actively planning or pursuing a business relationship at or before the date of termination of the Executive's employment.

(i) *Irreparable Harm.* The Executive acknowledges that: (i) the Executive's compliance with this Section is necessary to preserve and protect the Confidential Information, Inventions or Developments and the goodwill of the Company and its Affiliates as going concerns; (ii) any failure by the Executive to comply with the provisions of this Section will result in irreparable and continuing injury for which there will be no adequate remedy at law; and (iii) in the event that the Executive should fail to comply with the terms and conditions of this Section, the Company shall be entitled, in addition to such other relief as may be proper, to all types of equitable relief (including, but not limited to, the issuance of an injunction and/or temporary restraining order) as may be necessary to cause the Executive to comply with this Section, to restore to the Company its property, and to make the Company whole.

(j) *Survival.* The provisions set forth in this Section shall, as noted, survive termination of this Agreement.

(k) *Forfeiture.* If the Executive violates any provision of this Section, the Executive will forfeit the Executive's right to all payments and benefits under Section 5(d) and Section 6, except to the extent otherwise provided by law.

(l) *Unenforceability.* If any provision(s) of this Section shall be found invalid or unenforceable, in whole or in part, then such provision(s) shall be deemed to be modified or restricted to the extent and in the manner necessary to render the same valid and enforceable, or shall be deemed excised from this Agreement, as the case may require, and this Agreement shall be construed and enforced to the maximum extent permitted by law, as if such provision(s) had been originally incorporated herein as so modified or restricted, or as if such provision(s) had not been originally incorporated herein, as the case may be.

8. **Release.** Any and all amounts payable and benefits or additional rights provided pursuant to this Agreement beyond those in Section 5(a), shall only be payable if the Executive delivers to the Company an original, signed release of claims of Executive occurring up to the release date, in

a form provided by the Company (the "Release"). The Company shall deliver the Release to the Executive within ten (10) calendar days of the date the Executive's employment terminates and the Executive must deliver to the Company and not revoke an executed and enforceable Release no later than sixty (60) calendar days after the date Executive's employment terminates (the "Release Deadline"). Payment of the amounts described in Sections 5 and 6 shall commence no earlier than the date on which the Executive delivers to the Company and does not revoke an executed and enforceable Release as described herein. Payment of any severance or benefits that are not exempt from Code Section 409A shall be delayed until the Release Deadline, irrespective of when the Executive executes the Release; provided, however, that where the Executive's termination of employment and the Release Deadline occur within the same calendar year, the payment may be made up to thirty (30) calendar days prior to the Release Deadline, and provided further that where Executive's termination of employment and the Release Deadline occur in two separate calendar years, payment may not be made before the later of January 1 of the second year or the date that is thirty (30) calendar days prior to the Release Deadline. As part of the Release, the Executive shall affirm that the Executive (i) has advised the Company in writing, of any facts that Executive is aware of that constitute or might constitute a violation of any ethical, legal, or contractual standards or obligations of the Company, and (ii) is not aware of any existing or threatened claims, charges, or lawsuits that the Executive has not disclosed to the Company.

9. **Compensation Recovery Policy.** Notwithstanding any provision in this Agreement to the contrary, payments under this Agreement will be subject to any Compensation Recovery Policy established by the Company and amended from time to time.

10. **Assignment; Successors.** This Agreement shall inure to the benefit of and be binding upon the Company and its successors. The Company may not assign this Agreement without the Executive's written consent, except that the Company's obligations under this Agreement shall be the binding legal obligations of any successor to the Company by sale, and in the event of any transaction that results in the transfer of substantially all of the assets or business of the Company, the Company will use its best efforts to cause the transferee to assume the obligations of the Company under this Agreement. The Executive may not assign this Agreement during the Executive's life. Upon the Executive's death this Agreement will inure to the benefit of Executive's heirs, legatees and legal representatives of the Executive's estate.

11. **Interpretation.** The laws of the State of _____ shall govern the validity, interpretation, construction and performance of this Agreement, without regard to the conflict of laws principles thereof. The jurisdiction and venue for any disputes arising under, or any action

brought to enforce (or otherwise relating to), this Agreement shall be exclusively in the courts in the State of _____, County of _____, including the Federal Courts located therein (should Federal jurisdiction exist).

12. **Withholding.** The Company may withhold from any payment that it is required to make under this Agreement amounts sufficient to satisfy applicable withholding requirements under any federal, state or local law.

13. **Amendment or Termination.** This Agreement may be amended at any time by written agreement between the Company and the Executive.

14. **Notices.** Notices given pursuant to this Agreement shall be in writing (including electronic) and shall be deemed received when personally delivered, or on the date of written confirmation of receipt by (i) overnight carrier, (ii) telecopy, (iii) registered or certified mail, return receipt requested, addressee only, postage prepaid, or (iv) such other method of delivery that provides a written confirmation of delivery. Notice to the Company shall be directed to:

ABC Corporation

_____

Attention: General Counsel

The Company may change the person and/or address to whom the Executive must give notice under this Section by giving the Executive written notice of such change, in accordance with the procedures described above. Notices to or with respect to the Executive will be directed to the Executive, or to the Executive's executors, personal representatives or distributees, if the Executive is deceased, or the assignees of the Executive, at the Executive's home address on the records of the Company.

15. **Removal from Any Boards and Positions.** Effective as of the Executive's date of termination for any reason whatsoever, Executive shall be deemed to resign (i) if a member, from the Board, or any other board to which Executive has been appointed or nominated by or on behalf of the Company and (ii) from any position or office with the Company.

16. **Code Section 409A.** If any payment under Section 5(d) or 6(a), does not qualify as a short-term deferral under Code Section 409A and Treas. Reg. § 1.409A-1(b)(4) (or any similar or successor provisions), and Executive is a Specified Employee as of the Termination Date, the Company will not make that payment to Executive before the date that is six months after Executive's Termination Date or, if earlier, the date of Executive's death (the "Six-Month Delay Rule"). Payments to which Executive otherwise would be entitled during the first six months following the Termination Date (the "Six-Month Delay") will be accumulated and paid on the first

day of the seventh month following the Termination Date. Notwithstanding the Six-Month Delay Rule set forth in this Section 16:

(a) To the maximum extent permitted under Code Section 409A and Treas. Reg. § 1.409A-1(b)(9)(iii) (or any similar or successor provisions), during each month of the Six-Month Delay, the Company will pay Executive an amount equal the lesser of (i) the monthly severance provided under Section 5(d) or 6(a), or (ii) one-sixth of the lesser of (1) the maximum amount that may be taken into account under a qualified plan pursuant to Code Section 401(a)(17) for the year in which Executive's date of termination occurs, and (2) the sum of Executive's annualized compensation based upon the annual rate of pay for services provided to the Company for the taxable year of Executive preceding the taxable year of Executive in which Executive's date of termination occurs (adjusted for any increase during that year that was expected to continue indefinitely if Executive had not had a termination); provided that amounts paid under this sentence will count toward, and will not be in addition to, the total payment amount required to be made to Executive by the Company under Section 5(d) or 6(a); and

(b) To the maximum extent permitted under Code Section 409A and Treas. Reg. § 1.409A-1(b)(9)(v)(D) (or any similar or successor provisions), within ten (10) days of the Termination Date, the Company will pay Executive an amount equal to the applicable dollar amount under Code Section 402(g)(1)(B) for the year of Executive's termination; provided that the amount paid under this sentence will count toward, and will not be in addition to, the total payment amount required to be made to Executive by the Company under Section 5(d) or 6(a).

(c) "Specified Employee" shall have the meaning, for purposes of this Agreement, given that term in Code Section 409A and Treas. Reg. § 1.409A-1(c)(i) (or any similar or successor provisions). The Company's "specified employee identification date" (as described in Treas. Reg. § 1.409A-1(c)(i)(3)) will be December 31 of each year, and the Company's "specified employee effective date" (as described in Treas. Reg. § 1.409A-1(c)(i)(4) or any similar or successor provisions) will be the specified employee effective date set forth in the Non-Qualified Deferred Compensation Plan or, if the Non-Qualified Plan does not set forth a specified employee effective date, February 1 of each succeeding year.

Notwithstanding any provision of this Agreement to the contrary, this Agreement is intended to be exempt from or, in the alternative, comply with Code Section 409A and the interpretive guidance thereunder, including the exceptions for short-term deferrals, separation pay arrangements, reimbursements, and in-kind distributions. It is intended that this Agreement and the Company's and Executive's exercise of authority or discretion hereunder shall comply with the provisions of Code Section 409A and the treasury regulations relating thereto so as not to subject Executive to the payment of interest and tax penalty which may be imposed under Code Section 409A. The Agreement shall be construed and interpreted in accordance with such intent.

17. **Severability.** If any provision(s) of this Agreement shall be found invalid or unenforceable by a court of competent jurisdiction, in whole or in part, then it is the parties' mutual desire that such court modify such provision(s) to the extent and in the manner necessary to render the same valid and enforceable, and this Agreement shall be construed and enforced to the maximum extent permitted by law, as if such provision(s) had been originally incorporated herein as so modified or restricted, or as if such provision(s) had not been originally incorporated herein, as the case may be.

18. **Entire Agreement.** This Agreement sets forth the entire agreement and understanding between the Company and the Executive and supersedes all prior agreements and understandings, written or oral, relating to the subject matter hereof.

19. **Consultation With Counsel.** The Executive acknowledges that the Executive has had a full and complete opportunity to consult with counsel of Executive's own choosing concerning the terms, enforceability and implications of this Agreement, and the Company has made no representations or warranties to Executive concerning the terms, enforceability or implications of this Agreement other than as are reflected in this Agreement.

20. **No Waiver.** No failure or delay by the Company or the Executive in enforcing or exercising any right or remedy hereunder shall operate as a waiver thereof. No modification, amendment or waiver of this Agreement nor consent to any departure by the Executive from any of the terms or conditions thereof, shall be effective unless in writing and signed by the Chairman of the Company's Board. Any such waiver or consent shall be effective only in the specific instance and for the purpose for which given.

21. **Mitigation and Set-Off.** The Executive will not be required to mitigate Executive's damages by seeking other employment or otherwise. Except as provided in Section 5(d)(ii), the Company's obligations under this Agreement shall not be reduced in any way by reason of any compensation or benefits received or foregone by Executive from sources other than the Company after Executive's employment termination, or any amounts that might have been received by Executive in other employment had Executive sought such other employment. Executive's entitlement to benefits and coverage under this Agreement shall continue after, and shall not be affected by Executive's obtaining other employment after, Executive's employment termination. Executive agrees that (i) any sums owed or owing in the future to the Company by Executive may be

deducted from Executive's paychecks or any bonus checks in amounts that are in accordance with applicable law, (ii) any sums owed to Executive's corporate charge card for reasons personal to Executive upon the termination of Executive's employment may be deducted by the Company from any outstanding paycheck in amounts that are in accordance with applicable law to make payments to the credit card company on Executive's behalf, and (iii) Executive will execute such authorizations as may be required by law, if any, to permit and effectuate such deductions.

22. **Survival.** All Sections of this Agreement survive beyond the Term except as otherwise specifically stated.

23. **Headings.** The headings in this Agreement are for convenience of reference only and shall not limit or otherwise affect the meaning thereof.

24. **Counterparts.** The parties may execute this Agreement in one or more counterparts, all of which together shall constitute but one Agreement.

IN WITNESS WHEREOF, the parties have executed this Agreement effective as of the date first above written.

	ABC Corporation
_____	By: _____
Executive D	Its: _____

¶10,020 CHECKLIST—Employment Agreement Checklist

The following is a checklist of many of the issues that an employment agreement could cover. The final agreement could cover as many or as few aspects of the employment relationship as the parties desire. The determination of which provisions to include in an employment agreement is a matter of business judgment for the board of directors and senior management, and subject to negotiation with the executive. For a discussion of executive employment agreements, see ¶101 *et seq.* For a discussion of parachute payment calculations, see ¶275.

EMPLOYMENT AGREEMENT CHECKLIST

_____ 1.   Title(s): _____

Board Membership?_____

_____ 2.   Office(s): _____

_____ 3.   Duties: _____

a.   May be increased? _____
b.   Carve out for other positions and fees? _____
c.   Location of duties: _____
d.   Travel Required? _____

_____ 4.   Term (automatic renewal?): _____
_____ 5.   Base Salary: _____

a.   automatic annual increases? _____
b.   annual board review to determine increases?_____
c.   May be increased but not decreased? _____

_____ 6.   Equity Compensation: _____
_____ 7.   Bonus(es) (signing bonus, guarantee of first year bonus?): _____
_____ 8.   Other Incentive Compensation (profit sharing, LTIP): _____
_____ 9.   Stock or Home Purchase Loan: _____
_____ 10.   Standard Benefits: _____

		Description, Amount, Limitations
a.	Medical insurance	
b.	Dental insurance	
c.	Vision insurance	
d.	Life insurance	
e.	Long-and short-term disability insurance	
f.	Qualified Retirement Plan(s) (401(k), pension plan)	

		Description, Amount, Limitations
g.	Nonqualified Retirement Plans(Deferred compensation, SERP)	
h.	Vacation	
i.	Reimbursement of expenses	
j.	Indemnification and D&O Insurance	
k.	Relocation assistance	

_____ 11. **Special Benefits Required for this Position:** (*e.g.*, cell phone, professional memberships and subscriptions, home computer equipment and connectivity)_____

_____ 12. **Other Benefits and Perquisites:** _____

		Yes - Amount	No
a.	Supplemental medical insurance		
b.	Executive physicals		
c.	Supplemental life insurance		
d.	Supplemental long- and short-term disability insurance		
e.	Employee stock purchase plan		
f.	Retiree Medical and Life Insurance		
g.	Company car, Limousine or Chauffeur (also discussed below)		
h.	Use of Company Aircraft		
i.	Spouse Travel (not deductible by employer)		
j.	Income Tax Preparation, Financial Counseling/Planning, Estate Planning		
k.	Club dues/fees (Employer's deduction disallowed for dues it pays to social, athletic, sporting and luncheon clubs, and airline, hotel and business clubs.)		
l.	Professional organization fees		
m.	Outplacement Services (also discussed below)		
n.	On-Premises Athletic Facilities (also discussed below)		
o.	Others		

_____ 13. **Special Tax-Favored Benefits and Perquisites:** _____
   a. Bona fide business-oriented security concern (Reg. § 1.132-5(m)): Car, Plane, Home? _____
   b. Company car:_____
   The amount of business use is excludable as a working condition fringe benefit. Personal use is taxable, generally based on the "annual lease value." Chauffeurs must be valued separately from the vehicle they drive.

    c.   Employer-provided meals: Meals furnished in-kind, from an eating facility owned or leased by the employer, located on the employer's premises, for the employer's convenience, during or immediately before or after the employees' workday, may be excludable from income.

    d.   Outplacement Services (excludable from executive's income as a working condition fringe)

    e.   On-Premises Athletic Facilities. Nontaxable.

    f.   Nontaxable Fringe Benefits: _____

_____ 14.   **Grounds for Termination: Severance Payments/Benefits upon Termination:**

    a.   Termination due to Death: _____

    b.   Termination due to Disability: _____

       i.   Defined: _____

       ii.   Who determines? If automatic, after how long? _____

       iii.   What result? _____

    c.   Termination by Company for Cause: _____

       i.   Defined: _____

       ii.   Who determines? Hearing? _____

       iii.   Notice and Opportunity to Cure? _____

       iv.   What result? _____

    d.   Termination by Company upon written notice (without Cause): _____

    e.   Termination by employee upon written notice: _____

    f.   Termination by Mutual Agreement: _____

    g.   Termination by Executive for Good Reason: _____

       i.   Defined: _____

       ii.   Notice and Opportunity to Cure? _____

       iii.   What result? _____

    h.   Termination by Executive following Company's notice of non-renewal: _____

    i.   Other: _____

_____ 15.   **Release of Claims Required to Receive Severance**

_____ 16.   **Change in Control Provision:** _____

    a.   Definition of "Change": _____

    b.   Single, double or modified trigger: _____

    c.   Protected Period after (and before) Change: _____

    d.   Payout Multiple: _____

    e.   Other Benefits: _____

    f.   Cause: _____

    g.   Good Reason: _____

    h.   Gross Up? _____

    i.   For private companies: consider whether the executive should have a right of first refusal to purchase company himself.

_____ 17.   **Code Section 409A Issues**

a.		Will severance payments qualify for an exception to the six-month delay rule of Code Sec. 409A?
b.		If not, how will the agreement apply the six-month delay rule of Code Sec. 409A?
_____ 18.		**Restrictive Covenants:**
	a.	Noncompete
	i.	duration: _____
	ii.	geographic scope: _____
	iii.	definition of "business conducted:" _____
	iv.	exceptions to application: _____
	b.	Nonsolicitation/employees (Y/N; duration) _____
	c.	Nonsolicitation/customers (Y/N; duration) _____
	d.	Confidential information (description of): _____
	e.	Inventions
_____ 19.		**Representations by Executive:**
_____ 20.		**Legal Fees to Negotiate Agreement?**
_____ 21.		**Expenses of Litigation of Arbitration?**
_____ 21.		**Choice of Law:** _____
_____ 23.		**Choice of Forum:** _____
_____ 24.		**Arbitration Provision:** _____
_____ 25.		**Provision to Limit Time for Filing Claims; superseding the otherwise applicable statute of limitations:**
_____ 26.		**Cooperation:**
_____ 27.		**Opportunity to Consult Legal Counsel:**
_____ 28.		**Successors:** (Will the contract be binding on the employer's successors or assigns?)
_____ 29.		**Drafting:** When representing Employer: Both parties participated.
_____ 30.		**Persons to Whom Notices Should Be Sent:**

Consider requiring Notice to Company's outside legal counsel.

_____ 31.		**Employment "At Will:"**
_____ 32.		**Severance Taxation Issues:**
_____ 33.		**Counterparts:** Each signed copy of the agreement is treated as an original:

¶10,030 CHECKLIST—Change in Control Agreements Checklist

The following is a checklist of many of the issues that a change in control or "golden parachute" agreement between a company and an executive could cover. Like an employment agreement, the change in control agreement will be a legal contract between the company and the executive, which sets forth the compensation and benefits payable to legal and business terms of the employment relationship. Either a public or a private company could use the provisions in this checklist. For a discussion of change in control, see ¶285.

CHECKLIST FOR CHANGE IN CONTROL AGREEMENTS

1. **Purpose**. The Company offers a change in control agreement to selected Executives ("Executive"). The agreement could specify the precise type of change in control the parties expect, or simply provide protection to the Executive in the event of any "Change in Control."

2. **Term of the Agreement**. Many change in control agreements provide for a fixed term of years. Many others provide for automatic extension for one or more years on each anniversary of the agreement's effective date, unless either party gives notice at least 180 days prior to end of year. Some agreements continue indefinitely, but provide that the Company could terminate it by giving notice to the Executive at least eighteen or twenty-four months prior to such termination.

3. **Single or Double Trigger**. Nearly all change in control agreements are so-called "double trigger" agreements. Double trigger agreements provide that the Company will pay only if the Company terminates the Executive's employment without "cause" or Executive terminates the Executive's employment with "Good Reason" after the change in control.

Investors and proxy advisory firms loathe "single trigger" agreements, which provide all amounts and benefits become payable upon the change in control, regardless of whether the Executive's employment is terminated. Some agreements contain a so-called modified trigger that provides a window period following a change in control during which the Executive can voluntarily terminate employment for any reason whatever, but investors and proxy advisory firms also loathe this feature. The window is generally open for thirty days, beginning six or twelve months after the change in control.

4. **Payment Amount/Period**. Another of the most significant design decisions in preparing a change in control agreement is the amount of payments. Most agreements provide for the Company to make payments equal to a multiple of the Executive's compensation, *e.g.*, one, two or three times.

    (a) The agreement should specify whether this multiple applies to the Executive's base salary only, or to the Executive's total annual compensation (including bonuses).

    (b) The agreement should specify whether the Company will (i) make payment in a single lump sum following Executive's qualifying employment termination, or (ii) continue the Executive's compensation for a specified period of time (*e.g.*, twelve, twenty-four, thirty-six months) at the same time and in the same manner before termination (possibly including the right to defer such amounts under the Company's deferred compensation program). Some agreements give the Executive an election as to whether to have salary continuation or payment of the lump sum present value.

5. **Parachute Payment Limits: Gross-Up, Best-After Tax, or Cap.** Another important issue in the design and drafting of change in control agreements is how to deal with the possibility of an excess parachute payment. As discussed in Chapter 2 (¶201, *et seq.*), the punitive effects of Code Sec. 280G and Code Sec. 4999 are so severe that the Company and the Executive nearly always deal with the possibility of an excess parachute payment in advance. Some change in control agreements are silent on the issue, but most deal with nondeductibility and excise tax limits in one of three ways:

(a) The Company's payments made under the agreement are limited to an amount that, when combined with all other payments to the Executive upon the change in control, would be $1 less than the amount that would constitute an excess parachute payment.

(b) The agreement contains a so-called best-after tax result feature, which provides that the agreement will pay the either (1) $1 less than the amount that would constitute an excess parachute payment, or (2) the uncapped amount with no gross up, which results in the Executive retaining the greater after-tax amount.

(c) The agreement requires the Company to make a gross up payment if payments under the agreement result in excess parachute payments, and the Executive is liable for the payment of an excise tax under Code Sec. 4999. However, investors and proxy advisory firms strongly disapprove of the gross-up feature.

6. **Protected Period**. The agreement would provide that if the Company terminates the Executive's employment without "cause" or Executive terminates the Executive's employment with "good reason" within a specified period after the change in control, *e.g.*, twelve, twenty-four, or thirty-six months, the Company must pay or provide specified benefits or amounts.

The agreement also should protect the Executive if the Company terminates the Executive's employment without cause or Executive terminates employment with good reason prior to the change in control, *e.g.*, during the period after the approval by the Company's stockholders and prior to the effective time of any transaction. This is to avoid the possibility that an acquirer will pressure the Company to terminate an Executive prior to the change in control to avoid payments.

7. **Payment/Continuation of Other Benefits and Amounts**. Among the amounts and benefits agreements commonly provide are the following:

• *Health and Welfare Benefits*. Most agreements provide for continued coverage by the medical [and other welfare] benefit plans maintained by the

Company, on the same basis and at the same cost to Executive as immediately before the change in control, until the earlier of (i) expiration of the severance period, or (ii) the date the Executive becomes covered by a plan that provides coverage or benefits at least equal to the applicable Company plan.

- *Nonqualified Plans.* Some agreements provide that the Company will pay the Executive a lump sum amount equal to the present value of the additional benefit that the Executive would have accrued under the Company's qualified and nonqualified retirement plans had the Executive continued to receive benefits thereunder from the date of termination through the last day of the benefit continuation period. Some agreements provide that the Company will fully vest all benefits under the Company's nonqualified retirement plans (to the extent not vested upon the change in control). Some agreements provide that the Company will add years to the Executive's age and years of service for purposes of determining the Executive's eligibility for and benefits under such plans.

- *Retiree Medical and Life Benefits.* Some agreements provide that the Company will add years to the Executive's age and benefit service for purposes of determining Executive's eligibility for and benefits under the Company's retiree medical and/or life insurance plan.

- *Outplacement.* Some agreements provide that the Company will provide outplacement services for a period of months.

8. Lapse of Stock Vesting Restrictions. Most agreements would provide that, upon a change in control, all restrictions lapse under any Executive compensation programs applicable to the Executive, including stock options, restricted stock, performance shares, and any amounts under a long-term incentive plan. These would be "single trigger" benefits.

9. Incentive Plans. Many agreements will provide for an accelerated or guaranteed lump sum cash payment to the Executive with respect to the Company's annual and long-term incentive plans. The agreement may provide that the Company will make a cash payment equal to the greater of: (i) the greatest annual bonus the Executive received during any of the three years preceding the change in control; (ii) the target bonus under the plan for the year of the change in control; or (iii) the average of the annual bonuses the Executive received during the three years preceding the change in control.

10. Retention Bonus (or Golden Handcuff). Some agreements would also provide that the Company will pay to the Executive a lump sum cash bonus after a change in control as a form of success fee or incentive to ensure the transaction closes.

11. Definitions. The change in control agreement should define a number of key terms, including "cause," "good reason," and "change in control." These definitions are critical to determining whether the agreement is more favorable to the Executive or the Company.

12. Miscellaneous.

(a) *Restrictive Covenants.* Most change in control agreements include the covenants of noncompetition, nondisclosure, nonsolicitation, nondisparagament, and/or cooperation in the agreements. This is partly to make them more palatable to a prospective purchaser. More importantly, however, restrictive covenants can count as "reasonable compensation for services rendered following a change in control" – in this case agreeing to forego the rendering of services – and, thus, reduce the amount of the total payment made to the Executive that will be counted as "parachute payments."

(b) *Arbitration.* Some change in control agreements require that the parties resolve any dispute or controversy arising under or in connection with the agreement by arbitration.

(c) *Litigation/Arbitration Expenses.* Some change in control agreements provide that the Company will pay to the Executive all out-of-pocket expenses, including attorneys' fees, incurred by the Executive in the event the Executive successfully enforces any provision of the agreement in any action, arbitration, or lawsuit.

(d) *Mitigation.* Some change in control agreements provide that the Executive need not mitigate the Executive's damages or seek other employment after termination following a change in control.

(e) *Continued Indemnification.* Some agreements provide that, following Executive's employment termination, the Company will (i) indemnify Executive for all acts and omissions of Executive that relate to Executive's employment with the Company, to the maximum extent permitted by law; and (ii) continue Executive's coverage under the directors' and officers' liability coverage maintained by the Company, as in effect from time to time, to the same extent as other current or former senior Executive officers and directors of the Company.

(f) *All Prior Agreements Superseded.* The Agreement would supersede and cancel any prior Severance Agreements between the Company and the Executive.

(g) *Choice of Law; Choice of Forum.* The agreement should specify the state law that would govern in the event of any disputes and county and state where any disputes must be resolved.

(h) *Future Amendments.* The agreement should provide that it can only be amended by written agreement between the Company and the Executive.

¶10,040 SAMPLE LEGAL AGREEMENT—Consulting/ Independent Contractor Agreement

The following is a sample consulting agreement between a company and an independent contractor, which sets forth the legal and business terms of the consulting/contracting relationship. No law requires a company and a consultant to set forth the terms of their relationship in a written agreement. However, many companies and consultants feel it is necessary to have some form of written agreement for their mutual protection. Either a public or private company or other business entity could use this sample agreement. For a discussion of consulting agreement provisions, see ¶325.

CONSULTING/INDEPENDENT CONTRACTOR AGREEMENT

This Consulting Agreement ("Agreement") is entered into effective as of this _____ day of _____, [year], between ABC Corporation ("Company") an [State] corporation, and _____ ("Consultant").

WHEREAS, Company wishes to enter into a consulting relationship with Consultant; and

WHEREAS, Consultant desires to enter into a consulting relationship with Company upon the terms and conditions hereinafter contained;

NOW, THEREFORE, in consideration of the covenants and agreements herein set forth and of the mutual benefits accruing to Company and to Consultant from the consulting relationship to be established between the parties by the terms of this Agreement, Company and Consultant agree as follows:

1. **Consulting Relationship.** Company hereby retains Consultant, and Consultant hereby agrees to be retained by Company, as an independent consultant, and not as an employee.

2. **Consulting Services.** Consultant agrees that during the term of this Agreement:

    (a) Consultant will devote his/her best efforts to his/her position as an independent consultant and will perform such duties and execute the policies of Company as determined by its board of directors; [provided that said duties and policies will not be inconsistent with the nature of the duties performed by Consultant during his/her active service with Company as an officer and employee thereof;]

    (b) Consultant shall exercise a reasonable degree of skill and care in performing the services referred to in paragraph (a) above;

    (c) Consultant shall give Company a list of all other companies, organizations or persons for whom Consultant currently performs services and shall continually update that list during the consulting relationship provided for by this Agreement;

    (d) Consultant shall be available to render services to Company under this Agreement for a minimum of at least _____ days during any 12-month period commencing on the date of this Agreement, or any anniversary thereof and shall not be obligated to render in excess of days of service during any such 12-month period. Consultant shall not be obligated to render any services under this Agreement during any such period when he/she is unable to do so due to illness, disability or injury; and

(e) Consultant shall be available for service hereunder upon receipt of five days' written notice from Company.

3. **Compensation.** Company agrees to pay Consultant for his/her services performed under this Agreement at the rate of $____ per month whether or not services are actually rendered hereunder. In addition, Company agrees to pay Consultant at the rate of $_____ per day for services actually rendered hereunder, payable in monthly or more frequent installments. Consultant shall also be entitled to reimbursement for expenses authorized in writing by Company in advance and incurred by Consultant in the performance of his/her duties hereunder. Consultant shall not be entitled to participate in or receive benefits under any Company programs maintained for its employees, including, without limitation, life, medical and disability benefits, pension, profit sharing or other retirement plans or other fringe benefits. If Consultant is subsequently classified by the IRS as a common law employee, Consultant expressly waives his/her rights to any benefits to which he/she was, or might have become, entitled.

4. **Other Conditions.** Company shall, at its expense, provide Consultant with appropriate and sufficient space in order to allow Consultant to perform his/her duties hereunder. Consultant shall have no authority over any employee or officer of Company, except as may be necessary in the routine performance of his/her duties hereunder, nor shall Company be required in any manner to implement any plans or suggestions Consultant may provide.

5. **Support, Supplies and Office Space.** [ONLY For Very Favored Consultants, *e.g.*, Former CEO] Company will provide Consultant with suitable administrative support during the Term including, among other things, secretarial support, photocopying and facsimile services, voice mail access, remote e-mail access, message taking services, mail receipt, office furniture, utilities, office equipment, and office supplies.

6. **Term.** The term of this Agreement shall begin on the date first written above and shall continue until terminated in accordance with the provisions set forth below.

(a) *Notice.* This Agreement may be terminated by either party by not less than two weeks' prior written notice except as provided in the Letter Agreements.

(b) *Breach or Injurious Conduct.* Company may terminate this Agreement at any time without notice if (i) Consultant breaches any provision of this Agreement or (ii) Consultant engages in conduct which, in the judgment of the President of Company, is injurious to Company.

(c) *Death or Disability*. In the event of Consultant's death or total disability this Agreement shall terminate as of the date of death or disability.

7. **Restrictive Covenants**. In the course of Consultant's consulting services hereunder, Consultant will acquire valuable trade secrets, proprietary data and other confidential information, with respect to Company's business. The parties hereto agree that such trade secrets, proprietary data and other confidential information include but are not limited to the following: the inventions, models, processes, patents, copyrights, and improvements thereon, Company's business and financial methods and practices, pricing and selling techniques, file or data base materials, price lists, software listings or printouts, computer programs, lists of Company's clients, client record cards, client files, credit and financial data of Company's suppliers and present and prospective clients, and particular business requirements of Company's present and prospective clients, as well as similar information relating to the parent, subsidiaries and affiliates of Company. In addition, Consultant, on behalf of Company, may develop a personal acquaintance with clients and prospective clients of Company, its parent, subsidiaries and affiliates. As a consequence thereof, the parties hereto acknowledge that Consultant will occupy a position of trust and confidence with respect to Company's affairs, products and services.

In view of the foregoing and in consideration of the remuneration to be paid to Consultant, Consultant acknowledges that it is reasonable and necessary for the protection of the goodwill and business of Company that Consultant make the covenants contained in this section regarding the conduct of Consultant during and subsequent to Consultant's rendering of services to Company, and that Company will suffer irreparable injury if Consultant engages in conduct prohibited thereby. Consultant represents that his/her experience and abilities are such that observance of the aforementioned covenants will not cause Consultant any undue hardship or unreasonably interfere with Consultant's ability to earn a livelihood.

The covenants contained in this section shall each be construed as a separate agreement independent of any other provisions of this Agreement, and the existence of any claim or cause of action of Consultant against Company, whether predicated on this Agreement or otherwise, shall not constitute a defense to the enforcement by Company of any of those covenants.

(a) *Trade Secrets and Confidential Information*. Consultant, during the term of the Agreement or at any time thereafter, will not, without the express written consent of Company, directly or indirectly communicate or divulge to, or use for his/her own benefit or for the benefit of any other person, firm, association or corporation, any of Company's or its parent's or subsidiaries' or affiliates' trade secrets, proprietary data or other confidential information including, which trade secrets, proprietary data and other confidential information were communicated to or otherwise learned or acquired by Consultant in the course of the consulting relationship covered by this Agreement, except that Consultant may disclose such matters to the extent that disclosure is required (i) in the course of the consulting relationship with Company or (ii) by a court or other governmental agency of competent jurisdiction. As long as such matters remain trade secrets, proprietary data or other confidential information, Consultant will not use such trade secrets, proprietary data or other confidential information in any way or in any capacity other than as a consultant of Company and to further Company's interests.

(b) *Company Clientele.* For a period of two years following the termination of this Agreement for any reason whatsoever (or if this period shall be unenforceable by law, then for such period as shall be enforceable), Consultant will not contact (with a view towards selling any product or service competitive with any product or service sold or proposed to be sold by Company or its parent or any subsidiary or affiliate of Company at the time of termination of this Agreement) any person, firm, association or corporation (i) to which Company or its parent or any subsidiary or affiliate of Company sold any product or service, (ii) which Consultant solicited, contacted or otherwise dealt with on behalf of Company or its parent or any subsidiary or affiliate of Company, or (iii) which Consultant was otherwise aware was a client of Company or its parent or any subsidiary or affiliate of Company, during the year preceding the termination of this Agreement. Consultant will not directly or indirectly make any such contact, either for his/her own benefit or for the benefit of any other person, firm, association, or corporation, and Consultant will not in any manner assist any person, firm, association, or corporation to make any such contact.

(c) *Nonsolicitation.* For a period of two years following the termination of this Agreement for any reason whatsoever (or if this period shall be unenforceable by law, then for such period as shall be enforceable), Consultant shall not induce or attempt to induce any employee, consultant or independent contractor of Company to leave the service of Company, or in any way interfere with the relationship between Company and any employee, consultant or independent contractor.

(d) *Judicial Modification.* If the final judgment of a court of competent jurisdiction declares that any term or provision of this Section is invalid or unenforceable, the parties agree that (i) the court making the determination of invalidity or unenforceability shall have the power to reduce the scope, duration, or geographic area of the term or provision, to delete specific words or phrases, or to replace any invalid or unenforceable term or provision with a term or provision that is valid and enforceable and that comes closest to expressing the intention of the invalid or unenforceable term or provision, (ii) the parties shall request that the court exercise that power, and (iii) this Agreement shall be enforceable as so modified after the expiration of the time within which the judgment or decision may be appealed.

(e) *Relief.* In the event of a breach or a threatened or intended breach of this Agreement by Consultant, Company shall be entitled, in addition to remedies otherwise available to Company at law or in equity, to the following particular forms of relief:

  (i) In the event Consultant breaches the restrictive covenants of paragraph (a), (b) or (c), Company shall be entitled to injunctions, both preliminary and permanent, enjoining such breach or threatened or intended breach, and Consultant hereby consents to the issuance thereof forthwith in any court of competent jurisdiction.

  (ii) In the event Company shall enforce any part of this Agreement through legal proceedings, Consultant agrees to pay to Company any costs and attorney's fees reasonably incurred by Company in connection therewith.

(f) *Blue Pencil.* The Consultant acknowledges and agrees that the non-competition non-solicitation and other restrictive covenant provisions contained herein are reasonable and valid in geographic, temporal and subject matter scope and in all other respects, and do not impose limitations greater than are necessary to protect the goodwill, Secret or Confidential Information and other business interests of the Company. Nevertheless, if any court or arbitrator determines that any of said non-competition, non-solicitation, or other restrictive covenants and agreements, or any provision thereof, is unenforceable because of the duration or geographic scope of such provision, such court or arbitrator will have the power to reduce the duration, geographic scope, or other scope of such provision, as the case may be; and, in its reduced form, such provision will then be enforceable to the maximum extent permitted by applicable law.

(g) *Tolling of Restrictive Periods.* If Consultant breaches any of the restrictions set forth in this Section above and the Company commences a legal proceeding in connection therewith, the time period applicable to each such restriction shall be tolled and extended for a period of time equal to the period of time during which the Consultant is determined by a court of competent jurisdiction to be in non-compliance or breach (not to exceed the duration set forth in the applicable restriction) commencing on the date of such determination.

(h) *Protected Rights.* Consultant understands that nothing contained in this Agreement limits Consultant ability to file a charge or complaint with the Equal Employment Opportunity Commission, the National Labor Relations Board, the Occupational Safety and Health Administration, the Securities and Exchange Commission or any other federal, state or local governmental agency or commission ("Government Agencies"). Consultant further understands that this Agreement does not limit the Consultant's ability to communicate with any Government Agencies or otherwise participate in any investigation or proceeding that may be conducted by any Government Agency, including providing documents or other information, without notice to the Company. This Agreement does not limit the Consultant's right to receive an award for information provided to any Government Agencies.

The taking of any action by Company or the forbearance of Company to take any action shall not constitute a waiver by Company of any of its rights to remedies or relief under this Agreement or under law or equity.

8. **Title to Certain Tangible Property**. All tangible materials (whether original or duplicates) including, but not in any way limited to, equipment purchase agreements, file or data base materials in whatever form, books, manuals, sales literature, equipment price lists, training materials, client record cards, client files, correspondence, documents, contracts, orders, messages, memoranda, notes, agreements, invoices, receipts, lists, software listings or printouts, specifications, models, computer programs, and records of any kind in the possession or control of Consultant which in any way relate or pertain to Company's business, including the business of the parent or subsidiaries or affiliates of Company, whether furnished to Consultant by Company or prepared, compiled or acquired by Consultant during his/her consulting relationship with Company, shall be the sole property of Company. At any time upon request of Company, and in any event promptly upon termination of this Agreement, Consultant shall deliver all such materials to Company. Company shall be under no obligation to pay to Consultant any sums of money then due Consultant or becoming due thereafter until Consultant has complied with the provisions of this section.

9. **Title to Certain Intangible Property**. Consultant shall immediately disclose and assign to Company all his/her right, title and interest in any inventions, models, processes, patents, copyrights and improvements thereon relating to services or processes or products of Company that he/she conceives or acquires during any consulting relationship with Company or that he/she may conceive or acquire during a period of one year after termination of this Agreement.

¶ 10,040

10. **Consultant's Representations.** Consultant hereby represents to Company that he/she: (1) is not a party to any contract that would preclude him from accepting this position, and (2) has no reason to believe that accepting Company position would inevitably result in a disclosure of any confidential information of any prior employer.

11. **Indemnity and Insurance.** [ONLY For Very Favored Consultants, *e.g.*, Former CEO] To the fullest extent permitted by law, Consultant shall indemnify and hold harmless Company against all claims, damages, losses (including but not limited to the loss of use of property) and expenses (including but not limited to attorneys' fees) arising out of or resulting from the performance of consulting services covered by this Agreement caused in whole or in part by any negligent or willful act or omission of Consultant.

12. **General.**

    (a) *Entire Agreement.* Any existing understandings or agreements between Company and Consultant are fully superseded by this Agreement and are null and void. Consultant and Company warrant that no promise or inducement has been offered or made except as herein set forth and that the consideration stated herein is the sole consideration for this Agreement. This Agreement constitutes the entire agreement between Company and Consultant, and states fully all agreements, understandings, promises and commitments between the parties.

    (b) *Amendment.* This Agreement may only be amended by written agreement between Company and Consultant.

    (c) *Notices.* Any notice or request specifically provided for or permitted to be given under this Agreement must be in writing (including electronic). Notice may be served in any manner, including by facsimile or nationally recognized overnight courier service, but shall be deemed delivered and effective as of the time of actual delivery thereof to the addressee. For purposes of notice, the addresses of the parties shall be as follows:

If to Company, to

ABC Corporation

_____

_____

Attention: _____

If to Consultant, to

_____

_____

_____

Each party named above may change its address and that of its representative for notice by the giving of notice thereof in the manner hereinabove provided.

(d) *Assignability.* This Agreement may not be assigned by either party without the prior written consent of the other party, except that no consent is necessary for Company to assign this Agreement to a corporation succeeding to substantially all the assets or business of Company whether by merger, consolidation, acquisition, or otherwise. This Agreement shall be binding upon Consultant, his/her heirs and permitted assigns and Company, its successors and permitted assigns.

(e) *Severability.* Each of the sections in this Agreement shall be enforceable independently of every other section in this Agreement, and the invalidity or nonenforceability of any section shall not invalidate or render nonenforceable any other section contained herein. If any section or provision in a section is found invalid or unenforceable, it is the intent of the parties that a court of competent jurisdiction shall reform the section or provisions to produce its nearest enforceable economic equivalent.

(f) *Applicable Law.* This Agreement will be governed by and construed under the laws of the State of _____, determined without regard to its conflicts of law rules, except as such laws are preempted by the laws of the United States. If any provision of this Agreement shall be held by a court of competent jurisdiction to be invalid or unenforceable, the remaining provisions hereof shall continue to be fully effective. The jurisdiction and venue for any disputes arising under, or any action brought to enforce (or otherwise relating to), this Agreement shall be exclusively in the courts in the State of _____, County of _____, including the Federal Courts located therein (should Federal jurisdiction exist).

(g) *Construction.* The headings in this Agreement are inserted for convenience and identification only and are not intended to describe, interpret, define or limit the scope, extent, or intent of this Agreement or any provision hereof. Each party has cooperated in the preparation of this Agreement. As a result, this Agreement shall not be construed against any party on the basis that the party was the draftsperson.

(h) *Arbitration.* Except for action by Company to enforce the restrictive covenants of Section 6, any dispute, controversy or difference which may arise between the parties hereto out of or in relation to or in connection with this Agreement or for the breach thereof which cannot be settled amicably by the parties within thirty (30) days shall be finally and exclusively settled by arbitration in _____, in accordance with the Commercial Arbitration Rules of the American Arbitration Association then in effect.

(i) *Taxes and Statutory Obligations.* As an independent contractor, Consultant will be solely responsible for all taxes, withholdings, and other similar statutory obligations, relating to his/her service and compensation under this Agreement, including, but not limited to, workers' compensation insurance laws if and to the extent applicable. No regular deductions or withholdings will be made from any payment to Consultant in his/her role as Consultant. For all purposes, including, but not limited to, deductions and payments pursuant to the Internal Revenue Code, the Federal Insurance Contributions Act, the Social Security Act, the Federal Unemployment Tax Act, _____ state income tax withholding, _____ unemployment taxes, _____ state disability insurance, and all other federal, state and local laws, rules and regulations, Consultant shall be treated as an independent contractor and not as an employee. Consultant shall file all tax returns, tax declarations and tax schedules, and pay all taxes required, when due, with respect to the consulting fees payable to him under this Agreement. Company will not withhold any employment taxes from the consulting fees payable to Consultant under this Agreement. Rather, Company will report the amounts it pays Consultant (or his/her designee) on an IRS Form 1099 or other similar, legally applicable form, to the extent required to do so under applicable Internal Revenue Code provisions and/or state or local law. Consultant shall indemnify Company against any liabilities or debts it may incur or suffer arising out of Consultant's failure to properly withhold or pay any applicable taxes.

(j) *Section 409A.* This Agreement is intended to be exempt from, or compliant with, Code Section 409A. Notwithstanding the foregoing or any provision of this Agreement, if any provision of this Agreement contravenes Code Section 409A or could cause Company or Consultant to incur any tax, interest or penalties under Code Section 409A, Company may, in its sole discretion and without Consultant's consent, modify such provision to (i) comply with, or avoid being subject to, Code Section 409A, or to avoid the incurrence of taxes, interest and penalties under Code Section 409A, and/or (ii) maintain, to the maximum extent practicable, the original intent and economic benefit to Consultant of the applicable provision without materially increasing the cost to Company or contravening the provisions of Code Section 409A. Company does not guarantee that any payments under this Agreement will not be subject to interest and penalties under Code Section 409A.

(k) *Survival.* All Sections of this Agreement survive beyond the Consulting Term except as otherwise specifically stated.

(l) *Counterparts.* This Agreement may be executed in any number of counterparts with the same effect as if each of the parties had signed the same document. All counterparts shall be construed together and shall constitute one and the same instrument.

IN WITNESS WHEREOF, the parties hereto have executed this Agreement as of the day and the year first above written.

_____   **ABC Corporation**

Consultant   By:_____

Its:_____

¶10,060 SAMPLE CORRESPONDENCE—Sample Offer Letter

The following is a sample of a letter by which a company could offer employment to an executive candidate. Because the offer letter is a form of enforceable employment agreement, it should cover the most significant aspects of the future employment relationship, including matters that the employment agreement will spell out in detail. Either a public or private company or other business entity could use this sample letter. For a discussion of offer letters, see ¶195.

SAMPLE OFFER LETTER

[ABC Corporation Letterhead]

_____, 2018

Mr/s. Executive

_____

_____

_____

_____

RE: ___ Offer of Employment

Dear _____:

We are all very excited about your interest in ABC Corporation and the prospects for a great future for ABC Corporation under your leadership. Accordingly, we are offering employment to you on the following terms:

1. **Title**. The offer is to become ABC Corporation [President and Chief Executive Officer.] [ABC Corporation also would appoint you as a member of its board of directors.]

2. **Employment Contract**. Your employment contract would provide for an initial term of three years. Thereafter, the contract would automatically continue from year to year unless either you or ABC gives notice of the intention not to renew the contract at least 90 days before the end of the year. The contract would provide that, if ABC Corporation terminates your employment without cause (or you resign due to a diminution of your duties), you would receive two year's continuation of salary, bonus, and benefits.

3. **Annual Salary**. Your annual salary would be [$_____]. Each year, beginning January 1, [year], the Board would meet to consider an increase in your base salary.

4. **Annual Incentive Bonus**. You would be eligible for an annual cash bonus, based on performance, and calculated as a percentage of your base salary. The target bonus level would be [50%] of your annual base salary. The maximum bonus opportunity would be [100%] of your annual base salary. ABC Corporation Board of Directors will set the threshold, target, and maximum performance levels, after consultation

with you. Your bonus for [year] will be at least [25%] of your annual base salary.

5. **Long-Term Incentive**. ABC Corporation would initially grant you a nonqualified stock option to purchase [10,000] shares of its common stock. The options' exercise price will be the fair market value of a share of ABC Corporation stock. The options would become vested as follows: 20% immediately on the grant date, and 20% on each anniversary of the grant date (full vesting on the fourth anniversary of the grant date). The options also would become fully vested on the effective date of a change in control of ABC. ABC Corporation would consider granting additional options in future years.

6. **Change in Control Protection**. Your employment contract would provide that, if your employment is terminated without cause (or constructively terminated) within two years following a change in control of ABC Corporation, you would receive two years continuation of salary, bonus, and benefits.

7. **Qualified Retirement Plan**. You will be eligible to participate in the ABC Corporation 401(k) Plan, which provides for a [50% matching contribution up to the first 4%] of a participant's contribution, subject to Internal Revenue Code limits.

8. **Nonqualified Retirement Plan**. ABC Corporation will establish a Supplemental Executive Retirement Plan that pays you an annual retirement benefit of [$_____], beginning at age 65 and continuing for ten years. You will be fully and immediately vested in this benefit.

9. **Health and Welfare Benefits**. You would be covered by ABC Corporation medical and dental benefit plans, and life and short- and long-term disability insurance plans.

10. **Vacation**. You will be entitled to [four] weeks paid vacation.

11. **Automobile Allowance**. ABC Corporation will pay you an automobile allowance of up to [$___] per month.

12. **Relocation Benefit**. ABC Corporation will reimburse your reasonable expenses in relocating to [City, State] metropolitan area from _____, including: (i) moving expenses, (ii) "home visit" expenses, and (iii) real estate commissions on the sale of your current residence (if you are able to sell your current residence without a real estate broker, ABC Corporation will discuss with you some other form of compensation).

13. **Restrictive Covenants**. In your employment contract, you must represent to ABC Corporation that you: (1) are not a party to any contract that would preclude you from accepting this position, and (2) have no reason to believe that accepting the ABC Corporation job would inevitably result in a disclosure of any confidential information of any prior employer. Your employment contract and any other agreements would provide the following restrictive covenants:

¶10,060

    (a) A noncompete provision that continues as long as the remaining contract period; and

    (b) A standard confidentiality provision.

14. **Prior Employment**. You will not use during your ABC Corporation employment, disclose to ABC Corporation, bring onto ABC Corporation's premises, or access using ABC Corporation systems or equipment any trade secret or other information that you are required to keep confidential relating to your former employer(s).

15. **Background Verification**. ABC Corporation's offer of employment is conditioned upon a completion of a background check (which may include a criminal history check, confirmation of prior employment, credit check, and confirmation of educational background), the results of which must be satisfactory to ABC in its sole discretion. You agree to execute all documentation and take all actions necessary for completion of the background check. You understand that your offer of employment can be rescinded, or your employment can be terminated, based on your background check results.

16. **U.S. Employment Authorization**. Verification of your authorization to work in the United States is required for your position, and you understand that you must complete a Form I-9, Employee Eligibility Verification, within the first three days of your employment.

17. **ABC Corporation's Code of Conduct**. Ongoing compliance with ABC Corporation's Code of Conduct, including its provisions prohibiting conflicts of interest, is required. ABC requires annual Code of Conduct training and that new hires complete Code of Conduct training within the first 30 days of employment.

This offer is contingent on ABC Corporation obtaining verification of the representations you have made to us regarding your employment with XYZ, Inc.

I believe this offer reflects our collective understanding of your expectations and I look forward to hearing from you. In that regard, we will need to have your response by 5 p.m. C.S.T., Friday, _____, [year].

Cordially yours,

Chairman of the Board,

ABC Corporation

cc. [Company Counsel]

¶10,100 SAMPLE LEGAL AGREEMENT—Sample Retention Payment Plan

The following is a sample of a retention payment plan. An employer may decide to establish a retention plan during a period of uncertainty or transition, such as an acquisition or bankruptcy. The plan should set forth the legal rights and obligation of the employer and of covered employees. Either a public or private company or other business entity could use this sample plan. A "decision tree" to assist the employer in making critical design decisions for its retention plan can be found at ¶10,120. For a discussion of retention benefit plans, see ¶1425.

SAMPLE RETENTION PAYMENT PLAN

ABC Corporation Retention Payment Plan

ABC Corporation ("ABC") hereby adopts this ABC Corporation Retention Bonus Plan (the "Plan") for its eligible employees and the eligible employees of its Subsidiaries, effective as of _____, [year] (the "Effective Date"). The purpose of the Plan is to encourage eligible employees to continue their employment with ABC and its Subsidiaries during the transition of ABC ownership to Acquiror Company ("Acquiror").

Article I — Definitions

Wherever used herein the following terms shall have the meanings hereinafter set forth:

1.1. "Board" means the Board of Directors of ABC.

1.2. "Committee" means the ABC Benefit Administration Committee, which is responsible for the administration of the Plan.

1.3. "Disability" means an Eligible Employee becomes: (i) entitled to benefits under ABC's group long-term disability plan; or (ii) permanently and totally disabled as determined in the sole discretion of the Committee.

1.4. "Eligible Employee" means each employee of ABC and its Subsidiaries occupying, on the Effective Date, a position in [salary grades C through G], as such salary grades are designated in the salary matrix approved by the Board in [year]. The Committee from time to time shall have the discretion to designate additional key employees of ABC or its Subsidiaries as Eligible Employees for purposes of the Plan. An Eligible Employee who is demoted out of a covered salary grade will continue as an Eligible Employee.

1.5. "ABC" means ABC Corporation, a [Delaware] corporation, or, to the extent provided in Section 3.8 below, any successor corporation or other entity resulting from a merger or consolidation into or with ABC or a transfer or sale of substantially all of the assets of ABC.

1.6. "Retention Payment" means the amount payable to an Eligible Employee under the terms of the Plan.

1.7. "Retention Payment Pool" means the amount ABC establishes for paying Retention Payments, including Special Retention Payments. The Retention Payment Pool is [$_____.]

1.8. "Special Retention Payment" means an amount payable to an Eligible Employee or other management employee of ABC (not limited to employees in the Alpha grade ranks) in special situations.

1.9. "Special Retention Payment Pool" means a portion of the Retention Payment Pool equal to [$_____].

1.10. "Subsidiary" means a business entity that is a direct or indirect, wholly-owned subsidiary of ABC.

Article II — Amount of Retention Payment

2.1. *Amount of Retention Payment.* The amount of each Eligible Employee's Retention Payment will be determined as follows:

Salary Grade	Retention Payment
C	$300,000
D	250,000
E	200,000
F	150,000
G	131,250

If the Committee designates any other key employee of ABC or its Subsidiaries as an Eligible Employee for purposes of the Plan, the Board designation also shall specify the total Retention Payment amount or Special Retention Payment amount to be paid to such Eligible Employee from the Retention Payment Pool or from the Special Retention Payment Pool.

2.2. *Payment of Retention Payment.* The Retention Payment will be paid in two approximately equal installments to each Eligible Employee who is still employed by ABC or its Subsidiaries on the date of such installment, as follows:

(a) The first installment will be paid on the earlier of the date of United States approves (subject to conditions acceptable to Acquiror) of the merger of ABC into Acquiror (the "Control Date"), or [date]; and

(b) The second installment will be paid on [date].

Notwithstanding the foregoing, a Retention Payment will be paid to an Eligible Employee whose employment with ABC and its Subsidiaries is terminated under the following circumstances: death, Disability, transfer to employment within the Acquiror controlled group, by ABC or Acquiror, without Cause, or by the Eligible Employee with Good Reason. The terms "Cause" and "Good Reason" will have the same meanings as defined in the ABC Corporation 2018 Stock Incentive Plan, as amended.

2.3. *Payment of Special Retention Payment.* A Special Retention Payment may be paid from the Special Retention Payment Pool in special situations that arise among management employees of ABC and its Subsidiaries (not limited to employees in the Alpha grade ranks). A Special Retention Payment may be used to encourage an employee to remain employed by ABC. In the event a situation arises where a Special Retention Payment may be appropriate, requests may be made to the Committee for its deliberation and approval. The Retention Payment may be paid in a single sum or in approximately equal installments, as determined by the Committee. The Committee's determination as to the amount and payment of any Special Retention Payment will be final.

2.4. *Reallocation of Forfeited Retention Payment Amounts.* The amount of any Retention Payment that is not paid to any Eligible Employee due to such Eligible Employee's termination of employment from ABC or its Subsidiaries prior to the date of one or both of the installments payable under Section 2.1, and for a reason other than those described in Section 2.2, shall be credited to the Retention Payment Pool and allocated among Eligible Employees in a manner determined by the Board in its sole discretion.

Article III — General Provisions

3.1. *Administration by the Committee.* The Committee shall administer the Plan in accordance with its terms and shall have all powers necessary to carry out the provisions of the Plan. The Committee shall interpret the Plan and shall determine all questions arising in the administration, interpretation, and application of the Plan, including but not limited to, questions of eligibility and the status and rights of employees, Eligible Employees and other persons. Any such determination by the Committee shall presumptively be conclusive and binding on all persons.

3.2. *Amendment or Termination.* ABC may amend the Plan by resolution of the Board, provided that no amendment of the Plan will reduce the amount of Retention Payment payable to an Eligible Employee without the written consent of that Eligible Employee.

3.3. *Compensation Recovery Policy.* Notwithstanding any provision in the Plan or any Agreement to the contrary, payments under the Plan will be subject to any Compensation Recovery Policy established by ABC Corporation and amended from time to time.

3.4. *No Enlargement of Employee Rights.* Establishment of the Plan shall not be construed to give any Eligible Employee the right to be retained in the service of ABC or its Subsidiaries.

3.5. *Spendthrift Provision.* No interest of any person or entity in, or right to receive a distribution under, the Plan shall be subject in any manner to sale, transfer, assignment, pledge, attachment, garnishment, or other alienation or encumbrance of any kind; nor may such interest or right to receive a distribution be taken, either voluntarily or involuntarily for the satisfaction of the debts of, or other obligations or claims against, such person or entity, including claims for alimony, support, separate maintenance and claims in bankruptcy proceedings.

3.6. *Applicable Law.* To the extent not preempted by federal law, the Plan shall be construed, administered and governed in all respects under and by the laws of the State of _____, without giving effect to its conflict of laws principles. If any provision of the Plan shall be held by a court of competent jurisdiction to be invalid or unenforceable, the remaining provisions hereof shall continue to be fully effective. The jurisdiction and venue for any disputes arising under, or any action brought to enforce (or otherwise relating to), the Plan shall be exclusively in the courts in the State of _____, County of _____, including the Federal Courts located therein (should Federal jurisdiction exist).

3.7. *Incapacity of Recipient.* Subject to applicable state law, if any person entitled to a payment under the Plan is deemed by the Committee to be incapable of personally receiving and giving a valid receipt for such payment, then, unless and until claim therefor shall have been made by a duly appointed guardian or other legal representative of such person, the Committee may provide for such payment or any part thereof to be made to any other person or institution then contributing toward or providing for the care and maintenance of such person. Any such payment shall be a payment for the account of such person and a complete discharge of any liability of ABC and the Plan therefor.

3.8. *Corporate Successors.* The Plan shall be continued after the merger or consolidation of ABC into or with any other corporation or other entity.

3.9. *Limitations on Liability.* Notwithstanding any of the preceding provisions of the Plan, neither any member of the Board or the Committee, nor any individual acting as an employee or agent of ABC or the Committee, shall be liable to any Eligible Employee or any beneficiary or other person for any claim, loss, liability or expense incurred in connection with the Plan.

3.10. *Code Section 409A.* This Plan and any Retention Payments made hereunder are intended to comply with Code Section 409A and the interpretative guidance thereunder, including the exceptions for short-term deferrals, separation pay arrangements, reimbursements, and in-kind distributions, and shall be administered accordingly. This Plan and any Retention Payments shall be construed and interpreted with such intent. Each Retention Payment under the Plan or any ABC Corporation benefit plan is intended to be treated as one of a series of separate payments for purposes of Code Section 409A and Treasury Regulation § 1.409A-2(b)(2)(iii). Any Retention Payment under the Plan that is subject to Code Section 409A will not be made before the date that is six (6) months after the date of termination or, if earlier, the date of the Eligible Employee's death (the "Six-Month Delay Rule") if the Eligible Employee is a Specified Employee (as defined below) as of the Eligible Employee's termination of employment. Payments to which the Eligible Employee otherwise would be entitled during the first six months following the Eligible Employee's termination of employment (the "Six-Month Delay") will be accumulated and paid on the first day of the seventh month following the Eligible Employee's termination of employment. Notwithstanding the Six-Month Delay Rule, to the maximum extent permitted under Code Section 409A and Treasury Regulation § 1.409A-1(b)(9)(iii) (or any similar or successor provisions), during the Six-Month Delay, the Corporation will pay the Eligible Employee an amount equal to the lesser of (A) the total amount scheduled to be provided under Section 2.1 above, or (B) two times the lesser of (1) the maximum amount that may be taken into account under a qualified plan pursuant to Code Section 401(a)(17) for the year in which the Eligible Employee's termination of employment occurs, and (2) the sum of the Eligible Employee's annualized compensation based upon the annual rate of pay for services provided to the Corporation for the taxable year of the Eligible Employee preceding the taxable year of the Eligible Employee in which termination of employment occurs; provided that amounts paid under this sentence will count toward, and will not be in addition to, the total payment amount required to be made to the Eligible Employee by the Corporation under Section 2.1 above. For purposes of this Agreement, the term "Specified Employee" has the meaning given to that term in Code Section 409A and Treasury Regulation § 1.409A-1(i) (or other similar or successor provisions). ABC Corporation's "specified employee identification date" (as described in Treasury Regulation § 1.409A-1(i)(3) or any similar or successor provisions) will be December 31 of each year, and ABC Corporation's "specified employee effective date" (as described in Treasury Regulation § 1.409A-1(i)(4) or any similar or successor provisions) will be April 1 of each succeeding year.

¶10,110 SAMPLE LEGAL AGREEMENT—Sample Retention Payment Letter Agreement

The following is a sample of a retention letter agreement. Employers may use a retention letter agreement for employees outside of the executive group. Because a letter agreement is a form of enforceable contract, the letter should cover all significant aspects of the retention arrangement, including both compensation and duration. Either a public or private company or other business entity could use this sample agreement. For a discussion of retention benefit plans, see ¶1425.

[ABC Corporation Letterhead]

_____, 2018

_____

_____

_____

_____

        Dear _____:

The following Letter Agreement (the "Agreement") is to confirm our agreement concerning your continued employment with ABC Corporation and its successors (the "Company"), including retention payments.

1. The Company will continue to employ you as its [Chief Financial Officer]. You will report directly to the Company's [Chief Executive Officer]. You will devote your full time and efforts to the business of the Company and will not engage in consulting work or any trade or business for your own account or for or on behalf of any other person, firm or company that competes, conflicts or interferes with the performance of your duties for the Company in any way.

2. Subject to Section 4, the Company will pay you up to [$_____] (the "Retention Payment"), in five equal annual installments, beginning [May 1, 2019], if you remain continuously employed by the Company until the date of each installment. Accordingly, the Company will pay you the following amounts on the following dates:

> [$60,000 on May 1, 2019], if you remain continuously employed by the Company until that date,
>
> [$60,000 on May 1, 2020], if you remain continuously employed by the Company until that date,
>
> [$60,000 on May 1, 2021], if you remain continuously employed by the Company until that date,
>
> [$60,000 on May 1, 2022], if you remain continuously employed by the Company until that date, and
>
> [$60,000 on May 1, 2023], if you remain continuously employed by the Company until that date.

3. Subject to Section 4, if the Company terminates your employment without Cause prior to [May 1, 2019], the Company will pay you the specified amounts

on the specified dates, regardless of the fact that you have not remained continuously employed by the Company until each such date.

4. Notwithstanding the foregoing, in the event of a Sale of the Company, the Company (or its successor) will pay you the full amount of the Retention Payment then unpaid within 10 days of the Sale of the Company.

5. This Agreement constitutes the entire agreement of the parties with respect to the subject matter hereof, and may not be modified except by a writing signed by you and the [Chairman of the Board] or [Chief Executive Officer] of the Company. The laws of the State of _____ shall govern the validity, interpretation, construction and performance of this Agreement, without regard to the conflict of laws principles thereof. If any provision of this Agreement shall be held by a court of competent jurisdiction to be invalid or unenforceable, the remaining provisions hereof shall continue to be fully effective. The parties agree that the jurisdiction and venue for any disputes arising under, or any action brought to enforce (or otherwise relating to), this Agreement shall be exclusively in the courts in the State of _____, County of _____, including the Federal Courts located therein (should Federal jurisdiction exist).

6. You understand and agree that this agreement is not a guarantee of continued employment and that your employment is at will. This means you are free to terminate your employment at any time, for any or no reason, and that the Company retains the same right.

7. By signing this Agreement, you expressly acknowledge and agree that you have read and fully understand the terms of this Agreement; that you have cooperated in the preparation of this Agreement and, as a result, this Agreement shall not be construed against any party on the basis that the party was the draftsperson; and you have knowingly and voluntarily entered this Agreement, without any duress, coercion or undue influence by anyone.

8. **Counterparts**. This Agreement may be signed in single or separate counterparts, each of which shall constitute an original.

If the foregoing accurately sets forth our understanding, please execute the enclosed copy of this letter and return it to the Secretary of the Company.

Sincerely yours,

ABC CORPORATION

By: _____

Its: Chief Executive Officer

ACCEPTED AND AGREED AS OF

this ____ day of _____ 2018:

_____

_____

¶10,120 DECISION TREE—Retention Payment Program Decision Tree

The most critical issues surrounding a retention payment program relate to the design of the program. If the employer does not design its retention payment program to satisfy employees' concerns, or extend coverage to the right employees, the employer could find its ability to run its business crippled by early departures. The following is a form of issues list or is a "decision tree" to assist the employer in making several critical design decisions when drafting a retention payment plan (a sample retention payment plan document can be found at ¶10,100). Either a public or private company or other business entity could use this decision tree. For a discussion of retention benefit plans, see ¶1425.

1. The first question is whether the employer is considering a retention payment program due to uncertainty over a possible acquisition or to limit key employee departures during a period when equity and cash incentive payouts haven fallen below competitive levels due to financial underperformance. In the latter situation, the employer also must consider the reaction of investors and proxy advisory firms to the additional compensation promises.

2. The employer should consider how deep into the organization and to which employees it needs to offer retention payments.

    (a) Employees with change in control or employment agreement protection probably do not need additional retention benefits.

    (b) The employer may need to promise additional retention benefits (*e.g.*, a payment that is made upon closing of a transaction (including all regulatory approvals, even if the employee is not terminated) to employees who possess critical skills and/or are particularly marketable.

    (c) A promise of severance payments may be sufficient to protect, calm, and retain other employees.

3. The employer should consider whether it needs to provide:

    (a) A generous severance amount (so employees can go about their jobs assured that if they lose their jobs, they would be paid while they look for new ones);

    (b) A cash bonus payable only if the employees remain with the employer until the end of a specified period (or periods); or

    (c) A payment that is based on the sales price, to motivate the executive to work toward the highest price and best deal.

4. The employer company should consider whether it needs to provide one or two payments. Some retention plans provide for one payment if the employee remains until the end of one period, and another if the employee remains employed with the employer until a later period. Providing retention payments in two installments can be useful in situations where:

(a) there will be a time lag between two critical stages in the process of a transaction, such as the execution of a purchase/merger agreement and the receipt of regulatory approval, or

(b) the parties recognize the need for the assistance of certain executives and employees during a post-closing transition period.

Different employees in different positions may need different structure.

5. For employees who stand to lose bonus or commission compensation because of the transaction (*e.g.*, because of the disruption or additional costs of a mid-year transaction), the employer should consider:

(a) a guaranteed compensation amount; or

(b) a retention bonus amount that is offset by any bonus or commission income they receive in the ordinary course.

Again, different employees in different positions may need different structure.

6. The employee must determine in what form to make payment(s):

- Cash payments, based on current compensation level, perceived importance to the company, and/or longevity with the company

- Equity incentives, which conserve cash and include a performance incentive

- Continuing coverage under group health (and other) benefit plan

- Acquirer stock or stock awards

- Pension credit/Nonqualified plan credit for contribution, years of service and/or vesting purposes

- Outplacement services

7. The employer must determine the amount of retention payments to offer:

(a) "Stupid to leave" amount; or

(b) "Think twice" amount.

Employers usually base the amount and/or duration of payments on the individual employee's current compensation level, his or her perceived importance to the employer, and/or the employee's longevity with the company.

Additionally, employers need to be cognizant of the possibility that a prospective employer will "buy out" the retention payment amount that employees will lose by leaving the employer, which has become an increasingly common practice, particularly for executive hires.

8. Until what time should the employer require covered employees to stay in order to receive retention payment:

(a) until closing of the transaction (including all regulatory approvals);

(b) for at least 3/6/12 months after closing (unless sooner terminated).

¶10,120

9. The employer should consider whether to provide for full or partial payment if the employer or the acquirer terminates the covered employee without "Cause" or the employee terminates employment for "Good Reason" prior to the end of the required stay period. Most retention plans and agreements provide this protection.

10. Protection against termination without cause or termination for good reason prior to end of required stay period.

11. Should the employer "fund" the program, *e.g.*, through a letter of credit, VEBA or rabbi trust? (Maybe fund a limited amount in case the deal doesn't go through.)

12. The employer should consider the legal issues raised by various form of retention bonus agreements, including the application of Code Section 409A and, for public companies, securities law reporting requirements.

13. Will the purchaser/acquirer pay some of the retention costs? It may if it recognizes the necessity to retain the employees.

14. Will the buyer pay some of these costs? Is buyer sufficiently eager to retain the employees?

¶10,130 SAMPLE LEGAL AGREEMENT—Sample Restricted Stock Unit Agreement

The following is a sample Restricted Stock Unit Agreement, pursuant to which a company could award an executive Restricted Stock Units ("RSUs"). The RSU Agreement will set forth the rights and obligations of both the company and the executive. An award of RSUs is structured like an award of restricted stock. The company's stock incentive plan must permit the company or its board of directors or compensation committee to award RSUs. The award agreement specifies the number of RSUs awarded, the vesting restrictions and any other terms and conditions the company deems necessary or appropriate for its award agreements. Either a public or private company or other business entity could use this sample agreement. For a discussion of restricted stock units, see ¶845.

SAMPLE RESTRICTED STOCK UNIT AGREEMENT

This Restricted Stock Unit Agreement (the "Agreement") is entered into effective as of _____, [year] (the "Award Date"), by and between ABC Corporation, a Delaware corporation (the "Company"), and [_____], a member of the Company's Board of Directors (the "Participant"). Any term capitalized but not defined in this Agreement will have the meaning set forth in the ABC Corporation 2018 Stock Incentive Plan (the "Plan").

The Plan provides for the grant of Restricted Stock Units to Directors of the Company or its Affiliates as approved by the Committee. In exercise of its discretion under the Plan, the Committee has determined that the Participant should receive a restricted stock award under the Plan and, accordingly, the Company and the Participant hereby agree as follows:

This RSU Award must be electronically accepted by the Participant. If the Participant fails to accept this RSU Award within sixty (60) calendar days of the Award Date, this RSU Award shall be null and void. By accepting this Agreement, the Participant consents to the electronic delivery of prospectuses, annual reports and other information required to be delivered by Securities and Exchange Commission rules (which consent may be revoked in writing by the Participant at any time upon three (3) business days' notice to the Company, in which case subsequent prospectuses, annual reports and other information will be delivered in hard copy to the Participant.

1. *Purpose.* The purpose of this Agreement is to provide compensation to the independent directors of the Company, including the Participant, for service in the form of a stock equivalent ownership interest in the Company. The award contemplated by this Agreement represents a portion of the Participant's total compensation for serving on the Company's Board, and the form is intended to serve as a longer-term incentive to the Participant and to further align the Participant's interests with those of the Company's stockholders.

2. *Award.* In accordance with the terms of the Plan and subject to the terms and conditions of this Agreement, the Company hereby awards the Participant

one thousand (1,000) Restricted Stock Units, effective as of the Award Date in respect of the Participant's service for the 12-month period ending on the Award Date. The number of Restricted Stock Units granted is equal to the whole number of share of the Common Stock.

3. *Restricted Stock Units.* The Company will credit the Restricted Stock Units contemplated by this Agreement to a Restricted Stock Unit Account (the "Account") established and maintained for the Participant. The Account shall be the record of Restricted Stock Units awarded to the Participant under the Agreement, is solely for accounting purposes and shall not require a segregation of any Company assets.

4. *Vesting of Restricted Stock Units.* All Restricted Stock Units granted to the Participant will be fully vested at all times.

5. *Distribution of Common Stock.*

(a) The Company will distribute to the Participant a whole number shares of Common Stock equal to the whole number of the Participant's Restricted Stock Units on the date that is six months after the day the Participant's Service on the Board terminates for any reason (or, if such day is not a trading day, on the next succeeding trading day) (the "Distribution Date"). On the Distribution Date, the Company will also pay to the Participant in cash an amount in lieu of any fractional Restricted Stock Unit in the Account, based on the closing price of the Common Stock on the trading day prior to the Distribution Date.

(b) In the event of the Participant's death, distribution of the Common Stock due under this Agreement shall be made to the appointed and qualified executor or other personal representative of the Participant to be distributed in accordance with the Participant's will or applicable intestacy law; or in the event that there shall be no such representative duly appointed and qualified within six months after the date of the Participant's death, then to such persons as, at the date of the Participant's death, would be entitled to share in the distribution of the Participant's personal estate under the provisions of the applicable statute then in force governing the descent of intestate property, in the proportion specified in such statute.

(c) In the event of a Change in Control that also constitutes a change in the ownership or effective control of the Company, or in the ownership of a substantial portion of the assets of the Company for purposes of Code Section 409A, all Common Stock not previously distributed shall be immediately distributed to the Participant.

6. *Dividends on Restricted Stock Units.* If the Company pays a dividend on shares of Common Stock, the Company will

(a) To the extent the Company pays the dividend in cash, credit the Account with additional Restricted Stock Units in an amount equal to number of shares of Common Stock (including fractions thereof) with a value equal to the value of the dividend that would have been paid to the Participant if each Restricted Stock Unit was a share of Common Stock, based on the closing price of the Common Stock on the payment date for the cash dividend.

(b) To the extent the Company pays the dividend in the form of additional shares of Common Stock, credit the Account with additional Restricted Stock Units in an amount equal to the number of shares of Common Stock (including fractions thereof) that would have been paid to the Participant if each Restricted Stock Unit was a share of Common Stock.

Prior to the distribution of shares of Common Stock, the Participant shall not be entitled to any voting rights with respect to the Restricted Stock Units.

7. *Confidentiality, Competition, and Nonsolicitation.* The Participant is voluntarily willing to enter into the following restrictive covenants in exchange for this Award.

(a) **Nondisclosure and Nonuse of Confidential Information.** The Participant shall not disclose or use at any time, either during the Participant's Service or thereafter, any Confidential Information (as defined below) of which the Participant is or becomes aware, whether or not such information is developed by the Participant, except to the extent that such disclosure or use is directly related to and required by the Participant's performance of duties assigned to the Participant by the Company or any of its Affiliates. The Participant shall take all appropriate steps to safeguard Confidential Information and to protect it against disclosure, misuse, espionage, loss and theft. For purposes of this Agreement, the term "Confidential Information" is defined to include all information, in whatever form recorded or transmitted, related to or coming within the past, present or future business affairs of the Company or any of its Affiliates, or other parties whose information the Company has in its possession under obligations of confidentiality, including, without limitation, all business plans, customer lists or information, data, designs, developments, discoveries, expressions (in any medium), ideas, improvements, innovations, inventions, marketing materials, methods, operations, processes, product development processes, programs, research, systems, techniques, financial information, employee compensation and benefits, personnel records and information, promotional materials and methods, trademarks, or trade secrets, having commercial or proprietary value, and of a secret or confidential nature or otherwise not readily available to members of the general public.

(b) **Forfeiture for Competition.** The Participant acknowledges and agrees that (i) in the course of the Participant's Service the Participant shall become familiar with the trade secrets of the Company and its Affiliates and with other Confidential Information concerning the Company and its Affiliates, (ii) the Participant's services to the Company are unique in nature and of an extraordinary value to the Company, and (iii) the Company and its Affiliates could be irreparably damaged if the Participant were to provide similar services to any person or entity competing with the Company or any of its Affiliates or engaged in a similar business. In connection with the issuance to the Participant of the Restricted Stock Units hereunder, and in consideration for and as an inducement to the Company to enter into this Agreement, the Participant covenants and agrees that during the period beginning on the Award Date and ending on the second anniversary of the date of the termination of the Participant's Service (the "Restricted Period"), the Participant shall not, directly or indirectly, either for himself or herself or for or through any other Person, participate in any business or enterprise that provides or proposes to provide _____ of the type the Company provides. Without limiting the generality of the foregoing, the Participant agrees that, during the Restricted Period, the Participant shall not compete against the Company or any of its Affiliates by soliciting any customer or prospective customer of the Company with whom the Company had any business dealings or contracts. The Participant agrees that this covenant is reasonable with respect to its duration, geographical area and scope. For purposes of this Agreement, the term "participate in" includes having any direct or indirect interest in any Person, whether as a sole proprietor, owner, stockholder, partner, joint venture, creditor or otherwise, or rendering any direct or indirect service or assistance to any Person (whether as a director, officer, manager, supervisor, employee, agent, consultant or otherwise), other than owning up to 2% of the outstanding stock of any class that is publicly traded.

(c) **Nonsolicitation.** During the Restricted Period, the Participant shall not induce or attempt to induce to leave the Service of the Company or any of its Affiliates or hire any Employee, Director or Advisor of the Company or any of its Affiliates, or in any way interfere with the relationship between the Company and any Employee, Director or Advisor thereof. During the Restricted Period, the Participant shall not call on, solicit or service any customer, supplier, licensee, licensor or other business relation of the Company in order to induce or attempt to induce any such Person to cease doing business with the Company, or in any way interfere with the relationship between any such customer, supplier, licensee or business relation and the Company (including making any negative statements or communications concerning any of the Company or its Employees, Directors or Advisors).

(d) **Judicial Modification.** If the final judgment of a court of competent jurisdiction declares that any term or provision of this Section is invalid or unenforceable, the parties agree that (i) the court making the determination of invalidity or unenforceability shall have the power to reduce the scope, duration, or geographic area of the term or provision, to delete specific words or phrases, or to replace any invalid or unenforceable term or provision with a term or provision that is valid and enforceable and that comes closest to expressing the intention of the invalid or unenforceable term or provision, (ii) the parties shall request that the court exercise that power, and (iii) this Agreement shall be enforceable as so modified after the expiration of the time within which the judgment or decision may be appealed.

(e) **Remedy for Breach.** The Participant agrees that in the event of a breach or threatened breach of any of the covenants contained in this Section, in addition to any other penalties or restrictions that may apply under any employment agreement, state law, or otherwise, the Participant shall forfeit, upon written notice to such effect from the Company:

    (i) any and all Restricted Stock Units granted to the Participant under the Plan and this Agreement, including vested Restricted Stock Units; and

    (ii) the profit the Participant has realized on the sale of any shares of Common Stock received by the Participant upon the vesting of Restricted Stock Units and distribution of Common Stock (which the Participant may be required to repay to the Company).

The forfeiture provisions of this Section shall continue to apply, in accordance with their terms, after the provisions of any employment or other agreement between the Company and the Participant have lapsed.

(f) **Blue Pencil.** The Participant acknowledges and agrees that the non-competition non-solicitation and other restrictive covenant provisions contained herein are reasonable and valid in geographic, temporal and subject matter scope and in all other respects, and do not impose limitations greater than are necessary to protect the goodwill, Secret or Confidential Information and other business interests of the Company. Nevertheless, if any court or arbitrator determines that any of said non-competition, non-solicitation, or other restrictive covenants and agreements, or any provision thereof, is unenforceable because of the duration or geographic scope of such provision, such court or arbitrator will have the power to reduce the duration, geographic scope, or other scope of such provision, as the case may be; and, in its reduced form, such provision will then be enforceable to the maximum extent permitted by applicable law.

(g) **Tolling of Restrictive Periods.** If the Participant breaches any of the restrictions set forth in this Section above and the Company commences a legal proceeding in connection therewith, the time period applicable to each such restriction shall be tolled and extended for a period of time equal to the period of time during which the Participant is determined by a court of competent jurisdiction to be in non-compliance or breach (not to exceed the duration set forth in the applicable restriction) commencing on the date of such determination.

(h) **Protected Rights.** The Participant understands that nothing contained in this Agreement limits the Participant's ability to file a charge or complaint with the Equal Employment Opportunity Commission, the

National Labor Relations Board, the Occupational Safety and Health Administration, the Securities and Exchange Commission or any other federal, state or local governmental agency or commission ("Government Agencies"). The Participant further understands that this Agreement does not limit the Participant's ability to communicate with any Government Agencies or otherwise participate in any investigation or proceeding that may be conducted by any Government Agency, including providing documents or other information, without notice to the Company. This Agreement does not limit the Participant's right to receive an award for information provided to any Government Agencies.

8. *Clawback/Forfeiture.* Notwithstanding anything to the contrary contained herein, the Committee may, in its sole discretion, cancel the Restricted Stock Unit if the Participant, without the consent of the Company, while employed by or providing Service to the Company or any Affiliate or after termination of such employment or Service, violates a non-competition, non-solicitation, non-disparagement or non-disclosure covenant or agreement, or otherwise has engaged in or engages in activity that is in conflict with or adverse to the interest of the Company or any Affiliate, including fraud or conduct contributing to any financial restatements or irregularities, as determined by the Committee in its sole discretion. Further, if the Participant otherwise has engaged in or engages in any activity referred to in the preceding sentence, the Participant shall forfeit any compensation, gain or other value realized thereafter on the vesting, exercise or settlement of such Restricted Stock Units, the sale or other transfer of such Restricted Stock Units, or the sale of shares of Common Stock acquired in respect of such Restricted Stock Units, and must promptly repay such amounts to the Company. In addition, if the Participant receives any amount in excess of what the Participant should have received under the terms of this Award for any reason (including without limitation by reason of a financial restatement, mistake in calculations or other administrative error), all as determined by the Committee in its sole discretion, then the Participant shall be required to promptly repay any such excess amount to the Company. To the extent required by applicable law (including without limitation Section 304 of the Sarbanes-Oxley Act and Section 954 of the Dodd-Frank Wall Street Reform and Consumer Protection Act) and/or the rules and regulations of the NYSE or other securities exchange or inter-dealer quotation system on which the Common Stock is listed or quoted, or if so required by the Company's Compensation Recoupment Policy, or pursuant to any similar written policy adopted by the Company, the Restricted Stock Units shall be subject (including on a retroactive basis) to clawback, forfeiture or similar requirements (and such requirements shall be deemed incorporated by reference into this Agreement).

9. *No Right to Employment or Service.* Nothing in the Plan or this Agreement will be construed as creating any right in the Participant to be continued in employment or Service in any position, as an employee, consultant or director of the Company or its Affiliates or as altering or amending the existing terms and conditions of the Participant's employment or Service, or shall interfere with or

restrict in any way the rights of the Company or its Affiliates, which are hereby expressly reserved, to remove, terminate, or discharge the Participant at any time for any reason whatsoever.

10. *Nontransferability.* No interest of the Participant or any beneficiary in or under this Agreement will be assignable or transferable by voluntary or involuntary act or by operation of law, other than by testamentary bequest or devise or the laws of descent or distribution. Distribution of Common Stock will be made only to the Participant; or, if the Committee has been provided with evidence acceptable to it that the Participant is legally incompetent, the Participant's personal representative; or, if the Participant is deceased, to the beneficiaries or personal representative that the Participant has designated in the manner required by the Committee. The Committee may require personal receipts or endorsements of a Participant's personal representative or beneficiaries. Any effort to assign or transfer the rights under this Agreement will be wholly ineffective, and will be grounds for termination by the Committee of all rights of the Participant and the Participant's beneficiary in and under this Agreement.

11. *Administration.* The Board will administer this Agreement, provided that Participant and other independent Board members party to these arrangements shall not participate in the administration of this Agreement. The Board shall have authority to interpret the Agreement, to adopt and revise rules and regulations relating to the Agreement and to make any other determinations that it believes necessary or advisable for the administration of the Agreement. Determinations by the Board shall be final and binding on all parties with respect to all matters relating to the Agreement.

12. *Governing Law; Choice of Venue.* This Agreement will be governed by and construed under the laws of the State of ____, determined without regard to its conflicts of law rules, except as such laws are preempted by the laws of the United States. If any provision of this Agreement shall be held by a court of competent jurisdiction to be invalid or unenforceable, the remaining provisions hereof shall continue to be fully effective. The jurisdiction and venue for any disputes arising under, or any action brought to enforce (or otherwise relating to), this Agreement shall be exclusively in the courts in the State of _____, County of ____, including the Federal Courts located therein (should Federal jurisdiction exist).

13. *Securities Laws.* The Participant agrees that the obligation of the Company to issue Common Stock shall also be subject, as conditions precedent, to compliance with applicable provisions of the Securities Act of 1933, as amended, the Securities Exchange Act of 1934, as amended, state securities or corporation laws, rules and regulations under any of the foregoing and applicable requirements of any securities exchange upon which the Company's securities shall be listed.

14. *Successors.* All obligations of the Company under this Agreement will be binding on any successor to the Company, whether the existence of the successor results from a direct or indirect purchase of all or substantially all of the business of the Company, or a merger, consolidation, or otherwise.

15. *Section 409A.* This Agreement is intended to be exempt from, or compliant with, Code Section 409A. Notwithstanding the foregoing or any provision of the Plan or this Agreement, if any provision of the Plan or this Agreement contravenes Code Section 409A or could cause the Participant to incur any tax, interest or penalties under Code Section 409A, the Committee may, in its sole discretion and without the Participant's consent, modify such provision to (i) comply with, or avoid being subject to, Code Section 409A, or to avoid the incurrence of taxes, interest and penalties under Code Section 409A, and/or (ii) maintain, to the maximum extent practicable, the original intent and economic benefit to the Participant of the applicable provision without materially increasing the cost to the Company or contravening the provisions of Code Section 409A. This Section does not create an obligation on the part of the Company to modify the Plan or this Agreement and does not guarantee that the Agreement will not be subject to interest and penalties under Code Section 409A.

16. *Sole Agreement.* This Award is in all respects subject to the provisions set forth in the Plan to the same extent and with the same effect as if set forth fully herein. In the event that the terms of this Award conflict with the terms of the Plan, the Plan shall control. This Agreement is the entire Agreement and understanding between the parties to it, and supersedes all prior communications, representations, and negotiations, oral or written in respect thereto.

17. *Waiver.* Any right of the Company contained in this Agreement may be waived in writing by the Committee. No waiver of any right hereunder by any party shall operate as a waiver of any other right, or as a waiver of the same right with respect to any subsequent occasion for its exercise, or as a waiver of any right to damages. No waiver by any party of any breach of this Agreement shall be held to constitute a waiver of any other breach or a waiver of the continuation of the same breach.

18. *Amendment of the Agreement.* The Company and the Participant may amend this Agreement only by a written instrument signed by both parties. No change, modification, or waiver of any provision of this Agreement shall be valid unless in writing and signed by the parties hereto.

19. *Severability.* The invalidity or unenforceability of any provision of this Agreement shall not affect the validity or enforceability of any other provision of this Agreement and each other provision of this Agreement shall be severable and enforceable to the extent permitted by law.

20. *Headings.* The headings of the Sections hereof are provided for convenience only and are not to serve as a basis for interpretation or construction, and shall not constitute a part, of this Agreement.

21. *Counterparts.* The parties may execute this Agreement in one or more counterparts, all of which together shall constitute but one Agreement.

* * *

IN WITNESS WHEREOF, the Company and the Participant have executed this Agreement effective as of the date first above written.

ABC Corporation

_____

Participant

By: _____

Its: _____

¶10,150 SAMPLE LEGAL AGREEMENT—Stock Appreciation Rights Agreement

The following is a sample Stock Appreciation Rights (SAR) Agreement, pursuant to which a company could give an executive the right to receive the appreciated value of the company's stock when the right vests and the executive exercises it. This Agreement sets forth the rights of both the company and the executive.

This form of SAR Agreement is designed for a privately held company. Some companies would award SARs under an "omnibus stock incentive plan" (see ¶10,310) that permits the company to grant a wide variety of stock-based awards. For a discussion of stock appreciation rights, see ¶925.

Stock Appreciation Rights Agreement

This Stock Appreciation Rights Agreement (the "Agreement") is entered into effective as of _____, [year] (the "Award Date"), by and between ABC Corporation (the "Company"), and [_____] (the "Participant"). Any term capitalized but not defined in this Agreement will have the meaning set forth in the ABC Corporation 2018 Stock Incentive Plan (the "Plan").

The Plan provides for the award of Stock Appreciation Rights to key employees of the Company or its Affiliates as approved by the Committee. In exercise of its discretion under the Plan, the Committee has determined that the Participant should receive a restricted stock award under the Plan and, accordingly, the Company and the Participant hereby agree as follows:

This SAR Award must be electronically accepted by the Participant. If the Participant fails to accept this SAR Award within sixty (60) calendar days of the Award Date, this SAR Award shall be null and void. By accepting this Agreement, the Participant consents to the electronic delivery of prospectuses, annual reports and other information required to be delivered by Securities and Exchange Commission rules (which consent may be revoked in writing by the Participant at any time upon three (3) business days' notice to the Company, in which case subsequent prospectuses, annual reports and other information will be delivered in hard copy to the Participant.

1. *Purpose.* The purpose of this Agreement is to provide compensation to key employees of the Company, including the Participant, for service in the form of a stock equivalent ownership interest in the Company. The award contemplated by this Agreement represents a portion of the Participant's total compensation for Service to the Company, and the form is intended to serve as a longer-term incentive to the Participant and to further align the Participant's interests with those of the Company's stockholders

2. *Stock Appreciation Rights Award.* Subject to the terms and conditions of this Agreement, the Company hereby awards to the Participant an aggregate of [_____] Stock Appreciation Rights, which is equal to 0.2% (two-tenths of one percent) of the total number of outstanding shares of Company Stock, counting, for this purpose, all Stock Appreciation Rights issued to the Participant

and any other employee as issued and outstanding]. The Award Value of each Stock Appreciation Right awarded under this Agreement is $[10.00].

3. *Stock Appreciation Rights.* Each Stock Appreciation Right entitles the Participant, upon the proper exercise of the Stock Appreciation Right, and subject to the vesting restrictions of Section 4, to the difference between the Award Value of the Stock Appreciation Right and the Fair Market Value of a share of Company Stock.

4. *Term, Vesting of the Stock Appreciation Rights.* The Stock Appreciation Rights will expire on the fifteenth anniversary of the Award Date (the "Expiration Date").The Stock Appreciation Rights will vest on the fifth anniversary of the Award Date, if the Participant has remained in Service continuously until that date. [In installments, one-fifth (1/5) on each anniversary of the Award Date, if the Participant has remained in Service continuously until that date, so that the Stock Appreciation Rights will be one hundred percent (100%) vested on the fifth anniversary of the Award Date.] The Participant may exercise the Stock Appreciation Rights only after they have become vested in accordance with the provisions of this Section. While the Participant is in Service, and after the fifth anniversary of the Award Date, the Participant will have a right to exercise the Participant's vested Stock Appreciation Rights, by written notice to the Company indicating the number of Stock Appreciation Rights being exercised; provided that, during any 12-consecutive month period, the Participant may not exercise more than twenty percent (20%) of the Participant's vested Stock Appreciation Rights (measured as of the first date on which the Participant exercises the Participant's Stock Appreciation Rights, but adjusted to reflect the acquisition of any additional vested Stock Appreciation Rights). The Participant must sign the notice.

5. *Termination of Service.* If the Participant's Service terminates, for any reason and before all of the Participant's SAR has become vested under this Agreement, the Participant: (a) will forfeit any Stock Appreciation Right to the extent that it was not vested on the date of the termination; and (b) the Redemption Value of the Participant's vested Stock Appreciation Rights will be paid according to Sections 8 and 9. The Participant will be deemed to have exercised the Participant's Stock Appreciation Rights upon the Participant's termination Service date. Notwithstanding any other provision of this Agreement, if the Company terminates the Participant's Service for Cause, the Participant will forfeit the Participant's right to exercise the Stock Appreciation Rights, whether or not it has already vested.

6. *Redemption Value.* The Redemption Value of the Participant's exercised Stock Appreciation Rights will be equal to the product of (a) the aggregate number of the Participant's vested and exercised Stock Appreciation Rights, multiplied by (b) the difference between the Award Value of the Stock Appreciation Rights and Fair Market Value of such Stock Appreciation Rights determined as of (i) the last day of the calendar month ending on or immediately preceding the date on which the Participant exercises the Participant's vested Stock Appre-

ciation Rights, or (ii) the end of the Company's most recently concluded Fiscal Year, whichever date produces the lower Fair Market Value figure.

7. *Commencement of Participant's Distributions.* Subject to the conditions of Section 9, distribution of the Participant's Redemption Value will be made to the Participant no earlier than 60 days after the latest of: (i) the Settlement Date, or (ii) the fifth anniversary of the Award Date.

8. *Form and Amount of Distribution.* The Redemption Value of the vested Stock Appreciation Rights the Participant exercises will be paid immediately in a lump sum. If the Participant dies before distribution of the Participant's Redemption Value, the remaining amount in the Account will be distributed to the Participant's Beneficiary over the same period as distributions were being made to the Participant.

9. *Withholding.* Payments made under this Agreement will be net of any amounts sufficient to satisfy all federal, state, local and other withholding tax requirements.

10. *Participant to Have No Rights as a Stockholder.* The holder of any Stock Appreciation Rights will have no rights as a stockholder with respect to those Stock Appreciation Rights.

11. *Confidentiality, Noncompete, and Nonsolicitation.* The Participant is voluntarily willing to enter into the following restrictive covenants in exchange for this Award.

    (a) **Nondisclosure and Nonuse of Confidential Information.** The Participant shall not disclose or use at any time, either during the Participant's Service or thereafter, any Confidential Information (as defined below) of which the Participant is or becomes aware, whether or not such information is developed by the Participant, except to the extent that such disclosure or use is directly related to and required by the Participant's performance of duties assigned to the Participant by the Company or any of its Affiliates. The Participant shall take all appropriate steps to safeguard Confidential Information and to protect it against disclosure, misuse, espionage, loss and theft. For purposes of this Agreement, the term "Confidential Information" is defined to include all information, in whatever form recorded or transmitted, related to or coming within the past, present or future business affairs of the Company or any of its Affiliates, or other parties whose information the Company has in its possession under obligations of confidentiality, including, without limitation, all business plans, customer lists or information, data, designs, developments, discoveries, expressions (in any medium), ideas, improvements, innovations, inventions, marketing materials, methods, operations, processes, product development processes, programs, research, systems, techniques, financial information, employee compensation and benefits, personnel records and information, promotional materials and methods, trademarks, or trade secrets, having commercial or proprietary value, and of a secret or confidential nature or otherwise not readily available to members of the general public.

(b) **Forfeiture for Competition.** The Participant acknowledges and agrees that (i) in the course of the Participant's Service the Participant shall become familiar with the trade secrets of the Company and its Affiliates and with other Confidential Information concerning the Company and its Affiliates, (ii) the Participant's services to the Company are unique in nature and of an extraordinary value to the Company, and (iii) the Company and its Affiliates could be irreparably damaged if the Participant were to provide similar services to any person or entity competing with the Company or any of its Affiliates or engaged in a similar business. In connection with the issuance to the Participant of the Stock Appreciation Rights hereunder, and in consideration for and as an inducement to the Company to enter into this Agreement, the Participant covenants and agrees that during the period beginning on the Award Date and ending on the second anniversary of the date of the termination of the Participant's Service (the "Restricted Period"), the Participant shall not directly or indirectly, either for himself or herself or for or through any other Person, participate in any business or enterprise that provides or proposes to provide _____ of the type the Company provides. Without limiting the generality of the foregoing, the Participant agrees that, during the Restricted Period, the Participant shall not compete against the Company or any of its Affiliates by soliciting any customer or prospective customer of the Company with whom the Company had any business dealings or contracts. The Participant agrees that this covenant is reasonable with respect to its duration, geographical area and scope. For purposes of this Agreement, the term "participate in" includes having any direct or indirect interest in any Person, whether as a sole proprietor, owner, stockholder, partner, joint venture, creditor or otherwise, or rendering any direct or indirect service or assistance to any Person (whether as a director, officer, manager, supervisor, employee, agent, consultant or otherwise), other than owning up to 2% of the outstanding stock of any class that is publicly traded.

(c) **Nonsolicitation.** During the Restricted Period, the Participant shall not induce or attempt to induce any employee, director or advisor of the Company to leave the Service of the Company or any of its Affiliates or hire any employee, director or advisor of the Company or any of its Affiliates, or in any way interfere with the relationship between the Company and any employee, director or advisor thereof. During the Restricted Period, the Participant shall not call on, solicit or service any customer, supplier, licensee, licensor or other business relation of the Company in order to induce or attempt to induce any such Person to cease doing business with the Company, or in any way interfere with the relationship between any such customer, supplier, licensee or business relation and the Company (including making any negative state-

¶10,150

ments or communications concerning any of the Company or its employees, directors or advisors).

(d) **Judicial Modification.** If the final judgment of a court of competent jurisdiction declares that any term or provision of this Section is invalid or unenforceable, the parties agree that (i) the court making the determination of invalidity or unenforceability shall have the power to reduce the scope, duration, or geographic area of the term or provision, to delete specific words or phrases, or to replace any invalid or unenforceable term or provision with a term or provision that is valid and enforceable and that comes closest to expressing the intention of the invalid or unenforceable term or provision, (ii) the parties shall request that the court exercise that power, and (iii) this Agreement shall be enforceable as so modified after the expiration of the time within which the judgment or decision may be appealed.

(e) **Remedy for Breach.** The Participant agrees that in the event of a breach or threatened breach of any of the covenants contained in this Section, in addition to any other penalties or restrictions that may apply under any employment agreement, state law, or otherwise, the Participant shall forfeit, upon written notice to such effect from the Company:

(i) any and all Stock Appreciation Rights awarded to the Participant under this Agreement, including vested Stock Appreciation Rights; and

(ii) any distributions previously made to the Participant (which may require the Participant to repay such amounts to the Company);

The forfeiture provisions of this Section shall continue to apply, in accordance with their terms, after the provisions of any employment or other agreement between the Company and the Participant have lapsed.

(f) **Blue Pencil.** The Participant acknowledges and agrees that the non-competition non-solicitation and other restrictive covenant provisions contained herein are reasonable and valid in geographic, temporal and subject matter scope and in all other respects, and do not impose limitations greater than are necessary to protect the goodwill, Secret or Confidential Information and other business interests of the Company. Nevertheless, if any court or arbitrator determines that any of said non-competition, non-solicitation, or other restrictive covenants and agreements, or any provision thereof, is unenforceable because of the duration or geographic scope of such provision, such court or arbitrator will have the power to reduce the duration, geographic scope, or other scope of such provision, as the case may be; and, in its reduced form, such provision will then be enforceable to the maximum extent permitted by applicable law.

(g) **Tolling of Restrictive Periods.** If the Participant breaches any of the restrictions set forth in this Section above and the Company commences a legal proceeding in connection therewith, the time period applicable to each such restriction shall be tolled and extended for a period of time equal to the period of time during which the Participant is determined by a court of competent jurisdiction to be in non-compliance or breach (not to exceed the duration set forth in the applicable restriction) commencing on the date of such determination.

(h) **Protected Rights.** The Participant understands that nothing contained in this Agreement limits the Participant's ability to file a charge or complaint with the Equal Employment Opportunity Commission, the National Labor Relations Board, the Occupational Safety and Health Administration, the Securities and Exchange Commission or any other federal, state or local governmental agency or commission ("Government Agencies"). The Participant further understands that this Agreement does not limit the Participant's ability to communicate with any Government Agencies or otherwise participate in any investigation or proceeding that may be conducted by any Government Agency, including providing documents or other information, without notice to the Company. This Agreement does not limit the Participant's right to receive an award for information provided to any Government Agencies.

12. *Clawback/Forfeiture.* Notwithstanding anything to the contrary contained herein, the Committee may, in its sole discretion, cancel the SAR if the Participant, without the consent of the Company, while employed by or providing Service to the Company or any Affiliate or after termination of such employment or Service, violates a non-competition, non-solicitation, non-disparagement or non-disclosure covenant or agreement, or otherwise has engaged in or engages in activity that is in conflict with or adverse to the interest of the Company or any Affiliate, including fraud or conduct contributing to any financial restatements or irregularities, as determined by the Committee in its sole discretion. Further, if the Participant otherwise has engaged in or engages in any activity referred to in the preceding sentence, the Participant shall forfeit any compensation, gain or other value realized thereafter on the vesting, exercise or settlement of such SAR, the sale or other transfer of such SAR, or the sale of shares of Common Stock acquired in respect of such SAR, and must promptly repay such amounts to the Company. In addition, if the Participant receives any amount in excess of what the Participant should have received under the terms of the SAR for any reason (including without limitation by reason of a financial restatement, mistake in calculations or other administrative error), all as determined by the Committee in its sole discretion, then the Participant shall be required to promptly repay any such excess amount to the Company. To the extent required by applicable law (including without limitation Section 304 of the Sarbanes-Oxley Act and Section 954 of the Dodd-Frank Wall Street Reform and Consumer Protection Act) and/or the rules and regulations of the NYSE or other securities exchange or inter-dealer quotation system on which the Common Stock is listed or quoted, or if so required by the Company's Incentive Compensation Recoupment Policy, or pursuant to any similar written policy adopted by the Company, the SAR shall

be subject (including on a retroactive basis) to clawback, forfeiture or similar requirements (and such requirements shall be deemed incorporated by reference into this Agreement).

13. *Nontransferability of Stock Appreciation Rights.* The Participant may not sell, transfer, pledge, assign or otherwise alienate or hypothecate the Stock Appreciation Rights. Stock Appreciation Rights will be exercisable during the Participant's lifetime only by the Participant or the Participant's guardian or legal representative. The Committee may, in its discretion, require the Participant's guardian or legal representative to supply it with the evidence the Committee deems necessary to establish the authority of the guardian or legal representative to act on behalf of the Participant.

14. *Administration.* The Committee administers the Plan. The Participant's rights under this Agreement are expressly subject to the terms and conditions of the Plan, including continued shareholder approval of the Plan, and to any guidelines the Committee adopts from time to time. The Participant hereby acknowledges receipt of a copy of the Plan. Any interpretation by the Committee of the terms and conditions of the Plan or this Agreement will be final.

15. *No Limitation on Rights of the Company.* The award of the Stock Appreciation Rights does not and will not in any way affect the right or power of the Company to make adjustments, reclassifications or changes in its capital or business structure, or to merge, consolidate, dissolve, liquidate, sell or transfer all or any part of its business or assets.

16. *Plan and Agreement Not a Contract of Employment or Service.* Neither the Plan nor this Agreement is a contract of employment or Service, and no terms of the Participant's employment or Service will be affected in any way by the Plan, this Agreement or related instruments, except to the extent specifically expressed therein. Neither the Plan nor this Agreement will be construed as creating any right in the Participant to be continued in employment or Service in any position, as an employee, consultant or director of the Company or its Affiliates or as altering or amending the existing terms and conditions of the Participant's employment or Service, or shall interfere with or restrict in any way the rights of the Company or its Affiliates, which are hereby expressly reserved, to remove, terminate, or discharge the Participant at any time for any reason whatsoever.

17. *Notice.* Any notice or other communication required or permitted under this Agreement must be in writing (including electronic) and must be delivered personally, sent by certified, registered or express mail, or sent by overnight courier, at the sender's expense. Notice will be deemed given when delivered personally or, if mailed, three days after the date of deposit in the United States mail or, if sent by overnight courier, on the regular business day following the date sent. Notice to the Company should be sent to ABC Corporation, _____, Attention: President. Notice to the Participant should be sent to the address set forth on the signature page below. Either party may change the person and/or address to whom the other party must give notice under this Section by giving such other party written notice of such change, in

accordance with the procedures described above. Any reference in the Plan or this Agreement, or to a written document includes without limitation any document delivered electronically or posted on the Company's intranet or other shared electronic medium controlled by the Company.

18. *Governing Law; Choice of Venue.* This Agreement will be governed by and construed under the laws of the State of _____, determined without regard to its conflicts of law rules, except as such laws are preempted by the laws of the United States. If any provision of this Agreement shall be held by a court of competent jurisdiction to be invalid or unenforceable, the remaining provisions hereof shall continue to be fully effective. The jurisdiction and venue for any disputes arising under, or any action brought to enforce (or otherwise relating to), this Agreement shall be exclusively in the courts in the State of _____, County of _____, including the Federal Courts located therein (should Federal jurisdiction exist).

19. *Requirements of Law.* The awarding of Stock Appreciation Rights and/or cash payouts under the Agreement will be subject to all applicable laws, rules, and regulations, and to any approvals by governmental agencies or national securities exchanges as may be required.

20. *Securities Law Requirements.* If at any time the Committee determines that exercising the SAR or issuing shares of Common Stock would violate applicable securities laws, the SAR will not be exercisable, and the Company will not be required to issue shares of Common Stock. The Committee may declare any provision of this Agreement or action of its own null and void, if it determines the provision or action fails to comply with the short-swing trading rules. As a condition to exercise, the Company may require the Participant to make written representations it deems necessary or desirable to comply with applicable securities laws. No person who acquires shares under this Agreement may sell the shares of Common Stock, unless they make the offer and sale pursuant to an effective registration statement under the Securities Exchange Act, which is current and includes the shares of Common Stock to be sold, or an exemption from the registration requirements of that Act.

21. *Successors.* All obligations of the Company under this Agreement will be binding on any successor to the Company, whether the existence of the successor results from a direct or indirect purchase of all or substantially all of the business of the Company, or a merger, consolidation, or otherwise.

22. *Section 409A.* The SAR is intended to be exempt from, or compliant with, Code Section 409A. Notwithstanding the foregoing or any provision of the Plan or this Agreement, if any provision of the Plan or this Agreement contravenes Code Section 409A or could cause the Participant to incur any tax, interest or penalties under Code Section 409A, the Committee may, in its sole discretion and without the Participant's consent, modify such provision to (i) comply with, or avoid being subject to, Code Section 409A, or to avoid the incurrence of taxes, interest and penalties under Code Section 409A, and/or (ii) maintain, to the maximum extent practicable, the original intent and economic benefit to the

Participant of the applicable provision without materially increasing the cost to the Company or contravening the provisions of Code Section 409A. This Section does not create an obligation on the part of the Company to modify the Plan or this Agreement and does not guarantee that the SAR will not be subject to interest and penalties under Code Section 409A.

23. *Sole Agreement.* This Award is in all respects subject to the provisions set forth in the Plan to the same extent and with the same effect as if set forth fully herein. In the event that the terms of this Award conflict with the terms of the Plan, the Plan shall control. This Agreement is the entire Agreement and understanding between the parties to it, and supersedes all prior communications, representations, and negotiations, oral or written in respect thereto.

24. *Waiver.* Any right of the Company contained in this Agreement may be waived in writing by the Committee. No waiver of any right hereunder by any party shall operate as a waiver of any other right, or as a waiver of the same right with respect to any subsequent occasion for its exercise, or as a waiver of any right to damages. No waiver by any party of any breach of this Agreement shall be held to constitute a waiver of any other breach or a waiver of the continuation of the same breach.

25. *Amendment of the Agreement.* The Company and the Participant may amend this Agreement only by a written instrument signed by both parties. No change, modification, or waiver of any provision of this Agreement shall be valid unless in writing and signed by the parties hereto.

26. *Severability.* The invalidity or unenforceability of any provision of this Agreement shall not affect the validity or enforceability of any other provision of this Agreement and each other provision of this Agreement shall be severable and enforceable to the extent permitted by law.

27. *Headings.* The headings of the Sections hereof are provided for convenience only and are not to serve as a basis for interpretation or construction, and shall not constitute a part of this Agreement.

28. *Counterparts.* The parties may execute this Agreement in one or more counterparts, all of which together shall constitute but one Agreement.

* * *

IN WITNESS WHEREOF, the Company and the Participant have duly executed this Agreement effective as of the date first above written.

ABC Corporation

_____

(Participant's Signature)

By: _____

Its: _____

Participant's Name and Address for notices

_____

_____

¶10,190 SAMPLE LEGAL AGREEMENT—Annual Incentive Compensation Plan

The following is a sample Annual Incentive Compensation Plan under which the company promises to reward covered employees if certain specified performance targets are met. Once the company and the covered employee have satisfied the performance targets, the company will make a cash payment. For a discussion of structuring incentive compensation, see ¶1535.

Sample Incentive Compensation Plan

ABC Corporation (the "Company") has established this ABC Corporation Annual Incentive Compensation Plan ("Plan") effective as of _____, [year] (the "Effective Date"), to further the objectives of the Company through awards of annual incentive compensation, to attract, retain and motivate qualified executive employees.

SECTION 1
DEFINITIONS

1.1 "Annual Base Salary" shall mean, unless the Committee determines otherwise, for any Participant, an amount equal to the rate of annual base salary in effect at year-end for the year in which the Performance Period commences, including any base salary that otherwise would be payable to the Participant during the Performance Period but for his or her election to defer receipt thereof.

1.2 "Applicable Period" means, with respect to any Performance Period, a period commencing on or before the first day of the Performance Period and ending not later than the earlier of (i) ninety (90) calendar days after the commencement of the Performance Period and (ii) the date on which twenty-five percent (25%) of the Performance Period has been completed.

1.3 "Board" shall mean the Board of Directors of the Company or the successor thereto.

1.4 "Code" shall mean the Internal Revenue Code of 1986, as amended.

1.5 "Committee" shall mean the Compensation Committee of the Board or such other committee or subcommittee designated by the Board that satisfies any then applicable requirements of any established stock exchange or national market system on which the common stock of the Company is then listed to constitute a compensation committee, and which, as to any compensation intended to qualify as performance-based compensation under Section 162(m), shall consist solely of two or more members, each of whom is an "outside director" within the meaning of Section 162(m), and the applicable rules and regulations promulgated thereunder.

1.6 "Company" shall mean ABC Corporation, a Delaware corporation, or any successor thereto.

1.7 "Individual Award Opportunity" shall mean the potential of a Participant to receive an incentive payment if the Performance Goals for a Performance

Period have been satisfied. An Individual Award Opportunity may be expressed in U.S. dollars or pursuant to a formula that is consistent with the provisions of the Plan.

1.8 "Participant" shall mean, for each Performance Period, each Company employee who is or becomes [an executive officer of the Company or a Subsidiary during a specified Performance Period, as defined by the Securities Exchange Act of 1934, Rule 3b-7, as that definition may be amended from time to time], unless the Committee excludes such employee from participation in the Plan for a specified Performance Period.

1.9 "Performance Goals" shall mean one or more objective Performance Goals for each Participant or for any group of Participants (or both), established by the Committee in accordance with Section 4.1.

1.10 "Performance Period" shall mean the Company's fiscal year or any other period designated by the Committee with respect to which Performance Goals are established pursuant to Section 4.

1.11 "Plan" shall mean this ABC Corporation Annual Incentive Compensation Plan, as amended from time to time.

1.12 "Section 162(m)" means Section 162(m) of the Code, as amended from time to time, and the applicable rules and regulations promulgated thereunder.

1.13 "Section 409A" means Section 409A of the Code, as amended from time to time, and the applicable rules and regulations promulgated thereunder.

1.14 "Subsidiary" shall mean any entity that is directly or indirectly controlled by the Company or any entity in which the Company directly or indirectly has at least a fifty percent (50%) equity interest.

SECTION 2
ADMINISTRATION

2.1 *General.* The Plan shall be administered by the Committee, which shall have full authority to interpret the Plan, to establish rules and regulations relating to the operation of the Plan, to select Participants, to determine the Individual Award Opportunity and to make all determinations and take all other actions necessary or appropriate for the proper administration of the Plan. The Committee's interpretation of the Plan, and all actions taken within the scope of its authority, shall be final and binding on the Company, its stockholders, Participants, and former Participants and their respective successors and assigns. The Committee may delegate its authority hereunder as it deems appropriate. No member of the Committee shall be eligible to participate in the Plan.

2.2 *Powers and Responsibilities.* The Committee shall have the following discretionary powers, rights and responsibilities in addition to those described in Section 3.1:

(a) to designate within the Applicable Period, the Participants for a Performance Period;

(b) to establish within the Applicable Period the Performance Goals and other terms and conditions that are to apply to each Participant's Individual Award Opportunity, including: (A) the extent to which any incentive payment shall be made to a Participant in the event of the Participant's termination of employment with or service to the Company due to death, disability, or retirement based on actual performance, or any other reason, or transfer to an ineligible position; (B) the extent to which any incentive payment shall be made to a Participant in the event of a change in control; (C) in the case of an individual who is hired by the Company or a Subsidiary or who is promoted or becomes an executive officer after the beginning of a Performance Period, the Committee may designate such individual as a Participant in the Plan for that Performance Period, provided that the Committee may specify that such Participant's Individual Award Opportunity shall be determined only with respect to the portion of the Performance Period during which the Participant is employed by the Company or Subsidiary in the eligible position; (D) the rules that apply to Participants who are transferred from one eligible position to another during a Performance Period; and (E) the rules that apply to Participants who are on a leave of absence at any time during the Performance Period;

(c) to determine whether the Performance Goals for a Performance Period and any other material terms and conditions applicable to the Individual Award Opportunities have been satisfied;

(d) to decide whether, and under what circumstances and subject to what terms, Individual Award Opportunities are to be paid on a deferred basis, including whether such a deferred payment shall be made solely at the Committee's discretion or whether a Participant may elect deferred payment, in each case, so long as such deferral or deferral election is permissible under, and complies with the requirements set forth in Section 409A; provided, that any deferral contemplated by the Plan must be permitted by, and shall be governed by, the terms of any applicable deferred compensation plan of the Company; and

(e) to adopt, revise, suspend, waive or repeal, when and as appropriate, in its sole and absolute discretion, such administrative rules, guidelines and procedures for the Plan as it deems necessary or advisable to implement the terms and conditions of the Plan.

2.3 *Delegation of Power.* The Committee may delegate some or all of its power and authority hereunder to any officer of the Company as the Committee deems appropriate. Notwithstanding the foregoing, no Participant shall make decisions under the Plan with respect to his or her own compensation, including, without limitation, regarding his or her own Individual Award Opportunity.

SECTION 3
PERFORMANCE GOALS

3.1 *Establishing Performance Goals.* The Committee shall establish within the Applicable Period of each Performance Period one or more objective Performance Goals for each Participant or for any group of Participants (or both), provided that the outcome of each goal is substantially uncertain at the time the Committee establishes such goal. Performance Goals shall be based exclusively on one or more of the following objective corporate-wide or Subsidiary, division, operating unit or individual measures: (a) net or operating income (before or after taxes); (b) earnings before taxes, interest, depreciation, and/or amortization ("EBITDA"); (c) EBITDA excluding charges for stock compensation, management fees, restructurings and impairments ("Adjusted EBITDA"), Adjusted EBITDA growth/sales growth, operating leverage; (d) basic or diluted earnings per share or improvement in basic or diluted earnings per share; (e) sales (including, but not limited to, total sales, net sales, sales growth in excess of market growth, or revenue growth); (f) net operating profit; (g) financial return measures (including, but not limited to, return on assets, capital, invested capital, equity, sales, or revenue); (h) cash flow measures (including, but not limited to, operating cash flow, free cash flow, cash flow return on equity, cash flow return on investment, cash conversion, pre-tax, pre-interest cash flow/Adjusted EBITDA); (i) productivity ratios (including but not limited to measuring liquidity, profitability or leverage); (j) share price (including, but not limited to, growth measures and total shareholder return); (k) expense/cost management targets; (l) margins (including, but not limited to, operating margin, net income margin, cash margin, gross, net or operating profit margins, EBITDA margins, Adjusted EBITDA margins); (m) operating efficiency; (n) market share or market penetration; (o) customer targets (including, but not limited to, customer growth or customer satisfaction); (p) working capital targets or improvements; (q) economic value added; (r) balance sheet metrics (including, but not limited to, inventory, inventory turns, receivables turnover, net asset turnover, debt reduction, retained earnings, year-end cash, cash conversion cycle, ratio of debt to equity or to EBITDA); (s) workforce targets (including but not limited to diversity goals, employee engagement or satisfaction, employee retention, and workplace health and safety goals); (t) implementation, completion or attainment of measurable objectives with respect to research and development, key products or key projects, lines of business, acquisitions and divestitures and strategic plan development and/or implementation; (u) comparisons with various stock market indices, peer companies or industry groups or classifications with regard to one more of these criteria, or (v) for any period of time in which Section 162(m) is not applicable to the Company and the Plan, such other criteria as may be determined by the Administrator. Each such goal may be expressed in absolute terms, or relative to (i) current internal targets or budgets, (ii) the past performance of the Company (including the performance of one or more Subsidiaries, divisions, or operating units), (iii) the performance of one or more similarly situated companies, (iv) the performance of an index covering a peer group of companies, or (v) other external measures of the selected performance criteria. In the case of earnings-based measures, Performance Goals may include comparisons relating to capital (including, but not limited to, the cost of capital), shareholders' equity, shares outstanding, assets or net assets, or any combination thereof. The Committee may provide for a threshold level of performance below which no amount of compensation will be paid and a maximum level of performance above which no additional amount of compensation will be paid, and it may provide for the payment of differing amounts of compensation for different levels of performance. Performance Goals shall be subject to such other special rules and conditions as the Committee may establish at any time within the Applicable Period.

¶10,190

3.2 *Adjustments.* At the time the Committee determines and certifies in writing the extent to which the applicable Performance Goals for such Performance Period have been satisfied in accordance with Section 4.1, the Committee also shall take into account the following inclusion(s) or exclusion(s), as the Committee deems appropriate, for purposes of measuring performance against the applicable Performance Targets:

(a) for those occurring within such Performance Period, restructuring, reorganizations, discontinued operations, acquisitions, dispositions, or any other unusual, infrequently occurring, nonrecurring or non-core items;

(b) the aggregate impact in any Performance Period of accounting changes, in each case as those terms are defined under generally accepted accounting principles and provided in each case that such items are objectively determinable by reference to the Company's financial statements, notes to the Company's financial statements and/or management's discussion and analysis of financial condition and results of operations, appearing in the Company's Annual Report on Form 10-K for the applicable year;

(c) foreign exchange gains or losses;

(d) impairments of goodwill and other intangible assets, asset write downs, charges or expenses related to capital structure changes, or payments of bonuses or other financial and general and administrative expenses for the Performance Period;

(e) environmental or litigation reserve adjustments, litigation or claim judgments or settlements;

(f) any adjustments for other unusual or infrequently occurring items, discrete tax items, strike and/or strike preparation costs, business interruption, curtailments, natural disasters, force majeure events; or

(g) mark-to-market gains or losses.

If the Committee determines that a change in the business, operations, corporate structure or capital structure of the Company, or the manner in which it conducts its business, or other events or circumstances, render previously established Performance Goals unsuitable, the Committee may, in its discretion, modify such Performance Goals, in whole or in part, as the Committee deems appropriate and equitable.

3.3 *Capital Adjustments.* To the extent that a Performance Goal under an Individual Award Opportunity relates to the common stock of the Company, then, in the event of any stock dividend, stock split, combination of shares, recapitalization or other change in the capital structure of the Company, any merger, consolidation, spinoff, reorganization, partial or complete liquidation or other distribution of assets (other than a normal cash dividend), issuance of rights or warrants to purchase securities or any other corporate transaction having an effect similar to any of the foregoing, the Committee may make or provide for such adjustments in such Performance Goals as the Committee in its sole discretion may in good faith determine to be equitably required in order to prevent dilution or enlargement of the rights of Participants.

SECTION 4
INDIVIDUAL AWARD OPPORTUNITIES

4.1 *Terms*. At the time Performance Goals are established for a Performance Period, the Committee also shall establish an Individual Award Opportunity for each Participant or group of Participants, which shall be based on the achievement of one or more specified targets or Performance Goals. The targets shall be expressed in terms of an objective formula or standard which may be based upon the Participant's Annual Base Salary or a multiple or percentage thereof. In all cases the Committee shall have the sole and absolute discretion to: (A) reduce the amount of any payment under any Individual Award Opportunity that would otherwise be made to any Participant or to decide that no payment shall be made, and (B) determine that all or a portion of any Individual Award Opportunity shall be deemed to be earned based on such criteria as the Committee deems appropriate, including without limitation individual performance. No Participant shall receive a payment under the Plan with respect to any Performance Period in excess of $5,000,000, which maximum amount shall be prorated with respect to Performance Periods that are less than one year in duration.

4.2 *Incentive Payments*. No payment shall be made under the Plan unless and until the Committee, based to the extent applicable on the Company's audited consolidated financial statements for such Performance Period (as prepared and reviewed by the Company's independent public accountants), has certified in writing the extent to which the applicable Performance Goals for such Performance Period have been satisfied. Payments under Individual Award Opportunities shall be in cash. Payments under Individual Award Opportunities to any Participant who was an executive officer for less than the entire Performance Period shall be prorated based on the number of calendar days such Participant was an executive officer during the Performance Period. Participants must be employed on the date of payment unless determined otherwise by the Committee or the Board, provided that, in the event of termination of employment during the Performance Period due to death, disability or retirement, the Participant shall be entitled to a prorated payment for earned Individual Award Opportunities based on actual performance in accordance with Section 4.3. Incentive payments under this Plan will be made no event later than two and one-half ($2^1/2$) months after the close of the calendar year in which the Participant's right to the payment is no longer subject to a substantial risk of forfeiture or the 15th day of the third month following the end of the Company's first taxable year in which the right to the payment is no longer subject to a substantial risk of forfeiture.

4.3 *Proration Events*. If a Participant experiences any of the following events, the Participant's payout will be prorated to take such event into account: (i) time in eligible position, including periods of ineligibility pursuant to the terms of the Company's leave of absence policies; (ii) movement between business units or functions; (iii) termination of employment due to death, disability or retirement, other than a termination for cause as determined by the Company in its sole discretion, but in each case, based on actual performance. For this purpose, (A) "disability" shall have the meaning ascribed to such term by the ABC Corporation Stock Incentive Plan; and (B) retirement means termination of employment, other than for cause as determined by the Committee in its sole discretion, at or after attainment of age 62 with at least five years of continuous service with the Company.

SECTION 5
GENERAL

5.1 *Effective Date.* The Plan is adopted subject to the approval of Company stockholders at the Company's 2019 Annual Meeting, and no payment shall be made under the Plan to any Participant absent such stockholder approval. The Plan is effective when it is adopted by the Board and approved by Company stockholders.

5.2 *Amendment and Termination.* The Board or the Committee may at any time amend, suspend, discontinue or terminate the Plan.

5.3 *Non-Transferability of Awards.* No award under the Plan shall be transferable other than by will, the laws of descent and distribution or pursuant to beneficiary designation procedures approved by the Company. Except to the extent permitted by the foregoing sentence, no award may be sold, transferred, assigned, pledged, hypothecated, encumbered or otherwise disposed of (whether by operation of law or otherwise) or be subject to execution, attachment or similar process. Upon any attempt to sell, transfer, assign, pledge, hypothecate, encumber or otherwise dispose of any such award, such award and all rights thereunder shall immediately become null and void.

5.4 *Tax Withholding.* The Company shall have the right to require, prior to the payment of any amount pursuant to an award made hereunder, payment by the Participant of any federal, state, local or other taxes which may be required to be withheld or paid in connection with such award.

5.5 *Payment by a Subsidiary.* The Company may satisfy its obligations under the Plan with respect to a Participant by causing any Subsidiary to make the payment to which such Participant is entitled under the Plan.

5.6 *No Right of Participation or Employment.* No person shall have any right to participate in the Plan. Neither the Plan nor any award made hereunder shall confer upon any person any right to continued employment by the Company, any Subsidiary or any affiliate of the Company or affect in any manner the right of the Company, any Subsidiary or any affiliate of the Company to terminate the employment of any person at any time without liability hereunder.

5.7 *Beneficiary.* In the event of a Participant's death, any amount owing to the Participant, as determined by the Company in its sole discretion, shall be paid to the Participant's survivors in the following priority: (i) the Participant's surviving spouse, or surviving domestic partner who is eligible for coverage under the Company's healthcare plan or would be eligible but for the fact that the partner had coverage under another plan; or (ii) to the Participant's estate if a legal representative has been appointed, provided that, no payment shall be made if no legal representative has been appointed.

5.8 *Other Plans*. Payments under Individual Award Opportunities shall not be treated as compensation for purposes of any other compensation or benefit plan, program or arrangement of the Company or any of its subsidiaries, unless either (i) such other plan provides compensation such as payments made pursuant to Individual Award Opportunities are to be considered as compensation thereunder or (ii) the Board or the Committee so determines in writing. Neither the adoption of the Plan nor the submission of the Plan to the Company's stockholders for their approval shall be construed as limiting the power of the Board or the Committee to adopt such other incentive arrangements as it may otherwise deem appropriate.

5.9 *Binding Effect*. The Plan shall be binding upon the Company and its successors and assigns and the Participants and their beneficiaries, personal representatives and heirs. If the Company becomes a party to any merger, consolidation or reorganization, then the Plan shall remain in full force and effect as an obligation of the Company or its successors in interest, unless the Plan is amended or terminated pursuant to Section 5.2.

5.10 *Forfeiture of Individual Awards under Applicable Laws or Regulations*. The Company may (i) cancel, reduce, or require a Participant to forfeit any Individual Award Opportunity granted under the Plan or (ii) require a participant to reimburse or disgorge to the Company any amounts received pursuant to the payment of an award granted under the Plan, in each case, to the extent permitted or required by Company clawback policy, or by applicable law, regulation or stock exchange rule in effect on or after the effective date of the Plan.

5.11 *Unfunded Plan; Plan Not Subject to ERISA*. The Plan is an unfunded plan and Participants shall have the status of unsecured creditors of the Company. The Plan is not intended to be subject to the Employee Retirement Income and Security Act of 1974, as amended.

5.12 *Limitation Period for Claims*. Any person who believes he or she is being denied any benefit or right under the Plan may file a written notice with the Committee. Any claim must be delivered to the Committee within forty-five (45) calendar days of the later of the payment date of the award or the specific event giving rise to the claim. The Committee will notify the Participant of its decision in writing as soon as administratively practicable. Claims not responded to by the Committee in writing within one hundred twenty (120) calendar days of the date the written claim is delivered to the Committee shall be deemed denied. The Committee's decision is final and conclusive and binding on all persons. No lawsuit relating to the Plan may be filed before a written claim is filed with the Committee and is denied or deemed denied and any lawsuit must be filed within one year of such denial or deemed denial or be forever barred.

5.13 *Governing Law and Venue*. To the extent not preempted by federal law, the Plan shall be construed in accordance with and governed by the laws of the

State of Delaware regardless of the application of rules of conflict of law that would apply the laws of any other jurisdiction. Any and all claims and disputes of any kind whatsoever arising out of or relating to the Plan shall only be brought in the Delaware Chancery Court. The Participant or Person hereby waives any objection which it may now have or may hereafter have to the foregoing choice of venue and further irrevocably submits to the exclusive jurisdiction of the Delaware Chancery Court in any such claim or dispute.

5.14 *409A Compliance.* The Plan is intended to provide for payments that are exempt from the provisions of Section 409A to the maximum extent possible and otherwise to be administered in a manner consistent with the requirements, where applicable, of Section 409A. Where reasonably possible and practicable, the Plan shall be administered in a manner to avoid the imposition on Participants of immediate tax recognition and additional taxes pursuant to Section 409A. Notwithstanding the foregoing, neither the Company nor the Committee, nor any of the Company's directors, officers or employees shall have any liability to any person in the event Section 409A applies to any payment or right under the Plan in a manner that results in adverse tax consequences for the Participant or any of his beneficiaries or transferees. Notwithstanding any provision of the Plan to the contrary, the Board or the Committee may unilaterally amend, modify or terminate the Plan or any right hereunder if the Board or Committee determines, in its sole discretion, that such amendment, modification or termination is necessary or advisable to comply with applicable U.S. law, as a result of changes in law or regulation or to avoid the imposition of an additional tax, interest or penalty under Section 409A.

5.15 *Severability.* If any provision of the Plan is held unenforceable, the remainder of the Plan shall continue in full force and effect without regard to such unenforceable provision and shall be applied as though the unenforceable provision were not contained in the Plan.

*** *** *** ***

¶10,220 SAMPLE LANGUAGE—Qualified Retirement Plan Provisions

Qualified retirement plans are the last, best tax-favored form of compensation available. The employer's contributions are immediately deductible, yet not taxed to plan participants until eventually distributed. Some plans even permit a participant to make pre-tax salary reduction contributions. All contributions are held in a tax-exempt trust, which is protected from both the creditors of the employee/participant and creditors of the employer/plan sponsor. A qualified retirement plan must contain most of the qualification requirements and limitations applicable to such plans under the Internal Revenue Code, in addition to the provisions describing eligibility and benefits. The following are some of the key provisions from the two main types of qualified retirement plans: defined benefit pension plans and defined contribution plans. The provisions shown below could be used in the qualified plan of either a public or private company or other business entity. Limitations on qualified plan benefits are discussed in ¶1655.

Sample Qualified Retirement Plan Provisions

Defined Benefit Pension Plan

Eligibility:

(c) "Covered Employee" means any Employee employed by an Employer in a group of Employees to whom the Plan has been extended by action of the Board in accordance with section 12.1, but excluding any Employee who is included in a unit of Employees covered by a collective bargaining agreement between Employee representatives and an Employer, if retirement benefits were the subject of good faith bargaining between such Employee representatives and an Employer, and if as a result of such negotiations there has been no agreement between such parties for the Employee's coverage under this Plan.

Benefits:

(a) Normal Retirement Benefit. The monthly Normal Retirement Benefit payable upon actual retirement at or after Normal Retirement Age shall be equal to one-twelfth of the sum of three-fourths of 1 percent of the Employee's Compensation up to $6,600, plus 1 1/2 percent of such Compensation in excess of $6,600 for each year of the Employee's Credited Service.

Contributions:

6.1 Employer Contributions. The Company and each other Employer who may make a contribution shall make such contributions to the Trust Fund as shall be required under accepted actuarial principles to at least be sufficient to maintain the Plan as a qualified employee defined benefit plan meeting the minimum funding standard requirements of the Code with respect to its Participants under the Plan. Forfeitures of an Employer's Participants arising under the Plan for any reason shall be used as soon as possible to reduce the Employer's contributions under the Plan.

6.2 Participant Contributions. No Participant shall make contributions to the Plan.

Distributions:

(a) Commencement of Normal Retirement Benefit. A Participant's monthly Normal Retirement Benefit shall commence as of the first day of the month following his/her Normal Retirement Date.

Restrictions and Limitations:

Code Sec. 415

5.10 Maximum Annual Benefits. Notwithstanding any other provisions of this Plan to the contrary, the annual benefit provided under the Plan for any Participant for any Plan Year shall not exceed the lesser of: (1) $220,000 (or such higher amount as may be fixed by Treasury Regulations) (the "dollar limitation") or (2) 100% of the Participant's Section 415 Compensation for the period of three consecutive years during which the Participant both was an active participant in the Plan and had the greatest aggregate compensation from the Affiliate (the "highest average limitation"). In determining a Participant's highest three years, any 12-month period may be used, provided it is uniformly and consistently applied. In the case of a benefit beginning before age 62, the dollar limitation will be reduced so that it is the actuarial equivalent of a $220,000 Annual Benefit (as adjusted for cost of living adjustments) at age 62. In the event of a benefit commencing after age 65, the dollar limitation will be increased so that it is the actuarial equivalent of the $220,000 Annual Benefit (as adjusted for cost of living adjustments) at age 65. In the computation of the actuarial equivalent for this provision, the interest rate assumption will be seven percent in the case of a benefit beginning before age 62 and five percent in the case of a benefit beginning after age 65. In the case of a Participant who has fewer than 10 years of participation in the Plan, the dollar limitation shall be multiplied by a fraction, (i) the numerator of which is the number of years (or part thereof) of participation in the Plan and (ii) the denominator of which is 10.

Code Sec. 401(a)(17)

(a) For Plan Years beginning on or after January 1, 2018, the annual Compensation taken into account under the Plan for any Plan Year shall not exceed $275,000, adjusted each year to take into account any cost-of-living increase for such year pursuant to Code Sec. 401(a)(17)(B).

Top-25 Limitation

11.1 Restriction on Payments to Certain Highly Compensated Employees. This section 11.1 shall apply to restrict lump sum benefits payable prior to Plan termination to those 25 Highly Compensated Employees whose compensation (as defined in Code Sec. 414(s) and regulations thereunder) is the highest in the current or any prior Plan Year (the "Restricted Participants"), but only if both paragraphs (1) and (2) apply.

(1) If after payment of benefits to the Restricted Participant, the value of Plan assets would be less than 110 percent of the value of current liabilities, as the latter term is defined in Code Sec. 412(l)(7); and

(2) If the value of benefits payable to the Restricted Participant is 1 percent or more of the value of such current liabilities.

If paragraphs (1) and (2) apply, the annual payments to a Restricted Participant shall not exceed the annual payments that would be made to such person under a single life annuity that is the actuarial equivalent of the sum of the Restricted Participant's accrued benefit and other benefits under the Plan.

If a Participant's payment under the lump sum optional form of payment is restricted under this Section, a lump sum payment may nevertheless be made if the Restricted Participant enters into an agreement with the Trustee providing for repayment of any part of the distribution which is restricted hereunder in the event the Plan is terminated while such restrictions apply. The agreement shall provide for adequate security for the obligation of repayment, such as a bond, a segregated individual retirement account, or other security for repayment as may be acceptable to the Committee until either of the conditions in (1) and (2) above no longer applies.

The above restrictions shall also be applied to restrict the benefits to be provided with any amount transferred to the Plan from any prior plan attributable to Employer contributions.

Benefit Protections:

9.7 Nonalienation of Benefits.

(a) Assignment and Levy. To the maximum extent permissible at law, no benefit under this Plan shall be subject in any manner to anticipation, alienation, sale, transfer, assignment, pledge, encumbrance, levy, or charge, and any attempt so to anticipate, alienate, sell, transfer, assign, pledge, encumber, levy upon, or charge the same shall be void; nor shall any such benefit be in any manner liable for or subject to the debts, contracts, liabilities, engagements, or torts of the person entitled to such benefit.

(b) Alternate Application. If any Member or Beneficiary under this Plan becomes bankrupt or attempts to anticipate, alienate, sell, transfer, assign, pledge, encumber, or charge any benefit under this Plan, except as specifically provided herein, or if any benefit shall be levied upon, garnished, or attached, then the Retirement Committee may hold or apply the same or any part thereof to or for the benefit of such Member or Beneficiary, his/her spouse, children or other dependents, or any of them in such manner and in such proportion as the Retirement Committee may deem proper or as the court shall direct.

(c) Qualified Domestic Relations Orders. Notwithstanding (a) and (b) above, effective as of January 1, 1985, the Retirement Committee shall direct the Trustee to make all payments required by a qualified domestic relations order within the meaning of Code Sec. 414(p). The Retirement Committee shall establish reasonable procedures to determine the qualified status of domestic relations orders and to administer distributions under such orders.

(d) Judgments, Orders and Decrees. Notwithstanding (a) and (b) above, a Member's benefit under the Plan may be offset against an amount the Member is ordered or required to pay to the Plan under a judgment, order, decree, or settlement agreement that meets the requirements as set forth in Code Sec. 401(a)(13).

Roll over:

5.12 Direct Roll Overs of Eligible Roll Over Distributions. The Committee shall establish procedures under which a Participant, former Participant, or surviving spouse entitled to a single sum payment, a small amount under section 5.8, or any other "eligible roll over distribution" as defined in Code Sec.

402(c)(4) that equals $200 or more may authorize a direct roll over of all of such distribution, or part of such distribution if the amount rolled over is at least $500, excluding any employee contributions, in cash to a single individual retirement account established by the recipient or to a single qualified defined benefit or defined contribution plan maintained by the Participant's successor employer. Effective for distributions made after December 31, 2001, the Committee shall establish procedures under which a Participant, former Participant or surviving spouse may authorize direct roll overs to any 'eligible retirement plan' that accepts the distributee's eligible roll over distribution, so long as the other requirements of the preceding sentence are satisfied. An "eligible retirement plan" is an individual retirement account described in Code Sec. 408(a), an individual retirement annuity described in Code Sec. 408(b), an annuity plan described in Code Sec. 403(a), or a qualified trust described in Code Sec. 401(a), an annuity contract described in Code Sec. 403(b) and an eligible plan under Code Sec. 457(b) which is maintained by a state, political subdivision of a state, or any agency or instrumentality of a state or political subdivision of a state and which agrees to separately account for amounts transferred into such plan from this Plan. The definition of eligible retirement plan shall apply in the case of a distribution to a surviving spouse, or to a spouse or former spouse who is the alternate payee under a qualified domestic relation order, as defined in Code Sec. 414(p).

The Committee intends to provide a written explanation which summarizes appropriate tax, roll over, and withholding rules, as further described in Code Sec. 402(f), to each Participant, Beneficiary (if applicable), or alternate payee who receives an eligible roll over distribution. Such written explanation shall be provided by mail or personal delivery between 30 and 90 days before a distribution is paid out from the Plan, if such distribution constitutes an eligible roll over distribution.

Defined Contribution Plans

Eligibility:

2.1 Eligibility. Subject to the terms of the Plan, each Employee shall participate in the Plan on the first Entry Date coincident with or next following the date the Employee meets all of the following requirements:

    (i) the Employee is credited with one Year of Service;

    (ii) the Employee has attained age 18 years; and

    (iii) the Employee is not a member of a collective bargaining unit unless the collective bargaining agreement between the Employer and the union provides for participation in this Plan.

"Employee" means each and every person employed by an Employer who is classified by an Employer as a common law employee; provided that, only individuals who are paid as common law employees from the payroll of an Employer shall be deemed to be Employees for purposes of the Plan. Any person who agrees with an Employer that he/she will not be a Participant will not be eligible to participate in the Plan.

For purposes of this definition of Employee, and notwithstanding any other provisions of the Plan to the contrary, individuals who are not classified by an Employer, in its discretion, as employees under Code Sec. 3121(d) (including, but not limited to, individuals classified by the Employer as independent contractors and nonemployee consultants) and individuals who are classified by an Employer, in its discretion, as employees of any entity other than an Employer do not meet the definition of Employee and are ineligible for benefits under the Plan, even if the classification by the Employer is determined to be erroneous, or is retroactively revised. In the event the classification of an individual who is excluded from the definition of Employee under the preceding sentence is determined to be erroneous or is retroactively revised, the individual shall nonetheless continue to be excluded from the definition of Employee and shall be ineligible for benefits for all periods prior to the date the Employer determines its classification of the individual is erroneous or should be revised. The foregoing sets forth a clarification of the intention of the Company regarding participation in the Plan for any Plan Year, including Plan Years prior the amendment of this definition of Employee.

No person classified by an Employer as a temporary, seasonal or summer employee shall be deemed to be an Employee. No person who is classified by an Employer as an independent contractor shall be deemed to be an Employee. No person who is classified by an Employer as a "leased employee" shall be deemed to be an Employee. "Leased employee" shall mean any person who is not an Employee but who provides services to an Employer if:

(a) such services are provided pursuant to an agreement between the Employer and any leasing organization;

(b) such person has performed services for the Employer (or for the Employer and any related person within the meaning of Code Sec. 414(n)(6)) on a substantially full-time basis for a period of at least one (1) year; and

(c) such services are performed under the primary direction or control of the Employer.

Except as provided below, a "leased employee" shall be treated as an employee of an Employer for nondiscrimination testing and other purposes specified in Code Sec. 414(n). However, contributions or benefits provided by the leasing organization that are attributable to services performed for an Employer shall be treated as provided by the Employer. A "leased employee" shall not be treated as an employee if such "leased employee" is covered by a money purchase pension plan of the leasing organization, and the number of leased employees does not constitute more than 20% of the Employers' "nonhighly compensated work force" as defined by Code Sec. 414(n)(5)(C). The money purchase pension plan of the leasing organization must provide benefits equal to or greater than: (i) a nonintegrated employer contribution rate of at least 10% of compensation, (ii) immediate participation, and (iii) full and immediate vesting.

Employee Contributions:

3.4 Compensation Deferral Contributions. Each Employee who becomes eligible to participate may elect to defer a percentage of his/her Annual Compensation for each pay period that he/she remains a Participant in accordance with procedures established by the Plan Administrator. The Participant's election shall be made at such time and in such manner as the Plan Administrator shall determine. The Participant's election shall remain in effect until revoked or superseded by a subsequent election pursuant to procedures established by the Plan Administrator. A Participant may specify a Compensation Deferral Contribution amount equal to any whole percentage of his/her Annual Compensation, not less than 1% thereof; except that the Plan Administrator may specify a lower percentage amount of contribution from time to time in order to prevent excess contributions. A Participant may change the specified percentage of Compensation Deferral Contributions at any time, but not retroactively, by making a revised election, unless the Plan Administrator shall specify that changes are permitted less frequently.

* * *

3.10 Catch-Up Contributions. The Plan permits each "Catch-Up Eligible Participant" to make Compensation Deferral Contributions in excess of the applicable limits set forth in paragraph (c) below ("Catch-Up Contributions") in any Plan Year.

    (a) The Plan shall not permit a Participant to make Catch-Up Contributions in any Plan Year that exceed the lesser of:

        (i) the applicable dollar limit prescribed by Code Sec. 414(v) (*e.g.*, $6,000 for Plan Year 2018); and

        (ii) the excess (if any) of (A) the Participant's compensation (as defined in Code Sec. 415(c)(3)) for the year, over (B) any other Compensation Deferral Contributions the Catch-Up Eligible Participant makes for the Plan Year, other than Catch-Up Contributions under this Section 3.14.

    (b) Catch-Up Contributions to the Plan under this Section 3.14 shall not, with respect to the Plan Year in which the contribution is made:

        (i) be taken into account in applying the limits of Code Sec. 401(a)(30), Code Sec. 401(k)(11), Code Sec. 402(h), Code Sec. 402A(c)(2), Code Sec. 403(b)(1)(E), Code Sec. 404(h), Code Sec. 408(k), Code Sec. 408(p), Code Sec. 415 or Code Sec. 457 to other contributions or benefits under the Plan or under any other plan of the Employers;

        (ii) cause the Plan to be treated as failing to meet the requirements of Code Sec. 401(a)(4), Code Sec. 401(k)(3), Code Sec. 401(k)(8), Code Sec. 402(g), Code Sec. 403(b)(12), Code Sec. 408(k), Code Sec. 410(b) or Code Sec. 416 by reason of the making of (or the right to make) Catch-Up Contributions.

        For all other purposes of the Plan, Catch-Up Contributions shall be treated as Compensation Deferral Contributions.

    (c) For purposes of this Section 3.14, the term "Catch-Up Eligible Participant" means, with respect to any Plan Year, each Participant in the Plan who: (i) has attained, or will attain, age 50 before the close of the Plan Year, and (ii) who is otherwise eligible to make Compensation Deferral Elections during the Plan Year, except by reason of the application of any limitation or other restriction described in Code Sec. 401(a)(30), Code Sec. 402(h), Code Sec. 403(b)(1)(E), Code Sec. 404(h), Code Sec. 408(k), Code Sec. 408(p), Code Sec. 415, Code Sec. 457, Code Sec. 401(k)(8)(C) or Code Sec. 408(k)(6) or any comparable limitation or restriction contained in the terms of the Plan.

Employer Contributions:

3.1 Employer Contributions. The Plan is designed to qualify as a profit sharing plan for purposes of Code Sec. 401(a), Code Sec. 402, Code Sec. 412 and Code Sec. 417. The Employer may make contributions to the Plan without regard to current or accumulated earnings and profits for any taxable year or years ending with or within such Plan Year.

3.2 Matching Contributions. For each pay period beginning on or after the first Entry Date on which the Participant has satisfied the eligibility requirements of Section 2.1, the Employer shall contribute to the Trust Fund on behalf of each Participant an amount equal to 100% of the first 3% of the Participant's Compensation Deferral Contributions for the pay period, to a maximum of 3% of such Participant's Annual Compensation for such pay period. The Matching Contribution shall be contributed to the Trust Fund on behalf of each Participant who is eligible to receive such Contribution in accordance with Section 2.1, and allocated among the Investment Funds according to the Participant's election.

3.3 Profit Sharing Contributions. Each year the Employers may make a Profit Sharing Contribution to the Trust Fund in such amounts as the Company, in its sole discretion, shall determine. Employer Profit Sharing Contributions shall be held and administered in trust by the Trustee according to the terms and conditions of the Plan and Trust. Employer contributions may be paid in cash. To the extent that the Trust has obligations arising from an extension of credit of the Trust that is payable in cash within one year of the date of the Employer's contribution is made, such contribution will be paid to the Trust in cash. Any such contribution shall be allocated in accordance with Section 4.2 hereof, to those Participants eligible to receive such contribution.

Distributions:

6.1 Commencement of Benefits. The Plan shall distribute a Participant's Account in a single lump sum payment as soon as administratively feasible after the Participant's termination of employment, except as provided below. If the nonforfeitable portion of the Participant's Account exceeds (or at the time of any prior, periodic distribution ever exceeded) $5,000, the Plan shall not distribute the Participant's Account before the Participant attains Normal Retirement Date, unless the Participant consents to such distribution in writing. The Plan Administrator shall notify the Participant of the right to defer the distribution of his/her Account, subject to the limitations of Section 6.06 below. The value of a Participant's nonforfeitable Account shall be determined without regard to that portion of his/her Account that is attributable to roll over contributions (and earnings allocable thereto) within the meaning of Code Sec. 402(c), Code Sec. 403(a)(4), Code Sec. 403(b)(8), Code Sec. 408(d)(3)(A)(ii) and Code Sec. 457(e)(16).

Restrictions and Limitations:

Code Sec. 415

7.02 Limitation on Annual Additions. Any other provision of this Plan to the contrary notwithstanding, the maximum Annual Addition to the Accounts of any Participant under the Plan and any other Defined Contribution Plan maintained by an Employer may not exceed the lesser of:

    (a) $55,000 (as adjusted for cost of living increases pursuant to Code Section 415(d)), or

    (b) 100% of the Participant's Compensation for the Limitation Year.

"Annual Addition" means for each Plan Year the sum of the following amounts credited to a Participant's Accounts for the Limitation Year under all Defined Contribution Plans maintained by the Employer: (i) Employer contributions, (ii) Employee contributions, (iii) Forfeitures, and (iv) Any amounts allocated to an individual medical account (as defined in Code Sec. 415(l)(2)) that is part of any pension or annuity plan maintained by the Employer are treated as Annual Additions to a Defined Contribution Plan.

Code Sec. 401(a)(17)

1.5 Limit on Includible Compensation. The Annual Compensation of each Participant taken into account under the Plan for any Plan Year beginning after December 31, 2017, shall not exceed $275,000, as adjusted for cost-of-living increases in accordance with Code Sec. 401(a)(17)(B).

Code Sec. 402(g)

3.5 Annual Limitation on Compensation Deferral Contributions. In no event shall a Participant's Compensation Deferral Contributions to the Plan for any calendar year exceed $18,500 (for 2018). The Employer shall automatically discontinue Compensation Deferral Contributions for the remainder of the year on behalf of a Participant who reaches this limitation. If due to a mistake in fact, a Compensation Deferral Contribution in excess of $18,500 is allocated in a calendar year to the Compensation Deferral Contribution Account of any Participant, the Trustee shall return to such Participant the portion of his/her Compensation Deferral Contribution in excess of $18,500 plus any earnings and less any losses attributable to such excess not later than the April 15 immediately following the calendar year during which such excess contribution was made. If in a calendar year a Participant's Compensation Deferral Contributions under the Plan, when aggregated with any other elective deferrals made by such Participant in such calendar year to any other qualified retirement plan under Code Sec. 401(k), Code Sec. 403(b) and Code Sec. 408(k), whether or not maintained by an Employer, would otherwise exceed $18,500, such Participant may before the March 1 immediately following such calendar year notify the Plan Administrator in writing as to the portion of the amount in excess of $18,500 to be allocated to the Plan, and the Plan Administrator may, but is not required to, direct the Trustee to pay to such Participant the amount of the excess that was allocated to the Plan by such Participant plus any earnings allocated to such excess amount before the April 15 immediately following the calendar year during which the excess contribution was made. The $18,500 limitation contained in this Section shall be automatically adjusted in accordance with Code Sec. 402(g)(5) and Code Sec. 415(d).

Code Sec. 401(k)(3)

8.2 Nondiscrimination Requirements for Compensation Deferral Contributions. In no event shall the Actual Deferral Percentage of Participants who are HCEs exceed the Actual Deferral Percentage of the Participants who are Non-HCEs by more than the greater of (a) or (b):

    (a) 125% of the Actual Deferral Percentage for Participants who are Non-HCEs, or

    (b) The lesser of 200% of the Actual Deferral Percentage for Participants who are Non-HCEs or two percentage points higher than the Actual Deferral Percentage for Participants who are Non-HCEs.

"Highly Compensated Employee" means, effective January 1, 2018, an Employee who:

    (1) at any time during the Plan Year or the preceding Plan Year owns (or is considered under Code Sec. 318 to own) more than five percent of the Company or an Affiliate; or

    (2) had more than $120,000 in compensation from the Company and all Affiliates during the preceding Plan Year.

A former Employee of the Company or Affiliate is a Highly Compensated Employee for a given Plan Year if he/she separated from service (or was deemed to have separated) before the Plan Year, performs no service for the

Company or Affiliate during the Plan Year, and was a Highly Compensated Employee for the Plan Year during which he/she separated from service (or was deemed to have separated) or for any Plan Year ending on or after his/her 55th birthday.

For purposes of determining whether an individual is a Highly Compensated Employee, "compensation" means an Employee's compensation within the meaning of Code Sec. 415(c)(3).

Vesting:

5.03 Nonforfeitable Interest Upon Termination of Employment. Upon termination of a Participant's employment for any reason other than Disability, death or termination of employment after attaining the Normal Retirement Age, the Trustee shall, in accordance with the provisions of Section 6.01 of the Plan and at the instruction of the Plan Administrator, distribute to the Participant the entire interest then constituting his/her Compensation Deferral Contributions Account and Roll over Contributions Account, which are always nonforfeitable, and the nonforfeitable interest in the Participant's Matching Contributions Account, Profit Sharing Contributions Account, Frozen Plan Account and Prior Plan Account based on the Participant's Years of Service determined in accordance with the applicable schedule below:

Years of Service	Nonforfeitable Interest
Less than 2	0%
2 but less than 3	40%
3 but less than 4	60%
4 but less than 5	80%
5 or more	100%

Benefit Protections:

14.2 Assignment or Alienation of Benefits.

   (a) No benefit or interest available hereunder will be subject to assignment or alienation, either voluntarily or involuntarily.

   (b) The preceding subsection (a) shall also apply to the creation, assignment, or recognition of a right to any benefit with respect to a participant pursuant to a domestic relations order that is not a Qualified Domestic Relations Order. For purposes of this Section 14.2, "Qualified Domestic Relations Order" means any domestic relations order that creates or recognizes the existence of an alternate payee's right to, or assigns to an alternate payee the right to, receive all or a portion of the benefits payable with respect to a Participant, and that otherwise meets the requirements of Code Sec. 414(p). As soon as practical after receipt of a domestic relations order, the Plan Administrator shall determine whether it is a Qualified Domestic Relations Order. If the domestic relations order is determined to be a Qualified Domestic Relations Order, the Plan Administrator shall be permitted, in accordance with rules and regulations promulgated by the Internal Revenue Service and the rules and regulations established by the Plan Administrator, to direct the Trustee to make an immediate distribution to the alternate payee (i) if the amount is less than $5,000, (ii) as provided in any such Order, or (iii) as elected by the alternate payee. Such distribution shall be permitted regardless of the age or employment of the Participant and regardless of whether not the Participant is otherwise entitled to a distribution, but only from the Participant's vested Accounts.

(c) In addition, the prohibition of this Section 14.2 will not apply to any offset of a Participant's benefit under the Plan against an amount the Participant is ordered or required to pay to the Plan under a judgment, order, decree or settlement agreement that meets the requirements as set forth in this Section 14.2. The Participant must be ordered or required to pay the Plan under a judgment of conviction for a crime involving the Plan, under a civil judgment (including a consent order or decree) entered by a court in an action brought in connection with a violation (or alleged violation) of part 4 of subtitle B of title I of ERISA, or pursuant to a settlement agreement between the Secretary of Labor and the Participant in connection with a violation (or alleged violation) of that part 4. This judgment, order, decree or settlement agreement must expressly provide for the offset of all or part of the amount that must be paid to the Plan against the Participant's benefit under the Plan.

Roll Over:

6.8 Right to Have Accounts Transferred. Notwithstanding any provision of the Plan to the contrary that would otherwise limit an "eligible distributee" election under this Article VI, an eligible distributee may elect, at the time and in the manner prescribed by the Plan Administrator, to have any portion of an "eligible roll over distribution" paid directly to an "eligible retirement plan" specified by the eligible distributee in a "direct roll over."

(a) "Eligible roll over distribution" means any distribution of all or any portion of the balance to the credit of the eligible distributee, except that an eligible roll over distribution shall not include: (i) any distribution that is one of a series of substantially equal periodic payments (not less frequently than annually) made for the life (or life expectancy) of the distributee or the joint lives (or joint life expectancies) of the eligible distributee and the eligible distributee's designated beneficiary, or for a specified period of ten years or more; (ii) any distribution to the extent such distribution is required under Code Sec. 401(a)(9); (iii) any hardship distribution described in Code Sec. 401(k)(2)(B)(i)(IV); and (iv) the portion of any distribution that is not includible in gross income (determined without regard to the exclusion for net unrealized appreciation with respect to employer securities).

(b) "Eligible retirement plan" means an individual retirement account described in Code Sec. 408(a), an individual retirement annuity described in Code Sec. 408(b), an annuity plan described in Code Sec. 403(a), or a qualified trust described in Code Sec. 401 (a), that accepts the eligible distributee's roll over distribution. However, in the case of an eligible roll over distribution to the surviving spouse, an eligible retirement plan shall only be an individual retirement account or individual retirement annuity. "Eligible retirement plan" shall also mean an annuity contract described in Code Sec. 403(b) and an eligible plan under Code Sec. 457(b) that is maintained by a state, political subdivision of a state, or any agency or instrumentality of a state or political subdivision of a state.

(c) An "eligible distributee" means Employee or former Employee. In addition, the Employee's or former Employee's surviving spouse and the Employee's or former Employee's spouse who is the alternate payee under a qualified domestic relations order, as defined in

Sec. 414(p), are eligible distributees with regard to the interest of the spouse or former spouse.

(d) A "direct roll over" means a payment by the plan to the eligible retirement plan specified by the eligible distributee.

If a distribution is one to which Code Sec. 401(a)(11) and Code Sec. 417 do not apply, such distribution may commence less than 30 days after the notice required under Reg. § 1.411(a)-11(c) is given, provided that: (i) the Plan Administrator clearly informs the Participant that the Participant has a right to a period of at least 30 days after receiving the notice to consider the decision of whether or not to elect a distribution (and, if applicable, a particular distribution option); and (ii) the Participant, after receiving the notice, affirmatively elects a distribution.

¶10,230 SAMPLE LEGAL AGREEMENT—Sample Nonqualified Retirement Plan

The following is a sample of a nonqualified deferred compensation plan under which an employer could provide benefits and permit employee contributions in excess of those permitted under a "qualified" plan by the Internal Revenue Code. The nonqualified plan document would set forth the terms and conditions applicable to plan benefits, including the categories of employees eligible to participate in the plan, the benefits or contributions provided for under the plan, and any vesting or other restrictions. Either a public or private company or other business entity could use this sample plan. For a discussion of other nonqualified plan design issues, see ¶1755.

ABC Corporation Executive Deferred Compensation Plan

ABC Corporation has established the ABC Corporation Executive Deferred Compensation Plan effective September 1, [year], for the benefit of its executive and management employees. The Plan's purpose is to permit eligible employees to contribute a portion of their Compensation on a pre-tax basis toward retirement benefits, to provide a Plan that replicates the benefits of the ABC Corporation Retirement Savings Plan, to enhance the overall effectiveness of the ABC Corporation executive compensation program, and to attract, retain and motivate the executive and management employees.

The Plan is intended to be an unfunded plan maintained solely for the purpose of providing deferred compensation for a select group of management or highly compensated employees for purposes of Title I of ERISA. The Plan shall be administered and interpreted to the extent possible in a manner consistent with that intent.

Accordingly, ABC Corporation hereby adopts the Plan pursuant to the terms and provisions set forth below:

ARTICLE I
DEFINITIONS

Wherever used herein the following terms shall have the meanings hereinafter set forth:

1.1. *Account or Accounts.* The account or accounts maintained by the Company in the name of a Participant, including the Participant's Employer Matching Contribution Account, Employer Discretionary Contribution Account, Compensation Deferral Account and Transfer Account.

1.2. *Annual Incentive Award.* The annual bonus or compensation in addition to Salary paid to a Participant in a Plan Year, determined without regard to any deferrals elected under this Plan.

1.3. *Board.* The Board of Directors of the Company.

1.4. *Code.* The Internal Revenue Code of 1986, as amended, or as it may be amended from time to time, and all formal regulations and rulings issued thereunder.

1.5. *Committee.* The ABC Corporation Plan Administrative Committee, which is responsible for administration of the Plan. The Committee may delegate to any person or persons any of its responsibilities under the Plan.

1.6. *Company.* ABC Corporation, a Delaware corporation, or, to the extent provided in Section 7.7 below, any successor corporation or other entity resulting from a merger or consolidation into or with the Company or a transfer or sale of substantially all of the assets of the Company.

1.7. *Compensation.* A Participant's total cash compensation in any calendar year from the Employer, including, but not limited to, Salary and any Annual Incentive Award, and determined without regard to any deferrals under this Plan or the Qualified Saving Plan. Except as required by applicable law, Compensation Deferrals elected under this Plan shall not affect the determination of compensation or earnings for purposes of any other plan, policy or program maintained by an Employer.

1.8. *Compensation Deferral Account.* The account or accounts maintained under the Plan by the Company in the name of the Participant to which the Participant's Compensation Deferral Contributions are credited in accordance with the Plan.

1.9. *Compensation Deferral Contribution.* The amount of Compensation a Participant elects to defer under Section 2.1 of the Plan.

1.10. *Disability.* Total and permanent disability as a result of sickness or injury, to the extent that the Participant is prevented from engaging in any substantial gainful activity, and is eligible for and receives disability under a long-term disability insurance plan maintained by an Employer or Title II of the Federal Social Security Act.

1.11. *Employer.* The Company or any Affiliated Company that adopts the Plan with the Company's consent. An Affiliated Company is any entity that, together with an Employer, constitutes a member of a controlled group of corporations that includes, or a group of trades of businesses under common control with, the Company (as such terms are defined in Code Sec. 414). An Affiliated Company may adopt the Plan on behalf of its Executive Employees by resolution of its board of directors, or body with comparable powers if the Affiliated Company is not a corporation, subject to approval in writing by the Company.

1.12. *Employer Discretionary Contribution.* A discretionary contribution made by an Employer on behalf of one or more Participants and governed by the terms of the Plan.

1.13. *Employer Discretionary Contributions Account.* The account established for a Participant under the Plan that is credited with Employer Discretionary Contributions under Section 2.5 of the Plan.

1.14. *Employer Matching Contribution Account.* The account or accounts maintained under the Plan by the Company in the name of the Participant to which Employer Matching Contributions are credited in accordance with the Plan.

1.15. *Employer Matching Contribution.* The contribution made by each Employer under the Plan based on a Participant's Compensation Deferral Contributions, according to Section 2.2 of the Plan.

1.16. *Executive Employee.* Each employee who is an officer of the Employer with a rank of Vice President or above. The Committee from time to time shall have the discretion to designate additional individuals as Executive Employees for purposes of the Plan. An existing employee who becomes an Executive Employee during a Plan Year will be eligible to participate in the Plan at the beginning of the next Plan Year. Notwithstanding the foregoing, if the Committee determines that the inclusion of a Executive Employee will jeopardize the status of the plan as an unfunded plan maintained solely for the purposes of providing deferred compensation for a select group of management or highly compensated employees for purposes of Title I of ERISA such Executive Employees shall cease to be eligible to make Compensation Deferral Contributions.

1.17. *Key Employee.* Key Employee means, for purposes of this Plan, a Participant who, at the time of his or her distribution, is a "specified employee" as defined in Code Section 409A and Treas. Reg. Section 1.409A-1(c)(i) (or any similar or successor provisions). For purposes of determining whether a Participant is a "specified employee", the amount of compensation to be considered shall be the amount set forth in Box 1 of the Participant's Form W-2. Key Employees will be identified as of the 12-month period ending on each December 31 (the "Identification Date" as described in Treas. Reg. Section 1.409A-1(c)(i)(3)), and will be considered Key Employees for the 12-month period beginning on April 1 of the year following the Identification Date and ending on the following March 31.

1.18. *Investment Funds.* Any investment funds established and maintained under a Trust.

1.19. *Participant.* An Executive Employee of an Employer who is eligible for participation pursuant to Section 1.16 and who has completed the election and enrollment forms provided by the Committee.

1.20. *Plan.* The ABC Corporation Executive Deferred Compensation Plan, as set forth herein and as hereinafter amended from time to time.

1.21. *Plan Year.* The Plan Year shall be the calendar year; except that, the period from the September 1, [year] effective date of the Plan to December 31, [year], shall be a short Plan Year.

1.22. *Retirement Date.* The first day of the calendar month coincident with or next following the date on which the Participant attains age sixty-five (65) years.

1.23. *Qualified Savings Plan.* The ABC Corporation Retirement Savings Plan, as amended from time to time.

1.24. *Salary.* A Participant's annual base salary rate for the Plan Year, as specified by an Employer prior to each Plan Year, and determined without regard to any deferrals elected under this Plan or the Qualified Savings Plan.

1.25. *Sale of the Company.* A "Sale of the Company" means either (i) the sale, lease, transfer, conveyance or other disposition, in one or a series of related transactions, of all or substantially all of the assets of the Company (other than a collateral assignment by the Company of such assets to any lender as security for the Company's obligations to such lender), or (ii) a transaction or series of transactions (including by way of merger, consolidation, sale of equity, recapitalization or otherwise) the result of which is that (A) any "person or "group" (as such terms are used in Section 13(d)(3) of the Securities Exchange Act of 1934) other than the Company Parties becomes the "beneficial owner" (as such term is defined in Rule 13d-3 and Rule 13d-5 promulgated under the Securities Exchange Act of 1934), directly or indirectly through one or more intermediaries, of more than 50% of the voting power of the outstanding equity of the Company or (B) the beneficial owners of the Company's outstanding equity immediately prior to the transaction cease to own directly or indirectly at least 50% of the voting power of the outstanding equity of the Company other than as a result of a sale of stock that is a Public Offering.

1.26 "Separation from Service" means the Participant's separation from service with the Employer for any reason whatsoever, within the meaning of Code Sec. 409A and Treas. Reg. Section 1.409A-1(h). If an Eligible Employee terminates employment with an Employer but continues in service as a Director, the Committee will not automatically consider the Participant to have incurred a Separation from Service.

1.27. *Transfer Account.* An account representing funds transferred to the Plan on behalf of a Participant through a trust to trust transfer.

1.28. *Trust.* A trust agreement entered into by the Company under which the Employers agree to contribute to the Trust for the purpose of accumulating assets to assist the Employers in fulfilling their obligations to Participants hereunder. Such Trust agreement shall be substantially in the form of the model trust agreement set forth in Internal Revenue Service Revenue Procedure 92-64, or any subsequent Internal Revenue Service Revenue Procedure, and shall include provisions required in such model trust agreement that all assets of the Trust shall be subject to the creditors of the Employers in the event of insolvency.

1.29. *Year of Service.* Each 12-consecutive month period of an Executive Employee's continuous employment with the Employers, including period before the effective date of this Plan.

1.30. *Construction.* Words in the masculine gender shall include the feminine and the singular shall include the plural, and vice versa, unless qualified by the context. Any headings used herein are included for ease of reference only and are not to be construed so as to alter the terms hereof.

ARTICLE II
COMPENSATION DEFERRAL CONTRIBUTIONS AND EMPLOYER CONTRIBUTIONS

2.1. *Compensation Deferral Elections.* Any Executive Employee may elect to become a Participant under the Plan by completing the election form provided by the Committee. A Participant may elect to defer annually the receipt of a portion of the Compensation otherwise payable to the Participant by an Employer in any Plan Year. The amount of Compensation deferred by a Participant shall be a percentage of such Compensation, but shall not exceed: (i) fifty percent (50%) of the Participant's Salary for the Plan Year; (ii) one hundred percent (100%) of the Participant's Annual Incentive Award; and (iii) one hundred percent (100%) of any other bonus or incentive to be paid in cash to the Participant. A Participant's Compensation Deferral Election as to an Annual Incentive Award or other bonus or incentive may specify a percentage that varies depending upon the amount of the Annual Incentive Award or other bonus or incentive made to the Participant in the Plan Year.

The election by which a Participant elects to defer Compensation as provided in this Plan shall be in writing, signed by the Participant, and delivered to the Committee prior to the beginning of the period of service for which the Compensation to be deferred is otherwise payable to the Participant; except that:

(a) in the year in which the Plan is initially implemented, a Participant may make an election, no later than 30 days after the effective date of the Plan, to defer Compensation for services to be performed subsequent to the election; and

(b) in the year in which an Executive Employee first becomes eligible to participate in the Plan, such Executive Employee may make an election, no later than 30 days after such initial eligibility, to defer Compensation for services to be performed subsequent to the election.

The Participant's deferral election may not be changed, but may be revoked by written election to the Committee, effective as to Compensation earned and payable after the date of the election. Following any such revocation, no new Compensation deferral election by the Participant may be effective until the first day of the Plan Year next following the date of revocation. For purposes of this Section 2.1, "writing" includes, without limitation facsimile and other electronic transmission, and signatures includes, without limitation, an electronic signature.

Notwithstanding the foregoing, if the Participant's Annual Incentive Award qualifies as "Performance-Based Compensation" within the meaning of Code Sec. 409A and Treas. Reg. § 1.409A-1(e), the Participant will be permitted to make such a deferral election no later than June 30 of the Plan Year in which the Bonus is earned.

2.2. *Employer Matching Contributions.* An Employer shall make a matching contribution on behalf of Participants in its employ who have elected to make Compensation Deferral Contributions from Salary. The amount of the Employer Matching Contribution made on behalf of each Participant for any period shall equal fifty percent (50%) of the portion of the Participant's Compensation Deferral Contributions made from such Participant's Salary for such period, with a maximum Employer Matching Contribution equal to three percent (3%) of such Participant's Salary. No Employer Matching Contribution shall be based on a Participant's Deferral Contributions from Annual Incentive Award or other bonus or incentive pay.

2.3. *Investment of Participants' Accounts.* If the Company establishes a Trust in connection with the Plan, Participants' Compensation Deferral Contributions, Employer Matching Contributions and Employer Discretionary Contributions shall be contributed by the Employers to, and held and invested under, the Trust. Participants' Compensation Deferral Accounts, Employer Matching Contribution Accounts, Employer Discretionary Contributions Accounts, and Transfer Accounts, if any, shall be invested under the Trust until such amounts are distributed to the Participant in accordance with the provisions of Article IV of the Plan. The Company shall provide each Participant with a written statement of his/her Accounts at least annually.

2.4. *Cessation of Deferrals.* All Compensation Deferral Contributions, Employer Matching Contributions and Employer Discretionary Contributions shall cease upon a Participant's Separation from Service.

2.5. *Employer Discretionary Contributions.* An Employer may in its sole discretion contribute to the Account of a Participant an amount that it may from time to time deem advisable. Such discretionary contributions shall be credited to the Employer Discretionary Contributions Account maintained for the Participant.

ARTICLE III
VESTING OF PARTICIPANTS' ACCOUNTS

3.1. *Vesting of Participants' Accounts.* A Participant shall be fully vested in the amount in his/her Compensation Deferral Account and Transfer Account, if any, at all times.

3.2. *Vesting of Employer Discretionary and Matching Contributions Accounts.* Except as provided in the following sentence, a Participant shall be vested in his/her Employer Discretionary and Matching Contributions Accounts at a rate of twenty percent (20%) per Year of Service, according to the following schedule.

Years of Service	Vested Percentage
Less than 1 year	0%
1 year but less than 2 years	20%
2 years but less than 3 years	40%
3 years but less than 4 years	60%
4 years but less than 5 years	80%
5 years or more	100%

Notwithstanding the foregoing, the Committee, in its sole discretion, may specify in writing, a different vesting schedule applicable to any Participant or group of Participants, and/or any particular Employer Discretionary Contributions Account.

3.3. *Forfeiture Due to Competition or Breach of Confidentiality.* A Participant may not, except with the express prior written consent of the Company, for a period of two (2) years after the Participant's Separation from Service, directly or indirectly compete with the business of the Employers, including, but not by way of limitation, by directly or indirectly owning, managing, operating, controlling, financing, or by directly or indirectly serving as an employee, officer or director of or consultant to, or by soliciting or inducing, or attempting to solicit or induce, any employee or agent of an Employer to terminate employment with the Employer and become employed by any person, firm, partnership, corporation, trust or other entity that owns or operates, a [competing business] (the "Restrictive Covenant"). The foregoing Restrictive Covenant shall not prohibit a Participant from owning directly or indirectly capital stock or similar securities which are listed on a securities exchange, which do not represent more than one percent (1%) of the outstanding capital stock of any [ ] company.

If a Participant violates the Restrictive Covenant or the Company's Business Code of Conduct (or any successor code of conduct), all amounts in the Participant's Employer Discretionary and Matching Contribution Accounts shall be forfeited; except that this Section shall become ineffective upon a Sale of the Company.

3.4. *Full Vesting Provisions.* Notwithstanding the foregoing, a Participant shall be fully vested in his/her entire Account upon: (i) the date of the Participant's Separation from Service on account of death or Disability; (ii) the Participant's Retirement Date; or (iii) a Sale of the Company.

3.5. *Forfeiture.* A Participant whose Separation from Service occurs prior to the full vesting of his/her Account will forfeit the portion of his/her Account that is not vested. The Company may use any forfeiture under any Section of the Plan to reduce future Employer contributions or pay the Plan's administrative expenses.

ARTICLE IV
DISTRIBUTION OF PARTICIPANTS' ACCOUNTS

4.1. *Distribution of Participants' Accounts.* The Participant's Compensation Deferral, Employer Matching, Employer Discretionary Contribution, and Transfer Accounts, if any, shall be distributed to the Participant in accordance with Sections 4.2 and 4.3 below. A Participant's Accounts shall be distributed in cash.

4.2. *Form of Distribution.* Each Participant shall elect, at the time the Participant elects Compensation Deferral Contributions under Section 2.1 above, the form and timing of the distribution of his/her Compensation Deferral, Employer Matching Contribution, Employer Discretionary Contribution, and Transfer Accounts, if any, as follows:

    (a) in a lump sum distribution as soon as practicable after the Participant's Separation from Service; or

    (b) in substantially equal annual installment payments (as determined by the Committee) over a fixed period of 5 or 10 years, beginning as of the

January 1 coincident with or next following the Participant's Separation from Service. The entitlement to a series of installment payments will be deemed as the entitlement to a single payment.

Notwithstanding the foregoing, if the value of a Participant's Accounts is less than $5,000 at any time after the Participant's Separation from Service, such Accounts shall be distributed to the Participant in a single lump sum distribution, as soon as practicable. If a Participant does not make a valid distribution election, or if the Participant fails to elect the form or period of distribution, then the manner of payment and date for commencement of payment of the Participant's Account shall be a single lump sum payment, as soon as practicable but no later than December 31 of the calendar year of the Participant's Separation from Service or 2 1/2 months after the Participant's Separation from Service, whichever is later.

4.3. Timing of Distribution. The balance of a Participant's Accounts shall be distributed to or with respect to the Participant only: (i) upon Separation from Service; (ii) upon any date before Separation from Service that is specified by the Participant at least 12 months prior to such date, in accordance with subparagraph (d) below; (iii) upon the Participant's death; or (iv) as a result of an unforeseeable emergency in accordance with Section 4.6.

(a) Notwithstanding the Participant's election, distributions to a Participant will not begin sooner than 12 months following his or her election as to the form and timing of such distributions unless the Participant's Separation from Service is due to the Participant's death.

(b) Notwithstanding anything in this Section to the contrary, the balance of a Participant's Stock Option Deferral Account may not be distributed to or with respect to the Participant until a date that is at least 12 months from the date of deferral of the applicable Option.

(c) If the Participant modifies his or her election as to the form or timing of a distribution not related to a distribution due to death or unforeseeable emergency, the first payment with respect to such election must be deferred for a period not less than 5 years from the date the payment would have otherwise been made if not for the modification. A change in distribution election will not be effective unless the Participant files such change in writing with the Committee at least 12 months prior to the date that distribution of his or her Accounts is otherwise scheduled to commence.

(d) A Participant may elect at the time of his or her initial Deferral Agreement, to receive an in-service lump sum distribution of all or a portion of his or her Accounts, as of any date specified by the Participant. An election made in accordance with this subsection (d) will apply only to distributions of the Participant's Account made prior to the date of the Participant's Separation from Service.

(e) Notwithstanding the Participant's election, distribution of a Participant's Accounts will begin as soon as practicable after the Participant's death.

4.4. *Distributions to Key Employees Upon Separation from Service.* Notwithstanding anything in this Article to the contrary, if the Participant is a Key Employee, distribution of the Participant's Accounts upon Separation from Service will begin no sooner than 6 months after the Participant's Separation from Service, unless such Separation from Service is due to the Participant's death.

4.5. *Distribution Due to Death.* A Participant may designate a beneficiary or beneficiaries to whom the Participant's Account shall be distributed in the event such Participant dies before complete distribution of his/her Accounts. All distributions upon a Participant's death will be made in a single lump sum no later than the later of (i) December 31 of the year in which the Participant dies and (ii) the 15th day of the third month following the Participant's death. If the Participant has commenced receiving a distribution in substantially equal annual installments and dies before completing the receipt of all distributions, the remaining amount in his/her Accounts will be distributed in a lump sum no later than the later of (i) December 31 of the year in which the Participant dies and (ii) the 15th day of the third month following the Participant's death. Any such designation shall be made in writing on a form providing by the Committee. A Participant may make or change the beneficiary designation under this Section at any time prior to death. If a Participant has not designated a beneficiary under the Plan, or if no designated beneficiary is living on the date of distribution hereunder, amounts distributable pursuant to this Section shall be distributed to the Participant's spouse, if any, or to the Participant's estate. If the Committee has any doubt as to the proper beneficiary to receive payments under the Plan, the Committee shall have the right, exercisable in its discretion, to cause the Employer to withhold such payments until the matter is resolved to the Committee's satisfaction.

4.6. *Distributions Due to an Unforeseeable Emergency.* In the discretion of the Committee and at the written request of a Participant, an amount up to 100 percent of his or her vested Account may be distributed to a Participant in the case of an "unforeseeable emergency," subject to the limitations set forth below. For purposes of this Section 4.6, and in accordance with Treas. Reg. Section 1.409A-3(i)(3), an "unforeseeable emergency" is a severe financial hardship to the Participant resulting from an illness or accident of the Participant or of a dependent (as defined in Code Sec. 152(a)) of the Participant, loss of the Participant's property due to casualty, or other similar extraordinary and unforeseeable circumstances arising as a result of events beyond the control of the Participant. The circumstances that will constitute an unforeseeable emergency will depend upon the facts of each case, but, in any case, payment may not be made to the extent that such hardship is or may be relieved:

(a) through reimbursement or compensation by insurance or otherwise;

(b) by liquidation of the Participant's assets, to the extent the liquidation of such assets would not itself cause severe financial hardship; or

(c) by cessation of Deferral Contributions under the Plan.

Only one distribution on account of an unforeseeable emergency shall be permitted during a Plan Year. A Participant's request for such a distribution must be accompanied or supplemented by such evidence that the Committee or its designee may reasonably require. Withdrawals of amounts due to an unforeseeable emergency shall be permitted only to the extent reasonably needed to satisfy the unforeseeable emergency need and to pay taxes reasonably anticipated as a result of the distribution.

4.7. *Tax Effect.* Neither the Employer, the Committee, nor any firm, person, or corporation, represents or guarantees that any particular federal, state or local tax consequences will occur as a result of any Participant's participation in this Plan. Each Participant shall consult with his or her own advisers regarding the tax consequences of participation in this Plan. Notwithstanding anything to the contrary contained herein, and subject to the provisions of Code Sec. 409A, if (i) the Internal Revenue Service (IRS) prevails in its claim that all or a portion of the amounts contributed to the Plan, and/or earnings thereon, constitute taxable income to a Participant or beneficiary for any taxable year that is prior to the taxable year in which such contributions and/or earnings are actually distributed to such Participant or beneficiary, or (ii) legal counsel selected by the Committee advises the Committee that the IRS would likely prevail in such claim, the applicable Account balance shall be immediately distributed to the Participant or beneficiary. For purposes of this Section, the IRS shall be deemed to have prevailed in a claim if such claim is upheld by a court of final jurisdiction, or if the Committee, based upon the advice of legal counsel selected by the Committee, fails to appeal a decision of the IRS, or a court of applicable jurisdiction, with respect to such claim, to an appropriate IRS appeals authority or to a court of higher jurisdiction within the appropriate time period. The timing or schedule of a payment to a Participant under the Plan may be accelerated at any time the arrangement fails to meet the requirements of Code Sec. 409A. Such payment may not exceed the amount required to be included in income as a result of the failure to comply with the requirements of Code Sec. 409A and the regulations.

4.8. *Limitation on Distribution.* Notwithstanding the foregoing provisions of the Plan relating to distribution of Participant's Accounts, if distribution of a Participant's Accounts in any calendar year would not be deductible by an Employer because of the limitations of Code Sec. 162(m), such distribution shall be postponed in whole or in part, in the sole discretion of the Committee, until the first calendar year in which such distribution would not be limited as to deductibility by Code Sec. 162(m). For purposes of determining whether such distribution would be deductible, it shall be assumed that the Participant has received all other distributions to which he/she would be entitled during the year.

ARTICLE V
ADMINISTRATION OF THE PLAN

5.1. *Administration by the Committee.* The Committee shall be responsible for the general operation and administration of the Plan and for carrying out the provisions thereof.

5.2. *Powers and Duties of Committee.* The Committee shall administer the Plan in accordance with its terms and shall have all powers necessary to carry out the provisions of the Plan. The Committee shall interpret the Plan and shall have the discretion determine all questions arising in the administration, interpretation, and application of the Plan, whether of law or of fact including but not limited to, questions of eligibility and the status and rights of employees, Participants and other persons. Any such determination by the Committee shall be conclusive and binding on all persons. The regularly kept records of the Company shall be conclusive and binding upon all persons with respect to a Participant's date and length of employment, time and amount of Compensation and the manner of payment thereof, type and length of any absence from work and all other matters contained therein relating to Participants.

ARTICLE VI
AMENDMENT OR TERMINATION

6.1. *Amendment or Termination.* The Company intends the Plan to be permanent but reserves the right to amend or terminate the Plan. Any such amendment or termination shall be made pursuant to a written resolution of the Board.

6.2. *Effect of Amendment or Termination.* No amendment or termination of the Plan shall divest any Participant or beneficiary of the amount in the Participant's Accounts, including Employer Matching and Employer Discretionary Contributions, or of any rights to which the Participant would have been entitled if the Plan had been terminated immediately prior to the effective date of such amendment or termination. Upon termination of the Plan, distribution of Participants' Accounts shall be made to Participants or their beneficiaries in the manner elected by such Participants, unless the Committee determines to distribute all Accounts in lump sum distributions. No Compensation Deferral, Employer Matching, or Employer Discretionary Contributions shall be permitted after termination of the Plan. The time and form of a payment to a Participant under the Plan may be accelerated where the right to the payment arises due to a termination of the arrangement, in accordance with the provisions of Treas. Reg. Section 1.409A-3(j)(4)(ix) or any successor provisions thereto.

ARTICLE VII
GENERAL PROVISIONS

7.1. *Participants' Rights Unsecured.* Except as set forth in Section 2.3, the Plan at all times shall be entirely unfunded and no provision shall at any time be made with respect to segregating any assets of an Employer for payment of any benefits hereunder. The right of a Participant or the Participant's beneficiary to receive a distribution of the Participant's Accounts hereunder shall be an unsecured claim against the general assets of the Employers, and neither the Participant nor a beneficiary shall have any rights in or against any specific assets of any Employers.

7.2. *No Guaranty of Benefits.* Nothing contained in the Plan shall constitute a guaranty by the Employers or any other person or entity that the assets of the Employers will be sufficient to pay any benefit hereunder. No Participant or other person shall have any right to receive a benefit or a distribution of Accounts under the Plan except in accordance with the terms of the Plan.

7.3. *No Enlargement of Employee Rights.* Establishment of the Plan shall not be construed to give any Participant the right to be retained in the service of an Employer.

7.4. *Spendthrift Provision.* No interest of any person or entity in, or right to receive a distribution under, the Plan shall be subject in any manner to sale, transfer, assignment, pledge, attachment, garnishment, or other alienation or encumbrance of any kind; nor may such interest or right to receive a distribution be taken, either voluntarily or involuntarily for the satisfaction of the debts of, or other obligations or claims against, such person or entity, including claims for alimony, support, separate maintenance, whether pursuant to an order that purports to be a qualified domestic relations order under Code Sec. 414(p) or otherwise and claims in bankruptcy proceedings.

7.5. *Applicable Law; Choice of Forum.* The Plan shall be construed and administered under the laws of the State of _____ (without regard to its conflicts of law principles) except to the extent preempted by federal law. Any action or proceeding seeking to enforce any provision of, or based on any right arising out of, the Plan must be brought against any of the parties in the courts of the State of _____, county of _____or, if it has or can acquire jurisdiction, in the United States District Court for the District of _____, and each of the Company and Participants expressly consent to the jurisdiction of such courts (and of the appropriate appellate courts) in any such action or proceeding and waives any objection to venue laid therein. Process in any action or proceeding referred to in the preceding sentence may be served on any party anywhere in the world.

7.6. *Incompetency or Incapacity of Recipient.* Subject to applicable state law, if any person entitled to a payment under the Plan is deemed by the Committee to be incompetent or incapable of personally receiving and giving a valid receipt for such payment, then, unless and until claim therefor shall have been made by a duly appointed guardian or other legal representative of such person, the Committee may provide for such payment or any part thereof to be made to any other person or institution then contributing toward or providing for the care and maintenance of such person. Any such payment shall be a payment for the account of such person and a complete discharge of any liability of the Committee, and the Plan therefor. The Committee may require proof of incompetency, incapacity, guardianship or legal representation as it may deem appropriate prior to the distribution of any benefit.

7.7. *Corporate Successors.* The provisions of this Plan shall be binding upon the Company and its successors and assigns. The Plan shall not be automatically terminated by a transfer or sale of assets of the Company, or by the merger or consolidation of the Company into or with any other corporation or other entity, but the Plan shall be continued after such sale, merger or consolidation only if and to the extent that the transferee, purchaser or successor entity agrees to continue the Plan. In the event that the Plan is not continued by the transferee, purchaser or successor entity, the Plan shall terminate subject to the provisions of Section 6.2.

7.8. *Unclaimed Benefit.* Each Participant or beneficiary shall keep the Employer informed of his/her current address. The Committee shall not be obligated to search for the whereabouts of any person. If the location of a Participant is not made known to the Committee within three years after the date on which payment of the Participant's benefits under the Plan may first be made, payment may be made as though the Participant had died at the end of the three-year period. If, within one additional year after such three-year period has elapsed, or, within three years after the actual death of a Participant, the Committee is unable to locate any beneficiary of the Participant, then the Committee shall have no further obligation to pay any benefit hereunder to such Participant or beneficiary or any other person and such benefit shall be irrevocably forfeited.

7.9. *Limitations on Liability.* Notwithstanding any of the preceding provisions of the Plan, none of the Employers nor any individual acting as an employee or agent of an Employer, shall be liable to any Participant, former Participant or any beneficiary or other person for any claim, loss, liability or expense incurred in connection with the Plan, other than the payment of benefits hereunder.

7.10. *Special Distribution Provision.* Notwithstanding anything to the contrary contained herein, in the event that (i) the Internal Revenue Service (IRS) prevails in a claim that all or any portion of a Participant's Account constitutes taxable income to the Participant for any taxable year of such Participant prior to the taxable year in which such amount is distributed to him or her, or (ii) legal counsel satisfactory to the Company and the applicable Participant renders an opinion that IRS would likely prevail in such a claim, the affected portion of the Participant's Account shall be immediately distributed to the Participant (or his/her beneficiary). The Committee, in its sole discretion, also may order distributions to all similarly situated Participants and beneficiaries. For purposes of this Section, IRS shall be deemed to have prevailed in a claim if such claim is upheld by a court of final jurisdiction, or if the Company or Participant, based upon an opinion of legal counsel satisfactory to the Company and the Participant fails to appeal a decision of IRS, or a court of applicable jurisdiction, with respect to such claim, to an appropriate IRS appeals authority or to a court of higher jurisdiction within the appropriate time period.

7.11. *Notice.* Any notice or filing required or permitted to be given to the Committee under this Plan shall be sufficient if in writing and hand-delivered, or sent by registered or certified mail, to the address below:

The ABC Corporation Plan Administrative Committee
c/o ABC Corporation
123 Main Street
Anytown, AnyState 77777

Such notice shall be deemed given as of the date of delivery or, if delivery is made by mail, as of the date shown on the postmark on the receipt for registration or certification.

Any notice or filing required or permitted to be given to a Participant under this Plan shall be sufficient if in writing and hand-delivered, or sent by mail, to the last know address of the Participant.

7.12. *Transfer Account.* If a Participant has an account balance in a nonqualified deferred compensation program maintained by an affiliate of the Company, which has a transfer provision, the Participant may request that such account be transferred to this Plan in a direct trust-to-trust transfer. The amount transferred shall be added to the Participant's Account under the Plan, and shall thereafter be governed by the terms and conditions of this plan, and shall be referred to as the Transfer Account.

7.13. *FICA and Other Taxes.* The Employer shall withhold, in a manner determined by the Employer, the Participant's share of FICA and other employment taxes on Company Deferral Contributions, Employer Matching Contributions, and Employer Discretionary Contributions. The Participant's Employer, or the trustee of the Trust, shall withhold from all payments made to a Participant or beneficiary under the Plan all federal, state, and local income, employment and other taxes required to be withheld by the Employer or the trustee of the Trust, in connection with such payments, in amounts and in a manner to be determined in the sole discretion of the Employees and the trustees of the Trust.

7.14. *Indemnification.* The Employer shall indemnify and hold harmless each member of the Committee, or any employee of the Employer, or any individual acting as an employee or agent of either of them (to the extent not indemnified or saved harmless under any liability insurance or any other indemnification arrangement) from any and all claims, losses, liabilities, costs and expenses (including attorneys' fees) arising out of any actual or alleged act or failure to act made in good faith pursuant to the provisions of the Plan or the Trust, including expenses reasonably incurred in the defense of any claim relating thereto with respect to the administration of the Plan or the Trust, except that no indemnification or defense shall be provided to any person with respect to any conduct that has been judicially determined, or agreed by the parties, to have constituted willful misconduct on the part of such person, or to have resulted in his or her receipt of personal profit or advantage to which he or she is not entitled.

7.15. *Cooperation.* A Participant must cooperate with the Employer and the Committee by furnishing any and all information reasonably requested by the Employer or the Committee, in order to facilitate the payment of benefits hereunder, and taking such other actions as may be requested by the Employer.

If a Participant refuses to cooperate, the Employer shall have no further obligation to such Participant under the Plan.

7.16. *Compensation Recovery Policy.* Notwithstanding any provision in this Plan to the contrary, payments under the Plan will be subject to any compensation recovery policy established by the Employer and amended from time to time.

ARTICLE VIII
CLAIMS PROCEDURES

8.1. *Claims Procedures.* The Committee generally will distribute a Participant's Account in accordance with the Participant's election without the necessity of a formal written claim by the Participant. However, if any person believes he or she is being denied any rights or benefits under the Plan, such person (or the person's duly authorized representative) may file a claim in writing with the Committee within ninety (90) calendar days following the applicable Participant's date of termination. If any such claim is wholly or partially denied, the Committee will notify the claimant of its decision in writing. The notification will set forth, in a manner calculated to be understood by the claimant, the following: (a) the specific reason or reasons for the adverse determination, (b) reference to the specific Plan provisions on which the determination is based, (c) a description of any additional material or information necessary for the claimant to perfect the claim and an explanation of why such material or information is necessary, and (d) a description of the Plan's review procedures and the time limits applicable to such procedures, including a statement of the claimant's right to bring a civil action under ERISA Section 502(a) following an adverse benefit determination on review. Such notification will be given within ninety (90) calendar days after the claim is received by the Committee, or within one-hundred eighty (180) calendar days, if the Committee determines that special circumstances require an extension of time for processing the claim. If the Committee determines that an extension of time for processing is required, written notice of the extension will be furnished to the claimant prior to the termination of the initial ninety (90) day period. The extension notice will indicate the special circumstances requiring an extension of time and the date by which the Committee expects to render a benefit determination.

8.2. *Review Procedures.* Within sixty (60) calendar days after the receipt of notification of an adverse benefit determination, a claimant (or the claimant's duly authorized representative) may file a written request with the Committee for a review of the claimant's adverse benefit determination and submit written comments, documents, records, and other information relating to the claim for benefits. A request for review will be deemed filed as of the date of receipt of such written request by the Committee. A claimant will be provided, upon request and free of charge, reasonable access to, and copies of, all documents, records, and other information relevant to the claimant's claim for benefits. The Committee shall take into account all comments, documents, records, and other information submitted by the claimant relating to the claim, without regard to whether such information was submitted or considered in the initial benefit determination. The Committee will notify the claimant of its decision on review in writing. Such notification will be written in a manner calculated to be understood by the claimant and will contain the following: (a) the specific reason or reasons for the adverse determination, (b) reference to the specific Plan provisions on which the benefit determination is based, (c) a statement that the claimant is entitled to receive, upon request and free of charge, reasonable access to, and copies of, all documents, records, and other information relevant to the claimant's claim for benefits, and (d) a statement of the claimant's right to bring a civil action under ERISA Section 502(a). The decision on review will be made within sixty (60) calendar days after the request for review is received by the Committee, or within one-hundred twenty (120) calendar days if the Committee determines that special circumstances require an extension of time for processing the claim. If the Committee determines that an extension of time for processing is required, written notice of the extension will be furnished to the claimant prior to the termination of the initial sixty (60) day period. The extension notice will indicate the special circumstances requiring an extension of time and the date by which the Committee expects to render the determination on review.

8.3. *Disability Claims and Review Procedures.* If a claim involves a Disability determination, the claims and review procedures described in Sections 8.1 and 8.2 herein will apply but the time limits will differ. The Committee will have forty-five (45) calendar days to respond to the initial claim, and may extend the forty-five (45) calendar day period by up to thirty (30) calendar days if an extension is necessary and the Committee notifies the Participant during the forty-five (45) calendar day period of the reasons for the extension and the date by which the Committee expects to make a decision. The response deadline may be extended for an additional thirty (30) calendar day period if the Committee requires more time and notifies the Participant during the first thirty (30) calendar day extension period of the reasons for the extension and the date by which the Committee expects to make a decision.

The Participant will have one-hundred eighty (180) calendar days after receiving a notice of adverse benefit determination involving a Disability determination in which to submit a request for review of the adverse determination. The Committee shall reach a final decision and notify the Participant in writing of the decision within forty-five (45) calendar days after the date it receives the Participant's request for review, provided that the Committee may extend the response time by up to an additional forty-five (45) calendar days by notifying the Participant in writing of the extension.

8.4. *Legal Actions.* The claims and review procedures described in this Article VIII must be utilized before a legal action may be brought against the Company, the Committee, or the Plan. Any legal action must be filed within one (1) year of receiving final notice of a denied claim.

¶10,260 SAMPLE LEGAL AGREEMENT—Severance Pay Plan

The following is a sample Severance Pay Plan that sets forth the terms and conditions under which the employer would pay severance. This plan is not intended to cover change in control terminations. This plan is designed for any form of employer. The employer would also receive a release of claims from the terminating employee, which would be a separate document. This sample is designed to constitute both the legal plan document and the summary plan description. For a discussion of severance plan design, see ¶1415.

Sample Severance Pay Plan

ABC Corporation (the "Company") has established this ABC Corporation Severance Plan (the "Plan"), for the benefit of its eligible employees and the eligible employees of Affiliates. The purpose of the Plan is to provide Severance Benefits in accordance with the terms of the Plan. No individuals other than the Participants shall be eligible to receive Severance Benefits, and, unless otherwise specifically set forth herein, Severance Benefits for the Participants will be determined exclusively under the Plan. The Plan, as set forth herein, is an "employee welfare benefit plan" within the meaning of ERISA Section 3(1), and the Company intends that the Plan be administered in accordance with the applicable requirements of ERISA. This Plan document, including the information provided in Appendix A hereto, is also the summary plan description for the Plan, providing a non-technical summary of the Plan's main features and other information relating to the administration of the Plan. The Plan shall continue in effect until terminated by the Company, subject to Section 6.1 herein.

For purposes of the Plan, words in the masculine gender shall include the feminine and the singular shall include the plural, and vice versa, unless qualified by the context. Any headings used herein are included for case of reference only and are not to be construed so as to alter the terms hereof.

ARTICLE I
DEFINITIONS

Capitalized terms used in the Plan shall have the meanings set forth below, unless otherwise defined in the text of the Plan:

1.1 "Affiliate" means a Person that directly or indirectly through one or more intermediaries, controls, is controlled by, or is under common control with, the Company. For purposes of the preceding sentence, the word "control" (by itself and as used in the terms "controlling," "controlled by," and "under common control with") means the possession, direct or indirect, of the power to direct or cause the direction of the management and policies of a Person, whether through the ownership of voting securities, by contract, or otherwise.

1.2 "Alternative Benefits" has the meaning given to such term in Section 2.2(a) herein.

1.3 "Base Pay" means, at any time, the weekly base pay rate (based on a Participant's annual salary or hourly wage rate) shown in the Employer's records

¶10,260

as of the effective date of a Participant's termination of employment, excluding any (a) incentive, bonus, non-cash, equity or similar compensation or awards, (b) shift differentials and overtime, and (c) Retirement Benefit Plan and/or Health and Welfare Benefit Plan contributions made by the Employer.

1.4 "Board" means the Board of Directors of the Company.

1.5 "Cash Payment" has the meaning given to such term in Section 2.5(a) herein.

1.6 "Cause" means (a) such term as defined in any employment, consulting, change in control, severance, or other agreement between the Participant and the Company in effect at the time of the Committee's determination as to whether Cause exists, or (b) in the absence of any such agreement defining Cause, the Participant's (i) willful and continuing failure to reasonably perform his or her duties to the Company or an Affiliate, or willful failure to follow the lawful instructions of the Board or his or her direct superiors, in each case, other than as a result of the Participant's incapacity due to physical or mental illness or injury, and such failure has resulted or could reasonably be expected to result in harm (whether financially, reputationally, or otherwise) to the Company or an Affiliate; (ii) engaging in conduct that is materially harmful or detrimental (whether financially, reputationally, or otherwise) to the Company or an Affiliate; (iii) conviction of, or plea of guilty or no contest to, a felony or any crime involving as a material element fraud or dishonesty or moral turpitude; (iv) willful misconduct, gross neglect, or willful violation of the Company's written policies, in each case, which has resulted or could reasonably be expected to result in material harm (whether financially, reputationally, or otherwise) or detriment to the Company or an Affiliate; (v) fraud or misappropriation, embezzlement, or misuse of funds or property belonging to the Company or an Affiliate; (vi) act of personal dishonesty that involves personal profit in connection with the Participant's employment or service with the Company or an Affiliate; or (vii) willful breach of fiduciary duty owed to the Company or an Affiliate; provided, however, that the Participant shall be provided written notice thereof and a ten (10) calendar day period to cure any of the events or occurrences described in the immediately preceding clause (b) hereof, to the extent capable of cure during such period. In addition, a Participant's termination of employment shall be deemed to have been for Cause if, after the Participant's employment has terminated, facts and circumstances are discovered that would have justified a termination for Cause. Any determination of whether Cause exists shall be made by the Committee in its sole discretion.

1.7 "Code" means the U.S. Internal Revenue Code of 1986 and the regulations thereunder, as amended from time to time.

1.8 "Committee" means the ABC Corporation Benefit Plans Committee, which is the plan administrator of the Plan.

1.9 "Company" means ABC Corporation, a Delaware corporation, and any successor thereto as provided in Section 7.8 herein.

1.10 "Company Group" means, collectively, the Company and its Affiliates.

1.11 "Competing Entity" has the meaning given to such term in Section 3.4(c) herein.

1.12 "Competitive Activity" has the meaning given to such term in Section 3.4(c) herein.

1.13 "Confidential Information" has the meaning given to such term in Section 3.1 herein.

1.14 "Employer" means, as applicable, the Company or the Affiliate thereof that employs a Participant and that has adopted the Plan.

1.15 "ERISA" means the Employee Retirement Income Security Act of 1974 and the regulations thereunder, as amended from time to time.

1.16 "Health and Welfare Benefit Plan" means (a) any health and dental plan, disability plan, accidental death and dismemberment plan, survivor income plan, and life insurance plan or arrangement made available by the Employer for its employees, and (b) any such additional or substitute plan or arrangement that the Employer may make available in the future and during the term of the Plan for its employees, in each case that is a "welfare plan" (as such term is defined in ERISA Section 3(1)).

1.17 "Involuntary Termination" has the meaning given to such term in Section 2.3 herein.

1.18 "Participant" means a regular, full-time salaried (*e.g.*, exempt or non-exempt) employee of the Employer or a regular, full-time hourly employee of the Employer, other than an employee that is covered by a collective bargaining agreement. Notwithstanding anything herein to the contrary, any individual that is a party or subject to a written employment agreement or other written agreement, arrangement or policy with any entity within the Company Group (collectively, a "Written Arrangement"), that provides for Alternative Benefits may receive Severance Benefits under the Plan only under the circumstances described in Section 2.2 herein. Any individual who is not treated as an employee for purposes of the tax reporting of wages by the Employer and who is subsequently reclassified as an employee for such purposes shall not be considered a "Participant" for the period during which he or she was not classified as an employee by the Employer.

1.19 "Person" has the meaning given to such term in Sections 13(d) and 14(d)(2) of the Securities Exchange Act of 1934 and the regulations thereunder, as amended from time to time.

1.20 "Plan" means the ABC Corporation Severance Plan, as set forth herein and as amended from time to time.

1.21 "Plan Year" means the twelve (12) month period that begins each January 1 and ends on the next December 31.

1.22 "Release" has the meaning given to such term in Section 2.8 herein.

1.23 "Release Deadline" means the date that is (a) if the Participant is under forty (40) years of age as of the Participant's termination date, twenty-eight (28) calendar days after a Participant's termination of employment, or (b) if the Participant is forty (40) years of age or more as of the Participant's termination date, fifty-two (52) calendar days after a Participant's termination of employment.

1.24 "Restricted Period" means a period of time equal to (a) the number of weeks of Base Pay used in the calculation to determine the Cash Payment in accordance with Section 2.5(a), plus (b) the number of days elapsed between the date of the Participant's termination and the expiration of the period during which the Participant may revoke his/her acceptance and execution of the Release.

1.25 "Retirement Benefit Plan" means (a) any qualified or non-qualified retirement, savings or deferred compensation plan, program or arrangement currently made available by the Employer for its employees, and (b) any such additional or substitute plan, program or arrangement that the Employer may make available in the future and during the term of the Plan for its employees, in each case that is a "pension plan" (as such term is defined in ERISA Section 3(2)).

1.26 "Separation from Service" means a Participant's termination of employment with the Company and all Affiliates in a manner such as to constitute a separation from service as defined under Code Section 409A. For purposes of this Section, and in accordance with Treasury Regulation § 1.409A-1(h)(1)(ii) (or any similar or successor provisions), a Separation from Service shall be deemed to occur, without limitation, if the Company and the Participant reasonably anticipate that the level of bona fide services the Participant will perform after a certain date (whether as an employee or an independent contractor) will permanently decrease to less than fifty percent (50%) of the average level of bona fide services provided by the Participant in the immediately preceding thirty-six (36) months.

1.27 "Severance Benefits" has the meaning given to such term in Section 2.5 herein.

1.28 "Severance Pay Period" means any period during which a Participant is eligible to receive a payment or benefit under the Plan.

1.29 "Suitable Position" has the meaning given to such term in Section 2.3 herein.

1.30 "Years of Service" means a Participant's aggregate period of employment with an Employer as an employee divided into whole years, subject to the following rules: (a) any absence from employment for a period of twelve (12) or more successive months will be excluded; (b) any remaining partial period of employment of at least six (6) months will be rounded up to be considered as a full Year of Service; and (c) any remaining partial period of employment of less than six (6) months will not be included when calculating Years of Service. Notwithstanding the foregoing, and unless otherwise set forth in any Written Arrangement, if a Participant was previously eligible for severance benefits under the Plan or any other plan, program, policy or arrangement sponsored by an Employer and is subsequently rehired by an Employer, such Participant's

Years of Service shall be cancelled in an amount determined by the Company as appropriate to avoid duplication of the payment of severance benefits related to the period of employment prior to such Participant's rehire for which severance benefits were earlier paid.

ARTICLE II
SEVERANCE BENEFITS

2.1 Eligibility for Severance Benefits. Subject to the conditions and limitations of the Plan (including without limitation adherence to and compliance with the restrictive covenants set forth in Article III herein), a Participant who experiences an Involuntary Termination (as defined below) shall be entitled to receive Severance Benefits as set forth below. For purposes of the Plan, a Participant's employment with the Employer shall be terminated when the Participant has a Separation from Service and references to termination of employment shall be deemed to refer to such a Separation from Service. Upon a Participant's Separation from Service for any reason, such Participant will be deemed to have resigned as of the date of such Participant's Separation from Service from all offices, directorships, and fiduciary positions with the Company Group and employee benefit plans, if any, held by such Participant. Notwithstanding the foregoing or anything contained herein to the contrary, in the event that a Participant is a party or subject to a Written Arrangement, and such Participant experiences an Involuntary Termination and/or any other cessation of Participant's employment addressed in or covered by such Written Arrangement, the terms of such Written Arrangement shall control and, except for Section 2.2 below, the remaining terms of this Plan shall not apply.

2.2 Eligibility for Alternative Benefits; No Duplication of Benefits.

(a) Notwithstanding anything in the Plan to the contrary, if a Participant is eligible for severance-type benefits under a Written Arrangement or any other written plan with a member of the Company Group ("Alternative Benefits"), then such Participant shall remain and be eligible for those benefits; provided that (i) if the amount of the Alternative Benefits would be less than the aggregate Cash Payment that the Participant would otherwise be eligible to receive under the Plan, then the Cash Payment will be offset on a dollar-for-dollar basis by the amount of such Alternative Benefits and (ii) if the amount of the Alternative Benefits would be greater in the aggregate than the Cash Payment that the Participant would otherwise be eligible to receive under the Plan, then the Participant shall not receive benefits under this Plan, but instead shall be entitled to receive solely such Alternative Benefits.

(b) In no event shall a Participant be entitled to receive both Severance Benefits under the Plan and Alternative Benefits, except as offset pursuant to Section 2.2(a) herein. The obligation of the Employer to make payments or provide benefits hereunder is expressly conditioned upon the Participant not receiving duplicate benefits.

2.3 Termination of Employment. A Participant shall be entitled to receive Severance Benefits under the Plan only if his or her employment with the Employer is terminated involuntarily by the Employer and not as a result of the following (an "Involuntary Termination"):

(a) a resignation by the Participant for any reason, including retirement or any other voluntary termination of employment;

(b) the Participant's death or disability (as defined in an applicable long-term disability plan of the Employer);

(c) in connection with the Participant's termination of employment, the Participant is offered employment in a Suitable Position (as defined below) at any facility or place of business of a member of the Company Group;

(d) the Participant's termination of employment is in conjunction with the sale or transfer, whether of stock or assets, of all or part of the Participant's Employer, and the Participant is offered a Suitable Position with the entity acquiring the stock or assets, or with the transferred entity;

(e) the Employer terminates the Participant's employment for failure to meet expectations with respect to the Participant's performance; provided, however, that the Participant shall be provided written notice thereof and a ten (10) calendar day period to cure such performance failure, to the extent capable of cure during such period. In all cases, the Employer will determine, in good faith and in the exercise of its discretion, and designate whether a Participant is terminated for same; or

(f) a termination by the Employer for Cause.

For purposes of the Plan, a "Suitable Position" is one for which the Participant is reasonably qualified in terms of skills, performance, experience, training or education, regardless of which member of the Company Group or for which business group within a member of the Company Group it is offered.

For the avoidance of doubt, a Participant shall not be entitled to receive any Severance Benefits, and the Company Group shall have no further obligations under the Plan (other than to pay any Accrued Benefits, as defined below), if the Participant's employment is terminated for any of the reasons set forth in clauses (a) through (f) immediately above.

2.4 Accrued Benefits. In the event that a Participant experiences a termination of employment for any reason, such Participant shall receive (a) accrued but unpaid Base Pay through the date of termination, payable in accordance with the Employer's normal payroll practice; (b) accrued but unused vacation through the date of termination, in accordance with the Employer's vacation policy as in effect from time to time and with applicable law; and (c) other benefits mandated under the terms of any of the Employer's employee plans or programs (collectively, the "Accrued Benefits").

2.5 Severance Benefits. In the event that a Participant experiences an Involuntary Termination, provided that such Participant executes and does not revoke a Release in accordance with Section 2.8 herein and, to the extent permitted by law, complies with the provisions of Article III herein and with any other written restrictive covenant agreements in place between the Participant and a member of the Company Group, the Employer shall provide the Participant with severance benefits set forth in clauses (a), (b) and (c) below (collectively, the "Severance Benefits"):

(a) A Participant shall be provided a cash severance payment payable in a single lump sum after the expiration of the Release Deadline, calculated as a certain number of weeks of Base Pay, subject to Section 2.8 herein, determined as follows (the "Cash Payment"):

Job Level	Formula	Maximum Severance Benefit

provided, however, that the minimum Cash Payment for any Participant shall be four (4) weeks of Base Pay for all Job Levels.

(b) To the extent that the Participant is participating in the Employer's group health, dental, vision, prescription drug, health care spending accounts and/or the employee assistance program on the date of his or her Involuntary Termination, the Employer shall offer such Participant and his or her eligible dependents COBRA continuation coverage in accordance with the terms of such plans and, if the Participant timely elects COBRA continuation coverage, the Employer shall continue the Participant's coverage for one full calendar month following the month of the Participant's Involuntary Termination, at the same level of Participant contribution as the Participant was paying immediately prior to the Involuntary Termination (the "COBRA Benefit"). By way of example only, if a Participant's Involuntary Termination occurred on June 15, 2018, the COBRA Benefit would end on July 31, 2018.

All Employee classifications are determined based on the Company's internal practices and procedures. Notwithstanding the foregoing, the Committee may choose, in its sole discretion, to pay the Severance Benefits in equal installments during the Severance Pay Period in accordance with the Employer's normal payroll practice and commencing upon the expiration of the Release Deadline, but only if and to the extent that such installments would not cause the Severance Benefits to be subject to tax under Code Section 409A. The Severance Benefits will not be deemed compensation for purposes of any Retirement Benefit Plan, provided that the Severance Benefits will be deemed compensation for purposes of any tax-qualified Retirement Benefit Plan only to the extent permitted by the terms of such Retirement Benefit Plan and by the applicable provisions of the Code.

2.6 Certain Reductions. The Severance Benefits shall be in lieu of and reduced by any severance, notice, termination pay or the like that may be payable under any plan or practice of the Employer, or that may be payable by any Federal, state, local, or foreign law, statute, regulation, ordinance, or the like (including the U.S. Worker Adjustment and Retraining Notification Act or any similar state or foreign law). Any Severance Benefits will be offset against any severance, notice, or termination pay required to be paid by a member of the Company Group pursuant to federal, state, or local law or ordinance. In addition, the Severance Benefits shall be reduced by any amount owed by the Participant to any member of the Company Group (such as cash advances, outstanding loans, relocation and education assistance reimbursements, etc.) and by any severance payment received by such Participant with respect to a prior termination of employment with the Employer or any other member of the Company

Group, to the extent the prior service relating to such severance payment is included in applicable service for the current calculation (unless such reduction would result in Severance Benefits less than the amount that would be determined without taking into account such prior service).

2.7 Notice of Termination. Any termination of the Participant's employment by the Employer for Cause shall be communicated by a written notice to the Participant that indicates the specific termination provision in the Plan relied upon and sets forth in reasonable detail the facts and circumstances claimed to provide a basis for termination of the Participant's employment under the provision so indicated.

2.8 Release. Notwithstanding anything in the Plan to the contrary, as a condition to receiving any Severance Benefits, the Participant shall execute a comprehensive separation agreement and release and waiver of claims in favor of the Employer, including confidentiality, non-competition, non-solicitation, and non-disparagement covenants, in the form provided by the Employer (the "Release"). The Employer shall deliver the Release to the Participant within ten (10) calendar days of the Participant's termination of employment. The Participant must deliver to the Employer an original, signed Release and the revocability period (if any) must elapse by the Release Deadline. Payment of any Severance Benefits that are not exempt from Code Section 409A shall be delayed until the Release Deadline, irrespective of when the Participant executes the Release; provided, however, that where the Participant's termination of employment and the Release Deadline occur within the same calendar year, the payment may be made up to thirty (30) calendar days prior to the Release Deadline, and provided further that where the Participant's termination of employment and the Release Deadline occur in two separate calendar years, payment may not be made before the later of January 1 of the second year or the date that is thirty (30) calendar days prior to the Release Deadline. If the Participant does not deliver an original, signed Release to the Employer by the Release Deadline, (a) the Participant's rights shall be limited to the Accrued Benefits, and (b) the Employer shall have no obligation otherwise to provide the Participant any Severance Benefits or any other monies on account of the termination of the Participant's employment.

By accepting the Severance Benefits, the Participant acknowledges and agrees that if the Participant files a lawsuit or accepts recoveries, payments, or benefits based on any claims that the Participant has released under the Release, as a condition precedent for maintaining or participating in any lawsuit or claim, or accepting any recoveries, payments, or benefits, the Participant shall forfeit immediately such Severance Benefits and reimburse the Employer for any Severance Benefits already provided.

2.9 No Further Obligations. Except as provided in the Plan or in any Retirement Benefit Plan or Health and Welfare Benefit Plan, neither the Employer nor any other member of the Company Group shall have any obligation to the Participant following the Participant's termination of employment for any reason, including any obligation for severance payments or benefits. Except as provided in the Plan, the provision of Severance Benefits shall have no effect upon the Participant's rights under any Retirement Benefit Plan, Health and Welfare Benefit Plan, or other employee policy or practice of the Employer applicable to the Participant's termination for any reason.

ARTICLE III
RESTRICTIVE COVENANTS

3.1 Confidentiality. No Participant shall ever, directly or indirectly: (i) use or disclose, for the benefit of any person, firm, or entity other than a member of the Company Group, the Confidential Information of the Company Group; (ii) distribute or disseminate in any way to anyone other than an Employer's employees with a "need to know," any Confidential Information in any form whatsoever; (iii) copy any Confidential Information other than for use by an Employer or the Participant in the ordinary course of performing his/her job; (iv) misappropriate any Confidential Information of a member of the Company Group; and (v) fail to safeguard all confidential and/or classified documents. For purposes of this Agreement, "Confidential Information" means information or material that is not generally available to or used by others or the utility or value of which is not generally known or recognized as a standard practice, whether or not the underlying details are in the public domain, including but not limited to computerized and manual systems, procedures, reports, client lists, review criteria and methods, financial methods and practices, plans, pricing and marketing techniques, business methods and procedures, and other valuable and proprietary information relating to the pricing, marketing, design, manufacture, and formulation of the products of any member of the Company Group, as well as information regarding the past, present, and prospective customers of any member of the Company Group and their particular needs and requirements, and their own confidential information.

3.2 Return of Company Property. Upon a Participant's termination of employment for any reason, the Participant shall return to the Employer all policy and procedure manuals, records, notes, data, memoranda, and reports of any nature (including computerized and electronically stored information) that are in the Participant's possession and/or control that relate to any (i) Confidential Information, or (ii) business activities or facilities of a member of the Company Group, or past, present, or prospective customers of any member of the Company Group, as well as any original documents related to the Participant's employment, other than the Participant's copy of the Plan.

3.3 Non-Disparagement. No Participant shall ever, in any manner, directly or indirectly, take any action that disparages, adversely affects or places in a false or negative light any member of the Company Group or any of such member's officers, directors, owners, employees, members, agents, advisors, consultants, insurers, attorneys, successors, and/or assigns of any of the foregoing; provided that the Participant shall not be required to make any untruthful statement or to violate any law.

3.4 Non-Solicitation; Non-Competition.

(a) During a Participant's employment with the Employer and continuing until the expiration of the Restricted Period, the Participant shall not directly or indirectly solicit, induce or retain, or assist any third party in soliciting, inducing, or retaining, any current or former employee of any member of the Company Group to become associated with, or to perform services on behalf of, the Participant or any Competing Entity, or otherwise disrupt, impair, damage, or interfere with such member of the Company Group's relationships with its employees.

(b) To the extent permitted by law, during the Restricted Period, a Participant shall not associate, directly or indirectly, as an employee, officer, director, agent, partner, owner, stockholder, representative, consultant, for, or on behalf of any Competing Entity. The restrictions in the foregoing sentence shall apply to the Participant's direct and indirect performance of the same or similar activities the Participant has performed for the Employer or any other member of the Company Group and to all other activities that reasonably could lead to the use or the disclosure of Confidential Information. The Participant will not have violated this Section 3.4(b) solely as a result of the Participant's investment in capital stock or other securities of a Competing Entity listed on a national securities exchange or actively traded in the over-the-counter market if the Participant and the members of the Participant's immediate family do not, directly or indirectly, hold more than one percent (1%) of all such shares of capital stock or securities issued and outstanding.

(c) For purposes of this Agreement, (i) "Competing Entity" means any person or entity engaged in or about to become engaged in any Competitive Activity, and (ii) "Competitive Activity" means any business, work, or other activity (x) that competes in any way, in any geographic market in which the Participant worked or for which the Participant had responsibility during the last two (2) years of his or her employment with the Employer or any other member of the Company Group, with any product, service, or business of Employer or such member of the Company Group with which the Participant worked or for which the Participant had responsibility at any time during the Participant's employment or (y) that involves or would inevitably involve the disclosure or use of Confidential Information.

3.5 Non-Solicitation. During the Restricted Period, the Participant shall not directly or indirectly solicit, induce, or influence, or attempt to solicit, induce, or influence, any customer, prospective customer, supplier, or vendor of the Employer or any other member of the Company Group to divert his, her, or its business away from any member of the Company Group to any Competing Entity, or otherwise disrupt, impair, damage or interfere with any of the Employer's or such member of the Company Group's contractual or business relationships, including without limitation with respect to any of its customers, suppliers, or vendors. For purposes of this Agreement, a "prospective" customer shall be one with respect to whom or which the Participant had contact or participated in any proposal to provide products or services during the last two (2) years of Participant's employment with the Employer or any other member of the Company Group.

3.6 Exception. Notwithstanding the foregoing, a Participant's obligations under Sections 3.1 through 3.3 shall not (a) prohibit the Participant from disclosing matters that are protected under any applicable whistleblower laws, including reporting possible violations of laws or regulations, or responding to inquiries from, or testifying before, any governmental agency or self-regulating authority, all without notice to or consent from the Company, or (b) limit the Participant's ability the Participant to file a charge or complaint with any governmental agency or to participate in any investigation or proceeding that may be conducted by any governmental agency.

ARTICLE IV
ADMINISTRATION OF THE PLAN

4.1 Administration by the Committee. The Committee shall be responsible for the general operation and administration of the Plan and for carrying out the provisions thereof.

4.2 Powers and Duties of Committee. The Committee shall administer the Plan in accordance with its terms and shall have all powers necessary to carry out the provisions of the Plan. The Committee shall interpret the Plan and shall determine all questions arising in the administration, interpretation, and application of the Plan, including, but not limited to, questions of eligibility and the status and rights of employees, Participants, and other persons. Any such determination by the Committee shall be conclusive and binding on all persons. The regularly kept records of the Committee shall be conclusive and binding upon all persons with respect to a Participant's date and length of employment, Years of Service, time and amount of Compensation, and the manner of payment thereof, type and length of any absence from work and all other matters contained therein relating to Participants.

4.3 Code Section 409A. Notwithstanding any other provision herein, the Plan is intended to comply with or be exempt from Code Section 409A, including the exceptions for short-term deferrals, separation pay arrangements, reimbursements, and in-kind distributions, and shall at all times be interpreted and administered in accordance with such intent. To the extent that any provision of the Plan violates Code Section 409A, such provision shall be automatically reformed, if possible, to comply with Code Section 409A or stricken from the Plan.

(a) To the extent that a distribution is on account of a Participant's Separation from Service and the Participant is a Specified Employee (as defined below) as of the date of Separation from Service, distributions to the Participant that are not otherwise excluded under Code Section 409A under the exception for short-term deferrals, separation pay arrangements, reimbursements, in-kind distributions, or any otherwise applicable exemption, may not be made before the date that is six (6) months after the date of Separation from Service (the "Six Month Delay") or, if earlier, the date of the Participant's death. Payments to which the Participant otherwise would be entitled during the Six Month Delay will be accumulated and paid on the first day of the seventh (7th) month following the Separation from Service or, if earlier, the date of the Participant's death. For purposes of the Plan, the term "Specified Employee" has the meaning given to that term in Code Section 409A and Treasury Regulation § 1.409A-1(i) (or any similar or successor provisions).

(b) Each payment under the Plan or any Employer benefit plan is intended to be treated as one of a series of separate payments for purposes of Code Section 409A.

(c) To the extent any reimbursements or in-kind benefit payments under the Plan are subject to Code Section 409A, such reimbursements and in-kind benefit payments will be made in accordance with Treasury Regulation Section 1.409A-3(i)(1)(iv) (or any similar or successor provisions).

(d) The Company may amend the Plan to the minimum extent necessary to satisfy the applicable provisions of Code Section 409A.

(e) Nothing in the Plan shall be construed as a guarantee of any particular tax effect for Participants.

(f) Notwithstanding any other provision of the Plan, no election shall be permitted, and no payment shall be made that would violate the requirements of or cause taxation to any person under Code Section 409A. All provisions of the Plan shall be interpreted in a manner consistent with Code Section 409A and the regulations and other guidance promulgated thereunder.

(g) The Company cannot and does not guarantee that the Severance Benefits provided under the Plan will satisfy all applicable provisions of Code Section 409A.

ARTICLE V
CLAIMS PROCEDURES

5.1 Claims Procedures. The Employer will provide Severance Benefits without the necessity of a formal written claim by the Participant. However, if any person believes he or she is being denied any rights or benefits under the Plan, or receives an adverse benefit determination, such person (or the person's duly authorized representative) may file a claim in writing with the Committee within ninety (90) calendar days following the applicable Participant's date of termination.

5.2 Non-Disability Related Claims. If any such claim is wholly or partially denied, the Committee will notify the claimant of its decision in writing. The notification will set forth, in a manner calculated to be understood by the claimant, the following: (a) the specific reason or reasons for the adverse determination, (b) reference to the specific Plan provisions on which the determination is based, (c) a description of any additional material or information necessary for the claimant to perfect the claim and an explanation of why such material or information is necessary, and (d) a description of the Plan's review procedures and the time limits applicable to such procedures, including a statement of the claimant's right to bring a civil action under ERISA Section 502(a) following an adverse benefit determination on review. Such notification will be given within ninety (90) calendar days after the claim is received by the Committee, or within one-hundred eighty (180) calendar days, if the Committee determines that special circumstances require an extension of time for processing the claim. If the Committee determines that an extension of time for processing is required, written notice of the extension will be furnished to the claimant prior to the termination of the initial ninety (90) day period. The extension notice will indicate the special circumstances requiring an extension of time and the date by which the Committee expects to render a benefit determination.

5.3 Review Procedures. Within sixty (60) calendar days after the receipt of notification of an adverse benefit determination, a claimant (or the claimant's duly authorized representative) may file a written request with the Committee for a review of the claimant's adverse benefit determination and submit written comments, documents, records, and other information relating to the claim for benefits. A request for review will be deemed filed as of the date of receipt of such written request by the Committee. A claimant will be provided, upon request and free of charge, reasonable access to, and copies of, all documents, records, and other information relevant to the claimant's claim for benefits. The Committee shall take into account all comments, documents, records, and other information submitted by the claimant relating to the claim, without regard to whether such information was submitted or considered in the initial benefit determination. The Committee will notify the claimant of its decision on review in writing. Such notification will be written in a manner calculated to be understood by the claimant and will contain the following: (a) the specific reason or reasons for the adverse determination, (b) reference to the specific Plan provisions on which the benefit determination is based, (c) a statement that the claimant is entitled to receive, upon request and free of charge, reasonable access to, and copies of, all documents, records, and other information relevant to the claimant's claim for benefits, and (d) a statement of the claimant's right to bring a civil action under ERISA Section 502(a). The decision on review will be made within sixty (60) calendar days after the request for review is received by the Committee or within one-hundred twenty (120) calendar days if the Committee determines that special circumstances require an extension of time for processing the claim. If the Committee determines that an extension of time for processing is required, written notice of the extension will be furnished to the claimant prior to the termination of the initial sixty (60) day period. The extension notice will indicate the special circumstances requiring an extension of time and the date by which the Committee expects to render the determination on review.

5.4 Disability Claims and Review Procedures. If a claim involves a disability determination, the claims and review procedures described in Sections 5.1 through 5.3 above will apply but the time limits will differ. If a claim involves a disability determination, the claims and review procedures described in Sections 5.4(a) and (b) will apply.

(a) Disability Related Claims. If any such claim is a disability related determination and is approved or wholly or partially denied, the Committee will notify the claimant of its decision in writing. The notification shall be provided in a culturally and linguistically appropriate manner) and will contain the following:

(i) the specific reason or reasons for the adverse determination, including the basis for disagreeing with or not following (if applicable) (1) the views presented by the claimant to the Committee of health care professionals treating the claimant and vocational professionals who evaluated the claimant; (2) the views of medical or vocational experts whose advice was obtained on behalf of the Plan in connection with a claimant's adverse benefit determination, without regard to whether the advice was relied upon in making the benefit determination; and (3) a disability determination regarding the claimant presented by the claimant to the Plan made by the Social Security Administration,

(ii) reference to the specific Plan provisions on which the benefit determination is based,

(iii) a statement that the claimant is entitled to receive, upon written request to the Committee and free of charge, reasonable access to, and copies of, all documents, records, and other information relevant to the claimant's claim for benefits,

(iv) if an internal rule, guideline, protocol or similar criterion was relied on in making the decision, a copy of that document will be furnished, free of charge, upon written request to the Committee (if no internal rule, guideline, protocol or similar criterion was relied on in making the decision, a statement that no such document was relied upon will be furnished),

(v) if the adverse benefit determination is based on a medical necessity or experimental treatment or similar exclusion or limit, the scientific or clinical judgment for the determination, applying the terms of the Plan to the claimant's medical circumstances will be furnished, free of charge, upon written request to the Committee, and

(vi) a statement of the claimant's right to bring a civil action under ERISA Section 502(a) following the final benefit determination on appeal, or if the claim appeal occurs on or after April 1, 2018, and the Committee failed to comply with the Claims Procedures herein, (unless the failure is due to a minor error). Similar to the above, notification will be given within a reasonable period of time, but not later than forty-five (45) calendar days after the claim is received by the Committee, or within ninety (90) calendar days, if the Committee determines that special circumstances require an extension of time for processing the claim.

If the Committee determines that an extension of time for processing is required, it will furnish written notice of the extension to the claimant prior to the termination of the initial forty-five (45) day period. The extension notice shall indicate the special circumstances requiring an extension of time and the date by which the Committee expects to render a benefit determination.

(b) Disability Related Appeals. Within one hundred and eighty (180) calendar days after the receipt of notification of an adverse benefit determination, a claimant (or the claimant's duly authorized representative) may file a written request with the Committee for an appeal. An adverse benefit determination is a denial, reduction, or termination of, rescission (including for a disability claim, a retroactive termination), or a failure to provide or make payment (in whole or in part) for, a benefit, including any such denial, reduction, termination, or failure to provide or make payment that is based on a determination of a participant's or beneficiary's eligibility to participate in the Plan. The claimant may submit written comments, documents, records, and other information relating to the claim for benefits. A request for review shall be deemed filed as of the date of receipt of such written request by the Committee. A claimant shall be provided, upon request and free of charge, reasonable access to, and copies of, all documents, records, and other information relevant to the claimant's claim for benefits. The Committee will take into account all comments, documents, records, and other information submitted by the claimant relating to the claim, without regard to whether such information was submitted or considered in the initial benefit determination. The Committee will notify the claimant of its decision on review in writing, however prior to issuing such a decision for a claim determination, the Committee will provide the claimant, free of charge, with any new or additional evidence or any new or additional rationale considered, relied upon, or generated by the Plan or person making the benefit determination, as soon as possible in advance of the date on which the benefit decision shall be made, and the claimant shall be provided a reasonable opportunity to respond prior to that date. Such notification will be written in a manner calculated to be understood by the claimant and the notification shall also be provided in a culturally and linguistically appropriate manner) and will contain the following: (1) the specific reason or reasons for the adverse determination including the basis for disagreeing with or not following (if applicable) (i) the views presented by the claimant to the Committee of health care professionals treating the claimant and vocational professionals who evaluated the claimant; (ii) the views of medical or vocational experts whose advice was obtained on behalf of the Plan in connection with a claimant's adverse benefit determination, without regard to whether the advice was relied upon in making the benefit determination; and (iii) a disability determination regarding the claimant presented by the claimant to the Plan made by the Social Security Administration, (2) reference to the specific Plan provisions on which the benefit determination is based, (3) a statement that the claimant is entitled to receive, upon written request to the Committee and free of charge, reasonable access to, and copies of, all documents, records, and other information relevant to the claimant's claim for benefits, (4) if an internal rule, guideline, protocol or similar criterion was relied on in making the decision, a copy of that document will be furnished, free of charge, upon written request to the Committee. If no internal rule, guideline, protocol or similar criterion was relied on in making the decision, a statement that no such document was relied upon will be furnished, (5) if the adverse benefit determination is based on a medical necessity or experimental treatment or similar exclusion or limit, the scientific or clinical judgment for the determination, applying the terms of the Plan to the claimant's medical circumstances will be furnished, free of charge, upon written request to the Committee, and (6) a statement of the claimant's right to bring a civil action under ERISA Section 502(a) if the Committee failed to comply with the Claims Procedures herein, (unless the failure is due to a minor error) or following the final benefit determination on appeal. Such notification will be given within a reasonable period of time, but not later than forty-five (45) calendar days after the claim is received by the Committee, or within ninety (90) calendar days, if the Committee determines that special circumstances require an extension of time for processing the claim. If the Committee determines that an extension of time for processing is required, it will furnish written notice of the extension to the claimant prior to the termination of the initial forty-five (45) day period. The extension notice shall indicate the special circumstances requiring an extension of time and the date by which the Committee expects to render a benefit determination.

5.5 Legal Actions. The claims and review procedures described in this Article 5 must be utilized before a legal action may be brought against the Company, the Committee, an Employer, or the Plan. If the claim is a disability claim appeal and the claimant believes that the Committee failed to comply with the Claims Procedures herein, the claimant may request a written explanation of the violation from the Committee, and the Committee will provide such explanation within ten (10) calendar days, including a specific description of its basis, if any, for asserting that the violation should not cause the administrative remedies available under the Plan to be deemed exhausted. Any legal action must be filed within one (1) year of receiving final notice of a denied claim.

ARTICLE VI
AMENDMENT AND TERMINATION

6.1 Amendment and Termination. The Company reserves the right, on a case-by-case basis or on a general basis, to amend the Plan at any time and to thereby alter, reduce, or eliminate any benefit under the Plan, in whole or in part, at any time; provided that no such amendment shall reduce the Severance Benefits of a Participant who has begun receiving Severance Benefits on or before the date of the amendment.

6.2 Notice of Amendment or Termination. The Company will notify the Participants, including, but not limited to, Participants receiving Severance Benefits, of any material amendment to or termination of the Plan within a reasonable time.

ARTICLE VII GENERAL PROVISIONS

7.1 Employment Status. The Plan is not a contract of employment, and eligibility under the Plan does not give the Participant the right to be rehired or retained in the employ of the Employer on a full-time, part-time or any other basis, or to receive any benefit under any other plan of the Employer. Eligibility under the Plan does not give the Participant any right, claim, or legal entitlement to any Severance Benefits, unless that right or claim has specifically accrued under the terms of the Plan.

7.2 No Reinstatement. By accepting Severance Benefits, the Participant waives any reinstatement or future employment with the Employer and agrees never to apply for employment or otherwise seek to be hired, rehired, employed, reemployed, or reinstated by the Employer.

7.3 Effect of Receiving Severance Benefits. A Participant's receipt of Severance Benefits does not constitute any sort of extension or perpetuation of employment beyond the Participant's actual date of employment termination.

7.4 Ethical Standards. By accepting Severance Benefits, the Participant acknowledges and agrees that he or she has been given an adequate opportunity to advise the Employer's human resources, legal, or other relevant management division, and has so advised such division in writing, of any facts that the Participant is aware of that constitute or might constitute a violation of any ethical, legal, or contractual standards or obligations of the Company Group. The Participant further acknowledges and agrees that the Participant is not aware of any existing or threatened claims, charges, or lawsuits that he or she has not disclosed to the Employer.

7.5 Spendthrift Provision. No interest of any person or entity in, or right to receive a distribution under, the Plan shall be subject in any manner to sale, transfer, assignment, pledge, attachment, garnishment, or other alienation or encumbrance of any kind; except as may be required by the tax withholding provisions of the Code or any state's income tax act, or pursuant to an agreement between the Participant and the Company, nor may such interest or right to receive a distribution be taken, either voluntarily or involuntarily for the satisfaction of the debts of, or other obligations or claims against, such person or entity, including claims for alimony, support, separate maintenance, and claims in bankruptcy proceedings.

7.6 Entire Plan. The Plan, including the appendices, contains the entire understanding of the Employer and the Participant with respect to the subject matter herein. Except as set forth in Sections 2.1 and 2.2, the Plan supersedes any other generally applicable severance-related plan or policy of the Employer in effect on the date the Company adopts the Plan. Payments or benefits provided to a Participant under any Written Arrangement, Retirement Benefit Plan, Health and Welfare Benefit Plan or other employee benefit plan are governed solely by the terms of that Written Arrangement, plan, arrangement or policy. Any obligations or duties of a Participant pursuant to any separate non-competition or other agreement with a member of the Company Group will be governed solely by the terms of that agreement, and will not be affected by the terms of the Plan, except to the extent that agreement expressly provides otherwise. Severance Benefits are not taken into account for purposes of contributions or benefits under any other employee benefit plans. Further, the period of coverage under any employee benefit plan is not extended due to the provision of Severance Benefits.

7.7 Notices. All notices, requests, demands, and other communications hereunder shall be sufficient if in writing and shall be deemed to have been duly given if delivered by hand or if sent by registered or certified mail to the Participant at the last address the Participant has filed in writing with the Employer or, in the case of the Employer, at the Company's principal offices, with attention to "ABC Corporation Benefit Plans Committee."

7.8 Successors to the Company. The Company shall require any successor (whether direct or indirect, by purchase, merger, reorganization, consolidation, acquisition of property or stock, liquidation, or otherwise) of all or a significant portion of the stock or assets of the Company by agreement, to expressly assume and agree to maintain the Plan in the same manner and to the same extent that the Company would be required to perform if no such succession had taken place, subject to Section 6.1 herein. Regardless of whether such agreement is executed, the Plan will be binding upon any successor in accordance with the operation of law and such successor shall be deemed the "Company" for purposes of the Plan.

7.9 Tax Withholding. The Employer shall withhold from any Severance Benefits all Federal, state, city, or other taxes as legally required to be withheld, as well as any other amounts authorized or required by policy, including, but not limited to, withholding for garnishments and judgments or other court orders.

7.10 Severability. In the event any provision of the Plan shall be held illegal or invalid for any reason, the illegality or invalidity will not affect the remaining parts of the Plan, and the Plan must be construed and enforced as if the illegal or invalid provision had not been included. Further, the captions of the Plan are not part of the provisions herein and will have no force or effect. Notwithstanding anything in the Plan to the contrary, the Employer shall have no obligation to provide any Severance Benefits to the Participant hereunder to the extent, but only to the extent, that such provision is prohibited by the terms of any final order of a Federal, state, or local court or regulatory agency of competent jurisdiction, provided that such an order shall not affect, impair, or invalidate any provision of the Plan not expressly subject to such order.

7.11 Applicable Law; Choice of Forum. The Plan shall be construed and administered under the laws of the State of _____ except to the extent preempted by federal law. Any action or proceeding seeking to enforce any provision of, or based on any right arising out of, the Plan must be brought against any of the parties in the courts of the State of _____ or, if it has or can acquire jurisdiction, in the United States District Court for the District of _____, and each of the Company and Participants expressly consent to the jurisdiction of such courts (and of the appropriate appellate courts) in any such action or proceeding and waives any objection to venue laid therein. Process in any action or proceeding referred to in the preceding sentence may be served on any party anywhere in the world.

7.12 Limitations on Liability. Notwithstanding any of the preceding provisions of the Plan, the Company, the Committee, and any individual acting as an employee or agent of the Company, shall not be liable to any Participant, former Participant, or any beneficiary or other person for any claim, loss, liability, or expense incurred in connection with the Plan.

7.13 Action by the Company. Any action required of or permitted to be taken by the Company under the Plan must be by written resolution of the Board, by written resolution of a duly authorized committee of the Board, by a person or persons authorized by resolutions of the Board, or by a duly authorized committee.

7.14 Plan Funding. The Employer will provide all Severance Benefits due and owing directly out of its general assets. To the extent that a Participant acquires a right to receive Severance Benefits, such right shall be no greater than the right of an unsecured general creditor of the Employer. Nothing herein contained may require or be deemed to require, or prohibit or be deemed to prohibit, the Employer to segregate, earmark, or otherwise set aside any funds or other assets, in trust or otherwise, to provide for any Severance Benefits.

7.15 Cooperation. A Participant must cooperate with the Company and the Committee by furnishing any and all information reasonably requested by the Company or the Committee, in order to facilitate the payment of benefits hereunder, and taking such other actions as may be requested by the Company. If a Participant refuses to cooperate, the Company shall have no further obligation to such Participant under the Plan.

7.16 Compensation Recovery Policy. Notwithstanding any provision in the Plan to the contrary, payments under the Plan will be subject to any compensation recovery policy established by the Company and amended from time to time.

Appendix A

ADDITIONAL INFORMATION FOR SUMMARY PLAN DESCRIPTION

This Appendix A, together with the Plan document, constitutes the summary plan description of the Plan. References in this Appendix A to "you" or "your" are references to the Participant. Any term capitalized but not defined in this Appendix A will have the meaning set forth in the Plan. To the extent that any of the information contained in this Appendix A or any information you receive orally is inconsistent with the official plan document, the provisions set forth in the plan document will govern in all cases.

YOUR RIGHTS UNDER ERISA

As a participant in the Plan, you are entitled to certain rights and protections under ERISA. ERISA provides that all Plan Participants shall be entitled to:

- Receive information about the Plan and benefits offered under the Plan.
- Examine, without charge, at the Committee's office and at other specified locations, all documents governing the Plan, and a copy of the latest annual report filed by the Plan with the U.S. Department of Labor and available at the Public Disclosure Room of the Employee Benefit Security Administration.
- Obtain, upon written request to the Committee, copies of documents governing the operation of the Plan, and copies of the latest annual report and updated summary plan description. The Committee may make a reasonable charge for the copies.
- Receive a summary of the Plan's annual financial report. The Committee is required by law to furnish each Participant with a copy of this summary annual report.

PRUDENT ACTION BY PLAN FIDUCIARIES

In addition to creating rights for Plan Participants, ERISA imposes duties upon the people who are responsible for the operation of the Plan. The people who operate your Plan, called fiduciaries of the Plan, have a duty to do so prudently and in the interest of you and other Plan Participants and beneficiaries. No one, including the Employer, or any other person, may fire you or otherwise discriminate against you in any way to prevent you from obtaining a benefit or exercising your rights under ERISA.

ENFORCE YOUR RIGHTS

If your claim for a benefit is denied or ignored in whole or in part, you have a right to know why this was done, to obtain copies of documents relating to the decision without charge, and to appeal any denial, all within certain time schedules.

Under ERISA, there are steps you can take to enforce the above rights. For instance, if you request a copy of Plan documents or the latest annual report from the Plan and do not receive them within 30 calendar days, you may file suit in a Federal court. In such a case, the court may require the Committee to provide the materials and pay you up to $147 a day until you receive the materials, unless the materials were not sent because of reasons beyond the control of the Committee. If you have a claim for benefits that is denied or ignored, in whole or in part, you may file suit in a state or Federal court. If you are discriminated against for asserting your rights, you may seek assistance from the U.S. Department of Labor, or you may file suit in a Federal court. The court will decide who should pay court costs and legal fees. If you are successful, the court may order the person you have sued to pay these costs and fees. If you lose, the court may order you to pay these costs and fees, for example, if it finds your claim is frivolous. However, no legal action may be commenced or maintained against the Plan prior to your exhaustion of the Plan's claims procedures described in this SPD.

ASSISTANCE WITH YOUR QUESTIONS

If you have any questions about the Plan, you should contact the Committee. If you have any questions about this statement or about your rights under ERISA, or if you need assistance in obtaining documents from the Committee, you should contact the nearest office of the Employee Benefits Security Administration, U.S. Department of Labor, listed in your telephone directory or the Division of Technical Assistance and Inquiries, Employee Benefits Security Administration, U.S. Department of Labor, 200 Constitution Avenue N.W., Washington, D.C. 20210. You also may obtain certain publications about your rights and responsibilities under ERISA by calling the publications hotline of the Employee Benefits Security Administration.

General Plan Information

Employer/Plan Sponsor:	ABC Corporation _____ (__) ___-___
Plan Name:	ABC Corporation Severance Plan
Type of Plan:	Welfare benefit plan
Source of Funds:	The Employer will pay all benefits due and owing under the Plan directly out of its general assets. To the extent that a Participant acquires a right to receive benefits under the Plan, such right shall be no greater than the right of an unsecured general creditor of the Employer.
Plan Number:	This Plan is a sub-plan of the ABC Corporation Health and Welfare Benefit Plan, Plan No. 501
Company's Employer Identification Number:	
Committee:	ABC Corporation Benefit Plans Committee ABC Corporation _____ (__) ___-___
Agent for Service of Legal Process:	The Committee
Plan Year:	The calendar year (January 1 – December 31)
Successors:	The Company shall cause the Plan to be assumed by any successor of the Company, whether such succession occurs by merger, asset acquisition or otherwise, unless such assumption would occur by operation of law.
Binding Legal Contract:	The Plan shall be a binding legal contract between the Employer and the Participant, subject to amendment or termination by the Employer.

¶10,270 SAMPLE LEGAL AGREEMENT—Model Rabbi Trust

The following is the model rabbi trust published and approved by the IRS in Rev. Proc. 92-64 (and the IRS has reaffirmed its approval several times since then). Many employers use a rabbi trust to "informally" fund nonqualified plans. A rabbi trust is the most effective and well-known method of "securing" deferred compensation from employer changes in management or control. Either a public or private company or other business entity could use this sample trust. For a discussion of rabbi trusts, see ¶1765.

TRUST UNDER _____ PLAN.

[Optional]

(a) THIS AGREEMENT, made this ____ day of _____, by and between (the "Company") and (the "Trustee"),

WITNESSETH:

[Optional]

(b) WHEREAS, the Company has adopted the nonqualified deferred compensation Plan(s) as listed in Appendix ____.

[Optional]

    (a) WHEREAS, the Company has incurred or expects to incur liability under the terms of such Plan(s) with respect to the individuals participating in such Plan(s);

    (b) WHEREAS, the Company wishes to establish a trust (hereinafter called "the Trust") and to contribute to the Trust assets that shall be held therein, subject to the claims of the Company's creditors in the event of the Company's Insolvency, as herein defined, until paid to Plan participants and their beneficiaries in such manner and at such times as specified in the Plan(s);

    (c) WHEREAS, it is the intention of the parties that this Trust shall constitute an unfunded arrangement and shall not affect the status of the Plan(s) as an unfunded plan maintained for the purpose of providing deferred compensation for a select group of management or highly compensated employees for purposes of Title I of the Employee Retirement Income Security Act of 1974;

    (d) WHEREAS, it is the intention of the Company to make contributions to the Trust to provide itself with a source of funds to assist it in the meeting of its liabilities under the Plan(s);

NOW, THEREFORE, the parties do hereby establish the Trust and agree that the Trust shall be comprised, held and disposed of as follows:

Section 1
Establishment of Trust

(a) The Company hereby deposits with the Trustee in trust $_____ [insert amount deposited], which shall become the principal of the Trust to be held, administered and disposed of by the Trustee as provided in this Trust Agreement.

[Alternatives—Select one provision.]

(b) The Trust hereby established shall be revocable by the Company.

(b) The Trust hereby established shall be irrevocable.

(b) The Trust hereby established is revocable by the Company; it shall come irrevocable upon a Change of Control, as defined herein.

(b) The Trust shall become irrevocable _____ [insert number] days following the issuance of a favorable private letter ruling regarding the Trust from the Internal Revenue Service.

(b) The Trust shall become irrevocable upon approval by the Board of Directors.

(c) The Trust is intended to be a grantor trust, of which the Company is the grantor, within the meaning of subpart E, part I, subchapter J, chapter 1, subtitle A of the Internal Revenue Code of 1986, as amended, and shall be construed accordingly.

(d) The principal of the Trust, and any earnings thereon shall be held separate and apart from other funds of the Company and shall be used exclusively for the uses and purposes of Plan participants and general creditors as herein set forth. Plan participants and their beneficiaries shall have no preferred claim on, or any beneficial ownership interest in, any assets of the Trust. Any rights created under the Plan(s) and this Trust Agreement shall be mere unsecured contractual rights of Plan participants and their beneficiaries against the Company. Any assets held by the Trust will be subject to the claims of the Company's general creditors under federal and state law in the event of Insolvency, as defined in Section 3(a) herein.

[Alternatives—Select one or more provisions, as appropriate.]

(e) The Company, in its sole discretion, may at any time, or from time to time, make additional deposits of cash or other property in trust with the Trustee to augment the principal to be held, administered and disposed of by the Trustee as provided in this Trust Agreement. Neither the Trustee nor any Plan participant or beneficiary shall have any right to compel such additional deposits.

(e) Upon a Change of Control, the Company shall, as soon as possible, but in no event longer than _____ [fill in blank] days following the Change of Control, as defined herein, make an irrevocable contribution to the Trust in an amount that is sufficient to pay each Plan participant or beneficiary the benefits to which Plan participants or their beneficiaries would be entitled pursuant to the terms of the Plan(s) as of the date on which the Change of Control occurred.

(e) Within _____ [fill in blank] days following the end of the Plan year(s), ending after the Trust has become irrevocable pursuant to Section 1(b) hereof, the Company shall be required to irrevocably deposit additional cash or other property to the Trust in an amount sufficient to pay each Plan participant or beneficiary the benefits payable pursuant to the terms of the Plan(s) as of the close of the Plan year(s).

Section 2
Payments to Plan Participants and Their Beneficiaries

(a) The Company shall deliver to the Trustee a schedule (the "Payment Schedule") that indicates the amounts payable in respect of each Plan participant and his/her beneficiaries), that provides a formula or other instructions acceptable to the Trustee for determining the amounts so payable, the form in which such amount is to be paid (as provided for or available under the Plan(s)), and the time of commencement for payment of such amounts. Except as otherwise provided herein, the Trustee shall make payments to the Plan participants and their beneficiaries in accordance with such Payment Schedule. The Trustee shall make provision for the reporting and withholding of any federal, state or local taxes that may be required to be withheld with respect to the payment of benefits pursuant to the terms of the Plan(s) and shall pay amounts withheld to the appropriate taxing authorities or determine that such amounts have been reported, withheld and paid by the Company.

(b) The entitlement of a Plan participant or his/her beneficiaries to benefits under the Plan(s) shall be determined by the Company or such party as it shall designate under the Plan(s), and any claim for such benefits shall be considered and reviewed under the procedures set out in the Plan(s).

(c) The Company may make payment of benefits directly to Plan participants or their beneficiaries as they become due under the terms of the Plan(s). The Company shall notify the Trustee of its decision to make payment of benefits directly prior to the time amounts are payable to participants or their beneficiaries. In addition, if the principal of the Trust, and any earnings thereon, are not sufficient to make payments of benefits in accordance with the terms of the Plan(s), the Company shall make the balance of each such payment as it falls due. The Trustee shall notify the Company where principal and earnings are not sufficient.

Section 3
Trustee Responsibility Regarding Payments
to Trust Beneficiary When Company is Insolvent

(a) The Trustee shall cease payment of benefits to Plan participants and their beneficiaries if the Company is Insolvent. The Company shall be considered "Insolvent" for purposes of this Trust Agreement if (i) the Company is unable to pay its debts as they become due, or (ii) the Company is subject to a pending proceeding as a debtor under the United States Bankruptcy Code.

[Optional]

, or (iii) the Company is determined to be Insolvent by _____ [insert names of applicable federal and/or state regulatory agency].

(a) At all times during the continuance of this Trust, as provided in Section 1(d) hereof, the principal and income of the Trust shall be subject to claims of general creditors of the Company under federal and state law as set forth below.

(1) The Board of Directors and the Chief Executive Officer [or substitute the title of the highest ranking officer of the Company] of the Company shall have the duty to inform the Trustee in writing of the Company's Insolvency. If a person claiming to be a creditor of the Company alleges in writing to the Trustee that the Company has become Insolvent, the Trustee shall determine whether the Company is Insolvent and, pending such determination, the

Trustee shall discontinue payment of benefits to Plan participants or their beneficiaries.

(2) Unless the Trustee has actual knowledge of the Company's Insolvency, or has received notice from the Company or a person claiming to be a creditor alleging that the Company is Insolvent, the Trustee shall have no duty to inquire whether the Company is Insolvent. The Trustee may in all events rely on such evidence concerning the Company's solvency as may be furnished to the Trustee and that provides the Trustee with a reasonable basis for making a determination concerning the Company's solvency.

(3) If at any time the Trustee has determined that the Company is Insolvent, the Trustee shall discontinue payments to Plan participants or their beneficiaries and shall hold the assets of the Trust for the benefit of the Company's general creditors. Nothing in the Trust Agreement shall in any way diminish any rights of Plan participants or their beneficiaries to pursue their rights as general creditors of the Company with respect to benefits due under the Plan(s) or otherwise.

(4) The Trustee shall resume the payment of benefits to Plan participants or their beneficiaries in accordance with Section 2 of this Trust Agreement only after the Trustee has determined that the Company is not Insolvent (or is no longer Insolvent).

(b) Provided that there are sufficient assets, if the Trustee discontinues the payment of benefits from the Trust pursuant to Section 3(b) hereof and subsequently resumes such payments, the first payment following such discontinuance shall include the aggregate amount of all payments due to Plan participants or their beneficiaries under the terms of the Plan(s) for the period of such discontinuance, less the aggregate amount of any payments made to Plan participants or their beneficiaries by the Company in lieu of the payments provided for hereunder during any such period of discontinuance.

Section 4
Payments to the Company

[The following need not be included if the first alternative under 1(b) is selected.]

Except as provided in Section 3 hereof, after the Trust has become irrevocable, the Company shall have no right or power to direct the Trustee to return to the Company or to divert to others any of the Trust assets before all payment of benefits have been made to Plan participants and their beneficiaries pursuant to the terms of the Plan(s).

Section 5
Investment Authority

[Alternatives—Select one provision, as appropriate.]

(a) In no event may the Trustee invest in securities (including stock or rights to acquire stock) or obligations issued by the Company, other than a de minimis amount held in common investment vehicles in which the Trustee invests. All rights associated with assets of the Trust shall be exercised by the Trustee or the person designated by the Trustee, and shall in no event be exercisable by or rest with Plan participants.

(a) The Trustee may invest in securities (including stock or rights to acquire stock) or obligations issued by the Company. All rights associated with assets of the Trust shall be exercised by the Trustee or the person designated by the Trustee, and shall in no event be exercisable by or rest with Plan participants.

[Optional]

, except that voting rights with respect to Trust assets will be exercised by the Company.

[Optional]

, except that dividend rights with respect to Trust assets will rest with the Company.

[Optional]

The Company shall have the right, at any time, and from time to time in its sole discretion, to substitute assets of equal fair market value for any asset held by the Trust.

[If the second Alternative 5(a) is selected, the trust must provide either (1) that the trust is revocable under Alternative 1(b), or (2) the following provision must be included in the Trust]:

"The Company shall have the right at any time, and from time to time in its sole discretion, to substitute assets of equal fair market value for any asset held by the Trust. This right is exercisable by the Company in a nonfiduciary capacity without the approval or consent of any person in a fiduciary capacity."

Section 6
Disposition of Income

[Alternatives—Select one provision.]

(a) During the term of this Trust, all income received by the Trust, net of expenses and taxes, shall be accumulated and reinvested.

(a) During the term of this Trust, all, or _____[insert amount] part of the income received by the Trust, net of expenses and taxes, shall be returned to the Company.

Section 7
Accounting by the Trustee

[Optional]

The Trustee shall keep accurate and detailed records of all investments, receipts, disbursements, and all other transactions required to be made, including such specific records as shall be agreed upon in writing between the Company and the Trustee. Within ____ [insert number] days following the close of each calendar year and within ____ [insert number] days after the removal or resignation of the Trustee, the Trustee shall deliver to the Company a written account of its administration of the Trust during such year or during the period from the close of the last preceding year to the date of such removal or resignation, setting forth all investments, receipts, disbursements and other transactions effected by it, including a description of all securities and investments purchased and sold with the cost or net proceeds of such purchases or sales (accrued interest paid or receivable being shown separately), and showing all cash, securities and other property held in the Trust at the end of such year or as of the date of such removal or resignation, as the case may be.

Section 8
Responsibility of the Trustee

[Optional]

(a) The Trustee shall act with the care, skill, prudence and diligence under the circumstances then prevailing that a prudent person acting in like capacity and familiar with such matters would use in the conduct of an enterprise of a like character and with like aims, provided, however, that the Trustee shall incur no liability to any person for any action taken pursuant to a direction, request or approval given by the Company which is contemplated by, and in conformity with, the terms of the Plan(s) or this Trust and is given in writing by the Company. In the event of a dispute between the Company and a party, the Trustee may apply to a court of competent jurisdiction to resolve the dispute.

[Optional]

(b) If the Trustee undertakes or defends any litigation arising in connection with this Trust, the Company agrees to indemnify the Trustee against the Trustee's costs, expenses and liabilities (including, without limitation, attorneys' fees and expenses) relating thereto and to be primarily liable for such payments. If Company does not pay such costs, expenses and liabilities in a reasonably timely manner, the Trustee may obtain payment from the Trust.

[Optional]

(c) The Trustee may consult with legal counsel (who may also be counsel for the Company generally) with respect to any of its duties or obligations hereunder.

[Optional]

(d) The Trustee may hire agents, accountants, actuaries, investment advisors, financial consultants or other professionals to assist it in performing any of its duties or obligations hereunder.

(e) The Trustee shall have, without exclusion, all powers conferred on Trustees by applicable law, unless expressly provided otherwise herein, provided, however, that if an insurance policy is held as an asset of the Trust, the Trustee shall have no power to name a beneficiary of the policy other than the Trust, to assign the policy (as distinct from conversion of the policy to a different form) other than to a successor Trustee, or to loan to any person the proceeds of any borrowing against such policy.

[Optional]

(f) However, notwithstanding the provisions of Section 8(e) above, the Trustee may loan to the Company the proceeds of any borrowing against an insurance policy held as an asset of the Trust.

(g) Notwithstanding any powers granted to the Trustee pursuant to this Trust Agreement or to applicable law, the Trustee shall not have any power that could give this Trust the objective of carrying on a business and dividing the gains therefrom, within the meaning of section 301.7701-2 of the Procedure and Administrative Regulations promulgated pursuant to the Internal Revenue Code.

Section 9
Compensation and Expenses of the Trustee

[Optional]

The Company shall pay all administrative and the Trustee's fees and expenses. If not so paid, the fees and expenses shall be paid from the Trust.

Section 10
Resignation and Removal of the Trustee

(a) The Trustee may resign at any time by written notice to the Company, which shall be effective _____ [insert number] days after receipt of such notice unless the Company and the Trustee agree otherwise.

[Optional]

(b) The Trustee may be removed by the Company on ____ [insert number] days notice or upon shorter notice accepted by the Trustee.

[Optional]

(c) Upon a Change of Control, as defined herein, the Trustee may not be removed by the Company for ____ [insert number] year(s).

[Optional]

(d) If the Trustee resigns within ____ [insert number] year(s) after a Change of Control, as defined herein, the Company shall apply to a court of competent jurisdiction for the appointment of a successor Trustee or for instructions.

[Optional]

(e) If the Trustee resigns or is removed within ____ [insert number] year(s) of a Change of Control, as defined herein, the Trustee shall select a successor Trustee in accordance with the provisions of Section 11(b) hereof prior to the effective date of the Trustee's resignation or removal.

(f) Upon resignation or removal of the Trustee and appointment of a successor Trustee, all assets shall subsequently be transferred to the successor Trustee. The transfer shall be completed within ____ [insert number] days after receipt of notice of resignation, removal or transfer, unless Company extends the time limit.

(g) If the Trustee resigns or is removed, a successor shall be appointed, in accordance with Section 11 hereof, by the effective date of resignation or removal under paragraph(s) (a) [or (b)] of this section. If no such appointment has been made, the Trustee may apply to a court of competent jurisdiction for appointment of a successor or for instructions. All expenses of the Trustee in connection with the proceeding shall be allowed as administrative expenses of the Trust.

Section 11
Appointment of Successor

(a) If the Trustee resigns [or is removed] in accordance with Section 10(a) [or (b)] hereof, the Company may appoint any third party, such as a bank trust department or other party that may be granted corporate trustee powers under state law, as a successor to replace the Trustee upon resignation or removal. The appointment shall be effective when accepted in writing by the new Trustee, who shall have all of the rights and powers of the former Trustee, including ownership rights in the Trust assets. The former Trustee shall execute any instrument necessary or reasonably requested by the Company or the successor Trustee to evidence the transfer.

[Optional]

(b) If the Trustee resigns or is removed pursuant to the provisions of Section 10(e) hereof and selects a successor Trustee, the Trustee may appoint any third party such as a bank trust department or other party that may be granted corporate trustee powers under state law. The appointment of a successor Trustee shall be effective when accepted in writing by the new Trustee. The new Trustee shall have all the rights and powers of the former Trustee, including ownership rights in Trust assets. The former Trustee shall execute any instrument necessary or reasonably requested by the successor Trustee to evidence the transfer.

[Optional]

(c) The successor Trustee need not examine the records and acts of any prior Trustee and may retain or dispose of existing Trust assets, subject to Sections 7 and 8 hereof. The successor Trustee shall not be responsible for and the Company shall indemnify and defend the successor Trustee from any claim or liability resulting from any action or inaction of any prior Trustee or from any other past event, or any condition existing at the time it becomes successor Trustee.

Section 12
Amendment or Termination

(a) This Trust Agreement may be amended by a written instrument executed by the Trustee and the Company. [Unless the first alternative under 1(b) is selected, the following sentence must be included.] Notwithstanding the foregoing, no such amendment shall conflict with the terms of the Plan(s) or shall make the Trust revocable after it has become irrevocable in accordance with Section 1(b) hereof.

(b) The Trust shall not terminate until the date on which Plan participants and their beneficiaries are no longer entitled to benefits pursuant to the terms of the Plan(s) [unless the second alternative under 1(b) is selected, the following must be included:], "unless sooner revoked in accordance with Section 1(b) hereof." Upon termination of the Trust any assets remaining in the Trust shall be returned to the Company.

[Optional]

(c) Upon written approval of participants or beneficiaries entitled to payment of benefits pursuant to the terms of the Plan(s), the Company may terminate this Trust prior to the time all benefit payments under the Plan(s) have been made. All assets in the Trust at termination shall be returned to the Company.

[Optional]

(d) Section(s) _____ [insert number(s)] of this Trust Agreement may not be amended by the Company for ____ [insert number] year(s) following a Change of Control, as defined herein.

Section 13
Miscellaneous

(a) Any provision of this Trust Agreement prohibited by law shall be ineffective to the extent of any such prohibition, without validating the remaining provisions hereof.

(b) Benefits payable to Plan participants and their beneficiaries under this Trust Agreement may not be anticipated, assigned (either at law or in equity), alienated, pledged, encumbered or subjected to attachment, garnishment, levy, execution or other legal or equitable process.

(c) This Trust Agreement shall be governed by and construed in accordance with the laws of _____.

[Optional]

(d) For purposes of this Trust, Change of Control shall mean: [insert objective definition such as: "the purchase or other acquisition by any person, entity or group of persons, within the meaning of section 13(d) or 14(d) of the Securities Exchange Act of 1934 (the 'Act'), or any comparable successor provisions, of beneficial ownership (within the meaning of Rule 13d-3 promulgated under the Act) of 30 percent or more of either the outstanding shares of common stock or the combined voting power of the Company's then outstanding voting securities entitled to vote generally, or the approval by the stockholders of the Company of a reorganization, merger, or consolidation, in each case, with respect to which persons who were stockholders of the Company immediately prior to such reorganization, merger or consolidation do not, immediately thereafter, own more than 50 percent of the combined voting power entitled to vote generally in the election of directors of the reorganized, merged or consolidated Company's then outstanding securities, or a liquidation or dissolution of the Company or of the sale of all or substantially all of the Company's assets"].

Section 14
Effective Date

The effective date of this Trust Agreement shall be , [year].

¶10,290 SAMPLE LANGUAGE—Sample Provisions for Merger and Purchase Agreements

The following is a sample of provisions that counsel could add to a merger or purchase agreement. The merger or purchase agreement first must disclose all executive compensation plans, programs, arrangements and liabilities. The agreement then must set forth the negotiated treatment of the plans and liabilities at the time of the transaction and into the near future. These sample provisions generally could be used in a merger or stock purchase agreement among public or private companies or other business entities. For a discussion of executive compensation in mergers and acquisitions, see Chapter 25 (¶2501 *et seq.*)

AGREEMENT AND PLAN OF MERGER

AGREEMENT AND PLAN OF MERGER, dated as of _____, [year] (this "*Agreement*"), by and among [**Parent**] Corporation, a corporation ("*Parent*"), Acquisition Corp., a _____ corporation and wholly-owned subsidiary of Parent ("*Merger Sub*"), and [**XYZ**], Inc., a [Delaware] corporation (the "*Company*").

***

ARTICLE II
CONVERSION OF SECURITIES; EXCHANGE OF CERTIFICATES

***

Section 2.1 *Stock Awards*. At the Effective Time, each holder of an outstanding Stock Award granted under the Company Stock Incentive Plan or otherwise (each, a "*Stock Award*"), whether or not vested, shall be entitled to receive, in full satisfaction of such Stock Award, cash in an amount equal to the product of (A) the Offer Price and (B) the number of shares of Company Common Stock subject to such Stock Award, less Applicable Withholding.

OR

Section 2.1 *Stock Awards*. Prior to the Effective Time, the Company and Parent shall take such action as may be necessary to cause each outstanding Stock Award granted under the Company Stock Incentive Plan or otherwise (each, a "*Stock Award*"), to be converted into an award relating to Parent Common Stock by the Common Stock Exchange Ratio (rounded down to the nearest whole number of shares of Parent Common Stock). Such Stock Award shall otherwise be subject to the same terms and conditions (including provisions regarding vesting and the acceleration thereof) as in effect at the Effective Time, including the date of grant. At the Effective Time, (1) all references in the Company Stock Incentive Plan and in the related stock award agreements to the Company shall be deemed to refer to Parent and (2) Parent shall assume all of the Company's obligations with respect to Stock Awards as so amended. Promptly after the Effective Time, to the extent necessary to provide for registration of shares of Parent Common Stock subject to such Stock Awards, Parent shall file a registration statement on Form S-8 (or any successor form) with respect to such shares of Parent Common Stock and shall use its best efforts to maintain such registration statement (or any successor form), including the current status of any related prospectus or prospectuses, for so long as the Stock Awards remain outstanding. Prior to the Effective Time, the Company shall adopt an amendment to the Company Stock Incentive Plan, which amendment shall be approved by Parent (such approval to not be unreasonably withheld.

Section 2.2 *Stock Options.* At the Effective Time, each holder of outstanding and unexercised options to purchase shares of Company Common Stock granted under the Company's Stock Incentive Plan or otherwise (each, a *"Stock Option"*), whether or not exercisable or vested, shall be entitled to receive, in full satisfaction of such Stock Option, cash in an amount equal to the product of (A) the excess, if any, of the Offer Price over the exercise price per share thereof and (B) the number of shares of Company Common Stock subject to such Stock Option, less Applicable Withholding.

OR

Section 2.2 *Stock Options.* Prior to the Effective Time, the Company and Parent shall take such action as may be necessary to cause each unexpired and unexercised option to purchase shares of Company Common Stock (each, a *"Stock Option"*) under the [year] Stock Incentive Plan, a true and complete copy of which has heretofore been provided to Parent by the Company, to be exercisable solely for such number of shares of Parent Common Stock as is equal to the number of shares of Company Common Stock that could have been purchased under such Stock Option immediately prior to the Effective Time multiplied by the Common Stock Exchange Ratio (rounded down to the nearest whole number of shares of Parent Common Stock), at a price per share of Parent Common Stock equal to the per-share option exercise price specified in the Stock Option divided by the Common Stock Exchange Ratio (rounded down to the nearest whole cent). Such Stock Option shall otherwise be subject to the same terms and conditions (including provisions regarding vesting and the acceleration thereof) as in effect at the Effective Time, including the date of grant. At the Effective Time, (1) all references in the Company Stock Incentive Plan and in the related stock option agreements to the Company shall be deemed to refer to Parent and (2) Parent shall assume all of the Company's obligations with respect to Stock Options as so amended. Promptly after the Effective Time, to the extent necessary to provide for registration of shares of Parent Common Stock subject to such Stock Options, Parent shall file a registration statement on Form S-8 (or any successor form) with respect to such shares of Parent Common Stock and shall use its best efforts to maintain such registration statement (or any successor form), including the current status of any related prospectus or prospectuses, for so long as the Stock Options remain outstanding. Prior to the Effective Time, the Company shall adopt an amendment to the Company Stock Incentive Plan, which amendment shall be approved by Parent (such approval to not be unreasonably withheld), to provide that one-half of any Stock Options that are unvested prior to the Effective Time and held by any person employed by or providing services to the

Company at the Effective Time shall become fully vested and exercisable as of the Effective Time, and the other one-half of such Stock Options shall become vested over the 12-month period immediately following the Effective Time in equal amounts on a monthly basis.

***

ARTICLE IV

REPRESENTATIONS AND WARRANTIES OF THE COMPANY

The Company represents and warrants to Parent and Merger Sub that, except as set forth in the disclosure schedule dated as of the date hereof delivered by the Company to Parent and Merger Sub (the *"Company Disclosure Schedule"*):

***

Section 4.2 *Capitalization.* (a) The Company represents and warrants to Parent that the authorized capital stock of the Company consists of [___],000,000 shares of Company Common Stock. As of _____, [year], (i) [_____] shares of Company Common Stock were reserved for issuance upon vesting of Stock Awards or the exercise of Stock Options issued and outstanding under the Company Stock Incentive Plan; (ii) [_____] shares of Company Common Stock were reserved for issuance under the Company's 401(k) Retirement Savings Plan (the "401(k) Plan"), (iii) [_____] shares of Company Common Stock were reserved for issuance under the Company's Employee Stock Purchase Plan (the "ESPP"), and (iv) [_____] shares of Company Common Stock were reserved for issuance under the Company's Directors' Deferral Plan (the "Directors' Plan"). Since _____, [year] through the date hereof, except as permitted by this Agreement, (i) no shares of Company Common Stock have been issued, except in connection with the vesting of Stock Awards or the exercise of Stock Options issued and outstanding and except for shares of Company Common Stock required to be issued in connection with the Company Stock Incentive Plan, the Company's 401(k), the Company's ESPP, and the Company's Directors' Plan and (ii) no options, warrants, securities convertible into, or commitments with respect to the issuance of, shares of capital stock of the Company have been issued, granted or made except Company Rights in accordance with the terms of the Company Rights Agreement.

(b) Except for Stock Awards and Stock Options issued and outstanding under the Company Stock Incentive Plan, and (iii) rights under the 401(k) Plan, the ESPP, and the Directors' Plan, as of the date hereof, there were no outstanding subscriptions, options, calls, contracts, commitments, understandings, restrictions, arrangements, rights or warrants, including any right of conversion or exchange under any outstanding security, instrument or other agreement and also including any rights plan or other anti-takeover agreement, obligating the Company or any subsidiary of the Company to issue, deliver or sell, or cause to be issued, delivered or sold, additional shares of Company Common Stock or obligating the Company or any subsidiary of the Company to grant, extend or enter into any such agreement or commitment. As of the date hereof, there are no obligations, contingent or otherwise, of the Company to (i) repurchase, redeem or otherwise acquire any shares of Company Common Stock or the capital stock or other equity interests of any subsidiary of the Company except in connection with the exercise of Company Stock Options issued and outstanding or (ii) (other than advances to subsidiaries in the ordinary course of business) provide material funds to, or make any material investment in (in the form of a loan, capital contribution or otherwise), or provide any guarantee with respect to the obligations of, any subsidiary of the Company or any other person. There are no bonds, debentures, notes or other indebtedness of the Company having the right to vote (or convertible into, or exchangeable for, securities having the right to vote) on any matters on which stockholders of the Company may vote. Except as otherwise contemplated by this Agreement there are no voting trusts, irrevocable proxies or other agreements or understandings to which the Company or any subsidiary of the Company is a party or is bound with respect to the voting of any shares of Company Common Stock.

(c) The Company has filed with the SEC or previously made available to Parent complete and correct copies of the Company Stock Incentive Plan, including all amendments thereto. *Section 4.02(c)* of the Company Disclosure Schedule contains a correct and complete list as of _____, **[year]** of each outstanding Company Stock Option, including the holder, date of grant, number of shares and, with respect to Stock Options, the exercise price of Company Common Stock subject thereto, and setting forth the weighted average exercise price for all outstanding Stock Options.

***

Section 4.10 *Employee Benefit Plans; ERISA.* (a) Section 4.10(a) of the Company Disclosure Schedule includes a complete list of each employee benefit plan, program or policy providing benefits to any current or former employee, officer or director of the Company or any of its subsidiaries or any beneficiary or dependent thereof that is sponsored or maintained by the Company or any of its subsidiaries or to which the Company or any of its subsidiaries contributes or is obligated to contribute (other than those programs or policies that do not provide material benefits), including without limitation any employee welfare benefit plan within the meaning of Section 3(1) of ERISA, any employee pension benefit plan within the meaning of Section 3(2) of ERISA (whether or not such plan is subject to ERISA, and including any "multiemployer plan" within the meaning of Section 4001(a)(3) of ERISA (a "Multiemployer Plan")) and any material bonus, incentive, deferred compensation, vacation, stock purchase, stock option, stock based, severance, employment, change of control or fringe benefit agreement, plan, program or policy (collectively, the "Company Employee Benefit Plans").

(b) With respect to each Company Employee Benefit Plan other than a Multiemployer Plan (a "Company Plan"), the Company has delivered or made available to Parent a true, correct and complete copy of: (i) all plan documents and trust agreements; (ii) the most recent Annual Report (Form 5500 Series) and accompanying schedule, if any; (iii) the current summary plan description, if any; (iv) the most recent annual financial report, if any; (v) the most recent actuarial report, if any; and (vi) the most recent determination letter from the IRS, if any. Except as specifically provided in the foregoing documents, or in other documents, delivered or made available to Parent, there are no amendments to any Company Plan that have been adopted or approved.

(c) The IRS has issued a favorable determination letter with respect to each Plan that is intended to be a "qualified plan" within the meaning of Code Sec. 401(a) (a "Qualified Plan") and its related trust that has not been revoked, and there are no circumstances and no events have occurred that would reasonably be expected to result in a revocation of such letter, which cannot be cured without a Company Material Adverse Effect.

(d) Except as is not reasonably likely to have, individually or in the aggregate, a Company Material Adverse Effect: (i) the Company and its subsidiaries have complied, and are now in compliance, with all provisions of ERISA, the Code and all laws and regulations applicable to the Company Employee Benefit Plans and each Company Plan has been administered in all material respects in accordance with its terms; (ii) none of the Company and its subsidiaries nor any other person, including any fiduciary, has engaged in any "prohibited transaction" (as defined in Code Sec. 4975 or Section 406 of ERISA), which could subject any of the Company Employee Benefit Plans or their related trusts, the Company, any of its subsidiaries or any person that the Company or any of its subsidiaries has an obligation to indemnify, to any tax or penalty imposed under Code Sec. 4975 or Section 502 of ERISA; (iii) there are no pending or, to the Company's knowledge, threatened claims (other than claims for benefits in the ordinary course), lawsuits or arbitrations which have been asserted or instituted against the Company Plans, any fiduciaries thereof with respect to their duties to the Company Plans or the assets of any of the trusts under any of the Company Plans which could reasonably be expected to result in any liability of the Company or any of its subsidiaries to the Pension Benefit Guaranty Corporation, the Department of Treasury, the Department of Labor, any Multiemployer Plan or any Plan.

(e) Neither the execution and delivery of this Agreement nor the consummation of the transactions contemplated hereby will result in, cause the accelerated vesting, funding or delivery of, or increase the amount or value of, any material payment or benefit to any employee, officer or director of the Company or any of its subsidiaries, or result in any limitation on the right of the Company or any of its subsidiaries to amend, merge, terminate or receive a reversion of assets from any Company Employee Benefit Plan or related trust.

(f) No Company Plan is subject to Title IV or Section 302 of ERISA or Code Sec. 412 or Code Sec. 4971, and none of the Company and its subsidiaries, nor any of their respective ERISA Affiliates, has, at any time during the last six years contributed to or been obligated to contribute to any plan subject to Title IV of ERISA.

(g) No Company Employee Benefit Plan is a Multiemployer Plan, none of the Company and its subsidiaries nor any of their respective ERISA Affiliates has, at any time during the last six years, contributed to or been obligated to contribute to any Multiemployer Plan, and none of the Company and its subsidiaries nor any ERISA Affiliates has incurred any withdrawal liability to a Company Multiemployer Plan that has not been satisfied in full.

(h) Neither the Company nor any of its subsidiaries has any obligations for retiree health and life benefits under any Company Employee Benefit Plan, except as set forth in Section 4.13(h) of the Company Disclosure Schedule and except for obligations under Section 601 et. seq. of ERISA and Code Sec. 4980B ("COBRA").

(i) There is no contract, agreement, plan or arrangement covering any employee or former employee of Company that, individually or collectively, could give rise to the payment by Company of any amount that would not be deductible by reason of Code Sec. 280G.

(j) Each contract, agreement, plan or arrangement to which the Company is a party is exempt from or in compliance with Code Sec. 409A.

***

ARTICLE V
COVENANTS

***

5.2 *Conduct of Business Pending the Merger.* Except as otherwise contemplated by this Agreement, required by law or disclosed in Section 5.01 of the Company Disclosure Schedule, and except within the amounts and pursuant to the time schedules contemplated by the Company's annual budget or capital budget (copies of which have been delivered to Parent on or prior to the date of this Agreement), after the date hereof and prior to the Effective Time, without Parent's consent (which shall not be unreasonably withheld), the Company shall, and shall cause its subsidiaries to:

***

(c) not issue, sell, pledge or dispose of, or agree to issue, sell, pledge or dispose of, any additional shares of, or any options, warrants or rights of any kind to acquire any shares of their capital stock of any class or any debt or equity securities convertible into or exchangeable for such capital stock, except that (i) the Company may issue shares of capital stock of the Company (A) upon exercise of Company Stock Options outstanding on the date hereof or hereafter granted in accordance with the provisions of subclause (ii) or (iii) of this clause (c), and (B) in accordance with the 401(k) Plan, the ESPP, and the Directors' Plan as in effect on the date hereof, and (ii) the Company may grant Company Stock Options to purchase in the aggregate with respect to all such Company Stock Options [_____] shares of Company Common Stock in accordance with the terms of the Company Stock Incentive Plans to persons who are not currently directors or officers of the Company or its subsidiaries consistent with past practice and with an exercise price per share of Company Common Stock no less than the fair market value of a share of Company Common Stock as of the date of grant and no new options will be allowed to accelerate as a result of the change of control caused by consummation of the Offer or the Merger;

***

(f) not enter into or amend any employment, severance, special pay arrangement with respect to termination of employment or other similar arrangements or agreements with any directors, officers or key employees or with any other persons, except pursuant to (i) applicable law; (ii) previously existing contractual arrangements or policies or (iii) employment agreements entered into with a person who is hired or promoted by the Company or one of its subsidiaries after the date hereof in the ordinary course of business;

(g) not materially increase the salary or monetary compensation of any person except for increases in the ordinary course of business consistent with past practice or except pursuant to previously existing contractual arrangements;

(h) not adopt, enter into or amend to materially increase benefits or obligations of any Company Plan, except (i) any of the foregoing involving any such then existing plans, agreements, trusts, funds or arrangements of any company acquired after the date hereof or (ii) as required pursuant to existing contractual arrangements or this Agreement;

***

Section 5.10 *Employee Benefits.* (a) Parent agrees that the Company will honor, and from and after the Effective Time, Parent and its Affiliates shall honor, all Company Employee Benefit Plans in accordance with their terms as in effect immediately before the Acceptance Date, subject to any amendment or termination thereof that may be permitted by such terms and provided that nothing in this sentence shall prevent Parent or the Surviving Corporation from replacing the Company's existing Company Employee Benefit Plans as contemplated by and in accordance with the following sentence. Until the date that is two (2) years from the Effective Date, Parent shall provide, or shall cause to be provided, to current and former employees of the Company and its subsidiaries (the "Company Employees") compensation and employee benefits that are, in the aggregate, not less favorable than those provided to Company Employees immediately before the Acceptance Date. The foregoing shall not be construed to prevent the termination of employment of any Company Employee or the amendment or termination of any particular Company Employee Benefit Plan to the extent permitted by its terms as in effect immediately before the Acceptance Date.

(b) For purposes of eligibility and vesting and levels of benefits under the employee benefit plans of Parent and its Affiliates providing benefits to any Company Employees after the Acceptance Date (the "New Plans"), each Company Employee shall be credited with his/her years of service with the Company and its Affiliates before the Effective Time, to the same extent as such Company Employee was entitled, before the Effective Time, to credit for such service under any similar Company Employee Benefit Plans, except to the extent such credit would result in a duplication of benefits. In addition, and without limiting the generality of the foregoing: (i) each Company Employee shall be immediately eligible to participate, without any waiting time, in any and all New Plans to the extent coverage under such New Plan replaces coverage under a comparable Company Employee Benefit Plan in which such Company Employee participated immediately before the Effective Time (such plans, collectively, the "Old Plans"); and (ii) for purposes of each New Plan providing medical, dental, pharmaceutical and/or vision benefits to any Company Employee, Parent shall cause all pre-existing condition exclusions and actively-at-work requirements of such New Plan to be waived for such employee and his/her covered dependents, and Parent shall cause any eligible expenses incurred by such employee and his/her covered dependents during the portion of the plan year of the Old Plan ending on the date such employee's participation in the corresponding New Plan begins to be taken into account under such New Plan for purposes of satisfying all deductible, coinsurance and maximum out-of-pocket requirements applicable to such employee and his/her covered dependents for the applicable plan year as if such amounts had been paid in accordance with such New Plan.

(c) Parent hereby acknowledges that the transactions contemplated by this Agreement shall constitute a "change of control" under the Company Employee Benefit Plans, as applicable.

***

Section 8.02. *Nonsurvivable of Representations and Warranties.* No representations or warranties in this Agreement or in any instrument delivered pursuant to this Agreement shall survive the Acceptance Date, with respect to representations and warranties of the Company, or the Effective Time, with respect to representations and warranties of Parent and Merger Sub. This Section 8.02 shall not limit any covenant or agreement of the parties which by its terms contemplates performance after such time.

***

Section 10. *Definitions.*

"Applicable Withholding" means any amount that may be required to be withheld under any federal, state, or local taxing authority.

"COBRA" means the requirements of Part 6 of Subtitle B of Title I of ERISA and Code Sec. 4980B.

"Code" means the Internal Revenue Code of 1986, as amended or now in effect or as hereafter amended, including but not limited to, any successor or substitute Federal tax codes or legislation.

"Company Stock Incentive Plan" means the ABC Corporation 2018 Stock Incentive Plan.

"Employee Benefit Plan" means any "employee benefit plan" (as such term is defined in ERISA Section 3(3)) and any other material employee benefit plan, program or arrangement of any kind.

"Employee Pension Benefit Plan" has the meaning set forth in ERISA Section 3(2).

"Employee Welfare Benefit Plan" has the meaning set forth in ERISA Section 3(1).

"ERISA" means the Employee Retirement Income Security Act of 1974, as amended.

"ERISA Affiliate" means each entity that is treated as a single employer with Company for purposes of Code Sec. 414.

"Exchange Act" means the Securities Exchange Act of 1934, as amended.

"Fiduciary" has the meaning set forth in ERISA Section 3(21).

"Multiemployer Plan" has the meaning set forth in ERISA Section 3(37).

"PBGC" means the Pension Benefit Guaranty Corporation.

"Prohibited Transaction" has the meaning set forth in ERISA Section 406 and Code Sec. 4975.

"Securities Act" means the Securities Act of 1933, as amended.

"Stock Option Cancellation Agreement" means the Stock Option Cancellation Agreement attached hereto as [Exhibit M].

"Stock Option Cancellation Payment" means with respect to each Stock Option an amount in cash equal to the Per Share Option Purchase Price *less* the exercise price for each Stock Option held by such Stock Optionee as further specified in each Stock Optionee's Stock Option Cancellation Agreement.

"Stock Optionee" has the meaning set forth in Section 1(f).

¶10,300 SAMPLE LEGAL DOCUMENT—Sample Compensation Committee Charter

The following is a sample charter for the compensation committee of a board of directors. The board of directors is responsible for selecting and compensating the corporation's chief executive officer. A good start to better performance of these functions, and better corporate governance overall, is a charter setting forth the duties and responsibilities of the compensation committee. Either a public or a private company could use this sample charter. For a discussion of director liability for excessive executive compensation, see ¶2125.

Sample Compensation Committee Charter

I. PURPOSE

The Compensation Committee (the "Committee") is appointed by the Board to discharge the Board's responsibilities relating to compensation of the Company's senior executives (collectively the "Subject Employees") and directors. The Committee has overall responsibility for approving and evaluating all compensation plans, policies and programs of the Company and its subsidiaries as they apply to the Subject Employees. For this purpose, compensation shall include:

- annual base salary;
- annual incentive opportunity;
- stock option or other equity participation plans;
- long-term incentive opportunity;
- the terms of employment agreements, severance arrangements, change in control plans and agreements, and other similar agreements, in each case as, when and if appropriate;
- any special or supplemental benefits; and
- any other payments or benefits that are deemed compensation under applicable rules and regulations of the U.S. Securities and Exchange Commission (the "SEC") and the New York Stock Exchange (the "NYSE").

Also, the Compensation Committee has overall responsibility to produce the annual report on executive compensation for inclusion in the Company's proxy statement in accordance with applicable rules and regulations.

II. COMPENSATION COMMITTEE MEMBERSHIP

The Committee shall consist of no fewer than three members of the Board, each of whom shall satisfy the applicable independence requirements of the Company's corporate governance guidelines, the NYSE and any other regulatory requirements. Each member shall also be an outside director for purposes of Section 162(m) of the U.S. Internal Revenue Code of 1986, as amended, and the rules and regulations promulgated thereunder, including Treasury Regulations Section 1.162-27, a non-employee director for purposes of Section 16, and inde-

¶10,300

pendent for purposes of Section 10C(a), of the U.S. Securities Exchange Act of 1934, as amended, and the rules and regulations promulgated thereunder (the "Exchange Act"). The members of the Committee shall be appointed by the Board on the recommendation of the Nominating and Governance Committee.

One member of the Committee shall be appointed as Committee Chairperson by the Board. Unless a Chairperson of the Committee is selected by the Board, the members of the Committee shall select an acting Committee Chairperson by majority vote of the full Committee. Committee members may be replaced by the Board.

III. MEETINGS

The Committee shall meet as often as necessary to carry out its responsibilities but no less than quarterly. The Committee Chairperson shall preside at each meeting. In the event the Committee Chairperson is not present at a meeting, the Committee members present at that meeting shall designate one of its members as the acting chair of such meeting. A majority of the members of the Committee shall constitute a quorum. Without a meeting, the Committee may act by unanimous written consent of all members. The Committee shall determine its own rules and procedures, including designation of a secretary. The secretary need not be a member of the Committee and shall attend Committee meetings and prepare minutes. The Committee shall keep written minutes of its meetings, which shall be recorded or filed with the books and records of the Company. Any member of the Board shall be provided with copies of such Committee minutes if requested.

No Subject Employee should attend that portion of any meeting where the Subject Employee's performance or compensation is discussed, unless specifically invited by the Committee. Meetings to determine the compensation of the CEO must be held in executive session. Meetings to determine the compensation of Subject Employees other than the CEO may be attended by the CEO, but the CEO may not vote on these matters.

IV. COMMITTEE RESPONSIBILITIES AND AUTHORITY

1. The Committee shall review the compensation philosophy and strategy of the Company and its subsidiaries and consult with the CEO, as needed, regarding the role of the Company's compensation strategy in achieving the Company's objectives and performance goals and long-term interests of the Company's stockholders. Consistent with this strategy the Committee will develop the Company's overall compensation policies as they affect Subject Employees, including, without limitation, determining the appropriate balance among base salary, annual bonus and long term incentive awards, and establish performance-based incentives. Once developed and established, the Committee shall monitor, review, evaluate and, at its discretion, revise such policies and incentives.

2. The Committee shall annually review and approve corporate goals and objectives relevant to CEO compensation, evaluate the CEO's perform-

ance in light of those goals and objectives, and determine and approve the CEO's compensation level based on this evaluation. In determining the incentive components of CEO compensation, the Committee may consider a number of factors, including, but not limited to, the Company's performance and relative shareholder return, the value of similar incentive awards to CEOs at comparable companies, and awards given to the CEO in past years.

3. The Committee shall, at least annually, review and approve the annual base salaries and annual incentive opportunities of the Subject Employees.

4. The Committee shall, periodically and as and when appropriate, review and approve the following as they affect the Subject Employees:

   a. All other incentive awards and opportunities, including both cash-based and equity-based awards and opportunities;

   b. Any employment agreements and severance arrangements;

   c. Any change in control agreements and change in control provisions affecting any elements of compensation and benefits; and

   d. Any special or supplemental compensation and benefits for the Subject Employees and individuals who formerly served as Subject Employees, including supplemental retirement benefits and the perquisites provided to them during and after employment.

5. The Committee shall make recommendations to the Board with respect to the Company's incentive-compensation plans and equity-based compensation plans and approve for submission to stockholders all new equity compensation plans. The Committee shall administer all Company plans that provide for awards of equity compensation, including plans that provide awards to directors, unless otherwise provided for in the plans. In that regard, the Committee (or its designee), shall:

   a. Determine (i) the individuals to whom grants shall be awarded under such plans, (ii) the number of shares to be covered by such awards, and (iii) the time or times at which such awards shall be made;

   b. Consider the recommendations of senior management as to the individuals to whom grants shall be awarded and the number of shares to be covered by such awards, except with respect to the CEO;

   c. Interpret such plans; and

   d. Adopt, amend and rescind any rules and regulations pertaining to such plans as the Committee deems appropriate.

The Committee shall not set the grant date of its stock option grants to executives in coordination with the release of material non-public information, except in extraordinary circumstances and with full disclosure to stockholders and the public.

¶10,300

6. Except as otherwise determined by the Board, the Committee shall review and monitor the other compensation plans of the Company as they affect the Subject Employees, in light of Company and plan objectives, needs, and current benefit levels, and, at the discretion of the Committee or direction of the Board, make changes in the management of such plans, and approve any amendments thereto.

7. The Committee shall review and discuss the Compensation Discussion and Analysis (the "CD&A") required to be included in the Company's proxy statement and annual report on Form 10-K by the rules and regulations of the SEC with management, and, based on such review and discussion, determine whether or not to recommend to the Board that the CD&A be so included.

8. The Committee shall produce any annual Compensation Committee Report required to be included in the Company's proxy statement and annual report on Form 10-K in compliance with the rules and regulations promulgated by the SEC.

9. The Committee shall oversee the Company's compliance with the requirement under NYSE rules that, subject to limited exceptions, stockholders approve equity compensation plans.

10. The Committee shall receive periodic reports on the Company's compensation programs as they affect all employees.

11. The Committee shall establish and periodically review policies concerning perquisite benefits.

12. The Committee shall review and recommend to the Board for approval the compensation of directors for their services to the Board.

13. The Committee shall make regular reports to the Board.

14. The Committee shall annually review its own performance and review and reassess the adequacy of this Charter.

15. The Committee shall have the sole authority to, and in its sole discretion may, retain or obtain the advice of or terminate any compensation consultant, independent legal counsel or other adviser to assist it in the evaluation of Subject Employee and director compensation. The Committee shall be directly responsible for the appointment, compensation, and oversight of the work of any compensation consultant, independent legal counsel or other adviser retained by the Committee. The Company must provide for appropriate funding, as determined by the Committee, for payment of reasonable compensation to a compensation consultant, independent legal counsel or any other adviser retained by the Committee. The Committee may select a compensation consultant, legal counsel or other adviser only after taking into consideration all factors relevant to that person's independence from management and from the Committee, including the factors identified by the SEC and NYSE. Nothing in this paragraph shall be construed:

a. To require the Committee to implement or act consistently with the advice or recommendations of the compensation consultant, independent legal counsel or other adviser; or

b. To affect the ability or obligation of the Committee to exercise its own judgment in fulfillment of its duties.

16. The Committee may form and delegate authority to subcommittees, including committees whose members are not members of the Board, as it deems appropriate.

17. The Committee shall annually review, along with the Audit Committee, the Company's CFO and the Company's senior risk officers, the Company's employee compensation programs as they relate to risk management and risk-taking incentives in order to determine whether any risk arising from such compensation programs is reasonably likely to have a material adverse effect on the Company. The Committee shall prepare, along with the Audit Committee, the Company's CFO and the Company's senior risk officers, any disclosure in respect of such risks required to be included in the Company's annual proxy statement or annual report on Form 10-K filed with the SEC.

18. The Committee may adopt policies regarding the adjustment or recovery of incentive awards or payments if the relevant Company performance measures upon which such incentive awards or payments were based are restated or otherwise adjusted in a manner that would reduce the size of an award or payment, consistent with Section 10D of the Exchange Act.

19. The Committee may adopt policies regarding the ability of any employee or Board member, or any designee of such employee or member, to purchase financial instruments that are designed to hedge or offset any decrease in the market value of equity securities (i) granted to the employee or Board member by the Company as part of the compensation of the employee or Board member; or (ii) held, directly or indirectly, by the employee or Board member, consistent with Section 14 of the Exchange Act.

V. MISCELLANEOUS

Nothing contained in this Charter is intended to expand applicable standards of liability under statutory or regulatory requirements for the directors of the Company or members of the Committee. The purposes and responsibilities outlined in this Charter are meant to serve as guidelines rather than as inflexible rules, and the Committee is encouraged to adopt such additional procedures and standards as it deems necessary from time to time to fulfill its responsibilities. This Charter, and any amendments thereto, shall be displayed on the Company's website, and a printed copy of such shall be made available to any stockholder of the Company who requests it.

¶10,310 SAMPLE LEGAL AGREEMENT—Stock Incentive Plan

The following is a sample Stock Incentive Plan that allows the company to award qualified and nonqualified stock options, restricted stock, performance shares and performance units. We sometimes call this form of stock incentive plan an "omnibus plan" because it permits the company to grant a wide variety of stock-based awards. This plan is designed for a publicly held company.

The company would use a separate Award Agreement to award Stock Options, Stock Appreciation Rights, Restricted Stock, Restricted Stock Units, or Performance Shares or Performance Units. Sample award agreements are found in ¶10,320, ¶10,330 and ¶10,340.

Sample Stock Incentive Plan

ABC Corporation (the "Company") has established this ABC Corporation 2018 Stock Incentive Plan (the "Plan") for the following purposes: (i) to promote the growth and success of the Company by linking a significant portion of Participant compensation to the increase in value of the Company's Common Stock; (ii) to attract and retain top quality, experienced executive officers and employees by offering a competitive incentive compensation program; (iii) to reward innovation and outstanding performance as important contributing factors to the Company's growth and progress; (iv) to align the interests of executive officers, Employees, Directors and Consultants with those of the Company's stockholders by reinforcing the relationship between Participant rewards and stockholder gains obtained through the achievement by Plan Participants of short-term objectives and long-term goals; and (v) to encourage executive officers, Employees, Directors and Consultants to obtain and maintain an equity interest in the Company.

ARTICLE I
DEFINITIONS

Whenever the following terms are used in the Plan, they shall have the meanings specified below unless the context clearly indicates to the contrary. The singular pronoun shall include the plural where the context so indicates.

Section 1.1 "Affiliate" shall mean, with respect to any Person, any other Person directly or indirectly controlling, controlled by or under common control with, such Person where "control" shall have the meaning given such term under Rule 405 of the Securities Act.

Section 1.2 "Applicable Laws" shall mean the requirements relating to the administration of stock option, restricted stock, restricted stock unit and other equity-based compensation plans under U.S. state corporate laws, U.S. federal and state securities laws, the Code, any stock exchange or quotation system on which the Common Stock is listed or quoted and the applicable laws of any other country or jurisdiction where Awards are granted under the Plan.

Section 1.3 "Award" shall mean any Option, Restricted Stock, Restricted Stock Unit, Performance Share, Performance Unit, SAR, Dividend Equivalent,

Cash Incentive Award, or other Stock-Based Award granted to a Participant pursuant to the Plan, including an Award combining two or more types of Awards into a single grant.

Section 1.4 "Award Agreement" shall mean any written agreement, contract or other instrument or document evidencing an Award and setting forth the terms and conditions of the Award, including through an electronic medium. The Committee may provide for the use of electronic, internet or other non-paper Award Agreements, and the use of electronic, internet or other non-paper means for the Participant's acceptance of, or actions under, an Award Agreement unless otherwise expressly specified herein. In the event of any inconsistency or conflict between the express terms of the Plan and the express terms of an Award Agreement, the express terms of the Plan shall govern.

Section 1.5 "Base Price" shall have the meaning set forth in Section 1.49.

Section 1.6 "Board" shall mean the Board of Directors of the Company.

Section 1.7 "Cause" shall mean: (a) if the Participant is party to an effective employment, consulting, severance or other similar agreement with the Company, a Subsidiary, or Affiliate, and such term is defined therein, "Cause" shall have the meaning provided in such agreement; (b) if the applicable Participant is not a party to an effective employment, consulting, severance or other similar agreement or if no definition of "Cause" is set forth in the applicable employment, consulting, severance or other similar agreement, then "Cause" shall mean, as determined by the Committee in its sole discretion, the Participant's (i) willful misconduct or gross negligence in connection with the performance of the Participant's material employment-related duties for the Company or any of its Subsidiaries or Affiliates; (ii) conviction of, or a plea of guilty or *nolo contendere* to, a felony or a crime involving fraud or moral turpitude; (iii) engaging in any business that directly or indirectly competes with the Company or any of its Subsidiaries or Affiliates; or (iv) disclosure of trade secrets, customer lists or confidential information of the Company or any of its Subsidiaries or Affiliates to any unauthorized Person; (v) engaging in willful or serious misconduct that has caused or could reasonably be expected to result in material injury to the Company or any of its Subsidiaries or Affiliates, including, but not limited to by way of damage to the Company's, Subsidiary's, or Affiliate's reputation or public standing or material violation of any Company policy; or (vi) failure to reasonably cooperate with the Company in any internal investigation or administrative, regulatory or judicial proceeding, after notice thereof from the Board or the Committee to the Participant and a reasonable opportunity for the Participant to cure such non-cooperation. The Participant's employment shall be deemed to have terminated for Cause if, after the Participant's employment or service has terminated, facts and circumstances are discovered that would have justified a termination for Cause. For purposes of the Plan, no act or failure to act on the Participant's part shall be considered "willful" unless it is done, or omitted to be done, by the Participant in bad faith or without reasonable belief that such action or omission was in the best interests of the Company. Notwithstanding the foregoing, neither the Plan or this provision is intended to, and shall not be interpreted in a manner that limits or restricts a Participant from exercising any legally protected whistleblower rights (including pursuant to Rule 21F under the Exchange Act.

Section 1.8 "Change in Control" shall mean the first to occur of any of the following events after the Effective Date, whether such event occurs as a single transaction or as a series of related transactions (unless otherwise provided in an Award Agreement):

(a) The acquisition, directly or indirectly, by any Person, entity or "group" (as used in Section 13(d) of the Exchange Act) (other than (i) the Company, (ii) any trustee or other fiduciary holding securities under an employee benefit plan of the Company or an Affiliate, or (iii) any company owned, directly or indirectly, by the stockholders of the Company in substantially the same proportions as their ownership of the voting power of the securities eligible to vote for the election of the Board ("Company Voting Securities")) becomes the beneficial owner, directly or indirectly, of securities of the Company representing fifty percent (50%) or more of the combined voting power of the Company Voting Securities; provided, however, that for purposes of this Section 1.9(a), the following acquisitions shall not constitute a Change in Control: (w) any acquisition directly from the Company, (x) any acquisition by any employee benefit plan (or related trust) sponsored or maintained by the Company or an Affiliate, (y) any acquisition by an underwriter temporarily holding such Company Voting Securities pursuant to an offering of such securities or any acquisition by a pledgee of Company Voting Securities holding such securities as collateral or temporarily holding such securities upon foreclosure of the underlying obligation or (z) any acquisition pursuant to a Reorganization or Sale (each as defined below) that does not constitute a Change in Control for purposes of Section 1.9(b) or (e) below;

(b) The consummation of a merger, consolidation, statutory share exchange or similar form of corporate transaction involving the Company (each of the events referred to in this sentence being hereinafter referred to as a "Reorganization"), as a result of which Persons who were the "beneficial owners" (as such term is defined in Rule 13d-3 under the Exchange Act (or a successor rule thereto)) of Company Voting Securities immediately prior to such Reorganization do not immediately thereafter, beneficially own, directly or indirectly, more than fifty percent (50%) of the combined voting power of the then outstanding voting securities of the corporation or other entity resulting from such Reorganization (including a corporation that, as a result of such transaction, owns the Company or all or substantially all of the Company's assets either directly or through one or more subsidiaries);

(c) Within any twenty-four (24)-month period, individuals who were directors of the Company on the first days of such period (the "Incumbent Directors") shall cease for any reason to constitute at least a majority of the Board, provided that any individual becoming a director subsequent to the first day of such period whose election, or nomination by the Board for election by the Company's stockholders, was approved by a vote of at least a majority of the Incumbent Directors shall be considered as though such individual were an Incumbent Director, but excluding for this purpose, any such individual whose initial assumption of office occurs as a result of an actual or threatened election contest with respect to the election or removal of directors or other actual or threatened solicitation of proxies or consents by or on behalf of a Person other than the Board (including without limitation any settlement thereof);

(d) The approval by the Company's stockholders of the liquidation or dissolution of the Company other than a liquidation of the Company into any Subsidiary or Affiliate or a liquidation as a result of which Persons who were holders of voting securities of the Company immediately prior to such liquidation, own, directly or indirectly, more than fifty percent (50%) of the combined voting power entitled to vote generally in the election of directors of the entity that holds substantially all of the assets of the Company following such event; or

(e) The consummation of the sale, transfer or other disposition of all or substantially all of the assets of the Company to one or more Persons or entities that are not, immediately prior to such sale, transfer or other disposition, Subsidiaries or Affiliates of the Company (a "Sale");

in each case, provided that, as to Awards subject to Section 409A, such event also constitutes a "change in control event" within the meaning of Section 409A. In addition, notwithstanding the foregoing, a "Change in Control" shall not be deemed to occur if the Company files for bankruptcy, liquidation, or reorganization under the United States Bankruptcy Code or as a result of any restructuring that occurs as a result of any such proceeding.

Section 1.9 "Code" shall mean the Internal Revenue Code of 1986, as amended. Any reference to a specific provision of the Code includes any successor provision and the regulations promulgated under such provision.

Section 1.10 "Committee" shall mean the Compensation Committee of the Board, which shall consist of two or more members, each of whom is a "Non-Employee Director" within the meaning of Rule 16b-3, as promulgated under the Exchange Act, and an "outside director" within the meaning of Section 162(m).

Section 1.11 "Common Stock" shall mean the common stock, par value $0.0001 per share, of the Company and such other stock or securities into which such common stock is hereafter converted or for which such common stock is exchanged.

Section 1.12 "Company" shall mean ABC Corporation, a Delaware corporation, and any successor.

Section 1.13 "Competitive Activity" shall mean a Participant's material breach of restrictive covenants relating to noncompetition, nonsolicitation (of customers or employees), preservation of confidential information, or other covenants having the same or similar scope, included in an Award Agreement or other agreement to which the Participant and the Company or any of its Subsidiaries or Affiliates is a party.

Section 1.14 "Consultant" shall mean any individual or entity who is engaged by the Company or any of its Subsidiaries or Affiliates to render consulting or advisory services to such entity.

Section 1.15 "Corporate Event" shall mean, as determined by the Committee in its sole discretion, any transaction or event described in Section 4.5(a) or any unusual or infrequently occurring or nonrecurring transaction or event affecting the Company, any Subsidiary or Affiliate of the Company, or the financial statements of the Company or any of its Subsidiaries or Affiliates, or any changes in Applicable Laws, regulations or accounting principles (including, without limitation, a recapitalization of the Company).

Section 1.16 "Director" shall mean a member of the Board or a member of the board of directors of any Subsidiary or Affiliate of the Company.

Section 1.17 "Disability" shall mean (x) with respect to an Incentive Stock Option, the meaning given in Code Section 22(e)(3), and (y) for Awards that are subject to Section 409A, "disability" shall have the meaning set forth in Section 409A(a)(2)(c); provided that, with respect to Awards that are not subject to Section 409A, in the case of any Participant who, as of the date of determination, is a party to an effective services, severance, consulting or employment agreement with the Company or any Subsidiary or Affiliate of the Company that employs such individual, "Disability" shall have the meaning, if any, specified in such agreement.

Section 1.18 "Dividend Equivalent" shall mean the right to receive payments, in cash or in Shares, based on dividends paid with respect to Shares.

Section 1.19 "Effective Date" shall have the meaning set forth in Section 13.7.

Section 1.20 "Eligible Representative" for a Participant shall mean such Participant's personal representative or such other person as is empowered under the deceased Participant's will or the then Applicable Laws of descent and distribution to represent the Participant hereunder. If a Participant dies, amounts payable with respect to an Award, if any, due under the Plan upon the Participant's death will be paid to the beneficiary designated by the Participant for the Company's 401(k) plan or, if none, the Participant's spouse, or if the Participant is otherwise unmarried at the time of death, the Participant's Eligible Representative.

Section 1.21 "Employee" shall mean any individual classified as an employee by the Company or one of its Subsidiaries or Affiliates, whether such employee is so employed at the time the Plan is adopted or becomes so employed subsequent to the adoption of the Plan, including any person to whom an offer of employment has been extended (except that any Award granted to such person shall be conditioned on his or her commencement of service). A person shall not cease to be an Employee in the case of (a) any leave of absence approved by the Company or required by law or (b) transfers between locations of the Company or between the Company, any of its Subsidiaries or Affiliates, or any successor to the foregoing. For purposes of Incentive Stock Options, no such leave may exceed three (3) months, unless reemployment upon expiration of such leave is guaranteed by statute or contract. If reemployment upon expiration of a leave of absence approved by the Company is not so guaranteed, the employment relationship shall be deemed to have terminated on the first day immediately following such three (3)-month period, and such Incentive Stock Option held by the Optionee shall cease to be treated as an Incentive Stock Option and shall be treated for tax purposes as a Non-Qualified Stock Option on the first day immediately following a three (3)-month period from the date the employment relationship is deemed terminated.

¶10,310

Section 1.22 "Exchange Act" shall mean the Securities Exchange Act of 1934, as amended. Any reference to a specific provision of the Exchange Act includes any successor provision and the regulations and rules promulgated under such provision.

Section 1.23 "Executive Officer" shall mean each person who is an officer of the Company or any Subsidiary or Affiliate and who is subject to the reporting requirements under Section 16(a) of the Exchange Act.

Section 1.24 "Exercise Price" shall have the meaning set forth in Section 6.3.

Section 1.25 "Fair Market Value" of a Share as of any date of determination means the last sales price on such date on the Nasdaq Stock Market, as reported in The Wall Street Journal, or if no sales of Common Stock occur on the date in question, on the last preceding date on which there was a sale on such market. If the Shares are not listed on the [NYSE/Nasdaq Stock Market], but are traded on a national securities exchange or in another over-the-counter market, the last sales price (or, if there is no last sales price reported, the average of the closing bid and asked prices) for the Shares on the particular date, or on the last preceding date on which there was a sale of Shares on that exchange or market, will be used, unless otherwise specified by the Committee. If the Shares are neither listed on a national securities exchange nor traded in an over-the-counter market, the price determined by the Committee, in its discretion, will be used.

Section 1.26 "Good Reason" shall have the meaning set forth in the Participant's employment agreement with the Company. If the Participant is not a party to an employment agreement with the Company or such employment agreement does not define "Good Reason," then "Good Reason" means, without the Participant's written consent, the occurrence of any of the following conditions, unless such condition is fully corrected within sixty (60) days after written notice thereof:

(a) The material reduction of the Participant's authorities, duties, or responsibilities with the Company;

(b) A material reduction by the Company of the Participant's Base Salary;

(c) A relocation of the offices of the Participant to a place greater than fifty (50) miles in distance from the current executive offices of the Company in _____; or

(d) Any action or inaction that constitutes a material breach by the Company of the Participant's employment or other written agreement with the Company.

Notwithstanding anything in the Plan to the contrary, a termination of employment due to Good Reason must occur, if at all, within one hundred twenty (120) days after the Company receives written notice of any one or more of the conditions set forth in this Section. The Participant must provide the Company with written notice of any one or more of the conditions set forth in this Section within ninety (90) days of the initial existence of the condition in order for such condition to constitute Good Reason under the Plan.

Section 1.27 "Incentive Stock Option" shall mean an Option that qualifies under Code Section 422, and is expressly designated as an Incentive Stock Option in the Award Agreement.

Section 1.28 "Non-Qualified Stock Option" shall mean an Option that is not an Incentive Stock Option.

Section 1.29 "Non-U.S. Awards" shall have the meaning set forth in Section 2.5.

Section 1.30 "Option" shall mean an option to purchase Common Stock granted under the Plan at a stated Exercise Price. The term "Option" includes both an Incentive Stock Option and a Non-Qualified Stock Option.

Section 1.31 "Optionee" shall mean a Participant to whom an Option or SAR is granted under the Plan.

Section 1.32 "Participant" shall mean any Service Provider who has been granted an Award pursuant to the Plan.

Section 1.33 "Performance Award" shall mean Performance Shares, Performance Units, and all other Awards that vest (in whole or in part) upon the achievement of specified Performance Goals.

Section 1.34 "Performance Goals" means the objectives established by the Committee for a Performance Period pursuant to Section 10.3(b) for the purpose of determining the extent to which a Performance Award has been earned or vested.

Section 1.35 "Performance Period" shall mean the period of time selected by the Committee during which performance is measured for the purpose of determining the extent to which a Performance Award has been earned or vested.

Section 1.36 "Performance Share" means an Award granted pursuant to Article IX of the Plan of a contractual right to receive a Share (or the cash equivalent thereof) upon the achievement, in whole or in part, of the applicable Performance Goals.

Section 1.37 "Performance Unit" means a U.S. Dollar-denominated unit (or a unit denominated in the Participant's local currency) granted pursuant to Article VIII of the Plan, payable upon the achievement, in whole or in part, of the applicable Performance Goals.

Section 1.38 "Person" shall have the meaning given in Section 3(a)(9) of the Exchange Act, as modified and used in Sections 13(d) and 14(d) thereof, including any individual, partnership, corporation, limited liability company, business trust, joint stock company, trust, unincorporated association, joint venture, governmental authority, or any other entity of whatever nature.

Section 1.39 "Plan" shall mean the ABC Corporation 2018 Stock Incentive Plan, as amended and restated herein, and as may be further amended from time to time.

Section 1.40 "Qualifying Termination" means a Participant's termination of service due to the Participant's death, Disability, termination by the Participant for Good Reason or termination by the Company without Cause that occurs upon or within twenty-four (24) months of the consummation of a Change in Control.

Section 1.41 "Replacement Awards" shall mean Shares issued in assumption of, or in substitution for, any outstanding awards of any entity acquired in any form or combination by the Company or any of its Subsidiaries or Affiliates.

Section 1.42 "Restricted Stock" shall mean an Award of Shares granted pursuant to Section 7.1, which is subject to a risk of forfeiture, restrictions on transfer, or both a risk of forfeiture and restrictions on transfer.

Section 1.43 "Restricted Stock Unit" shall mean an Award granted pursuant to Section 7.2, which is a contractual right to receive a number of Shares or an amount of cash equal to the value of that number of Shares corresponding to the number of units granted to a Service Provider without payment, as compensation for services to the Company or its Subsidiaries or Affiliates, which right is subject to performance or time-based vesting restrictions.

Section 1.44 "Section 162(m)" shall mean Code Section 162(m).

Section 1.45 "Section 409A" shall mean Code Section 409A.

Section 1.46 "Securities Act" shall mean the Securities Act of 1933, as amended.

Section 1.47 "Service Provider" shall mean an Employee, Consultant, or Director.

Section 1.48 "Share" shall mean a share of Common Stock.

Section 1.49 "Stock Appreciation Right" or "SAR" shall mean the right to receive a payment from the Company in cash and/or Shares equal to the product of (i) the excess, if any, of the Fair Market Value of one Share on the exercise date over a specified price (the "Base Price") fixed by the Committee on the grant date (which specified price shall not be less than the Fair Market Value of one Share on the grant date), multiplied by (ii) a number of Shares stated in the Award Agreement.

Section 1.50 "Stock-Based Award" shall have the meaning set forth in Section 9.1.

Section 1.51 "Subplans" shall have the meaning set forth in Section 3.5.

Section 1.52 "Subsidiary" of any entity shall mean any entity that is directly or indirectly controlled by the Company or any entity in which the Company has at least a 50% equity interest, provided that, to the extent required under Code Section 422 when granting an Incentive Stock Option, Subsidiary shall mean any corporation in an unbroken chain of corporations beginning with such entity if each of the corporations other than the last corporation in the unbroken chain then owns stock possessing fifty percent (50%) or more of the total combined voting power of all classes of stock in one of the other corporations in such chain.

Section 1.53 "Termination of employment," "termination of service" and any similar term or terms shall mean, with respect to a Director who is not an

Employee of the Company or any of its Subsidiaries or Affiliates, the date upon which such Director ceases to be a member of the Board, with respect to a Consultant who is not an Employee of the Company or any of its Subsidiaries or Affiliates, the date upon which such Consultant ceases to provide consulting or advisory services to the Company or any of its Subsidiaries or Affiliates, and, with respect to an Employee, the date the Participant ceases to be an Employee; provided, that, with respect to any Award subject to Section 409A, such terms shall mean "separation from service," as defined in Section 409A and the rules, regulations and guidance promulgated thereunder.

(a) A Participant who ceases to be a Non-Employee Director because he or she becomes an employee of the Company or a Subsidiary or Affiliate shall not be considered to have ceased service as a Non-Employee Director with respect to any Award until such Participant's termination of employment with the Company and its Subsidiaries;

(b) A Participant who ceases to be employed by the Company or a Subsidiary or Affiliate, and immediately thereafter becomes a Non-Employee Director, a non-employee director of a Subsidiary or Affiliate, or a consultant to the Company or any Subsidiary or Affiliate shall not be considered to have terminated employment until such Participant's service as a director of, or consultant to, the Company and its Subsidiaries or Affiliates has ceased; and

(c) A Participant employed by a Subsidiary or Affiliate will be considered to have terminated employment when such entity ceases to be a Subsidiary or Affiliate.

Section 1.54 "Withholding Taxes" shall mean any federal, state, local or foreign income taxes, withholding taxes or employment taxes required to be withheld under Applicable Law, not exceeding the maximum individual statutory tax rate in a given jurisdiction (or such lower mount as may be necessary to avoid liability award accounting, or any other accounting consequence or cost, as determined by the Committee, and in any event in accordance with Company policies.

ARTICLE II
ADMINISTRATION

Section 2.1 Committee. The Plan shall be administered by the Committee, which, unless otherwise determined by the Board, shall be constituted to comply with Applicable Laws, including, without limitation, Section 16 of the Exchange Act and Section 162(m).

Section 2.2 Powers of the Committee. Subject to the provisions of the Plan, including, but not limited to Sections 3.8, 3.9, and 3.10, the Committee shall have the authority in its discretion to:

(a) Determine the type or types of Awards to be granted to each Participant;

(b) Select the Service Providers to whom Awards may from time to time be granted hereunder;

(c) Determine all matters and questions related to the termination of service of a Service Provider with respect to any Award granted to him or her hereunder, including, but not by way of limitation of, all questions of whether a particular Service Provider has taken a leave of absence, all questions of whether a leave of absence taken by a particular Service Provider constitutes a termination of service, and all questions of whether a termination of service of a particular Service Provider resulted from discharge for Cause;

(d) Determine the number of Awards to be granted and the number of Shares to which an Award will relate;

(e) Approve forms of Award Agreement for use under the Plan, which need not be identical for each Service Provider or each Award type;

(f) Determine the terms and conditions of any Awards granted hereunder (including, without limitation, the Exercise Price, the time or times when Awards may be exercised (which may be based on performance criteria), any vesting acceleration or waiver of forfeiture restrictions and any restriction or limitation regarding any Awards or the Common Stock relating thereto) based in each case on such factors as the Committee determines appropriate, in its sole discretion;

(g) Prescribe, amend and rescind rules and regulations relating to the Plan, including rules and regulations relating to Subplans established for the purpose of satisfying applicable foreign laws;

(h) Determine whether, to what extent, and pursuant to what circumstances an Award may be settled in, or the exercise or purchase price of an Award may be paid in, cash, Common Stock, other Awards, or other property, or an Award may be canceled, forfeited or surrendered;

(i) Modify the terms of any Award, and authorize the exchange or replacement of Awards; provided, however, that (i) no such modification, exchange or substitution shall be to the detriment of a Participant with respect to any Award previously granted without the affected Participant's written consent, (ii) in no event shall the Committee be permitted to, without prior stockholder approval, cancel an Option or SAR in exchange for cash, reduce the Exercise Price of any outstanding Option or grant price of any SAR or exchange or replace an outstanding Option with a new Award or Option with a lower Exercise Price or exchange or replace an outstanding SAR with a new Award or SAR with a lower grant price, except pursuant to Section 4.5 or Article XIII, and (iii) any such modification, exchange or substitution shall not violate Section 409A (it is not an extension of a stock right if the expiration of the Option or SAR is tolled while the Option or SAR is unexercisable because an exercise would violate applicable securities laws, provided that the period during which the Option or SAR may be exercised is not extended more than thirty (30) calendar days after the exercise of the Option or SAR first would no longer violate applicable securities laws);

(j) Construe and interpret the terms of the Plan and Awards granted pursuant to the Plan; and

(k) Make all other decisions and determinations that may be required pursuant to the Plan or as the Committee deems necessary or advisable to administer the Plan.

Section 2.3 Delegation by the Committee. The Committee may delegate, subject to such terms or conditions or guidelines as it shall determine, to any officer or group of officers, or Director or group of Directors of the Company or its Subsidiaries any portion of its authority and powers under the Plan with respect to Participants who are not executive officers, as defined by the Securities Exchange Act of 1934, Rule 3b-7, as that definition may be amended from time to time, or Non-Employee Directors; provided, that any delegation to one or more officers of the Company shall be subject to and comply with Section 152 and Section 157(c) of the Delaware General Company Law (or successor provisions). In addition, (i) with respect to any Award intended to qualify as "performance-based" compensation under Section 162(m), the Committee shall mean the Compensation Committee of the Board or such other committee or subcommittee of the Board or the Compensation Committee as the Board or the Compensation Committee of the Board shall designate, consisting solely of two or more members, each of whom is an "outside director" within the meaning of Section 162(m) and (ii) with respect to any Award intended to qualify for the exemption contained in Rule 16b-3 promulgated under the Exchange Act, the Committee shall consist solely two or more Non-Employee Directors or, in the alternative, the entire Board.

Section 2.4 Compensation, Professional Assistance, Good Faith Actions. The Committee may receive such compensation for its services hereunder as may be determined by the Board. All expenses and liabilities incurred by the Committee in connection with the administration of the Plan shall be borne by the Company. The Committee, in its sole discretion, may elect to engage the services of attorneys, consultants, accountants, appraisers, brokers or other persons. The Committee, the Company and its officers and Directors shall be entitled to rely upon the advice, opinions, or valuations of any such persons. All actions taken and all interpretations, decisions and determinations made by the Committee, in good faith shall be final and binding upon all Participants, the Company and all other interested persons. The Committee's determinations under the Plan need not be uniform and may be made by the Committee selectively among persons who receive, or are eligible to receive, Awards under the Plan, whether or not such persons are similarly situated. The Committee shall not be personally liable for any action, determination, or interpretation made with respect to the Plan or the Awards, and the Committee shall be fully indemnified and protected by the Company with respect to any such action, determination, or interpretation. For the purposes of this Section 2.4, "Committee" shall be deemed to include any person to whom the Committee has delegated its responsibilities in accordance with Section 2.3.

Section 2.5 Participants Based Outside the United States. To conform with the provisions of local laws and regulations, or with local compensation practices and policies, in foreign countries in which the Company or any of its Subsidiaries or Affiliates operate, but subject to the limitations set forth herein regarding the maximum number of shares issuable hereunder and the maximum award to any single Participant, the Committee may (i) modify the terms and conditions of Awards granted to Participants employed outside the United States ("Non-U.S. Awards"), (ii) establish subplans with such modifications as may be necessary or advisable under the circumstances ("Subplans") and (iii) take any action which it deems advisable to obtain, comply with or otherwise reflect any necessary governmental regulatory procedures, exemptions or approvals with respect to the Plan.

(a) The Committee's decision to grant Non-U.S. Awards or to establish Subplans is entirely voluntary, and at the complete discretion of the Committee.

The Committee may amend, modify, or terminate any Subplans at any time, and such amendment, modification, or termination may be made without prior notice to the Participants. The Company, Subsidiaries, Affiliates, and members of the Committee shall not incur any liability of any kind to any Participant as a result of any change, amendment, or termination of any Subplan at any time. The benefits and rights provided under any Subplan or by any Non-U.S. Award (x) are wholly discretionary and, although provided by either the Company, a Subsidiary, or Affiliate, do not constitute regular or periodic payments and (y) except as otherwise required under Applicable Laws, are not to be considered part of the Participant's salary or compensation under the Participant's employment with the Participant's local employer for purposes of calculating any severance, resignation, redundancy or other end of service payments, vacation, bonuses, long-term service awards, indemnification, pension or retirement benefits, or any other payments, benefits or rights of any kind. If a Subplan is terminated, the Committee may direct the payment of Non-U.S. Awards (or direct the deferral of payments whose amount shall be determined) prior to the dates on which payments would otherwise have been made, and, in the Committee's discretion, such payments may be made in a lump sum or in installments.

(b) If an Award is held by a Participant who is employed or residing in a foreign country and the amount payable or Shares issuable under such Award would be taxable to the Participant under Code Section 457A in the year such Award is no longer subject to a substantial risk of forfeiture, then the amount payable or Shares issuable under such Award shall be paid or issued to the Participant as soon as practicable after such substantial risk of forfeiture lapses (or, for Awards that are not considered nonqualified deferred compensation subject to Section 409A, no later than the end of the short-term deferral period permitted by Code Section 457A) notwithstanding anything in the Plan or the Award Agreement to contrary.

ARTICLE III
SHARES SUBJECT TO PLAN

Section 3.1 Shares Subject to Plan. Subject to Section 3.5, the aggregate number of Shares that may be issued under the Plan shall be equal to the sum of (i) [___] million (__,000,000] Shares; and (ii) any Shares subject to an Award under the Plan that expire without being exercised, or are forfeited, or canceled, without a distribution of Shares to the Participant. No more than _____ Hundred Thousand (__00,000) Shares may be issued in the form of Incentive Stock Options under the Plan. The Shares issued under the Plan may be authorized but unissued or reacquired Common Stock. No provision of the Plan shall be construed to require the Company to maintain the Shares in certificated form.

Section 3.2 Adjustments to Authorized Share Pool. Upon the grant of an Award, the maximum number of Shares set forth in Section 3.1 shall be reduced by the maximum number of Shares that are issued or may be issued pursuant to such Award. If any such Award or portion thereof is for any reason forfeited, canceled, expired, or otherwise terminated without the issuance of Shares, the Shares subject to such forfeited, canceled, expired or otherwise terminated Award or portion thereof shall again be available for grant under the Plan. Notwithstanding the foregoing, the following Shares shall not again be available for grant under the Plan: (i) Shares that are tendered or withheld from issuance with respect to an Award in satisfaction of any tax withholding or similar obligations, (ii) Shares purchased on the open market with the cash proceeds from the exercise of Options or SARs, and (iii) Shares tendered to the Company by the Participant or withheld by the Company in payment of the Exercise Price of an Option or SAR. Except to the extent required by Applicable Law, Replacement Awards shall not be counted against Shares available for grant pursuant to the Plan (and shall not be added back under this Section 4.2).

Section 3.3 Individual Award Limitations. Subject to Section 3.1 and Section 3.5, the following individual Award limits shall apply:

(a) No Participant may be granted more than ____ Million (__,000,000) Options or SARs in the aggregate under the Plan in any calendar year.

(b) No Participant may be granted more than ____ Million (__,000,000) Performance Shares, shares of performance-based Restricted Stock, performance-based Restricted Stock Units or performance-based Dividend Equivalents under the Plan in any calendar year.

Section 3.4 Limitations on Non-Employee Director Compensation. The aggregate value of cash compensation and the Fair Market Value of Shares subject to Awards that may be paid or granted by the Company during any Board compensation year to any Non-Employee Director for Board service shall not exceed Four Hundred Thousand U.S. Dollars ($400,000). The Board compensation year is the period between the dates of each annual meeting of the Company's stockholders. For the avoidance of doubt, compensation shall be counted towards this limit for the Board compensation year in which it is earned (and not when it is paid or settled in the event it is deferred).

Section 3.5 Changes in Common Stock; Disposition of Assets and Corporate Events.

(a) In the event of any stock dividend, stock split, spinoff, rights offering, extraordinary dividend, combination or exchange of Shares, recapitalization or other change in the capital structure of the Company constituting an "equity restructuring" within the meaning of Financial Accounting Standards Board ("FASB") Accounting Standards Codification Topic 718 ("FASB ASC Topic 718"), the Committee shall make or provide for equitable adjustments in (i) the number and type of shares or other securities covered by outstanding Awards, (ii) the prices specified therein (if applicable), and (iii) the kind of shares covered thereby (including shares of another issuer). The Committee in its sole discretion and in good faith should determine the form of the adjustment required to prevent dilution or enlargement of the rights of Participants and shall, in furtherance thereof, take such other actions with respect to any outstanding Award or the holder or holders thereof, in each case as it determines to be equitable, which may include a cash payment to the Participant equivalent to the value of any dilution of the rights of such Participant. In the event of any merger, consolidation, or any other corporate transaction or event having a similar effect that is not an "equity restructuring" with the meaning of FASB ASC Topic 718, the Committee in its sole discretion may, in addition to the actions permitted to be taken in respect of an equity restructuring, provide in substitution for any or all outstanding Awards under the Plan such alternative consideration as it may in good faith determine to be equitable under the circumstances and may require in connection with such alternative consideration the surrender of all Awards so replaced. After any adjustment made by the Committee pursuant to this Section 3.5, the number of shares subject to each outstanding Award shall be rounded down to the nearest whole number.

(b) Any adjustment of an Award pursuant to this Section 3.5 shall be effected in compliance with Code Sections 422 and 409A to the extent applicable.

Section 3.6 Dividend Equivalents. Dividend Equivalents may be granted to Participants at such time or times as shall be determined by the Committee, provided that: (i) no Dividend Equivalents shall be paid on unvested Awards but may be accumulated and paid once the underlying Award vests; and (ii) no Dividend Equivalents may be paid on Options or SARs. Dividend Equivalents may be granted in tandem with other Awards, in addition to other Awards, or freestanding and unrelated to other Awards. The grant date of any Dividend Equivalents under the Plan will be the date on which the Dividend Equivalent is awarded by the Committee, or such other date permitted by Applicable Laws as the Committee shall determine in its sole discretion. For the avoidance of doubt, Dividend Equivalents with respect to Performance Shares or Performance Units shall not be fully vested until the Performance Shares or Performance Units have been earned. Dividend Equivalents shall be evidenced in writing, whether as part of the Award Agreement governing the terms of the Award, if any, to which such Dividend Equivalent relates, or pursuant to a separate Award Agreement with respect to freestanding Dividend Equivalents, in each case, containing such provisions not inconsistent with the Plan as the Committee shall determine.

Section 3.7 Award Agreement Provisions. The Committee may include such further provisions and limitations in any Award Agreement as it may deem equitable and in the best interests of the Company and its Subsidiaries or Affiliates that are not inconsistent with the terms of the Plan.

Section 3.8 Limit on Award Shares Not Satisfying Minimum Vesting Requirement. The maximum number of Shares that may be granted to Participants with respect to Awards that do not satisfy the minimum vesting requirement set forth in Section 5.5 shall be five percent (5%) of the authorized share limit set forth in Section 3.1.

Section 3.9 Prohibition Against Repricing. Except to the extent (i) approved in advance by holders of a majority of the Shares entitled to vote generally in the election of directors or (ii) pursuant to Section 3.5 as a result of any Corporate Event, the Committee shall not have the power or authority to reduce, whether through amendment or otherwise, the Exercise Price of any outstanding Option or Base Price of any outstanding SAR or to grant any new Award, or make any cash payment, in substitution for or upon the cancellation of Options or SARs previously granted.

Section 3.10 Prohibition Against Option Reloads. Except to the extent approved in advance by holders of a majority of the Shares entitled to vote generally in the election of directors, the Committee shall not have the power or authority to include provisions in an Option Award Agreement that provides for the reload of the Option or SAR upon exercise or settlement.

ARTICLE IV

GRANTING OF OPTIONS AND SARS

Section 4.1 Eligibility. The Committee may grant Non-Qualified Stock Options and SARs to Service Providers. Subject to Section 4.2, Incentive Stock Options may only be granted to Employees.

Section 4.2 Qualification of Incentive Stock Options. No Employee may be granted an Incentive Stock Option under the Plan if such Employee, at the time the Incentive Stock Option is granted, owns stock possessing more than ten percent (10%) of the total combined voting power of all classes of stock of the Company or any then existing Subsidiary of the Company or "parent corporation" (within the meaning of Code Section 424(e)) unless such Incentive Stock Option conforms to the applicable provisions of Code Section 422.

Section 4.3 Granting of Options and SARs to Service Providers.

(a) Options and SARs. The Committee may from time to time:

(i) Select from among the Service Providers (including those to whom Options or SARs have been previously granted under the Plan) such of them as in its opinion should be granted Options and/or SARs;

(ii) Determine the number of Shares to be subject to such Options and/or SARs granted to such Service Provider, and determine whether such Options are to be Incentive Stock Options or Non-Qualified Stock Options; and

(iii) Determine the terms and conditions of such Options and SARs, consistent with the Plan.

(b) SARs may be granted in tandem with Options or may be granted on a freestanding basis, not related to any Option. Unless otherwise determined by the Committee at the grant date or determined thereafter in a manner more favorable to the Participant, SARs granted in tandem with Options shall have substantially similar terms and conditions to such Options to the extent applicable, or may be granted on a freestanding basis, not related to any Option.

(c) Upon the selection of a Service Provider to be granted an Option or SAR under this Section 4.3, the Committee shall issue, or shall instruct an authorized officer to issue, such Option or SAR and may impose such conditions on the grant of such Option or SAR, as it deems appropriate. Subject to Section 13.2 of the Plan, any Incentive Stock Option granted under the Plan may be modified by the Committee, without the consent of the Optionee, even if such modification would result in the disqualification of such Option as an "incentive stock option" under Code Section 422.

Section 4.4 Notification upon Disqualifying Disposition of an Incentive Stock Option. Each Participant awarded an Incentive Stock Option under the Plan shall notify the Company in writing immediately after the date he or she makes a disqualifying disposition of any Common Stock acquired pursuant to the exercise of such Incentive Stock Option. A disqualifying disposition is any disposition (including, without limitation, any sale) of such Common Stock before the later of (a) two (2) years after the grant date of the Incentive Stock Option or (b) one (1) year after the date of exercise of the Incentive Stock Option. The Company may, if determined by the Committee and in accordance with procedures established by the Committee, retain possession, as agent for the applicable Participant, of any Shares acquired pursuant to the exercise of an Incentive Stock Option until the end of the period described in the preceding sentence, subject to

¶10,310

complying with any instruction from such Participant as to the sale of such Shares.

ARTICLE V
TERMS OF OPTIONS AND SARS

Section 5.1 Award Agreement. Each Option and each SAR shall be evidenced by a written Award Agreement, which shall be executed by the Optionee and an authorized officer and which shall contain such terms and conditions as the Committee shall determine, consistent with the Plan. Award Agreements evidencing Incentive Stock Options shall contain such terms and conditions as may be necessary to qualify such Options as "incentive stock options" under Code Section 422. If for any reason an Option intended to be an Incentive Stock Option (or any portion thereof) shall not qualify as an Incentive Stock Option, then, to the extent of such non-qualification, such Option or portion thereof shall be regarded as a Non-Qualified Stock Option appropriately granted under the Plan.

Section 5.2 Exercisability and Vesting of Options and SARs.

(a) Each Option and SAR shall vest and become exercisable according to the terms of the applicable Award Agreement; provided, however, that by a resolution adopted after an Option or SAR is granted the Committee may, on such terms and conditions as it may determine to be appropriate consistent with the Plan, accelerate the time at which such Option or SAR or any portion thereof may be exercised.

(b) Except as otherwise provided by the Committee or in the applicable Award Agreement, no portion of an Option or SAR which is unexercisable on the date that an Optionee incurs a termination of service as a Service Provider shall thereafter become exercisable.

(c) The aggregate Fair Market Value (determined as of the time the Option is granted) of all Shares with respect to which Incentive Stock Options are first exercisable by a Service Provider in any calendar year may not exceed One Hundred Thousand U.S. Dollars ($100,000) or such other limitation as imposed by Code Section 422(d), or any successor provision. To the extent that Incentive Stock Options are first exercisable by a Participant in excess of such limitation, the excess shall be considered Non-Qualified Stock Options.

(d) SARs granted in tandem with an Option shall become vested and exercisable on the same date or dates as the Options with which such SARs are associated vest and become exercisable. SARs that are granted in tandem with an Option may only be exercised upon the surrender of the right to exercise such Option for an equivalent number of Shares, and may be exercised only with respect to the Shares for which the related Option is then exercisable.

Section 5.3 Exercise Price and Base Price. Excluding Replacement Awards, the per Share purchase price of the Shares subject to each Option (the "Exercise Price") and the Base Price of each SAR shall be set by the Committee and shall be not less than one hundred percent (100%) of the Fair Market Value of such Shares on the date such Option or SAR is granted.

Section 5.4 Expiration of Options and SARs. No Option or SAR may be exercised after the first to occur of the following events:

(a) The expiration of ten (10) years from the date the Option or SAR was granted; or

(b) With respect to an Incentive Stock Option in the case of an Optionee owning (within the meaning of Code Section 424(d)), at the time the Incentive Stock Option was granted, more than ten percent (10%) of the total combined voting power of all classes of stock of the Company or any Subsidiary, the expiration of five (5) years from the date the Incentive Stock Option was granted.

Section 5.5 Minimum Vesting Period. Notwithstanding any provision of this Plan to the contrary, except as provided in Section 3.8 (with respect to the 5% of Shares not subject to this requirement), Article XIII, or in the event of death or Disability, no Award Agreement may provide for partial or graduated vesting beginning less than one year from the Grant Date.

ARTICLE VI
EXERCISE OF OPTIONS AND SARS

Section 6.1 Person Eligible to Exercise. During the lifetime of the Optionee, only the Optionee may exercise an Option or SAR (or any portion thereof) granted to him or her; provided, however, that the Optionee's Eligible Representative may exercise his or her Option or SAR or portion thereof during the period of the Optionee's Disability. After the death of the Optionee, any exercisable portion of an Option or SAR may, prior to the time when such portion becomes unexercisable under the Plan or the applicable Award Agreement, be exercised by his or her Eligible Representative.

Section 6.2 Partial Exercise. At any time and from time to time prior to the date on which the Option or SAR becomes unexercisable under the Plan or the applicable Award Agreement, the exercisable portion of an Option or SAR may be exercised in whole or in part; provided, however, that the Company shall not be required to issue fractional Shares and the Committee may, by the terms of the Option or SAR, require any partial exercise to exceed a specified minimum number of Shares.

Section 6.3 Manner of Exercise. Subject to any generally applicable conditions or procedures that may be imposed by the Committee, an exercisable Option or SAR, or any exercisable portion thereof, may be exercised solely by delivery to the Committee or its designee of all of the following prior to the time when such Option or SAR or such portion becomes unexercisable under the Plan or the applicable Award Agreement:

(a) Notice in writing signed by the Optionee or his or her Eligible Representative, stating that such Option or SAR or portion is being exercised, and specifically stating the number of Shares with respect to which the Option or SAR is being exercised (which form of notice shall be provided by the Committee upon request and may be electronic);

(b) (i) With respect to the exercise of any Option, full payment (in cash (through wire transfer only) or by personal, certified, or bank cashier check) of the aggregate Exercise Price of the Shares with respect to which such Option (or portion thereof) is thereby exercised; or

(ii) With the consent of the Committee, (A) Shares owned by the Optionee duly endorsed for transfer to the Company or (B) Shares issuable to the Optionee upon exercise of the Option, with a Fair Market Value on the date of Option exercise equal to the aggregate Exercise Price of the Shares with respect to which such Option (or portion thereof) is thereby exercised; or

(iii) With the consent of the Committee, payment of the Exercise Price through a broker-assisted cashless exercise program established by the Company; or

(iv) With the consent of the Committee, any form of payment of the Exercise Price permitted by Applicable Laws and any combination of the foregoing methods of payment.

(c) Full payment to the Company (in cash or by personal, certified or bank cashier check or by any other means of payment approved by the Committee) of all amounts necessary to satisfy any and all Withholding Taxes arising in connection with the exercise of the Option or SAR (notice of the amount of which shall be provided by the Committee as soon as practicable following receipt by the Committee of the notice of exercise);

(d) In the event that the Option or SAR or portion thereof shall be exercised as permitted under Section 6.1 by any person or persons other than the Optionee, appropriate proof of the right of such person or persons to exercise the Option or SAR or portion thereof.

Section 6.4 Settlement of SARs. Unless otherwise determined by the Committee, upon exercise of a SAR, the Participant shall be entitled to receive payment in the form, determined by the Committee and set forth in the Award Agreement, of Shares, or cash, or a combination of Shares and cash having an aggregate value equal to the amount determined by multiplying: (a) any increase in the Fair Market Value of one Share on the exercise date over the Base Price of such SAR, by (b) the number of Shares with respect to which such SAR is exercised; provided, however, that on the grant date, the Committee may establish, in its sole discretion, a maximum amount per Share that may be payable upon exercise of a SAR, and provided, further, that in no event shall the value of the Common Stock or cash delivered on exercise exceed the excess of the Fair Market Value of the Shares with respect to which the SAR is exercised over the Fair Market Value of such Shares on the grant date of such SAR.

Section 6.5 Conditions to Issuance of Shares. The Company shall evidence the issuance of Shares delivered upon exercise of an Option or SAR in the books and records of the Company or in a manner determined by the Company. Notwithstanding the above, the Company shall not be required to effect the issuance of any Shares purchased upon the exercise of any Option or SAR or portion thereof prior to fulfillment of all of the following conditions:

(a) The admission of such Shares to listing on any and all stock exchanges on which such class of Common Stock is then listed;

(b) The completion of any registration or other qualification of such Shares under any state or federal law or under the rulings or regulations of the U.S. Securities and Exchange Commission or any other governmental regulatory body, which the Committee shall, in its sole discretion, deem necessary or advisable;

(c) The obtaining of any approval or other clearance from any state or federal governmental agency which the Committee shall, in its sole discretion, determine to be necessary or advisable and

(d) The payment to the Company (or its Subsidiary or Affiliate, as applicable) of all amounts which it is required to withhold under Applicable Law in connection with the exercise of the Option or SAR.

The Committee shall not have any liability to any Optionee for any delay in the delivery of Shares to be issued upon an Optionee's exercise of an Option or SAR.

Section 6.6 Rights as Stockholders. The holder of an Option or SAR shall not be, nor have any of the rights or privileges of, a stockholder of the Company in respect of any Shares purchasable upon the exercise of any part of an Option or SAR.

Section 6.7 Transfer Restrictions. The Committee, in its sole discretion, may set forth in an Award Agreement such further restrictions on the transferability of the Shares purchasable upon the exercise of an Option or SAR, as it deems appropriate. Any such restriction may be referred to in the Share register maintained by the Company or otherwise in a manner reflecting its applicability to the Shares. The Committee may require the Employee to give the Company prompt notice of any disposition of Shares acquired by exercise of an Incentive Stock Option, within two (2) years from the grant date of such Option or one (1) year after the transfer of such Shares to such Employee. The Committee may cause the Share register maintained by the Company to refer to such requirement.

ARTICLE VII
RESTRICTED STOCK AWARDS AND RESTRICTED STOCK UNIT AWARDS

Section 7.1 Restricted Stock.

(a) Grant of Restricted Stock. The Committee is authorized to make Awards of Restricted Stock to any Service Provider selected by the Committee in such amounts and subject to such terms and conditions as determined by the Committee. All Awards of Restricted Stock shall be evidenced by an Award Agreement.

(b) Issuance and Restrictions. Restricted Stock shall be subject to such restrictions on transferability and other restrictions as the Committee may impose (including, without limitation, limitations on the right to vote Restricted Stock or limitations on the right to pay dividends or Dividend Equivalents on Restricted Stock before said Restricted Stock vests); provided, however, that any cash or shares of Common Stock distributed as a dividend or otherwise with respect to any Restricted Stock as to which the restrictions have not yet lapsed, shall be subject to the same restrictions as such Restricted Stock and held or restricted as provided in this Section. These restrictions may lapse separately or in combination at such times, pursuant to such circumstances, in such installments, or otherwise, as the Committee determines at the time of the grant of the Award or thereafter.

(c) Issuance of Restricted Stock. The issuance of Restricted Stock granted pursuant to the Plan may be evidenced in such manner as the Committee shall determine.

Section 7.2 Restricted Stock Units. The Committee is authorized to make Awards of Restricted Stock Units to any Service Provider selected by the Committee in such amounts and subject to such terms and conditions as determined by the Committee. At the time of grant, the Committee shall specify the date or dates on which the Restricted Stock Units shall become fully vested and nonforfeitable, and may specify such conditions to vesting as it deems appropriate. At the time of grant, the Committee shall specify the settlement date applicable to each grant of Restricted Stock Units which shall be no earlier than the vesting date or dates of the Award and may be determined at the election of the grantee. On the settlement date, the Company shall, subject to the terms of the Plan, transfer to the Participant one Share for each Restricted Stock Unit scheduled to be paid out on such date and not previously forfeited.

Section 7.3 Rights as a Stockholder. A Participant shall not be, nor have any of the rights or privileges of, a stockholder in respect of Restricted Stock Units awarded pursuant to the Plan, except as the Committee may provide under Section 3.6.

ARTICLE VIII
PERFORMANCE SHARES AND PERFORMANCE UNITS

Section 8.1 Grant of Performance Shares or Performance Units. The Committee is authorized to make Awards of Performance Shares and Performance Units to any Participant selected by the Committee in such amounts and subject to such terms and conditions as determined by the Committee. All Performance Shares and Performance Units shall be evidenced by an Award Agreement.

Section 8.2 Issuance and Restrictions. The Committee shall have the authority to determine the Participants who shall receive Performance Shares and Performance Units, the number of Performance Shares and the number and value of Performance Units each Participant receives for any Performance Period and the Performance Goals applicable in respect of such Performance Shares and Performance Units for each Performance Period. The Committee shall determine the duration of each Performance Period (the duration of Performance Periods may differ from one another), and there may be more than one Performance Period in existence at any one time. An Award Agreement evidencing the grant of Performance Shares or Performance Units shall specify the number of Performance Shares and the number and value of Performance Units awarded to the Participant, the Performance Goals applicable thereto, and such other terms and conditions not inconsistent with the Plan, as the Committee shall determine. No Common Stock will be issued at the time an Award of Performance Shares is made, and the Company shall not be required to set aside a fund for the payment of Performance Shares or Performance Units.

Section 8.3 Earned Performance Shares and Performance Units. Performance Shares and Performance Units shall become earned, in whole or in part, based upon the attainment of specified Performance Goals or the occurrence of any event or events, as the Committee shall determine, either in an Award Agreement or thereafter on terms more favorable to the Participant to the extent consistent with Section 162(m). In addition to the achievement of the specified Performance Goals, the Committee may condition payment of Performance Shares and Performance Units on such other conditions as the Committee shall specify in an Award Agreement. The Committee may also provide in an Award

Agreement for the completion of a minimum period of service (in addition to the achievement of any applicable Performance Goals) as a condition to the vesting of any Performance Share or Performance Unit Award.

Section 8.4 Rights as a Stockholder. A Participant shall not have any rights as a stockholder in respect of Performance Shares or Performance Units awarded pursuant to the Plan, except as the Committee may provide under Section 3.6. Performance Shares shall be subject to such restrictions on transferability and other restrictions as the Committee may impose (including, without limitation, limitations on the right to vote Performance Shares or limitations on the right to pay dividends or Dividend Equivalents on Performance Shares before said Performance Shares vest); provided, however, that any cash or shares of Common Stock distributed as a dividend or otherwise with respect to any Performance Shares as to which the restrictions have not yet lapsed, shall be subject to the same restrictions as such Performance Shares and held or restricted as provided in this Section. These restrictions may lapse separately or in combination at such times, pursuant to such circumstances, in such installments, or otherwise, as the Committee determines at the time of the grant of the Award or thereafter.

Section 8.5 Performance Goals. The Committee shall establish the Performance Goals that must be satisfied in order for a Participant to receive an Award for a Performance Period or for an Award of Performance Shares or Performance Units (or other Award subject to performance conditions) to be earned or vested. At the discretion of the Committee, the Performance Goals may be based upon (alone or in combination): (a) net or operating income (before or after taxes); (b) earnings before taxes, interest, depreciation, and/or amortization ("EBITDA"); (c) EBITDA excluding charges for stock compensation, management fees, restructurings and impairments ("Adjusted EBITDA"), and operating leverage or Adjusted EBITDA growth/sales growth; (d) basic or diluted earnings per share or improvement in basic or diluted earnings per share; (e) sales (including, but not limited to, total sales, net sales, revenue growth, or sales growth in excess of market growth); (f) net operating profit; (g) financial return measures (including, but not limited to, return on assets, capital, invested capital, equity, sales, or revenue); (h) cash flow measures (including, but not limited to, operating cash flow, free cash flow, cash flow return on equity, cash flow return on investment, cash conversion, or pre-tax, pre-interest cash flow/Adjusted EBITDA); (i) productivity ratios (including but not limited to measuring liquidity, profitability or leverage); (j) share price (including, but not limited to, growth measures and total stockholder return); (k) expense/cost management targets; (l) margins (including, but not limited to, operating margin, net income margin, cash margin, gross, net or operating profit margins, EBITDA margins, Adjusted EBITDA margins); (m) operating efficiency; (n) market share or market penetration; (o) customer targets (including, but not limited to, customer growth or customer satisfaction); (p) working capital targets or improvements; (q) economic value added; (r) balance sheet metrics (including, but not limited to, inventory, inventory turns, receivables turnover, net asset turnover, debt reduction, retained earnings, year-end cash, cash conversion cycle, ratio of debt to equity or to EBITDA); (s) workforce targets (including but not limited to diversity goals, employee engage-

¶10,310

ment or satisfaction, employee retention, and workplace health and safety goals); (t) implementation, completion or attainment of measurable objectives with respect to research and development, key products or key projects, lines of business, acquisitions and divestitures and strategic plan development and/or implementation; (u) comparisons with various stock market indices, peer companies or industry groups or classifications with regard to one more of these criteria, or (v) for any period of time in which Section 162(m) is not applicable to the Company and the Plan, or at any time in the case of (A) persons who are not "covered employees" under Section 162(m) or (B) Awards (whether or not to "covered employees") not intended to qualify as performance-based compensation under Section 162(m), such other criteria as may be determined by the Committee. Performance Goals may be established on a Company-wide basis or with respect to one or more business units, divisions, Subsidiaries or Affiliates, or products and may be expressed in absolute terms, or relative to (i) current internal targets or budgets, (ii) the past performance of the Company (including the performance of one or more Subsidiaries, Affiliates, divisions, or operating units), (iii) the performance of one or more similarly situated companies, (iv) the performance of an index covering a peer group of companies, or (v) other external measures of the selected performance criteria. Any performance goals that are financial metrics, may be determined in accordance with U.S. Generally Accepted Accounting Principles ("GAAP"), in accordance with accounting principles established by the International Accounting Standards Board ("IASB Principles"), or may be adjusted when established to include or exclude any items otherwise includable or excludable under GAAP or under IASB Principles. Any performance objective may measure performance on an individual basis, as appropriate. The Committee may provide for a threshold level of performance below which no Shares or compensation will be granted or paid in respect of Performance Shares or Performance Units, and a maximum level of performance above which no additional Shares or compensation will be granted or paid in respect of Performance Shares or Performance Units, and it may provide for differing amounts of Shares or compensation to be granted or paid in respect of Performance Shares or Performance Units for different levels of performance. The Committee may provide for exclusion of the impact of an event or occurrence which the Committee determines should appropriately be excluded, including but not limited to unusual and/or infrequently occurring or nonrecurring items as determined under U.S. generally accepted accounting principles and as identified in the financial statements, notes to the financial statements or management's discussion and analysis in the annual report, including, without limitation, the charges or costs associated with restructurings of the Company, discontinued operations, capital gains and losses, dividends, Share repurchase, other unusual or non-recurring items, and the cumulative effects of accounting changes.

Section 8.6 Special Rule for Performance Goals. If, at the time of grant, the Committee intends any Award to qualify as performance-based compensation within the meaning of Section 162(m) (except with respect to Options or SARs), the Committee must establish Performance Goals (and any exclusions) for the applicable Performance Period prior to the 91st day of the Performance Period (or by such other date as may be required under Section 162(m)) but not later than the date on which twenty-five percent (25%) of the Performance Period has elapsed.

Section 8.7 Negative Discretion. Notwithstanding anything in this Article VIII to the contrary, the Committee shall have the right, in its absolute discretion, (i) to reduce or eliminate the amount otherwise payable to any Participant under Section 8.9 based on individual performance or any other factors that the Committee, in its discretion, shall deem appropriate and (ii) to establish rules or procedures that have the effect of limiting the amount payable to each Participant to an amount that is less than the maximum amount otherwise authorized under the Award or under the Plan.

Section 8.8 Affirmative Discretion. Notwithstanding any other provision in the Plan to the contrary, but subject to the maximum number of Shares available for issuance under Article IV of the Plan, the Committee shall have the right, in its discretion, to grant an Award in cash, Shares or other Awards, or in any combination thereof, to any Participant (except for Awards intend to qualify as performance-based compensation under Section 162(m), to the extent Section 162(m) is applicable to the Company and the Plan) in a greater amount than would apply under the applicable Performance Goals, based on individual performance or any other criteria that the Committee deems appropriate. Notwithstanding any provision of the Plan to the contrary, in no event shall the Committee have, or exercise, discretion with respect to an Award intended to qualify as performance-based compensation under Section 162(m) if such discretion or the exercise thereof would cause such qualification not to be available.

Section 8.9 Certification of Attainment of Performance Goals. As soon as practicable after the end of a Performance Period and prior to any payment or vesting in respect of such Performance Period, the Committee shall certify in writing the number of Shares, units, and/or amount of cash that have been earned or vested on the basis of performance in relation to the established Performance Goals. If the Committee determines that a change in the business, operations, corporate structure or capital structure of the Company, or the manner in which it conducts its business, or other events or circumstances, render previously established Performance Goals unsuitable, the Committee may, in its discretion, modify such Performance Goals, in whole or in part, as the Committee deems appropriate and equitable; provided that, unless the Committee determines otherwise, no such action shall be taken if and to the extent it would result in the loss of an otherwise available exemption of the Award under Section 162(m).

Section 8.10 Payment of Awards. Payment or delivery of Common Stock and/or cash with respect to earned Performance Shares and earned Performance Units shall be made to the Participant or, if the Participant has died, to the Participant's Eligible Representative, as soon as practicable after the expiration of the Performance Period and the Committee's certification under Section 8.9 and (unless an applicable Award Agreement shall set forth one or more other dates or unless otherwise deferred in accordance with Company policies) in any event no later than the earlier of (i) ninety (90) calendar days after the end of the fiscal year in which the Performance Period has ended and (ii) ninety (90) calendar days after the expiration of the Performance Period. The Committee shall determine and set forth in the applicable Award Agreement whether earned Performance Shares and the value of earned Performance Units are to be distributed in the form of cash, Shares or in a combination thereof, with the value or number of Shares payable to be determined based on the Fair Market Value of the Common Stock on the date of the Committee's certification under Section 8.9 or such other date specified in the Award Agreement. The Committee may, in an Award Agreement with respect to the award or delivery of Shares or cash, condition the vesting of such Shares or cash on the performance of additional service.

Section 8.11 Newly Eligible Participants. Notwithstanding anything in this Article VIII to the contrary, the Committee shall be entitled to make such rules, determinations and adjustments, as it deems appropriate with respect to any Participant who becomes eligible to receive Performance Shares, Performance Units, or other Performance Awards after the commencement of a Performance Period.

ARTICLE IX
OTHER STOCK-BASED AWARDS

Section 9.1 Grant of Stock-Based Awards. The Committee is authorized to make Awards of other types of equity-based or equity-related awards ("Stock-Based Awards") not otherwise described by the terms of the Plan in such amounts and subject to such terms and conditions as the Committee shall determine. All Stock-Based Awards shall be evidenced by an Award Agreement. Such Stock-Based Awards may be granted as an inducement to enter the employ of the Company or any Subsidiary or Affiliate or in satisfaction of any obligation of the Company or any Subsidiary or Affiliate to an officer or other key employee, whether pursuant to the Plan or otherwise, that would otherwise have been payable in cash or in respect of any other obligation of the Company. Such Stock-Based Awards may entail the transfer of actual Shares, or payment in cash or otherwise of amounts based on the value of Shares and may include, without limitation, Awards designed to comply with or take advantage of the applicable local laws of jurisdictions other than the United States.

Section 9.2 Automatic Grants for Directors. Subject to Section 3.3, the Committee may institute, by resolution, grants of automatic Awards to new and continuing Directors, with the number and type of such Awards, the frequency of grant and all related terms and conditions, including any applicable vesting conditions, as determined by the Committee in its sole discretion.

ARTICLE X
CASH INCENTIVE AWARDS

Section 10.1 Cash Incentive Awards. The Committee may grant Awards that may be earned in whole or in part based on the attainment of the Performance

Goals ("Cash Incentive Awards"). In the event the Committee deems it appropriate that the Company's short-term cash incentives for executive officers of the Company who are from time to time determined by the Committee to be "covered employees" for purposes of Section 162(m), qualify for deductibility under the "performance-based" compensation exception contained in Section 162(m), the provisions of this Section 10 shall apply to such Cash Incentive Awards.

Section 10.2 Eligibility and Participation. All Section 16 Participants of the Company shall be eligible to receive Cash Incentive Awards under the Plan.

Section 10.3 Terms of Cash Incentive Awards.

(a) Performance Targets and Maximum Cash Incentive Awards. For each Performance Period, the Committee shall establish objective performance targets based on specified levels of one or more of the Performance Goals. The maximum aggregate dollar amount that may be paid with respect to Cash Incentive Awards during any one calendar year to any one Section 16 Participant pursuant to this Section 10 shall be $3,000,000.

(b) Performance Period. Within ninety (90) calendar days after the commencement of each fiscal year or, if earlier, by the expiration of twenty-five percent (25%) of a Performance Period, the Committee will designate one or more Performance Periods and establish the performance targets for determining the Cash Incentive Award for each Section 16 Participant or the Section 16 Participants as a group for the Performance Period(s). The time period during which the achievement of the performance goals is to be measured shall be determined by the Committee, but may be no longer than five (5) years and no less than six (6) months.

(c) Certification. Following the close of each Performance Period and prior to payment of any amount to any Section 16 Participant under this Section 10, the Committee will certify in writing as to the attainment of the Performance Goals and the amount of the Cash Incentive Award.

(d) Discretionary Adjustment. Except as permitted under Section 162(m), the Committee may not increase the amount payable under this Section 10 or with respect to a Cash Incentive Award pursuant to Section 10.3(a), but, except as prohibited under Section 162(m), the Committee may, at the time a Cash Incentive Award is made or at any time before a Cash Incentive Award is payable in full (or would be so payable but for deferral thereof in accordance with Section 10.3(f)) but before the occurrence of a Change in Control, reduce the amount of any Cash Incentive Award in its sole discretion. The Committee may establish factors to take into consideration in implementing its discretion, including, but not limited to, corporate or business unit performance against budgeted financial goals (e.g., operating income or revenue), achievement of non-financial goals, economic and relative performance considerations, and assessments of individual performance. The amount by which any Cash Incentive Award is so reduced shall not be paid to any other Participant. Notwithstanding any provision of the Plan to the contrary, in no event shall the Committee have, or exercise, discretion with respect to a Cash Incentive Award intended to qualify as performance-based compensation under Section 162(m) if such discretion or the exercise thereof would cause such qualification not to be available.

(e) Form of Payment. Each Cash Incentive Award under this Section 10 shall be paid in cash or its equivalent. The Committee in its discretion may determine that all or a portion of a Cash Incentive Award shall be paid in

Common Stock, Restricted Stock, Restricted Stock Units, Options, Stock Appreciation Rights or other stock-based awards or stock-denominated units, as permitted by the Plan.

(f) Timing of Payment. Subject to the immediately following sentence, payment of Cash Incentive Awards will be made as soon as practicable following determination of and certification of the Cash Incentive Award, but in no event more than two and one half (2 $1/2$) months after the close of the calendar year in which Participant becomes vested in such Cash Incentive Award, and is intended to qualify for the short-term deferral exception to Section 409A, unless the Section 16 Participant has, prior to the grant of a Cash Incentive Award, submitted an election to defer receipt of such Cash Incentive Award in accordance with a deferred compensation plan approved by the Committee. Notwithstanding the foregoing, any Cash Incentive Award (or portion thereof) determined to be paid in Common Stock, Restricted Stock, Restricted Stock Units, Options, Stock Appreciation Rights or other stock-based awards or stock-denominated units pursuant to the Plan may be issued to the Participant at any time following determination and certification of the Cash Incentive Award and prior to the last day of the fiscal year following the fiscal year with respect to which such Cash Incentive Award relates.

Section 10.4 New Hires, Promotions, and Terminations. Unless otherwise provided in an Award Agreement, Company policy, or other agreement between the Company or Affiliate and a Participant, the following rules shall apply:

(a) New Participants During the Performance Period. If an individual is newly hired or promoted during a Performance Period into a position eligible for a Cash Incentive Award as a Section 16 Participant under this Section 10, he or she shall be eligible (but not guaranteed) to receive a Cash Incentive Award under this Section 10 for the Performance Period, prorated for the portion of the Performance Period following the date of eligibility for a Cash Incentive Award hereunder.

(b) Disability or Death. A Section 16 Participant who terminates employment with the Company due to Disability or death during a Performance Period shall be eligible (but not guaranteed) to receive a Cash Incentive Award prorated for the portion of the Performance Period prior to termination of employment. A Participant who terminates employment with the Company due to Disability or death following the end of a Performance Period but before Cash Incentive Awards relating to such Performance Period are paid shall be eligible (but not guaranteed) to receive the full Cash Incentive Award for such Performance Period. Cash Incentive Awards payable in the event of death, if paid, shall be paid to the Section 16 Participant's estate. Any such Cash Incentive Award shall be payable at the same time as other Cash Incentive Awards are paid for the relevant year.

(c) Termination of Employment. Subject to Section 10.4(b), if a Participant's employment with the Company terminates for any reason (whether voluntarily or involuntarily) either during a Performance Period or following the end of a Performance Period but before Cash Incentive Awards relating to such Performance Period are paid, unless otherwise determined by the Committee, no Cash Incentive Award (or portion thereof) shall be payable or earned with respect to such Performance Period.

Section 10.5 Change in Control. Notwithstanding any other provision of the Plan, upon a Change in Control, the amount of the Cash Incentive Award shall be determined as if the Performance Goals had been achieved at the performance target level and Cash Incentive Awards shall be paid as if the date of the Change in Control were the last day of the Performance Period during which such Change in Control occurs.

Section 10.6 General. The provisions of this Section 10 are intended to ensure that Cash Incentive Awards granted to Section 16 Participants hereunder that are intended to qualify as "performance-based compensation" (within the meaning of Section 162(m)) satisfy the exemption from the limitation on deductibility imposed by Section 162(m) that is set forth in Section 162(m)(4)(C), and this Section 10 and the Plan shall be interpreted and operated consistent with that intention to the extent applicable. Notwithstanding the foregoing, neither the adoption and operation of this Section 10 by the Board nor its submission to (or approval by) the stockholders of the Company shall be construed as having created any limitations on the power of Board or the Committee to adopt such other incentive arrangements as either may deem desirable, including, without limitation, cash or equity-based compensation arrangements, whether tied to performance or otherwise, and the adoption and operation of this Section 10 shall not preclude the Board or the Committee from approving other Cash Incentive Awards or short-term incentive compensation arrangements for the benefit of individuals who are Participants hereunder, whether or not such Participants are Section 16 Participants, as the Committee deems appropriate and in the best interests of the Company.

ARTICLE XI
TERMINATION AND FORFEITURE

Section 11.1 Termination for Cause. Unless otherwise determined by the Committee at the grant date and set forth in the Award Agreement covering the Award or otherwise in writing or determined thereafter in a manner more favorable to the Participant, if a Participant's employment or service terminates for Cause, all Options and SARs, whether vested or unvested, and all other Awards that are unvested or unexercisable or otherwise unpaid (or were unvested or unexercisable or unpaid at the time of occurrence of Cause) shall be immediately forfeited and canceled, effective as of the date of the Participant's termination of service.

Section 11.2 Clawback. Awards and Common Stock that has been distributed pursuant to Awards shall be subject to any clawback policy adopted by the Committee, the Board, or the Company, including any such policy adopted to comply with Applicable Law.

Section 11.3 Termination for Any Other Reason. Unless otherwise determined by the Committee at the grant date and set forth in the Award Agreement covering the Award or otherwise in writing or determined thereafter in a manner more favorable to the Participant, or otherwise as may be provided in an agreement between a Participant and the Company, if a Participant's employment or service terminates for any reason other than Cause:

(a) All Awards that are unvested or unexercisable shall be immediately forfeited and canceled, effective as of the date of the Participant's termination of service;

(b) All Options and SARs that are vested shall remain outstanding until (w) in the case of termination for death or Disability, the 180th calendar day following the date of the Participant's death, Disability, (x) in the case of retirement at normal retirement age (and, for purposes of the Plan, "normal retirement age" shall have the meaning set forth in the applicable Award Agreement or, if not defined in the Award Agreement, pursuant to the customary policies of the Company), (I) for Options and SARs that are vested at the date of retirement, the 180th calendar day following the date of the Participant's retirement, and (II) for Options and SARs that become vested following the Participant's retirement (if any), the 90th calendar day following such post-termination vesting date, (y) the expiration of three months following the effective date of the Participant's termination for any reason other than death, Disability or retirement at normal retirement age or (z) the Award's normal expiration date, whichever is earlier, after which any unexercised Options and SARs shall immediately terminate; provide that, if the exercise period of an Option or SAR would expire at a time when trading in the Common Stock is prohibited by federal securities law or the Company's insider trading policy, the expiration of the Option or SAR shall be automatically extended until the thirtieth (30th) calendar day following the expiration of such prohibition (so long as such extension shall not violate Section 409A); and

(c) All Awards other than Options and SARs that are vested shall be treated as set forth in the applicable Award Agreement (or in any more favorable manner determined by the Committee).

Section 11.4 Post-Termination Informational Requirements. Before the settlement of any Award following termination of employment or service, the Committee may require the Participant (or the Participant's Eligible Representative, if applicable) to make such representations and provide such documents as the Committee deems necessary or advisable to effect compliance with Applicable Law and determine whether the provisions of Section 11.1 or Section 11.4 may apply to such Award.

Section 11.5 Forfeiture of Awards. Awards granted under the Plan (and gains earned or accrued in connection with Awards) shall be subject to such generally applicable policies as to forfeiture and recoupment (including, without limitation, upon the occurrence of material financial or accounting errors, financial or other misconduct or Competitive Activity) as may be adopted by the Committee or the Board from time to time and set forth in the Award Agreement communicated to Participants. Any such policies may (in the discretion of the Committee or the Board) be applied to outstanding Awards at the time of adoption of such policies, or on a prospective basis only. The Participant shall also forfeit and disgorge to the Company any Awards granted or vested and any gains earned or accrued due to the exercise of Options or SARs or the sale of any Common Stock to the extent required by Applicable Law or regulations in effect on or after the Effective Date, including Section 304 of the Sarbanes-Oxley Act of 2002 and Section 10D of the Exchange Act. For the avoidance of doubt, the Committee shall have full authority to implement any policies and procedures necessary to comply with Section 10D of the Exchange Act and any rules promulgated thereunder. The implementation of policies and procedures pursuant to this Section 11.5 and any modification of the same shall not be subject to any restrictions on amendment or modification of Awards.

ARTICLE XII

CHANGE IN CONTROL

Section 12.1 Change in Control Where Awards Assumed or Replaced. In the event of a Change in Control in which the Company is the surviving entity and any adjustments necessary to preserve the value of the Participants' outstanding Awards have been made, or the Company's successor at the time of the Change in Control irrevocably assumes the Company's obligations under the Plan or replaces each Participant's outstanding Award with an award of equal or greater value and having terms and conditions no less favorable to the Participant than those applicable to the Participant's Award immediately prior to the Change in Control, there will be no accelerated vesting of Participants' Awards on account of the Change in Control unless a Participant experiences a Qualifying Termination.

Section 12.2 Acceleration of Exercisability and Lapse of Restrictions Upon a Qualifying Termination. Upon the date of a Participant's Qualifying Termination:

(a) All Awards with time-based vesting conditions or restrictions shall become fully vested (and Options or SARs exercisable) at the time of such Qualifying Termination; and

(b) All Performance Shares, Performance Units, and any other performance-based Awards with respect to which the vesting or amount is based on the satisfaction or achievement of Performance Goals or other performance-based criteria, shall become earned and vested and the performance criteria shall be deemed to be achieved or fulfilled, at the greater of (i) the actual performance achieved or (ii) the target level of performance applicable to the Award, but prorated based on the elapsed proportion of the Performance Period as of the Qualified Termination.

Section 12.3 Vesting Where Awards Not Assumed or Replaced. In the event of a Change in Control, unless the Company is the surviving entity and any adjustments necessary to preserve the value of Participants' outstanding Awards have been made, or the Company's successor at the time of the Change in Control irrevocably assumes the Company's obligations under the Plan or re-places each Participant's outstanding Award with an award of equal or greater value and having terms and conditions no less favorable to the Participant than those applicable to the Participant's Award immediately prior to the Change in Control:

(a) All Awards with time-based vesting conditions or restrictions shall become fully vested (and Options or SARs exercisable) at the time of such Change in Control; and

(b) All Performance Shares, Performance Units, and any other performance-based Awards with respect to which the vesting or amount is based on the satisfaction or achievement of Performance Goals or other performance-based criteria, shall become earned and vested as of the Change in Control, and the performance criteria shall be deemed to be achieved or fulfilled, at the greater of (i) the actual performance achieved or (ii) the target level of performance applicable to the Award, but prorated based on the elapsed proportion of the Performance Period as of the Change in Control.

Section 12.4 Certain Covered Transactions. In the event of a Change in Control that is a merger or consolidation in which the Company is not the surviving corporation or that results in the acquisition of substantially all the Company's outstanding Shares by a Person or group of Persons or entities acting in concert, or in the event of a sale or transfer of all or substantially all of the Company's assets (a "Covered Transaction"), the Committee shall have the discretion to provide for the termination of all outstanding Options and SARs as of the effective date of the Covered Transaction; provided, that, no Option or SAR will be so terminated (without the consent of the Participant) prior to the expiration of twenty (20) calendar days following the later of (i) the date on which the Award became fully exercisable and (ii) the date on which the Participant received written notice of the Covered Transaction. In the event of a Change in Control that involves a purchase of Shares for cash, the Board can implement or negotiate a procedure whereunder all Participants' unexercised Options or SARs may be cashed out as part of the purchase transaction, without requiring exercise, for the difference between the purchase price and the Exercise Price.

ARTICLE XIII
OTHER PROVISIONS

Section 13.1 Awards Not Transferable. Unless otherwise agreed to in writing by the Committee, no Award or interest or right therein or part thereof shall be liable for the debts, contracts or engagements of the Participant or his or her successors in interest or shall be subject to disposition by transfer, alienation, anticipation, pledge, encumbrance, assignment or any other means whether such disposition be voluntary or involuntary or by operation of law, by judgment, levy, attachment, garnishment or any other legal or equitable proceedings (including bankruptcy), and any attempted disposition thereof shall be null and void and of no effect; provided, however, that nothing in this Section 13.1 shall prevent transfers by will or by the Applicable Laws of descent and distribution.

If allowed by the Committee, a Participant may transfer the ownership of some or all of the vested or earned Awards granted to such Participant, other than Incentive Stock Options to (i) the spouse, children or grandchildren of such Participant (the "Family Members"), (ii) a trust or trusts established for the exclusive benefit of such Family Members, or (iii) a partnership in which such Family Members are the only partners. Notwithstanding the foregoing:

(a) Under no circumstances will a Participant be permitted to transfer a stock option to a third-party financial institution without prior stockholder approval, and

(b) Vested or earned Awards may be transferred without the Committee's pre-approval if the transfer is made incident to a divorce as required pursuant to the terms of a "domestic relations order" as defined in Code Section 414(p); provided that no such transfer will be allowed with respect to Incentive Stock Options if such transferability is not permitted by Code Section 422.

Any such transfer shall be without consideration and shall be irrevocable. No Award so transferred may be subsequently transferred, except by will or applicable laws of descent and distribution. The Committee may create additional conditions and requirements applicable to the transfer of Awards. Following the allowable transfer of a vested Option, such Option shall continue to be subject to the same terms and conditions as were applicable to the Option immediately prior to the transfer. For purposes of settlement of the Award, delivery of Stock upon exercise of an Option, and the Plan's Change in Control provisions, however, any reference to a Participant shall be deemed to refer to the transferee.

Section 13.2 Amendment, Suspension or Termination of the Plan or Award Agreements.

(a) The Plan may be wholly or partially amended or otherwise modified, suspended or terminated at any time or from time to time by the Committee; provided that without the approval by a majority of the shares entitled to vote at a duly constituted meeting of stockholders of the Company, no amendment or modification to the Plan may (i) except as otherwise expressly provided in Section 3.5, increase the number of Shares subject to the Plan specified in Section 3.1 or the individual Award limitations specified in Section 3.3; (ii) modify the class of persons eligible for participation in the Plan or (iii) materially modify the Plan in any other way that would require stockholder approval under Applicable Law.

(b) Except as provided otherwise expressly provided in the Plan, neither the amendment, suspension nor termination of the Plan shall, without the consent of the holder of the Award, adversely alter or impair any rights or obligations under any Award theretofore granted. Except as provided by Section 4.5, notwithstanding the foregoing, the Committee at any time, and from time to time, may amend the terms of any one or more existing Award Agreements, provided, however, that the rights of a Participant under an Award Agreement shall not be adversely impaired without the Participant's written consent. The Company shall provide a Participant with notice of any amendment made to such Participant's existing Award Agreement in accordance with the terms of this Section 13.2(b).

(c) Notwithstanding any provision of the Plan to the contrary, in no event shall adjustments made by the Committee pursuant to Section 3.5 or the application of Section 11.4, 12.1, 12.2, 13.6 or 13.12 to any Participant constitute an amendment of the Plan or of any Award Agreement requiring the consent of any Participant.

(d) No Award may be granted during any period of suspension or after termination of the Plan, and in no event may any Award be granted under the Plan after the expiration of ten (10) years from the Effective Date (provided that no incentive stock options may be granted after ten (10) years from the date the Board approves the Plan).

Section 13.3 Effect of Plan upon Other Award and Compensation Plans. The adoption of the Plan shall not affect any other compensation or incentive plans in effect for the Company or any of its Subsidiaries or Affiliates. Nothing in the Plan shall be construed to limit the right of the Company or any of its Subsidiaries or Affiliates (a) to establish any other forms of incentives or compensation for Service Providers or (b) to grant or assume options or restricted stock other than under the Plan in connection with any proper corporate purpose, including, but not by way of limitation, the grant or assumption of options or restricted stock in connection with the acquisition by purchase, lease, merger, consolidation or otherwise, of the business, stock or assets of any corporation, firm or association.

Section 13.4 At-Will Employment. Nothing in the Plan or any Award Agreement hereunder shall confer upon the Participant any right to continue as a Service Provider of the Company or any of its Subsidiaries or Affiliates or shall interfere with or restrict in any way the rights of the Company and any of its Subsidiaries or Affiliates, which are hereby expressly reserved, to discharge any Participant at any time for any reason whatsoever, with or without Cause.

Section 13.5 Titles. Titles are provided herein for convenience only and are not to serve as a basis for interpretation or construction of the Plan.

Section 13.6 Conformity to Securities Laws. The Plan is intended to conform to the extent necessary with all provisions of the Securities Act and the Exchange Act and any and all regulations and rules promulgated under any of the foregoing, to the extent the Company, any of its Subsidiaries or Affiliates, or any Participant is subject to the provisions thereof. Notwithstanding anything herein to the contrary, the Plan shall be administered, and Awards shall be granted and may be exercised, only in such a manner as to conform to such laws, rules, and regulations. To the extent permitted by applicable law, the Plan and Awards granted hereunder shall be deemed amended to the extent necessary to conform to such laws, rules, and regulations.

Section 13.7 Term of Plan. The Plan, as amended and restated herein, shall become effective on the date that it is approved by the Board and approved by Company stockholders at the Company's 2018 Annual Meeting of Stockholders on June ___, 2018 (the "Effective Date") and shall continue in effect, unless sooner terminated pursuant to Section 13.2, until the tenth (10th) anniversary of the Effective Date. The provisions of the Plan shall continue thereafter to govern all outstanding Awards.

Section 13.8 Governing Law and Venue. To the extent not preempted by federal law, the Plan shall be construed in accordance with and governed by the laws of the State of Delaware regardless of the application of rules of conflict of law that would apply the laws of any other jurisdiction. Any and all claims and disputes of any kind whatsoever arising out of or relating to the Plan shall only be brought in the Delaware Chancery Court. The Participant or Person hereby waives any objection which it may now have or may hereafter have to the foregoing choice of venue and further irrevocably submits to the exclusive jurisdiction of the Delaware Chancery Court in any such claim or dispute.

Section 13.9 Severability. In the event any portion of the Plan or any action taken pursuant thereto shall be held illegal or invalid for any reason, the illegality or invalidity shall not affect the remaining parts of the Plan, and the Plan shall be construed and enforced as if the illegal or invalid provisions had not been included, and the illegal or invalid action shall be null and void.

Section 13.10 Governing Documents. In the event of any express contradiction between the Plan and any Award Agreement or any other written agreement between a Participant and the Company or any Subsidiary or Affiliate of the

Company that has been approved by the Committee, the express terms of the Plan shall govern, unless it is expressly specified in such Award Agreement or other written document that such express provision of the Plan shall not apply.

Section 13.11 Withholding Taxes. In addition to any rights or obligations with respect to Withholding Taxes under the Plan or any applicable Award Agreement, the Company or any Subsidiary or Affiliate employing a Service Provider shall have the right to withhold from the Service Provider, or otherwise require the Service Provider or an assignee to pay, any Withholding Taxes arising as a result of grant, exercise, vesting or settlement of any Award or any other taxable event occurring pursuant to the Plan or any Award Agreement, including, without limitation, to the extent permitted by law, the right to deduct any such Withholding Taxes from any payment of any kind otherwise due to the Service Provider or to take such other actions (including, without limitation, withholding any Shares or cash deliverable pursuant to the Plan or any Award) as may be necessary to satisfy such Withholding Taxes; provided, however, that in the event that the Company withholds Shares issued or issuable to the Participant to satisfy all or any portion of the Withholding Taxes, the Company shall withhold a number of whole Shares having a Fair Market Value, determined as of the date of withholding, not in excess of the amount required to be withheld by law, not exceeding the maximum individual statutory tax rate in a given jurisdiction (or such lower mount as may be necessary to avoid liability award accounting, or any other accounting consequence or cost, as determined by the Committee, and in any event in accordance with Company policies), and any remaining amount shall be remitted in cash or withheld; and provided, further, that with respect to any Award subject to Section 409A, in no event shall Shares be withheld pursuant to this Section 13.11 (other than upon or immediately prior to settlement in accordance with the Plan and the applicable Award Agreement) other than to pay taxes imposed under the U.S. Federal Insurance Contributions Act (FICA) and any associated U.S. federal withholding tax imposed under Code Section 3401 and in no event shall the value of such Shares (other than upon immediately prior to settlement) exceed the amount of the tax imposed under FICA and any associated U.S. federal withholding tax imposed under Code Section 3401. The Participant shall be responsible for all Withholding Taxes and other tax consequences of any Award granted under the Plan.

Section 13.12 Section 409A. To the extent that the Committee determines that any Award granted under the Plan is subject to Section 409A, the Award Agreement evidencing such Award shall incorporate the terms and conditions required by Section 409A. To the extent applicable, the Plan and Award Agreements shall be interpreted in accordance with Section 409A and Department of Treasury regulations and other interpretive guidance issued thereunder, including without limitation any such regulations or other guidance that may be issued after the adoption of the Plan. Notwithstanding any provision of the Plan to the contrary, in the event that following the adoption of the Plan, the Committee determines that any Award may be subject to Section 409A and related regulations and Department of Treasury guidance (including such Department of Treasury guidance as may be issued after the adoption of the Plan), the Commit-

Company and any Employee, Director or Advisor thereof. During the Restricted Period, the Participant shall not call on, solicit or service any customer, supplier, licensee, licensor or other business relation of the Company in order to induce or attempt to induce any such Person to cease doing business with the Company, or in any way interfere with the relationship between any such customer, supplier, licensee or business relation and the Company (including making any negative statements or communications concerning any of the Company or its Employees, Directors or Advisors).

(d) *Judicial Modification.* If the final judgment of a court of competent jurisdiction declares that any term or provision of this Section is invalid or unenforceable, the parties agree that (i) the court making the determination of invalidity or unenforceability shall have the power to reduce the scope, duration, or geographic area of the term or provision, to delete specific words or phrases, or to replace any invalid or unenforceable term or provision with a term or provision that is valid and enforceable and that comes closest to expressing the intention of the invalid or unenforceable term or provision, (ii) the parties shall request that the court exercise that power, and (iii) this Agreement shall be enforceable as so modified after the expiration of the time within which the judgment or decision may be appealed.

(e) *Remedy for Breach.* The Participant agrees that in the event of a breach or threatened breach of any of the covenants contained in this Section, in addition to any other penalties or restrictions that may apply under any employment agreement, state law, or otherwise, the Participant shall forfeit, upon written notice to such effect from the Company:

 (i) any and all Options granted to him or her under the Plan and this Agreement, including vested Options; and

 (ii) the profit the Participant has realized on the exercise of any Options, which is the difference between (A) the Exercise Price of any Options the Participant exercised after terminating Service and within the six-month period immediately preceding the Participant's termination of Service and (B) the Fair Market Value of the shares of Common Stock purchased under such Options (which difference the Participant may be required to repay to the Company).

(f) The forfeiture provisions of this Section shall continue to apply, in accordance with their terms, after the provisions of any employment or other agreement between the Company and the Participant have lapsed.

(g) *Blue Pencil.* The Participant acknowledges and agrees that the non-competition non-solicitation and other restrictive covenant provisions contained herein are reasonable and valid in geographic, temporal and subject matter scope and in all other respects, and do not impose limitations greater than are necessary to protect the goodwill, Secret or

Confidential Information and other business interests of the Company. Nevertheless, if any court or arbitrator determines that any of said non-competition, non-solicitation, or other restrictive covenants and agreements, or any provision thereof, is unenforceable because of the duration or geographic scope of such provision, such court or arbitrator will have the power to reduce the duration, geographic scope, or other scope of such provision, as the case may be; and, in its reduced form, such provision will then be enforceable to the maximum extent permitted by applicable law.

(h) *Tolling of Restrictive Periods.* If the Participant breaches any of the restrictions set forth in this Section above and the Company commences a legal proceeding in connection therewith, the time period applicable to each such restriction shall be tolled and extended for a period of time equal to the period of time during which the Participant is determined by a court of competent jurisdiction to be in non-compliance or breach (not to exceed the duration set forth in the applicable restriction) commencing on the date of such determination.

(i) *Protected Rights.* The Participant understands that nothing contained in this Agreement limits the Participant's ability to file a charge or complaint with the Equal Employment Opportunity Commission, the National Labor Relations Board, the Occupational Safety and Health Administration, the Securities and Exchange Commission or any other federal, state or local governmental agency or commission ("Government Agencies"). The Participant further understands that this Agreement does not limit the Participant's ability to communicate with any Government Agencies or otherwise participate in any investigation or proceeding that may be conducted by any Government Agency, including providing documents or other information, without notice to the Company. This Agreement does not limit the Participant's right to receive an award for information provided to any Government Agencies.

10. *Clawback/Forfeiture.* Notwithstanding anything to the contrary contained herein, the Committee may, in its sole discretion, cancel the Option if the Participant, without the consent of the Company, while employed by or providing Services to the Company or any Affiliate or after termination of such employment or Service, violates a non-competition, non-solicitation, non-disparagement or non-disclosure covenant or agreement, or otherwise has engaged in or engages in activity that is in conflict with or adverse to the interest of the Company or any Affiliate, including fraud or conduct contributing to any financial restatements or irregularities, as determined by the Committee in its sole discretion. Further, if the Participant otherwise has engaged in or engages in any activity referred to in the preceding sentence, the Participant shall forfeit any compensation, gain or other value realized thereafter on the vesting, exercise or settlement of such Option, the sale or other transfer of such Option, or the sale of shares of Common Stock acquired in respect of such Option, and must promptly

repay such amounts to the Company. In addition, if the Participant receives any amount in excess of what the Participant should have received under the terms of the Option for any reason (including without limitation by reason of a financial restatement, mistake in calculations or other administrative error), all as determined by the Committee in its sole discretion, then the Participant shall be required to promptly repay any such excess amount to the Company. To the extent required by applicable law (including without limitation Section 304 of the Sarbanes-Oxley Act and Section 954 of the Dodd-Frank Wall Street Reform and Consumer Protection Act) and/or the rules and regulations of the NYSE or other securities exchange or inter-dealer quotation system on which the Common Stock is listed or quoted, or if so required by the Company's Incentive Compensation Recoupment Policy, or pursuant to any similar written policy adopted by the Company, the Option shall be subject (including on a retroactive basis) to clawback, forfeiture or similar requirements (and such requirements shall be deemed incorporated by reference into this Agreement).

11. *Transferability of Option and Common Stock Acquired Upon Exercise of Option.* The Participant may not sell, transfer, pledge, assign or otherwise alienate or hypothecate the Option. The Company will not be required (i) to transfer on its books any Options or shares of Common Stock that have been sold or transferred, or (ii) to treat as owner of such Options or shares of Common Stock, to accord the right to vote as such owner or to pay dividends to any transferee to whom such Options or shares of Common Stock have been transferred, in violation of the Plan or this Agreement. During the Participant's lifetime, only the Participant or the Participant's guardian or legal representative may exercise the Option. The Committee may, in its discretion, require a guardian or legal representative to supply it with the evidence the Committee reasonably deems necessary to establish the authority of the guardian or legal representative to exercise the Option on behalf of the Participant or transferee, as the case may be.

12. *Administration.* The Committee administers the Plan. The Participant's rights under this Agreement are expressly subject to the terms and conditions of the Plan, including continued shareholder approval of the Plan, and to any guidelines the Committee adopts from time to time. The Participant hereby acknowledges receipt of a copy of the Plan. Any interpretation by the Committee of the terms and conditions of the Plan or this Agreement will be final.

13. *No Limitation on Rights of the Company.* The award of the Option does not and will not in any way affect the right or power of the Company to make adjustments, reclassifications or changes in its capital or business structure, or to merge, consolidate, dissolve, liquidate, sell or transfer all or any part of its business or assets.

14. *Plan and Agreement Not a Contract of Employment or Service.* Neither the Plan nor this Agreement is a contract of employment or Service, and no terms of the Participant's employment or Service will be affected in any way by the Plan, this Agreement or related instruments, except to the extent specifically expressed therein. Neither the Plan nor this Agreement will be construed as creating any right in the Participant to be continued in employment or Service in any position,

as an employee, consultant or director of the Company or its Affiliates or as altering or amending the existing terms and conditions of the Participant's employment or Service, or shall interfere with or restrict in any way the rights of the Company or its Affiliates, which are hereby expressly reserved, to remove, terminate, or discharge the Participant at any time for any reason whatsoever.

15. *Notice.* Any notice or other communication required or permitted under this Agreement must be in writing (including electronic) and must be delivered personally, sent by certified, registered or express mail, or sent by overnight courier, at the sender's expense. Notice will be deemed given when delivered personally or, if mailed, three days after the date of deposit in the United States mail or, if sent by overnight courier, on the regular business day following the date sent. Notice to the Company should be sent to ABC Corporation, _____, Attention: President. Notice to the Participant should be sent to the address set forth on the signature page below. Either party may change the person and/or address to whom the other party must give notice under this Section by giving such other party written notice of such change, in accordance with the procedures described above. Any reference in the Plan or this Agreement, or to a written document includes without limitation any document delivered electronically or posted on the Company's intranet or other shared electronic medium controlled by the Company.

16. *Governing Law; Choice of Venue.* This Agreement will be governed by and construed under the laws of the State of _____, determined without regard to its conflicts of law rules, except as such laws are preempted by the laws of the United States. If any provision of this Agreement shall be held by a court of competent jurisdiction to be invalid or unenforceable, the remaining provisions hereof shall continue to be fully effective. The jurisdiction and venue for any disputes arising under, or any action brought to enforce (or otherwise relating to), this Agreement shall be exclusively in the courts in the State of _____, County of _____, including the Federal Courts located therein (should Federal jurisdiction exist).

17. *Securities Law Requirements.* If at any time the Committee determines that exercising the Option or issuing shares of Common Stock would violate applicable securities laws, the Option will not be exercisable, and the Company will not be required to issue shares of Common Stock. The Committee may declare any provision of this Agreement or action of its own null and void, if it determines the provision or action fails to comply with the short-swing trading rules. As a condition to exercise, the Company may require the Participant to make written representations it deems necessary or desirable to comply with applicable securities laws. No person who acquires shares under this Agreement may sell the shares of Common Stock, unless they make the offer and sale pursuant to an effective registration statement under the Securities Exchange Act, which is current and includes the shares of Common Stock to be sold, or an exemption from the registration requirements of that Act.

18. *Successors.* All obligations of the Company under this Agreement will be binding on any successor to the Company, whether the existence of the successor

results from a direct or indirect purchase of all or substantially all of the business of the Company, or a merger, consolidation, or otherwise.

19. *Section 409A.* The Option is intended to be exempt from, or compliant with, Code Section 409A. Notwithstanding the foregoing or any provision of the Plan or this Agreement, if any provision of the Plan or this Agreement contravenes Code Section 409A or could cause the Participant to incur any tax, interest or penalties under Code Section 409A, the Committee may, in its sole discretion and without the Participant's consent, modify such provision to (i) comply with, or avoid being subject to, Code Section 409A, or to avoid the incurrence of taxes, interest and penalties under Code Section 409A, and/or (ii) maintain, to the maximum extent practicable, the original intent and economic benefit to the Participant of the applicable provision without materially increasing the cost to the Company or contravening the provisions of Code Section 409A. This Section does not create an obligation on the part of the Company to modify the Plan or this Agreement and does not guarantee that the Option will not be subject to interest and penalties under Code Section 409A.

20. *Sole Agreement.* This Award is in all respects subject to the provisions set forth in the Plan to the same extent and with the same effect as if set forth fully herein. In the event that the terms of this Award conflict with the terms of the Plan, the Plan shall control. This Agreement is the entire Agreement and understanding between the parties to it, and supersedes all prior communications, representations, and negotiations, oral or written in respect thereto.

21. *Waiver.* Any right of the Company contained in this Agreement may be waived in writing by the Committee. No waiver of any right hereunder by any party shall operate as a waiver of any other right, or as a waiver of the same right with respect to any subsequent occasion for its exercise, or as a waiver of any right to damages. No waiver by any party of any breach of this Agreement shall be held to constitute a waiver of any other breach or a waiver of the continuation of the same breach.

22. *Amendment of the Agreement.* The Company and the Participant may amend this Agreement only by a written instrument signed by both parties. No change, modification, or waiver of any provision of this Agreement shall be valid unless in writing and signed by the parties hereto.

23. *Severability.* The invalidity or unenforceability of any provision of this Agreement shall not affect the validity or enforceability of any other provision of this Agreement and each other provision of this Agreement shall be severable and enforceable to the extent permitted by law.

24. *Headings.* The headings of the Sections hereof are provided for convenience only and are not to serve as a basis for interpretation or construction, and shall not constitute a part, of this Agreement.

25. *Counterparts.* The parties may execute this Agreement in one or more counterparts, all of which together shall constitute but one Agreement.

***

IN WITNESS WHEREOF, the Company and the Participant have duly executed this Agreement effective as of the date first above written.

ABC Corporation

_____
(Participant's Signature)

By_____

Its_____   Participant's Name and Address for notices

Sample Option Exercise Form

The undersigned holder of an option to purchase shares of ABC Corporation, Inc. shares pursuant to a Stock Option Award Agreement under the ABC Corporation 2018 Stock Incentive Plan, effective _____, [year], hereby exercises the Participant's Option to purchase _____ of such shares of Common Stock, at the Option price of $_____ per share, in accordance with the terms and conditions of such Option Award Agreement.

I hereby agree to be bound by all of the provisions of, and to execute any applicable stockholders agreement or related document required by the Company.

Date of Exercise

_____

_____
Signature of Person Exercising Option

Please type or print legibly your name, as you want it to appear on your stock certificate, your address and your social security number in the space provided below.

Name: _____

Address: _____

(Street)

_____

(City)_____ (State)_____(Zip Code)

Social Security Number: _____

¶10,330 SAMPLE LEGAL AGREEMENT—Restricted Stock Award Agreement

The following is a sample Restricted Stock Award Agreement in which the company sets forth the specific terms and conditions applicable to the particular employee (or other award recipient). This sample agreement sets forth the obligations of both the employee and the Company. This award agreement is designed for a publicly held company to award restricted stock under an "omnibus plan." The legal terms of the omnibus plan would be contained in a separate Stock Incentive Award Plan document, a sample of which is found at ¶10,310. For a discussion of plan provisions unique to stock option plans and awards, see ¶675.

Sample Restricted Stock Award Agreement

This Restricted Stock Award Agreement (the "Agreement") is entered into effective as of _____, [year] (the "Award Date"), by and between ABC Corporation (the "Company") and _____ (the "Participant"). Any term capitalized but not defined in this Agreement will have the meaning set forth in the ABC Corporation 2018 Stock Incentive Plan (the "Plan").

The Plan provides for the grant of Restricted Stock to key employees of the Company or its Affiliates as approved by the Committee. In exercise of its discretion under the Plan, the Committee has determined that the Participant should receive a restricted stock award under the Plan and, accordingly, the Company and the Participant hereby agree as follows:

This Restricted Stock Award must be electronically accepted by the Participant. If the Participant fails to accept this Restricted Stock Award within sixty (60) calendar days of the Award Date, this Restricted Stock Award shall be null and void. By accepting this Agreement, the Participant consents to the electronic delivery of prospectuses, annual reports and other information required to be delivered by Securities and Exchange Commission rules (which consent may be revoked in writing by the Participant at any time upon three (3) business days' notice to the Company, in which case subsequent prospectuses, annual reports and other information will be delivered in hard copy to the Participant.

1. *Purpose.* The purpose of this Agreement is to provide compensation to key employees of the Company, including the Participant, for service in the form of a stock equivalent ownership interest in the Company. The award contemplated by this Agreement represents a portion of the Participant's total compensation for Service to the Company, and the form is intended to serve as a longer-term incentive to the Participant and to further align the Participant's interests with those of the Company's stockholders.

2. *Award.* The Company hereby grants to the Participant a Restricted Stock Award (the "Award") of _____ shares of Common Stock. This Award will be subject to the terms and conditions of the Plan and this Agreement. This Award constitutes the right, subject to the terms and conditions of the Plan and this Agreement, to distribution of the shares (known as "Restricted Stock").

3. *Vesting; Effect of Termination of Employment.* The Participant's Restricted Stock will become vested as to twenty-five percent (25%) of the Restricted Stock on the Award Date and an additional twenty-five percent (25%) of the Restricted Stock on each of the first, second and third anniversaries of the Award Date, provided the Participant remains continuously employed by the Company or an Affiliate until each such dates. If the application of this Section would result in the Participant vesting in a fraction of a share, such fractional share shall be rounded up to the next whole share.

If the Participant terminates Service with the Company and all Affiliates for any reason and before all of the Participant's Restricted Stock has become vested under this Agreement, the Participant's Restricted Stock that has not become vested will be forfeited on and after the effective date of the termination. Neither the Company nor any Affiliate will have any further obligations to the Participant under this Agreement when the Participant's Restricted Stock is forfeited.

4. *Terms and Conditions of Distribution.* The Company will distribute shares of Common Stock as soon as practicable after the Restricted Stock becomes vested.

    (a) *Death.* If the Participant dies before the Company has distributed any vested Restricted Stock, the Company will distribute shares to the beneficiary designated by the Participant or, if the Participant failed to designate a beneficiary, to the Participant's surviving spouse or, if no spouse survives the Participant, to the Participant's estate. The Company will distribute shares of Common Stock no later than six months after the Participant's death.

    (b) *Tax Withholding.* Vesting and settlement of the Restricted Stock shall be subject to the Participant satisfying any applicable federal, state, local, and foreign tax withholding obligations. The Company may withhold shares of Common Stock from all amounts payable to the Participant in connection with the Restricted Stock to satisfy any applicable taxes required by law.

5. *Issuance.* The Restricted Stock shall be issued by the Company and shall be registered in the Participant's name on the stock transfer books of the Company promptly after the date hereof in book-entry form, subject to the Company's directions at all times prior to the date the Restricted Stock vests. The Company may, but shall not be required to, issue certificates for the Restricted Stock in the Participant's name. If the Company issues certificates for the Restricted Stock, the Secretary of the Company will hold the certificates until the Restricted Stock is either (i) forfeited or (ii) vested. As a condition to the receipt of the Restricted Stock, the Participant shall at the request of the Company deliver to the Company one or more stock powers, duly endorsed in blank, relating to the Restricted Shares. The Committee may cause a legend or legends to be put on any stock certificate relating to the Restricted Shares to make appropriate reference to such restrictions as the Committee may deem advisable under the Plan or as may be required by the rules, regulations, and other requirements of the Securities and Exchange Commission, any exchange that lists the Restricted Stock, and any applicable federal or state laws.

6. *Rights as Stockholder.* On and after the Award Date, and except to the extent provided in Section 8, the Participant will be entitled to all of the rights of a stockholder with respect to the Restricted Stock, including the right to vote the Restricted Stock and to receive dividends and other distributions payable with respect to the Restricted Stock upon vesting of such Restricted Stock, subject to the restrictions set forth in the Plan and this Agreement. Dividends payable on unvested Restricted Stock shall be withheld by the Company in a separate book-entry account maintained for the Participant on the books of the Company, and shall be distributed (without interest) to the Participant at the same time as the underlying Common Stock is settled and delivered upon vesting of such Restricted Stock and, if such Restricted Stock is forfeited, the Participant shall have no right to such dividends. If the Participant forfeits any rights the Participant may have under this Award in accordance with Section 3, the Participant shall, on the day following the event of forfeiture, no longer have any rights as a stockholder with respect to the Restricted Stock or any interest therein and the Participant shall no longer be entitled to receive dividends on such stock.

7. *Confidentiality, Competition, and Nonsolicitation.* The Participant is voluntarily willing to enter into the following restrictive covenants in exchange for this Award.

(a) *Nondisclosure and Nonuse of Confidential Information.* The Participant shall not disclose or use at any time, either during the Participant's Service or thereafter, any Confidential Information (as defined below) of which the Participant is or becomes aware, whether or not such information is developed by the Participant, except to the extent that such disclosure or use is directly related to and required by the Participant's performance of duties assigned to the Participant by the Company or any of its Affiliates. The Participant shall take all appropriate steps to safeguard Confidential Information and to protect it against disclosure, misuse, espionage, loss and theft. For purposes of this Agreement, the term "Confidential Information" is defined to include all information, in whatever form recorded or transmitted, related to or coming within the past, present or future business affairs of the Company or any of its Affiliates, or other parties whose information the Company has in its possession under obligations of confidentiality, including, without limitation, all business plans, customer lists or information, data, designs, developments, discoveries, expressions (in any medium), ideas, improvements, innovations, inventions, marketing materials, methods, operations, processes, product development processes, programs, research, systems, techniques, financial information, employee compensation and benefits, personnel records and information, promotional materials and methods, trademarks, or trade secrets, having commercial or proprietary value, and of a secret or confidential nature or otherwise not readily available to members of the general public.

(b) *Forfeiture for Competition.* The Participant acknowledges and agrees that (i) in the course of the Participant's Service the Participant shall become familiar with the trade secrets of the Company and its Affiliates and with other Confidential Information concerning the Company and its Affiliates, (ii) the Participant's services to the Company are unique in nature and of an extraordinary value to the Company, and (iii) the Company and its Affiliates could be irreparably damaged if the Participant were to provide similar services to any person or entity competing with the Company or any of its Affiliates or engaged in a similar business. In connection with the issuance to the Participant of the Restricted Stock hereunder, and in consideration for and as an inducement to the Company to enter into this Agreement, the Participant covenants and agrees that during the period beginning on the Award Date and ending on the second anniversary of the date of the termination of the Participant's Service (the "Restricted Period"), the Participant shall not, directly or indirectly, either for himself or herself or for or through any other Person, participate in any business or enterprise that provides or proposes to provide _____ of the type the Company provides. Without limiting the generality of the foregoing, the Participant agrees that, during the Restricted Period, the Participant shall not compete against the Company or any of its Affiliates by soliciting any customer or prospective customer of the Company with whom the Company had any business dealings or contracts. The Participant agrees that this covenant is reasonable with respect to its duration, geographical area and scope. For purposes of this Agreement, the term "participate in" includes having any direct or indirect interest in any Person, whether as a sole proprietor, owner, stockholder, partner, joint venture, creditor or otherwise, or rendering any direct or indirect service or assistance to any Person (whether as a director, officer, manager, supervisor, employee, agent, consultant or otherwise), other than owning up to 2% of the outstanding stock of any class that is publicly traded.

(c) *Nonsolicitation.* During the Restricted Period, the Participant shall not induce or attempt to induce to leave the Service of the Company or any of its Affiliates or hire any Employee, Director or Advisor of the Company or any of its Affiliates, or in any way interfere with the relationship between the Company and any Employee, Director or Advisor thereof. During the Restricted Period, the Participant shall not call on, solicit or service any customer, supplier, licensee, licensor or other business relation of the Company in order to induce or attempt to induce any such Person to cease doing business with the Company, or in any way interfere with the relationship between any such customer, supplier, licensee or business relation and the Company (including making any negative statements or communications concerning any of the Company or its Employees, Directors or Advisors).

(d) *Judicial Modification.* If the final judgment of a court of competent jurisdiction declares that any term or provision of this Section is invalid or unenforceable, the parties agree that (i) the court making the determination of invalidity or unenforceability shall have the power to reduce the scope, duration, or geographic area of the term or provision, to delete specific words or phrases, or to replace any invalid or unenforceable term or provision with a term or provision that is valid and enforceable and that comes closest to expressing the intention of the invalid or unenforceable term or provision, (ii) the parties shall request that the court exercise that power, and (iii) this Agreement shall be enforceable as so modified after the expiration of the time within which the judgment or decision may be appealed.

(e) *Remedy for Breach.* The Participant agrees that in the event of a breach or threatened breach of any of the covenants contained in this Section, in addition to any other penalties or restrictions that may apply under any employment agreement, state law, or otherwise, the Participant shall forfeit, upon written notice to such effect from the Company:

    (i) any and all Restricted Stock granted to the Participant under the Plan and this Agreement, including vested Restricted Stock; and

    (ii) the profit the Participant has realized on the sale of any shares of Common Stock received by the Participant upon the vesting of Restricted Stock (which the Participant may be required to repay to the Company).

(f) The forfeiture provisions of this Section shall continue to apply, in accordance with their terms, after the provisions of any employment or other agreement between the Company and the Participant have lapsed.

(g) *Blue Pencil.* The Participant acknowledges and agrees that the non-competition non-solicitation and other restrictive covenant provisions contained herein are reasonable and valid in geographic, temporal and subject matter scope and in all other respects, and do not impose limitations greater than are necessary to protect the goodwill, Secret or Confidential Information and other business interests of the Company. Nevertheless, if any court or arbitrator determines that any of said non-competition, non-solicitation, or other restrictive covenants and agreements, or any provision thereof, is unenforceable because of the duration or geographic scope of such provision, such court or arbitrator will have the power to reduce the duration, geographic scope, or other scope of such provision, as the case may be; and, in its reduced form, such provision will then be enforceable to the maximum extent permitted by applicable law.

(h) *Tolling of Restrictive Periods.* If the Participant breaches any of the restrictions set forth in this Section above and the Company commences a legal proceeding in connection therewith, the time period applicable to each such restriction shall be tolled and extended for a period of time equal to the period of time during which the Participant is determined by a court of competent jurisdiction to be in non-compliance or breach (not to exceed the duration set forth in the applicable restriction) commencing on the date of such determination.

(i) *Protected Rights.* The Participant understands that nothing contained in this Agreement limits the Participant's ability to file a charge or complaint with the Equal Employment Opportunity Commission, the National Labor Relations Board, the Occupational Safety and Health Administration, the Securities and Exchange Commission or any other federal, state or local governmental agency or commission ("Government Agencies"). The Participant further understands that this Agreement does not limit the Participant's ability to communicate with any Government Agencies or otherwise participate in any investigation or proceeding that may be conducted by any Government Agency, including providing documents or other information, without notice to the Company. This Agreement does not limit the Participant's right to receive an award for information provided to any Government Agencies.

8. *Clawback/Forfeiture.* Notwithstanding anything to the contrary contained herein, the Committee may, in its sole discretion, cancel the Restricted Stock if the Participant, without the consent of the Company, while employed by or providing Service to the Company or any Affiliate or after termination of such employment or Service, violates a non-competition, non-solicitation, non-disparagement or non-disclosure covenant or agreement, or otherwise has engaged in or engages in activity that is in conflict with or adverse to the interest of the Company or any Affiliate, including fraud or conduct contributing to any financial restatements or irregularities, as determined by the Committee in its sole discretion. Further, if the Participant otherwise has engaged in or engages in any activity referred to in the preceding sentence, the Participant shall forfeit any compensation, gain or other value realized thereafter on the vesting, exercise or settlement of such Restricted Stock, the sale or other transfer of such Restricted Stock, or the sale of shares of Common Stock acquired in respect of such Restricted Stock, and must promptly repay such amounts to the Company. In addition, if the Participant receives any amount in excess of what the Participant should have received under the terms of this Award for any reason (including without limitation by reason of a financial restatement, mistake in calculations or other administrative error), all as determined by the Committee in its sole discretion, then the Participant shall be required to promptly repay any such excess amount to the Company. To the extent required by applicable law (including without limitation Section 304 of the Sarbanes-Oxley Act and Section 954 of the Dodd-Frank Wall Street Reform and Consumer Protection Act) and/or the rules and regulations of the NYSE or other securities exchange or inter-dealer quotation system on which the Common Stock is listed or quoted, or if so required by the Company's Compensation Recoupment Policy, or pursuant to any similar written policy adopted by the Company, the Restricted Stock shall be subject (including on a retroactive basis) to clawback, forfeiture or similar requirements (and such requirements shall be deemed incorporated by reference into this Agreement).

9. *No Right to Employment or Service.* Nothing in the Plan or this Agreement will be construed as creating any right in the Participant to be continued in employment or Service in any position, as an employee, consultant or director of the Company or its Affiliates or as altering or amending the existing terms and conditions of the Participant's employment or Service, or shall interfere with or restrict in any way the rights of the Company or its Affiliates, which are hereby expressly reserved, to remove, terminate, or discharge the Participant at any time for any reason whatsoever.

10. *Nontransferability.* No interest of the Participant or any beneficiary in or under this Agreement will be assignable or transferable by voluntary or involuntary act or by operation of law, other than by testamentary bequest or devise or the laws of descent or distribution. Distribution of Common Stock will be made only to the Participant; or, if the Committee has been provided with evidence acceptable to it that the Participant is legally incompetent, the Participant's personal representative; or, if the Participant is deceased, to the beneficiaries or personal representative that the Participant has designated in the manner required by the Committee. The Committee may require personal receipts or endorsements of a Participant's personal representative or beneficiaries. Any effort to assign or transfer the rights under this Agreement will be wholly ineffective, and will be grounds for termination by the Committee of all rights of the Participant and the Participant's beneficiary in and under this Agreement.

11. *Administration.* The Committee administers the Plan. The Participant's rights under this Agreement are expressly subject to the terms and conditions of the Plan, including continued stockholder approval of the Plan, and to any guidelines the Committee adopts from time to time. The Participant hereby acknowledges receipt of a copy of the Plan. Any interpretation by the Committee of the terms and conditions of the Plan or this Agreement will be final.

12. *Governing Law; Choice of Venue.* This Agreement will be governed by and construed under the laws of the State of _____, determined without regard to its conflicts of law rules, except as such laws are preempted by the laws of the United States. If any provision of this Agreement shall be held by a court of competent jurisdiction to be invalid or unenforceable, the remaining provisions hereof shall continue to be fully effective. The jurisdiction and venue for any disputes arising under, or any action brought to enforce (or otherwise relating to), this Agreement shall be exclusively in the courts in the State of _____, County of _____, including the Federal Courts located therein (should Federal jurisdiction exist).

13. *Securities Laws.* The Participant agrees that the obligation of the Company to issue Common Stock shall also be subject, as conditions precedent, to compliance with applicable provisions of the Securities Act of 1933, as amended, the Securities Exchange Act of 1934, as amended, state securities or corporation laws, rules and regulations under any of the foregoing and applicable requirements of any securities exchange upon which the Company's securities shall be listed.

14. *Successors.* All obligations of the Company under this Agreement will be binding on any successor to the Company, whether the existence of the successor results from a direct or indirect purchase of all or substantially all of the business of the Company, or a merger, consolidation, or otherwise.

15. *Section 409A.* This Agreement is intended to be exempt from, or compliant with, Code Section 409A. Notwithstanding the foregoing or any provision of the Plan or this Agreement, if any provision of the Plan or this Agreement contravenes Code Section 409A or could cause the Participant to incur any tax, interest or penalties under Code Section 409A, the Committee may, in its sole discretion and without the Participant's consent, modify such provision to (i) comply with, or avoid being subject to, Code Section 409A, or to avoid the incurrence of taxes, interest and penalties under Code Section 409A, and/or (ii) maintain, to the maximum extent practicable, the original intent and economic benefit to the Participant of the applicable provision without materially increasing the cost to the Company or contravening the provisions of Code Section 409A. This Section does not create an obligation on the part of the Company to modify the Plan or this Agreement and does not guarantee that the Award will not be subject to interest and penalties under Code Section 409A.

16. *Sole Agreement.* This Award is in all respects subject to the provisions set forth in the Plan to the same extent and with the same effect as if set forth fully herein. In the event that the terms of this Award conflict with the terms of the Plan, the Plan shall control. This Agreement is the entire Agreement and understanding between the parties to it, and supersedes all prior communications, representations, and negotiations, oral or written in respect thereto.

17. *Waiver.* Any right of the Company contained in this Agreement may be waived in writing by the Committee. No waiver of any right hereunder by any party shall operate as a waiver of any other right, or as a waiver of the same right with respect to any subsequent occasion for its exercise, or as a waiver of any right to damages. No waiver by any party of any breach of this Agreement shall be held to constitute a waiver of any other breach or a waiver of the continuation of the same breach.

18. *Amendment of the Agreement.* The Company and the Participant may amend this Agreement only by a written instrument signed by both parties. No change, modification, or waiver of any provision of this Agreement shall be valid unless in writing and signed by the parties hereto.

19. *Severability.* The invalidity or unenforceability of any provision of this Agreement shall not affect the validity or enforceability of any other provision of this Agreement and each other provision of this Agreement shall be severable and enforceable to the extent permitted by law.

20. *Headings.* The headings of the Sections hereof are provided for convenience only and are not to serve as a basis for interpretation or construction, and shall not constitute a part, of this Agreement.

21. *Counterparts.* The parties may execute this Agreement in one or more counterparts, all of which together shall constitute but one Agreement.

IN WITNESS WHEREOF, the Company and the Participant have duly executed this Agreement effective as of the date first above written.

ABC Corporation   [Participant's Signature]

_____ By:_____

[Participant's Name]   Its:_____

¶10,340 SAMPLE LEGAL AGREEMENT—Performance Share Award Agreement

The following is a sample Performance Share Award Agreement in which the company sets forth the specific terms and conditions applicable to the particular employee (or other award recipient). This sample agreement sets forth the obligations of both the employee and the Company. This award agreement is designed for a publicly held company to award Performance Shares under an "omnibus plan." The legal terms of the omnibus plan would be contained in a separate Stock Incentive Award Plan document, a sample of which is found at ¶10,310. For a discussion of plan provisions unique to performance share plans and awards, see ¶675.

Sample Performance Share Award Agreement

This Performance Share Award Agreement (the "Agreement") is entered into effective as of _____, [year] (the "Award Date"), by and between ABC Corporation (the "Company") and _____ (the "Participant"). Any term capitalized but not defined in this Agreement will have the meaning set forth in the ABC Corporation 2018 Stock Incentive Plan (the "Plan").

The Plan provides for the grant of Performance Shares to key employees of the Company or its Affiliates as approved by the Committee. In exercise of its discretion under the Plan, the Committee has determined that the Participant should receive a Performance Share award under the Plan and, accordingly, the Company and the Participant hereby agree as follows:

This Performance Share Award must be electronically accepted by the Participant. If the Participant fails to accept this Performance Share Award within sixty (60) calendar days of the Award Date, this Performance Share Award shall be null and void. By accepting this Agreement, the Participant consents to the electronic delivery of prospectuses, annual reports and other information required to be delivered by Securities and Exchange Commission rules (which consent may be revoked in writing by the Participant at any time upon three (3) business days' notice to the Company, in which case subsequent prospectuses, annual reports and other information will be delivered in hard copy to the Participant.

1. *Purpose.* The purpose of this Agreement is to provide compensation to key employees of the Company, including the Participant, for service in the form of a stock equivalent ownership interest in the Company. The award contemplated by this Agreement represents a portion of the Participant's total compensation for Service to the Company, and the form is intended to serve as a longer-term incentive to the Participant and to further align the Participant's interests with those of the Company's stockholders.

2. *Award.* The Company hereby grants to the Participant a Performance Share Award (the "Award") of _____ shares of Common Stock. This Award will be subject to the terms and conditions of the Plan and this Agreement. This

Award constitutes the right, subject to the terms and conditions of the Plan and this Agreement, to distribution of the shares (known as "Performance Shares").

3. *Vesting; Effect of Termination of Employment.* The Participant's Performance Shares will vest in installments as follows:

(a) one-third of the Performance Shares granted shall vest on January 1, [2019], if the Company has attained both the projected revenue and Adjusted EBITDA targets specified below for [2018], and if the Participant has remained in Service with the Company or any of the Company Parties continuously until that date;

(b) an additional one-third of the Performance Shares granted shall vest on January 1, [2020], if the Company has attained both the Revenue and Adjusted EBITDA targets specified below for [2019], and if the Participant has remained in Service with the Company or any of the Company Parties continuously until that date; and

(c) an additional one-third of the Performance Shares granted shall vest on January 1, [2021], if the Company has attained both the Revenue and Adjusted EBITDA targets specified below for [2020], and if the Participant has remained in Service with the Company or any of the Company Parties continuously until that date.

The Revenue and Adjusted EBITDA amounts in and for [2018] through [2020] are as follows (numbers are in millions):

	[2018]	[2019]	[2020]
Revenue	$18.0	$27.0	$39.0
Adjusted EBITDA	$5.7	$6.5	$7.4

If the application of this Section would result in the Participant vesting in a fraction of a share, such fractional share shall be rounded up to the next whole share.

If the Participant terminates Service with the Company and all Affiliates for any reason and before all of the Participant's Performance Shares have become vested under this Agreement, the Participant's Performance Shares that have not become vested will be forfeited on and after the effective date of the termination. Neither the Company nor any Affiliate will have any further obligations to the Participant under this Agreement when the Participant's Performance Shares are forfeited.

4. *Terms and Conditions of Distribution.* The Company will distribute shares of Common Stock as soon as practicable after the Performance Shares become vested.

(a) *Death.* If the Participant dies before the Company has distributed any vested Performance Shares, the Company will distribute shares to the beneficiary designated by the Participant or, if the Participant failed to designate a beneficiary, to the Participant's surviving spouse or, if no spouse survives the Participant, to the Participant's estate. The Company will distribute shares of Common Stock no later than six months after the Participant's death.

(b) *Tax Withholding*. Vesting and settlement of the Performance Shares shall be subject to the Participant satisfying any applicable federal, state, local, and foreign tax withholding obligations. The Company may withhold shares of Common Stock from all amounts payable to the Participant in connection with the Restricted Stock to satisfy any applicable taxes required by law.

5. *Rights as a Stockholder*. The Participant shall not be deemed for any purpose to be the owner of any shares of Common Stock underlying the Performance Shares unless, until and to the extent that (i) the Company shall have issued and delivered to the Participant the shares of Common Stock underlying the Performance Shares and (ii) the Participant's name shall have been entered as a stockholder of record with respect to such shares on the books of the Company.

6. *Dividend Equivalents*. Each Performance Share shall be credited with Dividend Equivalents, which shall be withheld by the Company in a separate book-entry account maintained for the Participant on the books of the Company. Dividend Equivalents credited to the Participant's account and attributable to a Performance Share shall be distributed (without interest) to the Participant at the same time as the underlying Common Stock is delivered upon settlement of such Performance Share and, if such Performance Share is forfeited, the Participant shall have no right to such Dividend Equivalents.

7. *Confidentiality, Competition, and Nonsolicitation*. The Participant is voluntarily willing to enter into the following restrictive covenants in exchange for this Award.

(a) *Nondisclosure and Nonuse of Confidential Information*. The Participant shall not disclose or use at any time, either during the Participant's Service or thereafter, any Confidential Information (as defined below) of which the Participant is or becomes aware, whether or not such information is developed by the Participant, except to the extent that such disclosure or use is directly related to and required by the Participant's performance of duties assigned to the Participant by the Company or any of its Affiliates. The Participant shall take all appropriate steps to safeguard Confidential Information and to protect it against disclosure, misuse, espionage, loss and theft. For purposes of this Agreement, the term "Confidential Information" is defined to include all information, in whatever form recorded or transmitted, related to or coming within the past, present or future business affairs of the Company or any of its Affiliates, or other parties whose information the Company has in its possession under obligations of confidentiality, including, without limitation, all business plans, customer lists or information, data, designs, developments, discoveries, expressions (in any medium), ideas, improvements, innovations, inventions, marketing materials, methods, operations, processes, product development processes, programs, research, systems, techniques, financial information, employee compensation and benefits, personnel records and information, promotional materials and methods, trademarks, or trade secrets, having commercial or proprietary value, and of a secret or confidential nature or otherwise not readily available to members of the general public.

(b) *Forfeiture for Competition.* The Participant acknowledges and agrees that (i) in the course of the Participant's Service the Participant shall become familiar with the trade secrets of the Company and its Affiliates and with other Confidential Information concerning the Company and its Affiliates, (ii) the Participant's services to the Company are unique in nature and of an extraordinary value to the Company, and (iii) the Company and its Affiliates could be irreparably damaged if the Participant were to provide similar services to any person or entity competing with the Company or any of its Affiliates or engaged in a similar business. In connection with the issuance to the Participant of the Performance Shares hereunder, and in consideration for and as an inducement to the Company to enter into this Agreement, the Participant covenants and agrees that during the period beginning on the Award Date and ending on the second anniversary of the date of the termination of the Participant's Service (the "Restricted Period"), the Participant shall not, directly or indirectly, either for himself or herself or for or through any other Person, participate in any business or enterprise that provides or proposes to provide _____ of the type the Company provides. Without limiting the generality of the foregoing, the Participant agrees that, during the Restricted Period, the Participant shall not compete against the Company or any of its Affiliates by soliciting any customer or prospective customer of the Company with whom the Company had any business dealings or contracts. The Participant agrees that this covenant is reasonable with respect to its duration, geographical area and scope. For purposes of this Agreement, the term "participate in" includes having any direct or indirect interest in any Person, whether as a sole proprietor, owner, stockholder, partner, joint venture, creditor or otherwise, or rendering any direct or indirect service or assistance to any Person (whether as a director, officer, manager, supervisor, employee, agent, consultant or otherwise), other than owning up to 2% of the outstanding stock of any class that is publicly traded.

(c) *Nonsolicitation.* During the Restricted Period, the Participant shall not induce or attempt to induce to leave the Service of the Company or any of its Affiliates or hire any Employee, Director or Advisor of the Company or any of its Affiliates, or in any way interfere with the relationship between the Company and any Employee, Director or Advisor thereof. During the Restricted Period, the Participant shall not call on, solicit or service any customer, supplier, licensee, licensor or other business relation of the Company in order to induce or attempt to induce any such Person to cease doing business with the Company, or in any way interfere with the relationship between any such customer, supplier, licensee or business relation and the Company (including making any negative statements or communications concerning any of the Company or its Employees, Directors or Advisors).

(d) *Judicial Modification.* If the final judgment of a court of competent jurisdiction declares that any term or provision of this Section is invalid or unenforceable, the parties agree that (i) the court making the determination of invalidity or unenforceability shall have the power to reduce the scope, duration, or geographic area of the term or provision, to delete specific words or phrases, or to replace any invalid or unenforceable term or provision with a term or provision that is valid and enforceable and that comes closest to expressing the intention of the invalid or unenforceable term or provision, (ii) the parties shall request that the court exercise that power, and (iii) this Agreement shall be enforceable as so modified after the expiration of the time within which the judgment or decision may be appealed.

(e) *Remedy for Breach.* The Participant agrees that in the event of a breach or threatened breach of any of the covenants contained in this Section, in addition to any other penalties or restrictions that may apply under any employment agreement, state law, or otherwise, the Participant shall forfeit, upon written notice to such effect from the Company:

(i) any and all Performance Shares granted to the Participant under the Plan and this Agreement, including vested Performance Shares; and

(ii) the profit the Participant has realized on the sale of any shares of Common Stock received by the Participant upon the vesting of Performance Shares (which the Participant may be required to repay to the Company).

(f) The forfeiture provisions of this Section shall continue to apply, in accordance with their terms, after the provisions of any employment or other agreement between the Company and the Participant have lapsed.

(g) *Blue Pencil.* The Participant acknowledges and agrees that the non-competition non-solicitation and other restrictive covenant provisions contained herein are reasonable and valid in geographic, temporal and subject matter scope and in all other respects, and do not impose limitations greater than are necessary to protect the goodwill, Secret or Confidential Information and other business interests of the Company. Nevertheless, if any court or arbitrator determines that any of said non-competition, non-solicitation, or other restrictive covenants and agreements, or any provision thereof, is unenforceable because of the duration or geographic scope of such provision, such court or arbitrator will have the power to reduce the duration, geographic scope, or other scope of such provision, as the case may be; and, in its reduced form, such

¶10,340

provision will then be enforceable to the maximum extent permitted by applicable law.

(h) *Tolling of Restrictive Periods.* If the Participant breaches any of the restrictions set forth in this Section above and the Company commences a legal proceeding in connection therewith, the time period applicable to each such restriction shall be tolled and extended for a period of time equal to the period of time during which the Participant is determined by a court of competent jurisdiction to be in non-compliance or breach (not to exceed the duration set forth in the applicable restriction) commencing on the date of such determination.

(i) *Protected Rights.* The Participant understands that nothing contained in this Agreement limits the Participant's ability to file a charge or complaint with the Equal Employment Opportunity Commission, the National Labor Relations Board, the Occupational Safety and Health Administration, the Securities and Exchange Commission or any other federal, state or local governmental agency or commission ("Government Agencies"). The Participant further understands that this Agreement does not limit the Participant's ability to communicate with any Government Agencies or otherwise participate in any investigation or proceeding that may be conducted by any Government Agency, including providing documents or other information, without notice to the Company. This Agreement does not limit the Participant's right to receive an award for information provided to any Government Agencies.

8. *Clawback/Forfeiture.* Notwithstanding anything to the contrary contained herein, the Committee may, in its sole discretion, cancel the Performance Shares if the Participant, without the consent of the Company, while employed by or providing Service to the Company or any Affiliate or after termination of such employment or Service, violates a non-competition, non-solicitation, non-disparagement or non-disclosure covenant or agreement, or otherwise has engaged in or engages in activity that is in conflict with or adverse to the interest of the Company or any Affiliate, including fraud or conduct contributing to any financial restatements or irregularities, as determined by the Committee in its sole discretion. Further, if the Participant otherwise has engaged in or engages in any activity referred to in the preceding sentence, the Participant shall forfeit any compensation, gain or other value realized thereafter on the vesting, exercise or settlement of such Performance Shares, the sale or other transfer of such Performance Shares, or the sale of shares of Common Stock acquired in respect of such Performance Shares, and must promptly repay such amounts to the Company. In addition, if the Participant receives any amount in excess of what the Participant should have received under the terms of the Performance Shares for any reason (including without limitation by reason of a financial restatement, mistake in calculations or other administrative error), all as determined by the Committee in its sole discretion, then the Participant shall be required to promptly repay any such excess amount to the Company. To the extent required by applicable law

(including without limitation Section 304 of the Sarbanes-Oxley Act and Section 954 of the Dodd-Frank Wall Street Reform and Consumer Protection Act) and/or the rules and regulations of the NYSE or other securities exchange or inter-dealer quotation system on which the Common Stock is listed or quoted, or if so required by the Company's Incentive Compensation Recoupment Policy, or pursuant to any similar written policy adopted by the Company, the Performance Shares shall be subject (including on a retroactive basis) to clawback, forfeiture or similar requirements (and such requirements shall be deemed incorporated by reference into this Agreement).

9. *No Right to Employment or Service.* Nothing in the Plan or this Agreement will be construed as creating any right in the Participant to be continued in employment or Service in any position, as an employee, consultant or director of the Company or its Affiliates, or as altering or amending the existing terms and conditions of the Participant's employment or Service, or shall interfere with or restrict in any way the rights of the Company or its Affiliates, which are hereby expressly reserved, to remove, terminate, or discharge the Participant at any time for any reason whatsoever.

10. *Nontransferability.* No interest of the Participant or any beneficiary in or under this Agreement will be assignable or transferable by voluntary or involuntary act or by operation of law, other than by testamentary bequest or devise or the laws of descent or distribution. Distribution of Common Stock will be made only to the Participant; or, if the Committee has been provided with evidence acceptable to it that the Participant is legally incompetent, the Participant's personal representative; or, if the Participant is deceased, to the beneficiaries or personal representative that the Participant has designated in the manner required by the Committee. The Committee may require personal receipts or endorsements of a Participant's personal representative or beneficiaries. Any effort to assign or transfer the rights under this Agreement will be wholly ineffective, and will be grounds for termination by the Committee of all rights of the Participant and the Participant's beneficiary in and under this Agreement.

11. *Administration.* The Committee administers the Plan. The Participant's rights under this Agreement are expressly subject to the terms and conditions of the Plan, including continued stockholder approval of the Plan, and to any guidelines the Committee adopts from time to time. The Participant hereby acknowledges receipt of a copy of the Plan. Any interpretation by the Committee of the terms and conditions of the Plan or this Agreement will be final.

12. *Governing Law; Choice of Venue.* This Agreement shall be governed by and construed under the laws of the State of _____, determined without regard to its conflicts of law rules, except as such laws are preempted by the laws of the United States. If any provision of this Agreement shall be held by a court of competent jurisdiction to be invalid or unenforceable, the remaining provisions hereof shall continue to be fully effective. The jurisdiction and venue for any disputes arising under, or any action brought to enforce (or otherwise relating to), this Agreement shall be exclusively in the courts in the State of _____,

County of _____, including the Federal Courts located therein (should Federal jurisdiction exist).

13. *Securities Laws.* The Participant agrees that the obligation of the Company to issue Common Stock shall also be subject, as conditions precedent, to compliance with applicable provisions of the Securities Act of 1933, as amended, the Securities Exchange Act of 1934, as amended, state securities or corporation laws, rules and regulations under any of the foregoing and applicable requirements of any securities exchange upon which the Company's securities shall be listed.

14. *Successors.* All obligations of the Company under this Agreement will be binding on any successor to the Company, whether the existence of the successor results from a direct or indirect purchase of all or substantially all of the business of the Company, or a merger, consolidation, or otherwise.

15. *Section 409A.* This Agreement is intended to be exempt from, or compliant with, Code Section 409A. Notwithstanding the foregoing or any provision of the Plan or this Agreement, if any provision of the Plan or this Agreement contravenes Code Section 409A or could cause the Participant to incur any tax, interest or penalties under Code Section 409A, the Committee may, in its sole discretion and without the Participant's consent, modify such provision to (i) comply with, or avoid being subject to, Code Section 409A, or to avoid the incurrence of taxes, interest and penalties under Code Section 409A, and/or (ii) maintain, to the maximum extent practicable, the original intent and economic benefit to the Participant of the applicable provision without materially increasing the cost to the Company or contravening the provisions of Code Section 409A. This Section does not create an obligation on the part of the Company to modify the Plan or this Agreement and does not guarantee that the Award will not be subject to interest and penalties under Code Section 409A.

16. *Sole Agreement.* This Award is in all respects subject to the provisions set forth in the Plan to the same extent and with the same effect as if set forth fully herein. In the event that the terms of this Award conflict with the terms of the Plan, the Plan shall control. This Agreement is the entire Agreement and understanding between the parties to it, and supersedes all prior communications, representations, and negotiations, oral or written in respect thereto.

17. *Waiver.* Any right of the Company contained in this Agreement may be waived in writing by the Committee. No waiver of any right hereunder by any party shall operate as a waiver of any other right, or as a waiver of the same right with respect to any subsequent occasion for its exercise, or as a waiver of any right to damages. No waiver by any party of any breach of this Agreement shall be held to constitute a waiver of any other breach or a waiver of the continuation of the same breach.

18. *Amendment of the Agreement.* The Company and the Participant may amend this Agreement only by a written instrument signed by both parties. No change, modification, or waiver of any provision of this Agreement shall be valid unless in writing and signed by the parties hereto.

¶10,340

19. *Severability.* The invalidity or unenforceability of any provision of this Agreement shall not affect the validity or enforceability of any other provision of this Agreement and each other provision of this Agreement shall be severable and enforceable to the extent permitted by law.

20. *Headings.* The headings of the Sections hereof are provided for convenience only and are not to serve as a basis for interpretation or construction, and shall not constitute a part, of this Agreement.

21. *Counterparts.* The parties may execute this Agreement in one or more counterparts, all of which together shall constitute but one Agreement.

IN WITNESS WHEREOF, the Company and the Participant have duly executed this Agreement effective as of the date first above written.

ABC Corporation

———————————
[Participant's Name]

By:———————

Its:———————

———————————
[Participant's Signature]

¶10,350 ILLUSTRATION—Examples of Incentive Stock Option Tax Treatment

The following is an example of the tax treatment of an incentive stock option to both the company and the employee/optionee, under the current tax rules. If the option plan and the award satisfy the ISO requirements, the employee will not recognize income when he or she is awarded the ISO or when he or she exercises the ISO. At the time of exercise, the difference between the ISO's exercise price and the fair market value of the company's stock is not taxed (unless the optionee is subject to the alternative minimum tax). The optionee does not incur any taxable income until the optionee sells or otherwise disposes of the shares of stock purchased when he or she exercised the option. If the optionee holds the shares of stock long enough, the difference between the option exercise price and the price at which the optionee sells or otherwise disposes of the stock will be long-term capital gain or loss. For a discussion of incentive stock options, see ¶725.

Examples of Incentive Stock Option Tax Treatment

Hypothetical: ABC Corporation grants an Incentive Stock Option on January 1, 2019, to purchase 1,000 shares at $4.00 per share exercise price with the following Vesting Schedule:

250 - 1/1/2020

250 - 1/1/2021

250 - 1/1/2022

250 - 1/1/2023

(a) Fair market value at exercise (FMV):	$10.00
(b) Sale Price:	$15.00
(c) Spread	$6.00 (FMV minus exercise price)
(d) Gain between exercise date FMV and sale price	$5.00 (sale price minus FMV)
(e) Gain between exercise price and sale price	$11.00 (sale price minus exercise price)

Example 1: ISO exercised and held for required holding periods. Total income is taxable at lower long term capital gain rates because shares were sold more than two years after grant and more than one year after exercise.

250 shares @ $4.00	$1,000
Grant Date:	1/1/19
Vest Date:	1/1/20
Exercise Date:	1/1/21
Date Stock Sold:	1/2/22

Taxable Income:	250 × $11.00 = $2,750 Long Term Capital Gain in 2022

Example 2: A disqualifying disposition on the ISO within same calendar year (no alternative minimum tax calculation required).

250 shares @ $4.00	$1,000
Grant Date:	1/1/19
Vest Date:	1/1/20
Exercise Date:	6/1/20
Date Stock Sold:	12/30/20
Taxable Income:	250 × $6.00 = $1,500 Ordinary Income in 2020
	250 × $5.00 = $1,250 Short-Term Capital Gain in 2020

- Spread is ordinary income because shares were sold within one year from purchase date and/or within two years from grant.

- Additional gain is short-term capital gain because shares not held for more than one year from purchase date.

Example 3: A disqualifying disposition of an ISO in subsequent calendar year (alternative minimum tax calculation required in year that shares are purchased).

250 shares @ $4.00	$1,000
Grant Date:	1/1/19
Vest Date:	1/1/20
Exercise Date:	6/1/20
Date Stock Sold:	1/1/21
Taxable Income:	250 × $6.00 = $1,500 Ordinary Income in 2021
	250 × $5.00 = $1,250 Short-Term Capital Gain in 2021

- Spread is ordinary income because shares were sold within one year from purchase.

- Additional gain is short-term capital gain because shares not held for more than one year from purchase.

- Alternative minimum tax calculation required in 2020.

Taxable Income	250 × $11.00 = $2,750 Long-Term Capital Gain in 2020

$10,350

Index

All references are to paragraph (¶) numbers.

All references are to paragraph (¶) numbers.

All references are to paragraph (¶) numbers.

All references are to paragraph (¶) numbers.

CO

All references are to paragraph (¶) numbers.

All references are to paragraph (¶) numbers.

All references are to paragraph (¶) numbers.

All references are to paragraph (¶) numbers.

All references are to paragraph (¶) numbers.

All references are to paragraph (¶) numbers.

All references are to paragraph (¶) numbers.

All references are to paragraph (¶) numbers.

All references are to paragraph (¶) numbers.

All references are to paragraph (¶) numbers.

All references are to paragraph (¶) numbers.

All references are to paragraph (¶) numbers.

All references are to paragraph (¶) numbers.

Qualified retirement plans—continued
. bankruptcy of employers or participants in—continued
    2401.03, 2435–2435.01, 2455–2455.01, 2455.02
. common law employees allowed to participate in . . . 325.06
. defined benefit. *See* Defined benefit plans
. defined contribution. *See* Defined contribution plans
. distributions from . . . 1615.03
. employee taxation upon payments from . . . 1601.02, 1625
. employer immediate tax deduction of contributions to . . . 1601.02, 1615.04, 1625, 1725.01
. ERISA and Internal Revenue Code of 1986 governing . . . 1601.03, 1601.07, 1615.03–1615.04, 1615.06, 1615.09, 1655–1655.04, 1665–1665.02
. excise penalty for premature distributions from . . . 1615.03
. of insolvent employers . . . 1615.05
. investments in employer stock in . . . 1645.01, 1645.02
. limitations on . . . 1601.07, 1655–1655.04, 1701.01, 1715–1715.06, 1745.01
. loans from . . . 1125.03
. misconduct of participant in . . . 1665.09
. nondiscrimination in eligibility and benefits for . . . 1601.07, 1615.01, 1715.04
. for non-U.S. citizens working for U.S. employers . . . 2325
. plan and trust documents for . . . 1615.07
. pre-tax salary reduction contributions to. *See* 401(k) plans
. remedies for participants in . . . 1615.09
. reporting and disclosure requirements for . . . 1615.07
. requirements to become qualified for . . . 1601.01, 1615–1615.09
. securities law compliance issues for . . . 1201–1285, 1685–1685.05
. service or benefit credits in, additional . . . 1425.08
. specified in executive employment agreements . . . 155
. state taxation of . . . 1695
. summary annual report to participants in . . . 1615.07

Qualified retirement plans—continued
. tax treatment of . . . 1625, 1725.01
. tax-exempt Code Sec. 501(c) trust holding contributions to . . . 1601.07, 1625, 1725.01
. for U.S. executives working abroad . . . 2301.02, 2325.01

Qualified Supplemental Executive Retirement Plan (QSERP) . . . 1745.07

Qualifying event for COBRA . . . 1925.04

R

Rabbi trust agreement, sample model . . . 10,270

Rabbi trusts
. differences between secular trusts and . . . 2435.03
. executives not protected from company's insolvency by . . . 2401.03
. to hold mirror 401(k) contributions . . . 1745.05
. to informally fund nonqualified plan . . . 1701.07, 1725.02, 1765.01, 2435.03, 2525.03
. insurance contracts to fund . . . 1765.05
. IRS model . . . 1765.01
. life insurance contract payments from . . . 1865
. parent company stock of subsidiary's . . . 1765.07
. to protect nonqualified plan benefits . . . 1755.14
. springing . . . 1765.08
. tax treatment of . . . 1765.02

Real estate investment trusts (REITs) under Code Sec. 856(a) as subject to Code Sec. 280G DI treatment . . . 201.04
. use of profits interests . . . 925.03

Reasonableness test of compensation required for deduction . . . 2201.02, 2225–2225.06
. Code Sec. 162(a)(1) definition of reasonable compensation for . . . 2225
. determination of reasonable compensation in, factors for . . . 2225.02
. independent investor test for analysis in . . . 2225.03
. services requirement of . . . 2225.01

All references are to paragraph (¶) numbers.

All references are to paragraph (¶) numbers.

All references are to paragraph (¶) numbers.

All references are to paragraph (¶) numbers.

All references are to paragraph (¶) numbers.

All references are to paragraph (¶) numbers.

All references are to paragraph (¶) numbers.

All references are to paragraph (¶) numbers.

SU

All references are to paragraph (¶) numbers.